Criminal Law

Criminal Law

EIGHTH EDITION

Paul Marcus
William and Mary Law School

Linda A. Malone
William and Mary Law School

Geraldine Szott Moohr
University of Houston Law Center

Cara H. Drinan
Catholic University of America

Carolina Academic Press
Durham, North Carolina

ISBN: 978-1-5221-0547-3
ebook ISBN: 978-1-5310-0042-4
LCCN: 2016956307

Carolina Academic Press, LLC
700 Kent Street
Durham, North Carolina 27701
Telephone (919) 489-7486
Fax (919) 493-5668
www.cap-press.com

Printed in the United States of America

Contents

Table of Cases

H

Q

R

Preface

Substantive criminal law has traditionally been a very important part of the first-year curriculum. The course introduces the student to the criminal justice system, raises the question of why and how we punish, and enables instructors to discuss with students the thorny problem of the relationship between the state and the individual. In preparing the latest edition of these materials, we have once again attempted to produce a casebook of reasonable length which can be completely covered in a one semester course. Problems have been developed to demonstrate the difficulties discussed above and many modern issues have been emphasized to stimulate student interest in the course.

Many fine people assisted us in the preparation of the various editions of these classroom materials, from Catholic University, the College of William and Mary and the University of Houston. We thank them all for their wonderful assistance.

Cara Drinan, Washington, D.C.
Linda Malone, Williamsburg, Virginia
Paul Marcus, Williamsburg, Virginia
Geraldine Szott Moohr, Houston, Texas

March 2016

Criminal Law

Chapter 1

The Province and Limits of the Criminal Law

§ 1.01 The Decision to Criminalize

Commonwealth v. Jones

Supreme Court of Kentucky
880 S.W.2d 544 (1994)

REYNOLDS, JUSTICE.

The Court of Appeals reversed a Jefferson Circuit Court order which affirmed a district court judgment of conviction of disorderly conduct. We reverse, as this is not solely a content of speech case.

Appellee was in attendance at the 1991 Pegasus Parade. It was Derby Week in Louisville, Kentucky, and General Schwarzkopf was performing as the Grand Marshal of the event. City Police Officer Phillips received a complaint from a mother, who was accompanied by four infant children, regarding appellee shouting obscenities at the military components of the parade. The officer investigated and then told appellee that such language was impermissible and to move out of the red-lined "safety zone" designated around the judges' stand located at the Floyd/Broadway intersection. Appellee refused to move from the zone and called the officer a "Nazi pig motherfucker." Appellee was charged with disorderly conduct and placed under arrest. During trial the district court jury was instructed that it would find the defendant guilty "... only if, you believe from the evidence beyond a reasonable doubt that ... she [Jones], with the intent to cause public inconvenience, annoyance and or alarm, or wantonly created a risk thereof, did (a) Make an unreasonable noise or (b) Created [sic] a hazardous or physically offensive condition by an act that served no legitimate purpose." The language of the instruction followed KRS § 525.060(1)(b) and (d). The verdict of guilty, however, did not specify under which subsection the appellee's conduct fell. The disorderly conduct statute, KRS § 525.060, provides as follows:

> **525.060 Disorderly conduct**
>
> (1) A person is guilty of disorderly conduct when in a public place and with intent to cause public inconvenience, annoyance or alarm, or wantonly creating a risk thereof, he:

(a) Engages in fighting or in violent, tumultuous or threatening behavior; or

(b) Makes unreasonable noise; or

(c) Refuses to obey an official order to disperse issued to maintain public safety in dangerous proximity to a fire, hazard or other emergency; or

(d) Creates a hazardous or physically offensive condition by any act that serves no legitimate purpose.

(2) Disorderly conduct is a Class B misdemeanor.

Commentary to subsection (1)(b) prohibits unreasonable noise. "Reasonable" in this context depends upon the time, place, nature and purpose of the noise. "Unreasonable" was preferred over "loud" because loud noises may be appropriate in some places and on some occasions.... It was for the jury, therefore, to determine whether appellee's "noise" was reasonable considering the circumstances under which it was made. There was sufficient evidence for a jury's determination of "unreasonable noise" as the officer testified to appellee's volume of speech.

...

"The ... [reviewing] court does not have authority to consider matters on appeal de novo. The ... court acting as an appellate court cannot reevaluate the evidence or substitute its judgment as to the credibility of a witness for that of the trial court and the jury." *Commonwealth v. Bivins, Ky.*, 740 S.W.2d 954, 956 (1987). There was sufficient evidence before the jury for a determination of "unreasonable noise" as Officer Phillips testified as to appellee's volume of speech being greater than a normal speaking voice. This was reinforced by Jones's statement that she was yelling no louder than the parade itself.[1] Jones, who continued to position herself within the safety zone, was asked to calm down, and the result was a voice escalation. Content, volume and surrounding circumstances may be considered together when making a determination of reasonableness.

We also consider Jones's conviction in light of KRS § 525.060(1)(d) which is a catch-all provision prohibiting the creation of a hazardous or physically offensive condition that has no legitimate purpose.

The evidence adduced at trial was sufficient to submit this case to the jury as to a violation of either or both of the statutory subsections, and to denote that a criminalization of speech did not occur. Such evidence, to a jury, was sufficient to substantiate that Jones's speech served no legitimate purpose and that such "action" resulted in the creation of the "hazardous or physically offensive condition." The content of the noise, however distasteful, is not punishable. Some of the key elements may be public inconvenience, alarm or annoyance. As the parties concede, the constitutionality of the statute is not at issue for, on its face, it rises to meet constitutional

---

1. Jones also testified, "Why are you singling me out, why aren't you telling the other people around me who are also yelling and clapping, why aren't you telling them to be quiet?"

measurements. Herein, there is a distinguishing difference from the case of *Musselman v. Commonwealth, Ky.*, 705 S.W.2d 476 (1986).

The opinion of the Court of Appeals is reversed and the Jefferson District Court judgment is affirmed.

STUMBO, JUSTICE dissenting.

... Appellee testified that the purpose of her verbal comments was to express opposition to the presence of military personnel and armor in the annual Pegasus parade. The police officer who arrested Appellee did so after he received a complaint that appellee was shouting obscenities directed at the military displays, and after he was himself called an obscene name.

... Certainly a parade is an appropriate place to express oneself loudly, be it with approval or disapproval of the displays in the parade. The arresting officer testified only that appellee spoke in a volume greater than a normal speaking voice, not that she was unreasonably loud given the circumstances. As the Court of Appeals concluded, appellee was arrested partly due to the expression of her ideas regarding the military and partly due to the content of her speech directed at the officer. Subsection (1)(b) was intended to regulate volume, not content.

Subsection (1)(d) prohibits the creation of "a hazardous or physically offensive condition by any act that serves no legitimate purpose." I simply cannot envision how yelling at a parade could conceivably create either, unless the content of what is yelled is considered. As the majority correctly noted, "[t]he content of the noise, however distasteful, is not punishable."

I would affirm.

Comments and Questions

(1) *Defining the Crime.* It is a matter of virtually universal agreement that homicides, aggravated assaults, thefts, etc., should be prohibited by law and perpetrators of these offenses should be punished. There is, of course, considerable disagreement regarding the circumstances under which exceptions should be made. But offenses such as these, which were recognized as felonies at common law, are but a small part of the forms of conduct outlawed in contemporary criminal codes. Why has the state of Kentucky (first through its legislature, then through its law enforcement apparatus, and finally through its courts) determined that the behavior of Christine Jones is a Class B misdemeanor, for which she could be imprisoned for up to 90 days?

Suppose Kentucky law had provided:

> A person is guilty of a Class B misdemeanor when in a public place he refers to another person as a "Nazi pig motherfucker."

Presumably, such a law would violate the First Amendment of the United States Constitution in that it enjoins expression on the basis of its content. Should the fact that the state has reached the same end by a more circuitous route affect the outcome? *Compare Cohen v. California*, 403 U.S. 15, 91 (1971), in which the defendant was convicted under a statute comparable to that in the *Jones* case for wearing a jacket in a Los Angeles courthouse corridor which bore the words "Fuck the Draft." The Supreme Court reversed the conviction.

What legitimate societal interests are served by the Kentucky disorderly conduct statute? What interests are served by applying the statute to the conduct of this defendant?

(2) *Proving the Crime.* Persons accused of crime in Anglo-American legal systems are presumed to be innocent, which means that the prosecution must prove every element of the offense charged beyond a reasonable doubt. Thus, in the present case it must first demonstrate that Ms. Jones had the "intent to cause public inconvenience, annoyance or alarm, or wantonly creat[ed] a risk thereof." Absent an admission by the defendant to this effect, as a prosecutor in this case, how would you go about convincing the fact-finder that Ms. Jones had the requisite intent?

Assuming the prosecution gets over this hurdle, it then is incumbent upon it to demonstrate that the defendant engaged in one of the four types of conduct enumerated in the statute, two of which (a and c) afford scant possibilities. Thus, the prosecution must convince the fact-finder that Ms. Jones either (b) made an "unreasonable noise" or (d) "[c]reate[d] a hazardous or physically offensive condition by any act that serve[d] no legitimate purpose."

Is there any objectively convincing way to define "unreasonable noise"? Or is it enough to say, paraphrasing the words of Justice Stewart in *Jacobellis v. Ohio*, 378 U.S. 184, 197 (1964), a notorious obscenity decision, "I know it when I hear it?" The Kentucky Supreme Court says that all loud noise is not unreasonable, but that some loud noise is, "considering the circumstances under which it was made." Is this anything more than an *ipse dixit*?

Moreover, does volume have anything to do with it? If instead Ms. Jones, when asked to move out of the red-lined safety zone, had simply turned to the mother of four and said in a conversational tone, "That gentleman is a Nazi pig motherfucker," would the outcome of the case necessarily be any different?

If subsection (b) proves to be too hazardous for the prosecution, what about (d)? Has Ms. Jones created a "physically offensive condition"? What does *that* mean? Furthermore, is it not plausible to say that the defendant, however crudely, is expressing a political opinion, thus belying the suggestion that the act "serve[s] no legitimate purpose." (*See Cohen v. California, supra.*) If this much is true, then once again we find ourselves firmly enmeshed in the core protection of the First Amendment.

(3) *The Question of Selective Enforcement of the Law.* Look at the footnote in the majority opinion in *Jones.* Suppose that Ms. Jones had shouted "Schwarzkopf for President," or "Dan Quayle for President," and a bystander had expressed their annoyance to Officer Phillips. Is it likely that she would have been arrested? If not, why not? And query, apropos of the above, if she were arrested, would her conduct fall within the statute, or would it be considered "reasonable noise" within the milieu of a parade?

Which of the following may have influenced the decision to arrest: (a) The defendant had refused the officer's request to move. (b) The defendant's conduct was within the purview of the judge's stand. (c) The officer received a complaint. (d) The defendant's conduct was within the presence of four infant children. (e) The defendant was female?

(4) *The Art of Distinguishing Precedent.* In the *Musselman* case, cited by the court, the statute provided:

> (1) A person is guilty of harassment when with the intent to harass, annoy or alarm another person he:
>
> . . .
>
> (b) In a public place, makes an offensively coarse utterance, gesture or display, or addresses abusive language to any person present.

The defendant in that case had been stopped for speeding and, in the words of the court of appeals, he called the officer "a little, fat person who had a continuing incestuous relationship with his mother. Unfortunately in doing so he employed a coarse phrase that is the vernacularism for the relationship he had in mind." The Supreme Court of Kentucky, while finding the conduct of the defendant "deplorable," nonetheless concluded that as written the statute was vague and overbroad.

The defendant in *Jones* conceded the constitutionality of the disorderly conduct statute. Was that a mistake? Had she challenged it, could the court have found a "distinguishing difference" from the statute invalidated in *Musselman*?

In referring to the defendant's verbal assault on the officer, the *Musselman* court said that "[s]uch words delivered in these circumstances would constitute a violation of a statute written narrowly enough to provide criminal penalty without infringing upon the right of free speech as guaranteed by the United States and Kentucky Constitutions." Can you articulate such a statute?

(5) *A Communitarian Counterpoint.* Notwithstanding all of the foregoing, one may still be persuaded intuitively that the decision in *Jones* is correct, for, she may say, there must be more to life than the strident pursuit of constitutional rights. It is springtime in Kentucky, and a mother has brought her four small children—each perhaps bandying a little American flag—to see the Pegasus Parade, only to have what should have been a felicitous outing for all marred by a rude and vulgar protester. Is there no place left for decency, one ponders. Such a view might be espoused by communitarian legal theorists who maintain, *inter alia*, that in our unrelenting efforts to maximize individual liberty and equality something has been lost. For the communitarian perspective on a wide range of topics, see the legal journal, *The Responsive Community*.

D.P. v. State

District Court of Appeal of Florida, Third District
705 So. 2d 593 (1997), *cert. denied*, 525 U.S. 1028 (1998)

COPE, JUDGE

Dade County passed a comprehensive anti-graffiti ordinance which forbids the sale to minors of spray paint cans and broad-tipped markers ("jumbo markers").

The ordinance provides that minors can possess spray paint or jumbo markers on public property only if accompanied by a responsible adult. On private property, the minor must have the consent of the property owner, but need not be accompanied by an adult. It is a misdemeanor for a minor to possess spray paint or a jumbo marker without the required supervision or consent.

D.P. challenges the facial constitutionality of the provisions of the anti-graffiti ordinance that restrict minors' possession of spray paint or jumbo markers. We conclude that the ordinance is constitutional and affirm the adjudication of delinquency.

I.

In 1994, Dade County enacted a comprehensive anti-graffiti ordinance.... The ordinance prohibits the making of graffiti and establishes the responsibility of property owners to remove graffiti promptly....

The ordinance prohibits the sale of spray paint or broad-tipped markers to minors.... A broad-tipped marker is an indelible felt tip marker having a writing surface of one-half inch or greater.... This is a so-called jumbo marker. The ordinance does not prohibit the possession of ordinary-sized felt tip markers.

Sellers of spray paint and jumbo markers are required to keep them in a place not accessible to the public, such as a locked display case.... Alternatively, the goods must be stored within sight of a work station which is continuously occupied while the store is open.... The rationale evidently is that graffiti artists frequently obtain spray paint and jumbo markers by shoplifting. *See Sherwin-Williams Co. v. City and County of San Francisco*, 857 F. Supp. 1355, 1361–62 (N.D. Cal. 1994). The ordinance makes it a misdemeanor to possess spray paint or jumbo markers with intent to make graffiti.... That portion of the ordinance applies to all persons, be they adult or minor.

The ordinance then sets forth special provisions pertaining to minors. Subdivision (e)(2) of the ordinance addresses possession of spray paint and jumbo markers by minors on public property, while subdivision (e)(3) addresses possession on private property:

> (e) Possession of Spray Paint and Markers
>
> ...
>
> (2) Possession of spray paint and markers by minors on public property prohibited. No person under the age of eighteen (18) shall have in his or her possession any aerosol container or spray paint or broad-tipped indelible marker while on any public property, highway, street, alley or way except in the company of a supervising adult.
>
> (3) Possession of spray paint and markers by minors on private property prohibited without consent of owner. No person under the age of eighteen (18) shall have in his or her possession any aerosol container of spray paint or broad-tipped indelible marker while on any private property unless the owner, agent, or manager, or person in possession of the property knows of

the minor's possession of the aerosol container or marker and has consented to the minor's possession while on his or her property.

. . .

A petition of delinquency was filed against D.P., alleging violations of subdivisions (e)(2) and (3). D.P. entered a plea of no contest, reserving the right to appeal the trial court order holding the ordinance constitutional.

II.

D.P. argues that the ordinance violates the due process clauses of the state and federal constitutions because the ordinance imposes a criminal penalty for a minor's possession of spray paint or jumbo markers without the State being required to show that the minor had any criminal intent. D.P. reasons that spray paint and jumbo markers are ordinary household items that have legitimate uses. D.P. urges that it is impermissible for the County to criminalize simple possession of ordinary household objects.

D.P. suggests that in its attack on graffiti, the County has two viable alternatives. First, the County can impose a criminal penalty for possession of spray paint or jumbo markers with intent to make graffiti. The anti-graffiti ordinance already does this....

Alternatively, D.P. states that the County could constitutionally place a total ban on possession and sale of spray paint and jumbo markers by anyone, adult or minor. This is an approach that was taken in the City of Chicago and was held constitutional. *See National Paint & Coatings Association v. City of Chicago*, 45 F.3d 1124, 1126 (7th Cir. 1995). D.P. reasons that if spray paint and jumbo markers cannot legally be purchased or possessed by anyone, then there would be no such thing as innocent possession of spray paint or jumbo markers. It would follow, therefore, that a criminal penalty could be imposed for possession of the forbidden objects. D.P. reasons, however, that so long as spray paint and jumbo markers are available in households in Dade County (because spray paint and jumbo markers can be lawfully purchased by adults), it follows that the county cannot impose a criminal penalty on minors for possession of the same household objects.

A.

D.P. relies on a line of Florida cases that has struck down statutes and ordinances that have imposed a criminal penalty for ordinary innocent conduct.

In *State v. Saiez*, 489 So. 2d 1125 (Fla. 1986), the court struck down a statute which imposed a criminal penalty for the possession of credit card embossing machines, regardless of whether the machines were being used legitimately.... The court explained that "the guarantee of due process requires that the means selected shall have a reasonable and substantial relation to the object sought to be attained and shall not be unreasonable, arbitrary, or capricious." ...

Other examples relied on by D.P. include *Robinson v. State*, 393 So. 2d 1076, 1077 (Fla. 1980) (invalidating statute prohibiting wearing of mask or hood because "this law is susceptible of application to entirely innocent activities ... so as to create prohibitions that completely lack any rational basis"); *Foster v. State*, 286 So. 2d 549, 551 (Fla. 1973) (prohibiting punishment of possession of a simple screwdriver as being a burglary tool, without any showing of criminal intent);....

B.

In our view, the anti-graffiti ordinance passes constitutional muster.

In the first place, this ordinance does not place an outright ban on possession of spray paint or jumbo markers by minors....

Furthermore, the cases relied on by D.P. involve situations in which a statute or ordinance made it a crime for defendant to possess certain property ... even though it was legal for the defendant to purchase the same property. In the present case, it is unlawful for a minor to purchase spray paint or jumbo markers at all, and lawful to possess only if the minor is under supervision.[1]

D.P. suggests that it is impermissible to treat minors differently than adults. That suggestion is clearly incorrect. There are many activities that are legal for adults but prohibited to minors: drinking, and driving under legal age, being the most obvious examples. Some supervisory requirements apply to minors that do not apply to adults, such as compulsory school attendance and the curfew ordinance....

We concur with the trial court's ruling that the statute is constitutional.

GREEN, JUDGE, dissenting.

... [A] minor is subject to criminal penalties under the challenged subsections when traveling between two points where his or her possession of spray paint and jumbo markers is permissible. For example, the minor science student or school pep squad member who is given spray paint or markers by a teacher to complete a school project at home is subject to being fined and/or jailed under the graffiti ordinance if the student is stopped by a police officer en route home without being accompanied by an adult. Further, a minor who may be spotted by an officer in the minor's own yard spray painting a go-cart or model airplane is subject to having his or her actions criminalized under the ordinance if his or her parents are unaware of this activity or have not consented to the same. Aside from the absurdity of these results under the ordinance, the ordinance violates the substantive due process rights of these minors in that it criminalizes the mere possession of inherently innocent items without requiring the state to show any intent to violate the county's anti-graffiti ordinance....

The challenged subsections of the graffiti ordinance are virtually indistinguishable from the statutes and ordinances repeatedly struck down under the "innocent acts doctrine" with one exception; the challenged subsections under the graffiti ordinance pertain solely to minors. For this reason, I believe that the central issue in this case

1. The trial court noted that based on anecdotal evidence, the graffiti problem appeared to be concentrated in the fifteen-, sixteen-, and possibly seventeen-year-old age group. *See also* Sherwin-Williams Co. v. City & County of San Francisco, 857 F. Supp. at 1360 (suggesting age range from twelve to twenty).

is whether minors possess diminished substantive due process rights when it comes to statutes or ordinances that seek to criminalize the possession of inherently innocent items which can be used in criminal endeavors. Neither our state nor the federal supreme court appears to have squarely addressed this issue, but I do not believe that existing law supports the notion that the substantive due process rights of minors are not co-equal to those of adults under the "innocent acts doctrine." To begin with, all of the statutes, ordinances, etc., which were struck down as unconstitutional by our state supreme court ... were applicable to adults and minors alike. Thus, it could scarcely be argued that in the aftermath of these decisions, state and local legislative bodies could constitutionally reenact any such laws to pertain solely to minors.

...

The majority points out that it is not constitutionally impermissible to treat minors differently from adults.... While that is certainly true, it is true only in some delineated areas. Our United States Supreme Court has recognized as a general proposition, that "[a] child, merely on account of his [or her] minority, is not beyond the protection of the Constitution." *Bellotti v. Baird*, 443 U.S. 622, 633, 99 S. Ct. 3035, 3043, 61 L. Ed. 2d 797 (1979); *see also In re Gault*, 387 U.S. 1, 13, 87 S. Ct. 1428, 1436, 18 L. Ed. 2d 527 (1967) ("[W]hatever may be their precise impact, neither the Fourteenth Amendment nor the Bill of Rights is for adults alone.").... The *Bellotti* court cited three reasons for not equating the constitutional rights of children with those of adults, namely, "the peculiar vulnerability of children; their inability to make critical decisions in an informed, mature manner, and the importance of the parental role in child rearing." ... The central rationale for finding diminished constitutional rights of minors, in limited circumstances, appears to be for the personal protection of the child or the personal protection of others from the acts of minors....

... The purpose of the challenged subsections of the graffiti ordinance is wholly unrelated to the personal protection of minors or others. The county's sole aim is to protect property from graffiti artists. While that is certainly a legitimate and laudable objective, I do not believe that it can be pursued by the county at the expense and deprivation of fundamental due process rights which both adults and minors share....

Comments and Questions

(1) Why do you suppose the legislature chose not to include an element of intent in the statute—for example, that the spray paint or marker be possessed with the intent to deface public or private property? If the problem is the difficulty of proving intent, would it be an improvement if the statute presumed wrongful intent, but permitted the party charged to show as a matter of defense that she had a legitimate purpose?

(2) Usually, age classifications in prohibitions are recognition of the fact that the possession and use of certain things are associated with a level of maturity, however roughly calculated, *e.g.*, drinking, smoking, driving, sexually explicit publications, etc. In all such cases, there is a greater potential for harm when indulged by youth. Here, however, the potential harm is undifferentiated by 20-year-old (or 50-year-old) graffiti artists cause no less damage than those in the targeted group. Does a law need

a better justification for singling out a sub-group of the population for criminal sanction than the fact that the offense is most prevalent among members of that group?

(3) The court says that the examples cited by the defense of statutes declared unconstitutional—wearing a mask or possessing a screwdriver—are distinguishable from the present case, because in those cases it was not illegal for the party to purchase the item. Is this a logical distinction? Is the implication of this argument that the state could legitimately outlaw the sale and purchase of masks and screwdrivers? Or could outlaw their purchase by those age groups most likely to use them for criminal purposes?

(4) A similar New York City ordinance prohibits the sale of aerosol paint containers and broad tipped indelible markers to persons under 21 years of age. In an action brought by graffiti artists challenging the constitutionality of the law, the Court of Appeals for the Second Circuit has entered a preliminary injunction prohibiting enforcement against persons between the ages of 18 and 21. *Vincenty v. Bloomberg*, 476 F.3d 74 (2d Cir. 2007).

Problem

The city of York, Pennsylvania, enacted an ordinance prohibiting "cruising" or "unnecessary repetitive driving," defined as "driving a motor vehicle on a street past a traffic control point, as designated by the York City Police Department, more than twice in any two (2) hour period, between the hours of 7:00 p.m. and 3:30 a.m." Plaintiffs brought an action for declaratory and injunctive relief against enforcement of the ordinance on the grounds that it violated their right to travel and was overbroad. Is their argument persuasive? *See Lutz v. City of York, Pa.*, 899 F.2d 255 (3d Cir. 1990).

Lawrence v. Texas

Supreme Court of the United States
539 U.S. 558 (2003)

Justice Kennedy delivered the opinion of the Court.

Liberty protects the person from unwarranted government intrusions into a dwelling or other private places. In our tradition the State is not omnipresent in the home. And there are other spheres of our lives and existence, outside the home, where the State should not be a dominant presence. Freedom extends beyond spatial bounds. Liberty presumes an autonomy of self that includes freedom of thought, belief, expression, and certain intimate conduct. The instant case involves liberty of the person both in its spatial and in its more transcendent dimensions.

I

The question before the Court is the validity of a Texas statute making it a crime for two persons of the same sex to engage in certain intimate sexual conduct.

In Houston, Texas, officers of the Harris County Police Department were dispatched to a private residence in response to a reported weapons disturbance. They entered an apartment where one of the petitioners, John Geddes Lawrence, resided. The right of the police to enter does not seem to have been questioned. The officers observed

Lawrence and another man, Tyron Garner, engaging in a sexual act. The two petitioners were arrested, held in custody overnight, and charged and convicted before a Justice of the Peace.

The complaints described their crime as "deviate sexual intercourse, namely anal sex, with a member of the same sex (man)." App. to Pet. for Cert. 127a, 139a. The applicable state law is Tex. Penal Code Ann. § 21.06(a) (2003). It provides: "A person commits an offense if he engages in deviate sexual intercourse with another individual of the same sex." The statute defines "[d]eviate sexual intercourse" as follows:

> "(A) any contact between any part of the genitals of one person and the mouth or anus of another person; or
>
> "(B) the penetration of the genitals or the anus of another person with an object." § 21.01(1).

The petitioners exercised their right to a trial *de novo* in Harris County Criminal Court. They challenged the statute as a violation of the Equal Protection Clause of the Fourteenth Amendment and of a like provision of the Texas Constitution. Tex. Const., Art. 1, § 3a. Those contentions were rejected. The petitioners, having entered a plea of *nolo contendere*, were each fined $200 and assessed court costs of $141.25....

The Court of Appeals for the Texas Fourteenth District considered the petitioners' federal constitutional arguments under both the Equal Protection and Due Process Clauses of the Fourteenth Amendment. After hearing the case en banc the court, in a divided opinion, rejected the constitutional arguments and affirmed the convictions. 41 S.W.3d 349 (2001). The majority opinion indicates that the Court of Appeals considered our decision in *Bowers v. Hardwick*, 478 U.S. 186, 106 S. Ct. 2841, 92 L. Ed. 2d 140 (1986), to be controlling on the federal due process aspect of the case. *Bowers* then being authoritative, this was proper.

...

II

... We conclude the case should be resolved by determining whether the petitioners were free as adults to engage in the private conduct in the exercise of their liberty under the Due Process Clause of the Fourteenth Amendment to the Constitution. For this inquiry we deem it necessary to reconsider the Court's holding in *Bowers*.

There are broad statements of the substantive reach of liberty under the Due Process Clause in earlier cases, including *Pierce v. Society of Sisters*, 268 U.S. 510, 45 S. Ct. 571, 69 L. Ed. 1070 (1925), and *Meyer v. Nebraska*, 262 U.S. 390, 43 S. Ct. 625, 67 L. Ed. 1042 (1923); but the most pertinent beginning point is our decision in *Griswold v. Connecticut*, 381 U.S. 479, 85 S. Ct. 1678, 14 L. Ed. 2d 510 (1965).

In *Griswold* the Court invalidated a state law prohibiting the use of drugs or devices of contraception and counseling or aiding and abetting the use of contraceptives. The Court described the protected interest as a right to privacy and placed emphasis on the marriage relation and the protected space of the marital bedroom. Id., at 485, 85 S. Ct. 1678.

After *Griswold* it was established that the right to make certain decisions regarding sexual conduct extends beyond the marital relationship. In *Eisenstadt v. Baird*, 405 U.S. 438, 92 S. Ct. 1029, 31 L. Ed. 2d 349 (1972), the Court invalidated a law prohibiting the distribution of contraceptives to unmarried persons. The case was decided under the Equal Protection Clause, *id.*, at 454, 92 S. Ct. 1029; but with respect to unmarried persons, the Court went on to state the fundamental proposition that the law impaired the exercise of their personal rights, *ibid.* It quoted from the statement of the Court of Appeals finding the law to be in conflict with fundamental human rights, and it followed with this statement of its own:

> "It is true that in *Griswold* the right of privacy in question inhered in the marital relationship.... If the right of privacy means anything, it is the right of the *individual*, married or single, to be free from unwarranted governmental intrusion into matters so fundamentally affecting a person as the decision whether to bear or beget a child." *Id.*, at 453, 92 S. Ct. 1029.

The opinions in *Griswold* and *Eisenstadt* were part of the background for the decision in *Roe v. Wade*, 410 U.S. 113, 93 S. Ct. 705, 35 L. Ed. 2d 147 (1973). As is well known, the case involved a challenge to the Texas law prohibiting abortions, but the laws of other States were affected as well. Although the Court held the woman's rights were not absolute, her right to elect an abortion did have real and substantial protection as an exercise of her liberty under the Due Process Clause. The Court cited cases that protect spatial freedom and cases that go well beyond it. *Roe* recognized the right of a woman to make certain fundamental decisions affecting her destiny and confirmed once more that the protection of liberty under the Due Process Clause has a substantive dimension of fundamental significance in defining the rights of the person.

In *Carey v. Population Services Int'l*, 431 U.S. 678, 97 S. Ct. 2010, 52 L. Ed. 2d 675 (1977), the Court confronted a New York law forbidding sale or distribution of contraceptive devices to persons under 16 years of age. Although there was no single opinion for the Court, the law was invalidated. Both *Eisenstadt* and *Carey*, as well as the holding and rationale in *Roe*, confirmed that the reasoning of *Griswold* could not be confined to the protection of rights of married adults. This was the state of the law with respect to some of the most relevant cases when the Court considered *Bowers v. Hardwick*.

The facts in *Bowers* had some similarities to the instant case. A police officer, whose right to enter seems not to have been in question, observed Hardwick, in his own bedroom, engaging in intimate sexual conduct with another adult male. The conduct was in violation of a Georgia statute making it a criminal offense to engage in sodomy. One difference between the two cases is that the Georgia statute prohibited the conduct whether or not the participants were of the same sex, while the Texas statute, as we have seen, applies only to participants of the same sex. Hardwick was not prosecuted, but he brought an action in federal court to declare the state statute invalid. He alleged he was a practicing homosexual and that the criminal prohibition violated rights guaranteed to him by the Constitution. The Court, in an opinion by Justice White, sustained the Georgia law. Chief Justice Burger and Justice Powell joined the opinion of the Court and filed separate, concurring opinions. Four Justices dissented....

The Court began its substantive discussion in *Bowers* as follows: "The issue presented is whether the Federal Constitution confers a fundamental right upon homosexuals to engage in sodomy and hence invalidates the laws of the many States that still make such conduct illegal and have done so for a very long time." *Id.*, at 190, 106 S. Ct. 2841. That statement, we now conclude, discloses the Court's own failure to appreciate the extent of the liberty at stake. To say that the issue in *Bowers* was simply the right to engage in certain sexual conduct demeans the claim the individual put forward, just as it would demean a married couple were it to be said marriage is simply about the right to have sexual intercourse. The laws involved in *Bowers* and here are, to be sure, statutes that purport to do no more than prohibit a particular sexual act. Their penalties and purposes, though, have more far-reaching consequences, touching upon the most private human conduct, sexual behavior, and in the most private of places, the home. The statutes do seek to control a personal relationship that, whether or not entitled to formal recognition in the law, is within the liberty of persons to choose without being punished as criminals.

This, as a general rule, should counsel against attempts by the State, or a court, to define the meaning of the relationship or to set its boundaries absent injury to a person or abuse of an institution the law protects. It suffices for us to acknowledge that adults may choose to enter upon this relationship in the confines of their homes and their own private lives and still retain their dignity as free persons. When sexuality finds overt expression in intimate conduct with another person, the conduct can be but one element in a personal bond that is more enduring. The liberty protected by the Constitution allows homosexual persons the right to make this choice.

Having misapprehended the claim of liberty there presented to it, and thus stating the claim to be whether there is a fundamental right to engage in consensual sodomy, the *Bowers* Court said: "Proscriptions against that conduct have ancient roots." *Id.*, at 192, 106 S. Ct. 2841. In academic writings, and in many of the scholarly *amicus* briefs filed to assist the Court in this case, there are fundamental criticisms of the historical premises relied upon by the majority and concurring opinions in *Bowers*....

At the outset it should be noted that there is no longstanding history in this country of laws directed at homosexual conduct as a distinct matter. Beginning in colonial times there were prohibitions of sodomy derived from the English criminal laws passed in the first instance by the Reformation Parliament of 1533. The English prohibition was understood to include relations between men and women as well as relations between men and men. *See, e.g.*, *King v. Wiseman*, 92 Eng. Rep. 774, 775 (K.B. 1718) (interpreting "mankind" in Act of 1533 as including women and girls). Nineteenth-century commentators similarly read American sodomy, buggery, and crime-against-nature statutes as criminalizing certain relations between men and women and between men and men. See, *e.g.*, 2 J. Bishop, Criminal Law § 1028 (1858); 2 J. Chitty, Criminal Law 47–50 (5th Am. ed. 1847); R. Desty, A Compendium of American Criminal Law 143 (1882); J. May, The Law of Crimes § 203 (2d ed. 1893).

The absence of legal prohibitions focusing on homosexual conduct may be explained in part by noting that according to some scholars the concept of the homosexual as a distinct category of person did not emerge until the late 19th century. See, *e.g.*, J. Katz, The Invention of Heterosexuality 10 (1995); J. D'Emilio & E. Freedman, Intimate Matters: A History of Sexuality in America 121 (2d ed. 1997) ("The modern terms *homosexuality* and *heterosexuality* do not apply to an era that had not yet articulated these distinctions"). Thus early American sodomy laws were not directed at homosexuals as such but instead sought to prohibit nonprocreative sexual activity more generally. This does not suggest approval of homosexual conduct. It does tend to show that this particular form of conduct was not thought of as a separate category from like conduct between heterosexual persons.

Laws prohibiting sodomy do not seem to have been enforced against consenting adults acting in private. A substantial number of sodomy prosecutions and convictions for which there are surviving records were for predatory acts against those who could not or did not consent, as in the case of a minor or the victim of an assault. As to these, one purpose for the prohibitions was to ensure there would be no lack of coverage if a predator committed a sexual assault that did not constitute rape as defined by the criminal law. Thus the model sodomy indictments presented in a 19th-century treatise, see 2 Chitty, *supra*, at 49, addressed the predatory acts of an adult man against a minor girl or minor boy. Instead of targeting relations between consenting adults in private, 19th-century sodomy prosecutions typically involved relations between men and minor girls or minor boys, relations between adults involving force, relations between adults implicating disparity in status, or relations between men and animals.

To the extent that there were any prosecutions for the acts in question, 19th-century evidence rules imposed a burden that would make a conviction more difficult to obtain even taking into account the problems always inherent in prosecuting consensual acts committed in private. Under then—prevailing standards, a man could not be convicted of sodomy based upon testimony of a consenting partner, because the partner was considered an accomplice. A partner's testimony, however, was admissible if he or she had not consented to the act or was a minor, and therefore incapable of consent. See, *e.g.*, F. Wharton, Criminal Law 443 (2d ed. 1852); 1 F. Wharton, Criminal Law 512 (8th ed. 1880). The rule may explain in part the infrequency of these prosecutions. In all events that infrequency makes it difficult to say that society approved of a rigorous and systematic punishment of the consensual acts committed in private and by adults. The longstanding criminal prohibition of homosexual sodomy upon which the *Bowers* decision placed such reliance is as consistent with a general condemnation of nonprocreative sex as it is with an established tradition of prosecuting acts because of their homosexual character.

The policy of punishing consenting adults for private acts was not much discussed in the early legal literature. We can infer that one reason for this was the very private nature of the conduct. Despite the absence of prosecutions, there may have been periods in which there was public criticism of homosexuals as such and an insistence that the criminal laws be enforced to discourage their practices. But far from possessing "ancient roots," *Bowers*, 478 U.S. at 192, 106 S. Ct. 2841, American laws targeting same-sex couples did not develop until the last third of the 20th century. The reported decisions concerning the prosecution of consensual, homosexual sodomy between adults for the years 1880–1995 are not always clear in the details, but a significant number involved conduct in a public place....

In summary, the historical grounds relied upon in *Bowers* are more complex than the majority opinion and the concurring opinion by Chief Justice Burger indicate. Their historical premises are not without doubt and, at the very least, are overstated.

It must be acknowledged, of course, that the Court in *Bowers* was making the broader point that for centuries there have been powerful voices to condemn homosexual conduct as immoral. The condemnation has been shaped by religious beliefs, conceptions of right and acceptable behavior, and respect for the traditional family. For many persons these are not trivial concerns but profound and deep convictions accepted as ethical and moral principles to which they aspire and which thus determine the course of their lives. These considerations do not answer the question before us, however. The issue is whether the majority may use the power of the State to enforce these views on the whole society through operation of the criminal law. "Our obligation is to define the liberty of all, not to mandate our own moral code." *Planned Parenthood of Southeastern Pa. v. Casey*, 505 U.S. 833, 850, 112 S. Ct. 2791, 120 L. Ed. 2d 674 (1992).

...

Bowers was not correct when it was decided, and it is not correct today. It ought not to remain binding precedent. *Bowers v. Hardwick* should be and now is overruled.

... The present case does not involve minors. It does not involve persons who might be injured or coerced or who are situated in relationships where consent might not easily be refused. It does not involve public conduct or prostitution. It does not involve whether the government must give formal recognition to any relationship that homosexual persons seek to enter. The case does involve two adults who, with full and mutual consent from each other, engaged in sexual practices common to a homosexual lifestyle. The petitioners are entitled to respect for their private lives. The State cannot demean their existence or control their destiny by making their private sexual conduct a crime. Their right to liberty under the Due Process Clause gives them the full right to engage in their conduct without intervention of the government. "It is a promise of the Constitution that there is a realm of personal liberty which the government may not enter." *Casey, supra*, at 847, 112 S. Ct. 2791. The Texas statute furthers no legitimate state interest which can justify its intrusion into the personal and private life of the individual.

Had those who drew and ratified the Due Process Clauses of the Fifth Amendment or the Fourteenth Amendment known the components of liberty in its manifold possibilities, they might have been more specific. They did not presume to have this insight. They knew times can blind us to certain truths and later generations can see that laws once thought necessary and proper in fact serve only to oppress. As the Constitution endures, persons in every generation can invoke its principles in their own search for greater freedom.

The judgment of the Court of Appeals for the Texas Fourteenth District is reversed, and the case is remanded for further proceedings not inconsistent with this opinion.

It is so ordered.

[JUSTICE O'CONNOR, concurring opinion, is included in the Equal Protection section, *infra* page 72.]

...

JUSTICE SCALIA, with whom THE CHIEF JUSTICE and JUSTICE THOMAS join, dissenting.

...

III

...

Bowers held, first, that criminal prohibitions of homosexual sodomy are not subject to heightened scrutiny because they do not implicate a "fundamental right" under the Due Process Clause, 478 U.S., at 191–194, 106 S. Ct. 2841. Noting that "[p]roscriptions against that conduct have ancient roots," *id.*, at 192, 106 S. Ct. 2841, that "[s]odomy was a criminal offense at common law and was forbidden by the laws of the original 13 States when they ratified the Bill of Rights," *ibid.*, and that many States had retained their bans on sodomy, *id.*, at 193, *Bowers* concluded that a right to engage in homosexual sodomy was not " 'deeply rooted in this Nation's history and tradition,' " *id.*, at 192, 106 S. Ct. 2841.

The Court today does not overrule this holding. Not once does it describe homosexual sodomy as a "fundamental right" or a "fundamental liberty interest," nor does it subject the Texas statute to strict scrutiny. Instead, having failed to establish that the right to homosexual sodomy is " 'deeply rooted in this Nation's history and tradition,' " the Court concludes that the application of Texas's statute to petitioners' conduct fails the rational-basis test, and overrules *Bowers*' holding to the contrary, see *id.*, at 196, 106 S. Ct. 2841. "The Texas statute furthers no legitimate state interest which can justify its intrusion into the personal and private life of the individual." *Ante*, at 2484.

...

IV

I turn now to the ground on which the Court squarely rests its holding: the contention that there is no rational basis for the law here under attack. This proposition is so out of accord with our jurisprudence—indeed, with the jurisprudence of *any* society we know—that it requires little discussion.

The Texas statute undeniably seeks to further the belief of its citizens that certain forms of sexual behavior are "immoral and unacceptable," *Bowers, supra*, at 196, 106 S. Ct. 2841—the same interest furthered by criminal laws against fornication, bigamy, adultery, adult incest, bestiality, and obscenity. *Bowers* held that this *was* a legitimate state interest. The Court today reaches the opposite conclusion. The Texas statute, it says, "furthers *no legitimate state interest* which can justify its intrusion into the personal and private life of the individual," *ante*, at 2484 (emphasis added). The Court embraces instead Justice STEVENS' declaration in his *Bowers* dissent, that " 'the fact that the governing majority in a State has traditionally viewed a particular practice as immoral is not a sufficient reason for upholding a law prohibiting the practice,' " *ante*, at 2483. This effectively decrees the end of all morals legislation. If, as the Court asserts, the promotion of majoritarian sexual morality is not even a *legitimate* state interest, none of the above-mentioned laws can survive rational-basis review.

...

JUSTICE THOMAS, dissenting.

I join Justice SCALIA's dissenting opinion. I write separately to note that the law before the Court today "is ... uncommonly silly." *Griswold v. Connecticut*, 381 U.S. 479, 527, 85 S. Ct. 1678, 14 L. Ed. 2d 510 (1965) (Stewart, J., dissenting). If I were a member of the Texas Legislature, I would vote to repeal it. Punishing someone for expressing his sexual preference through noncommercial consensual conduct with another adult does not appear to be a worthy way to expend valuable law enforcement resources.

Notwithstanding this, I recognize that as a Member of this Court I am not empowered to help petitioners and others similarly situated. My duty, rather, is to "decide cases 'agreeably to the Constitution and laws of the United States.' " *Id.*, at 530, 85 S. Ct. 1678. And, just like Justice Stewart, I "can find [neither in the Bill of Rights nor any other part of the Constitution a] general right of privacy," *ibid.*, or as the Court terms it today, the "liberty of the person both in its spatial and more transcendent dimensions," *ante*, at 2475.

Comments and Questions

(1) As the Court notes, the point of departure on the development of the constitutional right of privacy is *Griswold v. Connecticut*, which has had a wide-ranging and profound impact, perhaps most significantly in the evolving standards of protection against arrest, search and seizure under the Fourth Amendment. Most famously, *Griswold* provided the constitutional underpinning in *Roe v. Wade*, which invalidated prohibitory abortion statutes. More recently, in *Cruzan v. Director, Mo. Dep't of Health*, 497 U.S. 261, 279 (1990), the Court assumed that "the United States Constitution would grant a competent person a constitutionally protected right to refuse lifesaving hydration and nutrition." Given that assumption, it held that the state had the power to require evidence of the patient's wishes, not basing its decision solely on the wishes of family members. Lower courts have not interpreted *Cruzan* to recognize a terminally ill person's right to a physician-assisted suicide. *See, e.g., People v. Kevorkian*, 527 N.W.2d 714 (Mich. 1994), *cert. denied*, Hobbins v. Kelley, 514 U.S. 1083 (1995).

(2) Perhaps the largest hurdle for the parties attempting to attack the anti-contraceptive statute in *Griswold* was the failure to enforce the law, which made it

difficult to get the question before the courts. Similarly, in *Lawrence*, Justice Kennedy notes that "[l]aws prohibiting sodomy do not seem to have been enforced against consenting adults acting in private." In this case, an arrest was made by virtue of the fortuitous observation of the conduct of the defendant in the course of an investigation of "a reported weapons disturbance." If in fact a law is not being enforced (at least under some circumstances in which it could be), is a determination of its constitutional validity still important?

(3) Justice Scalia opines that in light of the Court's rationale in *Lawrence*, "criminal laws against fornication, bigamy, adultery, adult incest, bestiality, and obscenity" cannot survive rational basis review. Do you agree? If consensual sodomy is constitutionally protected, what about solicitation for such an act in a public restroom?

(4) As Justice Scalia observes, *Bowers* held that furthering the belief that certain forms of sexual behavior are "immoral and unacceptable" was a legitimate state interest. *Lawrence* adopts the view of Justice Stevens in *Bowers* that it is not. If this is the controlling question in the case, with implications for future cases, how does (should) the Court resolve it?

(5) For commentary on *Lawrence* and its aftermath, see Franke, *The Domesticated Liberty of* Lawrence v. Texas, 104 Colum. L. Rev. 1399 (2004); Sunstein, *Liberty After* Lawrence, 65 Ohio St. L.J. 1059 (2004); Strahilevitz, *Consent, Aesthetics, and the Boundaries of Sexual Privacy After* Lawrence v. Texas, 54 DePaul L. Rev. 671 (2005); Loewy, *Statutory Rape in a Post* Lawrence v. Texas *World*, 58 SMU L. Rev. 77 (2005); Leonard, *Thoughts on* Lawrence v. Texas, 11 Widener L. Rev. 171 (2005); Cruz, *Spinning* Lawrence, *or* Lawrence v. Texas *and the Promotion of Heterosexuality*, 11 Widener L. Rev. 249 (2005); Note, *Unfixing* Lawrence, 118 Harv. L. Rev. 2858 (2005).

(6) In an amicus brief in the *Bowers* case, Professor David Robinson, Jr., contended that the danger to public health threatened by AIDS was in itself ample justification for the prohibition of sodomy. This argument was not addressed by the Court. One lower court, however, acknowledged the relevance of such facts to the legitimacy of the legislative decision. *See State v. Walsh*, 713 S.W.2d 508 (Mo. 1986). Should this rationale satisfy rational basis review? *See generally* McGuigan, *The AIDS Dilemma: Public Health v. Criminal Law*, 4 L. & Inequality 545 (1986); Comment, *AIDS—New Reason to Regulate Homosexuality?*, 11 J. Contemp. L. 315 (1984); Carpenter, *Is* Lawrence *Libertarian?*, 88 Minn. L. Rev. 1140, 1159 (2004).

§ 1.02 The Decision to Punish

Regina v. Jones

Ontario Court of Appeal
115 Can. Crim. Cases 273 (1956)

Pickup, C.J.O.:—The Attorney—General appeals to this Court from sentences imposed by Magistrate Blain at Cooksville on January 17, 1956. The respondent pleaded guilty, on October 25, 1955, to three charges of indecent assault involving three young girls aged 6, 7 and 8 years respectively. The learned magistrate, after giving the matter careful consideration, considered that the ends of justice would be met by the imposition of a fine. We accordingly imposed a fine of $150 and costs on respect of each offence.

...

For the respondent it is urged that a prison sentence is not appropriate in the circumstances of this case. The reasons urged by counsel for the respondent against imposing a term of imprisonment are that the respondent is suffering from a form of sex perversion which Dr. McLarty, one of the psychiatrists, describes as sexual repression, that there is not much likelihood of a recurrence of the offence by the respondent, and that a prison term will be definitely detrimental to the respondent's condition. These are all considerations relating to the rehabilitation of the respondent and, in my opinion, entirely overlook the element of deterrence to others in the imposition of sentence for a criminal offence. It may be that this particular respondent, after continuation of psychiatric treatment, will not repeat the offence and there is a possibility of his being cured of his condition by such psychiatric treatment, but these are matters of grave uncertainty. I think I would agree that, so far as the condition of this particular respondent is concerned, a prison term may be detrimental to his recovery, but in my opinion the offence is too serious for punishment by a fine or by suspending sentence and placing the respondent upon probation. It is said that the prison term will not have any deterrent effect upon other persons who are truly sexual perverts. That may be so, but I do not think it justifies disregarding the deterrent effect upon those persons whom sentence will deter and who might be disposed to commit an assault of this character.

...

After giving the matter the best consideration I can, I have come to the conclusion that a definite prison sentence plus a longer indeterminate sentence should have been imposed in this case. I would therefore allow the appeal and substitute for the sentence imposed by the learned Magistrate a 6 month term of imprisonment plus an indeterminate term of 12 month imprisonment, this is to be the sentence on each of the three counts in the indictment but the three sentences so imposed to run concurrently. I do not suppose that the respondent has paid the fines imposed upon him by the learned Magistrate, but if he has they must of course be refunded.

...

LAIDLAW, J.A. (dissenting)

...

... [W]hat is best in this case from the standpoint of the safety of the public, both now and in the future? If the evidence satisfied me that there was a reasonable probability that the respondent would commit another sexual offence or that danger to the public would be appreciable if he were left at large, I would not hesitate to say that he should be detained in a safe place so that he could not do harm. In the absence of a suitable place of detention he would in such a case be imprisoned. But the respondent is not a true sex pervert; he is not a chronic sex deviate and he has not developed a "repetitive sexual deviation." On the contrary, it appeared to Dr. McLarty that the episode leading to his conviction was a "sporadic outburst." The respondent suffers from a mental illness or maladjustment, and one cannot be absolutely certain that he will not commit another sexual offence if permitted to be at liberty, but I give weight to his history and to the opinion of eminent psychiatrists, and I give to him the benefit of a reasonable doubt as to his ability to control his emotions while under treatment as an out-patient. I feel that the present danger to society is minimal.

On the other hand, I am not persuaded that prison is a curative institution. I think prison life would impede treatment and probably aggravate the respondent's condition of maladjustment. I think the needs of the respondent cannot be met by prison life. The nature of prison environment renders questionable the efficacy of treatment in that institution. The prisoner is under stress; he is deprived of the comfort and encouragement of friends and of opportunities to test the progress made and is subject to conditions which are often disadvantageous in other ways.

Counsel for the Crown stated that treatment is available and afforded to the inmates of the reformatory in this Province and that such treatment is given in groups. It is my view that to put this respondent in such a group with so-called sexual psychopaths—which is a nebulous term to describe persons, including sex perverts, who are a menace to society—and with other persons who have practiced sex perversion would be extremely harmful to him and perhaps destroy the probability of his complete recovery. In 9 *Rutgers Law Review*, 1954–55, p. 574, note 40, there is a statement to the effect that "experience has shown that it is neither practical nor conscionable to mix sexual psychopaths with non-psychopathic inmates, for such mingling greatly increases the danger of sex offences against innocent victims in the future." Finally, Dr. McLarty has expressed the opinion that "a jail sentence would be definitely detrimental to his condition."

From the standpoint of the safety of the public I am satisfied that no purpose would be served by sending the respondent to prison, but, on the contrary, there is substantial likelihood of detriment to him and increased danger to society upon his release.

Then, would a term of imprisonment imposed on the respondent in the unusual circumstances of this case deter others from committing criminal acts of sexual misbehavior? In my opinion it would not. Certainly it would not restrain others who suffer from mental maladjustment or illness of a kind that makes them unable to resist the driving and overpowering sexual impulse to do a wrongful act, nor in my opinion would it be any appreciable restraint or deterrent on those persons who are vaguely and inaccurately described as "ordinary" or "normal," over and above their certain knowledge, and the warning given now and many times before by the Courts that their willful sexual misbehavior will certainly be punished by imprisonment except in the most unusual and extreme circumstances. Moreover, my view finds support in the experience of many of the United States where provision is made by law for imprisonment of sexual offenders, and it has been found that the existence of such a penalty has not decreased the number of offences of this kind: *See* 37 *Massachusetts Law Quarterly*, Part 1, April 1952, p. 61. Finally, it is my view that in the extraordinary circumstances of this case the other considerations affecting the question of sentence, *i.e.*, the safety of the public, punishment, reformation and rehabilitation of the offender, far outweigh the doubtful benefit of deterrence.

...

Comments and Questions

(1) On the record, a prison term will do nothing to deter the respondent from committing this offense again. Indeed, Judge Pickup acknowledges that "so far as this particular respondent is concerned, a prison term may be detrimental to his recovery." To express it differently, it is possible that the respondent will be more likely to repeat the offense after serving a prison term than before he went in. Yet, the court imposes a sentence to deter others, albeit others *not* like the respondent, for it is conceded that those with his mental makeup will not be deterred in any event. Is this a legitimate use of the criminal law? Is the respondent being used as a means to an end? Is that important?

(2) What are the respective positions of Judge Pickup and Judge Laidlaw on the purpose of punishment? Are there additional reasons, other than those discussed by the judges, why the respondent should (not) be incarcerated?

Regina v. Dudley & Stephens

Queen's Bench Division
14 Q.B. 273 (1884)

Indictment for the murder of Richard Parker on the high seas within the jurisdiction of the Admiralty.

At the trial before Huddleston, B., at the Devon and Cornwall Winter Assizes, November 7, 1884, the jury, at the suggestion of the learned judge, found the facts of the case in a special verdict which stated "that on July 5, 1884, the prisoners, Thomas Dudley and Edward Stephens, with one Brooks, all able-bodied English seamen, and the deceased also an English boy, between seventeen and eighteen years of age, the crew of an English yacht, a registered English vessel, were cast away in a storm on the high seas 1600 miles from the Cape of Good Hope, and were compelled to put into an open boat belonging to said yacht. That in this boat they had no supply of water and no supply of food, except for 1 lb. of turnips, and for three days they had nothing else to subsist upon. That on the fourth day they caught a small turtle, upon which they subsisted for a few days, and this was the only food they had up to the twentieth day when the act now in question was committed. That on the twelfth day the remains of the turtle were entirely consumed, and for the next eight days they had nothing to eat. That they had no fresh water, except such rain as they from time to time caught in their oilskin capes. That the boat was drifting on the ocean, and was probably more than 1000 miles away from land. That on the eighteenth day, when they had been seven days without food and five without water, the prisoners spoke to Brooks as to what should be done if no succor came, and suggested that someone should be sacrificed to save the rest, but Brooks dissented, and the boy, by whom they were understood to refer, was not consulted. That on the 24th day of July, the day before the act now in question, the prisoner Dudley proposed to Stephens and Brooks that lots should be cast who should be put to death to save the rest, but Brooks refused to consent, and it was not put to the boy, and in point of fact there was no drawing of lots. That on that day the prisoners spoke of their having families, and suggested it would be better to kill the boy that their lives should be saved, and Dudley proposed that if there was no vessel in sight by the morrow morning the boy should be killed. That next day, the 25th of July, no vessel appearing, Dudley told Brooks that he had better go and have a sleep, and under signs to Stephens and Brooks that the boy had better be killed. The prisoner Stephens agreed to the act, but Brooks dissented from it. That the boy was then lying at the bottom of the boat quite helpless, and extremely weakened by famine and by drinking sea water, and unable to make any resistance, nor did he ever assent to his being killed. The prisoner Dudley offered a prayer asking forgiveness for them all if either of them should be tempted to commit a rash act, and that their souls might be saved. That Dudley, with the assent of Stephens, went to the boy, and telling him that his time was come, put a knife into his throat and killed him then and there; that the three men fed upon the body and blood of the boy for four days; that on the fourth day after the act had been committed the boat was picked up by a passing vessel, and the prisoners were rescued, still alive, but in the lowest state of prostration. That they were carried to the port of Falmouth, and committed for trial at Exeter. That if the men had not fed upon the body of the boy they would probably not have survived to be so picked up and rescued, but would within the four days died of famine. That the boy, being in a much weaker condition, was likely to have died before them. That at the time of the act in question there was no sail in sight, nor any reasonable prospect of relief. That under these circumstances there appeared to the prisoners every probability that unless they then fed or very soon fed upon the boy or one of themselves they would die of starvation. That there was no appreciable chance of saving life except by killing someone for the others to eat. That assuming any necessity to kill anybody, there was no greater necessity for killing the boy than any of the other three men. But whether upon the whole matter by the jurors found the killing of Richard Parker by Dudley and Stephens be felony and murder the jurors are ignorant, and pray the advise of the Court thereupon, and if upon the whole matter the Court shall be of opinion that the killing of Richard Parker be felony and murder, then the jurors say that Dudley and Stephens were each guilty of felony and murder as alleged in the indictment."

Lord Coleridge C.J....

Though law and morality are not the same, and many things may be immoral which are not necessarily illegal, yet the absolute divorce would follow if the temptation to murder in this case were to be held by law an absolute defence of it. It is not so. To preserve one's life is generally a duty, but it may be the plainest and the highest duty to sacrifice it. War is full of instances in which it is a man's duty not to live, but to die. The duty, in case of shipwreck, of a captain to his crew, of the crew to the passengers, of soldiers to women and children, as in the noble case of the *Birkenhead*, these duties impose on men the moral necessity, not of the preservation, but of the sacrifice of their lives for others, from which in no country, least of all, it is to be hoped, in England, will men ever shrink, as indeed, they have not shrunk. It is not correct, therefore, to say that there is any absolute or unqualified necessity to preserve one's life. "*Necesso est ut cam, not ut vivam*," is a saying of a Roman officer quoted by Lord Bacon himself with high eulogy in the very chapter on necessity to which so much reference has been made. It would be a very easy and cheap display of commonplace learning to quote from Greek and Latin authors, from Horace, from Juvenal, from Cicero, from Euripides, passage after passage, in which the duty of dying for others has been laid down in glowing and emphatic language as resulting from the principles of heathen ethics; it is enough in a Christian country to remind ourselves of the Great Example whom we profess to follow. It is not needful to point out the awful danger of admitting the principle which has been contended for. Who is to be the judge of this sort of necessity? By what measure is the comparative value of lives to be measured? Is it to be strength, or intellect, or what? It is plain that the principle leaves to him who is to profit by it to determine the necessity which will justify him in deliberately taking another's life to save his own. In this case the weakest, the youngest, the most unresisting was chosen. Was it more necessary to kill him than one of the grown men? The answer must be "No."

So spake the Fiend, and with necessity,

The tyrant's plea, excused his devilish deeds.

It is not suggested that in this particular case the deeds were "devilish," but it is quite plain that such a principle once admitted might be made the legal cloak for unbridled passion and atrocious crime. There is no safe path for judges to tread but to ascertain the law to the best of their ability and to declare it according to their judgment; and if in any case the law appears to be too severe on individuals, to leave it to the Sovereign to exercise that prerogative or mercy which the Constitution has intrusted to the hands fittest to dispense it.

It must not be supposed that in refusing to admit temptation to be an excuse for crime it is forgotten how terrible the temptation was; how awful the suffering; how hard in such trials to keep the judgment straight and the conduct pure. We are often compelled to set up standards we cannot reach ourselves, and to lay down rules which we could not ourselves satisfy. But a man has no right to declare temptation to be an excuse, though he might himself have yielded to it, nor allow compassion for the criminal to change or weaken in any manner the legal definition of the crime. It is therefore our duty to declare that the prisoners' act in this case was willful murder, that the facts as stated in the verdict are no legal justification of the homicide; and to say that in our unanimous opinion the prisoners are upon this special verdict guilty of murder.

Comments and Questions

(1) The defendants were sentenced to death, but the punishment was commuted by the Crown to six months imprisonment. What significance may be attributed to that? For additional facts of the case, see Mallin, *In Warm Blood: Some Historical and Procedural Aspects of* Regina v. Dudley & Stephens, 34 U. Chi. L. Rev. 387 (1967).

(2) The American counterpart of *Dudley & Stephens* is *United States v. Holmes*, 26 F. Cas. 360, 1 Wall. Jr. 1 (C.C.E.D. Pa. 1842) (No. 15,383), in which a passenger ship struck an iceberg, and nine crew members and 32 passengers got into the ship's longboat. Twenty-four hours later, the longboat began to sink, and the first mate directed that some of the passengers be thrown overboard to lessen the load. He instructed the crew not to part man and wife, and not to sacrifice any women. A total of 16 males were thrown overboard, including no members of the crew. (Two women were believed to have jumped overboard.) The remainder were rescued, and the defendant, one of the crewmen, was convicted of manslaughter. A principle concern of the court was the method by which the victims to be sacrificed were selected. The jury was instructed that the crew, but for a sufficient number to manage the ship, must go first. Further, "There should be consultation, and some mode of selection fixed, by which those in equal relations may have equal chance for their life." The defendant was sentenced to a term of six months and a fine of $20.00. A note appears at the end of the case report: "Considerable sympathy having been excited in favour of Holmes, by the popular press, an effort was made by several persons, and particularly by the Seamen's Friend Society, to obtain a pardon from the executive. President Tyler refused, however, to grant any pardon, in consequence of the court's not uniting in the application. The penalty was subsequently remitted."

(3) The *Dudley & Stephens* and *Holmes* cases inspired Professor Lon Fuller's famous jurisprudential puzzle, *The Case of the Speluncean Explorers*, 62 Harv. L. Rev. 616 (1949).

Kant, The Metaphysical Elements of Justice

138–39

Judicial punishment (*poena forensis*) is entirely distinct from natural punishment (*poena naturalis*). In natural punishment, vice punishes itself, and this fact is not taken into consideration by the legislator. Judicial punishment can never be used merely as a means to promote some other good for the criminal himself or for civil society, but instead it must in all cases be imposed on him only on the ground that he has committed a crime; for a human being can never be manipulated merely as a means to the purposes of someone else and can never be confused with the objects of the Law of things [Sachenrecht]. His innate personality [that is, his right as a person] protects him against such treatment, even though he may indeed be condemned to lose his civil personality. He must first be found to be deserving of punishment before any consideration is given to the utility of this punishment for himself or for his fellow citizens. The law concerning punishment is a categorical imperative, and woe to him who rummages around in the winding paths of a theory of happiness looking for some advantage to be gained by releasing the criminal from punishment or by reducing the amount of it—in keeping with the Pharisaic motto: "It is better that one man should die than that the whole people should perish." If legal justice perishes, then it is no longer worthwhile for men to remain alive on this earth. If this is so, what should one think of the proposal to permit a criminal who has been condemned to death to remain alive, if, after consenting to allow dangerous experiments to be made on him, he happily survives such experiments and if doctors thereby obtain new information that benefits the community? Any court of justice would repudiate such a proposal with scorn if it were suggested by a medical college, for [legal] justice ceases to be justice if it can be bought for a price.

What kind and what degree of punishment does public legal justice adopt as its principle and standard? None other than the principle of equality (illustrated by the pointer on the scales of justice), that is, the principle of not treating one side more favorably than the other. Accordingly, any undeserved evil that you inflict on someone else among the people is one that you do to yourself. If you vilify him, you vilify yourself; if you steal from him, you steal from yourself; if you kill him, you kill yourself. Only the Law of retribution (*jus talionis*) can determine exactly the kind and degree of punishment; it must be well understood, however, that this determination [must be made] in the chambers of a court of justice (and not in your private judgment). All other standards fluctuate back and forth and, because extraneous considerations are mixed with them, they cannot be compatible with the principle of pure and strict legal justice.

United States v. Bergman

United States District Court, Southern District of New York
416 F. Supp. 496 (1976)

Sentencing Memorandum

FRANKEL, DISTRICT JUDGE.

Defendant is being sentenced upon his plea of guilty to two counts of an 11-count indictment. The sentencing proceeding is unusual in some respects. It has been the subject of more extensive submissions, written and oral, than this court has ever received upon such an occasion. The court has studied some hundreds of pages of memoranda and exhibits, plus scores of volunteered letters. A broad array of issues has been addressed. Imaginative suggestions of law and penology have been tendered. A preliminary conversation with counsel, on the record, preceded the usual sentencing hearing. Having heard counsel again and the defendant speaking for himself, the court postponed the pronouncement of sentence for further reconsideration of thoughts generated during the days of studying the briefs and oral pleas. It seems fitting now to report in writing the reasons upon which the court concludes that defendant must be sentenced to a term of four months in prison.[1]

1. The court considered, and finally rejected, imposing a fine in addition to the prison term. Defendant seems destined to pay hundreds of thousands of dollars in restitution. The amount is being

I. Defendant and His Crimes

Defendant appeared until the last couple of years to be a man of unimpeachably high character, attainments, and distinction. A doctor of divinity and an ordained rabbi, he has been acclaimed by people around the world for his works of public philanthropy, private charity, and leadership in educational enterprises. Scores of letters have come to the court from across this and other countries reporting debts of personal gratitude to him for numerous acts of extraordinary generosity. (The court has also received a kind of petition, with fifty-odd signatures, in which the signers, based upon learning acquired as newspaper readers, denounce the defendant and urge a severe sentence. Unlike the pleas for mercy, which appear to reflect unquestioned facts inviting compassion, this document should and will be disregarded.) In addition to his good works, defendant has managed to amass considerable wealth in the ownership and operation of nursing homes, in real estate ventures, and in a course of substantial investments.

Beginning about two years ago, investigations of nursing homes in this area, including questions of fraudulent claims for Medicaid funds, drew to a focus upon this defendant among several others. The results that concern us were the present indictment and two state indictments. After extensive pretrial proceedings, defendant embarked upon the elaborate plea negotiations with both state and federal prosecutors. A state guilty plea and the instant plea were entered in March of this year. (Another state indictment is expected to be dismissed after defendant is sentenced on those to which he has pled guilty.) As part of the detailed plea arrangements, it is expected that the prison sentence imposed by this court will comprise the total covering the state as well as the federal convictions.[2]

For purposes of the sentence now imposed, the precise details of the charges, and of defendant's carefully phrased admissions of guilt, are not matters of prime importance. Suffice it to say that the plea on Count One (carrying a maximum of five years in prison and a $10,000 fine) confesses defendant's knowing and willful participation in a scheme to defraud the United States in various ways, including the presentation of wrongfully padded claims for payments under the Medicaid program to defendant's nursing homes. Count Three, for which the guilty plea carries a theoretical maximum of three more years in prison and another $5,000 fine, is a somewhat more "technical" charge. Here, defendant admits to having participated in the filing of a partnership return which was false and fraudulent in failing to list people who had bought partnership interests from him in one of his nursing homes, had paid for such interests, and had made certain capital withdrawals.

The conspiracy to defraud, as defendant has admitted it, is by no means the worst of its kind; it is by no means as flagrant or extensive as has been portrayed in the

---

worked out in connection with a state criminal indictment. Apart from defendant's further liabilities for federal taxes, any additional money exaction is appropriately left for the state court.

2. This is not absolutely certain. Defendant has been told, however, that the imposition of any additional prison sentence by the state court will be an occasion for reconsidering today's judgment.

press; it is evidently less grave than other nursing-home wrongs for which others have been convicted or publicized. At the same time, the sentence, as defendant has acknowledged, is imposed for two federal felonies including, as the more important, a knowing and purposeful conspiracy to mislead and defraud the Federal Government.

II. The Guiding Principles of Sentencing

Proceeding through the short list of the supposed justifications for criminal sanctions, defense counsel urge that no licit purpose could be served by defendant's incarceration. Some of these arguments are plainly sound; others are not.

The court agrees that this defendant should not be sent to prison for "rehabilitation." Apart from the patent inappositeness of the concept to this individual, this court shares the growing understanding that no one should ever be sent to prison *for rehabilitation.* That is to say, nobody who would not otherwise be locked up should suffer that fate on the incongruous premise that it will be good for him or her. Imprisonment is punishment. Facing the simple reality should help us to be civilized. It is less agreeable to confine someone when we deem it an affliction rather than a benefaction. If someone must be imprisoned—for other, valid reasons—we should seek to make rehabilitative resources available to him or her. But the goal of rehabilitation cannot fairly serve in itself as grounds for the sentence to confinement.[3]

Equally clearly, this defendant should not be confined to incapacitate him. He is not dangerous. It is most improbable that he will commit similar, or any, offenses in the future. There is no need for "specific deterrence."

Contrary to counsel's submissions, however, two sentencing considerations demand a prison sentence in this case:

> *First,* the aim of *general deterrence,* the effort to discourage similar wrongdoing by others through a reminder that the law's warnings are real and that the grim consequence of imprisonment is likely to follow from crimes of deception for gain like those defendant has admitted.
>
> *Second,* the related, but not identical, concern that any lesser penalty would, in the words of the Model Penal Code, 7.01(1)(c), "depreciate the seriousness of the defendant's crime."

Resisting the first of these propositions, defense counsel invoke Immanuel Kant's axiom that "one man ought never to be dealt with merely as a means subservient to the purposes of another."[4]

In a more novel, but equally futile, effort, counsel urge that a sentence for general deterrence "would violate the Eighth Amendment proscription against cruel and unusual punishment." Treating the latter point first, because it is a short subject, it may be observed simply that if general deterrence as a sentencing purpose were now to

---

3. This important point, correcting misconceptions still widely prevalent, is developed more fully by Dean Norval Morris in *The Future of Imprisonment* (1974).

4. Quoting from I. Kant, *Philosophy of Law* 1986 (Hastie Trans. 1887).

be outlawed, as against a near unanimity of views among state and federal jurists, the bolt would have to come from a place higher than this.[5]

As for Dr. Kant, it may well be that defense counsel mistake his meaning in the present context.[6]

Whether or not that is so, and without pretending to have authority on that score, we take the widely accepted stance that a criminal punished in the interest of general deterrence is not being employed "*merely* as a means...." Reading Kant to mean that every man must be deemed *more* than the instrument of others, and must "always be treated as an end in himself,"[7] the humane principle is not offended here. Each of us is served by the enforcement of the law—not least a person like the defendant in this case, whose wealth and privileges, so long enjoyed, are so much founded upon law. More broadly, we are driven regularly in our ultimate interests as members of the community to use ourselves and each other, in war and in peace, for social ends. One who has transgressed against the criminal laws is certainly among the more fitting candidates for a role of this nature. This is no arbitrary selection. Warned in advance of the prospect, the transgressor has chosen, in the law's premises, "between keeping the law required for society's protection or paying the penalty."[8]

But the whole business, defendant argues further, is guesswork; we are by no means certain that deterrence "works." The position is somewhat overstated; there is, in fact, some reasonably "scientific" evidence for the efficacy of criminal sanctions as deterrents, at least as against some kinds of crimes.[9] Moreover, the time is not yet here when all we can "know" must be quantifiable and digestible by computers. The shared wisdom of generations teaches meaningfully, if somewhat amorphously, that the utilitarians have a point; we do, indeed, lapse often into rationality and act to seek pleasure and avoid pain.[10] It would be better, to be sure, if we had more certainty and precision. Lacking these comforts, we continue to include among our working hypotheses a belief (with some concrete evidence in its support) that crimes like those in this case—deliberate, purposeful, continuing, non-impulsive, and committed for profit—are among those most likely to be generally deterrable by sanctions most shunned by those exposed to temptation.[11]

---

5. To a large extent the defendant's eighth amendment argument is that imprisoning him because he has been "newsworthy" would be cruelly wrong. This thought is accepted by the court without approaching the Constitution. (See below.) The reference at this point is meant to acknowledge, if only to reject, a seemingly broader submission.

6. *See* H. L. A. Hart, *Punishment and Responsibility* 243–44 (1968).

7. Andenaes, *The Morality of Deterrence*, 37 U. Chi. L. Rev. 649 (1970). *See also* O. Holmes, *Common Law* 43–44, 46–47 (1881).

8. H. L. A. Hart, *supra* note 6, at 23.

9. *See, e.g.*, F. Zimring and G. Hawkins, *Deterrence* 168–71, 282 (1973).

10. *See* Andenaes, *supra* note 7, at 663–64.

11. For some supporting evidence that "white-collar" offenses are somewhat specially deterrable, *see* Chambliss, *Types of Deviance and the Effectiveness of Legal Sanctions*, 1967 Wis. L. Rev. 703, 708–10.

The idea of avoiding depreciation of the seriousness of the offense implicates two or three thoughts, not always perfectly clear or universally agreed upon, beyond the idea of deterrence. It should be proclaimed by the court's judgment that the offenses are grave, not minor or purely technical. Some attention must be paid to the demand for equal justice; it will not do to leave the penalty of imprisonment a dead letter as against "privileged" violators while it is employed regularly, and with vigor, against others. There probably is in these conceptions an element of retributiveness, as counsel urge. And retribution, so denominated, is in some disfavor as a reason for punishment. It remains a factor, however, as Holmes perceived,[12] and as is known to anyone who talks to judges, lawyers, defendants, or people generally. It may become more palatable, and probably more humanely understood, under the rubric of "deserts" or "just deserts [sic]."[13] However the concept is formulated, we have not yet reached a state, supposing we ever should, in which the infliction of punishments for crime may be divorced generally from ideas of blame-worthiness, recompense, and proportionality.

Comments

(1) *Cf. United States v. Rannazzisi*, 434 F. Supp. 619 (S.D.N.Y. 1977), where the sentence of a government meat inspector convicted of accepting bribes from dealers was reduced from 18 months to one year. In support of his motion to reduce the sentence, defendant urged "(1) the hardship that the sentence has brought his family; (2) that it will prevent his attendance at the forthcoming wedding of his daughter in early next September; (3) that mortgage payments and other indebtedness cannot be met unless he is in a position to earn money; and (4) that he cooperated with the office of the United States Attorney in its endeavor to learn the full extent of the culpability of other meat inspectors and meat packers constantly engaged in the nefarious practice of what in essence amounts to bribe giving and bribe taking between the two." *Id.* at 620. The court found the request "totally without merit and accordingly den[ied] it in all respects," but nevertheless concluded that "[b]ased exclusively on our independent study of the family here involved, and the almost disastrous effects on them of the sentence imposed, we regard it only meet and proper, on the Court's own motion, to reduce the sentence to one year." *Id.* at 625. The court also ordered that the defendant be given four days leave from the prison to attend his daughter's wedding.

(2) "Kant ... does not opt for retributivism as a bit of intuitive moral knowledge. Rather he offers a theory of punishment that is based on his general view that political obligation is to be analyzed, quasi-contractually, in terms of reciprocity. If the law is to remain just, it is important to guarantee that those who disobey it will not gain an unfair advantage over those who do obey voluntarily. It is important that no man profit from his own criminal wrongdoing, and a certain kind of 'profit' (*i.e.*, not bearing the burden of self-restraint) is intrinsic in wrongdoing. Criminal punishment, then, has as its object the restoration of a proper balance between benefit and obe-

12. *See* O. Holmes, *Common Law* 41–42, 45 (1881).

13. *See* A. von Hirsch, *Doing Justice* 45–55 (1976); *see also* N. Norris, *The Future of Imprisonment* 73–77 (1974).

dience. The criminal himself has no complaint, because he has rationally consented to or willed his own punishment. That is, those very rules which he has broken work, when they are obeyed by others, to his own advantage as a citizen. He would have chosen such rules for himself and others in the original position of choice. And, since he derives and voluntarily accepts benefits from their operation, he owes his own obedience as a debt to his fellow-citizens for their sacrifices in maintaining them." Murphy, *Marxism and Retribution*, 2 Phil. & Pub. Affairs 217, 228 (1973).

(3) "I cannot reconcile a policy of sending poorly educated burglars from the ghetto to jail when men in the highest positions of public trust and authority receive judicial coddling when they are caught fleecing their constituencies. Penology's recent enchantment with rehabilitation as a wholesale justification for imprisonment has dissolved in the face of numerous studies proving that rehabilitation rarely occurs. A minority of the prison population are rightfully locked up because they are too dangerous to release. If we are to justify imprisonment for the rest, it must be on the grounds of punishment or deterrence. And if this is our premise, the white-collar criminal must come to expect equal or greater treatment than the common, non-violent thief. The consequences of a white-collar property crime tend to reach a higher magnitude in direct proportion to the level of status and power held by the criminal involved." District Judge Skopil in *Browder v. United States*, 398 F. Supp. 1042, 1046 (D. Or. 1975), *aff'd*, 544 F.2d 525 (9th Cir. 1976).

United States v. Jackson

United States Court of Appeals, Seventh Circuit
835 F.2d 1195 (1987), *cert. denied*, 485 U.S. 969 (1988)

EASTERBROOK, CIRCUIT JUDGE.

Thirty minutes after being released from prison, to which he had been sent on conviction of two bank robberies, Dwight Jackson robbed another bank. He was let out as part of a "work release" program and returned to his old line of work. Told to get a job, he decided to do a bank job.... Jackson was back in prison before the sun set on the day of his release....

The imposition of life in prison on Jackson was permissible. The selection of a sentence within the statutory range is essentially free of appellate review.... Armed bank robbery on the day of release—following earlier armed robbery convictions back to 1973—marked Jackson as a career criminal. Special deterrence had failed. The court was entitled to consider general deterrence and incapacitation. Although life without possibility of parole is the upper end of the scale of sanctions (short of capital punishment), the statute reflects a judgment that career criminals who persist in possessing weapons should be dealt with most severely.... If this sentence is unduly harsh, the holder of the clemency power may supply a remedy....

POSNER, CIRCUIT JUDGE, concurring.

I join the opinion and judgment of the court; but I think the sentence Jackson received is too harsh and I think it appropriate to point this out even though he presents no ground on which we are authorized to set aside an excessively severe sentence.

Jackson is unquestionably a dangerous and hardened criminal. He has been convicted of armed robbery four times (three were bank robberies—all of the same bank!); in each robbery he was carrying a loaded gun. I do not mean to denigrate the gravity of his offenses by pointing out that he has never inflicted a physical injury; but that fact is relevant to deciding whether the sheer enormity of his conduct warrants imprisonment for the rest of his life as a matter of retributive justice. It does not. Few murderers, traitors, or rapists are punished so severely—a good example being the life sentences, with parole eligibility after 10 years, imposed on two federal prisoners for first-degree murder, each having previously murdered three people, in *United States v. Fountain*, 768 F.2d 790, 799–800 (7th Cir. 1985). The grounds for the sentence in this case must be sought elsewhere.

One ground, the one articulated by the district judge, is the need to prevent Jackson from committing further crimes. There is little doubt that if he were released tomorrow he would commit a bank robbery, perhaps the same day. But it is extremely unlikely that if he were released 25 or 30 years from now (he is 35 years old) he would resume his career as a bank robber. We know that criminal careers taper off with age, although with the aging of the population and the improvements in the health of the aged the fraction of crimes committed by the elderly is rising. *See* Newman et al., *Elderly Criminals*, ch. 2 (1984). Crimes that involve a risk of physical injury to the criminal are especially a young man's game. In 1986 more than 62 percent of all persons arrested for robbery (any sort of robbery—I can find no breakdown by type of robbery) were below the age of 25, and only 3.4 percent were 60 years old or older. FBI, *Uniform Crime Reports*, 20, 174–75, 180 (1986). The only age group that accounted for a smaller percentage of arrests for robbery than persons 60 to 64, or 65 and older, were children below the age of 10—and, remarkably, there were almost as many arrests in that group as there were of persons in the 65 and over group (199 versus 209). *Id.* at 174–75. Bank robbery in particular, I suspect, is a young man's crime. A bank robber must be willing to confront armed guards and able to make a quick getaway. To suppose that if Jackson is fortunate enough to live on in prison into his seventies or eighties it would still be necessary to detain him lest he resume his life of crime after almost a lifetime in prison is too speculative to warrant imprisoning him until he dies of old age....

The remaining possibility is that this savage sentence is proper *pour encourager les autres*. Indeed, deterrence is the surest ground for punishment, since retributive norms are so unsettled and since incapacitation may, by removing one offender from the pool of offenders, simply make a career in crime more attractive to someone else, who is balanced on the razor's edge between criminal and legitimate activity and who now faces reduced competition in the crime "market." *See* Ehrlich, *On the Usefulness of Controlling Individuals: An Economic Analysis of Rehabilitation, Incapacitation, and Deterrence*, 71 Am. Econ. Rev. 307 (1981). Thus, even if one were sure that Jackson would be as harmless as a mouse in the last 10, or 15, or 20 years of his life, his sentence might be justified if the example of it were likely to deter other people, similarly situated, from committing such crimes. This is possible, but speculative; it was not mentioned by the district judge.

We should ask how many 35 year olds would rob a bank if they knew that if they were caught it would mean 20 years in prison with no possibility of parole (the sentence I would have given Jackson if I had been the sentencing judge), compared to the number who would do so if it would mean life in prison. Probably very few would be deterred by the incremental sentence. Bank robbery is a crime of acquisition, not of passion; the only gains are financial—and are slight (in 1986 the average "take" from a bank robbery was $2,664, *see* Uniform Crime Reports, *supra*, at 18). The net gains, when the expected cost of punishment is figured in, must be very small indeed. Although I can find no statistics on clearance rates for bank robbery, my impression is that most bank robbers are caught; and certainly conviction rates are high (90 percent in federal prosecutions for bank robbery) and average punishments severe (more than 13 years for federal defendants), *see* U.S. Dep't. of Justice, Bureau of Justice Statistics, *Sourcebook of Criminal Justice Statistics*—1986, at 354, 356 (tabs. 5.15, 5.16). It's a losers' game at best. Persons who would go ahead and rob a bank in the face of my hypothetical 20-year sentence are unlikely to be deterred by tightening the punishment screws still further. A civilized society locks up such people until age makes them harmless but it does not keep them in prison until they die.

Comments and Questions

(1) Judge Posner acknowledges that Jackson presents no argument which would warrant the court of appeal's vacation of the sentence to life imprisonment without parole. His quarrel is with the judgment of the legislature which permits such a sentence to be imposed in this case, or at most, that had he been the sentencing judge he would have exercised his discretion differently. Do you agree that Judge Posner's critique of the law and its application is "appropriate"?

(2) In a subsequent proceeding, Jackson moved for a reduction of his sentence. *United States v. Jackson*, 780 F. Supp. 1508 (N.D. Ill. 1991). District Judge Duff noted that the sentencing recommendation of the probation officer included, *inter alia*, the fact that Jackson had persistently denied his guilt, had attempted to murder an army colonel in Vietnam and assaulted a sergeant, and had offered no clear response when asked what he would have done had he been confronted by a bank guard with his pistol drawn. He then took umbrage of Judge Posner's comments in the following passage:

> Judge Posner does not consider whether strong-arm robberies are more frequent than armed robberies, or whether old persons more frequently "snatch and run," or physically roll their victims, or beat them, *etc.*, than do younger, stronger, quicker men. Nor do the statistics offered suggest whether there are fewer recidivists on the streets because more of them are in jail in their later years. The Judge suspects that bank robbery is more of a young man's crime than an old man's crime because a bank robber must be willing to confront armed guards and able to make a quick getaway.... Well, a gun

> helps any robber, young or old, and a car helps any robber, young or old, but either a gun or a car tolerates the strong possibility of victims. It would appear that the Judge has never heard of the most famous bank robber of our time, the nefarious Willie Sutton, who when asked, in his seventies, why he continued to rob banks, replied "Because that's where the money is."
>
> ...
>
> The concurring opinion amazingly brings Law and Economics into the equation and suggests, apparently with careful thought, ... that incapacitation may, by imprisoning Mr. Jackson, "simply make a career in crime more attractive to someone else ... who now faces reduced competition in the crime 'market.'" ... Unless, of course, deterrence works, a proposition the concurring opinion finds possible but speculative. Taking the suggestion to heart, the court is deeply concerned that by sentencing Mr. Jackson to prison it may have seduced some irresolute person into the bank robbery "market."
>
> ...
>
> In concentrating on the issue of bank robberies from an economic standpoint, the concurring opinion notes that the gains from such crimes are slight.... The concurring opinion points out that in 1986 the average "take" from a bank robbery was $2,664.... It doesn't point out that bank robberies were ten times more lucrative that year than other robberies, or that the successive "takes" of this defendant were many thousands more than the average.... Many bank robbers are "green" and scared note-passers—Mr. Jackson was neither.

The court denied the motion for reduction of sentence, with the caveat that should Jackson maintain a good record in prison he might at some future date petition the President for clemency.

Posner, *Optimal Sentence for White-Collar Criminals*

17 Am. Crim. L. Rev. 409, 409–11, 414–15 (1980)

I shall ... use the term "white-collar crime" to refer to the nonviolent crimes typically committed by either (1) well-to-do individuals or (2) associations, such as business corporations and labor unions, which are generally "well-to-do" compared to the common criminal. White-collar crime in the sense I use it is illustrated by the criminal offenses created by the securities laws, the labor laws, the antitrust laws, other regulatory statutes, and the income-tax laws. But not every offender under such laws is a white-collar criminal as I use the term. A waitress, for example, could commit a criminal violation of the tax laws by not reporting her tips as income; but because ... the affluence of the offender is very important to the correct punishment for the offense, I would not describe *her* offense as a white-collar crime. Nor would a murder committed by a wealthy person—or by a criminal gang seeking to monopolize the garbage-collection business of a city, for example—be a white-collar crime.... To summarize, white-collar crimes are those more likely to be committed by the affluent than by the poor criminal—crimes that involve fraud, monopoly, and breach of faith rather than violence. The white-collar criminal is the affluent perpetrator of those crimes.

... [T]he white-collar criminal as I have defined him should be punished only by monetary penalties—by fines (where civil damages or penalties are inadequate or inappropriate), rather than by imprisonment or other "afflictive" punishments (save as they may be necessary to coerce payment of the monetary penalty). In a social cost-benefit analysis of the choice between fining and imprisoning the white-collar criminal, the cost side of the analysis favors fining because ... the cost of collecting a fine from one who can pay it (an important qualification) is lower than the cost of imprisonment. On the benefit side, there is no difference in principle between the sanctions. The fine for a white-collar crime can be set at whatever level imposes the same disutility on the defendant, and thus yield the same deterrence, as the prison sentence that would have been imposed instead. Hence, fining the affluent offender is preferable to imprisoning him from society's standpoint because it is less costly and no less efficacious.

The reason that the fine is the cheaper sanction is that, unlike imprisonment, it is a transfer payment. Because the dollars collected from the criminal as a fine show up on the benefit side of the social ledger, the net social cost is limited to the costs of collecting the fine. A term of imprisonment, on the other hand, yields no comparable social revenue if we disregard the negligible, and nowadays usually zero, output of the prisoner. On the contrary, to the social costs of imprisonment must be added the considerable sums spent on maintaining prisoners. To be sure, for a middle-class offender, a short prison term might be the deterrent equivalent of a large fine. But it would not follow that the social costs of the short prison term were correspondingly low, because the greater one's income, the greater is the cost of imprisonment in lost earnings. As long as these are earnings in legitimate occupations, their loss is a social cost similar to the cost of the prison guards. The large fine avoids these costs.

I anticipate relatively little disagreement with the proposition that fines are cheaper to society than imprisonment when the offender can pay the fine. I expect great resistance, however, to the proposition that the social *benefits* of punishment are no greater when punishment takes the form of imprisonment than when it takes the form of a fine. It will be argued that there is no monetary equivalent to the pain of imprisonment, perhaps especially to the affluent, educated, "sensitive" person—the white-collar criminal—that would be within his power to pay. (The offender here is necessarily an individual: a corporation or other "artificial" person cannot, of course, be punished by imprisonment.) But whether this is so depends, in a theoretical analysis, on the gravity of the crime in relation to the probability of apprehension and conviction, and, in a practical analysis, on the severity of the prison sentences actually imposed for white-collar crimes. As to the first, it is no doubt true that very few people would consider a fine of any size to be as severe a punishment as death, or imprisonment for life, or, perhaps, imprisonment for twenty years. Thus, if there are optimal punishments (putting aside the consideration that imprisonment is more costly to administer), it might indeed be difficult to find a monetary equivalent. Perhaps these are optimal punishments for some white-collar crimes. If so, my proposal to substitute fines for prison for white-collar criminals is in serious difficulty—but only in a rather academic sense. For whatever may be theoretically optimal, white-collar criminals, at least in this country, are not punished by death or long prison terms.... With the (surprising) exception of securities offenses, the prison sentences for white-collar crimes—when prison sentences are imposed on the perpetrators of such crimes—barely exceed two years. Even this figure greatly exaggerates the actual time served behind bars, which is shortened by parole and time off for good behavior.

Perhaps, as I have suggested, these prison terms are too short given the gravity of the crimes and the difficulty of detecting them. That is a large question that I do not propose to investigate here. I shall instead treat the existing level of imprisonment for white-collar crimes as part of the background of the analysis. Given that level, it is highly improbable that there is *no* fine equivalent to a prison sentence in the amount of disutility it imposes on the offender.

...

I turn now to what seems a separate, but is really the same, objection to substituting fines for imprisonment in white-collar crimes: namely, that a system in which poor offenders were usually imprisoned and rich offenders usually fined would be a system that discriminated against poor people. This argument is just a variant of the fallacy that imprisonment is inherently more punitive than fines. It gains some plausibility only from the ridiculous "rates of exchange" that used to be commonplace in crimes where the criminal had the option of paying a fine or going to jail, a practice that has been invalidated by the Supreme Court under the Equal Protection Clause of the fourteenth amendment. The assumption behind this argument, however, is false. For every prison sentence there is some fine equivalent; if the fine is so large that it cannot be collected, then the offender should be imprisoned. How then are the rich favored under such a system?

A possible answer is that the rich could "buy" more crime under a fine system than under an imprisonment system. Suppose that the expected cost to society of a crime is $100, the probability of apprehension and conviction is 10 percent, and therefore the fine is set at $1,000 so that expected punishment cost will be equal to the expected social cost. A rich man would not be deterred from committing this crime as long as the expected benefits to him were greater than $1,000. But now suppose that instead of a fine of $1,000, a prison term of one month is imposed for this crime based on a study which shows that the disutility of a month in prison to an average person is $1,000. Since the disutility of imprisonment rises with income, this form of punishment will deter the rich man more than the poor one. Stated differently, a nominally uniform prison term has the effect of price discrimination based on income.

But this is not to say that a system of fines discriminates against the poor. It is rather that a *uniform* prison term discriminates against the rich compared with a *uniform* fine. If we want to discriminate against the rich through a fine system, that is easily done by progressively varying the fine with the offender's income. If we want not to discriminate against the rich through an imprisonment system, we can make the length of the sentence inverse to the offender's income. In either case the choice to discriminate is independent of the form of punishment.

Richards, *Human Rights and the Moral Foundation of the Substantive Criminal Law**

13 Ga. L. Rev. 1395, 1414–20 (1979)

The Moral Foundations of the Criminal Law

It is an uncontroversial truth that the criminal law rests on the enforcement of public morality, *viz.*, that criminal penalties, *inter alia*, identify and stigmatize certain moral wrongs which society at large justifiably condemns as violations of the moral decency whose observance defines the minimum boundary conditions of civilized social life.[94] ... [L]ittle critical attention has yet been given in Anglo-American law to the proper explication of the public morality in light of considerations of human rights to which constitutional democracy is in general committed. Rather, legal theory and practice has tended to acquiesce in a quite questionable identification of the public morality with social convention.[95] We are now in a position to articulate an alternative account of the moral foundations of the substantive criminal law, which can illuminate various criminal law and related constitutional law doctrines and the proper direction of criminal law reform.

The substantive criminal law and cognate principles of constitutional law rest on the same ethical foundations: the fundamental ethical imperative that each person should extend to others the same respect and concern that one demands for one's self, as a free and rational being with the higher-order capacities to take responsibility for the form of one's life. Whether one uses Rawls's maximizing contractarian hypothesis or Gewirth's universalization of rationally autonomous people, the consequence is, for purposes of the criminal law, the same. Certain basic principles are agreed to or universalized, as basic principles of critical morality, because they secure, at little comparable cost to agents acting on them, forms of action or forbearance from action that rational persons would want guaranteed as minimal conditions of advancing the responsible pursuit of their ends, whatever they are; furthermore, these principles will be so fundamental in securing either a higher lowest (Rawls) or the conditions of rational autonomy (Gewirth) that, in general, coercion will be viewed as justified, as a last resort, in getting people to conform their conduct to these principles. Accordingly, these principles are commonly referred to as the ethical principles of obligation and duty, which define correlative rights.

---

94. Hart, *The Aims of the Criminal Law*, 23 Law & Contemp. Prob. 401 (1958); Feinberg, *The Expressive Function of Punishment*, in Doing and Deserving 95–118 (1970); Butler, *Upon Resentment*, in Fifteen Sermons at the Rolls Chapel 102 (1913); Stephen, *"Punishment and Public Morality,"* from 2 *A History of the Criminal Law of England* 30–37, 90–93 (1885).

95. Richards, *Unnatural Acts and the Constitutional Right to Privacy*, 45 Fordham L. Rev. 1281, 1334–46 (1977).

One fundamental distinction between these principles of obligation and duty is that some apply in a state of nature whether or not people are in institutional relations to one another, whereas others arise because of the special benefits that life in institutions and communities makes possible; I shall refer to the former as natural duties, the latter as institutional duties and obligations. With respect to natural duties, the principles include, at a minimum, a principle of nonmalfeasance (not killing, inflicting harm, or gratuitous cruelty), mutual aid (securing a great good, like saving life, at little cost to the agent), consideration (not annoying or gratuitously violating the privacy of others), and paternalism (saving a person from impaired or undeveloped rationality likely to result in death or severe and irreparable harm). With respect to institutional duties and obligations, the principles include basic principles of justice which regulate such institutions (legal and economic systems, conventions of promise-keeping and truth-telling, family and educational structure) and in appropriate circumstances require compliance with the requirements of such institutions (for example, respecting certain property rights). Now, all these principles of obligation and duty—natural and institutional—are formulated in quite complex terms; and priority relations are established among them to determine how, in general, conflicting obligations should be resolved and what the relative moral seriousness of offenses would be (the infliction of death, for example, is a graver violation of integrity than a minor battery). I shall touch on some of these complexities in the discussion below of particular criminal law doctrines. The general nature of such principles and their derivation from the moral imperative of treating persons as equals, however, seem clear: Such principles secure to all persons on fair terms basic forms of action and forbearance from action which rational persons would want enforceably guaranteed as conditions and ingredients of living a life of self-critical integrity and self-respect; correlatively, such principles define human or moral rights, whose weight as grounds for enforceable demands rests on the underlying moral principles of obligation and duty which justify such enforceable demands. Other moral principles are also agreed to or universalized, but they fall in an area, supererogation, which is not our present concern.

Because all the moral principles of obligation and duty are the proper objects of the use of force or coercion (an evil), ethical principles are agreed to or universalized that govern the distribution of this evil. Enforcement of such principles in the law takes place through the criminal law and the private remedies of the civil law (contracts, torts). While both the criminal and civil law rest on the moral foundations of the moral principles of obligation and duty, the grounds of enforcement differ in both cases: the criminal law rests on the punitive upholding of basic standards of moral decency, the civil law on moral principles of compensation. While some moral principles are enforced under both bodies of law (for example, the criminal and civil law of assault), others are enforced only under one body of law (for example, American law tends to prefer the civil law to remedy breaches of contract, where the promisee has the moral and legal right to extinguish or enforce the obligation). The concern here is only with the ethical principles relevant to the just imposition of criminal sanctions, *viz.*, the principles of punishment. Generally, at least four relevant principles regulate the use of criminal sanctions to enforce moral obligations and duties.

First, the Kantian interpretation of treating persons as equals importantly puts special constraints on the imposition of criminal penalties for violations of moral duties and obligations, namely, that sanctions be applied only to persons who broke a reasonably specific law, who had the full capacity and opportunity to obey the law, and who could reasonably have been expected to know that such a law existed. In this way, each person is guaranteed a greatest liberty, capacity, and opportunity for controlling and predicting the consequences of one's actions, compatible with a like liberty, capacity, and opportunity for all. Such a principle can be agreed to or universalized because it is a rational way to secure general respect for and compliance with moral principles at a tolerable cost. Because criminal sanctions are a form of humiliating stigma, persons in Rawls's original position or Gewirth's equivalent would limit the application of such sanctions in order to secure a higher lowest than that allowed by alternative principles; for these conditions provide the fullest possible opportunity for people to avoid these sanctions if they so choose, or, at least, the fullest possible opportunity within the constraint that some system of coercive enforcement is justified to insure compliance with moral principles of obligation and duty. This principle forbids the application of criminal sanctions to an innocent who has not broken the law or to persons lacking the liberty (the severely coerced), the capacity (the insane, infants, involuntary acts) or full opportunity (those not reasonably apprised of the law) to regulate conduct by the relevant principles, even where the application of sanctions might have some deterrent effect in better enforcing moral principles; it also tends to render immune from criminal sanctions those unintentional actions that result from quite unforeseeable and unavoidable accident, which there was no fair opportunity to avoid. In general, forms of mental state (intent, knowledge, and an individualized standard of negligence) are required as necessary moral conditions of just punishment because the presence of these mental states insures that the person may fairly be said to have the capacity and opportunity to conform conduct to law; to the extent that intentional as opposed to unintentionally negligent actions involve easier or fuller opportunities to regulate conduct by principles, a higher gradation of sanction would, on this view, justly be applied to the former than the latter, other things being equal.

Secondly, given that the application of criminal sanctions is regulated by the principle of equal liberty, capacity, and opportunity, such sanctions must also observe two ethical principles of proportionality. The first principle rests on the purpose of the criminal law to enforce moral principles of obligation and duty: levels of sanctions must reflect the relative moral gravity of underlying moral wrongs. For example, since murder is morally graver than a minor battery, the level of sanction for murder must be greater than that for battery. This proportionality principle says nothing about the level at which sanctions should be set; it requires only that whatever sanctions may be justified on other grounds must reflect relative gravities of underlying moral wrongs. The second moral principle of proportionality is more substantive.

Since, from the ethical point of view of treating persons as equals, persons agree to or universalize principles of just punishment whether they were on the giving or receiving end, rational persons so situated are concerned to place substantive upper limits on the level of sanction that could be applied for moral wrongs in general or certain moral wrongs in particular. For example, certain forms of torture, that are incompatible with respecting human dignity, are ruled out, absent very extreme circumstances. In addition, rational contractors or universalizers place upper limits on sanctions for certain wrongs: death, for example, is never acceptable as an appropriate sanction for a minor battery or theft; such an extreme sanction cannot be rationally acceptable to persons who might be on the giving or receiving end, for the gains in moral conformity are incommensurate to the risks in punishment.

Thirdly, within the constraints of all the above principles, criminal sanctions must satisfy the underlying purpose of affording an effective symbolic statement of minimal moral standards of decency. Effectiveness in this context should be measured by many factors—general deterrence (whether the public example of punishment for a certain crime tends to deter people in general from committing that crime), special deterrence (whether the punishment makes the offender less likely to commit the crime again), atonement and moral reform (whether the punishment leads the criminal to repent the wrongdoing and develop moral character). While theories of punishment commonly distinguish retributive and deterrence aims of criminal justice, I believe that these considerations are, within the constraints of the principles of equal liberty and proportionality, one: the justifying aim of criminal sanctions is to make a symbolic public statement about the importance of respecting certain basic human rights defined by moral principles of obligation and duty. There is, *pace* Kant, no necessary connection between this aim and any particular form or level of criminal sanctions, including prisons. From the point of view of treating persons as equals in which rational persons must agree to or universalize principles acceptable whether on the giving or receiving end, certain constraints are placed on criminal sanctions (including upper limits), but, from this point of view, there is no reason to accept intuitionistic notions of the intrinsic goodness of evil plus pain, or Kant's concept of the abstract obligation to punish evil in the exactly same kind. Rather, the central rational aim of criminal sanctions, from this point of view, is to make the required effective public statement justified by the special moral force of the underlying moral principles of obligation and duty and correlative moral rights. Which sanctions make this statement most effectively is a matter of humane empirical research among alternative forms of sanction to identify which ones best communicate respect for the underlying values of human dignity, including, of course, forms of sanction that respect the moral personality of offenders themselves. One corollary of this approach is that levels of sanctions must be rigorously scrutinized to insure that the same level of effectiveness is not achievable with less severe sanctions, or less severe sanctions more certainly imposed. Any surplusage of sanctions, above the level necessary for their effectiveness, is a morally gratuitous cruelty, because it is the infliction of pain not necessary to a purpose which rational persons would reciprocally agree to or universalize.

Fourthly, on the assumption that a generally just legal system exists, rational persons must agree or universalize that the use of coercion in enforcing moral principles of obligation and duty, justified in an institutional state of nature, must be restricted to the legal system, except for certain special cases discussed below (for example, self-defense). The reason for this has been a prominent point made by the contractarian tradition, especially Locke and Kant: *viz.*, when each individual person, in an institutional state of nature, himself acts as an enforcer of moral duties, he is judge, jury, and executioner in each case, including his own, and this judgment will often be distorted by personal interest and bias, selfish envy, and vindictiveness. The great virtue of a just legal system, where the final appeal in the exercise of coercive power is to a group of impartial interpreters and executors of the law, is that the distortions of judgment and execution, found with an individual in the state of nature, are significantly reduced. This is simply to say that such legal institutions tend to be more just in their distribution of punishment: the persons who violate moral duties and obligation, which the law enforces, are more likely to be punished than in the state of nature, where distortions of judgment lead to applying coercion to the innocent, or applying coercion to the guilty to a degree that is out of all relation to the requirements of effective deterrence. For this reason, when a just legal system exists, coercion is justified in enforcing moral duties and obligations, in general, only when these requirements can be effectively enforced by law; those duties and obligations which cannot be effectively enforced by law must be, at best, left to informal forms of criticism and blame.

Bibliographical Note

Students interested in the jurisprudential aspects of criminal law are encouraged to read Professor Richards' article in its entirety, only a small portion of which is here included. For a more wide-ranging analysis, see D. Richards, *The Moral Criticism of Law* (1977).

Professor Richards makes explicit reference to two prominent theorists in this excerpt. John Rawls is the author of *A Theory of Justice* (1971), which at an earlier point Richards describes as "the most serious and profound attack on utilitarianism since Kant." Alan Gewirth is the author of *Reason and Morality* (1978), which is largely an amplification and criticism of the Rawls treatise.

Other significant works include G. Fletcher, *Rethinking Criminal Law* (1978); R. Dworkin, *Taking Rights Seriously* (1978); and R. Nozick, *Anarchy, State, and Utopia* (1974).

Jones v. City of Los Angeles

United States Court of Appeals, Ninth Circuit
444 F.3d 1118 (2006)

Wardlaw, Circuit Judge.

Six homeless individuals, unable to obtain shelter on the night each was cited or arrested, filed this Eighth Amendment challenge to the enforcement of a City of Los Angeles ordinance that criminalizes sitting, lying, or sleeping on public streets and sidewalks at all times and in all places within Los Angeles's city limits. Appellants seek limited injunctive relief from enforcement of the ordinance during nighttime hours, i.e., between 9:00 p.m. and 6:30 a.m., or at any time against the temporarily infirm or permanently disabled. We must decide whether the Eighth Amendment right to be free from cruel and unusual punishment prohibits enforcement of that law as applied to homeless individuals involuntarily sitting, lying, or sleeping on the street due to the unavailability of shelter in Los Angeles.

Facts and Procedural Background

The facts underlying this appeal are largely undisputed. Edward Jones, Patricia Vinson, George Vinson, Thomas Cash, Stanley Barger, and Robert Lee Purrie ("Appellants") are homeless individuals who live on the streets of Los Angeles's Skid Row district. Appellees are the City of Los Angeles, Los Angeles Police Department ("L.A.P.D.") Chief William Bratton, and Captain Charles Beck ("Appellees" or "the City"). Federal law defines the term "homeless individual" to include

> (1) an individual who lacks a fixed, regular, and adequate nighttime residence; and
>
> (2) an individual who has a primary nighttime residence that is—
>
> > (A) a supervised publicly or privately operated shelter designed to provide temporary living accommodations (including welfare hotels, congregate shelters, and transitional housing for the mentally ill);
> >
> > (B) an institution that provides a temporary residence for individuals intended to be institutionalized; or
> >
> > (C) a public or private place not designed for, or ordinarily used as, a regular sleeping accommodation for human beings.

Stewart B. McKinney Homeless Assistance Act of 1987 § 103(a), 42 U.S.C. § 11302(a) (2000). Appellants are six of the more than 80,000 homeless individuals in Los Angeles County on any given night. *See* L.A. Homeless Servs. Auth., Los Angeles Continuum of Care, Exhibit 1 Narrative, at 2–17 (2001); *see also* Patrick Burns et al., Econ. Roundtable, Homeless in L.A.: A Working Paper for the 10-Year Plan to End Homelessness in Los Angeles County (2003) (estimating that more than 253,000 individuals were homeless in Los Angeles County at some point during 2002).

The term "Skid Row" derives from the lumber industry practice of building a road or track made of logs laid crosswise over which other logs were slid. Christine Ammer,

The American Heritage Dictionary of Idioms 382 (paperback ed. 2003). By the 1930s, the term was used to describe the area of town frequented by loggers and densely populated with bars and brothels. *Id.* Beginning around the end of the nineteenth century, the area now known as Los Angeles's Skid Row became home to a transient population of seasonal laborers as residential hotels began to develop. *See* Mayor's Citizens' Task Force on Cent. City East, To Build a Community 5 (1988). For decades Skid Row has been home for "the down and out, the drifters, the unemployed, and the chronic alcoholic[s]" of Los Angeles. *Id.* Covering fifty city blocks immediately east of downtown Los Angeles, Skid Row is bordered by Third Street to the north, Seventh Street to the south, Alameda Street to the east, and Main Street to the west.

Los Angeles's Skid Row has the highest concentration of homeless individuals in the United States. Charlie LeDuff, *In Los Angeles, Skid Row Resists an Upgrade*, N.Y. Times, July 15, 2003, at A1. According to the declaration of Michael Alvidrez, a manager of single-room-occupancy ("SRO") hotels in Skid Row owned by the Skid Row Housing Trust, since the mid-1970s Los Angeles has chosen to centralize homeless services in Skid Row. *See also* Edward G. Goetz, *Land Use and Homeless Policy in Los Angeles*, 16 Int'l. J. Urb. & Regional Res. 540, 543 (1992) (discussing the City's longstanding "policy of concentrating and containing the homeless in the Skid Row area"). The area is now largely comprised of SRO hotels (multi-unit housing for very low income persons typically consisting of a single room with shared bathroom), shelters, and other facilities for the homeless.

Skid Row is a place of desperate poverty, drug use, and crime, where Porta-Potties serve as sleeping quarters and houses of prostitution. Steve Lopez, *A Corner Where L.A. Hits Rock Bottom*, L.A. Times, Oct. 17, 2005, at A1. Recently, it has been reported that local hospitals and law enforcement agencies from nearby suburban areas have been caught "dumping" homeless individuals in Skid Row upon their release. Cara Mia DiMassa & Richard Winton, *Dumping of Homeless Suspected Downtown*, L.A. Times, Sept. 23, 2005, at A1. This led Los Angeles Mayor Antonio Villaraigosa to order an investigation into the phenomenon in September 2005. Cara Mia DiMassa & Richard Fausset, *Mayor Orders Probe of Skid Row Dumping*, L.A. Times, Sept. 27, 2005, at B1. L.A.P.D. Chief William Bratton, insisting that the Department does not target the homeless but only people who violate city ordinances (presumably including the ordinance at issue), has stated:

> "If the behavior is aberrant, in the sense that it breaks the law, then there are city ordinances.... You arrest them, prosecute them. Put them in jail. And if they do it again, you arrest them, prosecute them, and put them in jail. It's that simple."

Cara Mia DiMassa & Stuart Pfeifer, *2 Strategies on Policing Homeless*, L.A. Times, Oct. 6, 2005, at A1 [hereinafter DiMassa, *Policing Homeless*] (omission in original) (quoting Chief Bratton). This has not always been City policy. The ordinance at issue was adopted in 1968. *See* L.A., Cal., Ordinance 137,269 (Sept. 11, 1968). In the late 1980s, James K. Hahn, who served as Los Angeles City Attorney from 1985 to 2001 and subsequently as Mayor, refused to prosecute the homeless for sleeping in public unless the City provided them with an alternative to the streets. Frederick M. Muir, *No Place Like Home: A Year After Camp Was Closed, Despair Still Reigns on Skid Row*, L.A. Times, Sept. 25, 1988, §2 (Metro), at 1.

For the approximately 11,000–12,000 homeless individuals in Skid Row, space is available in SRO hotels, shelters, and other temporary or transitional housing for only 9000 to 10,000, leaving more than 1000 people unable to find shelter each night. *See* Mayor's Citizens' Task Force, *supra*, at 5. In the County as a whole, there are almost 50,000 more homeless people than available beds. *See* L.A. Homeless Servs. Auth., *supra*, at 2–14. In 1999, the fair market rent for an SRO room in Los Angeles was $379 per month. L.A. Housing Crisis Task Force, In Short Supply 6 (2000). Yet the monthly welfare stipend for single adults in Los Angeles County is only $221. *See* L.A. Homeless Servs. Auth., *supra*, at 2–10. Wait-lists for public housing and for housing assistance vouchers in Los Angeles are three- to ten-years long. *See* The U.S. Conference of Mayors, A Status Report on Hunger and Homelessness in America's Cities 101, 105 (2002) [hereinafter Homelessness Report];[1] L.A. Housing Crisis Task Force, *supra*, at 7.

The result, in City officials' own words, is that "'[t]he gap between the homeless population needing a shelter bed and the inventory of shelter beds is severely large.'" Homelessness Report, *supra*, at 80. As Los Angeles's homeless population has grown, *see id.* at 109 (estimating annualized growth of ten percent in Los Angeles's homeless population in the years up to and including 2003), the availability of low-income housing in Skid Row has shrunk, according to the declaration of Alice Callaghan, director of a Skid Row community center and board member of the Skid Row Housing Trust. According to Callaghan's declaration, at night in Skid Row, SRO hotels, shelters, and other temporary or transitional housing are the only alternatives to sleeping on the street; during the day, two small parks are open to the public. Thus, for many in Skid Row without the resources or luck to obtain shelter, sidewalks are the only place to be.

As will be discussed below, Appellants' declarations demonstrate that they are not on the streets of Skid Row by informed choice. In addition, the Institute for the Study of Homelessness and Poverty reports that homelessness results from mental illness, substance abuse, domestic violence, low-paying jobs, and, most significantly, the chronic lack of affordable housing. Inst. for the Study of Homelessness and Poverty, "Who Is Homeless in Los Angeles?" 3 (2000). It also reports that between 33% and 50% of the homeless in Los Angeles are mentally ill, and 76% percent of homeless adults in 1990 had been employed for some or all of the two years prior to becoming homeless. *Id.* at 2; *see also* Grace R. Dyrness et al., Crisis on the Streets: Homeless Women and Children in Los Angeles 14 (2003) (noting that approximately 14% of homeless individuals in Los Angeles are victims of domestic violence).

---

1. It is unclear on what basis the dissent asserts that this report "does not indicate that Los Angeles was among the cities surveyed," or that it "is the only study in the record." Throughout the report, including on page 96 and on the final page, Los Angeles is named as one of the twenty-five surveyed cities. The record includes more than a half dozen public reports Appellants filed in support of their motion for summary judgment, without objection.

Against this background, the City asserts the constitutionality of enforcing Los Angeles Municipal Code section 41.18(d) against those involuntarily on the streets during nighttime hours, such as Appellants. It provides:

> No person shall sit, lie or sleep in or upon any street, sidewalk or other public way.
>
> The provisions of this subsection shall not apply to persons sitting on the curb portion of any sidewalk or street while attending or viewing any parade permitted under the provisions of Section 103.111 of Article 2, Chapter X of this Code; nor shall the provisions of this subsection supply [sic] to persons sitting upon benches or other seating facilities provided for such purpose by municipal authority by this Code.

L.A., Cal., Mun. Code § 41.18(d) (2005). A violation of section 41.18(d) is punishable by a fine of up to $1000 and/or imprisonment of up to six months. *Id.* § 11.00(m).

Section 41.18(d) is one of the most restrictive municipal laws regulating public spaces in the United States. The City can secure a conviction under the ordinance against anyone who merely sits, lies, or sleeps in a public way at any time of day. Other cities' ordinances similarly directed at the homeless provide ways to avoid criminalizing the status of homelessness by making an element of the crime some conduct in combination with sitting, lying, or sleeping in a state of homelessness. For example, Las Vegas prohibits standing or lying in a public way only when it obstructs pedestrian or vehicular traffic. *See, e.g.*, Las Vegas, Nev., Mun. Code § 10.47.020 (2005) ("It is unlawful to intentionally obstruct pedestrian or vehicular traffic...."). Others, such as Portland, prohibit "camping" in or upon any public property or public right of way. *See, e.g.*, Portland, Or., Mun. Code §§ 14A.50.020,.030 (2006) (prohibiting obstruction of public sidewalks in a designated area or camping on public property). Still others contain safe harbor provisions such as limiting the hours of enforcement. *See, e.g.*, Seattle, Wash., Mun. Code § 15.48.040 (2005) ("No person shall sit or lie down upon a public sidewalk ... during the hours between seven (7:00) a.m. and nine (9:00) p.m. in the following zones...."); Tucson, Ariz., Mun. Code § 11-36.2(a) (2005) (same, except prohibition extended to 10:00 p.m.); Houston, Tex., Mun. Code § 40-352(a) (2006) (same, except prohibition extended to 11:00 p.m.). Other cities include as a required element sitting, lying, or sleeping in clearly defined and limited zones. *See, e.g.*, Philadelphia, Pa., Mun. Code § 10-611(1)(b)–(c), (2)(g)–(h) (2005) (prohibiting sitting or lying in certain designated zones only); Reno, Nev., Mun. Code § 8.12.015(b) (2005) (similar); Seattle, Wash., Mun. Code § 15.48.040 (similar). As a result of the expansive reach of section 41.18(d), the extreme lack of available shelter in Los Angeles, and the large homeless population, thousands of people violate the Los Angeles ordinance every day and night, and many are arrested, losing what few possessions they may have.[2]

---

2. During oral argument, the attorney for the City asserted that L.A.P.D. officers leaflet Skid Row the day before making their section 41.18(d) sweeps to warn the homeless, and do not cite or arrest

Appellants are among them.

Robert Lee Purrie is in his early sixties. He has lived in the Skid Row area for four decades. Purrie sleeps on the streets because he cannot afford a room in an SRO hotel and is often unable to find an open bed in a shelter. Early in the morning of December 5, 2002, Purrie declares that he was sleeping on the sidewalk at Sixth Street and Towne Avenue because he "had nowhere else to sleep." At 5:20 a.m., L.A.P.D. officers cited Purrie for violating section 41.18(d). He could not afford to pay the resulting fine.

Purrie was sleeping in the same location on January 14, 2003, when police officers woke him early in the morning and searched, handcuffed, and arrested him pursuant to a warrant for failing to pay the fine from his earlier citation. The police removed his property from his tent, broke it down, and threw all of his property, including the tent, into the street. The officers also removed the property and tents of other homeless individuals sleeping near Purrie. After spending the night in jail, Purrie was convicted of violating section 41.18(d), given a twelve-month suspended sentence, and ordered to pay $195 in restitution and attorneys' fees. Purrie was also ordered to stay away from the location of his arrest. Upon his release, Purrie returned to the corner where he had been sleeping on the night of his arrest to find that all the belongings he had left behind, including blankets, clothes, cooking utensils, a hygiene kit, and other personal effects, were gone.

Stanley Barger suffered a brain injury in a car accident in 1998 and subsequently lost his Social Security Disability Insurance. His total monthly income consists of food stamps and $221 in welfare payments. According to Barger's declaration, he "want[s] to be off the street" but can only rarely afford shelter. At 5:00 a.m. on December 24, 2002, Barger was sleeping on the sidewalk at Sixth and Towne when L.A.P.D. officers arrested him. Barger was jailed, convicted of violating section 41.18(d), and sentenced to two days time served.

When Thomas Cash was cited for violating section 41.18(d), he had not worked for approximately two years since breaking his foot and losing his job, and had been sleeping on the street or in a Skid Row SRO hotel. Cash suffers from severe kidney problems, which cause swelling of his legs and shortness of breath, making it difficult for him to walk. At approximately noon on January 10, 2003, Cash tired as he walked to the SRO hotel where he was staying. He was resting on a tree stump when L.A.P.D. officers cited him.

Edward Jones's wife, Janet, suffers serious physical and mental afflictions. Edward takes care of her, which limits his ability to find full-time work, though he has held various minimum wage jobs. The Joneses receive $375 per month from the Los Angeles County General Relief program, enabling them to stay in Skid Row SRO hotels for the first two weeks of each month. Because shelters separate men and women, and Janet's disabilities require Edward to care for her, the Joneses are forced to sleep on the streets every month after their General Relief monies run out. At 6:30

---

people for violating section 41.18(d) unless there are open beds in homeless shelters at the time of the violations. No evidence in the record supports these assertions.

a.m. on November 20, 2002, Edward and Janet Jones were sleeping on the sidewalk at the corner of Industrial and Alameda Streets when the L.A.P.D. cited them for violating section 41.18(d).

Patricia and George Vinson, a married couple, were looking for work and a permanent place to live when they were cited for violating section 41.18(d). They use their General Relief payments to stay in motels for part of every month and try to stay in shelters when their money runs out. On the night of December 2, 2002, they missed a bus that would have taken them to a shelter and had to sleep on the sidewalk near the corner of Hope and Washington Streets instead. At 5:30 a.m. the next morning, L.A.P.D. officers cited the Vinsons for violating section 41.18(d).

The record before us includes declarations and supporting documentation from nearly four dozen other homeless individuals living in Skid Row who have been searched, ordered to move, cited, arrested, and/or prosecuted for, and in some cases convicted of, violating section 41.18(d). Many of these declarants lost much or all of their personal property when they were arrested.

On February 19, 2003, Appellants filed a complaint in the United States District Court for the Central District of California pursuant to 42 U.S.C. § 1983. They seek a permanent injunction against the City of Los Angeles and L.A.P.D. Chief William Bratton and Captain Charles Beck (in their official capacities), barring them from enforcing section 41.18(d) in Skid Row between the hours of 9:00 p.m. and 6:30 a.m. Appellants allege that by enforcing section 41.18(d) twenty-four hours a day against persons with nowhere else to sit, lie, or sleep, other than on public streets and sidewalks, the City is criminalizing the status of homelessness in violation of the Eighth and Fourteenth Amendments to the U.S. Constitution, and Article I, sections 7 and 17 of the California Constitution, *see* Cal. Const. art I, § 7 (guaranteeing due process and equal protection); *id.* § 17 (prohibiting cruel and unusual punishment). Appellants abandoned their second claim pursuant to 42 U.S.C. § 1983, alleging violations of a Fourteenth Amendment substantive due process right to treatment for chronic illnesses while in police custody, in the district court. On cross-motions for summary judgment, the district court granted judgment in favor of the City. Relying heavily on *Joyce v. City & County of San Francisco*, 846 F. Supp. 843 (N.D. Cal. 1994), the district court held that enforcement of the ordinance does not violate the Eighth Amendment because it penalizes conduct, not status. This appeal timely followed.

...

The district court erred by not engaging in a more thorough analysis of Eighth Amendment jurisprudence under *Robinson v. California*, 370 U.S. 660, 82 S. Ct. 1417, 8 L. Ed. 2d 758 (1962), and *Powell v. Texas*, 392 U.S. 514, 88 S. Ct. 2145, 20 L. Ed. 2d 1254 (1968), when it held that the only relevant inquiry is whether the ordinance at issue punishes status as opposed to conduct, and that homelessness is not a constitutionally cognizable status.

The district court relied exclusively on the analysis of *Robinson* and *Powell* by another district court in *Joyce v. City and County of San Francisco*, in which plaintiffs challenged certain aspects of San Francisco's comprehensive homelessness program on Eighth Amendment grounds. 846 F. Supp. 843 (N.D. Cal. 1994). *Joyce*, however, was based on a very different factual underpinning than is present here. Called the "Matrix Program," the homelessness program was "'an interdepartmental effort ... [utilizing] social workers and health workers ... [and] offering shelter, medical care, information about services and general assistance.'" *Id.* at 847 (alterations and omissions in original). One element of the program consisted of the "Night Shelter Referral" program conducted by the Police Department, which handed out "referrals" to temporary shelters. *Id.* at 848. The City demonstrated that of 3820 referral slips offered to men, only 1866 were taken and only 678 used. *Id.*

The *Joyce* plaintiffs made only the conclusory allegation that there was insufficient shelter, *id.* at 849; they did not make the strong evidentiary showing of a substantial shortage of shelter Appellants make here. Moreover, the preliminary injunction plaintiffs sought in *Joyce* was so broad as to enjoin enforcement of prohibitions on camping or lodging in public parks and on "'life-sustaining activities *such as* sleeping, sitting or remaining in a public place,'" which might also include such antisocial conduct as public urination and aggressive panhandling. *Id.* at 851 (emphasis added). Reasoning that plaintiffs' requested injunction was too broad and too difficult to enforce, and noting the preliminary nature of its findings based on the record at an early stage in the proceedings, the district court denied the injunction. *Id.* at 851–53. The *Joyce* court also concluded that homelessness was not a status protectable under the Eighth Amendment, holding that it was merely a constitutionally noncognizable "condition." *Id.* at 857–58.

... We disagree with the analysis of *Robinson* and *Powell* conducted by both the district court in *Joyce* and the district court in the case at bar. The City could not expressly criminalize the status of homelessness by making it a crime to be homeless without violating the Eighth Amendment, nor can it criminalize acts that are an integral aspect of that status. Because there is substantial and undisputed evidence that the number of homeless persons in Los Angeles far exceeds the number of available shelter beds at all times, including on the nights of their arrest or citation, Los Angeles has encroached upon Appellants' Eighth Amendment protections by criminalizing the unavoidable act of sitting, lying, or sleeping at night while being involuntarily homeless. A closer analysis of *Robinson* and *Powell* instructs that the involuntariness of the act or condition the City criminalizes is the critical factor delineating a constitutionally cognizable status, and incidental conduct which is integral to and an unavoidable result of that status, from acts or conditions that can be criminalized consistent with the Eighth Amendment.

Our analysis begins with *Robinson*, which announced limits on what the state can criminalize consistent with the Eighth Amendment. In *Robinson*, the Supreme Court considered whether a state may convict an individual for violating a statute making it a criminal offense to "'be addicted to the use of narcotics.'" 370 U.S. at 660, 82 S. Ct. 1417 (quoting Cal. Health & Safety Code § 11721). The trial judge had instructed the jury that

> "[t]o be addicted to the use of narcotics is said to be a status or condition and not an act. It is a continuing offense and differs from most other offenses in the fact that [it] is chronic rather than acute; that it continues after it is complete and subjects the offender to arrest at any time before he reforms.... All that the People must show is ... that while in the City of Los Angeles [Robinson] was addicted to the use of narcotics...."

Id. at 662–63, 82 S. Ct. 1417 (second alteration and third omission in original). The Supreme Court reversed Robinson's conviction, reasoning:

> It is unlikely that any State at this moment in history would attempt to make it a criminal offense for a person to be mentally ill, or a leper, or to be afflicted with a venereal disease.... [I]n the light of contemporary human knowledge, a law which made a criminal offense of such a disease would doubtless be universally thought to be an infliction of cruel and unusual punishment in violation of the Eighth and Fourteenth Amendments.
>
> We cannot but consider the statute before us as of the same category. In this Court counsel for the State recognized that narcotic addiction is an illness. Indeed, it is apparently an illness which may be contracted innocently or involuntarily. We hold that a state law which imprisons a person thus afflicted as a criminal, even though he has never touched any narcotic drug within the State or been guilty of any irregular behavior there, inflicts a cruel and unusual punishment in violation of the Fourteenth Amendment.

Id. at 666–67, 82 S. Ct. 1417 (citation and footnotes omitted).

The Court did not articulate the principles that undergird its holding. At a minimum, *Robinson* establishes that the state may not criminalize "being"; that is, the state may not punish a person for who he is, independent of anything he has done. *See, e.g.*, *Powell*, 392 U.S. at 533, 88 S. Ct. 2145 (Marshall, J., plurality opinion) (stating that *Robinson* requires an *actus reus* before the state may punish). However, as five Justices would later make clear in *Powell*, *Robinson* also supports the principle that the state cannot punish a person for certain conditions, either arising from his own acts or contracted involuntarily, or acts that he is powerless to avoid. *Powell*, 392 U.S. at 567, 88 S. Ct. 2145 (Fortas, J., dissenting) (endorsing this reading of *Robinson*); *id.* at 550 n. 2, 88 S. Ct. 2145 (White, J., concurring in the judgment) (same, but only where acts predicate to the condition are remote in time); *see Robinson*, 370 U.S. at 666–67, 82 S. Ct. 1417 (stating that punishing a person for having a venereal disease would be unconstitutional, and noting that drug addiction "may be contracted innocently or involuntarily").

Six years after its decision in *Robinson*, the Supreme Court considered the case of Leroy Powell, who had been charged with violating a Texas statute making it a crime to "'get drunk or be found in a state of intoxication in any public place.'" *Powell*, 392 U.S. at 517, 88 S. Ct. 2145 (Marshall, J., plurality opinion) (quoting Tex. Penal Code Ann. art. 477 (Vernon 1952)). The trial court found that Powell suffered from the disease of chronic alcoholism, which "'destroys the afflicted person's will'" to resist drinking and leads him to appear drunk in public involuntarily. *Id.* at 521, 88 S. Ct. 2145. Nevertheless, the trial court summarily rejected Powell's constitutional defense and found him guilty. *See id.* at 558, 88 S. Ct. 2145 (Fortas, J., dissenting). On appeal to the United States Supreme Court, Powell argued that the Eighth Amendment prohibited "punish[ing] an ill person for conduct over which he has no control." Brief for Appellant at 6, *Powell*, 392 U.S. 514, 88 S. Ct. 2145, 20 L. Ed. 2d 1254.

In a 4-1-4 decision, the Court affirmed Powell's conviction. The four Justices joining the plurality opinion interpreted *Robinson* to prohibit only the criminalization of pure status and not to limit the criminalization of conduct. *Powell*, 392 U.S. at 533, 88 S. Ct. 2145 (Marshall, J., plurality opinion). The plurality then declined to extend the Cruel and Unusual Punishment Clause's protections to any involuntary conduct, citing slippery slope concerns, id. at 534–35, 88 S. Ct. 2145, and considerations of federalism and personal accountability, *id.* at 535–36, 88 S. Ct. 2145. Because Powell was convicted not for his status as a chronic alcoholic, but rather for his acts of becoming intoxicated and appearing in public, the *Powell* plurality concluded that the Clause as interpreted by *Robinson* did not protect him. *Id.* at 532, 88 S. Ct. 2145.

In contrast, the four Justices in dissent read *Robinson* to stand for the proposition that "[c]riminal penalties may not be inflicted on a person for being in a condition he is powerless to change." *Id.* at 567, 88 S. Ct. 2145 (Fortas, J., dissenting). Applying *Robinson* to the facts of Powell's case, the dissenters first described the predicate for Powell's conviction as "the mere *condition* of being intoxicated in public" rather than any "acts," such as getting drunk and appearing in public. *Id.* at 559, 88 S. Ct. 2145. Next and more significantly, the dissenters addressed the involuntariness of Powell's behavior, noting that Powell had "'an uncontrollable compulsion to drink' to the point of intoxication; and that, once intoxicated, he could not prevent himself from appearing in public places." *Id.* at 568, 88 S. Ct. 2145. Having found that the Cruel and Unusual Punishment Clause, as interpreted by Robinson, protects against the criminalization of being in a condition one is powerless to avoid, *see id.* at 567, 88 S. Ct. 2145, and because Powell was powerless to avoid public drunkenness, the dissenters concluded that his conviction should be reversed, *see id.* at 569–70, 88 S. Ct. 2145.

In his separate opinion, Justice White rejected the plurality's proposed status-conduct distinction, finding it similar to "forbidding criminal conviction for being sick with flu or epilepsy but permitting punishment for running a fever or having a convulsion." *Id.* at 548–49, 88 S. Ct. 2145 (White, J., concurring in the judgment). Justice White read *Robinson* to stand for the principle that "it cannot be a crime to have an irresistible compulsion to use narcotics," *id.* at 548, 88 S. Ct. 2145, and concluded that "[t]he proper subject of inquiry is whether volitional acts [sufficiently proximate to the condition] brought about the" criminalized conduct or condition, *id.* at 550 n. 2, 88 S. Ct. 2145.

Justice White concluded that given the holding in *Robinson*, "the chronic alcoholic with an irresistible urge to consume alcohol should not be punishable for drinking or being drunk." *Id.* at 549, 88 S. Ct. 2145. For those chronic alcoholics who lack homes,

> a showing could be made that resisting drunkenness is impossible and that avoiding public places when intoxicated is also impossible. As applied to them this statute is in effect a law which bans a single act for which they may not be convicted under the Eighth Amendment—the act of getting drunk.

Id. at 551, 88 S. Ct. 2145. This position is consistent with that of the *Powell* dissenters, who quoted and agreed with Justice White's standard, *see id.* at 568 n. 31, 88 S. Ct. 2145 (Fortas, J., dissenting), and stated that Powell's conviction should be reversed because his public drunkenness was involuntary, *id.* at 570, 88 S. Ct. 2145.

Justice White's *Powell* opinion also echoes his prior dissent in *Robinson*. In *Robinson*, Justice White found no Eighth Amendment violation for two reasons: First, because he did "not consider [Robinson's] conviction to be a punishment for having an illness or for simply being in some status or condition, but rather a conviction for the regular, repeated or habitual use of narcotics immediately prior to his arrest," *Robinson*, 370 U.S. at 686, 82 S. Ct. 1417 & nn.2–3 (White, J., dissenting) (discussing jury instructions regarding addiction and substantial evidence of Robinson's frequent narcotics use in the days prior to his arrest); and second, and most importantly, for understanding his opinion in *Powell*, because the record did not suggest that Robinson's drug addiction was involuntary, *see id.* at 685, 82 S. Ct. 1417. According to Justice White, "if [Robinson] was convicted for being an addict who had lost his power of self-control, I would have other thoughts about this case." *Id.*

Justice White and the *Powell* dissenters shared a common view of the importance of involuntariness to the Eighth Amendment inquiry. They differed only on two issues. First, unlike the dissenters, Justice White believed Powell had not demonstrated that his public drunkenness was involuntary. *Compare Powell*, 392 U.S. at 553, 88 S. Ct. 2145 (White, J., concurring in the judgment) ("[N]othing in the record indicates that [Powell] could not have done his drinking in private.... Powell had a home and wife, and if there were reasons why he had to drink in public or be drunk there, they do not appear in the record."), *with id.* at 568 n. 31, 88 S. Ct. 2145 (Fortas, J., dissenting) ("I believe these findings must fairly be read to encompass facts that my Brother White agrees would require reversal, that is, that for appellant Powell, 'resisting drunkenness' and 'avoiding public places when intoxicated' on the occasion in question were 'impossible.' ").

Second, Justice White rejected the dissent's attempt to distinguish conditions from acts for Eighth Amendment purposes. *See id.* at 550 n. 2, 88 S. Ct. 2145 (White, J., concurring in the judgment). We agree with Justice White that analysis of the Eighth Amendment's substantive limits on criminalization "is not advanced by preoccupation with the label 'condition'" *Id.* One could define many acts as being in the condition of engaging in those acts, for example, the act of sleeping on the sidewalk is indistinguishable from the condition of being asleep on the sidewalk. " 'Being' drunk in public is not far removed in time from the acts of 'getting' drunk and 'going' into public," and there is no meaningful "line between the man who appears in public drunk and that same man five minutes later who is then 'being' drunk in public." *Id.* The dissenters themselves undermine their proposed distinction by suggesting that criminalizing involuntary acts that "typically flow from ... the disease of chronic alcoholism" would violate the Eighth Amendment, as well as by stating that "[i]f an alcoholic should be convicted for criminal conduct which is *not* a characteristic and involuntary part of the pattern of the disease as it afflicts him, nothing herein would prevent his punishment." *Id.* at 559 n. 2, 88 S. Ct. 2145 (Fortas, J., dissenting) (emphasis added).

Notwithstanding these differences, five Justices in *Powell* understood *Robinson* to stand for the proposition that the Eighth Amendment prohibits the state from punishing an involuntary act or condition if it is the unavoidable consequence of one's status or being. *See id.* at 548, 550 n.2, 551, 88 S. Ct. 2145 (White, J., concurring in the judgment); *id.* at 567, 88 S. Ct. 2145 (Fortas, J., dissenting); *see also* Robert L. Misner, *The New Attempt Laws: Unsuspected Threat to the Fourth Amendment*, 33 Stan. L. Rev. 201, 219 (1981) ("[T]he consensus [of White and the dissenters apparently] was that an involuntary act does not suffice for criminal liability."). Although this principle did not determine the outcome in *Powell*, it garnered the considered support of a majority of the Court. Because the conclusion that certain involuntary acts could not be criminalized was not dicta, *see United States v. Johnson*, 256 F.3d 895, 914–16 (9th Cir. 2001) (en banc) (Kozinski, J., concurring) (narrowly defining dicta as "a statement [that] is made casually and without analysis, ... uttered in passing without due consideration of the alternatives, or ... merely a prelude to another legal issue that commands" the court's full attention), we adopt this interpretation of *Robinson* and the Cruel and Unusual Punishment Clause as persuasive authority. We also note that in the absence of any agreement between Justice White and the plurality on the meaning of *Robinson* and the commands of the Cruel and Unusual Punishment Clause, the precedential value of the *Powell* plurality opinion is limited to its precise facts. "When a fragmented Court decides a case and no single rationale explaining the result enjoys the assent of five Justices, the holding of the Court may be viewed as that position taken by those Members who concurred in the judgments on the narrowest grounds...." Marks v. United States, 430 U.S. 188, 193, 97 S. Ct. 990, 51 L. Ed. 2d 260 (1977) (omission in original) (internal quotation marks omitted); *see also* Kent Greenawalt, *"Uncontrollable" Actions and the Eighth Amendment: Implications of Powell v. Texas*, 69 Colum. L. Rev. 927, 931 (1969) ("[T]he dissent comes closer to speaking for a majority of the Court than does the plurality opinion.").

Following *Robinson*'s holding that the state cannot criminalize pure status, and the agreement of five Justices in *Powell* that the state cannot criminalize certain involuntary conduct, there are two considerations relevant to defining the Cruel and Unusual Punishment Clause's limits on the state's power to criminalize. The first is the distinction between pure status—the state of being—and pure conduct—the act of doing. The second is the distinction between an involuntary act or condition and a voluntary one. Accordingly, in determining whether the state may punish a particular involuntary act or condition, we are guided by Justice White's admonition that "[t]he proper subject of inquiry is whether volitional acts brought about the 'condition' and whether those acts are sufficiently proximate to the 'condition' for it to be permissible to impose penal sanctions on the 'condition.'" *Powell*, 392 U.S. at 550 n.2, 88 S. Ct. 2145 (White, J., concurring in the judgment); *see also Bowers v. Hardwick*, 478 U.S. 186, 202 n.2, 106 S. Ct. 2841, 92 L. Ed. 2d 140 (1986) (Blackmun, J., dissenting) (quoting and endorsing this statement in discussing whether the Eighth Amendment limits the state's ability to criminalize homosexual acts).

The *Robinson* and *Powell* decisions, read together, compel us to conclude that enforcement of section 41.18(d) at all times and in all places against homeless individuals who are sitting, lying, or sleeping in Los Angeles's Skid Row because they cannot obtain shelter violates the Cruel and Unusual Punishment Clause. As homeless individuals, Appellants are in a chronic state that may have been acquired "innocently or involuntarily." *Robinson*, 370 U.S. at 667, 82 S. Ct. 1417. Whether sitting, lying, and sleeping are defined as acts or conditions, they are universal and unavoidable consequences of being human. It is undisputed that, for homeless individuals in Skid Row who have no access to private spaces, these acts can only be done in public. In contrast to Leroy Powell, Appellants have made a substantial showing that they are "unable to stay off the streets on the night[s] in question." *Powell*, 392 U.S. at 554, 88 S. Ct. 2145 (White, J., concurring in the judgment).

In disputing our holding, the dissent veers off track by attempting to isolate the supposed "criminal conduct" from the status of being involuntarily homeless at night on the streets of Skid Row. Unlike the cases the dissent relies on, which involve failure to carry immigration documents, illegal reentry, and drug dealing, the conduct at issue here is involuntary and inseparable from status—they are one and the same, given that human beings are biologically compelled to rest, whether by sitting, lying, or sleeping. The cases the dissent cites do not control our reading of *Robinson* and *Powell* where, as here, an Eighth Amendment challenge concerns the *involuntariness* of a criminalized act or condition inseparable from status. *See Johnson*, 256 F.3d at 915 ("Where it is clear that a statement ... is uttered in passing without due consideration of the alternatives, ... it may be appropriate to re-visit the issue in a later case."). The City and the dissent apparently believe that Appellants can avoid sitting, lying, and sleeping for days, weeks, or months at a time to comply with the City's ordinance, as if human beings could remain in perpetual motion. That being an impossibility, by criminalizing sitting, lying, and sleeping, the City is in fact criminalizing Appellants' status as homeless individuals.

Similarly, applying *Robinson* and *Powell*, courts have found statutes criminalizing the status of vagrancy to be unconstitutional. For example, *Goldman v. Knecht* declared unconstitutional a Colorado statute making it a crime for "'[a]ny person able to work and support himself'" to "'be found loitering or strolling about, frequenting public places, ... begging or leading an idle, immoral or profligate course of life, or not having any visible means of support.'" 295 F. Supp. 897, 899 n. 2, 908 (D. Colo. 1969) (three-judge court); *see also Wheeler v. Goodman*, 306 F. Supp. 58, 59 n.1, 62, 66 (W.D.N.C. 1969) (three-judge court) (striking down as unconstitutional under *Robinson* a statute making it a crime to, *inter alia*, be able to work but have no property or "'visible and known means'" of earning a livelihood), *vacated on other grounds*,

401 U.S. 987, 91 S. Ct. 1219, 28 L. Ed. 2d 524 (1971). These cases establish that the state may not make it an offense to be idle, indigent, or homeless in public places. Nor may the state criminalize conduct that is an unavoidable consequence of being homeless—namely sitting, lying, or sleeping on the streets of Los Angeles's Skid Row. As Justice White stated in *Powell*, "[p]unishing an addict for using drugs convicts for addiction under a different name." 392 U.S. at 548, 88 S. Ct. 2145 (White, J., concurring in the judgment).

...

Homelessness is not an innate or immutable characteristic, nor is it a disease, such as drug addiction or alcoholism. But generally one cannot become a drug addict or alcoholic, as those terms are commonly used, without engaging in at least some voluntary acts (taking drugs, drinking alcohol). Similarly, an individual may become homeless based on factors both within and beyond his immediate control, especially in consideration of the composition of the homeless as a group: the mentally ill, addicts, victims of domestic violence, the unemployed, and the unemployable. That Appellants may obtain shelter on some nights and may eventually escape from homelessness does not render their status at the time of arrest any less worthy of protection than a drug addict's or an alcoholic's.

Undisputed evidence in the record establishes that at the time they were cited or arrested, Appellants had no choice other than to be on the streets. Even if Appellants' past volitional acts contributed to their current need to sit, lie, and sleep on public sidewalks at night, those acts are not sufficiently proximate to the conduct at issue here for the imposition of penal sanctions to be permissible. *See Powell v. Texas*, 392 U.S. 514, 550 n.2, 88 S. Ct. 2145, 20 L. Ed. 2d 1254 (1968) (White, J., concurring in the judgment). In contrast, we find no Eighth Amendment protection for conduct that a person makes unavoidable based on their own immediately proximate voluntary acts, for example, driving while drunk, harassing others, or camping or building shelters that interfere with pedestrian or automobile traffic.

Our holding is a limited one. We do not hold that the Eighth Amendment includes a *mens rea* requirement, or that it prevents the state from criminalizing conduct that is not an unavoidable consequence of being homeless, such as panhandling or obstructing public thoroughfares. *Cf.* United States v. Black, 116 F.3d 198, 201 (7th Cir. 1997) (rejecting convicted pedophile's Eighth Amendment challenge to his prosecution for receiving, distributing, and possessing child pornography because, *inter alia*, defendant "did not show that [the] charged conduct was involuntary or uncontrollable").

We are not confronted here with a facial challenge to a statute, cf. Roulette v. City of Seattle, 97 F.3d 300, 302 (9th Cir. 1996) (rejecting a facial challenge to a municipal ordinance that prohibited sitting or lying on public sidewalks); *Tobe v. City of Santa Ana*, 9 Cal. 4th 1069, 1080, 40 Cal. Rptr. 2d 402, 892 P.2d 1145 (1995) (finding a municipal ordinance that banned camping in designated public areas to be facially valid); nor a statute that criminalizes public drunkenness or camping, *cf. Joyce v. City and County of San Francisco*, 846 F. Supp. 843, 846 (N.D. Cal. 1994) (program at issue targeted public drunkenness and camping in public parks); or sitting, lying, or sleeping only at certain times or in certain places within the city. And we are not called upon to decide the constitutionality of punishment when there are beds available for the homeless in shelters. *Cf.* Joel v. City of Orlando, 232 F.3d 1353, 1357 (11th Cir. 2000) (affirming summary judgment for the City where "[t]he shelter has never reached its maximum capacity and no individual has been turned away for lack of space or for inability to pay the one dollar fee").

We hold only that, just as the Eighth Amendment prohibits the infliction of criminal punishment on an individual for being a drug addict, *Robinson v. California*, 370 U.S. 660, 667, 82 S. Ct. 1417, 8 L. Ed.2d 758 (1962); or for involuntary public drunkenness that is an unavoidable consequence of being a chronic alcoholic without a home, *Powell*, 392 U.S. at 551, 88 S. Ct. 2145 (White, J., concurring in the judgment); *id.* at 568 n.31, 88 S. Ct. 2145 (Fortas, J., dissenting); the Eighth Amendment prohibits the City from punishing involuntary sitting, lying, or sleeping on public sidewalks that is an unavoidable consequence of being human and homeless without shelter in the City of Los Angeles.

We do not suggest that Los Angeles adopt any particular social policy, plan, or law to care for the homeless. *See Johnson v. City of Dallas*, 860 F. Supp. 344, 350–51 (N.D. Tex. 1994), *rev'd on standing grounds*, 61 F.3d 442 (5th Cir. 1995). We do not desire to encroach on the legislative and executive functions reserved to the City Council and the Mayor of Los Angeles. There is obviously a "homeless problem" in the City of Los Angeles, which the City is free to address in any way that it sees fit, consistent with the constitutional principles we have articulated. *See id.* By our decision, we in no way dictate to the City that it must provide sufficient shelter for the homeless, or allow anyone who wishes to sit, lie, or sleep on the streets of Los Angeles at any time and at any place within the City. All we hold is that, so long as there is a greater number of homeless individuals in Los Angeles than the number of available beds, the City may not enforce section 41.18(d) at all times and places throughout the City against homeless individuals for involuntarily sitting, lying, and sleeping in public. Appellants are entitled at a minimum to a narrowly tailored injunction against the City's enforcement of section 41.18(d) at certain times and/or places.

We reverse the award of summary judgment to the City, grant summary judgment to Appellants, and remand to the district court for a determination of injunctive relief consistent with this opinion.

...

RYMER, J., dissenting:

There is no question that homelessness is a serious problem and the plight of the homeless, a cause for serious concern. Yet this does not give us license to expand the narrow limits that, in a "rare type of case," the Cruel and Unusual Punishment Clause of the Eighth Amendment places on substantive criminal law. The majority sees it differently, concluding that the Eighth Amendment forbids the City of Los Angeles from enforcing an ordinance which makes it unlawful to sit, sleep, or lie on sidewalks. It gets there by cobbling together the views of dissenting and concurring justices, creating a circuit conflict on standing, and overlooking both Supreme Court precedent, and our own, that restrict the substantive component of the Eighth Amendment to crimes not involving an act. I disagree, and therefore dissent, for a number of reasons.

Los Angeles Municipal Code (LAMC) § 41.18(d) does not punish people simply because they are homeless. It targets *conduct*—sitting, lying or sleeping on city sidewalks—that can be committed by those with homes as well as those without. Although the Supreme Court recognized in *Robinson v. California*, 370 U.S. 660, 82 S. Ct. 1417, 8 L. Ed. 2d 758 (1962), that there are substantive limits on what may be made criminal and punished as such, both the Court and we have constrained this category of Eighth Amendment violation to persons who are being punished for crimes that do not involve *conduct* that society has an interest in preventing. *See, e.g.*, *Powell v. Texas*, 392 U.S. 514, 531–33, 88 S. Ct. 2145, 20 L. Ed. 2d 1254 (1968) (Marshall J., plurality); *United States v. Ayala*, 35 F.3d 423, 426 (9th Cir. 1994).

Neither the Supreme Court nor any other circuit court of appeals has ever held that conduct derivative of a status may not be criminalized. The majority relies on the dissenting opinions and dicta in the concurring opinion in *Powell* (which involved a conviction for public drunkenness of an alcoholic who was to some degree compelled to drink), but not even the *Powell* dissent would go so far as to hold that conduct which is closely related to status may not constitutionally be punished unless the conduct is "a characteristic and involuntary part of the pattern of the [status] as it afflicts" the particular individual, 392 U.S. at 559, n.2 (FORTAS, J., dissenting). This is not the case with a homeless person who sometimes has shelter and sometimes doesn't.

Nor, until now, has the Supreme Court or any other circuit court of appeals intimated (let alone held) that status plus a condition which exists on account of discretionary action by someone else is the kind of "involuntary" condition that cannot be criminalized. Here, the majority holds that the Eighth Amendment "prohibits the City from punishing involuntary sitting, lying or sleeping on public sidewalks that is an unavoidable consequence of being human and homeless without shelter in the City of Los Angeles." Maj. Op. at 46. In other words, the City cannot penalize the status of being homeless plus the condition of being without shelter that exists by virtue of the City's failure to provide sufficient housing on any given night. The ramifications of so holding are quite extraordinary. We do not—and should not—immunize from criminal liability those who commit an act as a result of a condition that the government's failure to provide a benefit has left them in.

Comment

On January 30, 2007, the Inter-University Consortium Against Homelessness issued a petition titled "A Reality Based Approach to Ending Homelessness in Los Angeles." It proposed a five-point plan.

> 1. Help homeless people help themselves by generating jobs for them. Work is the surest way out of poverty, so a share of public-sector jobs—tree planting, highway construction, for example—should be set aside for home-

less people who are able to work. Such a program could be paid for with some of the infrastructure bond money approved in November by California voters.

2. Make sure that public assistance is enough to allow recipients to afford a roof over their heads. General Relief, the last-resort L.A. County program for unemployed and disabled people, amounts to $221 a month, the same as it was 25 years ago. Back then GR would let you rent a room for four weeks, today it buys only one week in the worst housing in the city. Many county assistance dollars could be saved if the homeless entitled to federal Social Security benefits and veterans' disability payments were helped in obtaining them. These savings could be used to raise General Relief payments.

3. Go beyond the shelter mentality to provide affordable housing and services for the homeless. This would be a relative bargain compared with the cost of warehousing people in jails, hospitals and emergency shelters. In Los Angeles a night in supportive housing costs approximately $30, compared with $37 in a shelter, $64 in jail, $85 in prison, $607 in a mental hospital, and $1474 in a general hospital.

4. Stop the flow of additional homeless people into Skid Row. Other municipalities must scrap zoning restrictions that make it possible for some neighborhoods to keep out low-income housing and essential public services. It makes sense to support a law on the lines of SB 1322, introduced in 2006 by state Sen. Gilbert Cedillo, that would require cities to include emergency shelters and special-needs facilities in their general plans. Homeless people discharged from hospitals and jail should not have to travel to Skid Row in search of a cot. They should be able to find social services, housing and health clinics in their own communities.

5. Be willing to spend the political capital necessary to end homelessness. Long-established divisions of political authority cannot be used as an excuse for inaction. The old ways are not the only ways. The mayor and City Council of L.A. and the county supervisors can no longer avoid working together to solve the problem. And Southland cities should stand up to NIMBYism.

§ 1.03 Making Conduct Criminal

[A] The Sources of the Criminal Law

Weishaupt v. Commonwealth

Supreme Court Virginia
315 S.E.2d 847 (1984)

THOMAS, JUSTICE.

This appeal raises an issue of first impression in the Commonwealth: whether a husband can be guilty of raping his wife, in violation of Code § 18.2-61, where, at the time of the alleged offense, the parties were living separate and apart.

Weishaupt was indicted for rape. He moved to dismiss the indictment on the ground that pursuant to common law principles, a husband cannot be convicted of raping his wife. The trial court rejected Weishaupt's argument and denied the motion. The case was tried to a jury which found Weishaupt guilty of attempted rape. Judgment was entered on the verdict and Weishaupt was sentenced to two years in prison....

Viewing the evidence in the light most favorable to the Commonwealth, we find the facts to be as follows: Janet and Ronald Weishaupt were married on July 19, 1980. One child was born of their marriage. On November 9, 1981, Janet moved out of the marital abode, taking with her the couple's infant child. From the time Janet moved out in November 1981, through the date of the attack in October 1982, the parties lived separate and apart and did not engage in any sexual relations. Their contacts were limited to telephone conversations about their child and chance meetings in public where they exchanged perfunctory greetings. During the eleven months prior to the attack, Janet consulted a lawyer regarding a divorce and was advised to wait until she had been separated for one year before filing any divorce papers.

On the night of October 16, 1982, Weishaupt saw his estranged wife at a bowling alley. She was part of a group consisting of three males and three females. Janet said a "simple hello" to Weishaupt "just to be friendly." Janet's group bowled until approximately 12:30 a.m. on October 17, 1982. Her group then made plans to leave the bowling alley and meet at the apartment of one of the other women. However, two of the couples wanted to go "four-wheel-driving" before continuing their evening. Janet and one of the men chose not to go driving. They decided to wait in the apartment until the others arrived.

Weishaupt, who left the bowling alley shortly after his estranged wife's group, was driving around when he encountered a vehicle containing the two couples whom he had seen bowling with Janet and her companion. Weishaupt flagged the car down, observed that Janet and one of the three men were no longer in the group, and demanded to know where she was. When no one responded, Weishaupt drove off in search of his wife. He went to the high-rise apartment building where Janet and her escort were waiting for the others. He proceeded to the sixth floor of the building and beat on the door to the apartment where he suspected Janet was located. Janet looked through the peephole and recognized Weishaupt but neither opened the door nor acknowledged that she was inside. For a while, Weishaupt continued to beat on the door and try the doorknob, but eventually he stopped. Janet peeped through a window and saw him getting into his car. She thought he had left.

A short time later, however, Weishaupt returned to the apartment building. This time, instead of going inside he climbed up the outside of the building, working his way vertically from balcony to balcony until he reached the balcony to the apartment where Janet was located. He pounded on the sliding glass door. Janet came to investigate the noise, recognized Weishaupt, and told her companion that Weishaupt was on the balcony. At the suggestion of her companion, Janet opened the balcony door.

As soon as the door was open, Weishaupt charged into the apartment, ran into the bedroom and leaped on top of Janet's companion, punching him and yelling that he had "caught" them. Weishaupt demanded that the other man "step outside." Janet ran to the kitchen to call the police but Weishaupt pursued her, ripped the phone from her hand, tore the cord from the phone, and shoved her away. He then continued his altercation with the other man. Janet tried to break up the fight by stepping between the men. This time, Weishaupt knocked her down.

Weishaupt continued to demand that the other man step outside. The other man finally agreed, but said he would step outside only to talk, not to fight. Weishaupt held the door open, the other man walked out first, whereupon Weishaupt slammed the door, leaving him in the apartment alone with Janet.

Standing on the other side of the door, Janet's companion could hear her inside screaming and telling Weishaupt to leave her alone. He tried to gain entry by knocking on the door and asking Weishaupt to let him in. He got no response. While he was standing outside the door a security guard walked up to investigate the ruckus.

In the apartment, Weishaupt turned his attention to Janet. He pushed, shoved, and dragged her into the bedroom. Though she resisted, he succeeded in forcing her into the room, then threw her on the bed. All the while she was screaming, "No, don't. I don't want to." She fought with him on the bed and they fell to the floor. Weishaupt landed on top. He pinned Janet's arms down with this knees then used his hands to choke her as he demanded to know whether she had been to bed with anyone. She said no. She pleaded with him to let her get a drink of water. Weishaupt released her momentarily. When she finished getting the water, he put her back on the bed and started to kiss her and undo her blouse. She fought with him again and again they fell to the floor. This time he got her pants down and in Janet's words, "proceed to have intercourse." With Janet on the floor beneath him Weishaupt stated, "I have to do this to find out if you've been to bed with anyone else."

Throughout this ordeal, Janet continued to scream and resist. When the apartment owner arrived to open the door for the security guard, she and others in the hallway could hear Janet's screams. The security guard heard Janet say "leave [me] alone, you're hurting me, get off of me." When the door was opened, Janet was found lying on the floor, at the foot of the bed, curled up in the fetal position with her pants and underpants down to her ankles. She had red marks on her back and was sobbing hysterically.

Weishaupt was standing nearby covered with perspiration. He was observed buckling up his pants. One of the women who came to Janet's assistance asked Weishaupt whether he had raped Janet. He replied, "yes, I tried."

Weishaupt admits that he and Janet were living separate and apart at the time of the attack. Nevertheless, he contends that he had an absolute right to do what he did. In making this argument he relies on the so-called "marital exemption" which he says developed in English common law and applies in Virginia because of Code § 1-10.[1] The source of the marital exemption is said to be a statement made by the seventeenth-century English jurist Sir Matthew Hale.[2] He wrote as follows:

> [T]he husband cannot be guilty of a rape committed by himself upon his lawful wife, for by their mutual matrimonial consent and contract the wife hath given up herself in this kind unto her husband, which she cannot retract.

1 M. Hale, *The History of the Pleas of the Crown* (1736) at 629. Weishaupt argues that Hale's rule is absolute and completely exonerates his conduct.

Weishaupt advances three arguments in support of his position. He contends first that Code § 18.2-61[3] does not alter the common law rule as stated by Hale because the statute does not state explicitly that the common law rule is no longer in effect. Second, he argues that Hale's rule was adopted in Virginia in cases that used the word "unlawful" in defining rape. Third, he argues that to permit a husband to be charged with raping his wife would be disruptive to marriages. In our opinion, all of Weishaupt's arguments are meritless. We will address the arguments *seriatim*.

Weishaupt's first argument relies upon an unstated assumption. His reasoning runs as follows: (1) Code § 1-10 causes the common law of England to apply in Virginia; (2) since Code § 18.2-61 does not state that it modifies the common law rule, that rule remains in effect; and (3) therefore, Weishaupt concludes, he cannot be

---

1. Code § 1-10 reads as follows:

> The common law of England, insofar as it is not repugnant to the principles of the Bill of Rights and Constitution of this State, shall continue in full force within the same, and be the rule of decision, except as altered by the General Assembly.

2. Hale was born in 1609, two years after the landing at Jamestown. He became Lord Chief Justice of the Court of King's Bench in 1671, a position he held until he resigned in 1675. He died in 1676. It is not certain when he wrote his now famous statement, but the book based on his manuscript was not published until 1736, 50 years after his death. At the time Hale wrote, marriage was irrevocable and women were deemed the property of their husbands. *See The Marital Rape Exemption*, 52 N.Y.U.L. Rev. 306 (1977). Thus, his statement may have been a reflection of a view of the world that existed before America was born.

3. Code § 18.2-61 reads in pertinent part as follows:

> If any person has sexual intercourse with a female or causes a female to engage in sexual intercourse with any person and such act is accomplished (I) against her will, by force, threat or intimidation, or (ii) through the use of the female's mental incapacity or physical helplessness, ... he or she shall, in the discretion of the court or jury, be punished with confinement in the penitentiary for life or for any term not less than five years.

convicted of raping his wife. The unstated assumption is that Hale's statement sets forth the common law of England. That assumption is mistaken.

Hale's statement was not law, common or otherwise. At best, it was Hale's pronouncement of what he observed to be a custom in seventeenth-century England. Yet, unlike other customs that form the basis of common law, it nowhere appears that Hale, in making his statement, set forth a general rule of conduct of such long-standing acceptability that "the memory of man runneth not to the contrary." *See* I W. Blackstone, *Commentaries on the Law of England* (1765) at 67. Moreover, Hale cites no authority for his view nor was it subsequently adopted, in its entirety, by the English courts.

...

It is apparent from the English cases that, contrary to Weishaupt's assumptions and representations, from earliest times, a wife who was separated from her husband was in a different position than a wife living with her husband. The separation served to cut off marital rights that her husband otherwise may have had. Thus, the true state of English common law was that marriage carried with it the implied consent to sexual intercourse; but that consent could be revoked. The requirement for revocation was that there exist either a court order of separation or one limiting contact, or that there exist a separation agreement entered into by both husband and wife. The English courts refused to accept a unilateral revocation of consent to marital sex by the wife even if that revocation was manifested by the wife's moving out and filing for divorce. Nevertheless, contrary to the position advanced by Weishaupt, under English common law, there never existed an absolute irrevocable marital exemption that would protect a husband from a charge of rape in all circumstances.

The actual English common law rule, if applied directly to the facts of this case, would require us to reverse Weishaupt's conviction. But such a direct application is not possible. Before English common law can be applied in Virginia it must be analyzed in light of Code § 1-10 and the cases interpreting that code section. According to the code, English common law cannot be applied if it is "repugnant to the principles of the Bill of Rights and the Constitution." Nor can it be applied if it is "altered by the General Assembly." In addition to the statutory provision, *Foster v. Commonwealth*, 96 Va. 306, 31 S.E. 503 (1898), sets forth yet another limitation on the use of English common law. In *Foster*, we considered the predecessor to Code § 1-10. We stated that though the statute, aside from its express limitations, appears to adopt English common law "generally, and without a qualification," that is not in fact the case.... The true rule is this:

> Such of [English common law] doctrines and principles as are *repugnant to the nature and character of our political system, or which the different and varied circumstances of our country render inapplicable to us*, are either not in force here, or must be so modified in their application as to adapt them to our condition.

96 Va. at 310, 31 S.E. at 505 (emphasis added). Thus, by statute and case law, we are free, in essence, to adopt from English common law those principles that fit our way of life and to reject those which do not.

We must decide, therefore, whether the English rule, which permits revocation of the implied consent to marital sex but which refuses to grant that power to a woman acting unilaterally, is repugnant to the nature and character of our political system, contrary to statute, or whether the circumstances existing in Virginia render it inapplicable.

The question whether a woman should be allowed to make a unilateral decision to withdraw consent to marital sex is bound up in the larger question of whether women are to be in independent control of their personal fates or whether they are to be under the control of others. At the time Hale wrote, this latter view was much in vogue. At that time, a woman was considered "the property of either her father or her husband." *The Marital Rape Exemption*, 52 N.Y.U. L. Rev. 306, 309 (1977). When a woman married in the 17th century her very legal existence was deemed "suspended during the marriage, or at least ... incorporated and consolidated into that of the husband, under whose wing, protection, and cover" she functioned. *Id.* at 310. No citation of authority is required to establish that these views of the dependence of women have long been cast aside.

... [W]e are of the further view that the Virginia no-fault divorce statute, Code § 20-91(9), embodies a legislative endorsement of a woman's unilateral right to withdraw an implied consent to marital sex. The no-fault statute requires that the parties live separate and apart without cohabitation for a specified time period as a prerequisite to securing a no-fault divorce. The very scheme of the statute contemplates a voluntary withdrawal, by either spouse, from the marital relationship. Stated differently, the statute contemplates a *de facto* termination of the marital relationship which after the X passage of time will be terminated *de jure.* If, in this case, we failed to recognize a wife's unilateral authority to withdraw the implied consent to marital sex our decision would be inconsistent with a wife's statutorily acknowledged right to make a *de facto* withdrawal from the marriage contract. Along the same lines, if a woman can unilaterally secure a divorce, thereby revoking the marriage contract in its entirety, then it is illogical to conclude that she cannot, by her own act, revoke a term of that contract.

... [The Attorney General contends, on the basis of Section 1 of the Virginia Bill of Rights,[4] that any concept of implied consent to intercourse growing out of the marital relationship is unconstitutional. The Attorney General submits that blanket consent to sexual intercourse implied from marriage runs counter to the Bill of Rights in that it impinges upon individual liberty. In essence, the Commonwealth urges us to adopt what would amount to a requirement of actual consent on the part of the wife before each act of intercourse. In our opinion, we do not have to reach this argument in order to decide the present case. This is so because the Commonwealth's argument concerns a situation where a husband and wife are living together in a more or less

4. Section 1 of the Virginia Bill of Rights, Va. Const. Art. I, § 1, reads as follows:

> That all men are by nature equally free and independent and have certain rights, of which, when they enter into a state of society, they cannot, by any compact, deprive or divest their posterity; namely, the enjoyment of life and liberty and possession of property, and pursuing and obtaining happiness and safety.

normal, on-going marital relationship. Here, by contrast, we are concerned with a situation where, among other things, a husband and wife have lived separate and apart for almost one year and have not engaged in sexual relations during that time period. We will base our decision on the facts before us, not on hypothetical facts.

... [W]e hereby reject so much of the English common law rule regarding a husband's marital exemption from a charge of raping his wife and the implied consent to marital intercourse as provides that a wife cannot unilaterally revoke her implied consent to marital intercourse. In light of this conclusion, it is plain that Weishaupt's first argument, *i.e.*, that Code § 18.2-61 does not alter the common law, cannot suffice to overturn his conviction.

Weishaupt's second argument is of no more merit than his first. In this argument he contends that though the Virginia rape statute has never used the word "unlawful" in defining rape, certain early cases from this Court used that term in defining rape. Weishaupt says that the use of the word unlawful by the Court means the Court adopted Hale's rule. Weishaupt submits that sex between married persons is lawful. Therefore, he reasons that the use of the word unlawful in defining rape must mean that the Court intended to exclude married couples. The Attorney General responds that whatever the reasons for the use of the word unlawful in early rape cases, that word has not been used, in our cases, since 1956, though this Court has handed down approximately 150 rape cases in that 28-year period. The result is that even if Weishaupt's argument had merit, the basis for his position has not existed for nearly three decades. Thus, by Weishaupt's own logic, if the use of the word unlawful meant acceptance of Hale's rule then the elimination of the word unlawful must have meant the rejection of Hale's rule. Consequently, by that logic, when Weishaupt attacked his wife there existed no marital exemption of any kind.

The Attorney General points out a second problem with Weishaupt's argument concerning the use of the word unlawful. He states that the issue of spousal rape was not present in any of the cases relied on by Weishaupt. Therefore, the Attorney General argues, it cannot be assumed that by the mere insertion of the word unlawful the Court intended to exclude the possibility of spousal rape. We find merit in both the Commonwealth's arguments in response to Weishaupt's second contention.

Weishaupt's third argument is that to allow a husband to be convicted of raping his wife will be disruptive to marriages. He contends that the possibility of reconciliation will be foreclosed. This argument is absurd. It is hard to imagine how charging a husband with the violent crime of rape can be more disruptive of a marriage than the violent act itself. Moreover, if the marriage has already deteriorated to the point where intercourse must be commanded at the price of violence we doubt that there is anything left to reconcile.

We hold, on the basis of all the foregoing considerations, that a wife can unilaterally revoke her implied consent to marital sex where, as here, she has made manifest her intent to terminate the marital relationship by living separate and apart from her husband; refraining from voluntary sexual intercourse with her husband; and, in light of all the circumstances, conducting herself in a manner that establishes a *de facto* end to the marriage. And, once the implied consent is revoked, the husband can be found guilty of raping his wife, if the evidence against him establishes a violation of Code § 18.2-61.

In the instant appeal, the facts establish Janet's intent to terminate the marital relationship. We are convinced that, prior to the attack, she withdrew any implied consent to marital intercourse. Finally, there is no challenge to the sufficiency of the evidence to prove the crime for which Weishaupt was convicted.

Comments and Questions

(1) As the *Weishaupt* opinion demonstrates, there are several sources of criminal law. In particular, the *Weishaupt* Court grapples with the interplay of the "common law" and statutory law. Each term warrants some discussion.

(2) Common Law: The term "common law" itself can have several meanings. In general, the term refers to judge-made law—law that results from judicial examination and decision-making in a particular case as opposed to prospective legislative enactments. As the late Professor Perkins explained: "In brief, all of that part of the authoritative materials, used to guide and direct the judicial and administrative organs of the state in the performance of their official functions, which is not found in legislative enactment (or written constitution) is called the 'common law' to distinguish it from the statutory law." Perkins on Criminal Law, 23–27 (2d ed. 1969). American criminal law in its earliest form relied upon English common law, but, over time, American courts refined, tweaked and adapted English common law to meet the circumstances and norms of a new nation. For a discussion of the states' adoption of English common law, *see* Herbert Pope, *The English Common Law in the United States*, 24 Harv. L. Rev. 6 (1910).

(3) Statutory Law: Beginning in the eighteenth century, there was a movement toward codifying criminal law in statutory form. Initially, state legislative bodies enacted penal codes to supplement the evolving body of common law. Over time, though, state legislatures passed criminal laws designed to supplant the common law. *See* Herbert Wechsler, *The Challenge of a Model Penal Code*, 65 Harv. L. Rev. 1097 (1952) (discussing the piecemeal and often problematic evolution of American statutory law). Modern criminal law is statutory law.

(4) The Interplay: Even though most jurisdictions have codified what were once common law crimes, the common law is still a valuable resource for courts. First, many statutes define crimes in exclusively common law terms, and in such cases, courts will treat the statutory law term as retaining its common law meaning. *See e.g., Keeler v. Superior Court*, 470 P.2d 617 (Ca. 1970) (where California homicide statute did not define term "human being," court deferred to common law definition of that term in use at the time of statute's enactment) (discussed in Chapter 5). Second, there may be gaps in a criminal law statute, and courts may rely upon common law concepts to fill such gaps. *See e.g., Morissette v. United States*, 342 U.S. 246 (1952) (federal criminal law was silent as to criminal intent and Supreme Court held that common law requirement of criminal intent would apply absent explicit con-

gressional intent to the contrary) (discussed in Chapter 3). The *Weishaupt* Court also grappled with the interplay of statutory and common law. Virginia had codified the crime of rape at the time of the defendant's trial, and yet the defendant argued that the English common law concept of "marital exemption" from rape insulated him from prosecution. Notice how his argument proceeds and how the Court reasons its way to rejecting his arguments.

(5) The Model Penal Code: With each state developing its own common law at its own pace and in its own fashion, it should come as no surprise that there emerged no "American criminal law." Recognizing this, the American Law Institute (ALI), comprised of highly regarded law professors, lawyers, and judges, sought to provide a coherent statement of American criminal law principles, or a model penal code. Begun in the 1930s and first completed in 1962, the Model Penal Code (MPC) today has provided the basis for a majority of state criminal codes, and, even where it has not been adopted as governing law, it is treated as highly persuasive authority by courts and lawmakers. For a summary of the MPC, *see* Paul H. Robinson and Markus D. Dubber, *The American Model Penal Code: A Brief Overview*, 10 New Crim. L. Rev. 319 (2007). The MPC is highlighted throughout this book.

[B] Constitutional Limitations

States are generally free to enact laws that protect the safety and welfare of their citizens. However, as you will come to learn in constitutional law, those state laws must comport with state and federal constitutional provisions. As the following cases demonstrate, criminal defendants may challenge their convictions by arguing that the law under which they have been prosecuted violates a right protected by the Constitution—for example, the right to free expression, the right to equal protection under the law, the right to Due Process, or the right to be free from cruel and unusual punishment.

[1] Free Expression

People v. Barton

Court of Appeals of New York
861 N.E.2d 75 (2006)

Read, J.

On August 4, 2004, defendant Michael Barton was ticketed for violating section 44-4 (H) of the Code of the City of Rochester when he allegedly waded into traffic on a highway exit ramp in downtown Rochester, soliciting money from motorists. Section 44-4 of the Code addresses aggressive panhandling, and subsection (H) specifies that "[n]o person on a sidewalk or alongside a roadway shall solicit from any occupant of a motor vehicle that is on a street or other public place." The Code defines "solicit" as "the spoken, written, or printed word or such other acts or bodily gestures as are conducted in furtherance of the purposes of immediately obtaining money or any other thing of value" (Rochester City Code § 44-4 [B]). Violations are punishable by fines ranging from $25 to $250, or an appropriate alternative sentence; a second conviction within a year could result in imprisonment for up to 15 days (Rochester City Code § 44-4 [I]).

Section 44-4, approved by the City Council and the Mayor of the City of Rochester in the spring of 2004, was nearly a decade in the making, spurred by the increasing incidence of panhandling in the downtown area and attendant citizen complaints. Subsection (A) of section 44-4, entitled "Legislative intent," states that this provision was

> "adopted in order to protect persons from threatening, intimidating or harassing behavior, to keep public places safe and attractive for use by all members of the community and to maintain and preserve public places where all of the community can interact in a peaceful manner. *This legislation is also intended to provide for the free flow of pedestrian and vehicular traffic on the streets and sidewalks in the City*, to promote tourism and business and preserve the quality of urban life" (emphasis added).

The Council loosely patterned section 44-4 after panhandling ordinances adopted in other cities, including Atlanta, Baltimore, Cincinnati, New Haven, New York City, Philadelphia, Portland, San Francisco, Seattle and Washington, D.C.

As the Council's President explained, subsection (H) of section 44-4 was "aimed at specific conduct, and not at any type of speech or expression," because "[the conduct itself is offensive, for it leads to an interference with the free flow of vehicular traffic and raises traffic safety and traffic congestion concerns." In particular,

> "[s]olicitation of contributions from occupants of motor vehicles is disruptive to the drivers of those vehicles and diverts their attention from the traffic on the street. Even if the vehicle is stopped, the driver is not paying attention to potential hazards in the road, observing traffic control signals, or preparing to move along the street or through the intersection."

Further, section 44-4 (H) treats all solicitation "the same whether it be for an individual or a charity, and whether the cause may be deemed by some to be favored or disfavored."

On August 31, 2004, defendant moved to dismiss the accusatory instrument lodged against him. He contended that section 44-4 (H) was overbroad in violation of the Free Speech clauses of the federal and New York State constitutions. Defendant did not argue that section 44-4 (H) was unconstitutional as applied to him. Rather, he complained that this provision impermissibly "impact[ed] activities beyond its intended reach" as it applied not only to aggressive panhandling, but "to anyone who would solicit" motorists from the sidewalk, including an individual holding up a sign simply stating "Food," or participating in the city firefighters' annual "Fill-the-Boot" fundraising campaign.

City Court agreed, declaring section 44-4 (H) unconstitutional and dismissing the accusatory instrument. The court cited *Perry Ed. Assn. v. Perry Local Educators' Assn.* (460 U.S. 37, 45 [1983]) for the relevant constitutional standard: "The state may ... enforce regulations of the time, place, and manner of expression which are content-neutral, are narrowly tailored to serve a significant government interest, and leave open ample alternative channels of communication." In City Court's view, section 44-4 (H) was content-neutral, but lacked narrow tailoring because it "allow[ed] for the prosecution of those ... guilty of nothing more than peacefully asking for assistance" (8 Misc 3d 291, 298 [Rochester City Ct 2004]).

County Court reversed, concluding that section 44-4 (H) was content-neutral, sufficiently narrowly tailored, and left open ample alternative channels of communication. The court observed that section 44-4 (H) was "aimed specifically at a certain type of conduct engaged in at a certain location"—the "use [of] spoken or written words or acts, for the purpose of immediately obtaining money or any other thing of value from an occupant of a motor vehicle that is on a street or other public place" (12 Misc 3d 322, 330 [Monroe County Ct 2006]). The court further pointed out that section 44-4 (H) was not overbroad because it applied to bona fide charitable canvassing as well as to defendant's soliciting. "Because a statute is evenhanded and applies equally to all persons conducting the same unwanted conduct does not make a statute overbroad" (*id.*) In short, section 44-4 (H)'s "overbreadth, if any, [was] not substantial when judged in relation to the [provision's] plainly legitimate sweep" (*id.*). Upon defendant's application, a Judge of this Court granted leave to appeal. We now affirm.

As an initial matter, for purposes of this appeal the People do not contest, and we therefore assume, that panhandling is speech or expressive conduct safeguarded by the First Amendment, entitled to protection tantamount to that afforded eleemosynary appeals by organized charities (*see Schaumburg v. Citizens for a Better Environment*, 444 U.S. 620 [1980] [holding that there is sufficient nexus between solicitation by organized charities and a variety of speech interests to implicate First Amendment]). The United States Supreme Court has yet to rule on this issue, and lower courts have expressed differing views (*e.g. compare Young v. New York City Tr. Auth.*, 903 F.2d 146, 154 [2d Cir 1990], *cert. denied*, 498 U.S. 984 [1990] [sustaining prohibition on begging in subways, reasoning that panhandling is not constitutionally protected speech or expressive conduct analogous to solicitation by organized charities: "Whether with or without words, the object of begging and panhandling is the transfer of money. Speech simply is not inherent to the act; it is not of the essence of the conduct"], *with Loper v. New York City Police Dept.*, 999 F2d 699, 704 [2d Cir 1993] [enjoining enforcement of statute prohibiting public loitering for purposes of begging, concluding that there is "little difference between those who solicit for organized charities and those who solicit for themselves in regard to the message conveyed," and that "(t)he distinction is not a significant one for First Amendment purposes"]). Second, even though defendant's own conduct may be unshielded by the First Amendment, he nonetheless may challenge section 44-4 (H) as overbroad on behalf of others provision's very existence (*Broadrick v. Oklahoma*, 413 U.S. 601, 610–13 [1973]).

The test for determining overbreadth is whether the law on its face prohibits a real and substantial amount of constitutionally protected conduct (*see Houston v. Hill*, 482 US 451, 458 [1987]; *Broadrick*, 413 U.S. at 615). "[The mere fact that one can conceive of some impermissible applications of a statute is not sufficient to render it susceptible to an overbreadth challenge" (*Members of City Council of Los Angeles v. Taxpayers for Vincent*, 466 US 789, 800 [1984]). Here, section 44-4 (H) reaches any solicitation intended to obtain immediate funds or things of value from occupants of motor vehicles in Rochester's streets or other public places. Defendant claims that because section 44-4 (H) on its face concededly reaches "passive" panhandling targeting motorists—specifically, someone standing mute on the sidewalk, facing traffic in the street and holding a sign requesting immediate money or food—it is unconstitutionally overbroad. According to defendant, section 44-4 (H) thus runs afoul of the First Amendment because it is not limited to panhandlers who act aggressively, or solicit motorists successfully or actually walk into a lane of stopped or moving traffic. As this appeal is presented to us then, the parties dispute whether section 44-4 (H) is a reasonable time, place and manner restriction once it sweeps defendant's hypothetical passive panhandler within its coverage.

...

In determining whether a regulation is content neutral, the principal inquiry is

> "whether the government has adopted a regulation of speech because of disagreement with the message it conveys. The government's purpose is the controlling consideration. A regulation that serves purposes unrelated to the content of expression is deemed neutral, even if it has an incidental effect on some speakers or messages but not others. Government regulation of expressive activity is content neutral so long as it is *justified* without reference to the content of the regulated speech" (*Ward v. Rock Against Racism*, 491 U.S. 781, 791 [1989] [internal quotation marks and citations omitted]).

Content neutrality is not negated because a sign must be read by the police in order to determine whether section 44-4 (H) has been violated (i.e., whether the sign's message seeks to obtain money or any other thing of value on the spot), as defendant argues. The Council's reason for adopting section 44-4 (H)—to promote the free and safe flow of traffic—is the relevant consideration, and the ban covers all those asking motorists for immediate donations, regardless of their message (*see Heffron v. International Soc. for Krishna Consciousness, Inc.*, 452 U.S. 640, 648–49 [1981] [speech restriction applying impartially to all persons or organizations, whether charitable or commercial, is content neutral]). Section 44-4 (H) does not attempt to silence one particular message; it does not frown on any particular viewpoint. Nor is it important that section 44-4 (H) may not reach every speech-related side-of-the-road distraction or source of traffic disruption in downtown Rochester; i.e., that it has "an incidental effect on some speakers or messages but not others."

Next, although "a regulation of the time, place, or manner of protected speech must be narrowly tailored to serve the government's legitimate, content-neutral interests ... it need not be the least restrictive or least intrusive means of doing so" (*Ward*, 491 U.S. at 798). Instead,

> "the requirement of narrow tailoring is satisfied so long as the ... regulation promotes a substantial government interest that would be achieved less ef-

> fectively absent the regulation.... So long as the means chosen are not substantially broader than necessary to achieve the government's interest ... the regulation will not be invalid simply because a court concludes that the government's interest could be adequately served by some less-speech-restrictive alternative. The validity of [time, place, or manner] regulations does not turn on a judge's agreement with the responsible decisionmaker concerning the most appropriate method for promoting significant government interests or the degree to which those interests should be promoted" (id. at 799–800 [internal quotation marks and citations omitted]).

Section 44-4 (H) was designed to address a specific problem brought to the Council's attention: individuals seeking handouts from occupants of motor vehicles on a public thoroughfare or place, thereby creating a hazard and slowing or snarling traffic. Because section 44-4 (H) focuses on specific conduct that the City has an interest in controlling in order to further a significant content-neutral government interest, it is narrowly tailored.

Accordingly, the order of County Court should be affirmed.

...

Potts v. United States

District of Columbia Court of Appeals

919 A.2d 1127 (2007)

Glickman, Associate Judge.

Appellants ask us to reverse their convictions after a bench trial of violating 40 U.S.C. §6135 by displaying, on the Supreme Court grounds, a banner or device "designed or adapted to bring into public notice a party, organization, or movement." Appellants challenge the jurisdiction of the Superior Court, the Constitutionality of the statute on its face and as applied to them, and the factual findings of the trial court. We reject appellants' arguments and affirm their convictions.

Appellants were at the Supreme Court on February 9, 2005, as part of a small group protesting the mistreatment of prisoners at the Abu Ghraib and Guantanamo Bay prisons and the appointment of Alberto Gonzales as Attorney General. To dramatize their cause, appellant Potts was wearing a black hood; appellant Barrows was wearing an orange jumpsuit and black hood; and appellant Perry was holding a sign over his head that read "no taxes for war or torture." In the course of the protest, appellants ascended several steps from the sidewalk to the plaza in front of the Supreme Court building. Supreme Court Police repeatedly asked appellants to return to the sidewalk and arrested them when they refused to do so.

...

... 40 U.S.C. §6135 does not violate the First Amendment, either on its face or as applied to appellants. We have held, contrary to appellants' contention, that "the Supreme Court plaza is a nonpublic forum." *Bonowitz v. United States*, 741 A.2d 18, 22 (D.C. 1999). As such, "the government can regulate speech [there] 'as long as the restrictions are reasonable and not an effort to suppress expression merely because public officials oppose the speaker's view.'" *Id.* at 21 (quoting *Cornelius v. NAACP Legal Def. & Educ. Fund*, 473 U.S. 788, 802, 105 S. Ct. 3439, 87 L. Ed.2d 567 (1985)). Both of those conditions are met in this case. The statutory restriction on expression at issue here is reasonable as a measure "to permit the unimpeded access and egress of litigants and visitors to the Court, and to preserve the appearance of the Court as a body not swayed by external influence." *United States v. Wall*, 521 A.2d 1140, 1144 (D.C. 1987); *see also United States v. Grace*, 461 U.S. 171, 182–83, 103 S. Ct. 1702, 75 L. Ed.2d 736 (1983). The general restriction is reasonable, and reasonably applied to appellants, even if they could show that their particular conduct did not threaten the harms sought to be avoided. *See Ward v. Rock Against Racism*, 491 U.S. 781, 801, 109 S. Ct. 2746, 105 L. Ed.2d 661 (1989) ("[T]he validity of the regulation depends on the relation it bears to the overall problem the government seeks to correct, not on the extent to which it furthers the government's interests in an individual case."). Moreover, the statute is viewpoint-neutral on its face, and there is no evidence that it was applied to appellants in a discriminatory manner.

... We likewise reject appellants' claim that the "display" clause of 40 U.S.C. §6135 is unconstitutionally vague. The Supreme Court's decision in *Grace*, coupled with the plain text of the statute, makes it clear that protestors may not demonstrate on the Supreme Court steps and plaza. Appellants' primary claim, that the term "movement" in 40 U.S.C. §6135 is impermissibly vague because it may be applied both to large, established political organizations and small, *ad hoc* groups of protestors who converge for a single occasion, is unconvincing. In context, juxtaposed with the words "party" and "organization," the term "movement" is not unduly vague; it encompasses any person or group seeking to advocate a cause or message. The breadth of this definition, which does not turn on the size, structure or other arbitrary characteristics of the demonstrators or their cause, avoids rather than threatens the dangers of uncertain, arbitrary or discriminatory application and enforcement. Thus, in *Grace*, the statute was challenged by solitary protestors, one who merely displayed a sign with the text of the First Amendment, and the other who merely distributed leaflets concerning oppression in Guatemala. The Supreme Court agreed "that almost any sign or leaflet carrying a communication, including Grace's picket sign and Zywicki's leaflets, would be 'designed or adapted to bring into public notice [a] party, organization or movement,'" noting that "[s]uch a construction brings some certainty to the reach of the statute and hence avoids what might be other challenges to its validity." 461 U.S. at 176, 103 S. Ct. 1702.

Finally, the trial court did not misconstrue the statute or clearly err in finding that appellants' costumes—the orange jumpsuit and the black hood—constituted "devices[s] designed or adapted to bring into public notice" a "movement." Merely because some distinctive clothing, such as religious attire, is not worn to promote a cause or position, does not mean that a garment cannot be a "device" within the coverage of 40 U.S.C. §6135. Whether appellants' display was expressive conduct to which the statute applied turned on whether an "intent to convey a particularized message was present, and [whether] the likelihood was great that the message would be understood by those who viewed it." *Texas v. Johnson*, 491 U.S. 397, 404, 109 S. Ct. 2533, 105 L. Ed.2d 342 (1989). In this case, the answer to those questions is not in doubt. Indeed, appellants themselves testified that they intended to symbolize their disgust with the current Administration's alleged complicity with torture and with the appointment of Mr. Gonzales.

Appellants' convictions are hereby *Affirmed*.

Comment and Questions

Citing an earlier decision, the court notes two purposes served by the statute which satisfy the reasonable regulation test: (1) "to permit the unimpeded access and egress of litigants and visitors to the Court," and (2) "to preserve the appearance of the Court as a body not swayed by external influence." The court then concedes that neither of these concerns is raised in the present case, but that it really does not matter. Is this a tacit recognition that the statute is overbroad? If (1) is a bona fide concern, would it not be simpler and more direct to prohibit impeding access and egress to the building? Presumably such a law would not unabashedly enjoin expressive behavior. Note that concern (2) is with preserving the *appearance* that the Court is not swayed, not with the possibility that the activities might actually influence the Court. Should such an appearance be sufficient to stifle otherwise constitutionally protected expression?

[2] Equal Protection

Lawrence v. Texas

Supreme Court of the United States
539 U.S. 558 (2003)

...

Justice O'Connor, concurring in the judgment.

The Court today overrules *Bowers v. Hardwick*, 478 U.S. 186, 106 S. Ct. 2841, 92 L. Ed. 2d 140 (1986). I joined *Bowers*, and do not join the Court in overruling it. Nevertheless, I agree with the Court that Texas' statute banning same-sex sodomy is unconstitutional. *See* Tex. Penal Code Ann. §21.06 (2003). Rather than relying on the substantive component of the Fourteenth Amendment's Due Process Clause, as the Court does, I base my conclusion on the Fourteenth Amendment's Equal Protection Clause.

The Equal Protection Clause of the Fourteenth Amendment "is essentially a direction that all persons similarly situated should be treated alike." *City of Cleburne v. Cleburne Living Center, Inc.*, 473 U.S. 432, 439, 105 S. Ct. 3249, 87 L. Ed. 2d 313 (1985); *see also Plyler v. Doe*, 457 U.S. 202, 216, 102 S. Ct. 2382, 72 L. Ed. 2d 786 (1982). Under our rational basis standard of review, "legislation is presumed to be valid and will be sustained if the classification drawn by the statute is rationally related to a legitimate state interest."

...

Laws such as economic or tax legislation that are scrutinized under rational basis review normally pass constitutional muster, since "the Constitution presumes that even improvident decisions will eventually be rectified by the democratic processes."

...

We have consistently held, however, that some objectives, such as "a bare ... desire to harm a politically unpopular group," are not legitimate state interests.

...

When a law exhibits such a desire to harm a politically unpopular group, we have applied a more searching form of rational basis review to strike down such laws under the Equal Protection Clause.

We have been most likely to apply rational basis review to hold a law unconstitutional under the Equal Protection Clause where, as here, the challenged legislation inhibits personal relationships. In *Department of Agriculture v. Moreno*, for example, we held that a law preventing those households containing an individual unrelated to any other member of the household from receiving food stamps violated equal protection because the purpose of the law was to "'discriminate against hippies.'" 413 U.S., at 534, 93 S. Ct. 2821. The asserted governmental interest in preventing food stamp fraud was not deemed sufficient to satisfy rational basis review. *Id.* at 535–538, 93 S. Ct. 2821. In *Eisenstadt v. Baird*, 405 U.S. 438, 447–55, 92 S. Ct. 1029, 31 L. Ed. 2d 349 (1972), we refused to sanction a law that discriminated between married and unmarried persons by prohibiting the distribution of contraceptives to single persons. Likewise, in *Cleburne v. Cleburne Living Center, supra*, we held that it was irrational for a State to require a home for the mentally disabled to obtain a special use permit when other residences—like fraternity houses and apartment buildings—did not have to obtain such a permit. And in *Romer v. Evans*, we disallowed a state statute that "impos[ed] a broad and undifferentiated disability on a single named group"—specifically, homosexuals. 517 U.S., at 632, 116 S. Ct. 1620.

The statute at issue here makes sodomy a crime only if a person "engages in deviate sexual intercourse with another individual of the same sex." Tex. Penal Code Ann. § 21.06(a) (2003). Sodomy between opposite-sex partners, however, is not a crime in Texas. That is, Texas treats the same conduct differently based solely on the participants. Those harmed by this law are people who have a same-sex sexual orientation and thus are more likely to engage in behavior prohibited by § 21.06.

The Texas statute makes homosexuals unequal in the eyes of the law by making particular conduct—and only that conduct—subject to criminal sanction. It appears that prosecutions under Texas' sodomy law are rare. *See State v. Morales*, 869 S.W.2d 941, 943 (Tex. 1994) (noting in 1994 that § 21.06 "has not been, and in all probability will not be, enforced against private consensual conduct between adults"). This case shows, however, that prosecutions under § 21.06 do occur. And while the penalty imposed on petitioners in this case was relatively minor, the consequences of conviction are not. It appears that petitioners' convictions, if upheld, would disqualify them from or restrict their ability to engage in a variety of professions, including medicine, athletic training, and interior design. *See, e.g.*, Tex. Occ. Code Ann. § 164.051(a)(2)(B) (2003 Pamphlet) (physician); § 451.251(a)(1) (athletic trainer); § 1053.252(2) (interior designer). Indeed, were petitioners to move to one of four States, their convictions would require them to register as sex offenders to local law enforcement. *See, e.g.*, Idaho Code § 18-8304 (Cum. Supp. 2002); La. Stat. Ann. § 15:542 (West Cum. Supp. 2003); Miss. Code Ann. § 45-33-25 (West 2003); S.C. Code Ann. § 23-3-430 (West Cum. Supp. 2002); cf. *ante*, at 2482.

And the effect of Texas' sodomy law is not just limited to the threat of prosecution or consequence of conviction. Texas' sodomy law brands all homosexuals as criminals, thereby making it more difficult for homosexuals to be treated in the same manner as everyone else. Indeed, Texas itself has previously acknowledged the collateral effects of the law, stipulating in a prior challenge to this action that the law "legally sanctions discrimination against [homosexuals] in a variety of ways unrelated to the criminal law," including in the areas of "employment, family issues, and housing." ...

... The only question in front of the Court in *Bowers* was whether the substantive component of the Due Process Clause protected a right to engage in homosexual sodomy.... *Bowers* did not hold that moral disapproval of a group is a rational basis under the Equal Protection Clause to criminalize homosexual sodomy when heterosexual sodomy is not punished.

This case raises a different issue than *Bowers*: whether, under the Equal Protection Clause, moral disapproval is a legitimate state interest to justify by itself a statute that bans homosexual sodomy, but not heterosexual sodomy. It is not. Moral disapproval of this group, like a bare desire to harm the group, is an interest that is insufficient to satisfy rational basis review under the Equal Protection Clause. *See, e.g., Department of Agriculture v. Moreno*, 413 U.S., at 534, 93 S. Ct. 2821; *Romer v. Evans*, 517 U.S. at 634–635, 116 S. Ct. 1620. Indeed, we have never held that moral disapproval, without any other asserted state interest, is a sufficient rationale under the Equal Protection Clause to justify a law that discriminates among groups of persons.

Moral disapproval of a group cannot be a legitimate governmental interest under the Equal Protection Clause because legal classifications must not be "drawn for the purpose of disadvantaging the group burdened by the law." *Id.*, at 633, 116 S. Ct. 1620. Texas' invocation of moral disapproval as a legitimate state interest proves nothing more than Texas' desire to criminalize homosexual sodomy. But the Equal Protection Clause prevents a State from creating "a classification of persons undertaken for its own sake." *Id.*, at 635, 116 S. Ct. 1620. And because Texas so rarely enforces its sodomy law as applied to private, consensual acts, the law serves more as a statement of dislike and disapproval against homosexuals than as a tool to stop criminal behavior. The Texas sodomy law "raise[s] the inevitable inference that the disadvantage imposed is born of animosity toward the class of persons affected." *Id.*, at 634, 116 S. Ct. 1620.

...

That this law as applied to private, consensual conduct is unconstitutional under the Equal Protection Clause does not mean that other laws distinguishing between heterosexuals and homosexuals would similarly fail under rational basis review. Texas cannot assert any legitimate state interest here, such as national security or preserving the traditional institution of marriage. Unlike the moral disapproval of same-sex relations—the asserted state interest in this case—other reasons exist to promote the institution of marriage beyond mere moral disapproval of an excluded group.

A law branding one class of persons as criminal based solely on the State's moral disapproval of that class and the conduct associated with that class runs contrary to the values of the Constitution and the Equal Protection Clause, under any standard of review. I therefore concur in the Court's judgment that Texas' sodomy law banning "deviate sexual intercourse" between consenting adults of the same sex, but not between consenting adults of different sexes, is unconstitutional.

...

[3] Due Process

Kolender v. Lawson

Supreme Court of the United States
461 U.S. 352 (1983)

Justice O'Connor delivered the opinion of the Court.

This appeal presents a facial challenge to a criminal statute that requires persons who loiter or wander on the streets to provide a "credible and reliable" identification and to account for their presence when requested by a peace officer under circumstances that would justify a stop....[1] We conclude that the statute as it has been construed is unconstitutionally vague within the meaning of the Due Process clause of the Fourteenth Amendment by failing to clarify what is contemplated by the requirement that a suspect provide a "credible and reliable" identification. Accordingly, we affirm the judgment of the court below.

I.

Appellee Edward Lawson was detained or arrested on approximately 15 occasions between March 1975 and January 1977 pursuant to Cal. Penal Code § 647(e).[2] Lawson was prosecuted only twice, and convicted once. The second charge was dismissed.

---

1. Cal. Penal Code § 647(e) (West 1970) provides:

> Every person who commits any of the following acts is guilty of disorderly conduct, a misdemeanor: ... (e) Who loiters or wanders upon the streets or from place to place without apparent reason or business and who refuses to identify himself and to account for his presence when requested by any peace officer to do so, if the surrounding circumstances are such as to indicate to a reasonable man that the public safety demands such identification.

2. The District Court failed to find facts concerning the particular occasions on which Lawson was detained or arrested under § 647(e). However, the trial transcript contains numerous descriptions of the stops given both by Lawson and by the police officers who detained him. For example, one police officer testified that he stopped Lawson while walking on an otherwise vacant street because it was late at night, the area was isolated, and the area was located close to a high crime area. Tr. 266–67. Another officer testified that he detained Lawson, who was walking at a late hour in a business area where some businesses were still open, and asked for identification because burglaries had been

Lawson then brought a civil action in the District Court for the Southern District of California seeking a declaratory judgment that § 647(e) is unconstitutional, a mandatory injunction seeking to restrain enforcement of the statute, and compensatory and punitive damages against the various officers who detained him. The District Court found that § 647(e) was overbroad because "a person who is stopped on less than probable cause cannot be punished for failing to identify himself." [The Court of Appeals for the Ninth Circuit affirmed the determination of unconstitutionality.]

II.

... As construed by the California Court of Appeal, § 647(e) requires that an individual provide "credible and reliable" identification when requested by a police officer who has reasonable suspicion of criminal activity sufficient to justify a *Terry* detention.[4] ... "Credible and reliable" identification is defined by the state Court of Appeal as identification "carrying reasonable assurance that the identification is authentic and providing means for later getting in touch with the person who has identified himself." ... In addition, a suspect may be required to "*account for his presence* ... to the extent that it assists in producing credible and reliable identification...." ... Under the terms of the statute, failure of the individual to provide "credible and reliable" identification permits the arrest.

III.

...

As generally stated, the void-for-vagueness doctrine requires that a penal statute define the criminal offense with sufficient definiteness that ordinary people can understand what conduct is prohibited and in a manner that does not encourage arbitrary and discriminatory enforcement.... Although the doctrine focuses both on actual notice to citizens and arbitrary enforcement, we have recognized recently that the more important aspect of vagueness doctrine "is not actual notice, but the other principal element of the doctrine—the requirement that a legislature establish minimal guidelines to govern law enforcement." ... Where the legislature fails to provide such minimal guidelines, a criminal statute may permit "a standardless sweep [that] allows policemen, prosecutors, and juries to pursue their personal predilections." ...

Section 647(e), as presently drafted and construed by the state courts, contains no standard for determining what a suspect has to do in order to satisfy the requirement to provide a "credible and reliable" identification. As such, the statute vests virtually complete discretion in the hands of the police to determine whether the suspect has satisfied the statute and must be permitted to go on his way in the absence of probable cause to arrest. An individual, whom police may think is suspicious but do

---

committed by unknown persons in the general area. Tr. 207. The appellee states that he has never been stopped by police for any reason apart from his detentions under § 647(e).

4. The reference is to Terry v. Ohio, 392 U.S. 1, 88 S. Ct. 1868, 20 L. Ed. 2d 889 (1968), the landmark decision establishing constitutional standards for field detentions under circumstances short of probable cause to arrest.

not have probable cause to believe has committed a crime, is entitled to continue to walk the public streets "only at the whim of any police officer" who happens to stop that individual under § 647(e).... Our concern here is based upon the "potential for arbitrarily suppressing First Amendment liberties...." ... In addition, § 647(e) implicates consideration of the constitutional right to freedom of movement....

Section 647(e) is not simply a "stop-and-identify" statute. Rather, the statute requires that the individual provide a "credible and reliable" identification that carries a "reasonable assurance" of its authenticity, and that provides "means for later getting in touch with the person who has identified himself." ... In addition, the suspect may also have to account for his presence "to the extent it assists in producing credible and reliable identification." ...

At oral argument, the appellants confirmed that a suspect violates § 647(e) unless "the officer [is] satisfied that the identification is reliable." ... In giving examples of how suspects would satisfy the requirement, appellants explained that a jogger, who was not carrying identification, could, depending on the particular officer, be required to answer a series of questions concerning the route that he followed to arrive at the place where the officers detained him, or could satisfy the identification requirement simply by reciting his name and address....

It is clear that the full discretion accorded to the police to determine whether the suspect has provided a "credible and reliable" identification necessarily "[entrusts] lawmaking 'to the moment-to-moment judgment of the policeman on his beat.'" ... Section 647(e) "furnishes a convenient tool for 'harsh and discriminatory enforcement by local prosecuting officials, against particular groups deemed to merit their displeasure,'" ... and "confers on police a virtually unrestrained power to arrest and charge persons with a violation." ... Appellants stress the need for strengthened law enforcement tools to combat the epidemic of crime that plagues our Nation. The concern of our citizens with curbing criminal activity is certainly a matter requiring the attention of all branches of government. As weighty as this concern is, however, it cannot justify legislation that would otherwise fail to meet constitutional standards for definiteness and clarity.... Section 647(e), as presently construed, requires that "suspicious" persons satisfy some undefined identification requirement, or face criminal punishment. Although due process does not require "impossible standards" of clarity, ... this is not a case where further precision in the statutory language is either impossible or impractical.

IV.

We conclude § 647(e) is unconstitutionally vague on its face because it encourages arbitrary enforcement by failing to describe with sufficient particularity what a suspect must do in order to satisfy the statute....

Comments

(1) As the *Kolender* Court explains, the concern with vague statutes, or those that fail to meet the constitutional requirement of definiteness, is twofold: (1) vague

statutes fail to give citizens fair notice regarding what conduct has been made criminal; and (2) vague statutes enable executive actors to enforce the law in an arbitrary, and potentially discriminatory, manner. The *Kolender* Court was particularly concerned with the second issue—that police enjoyed unfettered discretion to determine on an ad hoc basis whom to stop and whether that person provided reliable identification. For an example of a court addressing the fair notice aspect of a due process challenge, *see State v. Miranda*, 794 A.2d 506, *cert. denied*, 537 U.S. 902 (Conn. 2002) (rejecting defendant's Due Process challenge to his conviction for failure to render aid to abused stepdaughter).

(2) *Kolender v. Lawson* was the controlling precedent for declaring the Chicago Gang Congregation Ordinance void for vagueness in *City of Chicago v. Morales*, 527 U.S. 41 (1999). The ordinance provided:

> Whenever a police officer observes a person whom he reasonably believes to be a criminal street gang member loitering in any public place with one or more other persons, he shall order all such persons to disperse and remove themselves from the area. Any person who does not promptly obey such an order is in violation of this section.

Chicago Municipal Code §8-4-015. A majority of the Supreme Court held that the ordinance failed to respect the admonition of *Kolender* that the legislature establish minimal guidelines to govern law enforcement. The Court noted that the highest state court had interpreted the ordinance so as to authorize "absolute discretion to police officers to determine what activities constitute loitering," and the Court was bound by this construction. So construed, the Court concluded that the ordinance was too broad in its sweep to survive scrutiny under the due process clause.

(3) In *Johnson v. United States*, 135 S. Ct. 2551 (2015) the defendant pleaded guilty to being a felon in possession of a firearm. The government sought a sentencing enhancement under the Armed Career Criminal Act (ACCA), which permitted a more severe punishment for defendants with three or more previous convictions for a "violent felony." The ACCA further defined a "violent felony" as any felony that "involves conduct that presents a serious potential risk of physical injury to another." 18 U. S. C. §924(e)(2)(B). Writing for the majority, Justice Scalia found the statutory definition of a violent felony vague and in violation of the due process clause.

> The Fifth Amendment provides that "[n]o person shall ... be deprived of life, liberty, or property, without due process of law." Our cases establish that the Government violates this guarantee by taking away someone's life, liberty, or property under a criminal law so vague that it fails to give ordinary people fair notice of the conduct it punishes, or so standardless that it invites arbitrary enforcement. *Kolender v. Lawson*, 461 U.S. 352, 357–358, 103 S. Ct. 1855, 75 L.Ed.2d 903 (1983). The prohibition of vagueness in criminal statutes "is a well-recognized requirement, consonant alike with ordinary notions of fair play and the settled rules of law," and a statute that flouts it "violates the first essential of due process." *Connally v. General Constr. Co.*,

> 269 U.S. 385, 391, 46 S. Ct. 126, 70 L. Ed. 322 (1926). These principles apply not only to statutes defining elements of crimes, but also to statutes fixing sentences. *United States v. Batchelder*, 442 U.S. 114, 123, 99 S. Ct. 2198, 60 L.Ed.2d 755 (1979).
>
> In *Taylor v. United States*, 495 U.S. 575, 600, 110 S. Ct. 2143, 109 L.Ed.2d 607 (1990), this Court held that the Armed Career Criminal Act requires courts to use a framework known as the categorical approach when deciding whether an offense "is burglary, arson, or extortion, involves use of explosives, or otherwise involves conduct that presents a serious potential risk of physical injury to another." Under the categorical approach, a court assesses whether a crime qualifies as a violent felony "in terms of how the law defines the offense and not in terms of how an individual offender might have committed it on a particular occasion." *Begay, supra,* at 141, 128 S. Ct. 1581.
>
> Deciding whether the residual clause covers a crime thus requires a court to picture the kind of conduct that the crime involves in "the ordinary case," and to judge whether that abstraction presents a serious potential risk of physical injury. *James, supra,* at 208, 127 S. Ct. 1586. The court's task goes beyond deciding whether creation of risk is an element of the crime. That is so because, unlike the part of the definition of a violent felony that asks whether the crime "has *as an element* the use ... of physical force," the residual clause asks whether the crime "*involves conduct*" that presents too much risk of physical injury. What is more, the inclusion of burglary and extortion among the enumerated offenses preceding the residual clause confirms that the court's task also goes beyond evaluating the chances that the physical acts that make up the crime will injure someone. The act of making an extortionate demand or breaking and entering into someone's home does not, in and of itself, normally cause physical injury. Rather, risk of injury arises because the extortionist might engage in violence *after* making his demand or because the burglar might confront a resident in the home *after* breaking and entering.
>
> We are convinced that the indeterminacy of the wide-ranging inquiry required by the residual clause both denies fair notice to defendants and invites arbitrary enforcement by judges. Increasing a defendant's sentence under the clause denies due process of law.

Three members of the Court would have left the residual clause of the ACCA intact and would have resolved the vagueness challenge under the Court's prior framework. Justice Thomas, concurring in the judgment, wrote:

> It has long been understood that one of the problems with holding a statute "void for 'indefiniteness'" is that "'indefiniteness' ... is itself an indefinite concept," *Winters, supra,* at 524, 68 S. Ct. 665 (Frankfurter, J., dissenting), and we as a Court have a bad habit of using indefinite concepts—especially ones rooted in "due process"—to invalidate democratically enacted laws.

Is there are any truth to Justice Thomas's claim that "indefiniteness" is an "indefinite concept"? And if so, which branch of government is better suited to resolve the question of indefiniteness?

Justice Alito dissented, arguing that the Court was abandoning the doctrine of stare decisis and ignoring that a majority had found the same statutory language sufficiently definite in recent prior cases. Further, Justice Alito maintained that the violent felony definition in the Act was not unconstitutionally vague:

> The Fifth Amendment prohibits the enforcement of vague criminal laws, but the threshold for declaring a law void for vagueness is high. "The strong presumptive validity that attaches to an Act of Congress has led this Court to hold many times that statutes are not automatically invalidated as vague simply because difficulty is found in determining whether certain marginal offenses fall within their language." *United States v. National Dairy Products Corp.*, 372 U.S. 29, 32, 83 S. Ct. 594, 9 L.Ed.2d 561 (1963). Rather, it is sufficient if a statute sets out an "ascertainable standard." *United States v. L. Cohen Grocery Co.*, 255 U.S. 81, 89, 41 S. Ct. 298, 65 L. Ed. 516 (1921). A statute is thus void for vagueness only if it wholly "fails to provide a person of ordinary intelligence fair notice of what is prohibited, or is so standardless that it authorizes or encourages seriously discriminatory enforcement." *United States v. Williams*, 553 U.S. 285, 304, 128 S. Ct. 1830, 170 L.Ed.2d 650 (2008).
>
> The bar is even higher for sentencing provisions. The fair notice concerns that inform our vagueness doctrine are aimed at ensuring that a " 'person of ordinary intelligence [has] a reasonable opportunity to know what is prohibited, so that he may act accordingly.' " *Hoffman Estates v. Flipside, Hoffman Estates, Inc.*, 455 U.S. 489, 498, 102 S. Ct. 1186, 71 L.Ed.2d 362 (1982) (quoting *Grayned v. City of Rockford*, 408 U.S. 104, 108, 92 S. Ct. 2294, 33 L.Ed.2d 222 (1972)). The fear is that vague laws will " 'trap the innocent.' " 455 U.S., at 498, 102 S. Ct. 1186. These concerns have less force when it comes to sentencing provisions, which come into play only after the defendant has been found guilty of the crime in question. Due process does not require, as Johnson oddly suggests, that a "prospective criminal" be able to calculate the precise penalty that a conviction would bring.

Justice Alito seemed to question the reality that prospective criminals weigh their choices in light of potential sentences—let alone the claim that individuals have a right to make such a calculus. Do "prospective criminals" engage in that analysis? If you think they do not, then what is the purpose behind the requirement of definiteness?

[4] Freedom from Cruel and Unusual Punishment

Gregg v. Georgia

Supreme Court of the United States
428 U.S. 153 (1976)

Judgment of the Court, and opinion of Mr. Justice STEWART, Mr. Justice POWELL, and Mr. Justice STEVENS, announced by Mr. Justice STEWART.

The issue in this case is whether the imposition of the sentence of death for the crime of murder under the law of Georgia violates the Eighth and Fourteenth Amendments.

...

II

Before considering the issues presented it is necessary to understand the Georgia statutory scheme for the imposition of the death penalty. The Georgia statute, as amended after our decision in *Furman v. Georgia*, 408 U.S. 238, 92 S. Ct. 2726, 33 L.Ed.2d 346 (1972), retains the death penalty for six categories of crime: murder, kidnaping for ransom or where the victim is harmed, armed robbery, rape, treason, and aircraft hijacking. 6 Ga. Code Ann.§§ 26-1101, 26-1311, 26-1902, 26-2001, 26-2201, 26-3301 (1972). The capital defendant's guilt or innocence is determined in the traditional manner, either by a trial judge or a jury, in the first stage of a bifurcated trial.

... After a verdict, finding, or plea of guilty to a capital crime, a presentence hearing is conducted before whoever made the determination of guilt. The sentencing procedures are essentially the same in both bench and jury trials. At the hearing:

"(T)he judge (or jury) shall hear additional evidence in extenuation, mitigation, and aggravation of punishment, including the record of any prior criminal convictions and pleas of guilty or pleas of nolo contendere of the defendant, or the absence of any prior conviction and pleas: Provided, however, that only such evidence in aggravation as the State has made known to the defendant prior to his trial shall be admissible. The judge (or jury) shall also hear argument by the defendant or his counsel and the prosecuting attorney ... regarding the punishment to be imposed." s 27-2503. (Supp.1975).

The defendant is accorded substantial latitude as to the types of evidence that he may introduce.... Evidence considered during the guilt stage may be considered during the sentencing stage without being resubmitted....

In the assessment of the appropriate sentence to be imposed the judge is also required to consider or to include in his instructions to the jury "any mitigating circumstances or aggravating circumstances otherwise authorized by law and any of (10) statutory aggravating circumstances which may be supported by the evidence...." s 27-2534.1(b) (Supp.1975). The scope of the nonstatutory aggravating or mitigating circumstances is not delineated in the statute. Before a convicted defendant may be sentenced to death, however, except in cases of treason or aircraft hijacking, the jury, or the trial judge in cases tried without a jury, must find beyond a reasonable doubt one of the 10 aggravating circumstances specified in the statute. The sentence of death may be imposed only if the jury (or judge) finds one of the statutory aggravating circumstances and then elects to impose that sentence. s 26-3102 (Supp.1975). If the verdict is death, the jury or judge must specify the aggravating circumstance(s) found. s 27-2534.1(c) (Supp.1975). In jury cases, the trial judge is bound by the jury's recommended sentence. ss 26-3102, 27-2514 (Supp.1975)

In addition to the conventional appellate process available in all criminal cases, provision is made for special expedited direct review by the Supreme Court of Georgia of the appropriateness of imposing the sentence of death in the particular case. The court is directed to consider "the punishment as well as any errors enumerated by way of appeal," and to determine:

> (1) Whether the sentence of death was imposed under the influence of passion, prejudice, or anything arbitrary factor, and
>
> (2) Whether, in cases other than treason or aircraft hijacking, the evidence supports the jury's or judge's finding of a statutory aggravating circumstance as enumerated in section 27.2534.1(b), and
>
> (3) Whether the sentence of death is excessive or disproportionate to the penalty imposed in similar cases, considering both the crime and the defendant. s 27-2537 (Supp.1975).

If the court affirms a death sentence, it is required to include in its decision reference to similar cases that it has taken into consideration. s 27-2537(e) (Supp. 1975).

A transcript and complete record of the trial, as well as a separate report by the trial judge, are transmitted to the court for its use in reviewing the sentence. s 27-2537(a) (Supp. 1975). The report is in the form of a 6½ page questionnaire, designed to elicit information about the defendant, the crime, and the circumstances of the trial. It requires the trial judge to characterize the trial in several ways designed to test for arbitrariness and disproportionality of sentence. Included in the report are responses to detailed questions concerning the quality of the defendant's representation, whether race played a role in the trial, and, whether, in the trial court's judgment, there was any doubt about the defendant's guilt or the appropriateness of the sentence. A copy of the report is served upon defense counsel. Under its special review authority, the court may either affirm the death sentence or remand the case for resentencing. In cases in which the death sentence is affirmed there remains the possibility of executive clemency.

III

We address initially the basic contention that the punishment of death for the crime of murder is, under all circumstances, "cruel and unusual" in violation of the Eighth and Fourteenth Amendments of the Constitution. In Part IV of this opinion, we will consider the sentence of death imposed under the Georgia statutes at issue in this case.

The Court on a number of occasions has both assumed and asserted the constitutionality of capital punishment. In several cases that assumption provided a necessary foundation for the decision, as the Court was asked to decide whether a particular method of carrying out a capital sentence would be allowed to stand under the Eighth Amendment. But until *Furman v. Georgia*, 408 U.S. 238, 92 S. Ct. 2726, 33 L.Ed.2d

346 (1972), the Court never confronted squarely the fundamental claim that the punishment of death always, regardless of the enormity of the offense or the procedure followed in imposing the sentence, is cruel and unusual punishment in violation of the Constitution. Although this issue was presented and addressed in *Furman*, it was not resolved by the Court.... We now hold that the punishment of death does not invariably violate the Constitution.

A

The history of the prohibition of "cruel and unusual" punishment already has been reviewed at length. The phrase first appeared in the English Bill of Rights of 1689, which was drafted by Parliament at the accession of William and Mary. See Granucci, *"Nor Cruel and Unusual Punishments Inflicted:" The Original Meaning*, 57 CALIF. L. REV. 839, 852–853 (1969). The English version appears to have been directed against punishments unauthorized by statute and beyond the jurisdiction of the sentencing court, as well as those disproportionate to the offense involved. *Id.*, at 860. The American draftsmen, who adopted the English phrasing in drafting the Eighth Amendment, were primarily concerned, however, with proscribing "tortures" and other "barbarous" methods of punishment. *Id.*, at 842.

In the earliest cases raising Eighth Amendment claims, the Court focused on particular methods of execution to determine whether they were too cruel to pass constitutional muster. The constitutionality of the sentence of death itself was not at issue, and the criterion used to evaluate the mode of execution was its similarity to "torture" and other "barbarous" methods. See *Wilkerson v. Utah*, 99 U.S. 130, 136 (1879) ("(I)t is safe to affirm that punishments of torture ... and all others in the same line of unnecessary cruelty, are forbidden by that amendment ...")....

But the Court has not confined the prohibition embodied in the Eighth Amendment to "barbarous" methods that were generally outlawed in the 18th century. Instead, the Amendment has been interpreted in a flexible and dynamic manner. The Court early recognized that "a principle to be vital, must be capable of wider application than the mischief which gave it birth." *Weems v. United States*, 217 U.S. 349, 373, 30 S. Ct. 544, 551, 54 L. Ed. 793 (1910). Thus the Clause forbidding "cruel and unusual" punishments "is not fastened to the obsolete but may acquire meaning as public opinion becomes enlightened by a humane justice." *Id.*, at 378, 30 S. Ct., at 553....

In *Weems* the Court addressed the constitutionality of the Philippine punishment of Cadena temporal for the crime of falsifying an official document. That punishment included imprisonment for at least 12 years and one day, in chains, at hard and painful labor; the loss of many basic civil rights; and subjection to lifetime surveillance. Although the Court acknowledged the possibility that "the cruelty of pain" may be present in the challenged punishment, 217 U.S., at 366, 30 S. Ct., at 549, it did not rely on that factor, for it rejected the proposition that the Eighth Amendment reaches only punishments that are "inhuman and barbarous, torture and the like." *Id.*, at 368, 30 S. Ct., at 549. Rather, the Court focused on the lack of proportion between the crime and the offense:

"Such penalties for such offenses amaze those who have formed their conception of the relation of a state to even its offending citizens from the practice of the American commonwealths, and believe that it is a precept of justice that punishment for crime should be graduated and proportioned to offense." *Id.*, at 366–367, 30 S. Ct., at 549....

The substantive limits imposed by the Eighth Amendment on what can be made criminal and punished were discussed in *Robinson v. California*, 370 U.S. 660, 82 S. Ct. 1417, 8 L.Ed.2d 758 (1962). The Court found unconstitutional a state statute that made the status of being addicted to a narcotic drug a criminal offense. It held, in effect, that it is "cruel and unusual" to impose any punishment at all for the mere status of addiction. The cruelty in the abstract of the actual sentence imposed was irrelevant: "Even one day in prison would be a cruel and unusual punishment for the 'crime' of having a common cold." Id., at 667, 82 S. Ct. at 1421. Most recently, in Furman v. Georgia, supra, three Justices in separate concurring opinions found the Eighth Amendment applicable to procedures employed to select convicted defendants for the sentence of death.

It is clear from the foregoing precedents that the Eighth Amendment has not been regarded as a static concept. As Mr. Chief Justice Warren said, in an oft-quoted phrase, "(t)he Amendment must draw its meaning from the evolving standards of decency that mark the progress of a maturing society." *Trop v. Dulles, supra*, 356 U.S. at 101, 78 S. Ct., at 598.... Thus, an assessment of contemporary values concerning the infliction of a challenged sanction is relevant to the application of the Eighth Amendment. As we develop below more fully ... this assessment does not call for a subjective judgment. It requires, rather, that we look to objective indicia that reflect the public attitude toward a given sanction.

But our cases also make clear that public perceptions of standards of decency with respect to criminal sanctions are not conclusive. A penalty also must accord with "the dignity of man," which is the "basic concept underlying the Eighth Amendment." *Trop v. Dulles, supra*, 356 U.S., at 100, 78 S. Ct., at 597 (plurality opinion). This means, at least, that the punishment not be "excessive." When a form of punishment in the abstract (in this case, whether capital punishment may ever be imposed as a sanction for murder) rather than in the particular (the propriety of death as a penalty to be applied to a specific defendant for a specific crime) is under consideration, the inquiry into "excessiveness" has two aspects. First, the punishment must not involve the unnecessary and wanton infliction of pain.... Second, the punishment must not be grossly out of proportion to the severity of the crime ...

B

Of course, the requirements of the Eighth Amendment must be applied with an awareness of the limited role to be played by the courts. This does not mean that judges have no role to play, for the Eighth Amendment is a restraint upon the exercise of legislative power.

"Judicial review by definition, often involves a conflict between judicial and legislative judgment as to what the Constitution means or requires. In this respect,

Eighth Amendment cases come to us in no different posture. It seems conceded by all that the Amendment imposes some obligations on the judiciary to judge the constitutionality of punishment and that there are punishments that the Amendment would bar whether legislatively approved or not." *Furman v. Georgia*, 408 U.S., at 313–314, 92 S. Ct., at 2764 (White, J., concurring)....

But, while we have an obligation to insure that constitutional bounds are not overreached, we may not act as judges as we might as legislators.

"Courts are not representative bodies. They are not designed to be a good reflex of a democratic society. Their judgment is best informed, and therefore most dependable, within narrow limits. Their essential quality is detachment, founded on independence. History teaches that the independence of the judiciary is jeopardized when courts become embroiled in the passions of the day and assume primary responsibility in choosing between competing political, economic and social pressures." *Dennis v. United States*, 341 U.S. 494, 525, 71 S. Ct. 857, 875, 95 L. Ed. 1137 (1951) (FRANKFURTER, J., concurring in affirmance of judgment).

Therefore, in assessing a punishment selected by a democratically elected legislature against the constitutional measure, we presume its validity. We may not require the legislature to select the least severe penalty possible so long as the penalty selected is not cruelly inhumane or disproportionate to the crime involved. And a heavy burden rests on those who would attack the judgment of the representatives of the people.

This is true in part because the constitutional test is intertwined with an assessment of contemporary standards and the legislative judgment weighs heavily in ascertaining such standards. "(I)n a democratic society legislatures, not courts, are constituted to respond to the will and consequently the moral values of the people." *Furman v. Georgia, supra*, 408 U.S., at 383, 92 S. Ct., at 2800 (BURGER, C.J., dissenting). The deference we owe to the decisions of the state legislatures under our federal system, 408 U.S., at 465–470, 92 S. Ct., at 2842–2844 (Rehnquist, J., dissenting), is enhanced where the specification of punishments is concerned, for "these are peculiarly questions of legislative policy." *Gore v. United States*, 357 U.S. 386, 393, 78 S. Ct. 1280, 1285, 2 L.Ed.2d 1405 (1958).... Caution is necessary lest this Court become, "under the aegis of the Cruel and Unusual Punishment Clause, the ultimate arbiter of the standards of criminal responsibility ... throughout the country." *Powell v. Texas*, 392 U.S. 514, 533, 88 S. Ct. 2145, 2154, 20 L.Ed.2d 1254 (1968) (plurality opinion). A decision that a given punishment is impermissible under the Eighth Amendment cannot be reversed short of a constitutional amendment. The ability of the people to express their preference through the normal democratic processes, as well as through ballot referenda, is shut off. Revisions cannot be made in the light of further experience. See Furman v. Georgia, Supra, 408 U.S., at 461–462, 92 S. Ct., at 2839–2840 (POWELL, J., dissenting).

C

In the discussion to this point we have sought to identify the principles and considerations that guide a court in addressing an Eighth Amendment claim. We now consider specifically whether the sentence of death for the crime of murder is a *per se* violation of the Eighth and Fourteenth Amendments to the Constitution. We note first that history and precedent strongly support a negative answer to this question.

The imposition of the death penalty for the crime of murder has a long history of acceptance both in the United States and in England. The common-law rule imposed a mandatory death sentence on all convicted murderers. *McGautha v. California*, 402 U.S. 183, 197–198, 91 S. Ct. 1454, 1462–1463, 28 L.Ed.2d 711 (1971). And the penalty continued to be used into the 20th century by most American States, although the breadth of the common-law rule was diminished, initially by narrowing the class of murders to be punished by death and subsequently by widespread adoption of laws expressly granting juries the discretion to recommend mercy....

It is apparent from the text of the Constitution itself that the existence of capital punishment was accepted by the Framers. At the time the Eighth Amendment was ratified, capital punishment was a common sanction in every State. Indeed, the First Congress of the United States enacted legislation providing death as the penalty for specified crimes. C. 9, 1 Stat. 112 (1790). The Fifth Amendment, adopted at the same time as the Eighth, contemplated the continued existence of the capital sanction by imposing certain limits on the prosecution of capital cases:

> No person shall be held to answer for a capital, or otherwise infamous crime, unless on a presentment or indictment of a Grand Jury ... ; nor shall any person be subject for the same offense to be twice put in jeopardy of life or limb; ... nor be deprived of life, liberty, or property, without due process of law....

And the Fourteenth Amendment, adopted over three-quarters of a century later, similarly contemplates the existence of the capital sanction in providing that no State shall deprive any person of "life, liberty, or property" without due process of law.

For nearly two centuries, this Court, repeatedly and often expressly, has recognized that capital punishment is not invalid *per se*. In *Wilkerson v. Utah*, 99 U.S., at 134–135, where the Court found no constitutional violation in inflicting death by public shooting, it said:

> Cruel and unusual punishments are forbidden by the Constitution, but the authorities referred to are quite sufficient to show that the punishment of shooting as a mode of executing the death penalty for the crime of murder in the first degree is not included in that category, within the meaning of the eighth amendment.

Rejecting the contention that death by electrocution was "cruel and unusual," the Court in *In re Kemmler, supra*, 136 U.S., at 447, 10 S. Ct., at 933 reiterated:

> (T)he punishment of death is not cruel, within the meaning of that word as used in the Constitution. It implies there something inhuman and barbarous, something more than the mere extinguishment of life.

Again, in *Louisiana ex rel. Francis v. Resweber*, the Court remarked: "The cruelty against which the Constitution protects a convicted man is cruelty inherent in the method of punishment, not the necessary suffering involved in any method employed to extinguish life humanely." And in *Trop v. Dulles*, 356 U.S., at 99, 78 S. Ct., at 597, Mr. Chief Justice Warren, for himself and three other Justices, wrote:

> Whatever the arguments may be against capital punishment, both on moral grounds and in terms of accomplishing the purposes of punishment ... the death penalty has been employed throughout our history, and, in a day when it is still widely accepted, it cannot be said to violate the constitutional concept of cruelty.

Four years ago, the petitioners in *Furman* and its companion cases predicated their argument primarily upon the asserted proposition that standards of decency had evolved to the point where capital punishment no longer could be tolerated. The petitioners in those cases said, in effect, that the evolutionary process had come to an end, and that standards of decency required that the Eighth Amendment be construed finally as prohibiting capital punishment for any crime regardless of its depravity and impact on society. This view was accepted by two Justices. Three other Justices were unwilling to go so far; focusing on the procedures by which convicted defendants were selected for the death penalty rather than on the actual punishment inflicted, they joined in the conclusion that the statutes before the Court were constitutionally invalid.

The petitioners in the capital cases before the Court today renew the "standards of decency" argument, but developments during the four years since *Furman* have undercut substantially the assumptions upon which their argument rested. Despite the continuing debate, dating back to the 19th century, over the morality and utility of capital punishment, it is now evident that a large proportion of American society continues to regard it as an appropriate and necessary criminal sanction.

The most marked indication of society's endorsement of the death penalty for murder is the legislative response to *Furman*. The legislatures of at least 35 States have enacted new statutes that provide for the death penalty for at least some crimes that result in the death of another person. And the Congress of the United States, in 1974, enacted a statute providing the death penalty for aircraft piracy that results in death. These recently adopted statutes have attempted to address the concerns expressed by the Court in *Furman* Primarily (i) by specifying the factors to be weighed and the procedures to be followed in deciding when to impose a capital sentence, or (ii) by making the death penalty mandatory for specified crimes. But all of the post-Furman Statutes make clear that capital punishment itself has not been rejected by the elected representatives of the people....

The jury also is a significant and reliable objective index of contemporary values because it is so directly involved. See *Furman v. Georgia*, 408 U.S., at 439–440, 92 S. Ct., at 2828–2829 (Powell, J., dissenting). See generally Powell, *Jury Trial of Crimes*, 23 Wash. & Lee L. Rev. 1 (1966). The Court has said that "one of the most important functions any jury can perform in making ... a selection (between life imprisonment and death for a defendant convicted in a capital case) is to maintain a link between contemporary community values and the penal system." *Witherspoon v. Illinois*, 391

U.S. 510, 519 n. 15, 88 S. Ct. 1770, 1775, 20 L.Ed.2d 776 (1968). It may be true that evolving standards have influenced juries in recent decades to be more discriminating in imposing the sentence of death. But the relative infrequency of jury verdicts imposing the death sentence does not indicate rejection of capital punishment Per se. Rather, the reluctance of juries in many cases to impose the sentence may well reflect the humane feeling that this most irrevocable of sanctions should be reserved for a small number of extreme cases.... Indeed, the actions of juries in many States since Furman are fully compatible with the legislative judgments, reflected in the new statutes, as to the continued utility and necessity of capital punishment in appropriate cases. At the close of 1974 at least 254 persons had been sentenced to death since Furman, and by the end of March 1976, more than 460 persons were subject to death sentences.

As we have seen, however, the Eighth Amendment demands more than that a challenged punishment be acceptable to contemporary society. The Court also must ask whether it comports with the basic concept of human dignity at the core of the Amendment. *Trop v. Dulles*, 356 U.S., at 100, 78 S. Ct., at 597 (plurality opinion). Although we cannot "invalidate a category of penalties because we deem less severe penalties adequate to serve the ends of penology," *Furman v. Georgia, supra*, 408 U.S., at 451, 92 S. Ct., at 2834 (Powell, J., dissenting), the sanction imposed cannot be so totally without penological justification that it results in the gratuitous infliction of suffering....

The death penalty is said to serve two principal social purposes: retribution and deterrence of capital crimes by prospective offenders.

In part, capital punishment is an expression of society's moral outrage at particularly offensive conduct. This function may be unappealing to many, but it is essential in an ordered society that asks its citizens to rely on legal processes rather than self-help to vindicate their wrongs.

"The instinct for retribution is part of the nature of man, and channeling that instinct in the administration of criminal justice serves an important purpose in promoting the stability of a society governed by law. When people begin to believe that organized society is unwilling or unable to impose upon criminal offenders the punishment they 'deserve,' then there are sown the seeds of anarchy of self-help, vigilante justice, and lynch law." *Furman v. Georgia, supra*, 408 U.S., at 308, 92 S. Ct., at 2761 (Stewart, J., concurring).... Indeed, the decision that capital punishment may be the appropriate sanction in extreme cases is an expression of the community's belief that certain crimes are themselves so grievous an affront to humanity that the only adequate response may be the penalty of death.

Statistical attempts to evaluate the worth of the death penalty as a deterrent to crimes by potential offenders have occasioned a great deal of debate....

The value of capital punishment as a deterrent of crime is a complex factual issue the resolution of which properly rests with the legislatures, which can evaluate the results of statistical studies in terms of their own local conditions and with a flexibility of approach that is not available to the courts. *Furman v. Georgia, supra*, 408 U.S., at 403–405, 92 S. Ct., at 2810–2812 (Burger, C. J., dissenting). Indeed, many of the post-*Furman* statutes reflect just such a responsible effort to define those crimes and those criminals for which capital punishment is most probably an effective deterrent.

In sum, we cannot say that the judgment of the Georgia Legislature that capital punishment may be necessary in some cases is clearly wrong. Considerations of federalism, as well as respect for the ability of a legislature to evaluate, in terms of its particular State, the moral consensus concerning the death penalty and its social utility as a sanction, require us to conclude, in the absence of more convincing evidence, that the infliction of death as a punishment for murder is not without justification and thus is not unconstitutionally severe.

Finally, we must consider whether the punishment of death is disproportionate in relation to the crime for which it is imposed. There is no question that death as a punishment is unique in its severity and irrevocability.... When a defendant's life is at stake, the Court has been particularly sensitive to insure that every safeguard is observed. *Powell v. Alabama*, 287 U.S. 45, 71, 53 S. Ct. 55, 65, 77 L. Ed. 158 (1932); *Reid v. Covert*, 354 U.S. 1, 77, 77 S. Ct. 1222, 1262, 1 L.Ed.2d 1148 (1957) (Harlan, J., concurring in result). But we are concerned here only with the imposition of capital punishment for the crime of murder, and when a life has been taken deliberately by the offender, we cannot say that the punishment is invariably disproportionate to the crime. It is an extreme sanction, suitable to the most extreme of crimes.

We hold that the death penalty is not a form of punishment that may never be imposed, regardless of the circumstances of the offense, regardless of the character of the offender, and regardless of the procedure followed in reaching the decision to impose it.

IV

We now consider whether Georgia may impose the death penalty on the petitioner in this case.

A

While *Furman* did not hold that the infliction of the death penalty Per se violates the Constitution's ban on cruel and unusual punishments, it did recognize that the penalty of death is different in kind from any other punishment imposed under our system of criminal justice. Because of the uniqueness of the death penalty, Furman held that it could not be imposed under sentencing procedures that created a substantial risk that it would be inflicted in an arbitrary and capricious manner. Mr. Justice White concluded that "the death penalty is exacted with great infrequency even for the most atrocious crimes and ... there is no meaningful basis for distinguishing the few cases in which it is imposed from the many cases in which it is not." 408 U.S., at 313, 92 S. Ct., at 2764 (concurring). Indeed, the death sentences examined by the Court in *Furman* were "cruel and unusual in the same way that being struck by lightening is cruel and unusual. For, of all the people convicted of (capital crimes), many just as reprehensible as these, the petitioners (in Furman were) among a capriciously selected random handful upon whom the sentence of death has in fact been imposed.... (T)he Eighth and Fourteenth Amendments cannot tolerate the infliction of a sentence of death under legal systems that permit this unique penalty to be so wantonly and so freakishly imposed." Id., at 309–310, 92 S. Ct., at 2762 (STEWART, J., concurring).

Furman mandates that where discretion is afforded a sentencing body on a matter so grave as the determination of whether a human life should be taken or spared, that discretion must be suitably directed and limited so as to minimize the risk of wholly arbitrary and capricious action.

...

B

We now turn to consideration of the constitutionality of Georgia's capital-sentencing procedures. In the wake of Furman, Georgia amended its capital punishment statute, but chose not to narrow the scope of its murder provisions. See Part II, *supra*. Thus, now as before *Furman*, in Georgia "(a) person commits murder when he unlawfully and with malice aforethought, either express or implied, causes the death of another human being." Ga. Code Ann., s 26-1101(a) (1972). All persons convicted of murder "shall be punished by death or by imprisonment for life." s 26-1101(c) (1972).

Georgia did act, however, to narrow the class of murderers subject to capital punishment by specifying 10 statutory aggravating circumstances, one of which must be found by the jury to exist beyond a reasonable doubt before a death sentence can ever be imposed. In addition, the jury is authorized to consider any other appropriate aggravating or mitigating circumstances. s 27-2534.1(b) (Supp.1975). The jury is not required to find any mitigating circumstance in order to make a recommendation of mercy that is binding on the trial court, see s 27-2302 (Supp.1975), but it must find a *statutory* aggravating circumstance before recommending a sentence of death.

These procedures require the jury to consider the circumstances of the crime and the criminal before it recommends sentence. No longer can a Georgia jury do as Furman's jury did: reach a finding of the defendant's guilt and then, without guidance or direction, decide whether he should live or die. Instead, the jury's attention is directed to the specific circumstances of the crime: Was it committed in the course of another capital felony? Was it committed for money? Was it committed upon a peace officer or judicial officer? Was it committed in a particularly heinous way or in a manner that endangered the lives of many persons? In addition, the jury's attention is focused on the characteristics of the person who committed the crime: Does he have a record of prior convictions for capital offenses? Are there any special facts about this defendant that mitigate against imposing capital punishment (E.g., his youth, the extent of his cooperation with the police, his emotional state at the time of the crime). As a result, while some jury discretion still exists, "the discretion to be exercised is controlled by clear and objective standards so as to produce non-discriminatory application." *Coley v. State*, 231 Ga. 829, 834, 204 S.E.2d 612, 615 (1974).

As an important additional safeguard against arbitrariness and caprice, the Georgia statutory scheme provides for automatic appeal of all death sentences to the State's Supreme Court. That court is required by statute to review each sentence of death and determine whether it was imposed under the influence of passion or prejudice, whether the evidence supports the jury's finding of a statutory aggravating circumstance, and whether the sentence is disproportionate compared to those sentences imposed in similar cases. s 27-2537(c) (Supp.1975).

In short, Georgia's new sentencing procedures require as a prerequisite to the imposition of the death penalty, specific jury findings as to the circumstances of the crime or the character of the defendant. Moreover, to guard further against a situation comparable to that presented in Furman, the Supreme Court of Georgia compares each death sentence with the sentences imposed on similarly situated defendants to ensure that the sentence of death in a particular case is not disproportionate. On their face these procedures seem to satisfy the concerns of Furman. No longer should there be "no meaningful basis for distinguishing the few cases in which (the death penalty) is imposed from the many cases in which it is not." 408 U.S., at 313, 92 S. Ct., at 2764 (WHITE, J., concurring).

...

Finally, the Georgia statute has an additional provision designed to assure that the death penalty will not be imposed on a capriciously selected group of convicted defendants. The new sentencing procedures require that the State Supreme Court review every death sentence to determine whether it was imposed under the influence of passion, prejudice, or any other arbitrary factor, whether the evidence supports the findings of a statutory aggravating circumstance, and "(w)hether the sentence of death is excessive or disproportionate to the penalty imposed in similar cases, considering both the crime and the defendant." s 27-2537(c)(3) (Supp.1975). In performing a sentence-review function, the Georgia court has held that "if the death penalty is only rarely imposed for an act or it is substantially out of line with sentences imposed for other acts it will be set aside as excessive." *Coley v. State*, 231 Ga., at 834, 204 S.E.2d, at 616. The court on another occasion stated that "we view it to be our duty under the similarity standard to assure that no death sentence is affirmed unless in similar cases throughout the state the death penalty has been imposed generally...." *Moore v. State*, 233 Ga. 861, 864, 213 S.E.2d 829, 832 (1975). See also *Jarrell v. State*, *supra*, 234 Ga., at 425, 216 S.E.2d, at 270 (standard is whether "juries generally throughout the state have imposed the death penalty"); *Smith v. State*, 236 Ga. 12, 24, 222 S.E.2d 308, 318 (1976) (found "a clear pattern" of jury behavior).

...

The provision for appellate review in the Georgia capital-sentencing system serves as a check against the random or arbitrary imposition of the death penalty. In particular, the proportionality review substantially eliminates the possibility that a person will be sentenced to die by the action of an aberrant jury. If a time comes when juries generally do not impose the death sentence in a certain kind of murder case, the appellate review procedures assure that no defendant convicted under such circumstances will suffer a sentence of death.

V

The basic concern of *Furman* centered on those defendants who were being condemned to death capriciously and arbitrarily. Under the procedures before the Court in that case, sentencing authorities were not directed to give attention to the nature or circumstances of the crime committed or to the character or record of the defendant. Left unguided, juries imposed the death sentence in a way that could only be called freakish. The new Georgia sentencing procedures, by contrast, focus the jury's attention on the particularized nature of the crime and the particularized characteristics of the individual defendant. While the jury is permitted to consider any aggravating or mitigating circumstances, it must find and identify at least one statutory aggravating factor before it may impose a penalty of death. In this way the jury's discretion is channeled. No longer can a jury wantonly and freakishly impose the death sentence; it is always circumscribed by the legislative guidelines. In addition, the review function of the Supreme Court of Georgia affords additional assurance that the concerns that prompted our decision in *Furman* are not present to any significant degree in the Georgia procedure applied here.

For the reasons expressed in this opinion, we hold that the statutory system under which Gregg was sentenced to death does not violate the Constitution. Accordingly, the judgment of the Georgia Supreme Court is affirmed.

It is so ordered.

Comments and Questions

(1) The *Gregg* Court identified the two avenues for challenging a punishment as cruel and unusual. A punishment may violate the Eighth Amendment because it is a "barbarous" method of punishment. Or, as the Court has more recently recognized, a punishment may be unconstitutional because it is not proportionate to the offense committed. Eighth Amendment challenges to capital punishment receive by far the greatest attention, but theoretically defendants may challenge any sentence or method of punishment as either "barbarous" or disproportionate. *See e.g., State v. Lyle*, 854 N.W.2d 378 (Iowa 2014) (affirming juvenile defendant's Eighth Amendment challenge to mandatory ten-year prison sentence for second degree robbery); *Hope v. Pelzer*, 536 U.S. 730, 736–738 (2002) (handcuffing inmate to hitching post for seven hours without water or bathroom breaks violated Eighth Amendment because it was an "unnecessary and wanton infliction of pain."); *United States v. Gementera*, 379 F.3d 596 (9th Cir. 2004) (rejecting defendant's Eighth Amendment challenge to punishment requiring him to spend a day outside post office wearing a signboard stating, "I stole mail. This is my punishment.").

(2) As the *Gregg* Court discussed, the death penalty has been a long-standing and permitted component of the American criminal justice system. After centuries of the Court upholding the death penalty against Eighth Amendment challenges, in *Furman v. Georgia*, 408 U.S. 238 (1972), the Court held that the death penalty in Mr. Furman's case (and two companion cases) was unconstitutional. Two Justices on the Court at the time, Justices Brennan and Marshall, took the position that the death penalty in all instances violated the ban on cruel and unusual punishment. Three other Justices agreed with the judgment in the cases before them, finding that the statutes at issue led to arbitrary decision making in death penalty cases. In the wake of the Court's 1972 decision, state legislatures were forced to reconsider their capital sentencing schemes, and, as the *Gregg* Court noted, by 1976 at least 35 states had revised them in response to the Court's decision in *Furman*. After a brief hiatus, the *Gregg* opinion ushered in the modern era of American executions. Executions nationwide reached the high water mark in 1999: that year, 98 people were executed. The number of executions nationwide has been in fairly steady decline since 2000, and in 2014 there were 35 executions in only seven states. http://www.deathpenaltyinfo.org/number-executions-state-and-region-1976.

(3) Defendants have long argued that the death penalty is imposed in a racially discriminatory manner. The Supreme Court squarely confronted that issue in *McCleskey v. Kemp*, 481 U.S. 279 (1987). Petitioner McCleskey argued that his sentence violated the Eighth and Fourteenth Amendments because it had been imposed in a racially discriminatory manner. Specifically, McCleskey's counsel relied upon a study of more than 2,000 murder cases in Georgia during the 1970s. The study demonstrated that, among other things, even after accounting for non-racial variables, black defendants who killed white victims were most likely to receive the death penalty. Despite the rigor of the statistical evidence, the Supreme Court rejected McCleskey's challenge and held that petitioner had failed to demonstrate a discriminatory *purpose* on the state's part. Recall that the Supreme Court had invalidated many capital statutes in *Furman v. Georgia*, *supra*, because it deemed those statutes likely to lead to arbitrary and capricious death sentences. What additional evidence might a defendant mount to argue that death sentences were imposed in a racially discriminatory manner? To whom should defendants make such claims—courts or legislative bodies?

(4) In the last few decades, the Court has identified a handful of cases where the death penalty is categorically unconstitutional. In some cases, the Court held that capital punishment was unconstitutional given the *nature of the crime*. *See, e.g., Coker v. Georgia*, 433 U.S. 584 (1977) (death sentence for rape of an adult woman unconstitutional); *Enmund v. Florida*, 458 U.S. 782 (1982) (death sentence unconstitutional for co-defendant in felony murder case absent showing of defendant's culpable mental state); *Kennedy v. Louisiana*, 554 U.S. 407 (2008) (unconstitutional to execute defendant for rape of a child). In other cases, the Court held that capital punishment was unconstitutional given the *nature of the defendant* regardless of the crime. *See, e.g., Ford v. Wainwright*, 477 U.S. 399 (1986) (unconstitutional to execute an insane person); *Thompson v. Oklahoma*, 487 U.S. 815 (1988) (unconstitutional to execute

individual under 16 years at time of crime); *Atkins v. Virginia*, 536 U.S. 304 (2002) (unconstitutional to execute an intellectually disabled person).

Roper v. Simmons

Supreme Court of the United States
543 U.S. 551 (2005)

Justice Kennedy delivered the opinion of the Court.

This case requires us to address, for the second time in a decade and a half, whether it is permissible under the Eighth and Fourteenth Amendments to the Constitution of the United States to execute a juvenile offender who was older than 15 but younger than 18 when he committed a capital crime. In *Stanford v. Kentucky*, 492 U.S. 361, 109 S. Ct. 2969, 106 L.Ed.2d 306 (1989), a divided Court rejected the proposition that the Constitution bars capital punishment for juvenile offenders in this age group. We reconsider the question.

I

At the age of 17, when he was still a junior in high school, Christopher Simmons, the respondent here, committed murder. About nine months later, after he had turned 18, he was tried and sentenced to death. There is little doubt that Simmons was the instigator of the crime. Before its commission Simmons said he wanted to murder someone. In chilling, callous terms he talked about his plan, discussing it for the most part with two friends, Charles Benjamin and John Tessmer, then aged 15 and 16 respectively. Simmons proposed to commit burglary and murder by breaking and entering, tying up a victim, and throwing the victim off a bridge. Simmons assured his friends they could "get away with it" because they were minors.

The three met at about 2 a.m. on the night of the murder, but Tessmer left before the other two set out. (The State later charged Tessmer with conspiracy, but dropped the charge in exchange for his testimony against Simmons.) Simmons and Benjamin entered the home of the victim, Shirley Crook, after reaching through an open window and unlocking the back door. Simmons turned on a hallway light. Awakened, Mrs. Crook called out, "Who's there?" In response Simmons entered Mrs. Crook's bedroom, where he recognized her from a previous car accident involving them both. Simmons later admitted this confirmed his resolve to murder her.

Using duct tape to cover her eyes and mouth and bind her hands, the two perpetrators put Mrs. Crook in her minivan and drove to a state park. They reinforced the bindings, covered her head with a towel, and walked her to a railroad trestle spanning the Meramec River. There they tied her hands and feet together with electrical wire, wrapped her whole face in duct tape and threw her from the bridge, drowning her in the waters below.

By the afternoon of September 9, Steven Crook had returned home from an overnight trip, found his bedroom in disarray, and reported his wife missing. On the same afternoon fishermen recovered the victim's body from the river. Simmons, meanwhile, was bragging about the killing, telling friends he had killed a woman "because the bitch seen my face."

The next day, after receiving information of Simmons' involvement, police arrested him at his high school and took him to the police station in Fenton, Missouri. They read him his Miranda rights. Simmons waived his right to an attorney and agreed to answer questions. After less than two hours of interrogation, Simmons confessed to the murder and agreed to perform a videotaped reenactment at the crime scene.

The State charged Simmons with burglary, kidnaping, stealing, and murder in the first degree. As Simmons was 17 at the time of the crime, he was outside the criminal jurisdiction of Missouri's juvenile court system. See Mo. Rev. Stat. §§ 211.021 (2000) and 211.031 (Supp.2003). He was tried as an adult. At trial the State introduced Simmons' confession and the videotaped reenactment of the crime, along with testimony that Simmons discussed the crime in advance and bragged about it later. The defense called no witnesses in the guilt phase. The jury having returned a verdict of murder, the trial proceeded to the penalty phase.

The State sought the death penalty. As aggravating factors, the State submitted that the murder was committed for the purpose of receiving money; was committed for the purpose of avoiding, interfering with, or preventing lawful arrest of the defendant; and involved depravity of mind and was outrageously and wantonly vile, horrible, and inhuman. The State called Shirley Crook's husband, daughter, and two sisters, who presented moving evidence of the devastation her death had brought to their lives.

In mitigation Simmons' attorneys first called an officer of the Missouri juvenile justice system, who testified that Simmons had no prior convictions and that no previous charges had been filed against him. Simmons' mother, father, two younger half brothers, a neighbor, and a friend took the stand to tell the jurors of the close relationships they had formed with Simmons and to plead for mercy on his behalf. Simmons' mother, in particular, testified to the responsibility Simmons demonstrated in taking care of his two younger half brothers and of his grandmother and to his capacity to show love for them.

During closing arguments, both the prosecutor and defense counsel addressed Simmons' age, which the trial judge had instructed the jurors they could consider as a mitigating factor. Defense counsel reminded the jurors that juveniles of Simmons' age cannot drink, serve on juries, or even see certain movies, because "the legislatures have wisely decided that individuals of a certain age aren't responsible enough." Defense counsel argued that Simmons' age should make "a huge difference to [the jurors] in deciding just exactly what sort of punishment to make." In rebuttal, the prosecutor gave the following response: "Age, he says. Think about age. Seventeen years old. Isn't that scary? Doesn't that scare you? Mitigating? Quite the contrary I submit. Quite the contrary."

The jury recommended the death penalty after finding the State had proved each of the three aggravating factors submitted to it. Accepting the jury's recommendation, the trial judge imposed the death penalty.

Simmons obtained new counsel, who moved in the trial court to set aside the conviction and sentence. One argument was that Simmons had received ineffective assistance at trial. To support this contention, the new counsel called as witnesses Simmons' trial attorney, Simmons' friends and neighbors, and clinical psychologists who had evaluated him.

Part of the submission was that Simmons was "very immature," "very impulsive," and "very susceptible to being manipulated or influenced." The experts testified about Simmons' background including a difficult home environment and dramatic changes in behavior, accompanied by poor school performance in adolescence. Simmons was absent from home for long periods, spending time using alcohol and drugs with other teenagers or young adults. The contention by Simmons' postconviction counsel was that these matters should have been established in the sentencing proceeding.

The trial court found no constitutional violation by reason of ineffective assistance of counsel and denied the motion for postconviction relief. In a consolidated appeal from Simmons' conviction and sentence, and from the denial of postconviction relief, the Missouri Supreme Court affirmed. *State v. Simmons*, 944 S.W.2d 165, 169 (en banc), *cert. denied*, 522 U.S. 953, 118 S. Ct. 376, 139 L.Ed.2d 293 (1997). The federal courts denied Simmons' petition for a writ of habeas corpus. *Simmons v. Bowersox*, 235 F.3d 1124, 1127(CA8), *cert. denied*, 534 U.S. 924, 122 S. Ct. 280, 151 L.Ed.2d 206 (2001).

After these proceedings in Simmons' case had run their course, this Court held that the Eighth and Fourteenth Amendments prohibit the execution of a mentally retarded person. *Atkins v. Virginia*, 536 U.S. 304, 122 S. Ct. 2242, 153 L.Ed.2d 335 (2002). Simmons filed a new petition for state postconviction relief, arguing that the reasoning of Atkins established that the Constitution prohibits the execution of a juvenile who was under 18 when the crime was committed.

The Missouri Supreme Court agreed. *State ex rel. Simmons v. Roper*, 112 S.W.3d 397 (2003) (en banc). It held that since Stanford,

"a national consensus has developed against the execution of juvenile offenders, as demonstrated by the fact that eighteen states now bar such executions for juveniles, that twelve other states bar executions altogether, that no state has lowered its age of execution below 18 since *Stanford*, that five states have legislatively or by case law raised or established the minimum age at 18, and that the imposition of the juvenile death penalty has become truly unusual over the last decade." 112 S.W.3d, at 399.

On this reasoning it set aside Simmons' death sentence and resentenced him to "life imprisonment without eligibility for probation, parole, or release except by act of the Governor." *Id.*, at 413.

We granted certiorari ... and now affirm.

II

The Eighth Amendment provides: "Excessive bail shall not be required, nor excessive fines imposed, nor cruel and unusual punishments inflicted." The provision is applicable to the States through the Fourteenth Amendment.... As the Court explained in Atkins, the Eighth Amendment guarantees individuals the right not to be subjected to excessive sanctions. The right flows from the basic "'precept of justice that punishment for crime should be graduated and proportioned to [the] offense.'" ... By protecting even those convicted of heinous crimes, the Eighth Amendment reaffirms the duty of the government to respect the dignity of all persons.

The prohibition against "cruel and unusual punishments," like other expansive language in the Constitution, must be interpreted according to its text, by considering history, tradition, and precedent, and with due regard for its purpose and function in the constitutional design. To implement this framework we have established the propriety and affirmed the necessity of referring to "the evolving standards of decency that mark the progress of a maturing society" to determine which punishments are so disproportionate as to be cruel and unusual. *Trop v. Dulles*, 356 U.S. 86, 100–101, 78 S. Ct. 590, 2 L.Ed.2d 630 (1958) (plurality opinion).

In *Thompson v. Oklahoma*, 487 U.S. 815, 108 S. Ct. 2687, 101 L.Ed.2d 702 (1988), a plurality of the Court determined that our standards of decency do not permit the execution of any offender under the age of 16 at the time of the crime. Id., at 818–838, 108 S. Ct. 2687 (opinion of Stevens, J., joined by Brennan, Marshall, and Blackmun, JJ.). The plurality opinion explained that no death penalty State that had given express consideration to a minimum age for the death penalty had set the age lower than 16. *Id.*, at 826–829, 108 S. Ct. 2687. The plurality also observed that "[t]he conclusion that it would offend civilized standards of decency to execute a person who was less than 16 years old at the time of his or her offense is consistent with the views that have been expressed by respected professional organizations, by other nations that share our Anglo-American heritage, and by the leading members of the Western European community." Id., at 830, 108 S. Ct. 2687. The opinion further noted that juries imposed the death penalty on offenders under 16 with exceeding rarity; the last execution of an offender for a crime committed under the age of 16 had been carried out in 1948, 40 years prior. *Id.*, at 832–833, 108 S. Ct. 2687.

Bringing its independent judgment to bear on the permissibility of the death penalty for a 15-year-old offender, the Thompson plurality stressed that "[t]he reasons why juveniles are not trusted with the privileges and responsibilities of an adult also explain why their irresponsible conduct is not as morally reprehensible as that of an adult." *Id.*, at 835, 108 S. Ct. 2687. According to the plurality, the lesser culpability of offenders under 16 made the death penalty inappropriate as a form of retribution, while the low likelihood that offenders under 16 engaged in "the kind of cost-benefit analysis that attaches any weight to the possibility of execution" made the death penalty ineffective as a means of deterrence. *Id.*, at 836–838, 108 S. Ct. 2687. With Justice O'Connor concurring in the judgment on narrower grounds, id., at 848–859, 108 S. Ct. 2687, the Court set aside the death sentence that had been imposed on the 15-year-old offender.

The next year, in *Stanford v. Kentucky*, 492 U.S. 361, 109 S. Ct. 2969, 106 L.Ed.2d 306 (1989), the Court, over a dissenting opinion joined by four Justices, referred to contemporary standards of decency in this country and concluded the Eighth and Fourteenth Amendments did not proscribe the execution of juvenile offenders over 15 but under 18. The Court noted that 22 of the 37 death penalty States permitted the death penalty for 16-year-old offenders, and, among these 37 States, 25 permitted it for 17-year-old offenders. These numbers, in the Court's view, indicated there was no national consensus "sufficient to label a particular punishment cruel and unusual." *Id.*, at 370–371, 109 S. Ct. 2969. A plurality of the Court also "emphatically reject [ed]" the suggestion that the Court should bring its own judgment to bear on the acceptability of the juvenile death penalty. Id., at 377–378, 109 S. Ct. 2969 (opinion of SCALIA, J., joined by REHNQUIST, C.J., and WHITE and KENNEDY, JJ.); see also *id.*, at 382, 109 S. Ct. 2969 (O'CONNOR, J., concurring in part and concurring in judgment) (criticizing the plurality's refusal "to judge whether the '"nexus between the punishment imposed and the defendant's blameworthiness"' is proportional").

The same day the Court decided Stanford, it held that the Eighth Amendment did not mandate a categorical exemption from the death penalty for the mentally retarded. *Penry v. Lynaugh*, 492 U.S. 302, 109 S. Ct. 2934, 106 L.Ed.2d 256 (1989). In reaching this conclusion it stressed that only two States had enacted laws banning the imposition of the death penalty on a mentally retarded person convicted of a capital offense. *Id.*, at 334, 109 S. Ct. 2934. According to the Court, "the two state statutes prohibiting execution of the mentally retarded, even when added to the 14 States that have rejected capital punishment completely, [did] not provide sufficient evidence at present of a national consensus." *Ibid.*

Three Terms ago the subject was reconsidered in *Atkins*. We held that standards of decency have evolved since Penry and now demonstrate that the execution of the mentally retarded is cruel and unusual punishment. The Court noted objective indicia of society's standards, as expressed in legislative enactments and state practice with respect to executions of the mentally retarded. When *Atkins* was decided only a minority of States permitted the practice, and even in those States it was rare. 536 U.S., at 314–315, 122 S. Ct. 2242. On the basis of these indicia the Court determined that executing mentally retarded offenders "has become truly unusual, and it is fair to say that a national consensus has developed against it." Id., at 316, 122 S. Ct. 2242.

The inquiry into our society's evolving standards of decency did not end there. The *Atkins* Court neither repeated nor relied upon the statement in Stanford that the Court's independent judgment has no bearing on the acceptability of a particular punishment under the Eighth Amendment. Instead we returned to the rule, established in decisions predating Stanford, that "'the Constitution contemplates that in the end our own judgment will be brought to bear on the question of the acceptability of the death penalty under the Eighth Amendment.'" 536 U.S., at 312, 122 S. Ct. 2242 (quoting *Coker v. Georgia*, 433 U.S. 584, 597, 97 S. Ct. 2861, 53 L.Ed.2d 982 (1977) (plurality opinion)). Mental retardation, the Court said, diminishes personal culpability even if the offender can distinguish right from wrong. 536 U.S., at 318, 122 S. Ct. 2242. The impairments of mentally retarded offenders make it less defensible to impose the death penalty as retribution for past crimes and less likely that the death penalty will have a real deterrent effect. *Id.*, at 319–320, 122 S. Ct. 2242. Based on these considerations and on the finding of national consensus against executing the mentally retarded, the Court ruled that the death penalty constitutes an excessive sanction for the entire category of mentally retarded offenders, and that the Eighth Amendment " 'places a substantive restriction on the State's power to take the life' of a mentally retarded offender." *Id.*, at 321, 122 S. Ct. 2242 (quoting *Ford v. Wainwright*, 477 U.S. 399, 405, 106 S. Ct. 2595, 91 L.Ed.2d 335 (1986)).

Just as the *Atkins* Court reconsidered the issue decided in Penry, we now reconsider the issue decided in Stanford. The beginning point is a review of objective indicia of consensus, as expressed in particular by the enactments of legislatures that have addressed the question. These data give us essential instruction. We then must determine, in the exercise of our own independent judgment, whether the death penalty is a disproportionate punishment for juveniles.

III

A

The evidence of national consensus against the death penalty for juveniles is similar, and in some respects parallel, to the evidence *Atkins* held sufficient to demonstrate a national consensus against the death penalty for the mentally retarded. When Atkins was decided, 30 States prohibited the death penalty for the mentally retarded. This number comprised 12 that had abandoned the death penalty altogether, and 18 that maintained it but excluded the mentally retarded from its reach. 536 U.S., at 313–315, 122 S. Ct. 2242. By a similar calculation in this case, 30 States prohibit the juvenile death penalty, comprising 12 that have rejected the death penalty altogether and 18 that maintain it but, by express provision or judicial interpretation, exclude juveniles from its reach. See Appendix A, *infra*. *Atkins* emphasized that even in the 20 States without formal prohibition, the practice of executing the mentally retarded was infrequent. Since *Penry*, only five States had executed offenders known to have an IQ under 70. 536 U.S., at 316, 122 S. Ct. 2242. In the present case, too, even in the 20 States without a formal prohibition on executing juveniles, the practice is infrequent. Since Stanford, six States have executed prisoners for crimes committed as juveniles. In the past 10 years, only three have done so: Oklahoma, Texas, and Virginia.... In December 2003 the Governor of Kentucky decided to spare the life of Kevin Stanford, and commuted his sentence to one of life imprisonment without parole, with the declaration that " '[w]e ought not be executing people who, legally, were children.' " ... By this act the Governor ensured Kentucky would not add itself to the list of States that have executed juveniles within the last 10 years even by the execution of the very defendant whose death sentence the Court had upheld in *Stanford v. Kentucky*.

There is, to be sure, at least one difference between the evidence of consensus in Atkins and in this case. Impressive in *Atkins* was the rate of abolition of the death penalty for the mentally retarded. Sixteen States that permitted the execution of the mentally retarded at the time of Penry had prohibited the practice by the time we heard *Atkins*. By contrast, the rate of change in reducing the incidence of the juvenile death penalty, or in taking specific steps to abolish it, has been slower. Five States that allowed the juvenile death penalty at the time of Stanford have abandoned it in the intervening 15 years—four through legislative enactments and one through judicial decision....

Though less dramatic than the change from *Penry* to *Atkins* ... we still consider the change from Stanford to this case to be significant. As noted in Atkins, with respect to the States that had abandoned the death penalty for the mentally retarded since *Penry*, "[i]t is not so much the number of these States that is significant, but the consistency of the direction of change." 536 U.S., at 315, 122 S. Ct. 2242. In particular we found it significant that, in the wake of *Penry*, no State that had already prohibited the execution of the mentally retarded had passed legislation to reinstate the penalty. 536 U.S., at 315–316, 122 S. Ct. 2242. The number of States that have abandoned capital punishment for juvenile offenders since *Stanford* is smaller than the number of States that abandoned capital punishment for the mentally retarded after *Penry*; yet we think the same consistency of direction of change has been demonstrated. Since *Stanford*, no State that previously prohibited capital punishment for juveniles has reinstated it. This fact, coupled with the trend toward abolition of the juvenile death penalty, carries special force in light of the general popularity of anticrime legislation, *Atkins, supra*, at 315, 122 S. Ct. 2242, and in light of the particular trend in recent years toward cracking down on juvenile crime in other respects.... Any difference between this case and *Atkins* with respect to the pace of abolition is thus counterbalanced by the consistent direction of the change.

...

As in *Atkins*, the objective indicia of consensus in this case—the rejection of the juvenile death penalty in the majority of States; the infrequency of its use even where it remains on the books; and the consistency in the trend toward abolition of the practice—provide sufficient evidence that today our society views juveniles, in the words Atkins used respecting the mentally retarded, as "categorically less culpable than the average criminal." 536 U.S., at 316, 122 S. Ct. 2242.

B

A majority of States have rejected the imposition of the death penalty on juvenile offenders under 18, and we now hold this is required by the Eighth Amendment.

Because the death penalty is the most severe punishment, the Eighth Amendment applies to it with special force. *Thompson*, 487 U.S., at 856, 108 S. Ct. 2687 (-O'Connor, J., concurring in judgment). Capital punishment must be limited to those offenders who commit "a narrow category of the most serious crimes" and whose extreme culpability makes them "the most deserving of execution." *Atkins*, supra, at 319, 122 S. Ct. 2242. This principle is implemented throughout the capital sentencing process. States must give narrow and precise definition to the aggravating factors that can result in a capital sentence. *Godfrey v. Georgia*, 446 U.S. 420, 428–429, 100 S. Ct. 1759, 64 L.Ed.2d 398 (1980) (plurality opinion). In any capital case a defendant has wide latitude to raise as a mitigating factor "any aspect of [his or her] character or record and any of the circumstances of the offense that the defendant proffers as a basis for a sentence less than death." ... There are a number of crimes that beyond question are severe in absolute terms, yet the death penalty may not be imposed for their commission. *Coker v. Georgia*, 433 U.S. 584, 97 S. Ct. 2861, 53 L.Ed.2d 982 (1977) (rape of an adult woman); *Enmund v. Florida*, 458 U.S. 782, 102 S. Ct. 3368, 73 L.Ed.2d 1140 (1982) (felony murder where defendant did not kill, attempt to kill, or intend to kill). The death penalty may not be imposed on certain classes of offenders, such as juveniles under 16, the insane, and the mentally retarded, no matter how heinous the crime. *Thompson v. Oklahoma, supra*; *Ford v. Wainwright*, 477 U.S. 399, 106 S. Ct. 2595, 91 L.Ed.2d 335 (1986); *Atkins*, supra. These rules vindicate the underlying principle that the death penalty is reserved for a narrow category of crimes and offenders.

Three general differences between juveniles under 18 and adults demonstrate that juvenile offenders cannot with reliability be classified among the worst offenders. First, as any parent knows and as the scientific and sociological studies respondent and his amici cite tend to confirm, "[a] lack of maturity and an underdeveloped sense of responsibility are found in youth more often than in adults and are more understandable among the young. These qualities often result in impetuous and ill-considered actions and decisions." *Johnson, supra*, at 367, 113 S. Ct. 2658; see also *Eddings, supra*, at 115–116, 102 S. Ct. 869 ("Even the normal 16-year-old customarily lacks the maturity of an adult"). It has been noted that "adolescents are overrepresented statistically in virtually every category of reckless behavior." Arnett, *Reckless Behavior in Adolescence: A Developmental Perspective*, 12 Developmental Rev. 339 (1992). In recognition of the comparative immaturity and irresponsibility of juveniles, almost every State prohibits those under 18 years of age from voting, serving on juries, or marrying without parental consent. See Appendixes B–D, *infra*.

The second area of difference is that juveniles are more vulnerable or susceptible to negative influences and outside pressures, including peer pressure. *Eddings, supra*, at 115, 102 S. Ct. 869 ("[Y]outh is more than a chronological fact. It is a time and condition of life when a person may be most susceptible to influence and to psychological damage"). This is explained in part by the prevailing circumstance that juveniles have less control, or less experience with control, over their own environment. See Steinberg & Scott, *Less Guilty by Reason of Adolescence: Developmental Immaturity, Diminished Responsibility, and the Juvenile Death Penalty*, 58 Am. Psychologist 1009, 1014 (2003) (hereinafter Steinberg & Scott) ("[A]s legal minors, [juveniles] lack the freedom that adults have to extricate themselves from a criminogenic setting").

The third broad difference is that the character of a juvenile is not as well formed as that of an adult. The personality traits of juveniles are more transitory, less fixed. See generally E. Erikson, Identity: Youth and Crisis (1968).

These differences render suspect any conclusion that a juvenile falls among the worst offenders. The susceptibility of juveniles to immature and irresponsible behavior means "their irresponsible conduct is not as morally reprehensible as that of an adult." *Thompson, supra*, at 835, 108 S. Ct. 2687 (plurality opinion). Their own vulnerability and comparative lack of control over their immediate surroundings mean juveniles have a greater claim than adults to be forgiven for failing to escape negative influences in their whole environment. See *Stanford*, 492 U.S., at 395, 109 S. Ct. 2969 (Brennan, J., dissenting). The reality that juveniles still struggle to define their identity means it is less supportable to conclude that even a heinous crime committed by a juvenile is evidence of irretrievably depraved character. From a moral standpoint it would be misguided to equate the failings of a minor with those of an adult, for a greater possibility exists that a minor's character deficiencies will be reformed. Indeed, "[t]he relevance of youth as a mitigating factor derives from the fact that the signature qualities of youth are transient; as individuals mature, the impetuousness and recklessness that may dominate in younger years can subside." Johnson, supra, at 368, 113 S. Ct. 2658; see also Steinberg & Scott 1014 ("For most teens, [risky or antisocial] behaviors are fleeting; they cease with maturity as individual identity becomes settled. Only a relatively small proportion of adolescents who experiment in risky or illegal activities develop entrenched patterns of problem behavior that persist into adulthood").

In Thompson, a plurality of the Court recognized the import of these characteristics with respect to juveniles under 16, and relied on them to hold that the Eighth Amendment prohibited the imposition of the death penalty on juveniles below that age. 487 U.S., at 833–838, 108 S. Ct. 2687. We conclude the same reasoning applies to all juvenile offenders under 18.

Once the diminished culpability of juveniles is recognized, it is evident that the penological justifications for the death penalty apply to them with lesser force than to adults. We have held there are two distinct social purposes served by the death penalty: "'retribution and deterrence of capital crimes by prospective offenders.'".... As for retribution, we remarked in *Atkins* that "[i]f the culpability of the average murderer is insufficient to justify the most extreme sanction available to the State, the lesser culpability of the mentally retarded offender surely does not merit that form of retribution." 536 U.S., at 319, 122 S. Ct. 2242. The same conclusions follow from the lesser culpability of the juvenile offender. Whether viewed as an attempt to express the community's moral outrage or as an attempt to right the balance for the wrong to the victim, the case for retribution is not as strong with a minor as with an adult. Retribution is not proportional if the law's most severe penalty is imposed on one whose culpability or blameworthiness is diminished, to a substantial degree, by reason of youth and immaturity.

As for deterrence, it is unclear whether the death penalty has a significant or even measurable deterrent effect on juveniles, as counsel for petitioner acknowledged at oral argument.... In general we leave to legislatures the assessment of the efficacy of various criminal penalty schemes, see *Harmelin v. Michigan*, 501 U.S. 957, 998–999, 111 S. Ct. 2680, 115 L.Ed.2d 836 (1991) (Kennedy, J., concurring in part and concurring in judgment). Here, however, the absence of evidence of deterrent effect is of special concern because the same characteristics that render juveniles less culpable than adults suggest as well that juveniles will be less susceptible to deterrence. In particular, as the plurality observed in *Thompson*, "[t]he likelihood that the teenage offender has made the kind of cost-benefit analysis that attaches any weight to the possibility of execution is so remote as to be virtually nonexistent." 487 U.S., at 837,

108 S. Ct. 2687. To the extent the juvenile death penalty might have residual deterrent effect, it is worth noting that the punishment of life imprisonment without the possibility of parole is itself a severe sanction, in particular for a young person.

In concluding that neither retribution nor deterrence provides adequate justification for imposing the death penalty on juvenile offenders, we cannot deny or overlook the brutal crimes too many juvenile offenders have committed. See Brief for Alabama et al. as *Amici Curiae*. Certainly it can be argued, although we by no means concede the point, that a rare case might arise in which a juvenile offender has sufficient psychological maturity, and at the same time demonstrates sufficient depravity, to merit a sentence of death. Indeed, this possibility is the linchpin of one contention pressed by petitioner and his *amici*. They assert that even assuming the truth of the observations we have made about juveniles' diminished culpability in general, jurors nonetheless should be allowed to consider mitigating arguments related to youth on a case-by-case basis, and in some cases to impose the death penalty if justified. A central feature of death penalty sentencing is a particular assessment of the circumstances of the crime and the characteristics of the offender. The system is designed to consider both aggravating and mitigating circumstances, including youth, in every case. Given this Court's own insistence on individualized consideration, petitioner maintains that it is both arbitrary and unnecessary to adopt a categorical rule barring imposition of the death penalty on any offender under 18 years of age.

We disagree. The differences between juvenile and adult offenders are too marked and well understood to risk allowing a youthful person to receive the death penalty despite insufficient culpability. An unacceptable likelihood exists that the brutality or cold-blooded nature of any particular crime would overpower mitigating arguments based on youth as a matter of course, even where the juvenile offender's objective immaturity, vulnerability, and lack of true depravity should require a sentence less severe than death. In some cases a defendant's youth may even be counted against him. In this very case, as we noted above, the prosecutor argued Simmons' youth was aggravating rather than mitigating. Supra, at 1188–1189. While this sort of overreaching could be corrected by a particular rule to ensure that the mitigating force of youth is not overlooked, that would not address our larger concerns.

It is difficult even for expert psychologists to differentiate between the juvenile offender whose crime reflects unfortunate yet transient immaturity, and the rare juvenile offender whose crime reflects irreparable corruption. See Steinberg & Scott 1014–1016. As we understand it, this difficulty underlies the rule forbidding psychiatrists from diagnosing any patient under 18 as having antisocial personality disorder, a disorder also referred to as psychopathy or sociopathy, and which is characterized by callousness, cynicism, and contempt for the feelings, rights, and suffering of others. AMERICAN PSYCHIATRIC ASSOCIATION, DIAGNOSTIC AND STATISTICAL MANUAL OF MENTAL DISORDERS 701–706 (4th ed. text rev.2000); see also Steinberg & Scott 1015. If trained psychiatrists with the advantage of clinical testing and observation refrain, despite diagnostic expertise, from assessing any juvenile under 18 as having antisocial personality disorder, we conclude that States should refrain from asking jurors to issue a far graver condemnation—that a juvenile offender merits the death penalty. When a juvenile offender commits a heinous crime, the State can exact forfeiture of some of the most basic liberties, but the State cannot extinguish his life and his potential to attain a mature understanding of his own humanity.

Drawing the line at 18 years of age is subject, of course, to the objections always raised against categorical rules. The qualities that distinguish juveniles from adults do not disappear when an individual turns 18. By the same token, some under 18 have already attained a level of maturity some adults will never reach. For the reasons we have discussed, however, a line must be drawn. The plurality opinion in Thompson drew the line at 16. In the intervening years the Thompson plurality's conclusion that offenders under 16 may not be executed has not been challenged. The logic of Thompson extends to those who are under 18. The age of 18 is the point where society draws the line for many purposes between childhood and adulthood. It is, we conclude, the age at which the line for death eligibility ought to rest.

...

IV

Our determination that the death penalty is disproportionate punishment for offenders under 18 finds confirmation in the stark reality that the United States is the only country in the world that continues to give official sanction to the juvenile death penalty. This reality does not become controlling, for the task of interpreting the Eighth Amendment remains our responsibility. Yet at least from the time of the Court's decision in *Trop,* the Court has referred to the laws of other countries and to international authorities as instructive for its interpretation of the Eighth Amendment's prohibition of "cruel and unusual punishments." ...

As respondent and a number of *amici* emphasize, Article 37 of the United Nations Convention on the Rights of the Child, which every country in the world has ratified save for the United States and Somalia, contains an express prohibition on capital punishment for crimes committed by juveniles under 18....

Respondent and his *amici* have submitted, and petitioner does not contest, that only seven countries other than the United States have executed juvenile offenders since 1990: Iran, Pakistan, Saudi Arabia, Yemen, Nigeria, the Democratic Republic of Congo, and China. Since then each of these countries has either abolished capital punishment for juveniles or made public disavowal of the practice. Brief for Respondent 49–50. In sum, it is fair to say that the United States now stands alone in a world that has turned its face against the juvenile death penalty.

...

It is proper that we acknowledge the overwhelming weight of international opinion against the juvenile death penalty, resting in large part on the understanding that the instability and emotional imbalance of young people may often be a factor in the crime. See Brief for Human Rights Committee of the Bar of England and Wales et al. as *Amici Curiae* 10–11. The opinion of the world community, while not controlling our outcome, does provide respected and significant confirmation for our own conclusions.

Over time, from one generation to the next, the Constitution has come to earn the high respect and even, as Madison dared to hope, the veneration of the American people. See THE FEDERALIST No. 49, p. 314 (C. Rossiter ed.1961). The document sets forth, and rests upon, innovative principles original to the American experience, such as federalism; a proven balance in political mechanisms through separation of powers; specific guarantees for the accused in criminal cases; and broad provisions to secure individual freedom and preserve human dignity. These doctrines and guarantees are central to the American experience and remain essential to our present-day self-definition and national identity. Not the least of the reasons we honor the Constitution, then, is because we know it to be our own. It does not lessen our fidelity to the Constitution or our pride in its origins to acknowledge that the express affirmation of certain fundamental rights by other nations and peoples simply underscores the centrality of those same rights within our own heritage of freedom.

* * *

The Eighth and Fourteenth Amendments forbid imposition of the death penalty on offenders who were under the age of 18 when their crimes were committed. The judgment of the Missouri Supreme Court setting aside the sentence of death imposed upon Christopher Simmons is affirmed.

It is so ordered.

[JUSTICES STEVENS and GINSBURG concurred in the opinion].

JUSTICE O' CONNOR, dissenting.

The Court's decision today establishes a categorical rule forbidding the execution of any offender for any crime committed before his 18th birthday, no matter how deliberate, wanton, or cruel the offense. Neither the objective evidence of contemporary societal values, nor the Court's moral proportionality analysis, nor the two in tandem suffice to justify this ruling.

Although the Court finds support for its decision in the fact that a majority of the States now disallow capital punishment of 17-year-old offenders, it refrains from asserting that its holding is compelled by a genuine national consensus. Indeed, the evidence before us fails to demonstrate conclusively that any such consensus has emerged in the brief period since we upheld the constitutionality of this practice in *Stanford v. Kentucky*, 492 U.S. 361, 109 S. Ct. 2969, 106 L.Ed.2d 306 (1989).

Instead, the rule decreed by the Court rests, ultimately, on its independent moral judgment that death is a disproportionately severe punishment for any 17-year-old offender. I do not subscribe to this judgment. Adolescents as a class are undoubtedly less mature, and therefore less culpable for their misconduct, than adults. But the Court has adduced no evidence impeaching the seemingly reasonable conclusion reached by many state legislatures: that at least some 17-year-old murderers are sufficiently mature to deserve the death penalty in an appropriate case. Nor has it been shown that capital sentencing juries are incapable of accurately assessing a youthful defendant's maturity or of giving due weight to the mitigating characteristics associated with youth.

On this record—and especially in light of the fact that so little has changed since our recent decision in Stanford—I would not substitute our judgment about the moral propriety of capital punishment for 17-year-old murderers for the judgments of the Nation's legislatures. Rather, I would demand a clearer showing that our society truly has set its face against this practice before reading the Eighth Amendment categorically to forbid it.

...

JUSTICES SCALIA, with whom the CHIEF JUSTICE and JUSTICE THOMAS join, dissenting.

In urging approval of a constitution that gave life-tenured judges the power to nullify laws enacted by the people's representatives, Alexander Hamilton assured the citizens of New York that there was little risk in this, since "[t]he judiciary ... ha[s] neither FORCE nor WILL but merely judgment." The Federalist No. 78, p. 465 (C. Rossiter ed.1961). But Hamilton had in mind a traditional judiciary, "bound down by strict rules and precedents which serve to define and point out their duty in every particular case that comes before them." *Id.*, at 471. Bound down, indeed. What a mockery today's opinion makes of Hamilton's expectation, announcing the Court's conclusion that the meaning of our Constitution has changed over the past 15 years—not, mind you, that this Court's decision 15 years ago was *wrong*, but that the Constitution *has changed*. The Court reaches this implausible result by purporting to advert, not to the original meaning of the Eighth Amendment, but to "the evolving standards of decency," *ante*, at 1190 (internal quotation marks omitted), of our national society. It then finds, on the flimsiest of grounds, that a national consensus which could not be perceived in our people's laws barely 15 years ago now solidly exists. Worse still, the Court says in so many words that what our people's laws say about the issue does not, in the last analysis, matter: "[I]n the end our own judgment will be brought to bear on the question of the acceptability of the death penalty under the Eighth Amendment." *Ante*, at 1191–1192 (internal quotation marks omitted). The Court thus proclaims itself sole arbiter of our Nation's moral standards—and in the course of discharging that awesome responsibility purports to take guidance from the views of foreign courts and legislatures. Because I do not believe that the meaning of our Eighth Amendment, any more than the meaning of other provisions of our Constitution, should be determined by the subjective views of five Members of this Court and like-minded foreigners, I dissent.

...

Comments and Questions

(1) The majority finds some "confirmation" of its decision in international law. Is that an appropriate tool for constitutional interpretation? Justices O'Connor and Scalia dissent on different grounds. What is the difference between their objections?

(2) Since its 2005 decision in *Roper*, the Court has extended its special treatment of juveniles to the non-capital context. In *Graham v. Florida*, 560 U.S. 48 (2010), Mr.

Graham challenged his life without parole sentence for several juvenile, non-homicide offenses. The Supreme Court imported its death penalty jurisprudence into a non-capital context and held that his sentence was disproportionate and violated the Eighth Amendment. Writing for the Court, Justice Kennedy held:

> A State is not required to guarantee eventual freedom to a juvenile offender convicted of a nonhomicide crime. What the State must do, however, is give defendants like Graham some meaningful opportunity to obtain release based on demonstrated maturity and rehabilitation. It is for the State, in the first instance, to explore the means and mechanisms for compliance. It bears emphasis, however, that while the Eighth Amendment forbids a State from imposing a life without parole sentence on a juvenile nonhomicide offender, it does not require the State to release that offender during his natural life. Those who commit truly horrifying crimes as juveniles may turn out to be irredeemable, and thus deserving of incarceration for the duration of their lives. The Eighth Amendment does not foreclose the possibility that persons convicted of nonhomicide crimes committed before adulthood will remain behind bars for life. It does forbid States from making the judgment at the outset that those offenders never will be fit to reenter society.

Id. at 2030. *See generally*, Cara H. Drinan, *Graham on the Ground*, 87 Wash. L. Rev. 51 (2012) (discussing the *Graham* decision and its implementation by the states). Only two years later, the Court once again relied upon the diminished culpability of juveniles to find *mandatory* life without parole sentences unconstitutional for juveniles—even those convicted of homicide offenses. *Miller v. Alabama*, 132 S. Ct. 2455 (2012). Do you agree that "kids are different" from a constitutional standpoint? Are there other categories of individuals whom one may consider to be categorically different for sentencing purposes?

(3) Recall that the Eighth Amendment bars methods of punishment that inflict unnecessary cruelty and pain. While states have historically employed methods such as hanging, firing squad and the electric chair, since 1976, the dominant method of execution has been lethal injection. In *Baze v. Rees*, 553 U.S. 35 (2008), petitioners argued that Kentucky's three-drug lethal injection protocol presented the risk of significant pain and suffering and was unconstitutional. The Court rejected the Eighth Amendment challenge. Writing for the majority, Chief Justice Roberts held that "subjecting individuals to a risk of future harm—not simply actually inflicting pain—can qualify as cruel and unusual punishment" ... but that the constitution is only violated when there is a "substantial risk of serious harm," an "objectively intolerable risk of harm" that prevents prison officials from pleading that they were "subjectively blameless for purposes of the Eighth Amendment." *Id.* at 51 (citations omitted). In the wake of the *Baze* decision, lethal injection drug protocols continued to come under legal and practical attack. Several high-profile botched executions horrified citizens; drug companies began to refuse to supply the drugs for capital punishment purposes; and medical doctors and pharmacists questioned the ethics of their participation in any executions. In *Glossip v. Gross*, 135 S. Ct. 2726 (2015), death row

inmates in Oklahoma again argued that the state's lethal injection protocol presented an unacceptable risk of severe pain and violated the Eighth Amendment. Again, in a highly fragmented decision, a majority of the Court rejected the Eighth Amendment challenge, holding that "the prisoners failed to identify a known and available alternative method of execution that entails a lesser risk of pain," *Id.* at 2731, and that "because it is settled that capital punishment is constitutional, '[i]t necessarily follows that there must be a [constitutional] means of carrying it out.'" *Id.* at 2732–33.

(4) Capital punishment nationwide has come under judicial and legislative scrutiny in the last decade for a host of reasons: it is incredibly expensive to implement; it has had a disparate impact on poor people of color; it requires a heightened standard of legal representation that few defendants actually receive; and death row exonerations have caused voters to question its legitimacy altogether. While 31 states currently have the death penalty, in the last seven years, seven states have abolished the practice through legislative or judicial action. The American Law Institute, citing structural and procedural impediments to the fair administration of capital punishment, officially withdrew its death penalty provision from the Model Penal Code in 2009. *See generally* Carol S. Steiker and Jordan M. Steiker, *No More Tinkering: The American Law Institute and the Death Penalty Provisions of the Model Penal Code*, 89 TEX. L. REV. 353 (2010). Available at SSRN: http://ssrn.com/abstract=1991314. Most recently, in *Glossip v. Gross*, Justices Breyer and Ginsburg suggested that it is time for the Supreme Court to reconsider the question whether capital punishment is per se unconstitutional. 135 S. Ct. 2726, 2755 (2015) (Breyer, J., dissenting) ("rather than try to patch up the death penalty's legal wounds one at a time, I would ask for full briefing on a more basic question: whether the death penalty violates the Constitution."). Should the death penalty be abolished in light of concerns about the fairness of its implementation? If so, should that decision be left to state legislators? To the United States Supreme Court?

Chapter 2

The Act Requirement

§ 2.01 Introduction — Actus Reus: Of Acts and Omissions

Denno, *Crime and Consciousness: Science and Involuntary Acts**

87 Minn. L. Rev. 269, 270–75 (2002)

For most of the twentieth century, the topic of consciousness, apart from Freudian theory, was not considered fit for serious scientific study. Consciousness was the "ghost in the machine," an unobservable, immeasurable, phenomenon rendered irrelevant to objective science. Starting in the 1970s, however, interest in the topic surged to the current point of "explosion." The scientific "race" to understand consciousness is on and the potential for discovery seems boundless.

This race within science has far-reaching legal implications. Criminal law, in particular, presumes that most human behavior is voluntary and that individuals are consciously aware of their acts. On the other hand, it also presumes that individuals who act unconsciously, such as sleepwalkers, are not "acting" at all. Under the criminal law's voluntary act requirement, unconscious individuals can be totally acquitted even if their behavior causes serious harm.

In contrast to these legal "dichotomies" (voluntary/involuntary, conscious/unconscious), modern neuroscientific research has revealed a far more fluid and dynamic relationship between conscious and unconscious processes. If such fluidity exists, human behavior is not always conscious or voluntary in the "either/or" way that the voluntary act requirement presumes. Rather, consciousness manifests itself in degrees that represent varying levels of awareness.

...

Conventionally, analyses of criminal law and the mind have incorporated debates about free will versus determinism. This Article does not revisit this frequently examined issue, choosing instead to adopt the Model Penal Code's (MPC) stance that a focus on what is voluntary need not "inject into the criminal law questions about determinism and free will."

...

There are many line-drawing dilemmas throughout the criminal law. The problems with the voluntary act requirement are especially acute. First, the voluntary act requirement is the initial filter (at least conceptually) for all individuals potentially subject to the criminal justice system. The criminal justice system, therefore, has to assess actors with the widest possible range of mental states, behaviors, and potential defenses because it has yet to determine if they should proceed through the criminal justice system or be acquitted entirely. A forced voluntary/involuntary dichotomy amidst such heterogeneity can produce particularly artificial choices with potentially extreme variations in sanctions for similar types of behaviors depending on how they are categorized (e.g., involuntary, insane, voluntary, and dangerous). Second, other criminal law doctrines (such as *mens rea*) have a relatively broader line-drawing selection (e.g., the four mental states under the MPC) within a more homogenous group of individuals (persons who have already been determined to have committed only voluntary acts). Therefore, the line-drawing choices and their consequences are less extreme than those faced by voluntariness determinations. Third, voluntariness determinations are more prescriptive of the kinds of acts and mental states that constitute involuntariness in contrast to other kinds of binary doctrines—such as sanity/insanity or reasonableness/unreasonableness. While these doctrines can rely heavily on science, they do not specifically designate mental states or behaviors that, if proven, would legally justify a certain outcome (for example, acquittal due to the involuntariness of a sleepwalking defendant).

§ 2.02 The Voluntary Act

Kilbride v. Lake

Supreme Court of New Zealand
[1962] N.Z.L.R. 590

WOODHOUSE, JUSTICE.

On Thursday, 15 June 1961, the appellant drove his wife's car into Queen Street in the City of Auckland where he left it parked. He returned to it a short time later to find stuck to the inside of the windscreen a traffic offence notice drawing his attention to the fact that a current warrant of fitness was not displayed in terms of Reg. 52 of the Traffic Regulations 1956 (S.R. 1956/217). It was agreed before me that the warrant had been in its correct position when he left the vehicle, but that it could not be found upon his return. It was further agreed that during the period of his absence from the car the warrant had become detached from the windscreen in some way and been lost, or it had been removed by some person unknown. The fact that it was a current warrant was proved conclusively by records showing that on 13 April it had been issued by the Auckland Municipal Motor Vehicle Testing Station under No. 4513, and in respect of voucher No. 115456. Thus it had been issued for only two months, and four months would elapse before it required to be renewed. Despite a written explanation to this general effect which he had forwarded on the same day, a prosecution followed and he was convicted before Justices on an information alleging that he "did operate a motor vehicle ... and did fail to display in the prescribed manner a current warrant of fitness." The proceedings were defended, but no note of the evidence was taken and no reasons for the decision were given. In these circumstances the appeal was argued on agreed facts as I have summarized them.

So far as it is applicable the Regulation reads:

> (1) ... No person shall operate a motor vehicle ... unless there is carried on the vehicle a current warrant of fitness as described in subclause (2) of this Regulation.

Subclause (2) provides that in the case of a vehicle fitted with a windscreen the warrant shall be affixed to the inside of the windscreen. The word "operate" is defined in Reg. 3 as meaning

> to use or drive or ride, or cause or permit to be driven or ridden or to permit to be on any road whether the person operating is present in person or not.

The appeal was argued on the basis that the appellant operated the vehicle by permitting it to be on the road, and the facts do not support any wider application of the word "operate." Accordingly the regulation under review may be written, for the present purpose, as follows:

> No person shall permit a motor vehicle to be on a road whether the person operating it is present or not unless there is carried on the vehicle a current warrant of fitness....

The case for the appellant was that if he could show an absence of *mens rea*, then he could not be convicted, and he had succeeded in doing this as the warrant had disappeared without his knowledge during his absence from the car. On the other hand, it was claimed for the respondent that this statutory offence was one which excluded *mens rea* as an ingredient to be proved. On this basis it was submitted that the offence was one of strict liability, and therefore the knowledge or the intention of the appellant was irrelevant. The issue thus raised on these simple facts directly poses the important question as to whether something done perfectly lawfully by the appellant could become an offence on his part by reason of an intervening cause beyond his influence or control, and which produced an effect entirely outside his means of knowledge.

It has long been established, of course, that if there is an absolute prohibition, and the prohibited act is done by the defendant, then the absence of *mens rea* affords no defense. This principle derives its justification from the general public interest, and any consequential injustice which might seem to follow in individual cases has necessarily been accepted. In the present case the respondent has conceded that the appellant had no opportunity of dealing with the situation which arose. But, it is said, however unfair a conviction might be to him personally, this offence has been made one of absolute liability as it is essential to put strong pressure on drivers of motor vehicles to do their whole duty. He permitted the car to be on the road, it was found there without a warrant, and accordingly he is guilty of the offence. With all respect to the arguments of both counsel, however, I am of the opinion that the emphasis which has been put on the matter of *mens rea* has obscured the real issue in this case.

It is fundamental that quite apart from any need there might be to prove *mens rea*, "a person cannot be convicted of any crime unless he has committed an overt act prohibited by the law, or has made default in doing some act which there was a legal obligation upon him to do. The act or omission must be voluntary" (*10 Halsbury's Laws of England*, 3rd ed., 272). He must be shown to be responsible for the physical ingredient of the crime or offence. This elementary principle obviously involves the proof of something which goes behind any subsequent and additional inquiry that might become necessary as to whether *mens rea* must be proved as well. Until that initial proof exists, arguments concerning *mens rea* are premature. If the first decision to be made is that the offence excludes *mens rea*, then that finding is likely to disguise the fact that there is an absence of proof showing that the accused has done all that is charged against him, should this in fact be the case. The missing link in the chain of causation, if it is noticed at all, appears to be provided by notions of absolute liability. But it is impossible, of course, to prove the one ingredient by eliminating the need to prove another. It appears to me that this confusion has arisen in this case. The primary question arising on this appeal, in my opinion, is whether or not the physical element in the offence was produced by the appellant. This physical element may be described by the convenient term *actus reus*, in contrast to the mental element or *mens rea* which is also an ingredient of a crime or offence, unless expressly excluded by its statutory definition.

In considering whether the *actus reus* can be attributed to a defendant, it is important to recognize that this is something which occurs following acts or omissions. It is not the line of conduct which produces the prohibited event, but it is the event itself. It is an occurrence brought about by some activity or inactivity, or by both. The crime therefore (excluding for the moment the possible ingredient of *mens rea*) is constituted by the event, and not by the discrete acts or omissions which preceded it (*Russell on Crime*, 11th ed., pp. 25, *et seq.)*. Accordingly it is not sufficient to show by some single act or omission that the accused produced the event. It is this fact which produces difficulties of causation when attempting to attribute responsibility for the *actus reus* to a given person. It is easy to do this when the *actus reus* can result from a single act, as, for example, a death by shooting. When it depends, however, upon supervening acts, and particularly when omissions are added to them, then the difficulties tend to multiply. Of course, when *mens rea* is an ingredient to be proved against an accused person, all these difficulties disappear as soon as they arise because he usually cannot be proved to have intended acts done by others. He is thereupon acquitted on that ground. As *mens rea* is so frequently an ingredient of crimes and offences, this is a problem which rarely arises, and for that reason is not always recognised.

In the present case the definition of the offence takes the form of a prohibition followed by an exception. The prohibited event, however, in the sense of the term *actus reus*, is not merely to permit a vehicle to be on a road. It is the doing of that act accompanied by an omission to observe the obligation to carry the current warrant of fitness. The *actus reus* occurs only when the second of these factual ingredients coexists with the first. There must be the presence of the car combined with the absence of the warrant. Did this appellant produce that prohibited event, or did he merely set the stage?

There can be no doubt that the appellant permitted the vehicle to be on the road, and his conduct in this respect was a continuing act which did not end when he left the vehicle. Nevertheless, at this latter point of time the warrant was on the car, and there was no unlawful situation. Only when some extraneous cause subsequently removed the warrant did the event occur which the regulation is directed to prevent. If he is to be regarded as responsible for that *actus reus*, therefore, the decision must be made on the basis that he omitted immediately to replace the warrant.

It is, of course, difficult to demonstrate that an omission to act was not, in a causal sense, an omission which produced some event. All omissions result from inactivity, and in this matter of the warrant the appellant was necessarily inactive. But, in my opinion, it is a cardinal principle that, altogether apart from the mental element of intention or knowledge of the circumstances, a person cannot be made criminally responsible for an act or omission unless it was done or omitted in circumstances where there was some other course open to him. If this condition is absent, any act or omission must be involuntary, or unconscious, or unrelated to the forbidden event in any causal sense regarded by the law as involving responsibility. See for example *Salmond on Jurisprudence* 11th ed., 401, *Causation in the Law* by Hart and Honore 292, *et seq*., and the passage in *10 Halsbury's Laws of England*, 3rd ed., 272 cited above. In my opinion a correct emphasis is now given by this last paragraph to the need for the act or omission making up the *actus reus* to be voluntary, whereas in the corresponding paragraph of the second edition this distinction was blurred in discussion of *mens rea*. Naturally the condition that there must be freedom to take one course or another involves free and conscious exercise of will in the case of an act, or the opportunity to choose to behave differently in the case of omissions. But this mental stimulus required to promote acts or available to promote omissions if the matter is adverted to, and consequently able to produce some forbidden condition, is entirely distinct from the mental element contained in the concept of *mens rea*. The latter is the intention or the knowledge behind or accompanying the exercise of will, while the former is simply the spark without which the *actus reus* cannot be produced at all. In the present case there was no opportunity at all to take a different course, and any inactivity on the part of the appellant after the warrant was removed was involuntary and unrelated to the offence. In these circumstances I do not think it can be said that the *actus reus* was in any sense the result of his conduct, whether intended or accidental. There was an act of the appellant which led up to the prohibited event (the *actus reus*), and that was to permit the car to be on the road. The second factual ingredient was not satisfied until the warrant disappeared during his absence. The resulting omission to carry the warrant was not within his conduct, knowledge, or control: on these facts the chain of causation was broken.

For the foregoing reasons I am of the opinion that the physical ingredient of this charge was not proved against the appellant. Accordingly, I express no opinion on the submission that *mens rea* is excluded as an ingredient of the offence. On the view I have taken of the case the point does not arise.

Before I part with this appeal I think it should be said that the true purpose of the regulation is to ensure that motor vehicles are kept off the highway unless they are shown to be roadworthy by means of a current warrant of fitness. The additional requirement that the current warrant be displayed in a particular manner is, of course, an effective and sensible means of promoting that purpose. It keeps the matter before the notice of the driver, and also it enables traffic officers to check the position regularly, and with a minimum of difficulty. This latter fact, however, should not be elevated to such a level that charges are laid almost automatically against ordinary folks who have shown promptly and conclusively that a missing warrant was in fact current, and that there was an acceptable and proper explanation for its absence from the windscreen. As I have already stated, this appellant provided the Traffic Department of the Corporation concerned with a written explanation of the whole position on the day of the alleged offence, and he included in his letter all the numerical details concerning the issue of the warrant to which I have referred. I was informed by counsel that if he had also enclosed the voucher itself, his explanation would probably have been accepted and no further action would have been taken. If there was any real doubt in the mind of the officer concerned as to the currency of the warrant, it is a pity that he did not check with the Municipal Testing Station, or invite the appellant to produce the voucher. To the extent that this is a mandatory requirement it is a weapon intended to put appropriate pressure on people to do their duty. This general purpose is not likely to be promoted by prosecuting people who cannot reasonably be expected to do more than in fact they have done. It seems a proper case to award costs against the respondent, and accordingly I allow the appellant 10 guineas and disbursements. The appeal is allowed and the conviction quashed.

Comments and Questions

(1) The facts indicate that the accused did not intend to operate the vehicle without the proper certificate, nor did he have any knowledge of the absence of the certificate. Why does Judge Woodhouse choose to decide this case on the *actus reus* issue rather than the *mens rea* issue?

(2) In *State v. Bugger*, 483 P.2d 442 (Utah 1971), the defendant was discovered by an officer asleep in his automobile parked on the shoulder of a road. The officer awakened him and detected the smell of alcohol, whereupon the defendant was arrested and ultimately convicted for being "in actual physical control of any vehicle" while under the influence of intoxicating liquor. Conviction was reversed, because:

> [t]he defendant at the time of his arrest was *not* controlling the vehicle, nor was he exercising any dominion over it. It is noted that the cases cited by the plaintiff in support of its position in this matter deal with entirely different

> fact situations, such as the case where the driver was seated in his vehicle on the traveled portion of the highway; or where the motor of the vehicle was operating; or where the driver was attempting to steer the automobile while it was in motion; or where he was attempting to brake the vehicle to arrest its motion.

The dissent disagreed:

> It only takes a flick of the wrist to start the motor to engage the gears, and it requires only a moment of time to get under the wheel from the back seat. A drunk in control of a motor vehicle has such a propensity to cause harm that the statute intended to make it criminal for him to be in a position to do so.

See also State v. Taft, 102 S.E.2d 152 (W. Va. 1958). *But see Kozak v. Commissioner of Pub. Safety*, 359 N.W.2d 625 (Minn. Ct. App. 1984).

(3) The voluntary act required from criminal culpability need not be the act of the defendant. If, for example, the defendant induces another to commit a crime, albeit as an innocent agent, the act may be attributed to the defendant. *Heard v. State*, 267 S.W.2d 150 (Tex. Crim. App. 1954). More commonly, the act in furtherance of a conspiracy by one of the conspirators is attributable to the rest. *See Pinkerton v. United States*, 328 U.S. 640 (1946).

State v. Hinkle

Supreme Court of Appeals of West Virginia
489 S.E.2d 257 (1996)

CLECKLEY, JUSTICE.

...

On June 12, 1993, the defendant finished his work shift at the Ormet Corporation, an aluminum plant in Hannibal, Ohio, at approximately 4:00 p.m. He obtained a ride to the Village Inn Tavern in Paden City, West Virginia. At the tavern, the defendant made several telephone calls attempting to locate someone to give him a ride to his car. The defendant also ordered a can of beer, and drank approximately one-third of the beer. While at the tavern, the defendant complained of not feeling well, dizziness, and double vision. The tavern owner's daughter then agreed to take the defendant to retrieve his car. As he was leaving the bar, the defendant took an unopened can of beer with him.

At approximately 7:30 p.m., the defendant was traveling north on Route 2 in St. Marys, West Virginia. Robert Barrett was driving south on Route 2 with his wife, Charlotte Ann Barrett. It appears the defendant's car gradually crossed the centerline and traveled in a straight line for approximately two hundred yards in the southbound lane before it collided head-on with the Barrett automobile. As a result of the accident, the defendant and Mr. Barrett suffered severe injuries. Mrs. Barrett also sustained serious injuries, and died as a result of those injuries. Eyewitnesses reported the defendant crossed the centerline in a consistent, even fashion without attempting to swerve, brake, change directions, or stop. Witnesses also indicated that both the defendant and Mr. Barrett were traveling at the posted speed limit. A bystander stated the defendant was semi-conscious immediately after the accident, and his breath smelled of alcohol.

An investigation of the defendant's vehicle immediately after the accident revealed one open can of beer, which was one-half full, in the driver's door compartment; several empty beer cans on the passenger's floor; four full beer cans on the rear floor; three empty beer cans on the driver's floor; and an empty glass, which smelled of beer, on the ground near the car. The defendant was transported to Camden Clark Memorial Hospital where testing revealed he had a blood alcohol level of less than one hundredth of one percent. Officer Charles Templeton of the Pleasants County Sheriff's Department, who investigated the accident, also requested that a blood sample from the defendant be tested by the crime lab. The crime lab found the defendant's blood alcohol level to be less than one thousandth of one percent, well below the statutory definition of intoxication. While treating the defendant's injuries, he was given a Magnetic Resonance Imaging [MRI] scan to determine whether he had sustained any head injuries. The MRI results indicated the defendant had an undiagnosed brain disorder in the portion of his brain that regulates consciousness.

On September 13, 1993, a Pleasants County grand jury returned an indictment charging the defendant with the misdemeanor offense of involuntary manslaughter in violation of W. Va. Code § 61-2-5 (1923). The defendant stood trial, by jury, for this charge in Pleasants County on March 1, 1995. During the trial, the defendant's son testified that the defendant had been having memory loss for several months prior to the accident, and that he believed the defendant had seen a doctor in New Martinsville, West Virginia. Similarly, the tavern owner stated the defendant had complained of feeling ill during the months preceding the collision, and he had complained of dizziness, memory loss, and double vision on the night of the accident. She, too, believed the defendant recently had been treated by a physician.

...

The defendant argues he was entitled to an insanity instruction. Of course, the State contends otherwise. We agree partially with the State that technically the defense was one of unconsciousness as opposed to insanity. The law on the notion of unconsciousness in West Virginia is terribly undeveloped. This is, no doubt, the reason why the defendant requested an insanity instruction in this case, since that is where our older cases seem to place this claim.... Indeed there is only a paucity of American appellate courts that have discussed this defense. With regard to those jurisdictions, Section 44 of Wayne R. LaFave & Austin W. Scott, Jr., *Criminal Law* (1972), one of the few treatises that gives this defense any extensive coverage, states: "A defense related to but different from the defense of insanity is that of unconsciousness, often referred to as automatism: one who engages in what would otherwise be criminal conduct is not guilty of a crime if he does so in a state of unconsciousness or semi-consciousness." *Id.* at 337.

... [T]he most significant distinction between insanity and unconsciousness rests on the burden of proof issue. Because insanity leading to criminal behavior usually does not eliminate the mental state necessary for a finding of criminal culpability, the burden can be placed on the defendant to prove insanity.... On the contrary, unconsciousness eliminates one of the basic elements of the crime—either the mental state or the voluntary nature of the act. As such, once the issue of unconsciousness or automatism is raised by the defense, the State must disprove it beyond a reasonable doubt in order to meet its burden of proof with respect to the elements of the crime....

[I]t is better to view unconsciousness as eliminating the voluntary act requirement rather than negating the mental component of crimes. Thinking of unconsciousness in this conceptual fashion helps to avoid the temptation to collapse it into insanity which, of course, also deals with mental conditions. The defense of unconsciousness should be recognized in a criminal trial and equated with epilepsy rather than insanity. We believe this is the way the claim of unconsciousness should be viewed jurisprudentially in West Virginia.

...

Even if the trier of fact believes the defendant was unconscious at the time of the act, there is another consideration which occasionally arises. If the defendant was sufficiently apprised and aware of the condition and experienced recurring episodes of loss of consciousness, e.g., epilepsy, then operating a vehicle or other potentially destructive implement, with knowledge of the potential danger, might well amount to reckless disregard for the safety of others. Therefore, the jury should be charged that even if it believes that there is a reasonable doubt about the defendant's consciousness at the time of the event, the voluntary operation of a motor vehicle with knowledge of the potential for loss of consciousness can constitute reckless behavior.

...

Four considerations lead us to reverse the defendant's conviction. First, although the defendant failed to request a specific instruction on unconsciousness, such failure is understandable given the confusion in our cases, essentially equating this claim with insanity. The defendant did request, in fact, an insanity instruction, which was refused. Therefore we believe the claim to be adequately preserved for appeal.

Second, although the trial court instructed the jury that the defendant was suffering from a brain disorder, no further instruction was given (on insanity or otherwise) which required the jury carefully to focus on how the nature of the defendant's brain disorder related to the elements of the crime. The jury should have been told that, in light of the evidence of the defendant's brain disorder and apparent blackout, he could not be convicted unless the State proved beyond a reasonable doubt that his act was *voluntary and that he acted in reckless disregard of the safety* of others.

...

Third, irrespective of the foregoing, we would be inclined to reverse the defendant's conviction based on the absence of evidence justifying the "should have known" language in the charge. There is virtually no evidence in the record to indicate that the defendant knew (or reasonably should have known) that it would impair his ability to drive an automobile so as to endanger human life....

Finally, our conclusion about the weight of the evidence is buttressed by the fact that evidence of the presence of alcohol was admitted by the trial court even though contemporaneous blood tests indicated the defendant was clearly not intoxicated, and the trial court so instructed the jury. Under these circumstances, the marginal relevance of alcohol use may have been outweighed substantially by its potential to prejudice the jury, ... and may have obscured the jury's deliberations....

Based on the foregoing, the judgment of the Circuit Court of Pleasants County is *reversed*, and this case is *remanded* for a new trial.

Comments and Questions

(1) A voluntary act may not be found when the defendant acted under the compulsion of another. In *Martin v. State*, 17 So. 2d 427 (Ala. Ct. App. 1944), the defendant was convicted of public intoxication upon proof that he had been arrested in his home and taken by the officers onto the highway. In reversing the conviction, the court said, "[A]n accusation of drunkenness in a designated public place cannot be established by proof that the accused, while in an intoxicated condition, was involuntarily and forcibly carried to that place by the arresting officer." *See also People v. Newton*, 72 Misc. 2d 646, 340 N.Y.S.2d 77 (Sup. Ct. 1973). Cases of this nature may also be examined under the rubric of the defense of duress. *See infra.*

(2) Hypnotism was asserted as a defense in *People v. Marsh*, 338 P.2d 495 (Cal. App. 4th Dist. 1959). The court did not reach the merits of the defense because the defendant had failed to convince the jury that he had acted under hypnotic suggestion. If it is true, as generally believed, that an individual will not carry out a hypnotic suggestion which he or she finds repugnant in content, does this foreclose reliance upon hypnosis as a defense?

(3) In the notorious Washington, D.C. area sniper case in 2002, 17-year-old Lee Malvo asserted an insanity defense based on his being "brainwashed" as a teenager by John A. Muhammad, the alleged mastermind of the shootings by Malvo. The Virginia jury convicted Malvo of murder and terrorism, but sentenced him to life in prison rather than the death penalty. Liptak, *Younger Sniper Given Sentence of a Life Term*, N.Y. TIMES, Dec. 24, 2003. Is "brainwashing" a form of legal insanity, or more appropriately a defense of an involuntary act?

(4) Unconsciousness has been recognized as a defense to crimes committed while the accused was asleep. In *Fain v. Commonwealth*, 78 Ky. 183 (1879), the defendant fell asleep in a public room of a hotel. When a porter shook him in an effort to wake him up, the accused, apparently without regaining consciousness, drew a pistol and killed the porter. The court held that, if the accused was unconscious at the time the pistol was fired, he could not be convicted. *See also Bradley v. State*, 277 S.W. 147 (Tex. Crim. App. 1925).

(5) A different question is presented when the accused goes to sleep and thereby causes the harm, as in *State v. Olsen*, 160 P.2d 427 (Utah 1945), where the driver fell asleep and ran over a pedestrian. The court held, "While one cannot be liable for what he does during the unconsciousness of sleep, he is responsible for allowing himself to go to sleep to get into a condition where the accident could happen without his being aware of it."

Court Pours Cold Water on Hot Coffee Defense

> St. Paul, Minn. (AP)—Spilling hot coffee on yourself while driving is no excuse for speeding, the state Court of Appeals ruled Tuesday.
>
> A three-judge panel unanimously upheld the conviction of Minneapolis sales representative and law student Robert Miller, who received a ticket in November 1985 for going 40 mph in a 30 mph speed zone.
>
> Miller also argued that he did not have the necessary intent to commit a crime.
>
> However, the court said that Miller's decision to bring a cup of hot coffee into the car "set in motion the sequence of events leading to a violation of the statute."
>
> The court said Miller would have been right if the speeding had been beyond his control.
>
> For example, it said, a driver whose brakes fail would not be guilty of running a stop sign if he had no reason to suspect there was something wrong with the brakes.
>
> Miller, a student at the William Mitchell School of Law, was found guilty of a petty misdemeanor by Ramsey Municipal Judge Allan R. Markert in June. The judge waived the fine.

KNOXVILLE NEWS—SENTINEL, Nov. 5, 1986, at A7.

The case is reported in *State v. Miller*, 395 N.W.2d 431 (Minn. Ct. App. 1986).

§ 2.03 Act of Omission

Commonwealth v. Pestinikas

Superior Court of Pennsylvania
617 A.2d 1339 (1992)

WIEAND, JUDGE:

The principal issue in this appeal is whether a person can be prosecuted criminally for murder when his or her failure to perform a contract to provide food and medical care for another has caused the death of such other person. The trial court answered this question in the affirmative and instructed the jury accordingly. The jury thereafter found Walter and Helen Pestinikas guilty of murder of the third degree in connection with the starvation and dehydration death of ninety-two (92) year old Joseph Kly....

Joseph Kly met Walter and Helen Pestinikas in the latter part of 1981 when Kly consulted them about pre-arranging his funeral. In March, 1982, Kly, who had been living with a stepson, was hospitalized and diagnosed as suffering from Zenker's diverticulum, a weakness in the walls of the esophagus, which caused him to have trouble swallowing food. In the hospital, Kly was given food which he was able to swallow and, as a result, regained some of the weight which he had lost. When he was about to be discharged, he expressed a desire not to return to his stepson's home and sent word to appellants that he wanted to speak with them. As a consequence, arrangements were made for appellants to care for Kly in their home on Main Street in Scranton, Lackawanna County.

Kly was discharged from the hospital on April 12, 1982. When appellants came for him on that day they were instructed by medical personnel regarding the care which was required for Kly and were given a prescription to have filled for him. Arrangements were also made for a visiting nurse to come to appellants' home to administer vitamin B-12 supplements to Kly. Appellants agreed orally to follow the medical instructions and to supply Kly with food, shelter, care and the medicine which he required.

According to the evidence, the prescription was never filled, and the visiting nurse was told by appellants that Kly did not want the vitamin supplement shots and that her services, therefore, were not required. Instead of giving Kly a room in their home, appellants removed him to a rural part of Lackawanna County, where they placed him in the enclosed porch of a building, which they owned, known as the Stage Coach Inn. This porch was approximately nine feet by thirty feet, with no insulation, no refrigeration, no bathroom, no sink and no telephone. The walls contained cracks which exposed the room to outside weather conditions. Kly's predicament was compounded by appellants' affirmative efforts to conceal his whereabouts. Thus, they gave misleading information in response to inquiries, telling members of Kly's family that they did not know where he had gone and others that he was living in their home.

After Kly was discharged from the hospital, appellants took Kly to the bank and had their names added to his savings account. Later, Kly's money was transferred into an account in the names of Kly or Helen Pestinikas, pursuant to which money could be withdrawn without Kly's signature. Bank records reveal that from May, 1982, to July, 1983, appellants withdrew amounts roughly consistent with the three hundred ($300) dollars per month which Kly had agreed to pay for his care. Beginning in August, 1983 and continuing until Kly's death in November, 1984, however, appellants withdrew much larger sums so that when Kly died, a balance of only fifty-five ($55) dollars remained. In the interim, appellants had withdrawn in excess of thirty thousand ($30,000) dollars.

On the afternoon of November 15, 1984, when police and an ambulance crew arrived in response to a call by appellants, Kly's dead body appeared emaciated, with his ribs and sternum greatly pronounced. Mrs. Pestinikas told police that she and her husband had taken care of Kly for three hundred ($300) dollars per month and that she had given him cookies and orange juice at 11:30 a.m. on the morning of his death. A subsequent autopsy, however, revealed that Kly had been dead at that time and may have been dead for as many as thirty-nine (39) hours before his body was found. The cause of death was determined to be starvation and dehydration. Expert testimony opined that Kly would have experienced pain and suffering over a long period of time before he died.

At trial, the Commonwealth contended that after contracting orally to provide food, shelter, care and necessary medicine for Kly, appellants engaged in a course of conduct calculated to deprive Kly of those things necessary to maintain life and thereby cause his death. The trial court instructed the jury that appellants could not be found guilty of a malicious killing for failing to provide food, shelter and necessary medicines to Kly unless a duty to do so had been imposed upon them by contract....

The applicable law appears at 18 Pa. C.S. § 301(a) and (b) as follows:

> (a) General rule.—A person is not guilty of an offense unless his liability is based on conduct which includes a voluntary act or the omission to perform an act of which he is physically capable.
>
> (b) Omission as basis of liability.—Liability for the commission of an offense may not be based on an omission unaccompanied by action unless:
>
> > (1) the omission is expressly made sufficient by the law defining the offense; or
> >
> > (2) a duty to perform the omitted act is otherwise imposed by law.

With respect to subsection (b), Toll, in his invaluable work on the Pennsylvania Crimes Code, has commented

> [Subsection (b)] states the conventional position with respect to omissions unaccompanied by action as a basis of liability. Unless the omission is expressly made sufficient by the law defining the offense, a duty to perform the omitted act must have been otherwise imposed by law for the omission to have the same standing as a voluntary act for purposes of liability. It should, of course, suffice, as the courts now hold, that the duty arises under some branch of the civil law. If it does, this minimal requirement is satisfied, though whether the omission constitutes an offense depends as well on many other factors.

Toll, Pennsylvania Crimes Code Annotated, § 301, at p. 60, quoting Comment, Model Penal Code § 2.01 (emphasis added)....

... [W]e hold that when, in 18 Pa. C.S. § 301(b)(2), the statute provides that an omission to do an act can be the basis for criminal liability if a duty to perform the omitted act has been imposed by law, the legislature intended to distinguish between a legal duty to act and merely a moral duty to act. A duty to act imposed by contract is legally enforceable and, therefore, creates a legal duty. It follows that a failure to perform a duty imposed by contract may be the basis for a charge of criminal homicide if such failure causes the death of another person and all other elements of the offense are present. Because there was evidence in the instant case that Kly's death had been caused by appellants' failure to provide the food and medical care which they had agreed by oral contract to provide for him, their omission to act was sufficient to support a conviction for criminal homicide, and the trial court was correct when it instructed the jury accordingly.

Our holding is not that every breach of contract can become the basis for a finding of homicide resulting from an omission to act. A criminal act involves both a physical and mental aspect. An omission to act can satisfy the physical aspect of criminal conduct only if there is a duty to act imposed by law. A failure to provide food and medicine, in this case, could not have been made the basis for prosecuting a stranger who learned of Kly's condition and failed to act. Even where there is a duty imposed by contract, moreover, the omission to act will not support a prosecution for homicide in the absence of the necessary mens rea. For murder, there must be malice. Without a malicious intent, an omission to perform duties having their foundation in contract cannot support a conviction for murder. In the instant case, therefore, the jury was required to find that appellants, by virtue of contract, had undertaken responsibility for providing necessary care for Kly to the exclusion of the members of Kly's family. This would impose upon them a legal duty to act to preserve Kly's life. If they maliciously set upon a course of withholding food and medicine and thereby caused Kly's death, appellants could be found guilty of murder.

...

Having found no valid reason for disturbing the jury's verdicts, we conclude that the judgments of sentence must be, as they are,

Affirmed.

...

Del Sole, Judge, dissenting.

...

Duties which are "imposed by law" do not encompass those which arise out of a contract or agreement. A person who enters a contract does so freely. The duties contained in a contract are those which the person who is entering the contract agrees to undertake voluntarily in exchange for some other consideration. The duties themselves are not "imposed by law," they are assumed by the terms of the agreement. Although breach of the agreement may result in some legal recourse, the law will fashion a remedy only if the injured party seeks one. The Pestinikases' omissions which resulted in a breach of their agreement to care for Mr. Kly do not constitute an omission which could be the basis of liability under § 301(b)(2).

Comment

According to the "American bystander rule," a party is under no legal duty to rescue or summon aid for another at risk or in danger, even "when that aid can be rendered without danger or inconvenience to" the potential rescuer. *Pope v. State*, 396 A.2d 1054, 1064 (Md. 1979). "Thus, an Olympic swimmer may be deemed by the community as a shameful coward, or worse, for not rescuing a drowning child in the neighbor's pool, but she is not a criminal." *State ex rel. Kuntz v. Montana Thirteenth Judicial Dist. Court*, 995 P.2d 951 (Mont. 2000). There are exceptions to the rule, the most frequently cited being the existence of a personal relationship between the parties, such as parent-child or husband-wife. In the *Kuntz* case, the court considered another exception: the duty to render aid based on creation of the peril. The defendant, who was not married to the victim, but had lived with him for some six years (the court viewed the case indistinguishable from one involving marital partners), had justifiably used deadly force in self-defense. After stabbing him in the chest, she had failed to summon medical assistance, and he had died as a result of the wound. She was charged with negligent homicide. The court held that "to find a person who justifiably acts in self-defense criminally culpable for negligently causing the death of the aggressor, the failure to summon medical aid must be the 'cause in fact' of the original aggressor's death, not the justified use of force."

People v. Campbell

Court of Appeals of Michigan
335 N.W.2d 27 (1983)

HOEHN, JUDGE.

...

On October 4, 1980, Kevin Patrick Basnaw committed suicide. On the night in question, Steven Paul Campbell went to the home of the deceased. They were drinking quite heavily.

The testimony indicates that late in the evening the deceased began talking about committing suicide. He had never talked about suicide before.

About two weeks before, the defendant, Steven Paul Campbell, caught the deceased in bed with defendant's wife, Jill Campbell. Some time during the talk of suicide, Kevin said he did not have a gun. At first the defendant, Steven Paul Campbell, indicated Kevin couldn't borrow or buy one of his guns. Then he changed his mind and told him he would sell him a gun, for whatever amount of money he had in his possession. Then the deceased, Kevin Basnaw, indicated he did not want to buy a gun, but Steve Campbell continued to encourage Kevin to purchase a gun, and alternately ridiculed him.

The defendant and the deceased then drove to the defendant's parent's home to get the weapon, leaving Kimberly Cleland, the deceased's girlfriend, alone. Even though she knew of the plan, she did not call anyone during this period of time. She indicated she thought the defendant was saying this to get a ride home.

The defendant and the deceased returned in about fifteen minutes with the gun and five shells. The deceased told his girlfriend to leave with the defendant because he was going to kill himself. He put the shells and the gun on the kitchen table and started to write a suicide note.

The defendant and the deceased's girlfriend left about 3 to 3:30 a.m. When they left, the shells were still on the table.

Steven, out of Kevin's presence and hearing, told Kimberly not to worry, that the bullets were merely blanks and that he wouldn't give Kevin real bullets. Kimberly and Steven prepared to leave.

On the way home, Kimberly asked Steven if the bullets he had given Kevin were really blanks. Steven said that they were and said "besides, the firing pin doesn't work." The girlfriend indicated that both defendant and deceased were about equally intoxicated at this point. The deceased's blood alcohol was found to be .26 percent.

The deceased's girlfriend drove herself to the defendant's home and remained there overnight. The deceased's roommate, Alfred Whitcomb, arrived home at approximately 4 a.m. His testimony indicates that when he arrived home he looked for Kevin Basnaw throughout the home and was unable to find him, but he did see the suicide note on the kitchen table. He waited up about 20 to 30 minutes. The deceased did not come home, so he went to sleep on the couch.

Next morning, one Billy Sherman arrived at about 11:30 a.m. and he and the deceased's roommate found the deceased slumped at the kitchen table with the gun in his hand. Dr. Kopp, the county Pathologist, listed the cause of death as suicide; self-inflicted wound to the temple. No autopsy was performed. No time of death was established.

The prosecutor and the trial court relied on *People v. Roberts*, 211 Mich. 187, 178 N.W. 690 (1920), to justify trying defendant for open murder.

In that case, Mr. Roberts' wife had terminal multiple sclerosis. She was in great pain. In the past, she had unsuccessfully attempted suicide by ingesting carbolic acid. At his wife's request, Mr. Roberts made a potion of water and poison and placed it within her reach.

Defendant Roberts was convicted of murder in the first degree.

...

The prosecutor argues that inciting to suicide, coupled with the overt act of furnishing a gun to an intoxicated person, in a state of depression, falls within the prohibition, "or other willful, deliberate and premeditated killing."

There exists no statutory definition of the term "murder." That crime is defined in the common law.

"Homicide is the killing of one human being by another...."

The term suicide excludes by definition a homicide. Simply put, the defendant here did not kill another person.

...

Defendant had no present intention to kill. He provided the weapon and departed. Defendant hoped Basnaw would kill himself but hope alone is not the degree of intention requisite to a charge of murder.

The common law is an emerging process. When a judge finds and applies the common law, hopefully he is applying the customs, usuage [sic] and moral values of the present day. It is noted that in none of the cases decided since 1920 has a defendant, guilty of incitement to suicide, been found guilty of murder. Instead, they have been found guilty of crimes ranging from the equivalent of negligent homicide to voluntary manslaughter.

...

While we find the conduct of the defendant morally reprehensible, we do not find it to be criminal under the present state of the law.

Questions

(1) Clearly, criminal liability may be based on a failure to act: failure to register for the draft, failure to file an income tax return, failure to wear a motorcycle helmet, etc. Recall *Lambert v. California* and *Jones v. Los Angeles, supra.* Under *Lambert* and *Jones*, is the following statute constitutional?

Wisconsin Statutes Annotated

940.34.

Duty to aid victim or report crime

...

(2)

(a) Any person who knows that a crime is being committed and that a victim is exposed to bodily harm shall summon law enforcement officers or other assistance or shall provide assistance to the victim.

...

(d) A person need not comply with this subsection if any of the following apply:

1. Compliance would place him or her in danger.
2. Compliance would interfere with duties the person owes to others.
3. In the circumstances described under par. (a), assistance is being summoned or provided by others.

§ 2.04 Possession

People v. Valot

Michigan Court of Appeals
189 N.W.2d 873 (1971)

Churchill, J....

Three Redford Township policemen went to a motel in their township in response to a call from a motel employee. Upon answering they learned from the motel manager that he was concerned about the continued use of one of the motel rooms by a number of "hippie-type people." The room had been rented about three days before. The rent was paid until noon of that day. The police were called and arrived in the early afternoon. The officers examined the registration card and learned that the motel room was registered in the name of Harold Valot. One officer recognized the name as the name of an escapee from the Detroit House of Correction. They learned that an auto, identified on the registration card, was parked in the motel parking lot. They learned that a man answering Valot's description had been seen entering the room. They were unable to learn if he had left the room. The police were informed that efforts to contact the room by motel employees by telephone were unsuccessful.

The policemen went to the room with the motel manager. The manager knocked on the door. There was no response. The manager opened the door with a key. The manager and the policemen walked in and observed five persons in the room, all apparently asleep on or in beds. One of the officers recognized the defendant by description and the officers observed marijuana about the room. Defendant was arrested. The marijuana was seized....

Defendant personally registered for the room on September 27, 1968, three days before the arrest, and paid one day's room rent. A girl paid rent on the day before the arrest. Defendant testified that he rented the room for two other persons, and that he had been sleeping there since about 7 a.m. or 8 a.m. on the day of the arrest. He said that he knew that Paul Silver carried and used marijuana and that he, Valot, previously chased Silver out, but that Silver was there when he was aroused by the police. He said that he was unaware of the presence of marijuana in the room until that time.

The room, upon police entry, was in complete disarray. There was a strong odor of marijuana in the room. There were four hand rolled marijuana cigarettes and a brass water pipe of a type used for smoking marijuana on tables, including one on a table next to the bed occupied by defendant and another. Later examination disclosed traces of marijuana on the pipe. Two marijuana cigarette butts were in the room, one of them being on the floor beside defendant's bed. Defendant's record player was in the room....

The legislature used the words "possession" and "control" in the narcotics statute in their commonly understood sense, and not in a restricted, technical sense.... The trial judge conceded the possibility that someone, unbeknownst to defendant, brought the marijuana into the room, but nevertheless did not have a reasonable or fair doubt as to defendant's control thereof. It was a fact question. There was strong circumstantial evidence to support the court's findings. Defendant's control of the marijuana in the room was a fact reasonably inferred from the evidence....

Upon timely motion of either party, or on its own initiative, the trial court may correct the judgment to disclose that defendant was convicted of control rather than possession of marijuana....

His conviction is *affirmed.*

LEVIN, J. (*dissenting*). I dissent because it is not a crime to be in control of a room where marijuana is found and because the people failed to prove that the defendant, Harold Eugene Valot, Jr., was in possession or control of marijuana.

Time and again the courts of this and other states have ruled that where the people's case is based on circumstantial evidence the prosecution has the burden of proving "that there is no innocent theory possible which will, without violation of reason, accord with the facts"....

One or more of the persons in the room possessed or controlled the marijuana that was in it. There was, however, no evidence as to who brought the marijuana into the room or who used it. The people did not prove by direct or circumstantial evidence that Valot, rather than another person or persons in the room, was himself in actual possession of the marijuana found in the room. There was no evidence, direct or circumstantial, that Valot ever used marijuana or did so on this occasion. The trier of fact's disbelief of Valot's testimony does not support a conclusion that the opposite of his testimony is true in the absence of independent evidence affirmatively supporting that conclusion.

If Valot did not bring the marijuana into the room or smoke it—and, again, there was no evidence that he had—then someone else did. It is not reasonable to infer from Valot's *control of the room* and his knowledge that others in the room possessed or were using marijuana, and I quote from the majority opinion, that Valot, rather than one or another of the other persons in the room, was in "control of the marijuana in the room."

In *People v. Burrel*, 253 Mich. 321 (1931), the Supreme Court of Michigan held that the owner-driver of an automobile could not be convicted of statutory rape on evidence that he chauffeured his automobile while one of his boy friends had sexual intercourse with an under-age girl. Since the people had not shown that Burrel had knowledge that the offense was to be committed he could not be convicted as an accessory merely because he was aware of what was happening when the offense was being committed. Just as Burrel, although the owner of the automobile, and aware of what his boy friend was doing, was not under an obligation to control him, so Valot, although in control of the motel room and, no doubt, aware that marijuana was or had been used, was not under an obligation to control the users....

The legislature may, if it wishes, amend the statute to make presence in a room where marijuana is in use a crime.[9]

---

9. The Massachusetts legislature has so enacted. *See* 3A Annotated Laws of Massachusetts, 1970 Cum. Supp., C 94, §213A, which provides:

> Whoever is present at a place where he knows a narcotic drug is illegally kept or deposited, or whoever is in the company of a person, knowing that said person is illegally in possession of a narcotic drug, or whoever conspires with another person to violate the narcotic drugs law, may be arrested without a warrant by an officer or inspector whose duty it is to enforce the narcotic drugs law, and may be punished by imprisonment in the state prison for not more than five years, or by imprisonment in a jail or house of correction for not more than

In the meantime, enforcement of the law prohibiting possession and control of marijuana is not, in my opinion, of sufficient overriding public importance to justify departure from fundamental principles long established.

The legislature made possession and control of marijuana a crime. It is not a crime for one in possession or control of a motel room to invite or allow hippie types in the room or to fail to evict guests smoking marijuana. The legislature has not yet made a citizen responsible for the indulgence of others in his presence.

Comments and Questions

(1) If the accused knowingly possesses an object, is it necessary to show that she knew the object possessed was contraband? Suppose the accused receives a package in the mail, but she is arrested before she opens it. It is subsequently found to contain marijuana. What, if anything, should the prosecution be required to prove as to her knowledge of the contents of the package? *See Commonwealth v. Lee*, 117 N.E.2d 830 (Mass. 1954).

In *State v. Louali*, 716 S.E.2d 385 (N.C. Ct. App. 2011), the court decided that the statute governing the offense of receiving stolen goods did not require that specific words, such as "stolen," be used to satisfy the statute's requirement that the property be "explicitly represented" as stolen. The court explained that, despite the statute's language, the statute only requires that a person knowingly receive or possess property that was clearly expressed in word or conduct as stolen.

(2) In *Crawford v. United States*, 278 A.2d 125 (D.C. 1971), the court affirmed a conviction for possession of narcotics paraphernalia which was found protruding from beneath the driver's seat of an automobile. The court conceded that the accused "did not have actual possession of the needle and syringe at the time of his arrest."

> But appellant had been present in the automobile immediately before the officer noticed the paraphernalia protruding from under the seat where appellant had just been seated. He had been driving the car immediately prior to the time the articles were recovered in plain view from beneath the seat. He was the owner of the vehicle. The single needle and syringe were certainly within his reach. Additionally, puncture marks were found on his arm which indicated he was a user of drugs.... From these facts it was reasonable to infer that appellant had dominion and control over the needle and syringe under his seat.

In *State v. Billinger*, 714 S.E.2d 201 (N.C. Ct. App. 2011), the Court of Appeals of North Carolina held that a defendant could be found to have "constructively possessed" a blue sawed-off shotgun, even though he did not have actual possession of the shotgun. The court concluded that constructive possession of the weapon, necessary to support a conviction for possession of a weapon of mass death and destruction, could be established by evidence of the defendant's ownership of the gun.

---

two years or by a fine of not less than five hundred dollars nor more than five thousand dollars.

[*See Commonwealth v. Buckley, infra.*—Ed.]

(3) In *United States v. Velasquez*, 28 F.3d 2 (2d Cir. 1994), *cert. denied*, 513 U.S. 1064 (1994), the defendant had pled guilty to importing heroin, but at her sentencing hearing contended that the quantity of heroin found hidden in her shoes should not be taken into account, because she had no knowledge that it was there. The court rejected the argument on the ground that by pleading guilty the defendant had conceded knowing importation. The quantity of heroin imported went only to the matter of sentencing, and the defendant's ignorance of the amount was irrelevant.

(4) Computers have added an additional level of difficulty regarding what constitutes possession of contraband. In *People v. Marsh*, 2011 WL 6425492 (Colo. App. 2011), *cert. granted*, 2013 WL 225978 (Colo. 2013), the court decided that the presence of digital images of child pornography in the Internet cache on the defendant's computer was sufficient to constitute evidence of possession for the purpose of supporting a conviction of sexual exploitation of children. The court reasoned that the cache proved the defendant visited Web pages involving sexually exploitative material, which was sufficient to show a prior act of possession.

Commonwealth v. Buckley

Supreme Judicial Court of Massachusetts
238 N.E.2d 335 (1968)

CUTTER, J.

Buckley was indicted for being present where a narcotic drug was illegally kept and deposited. The defendant moved for dismissal of the indictment "because the charge is unconstitutionally vague and indefinite, and because it inflicts cruel and unusual punishment." This motion and a motion for a directed verdict of not guilty were denied. The case is before us only on exceptions to these denials.

On December 14, 1966, Lawrence MacNamara, a Boston police officer serving in the narcotics division, went with other officers to an apartment at 35 Revere Street with a search warrant. Jimmy Boyer Banks, "occupant and tenant of the premises," opened the door. The other officers "went ... into the parlor with" Banks. Officer MacNamara went into the kitchen. Buckley was seated at the kitchen table on which was a brown envelope, found later by analysis to contain marijuana, and a partly smoked, unlighted cigarette, also found later to contain marijuana. Buckley was placed under arrest. He stated that he had "arrived ... a few minutes before the police." Banks and Buckley were the only persons in the apartment....

The first clause of § 243A, if read literally, imposes strict criminal liability without regard to whether the accused had knowledge or *mens rea*. The provision cannot be construed as merely stating the circumstances which give rise to a *prima facie* case sufficient to establish guilt. Compare the statutes discussed in *Commonwealth v. Douglas*, 236 N.E.2d 865, and cases cited. We thus first consider whether a literal reading of the section as a "public welfare" statute, imposing strict liability "notwithstanding innocent intent," should be taken as reflecting the legislative purpose.

Statutes, purporting to create criminal offenses which may "impinge upon the public's access to constitutionally protected matter" (*see Demetropolos v. Commonwealth*, 342 Mass. 658, 661), have been construed to require knowledge by the accused of the facts giving rise to criminality. Such an interpretation is in part, at least, to preserve interests protected under the First Amendment to the Constitution of the United States. *See Commonwealth v. Corey*, 351 Mass. 331, 332–334. There is some indication that the due process clause of the Fourteenth Amendment may require knowledge in a range of situation[s] not limited to these which have First Amendment aspects. *See Lambert v. California*, 355 U.S. 225, 228–230 (failure of a person who had previously been convicted of a felony to register as required by a city ordinance, where such person had no knowledge of the ordinance). Generally, however, it has been held that the Legislature may make criminal an act or omission even where the person responsible has no "blameworthy condition of the mind." ...

Section 213A permits the imposition of a severe penalty, as much as five years in prison. It hardly can be regarded as a minor offense. Thus it would take unusually clear legislative language to lead us to the view that knowledge is not required for a conviction under the first clause (fn. 1 at [A]). In view of the *Lambert* case, 355 U.S. 225, any other interpretation would raise serious constitutional doubts....

Reading the first clause of § 213A as including a requirement that the accused be present where he knows a narcotic drug is illegally kept or deposited, we think that the words "[w]hoever is present" are not vague. These words, coupled with knowledge, do not import an unlimited area. The words must be given a reasonable interpretation which would permit the knowledge required to be proved. The language reasonably refers to a somewhat restricted space. *See Commonwealth v. Kane*, 173 Mass. 477, 481–482.

Buckley vaguely argues that (a) the first clause of the statute potentially interferes with the constitutional right of free association, and (b) that it imposes a cruel and unusual punishment. No such violation of constitutional interests can reasonably be found in view of the requirement in the first clause of § 213A, as interpreted by us, that there be proof of knowledge of facts constituting noncompliance with the statute.

We are of opinion that there was ample evidence from which the jury could find violation of § 213A as we interpret it. The section is not invalidly vague on its face. There were no exceptions to the judge's charge or to any failure to give requested instructions. The jury reasonably could infer, from Buckley's presence at a table on which were found plainly visible marijuana and a half smoked marijuana cigarette, that he knew about these items.

Problems

(1) Suppose *A* and *B*, two college students, share an apartment. *A* keeps marijuana in the commonly shared area of the apartment. *B* is aware of this fact, although *B* has never used or otherwise exercised dominion over the marijuana, and he has frequently asked *A* to remove it from the premises. Could *B* be convicted of possession of marijuana? What would you advise *B* to do? Suppose in *A*'s absence, *B* determines

to dispose of *A*'s marijuana. He is arrested in an alley while putting it in a garbage can. Is he guilty of possession? *See People v. Mijares*, 491 P.2d 1115 (Cal. 1971).

(2) The defendant was taken to a hospital following an automobile accident, and a lawfully obtained urine sample revealed traces of morphine. On the basis of this evidence, he was convicted for the unlawful possession of a controlled substance. Should the conviction stand? *See State v. Lewis*, 394 N.W.2d 212 (Minn. Ct. App. 1986).

Chapter 3

The Mental State

§ 3.01 Introduction

Morissette v. United States

Supreme Court of the United States
342 U.S. 246 (1952)

Mr. Justice Jackson delivered the opinion of the Court.

This would have remained a profoundly insignificant case to all except its immediate parties had it not been so tried and submitted to the jury as to raise questions both fundamental and far-reaching in federal criminal law, for which reason we granted certiorari.

On a large tract of uninhabited and untilled land in a wooded and sparsely populated area of Michigan, the Government established a practice bombing range over which the Air Force dropped simulated bombs at ground targets. These bombs consisted of a metal cylinder about forty inches long and eight inches across, filled with sand and enough black powder to cause a smoke puff by which the strike could be located. At various places about the range signs read 'Danger-Keep Out-Bombing Range.' Nevertheless, the range was known as good deer country and was extensively hunted.

Spent bomb casings were cleared from the targets and thrown into piles 'so that they will be out of the way.' They were not sacked or piled in any order but were dumped in heaps, some of which had been accumulating for four years or upwards, were exposed to the weather and rusting away.

Morissette, in December of 1948, went hunting in this area but did not get a deer. He thought to meet expenses of the trip by salvaging some of these casings. He loaded three tons of them on his truck and took them to a nearby farm, where they were flattened by driving a tractor over them. After expending this labor and trucking them to market in Flint, he realized $84.

Morissette, by occupation, is a fruit stand operator in summer and a trucker and scrap iron collector in winter. An honorably discharged veteran of World War II, he enjoys a good name among his neighbors and has had no blemish on his record more disreputable than a conviction for reckless driving.

The loading, crushing and transporting of these casings were all in broad daylight, in full view of passers-by, without the slightest effort at concealment. When an investigation was started, Morissette voluntarily, promptly and candidly told the whole story to the authorities, saying that he had no intention of stealing but thought the property was abandoned, unwanted and considered of no value to the Government. He was indicted, however, on the charge that he 'did unlawfully, wilfully and knowingly steal and convert' property of the United States of the value of $84, in violation of 18 U.S.C. §641, which provides that 'whoever embezzles, steals, purloins, or knowingly converts' government property is punishable by fine and imprisonment. Morissette was convicted and sentenced to imprisonment for two months or to pay a fine of $200. The Court of Appeals affirmed, one judge dissenting.

On his trial, Morissette, as he had at all times told investigating officers, testified that from appearances he believed the casings were cast-off and abandoned, that he did not intend to steal the property, and took it with no wrongful or criminal intent. The trial court, however, was unimpressed, and ruled: '(H)e took it because he thought it was abandoned and he knew he was on government property.... That is no defense.... I don't think anybody can have the defense they thought the property was abandoned on another man's piece of property.' The court stated: 'I will not permit you to show this man thought it was abandoned.... I hold in this case that there is no question of abandoned property.' The court refused to submit or to allow counsel to argue to the jury whether Morissette acted with innocent intention. It charged: 'And I instruct you that if you believe the testimony of the government in this case, he intended to take it. He had no right to take this property. (A)nd it is no defense to claim that it was abandoned, because it was on private property.... Petitioner's counsel contended, 'But the taking must have been with a felonious intent.' The court ruled, however: 'That is presumed by his own act.'

The Court of Appeals suggested that 'greater restraint in expression should have been exercised', but affirmed the conviction because, 'As we have interpreted the statute, appellant was guilty of its violation beyond a shadow of doubt, as evidenced even by his own admissions.' Its construction of the statute is that it creates several separate and distinct offenses, one being knowing conversion of government property. The court ruled that this particular offense requires no element of criminal intent. This conclusion was thought to be required by the failure of Congress to express such a requisite and this Court's decisions. in *United States v. Behrman*, 258 U.S. 280, and *United States v. Balint*, 258 U.S. 250.

In those cases this Court did construe mere omission from a criminal enactment of any mention of criminal intent as dispensing with it. If they be deemed precedents for principles of construction generally applicable to federal penal statutes, they authorize this conviction. Indeed, such adoption of the literal reasoning announced in those cases would do this and more—it would sweep out of all federal crimes, except when expressly preserved, the ancient requirement of a culpable state of mind. We think a resumé of their historical background is convincing that an effect has been ascribed to them more comprehensive than was contemplated and one inconsistent with our philosophy of criminal law.

The contention that an injury can amount to a crime only when inflicted by intention is no provincial or transient notion. It is as universal and persistent in mature systems of law as belief in freedom of the human will and a consequent ability and duty of the normal individual to choose between good and evil. A relation between some mental element and punishment for a harmful act is almost as instinctive as the child's familiar exculpatory 'But I didn't mean to,' and has afforded the rational basis for a tardy and unfinished substitution of deterrence and reformation in place of retaliation and vengeance as the motivation for public prosecution. Unqualified acceptance of this doctrine by English common law in the Eighteenth Century was indicated by Blackstone's sweeping statement that to constitute any crime there must first be a 'vicious will.' Common-law commentators of the Nineteenth Century early pronounced the same principle, although a few exceptions not relevant to our present problem came to be recognized.

Crime, as a compound concept, generally constituted only from concurrence of an evil-meaning mind with an evil-doing hand, was congenial to an intense individualism and took deep and early root in American soil. As the state codified the common law of crimes, even if their enactments were silent on the subject, their courts assumed that the omission did not signify disapproval of the principle but merely recognized that intent was so inherent in the idea of the offense that it required no statutory affirmation. Courts, with little hesitation or division, found an implication of the requirement as to offenses that were taken over from the common law. The unanimity with which they have adhered to the central thought that wrongdoing must be conscious to be criminal is emphasized by the variety, disparity and confusion of their definitions of the requisite but elusive mental element. However, courts of various jurisdictions, and for the purposes of different offenses, have devised working formulae, if not scientific ones, for the instruction of juries around such terms as 'felonious intent,' 'criminal intent,' 'malice aforethought,' 'guilty knowledge,' 'fraudulent intent,' 'wilfulness,' 'scienter,' to denote guilty knowledge, or 'mens rea,' to signify an evil purpose or mental culpability. By use or combination of these various tokens, they have sought to protect those who were not blameworthy in mind from conviction of infamous common-law crimes....

However, the *Balint* and *Behrman* offenses belong to a category of another character, with very different antecedents and origins. The crimes there involved depend on no mental element but consist only of forbidden acts or omissions. This, while not expressed by the Court, is made clear from examination of a century-old but accelerating tendency, discernible both here and in England, to call into existence new duties and crimes which disregard any ingredient of intent. The industrial revolution multiplied the number of workmen exposed to injury from increasingly powerful and complex mechanisms, driven by freshly discovered sources of energy, requiring higher precautions by employers. Traffic of velocities, volumes and varieties unheard of came to subject the wayfarer to intolerable casualty risks if owners and drivers were not to observe new cares and uniformities of conduct. Congestion of cities and crowding of quarters called for health and welfare regulations undreamed of in simpler times. Wide distribution of goods became an instrument of wide distribution of harm when those who dispersed food, drink, drugs, and even securities, did not comply with reasonable standards of quality, integrity, disclosure and care. Such dangers have engendered increasingly numerous and detailed regulations which heighten the duties of those in control of particular industries, trades, properties or activities that affect public health, safety or welfare.

While many of these duties are sanctioned by a more strict civil liability, lawmakers, whether wisely or not, have sought to make such regulations more effective by invoking criminal sanctions to be applied by the familiar technique of criminal prosecutions and convictions. This has confronted the courts with a multitude of prosecutions, based on statutes or administrative regulations, for what have been aptly called "public welfare offenses." These cases do not fit neatly into any of such accepted classifications of common-law offenses, such as those against the state, the person, property, or public morals. Many of these offenses are not in the nature of positive aggressions or invasions, with which the common law so often dealt, but are in the nature of neglect where the law requires care, or inaction where it imposes a duty. Many violations of such regulations result in no direct or immediate injury to person or property but merely create the danger or probability of it which the law seeks to minimize. While such offenses do not threaten the security of the state in the manner of treason, they may be regarded as offenses against its authority, for their occurrence impairs the efficiency of controls deemed essential to the social order as presently constituted. In this respect, whatever the intent of the violator, the injury is the same, and the consequences are injurious or not according to fortuity. Hence, legislation applicable to such offenses, as a matter of policy, does not specify intent as a necessary element. The accused, if he does not will the violation, usually is in a position to prevent it with no more care than society might reasonably expect and no more exertion than it might reasonably exact from one who assumed his responsibilities. Also, penalties commonly are relatively small, and conviction does no grave damage to an offender's reputation. Under such considerations, courts have turned to construing statutes and regulations which make no mention of intent as dispensing with it and holding that the guilty act alone makes out the crime....

Neither this Court nor, so far as we are aware, any other has undertaken to delineate a precise line or set forth comprehensive criteria for distinguishing between crimes that require a mental element and crimes that do not. We attempt no closed definition, for the law on the subject is neither settled nor static. The conclusion reached in the *Balint* and *Behrman* cases has our approval and adherence for the circumstances to which it was there applied. A quite different question here is whether we will expand the doctrine of crimes without intent to include those charged here.

Stealing, larceny, and its variants and equivalents, were among the earliest offenses known to the law that existed before legislation; they are invasions of rights of property which stir a sense of insecurity in the whole community and arouse public demand for retribution, the penalty is high and, when a sufficient amount is involved, the infamy is that of a felony, which, says Maitland, is '... as bad a word as you can give to man or thing.' State courts of last resort, on whom fall the heaviest burden of interpreting criminal law in this country, have consistently retained the requirement of intent in larceny-type offenses. If any state has deviated, the exception has neither been called to our attention nor disclosed by our research.

Congress, therefore, omitted any express prescription of criminal intent from the enactment before us in the light of an unbroken course of judicial decision in all constituent states of the Union holding intent inherent in this class of offense, even when not expressed in a statute. Congressional silence as to mental elements in an Act merely adopting into federal statutory law a concept of crime already so well defined in common law and statutory interpretation by the states may warrant quite contrary inferences than the same silence in creating an offense new to general law, for whose definition the courts have no guidance except the Act....

The government asks us by a feat of construction radically to change the weights and balances in the scales of justice. The purpose and obvious effect of doing away with the requirement of guilty intent is to ease the prosecution's path to conviction, to strip the defendant of such benefit as he derived at common law from innocence of evil purpose, and to circumscribe the freedom heretofore allowed juries. Such a manifest impairment to the immunities of the individual should not be extended to common-law crimes on judicial initiative.

The spirit of the doctrine which denies to the federal judiciary power to create crimes forthrightly admonishes that we should not enlarge the reach of enacted crimes by constituting them from anything less than the incriminating components contemplated by the words used in the statute. And where Congress borrows terms of art in which are accumulated the legal tradition and meaning of centuries of practice, it presumably knows and adopts the cluster of ideas that were attached to each borrowed word in the body of learning from which it was taken and the meaning its use will convey to the judicial mind unless otherwise instructed. In such case, absence of contrary direction may be taken as satisfaction with widely accepted definitions, not as a departure from them.

We hold that mere omission from section 641 of any mention of intent will not be construed as eliminating that element from the crimes denounced....

Comments and Questions

(1) As Justice Jackson observed, the actor's state of mind at the time he or she engaged in prohibited conduct is a necessary element of common law crimes. Without culpability, or *mens rea*, even harmful conduct does not usually merit punishment. Why is this so?

(2) A blameworthy mental state is central to both retributive and utilitarian theories of punishment. Proof of the *mens rea* required by the criminal statute ensures that only those who choose to break the law are punished. In ensuring just punishment, the *mens rea* element leads to deterrence because it encourages respect for law and informal enforcement by the community.

(3) The Court was careful to distinguish between offenses "new to general law" and those "incorporated from the common law." Congress may enact new offenses

that protect the public and may pass statutes that explicitly depart from common law concepts. Public welfare crimes, such as those that regulate food and drugs, are discussed later in this chapter.

United States v. Bailey

Supreme Court of the United States
444 U.S. 394 (1980)

Mr. Justice Rehnquist delivered the opinion of the Court.

In the early morning hours of August 26, 1976, respondents Clifford Bailey, James T. Cogdell, Ronald C. Cooley, and Ralph Walker, federal prisoners at the District of Columbia Jail, crawled through a window from which a bar had been removed, slid down a knotted bed sheet, and escaped from custody.... Upon their apprehension, they were charged with violating § 18 U.S.C. 731(a), which governs escape from federal custody.

...

... By a divided vote, the court of Appeals reversed each respondent's conviction and remanded for new trials. The majority concluded that the District court should have allowed the jury to consider the evidence of coercive conditions in determining whether the respondents had formulated the requisite ... intent to avoid confinement.

...

Few areas of criminal law pose more difficulty than the proper definition of the mens rea required for any particular crime. In 1970, the National Commission on Reform of Federal Criminal Laws decried the "confused and inconsistent ad hoc approach" of the federal courts to this issue and called for "a new departure." *See* 1 *Working Papers of the National Commission on Reform of Federal Criminal Laws* 123 (1970) (hereinafter Working Papers). Although the central focus of this and other reform movements has been the codification of workable principles for determining criminal culpability, a byproduct has been a general rethinking of traditional *mens rea* analysis.

At common law, crimes generally were classified as requiring either "general intent" or "specific intent." This venerable distinction, however, has been the source of a good deal of confusion. As one treatise explained:

> Sometimes "general intent" is used in the same way as "criminal intent" to mean the general notion of *mens rea*, while "specific intent" is taken to mean the mental state required for a particular crime. Or, "general intent" may be used to encompass all forms of the mental state requirement, while "specific intent" is limited to the one mental state of intent. Another possibility is that "general intent" will be used to characterize an intent to do something on an undetermined occasion, and "specific intent" to denote an intent to do that thing at a particular time and place.

W. LaFave & A. Scott, *Handbook on Criminal Law* § 28, at 201–202 (1972).

This ambiguity has led to a movement away from the traditional dichotomy of intent and toward an alternative analysis of *mens rea*. This new approach, exemplified in the American Law Institute's Model Penal Code, is based on two principles. First, the ambiguous and elastic term "intent" is replaced with a hierarchy of culpable states of mind. The different levels in this hierarchy are commonly identified, in descending order of culpability, as purpose, knowledge, recklessness, and negligence....

Perhaps the most significant, and most esoteric, distinction drawn by this analysis is that between the mental states of "purpose" and "knowledge." As we pointed out, a person who causes a particular result is said to act purposefully if " 'he consciously desires that result, whatever the likelihood of that result happening from his conduct[,]' " while he is said to act knowingly if he is aware " 'that the result is practically certain to follow from his conduct, whatever his desire may be as to that result.' "

In the case of most crimes, "the limited distinction between knowledge and purpose has not been considered important since 'there is good reason for imposing liability whether the defendant desired or merely knew of the practical certainty of the result[s].' " ...

In certain narrow classes of crimes, however, heightened culpability has been thought to merit special attention. Thus, the statutory and common law of homicide often distinguishes, either in setting the "degree" of the crime or in imposing punishment, between a person who knows that another person will be killed as the result of his conduct and a person who acts with the specific purpose of taking another's life.... Similarly, where a defendant is charged with treason, this Court has stated that the government must demonstrate that the defendant acted with a purpose to aid the enemy.... Another such example is the law of inchoate offenses such as attempt and conspiracy, where a heightened mental state separates criminality itself from otherwise innocuous behavior....

In a general sense, "purpose" corresponds loosely with the common-law concept of specific intent, while "knowledge" corresponds loosely with the concept of general intent.

Were this substitution of terms the only innovation offered by the reformers, it would hardly be dramatic. But there is another ambiguity inherent in the traditional distinction between specific intent and general intent. Generally, even time-honored common-law crimes consist of several elements, and complex statutorily defined crimes exhibit this characteristic to an even greater degree. Is the same state of mind required of the actor for each element of the crime, or may some elements require one state of mind and some another? ...

[T]he American Law Institute stated: "clear analysis requires that the question of the kind of culpability required to establish the commission of an offense be faced separately with respect to each material element of the crime[.]"

...

... [W]e believe that two observations are in order. First, ... courts obviously must follow Congress' intent as to the required level of mental culpability for any particular offense. Principles derived from common law as well as precepts suggested by the American Law Institute must bow to legislative mandates.

Second, while the suggested element-by-element analysis is a useful tool for making sense of an otherwise opaque concept, it is not the only principle to be considered. The administration of the federal system of criminal justice is confided to ordinary mortals, whether they be lawyers, judges, or jurors. This system could easily fall of its own weight if courts or scholars become obsessed with hair-splitting distinctions, either traditional or novel, that Congress neither stated nor implied when it made the conduct criminal.

As relevant to the charges against Bailey, Cooley, and Walker, § 751(a) required the prosecution to prove that (1) they had been in the custody of the Attorney General, (2) as the result of a conviction, and (3) that they had escaped from that custody. As for the charges against respondent Cogdell, § 751(a) required the same proof, with the exception that his confinement was based upon an arrest for a felony rather than a prior conviction. Although § 751(a) does not define the term "escape," courts and commentators are in general agreement that it means absenting one-self from custody without permission.

...

Respondents have not challenged the District Court's instructions on the first two elements of the crime defined by § 751(a). It is undisputed that, on August 26, 1976, respondents were in the custody of the Attorney General as the result of either arrest on charges of felony or conviction.... Here, the District Court clearly instructed the juries that the prosecution bore the burden of proving that respondents "knowingly committed an act which the law makes a crime" and that they acted "knowingly, intentionally, and deliberately...."

...

At a minimum, the juries had to find that respondents knew they were leaving the jail and that they knew they were doing so without authorization. The sufficiency of the evidence to support the juries' verdicts under this charge has never seriously been questioned, nor could it be.

...

As we stated earlier, the cases have generally held that, except in narrow classes of offenses, proof that the defendant acted knowingly is sufficient to support a conviction. Accordingly, we hold that the prosecution fulfills its burden under § 751(a) if it demonstrates that an escapee knew his actions would result in his leaving physical confinement without permission.

Comments

(1) Like the statute at issue in *Morissette*, the statute in *Bailey* did not contain a *mens rea* term. In considering the problem, the Court summarized the common law terms of specific intent to achieve a result (purpose) and a general intent to act. Which

did the Court require for conviction: purpose or knowing? Which level of culpability had the appellate court applied?

(2) The Court noted the "confused and inconsistent ad hoc approach" to *mens rea* issues in the federal criminal system. The proposed reforms of federal criminal law noted by the Court were not enacted. Among the consequences of this decision, unlike most state criminal codes, the mens rea elements of federal crimes do not have uniform definitions. This means that a culpability term, like *knowledge*, can have one definition in one criminal provision and another definition in other federal criminal statutes.

(3) For the response of the Supreme Court to the defense of necessity, see §7.02, *infra*.

Model Penal Code

In 1962, after 12 years of research and drafting, scholars at the American Law Institute (ALI) approved and published a model criminal code. The Model Penal Code (MPC) is just that, a "model," for states to consider. The majority of states have amended their state criminal laws to reflect all or parts of the model law.[1] As noted in *Bailey*, the federal government did not adopt it.

The MPC refers to the *mens rea* element as "culpability." The culpability provisions refined and organized common law *mens rea* doctrine. First, the MPC drafters reduced the many mental states used in common law, such as malice, scienter, willfulness, feloniously, and so on, to four mental states: purposely, knowingly, recklessly, and negligently. Second, the drafters carefully defined each term and provided guidance on how they should be applied. Third, the code includes a commentary that further explains nuances of the *mens rea* requirement. The culpability section is consistent with common law principles and provides a uniform standard among the states.

Section 2.02.*

General Requirements of Culpability

(1) Minimum Requirements of Culpability. Except as provided in Section 2.05, a person is not guilty of an offense unless he acted purposely, knowingly, recklessly or negligently, as the law may require, with respect to each material element of the offense.

(2) Kinds of Culpability Defined.

(a) *Purposely.*

A person acts purposely with respect to a material element of an offense when:

(i) if the element involves the nature of his conduct or a result thereof, it is his conscious object to engage in conduct of that nature or to cause such a result; and

---

1. *See generally,* Paul H. Robinson & Markus D. Dubber, *The American Model Penal Code: A Brief Overview*, 10 New Crim. L. Rev. 319 (2007).

(ii) if the element involves the attendant circumstances, he is aware of the existence of such circumstances or he believes or hopes that they exist.

(b) *Knowingly.*

A person acts knowingly with respect to a material element of an offense when:

(i) if the element involves the nature of his conduct or the attendant circumstances, he is aware that his conduct is of that nature or that such circumstances exist; and

(ii) if the element involves a result of his conduct, he is aware that it is practically certain that his conduct will cause such a result.

(c) *Recklessly.*

A person acts recklessly with respect to a material element of an offense when he consciously disregards a substantial and unjustifiable risk that the material element exists or will result from his conduct. The risk must be of such a nature and degree that, considering the nature and purpose of the actor's conduct and the circumstances known to him, its disregard involves a gross deviation from the standard of conduct that a law-abiding person would observe in the actor's situation.

(d) *Negligently.*

A person acts negligently with respect to a material element of an offense when he should be aware of a substantial and unjustifiable risk that the material element exists or will result from his conduct. The risk must be of such a nature and degree that the actor's failure to perceive it, considering the nature and purpose of his conduct and the circumstances known to him, involves a gross deviation from the standard of care that a reasonable person would observe in the actor's situation.

Commentary

Section 2.02. General requirements of culpability.

1. *Objective.* This section expresses the Code's basic requirement that unless some element of mental culpability is proved with respect to each material element of the offense, no valid criminal conviction may be obtained....

2. *Purpose and Knowledge.* In defining the kinds of culpability, the Code draws a narrow distinction between acting purposely and knowingly, one of the elements of ambiguity in legal usage of the term "intent." Knowledge of the requisite external circumstances is a common element in both conceptions. But action is not purposive with respect to the nature or result of the actor's conduct unless it was his conscious object to perform an action of that nature or to cause such a result. It is meaningful to think of the actor's attitude as different if he is simply aware that his conduct is of the required nature or that the prohibited result is practically certain to follow from his conduct.

It is true, of course, that this distinction is inconsequential for most purposes of liability; acting knowingly is ordinarily sufficient. But there are areas where the discrimination is required and is made under traditional law, which uses the awkward concept of "specific intent." ... Although in most instances either knowledge or purpose should suffice for criminal liability, articulating the distinction puts to the test the issue whether an actual purpose is required....

3. *Recklessness.* An important discrimination is drawn between acting either purposely or knowingly and acting recklessly. As the Code uses the term, recklessness involves conscious risk creation. It resembles acting knowingly in that a state of awareness is involved, but the awareness is of risk that is, of a probability less than substantial certainty; the matter is contingent from the actor's point of view....

The risk of which the actor is aware must of course be substantial in order for the recklessness judgment to be made. The risk must also be unjustifiable.... Describing the risk as "substantial" and "unjustifiable" is useful but not sufficient, for these are terms of degree, and the acceptability of a risk in a given case depends on a great many variables. Some standard is needed for determining *how* substantial and how unjustifiable the risk must be in order to warrant a finding of culpability.... The code proposes ... that the jury be asked to measure the substantiality and unjustifiability of the risk by asking whether its disregard, given the actor's perceptions, involved a gross deviation from the standard of conduct that a law-abiding person in the actor's situation would observe.

4. *Negligence.* Negligence is distinguished from purposeful, knowing or reckless action in that it does not involve a state of awareness. A person acts negligently under this subsection when he inadvertently creates a substantial and unjustifiable risk of which he ought to be aware. He is liable if given the nature and degree of the risk, his failure to perceive it is, considering the nature and purpose of the actor's conduct and the circumstances known to him, a gross deviation from the care that would be exercised by a reasonable person in his situation....

... The standard for ultimate judgment invites consideration of the "care that a reasonable person would observe in the actor's situation." There is an inevitable ambiguity in "situation." If the actor were blind or if he had just suffered a blow or experienced a heart attack, these would certainly be facts to be considered in a judgment involving criminal liability, as they would be under traditional law. But the heredity intelligence or temperament of the actor would not be held material in judging negligence, and could not be without depriving the criterion of all its objectivity. The Code is not intended to displace discriminations of this kind, but rather to leave the issue to the courts.

[A] Purposefulness

State v. Smith

Superior Court of New Jersey, Appellate Division
621 A.2d 493, *cert. denied*, 634 A.2d 523 (1993)

King, P.J.A.D.

Defendant was a county jail inmate at the time of the criminal episode on June 11, 1989. He had, and knew he had, the human immunodeficiency virus (HIV). On several occasions before June 11 he had threatened to kill corrections officers by biting or spitting at them. On that day he bit an officer's hand causing puncture wounds on the skin during a struggle which he had precipitated. The jury found him guilty of attempted murder, aggravated assault and terroristic threats. The judge imposed an aggregate 25-year term with a 12 1/2-year period of parole ineligibility.

On this appeal each of defendant's claims of error arises from his premises that (1) without dispute a bite cannot transmit HIV, and (2) defendant knew this when he bit the officers. From these premises defendant urges that he was wrongfully convicted of attempted murder because he knew that his bite could not kill the officer. He insists that he was convicted of such a serious charge because of society's discrimination against persons infected with this deadly virus. He claims that at worst he was guilty only of assaultive conduct and should have been sentenced, as a third-degree offender, to a relatively short custodial term.

From our review of this record, we conclude that neither of defendant's two premises has been established. First, if HIV cannot possibly be spread by a bite, the evidence at trial did not establish that proposition. Indeed, we doubt that the proposition is presently provable scientifically, given the current state of medical knowledge. The apparent medical consensus is that there has never been a controlled study of a sufficiently large number of cases to establish to any scientific certainty if transmission of HIV is possible by a bite, and if so, the percentage of likely infection. The proposition was surely disputed at this trial. Second, whether defendant actually believed that his bite could result in death was a question of his credibility, a question the jury obviously resolved against him.

We cannot and need not decide if a bite can transmit HIV. We have applied the elements of the attempted murder statute as we would in a case involving a more traditional criminal methodology. We conclude that the attempted murder verdict was supported by proof, which the jury reasonably could accept, that the defendant subjectively believed that his conduct could succeed in causing the officer's death, regardless of whether his belief was objectively valid. For this reason, we affirm the conviction.

...

II.

Defendant contends that Judge Mariano erroneously charged the jury that it could find him guilty of attempted murder upon proof that he intended to kill [Officer] Waddington by biting him, regardless of whether it was medically possible that the bite could have transmitted HIV. Instead of focusing on his subjective belief about the effect of the bite, defendant contends the judge should have charged an objective test. Defendant claims that he can be guilty only if a "reasonable person" would have believed that the bite could be fatal.

...

The statute governing criminal attempts is N.J.S.A. 2C:5-1. The pertinent part of that statute is the definitional subsection:

a. Definition of attempt. A person is guilty of an attempt to commit a crime if, acting with the kind of culpability otherwise required for commission of the crime, he:

(1) Purposely engages in conduct which would constitute the crime if the attendant circumstances were as a reasonable person would believe them to be;

(2) When causing a particular result is an element of the crime, does or omits to do anything with the purpose of causing such result without further conduct on his part; or

(3) Purposely does or omits to do anything which, under the circumstances as a reasonable person would believe them to be, is an act or omission constituting a substantial step in a course of conduct planned to culminate in his commission of the crime.

On its face this section creates three separate categories of attempt, two of which incorporate a reasonable-person standard-subsections (1) and (3)—and one of which looks only to defendant's own purpose—subsection (2) ... Judge Mariano charged on subsection (2) only, saying:

Our law provides that a person is guilty of an attempt to commit a crime if the person, acting with the same culpability or state of mind required for the commission of the substantive offense, the crime of murder in this case, does anything with the purpose of causing death, without any further conduct on his part.

The judge then explained that defendant must have "done all that he believes necessary to cause the particular result," here, the death of Waddington. Our Criminal Code "requires that to be guilty of attempted murder, a defendant must have purposely intended to cause the particular result that is the necessary element of the underlying offense—death." *State v. Rhett*, 127 N.J. 3, 7, 601 A.2d 689 (1992).

The judge then charged that it was irrelevant whether the jury found that a bite could succeed in transmitting HIV:

I must instruct you that impossibility is not a defense to the charge of attempted murder. That is because our law, our criminal statutes punish conduct based on state of mind. It punishes purposeful actions regardless of whether the result can be accomplished. And even if the result, which would be death in this case, was a scientific or factual impossibility. In this case if you should be convinced beyond a reasonable doubt by the State's evidence that Mr. Smith's purpose was to kill Sheriff's Officer Waddington by biting him it does not matter that the chances of spreading the virus were either remote or impossible. If the State has proven purposeful conduct beyond a reasonable doubt then the State has proven the essential elements of the crime attempted murder.

Defendant contends that the judge deprived him of the impossibility defense created by the "reasonable person" language of subsection (1), Defendant

> overlooks the separate and different standard announced in subsection (2), which was intended to eliminate an impossibility defense....

... [D]efendant contends "plain error" in the charge in barring the jury from considering the unlikelihood that the AIDS virus could be spread by a bite. Defendant reasons: "The court below should have instructed the jury that it should consider the unsuitability of the means chosen in its determination of whether Smith acted with the requisite purpose."

Defendant invokes the following excerpt from the commentary to the Model Penal Code as authority for his theory: "if the means selected were absurd, there is good ground for doubting that the actor really planned to commit a crime." Model Penal Code, ... 5.01, commentary at 315. Defendant equates his biting with a "voodoo incantation" which is medically incapable of causing death, regardless of whether a person believed to the contrary.

Again, defendant's theory founders on its premise. There was no proof at trial that biting could not possibly transmit HIV. Rather, the evidence was equivocal, with even defendant's expert conceding that there was at least a "remote" possibility of transmission. In any event, the objective likelihood of transmission is irrelevant to liability under N.J.S.A. 2C:5-1(a)(2). It is sufficient that defendant believed his attack would infect Waddington. Such a belief would not necessarily be "absurd" in the same way that the belief in the efficacy of a voodoo curse is unfounded.

Moreover, even if the voodoo analogy is apt, defendant could still be found guilty if the circumstances showed that defendant was "dangerous":

> Cases can be imagined in which it might well be accurate to say that the nature of the means selected, say black magic, substantially negates dangerousness of character. On the other hand, there are many cases as well where one who tries to commit a crime by what he later learns to be inadequate methods will recognize the futility of his course of action and seek more efficacious means. There are, in other words, many instances of dangerous character revealed by "impossible" attempts, and to develop a theory around highly exceptional situations ignores the propriety of convictions in these. [Model Penal Code, *supra*, 5.01, commentary at 316 n.88.]

In the present case defendant's violent assaults and venomous harangues before, during and after biting Waddington, all justified an inference that he bore the requisite criminal state of mind under N.J.S.A. 2C:5-1(a)(2). The judge did not err in failing to charge that the jury should consider the probable efficacy of a bite in spreading HIV.

III.

Defendant contends that the verdicts on Counts One and Six (attempted murder and aggravated assault of Waddington) were against the weight of the evidence, given the "wholly uncontroverted" evidence that defendant knew that AIDS could not be transmitted through biting or spitting. While he concedes the State's evidence shows that he repeatedly threatened to kill various officers by biting them or spitting at them, he contends that in view of his certain knowledge that neither kind of attack could spread AIDS, his only true motive was to take "advantage of the ignorance and fear of his jailors." He pleads that he should not be punished for exploiting that fear and ignorance.

... [T]he jury ... reasonably could have rejected defendant's claim that he "knew" biting or spitting could not spread HIV, especially in view of the conflict in the record between that claim and his conduct in jail over several months. Defendant repeatedly used his HIV infection to arm his verbal threats to kill. He threatened: to spit in an officer's mouth; to give an officer "what I have" if the officer tried to shackle him; to give Officer Snow HIV by biting him; to bite or spit at Snow and Waddington so that they would get HIV and die; and to kill another officer by biting him. Moreover, when defendant spit at Waddington's head he said, "now die, you pig, die from what I have."

Defendant now rationalizes this conduct, for purposes of appellate argument, as reflecting not his own belief that his bites could kill, but rather his realization that the officers' fear and ignorance would cause them to believe that the bites could be fatal. Defendant now terms this an "empowering experience" for him, allowing him to turn this nation's alleged hysteria over AIDS into a weapon against his aggressors.

Inventive as this theory may be, it requires far greater speculation than the jury had to indulge in when it found that defendant possessed the requisite mental state for attempted murder. If defendant were indeed motivated by the desire to take advantage of the correction officers' ignorance, he could have so testified. Even if defendant's personal conviction about society's indifference towards AIDS is correct, and it perhaps is, this does not exempt him from the crimes of attempted murder and aggravated assault under the criminal code.

Comments

(1) The issue in *Smith* is whether the defendant acted with the requisite *mens rea* to be found guilty of attempted murder. As in attempt crimes, the statute under which Smith was charged requires that the accused acted "purposely." Smith contended that he did not act with the purpose to murder because either (1) a reasonable person would know that an HIV-positive individual could not kill another by biting him, or (2) Smith himself knew that he could not kill anyone in that manner. The court holds that the first argument is irrelevant, because it is the defendant's state of mind that is at issue. The second argument is theoretically sound, but the defendant failed to prove it.

(2) The *mens rea* of attempt is a purposeful intention to commit another crime. The law of attempt is the subject of section 6.02, *infra*. The subject of impossible attempt is presented in section 6.02[E], *infra*.

People v. Hood

Supreme Court of California
462 P.2d 370 (1969)

TRAYNOR, CHIEF JUSTICE.

An indictment charged defendant in Count I with assault with a deadly weapon upon a peace officer, Alfred Elia, in Count II with battery upon a peace officer, Donald Kemper, and in Count III with assault with intent to murder Officer Elia. A jury found him guilty.... Defendant appeals.

On September 11, 1967, at about 2:00 a.m., defendant, his brother Donald, and a friend, Leo Chilton, all of whom had been drinking for several hours, knocked on the door of the house of Susan Bueno, defendant's former girlfriend, and asked if they could use the bathroom. Susan said no, but defendant forced his way in and started to hit her. He knocked her to the floor and kicked her. Donald Hood then took Susan aside, and defendant, Chilton, and Gene Saunders, a friend of Susan's who was staying at the house, went to the kitchen and sat down.

Gilbert A. Nielsen, Susan's next-door neighbor, was awakened by the sound of Susan's screams and called the police. Officers Elia and Kemper responded to his call. After talking to Nielsen, they went to Susan's house, knocked on the door, which was opened by Stella Gonzales, Susan's cousin, and asked if "Susie" was there. Miss Gonzales said, "Yes, just a minute," and in a few seconds Susan came running to the door crying. Officer Elia asked Susan if she had been beaten and who did it. She pointed to the kitchen and said, "They're in there right now." The two officers walked through the living room, where Susan, Susan's seven-year-old son Ronnie, and Stella remained, and went into the kitchen. There they observed defendant on the right-hand side of the room leaning against a door. On the left side of the kitchen, the three other men were seated at a table. Officer Elia walked to the middle of the room and questioned the men at the table. Defendant interrupted the questioning and asked Officer Elia if he had a search warrant. Officer Elia replied that he did not need one since the person who rented the house had given him permission to enter. Defendant then directed a stream of obscenities at Officer Elia, who turned and, according to his testimony, started to place defendant under arrest for a violation of Penal Code section 415 (using vulgar, profane, or indecent language within the presence or hearing of women or children). He got no further than to say, "Okay fella, you are...," when defendant swung at him with his fist. When Officer Kemper attempted to go to Officer Elia's assistance, Donald Hood jumped on him from behind. During the ensuing struggle, Officer Elia fell with defendant on top of him in a corner of a pantry adjoining the kitchen at the rear. While struggling on the floor, Officer Elia felt a tug at his gun belt and then heard two shots fired.

A third officer, Laurence Crocker, who had arrived at the house shortly after the other two officers, came into the kitchen as the scuffle between Officer Elia and defendant was beginning. After he had control of Donald Hood, he looked across the kitchen and saw defendant with a gun in his right hand. He testified that defendant pointed the gun towards Officer Elia's midsection and pulled the trigger twice.

Both Officers Crocker and Kemper testified that after the shots, defendant's arm came up over his head with the revolver in his hand. The struggle continued into the bathroom. Defendant was finally subdued when Officer Elia regained possession of the gun and held it against the side of defendant's neck. Officer Elia then noticed that defendant had shot him once in each leg.

The foregoing evidence is clearly sufficient to support the verdicts.

Defendant contends that the court failed properly to instruct the jury ... on the effect of intoxication with respect to the offenses charged in both Counts I and III.

...

The judgment must also be reversed as to Count III, for the court gave hopelessly conflicting instructions on the effect of intoxication. Although the court correctly instructed the jury to consider the evidence that defendant was intoxicated in determining whether he had the specific intent to commit murder, it followed that instruction with the complete text of CALJIC No. 78 (revised), which applies to crimes that require proof only of a general criminal intent. The court in no way made clear to the jury that the latter instruction did not apply to the charge of assault with intent to commit murder....

The distinction between specific and general intent crimes evolved as a judicial response to the problem of the intoxicated offender. That problem is to reconcile two competing theories of what is just in the treatment of those who commit crimes while intoxicated. On the one hand, the moral culpability of a drunken criminal is frequently less than that of a sober person effecting a like injury. On the other hand, it is commonly felt that a person who voluntarily gets drunk and while in that state commits a crime should not escape the consequences.

Before the nineteenth century, the common law refused to give any effect to the fact that an accused committed a crime while intoxicated. The judges were apparently troubled by this rigid traditional rule, however, for there were a number of attempts during the early part of the nineteenth century to arrive at a more humane, yet workable, doctrine. The theory that these judges explored was that evidence of intoxication could be considered to negate intent, whenever intent was an element of the crime charged. As Professor Hall notes, however, such an exculpatory doctrine could eventually have undermined the traditional rule entirely, since some form of mens rea is a requisite of all but strict liability offenses. (Hall, *Intoxication and Criminal Responsibility*, 57 HARV. L. REV. 1045, 1049.) To limit the operation of the doctrine and achieve a compromise between the conflicting feelings of sympathy and reprobation for the intoxicated offender, later courts both in England and this country drew a distinction between so-called specific intent and general intent crimes.

Specific and general intent have been notoriously difficult terms to define and apply, and a number of textwriters recommend that they be abandoned altogether.

Too often the characterization of a particular crime as one of specific or general intent is determined solely by the presence or absence of words describing psychological phenomena—"intent" or "malice," for example—in the statutory language of defining the crime. When the definition of a crime consists of only the description of a particular act, without reference to intent to do a further act or achieve a future consequence, we ask whether the defendant intended to do the proscribed act. This intention is deemed to be a general criminal intent. When the definition refers to defendant's intent to do some further act or achieve some additional consequence, the crime is deemed to be one of specific intent. There is no real difference, however, only a linguistic one, between an intent to do an act already performed and an intent to do that same act in the future.

The language of Penal Code section 22, drafted in 1872 when "specific" and "general" intent were not yet terms of art, is somewhat broader than those terms: "No act committed by a person while in a state of voluntary intoxication is less criminal by reason of his having been in such condition. But whenever the actual existence of any particular purpose, motive, or intent is a necessary element to constitute any particular species or degree of crime, the jury may take into consideration the fact that the accused was intoxicated at the time, in determining the purpose, motive, or intent with which he committed the act." Even this statement of the relevant policy is no easier to apply to particular crimes. We are still confronted with the difficulty of characterizing the mental element of a given crime as a particular purpose, motive, or intent necessary to constitute the offense, or as something less than that to which evidence of intoxication is not pertinent.

Even if we assume that the presence or absence of words clearly denoting mental activity is a valid criterion for determining the significance of intoxication, our present problem is not resolved. The difficulty with applying such a test to the crime of assault or assault with a deadly weapon is that no word in the relevant code provisions unambiguously denotes a particular mental element, yet the word "attempt" in Penal Code section 240 strongly suggests goal-directed, intentional behavior. This uncertainty accounts for the conflict over whether assault is a crime only of intention or also of recklessness.

We need not reconsider our position in *Carmen* [36 Cal. 2d 768, 228 P.2d 281 (1951)] that an assault cannot be predicated merely on reckless conduct. Even if assault requires an intent to commit a battery on the victim, it does not follow that the crime is one in which evidence of intoxication ought to be considered in determining whether the defendant had that intent. It is true that in most cases specific intent has come to mean an intention to do a future act or achieve a particular result, and that assault is appropriately characterized as a specific intent crime under this definition. An assault, however, is equally well characterized as a general intent crime under the definition of general intent as an intent merely to do a violent act. Therefore, whatever reality the distinction between specific and general intent may have in other contexts, the difference is chimerical in the case of assault with a deadly weapon or simple assault. Since the definitions of both specific intent and general intent cover the requisite intent to commit a battery, the decision whether or not to give effect to evidence of intoxication must rest on other considerations.

A compelling consideration is the effect of alcohol on human behavior. A significant effect of alcohol is to distort judgment and relax the controls on aggressive and antisocial impulses. Alcohol apparently has less effect on the ability to engage in simple goal-directed behavior, although it may impair the efficiency of that behavior. In other words, a drunk man is capable of framing an intent to do something simple, such as strike another, unless he is so drunk that he has reached the stage of unconsciousness. What he is not as capable as a sober man of doing is exercising judgment about the social consequences of his acts or controlling his impulses toward antisocial acts. He is more likely to act rashly and impulsively and to be susceptible to passion and anger. It would therefore be anomalous to allow evidence of intoxication to relieve a man of responsibility for the crimes of assault with a deadly weapon or simple assault, which are so frequently committed in just such a manner. As the court said in *Parker v. United States* (1966) 359 F.2d 1009, 1012–1013, 123 U.S. App. D.C. 343, "Whatever ambiguities there may be in distinguishing between specific and general intent to determine whether drunkenness constitutes a defense, an offense of this nature is not one which requires an intent that is susceptible to negation through a showing of voluntary intoxication."

Those crimes that have traditionally been characterized as crimes of specific intent are not affected by our holding here. The difference in mental activity between formulating an intent to commit a battery and formulating an intent to commit a battery for the purpose of raping or killing may be slight, but it is sufficient to justify drawing a line between them and considering evidence of intoxication in the one case and disregarding it in the other. Accordingly, on retrial the court should not instruct the jury to consider evidence of defendant's intoxication in determining whether he committed assault with a deadly weapon on a peace officer or any of the lesser assaults included therein.

Comments and Questions

(1) As in this case, intoxicated defendants can argue that they were too impaired to have acted purposefully or knowingly. In addition, in certain circumstances intoxication may excuse conduct. Note that an excuse does not negate a *mens rea* or justify conduct, but may mitigate punishment. *See* section 7.04, *infra*.

(2) The court, after discussing the perplexing role of intoxication, decided it was not relevant in this case. Why? If the statute had required a *mens rea* of purpose, would Hood have succeeded in having the jury consider the defense? If the *mens rea* of assault was knowledge?

[B] Knowledge

[1] In General

Fabritz v. Traurig

United States Court of Appeals, Fourth Circuit
583 F.2d 697 (1978), *cert. denied*, 443 U.S. 915 (1979)

Bryan, Senior Circuit Judge.

Habeas corpus was refused by the District Court to Virginia Fabritz, a 20-year old mother, who was imprisoned under a conviction and five-year sentence in a Maryland court for abuse—delayed medical attention—touching the death of her daughter, Windy, three years of age. Md. Code Ann. Art. 27, §35A(a) (Cum. Supp. 1975).[1] …

The evidence follows. Fabritz resided with her daughter, Windy, in the home of Thomas L. Crockett and his wife, Ann. The child was three years old when, on October 1, 1973, she was left with the Crocketts while her mother went to her grandfather's funeral in another county. She did not again see Windy until her return at one o'clock on the afternoon of October 3rd. She was met by Crockett with his motorcycle and with Windy riding in the side car. To the mother the child looked unwell. Crockett attributed this appearance to the bumpiness of the motorcycle ride.

On arrival home about 2:30 that afternoon, Windy began to suffer with cramps and to her mother seemed feverish with the flu. At this time she noted the bruises on her body. After bathing her, Fabritz put her to bed or on a couch. Soon afterwards, Windy was seen to have gotten up and curled herself in a blanket on the floor. At 5:00 the child was semiconscious and improved, sitting up for a brief interval after receiving some liquid nourishment. Near 6:00 that afternoon, Windy vomited and showed she was not feeling well. At 7:00 she was put back to bed. Believing the child to have a temperature, her mother sent for a thermometer. The little girl was given soda to settle her stomach, as well as more liquid nourishment, and placed in bed again around 7:30 or 8:00.

---

1. §35A. Causing abuse to child under eighteen.

…

(a) *Penalty*—Any parent, adoptive parent or other person who has the permanent or temporary care of custody or responsibility for the supervision of a minor child under the age of eighteen years *who causes abuse* to such minor child shall be guilty of a felony and upon conviction shall be sentenced to not more than fifteen years in the penitentiary. (Accent added).

…

(b) 7. *"Abuse"* shall mean any: (A) *physical injury or injuries* sustained by a child as a result of *cruel or inhumane treatment* or as a result of malicious act or acts by any parent, adoptive parent or other person who has the permanent or temporary care of custody or responsibility for supervision of a minor child (B) any sexual abuse of a child, whether physical injuries are sustained or not. (Accent added).

…

Fabritz twice telephoned Connie Schaeffer, a neighbor, for assistance, telling her of the child's flu and of her worsening condition. On arrival Schaeffer, too, saw that Windy had a fever. Asked about the bruises on Windy, the mother replied, "Tommy hits hard." They bathed her in alcohol and put her to bed. At this point the child appeared to Schaeffer to be half asleep, neither moaning nor crying.

Schaeffer testified at trial that she did not know what was the matter with Windy, and had left the Crockett house without suggesting medical assistance. Further testimony related that at this moment Ann Crockett arrived home and discussed with Fabritz the procurement of medical attention and Fabritz asked Ann to keep an eye on Windy. The two concluded it was necessary to seek help. Ann called the County Hospital, and was advised by the doctor that the women should bring the child to the hospital.

It was then that Ann, on entering the child's bedroom, perceived she was not breathing. Thereupon she sought an ambulance while Fabritz applied mouth-to-mouth resuscitation. The rescue ambulance took Windy, accompanied by Ann, to the hospital. Meanwhile, Schaeffer saw Fabritz in a hysterical condition, endeavored to calm her and drove her to the hospital, where they were informed the child had been declared dead on arrival at 10:35. In this state she told Schaeffer, "It is my fault, I killed her."

The medical opinion was that 18 to 24 hours before death—during Fabritz' absence from home—the child had been struck in the abdomen by a blunt instrument, possibly a fist, rupturing the duodenum and leading to death from peritonitis. No evidence intimated that Fabritz had knowledge that the person in whose custody Windy was left would abuse her.

At one juncture Fabritz remarked that she had not taken Windy to the hospital because Fabritz "was too ashamed of the bruises" on her body. On his trial Crockett was acquitted of any connection with the death. At her trial the prosecution conceded that Fabritz had not struck the child.

The Maryland Court of Appeals' conclusion was that Fabritz' "inaction amounted to child abuse;" that her "failure to obtain medical attention" constituted "cruel or inhumane treatment;" and that this treatment was a cause of the child's "physical injury." In determining to grant Fabritz habeas corpus, we accept the statute as valid, as did the Court of Appeals of Maryland and the District Court, and accept, too, their clear exposition of the critical words of the law. The statute simply was unconstitutionally applied.

Our conclusion does not affront the conclusion of the Maryland Court, nor that of the District Court. The three steps of the State Court's reasoning do not preclude a finding that the evidence is wholly wanting in proof of an indispensable factor: that during the three stages of the syllogism Fabritz had knowledge that she was risking the life of her child. That is the decisive issue here.

The evidence is utterly bare of proof of a consciousness of criminality during her bedside vigil. *Cf. Morissette v. United States*. This may have been an error of judgment, however dreadfully dear, but there was no awareness of wrongdoing on her part. The jury's contrary verdict on that question finds no warrant in the testimony. Fabritz' error amounted to a failure to procure medical attention in less than eight hours after her arrival at home. Without expert medical knowledge to place her on notice of the fatal nature of the child's illness, she treated her as best she knew. The misjudgment was only to the significance of the symptoms and of the immediacy of demand for professional care. In these circumstances the conviction cannot stand—without even so much as a murmur of evidential justification.

As the Court said in *Thompson v. Louisville*, 362 U.S. 199 (1960):

> The ultimate question presented to us is whether the charges against petitioner were so totally devoid of evidentiary support as to render his conviction unconstitutional under the Due Process Clause of the Fourteenth Amendment. Decision of this question turns not on the sufficiency of the evidence, but on whether this conviction rests upon any evidence at all.
>
> ...
>
> Just as conviction upon a charge not made would be sheer denial of due process, [s]o it is a violation of due process to convict and punish a man without evidence of his guilt.

It would be a radical overthrow of the universal understanding of motherly devotion, as well as the confidence gained by experience to be accorded the judgment of two women having the responsibility of a sick 3-year old, to hold the conduct of the mother or of her friend suspect. Especially is this true when it is remembered that although the child would have survived "had an operation been performed within at least twelve hours prior to death," Fabritz had not even then returned from her grandfather's funeral. The callings of nursing and baby-sitting ought not impose so frightening a trusteeship.

The judgment on appeal will be vacated and the case remanded to the District Court to grant the writ.

HAYNSWORTH, CHIEF JUDGE, dissenting.

I have a great deal of sympathy for this young woman who has spent a time in prison on a conviction of child abuse arising out of the death of her three-year old daughter, though generally the mother had been a loving and considerate one. My sympathy for the mother is enhanced by the fact that the person who inflicted the fatal injury upon the child has remained unpunished. I think, however, that the proof at trial did not permit a conclusion on our part that there was no evidence to support a finding of a violation of the statute by the mother.

Of course, a parent should not go to prison for an erroneous diagnosis of a child's illness, but the Court of Appeals of Maryland has clearly held that the statute is violated if a custodian of a child knowingly withholds medical assistance and if the child's condition is aggravated or if death ensues as a result of want of medical attention.

Indeed, Maryland has long embraced the common law doctrine that one who, through gross negligence, fails to perform a legal duty owing to another as a result of which the other dies is guilty of involuntary manslaughter.

There can be no doubt here that the multiple bruises were not symptomatic of influenza. When the neighbor saw the child, she was moaning in pain. That and her comatose condition should have signaled a more serious condition than the flu. That the mother recognized that there may have been internal injuries is supported by the testimony that she explained the child's bruised condition to the neighbor by saying, "Tommy hits hard."

One may suppose that this three-year old child had told her mother who had beaten her, and the record clearly indicates that Tommy Crockett was the lover of both of the women who shared the house with him. Thus, she explained to the neighbor that she had not sought a physician's help because she was ashamed of the bruised condition of the child's body and that if the child were seen by a physician she would have to explain the origin of the bruises.

I put no great weight on her exclamation after being informed that the child was dead, "I killed her," but her statements to the neighbor before the child was dead of her reasons for not having sooner sought medical help furnished support for a finding that for some hours the mother consciously refrained from seeking medical help to protect Crockett from possible criminal charges and to support her own ego. Though the mother was generally loving and protective of her daughter, a conscious indulgence of such a preference is in violation of Maryland's Child Abuse Law when earlier medical attention might have saved the child's life.

I cannot agree that this conviction was devoid of evidentiary support.

Comments and Questions

(1) What did the defendant have to know for this conviction to be sustained? That the child was injured? Severely injured? Mortally injured? Would it make a difference if Fabritz knew that Crockett had violent propensities? What of her statements that "Tommy hits hard," and that she "was too ashamed of the bruises" to take the child to the hospital?

(2) In this appeal from a state court conviction, the federal court accepted the validity of the Maryland statute and the state court's application of it. Why then did the court overturn the state court decision and grant Fabritz's appeal?

[2] Statutory Interpretation

Flores-Figueroa v. United States

Supreme Court of the United States
556 U.S. 646 (2009)

Justice Breyer delivered the opinion of the Court.

A federal criminal statute forbidding "[a]ggravated identity theft" imposes a mandatory consecutive 2-year prison term upon individuals convicted of certain other crimes *if*, during (or in relation to) the commission of those other crimes, the offender "*knowingly* transfers, possesses, or uses, without lawful authority, *a means of identification of another person.*" 18 U.S.C. § 1028A(a)(1) (emphasis added)....

I.

The statutory provision in question references a set of predicate crimes, including, for example, theft of government property, fraud, or engaging in various unlawful activities related to passports, visas, and immigration. It then provides that if any person who commits any of those other crimes (in doing so) "knowingly transfers, possesses, or uses, without lawful authority, a means of identification of another person," the judge must add two years' imprisonment to the offender's underlying sentence. All parties agree that the provision applies only where the offender knows that he is transferring, possessing, or using *something*. And the Government reluctantly concedes that the offender likely must know that he is transferring, possessing, or using that *something* without lawful authority. But they do not agree whether the provision requires that a defendant also know that the *something* he has unlawfully transferred is, for example, a real ID belonging to another person rather than, say, a fake ID (*i.e.*, a group of numbers that does not correspond to any real Social Security number).

Petitioner Ignacio Flores-Figueroa argues that the statute requires that the Government prove that he *knew* that the "means of identification" belonged to someone else, *i.e.*, was "a means of identification *of another person*." The Government argues that the statute does not impose this particular knowledge requirement. The Government concedes that the statute uses the word "knowingly," but that word, the Government claims, does not modify the statute's last phrase ("a means of identification of another person") or, at the least, it does not modify the last three words of that phrase ("of another person").

The facts of this case illustrate the legal problem. Ignacio Flores-Figueroa is a citizen of Mexico. In 2000, to secure employment, Flores gave his employer a false name, birth date, and Social Security number, along with a counterfeit alien registration card. The Social Security number and the number on the alien registration card were not those of a real person. In 2006, Flores presented his employer with new counterfeit Social Security and alien registration cards; these cards (unlike Flores' old alien registration card) used his real name. But this time the numbers on both cards were in fact numbers assigned to other people.

Flores' employer reported his request to U.S. Immigration and Customs Enforcement. Customs discovered that the numbers on Flores' new documents belonged to other people. The United States then charged Flores with two predicate crimes, namely, entering the United States without inspection and misusing immigration documents. And it charged him with aggravated identity theft, the crime at issue here.

Flores moved for a judgment of acquittal on the "aggravated identity theft" counts. He claimed that the Government could not prove that he *knew* that the numbers on the counterfeit documents were numbers assigned to other people. The Government replied that it need not prove that knowledge, and the District Court accepted the Government's argument. After a bench trial, the court found Flores guilty of the predicate crimes and aggravated identity theft. The Court of Appeals upheld the District Court's determination. And we granted certiorari to consider the "knowledge" issue—a matter about which the Circuits have disagreed.

II.

There are strong textual reasons for rejecting the Government's position. As a matter of ordinary English grammar, it seems natural to read the statute's word "knowingly" as applying to all the subsequently listed elements of the crime. The Government cannot easily claim that the word "knowingly" applies only to the statutes first four words, or even its first seven. It makes little sense to read the provision's language as heavily penalizing a person who "transfers, possesses, or uses, without lawful authority" a *something*, but does not know, at the very least, that the "something" (perhaps inside a box) is a "means of identification." Would we apply a statute that makes it unlawful "*knowingly* to possess drugs" to a person who steals a passenger's bag without knowing that the bag has drugs inside?

The Government claims more forcefully that the word "knowingly" applies to all but the statute's last three words, *i.e.*, "of another person." The statute, the Government says, does not require a prosecutor to show that the defendant *knows* that the means of identification the defendant has unlawfully used in fact belongs to another person. But how are we to square this reading with the statute's language?

In ordinary English, where a transitive verb has an object, listeners in most contexts assume that an adverb (such as knowingly) that modifies the transitive verb tells the listener how the subject performed the entire action, including the object as set forth in the sentence. Thus, if a bank official says, "Smith knowingly transferred the funds to his brother's account," we would normally understand the bank official's statement as telling us that Smith knew the account was his brother's. Nor would it matter if the bank official said "Smith knowingly transferred the funds to the account of his brother." In either instance, if the bank official later told us that Smith did not know the account belonged to Smith's brother, we should be surprised.

...

The manner in which the courts ordinarily interpret criminal statutes is fully consistent with this ordinary English usage. That is to say courts ordinarily read a phrase in a criminal statute that introduces the elements of a crime with the word "knowingly" as applying that word to each element.

...

Finally, and perhaps of greatest practical importance, there is the difficulty in many circumstances of proving beyond a reasonable doubt that a defendant has the necessary knowledge.

...

We do not find this argument sufficient, however, to turn the tide in the Government's favor. For one thing, in the classic case of identity theft, intent is generally not difficult to prove. For example, where a defendant has used another person's identification information to get access to that person's bank account, the Government can prove knowledge with little difficulty. The same is true when the defendant has gone through someone else's trash to find discarded credit card and bank statements, or pretends to be from the victim's bank and requests personal identifying information. Indeed, the examples of identity theft in the legislative history (dumpster diving, computer hacking, and the like) are all examples of the types of classic identity theft where intent should be relatively easy to prove, and there will be no practical enforcement problem. For another thing, to the extent that Congress may have been concerned about criminalizing the conduct of a broader class of individuals, the concerns about practical enforceability are insufficient to outweigh the clarity of the text. Similar interpretations that we have given other similarly phrased statutes also created practical enforcement problems. But had Congress placed conclusive weight upon practical enforcement, the statute would likely not read the way it now reads. Instead, Congress used the word "knowingly" followed by a list of offense elements. And we cannot find indications in statements of its purpose or in the practical problems of enforcement sufficient to overcome the ordinary meaning, in English or through ordinary interpretive practice, of the words that it wrote.

We conclude that § 1028A(a)(1) requires the Government to show that the defendant knew that the means of identification at issue belonged to another person. The judgment of the Court of Appeals is reversed, and the case is remanded for further proceedings consistent with this opinion.

[The concurring opinions of JUSTICES SCALIA and ALITO are omitted.]

Comments and Questions

(1) Under the Model Penal Code, how would this issue be resolved? *See* Model Penal Code § 2.02(4) (stating that when an offense does not distinguish among its material elements, the prescribed culpability term "shall apply to all the material elements of the offense, unless a contrary purpose plainly appears." The Court, however, reached its decision without reference to the MPC.

(2) Three concurring justices wrote specifically to critique the majority's statement that "it was ordinary practice" to apply the mens rea to every element of the offense. Justices Alito, Scalia and Thomas favored a more flexible approach. Which approach do you favor—a uniform rule or a case-by-case analysis?

United States v. International Minerals & Chemical Corp.

Supreme Court of the United States
402 U.S. 558 (1971)

MR. JUSTICE DOUGLAS delivered the opinion of the Court.

The information charged that appellee shipped sulfuric acid and hydrofluosilicic acid in interstate commerce and "did knowingly fail to show on the shipping papers the required classification of said property, to wit, Corrosive Liquid, in violation of 49 CFR 173.427."

Title 18 U.S.C. § 834(a) gives the Interstate Commerce Commission power to "formulate regulations for the safe transportation" of "corrosive liquids" and 18 U.S.C. § 834(f) states that whoever "knowingly violates any such regulation" shall be fined or imprisoned.

Pursuant to the power granted by § 834(a) the regulatory agency promulgated the regulation already cited which reads in part:

> Each shipper offering for transportation any hazardous material subject to the regulations in this chapter, shall describe that article on the shipping paper by the shipping name prescribed in § 172.5 of this chapter and by the classification prescribed in § 172.4 of this chapter, and may add a further description not inconsistent therewith. Abbreviations must not be used.

49 CFR § 173.427.

The District Court, relying primarily on *Boyce Motor Lines, Inc. v. United States*, 342 U.S. 337, ruled that the information did not charge a "knowing violation" of the regulation and accordingly dismissed the information.

...

Here as in *United States v. Freed*, 401 U.S. 601, which dealt with the possession of hand grenades, strict or absolute liability is not imposed; knowledge of the shipment of the dangerous materials is required. The sole and narrow question is whether "knowledge" of the regulation is also required. It is in that narrow zone that the issue of "*mens rea*" is raised; and appellee bears down hard on the provision in 18 U.S.C. § 834(f) that whoever "knowingly violates any such regulation" shall be fined, etc.

Boyce Motor Lines, Inc. v. United States, supra, on which the District Court relied, is not dispositive of the issue.

...

The "*mens rea*" that emerged [from *Boyce*] was not knowledge of the regulation but knowledge of the safer routes and those that were less safe within the meaning of the regulation. Mr. Justice Jackson, writing in dissent for himself, Mr. Justice Black, and Mr. Justice Frankfurter, correctly said:

> I do not suppose the Court intends to suggest that if petitioner knew nothing of the existence of such a regulation its ignorance would constitute a defense.

342 U.S. at 345.

...

The principle that ignorance of the law is no defense applies whether the law be a statute or a duly promulgated and published regulation. In the context of these proposed 1960 amendments we decline to attribute to Congress the inaccurate view that that Act requires proof of knowledge of the law, as well as the facts, and that it intended to endorse that interpretation by retaining the word "knowingly." We conclude that the meager legislative history of the 1960 amendments makes unwarranted the conclusion that Congress abandoned the general rule and required knowledge of both the facts and the pertinent law before a criminal conviction could be sustained under this Act.

So far as possession, say, of sulfuric acid is concerned the requirement of "*mens rea*" has been made a requirement of the Act as evidenced by the use of the word "knowingly." A person thinking in good faith that he was shipping distilled water when in fact he was shipping some dangerous acid would not be covered.

...

In *Balint* the Court was dealing with drugs, in *Freed* with hand grenades, in this case with sulfuric and other dangerous acids. Pencils, dental floss, paper clips may also be regulated. But they may be the type of products which might raise substantial due process questions if Congress did not require ... "*mens rea*" as to each ingredient of the offense. But where, as here and as in *Balint* and *Freed*, dangerous or deleterious devices or products or obnoxious waste materials are involved, the probability of regulation is so great that anyone who is aware that he is in possession of them or dealing with them must be presumed to be aware of the regulation.

Mr. Justice Stewart, with whom Mr. Justice Harlan and Mr. Justice Brennan join, dissenting.

This case stirs large questions—questions that go to the moral foundations of the criminal law. Whether postulated as a problem of "*mens rea*," of "*willfulness*," of "*criminal responsibility*," or of "*scienter*," the infliction of criminal punishment upon the unaware has long troubled the fair administration of justice. But there is no occasion here for involvement with this root problem of criminal jurisprudence, for it is evident to me that Congress made punishable only knowing violations of the regulation in question. That is what the law quite clearly says, what the federal courts have held, and what the legislative history confirms.

...

A final word is in order. Today's decision will have little practical impact upon the prosecution of interstate motor carriers or institutional shippers. For interstate motor carriers are members of a regulated industry, and their officers, agents, and employees are required by law to be conversant with the regulations in question. As a practical matter, therefore, they are under a species of absolute liability for violation of the regulations despite the "knowingly" requirement. This, no doubt, is as Congress intended it to be. Likewise, prosecution of regular shippers for violations of the regulations could hardly be impeded by the "knowingly" requirement, for triers of fact would have no difficulty whatever in inferring knowledge on the part of those whose business it is to know, despite their protestations to the contrary. The only real impact of this decision will be upon the casual shipper, who might be any man, woman, or child in the Nation. A person who had never heard of the regulation might make a single shipment of an article covered by it in the course of a lifetime. It would be wholly natural for him to assume that he could deliver the article to the common carrier and depend upon the carrier to see that it was properly labeled and that the shipping papers were in order. Yet today's decision holds that a person who does just that is guilty of a criminal offense punishable by a year in prison. This seems to me a perversion of the purpose of criminal law.

I respectfully dissent from the opinion and judgment of the Court.

Comments and Questions

(1) The issue in *International Minerals* was what the defendant had to have known to satisfy the *mens rea* element of "knowingly." The Supreme Court held that the statute required only knowledge of the fact that sulfuric acid was to be shipped—not, as the defendant argued, knowledge of the regulation that made such actions illegal.

(2) The regulation in *International Minerals* is typical of public welfare offenses (sometimes called regulatory crimes). The Supreme Court in *Morissette* noted that industrialization and urbanization made it necessary to pass "health and welfare regulations undreamed of in simpler times" to protect citizens who are unable to protect themselves against the risks created. *Morissette*, 342 U.S. 246. As Justice Jackson predicted, such offenses altered the common law requirement of a *mens rea*. In some situations, the gravity of harm justified strict liability offenses, relieving the government of proving any *mens rea*. *See infra* § 3.03 (discussing strict liability crimes). In others, the courts interpret the knowledge requirement broadly in order to achieve the purpose of the statute. Cases that follow in this chapter provide more examples of regulatory and public welfare offenses (*United States v. Hanousek, Ratzlaff v. United States*, and *Staples v. United States*).

[3] Willful Blindness

In some circumstances, little evidence or no evidence exists to show the defendant knew that a material fact incident to the crime even existed. A defendant may claim she did not know the van she was driving contained drugs when charged with "knowingly transporting drugs." The defendant is not guilty unless the government can prove she knew drugs were in the van.

In such cases, courts may instruct juries to consider whether the defendant was willfully blind or deliberately indifferent to the fact at issue. The instruction allows a jury to infer that the defendant acted with knowledge of the fact. As you read the following material, consider what "willfully blind" means and why the doctrine is controversial.

United States v. Giovannetti

United States Court of Appeals, Seventh Circuit
919 F.2d 1223 (1990)

Posner, Circuit Judge.

The government indicted fifteen men for offenses arising from their participation in an illegal gambling enterprise.... Nicholas Janis was convicted of conducting an illegal gambling business or aiding and abetting its conducting, and was sentenced to 60 days.

The head of the gambling enterprise was Thomas Orlando, one of the defendants who pleaded guilty. Active primarily in Bridgeview and other southwestern suburbs of Chicago between 1978 and 1987, the enterprise operated a succession of "wire-rooms," where bets on various sporting events were accepted over the telephone, and it also sponsored "smokers," or casino gambling nights, held at restaurants and bars, where guests played blackjack, craps, and poker. Giovannetti, and particularly Janis, had minor roles in the enterprise. Giovannetti was a bouncer, enforcer, and strong-arm collector of gambling debts owed the enterprise. Janis owned a house that the enterprise for a time used as its wireroom.

The evidence against Giovannetti was strong and the trial rulings of which he complains plainly correct, so we shall move directly to Janis's appeal, which raises some difficult questions. Janis was a gambler and knew members of the Orlando organization, including Orlando himself and Richard Merino, a bookmaker for the organization. Together with a real estate agent who has not been charged with any wrongdoing, Janis owned, as an investment, a lot in Bridgeview with two houses on it, one behind the other. In the fall of 1982, Merino, who unbeknownst to Janis was a government informant, went to Janis and said he wanted to rent the smaller of the houses, the one in the rear, for his friend Pluta, who was recently divorced. This was done. Pluta did not move in until the spring of the next year (1983), but from November 1982 until July 1983 the house was in continuous use as a wireroom, operated first (it appears) by Merino and then, after Pluta moved in, by Pluta. The house was not used in the gambling enterprise after that, but early the following year the government tape-recorded a telephone conversation between Janis and Orlando in which Janis offered Orlando a key to the house and asked him whether everything was all right. Orlando responded: "Yeah, yeah, they just wanted to get out of there. They spotted some guys out there I guess." Janis replied: "I know." Although Merino and then Pluta were the nominal tenants, often the rent was paid not by either of them but instead by Michael Gioringo, whom Janis knew to be an aide to Thomas Orlando.

...

Reference to Janis's knowledge brings us to the central issue in the case, the propriety of the judge's having given the "ostrich" instruction, on which see the thorough discussion in *United States v. Jewell*, 532 F.2d 697 (9th Cir.1976) (en banc). The instruction told the jury, "You may infer knowledge from a combination of suspicion and indifference to the truth. If you find that a person had a strong suspicion that things were not what they seemed or that someone had withheld some important facts, yet shut his eyes for fear that he would learn, you may conclude that he acted knowingly." There is no quarrel with the wording of the instruction, which is verbatim the instruction that we recommended to the district judges of this circuit; the question is whether it should have been given.

The ultimate question that the jury had to decide was whether Janis either had participated in conducting the Orlando gambling enterprise or, more plausibly, had aided and abetted the enterprise, by renting the house to Merino knowing it would be used as a wireroom. Now it is not the law that every time a seller sells something that he knows will be used for an illegal purpose he is guilty of aiding and abetting, let alone of actual participation in the illegal conduct. Aiding and abetting requires more; in Learned Hand's words, requires that the alleged aider and abettor "in some sort associate himself with the venture, that he participate in it as in something that he wishes to bring about, that he seek by his action to make it succeed." *United States v. Peoni*, 100 F.2d 401, 402 (2d Cir.1938)....

But Janis concedes that the rental of a house for gambling purposes is the type of assistance that brings the supplier within the field of the aider and abettor concept, provided that the landlord (Janis) knew what use his tenant (Merino) intended to put the rented house to. The reason for this concession may be that it would be difficult to conceal the purpose of such a rental from the landlord. If a gambling enterprise to succeed needs to enlist a landlord who knows the purpose of the rental, punishing him will make life significantly more difficult for the enterprise.

The tape-recorded conversation from which we quoted earlier makes clear that Janis learned of the house's use as a wireroom eventually, but possibly only after that use had ceased. It is true that he offered Orlando the key so that it could be reopened as a wireroom, but he was never taken up on his offer (perhaps because the FBI shut down Orlando's enterprise three weeks later) and the wireroom never was reopened in his house. There is considerable doubt whether that rather empty gesture of offering the key could be thought to aid and abet the enterprise—it sounds more like attempted aiding and abetting, a crime that the American Law Institute thinks should exist, Model Penal Code § 2.06(3)(a)(ii), but that probably does not exist under federal law because of the interpretation that the courts place on aiding and abetting, combined with the absence of a general federal attempt statute. A critical question, therefore, was whether Janis knew when he rented the house that it was destined for use as a wireroom. There was no direct evidence of his knowledge, but that was not necessary, and certainly it would have been proper to instruct the jury to this effect. The jury could have inferred from ... the recorded conversation with Orlando that Janis had known what use the rented house would be put to.

It is not the purpose of the ostrich instruction to tell the jury that it does not need direct evidence of guilty knowledge in order to find such knowledge beyond a reasonable doubt. Still less is it to enable conviction of one who merely suspects that he may be involved with wrongdoers. At times during the oral argument of this appeal the government's able lawyer came close to suggesting that the proper office of the ostrich instruction is to enable conviction upon the basis of constructive notice—if a reasonable man who knew what Janis knew would have inquired further and discovered the illegal activity, Janis is an aider and abettor. Not so. Aider and abettor liability is not negligence liability. The abettor and aider must know that he is assisting an illegal activity. We add that if it were the purpose of the ostrich instruction to enable conviction for mere negligence, the instruction would be worded differently.

The most powerful criticism of the ostrich instruction is, precisely, that its tendency is to allow juries to convict upon a finding of negligence for crimes that require intent. The criticism can be deflected by thinking carefully about just what it is that real ostriches do (or at least are popularly supposed to do). They do not just fail to follow through on their suspicions of bad things. They are not merely *careless* birds. They bury their heads in the sand so that they will not see or hear bad things. They *deliberately* avoid acquiring unpleasant knowledge. The ostrich instruction is designed for cases in which there is evidence that the defendant, knowing or strongly suspecting that he is involved in shady dealings, takes steps to make sure that he does not acquire full or exact knowledge of the nature and extent of those dealings. A deliberate effort to avoid guilty knowledge is all the guilty knowledge the law requires. "[T]o know, and to want not to know because one suspects, may be, if not the same state of mind, the same degree of fault."

The government points out that the rented house in Bridgeview was a short way down a side street from the thoroughfare on which Janis commuted to work daily. It would have been easy for him to drive by the house from time to time to see what was doing, and if he had done so he might have discovered its use as a wireroom. He did not do so. But this is not the active avoidance with which the ostrich doctrine is concerned. It would be if the house had been *on* the thoroughfare, and Janis, fearful of what he would see if he drove past it, altered his commuting route to avoid it. Janis failed to display curiosity, but he did nothing to prevent the truth from being communicated to him. He did not *act* to avoid learning the truth.

The critical question so far as Janis's guilt or innocence was concerned is simple (to pose, not necessarily to answer): what did Janis know? Did he know that he was renting his house for use as a wireroom, or did he believe that he was renting his house to the Orlando crew for some private purpose of theirs unconnected with gambling? (Even criminals have private lives.) The ostrich instruction did not advance this inquiry; it confused it, by pointing the jury to circumstances of deliberate avoidance of knowledge that did not exist. As we said in *United States v. Bigelow*, 914 F.2d 966, 971 (7th Cir.1990), when the facts require the jury to make a "binary choice" between "actual knowledge" and "complete innocence," the ostrich instruction should not be given.

...

Comments and Questions

(1) Judge Posner cited the danger that juries would find knowledge based on what the defendant should have known, a negligence standard. A similar concern is that willful blindness defines knowledge as being reckless as to whether the fact at issue existed or was true. The *mens rea* terms of recklessness and negligence are included in this chapter. *See* §§ 3.01[C] & 3.01[D], *infra*.

(2) The Ninth Circuit, whose decision in *Jewell* articulated the willful blindness doctrine, recently differentiated between willful blindness, recklessness and negligence:

> A willfully blind defendant is one who took deliberate actions to avoid confirming suspicion of criminality. A reckless defendant is one who merely knew of a substantial and unjustifiable risk that his conduct was criminal; a negligent defendant is one who should have had similar suspicions but, in fact, did not.

United States v. Heredia, 483 F.3d 913, 918 n.4 (9th Cir. 2007) (*en banc*). The court reiterated that willful blindness is tantamount to knowledge, nothing less. The dissent noted that a *Jewell* instruction makes defendants who "don't know because they don't want to know" ... "just as culpable as those who knowingly or intentionally act unlawfully." *Id.* at 932.

(3) The Model Penal Code defines knowledge to include deliberate ignorance:

> When knowledge of the existence of a particular fact is an element of an offense, such knowledge is established if a person is aware of a *high probability* of its existence, unless he actually believes that it does not exist.

Model Penal Code § 2.02(7) (emphasis added). The drafters of the Model Penal Code noted the "subtle but important question" of whether willful blindness was "acting recklessly or knowingly." As a consequence, they changed their initial formulation from "substantial probability" to "high probability."

See Model Penal Code § 2.02 cmt. 9 & n. 42.

(4) Judge Posner commented on the venerable ostrich in another case.

> The reference [to ostriches] of course is to the legend that ostriches when frightened bury their head in the sand. It is pure legend and a canard on a very distinguished bird. Zoological Society of San Diego, *Birds: Ostrich*, www.sandiegozoo.org/animalbytes/t-ostrich.html (visited June 12, 2008) ("When an ostrich senses danger and cannot run away, it flops to the ground and remains still, with its head and neck flat on the ground in front of it. Because the head and neck are lightly colored, they blend in with the color of the soil. From a distance, it just looks like the ostrich has buried its head in the sand, because only the body is visible"). It is too late, however, to correct this injustice....

United States v. Black, 530 F.3d 596 (7th Cir. 2008), *vacated and remanded on other grounds*, 130 S. Ct. 2963 (2010).

(5) The Supreme Court recently considered the willful blindness doctrine in *Global-Tech Appliances, Inc. v. SEB S.A.*, 131 S. Ct. 2060 (S. Ct. 2011). Although it is a civil case, the standard articulated in *Global-Tech* seems likely to apply to federal criminal cases. *See* United States v. Brooks, 681 F.3d 678 (5th Cir. 2012); United States v. Ferguson, 676 F.3d 260 (2d Cir. 2011); United States v. Butler, 646 F.3d 1038 (8th Cir. 2011). The Court stated:

> The doctrine of willful blindness is well-established in criminal law. Many criminal statutes require proof that a defendant acted knowingly or willfully, and courts applying the doctrine of willful blindness hold that defendants cannot escape the reach of these statutes by deliberately shielding themselves from clear evidence of critical facts that are strongly suggested by the circumstances. The traditional rationale for this doctrine is that defendants who behave in this manner are just as culpable as those who have actual knowledge. It is also said that persons who know enough to blind themselves

> to direct proof of critical facts in effect have actual knowledge of those facts. See *United States v. Jewell,* 532 F.2d 697, 700 (C.A.9 1976) (en banc).
>
> This Court's opinion more than a century ago in *Spurr v. United States,* 174 U.S. 728 (1899),[6] while not using the term "willful blindness," endorsed a similar concept.... Following our decision in *Spurr,* several federal prosecutions in the first half of the 20th century invoked the doctrine of willful blindness. Later, a 1962 proposed draft of the Model Penal Code, which has since become official, attempted to incorporate the doctrine by defining "knowledge of the existence of a particular fact" to include a situation in which "a person is aware of a high probability of [the fact's] existence, unless he actually believes that it does not exist." ALI, Model Penal Code § 2.02(7) (Proposed Official Draft 1962). Our Court has used the Code's definition as a guide in analyzing whether certain statutory presumptions of knowledge comported with due process. And every Court of Appeals—with the possible exception of the District of Columbia Circuit ... has fully embraced willful blindness, applying the doctrine to a wide range of criminal statutes.
>
> ...
>
> While the Courts of Appeals articulate the doctrine of willful blindness in slightly different ways, all appear to agree on two basic requirements: (1) the defendant must subjectively believe that there is a high probability that a fact exists and (2) the defendant must take deliberate actions to avoid learning of that fact. We think these requirements give willful blindness an appropriately limited scope that surpasses recklessness and negligence. Under this formulation, a willfully blind defendant is one who takes deliberate actions to avoid confirming a high probability of wrongdoing and who can almost be said to have actually known the critical facts. By contrast, a reckless defendant is one who merely knows of a substantial and unjustified risk of such wrongdoing and a negligent defendant is one who should have known of a similar risk but, in fact, did not.

Global Tech, 131 S. Ct. at 2068–70.

The *Global-Tech* decision is both expansive and narrow. It expansively endorses the notion of proving knowledge through the willful blindness doctrine. On the other hand, the Court's standard is high, "a willfully blind defendant is one *who takes deliberate actions to avoid* confirming a high probability of wrongdoing and who can almost be said to have actually known the critical facts." (emphasis added).

---

6. The doctrine emerged in English law almost four decades earlier and became firmly established by the end of the nineteenth century. In American law, one of the earliest references to the doctrine appears in an 1882 jury charge in a federal prosecution. In the charge, the trial judge rejected the "great misapprehension" that a person may "close his eyes, when he pleases, upon all sources of information, and then excuse his ignorance by saying that he does not see anything." See *United States v. Houghton,* 14 F. 544, 547 (D.C.N.J.).

(6) Justice Kennedy, as an appellate judge on the Ninth Circuit Court of Appeals, dissented in *Jewell* and again in *Global-Tech*:

> Having interpreted the statute to require a showing of knowledge, the Court holds that willful blindness will suffice. This is a mistaken step. Willful blindness is not knowledge; and judges should not broaden a legislative proscription by analogy. See *United States v. Jewell,* 532 F.2d 697, 706 (C.A.9 1976) (en banc) (Kennedy, J., dissenting) ("When a statute specifically requires knowledge as an element of a crime, however, the substitution of some other state of mind cannot be justified even if the court deems that both are equally blameworthy").
>
> The Court justifies its substitution of willful blindness for the statutory knowledge requirement in two ways, neither of which is convincing.
>
> First, the Court appeals to moral theory by citing the "traditional rationale" that willfully blind defendants "are just as culpable as those who have actual knowledge." But the moral question is a difficult one. Is it true that the lawyer who knowingly suborns perjury is no more culpable than the lawyer who avoids learning that his client, a criminal defendant, lies when he testifies that he was not the shooter? The answer is not obvious. Perhaps the culpability of willful blindness depends on a person's reasons for remaining blind. Or perhaps only the person's justification for his conduct is relevant. This is a question of morality and of policy best left to the political branches....
>
> Second, the Court appeals to precedent, noting that a "similar concept" to willful blindness appears in this Court's cases as early as 1899. But this Court has never before held that willful blindness can substitute for a statutory requirement of knowledge.... And although most Courts of Appeals have embraced willful blindness, counting courts in a circuit split is not this Court's usual method for deciding important questions of law.
>
> The Court appears to endorse the willful blindness doctrine here for all federal criminal cases involving knowledge. It does so in a civil case where it has received no briefing or argument from the criminal defense bar, which might have provided important counsel on this difficult issue.

Global-Tech, 131 S. Ct. at 2072–73 (Kennedy, J., dissenting).

[C] Recklessness

Commonwealth v. Welansky

Supreme Judicial Court of Massachusetts
55 N.E.2d 902 (1944)

LUMMUS, JUSTICE.

On November 28, 1942, and for about nine years before that day, a corporation named New Cocoanut Grove, Inc., maintained and operated a "night club" in Boston, having an entrance at 17 Piedmont Street, for the furnishing to the public for compensation of food, drink and entertainment, consisting of orchestra and band music, singing and dancing. It employed about eighty persons. The corporation, its officers and employees, and its business were completely dominated by the defendant Barnett Welansky, who is called in this opinion simply the defendant, since his codefendants were acquitted by the jury. He owned, and held in his own name or in the names of others, all the capital stock. He leased some of the land on which the corporate business was carried on, and owned the rest, although title was held for him by his sister. He was entitled to, and took, all the profits. Internally, the corporation was operated without regard to corporate forms, as though the business were that of the defendant as an individual. It was not shown that responsibility for the number or condition of safety exits had been delegated by the defendant to any employee or other person.

The defendant was accustomed to spend his evenings at the night club, inspecting the premises and superintending the business. On November 16, 1942, he became suddenly ill, and was carried to a hospital, where he was in bed for three weeks and remained until discharged on December 11, 1942. During his stay at the hospital, although employees visited him there, he did not concern himself with the night club, because, as he testified, he "knew it would be all right" and that "the same system … [he] had would continue" during his absence. There is no evidence of any act, omission or condition at the night club on November 28, 1942 (apart from the lighting of a match hereinafter described), that was not within the usual and regular practice during the time before the defendant was taken ill when he was at the night club nearly every evening. While the defendant was at the hospital, his brother James Welansky and an employee named Jacob Goldfine, who were made codefendants, assumed some of the defendant's duties at the night club, but made no change in methods. Under these circumstances the defendant was not entitled to a verdict of not guilty on the ground that any acts or omissions on the evening of November 28, 1942, were the transitory and unauthorized acts or omissions of servants or other persons, for which the defendant could not be held criminally responsible....

The physical arrangement of the night club on November 28, 1942, as well as on November 16, 1942, when the defendant last had personal knowledge of it, was as follows. The total area of the first or street floor was nine thousand seven hundred sixty-three square feet. Entering the night club through a single revolving door at 17 Piedmont Street, one found himself in a foyer or hall having an area of six hundred six square feet. From the foyer, there was access to small rooms used as toilets, to a powder room and a telephone room, to a small room for the checking of clothing, and to another room with a vestibule about five feet by six feet in size adjoining it, both of which were used as an office in the daytime and for the checking of clothing in the evening. In the front corner of the foyer, to the left, beyond the office, was a passageway leading to a stairway about four feet wide, with fifteen risers. That stairway led down to the Melody Lounge in the basement, which was the only room in the basement open to the public. There were to be found a bar, tables and chairs.

The extreme dimensions of the Melody Lounge were about thirty-six feet by fifty-five feet, and its area was one thousand eight hundred ninety-five square feet. It was separated from a narrow corridor leading to the kitchen (which was located under the main dining room) by a wooden partition. In that partition was a wooden door, two feet and two inches wide, which could have been found to be unmarked. Passing from the Melody Lounge through that door, and thus entering the narrow corridor, one could turn to the left and go to a door which swung inward and could be opened only to a width of eighteen inches, at the top of three steps. That door was barred by a wooden bar that had to be lifted off before the door could be opened at all. On opening that door, one could pass into an outdoor alley about three and one-half feet wide. That alley led to a yard, from which egress could be had through in-swinging doors into another passageway and thence to Shawmut Street.

If, instead, one passing from the Melody Lounge into the narrow corridor should turn to the right, he might pass, as employees were accustomed to do, through a door two and one-half feet wide swinging into the corridor from the kitchen. Once in the kitchen, he could traverse that room with all its equipment to the other end of it near Shawmut Street, and then go upstairs and through swinging doors into a corner of the main dining room.

It is evident that in an emergency escape from the Melody Lounge by either of these courses would be difficult for a patron not thoroughly familiar with parts of the premises not ordinarily open to him.

Returning to the foyer, and standing as though one had just entered it by the revolving door, to the right, in the front of the building on Piedmont Street, was a room called the Caricature Bar, with an area of one thousand three hundred ninety-nine square feet, containing two bars, stools and chairs. Toward Shawmut Street, and separated from the Caricature Bar by a railing, was the main dining room, with an area of three thousand seven hundred sixty-five square feet. The foyer opened into both the Caricature Bar and the main dining room. In the main dining room was a dance floor with an area of six hundred sixty square feet, and behind it, in the direction of Broadway, was a stage with an area of four hundred thirty-six square feet.

From the Caricature Bar and from the main dining room one could pass into a corridor near the stage, about four feet wide, up some steps, and through a passageway about seven feet wide into the new Cocktail Lounge, which was first opened on November 17, 1942, and which had an area of seven hundred eighty-one square feet. There one found a bar, stools, tables and seats, and also a check room and toilets. In the farther corner of the Cocktail Lounge was a door three feet wide, swinging inward, through which one could enter a small vestibule from which he could go through a pair of doors to Broadway at 59 Broadway.

That pair of doors, and the revolving door at 17 Piedmont Street, were the only entrances and exits intended for the ordinary use of patrons. Besides these doors, and the exit through the wooden partition from the Melody Lounge, already described, there were five possible emergency exits from the night club, all on the first or street floor. These will now be listed and described.

(1) A door, opening outward to Piedmont Street, two and one-half feet wide, at the head of the stairway leading to and from the basement of the Melody Lounge. That door apparently was not visible from the greater part of the foyer, for it was in a passageway that ran from one end of the foyer past the office to the stairway. That door was marked "Exit" by an electric sign. It was equipped with a "panic" or "crash" bar, intended to unbolt and open the door upon pressure from within the building. But on the evidence it could have been found that the device just mentioned was regularly made ineffective by having the door locked by a separate lock operated by a key that was kept in a desk in the office. Late in the evening of November 28, 1942, firemen found that door locked and had to force it open with an axe. The jury were entitled to disbelieve the testimony of the defendant that he had instructed the head waiter, who died in the occurrence of that evening, always to keep that door unlocked. It may be observed that if that door should be left so that it could be opened by means of the panic bar, a patron might leave through that door without paying his bill. It does not appear that anyone watched that door to prevent patrons from so doing.

(2) A door two and one-third feet wide leading from the foyer, near the revolving door, into the small vestibule adjoining the office, already described. From that vestibule another similar door, swinging inward, gave egress to Piedmont Street, near the revolving door. The door to Piedmont Street could not be opened fully, because of a wall shelf. And that door was commonly barred in the evening, as it was on November 28, 1942, by a removable board with clothing hooks on it, and by clothing, for in the evening the office and vestibule were used for checking clothing.

(3) A door, opening outward, from the middle of the wall of the main dining room to Shawmut Street, and marked "Exit" by an electric sign. The opening was about three and two-thirds feet wide. The defendant testified that this was the principal exit provided for emergencies. From the sides of the opening hung double doors, equipped with "panic" bars intended to unbolt and open the doors upon pressure from within. But on the evening of November 28, 1942, one of the two doors did not open upon pressure, and had to be hammered with a table before it would open. Besides, the "panic" doors were hidden from the view of diners by a pair of "Venetian" wooden doors, swinging inward, and fastened by a hook, which had to be opened before one could operate the "panic" doors. In addition, dining tables were regularly placed near the Venetian doors, one of them within two feet, and these had to be moved away in order to get access to the doors. That condition prevailed on the evening of November 28, 1942.

(4) The service door, two and one-half feet wide, swinging inward, leading to Shawmut Street at 8 Shawmut Street. This door was near the stage, at the foot of a stairway leading to dressing rooms on the second floor, and was in a part of the premises to which patrons were not admitted and which they could not see. This door was known to employees, but doubtless not to patrons. It was kept locked by direction of the defendant, and the key was kept in a desk in the office.

(5) The door, two and three-fourths feet wide, swinging inward, leading from a corridor into which patrons had no occasion to go, to Shawmut Street at 6 Shawmut Street. No patron was likely to know of this door. It was kept locked by direction of the defendant, but he ordered the key placed in the lock at seven every evening.

We now come to the story of the fire. A little after ten o'clock on the evening of Saturday, November 28, 1942, the night club was well filled with a crowd of patrons. It was during the busiest season of the year. An important football game in the afternoon had attracted many visitors to Boston. Witnesses were rightly permitted to testify that the dance floor had from eighty to one hundred persons on it, and that it was "very crowded." *Beverley v. Boston Elevated Railway*, 194 Mass. 450, 457, 80 N.E. 507. Witnesses were rightly permitted to give their estimates, derived from their observations, of the number of patrons in various parts of the night club. Upon the evidence it could have been found that at that time there were from two hundred fifty to four hundred persons in the Melody Lounge, from four hundred to five hundred in the main dining room and the Caricature Bar, and two hundred fifty in the Cocktail Lounge. Yet it could have been found that the crowd was no larger than it had been on other Saturday evenings before the defendant was taken ill, and that there had been larger crowds at earlier times. There were about seventy tables in the dining room, each seating from two to eight persons. There was testimony that all but two were taken. Many persons were standing in various rooms. The defendant testified that the reasonable capacity of the night club, exclusive of the new Cocktail Lounge, was six hundred fifty patrons. He never saw the new Cocktail Lounge with the furniture installed, but it was planned to accommodate from one hundred to one hundred twenty-five patrons.

A bartender in the Melody Lounge noticed that an electric light bulb which was in or near the cocoanut husks of an artificial palm tree in the corner had been turned off and that the corner was dark. He directed a sixteen year old bar boy who was waiting on customers at the tables to cause the bulb to be lighted. A soldier sitting with other persons near the light told the bar boy to leave it unlighted. But the bar boy got a stool, lighted a match in order to see the bulb, turned the bulb in its socket, and thus lighted it. The bar boy blew the match out, and started to walk away. Apparently the flame of the match had ignited the palm tree and that had speedily ignited the low cloth ceiling near it, for both flamed up almost instantly. The fire spread with great rapidity across the upper part of the room, causing much heat. The crowd in the Melody Lounge rushed up the stairs, but the fire preceded them. People got on fire while on the stairway. The fire spread with great speed across the foyer and into the Caricature Bar and the main dining room, and thence into the Cocktail Lounge. Soon after the fire started the lights in the night club went out. The smoke had a peculiar odor. The crowd were panic stricken, and rushed and pushed in every direction through the night club, screaming, and overturning tables and chairs in their attempts to escape.

The door at the head of the Melody Lounge stairway was not opened until firemen broke it down from outside with an axe and found it locked by a key lock, so that the panic bar could not operate. Two dead bodies were found close to it, and a pile of bodies about seven feet from it. The door in the vestibule of the office did not become open, and was barred by the clothing rack. The revolving door soon jammed, but was burst out by the pressure of the crowd. The head waiter and another waiter tried to get open the panic doors from the main dining room to Shawmut Street, and succeeded after some difficulty. The other two doors to Shawmut Street were locked, and were opened by force from outside by firemen and others. Some patrons escaped through them, but many dead bodies were piled up inside them. A considerable number of patrons escaped through the Broadway door, but many died just inside that door. Some employees, and a great number of patrons, died in the fire. Others were taken out of the building with fatal burns and injuries from smoke, and died within a few days....

II. The Principles Governing Liability.

The Commonwealth disclaimed any contention that the defendant intentionally killed or injured the persons named in the indictments as victims. It based its case on involuntary manslaughter through wanton or reckless conduct. The judge instructed the jury correctly with respect to the nature of such conduct.

Usually wanton or reckless conduct consists of an affirmative act, like driving an automobile or discharging a firearm, in disregard of probable harmful consequences to another. But whereas in the present case there is a duty of care for the safety of business visitors invited to premises which the defendant controls, wanton or reckless conduct may consist of intentional failure to take such care in disregard of the probable harmful consequences to them or of their right to care....

...

Sometimes the word "willful" is prefaced to the words "wanton" and "reckless" in expressing the concept. That only blurs it. Willful means intentional. In the phrase "willful, wanton or reckless conduct," if "willful" modifies "conduct" it introduces something different from wanton or reckless conduct, even though the legal result is the same. Willfully causing harm is a wrong, but a different wrong from wantonly or recklessly causing harm. If "willful" modifies "wanton or reckless conduct" its use is accurate. What must be intended is the conduct, not the resulting harm.... The words "wanton" and "reckless" are practically synonymous in this connection, although the word "wanton" may contain a suggestion of arrogance or insolence or heartlessness that is lacking in the word "reckless." But intentional conduct to which either word applies is followed by the same legal consequences as though both words applied.

The standard of wanton or reckless conduct is at once subjective and objective, as has been recognized ever since *Commonwealth v. Pierce*, 138 Mass. 165, 52 Am. Rep. 264. Knowing facts that would cause a reasonable man to know the danger is equivalent to knowing the danger....

The judge charged the jury correctly when he said, "To constitute wanton or reckless conduct, as distinguished from mere negligence, grave danger to others must have been apparent and the defendant must have chosen to run the risk rather than alter his conduct so as to avoid the act or omission which caused the harm. If the grave danger was in fact realized by the defendant, his subsequent voluntary act or omission which caused the harm amounts to wanton or reckless conduct, no matter whether the ordinary man would have realized the gravity of the danger or not. But even if a particular defendant is so stupid [or] so heedless ... that in fact he did not realize the grave danger, he cannot escape the imputation of wanton or reckless conduct in his dangerous act or omission, if an ordinary normal man under the same circumstances would have realized the gravity of the danger. A man may be reckless within the meaning of the law although he himself thought he was careful."

The essence of wanton or reckless conduct is intentional conduct, by way either of commission or of omission where there is a duty to act, which conduct involves a high degree of likelihood that substantial harm will result to another....

Wanton or reckless conduct amounts to what has been variously described as indifference to or disregard of probable consequences to that other....

The words "wanton" and "reckless" are thus not merely rhetorical or vituperative expressions used instead of negligent or grossly negligent. They express a difference in the degree of risk and in the voluntary taking of risk so marked, as compared with negligence, as to amount substantially and in the eyes of the law to a difference in kind....

To convict the defendant of manslaughter, the Commonwealth was not required to prove that he caused the fire by some wanton or reckless conduct. Fire in a place of public resort is an ever-present danger. It was enough to prove that death resulted from his wanton or reckless disregard of the safety of patrons in the event of fire from any cause....

The Commonwealth introduced evidence that the electrical system was defective and dangerous. Shortly after the fire started the electric lights went out, leaving the patrons struggling in the dark. What caused the lights to go out did not appear. There was no evidence that the defendant knew, or had reason to know, of any defect in the electrical system. There was no evidence that faulty wiring caused the fire, or bore any causal relation to the deaths. A verdict of guilty could not lawfully have been based upon any such defect. But when the evidence was introduced the judge could not foresee that knowledge on the part of the defendant and some causal relation would not be shown. He had a right to let the Commonwealth begin by proving defective wiring. If the defendant had a remedy, it was by asking the judge to strike out the evidence when it appeared that no causal relation existed and the defendant was not shown to be responsible for any such defect, or by asking the judge to instruct the jury that a verdict of guilty could not be based upon wanton or reckless conduct with respect to the electrical system. No such request was made....

Judgments affirmed.

Comments and Questions

(1) The distinction drawn between knowledge of the facts and estimate of the danger seems initially persuasive, and it may also survive critical exam-

> ination. But there is considerable vagueness in the ... opinion regarding these criteria. If Welansky had actually anticipated that a patron, desiring a dark corner of the premises, would turn off an electric light bulb, that a fire might start and spread with tremendous speed, that many persons would become panic-stricken and killed, etc., etc., he would certainly have taken action to prevent a tragedy such as that which occurred. No claim was made that Welansky was not a normal person. Yet the imputation to him of what the jury decided " 'the reasonable man' would estimate the danger to be" implies either that he actually did know the danger, which implication is excluded or, as the decision holds, that negligence in estimating danger is sufficient to support penal liability at least for manslaughter.

J. Hall, General Principles of Criminal Law 131–32 (2d ed. 1960).

(2) In *Commonwealth v. Huggins*, 836 A.2d 862 (Pa. 2003), the Supreme Court of Pennsylvania considered whether a defendant who had fallen asleep while driving, leading to a collision and the deaths of two children, should face charges of involuntary manslaughter. The trial and appellate courts ruled the state had failed to show the driver had consciously disregarded a substantial and unjustifiable risk that death would result from his actions. According to the court:

> The Crimes Code defines involuntary manslaughter as follows:
>
> > A person is guilty of involuntary manslaughter when as a direct result of the doing of an unlawful act in a reckless or grossly negligent manner, or the doing of a lawful act in a reckless or grossly negligent manner, he causes the death of another person.
>
> 18 Pa. C.S. § 2504(a).
>
> To decide the issue raised in this matter, we must analyze the Crimes Code's general definition of "recklessly," which reads as previously stated:
>
> > A person acts recklessly with respect to a material element of an offense when he consciously disregards a substantial and unjustifiable risk that the material element exists or will result from his conduct. The risk must be of such a nature and degree that, considering the nature and intent of the actor's conduct and the circumstances known to him, its disregard involves a gross deviation from the standard of conduct that a reasonable person would observe in the actor's situation.
>
> 18 Pa. C.S. § 302(b)(3).
>
> A motor vehicle can be a dangerous instrumentality. Driving is a correspondingly heavily regulated privilege, both as to licensure and the rules of the road, the regulation being a necessary concomitant of the dangers to self and others inherent in driving. The danger increases with the speed at which a vehicle is operated, since speed both reduces reaction times and heightens the consequences of any collision. The danger also may increase if other safety measures are ignored—whether those measures involve vehicle maintenance, internal safety features such as seating capacity or restraints, or the rules of the road....

> Losing consciousness at the wheel differs in kind from the acts of momentary inadvertence or inattention that often occasion car accidents and are commonly encompassed in the term "negligence" in the tort arena. A momentary lapse leaves the driver unprepared for the unexpected or extraordinary. A loss of consciousness, on the other hand, leaves one totally unprepared even for the ordinary requirements for safe driving. Drivers have an unflagging duty either to remain vigilant and awake or to immediately desist from driving....
>
> We need not resolve the question of whether falling asleep alone is enough to raise a jury question of recklessness, since the Commonwealth proved additional circumstances which revealed a conscious disregard of the serious risk involved here. Appellee allowed himself to fall asleep despite the fact that he was driving a van filled with children. The presence of these children would have led a prudent person to be extra-cautious; far from acting cautiously, however, appellee's van was filled to over-capacity and, in addition, the children were not secured with safety belts. Appellee elected to drive at an excessive rate of speed—at least twenty-three miles beyond the 55 m.p.h. speed limit—at the time he allowed himself to fall asleep. Each of these additional factors, beyond the mere fact of falling asleep at the wheel, increased the risk of collision, injury, and death. Moreover, each was a circumstance within appellee's knowledge and control. Viewed in their totality, the circumstances here reveal a pattern of conscious disregard for circumstances that placed the lives of these children in increasing danger. We are also satisfied that the Commonwealth proved that the circumstances here revealed a disregard of duty and risk which would warrant a jury in finding "a gross deviation from the standard of conduct that a reasonable person would observe in the actor's situation." Accordingly, we hold that the Commonwealth sufficiently proved a *prima facie* case of two counts of involuntary manslaughter so as to warrant submission of those charges to a jury.

Huggins, 836 A.2d at 869–871.

(3) According to *Huggins*, the *mens rea* terms of involuntary manslaughter, reckless, or grossly negligent, are equivalent standards. Thus, the Court considered whether evidence suggested reckless conduct. The Court suggested that a sleepy driver had "to remain vigilant and awake or to immediately desist from driving." What additional facts did the court consider to justify allowing a jury to consider an involuntary manslaughter charge? Would a driver typically be responsible for overcrowding? For the absence of seatbelts?

[D] Negligence

People v. Howk

Supreme Court of California
365 P.2d 426 (1961)

PETERS, JUSTICE.

Appeal by Horowitz

Facts.

Horowitz was convicted of involuntary manslaughter, an offense included within the charge of murder. So far as pertinent here, involuntary manslaughter is defined by section 192 of the Penal Code as:

> Manslaughter is the unlawful killing of a human being without malice. It is of three kinds:....
>
> 2. Involuntary—in the commission of an unlawful act, not amounting to felony; or in the commission of a lawful act which might produce death, in an unlawful manner, or without due caution and circumspection; ...
>
> The evidence against Horowitz consists of the testimony of Abdullah, statements given by Horowitz voluntarily on the day of the murder or shortly thereafter, and of the testimony of several witnesses, some of whom were friends or acquaintances of Abdullah, or of Horowitz, or of both. Horowitz did not testify on his own behalf.

Abdullah testified, as a witness in his own defense, that he had met Horowitz two or three months before July 13, 1960, and had seen him less than ten times before that date; that he knew Horowitz possessed some guns; that about eight days before July 13, 1960, he had a conversation with Horowitz and told him that he wanted to kill Sonja and needed a gun; that Horowitz stated to him that the best way to murder was to make it look like a hunting accident; that he would furnish a gun; that the two went to Horowitz's quarters and Horowitz gave him a gun; that he examined it and gave it back to Horowitz stating that he did not have the "guts" to use it; that on July 13, 1960, shortly after noon, he saw Horowitz going into a restaurant and followed him; that Horowitz told him that he had recently been dispossessed of his apartment; that he invited Horowitz to bring his suitcase and brief case to his apartment; that the two men proceeded to Abdullah's apartment; that he told Horowitz he wanted a gun to "protect" himself; that Horowitz said he might as well sell a gun to him; that he paid Horowitz $20 for the gun and promised to pay him an additional $20 later; that Horowitz delivered the gun to him; and told him that it was loaded; that he put the gun in his pocket while Horowitz was out of the room; then the two proceeded back to the restaurant and had some beer and then parted; that it was true that in his suicide note and in several statements to the police he had stated that he had stolen the gun from Horowitz but this was not true; that he had made such statements to protect Horowitz.

Several students who knew both Abdullah and Horowitz testified that they had heard Abdullah make threats about killing Sonja, and also knew Horowitz and knew that he possessed guns. One of them, Pieper by name, testified that about a week before July 13, 1960, he sought out Horowitz and expressed to him his concern about Abdullah's mental condition; that he warned Horowitz about giving Abdullah a gun; that Horowitz replied that if any of his friends needed anything he would give it to them. During the succeeding week this witness saw Abdullah, who again threatened to kill Sonja and stated that he needed and wanted a gun. On July 12th this witness observed Abdullah and Horowitz speaking privately, then leave the restaurant and then return; that he asked Horowitz if Abdullah now had the gun and Horowitz said no.

After the murder, Pieper and a friend saw Horowitz three times during the evening. Horowitz was obviously upset and nervous, and his answers to their questions were somewhat incoherent. On one occasion Horowitz expressed pride in Abdullah because he had "hit the target." In answer to repeated questions as to whether he had given Abdullah a gun, he replied that if it was a .38 "it is mine."

On the night of the murder Horowitz voluntarily reported to the campus police, and that night, and the next day, wrote out several statements, both prior and subsequent to his arrest. He was undoubtedly emotionally disturbed when he came to the police department, and many of his statements and replies were incoherent. But some of them made sense. He told the police that possibly the gun used in the shooting was his, and that he knew of at least four witnesses who had heard Abdullah threaten to "destroy" Sonja. Later he admitted the death weapon was in fact his gun, and the police records showed it was owned and registered to him. He then stated that several days before the killing Abdullah had been at his apartment and made various threats; that he had then given Abdullah a gun; that Abdullah had returned the gun to him saying he did not have the courage to use it; that because of this test he was sure in his own mind that Abdullah would not use a gun; that on July 11th, at Abdullah's request, he gave him a gun; that although on the prior occasion Abdullah had said he intended to kill Sonja, Horowitz did not believe that he had the courage to so use it; that he was "practicing psychology" on him but apparently, said Horowitz, he had "fell a little short in some respects." Horowitz admitted that on July 13th he was staying at Abdullah's apartment, and that his suitcase and brief case, in which he carried his guns, were there. He first stated that he had seen Abdullah on the afternoon of the murder and then stated that it was the day before.

On July 14th Horowitz was interviewed in jail by a newspaper reporter. The reporter testified that most of the statements of Horowitz were pretty rambling but that Horowitz did state that sometime before July 13th he had given Abdullah a gun and Abdullah had returned it to him. He later gave him a gun the second time believing that Abdullah would not use it, and would return it to him.

On this evidence Horowitz was convicted of involuntary manslaughter as defined in section 192 of the Penal Code. The jury was fully and fairly instructed on the elements of this offense and no complaint is raised on appeal in this respect. Under the section, criminal negligence can amount to lack of "due caution and circumspection" sufficient to constitute involuntary homicide within the meaning of the section (*People v. Penny*, 44 Cal. 2d 861, 871–80, 285 P.2d 926).

Certainly, the evidence of Abdullah, if believed by the jury, was sufficient to show the required criminal negligence, and this is conceded by Horowitz. This concession is in accord with the facts. Abdullah testified that Horowitz sold him the gun on the day of the killing; that this gun was used by him to kill Sonja and to attempt suicide; that about eight days prior to the killing he told Horowitz he wanted to kill Sonja and commit suicide; that in response to his request Horowitz gave him a gun but he returned it because he then did not have the courage to commit the acts. It was a possible and reasonable inference that Horowitz knew when he sold or gave the gun to Abdullah on the day of the killing, or shortly before, that Abdullah wanted it to kill Sonja.

Comments and Questions

(1) In providing a gun to the murderer, the defendant may have acted "without due caution and circumspection," thus acting with criminal negligence and subject to conviction for involuntary manslaughter. The statutory *mens rea* applied here is modeled after common law. It can be compared with the Model Penal Code definition of negligence, which uses an objective standard: "should be aware of a substantial and unjustifiable risk will result from his conduct." Model Penal Code § 2.02(2)(d). It further requires that the defendant's failure to perceive the risk shows a "gross deviation from the standard of care that a reasonable person would observe." *Id.* (defining negligence). Based only on language, which standard do you find most preferable for assigning criminal liability?

(2) Was the defendant's conduct tantamount to recklessness? Was there evidence that he had perceived and ignored a substantial and unjustifiable risk that a killing would result from his conduct? If so, was that subjective disregard of the risk a gross deviation from the standard of conduct that a law-abiding person would observe? *See supra*, § 2.02(2)(c) (defining recklessness).

Again, based only on language, which standard, the common law or the Model Penal Code, do you find preferable for distinguishing between reckless and negligent criminal conduct?

(3) Punishment for negligent acts remains controversial. The problems are: defining the term to avoid an objective standard, distinguishing between criminal negligence and recklessness, and using the civil negligent standard in criminal cases.

United States v. Hanousek

United States Court of Appeals, Ninth Circuit
176 F.3d 1116 (1998), *cert. denied*, 528 U.S. 1102 (2000)

David R. Thompson, Circuit Judge.

...

Hanousek was employed by the Pacific & Arctic Railway and Navigation Company (Pacific & Arctic) as roadmaster of the White Pass & Yukon Railroad, which runs between Skagway, Alaska, and Whitehorse, Yukon Territory, Canada. As roadmaster, Hanousek was responsible under his contract "for every detail of the safe and efficient maintenance and construction of track, structures and marine facilities of the entire railroad ... and [was to] assume similar duties with special projects."

One of the special projects under Hanousek's supervision was a rock-quarrying project at a site alongside the railroad referred to as "6-mile," located on an embankment 200 feet above the Skagway River. The project was designed to realign a sharp curve in the railroad and to obtain armor rock for a ship dock in Skagway. The project involved blasting rock outcroppings alongside the railroad, working the fractured rock toward railroad cars, and loading the rock onto railroad cars with a backhoe. Pacific & Arctic hired Hunz & Hunz, a contracting company, to provide the equipment and labor for the project.

At 6-mile, a high-pressure petroleum products pipeline owned by Pacific & Arctic's sister company, Pacific & Arctic Pipeline, Inc., runs parallel to the railroad at or above ground level, within a few feet of the tracks. To protect the pipeline during the project, a work platform of sand and gravel was constructed on which the backhoe operated to load rocks over the pipeline and into railroad cars. The location of the work platform changed as the location of the work progressed along the railroad tracks. In addition, when work initially began in April, 1994, Hunz & Hunz covered an approximately 300-foot section of the pipeline with railroad ties, sand, and ballast material to protect the pipeline, as was customary. After Hanousek took over responsibility for the project in May, 1994, no further sections of the pipeline along the 1000-foot work site were protected, with the exception of the movable backhoe work platform.

On the evening of October 1, 1994, Shane Thoe, a Hunz & Hunz backhoe operator, used the backhoe on the work platform to load a train with rocks. After the train departed, Thoe noticed that some fallen rocks had caught the plow of the train as it departed and were located just off the tracks in the vicinity of the unprotected pipeline. At this location, the site had been graded to finish grade and the pipeline was covered with a few inches of soil. Thoe moved the backhoe off the work platform and drove it down alongside the tracks between 50 to 100 yards from the work platform. While using the backhoe bucket to sweep the rocks from the tracks, Thoe struck the pipeline causing a rupture. The pipeline was carrying heating oil, and an estimated 1,000 to 5,000 gallons of oil were discharged over the course of many days into the adjacent Skagway River, a navigable water of the United States.

Following an investigation, Hanousek was charged with one count of negligently discharging a harmful quantity of oil into a navigable water of the United States, in violation of the Clean Water Act, 33 U.S.C. §§ 1319(c)(1)(A) & 1321(b)(3)....

After a twenty-day trial, the jury convicted Hanousek of negligently discharging a harmful quantity of oil into a navigable water of the United States.... The district court imposed a sentence of six months of imprisonment, six months in a halfway house and six months of supervised release, as well as a fine of $5,000. This appeal followed.

DISCUSSION

A. Negligence Jury Instruction

Hanousek contends the district court erred by failing to instruct the jury that, to establish a violation under 33 U.S.C. § 1319(c)(1)(A), the government had to prove that Hanousek acted with criminal negligence, as opposed to ordinary negligence, in discharging a harmful quantity of oil into the Skagway River. In his proposed jury instruction, Hanousek defined criminal negligence as "a gross deviation from the standard of care that a reasonable person would observe in the situation." *See* American Law Institute, *Model Penal Code* § 2.02(2)(d) (1985). Over Hanousek's objection, the district court instructed the jury that the government was required to prove only that Hanousek acted negligently, which the district court defined as "the failure to use reasonable care." ...

Statutory interpretation begins with the plain language of the statute. If the language of the statute is clear, we need look no further than that language in determining the statute's meaning.

Codified sections 1319(c)(1)(A) & 1321(b)(3) of the Clean Water Act work in tandem to criminalize the conduct of which Hanousek was convicted. Section 1319(c)(1)(A) provides that any person who negligently violates 33 U.S.C. § 1321(b)(3) shall be punished by fine or imprisonment, or both. Section 1321(b)(3) proscribes the actual discharge of oil in harmful quantities into navigable waters of the United States, adjoining shore lines or waters of a contiguous zone, as well as other specified activity.

Neither section defines the term "negligently," nor is that term defined elsewhere in the CWA. In this circumstance, we "start with the assumption that the legislative purpose is expressed by the ordinary meaning of the words used." The ordinary meaning of "negligently" is a failure to use such care as a reasonably prudent and careful person would use under similar circumstances.

If Congress intended to prescribe a heightened negligence standard, it could have done so explicitly, as it did in 33 U.S.C. § 1321(b)(7)(D). This section of the CWA provides for increased civil penalties "[i]n any case in which a violation was the result of gross negligence or willful misconduct." This is significant. "[W]here Congress includes particular language in one section of a statute but omits it in another section of the same Act, it is generally presumed that Congress acts intentionally and purposely in the disparate inclusion or exclusion."

Hanousek argues that Congress could not have intended to distinguish "negligently" in 33 U.S.C. § 1319(c)(1)(A) from "gross negligence" in 33 U.S.C. § 1321(b)(7)(D) because the phrase "gross negligence" was only recently added to the statute in 1990. We reject this argument because Congress is presumed to have known of its former legislation and to have passed new laws in view of the provisions of the legislation already enacted.

We conclude from the plain language of 33 U.S.C. § 1319(c)(1)(A) that Congress intended that a person who acts with ordinary negligence in violating 33 U.S.C. § 1321(b)(3) may be subject to criminal penalties. We next consider Hanousek's argument that, by imposing an ordinary negligence standard for a criminal violation, section 1319(c)(1)(A) violates the due process clause of the Constitution.

B. Due Process

The criminal provisions of the CWA constitute public welfare legislation. *See Weitzenhoff*, 35 F.3d at 1286 ("The criminal provisions of the CWA are clearly designed to protect the public at large from the potentially dire consequences of water pollution, and as such fall within the category of public welfare legislation."). Public welfare legislation is designed to protect the public from potentially harmful or injurious items, *see Staples v. United States*, and may render criminal "a type of conduct that a reasonable person should know is subject to stringent public regulation and may seriously threaten the community's health or safety," *see Liparota v. United States*, 471 U.S. 419 (1985).

It is well established that a public welfare statute may subject a person to criminal liability for his or her ordinary negligence without violating due process. *See United States v. Balint*, 258 U.S. 250, 252–53 (1922) ("[W]here one deals with others and his mere negligence may be dangerous to them, as in selling diseased food or poison, the policy of the law may, in order to stimulate proper care, require the punishment of the negligent person though he be ignorant of the noxious character of what he sells."); *see also Morissette v. United States*, 342 U.S. 246, 256 (1952) ("The accused, if he does not will the violation, usually is in a position to prevent it with no more care than society might reasonably expect and no more exertion than it might reasonably exact from one who assumed his responsibilities."); *United States v. Dotterweich*, 320 U.S. 277 (1943) ("In the interest of the larger good it puts the burden of acting at hazard upon a person otherwise innocent but standing in responsible relation to a public danger."); *Staples*, 511 U.S. at 607 n.3.

...

Hanousek argues that he was simply the roadmaster of the White Pass & Yukon railroad charged with overseeing a rock-quarrying project and was not in a position to know what the law required under the CWA. This is a distinction without a difference. In the context of a public welfare statute, "as long as a defendant knows he is dealing with a dangerous device of a character that places him 'in responsible relation to a public danger,' he should be alerted to the probability of strict regulation." *Staples*, 511 U.S. at 607, (quoting *Dotterweich*, 320 U.S. at 281). Although Hanousek was not a permittee under the CWA, he does not dispute that he was aware that a high-pressure petroleum products pipeline owned by Pacific & Arctic's sister company ran close to the surface next to the railroad tracks at 6-mile, and does not argue that he was unaware of the dangers a break or puncture of the pipeline by a piece of heavy machinery would pose. Therefore, Hanousek should have been alerted to the probability of strict regulation.

In light of our holding in *Weitzenhoff* that the criminal provisions of the CWA constitute public welfare legislation, and the fact that a public welfare statute may impose criminal penalties for ordinary negligent conduct without offending due process, we conclude that section 1319(c)(1)(A) does not violate due process by permitting criminal penalties for ordinary negligent conduct.

E. Sufficiency of the Evidence

...

The government presented evidence at trial that Hanousek was responsible for the rock-quarrying project at 6-mile; that the project involved the use of heavy equipment and machinery along the 1000-foot work site; that Hanousek directed the daily activities of Hunz & Hunz employees and equipment; and that it was customary to protect the pipeline with railroad ties and fill when using heavy equipment in the vicinity of the pipeline. The government also presented evidence that when work initially began in April, 1994, Hunz & Hunz covered an approximately 300-foot section of the pipeline with railroad ties, sand, and ballast material to protect the pipeline; that after Hanousek took over responsibility for the project in May, 1994, no further sections of the pipeline along the work site were protected; and that the section of the pipeline where the rupture occurred was not protected with railroad ties, sand or ballast. Finally, the government presented evidence that although the rock quarrying work had been completed in the location of the rupture, rocks would sometimes fall off the loaded railroad cars as they proceeded through the completed sections of the work site; that no policy prohibited the use of backhoes off the work platform for other activities; that a backhoe operator ruptured the unprotected pipeline while using a backhoe to remove a rock from the railroad tracks; and that a harmful quantity of oil was discharged into the Skagway River.

The totality of this evidence is sufficient to support Hanousek's conviction for negligently discharging a harmful quantity of oil into a navigable water of the United States, in violation of 33 U.S.C. §§ 1319(c)(1)(A) & 1321(b)(3).

Comments and Questions

(1) The Ninth Circuit upheld the use of ordinary negligence, a "failure to use reasonable care" to assign criminal liability and punishment in this case. Does this result accord with the Supreme Court's discussion of *mens rea* and public welfare offenses in *Morissette*? *See supra*, § 3.01.

(2) How is the statute at issue in *Hanousek* similar to the provision at issue in *International Minerals*? Are the decisions consistent?

(3) Justice Thomas (with Justice O'Connor) dissented from the Supreme Court's denial of *certiorari* in *Hanousek.* He noted that federal appellate courts are divided

on whether the Clean Water Act is a public welfare statute, and prior cases involving public welfare legislation required the existence of a dangerous and deleterious device. *Hanousek*, 528 U.S. 1102, 1106 (2000) (Thomas, J., dissenting).

(4) The decision in *Staples v. United States*, which presents a discussion of strict liability in the context of public welfare offenses, is provided in § 3.03 of this chapter.

§ 3.02 Mistake

[A] Mistake of Fact

In *Morissette v. United States*, *supra* § 3.01, the defendant mistakenly believed the bomb casings he loaded onto his truck had been abandoned. He was not aware, he did not realize, that they were the property of another. Thus, the jury was to be instructed that, if they believed the defendant's story, he could not have knowingly stolen the casings. In *Morissette*, the issue presented went directly to the *mens rea* of the crime.

The same principle applies in another form, referred to as a mistake of fact defense, where a defendant claims ignorance or mistake about a fact that relates to an element of the offense. If a jury finds that a good faith mistake is genuine, the error can negate the government's case that the defendant acted with purpose or knowledge.

Initially developed by common law courts, the mistake of fact doctrine was endorsed by the Model Penal Code.

Section 2.04.

Ignorance or Mistake

(1) Ignorance or mistake as to a matter of fact ... is a defense if

(a) the ignorance or mistake negatives the purpose, knowledge, belief, recklessness or negligence required to establish a material element of the offense.

California v. Russell

Court of Appeal, Sixth District, California
144 Cal.App.4th 1415 (2006)

Opinion, McAdams, J.

Defendant Philip Russell was convicted by jury of one count of receiving a stolen motor vehicle, a felony.

Facts

I. Prosecution Case

At about 4:00 p.m. on Sunday, March 6, 2005, Doug Foster was riding his 1982 Yamaha motorcycle on Highway 280 in San Jose when the motorcycle stopped running. Foster knew there was a motorcycle repair shop nearby. He pushed the motorcycle to the repair shop, which was located behind the Cycle Gear motorcycle accessories store on Parkmoor Avenue in San Jose. According to Foster, Cycle Gear and the repair shop were separate businesses.

When Foster arrived, the repair shop was closed. Foster parked the motorcycle next to a fenced area near the repair shop; trash bins were located inside the fenced area. Foster did not leave the keys with the motorcycle, however he did not lock the forks to the motorcycle. He went into Cycle Gear and told a salesperson he was leaving the motorcycle at the repair shop. The salesperson told him the repair shop was closed on Monday and suggested he call on Tuesday morning.

When Foster called the repair shop the following Tuesday about his motorcycle, the person he spoke to said, "What motorcycle?" Foster reported the motorcycle missing to the police either on Tuesday, March 8, 2005, or the following day. The officer told Foster he could not take a report until Foster went to the repair shop and confirmed the motorcycle was not there. This took some time and the police report was not completed until March 19, 2005....

On March 30, 2005, San Jose police officers Lisa Gannon and Ellen Ciaburro responded to a complaint about a homeless encampment near Parkmoor Avenue and Race Street in San Jose. The officers walked through a hole in a cyclone fence along Highway 280 and saw a tent in the foliage. Foster's motorcycle was parked in a parking lot 50 to 100 feet from the tent. The officers did a license plate check and discovered the motorcycle had been reported stolen....

As Officer Ciaburro exited the fenced area, defendant rode up on a bicycle. Officer Ciaburro, who was in plain clothes, showed defendant her badge and asked him what business he had in the area. He said he lived in the tent. The officer asked if he knew who the motorcycle belonged to and he said it was his. The officer placed defendant in handcuffs, told him the motorcycle had been reported stolen, and read him his *Miranda* rights. Defendant waived his *Miranda* rights and was eager to talk to the officer about the motorcycle.

Defendant told Officer Ciaburro he found the motorcycle around 4:00 a.m. on March 7, 2005, in a commercial parking lot near Parkmoor and Meridian. He said he contacted an employee in a nearby shop, who told him a man had left the motorcycle there. Defendant told the officer he did not have the keys to the motorcycle and had walked it back to his camp. He "punched the ignition," which is the same as hot-wiring a car, to get it running. Officer Ciaburro searched defendant and found a traffic citation dated March 14, 2005, for a traffic violation involving the motorcycle. The citation listed Foster as the registered owner of the motorcycle.

II. Defense Case

Defendant testified. In March 2005, he was homeless. He lived in the tent near Parkmoor Avenue and Race Street and operated a mobile bicycle repair business, repairing bicycles at his clients' homes or offices.

Defendant got up early on March 7, 2005, to recycle. At about 4:00 a.m., he saw the motorcycle sitting next to the dumpsters behind Cycle Gear and thought it was abandoned. The following factors led defendant to conclude the motorcycle was abandoned: (1) the front right turn signal was covered with packing tape; (2) there was rust on the mirror, the post to the mirror, the exhaust pipes, and fenders; (3) there were cobwebs and leaves in the front wheel; (4) the aluminum cast blocks on the motor were severely tarnished; (5) the motorcycle was located next to the trash area; (6) the registration tags had expired 22 months before; (7) the forks on the motorcycle were not locked. Defendant frequented the area and knew the repair shop's policy was to bring all the motorcycles that were being repaired inside the shop at night. Defendant testified he assumed someone left the motorcycle there for the repair shop to use for parts or that the owner had told the repair shop not to do the work because it was going to cost more than the motorcycle was worth. The motorcycle had been left in neutral, so defendant wheeled it to his camp.

At about 11:00 a.m. that morning, defendant went to Cycle Gear and spoke with a salesperson about the motorcycle. The salesperson told him it was not one of their motorcycles because the repair shop brings the motorcycles inside at night and said Cycle Gear was not responsible for things that are left behind.

During the week that followed, defendant took the battery out of the motorcycle and had the repair shop recharge it, replaced the spark plugs, changed the oil, drained and flushed the fuel tank, and tuned up the motorcycle.

On March 14, 2005, at about 5:30 a.m., defendant was riding the motorcycle with a friend on the back when he was pulled over by Officer Kate Reyes for a traffic violation. He told the officer he found the motorcycle behind Cycle Gear and had just gotten it running the night before. He told the officer he had "punched the ignition" to start the motorcycle. The officer ran the vehicle identification number (VIN) on the motorcycle and told defendant the motorcycle had not been reported stolen. Defendant told the officer he intended to fix the motorcycle and register it in his own name. The officer wrote up a traffic citation. Defendant asked her to put the name of the registered owner on the ticket. The officer let defendant keep the motorcycle as long as he promised to walk it and not ride it.

At 1:00 p.m. that same day, defendant went to Foster's apartment at the address listed on the citation. He wanted to register the motorcycle in his name and hoped Foster would sign the motorcycle over to him. Defendant spoke with Terry Stultz, the apartment manager, who told him Foster had not lived there for 18 months. Defendant told Stultz he had found Foster's motorcycle and hoped Foster would sign the motorcycle over to him. Stultz did not know Foster's new address.

Defendant testified regarding his encounter with Officers Gannon and Ciaburro on March 30, 2005. For the most part, his testimony was consistent with Officer Ciaburro's testimony. He told Officer Ciaburro he found the motorcycle, assumed it was abandoned, "punched the ignition," tried to contact Foster, and had been stopped by another officer, who told him the motorcycle was not stolen.

Defendant told the jury he had prior convictions for grand theft and robbery in 2001.

On cross-examination, defendant admitted that he knew the place where he found the motorcycle was a repair shop and that people take motorcycles there to be fixed. He agreed the motorcycle was intact when he found it. He never asked the salesperson at Cycle Gear whether someone had left the motorcycle there for repairs or whether someone was waiting to take parts from it. He thought Cycle Gear and the repair shop were "connected," and were not separate businesses. He did not contact the Department of Motor Vehicles (DMV), the phone company, or the police for help in finding Foster. He did not ask anyone in the repair shop about the motorcycle when he got the battery recharged.

. . .

C. Mistake-of-Fact Defense

To sustain a conviction for receiving stolen property, the prosecution must prove: (1) the property was stolen; (2) the defendant knew the property was stolen (hereafter the knowledge element); and, (3) the defendant had possession of the stolen property.

Although receiving stolen property has been characterized as a general intent crime, the second element of the offense is knowledge that the property was stolen, which is a specific mental state. With regard to the knowledge element, receiving stolen property is a "'specific intent crime.'" The defendant therefore should have an opportunity to request instructions regarding the lack of requisite knowledge.

At common law, an honest and reasonable belief in the existence of circumstances, which, if true, would make the act with which the person is charged an innocent act, was a good defense. A person who commits an act or makes an omission under a mistake of fact which disproves his or her criminal intent, is excluded from the class of persons who are capable of committing crimes.

. . .

Although the jury was not required to believe it, defendant presented substantial evidence from which the jury could have inferred that he had a good faith belief that the motorcycle was abandoned. First, defendant testified repeatedly that he thought the motorcycle was abandoned.

Second, the condition and location of the motorcycle supported an inference that it had been abandoned....

Third, defendant's conduct could lead the jury to conclude that he had a good faith belief the motorcycle had been abandoned....

. . .

In summary, defendant acted as if he believed he was entitled to possess the motorcycle. He did not behave in a furtive manner or attempt to conceal the fact that he had taken the motorcycle or punched its ignition. Moreover, this evidence was not minimal or insubstantial.

At trial, defendant's primary defense was that he did not know the motorcycle was a stolen vehicle because he believed the motorcycle had been abandoned. Defense counsel did not request mistake-of-fact or claim-of-right instructions. However, the trial court had a sua sponte duty to instruct on both of these defenses if it appeared defendant was relying on the defenses, or if there was substantial evidence supportive of the defenses and they were not inconsistent with defendant's theory of the case. [T]he mistake-of-fact defense was] implicated by defendant's claim that he did not have the requisite knowledge that the motorcycle was stolen because at all times he held a good faith belief that it had been abandoned.

For these reasons, we conclude there was substantial evidence that supported instructing the jury on the claim-of-right and mistake-of-fact defenses and that the trial court erred when it failed to instruct the jury on these defenses.

...

The judgment is reversed.

Comments and Questions

(1) The defendant in *Russell* had not requested the jury be instructed on his claim of mistake of fact. On appeal, Russell argued that the court should have given the instruction on its own initiative, *sua sponte*. The reviewing court agreed.

(2) In *People v. Navarro,* 99 Cal.App.3d Supp. 1 (1979), the defendant was charged with grand theft for taking four wooden beams from a construction site. There was evidence that defendant believed the wooden beams had been abandoned and that the owner had no objection to his taking them. The trial court instructed on the mistake of fact defense, but included the condition that the mistake had to be reasonable.

The appellate court reversed the conviction. It reasoned that even if the defendant's mistake was unreasonable, if it was a good faith belief, he lacked the specific intent required for the crime of theft. The court noted that if the jury thought the defendant's belief was unreasonable, it might infer that he did not in good faith hold such belief. If, however, the jury "concluded that defendant in good faith believed he had the right to take the beams, even though such belief was unreasonable as measured by the objective standard of a hypothetical reasonable man, defendant was entitled to an acquittal since the specific intent required to be proved as an element of the offense had not been established." *Navarro*, 99 Cal.App.3d Supp. at 11.

(3) In *California v. Lawson*, 155 Cal. Rptr. 3d 236 (2013), a sister court rejected the approach taken in *Russell.* The defendant paid a Wal-Mart clerk for cigarettes and gum, but did not offer or pay for a hoodie he had slung around his shoulders. He was convicted of theft by larceny, which required the defendant act with intent to steal. The defendant claimed he had forgotten about the hoodie and argued the trial court erred in not *sua sponte* instructing the jury on a mistake of fact. The appellate court disagreed, reasoning that the trial court's instruction on the *mens rea* element of larceny was adequate. A mistake involving a failure to remember negates the *mens rea* of intentional action. Because the claim contradicts the required *mens rea*, it is not a "true affirmative defense." Rather, "the 'I forgot about it' defense amounted to no more than a claim that defendant took the hoodie out of the store *without intending*

to steal it." *Lawson*, 135 Cal. Rptr. 3d at 241 (emphasis original) (questioning whether courts are obliged *sua sponte* to instruct the jury on mistake); *see also* California v. Anderson, 51 Cal. 4th 989 (2011).

(4) The "specific intent" required of larceny and offenses based on larceny is a further purpose beyond the physical act of taking. Thus, in addition to an intent to "take and carry away" casings or bicycles, larceny requires more: a purpose to deprive the owner of the property permanently. Under this formulation, if Morissette's mistaken assumption that the casings were abandoned was unreasonable, is he still innocent? *See Morissette, supra.*

Problem

Roy Rypinski was convicted of reckless assault in the first degree, defined as follows:

> A person is guilty of assault in the first degree when: … 3. Under circumstances evincing a depraved indifference to human life, he recklessly engages in conduct which creates a grave risk of death to another person, and thereby causes serious physical injury to another person.…

The appellate court provided a summary of the facts:

> The evidence established that defendant, who had been drinking all evening, shot Gordon Ulrich above the left knee in the early morning hours of January 1, 1985 after an argument concerning defendant's girlfriend. Prosecution witnesses testified that, before defendant got a rifle from his car, he threatened to blow the victim's brains out. They also testified that, after the gun discharged, defendant said "I'm sorry, it was an accident. I didn't mean to hurt anybody."
>
> Defendant testified that he was a member of a conservation society and used its rifle range. He said that he intended to go there on January 1st, that he had cleaned the rifle the day before, that he always kept three rounds of ammunition in the rifle (one in the chamber and two in the clip), and that he had removed and replaced the three rounds while cleaning the gun. He said he had thrown it in the back seat of his car because he was having trouble opening his trunk.
>
> He testified that he was drunk and that, when he knew there would be trouble, he pulled the rifle from the back seat of his car. He further testified that:
>
> … as I stood by the door, I ejected it three times. And the gun was unloaded as far as I knew because I always had the three rounds in it. And I turned away from my car. I had the rifle in my right hand, and I was hanging on to the car with my left as I was walking. I didn't even reach to the end of the car and the rifle discharged. I don't know how it went off. It was unloaded as far as I knew. And I was surprised as everybody else. I was in shock that it went off. I looked around. I heard people screaming, and I looked and I seen somebody on the ground. I walked over to the person and I seen him bleeding. I put my hand on him and I says, "I'm sorry, it was an accident."

> Defendant conceded that he did not look in the chamber to see whether the gun was unloaded. He testified that the only way the gun could have been loaded was that he had not put one bullet in the chamber and two "in the ready," as he thought, but had mistakenly put three "in the ready." If he had done that, there would still have been a bullet in the chamber after he cocked the rifle three times.

Rypinski contended that the jury should have been instructed on mistake of fact as a defense to a charge of reckless assault. Is that correct? *See People v. Rypinski*, 555 N.Y.S.2d 500 (App. Div. 1990) (yes, a mistake of fact can negate the subjective *mens rea* of reckless conduct, citing the Model Penal Code); *but see Leggio v. Leggio*, 737 N.Y.S.2d 259 (Fam. Ct. 2002) (disagreeing with *Rypinski* on basis of state case law).

[B] Mistake or Ignorance of Law

"Ignorance of the law is no defense" is a well-known legal principle. There are, however, exceptions to it. Three major exceptions involve mistakes of fact and mistakes of law. For instance, the Model Penal Code states:

> ... (3) a belief that conduct does not legally constitute an offense is a defense to a prosecution for that offense based upon such conduct when:
>
> (a) the statute or other enactment defining the offense is not known to the actor and has not been published or otherwise reasonably made available to the conduct alleged; or
>
> (b) he acts in reasonable reliance upon an official statement of the law, afterward determined to be invalid or erroneous, contained in ... an official interpretation of the public officer or body charged by law with responsibility for the interpretation; administration or enforcement of the law defining the offense.
>
> Model Penal Code, Section 2.04(3).

The cases in this part take up these two types of mistake of law.

United States v. Mancuso

United States Court of Appeals, Second Circuit
420 F.2d 556 (1970)

Irving R. Kaufman, Circuit Judge:

18 U.S.C. § 1407 requires any citizen convicted of narcotics or marijuana offenses, as well as those who are addicted to, or "use" narcotic drugs, to register with customs officials on leaving and entering the country. The only question on this appeal is whether one who violated the statute without knowledge or probability of knowledge of its provisions may be convicted under it.

On September 20, 1950, Thomas Mancuso was convicted of violating the federal narcotics laws, and sentenced to three years probation. Almost seventeen years later, on January 18, 1967, Mancuso boarded a British Overseas Airways Corporation plane at Kennedy Airport in New York and flew to England. He returned six days later. Neither on his departure or arrival at Kennedy did he fill out the registration forms required by the statute and the applicable regulations. While the prosecution did introduce evidence at trial showing that there were some signs at Kennedy Airport indicating the existence of the registration requirement, the indictment did not charge knowledge, and there were no signs at the BOAC terminal from which Mancuso departed. There can be no argument with the trial judge's conclusion that "[t]he court finds as a fact that the defendant did not have knowledge of the registration requirement in both of the instances as to which he is charged."

Mancuso, after his return to the United States on January 24, 1967, was charged with two counts of violating section 1407; one for leaving the country without registering, and one for entering without registering. He was convicted on both counts and sentenced to one year in jail and $1000 on count 1, and three years on count 2, to run consecutively after count 1. Sentence on count 2 was suspended, with five years probation.

Mancuso urges vigorously that *Lambert v. California*, 355 U.S. 225 (1957), controls. In *Lambert* the Supreme Court declared unconstitutional a Los Angeles statute requiring all convicted felons to register with the police department within five days after arriving in the city. The Court held that the lack of either notice or a showing of probability of knowledge of the statute, which permitted conviction of those who had no knowledge or reason to know of its provisions, violated fundamental precepts of due process....

The government stresses our holding in *United States v. Juzwiak*, 258 F.2d 844 (2d Cir. 1958), where we upheld a seaman's conviction under 18 U.S.C. § 1407 for entering and leaving the country without registering. This Court's decision in *Juzwiak* rested on two alternative grounds; the first, that *Lambert* was not controlling because it involved "nonfeasance" as opposed to Juzwiak's "misfeasance" in accepting employment on a ship traveling to Europe. The second, citing *Lambert*, explained that "there was a showing of the probability that the defendant [Juzwiak] had knowledge of his duty to register." Later, in *United States v. Jones*, 368 F.2d 795 (2d Cir. 1966), we expressly refused to decide whether or not knowledge of the statute, or reasonable probability of such knowledge, was a necessary element for conviction under section 1407. We also did not take issue with Judge Port in the District Court for charging that knowledge was required (despite *Juzwiak*). Since it would be sheer sophistry to attempt to distinguish *Lambert* by describing flying to London (Mancuso) as "misfeasance," while characterizing flying to Los Angeles (which *Lambert* would cover) as "nonfeasance," we regard the second ground in *Juzwiak* (that there was a showing of probability of knowledge on Juzwiak's part) as the holding in that case. Since the district court specifically found that there was "no knowledge" of the statute, we hold that Mancuso did not violate 18 U.S.C. § 1407. Our decision to so construe the statute is supported by a long line of Supreme Court precedents that urge construction of federal statutes, if possible, so as to avoid the question of their constitutionality.

Our determination to so interpret section 1407 is underscored by both precedent and practicality. The Supreme Court was faced with interpreting a criminal statute lacking of a specific requirement of wilfulness in *Morissette v. United States*. It considered the aim of the act (one punishing conversion of government property), and the common-law background in order to conclude that intent, although not specifically mentioned, must be read into it.

On practical, purposive grounds, it is difficult to understand how elimination of the requirement of knowledge would have furthered the Congressional aim to make detection of illegal narcotics importation easier....

The primary purpose of law, and the criminal law in particular, is to conform conduct to the norms expressed in that law. When there is no knowledge of the law's provisions, and no reasonable probability that knowledge might be obtained, no useful end is served by prosecuting the "violators." Since they could not know better, we can hardly expect that they should have been deterred. Similarly, it is difficult to justify application of criminal punishment on other traditional grounds such as retribution, rehabilitation or disablement. Without knowledge, the moral force of retribution is entirely spent; we do not rehabilitate conduct that is by hypothesis not faulty; and there is little to recommend incarcerating those who would obey the law if only they knew of its existence....

We emphasize these points not to argue that a court may simply rewrite a statute that it does not like, but rather to illustrate how self-frustrating the Congressional enactment would have been had it carried the interpretation urged by the government....

And finally, we are presented with that rare instance in which overturning a criminal conviction will in all probability lead to improved enforcement of the underlying act. The hallmark of this case is sloppiness on the part of those charged with responsibility for enforcing the statute. The total effort to inform those likely to be affected by the provisions of section 1407 seems to have consisted of a few signs posted in crew entrances at airports, in a few places near customs stations, and at other odd locations ill-designed to bring them to public notice of travelers generally. As the trial judge summarized the evidence before him:

> Incredible as it may seem, the Government in all the years since the enactment of the Narcotics Control Act of 1956 [citation omitted], has devised no better way to implement it than to tack up the aforesaid warning notices in various places (not including the departure areas for travelers at the John F. Kennedy Airport). It is obvious that a simple question and warning on applications for passports would accomplish the purpose perfectly....

Thus a simple notice provided with each passport application, or a printed form given to narcotics violators on their conviction, warning them of the requirement to register, would provide both the notice and knowledge necessary to sustain a criminal conviction, and to ensure that the aim of the statute would be fulfilled.

The judgment of the District Court is reversed and the indictment is dismissed.

Comments and Questions

(1) Did the court usurp Congress' function by adding the requirement of knowledge of the requirements to the statute? *See Mancuso*, 420 F.2d at 560 (Moore, J., concurring).

(2) What result under section 2.04(3) of the Model Penal Code? Federal law has not incorporated the code, and the court relied on its own precedents. The court suggested that upholding the conviction would raise constitutional issues, as in *Lambert.*

(3) Despite the holding in *Mancuso*, ignorance of the law is generally not a successful defense. The *Lambert* case remains an exception that has been confined to its peculiar posture, nonfeasance, because the defendant had no reason to know of the state law that required felons convicted in other states to register upon arrival in California.

Ratzlaf v. United States

United States Supreme Court
510 U.S. 135 (1994)

Justice Ginsburg delivered the opinion of the Court.

... Federal law requires banks and other financial institutions to file reports with the Secretary of the Treasury whenever they are involved in a cash transaction that exceeds $10,000. 31 U.S.C. § 5313; 31 CFR § 103.22(a) (1993). It is illegal to "structure" transactions—*i.e.*, to break up a single transaction above the reporting threshold into two or more separate transactions—for the purpose of evading a financial institution's reporting requirement. 31 U.S.C. § 5324. "A person willfully violating" this antistructuring provision is subject to criminal penalties. § 5322. This case presents a question on which Courts of Appeals have divided: Does a defendant's purpose to circumvent a bank's reporting obligation suffice to sustain a conviction for "willfully violating" the antistructuring provision? We hold that the "willfulness" requirement mandates something more. To establish that a defendant "willfully violat[ed]" the antistructuring law, the Government must prove that the defendant acted with knowledge that his conduct was unlawful.

...

On the evening of October 20, 1988, defendant-petitioner Waldemar Ratzlaf ran up a debt of $160,000 playing blackjack at the High Sierra Casino in Reno, Nevada. The casino gave him one week to pay. On the due date, Ratzlaf returned to the casino with cash of $100,000 in hand. A casino official informed Ratzlaf that all transactions involving more than $10,000 in cash had to be reported to state and federal authorities. The official added that the casino could accept a cashier's check for the full amount due without triggering any reporting requirement. The casino helpfully placed a limousine at Ratzlaf's disposal, and assigned an employee to accompany him to banks in the vicinity. Informed that banks, too, are required to report cash transactions in excess of $10,000, Ratzlaf purchased cashier's checks, each for less than $10,000 and each from a different bank. He delivered these checks to the High Sierra Casino.

Based on this endeavor, Ratzlaf was charged with "structuring transactions" to evade the banks' obligation to report cash transactions exceeding $10,000; this conduct, the indictment alleged, violated 31 U.S.C. §§ 5322(a) and 5324(3). The trial judge instructed the jury that the Government had to prove defendant's knowledge of the banks' reporting obligation and his attempt to evade that obligation, but did not have to prove defendant knew the structuring was unlawful. Ratzlaf was convicted, fined, and sentenced to prison.

...

Ratzlaf maintained on appeal that he could not be convicted of "willfully violating" the antistructuring law solely on the basis of his knowledge that a financial institution must report currency transactions in excess of $10,000 and his intention to avoid such reporting. To gain a conviction for "willful" conduct, he asserted, the Government must prove he was aware of the illegality of the "structuring" in which he engaged. The Ninth Circuit upheld the trial court's construction of the legislation and affirmed Ratzlaf's conviction.... We granted certiorari, ... and now conclude that, to give effect to the statutory "willfulness" specification, the Government had to prove Ratzlaf knew the structuring he undertook was unlawful. We therefore reverse the judgment of the Court of Appeals.

II

A

Congress enacted the Currency and Foreign Transactions Reporting Act (Bank Secrecy Act) in 1970, ... in response to increasing use of banks and other institutions as financial intermediaries by persons engaged in criminal activity. The Act imposes a variety of reporting requirements on individuals and institutions regarding foreign and domestic financial transactions. The reporting requirement relevant here, § 5313(a), applies to domestic financial transactions....

To deter circumvention of this reporting requirement, Congress enacted an antistructuring provision, 31 U.S.C. § 5324, as part of the Money Laundering Control Act of 1986, ... which Ratzlaf is charged with "willfully violating," reads:

> ...
>
> "No person shall for the purpose of evading the reporting requirements of section 5313(a) with respect to such transaction—
>
> ...
>
> "(3) structure or assist in structuring, or attempt to structure or assist in structuring, any transaction with one or more domestic financial institutions."

The criminal enforcement provision at issue, 31 U.S.C. § 5322(a), sets out penalties for "[a] person willfully violating," *inter alia*, the antistructuring provision. Section 5322(a) reads:

> "A person willfully violating this subchapter or a regulation prescribed under this subchapter ... shall be fined not more than $250,000, or [imprisoned] for not more than five years, or both."

B

... Section 5324 forbids structuring transactions with a "purpose of evading the reporting requirements of section 5313(a)." Ratzlaf admits that he structured cash transactions, and that he did so with knowledge of, and a purpose to avoid, the banks' duty to report currency transactions in excess of $10,000. The statutory formulation (§ 5322) under which Ratzlaf was prosecuted, however, calls for proof of "willful[ness]" on the actor's part. The trial judge in Ratzlaf's case, with the Ninth Circuit's approbation, treated § 5322(a)'s "willfulness" requirement essentially as surplusage—as words of no consequence. Judges should hesitate so to treat statutory terms in any setting, and resistance should be heightened when the words describe an element of a criminal offense....

...

... "Willful," this Court has recognized, is a "word of many meanings," and "its construction [is] often ... influenced by its context." *Spies v. United States*, 317 U.S. 492, 497 (1943). Accordingly, we view §§ 5322(a) and 5324(3) mindful of the complex of provisions in which they are embedded. In this light, we count it significant that § 5322(a)'s omnibus "willfulness" requirement, when applied to other provisions in the same subchapter, consistently has been read by the Courts of Appeals to require both "knowledge of the reporting requirement" *and* a "specific intent to commit the crime," *i.e.*, "a purpose to disobey the law."

...

C

... In § 5322, Congress subjected to criminal penalties only those "willfully violating" § 5324, signaling its intent to require for conviction proof that the defendant knew not only of the bank's duty to report cash transactions in excess of $10,000, but also of his duty not to avoid triggering such a report. There are, we recognize, contrary indications in the statute's legislative history. But we do not resort to legislative history to cloud a statutory text that is clear....

...

We do not dishonor the venerable principle that ignorance of the law generally is no defense to a criminal charge. In particular contexts, however, Congress may decree otherwise. That, we hold, is what Congress has done with respect to 31 U.S.C. § 5322(a) and the provisions it controls. To convict Ratzlaf of the crime with which he was charged, violation of 31 U.S.C. §§ 5322(a) and 5324(3), the jury had to find he knew the structuring in which he engaged was unlawful. Because the jury was not properly instructed in this regard, we reverse the judgment of the Ninth Circuit and remand this case for further proceedings consistent with this opinion.

...

Justice Blackmun, with whom The Chief Justice, Justice O'Connor, and Justice Thomas join, dissenting.

* * *

The petitioner in this case was informed by casino officials that a transaction involving more than $10,000 in cash must be reported, was informed by the various banks he visited that banks are required to report cash transactions in excess of $10,000, and then purchased $76,000 in cashier's checks, each for less than $10,000 and each from a different bank. Petitioner Ratzlaf, obviously not a person of limited intelligence, was anything but uncomprehending as he traveled from bank to bank converting his bag of cash to cashier's checks in $9,500 bundles. I am convinced that his actions constituted a "willful" violation of the antistructuring provision embodied in 31 U.S.C. § 5324. As a result of today's decision, Waldemar Ratzlaf—to use an old phrase—will be "laughing all the way to the bank."

The majority's interpretation of the antistructuring provision is at odds with the statutory text, the intent of Congress, and the fundamental principle that knowledge of illegality is not required for a criminal act. Now Congress must try again to fill a hole it rightly felt it had filled before. I dissent.

Comments and Questions

(1) "Willful" is a common law *mens rea* term that, in federal criminal law, can have one of several meanings, depending on the statute at issue. *Compare Cheek v. United States*, 498 U.S. 192 (1991) (criminal income tax case) (stating that willful is defined as a "voluntary, intentional violation of a known legal duty"), *with Bryan v. United States*, 524 U.S. 184 (1998) (statutory obligation that firearm dealers register) (stating that willful means the defendant must be aware that some aspect of his conduct was unlawful); *see also United States v. Griffin*, 84 F.3d 912, 925 (7th Cir. 1996) (discussing accepted definitions of willfulness in federal criminal law).

(2) Congress took the advice of Justice Blackmun and amended the structuring statutes. *See* 31 U.S.C. § 5322 (excepting §§ 5315 & 5324 from requirement of willful *mens rea*).

United States v. Clegg

United States Court of Appeals, Ninth Circuit
846 F.2d 1221 (1988)

PER CURIAM:

Eugene Ray Clegg is charged with exporting firearms in violation of 18 U.S.C. § 922(a)(1) (1982) and 22 U.S.C. § 2778(b)(2), (c) (1982)....

Prior to his arrest in September 1982, Clegg taught at an American school in Islamabad, Pakistan. According to Clegg, United States officials, affiliated with various agencies of our government, solicited, encouraged and assisted his efforts to supply weapons to Afghan rebels resisting Soviet occupation of their country. Believing that this solicitation, encouragement, and assistance constituted official permission to transport arms, Clegg smuggled arms through Pakistan to the Afghan rebels. He was arrested in Pakistan, where he was imprisoned. Upon his release, United States marshals escorted him back to this country. He returned home facing charges of exporting firearms in violation of federal law. In defense against these charges, Clegg seeks to prove that he acted in reasonable good-faith reliance on statements of United States officials that led him to believe he was lawfully transporting guns.

The acts on which Clegg claims to have relied include the following alleged events, occurrence of which Clegg proposes to prove at trial: (1) that Lieutenant Colonel Durham of the United States Army, second in command in Pakistan, informed Clegg that the United States supplied arms to Afghan rebels, and that the United States wanted Clegg to smuggle arms to the rebels; (2) that Durham offered to put Clegg in contact with the rebels, that he later became aware of Clegg's smuggling, that he helped Clegg to plan a large secret arms shipment which never took place, and that he supplied Clegg with arms for resale to Afghan rebels on one occasion; (3) that Colonel Maugher of the United States Army, who was director of military intelligence for the United States in Pakistan, knew of Clegg's activities, and that Maugher once sold ammunition to Clegg with the understanding that it was destined for resale to the rebels; and (4) that several other individual government officials, whose positions led Clegg to believe that they had power to authorize arms shipments to the rebels, knew of Clegg's shipments and on at least one occasion assisted Clegg in shipping arms.

...

This case is controlled by our recent decision in *United States v. Tallmadge*, 829 F.2d 767 (9th Cir. 1987). In *Tallmadge*, we reviewed a conviction for violation of 18 U.S.C. §922(h)(1) (1982), which prohibits convicted felons from receiving firearms. Tallmadge defended on the ground that his state felony conviction had been reduced to a misdemeanor. While that fact alone did not bring him outside the sweep of section 922, we exonerated Tallmadge because he had disclosed these facts to a licensed firearm dealer and the dealer had sold him the weapon anyway. *Id.* at 774. In reaching this conclusion, we reasoned as follows:

> ... Congress has not only granted certain persons the exclusive right to engage in the business of selling firearms, it has also given them the affirmative duty of inquiring of a prospective buyer whether he has a criminal record that would make it unlawful for him to purchase a firearm.... In addition, the Treasury Department requires licensees to inform buyers concerning the restrictions imposed by Congress on the purchase of firearms. Clearly, the United States Government has made licensed firearms dealers federal agents in connection with the gathering and dispensing of information on the purchase of firearms. Under these circumstances, we believe that a buyer has the right to rely on the representations of a licensed firearms dealer, who has been made aware of all the relevant historical facts, that a person may receive and possess a weapon if his felony conviction has been reduced to a misdemeanor.

Id.

We view this as an a fortiori case. Tallmadge was dealing with a licensed firearm dealer, a private party. Clegg alleges that he dealt not merely with government officials, but with officials of the highest rank. Moreover, Clegg, unlike Tallmadge, was operating far from the territory of the United States, in a place not obviously covered by American law. If Tallmadge was entitled to rely upon the representations of the gun dealer as a complete defense, we can hardly deny the same defense to Clegg. Whatever our disagreements may be with the court's ruling in *Tallmadge, see, e.g., id.* at 775–782 (Kozinski, J., dissenting), it is the law of the circuit and we are bound to follow it.

...

Skopil, Circuit Judge, dissenting.

I dissent from the majority's holding that Clegg is entitled to assert a mistake of law defense to the charges of exporting firearms without a license. Generally, ignorance of the law or a mistake as to the law's requirements cannot be a defense in a criminal prosecution. See United States v. International Minerals & Chemical Corp. An exception has been created to provide for the legitimate reliance on an official interpretation of law. *See, e.g.,* Cox v. Louisiana, 379 U.S. 559 (1965) (due process prevents conviction of individual advised by police chief to protest across the street to avoid prosecution under statute prohibiting demonstrations "near" the courthouse);.... Similarly, in *United States v. Tallmadge* ... we held that a purchaser of a gun could reasonably rely on the representations of a licensed firearms dealer who declared that the sale was lawful. We concluded that the conviction of someone misled by the affirmative statements of a government agent that certain conduct is lawful violates due process....

Nothing in my search of the record in this case discloses the requisite reliance on an official interpretation of the law. Even assuming that Clegg dealt with officials possessing the requisite authority to suspend the law, Clegg never alleges these officials authorized the unlawful conduct or told him that his activities were lawful. In fact, Clegg admits that he was involved in gun running activities before he ever became acquainted with these officials. As the majority notes in its summary of Clegg's allegations, various officials of the United States may have become aware of Clegg's activities. Moreover, several officials may have actually helped Clegg in his quest to supply arms to Afghan rebels. Liberally construed, the officials' conduct may amount to what the majority terms "solicitation, encouragement, and assistance" to Clegg. Nevertheless, in my opinion, there is still lacking any allegation of an official representation that Clegg's conduct was lawful.

Comments and Questions

(1) In dissent, Judge Skoph also raised the issue of what authority the official must possess:

> In *United States v. Barker*, 546 F.2d 940, 946–49 (D.C. Cir. 1976), Judge Wilkey approved the use of a mistake of law defense for someone who relies on the "apparent authority" of a government official. Other circuits have adopted a stricter standard by requiring that the government official have actual authority. *See* United States v. Duggan, 743 F.2d 59, 84 (2d Cir. 1984). In *Tallmadge*,

> we seemed to conclude that a licensed firearms dealer is an agent of the United States empowered by the statute to interpret the law.... Here, the majority simply notes that Clegg dealt with "officials of the highest rank" but does not decide whether such officials are empowered either to provide Clegg with a license to export arms or to suspend the license requirement.

Clegg, 846 F.2d at 1225.

(2) A claim of ignorance of the law that is based on an official interpretation requires that the official have responsibility for the interpretation or enforcement of the law defining the offense. *See Massachusetts v. Twitchell*, 617 N.E. 2d 609 (1993) (holding defendants were entitled to present letter of a state attorney general to the jury).

§ 3.03 Strict Liability

Staples v. United States

United States Supreme Court
511 U.S. 600 (1994)

Justice Thomas delivered the opinion of the Court.

The National Firearms Act makes it unlawful for any person to possess a machinegun that is not properly registered with the Federal Government. Petitioner contends that, to convict him under the Act, the Government should have been required to prove beyond a reasonable doubt that he knew the weapon he possessed had the characteristics that brought it within the statutory definition of a machinegun. We agree and accordingly reverse the judgment of the Court of Appeals.

...

According to the Government ... the nature and purpose of the Act suggest that the presumption favoring *mens rea* does not apply in this case. The Government argues that Congress intended the Act to regulate and restrict the circulation of dangerous weapons. Consequently, in the Government's view, this case fits in a line of precedent concerning what we have termed "public welfare" or "regulatory" offenses, in which we have understood Congress to impose a form of strict criminal liability through statutes that do not require the defendant to know the facts that make his conduct illegal. In construing such statutes, we have inferred from silence that Congress did not intend to require proof of *mens rea* to establish an offense.

For example, in [*United States v.] Balint* [258 U.S. 250 (1922)], we concluded that the Narcotic Act of 1914, which was intended in part to minimize the spread of addictive drugs by criminalizing undocumented sales of certain narcotics, required proof only that the defendant knew that he was selling drugs, not that he knew the specific items he had sold were "narcotics" within the ambit of the statute....

Such public welfare offenses have been created by Congress, and recognized by this Court, in "limited circumstances." ... Typically, our cases recognizing such offenses involve statutes that regulate potentially harmful or injurious items.... In such situations, we have reasoned that as long as a defendant knows that he is dealing with a dangerous device of a character that places him "in responsible relation to a public danger," ... he should be alerted to the probability of strict regulation, and we have assumed that in such cases Congress intended to place the burden on the defendant to "ascertain at his peril whether [his conduct] comes within the inhibition of the statute." ... Thus, we essentially have relied on the nature of the statute and the particular character of the items regulated to determine whether congressional silence concerning the mental element of the offense should be interpreted as dispensing with conventional *mens rea* requirements....

The Government argues that § 5861(d) defines precisely the sort of regulatory offense described in *Balint*. In this view, all guns, whether or not they are statutory "firearms," are dangerous devices that put gun owners on notice that they must determine at their hazard whether their weapons come within the scope of the Act....

The Government seeks support for its position from our decision in *United States v. Freed*, 401 U.S. 601 (1971), which involved a prosecution for possession of unregistered grenades under § 5861(d). The defendant knew that the items in his possession were grenades, and we concluded that § 5861(d) did not require the Government to prove the defendant also knew that the grenades were unregistered.... To be sure, in deciding that *mens rea* was not required with respect to that element of the offense, we suggested that the Act "is a regulatory measure in the interest of the public safety, which may well be premised on the theory that one would hardly be surprised to learn that possession of hand grenades is not an innocent act." ... Grenades, we explained, "are highly dangerous offensive weapons, no less dangerous than the narcotics involved in *United States v. Balint*." ... But that reasoning provides little support for dispensing with *mens rea* in this case.

As the Government concedes, *Freed* did not address the issue presented here. In *Freed*, we decided only that § 5861(d) does not require proof of knowledge that a firearm is *unregistered*. The question presented by a defendant who possesses a weapon that is a "firearm" for purposes of the Act, but who knows only that he has a "firearm" in the general sense of the term, was not raised or considered. And our determination that a defendant need not know that his weapon is unregistered suggests no conclusion concerning whether § 5861(d) requires the defendant to know of the features that make his weapon a statutory "firearm"; different elements of the same offense can require different mental states. *See Liparota*.... Moreover, our analysis in *Freed* likening the Act to the public welfare statute in *Balint* rested entirely on the assumption that the defendant *knew* that he was dealing with hand grenades—that is, that he knew he possessed a particularly dangerous type of weapon (one within the statutory definition of a "firearm"), possession of which was not entirely "innocent" in and of itself.... The predicate for that analysis is eliminated when, as in this case, the very question to be decided is *whether* the defendant must know of the particular characteristics that make his weapon a statutory firearm.

Notwithstanding these distinctions, the Government urges that *Freed*'s logic applies because guns, no less than grenades, are highly dangerous devices that should alert their owners to the probability of regulation. But the gap between *Freed* and this case is too wide to bridge. In glossing over the distinction between grenades and guns, the Government ignores the particular care we have taken to avoid construing a statute to dispense with *mens rea* where doing so would "criminalize a broad range of apparently innocent conduct." … In *Liparota*, we considered a statute that made unlawful the unauthorized acquisition or possession of food stamps. We determined that the statute required proof that the defendant knew his possession of food stamps was unauthorized, largely because dispensing with such a *mens rea* requirement would have resulted in reading the statute to outlaw a number of apparently innocent acts.… Our conclusion that the statute should not be treated as defining a public welfare offense rested on the commonsense distinction that a "food stamp can hardly be compared to a hand grenade." …

Neither, in our view, can all guns be compared to hand grenades. Although the contrast is certainly not as stark as that presented in *Liparota*, the fact remains that there is a long tradition of widespread lawful gun ownership by private individuals in this country. Such a tradition did not apply to the possession of hand grenades in *Freed* or to the selling of dangerous drugs that we considered in *Balint*.

…

The Government protests that guns, unlike food stamps, but like grenades and narcotics, are potentially harmful devices. Under this view, it seems that *Liparota*'s concern for criminalizing ostensibly innocuous conduct is inapplicable whenever an item is sufficiently dangerous—that is, dangerousness alone should alert an individual to probable regulation and justify treating a statute that regulates the dangerous device as dispensing with *mens rea*. But that an item is "dangerous," in some general sense, does not necessarily suggest, as the Government seems to assume, that it is not also entirely innocent. Even dangerous items can, in some cases, be so commonplace and generally available that we would not consider them to alert individuals to the likelihood of strict regulation. As suggested above, despite their potential for harm, guns generally can be owned in perfect innocence. Of course, we might surely classify certain categories of guns—no doubt including machineguns, sawed-off shotguns, and artillery pieces that Congress has subjected to regulation—as items the ownership of which would have the same quasi-suspect character we attributed to owning hand grenades in *Freed*. But precisely because guns falling outside those categories traditionally have been widely accepted as lawful possessions, their destructive potential, while perhaps even greater than that of some items we would classify along with narcotics and hand grenades, cannot be said to put gun owners sufficiently on notice of the likelihood of regulation to justify interpreting § 5861(d) as not requiring proof of knowledge of a weapon's characteristics.

On a slightly different tack, the Government suggests that guns are subject to an array of regulations at the federal, state, and local levels that put gun owners on notice that they must determine the characteristics of their weapons and comply with all legal requirements. But regulation in itself is not sufficient to place gun ownership in the category of the sale of narcotics in *Balint*. The food stamps at issue in *Liparota* were subject to comprehensive regulations, yet we did not understand the statute there to dispense with a *mens rea* requirement. Moreover, despite the overlay of legal restrictions on gun ownership, we question whether regulations on guns are sufficiently intrusive that they impinge upon the common experience that owning a gun is usually licit and blameless conduct. Roughly 50 percent of American homes contain at least one firearm of some sort, and in the vast majority of States, buying a shotgun or rifle is a simple transaction that would not alert a person to regulation any more than would buying a car.

If we were to accept as a general rule the Government's suggestion that dangerous and regulated items place their owners under an obligation to inquire at their peril into compliance with regulations, we would undoubtedly reach some untoward results. Automobiles, for example, might also be termed "dangerous" devices and are highly regulated at both the state and federal levels. Congress might see fit to criminalize the violation of certain regulations concerning automobiles, and thus might make it a crime to operate a vehicle without a properly functioning emission control system. But we probably would hesitate to conclude on the basis of silence that Congress intended a prison term to apply to a car owner whose vehicle's emissions levels, wholly unbeknownst to him, began to exceed legal limits between regular inspection dates.

...

We emphasize that our holding is a narrow one. As in our prior cases, our reasoning depends upon a commonsense evaluation of the nature of the particular device or substance Congress has subjected to regulation and the expectations that individuals may legitimately have in dealing with the regulated items. In addition, we think that the penalty attached to § 5861(d) suggests that Congress did not intend to eliminate a *mens rea* requirement for violation of the section. As we noted in *Morissette*: "Neither this Court nor, so far as we are aware, any other has undertaken to delineate a precise line or set forth comprehensive criteria for distinguishing between crimes that require a mental element and crimes that do not." ... We attempt no definition here, either. We note only that our holding depends critically on our view that if Congress had intended to make outlaws of gun owners who were wholly ignorant of the offending characteristics of their weapons, and to subject them to lengthy prison terms, it would have spoken more clearly to that effect.

[JUSTICES GINSBURG and O'CONNOR concurred in the judgment.]

JUSTICE STEVENS, with whom JUSTICE BLACKMUN joins, dissenting.

To avoid a slight possibility of injustice to unsophisticated owners of machineguns and sawed-off shotguns, the Court has substituted its views of sound policy for the judgment Congress made when it enacted the National Firearms Act (or Act). Because the Court's addition to the text of 26 U.S.C. § 5861(d) is foreclosed by both the statute and our precedent, I respectfully dissent.

The Court is preoccupied with guns that "generally can be owned in perfect innocence." ... This case, however, involves a semiautomatic weapon that was readily convertible into a machinegun—a weapon that the jury found to be "'a dangerous device of a type as would alert one to the likelihood of regulation.'" ... These are not guns "of some sort" that can be found in almost "50 percent of American homes." ... They are particularly dangerous—indeed, a substantial percentage of the unregistered machineguns now in circulation are converted semiautomatic weapons.

...

Contrary to the assertion by the Court, the text of the statute does provide "explicit guidance in this case." ... The relevant section of the Act makes it "unlawful for any person ... to receive or possess a firearm which is not registered to him in the National Firearms Registration and Transfer Record." 26 U.S.C. § 5861(d). Significantly, the section contains no knowledge requirement, nor does it describe a common-law crime.

The common law generally did not condemn acts as criminal unless the actor had "an evil purpose or mental culpability," *Morissette v. United States*, ... and was aware of all the facts that made the conduct unlawful, *United States v. Balint*.... In interpreting statutes that codified traditional common-law offenses, courts usually followed this rule. Even when the text of the statute contained no such requirement.... Because the offense involved in this case is entirely a creature of statute, however, "the background rules of the common law," ... do not require a particular construction, and critically different rules of construction apply....

[E]ven assuming that the Court is correct that the mere possession of an ordinary rifle or pistol does not entail sufficient danger to alert one to the possibility of regulation, that conclusion does not resolve this case. Petitioner knowingly possessed a semiautomatic weapon that was readily convertible into a machinegun. The "character and nature" of such a weapon is sufficiently hazardous to place the possessor on notice of the possibility of regulation.... No significant difference exists between imposing upon the possessor a duty to determine whether such a weapon is registered, *Freed*, ... and imposing a duty to determine whether that weapon has been converted into a machinegun.

...

The enforcement of public welfare offenses always entails some possibility of injustice. Congress nevertheless has repeatedly decided that an overriding public interest in health or safety may outweigh that risk when a person is dealing with products that are sufficiently dangerous or deleterious to make it reasonable to presume that he either knows, or should know, whether those products conform to special regulatory requirements. The dangerous character of the product is reasonably presumed to provide sufficient notice of the probability of regulation to justify strict enforcement against those who are merely guilty of negligent, rather than willful, misconduct. ... I would affirm the judgment of the Court of Appeals.

Comments and Questions

(1) Based on your understanding of *Staples*, how would you determine whether a criminal statute is a public welfare offense? Why is it important?

(2) As you read the following case, consider whether the statute at issue is a public welfare regulation. Applying the criteria noted in *Staples*, is it? Should it be?

State v. Miller

Supreme Court of Oregon
788 P.2d 974 (1990)

JONES, JUSTICE.

The issue is whether a defendant may be convicted of violating ORS 813.010 without proof of a culpable mental state as to the element of being under the influence of an intoxicant. We hold that being under the influence of an intoxicant is a strict liability element and, therefore, affirm the decision of the Court of Appeals.

On January 16, 1988, an Oregon State Police officer arrested defendant for Driving under the Influence of Intoxicants (DUII). An Intoxilizer test registered defendant's blood alcohol content (BAC) at 0.12 percent. Defendant waived his right to a jury trial, and the trial court found defendant guilty of DUII.

Defendant maintains that he had not been aware that he ingested an intoxicating beverage prior to driving on the date in question. Defendant states that at trial he made the following offer of proof:

> "Defendant stated that he had slept all [day on January 16, 1988]. About 9 p.m. he went out and found his friend at McDonald's. His friend had had about eight or nine beers, and so defendant did not want him to drive. They got in defendant's car, drove around town, got bored, rented some movies and then went to the friend's house to watch them. Defendant was sick, not having eaten anything for almost two days. His throat hurt, he couldn't breathe and couldn't taste anything. He said he didn't want to drink any beer. By 1:30 or 2:00 a.m., they had finished the first movie. They had been drinking coffee so as to stay awake while they watched the movies. Defendant's friend fixed him a special coffee drink that had a minty taste, and defendant drank a full coffee cup of it. His friend explained that this was coffee with some flavoring in it, a sort of home remedy that would make defendant feel better. Defendant did not know that the coffee drink contained any alcoholic beverage. He learned about that the next day, when he talked to his friend about the drink."

Defense counsel argued as follows to the trial court:

> "Your Honor, ... it does seem as a matter of fairness and due process of law that somebody should have to knowingly do something wrong or at least be criminally negligent.... There should be some kind of culpable mental state...."

... The DUII statute, ORS 813.010, provides:

> "(1) A person commits the offense of driving while under the influence of intoxicants if the person drives a vehicle while the person:
>
> "(a) Has .08 percent or more by weight of alcohol in the blood of the person as shown by chemical analysis of the breath or blood of the person ...
>
> "(b) Is under the influence of intoxicating liquor or a controlled substance; or
>
> "(c) Is under the influence of intoxicating liquor and a controlled substance...."

...

Having a certain BAC or being under the influence is a status, and a person's mental state has nothing to do with whether that status exists. The statute requires only that the state prove that a defendant had the status while driving, not that the defendant knew or should have known of it. One who drives after drinking intoxicating liquor takes the risk that his BAC violates the statute. The legislature made DUII an offense to keep dangerous drivers off the road. It was undoubtedly aware that experience has shown that dangerously intoxicated drivers often insist, at times sincerely, that the liquor they drank did not affect their driving ability. The statute, in the context of its history and surrounding circumstances, clearly indicates a legislative intent that the BAC element of DUII does not involve any culpable mental state.

...

FADELEY, JUSTICE, dissenting.

... As far as this court knows, defendant has been convicted of a crime because he drank a cup of coffee handed to him by a friend and thereafter drove a vehicle on the public way. After deliberation, I simply can't bring myself to believe that the legislature intended to prevent any jury consideration and determination of a defense of the character that defendant asserts in this case.

...

To what extent may the legislature or this court constitutionally prevent a jury from exercising any meaningful role in determining whether a person shall be declared to be a criminal or otherwise held criminally responsible by proscribing, as a crime, a status or act lacking any volitional component on the part of an accused defendant? May a jury be prevented from making a reasoned moral response to the question of criminal responsibility of a defendant found in a non-volitional status or performing a non-volitional act without knowledge that the act contributes to the person coming within the non-volitional status?

...

The majority points out the policy of society is "to get drunken drivers off Oregon highways." Again, I agree. Clearly, the police who apprehended defendant should have done so and should have arrested him and prevented his further driving. But that is not the issue. Rather, the question is whether that policy must mean that a person who asserts that he does not know he had anything at all alcoholic to drink should be prevented from telling that to the jury so it may decide whether he is truthful and, therefore, not a criminal. Even if one feels that it is not very likely that the jury will believe the defendant, that credibility question is what jurors and other triers of fact are to decide. Keeping drunken drivers off the road will not be achieved by convicting people who believed they drank coffee only.

Comments and Questions

(1) In *Commonwealth v. Olshefski*, 64 Pa. D. & C. 343 (1948), a driver for the defendant purchased a load of coal that was determined to weigh 15,200 pounds. A load of 15,750 pounds was permitted on the highway. The truck was stopped by an officer and directed to a weigh station, whereupon it was determined to be carrying 16,015 pounds. A conviction for violating the weight limit was affirmed, with punishment set at $25 and costs.

(2) In *State v. Williams*, 115 N.E.2d 36 (Ohio App. 1952), the defendant truck driver was charged with possession of undersized fish. He had no knowledge that his cargo consisted of undersize fish, and the truck was packed so that it would have been unreasonable and impractical for him to inspect it. In reversing his conviction, did the court read a requirement of knowledge into the statute?

§ 3.04 Vicarious Liability

> The imposition of liability on one person for the actionable conduct of another, based solely on a relationship between the two persons. Indirect or imputed legal responsibility for acts of another, for example, the liability of an employer for the acts of an employee, or, a principal for torts and contracts of an agent.

BLACK'S LAW DICTIONARY (6th ed. 1990).

Davis v. Peachtree City

Supreme Court of Georgia
304 S.E.2d 701 (1983)

BELL, JUSTICE.

This appeal arises out of a conviction of Melvin Davis, the appellant, for the offenses of the sale of alcoholic beverages to a minor and the sale of alcoholic beverages on a Sunday.

Davis is a resident of Bibb County, Georgia. He is president of Kwickie Food Stores, a chain of approximately one hundred convenience food stores, and holds a retail wine license for a Kwickie store in Peachtree City. On Sunday, August 16, 1981, Jim Renew, an employee of that store, sold wine to a minor. It is undisputed that Davis had no knowledge of and did not authorize this sale.

As a result of the sale by Renew, Davis was charged with sale of alcoholic beverages to a minor pursuant to § 3-60(a)(1) of the Code of Ordinances of Peachtree City and with the sale of wine on a Sunday pursuant to § 3-60(d) of the same code. Peachtree City contended that these code sections were applicable to Davis under § 3-87 of the City's Code, which provides that "The licensee is responsible for the conduct or actions of his employees while in his employment."

Davis was convicted of these crimes in the Municipal Court of Peachtree City, fined $200.00, and given 60 days in jail, with the confinement to be suspended upon the payment of the fine so long as David did not "again violate the laws of Georgia."

...

Davis first argues that these ordinances violate the due process clauses of the Georgia and United States Constitutions because they provide for the automatic criminal liability of a licensee for actions of his employees which are taken without his knowledge, consent, or authorization and which are not the result of negligence attributable to him. We agree.

... [T]he ordinances in question regulate the use and sale of intoxicating beverages. Specifically, the ordinances impose vicarious criminal liability on a licensee for the acts of the licensee's employees taken during the course of their employment. This means that a licensee, as Davis has been in this case, may be subject to criminal liability for acts not committed by him, not accomplished at his direction, not aided by his participation, and not done with his knowledge. In familiar criminal law language, Davis has no actus reus or mens rea; his criminal liability arose under the doctrine of respondeat superior....

It is clear that the use and sale of intoxicating beverages is an area the state has a legitimate interest in controlling. One purpose of ordinances regulating such activity is to encourage licensees who embark upon the enterprise of selling intoxicating beverages to assume a high degree of responsibility in regulating their business. It encourages them not only to regulate their actions in a manner consistent with the law subject to which they received their permit, but also to exercise due care in hiring individuals to whom they entrust the sale of alcoholic beverages, and to exercise sufficient control over their employees to assure their compliance with the applicable laws.[6] ... In other words, the objective of the use of vicarious criminal liability in such cases is one of deterrence. "To hold the master liable if he fails to prevent his servant from committing the prohibited conduct will have a powerful deterrent effect." Sayre, *Criminal Responsibility for Acts of Another*, 43 Harv. L. Rev. 689 (1930) p. 722. In fact, other related objectives, such as reform or rehabilitation, are inapplicable to vicarious liability cases because the licensee's own conduct has measured up to social

6. The record shows that Kwickie Food Stores took precautions to try to insure that its employees knew the law and would not violate it. Renew was required to fill out a thirteen page job application that inquired into his past work history and his attitudes about crime, and he also signed and read a company policy sheet explaining the law regarding beer and wine sales.

standards in that the licensee has in no way injured or menaced any social interest or engaged in any anti-social activity.

In addition, governing authorities and prosecuting officials have an interest in imposing vicarious liability because it facilitates the enforcement of legal requirements by dispensing with the sometimes difficult task of proving knowledge or authorization on the part of the employer....

In opposition to these interests of the public are those of the individual. In this case, we must examine the burden placed on Davis for an offense for which he was not morally blameworthy and which he did not commit. In this regard, Davis faces a possible restraint of his liberty, particularly if another employee fails to exercise good judgment; damage will be done to his good name by having a criminal record; and his future will be imperiled because of possible disabilities or legal disadvantages arising from the conviction.

In balancing this burden against the public's interests, we find that it cannot be justified under the due process clauses of the Georgia or United States Constitutions, regardless of Peachtree City's admittedly legitimate interests of deterring employers from allowing their employees to break the law and of facilitating the enforcement of these laws. This is especially true, when, as here, there are other, less onerous alternatives which sufficiently promote these interests.... The Model Penal Code recommends that civil violations providing civil penalties such as fines or revocation of licenses be used for offenses for which the individual was not morally blameworthy and does not deserve the social condemnation "implicit in the concept 'crime.'" Model Penal Code § 1.04(s), Comments, Tent. Draft No. 2, p. 7 (1954). The availability of such sanctions renders the use of criminal sanctions in vicarious liability cases unjustifiable.

Although some commentators and courts have found that vicarious criminal liability does not violate due process in misdemeanor cases which involve as punishment only a slight fine and not imprisonment, we decline to so hold. The damage done to an individual's good name and the peril imposed on an individual's future are sufficient reasons to shift the balance in favor of the individual. The imposition of such a burden on an employer "cannot rest on so frail a reed as whether his employee will commit a mistake in judgment," ... but instead can be justified only by the appropriate prosecuting officials proving some sort of culpability or knowledge by the employer.

Comment

(1) In the course of discussion, the court distinguished vicarious and strict criminal liability.

> Vicarious criminal liability must be distinguished from strict criminal liability. Although both are types of liability without fault, there is a difference. With strict liability, although it must be shown that the defendant committed the acts or omissions for which he is being held responsible, the requirement of proving mental fault or *mens rea* is dispensed with. With vicarious liability,

> there is no need to prove *actus reus* or mental fault on the part of the employer, whereas, it is usually necessary to prove both *actus reus* and *mens rea* on the part of the employee, although sometimes the latter requirement is also dispensed with, thus creating both a strict and vicarious liability statute.

Davis, 304 S.E.2d at 702, n.1.

State v. Zeta Chi Fraternity

Supreme Court of New Hampshire
696 A.2d 530, *cert. denied*, 522 U.S. 995 (1997)

HORTON, JUSTICE.

The defendant, Zeta Chi Fraternity, appeals its convictions and sentence on the charges of selling alcohol to a person under the age of twenty-one, RSA 179:5 (1994) (amended 1996), and prostitution, RSA 645:2, I(e) (1996). The defendant argues that the evidence was not sufficient to support the convictions.... Finally, the defendant challenges the constitutionality of its sentence for illegal sale of alcohol. We affirm the defendant's convictions but vacate and remand for resentencing.

On February 21, 1994, the defendant, a New Hampshire corporation and fraternity at the University of New Hampshire in Durham, held a "rush" at its fraternity house to attract new members. In order to encourage people to attend the rush, the defendant hired two female strippers to perform at the event. Fraternity brothers encouraged guests to give the strippers dollar bills so that they would continue to perform. The brothers also told guests that the more money the strippers were given, the more that they would do. One of the members of the fraternity was providing change for larger bills. As part of the performance, the dancers lay on a mattress brought out by members of the fraternity and simulated oral sex on each other. At one point, a guest gave five dollars to one of the strippers who sat on the guest's lap. When a brother moved the dancer along, the guest complained that he had given five dollars. The stripper took the guest to the mattress and pushed his head into her crotch. Two witnesses testified at trial that they saw guests being led to the mattress after they gave money, at which point the guests then performed oral sex on the dancer.

In addition, Andrew Strachan, a nineteen-year-old guest at the fraternity party, testified that at some point during the evening he learned that beer was available from a soda machine. He made his way to an apartment in another part of the fraternity house where the machine was located, waited in line with three or four other people, and purchased three to five cans of beer. Strachan also testified that he noticed someone making change for the machine. The fraternity's secretary testified that the fraternity members voted not to provide alcohol at the rush and that they moved the vending machine that contained beer to a separate apartment in another part of the fraternity house for the rush. He also testified, however, that the fraternity had control over the vending machine and its proceeds and that only fraternity members would have an interest in making change for the machine.

I. Sufficiency of Evidence

A. Illegal Sale of Alcohol

... We begin by noting that the only defendant in this case is a corporate entity.... A corporation may be held criminally liable for criminal acts performed on its behalf by agents or employees acting within the scope of their authority or employment.... The criminal conduct need not have been "performed, authorized, ratified, adopted or tolerated by the corporation['s] directors, officers, or other 'high managerial agents'" in order to be chargeable to the corporation....

In fact, a corporation can be convicted for actions of its agents even if it expressly instructed the agents not to engage in the criminal conduct.... The agents, however, must have been acting within the scope of their actual or apparent authority....

Evidence at trial indicates that the defendant had control over the apartment in which the vending machine was located, even though it had voted to make the apartment separate from the fraternity house. More importantly, however, witnesses testified that the defendant had control over the soda machine; that only the defendant had an interest in the proceeds from the machine; that only fraternity members had keys to the apartment in which the machine was located; that someone was making change for the machine; and that no one would have an interest in making change except a member of the fraternity. We believe that from these facts the jury could reasonably have found that an agent of the defendant sold beer from the vending machine and that this agent was acting on behalf of the corporation and within the scope of his authority....

The defendant next argues that the evidence was insufficient for the jury to find that the defendant acted recklessly, the *mens rea* charged in the indictment. Because the defendant is a corporation, its mental state depends on the knowledge of its agents.... "[T]he corporation is considered to have acquired the collective knowledge of its employees and is held responsible for their failure to act accordingly." ...

In this case, the jury could reasonably have found that the defendant acted recklessly from the facts that about 150 guests, many of them under the age of twenty-one, were at the rush party that had been widely publicized on campus; that it was the defendant's vending machine; that only fraternity members had keys to the apartment in which the machine was located; that party guests gained access to the machine; that someone was making change; and that a number of people were waiting in line to use the machine.

B. Prostitution

[The court held that the evidence was sufficient to support a finding that the premises had been used for prostitution.]

The defendant ... contends that the State failed to prove that the defendant knowingly allowed the prostitution and that if prostitution occurred, the individuals who allowed it were not acting within the scope of their authority. We will first address the issue of agency.

As noted above, in the context of corporate criminal liability, the corporation acts through its agents and those agents must be acting within the scope of either their actual or apparent authority in order for the corporation to be liable for their actions. The defendant asserts that because the members of the fraternity announced that guests were not allowed to touch the dancers and that, if the dancer stayed too long with one guest, members of the fraternity would move her along, this indicated the lack of actual or apparent authority.

... [T]here was testimony that the guests were told that if they paid more money the dancers would do more, that on more than one occasion guests were led to the mattress that was brought into the room by the brothers to perform oral sex in exchange for money; and that at least one guest performed oral sex on the dancer for "quite a while." From these facts the jury could reasonably have found that members of the fraternity acted within the scope of their authority and on behalf of the corporation in allowing oral sex to be performed in exchange for money.

Comments and Questions

(1) New Hampshire had adopted the Model Penal Code provision, which for corporate criminal liability requires participation of or ratification by a high managerial agent of the firm. *See* Model Penal Code § 2.07.

(2) The court buttressed its decision by referring to the common law *respondeat superior* doctrine, which is used in federal criminal law. Under that doctrine, corporations may be held criminally liable for the conduct of agents when agents act within the scope of their authority for the benefit of the corporation. The standard was articulated in 1909:

> [W]e see no good reason why corporations may not be held responsible for and charged with the knowledge and purposes of their agents, acting within the authority conferred upon them. If it were not so, many offenses might go unpunished and acts be committed in violation of the law.

New York Central & Hudson River R.R. v. United States, 212 U.S. 481, 494–95 (1909); *see also* Brickey, *Corporate Criminal Liability: A Primer for Corporate Counsel*, 40 Bus. Law. 129 (1984).

Which standard, the federal law's *respondeat superior* or state law ratification by a high managerial agent, reaches more corporate malfeasance? Which is more consistent with the criminal theory of personal responsibility for criminal acts?

(3) A few courts have found corporations criminally culpable for homicide. *See, e.g., Commonwealth v. McIlwain Sch. Bus Lines, Inc.*, 423 A.2d 413 (Pa. Super. 1980). Comment, *Corporate Criminal Liability for Homicide: Can the Criminal Law Control Corporate Behavior?*, 38 Sw. L.J. 1275 (1985).

Courts have rejected the notion that corporate criminal liability should be confined to crimes against property:

> This attempt to distinguish crimes against property from crimes against the person relies on the corporation's nature as an economically motivated entity. While a corporation may directly benefit from a crime against property,

> crimes against persons are not as directly linked to the profit motive. This argument is unsuccessful. It overlooks the substantial *indirect* economic benefits that may accrue to the corporation through crimes against the person. To get these economic benefits, corporate management may shortcut expensive safety precautions, respond forcibly to strikes, or engage in criminal anticompetitive behavior. If any such risk-taking is corporate action, the corporation becomes a proper criminal defendant.

Granite Constr. Co. v. Superior Court of Fresno County, 149 Cal. App. 3d 465, 197 Cal. Rptr. 3, 5 (1983).

(4) Under the *Pinkerton* doctrine, co-conspirators may be culpable for the act of any other co-conspirator if the act is the natural consequence of the object of the conspiracy, whether or not the criminal act was originally intended and irrespective of whether the party charged was present at the time of the act. Hence, conspirators may be held vicariously liable for crimes perpetrated by another conspirator. *See* Ch. 6, §6.03[D], *infra*.

Chapter 4

Parties to Crimes

Throughout much of this book we have been asking questions in order to determine whether certain acts should be criminally sanctioned: What is a crime? How should the criminal offender be punished? What are the constitutional limits on criminal law? In this chapter, the emphasis shifts. Here attention is focused on two questions: Which person can be convicted of criminal activities? With what crimes can particular persons be charged?

§4.01 The Old

At common law a rather detailed scheme was developed to decide which persons could be convicted of criminal activities. One was either a principal in the first degree, a principal in the second degree, or an accessory before the fact.[1] A principal in the first degree was the person at the scene of the crime who committed one of the elements of the criminal offense. A principal in the second degree was also at the scene of the crime; she, however, did not commit the crime, she assisted in the commission of the crime. The classic principal in the second degree was the look-out who was at the scene (at the place where the crime was being committed or in the immediate vicinity); she aided the principal in the first degree by watching for the victim or the police. An accessory before the fact provided aid to the principal in the first degree, like the principal in the second degree. Unlike the principal in the second degree, he was not at the scene of the crime. Very often it was the accessory before the fact who was the true "brains" behind the operation. He planned the crime and provided weapons and methods of escape. He could not be charged as a principal, however, because he did not go to the scene when the crime was being committed.

This scheme was well developed at common law, though numerous difficult issues plagued lawyers. For instance, what was "the scene of the crime"? Could an accessory be tried before the principal in the first degree? Under the modern view of parties to the crime, many of the formerly significant issues have become far less important. Because so very many states have adopted this modern view, little time will be spent exploring most of these issues. One issue, however, was troubling at common law and was resolved finally by the United States Supreme Court.

1. At common law, accessories after the fact were also part of this scheme if they aided escaping felons. Because this involvement arose after the commission of the crime, they were treated apart from the other three parties. *See* "After the Fact Assistance," *infra*.

Standefer v. United States

United States Supreme Court
447 U.S. 10 (1980)

MR. CHIEF JUSTICE BURGER delivered the opinion of the Court.

We granted certiorari in this case to decide whether a defendant accused of aiding and abetting in the commission of a federal offense may be convicted after the named principal has been acquitted of that offense.

I.

In June 1977, petitioner Standefer was indicted on four counts of making gifts to a public official, and on five counts of aiding and abetting a revenue official in accepting compensation in addition to that authorized by law. The indictment charged that petitioner, as head of Gulf Oil Company's tax department, had authorized payments for five vacation trips to Cyril Niederberger, who then was the Internal Revenue Service agent in charge of the audits of Gulf's federal income tax returns. Specifically, the indictment alleged that Gulf, on petitioner's authorization, had paid for vacations for Niederberger in Pompano Beach (July 1971), Miami (January 1973), Absecon (August–September 1973), Pebble Beach (April 1974), and Las Vegas (June 1974)....

Prior to the filing of this indictment, Niederberger was separately charged in a 10-count indictment—two counts for each of the five vacations. In February 1977, Niederberger was tried on these charges. He was convicted on four counts in connection with the vacations in Miami, Absecon, Pebble Beach, and Las Vegas and of two counts for the Pebble Beach and Las Vegas trips. He was acquitted on the count involving the Pompano Beach trip and on the three counts charging him with accepting payments from Gulf for trips to Pompano Beach, Miami, and Absecon.

In July 1977, following Niederberger's trial and before the trial in his own case commenced, petitioner moved to dismiss the counts which charged him with aiding and abetting Niederberger in connection with the Pompano Beach, Miami, and Absecon vacations. Petitioner argued that because Niederberger, the only named principal, had been acquitted of accepting unlawful compensation as to those vacations, he could not be convicted of aiding and abetting in the commission of those offenses. The District Court denied the motion.

Petitioner's case then proceeded to trial on all nine counts. At trial, petitioner admitted authorizing payment for all five vacation trips, but testified that the trips were purely social and not designed to influence Niederberger in the performance of his official duties. The jury returned guilty verdicts on all nine counts.[1]

Petitioner was sentenced to concurrent terms of six months' imprisonment followed by two years' probation; he was fined a total of $18,000–$2,000 on each count. Pe-

---

1. The jury was instructed that in order to render a guilty verdict it must determine (1) that Niederberger knowingly "received a fee, compensation or reward except as prescribed by law ... for the performance ... of any duty" and (2) that petitioner "willfully aided and abetted [him]."

titioner appealed his convictions claiming, *inter alia*, that he could not be convicted of aiding and abetting a principal, Niederberger, when that principal had been acquitted of the charged offense.

II.

Petitioner makes two main arguments: first, that Congress in enacting 18 U.S.C. § 2 did not intend to authorize prosecution of an aider and abettor after the principal has been acquitted of the offense charged; second, that, even if § 2 permits such a prosecution, the government should be barred from relitigating the issue of whether Niederberger accepted unlawful compensation in connection with the Pompano Beach, Miami, and Absecon vacations. The first contention relies largely on the common law as it prevailed before the enactment of 18 U.S.C. § 2. The second rests on the contemporary doctrine of nonmutual collateral estoppel.

A.

At common law, the subject of principals and accessories was riddled with "intricate" distinctions. In felony cases, parties to a crime were divided into four distinct categories: (1) principals in the first degree who actually perpetrated the offense; (2) principals in the second degree who were actually or constructively present at the scene of the crime and aided or abetted its commission; (3) accessories before the fact who aided or abetted the crime, but were not present at its commission; and (4) accessories after the fact who rendered assistance after the crime was complete. By contrast, misdemeanor cases "d[id] not admit of accessaries [*sic*] either before or after the fact;" instead, all parties to a misdemeanor, whatever their roles, were principals.

Because at early common law all parties to a felony received the death penalty, certain procedural rules developed tending to shield accessories from punishment. Among them was one of special relevance to this case: the rule that an accessory could not be convicted without the prior conviction of the principal offender. Under this rule, the principal's flight, death, or acquittal barred prosecution of the accessory. And if the principal were pardoned or his conviction reversed on appeal, the accessory's conviction could not stand. In every way, "an accessory follow[ed], like a shadow, his principal."

This procedural bar applied only to the prosecution of accessories in felony cases. In misdemeanor cases, where all participants were deemed principals, a prior acquittal of the actual perpetrator did not prevent the subsequent conviction of a person who rendered assistance. And in felony cases a principal in the second degree could be convicted notwithstanding the prior acquittal of the first-degree principal. Not surprisingly, considerable effort was expended in defining the categories—in determining, for instance, when a person was "constructively present" so as to be a second-degree principal. In the process, justice all too frequently was defeated.

To overcome these judge-made rules, statutes were enacted in England and in the United States. In 1848 the Parliament enacted a statute providing that an accessory before the fact could be "indicted, tried, convicted, and punished in all respects *like the Principal*." As interpreted, the statute permitted an accessory to be convicted "although the principal be acquitted." Several state legislatures followed suit. In 1899,

Congress joined this growing reform movement with the enactment of a general penal code for Alaska which abrogated the common-law distinctions and provided that "all persons concerned in the commission of a crime, whether it be felony or misdemeanor, and whether they directly commit the act constituting the crime or aid and abet in its commission, though not present, are principals, and to be tried and punished as such." In 1901 Congress enacted a similar provision for the District of Columbia.

The enactment of 18 U.S.C. § 2 in 1909 was part and parcel of this same reform movement. The language of the statute, as enacted, unmistakably demonstrates the point:

> "Whoever directly commits any act constituting an offense defined in any law of the United States, or aids, abets, counsels, commands, induces or procures its commission, *is a principal*."

The statute "abolishe[d] the distinction between principals and accessories and [made] them all principals." Read against its common-law background, the provision evinces a clear intent to permit the conviction of accessories to federal criminal offenses despite the prior acquittal of the actual perpetrator of the offense. It gives general effect to what had always been the rule for second-degree principals and for all misdemeanants.

B.

The doctrine of nonmutual collateral estoppel was unknown to the common law and to the Congress when it enacted § 2 in 1909. It emerged in a civil case. There, we held that a determination of patent invalidity in a prior infringement action was entitled to preclusive effect against the patentee in subsequent litigation against a different defendant. Just this past term we again applied the doctrine—this time "offensively"—to hold that a defendant who had had a "full and fair" opportunity to litigate issues of fact in a civil proceeding initiated by the Securities and Exchange Commission could be estopped from relitigating those issues in a subsequent action brought by a private plaintiff. In both cases, application of nonmutual estoppel promoted judicial economy and conserved private resources without unfairness to the litigant against whom estoppel was invoked.

Here, petitioner urges us to apply nonmutual estoppel against the government; specifically he argues that the government should be barred from relitigating Niederberger's guilt in connection with the vacation trips to Pompano Beach, Miami, and Absecon. That issue, he notes, was an element of his offense which was determined adversely to the government at Niederberger's trial.

This, however, is a criminal case, presenting different considerations. First, in a criminal case, the government is often without the kind of "full and fair opportunity to litigate" that is a prerequisite of estoppel. Several aspects of our criminal law make this so: the prosecution's discovery rights in criminal cases are limited, both by rules of court and constitutional privileges; it is prohibited from being granted a directed verdict or from obtaining a judgment notwithstanding the verdict no matter how clear the evidence in support of guilt, compare Fed. Rule Civ. Proc. 50; it cannot secure a new trial on the ground that an acquittal was plainly contrary to the weight of the evidence, compare Fed. Rule Civ. Proc. 59; and it cannot secure appellate review where a defendant has been acquitted.

The absence of these remedial procedures in criminal cases permits juries to acquit out of compassion or compromise or because of " 'their assumption of a power which they had no right to exercise, but to which they were disposed through lenity.' " It is of course true that verdicts induced by passion, and prejudice are not unknown in civil suits. But in civil cases, post-trial motions and appellate review provide an aggrieved litigant a remedy; in a criminal case the government has no similar avenue to correct errors. Under contemporary principles of collateral estoppel, this factor strongly militates against giving an acquittal preclusive effect....

Finally, this case involves the important federal interest in the enforcement of the criminal law. [Earlier cases] were disputes over private rights between private litigants. In such cases, no significant harm flows from enforcing a rule that affords a litigant only one full and fair opportunity to litigate an issue, and there is no sound reason for burdening the courts with repetitive litigation.

In short, this criminal case involves "competing policy considerations" that outweigh the economy concerns that undergird the estoppel doctrine.

III.

In denying preclusive effect to Niederberger's acquittal, we do not deviate from the sound teaching that "justice must satisfy the appearance of justice." This case does no more than manifest the simple, if discomforting, reality that "different juries may reach different results under any criminal statute. That is one of the consequences we accept under our jury system." While symmetry of results may be intellectually satisfying, it is not required.

Here, petitioner received a fair trial at which the Government bore the burden of proving beyond reasonable doubt that Niederberger violated 26 U.S.C. § 7214(a)(2) and that petitioner aided and abetted him in that venture. He was entitled to no less—and to no more.

The judgment of the Court of Appeals is *affirmed.*

Comments and Questions

(1) The court in *State v. Suites*, 427 S.E.2d 318, 321 (N.C. Ct. App. 1993), took the view that "the acquittal of the named principal operates as an acquittal of the accessory before the fact," setting aside the plea of guilty of the accessory. In Georgia the proposition does not operate as a per se rule of law but instead allows the trier of fact to consider the acquittal of the principal as relevant evidence as to the guilt or innocence of one charged as a party to the crime. *White v. State*, 356 S.E.2d 875 (Ga. 1987).

The dissenting circuit judge in the instant case remarked: "I insist that a small measure of consistency is essential, that there must be some dependency between aiding or abetting and the offense that is aided or abetted." Did the Chief Justice directly address this concern? What is an appropriate response?

(2) What would the result have been if the acquittal/conviction judgments had been the same but Standefer and Niederberger had been tried together, before the same jury? If there would be a different result, can that be rationalized against the result reached by the Court?

(3) The Supreme Court recently revisited accomplice liability doctrine, though in a somewhat more narrow setting, in *Rosemond v. United States,* 134 S. Ct. 1240, 1248 (2014). There the defendant was convicted of violating a provision of the U.S. Code that prohibits the use of a firearm during a crime of violence. The Justices had earlier required the government to show that, under the code section, the accomplice defendant had to have "foreknowledge" that someone would be using a gun during the commission of the act. The trial judge did not instruct specifically on this point; indeed, the government's view was that the defendant could be convicted "even if he became aware of the gun only after he realistically could have opted out of the crime." The Supreme Court rejected this view. The language of the opinion is of broad application:

> [The federal aiding and abetting statute] reflects a centuries-old view of culpability: that a person may be responsible for a crime he has not personally carried out if he helps another to complete its commission.
>
> We have previously held that ... "those who provide knowing aid to persons committing federal crimes, with the intent to facilitate the crime, are themselves committing a crime." [A] person is liable ... for aiding and abetting a crime if (and only if) he (1) takes an affirmative act in furtherance of that offense, (2) with the intent of facilitating the offense's commission....
>
> [A] person aids and abets a crime when (in addition to taking the requisite act) he intends to facilitate that offense's commission. An intent to advance some different or lesser offense is not, or at least not usually, sufficient: instead, the intent must go to the specific and entire crime charged. And the canonical formulation of that needed state of mind—later appropriated by this Court and oft-quoted in both parties' briefs—is Judge Learned Hand's: To aid and abet a crime, a defendant must not just "in some sort associate himself with the venture," but also "participate in it as in something that he wishes to bring about" and "seek by his action to make it succeed." We have previously found that intent requirement satisfied when a person actively participates in a criminal venture with full knowledge of the circumstances constituting the charged offense.

(4) What is the purpose of the doctrine of nonmutual collateral estoppel? Does the Court's opinion indicate that it could *never* be used in criminal cases? Should it?

§ 4.02 The New

As mentioned earlier, the common law scheme regarding parties to crimes has been largely rejected by those states which have reviewed their criminal law in recent times. In its place we have seen a much broader—and less technical—statement of accomplice liability. The modern approach focuses on the defendant's state of mind and the type of assistance she rendered. *See, e.g.*, Section 12.1-03-1 of the North Dakota Criminal Code:

> 1. A person may be convicted of an offense based upon the conduct of another when:
>
> a. Acting with the kind of culpability required for the offense, he causes the other to engage in such conduct;
>
> b. With intent of the offense committed, he commands, induces, procures, or aids the other to commit it, or having a statutory duty to prevent its commission, he fails to make proper effort to do so.

One court explained the principles:

> In order to prove aiding and abetting, the government must first establish the commission of the offense by the principal, and then prove that "the defendant consciously shared the principal's knowledge of the underlying criminal act, and intended to help the principal." [T]he government [must] show "that the defendant associated himself with the commission of the offense, participated in it as something that he wished to bring about, and sought by his actions to make it succeed."

United States v. Garcia-Carrasquillo, 483 F.3d 124, 130 (1st Cir. 2007).

[A] The State of Mind

[1] The Proof Problem

State v. Gladstone

Supreme Court of Washington
474 P.2d 274 (1970)

Hale, Justice.

One who aids or abets another in the commission of a crime is guilty as a principal under RCW 9.01.030, which says:

> Every person concerned in the commission of a felony, gross misdemeanor or misdemeanor, whether he directly commits the act constituting the offense, or aids or abets in its commission, and whether present or absent; and every person who directly or indirectly counsels, encourages, hires, commands, induces or otherwise procures another to commit a felony, gross misdemeanor or misdemeanor, is a principal, and shall be proceeded against and punished as such. The fact that the person aided, abetted, counseled, encouraged, hired, commanded, induced or procured, could not or did not entertain a criminal intent, shall not be a defense to any person aiding, abetting, counseling, encouraging, hiring, commanding, inducing or procuring him.

Gladstone's guilt as an aider and abettor in this case rests solely on evidence of a conversation between him and one Douglas MacArthur Thompson concerning the possible purchase of marijuana from one Robert Kent. There is no other evidence to connect the accused with Kent who ultimately sold some marijuana to Thompson.

When asked by Thompson—an agent of the police—where marijuana could be bought, the defendant did no more than name Kent as an individual who might be willing to sell some and draw a sketch of his location. There was no evidence whatever that the defendant had any association, understanding, agreement or arrangement, direct or indirect, tacit or express with Kent to aid or persuade him in any way in the sale of marijuana.

The conversation between defendant and Thompson occurred at defendant's residence. Douglas MacArthur Thompson, a 25-year-old student at the University of Puget Sound in Tacoma and an employee of the Internal Revenue Service of the United States, had done some investigative work for the government. From time to time, the Tacoma Police Department engaged him to investigate the use, possession and sale of narcotics, principally marijuana, among college students. When working for the Tacoma Police Department, he operated under the control and direction of the department's narcotics detail.

Thompson testified that Lieutenant Seymour and Detective Gallwas of the narcotics detail asked him to attempt a purchase of marijuana from Gladstone. During the evening of April 10, 1967—between 10 and 11 o'clock—the two officers and Thompson drove in a police car to the vicinity of defendant's apartment. Thompson went to Gladstone's door alone, beyond the hearing and out of the sight of the two officers. He knocked at the door and Gladstone responded. Thompson asked Gladstone if he would sell him some marijuana. Describing this incident, Thompson testified as follows:

> Well, I asked—at the time Gladstone told me that he was—he did not have enough marijuana on hand to sell me any, but he did know an individual who had quite a sufficient quantity and that was very willing to sell and he named the individual as Robert Kent, or Bob Kent as he put it, and he gave me directions to the residence and he—due to the directions I asked him if, you know, if he could draw me a map and he did.

When Thompson said he asked Gladstone to draw the map for him, he added, "I'm not sure whether he did give me the exact address or not, he told me where the residence was." He said that Gladstone then with pencil and paper sketched the location of Kent's place of residence. Thompson had no prior knowledge of where Kent lived, and did not know if he might have marijuana or that he had ever possessed it.

The two officers then took Thompson to Kent's residence where marijuana was purchased. The actual purchase was made by Thompson directly from Kent while Officer Gallwas and Lieutenant Seymour stayed in the police car. Kent was subsequently arrested and convicted of selling Thompson approximately 8 ounces of marijuana—the very sale which defendant here was convicted of aiding and abetting.

That ended the prosecution's case. Even if it were accorded all favorable inferences, there appears at this point a gap in the evidence which we feel as a matter of law is fatal to the prosecution's cause. Neither on direct examination nor under cross-examination did Thompson testify that he knew of any prior conduct, arrangements or communications between Gladstone and Kent from which it could be even remotely inferred that the defendant had any understanding, agreement, purpose, intention or design to participate or engage in or aid or abet any sale of marijuana by Kent. Other than to obtain a simple map from Gladstone and to say that Gladstone told him Kent might have some marijuana available, Thompson did not even establish that Kent and the defendant were acquainted with each other. Testimony of the brief conversation and Gladstone's very crude drawing consisting of 8 penciled lines indicating where Kent lived constitute the whole proof of the aiding and abetting presented.

Except for the conversation between Gladstone and Thompson and the map, the state showed only that the officers and their informant, Thompson, went to Kent's residence, more than 3 or 4 blocks from where Gladstone lived, bought some marijuana from him and proved that it was the substance known scientifically as cannabis. Thus, at the close of its case in chief, the state had failed to show any connection or association whatever between Gladstone and Kent or even that they knew each other, and at that juncture a motion for dismissal would lie.

At the conclusion of all the proof, the evidence still showed no more than a possible accommodation to someone who said he wanted to buy some marijuana, and no connection whatever between defendant and the seller. The gap in the evidence remained; the missing link was still missing.

If all reasonable inferences favorable to the state are accorded the evidence, it does not, in our opinion, establish the commission of the crime charged. That vital element—a nexus between the accused and the party whom he is charged with aiding and abetting in the commission of a crime—is missing. The record contains no evidence whatever that Gladstone had any communication by word, gesture or sign, before or after he drew the map, from which it could be inferred that he counseled, encouraged, hired, commanded, induced or procured Kent to sell marijuana to Douglas Thompson as charged, or took any steps to further the commission of the crime charged. He was not charged with aiding and abetting Thompson in the purchase of marijuana, but with Kent's sale of it.

Gladstone's culpability, if at all, must be brought within RCW 9.01.030, which makes a principal of one who aids and abets another in the commission of the crime. Although an aider and abettor need not be physically present at the commission of the crime to be held guilty as a principal, his conviction depends on proof that he did something in association or connection with the principal to accomplish the crime. Learned Hand, J., we think, hit the nail squarely when he wrote that, in order to aid and abet another to commit a crime, it is necessary that a defendant

> in some sort associate himself with the venture, that he participate in it as in something that he wishes to bring about, that he seek by his action to make it succeed. All the words used—even the most colorless, "abet"—carry an implication of purposive attitude towards it.

It would be a dangerous precedent indeed to hold that mere communications to the effect that another might or probably would commit a criminal offense amount to an aiding and abetting of the offense should it ultimately be committed.

There being no evidence whatever that the defendant ever communicated to Kent the idea that he would in any way aid him in the sale of any marijuana, or said anything to Kent to encourage or induce him or direct him to do so, or counseled Kent in the sale of marijuana, or did anything more than describe Kent to another person as an individual who might sell some marijuana, or would derive any benefit, consideration or reward from such a sale, there was no proof of an aiding and abetting, and the conviction should, therefore, be reversed as a matter of law. Remanded with directions to dismiss.

HAMILTON, JUSTICE (dissenting).

This state, in common with many jurisdictions, legislatively abolished the common law classifications of principals in the first and second degree and accessories before the fact by and through the enactment of RCW 9.01.030.

In the construction of this statute this court has said that each of the words of the statute, from which criminal culpability can flow, signifies the overt and affirmative doing or saying of something on the part of a person charged which directly *or indirectly* contributes to the commission of the primary crime.

As is apparent from its language, our statute does not require the presence at the scene of the crime of one aiding, abetting, counseling or inducing the commission of a crime. Neither does it require a community of intent, for by the last sentence it provides that absence of criminal intent on the part of the person aided, abetted or induced to commit the primary offense is no defense to the aider or abettor. The statutory language and the overt action it contemplates does, however, give rise to the requirement that the aider or abettor entertain a conscious intent, *i.e.*, knowledge and intent that his action will instigate, induce, procure or encourage perpetration of the primary crime.

The question to be resolved, then, in the instant case is whether the evidence sustains the jury's conclusion that the appellant entertained the requisite intent to render him culpable as an aider or abettor.

[T]he jury was entitled to believe that on April 10, 1967, one Robert Kent sold marijuana to Douglas Thompson, who at the time was acting as an undercover agent for and in concert with officers of the Tacoma Police Department; that appellant Gladstone, Kent, and Thompson were students at the same school in Tacoma; that prior to the evening of April 10, 1967, when Thompson talked to appellant, *Thompson and the Tacoma Police Department were unaware of Kent or his association with marijuana;* that appellant knew Kent, whom he met and associated with on the campus of the school they respectively attended; that both appellant and Kent lived off campus; that appellant knew where Kent lived and on at least one occasion had driven him home; that at the time in question the Tacoma Police Department had information that appellant was supposed to be holding a supply of marijuana for sale; that Thompson, who was but slightly acquainted with appellant, approached appellant at his residence about 10:50 p.m. on April 10, 1967, and asked appellant to sell him some marijuana; that appellant then stated that he did not have enough marijuana on hand to sell but that he knew an individual who did have an ample supply and who was willing to sell some and named the individual as Robert Kent; that upon request appellant orally gave Thompson directions to Kent's apartment and drew a map to aid Thompson in finding the address, utilizing as a reference point a building known to appellant to be a student rendezvous where drugs had been sold; that by using the map and oral directions Thompson and the police went to Kent's residence; *that Thompson approached Kent and told him "Gladstone had sent me" whereupon Kent invited him to a room and sold him some marijuana for $30;* and that Thompson and one of the police officers later returned to the Kent residence, after again visiting appellant, and made a second purchase of marijuana at which time Kent was arrested.

Based upon the foregoing circumstances and the inferences reasonably derivable therefrom, I am satisfied that the jury was fully warranted in concluding that appellant, when he affirmatively recommended Kent as a source and purveyor of marijuana, entertained the requisite conscious design and intent that his action would instigate, induce, procure or encourage perpetration of Kent's subsequent crime of selling marijuana to Thompson. Furthermore, insofar as an element of preconcert be concerned, certainly the readiness with which the passwords, "Gladstone had sent me," gained a stranger's late evening entree to Kent's domain and produced two illegal sales strongly suggests, if not conclusively establishes, the missing communal nexus which the majority belabors.

Comments and Questions

(1) Several times the court referred to "the missing link" or gap in the evidence. What was this missing link or gap? Was there truly a gap when the prosecutor showed that the defendant told Thompson of Kent, gave him directions and even drew him a map? Would the result change if it was clear that the next day Kent gave the defendant money? Suppose the defendant gave Thompson not a crudely written map, but a neatly photocopied map?

(2) The Court in *Brown v. Palmer*, 441 F.3d 347, 351–52 (6th Cir. 2006), laid out the government's case but found the evidence lacking.

> On appeal, the state relies on the following facts to argue that "the jury reasonably concluded from the circumstantial evidence presented ... that Petitioner intended to give aid or encouragement to the principal in committing the armed robbery and carjacking": (a) Brown was present before and during the carjacking, (b) he and the perpetrator were in the car together before the perpetrator committed the offenses, (c) he stared at the victims while the perpetrator fired the shots, (d) he never got gas even though he was parked near a gas pump, (e) he attempted to flee as soon as the perpetrator drove off in the car, and (f) he failed to contact the police to retrieve his car.

> [T]he evidence clearly demonstrates that Brown was present at the scene and had some acquaintance with the perpetrator. Beyond that, however, the evidence pointing to Brown's guilt becomes quite speculative. [B]eing present at the scene of the crime and having a brief relationship with the carjacker are insufficient facts to establish beyond a reasonable doubt that Brown aided and abetted the latter individual.

Was the prosecution's case stronger in *Brown* or in *Gladstone*?

(3) The defendant in *People v. Marshall*, 106 N.W.2d 842 (Mich. 1961), gave his car keys to his friend, with knowledge that his friend was drunk. The friend crashed head-on into another car, killing himself and the other driver. The court reversed the defendant's conviction for involuntary manslaughter, stating "the killing was not counseled by him, was not accomplished by another acting jointly with him, and did not occur in the attempted achievement of some common enterprise." Should it matter that the court affirmed the defendant's conviction for *knowingly* permitting his car to be driven by a person under the influence? In *People v. Germany*, 116 Cal. Rptr. 841, 845 (Ct. App. 1974), the court wrote: "[A]n aider and abettor need only have knowledge of the criminal purpose of the perpetrator and criminal intent and need not have the specific intent to commit the target crime." If Michigan followed the *Germany* case would the *Marshall* conviction have been reversed? Should it have?

(4) Most modern statutes *do* require more than mere knowledge for conviction under a complicity theory. Recall the N.D. Crim. Code, *supra*, § 12.01-03-01: "A person may be convicted of an offense based upon the conduct of another when with intent of the offense committed, he commands, induces..." In *Hicks v. United States*, 150 U.S. 442 (1893), the defendant was convicted of murder after he made statements to the other defendant Rowe and thereafter Rowe killed the victim. Hicks' conviction was reversed.

> We agree with the counsel for the plaintiff in error in thinking that this instruction was erroneous in two particulars. It omitted to instruct the jury that the acts or words of encouragement and abetting must have been used by the accused with the intention of encouraging and abetting Rowe. So far as the instruction goes, the words may have been used for a different purpose, and yet have had the actual effect of inciting Rowe to commit the murderous act. Hicks, indeed, testified that the expressions used by him were intended to dissuade Rowe from shooting. But the jury were left to find Hicks guilty as a principal because the effect of his words may have had the result of encouraging Rowe to shoot, regardless of Hicks' intention. In another part of the charge the learned judge did make an observation as to the question of intention in the use of the words, saying: "If the deliberate and intentional use of words has the effect to encourage one man to kill another, he who uttered these words is presumed by the law to have intended that effect, and is responsible therefor." This statement is itself defective in confounding the intentional use of the words with the intention as respects the effect to be produced. Hicks no doubt *intended* to use the words he did use, but did he thereby *intend* that they were to be understood by Rowe as an encouragement

> to act? However this may be, we do not think this expression of the learned judge availed to cure the defect already noticed in his charge, that the mere use of certain words would suffice to warrant the jury in finding Hicks guilty, regardless of the intention with which they were used.

(5) In California, the standard form jury instruction dealing with accomplice liability had read as follows:

> A person aids and abets the commission of a crime if, with knowledge of the unlawful purpose of the perpetrator of the crime, he aids, promotes, encourages or instigates by act or advice the commission of such crime.

Does this instruction—CALJIC 3.00—correctly state the law? Held, the instruction was improper for failing to define the intent element.

> The weight of authority and sound law require proof that an aider and abettor act with knowledge of the criminal purpose of the perpetrator *and* with an intent or purpose either of committing, or of encouraging or facilitating commission of, the offense. When the definition of the offense includes the intent to do some act or achieve some consequence beyond the *actus reus* of the crime, the aider and abettor must share the specific intent of the perpetrator.... [A]n aider and abettor will "share" the perpetrator's specific intent when he or she knows the full extent of the perpetrator's criminal purpose and gives aid or encouragement with the intent or purpose of facilitating the perpetrator's commission of the crime.

People v. Beeman, 674 P.2d 1318, 1325 (Cal. 1984). *See also State v. Gonzalez*, 87 A.3d 1101, 1111 (Conn. 2014), where the court succinctly stated the mental state requirement: "[T]o be guilty as an accessory one must share the criminal intent and community of unlawful purpose with the perpetrator of the crime and one must knowingly and wilfully assist the perpetrator in the acts which prepare for, facilitate or consummate it." The Supreme Court of Indiana agreed, even with an attempted murder charge, "an accomplice must have the specific intent to kill when he or she knowingly or intentionally aids, induces, or causes another to attempt to commit murder." *Rosales v. State*, 23 N.E.3d 8, 13 (Ind. 2015).

[B] What Is Enough Aid?

[1] The Proof Problem

United States v. Garguilo

United States Court of Appeals, Second Circuit
310 F.2d 249 (1962)

FRIENDLY, CIRCUIT JUDGE.

Ralph Garguilo and Joseph Macchia appeal from judgments of the District Court for the Southern District of New York, convicting them after a verdict under a single count indictment which charged the making of a likeness of a $10 bill in violation of 18 U.S.C. § 474. Because of a serious question raised by Macchia as to the sufficiency of the evidence against him, it is necessary to recount the testimony in some detail.

The Government's principal witnesses were Mario Villari, owner of Graphic Printing Company, a co-defendant who pleaded guilty, and Albert Della Monica, a photographer and long-time friend of the Garguilo family, whose innocence was not questioned. Villari first met Garguilo in Magistrate's Court on August 17, 1960, while both were waiting to pay traffic fines; Villari told Garguilo he was in the printing business and gave Garguilo his card. About a month later Garguilo came to Villari's shop on West 53rd Street in Manhattan. Joseph Macchia was with him. According to Villari, Garguilo introduced Macchia as "Tony," saying "that he is buddy-buddy, that they do everything together as a group." Garguilo took Villari "on the side," approximately 25 feet away from Macchia and, placing his arm around Villari's shoulder, asked Villari to join him in a counterfeiting endeavor; Villari said he was not interested and the two visitors left about ten minutes after they had arrived. There is no evidence that Macchia talked about counterfeiting or anything else.

Sometime during the summer of 1961, Garguilo came to Della Monica's photography studio in Brooklyn and asked to be taught how to develop a picture and make a copy. He came "several times," "about a week or so." He had Macchia with him "only once or two" of these times. Garguilo introduced Macchia to Della Monica as "my friend, Joe." After Garguilo had learned how to develop pictures, he "started to practice himself" and apparently did so regularly at Della Monica's studio; Macchia was there "two or three times" in all, never alone but always with Garguilo. Garguilo borrowed a camera and other photographic equipment from Della Monica, explaining that he was going into the advertising business and needed the camera to make copies. Inquiries by Della Monica as to Garguilo's progress produced no satisfactory response. There was no evidence that Macchia witnessed the loan of the equipment or participated in its use.

In July, 1961, Garguilo returned to Villari's printing shop. The record is not altogether plain whether there were two or three visits during July, but it is clear that Garguilo was alone on each of them. Assuming that there were three, the first was devoted to a general request for help, which Villari declined, as he had a year before; on the second, Garguilo asked Villari to check his negatives of $10 bills, which Villari again refused to do; on the third, Villari "succumbed," looked at the negatives, which Garguilo carried in a newspaper, through a "view box" and pronounced them too dark, whereupon Garguilo destroyed them.

Garguilo again came to Villari's shop in early August, 1961. This time Macchia accompanied him. Garguilo had brought some more negatives which Villari viewed and found "pretty good"—good enough so that he "burnt in" a plate. This was done with Macchia two or three feet away, "very close." The plate being blurred and inadequate, Garguilo erased it, whereupon he and Macchia "went away." Who carried the negatives is not clear. Villari testified this was the last he saw of Macchia.

Garguilo came to Villari's shop a few days later with some more negatives. Again a plate was "burnt in," found inadequate, and destroyed.

One of Garguilo's visits to the printing shop was witnessed by Secret Service Agent Motto. He testified that on August 11, 1961, he saw Garguilo and another man drive up in an automobile. Garguilo got out, carrying a newspaper wrapped tightly under his arm, and went into the building where Villari's shop was located. He remained for approximately one hour. Then he and Villari came out, got in the car in which the other man was seated, and drove off. Motto could not identify the man who stayed in the car; he did estimate the man's age, height and weight, but there is nothing to tell whether these estimates bear any correspondence with Macchia or whether the identified man was the driver. Toward the end of August, Secret Service Agents searched Villari's shop and found the erased plate of early August, which bore Garguilo's fingerprints.

The only other evidence against Macchia was that, when brought before an Assistant United States Attorney for questioning, he admitted that he knew Garguilo, that on several occasions he accompanied Garguilo to the photographer in Brooklyn, and that several times he went to a printing place with him. He claimed, however, "that he never went up to the printer's establishment but merely sat on the stoop." Macchia also admitted that he knew what was in the newspaper taken out of the car by Garguilo, but refused to say what this was.

Macchia claims that the evidence was insufficient to warrant submission to the jury of the case against him as an aider or abettor. Insofar as his claim relates to alleged lack of knowledge of the crime in which Garguilo was engaged, it is baseless—an inference of such knowledge would be not only permissible but virtually inescapable if the jury credited the testimony that Macchia was "very close" to Garguilo and Villari when the telltale plate was made, and that Macchia had admitted knowing what was in the newspaper that Garguilo had removed from the car. But knowledge that a crime is being committed, even when coupled with presence at the scene, is generally not enough to constitute aiding and abetting.

> In order to aid and abet another to commit a crime it is necessary that a defendant in some sort associate himself with the venture, that he participate in it as in something that he wishes to bring about, that he seek by his action to make it succeed.

It is true, as the Government urges, that evidence of an act of relatively slight moment may warrant a jury's finding participation in a crime. Thus it would have been enough here if the Government adduced evidence from which the jury could find, in addition to guilty knowledge, that Macchia had carried the negatives or driven the car. Perhaps the evidence is, in fact, susceptible of exactly such a construction. Villari testified that on the first unsuccessful plate burning, "They took the negatives with them and went away." And Motto's testimony, coupled with the evidence as to Macchia's admission of knowing what was in the paper that Garguilo took out of the car, would be consistent with Macchia's having been the driver on August 11, although if this was Garguilo's final visit, a finding of Macchia's presence on that occasion would run counter to Villari's testimony that the penultimate visit was the last time he saw Macchia. It is true also that participation may be proved by circumstantial evidence. There may even be instances where the mere presence of a defendant at the scene of a crime he knows is being committed will permit a jury to be convinced beyond a reasonable doubt that the defendant sought "by his action to make it succeed"—for example, the attendance of a 250-pound bruiser at a shakedown as a companion to the extortionist, or the maintenance at the scene of crime of someone useful as a lookout. Here, presence in the car on August 11 might be thought to have been for the latter purpose. Again, it is enough if the presence of the alleged aider and abettor has stimulated others to help the perpetrator, as, for example, if Macchia rather than Garguilo had been the friend of Della Monica, or perhaps simply on the sole basis that it is proved to have positively encouraged the perpetrator himself. Yet, even in an age when solitude is so detested and "togetherness" so valued, a jury could hardly be permitted to find that the mere furnishing of company to a person engaged in crime renders the companion an aider or abettor. Here, on every occasion that was the subject of testimony, Garguilo was the actor, often he was alone, and when he first propositioned Villari, he left Macchia to one side; any inference that Macchia had some role beyond that of a companion rested on the rather equivocal evidence just discussed and on the repetitive instances of his presence, all colored by Garguilo's unusual introduction of Macchia to Villari on their first visit to the print shop.

If the evidence against Macchia passed the test of sufficiency applicable in a criminal case, it did so "only by a hair's breadth." We are not here required to make so fine a judgment, since we believe reversal for a new trial to be called for in any event. If the evidence was insufficient it came near enough to the line to entitle the Government, if it desires, to an opportunity to put it across on a new trial. On the other hand, we would still be disposed to direct a new trial even though the evidence was sufficient. The closeness of the issue against Macchia imposed an obligation on the trial judge to instruct the jury with extreme precision, as he realized, and on us to review the charge with what, in a less doubtful case, would be undue meticulousness. Reading the entire charge, we cannot overcome a fear that the judge, quite unwittingly and simply by emphasis, may have led the jury to believe that a finding of presence and knowledge on the part of Macchia was enough for conviction. True, there is much in the charge that would argue against this. Turning to the case against Macchia, the judge began by stating the law as to aiding and abetting with entire correctness. However, when he came to apply these principles to the facts, very nearly the whole of his comment, and a vivid illustration that he used, related solely to the issue of "conscious, intelligent awareness of what was going on."[2] The jury evidenced its concern

2. The judge stated:
"Now let us take it from there, making those basic assumptions [that the jury believed Villari and Della Monica]. Was Mecchia [sic] close enough to the transactions, to the conversations, to the general atmosphere of the transactions to know what was going on? Did he have an intelligent, conscious awareness of what was going on? And if he did have that conscious intelligent awareness of what was going on, was it sufficient to constitute an aiding or abetting within the terms of the definition I gave you?" He then gave as an illustration the case of a man in the back seat of a car "who was fast asleep and all rolled up in a rug or with his overcoat over his head," who, even though introduced by the principal

over the case against Macchia by a request for further instructions as to what constituted aiding or abetting; although what the judge said would have been adequate, indeed excellent, in the usual trial, the contrasting hypothetical cases which he put to the jury turned on the issue of knowledge,[3] whereas his instructions with respect to purposive participation, although correct, were rather abstract. Never were the jurors told in plain words that mere presence and guilty knowledge on the part of Macchia would not suffice unless they were also convinced beyond a reasonable doubt that Macchia was doing something to forward the crime—that he was a participant rather than merely a knowing spectator. In the usual case we should not think of finding reversible error in such a charge when there was no objection, or perhaps even if there had been. However, in the exceptional circumstances here presented we believe that the interests of justice as between the Government and Macchia will be best served by reversal and remand for a new trial.

Lumbard, Chief Judge (concurring and dissenting).

As I believe that the jury may well have thought that knowledge by Macchia of what was afoot was sufficient to convict, I concur in the result which permits a retrial of the case against him. But I disagree with my brethren insofar as Judge Friendly's opinion implies that there was not enough evidence from which the jury could conclude that Macchia was guilty as an aider and abettor in the sense of wishing to see Garguilo succeed and assisting him by his actions. I think there was sufficient evidence to support a verdict of guilty upon a proper charge from the court.

There can be little doubt that when Macchia, together with Garguilo, visited Villari at his printing shop at 537 West 53rd Street, Manhattan, and Della Monica at his photography shop on New Utrecht Avenue in Brooklyn, they must have thought that Macchia was interested in Garguilo's business. Each of them saw him at least twice. The presence of a friend is not only an encouragement to the one who is accompanied but it may also be of assistance in persuading others to be of help. From these four or five visits which Macchia made with Garguilo to the business places of Villari and Della Monica, and from all the surrounding circumstances, and the admissions of Macchia, it seems to me that it was a question for the jury as to whether Macchia's accompanying Garguilo did not contribute to the likelihood of the success of Garguilo's efforts.

As Judge Friendly says, if Macchia had said one single word of encouragement to Villari or Della Monica, it would have been enough. I think the jury could construe his mere presence on these occasions as tantamount to such encouragement. It seems to me naive to suppose that the kind of company and moral (or immoral) support which Macchia gave to Garguilo by being with him was not of the kind which would

defendant as "my pal, my partner, and my co-conspirator," would not be an aider or abettor.

3. These cases concerned a taxi driver who drove a narcotics smuggler to an illegal appointment with special celerity and made a telephone call for him, without knowing that he was dealing with a narcotics smuggler, and another who performed the same acts with knowledge of the illegality of the venture.

help Garguilo in his business with Villari and Della Monica. While there is nothing to show that Macchia might have been a hoodlum or bodyguard, his presence certainly rendered it less likely that Villari or Della Monica might report the matter to the police. Moreover, Macchia's presence gave Garguilo an ally and at least a possible witness if any dispute had arisen. It is precisely because two persons together are more formidable than two persons acting separately in carrying out any illegal design that conspiracy has been made a crime even though it may not succeed.

Comments and Questions

(1) Much of the case turns on the jury instruction given by the trial judge. What would a proper instruction have been? Assuming a proper instruction, was there sufficient evidence to convict Macchia? Would the government's case be significantly stronger if Macchia "had said one single word of encouragement to Villari or Della Monica"? *See United States v. Bowen*, 527 F.3d 1065, 1078 (10th Cir. 2008):

> One need not participate in an important aspect of a crime to be liable as an aider and abetter; participation of "relatively slight moment" is sufficient. Even mere "words or gestures of encouragement" constitute affirmative acts capable of rendering one liable under this theory.

(2) In *Altamirano v. Gonzales*, 427 F.3d 586 (9th Cir. 2005), the court reviewed a deportation decision in which the key question was whether Altamirano had aided and abetted the illegal smuggling of an alien into the United States. Altamirano often drove into Mexico to visit family. On the day in question, she was at the border in the car with family members and in the trunk of the car was someone who was trying unlawfully to enter the U.S. Altamirano and the other people in the car all were aware of the person in the trunk, of that there was no doubt. The court found that the evidence against Altamirano was insufficient, for all it demonstrated was her "mere presence in the vehicle at the port of entry ... despite her knowledge that an alien was hiding in the trunk of the vehicle." Do you agree with the decision? Does your view change in light of this statement by the court:

> When questioned by immigration officers following the primary inspection of the vehicle, Altamirano informed the officers that she knew that her father-in-law had made plans with a friend to transport Martinez-Marin into the United States. She admitted that her husband had told her of the plan the night before. She also knew that Martinez-Marin was in the trunk when she got into the vehicle. Altamirano testified, however, that she did not see Martinez-Marin before they were detained; she did not know his name prior to their detention and she did not know his final destination.

Is that sufficient evidence under Judge Lumbard's view in *Garguilo*? Was the defendant not truly an accessory to the crime of alien smuggling?

(3) The cases are hardly consistent concerning the sufficiency of evidence for the aid requirement. See, for example, *United States v. Diaz-Boyzo*, 432 F.3d 1264 (11th Cir. 2005), where the government showed that the defendant was in a friend's car,

and the friend had drugs hidden inside a bag in the car. These facts alone were not sufficient to support a conviction, wrote the court. But, there was more, and it was enough to uphold a conviction for drug distribution under an aiding and abetting theory.

> First, Diaz-Boyzo rode with Eustolio Villa-Gamino to the initial meeting, the two apartment complexes for the drug pick-up, and the final delivery meeting. Second, when Agent Beard approached the car, Diaz-Boyzo was sitting in the passenger side of the truck and looking back toward Eustolio Villa-Gamino during the delivery of the drugs. Third, Diaz-Boyzo possessed a loaded firearm, which rested near his hands and in his lap, also during the delivery of the drugs. We believe these facts, especially in light of the firearm and its location, would allow a reasonable factfinder to conclude that Diaz-Boyzo served as lookout and protection for Eustolio Villa-Gamino in the transaction.

Was Diaz-Boyzo guilty? Was his conduct more culpable than Altamirano's? More culpable than Macchia's in the principal case? In *Commonwealth v. Raposo*, 595 N.E.2d 773 (Mass. 1992), the government showed that the defendant/mother knew of her boyfriend's intent to have sexual intercourse with her intellectually disabled daughter; she made no effort to enlist outside assistance to prevent the sexual intercourse, and did not immediately report the crime to the police. Held, the defendant was not an accomplice for she did not aid or assist in the commission of the offense. See also *Kelly v. Roberts*, 998 F.2d 802 (10th Cir. 1993), where the defendants robbed a restaurant and killed the manager. One defendant was not in the restaurant at the time, but was known to be acquainted with the robbers, and had been in the parking lot of the restaurant just before the robbery. The government argued this demonstrated that the defendant was "casing" the restaurant for the two robbers. The court on appeal reversed the conviction, finding that the government failed to show that the defendant had conveyed any information to the robbers prior to the robbery or that they were even in the vicinity at that time. "[The] testimony may raise a suspicion of guilt but is not sufficient to allow a rational jury to conclude beyond a reasonable doubt the [defendant] willfully intended to further the success of the unlawful venture." *Kelly*, at 809.

(4) In *People v. Stanciel*, 606 N.E.2d 1201 (Ill. 1992), the defendant was charged under the Illinois accountability statute with assisting in the killing of her young child. With knowledge of her boyfriend's prior brutal treatment toward her child, the defendant allowed the boyfriend to assume the role of disciplinarian over the child. The child died as a result of multiple blunt force injuries inflicted by the boyfriend. The Illinois statute requires the government to show that the defendant "with the intent to promote [the crime] ... aids, abets ... such other person in the ... commission of the offense." Would the evidence of the defendant's knowledge of prior physical treatment and her allowing her boyfriend to be alone with the child suffice? Held, the mother's conviction was valid, as the statute covers the situation of the parent who is not "actively participating in the overt act itself.... The delegation of exclusive control of the child to [a known abuser] constituted the act of aiding a prin-

cipal under the accountability statute." Does this evidence show that the defendant intentionally provided aid such as to justify conviction for the crime of murder?

(5) Can an accomplice be guilty of a greater crime than the person who actually committed the criminal act? Yes, said the court in *Taylor v. State*, 840 N.E.2d 324 (Ind. 2006). There the defendant was found guilty of murder, on an accomplice theory, and received a sentence of 60 years imprisonment. He argued on appeal that his conviction and sentence were improper because of a faulty jury instruction. The jury had been told that it could find such responsibility for Taylor even if it was unable to determine that the person who actually shot the victim had killed knowingly or intentionally. The keys, according to the court, were that the killer was found guilty of a homicide offense and that the jury decided that the accomplice truly did act in an intentional fashion even if the killer had not. "[A]n accomplice can be guilty of a greater homicide crime than the principal when the accomplice's mens rea is more culpable."

[2] Words Alone

United States v. Kelley

United States Court of Appeals, Fourth Circuit
769 F.2d 215 (1985)

HAYNSWORTH, SENIOR CIRCUIT JUDGE:

The defendant was convicted of conspiring to defraud the federal government and of aiding and assisting in the preparation of false W-4 forms. On appeal he advances several contentions, in none of which do we find any merit.

I.

Kelley was the organizer and leader of a group calling themselves the Constitutional Tax Association. With some irony, the doctrine embraced by the Constitutional Tax Association was that the federal income tax is unconstitutional as applied to wages. Kelley had done some research and prepared a legal brief in which he reasoned that wages are received for labor in exchange of equal value; since no party to the exchange realizes a profit, the exchange is not a taxable event or that there is no gain to be recognized.

Kelley solicited dues paying members. In exchange for their payments to him, he explained how the members might avoid all income tax withholding on their wages and obtain refunds of previously withheld wages. He provided forms for use by the members and gave them detailed instructions as to how they should be filled out. He provided paying members with W-4 forms for the claiming of exemptions from withholding and blank copies of refund claim forms. He provided detailed instructions for the preparation of W-4 and refund claim forms, while the members were instructed to report zero wages on their 1040A income tax return forms. The packet he provided the members contained what purported to be a legal brief in support of the position that wages were not subject to income taxation and that employers should not withhold anything for federal income taxes. Members were instructed to attach the brief to the W-4 forms.

He also instructed the members to destroy their credit cards and to deal only in cash so that they would leave no paper trails to be followed by the IRS agents.

As part of the consideration for the payments made to him, he held himself in readiness to talk to any employer that declined to honor the claimed withholding exemption form or who threatened to call the claimed exemption to the attention of the Internal Revenue Service.

There was a back-up plan. As he explained to undercover Revenue Agents posing as members of his Association, if an employer could not be persuaded to honor the exemption certificate without reporting it to the IRS, the member should file a W-4 form claiming twelve dependents. Kelley told them of his understanding that if fourteen or more dependents were claimed the employer was required to report the matter to the IRS, but that the employer would not do so if no more than twelve were claimed.

At each meeting with each group of members, Kelley explained that if the members followed his advice he would keep them out of trouble. That Kelley himself was not completely convinced of the legality or appropriateness of his advice, however, is strongly indicated by the fact that, while he was thus engaged in soliciting and advising members, in the spring of 1981 he filed his own income tax return in which he properly reported the wages he had received in 1980. He admitted that he had talked to a number of lawyers about his legal proposition and that none of them agreed with him.

II.

The defendant contends that he could not be lawfully convicted of aiding and abetting. He said he did not actually participate in the preparation of any of the tax forms but only gave advice that his listeners were free to accept or reject. The contention ignores reality, for he did participate in the preparation of the forms. He told the listeners what to do and how to prepare the forms. He did so with the intention that his advice be accepted, and the fact that the members paid him for the advice and promised assistance warranted an inference of an expectation that the advice would be followed. Moreover, he actually supplied forms and materials to be filed with W-4 forms. He did not take his pen in his hand to complete the forms, but his participation in their preparation was as real as if he had.

The claim of First Amendment protection of his speech is frivolous. His was no abstract criticism of income tax laws. His listeners were not urged to seek congressional action to exempt wages from income taxation. Instead, they were urged to file false returns, with every expectation that the advice would be heeded.

The cloak of the First Amendment envelops critical, but abstract, discussions of existing laws, but lends no protection to speech which urges the listeners to commit violations of current law. It was no theoretical discussion of non-compliance with laws; action was urged; the advice was heeded, and false forms were filed.

III.

Relying upon *United States v. Snider*, 502 F.2d 645 (4th Cir. 1974), the defendant contends that the forms actually filed were not potentially deceptive. In *Snider* a Quaker had filed a W-4 form in which he claimed three billion dependents. He attached a letter addressed to the Internal Revenue Service explaining that he felt a sense of responsibility for all of the people of the earth and a strong religious opposition to war. He decried this country's participation in the war in Southeast Asia and stated that he would not willingly pay federal income taxes as long as this country was engaged in that war. A divided panel of this court felt that no criminal sanctions should be imposed upon him, for there was no deceptiveness in the form as filed; it simply should have been treated by the employer as one claiming no dependents.

The holding in *Snider* has been criticized. Other courts have held that a false return is false within the meaning of the statute whether or not it is deceptive.

This case, however, occasions no reconsideration of *Snider*, even if this panel were authorized to reconsider. It is enough to observe that *Snider* was a rare case. Only one taxpayer was involved, and no employer would be expected to exempt Snider from income tax withholding on the basis of the filing. This case is quite different. It involves a number of taxpayers whose collective action was calculated to cause substantial disruption in the process of current collection of income taxes. While the legal argument that wages were not subject to taxation would not be embraced by any Internal Revenue Agent, the W-4 forms did carry a substantial potential of deception. They were addressed to employers, some of whom may have been unsophisticated. The testimony shows that Kelley's listeners found him persuasive. He was glib and articulate, and he claimed to have successfully persuaded employers to accept the W-4 forms without reporting them to the IRS. The symbolic protest involved in *Snider* was calculated to deceive no one; the false certificates that Kelley's clients filed at his behest were designed to deceive employers charged with the duty of withholding.

IV.

Finally, Kelley complains of selective prosecution. Those members of his organization who followed his advice were not prosecuted criminally, but Kelley was the instigator of the entire affair. There is no impermissible selectivity in a prosecutorial decision to prosecute the ringleader and instigator, without prosecuting his foolish followers, when a prosecution of the instigator can be expected to bring the whole affair to an end.

V.

We find no infirmity in Kelley's conviction.

Affirmed.

Comments and Questions

(1) In the prior cases the courts indicated that the defendant could be guilty of aiding if he specifically aided a particular individual. How can a defendant such as Kelley be guilty if it is alleged that he merely provided forms and instruction? In a case remarkably similar on the facts—*People v. Bohmer*, 120 Cal. Rptr. 136, 144 (Ct. App.), *cert. denied*, 423 U.S. 990 (1975)—the court affirmed the convictions, stating that the defendant's speech "was reasonably calculated to incite or produce imminent lawless action." See also *United States v. Knapp*, 25 F.3d 451 (7th Cir. 1994), where the defendant

> was a self-proclaimed expert on preserving personal assets through creative estate planning. Ostensibly through his unique understanding of the United States Constitution, the Tax Code, the Internal Revenue Service (IRS) and the structuring of estate trusts, Knapp taught people how to avoid paying income taxes.

He argued that because the basis of the charge against him was protected free speech his conviction was unlawful. The court on appeal disagreed.

> The proof at trial showed the jury that Knapp did, in fact, commit a criminal act as charged in the indictment: Knapp willfully assisted the preparation of a false return by advising the Hillmers' tax return preparer to claim a deduction on the Hillmers' 1985 tax return to the rental of business property in an amount sufficient to eliminate profit, while knowing that the Hillmers had not paid such rent and were not entitled to such a deduction. This conduct is well beyond the mere advocacy entitled to the protection of the First Amendment.

(2) The defendant in *United States v. Leitner*, 555 Fed. App'x 932 (11th Cir. 2014) used techniques similar to that found in *Kelley*. He was, perhaps, even more forceful with one of the defendant's communications, stating:

> Hi, my name is Mark Leitner and I am a consultant for the educational organization PQI. We are for expert consultation, education and services in the area of debt elimination, asset protection, and freedom and privacy.... If you are looking to reduce or eliminate your income tax burden legally and immediately, then this is information that can help you. Our education will blow your socks off and leave your toes smoking. And we have a money back guarantee to.... back that statement up.
>
> [Y]ou may also wish to be introduced to a few of the many people that have taken advantage of our services and who are now living a tax-free lifestyle, people like doctors, CPAs, attorneys, housewives, business executives, construction workers, nurses, and many other Americans just like you. We have helped tens of thousands. Our financial tools and processes are applicable to almost everyone. W-2 wage earners will be able to keep most of their paycheck in as soon as several weeks time. Our experts will handle all paperwork and correspondence for you.
>
> I am looking forward to speaking with you and hope to help you on your way to living completely income tax and debt free. You will find beyond a doubt that PQI's education services will elevate you above the vast majority of Americans in knowledge and financial freedoms. You will have many advantages and opportunities that most Americans will never know about.
>
> I look forward to speaking to you soon, prosperously yours, Mark Leitner.

Id. at 933–34. Leitner's conviction, too, was affirmed on appeal.

(3) The book *Final Exit* written by Derek Humphrey, a former president of the Hemlock Society, asserts the right of terminally ill patients to commit suicide. The book sold many copies and has been referred to as a "suicide manual." One of the

methods recommended in the book for terminally ill individuals who wish to end their lives is asphyxiation, "self-deliverance via the plastic bag." According to one report, in the year after the book's publication in March 1991, the number of suicides by asphyxiation rose to 33 in New York City, compared to eight in the year before the manual came out. While no direct evidence showed a clear link between the manual and the deaths, the New York medical examiner's office found in nine cases the book was at the scene of the suicide. Did the author and publisher of "Final Exit" subject themselves to criminal liability by publishing the book?

"Compassion" is a non-profit organization created to "support the right of terminally ill patients to choose to die without pain, without suffering, and with personal assistance." As stated in the organization's newsletter: "Compassion does not promote suicide. We see hastening death as a last resort when all other possibilities have been exhausted and where further suffering is intolerable. Compassion provides information and counseling during the period of decision-making, and emotional support and personal presence for patients who chose to hasten death. We do not administer lethal injections or 'kill' anyone." By providing counseling to individuals who later kill themselves, does Compassion commit any crimes? For a discussion of the legal issues involved with physician assisted suicides, see § 5.05[A], *infra*.

[3] Facilitation

The following case is a famous and important one for it explores criminal responsibility for the actions of others. It is not, however, the typical fact pattern involving a defendant assisting others in committing crimes against third parties. Consider the various ways the prosecution here could have gone forward on a theory of liability.

Commonwealth v. Feinberg

Supreme Court of Pennsylvania
253 A.2d 636 (1969)

Jones, Justice.

Appellant Max Feinberg owned and operated a cigar store in the skid row section of Philadelphia. One of the products he sold was Sterno, a jelly-like substance composed primarily of methanol and ethanol and designed for cooking and heating purposes. Sterno was manufactured and sold in two types of containers, one for home use and one for industrial use. Before September, 1963, both types of Sterno contained approximately 3.75% methanol, or wood alcohol, and 71% ethanol, or grain alcohol; of the two types of alcohols, methanol is far more toxic if consumed internally. Beginning in September of 1963, the Sterno company began manufacturing a new type of industrial Sterno which was 54% methanol. The cans containing the new industrial Sterno were identical to the cans containing the old industrial Sterno except in one crucial aspect: on the lids of the new 54% methanol Sterno were imprinted the words "Institutional Sterno. Danger. Poison. For use only as a Fuel. Not for consumer use. For industrial and commercial use. Not for home use." A skull and crossbones were also lithographed on the lid. The carton in which the new Sterno cans were packaged and shipped did not indicate that the contents differed in any respect from the old industrial Sterno.

According to its records, Sterno Corporation sent only one shipment of the new Sterno to the Philadelphia area; that shipment went to the Richter Paper Company and was received on December 17, 1963. Charles Richter, president of the firm, testified that his company, in turn, made only one sale of the new industrial Sterno, and that was to appellant. Richter testified that his records indicated that appellant received the Sterno on December 21 and, since Richter had not opened any of the cartons, he was unaware that he was selling appellant a new type of industrial Sterno. On December 27, Richter received a call from appellant informing him that the cartons contained a new type of Sterno and that appellant wished to return the portion of his order that he had not sold. The unused cartons were picked up by Richter's deliveryman the next day.

Meanwhile, between December 21 and December 28, appellant had sold approximately 400 cans of the new industrial Sterno. Between December 23 and December 30, thirty-one persons died in the skid-row area as a result of methanol poisoning. In many of the cases the source of the methanol was traced to the new industrial Sterno. Since appellant was the only retail outlet of this type of Sterno in Philadelphia, he was arrested and indicted on thirty-one counts charging involuntary manslaughter.

Appellant was convicted on seventeen counts of involuntary manslaughter.

The second issue in this case is whether appellant is guilty of involuntary manslaughter in each or any of the four appeals presently before us. The Penal Code defines involuntary manslaughter as a death "happening in consequence of an unlawful act, or the doing of a lawful act in an unlawful way...." When a death results from the doing of an act lawful in itself but done in an unlawful manner, in order to sustain a conviction for manslaughter the Commonwealth must present evidence to prove that the defendant acted in a rash or reckless manner. The conduct of the defendant resulting in the death must be such a departure from the behavior of an ordinary and prudent man as to evidence a disregard of human life or an indifference to the consequences. Furthermore, there must be a direct causal relationship between the defendant's act and the deceased's death.

We conclude that the Commonwealth has made out all the elements necessary to warrant a conviction for involuntary manslaughter. First, the record establishes that appellant sold the Sterno with the knowledge that at least some of his customers would extract the alcohol for drinking purposes. Witnesses for the Commonwealth testified that when they purchased the Sterno from appellant, they would merely say "make one" or hold up fingers to indicate how many cans they wanted; one witness testified that appellant referred to the Sterno as shoe polish and on one occasion shouted to him on the street asking how he and his wife were making out with their shoe polish; finally, the witnesses testified that appellant asked them to conceal the Sterno under their coats when leaving his store. Such conduct does not square with the conclusion that appellant was merely selling the Sterno for cooking and heating purposes. Second, appellant was aware, or should have been aware, that the Sterno he was selling was toxic if consumed. The new industrial Sterno was clearly marked as being poisonous. Even the regular Sterno is marked "Caution. Flammable. For Use only as a Fuel" and if consumed internally may have serious consequences. Furthermore, when appellant was informed about the first deaths from methanol poisoning, he told the boy who worked in his shop to tell any police who came around that there was no Sterno in the store. Appellant also told the police that he had never purchased any Sterno from the Richter Paper Company. This evidence indicates to us that appellant was aware that he was selling the Sterno for an illicit purpose.

Comments and Questions

(1) Could the manufacturer also have been found guilty of manslaughter? If the manufacturer had knowledge of Feinberg's activities, could the manufacturer have been convicted of aiding and abetting Feinberg's illegal acts? Could the wholesaler, Richter? Should the manufacturer, Richter, and Feinberg be treated differently?

> [T]hose who make a profit by furnishing to criminals, whether by sale or otherwise, the means to carry on their nefarious undertakings aid them just as truly as if they were actual partners with them, having a stake in the fruits of their enterprise. To say that the sale of goods is a normally lawful transaction is beside the point. The seller may not ignore the purpose for which the purchase is made if he is advised of that purpose, or wash his hands of the aid that he has given the perpetrator of a felony by the plea that he has merely made a sale of merchandise. One who sells a gun to another knowing that he is buying it to commit a murder, would hardly escape conviction as an accessory to the murder by showing that he received full price for the gun; and no difference in principle can be drawn between such a case and any other case of a seller who knows that the purchaser intends to use the goods which he is purchasing in the commission of felony. In any such case, not only does the act of the seller assist in the commission of the felony, but his will assents to its commission, since he could refuse to give the assistance by refusing to make the sale.

Backun v. United States, 112 F.2d 635, 637 (4th Cir. 1940). Under *Backun* would the owner of a pawn shop be convicted of a homicide offense if a licensed handgun he lawfully sold was fatally used in a holdup? Was used in a suicide?

(2) In *Regina v. Thomas*, 2 All ER 181 (1957), the defendant had rented an apartment to a prostitute. "He knew she was a prostitute, and knew that her purpose in securing the use of this room was to bring her clients there, and I think it is probably almost certain that he knew that she did a very satisfactory trade in this room." Was the defendant guilty of aiding and abetting the prostitute? Would it matter how much rent the defendant received for the room? In *Thomas* the rent was at "a grossly inflated rate." Would the prostitute's doctor also be guilty if he charged her more than the usual rate for her visits?

(3) Numerous statutory efforts have been made to deal with what is commonly known as criminal facilitation.

> A person is guilty of criminal facilitation ... when, believing it probable that he is rendering aid ... to a person who intends to commit a crime, he engages in conduct which provides such person with means or opportunity for the commission thereof and which in fact aids such person to commit a felony.

§ 115.00 of the New York Penal Law.

In *United States v. Zafiro*, 945 F.2d 881, 887 (7th Cir. 1991), *aff'd*, 506 U.S. 534 (1993), the court discussed the aiding and abetting issue as it relates to criminal facilitation, assisting in an otherwise lawful way the ultimate commission of crimes against others.

> To be proved guilty of aiding and abetting, still another element must be established: that the defendant desired the illegal activity to succeed. The purpose of this requirement is a little mysterious but we think it is to identify, and confine punishment to, those forms of assistance the prevention of which makes it more difficult to carry on the illegal activity assisted. A clerk in a clothing store who sells a dress to a prostitute knowing that she will be using it in plying her trade is not guilty of aiding and abetting. The sale makes no difference to her illegal activity. If the clerk didn't make the sale, she would buy, at some trivial added expense of time and money, an equivalent outfit from someone ignorant of her trade. That is where the requirement of proving the defendant's desire to make the illegal activities succeed cuts off liability. The boost of prostitution brought about by selling a prostitute a dress is too trivial to support an inference that the clerk actually wants to help the prostitute succeed in her illegal activity. If on the other hand he knowingly provides essential assistance, we can infer that he does want her to succeed for that is the natural consequence of his deliberate act.

With the traditional aiding and abetting analysis, is the court correct that the clerk could not be found guilty by providing such assistance? Will the result change under the criminal facilitation statute? Should it?

[C] The Scope of Responsibility

People v. Poplar

Court of Appeals of Michigan
173 N.W.2d 732 (1969)

J. H. Gillis, Presiding Judge.

Defendant was charged, as an aider and abettor, of breaking and entering, and of assault with intent to commit murder. Defendant was found guilty on both counts by a jury.

The breaking and entering was of the Oak Park recreation building in Flint and was carried out in the early morning of December 3, 1964, by Alfred Williams and

Clifford Lorrick. When the manager of the building discovered the two men, Williams shot him in the face with a shotgun. Defendant allegedly acted as a lookout.

Williams was tried as a codefendant and was convicted, along with this defendant, of breaking and entering and of assault with intent to commit murder.

Lorrick pled guilty to breaking and entering on January 25, 1965, and testified for the prosecution at defendant's trial. He stated that he met defendant and Williams in a bar the night before the breaking and entering and left with them and two others. The five men allegedly drove around for a while before stopping to pick up some tools. They then took the tools and placed them in back of the bowling alley. An unsuccessful attempt to enter was made at that time. The group continued to drive around and during that time a shotgun that was in the car accidentally discharged, blowing a hole in the windshield. Just before the actual breaking and entering, the defendant, after getting out of the car with Lorrick and Williams, proceeded to a house directly across from the bowling alley. Lorrick testified that defendant went to see if anybody was watching.

Defendant took the stand and testified that he was in no way involved in the plans of Lorrick and Williams. He stated that the purpose of his going to the house across the street was to seek a friend who he thought would help him find employment.

Since the jury found that defendant acted as a lookout, a more difficult question is whether defendant may be found guilty, as an aider and abettor, of assault with intent to commit murder.

"Where a crime requires the existence of a specific intent, an alleged aider and abettor cannot be held as a principal unless he himself possessed the required intent or unless he aided and abetted in the perpetration of the crime knowing that the actual perpetrator had the required intent."

"But it is the knowledge of the wrongful purpose of the actor plus the encouragement provided by the aider and abettor that makes the latter equally guilty. Although the guilt of the aider and abettor is dependent upon the actor's crime, the criminal intent of the aider and abettor is presumed from his actions with knowledge of the actor's wrongful purpose." ...

There was no evidence that defendant harbored any intent to commit murder. Therefore, "knowledge of the intent of Hill [Williams] to kill the deceased is a necessary element to constitute him [defendant] a principal. This, however, may be established either by direct or circumstantial evidence from which knowledge of the intent may be inferred."

A typical case of this kind is one where, as here, a crime not specifically within the common intent and purpose is committed during an escape. Convictions for aiding and abetting such crimes have been carefully scrutinized.

> *There can be no criminal responsibility for any thing not fairly within the common enterprise, and which might be expected to happen if occasion should arise for any one to do it.* In other words, the principle is quite analogous to that of agency, where the liability is measured by the express or implied

> authority. And the authorities are quite clear, and reasonable, which deny any liability for acts done in escaping, which were not within any joint purpose or combination.

Whether the crime committed was fairly within the scope of the common unlawful enterprise is a question of fact for the jury. In the present case, the evidence tends to show that the gun with which the victim was shot was removed from the trunk of the car to the front seat. It is not clear whether the defendant was present when the gun was moved but he was aware of its presence inside the car. Since the record also fails to reveal whether or not defendant knew that the gun was taken into the bowling alley, the question is whether it was proper for the jury to infer from the circumstantial evidence that the defendant entertained the requisite intent to render him liable as a principal for assault with intent to commit murder.

In our opinion the jury could reasonably infer from the defendant's knowledge of the fact that a shotgun was in the car that he was aware of the fact that his companions might use the gun if they were discovered committing the burglary or in making their escape. If the jury drew that inference, then it could properly conclude that the use of the gun was fairly within the scope of the common unlawful enterprise and that the defendant was criminally responsible for the use by his confederates of the gun in effectuating their escape.

Affirmed.

Comments and Questions

(1) What is the standard required to convict an accomplice of a particular crime? Must the prosecution show that the accomplice *intended* that the crime take place? *Knew* that it would take place? Or simply, that the crime was *reasonably foreseeable*? Does it matter? Which standard did the court in *Poplar* apply? *See* Minn. Stat. Ann §609.05:

> 1. A person is criminally liable for a crime committed by another if the person intentionally aids, advises, hires, counsels, or conspires with or otherwise procures the other to commit the crime.
>
> 2. A person liable under subdivision 1 is also liable for any other crime committed in pursuance of the intended crime if reasonably foreseeable by the person as a probable consequence of committing or attempting to commit the crime intended.

(2) Suppose the defendant hired an arsonist to burn down an expensive jewelry store. Suppose also, that the defendant knew the arsonist had previously been convicted of various theft offenses. If the arsonist burned the building down, and also stole jewelry, of what could the defendant be convicted? Would it matter if theft was ever discussed? Would it depend on what was said about theft?

(3) How can the government prove that an individual aided and abetted by being a "lookout" as opposed to simply being present at the scene? In *State v. Hoselton*, 371 S.E.2d 366 (W. Va. 1988), the court stated that a lookout is one who is "by prearrange-

ment, keeping watch to avoid interception or detection or to provide warning during the perpetration of the crimes.... The only evidence that suggested [the defendant] was a lookout was his response to the investigating officer's questioning: '[Question] Were you keeping a lookout? [Answer] You could say that. I just didn't want to go down in there.'" Such evidence appeared strong, but the testimony also showed that the defendant had no prior knowledge of his friends' intentions to steal, when he saw what his friends were doing he left the area and returned to his car, and he never received any of the stolen property unlike the other participants in the crime. Held, the state did not prove the accused was a lookout. "[T]he accused's response that 'you could say' he was a lookout, standing completely alone, does not establish that the accused was an aider and abettor by participating in, and wishing to bring about the entering with intent to commit larceny."

(4) The defendant in *People v. Chiu*, 325 P. 3d 972 (Cal. 2014) was convicted of first degree murder [premeditated killing, under California law] as an accomplice. The jury was instructed that he could be so held if either he aided the actual killers with intent, or if the premeditated killing was "a natural and probable consequence" of the premeditated killing. The state supreme court reversed the conviction, finding that an accomplice "may not be convicted of first degree premeditated murder under the natural and probable consequences doctrine. Rather, his or her liability for that crime must be based on direct aiding and abetting principles." *Id.* at 974. The majority explained its rationale.

> In the context of murder, the natural and probable consequences doctrine serves the legitimate public policy concern of deterring aiders and abettors from aiding or encouraging the commission of offenses that would naturally, probably, and foreseeably result in an unlawful killing. A primary rationale for punishing such aiders and abettors—to deter them from aiding or encouraging the commission of offenses—is served by holding them culpable for the perpetrator's commission of the nontarget offense of second degree murder....
>
> However, this same public policy concern loses its force in the context of a defendant's liability as an aider and abettor of a first degree premeditated murder. First degree murder, like second degree murder, is the unlawful killing of a human being with malice aforethought, but has the additional elements of willfulness, premeditation, and deliberation which trigger a heightened penalty. That mental state is uniquely subjective and personal. It requires more than a showing of intent to kill; the killer must act deliberately, carefully weighing the considerations for and against a choice to kill before he or she completes the acts that caused the death.

Id. at 979. The dissent was not persuaded.

> [T]he majority's reasoning proves too much. It precludes not only a first degree murder conviction based on the natural and probable consequences rule, but also a second degree murder conviction based on that rule. Yet the majority insists that holding defendants liable for second degree murder

> under the natural and probable consequences rule "serves the legitimate public policy concern of deterring aiders and abettors from aiding or encouraging the commission of offenses that would naturally, probably, and foreseeably result in an unlawful killing." Why is the mental state of malice foreseeable, but not the mental state of premeditation? The majority does not say. And why are the deterrent purposes of the natural and probable consequences rule served by applying it to second degree murder, but not to first degree.

Id. at 985. Are you persuaded by the majority?

[D] No Criminal Responsibility

[1] Withdrawal

State v. Formella

Supreme Court of New Hampshire
960 A.2d 722 (2008)

GALWAY, JUSTICE.

The defendant, Paul Formella, appeals his conviction ... for criminal liability for the conduct of another. See RSA 626:8 (2007). We affirm.

The relevant facts are not in dispute. On the afternoon of Wednesday, June 13, 2007, the defendant, then a junior at Hanover High School, and two friends, were studying at the Howe Library near the school. Wednesdays were typically early release days at the school, and students had been dismissed at 2:00 p.m. After studying for approximately two hours, the defendant and his friends returned to the school to retrieve some books from their second-floor lockers. Upon entering the school, they encountered another group of students who said they intended to steal mathematics exams from the third floor. The defendant and his companions were asked to serve as lookouts during the theft, which they agreed to do. They were instructed to yell something like "did you get your math book?" up to the third floor as a code to alert the thieves if someone was coming.

The defendant and his friends then proceeded to their second-floor lockers. The defendant testified that on their way to their lockers they looked around to "confirm or dispel" whether anyone was there. Once the defendant and his friends had retrieved their books, they "were all feeling like this was the wrong thing to do," and decided to head back down to the first floor to wait for the other group. On their way down the stairs, they encountered some janitors who told them that they ought to leave the school. The defendant and his friends left the school building, but waited in the parking lot for approximately five to ten minutes for the other group. Eventually, the other students exited the school with the stolen examinations and all of the students shared the exam questions.

The next week, someone informed the dean of students that some students had stolen the exams. The police were called, and in connection with their investigation they interviewed the defendant, who admitted his involvement in the theft. He was later charged with criminal liability for conduct of another. See RSA 626:8. Following his conviction, the defendant appealed to this court....

Before addressing the defendant's specific arguments, we must construe RSA 626:8. In matters of statutory interpretation, we are the final arbiters of the legislature's intent as expressed in the words of the statute considered as a whole. When examining the language of the statute, we ascribe the plain and ordinary meaning to the words used. We construe provisions of the Criminal Code according to the fair import of their terms and to promote justice. In doing so, we must first look to the plain language of the statute to determine legislative intent. Absent an ambiguity we will not look beyond the language of the statute to discern legislative intent.

RSA 626:8 provides, in relevant part, that an individual is criminally liable for the conduct of another when he acts as an accomplice in the commission of an offense. A person is an accomplice when with the purpose of promoting or facilitating the commission of an offense, he aids or agrees or attempts to aid another person in planning or committing the offense. RSA 626:8 further provides, however, that a person is not an accomplice if he "terminates his complicity prior to the commission of the offense and wholly deprives it of effectiveness in the commission of the offense or gives timely warning to the law enforcement authorities or otherwise makes proper effort to prevent the commission of the offense."

The defendant does not dispute that he became an accomplice in the first instance when he agreed to act as a lookout. Accordingly, we are concerned only with whether the defendant's later acts terminated his liability as an accomplice. We note that the defendant does not contend that he gave timely warning to law enforcement or otherwise made "proper effort" to prevent the offense. Thus, under RSA 626:8, VI(c) the defendant was not an accomplice if: (1) he terminated his complicity in the crime; (2) his termination occurred prior to the commission of the offense; and (3) he wholly deprived his complicity of effectiveness in the commission of the offense.

We conclude that the statute is ambiguous. As regards the third factor, for example, the statute does not define what is required for a person to "wholly deprive" his complicity of effectiveness in the commission of an offense. According to the State, an overt act aimed at undermining the prior complicity is required, while the defendant argues that, at least in this case, no such act is necessary. As the statute does not clarify whether such an act is necessary, we conclude that it is ambiguous, and we look to other sources to determine legislative intent.

RSA 626:8, like much of our criminal law, is based upon the Model Penal Code. Accordingly, we look to the Model Penal Code and its commentaries for guidance. Comment 9(c) to section 2.06 ... notes that the actions sufficient to deprive the prior complicity of effectiveness vary with the type of accessorial behavior. Relevant to the analysis here, the comment states that if "complicity inhered in request or encour-

agement, countermanding disapproval may suffice to nullify its influence, providing it is heard in time to allow reconsideration by those planning to commit the crime." The comments thus indicate that in order to deprive the prior complicity of effectiveness, one who has encouraged the commission of an offense may avoid liability by terminating his or her role in the commission of the crime and by making his or her disapproval known to the principals sufficiently in advance of the commission of the crime to allow them time to reconsider as well.

While there appears to be a paucity of authority on the issue, the view that an accomplice must make some affirmative act, such as an overt expression of disapproval to the principals, accords with that of other jurisdictions with statutes mirroring the provisions of the Model Penal Code. Additionally, the relevant authorities weigh in favor of requiring any withdrawal to be communicated far enough in advance to allow the others involved in the crime to follow suit.... "A mere change of heart, flight from the crime scene, apprehension by the police, or an uncommunicated decision not to carry out his part of the scheme will not suffice." This is not to say that the terminating accomplice must actually prevent the crime from occurring. Instead, he need only make some act demonstrating to the principals of the crime that he has withdrawn, and he must do so in a manner, and at such a time, that the principals could do likewise. We agree with the rationale of these authorities....

The relevant portion of the statute is phrased in the conjunctive. For a person not to be an accomplice he must terminate his complicity prior to the commission of the offense and wholly deprive that complicity of its effectiveness. Even assuming the defendant terminated his complicity prior to the commission of the offense, he did not wholly deprive his complicity of its effectiveness.

As stated above, to extricate himself from accomplice liability, the defendant needed to make an affirmative act, such as communicating his withdrawal to the principals. Here, the defendant made no such act. The defendant testified that he and his companions simply left the scene. He did not communicate his withdrawal, discourage the principals from acting, inform the custodians, or do any other thing which would deprive his complicity of effectiveness. In fact, the principals remained unaware of his exit. Thus, the defendant did not do that which was necessary to undo his complicity.

The defendant contends that because he had been acting as a lookout, leaving the scene so as to no longer be "looking out" deprived his complicity of its effectiveness, and, therefore, findings regarding the timing of the offense were required. We disagree. While at the point he left the scene he was no longer an effective lookout, the defendant did nothing to counter his prior complicity. According to the defendant, the principals had requested aid in committing the offense, he agreed to provide it, and he agreed to warn the principals if anyone approached, thus encouraging the act. Further, upon reaching the second floor the defendant looked around to "confirm or dispel" whether anyone was around who might have apprehended the thieves or otherwise spoiled the crime. Thus, it was the complicity of agreeing to aid the primary actors and then actually aiding them that needed to be undone; silently withdrawing from the scene did not, in any way, undermine the encouragement the defendant had provided....

Affirmed.

DALIANIS, JUSTICE, concurring specially.

... As the defendant concedes, he became an accomplice when he agreed to act as a lookout. He argues that the evidence compelled a finding that nonetheless he was immune from liability because he "terminate[d] his complicity prior to the commission of the offense and wholly deprive[d] it of effectiveness in the commission of the offense" when he left his lookout position. The State counters that merely abandoning his lookout post was insufficient to terminate his complicity. The State argues that to terminate his complicity, the defendant had to "make some effort to actually prevent the crime from occurring," which he did not do....

[F]or termination to be effective, it must, at a minimum, be communicated to the principal....

[T]he defendant did not terminate his complicity when he abandoned his lookout post. To terminate his complicity, the defendant had to wholly deprive his earlier aid to the principals of its effectiveness. His earlier assistance enabled the principals to commit the offense without fear of being caught. By merely abandoning his post as a lookout, the defendant did nothing to deprive his earlier assistance of its effectiveness. For all the principals knew, he was still acting as a lookout and they could continue committing the offense without fear of being caught. When he left his post, the defendant did nothing to dispel this belief. Had he done something to dispel this belief, such as announcing to the principals that he was leaving his post, the principals could have had an opportunity to reconsider their actions. Without at least informing them that he was leaving, the defendant did not wholly deprive his earlier assistance to the principals of its effectiveness.

Accordingly, I agree with the majority that the defendant's conviction for criminal liability for the conduct of another must be affirmed.

Comments and Questions

(1) Was the evidence—even with the defendant's own admission—sufficient to convict him? Assuming that it was, why was his withdrawal defense rejected? Was it because it was not timely? Not announced? Did not "neutralize the effects of his previous support"? If the last, what should the defendant have done to effectuate a lawful withdrawal? Simply tell the other students?

(2) A number of states use the withdrawal defense, but not looking to statutory authority. *See, e.g., State v. Thomas*, 356 A.2d 433 (N.J. Super. Ct. 1976), *rev'd on other grounds*, 387 A.2d 1187 (N.J. 1978). Others have adopted the withdrawal, or renunciation, principle in statutory form. In some, one additional element is present. *See, e.g.*, N.Y. Penal Law § 40.10:

> 1. In any prosecution for an offense, other than an attempt to commit a crime, in which the defendant's guilt depends upon his criminal liability for the conduct of another person pursuant to section 20.00, it is an affirmative defense that, under circumstances manifesting a voluntary and complete re-

> nunciation of his criminal purpose, the defendant withdrew from participation in such offense prior to the commission thereof and made a substantial effort to prevent the commission thereof.

Under this statute, would Formella's conviction be reversed had he told his friends he was leaving? The New York statute later defines "voluntary and complete renunciation."

> 5. A renunciation is not "voluntary and complete" within the meaning of this section if it is motivated in whole or in part by (a) a belief that circumstances exist which increase the probability of detection or apprehension of the defendant or another participant in the criminal enterprise, or which render more difficult the accomplishment of the criminal purpose, or (b) a decision to postpone the criminal conduct until another time or to transfer the criminal effort to another victim or another but similar objective.

What is the purpose of such a requirement? *See People v. Bauer*, 350 N.Y.S.2d 745, 746–47 (App. Div. 1974): "[There is no defense if] he was motivated by the suspicion that the authorities had been alerted and that he was in imminent danger of apprehension if he pursued the matter. There is no effective renunciation where it is prompted by fear of detection or arrest."

[2] Exceptions

Regina v. Tyrell

Court for Crown Cases Reserved
17 Cox Crim. Cas. 716 (1893)

The evidence for the prosecution proved conclusively that the defendant, who was under the age of sixteen, aided and abetted and solicited and incited Thomas Froud to have unlawful carnal connection with her, and the defendant was accordingly convicted.

I reserved, at the request of defendant's counsel, for the opinion of this Court the question,

Whether it is an offence for a girl between thirteen and sixteen years of age, to aid and abet a male person in the commission of the misdemeanour of having unlawful carnal connection with her, and to solicit and incite a male person to commit that misdemeanour.

By sec. 5 of the Criminal Law Amendment Act, 1885 (48 & 49 Vict. c. 69), it is enacted (*inter alia*) that:

> A person who unlawfully and carnally knows, or attempts to have unlawful carnal knowledge of any girl being of or above the age of thirteen years, and under the age of sixteen years ... shall be guilty of a misdemeanour.

Clarke Hall (with him *Campbell*), on behalf of the prisoner.

One of the consequences of upholding the conviction would be, that a girl who had been seduced could be convicted of aiding or abetting, or soliciting or procuring her seduction. The sole object of the enactment was to prevent its being considered that a girl of immature mind had consented to the act committed upon her. The 4th section shows that, if the contention of the prosecution were to be held to be correct the prisoner, had she been under the age of thirteen years, would have been liable to penal servitude for life. Were the construction put upon the Act which the prosecution sought to place upon it, it would be rendered practically inoperative, as it was not likely that parents would allow their children to run the risk of prosecution by giving information of offences committed upon them. Lastly, the Act having been passed expressly to prevent its being said when prosecuting the man that a girl under the age of sixteen could consent, it could not be construed as meaning that she could be considered to have consented for the purpose of herself being prosecuted.

Dutton, in support of the conviction, submitted that there was nothing in the Act to prevent a girl being convicted of the offence with which she was charged; and that the jury having found upon the clearest evidence that she did incite the boy to commit the act, the conviction should stand.

LORD COLERIDGE, C.J.—I believe that I am expressing the opinion of my learned brothers when I say that this conviction must be quashed. This Act of Parliament was passed, and enacted after a great deal of disputing and fighting in the House of Commons, and a great deal of controversy took place as to the point at which the age of consent was to be fixed. It ended in a compromise; and it is not for us to dispute whether it was wisely or unwisely fixed at the age of sixteen. What was intended by the Legislature was to protect girls against themselves, and it cannot be said that an Act which says nothing at all about the girl inciting or anything of that kind, and the whole object of which is to protect women against men, is to be construed so as to render a girl against whom an offence is committed equally liable with the man by whom the offence is committed. In my opinion this conviction cannot be sustained, and must therefore be quashed.

MATHEW, J.—I am of the same opinion. I fail to see how this argument on the construction of the statute can be supported. The consequences of upholding this conviction would, as has been pointed out in the course of the argument, be most serious, there being scarcely a section in the Act which would not, upon the construction sought to be put upon the Act, support a criminal prosecution against a girl. There is no trace anywhere in the Act of any intention on the part of the Legislature to deal with the woman as a criminal, and I am of opinion that the Act does not create the offence alleged in the indictment.

Conviction quashed.

Comments and Questions

(1) In *Gebardi v. United States*, 287 U.S. 112, 53 S. Ct. 35, 77 L. Ed. 206 (1932), the Supreme Court unanimously concluded that the Mann Act (transporting a woman in interstate commerce "for the purpose of prostitution or debauchery or for any other immoral purpose") could not be construed to allow the woman who willingly crossed state boundaries to be convicted under an aiding and abetting theory.

(2) In *State v. Bearcub*, 465 P.2d 252 (Or. Ct. App. 1970), the defendants were jointly indicted, before their marriage, under Or. Rev. Stat. §418.140, which provided:

> (1) No male person over the age of 18 years ... shall habitually accept subsistence or lodging in the dwelling place of any female householder, who is the recipient of aid....

The female defendant contended that only a male could be prosecuted under the statute. The government claimed that a female could be guilty of the crime by aiding and abetting the male who violated the statute. The defendant's demurrer to the charge was sustained by the trial judge. What result on appeal? See also *United States v. Farrar*, 281 U.S. 624 (1930), dealing with a provision of the National Prohibition Act:

> Since long before the adoption of the Eighteenth Amendment it has been held with practical unanimity that, in the absence of an express statutory provision to the contrary, the purchaser of intoxicating liquor, the sale of which was prohibited, was guilty of no offense. And statutes to the contrary have been the rare exception. Probably it was thought more important to preserve the complete freedom of the purchaser to testify against the seller than to punish him for making the purchase. However that may be, it is fair to assume that Congress, when it came to pass the Prohibition Act, knew this history and, acting in the light of it, deliberately and designedly omitted to impose upon the purchaser of liquor for beverage purposes any criminal liability. If aid were needed to support this view of the matter, it would be found in the fact, conceded by the government's brief, that during the entire life of the National Prohibition Act, a period of ten years, the executive departments charged with the administration and enforcement of the act have uniformly construed it as not including the purchaser in a case like the present; no prosecution until the present one has ever been undertaken upon a different theory; and Congress, of course well aware of this construction and practice, has significantly left the law in its original form. It follows that, since the indictment charges no offense, it was properly quashed.

[E] After the Fact Assistance

As indicated earlier, the person who knowingly aided a felon to escape was, at common law, considered an accessory after the fact. The modern statutes attempt to spell out in detail the nature of this offense.

New York Penal Law §205.50 Hindering prosecution; definition of term

> [A] person "renders criminal assistance" when, with intent to prevent, hinder or delay the discovery or apprehension of, or the lodging of a criminal charge against, a person who he knows or believes has committed a crime or is being sought by law enforcement officials for the commission of a crime, or with intent to assist a person in profiting or benefitting from the commission of a crime, he:

1. Harbors or conceals such person; or

2. Warns such person of impending discovery or apprehension; or

3. Provides such person with money, transportation, weapon, disguise or other means of avoiding discovery or apprehension; or

4. Prevents or obstructs, by means of force, intimidation or deception, anyone from performing an act which might aid in the discovery or apprehension of such person or in the lodging of a criminal charge against him; or

5. Suppresses, by any act of concealment, alteration or destruction, any physical evidence which might aid in the discovery or apprehension of such person or in the lodging of a criminal charge against him; or

6. Aids such person to protect or expeditiously profit from an advantage derived from such crime.

As stated in *United States v. De La Rosa*, 171 F.3d 215, 221 (5th Cir. 1999):

> [To convict an accused as] an accessory after the fact the government must prove: (1) the commission of an underlying offense against the United States; (2) the defendant's knowledge of that offense; and (3) assistance by the defendant in order to prevent the apprehension, trial, or punishment of the offender.

People v. Duty

California Court of Appeal

269 Cal. App. 2d 97, 74 Cal. Rptr. 606 (1969)

FRIEDMAN, ASSOCIATE JUSTICE.

After Barbara Jenner had been convicted of arson in wilfully setting fire to her home, a jury found defendant Earl Duty guilty as an accessory to Mrs. Jenner's crime. He appeals from the judgment.

Penal Code, section 32 defines an "accessory" as follows: "Every person who, after a felony has been committed, harbors, conceals or aids a principal in such felony, with the intent that said principal may avoid or escape from arrest, trial, conviction or punishment, having knowledge that said principal has committed such felony or has been charged with such felony or convicted thereof, is an accessory to such felony."

The constituent elements of the accessory offense have been summarized as follows: "The crime of being an accessory is a complex one, being composed of the following elements, each of which must be alleged and proved by the prosecution: (1) someone other than the accused, the principal to the crime, must have committed a specific, completed felony; (2) the accused must have harbored, concealed or aided the principal; (3) the element of *scienter* must be present in this, that the accused must have had knowledge that the principal has committed a felony, or has been charged or convicted thereof; (4) the element of specific intent must have been present, namely, that the accused must have harbored, concealed or aided with the intent that the principal may avoid or escape from arrest, trial, conviction or punishment."

Defendant charges absence of proof of *scienter* and specific intent. The test on appeal is whether there is substantial evidence, including inferences reasonably deduced from facts in evidence, to support the findings of guilt. State of mind, such as *scienter* or specific intent, is a question of fact, and if the evidence reasonably justifies the fact finder's inference that the state of mind existed, the finding will not be disturbed on appeal.

Mrs. Jenner's home in the city of Oroville was seriously damaged by a fire during the early morning hours of January 22, 1967. Uncontradicted evidence pointed to a fire which had been deliberately set. At approximately 2:45 a.m., before the fire's outbreak, George Kelly, a neighbor, noticed Mrs. Jenner's car parked in her driveway. Somewhat later, at 3:25 a.m., Officer Gerald Bryson noticed a car parked outside the Table Mountain Tavern. He looked it over, identified it as the car belonging to Mrs. Jenner and saw a table television set, blankets and household items in the back seat. The record does not indicate the distance between the Table Mountain Tavern and Mrs. Jenner's home. It does show that after Officer Bryson observed Mrs. Jenner's car, he drove away from the tavern, noticed a glow in the sky, drove toward it and found Mrs. Jenner's house in flames. Fire equipment arrived about five minutes later. A city fire marshal, Harold Ogle, also arrived. Bryson and Ogle conferred briefly. Ogle then left the fire scene and drove to the Table Mountain Tavern, where Bryson had seen Mrs. Jenner's car. He arrived there at about 3:45 a.m. Mrs. Jenner's automobile was no longer there.

Ogle testified that he had arrived at the fire at 3:35 a.m. In his opinion the fire had commenced approximately 15 minutes earlier.

The day after the fire Ogle interviewed Mrs. Jenner, who told him that she had been with defendant the previous night. Three days later, on January 25, Ogle called on defendant in company with William Hull, an insurance investigator. They told defendant they were investigating an "arson fire" at Mrs. Jenner's house. At their request, defendant gave them an oral statement describing his and Mrs. Jenner's activities on the night of the fire. Defendant had come to Mrs. Jenner's house that evening. They then drove to the Oroville Inn, defendant in his car and Mrs. Jenner in her own, arriving there about 8:30 p.m. Both parked outside the Inn. About 9 o'clock they left the Oroville Inn in defendant's car, leaving Mrs. Jenner's car where she had parked it earlier. They drove together to the Moose Lodge in Gridley, where defendant, a musician, was playing for a party, arriving there about 9:30 p.m. About 2:15 a.m. defendant and another musician took their musical equipment out to the former's car and found Mrs. Jenner asleep in the front seat. According to defendant's statement to the investigators, he then drove with Mrs. Jenner to San Francisco, registered at a motel, stayed there less than an hour, left about 6:30 or 7 a.m. and drove back to Oroville, arriving there at 10 or 10:30 a.m., found Mrs. Jenner's car parked in front of the Oroville Inn where they had left it the preceding evening.

Mrs. Jenner was called by the prosecution. She testified that she and defendant had left her car at the Oroville Inn and had driven to the Gridley Moose Lodge in his car, arriving there about 9:30 p.m. She drank liquor at the Moose Lodge and went outside to defendant's car, where she "passed out." Later she was conscious of being bumped in the head as defendant and a companion were loading equipment in the car. She went back to sleep and did not resume consciousness until about 11 o'clock in the morning. At that time, she testified, she and defendant were parked beside a highway. They drove to Oroville, where she picked up her car outside the Oroville Inn. She admitted that she had been convicted of the arson.

Defendant testified in his own defense. His description of the events on the night of the fire roughly paralleled Mrs. Jenner's testimony.

From the prosecution evidence the jury could reasonably infer that defendant and Mrs. Jenner had been together during the entire night; that Mrs. Jenner had left the Moose Lodge in Gridley with defendant about 2:15 a.m., picked up her car at the Oroville Inn, drove to her house, loaded the car with household goods, set the fire about 3:20 a.m. and drove away; that defendant had been with her during these activities. From this set of inferences several alternative corollaries were available: (a) Defendant actively aided and abetted the arson, incurring liability as a principal in the crime under Penal Code, section 31. (b) He aided and concealed Mrs. Jenner by assisting her to remove her household goods from the scene, incurring liability as an accessory under section 32. (c) He was nothing but a bystander, one who had an opportunity to act but did not. Evidentiary justification for one or another of these conclusions is not a problem, for the evidence goes farther. Suffice it to say that the prosecution evidence at this point supports a finding of the first element of the accessory offense, the principal's commission of a specific felony, arson.

The additional evidence is defendant's inferably false statement to Ogle, a public investigator. This statement placed defendant and Mrs. Jenner in his car en route to San Francisco at the time of the fire and placed her automobile at its parking place outside the Oroville Inn during the entire night and well into the morning. The prosecution evidence, in contrast, placed Mrs. Jenner's car at her house in Oroville at 2:45 a.m. approximately 35 minutes before the probable commencement of the fire, and put it outside the Table Mountain Tavern, loaded with her household goods, a few minutes later.

Whether a falsehood to the police or other public investigators may violate the accessory statute is a new question in California. According to some American decisions, the offense is not committed by passive failure to reveal a known felony, by refusal to give information to the authorities, or by a denial of knowledge motivated by self-interest. On the other hand, an affirmative falsehood to the public investigator, when made with the intent to shield the perpetrator of the crime, may form the aid or concealment denounced by the statute.

The gist of the offense described by section 32 of the California Penal Code is that the accused "harbors, conceals or aids" the principal with the requisite knowledge and intent. Any kind of overt or affirmative assistance to a known felon may fall within these terms. A person may be charged under section 32 when he aids the principal in concealing the latter's crime. "The test of an accessory after the fact is that, he renders his principal some personal help to elude punishment,—the kind of help being unimportant."

The evidence here shows more than passive nondisclosure. The jury could reasonably find that defendant had actively concealed or aided Mrs. Jenner by supplying an affirmative and deliberate falsehood to the public authorities, a false alibi which removed the principal from the scene of her crime and placed her on the highway en route to San Francisco at the time when the fire must have been set. In determining the knowledge and intent of the aider, the jury may consider such factors as his possible presence at the crime or other means of knowledge of its commission, as well as his companionship and relationship with the principal before and after the offense. The evidence provided a rational basis for the conclusion that defendant knew of Mrs. Jenner's arsonous activity at the time of the false alibi and supplied it with the specific intent of shielding her from prosecution and punishment. There was substantial evidence to prove all four elements of the accessory offense.

Comments and Questions

(1) If the defendant had not actively aided Mrs. Jenner but refused to tell the police what he knew, could he be convicted of any crime? What if he simply said he did not know Mrs. Jenner? *See United States v. Hodges*, 566 F.2d 674, 675 (9th Cir. 1977):

> Hodges has conceded that he failed to notify authorities. He argues, however, that he did not take an affirmative step to conceal the crime. We disagree. Although "mere silence" is insufficient (*i.e.*, there is no obligation to notify civil authorities), the giving of an untruthful statement to authorities is a sufficient act of concealment to sustain a conviction for misprision of felony.

Compare State v. McCusker, 503 P.2d 732, 733 (Or. Ct. App. 1972):

> We turn now to the accessory-after-the-fact conviction. On November 22, 1971, a group of people were at the defendant's residence. One Pomeroy assaulted one Pruitt with a knife. Later in the day the police received, from a woman who had been one of those present at the altercation, a report that Pruitt had been knifed at defendant's residence. When the police went to the scene, Pomeroy was still present, but Pruitt, the victim, was already gone. In response to police questioning the defendant told the police that nothing of consequence had happened at his house, and when asked by the police whether Pruitt had been there earlier, the defendant replied in the negative.
>
> The basis of the charge is that the defendant lied to the police about having recently seen the victim of a crime, and thus frustrated apprehension of the culprit, Pomeroy. In *State v. Clifford*, 263 Or. 436, 502 P.2d 1371 (1972), the Supreme Court held that falsely denying having recently seen a fugitive was in itself not sufficient evidence to constitute the crime of being an accessory after the fact. If it is not such crime to lie about having recently seen a criminal actor, it seems to follow that it is not such crime to lie about having recently seen the victim of a criminal act.

(2) The court in *Bowen v. State*, 791 So. 2d 44 (Fla. 2001) nicely laid out the issues here:

> The State must prove that Ms. Bowen provided some maintenance, assistance, or aid to Carr after he committed each crime. Although the common law recognized the crime of misprision of a felony for failing to report a felony to authorities, the substantive law of Florida does not recognize such a crime. Thus, the crime of accessory after the fact requires some overt action by the defendant (merely living with person, knowing that there is an active outstanding warrant for person's arrest, does not constitute crime of accessory after the fact).
>
> On the other hand, the State need not prove that Ms. Bowen's assistance was successful in allowing Carr to escape. It is sufficient for the State to prove that Ms. Bowen committed some overt act intending to assist Carr in avoiding or escaping detection, arrest, trial, or punishment, even though he was eventually apprehended.
>
> The type of overt act that will make one criminally responsible for this offense, however, is subject to some debate. In some jurisdictions, merely disavowing knowledge of a crime or of the perpetrator or his whereabouts is not enough to support a conviction for accessory after the fact. These cases are a logical extension of the principle that a person generally has no duty to report a crime or to respond to police inquiries.
>
> Other jurisdictions disagree whether a falsehood told to a police officer during his investigation of a crime will support a conviction as accessory after the fact, [as opposed to aid being given personally to perpetrator].
>
> We agree that certain falsehoods told to an officer seeking information, which go beyond merely disavowing knowledge or refusing to cooperate with an investigation, may support a conviction for accessory after the fact.

(3) If someone provides assistance to a fleeing murderer, is that person an accessory after the fact or punishable as a principal in the murder? See discussion in *United States v. Taylor*, 322 F.3d 1209, 1212 (9th Cir. 2003).

> When someone drives a get-away car, that person satisfies the plain language of the accessory after the fact statute because that person is "assist[ing] the offender in order to hinder or prevent his apprehension."
>
> We have held, however, that the escape phase of a crime is still part of the commission of the crime. Here, Taylor assisted in the escape of Waggoner, the offender. As a result, Taylor was found guilty of aiding and abetting; Taylor is an offender punishable as a principal to the murder....
>
> Because Taylor participated in the escape phase of the shooting, he is liable as a principal. Although the evidence is sufficient to show that Taylor violated the plain language of the accessory after the fact statute, the statute does not apply to Taylor given that he was found guilty as a principal to the crime.

Chapter 5

Principal Offenses

§ 5.01 Theft Offenses

[A] Larceny

English judges devised the offense of larceny, the first and most significant step in developing the common law. The initial purpose of this intervention was to avoid disturbances in the community when victims tried to recover their property; offering official recourse to victims of theft maintained peace and order.

Gradually, as cases were resolved, common law theft was expanded to include a greater range of conduct (larceny by trick, cheat) and to encompass more types of property. In the late the eighteenth century, English legislators enacted the criminal laws of false pretenses and embezzlement. American states incorporated English theft law, including common and statutory offenses, after the revolution.

The cases that follow provide common law approaches to thievery and current conceptions of the crime. They also present emerging issues that involve new types of property and white-collar crimes.

The theft materials begin, as does all theft law, with larceny. Common law larceny consists of several elements: (1) trespass, (2) taking, (3) asportation, (4) personal property, (5) and intent to deprive permanently.

[1] "Trespass"

Topolewski v. State

Supreme Court of Wisconsin
109 N.W. 1037 (1906)

The accused was charged with having stolen three barrels of meat, the property of the Plankinton Packing Company, of the value of $55.20, and was found guilty.

The evidence was to this effect: The Plankinton Packing Company suspected the accused of having by criminal means possessed himself of some of its property and of having a purpose to make further efforts to that end. A short time before the 14th day of October, 1905, one Mat Dolan, who was indebted to the accused in the sum of upwards of $100.00, was discharged from the company's employ. Shortly theretofore the accused pressed Dolan for payment of the aforesaid indebtedness and the latter, being unable to respond, the former conceived the idea of solving the difficulty by obtaining some of the company's meat products through Dolan's aid and by criminal means, Dolan to participate in the benefits of the transaction by having the value of the property credited upon his indebtedness. A plan was accordingly laid by the two to that end, which Dolan disclosed to the company. Such plan was abandoned. Thereafter various methods were discussed of carrying out the idea of the accused, Dolan participating with the knowledge and sanction of the company. Finally a meeting was arranged between Dolan and the accused to consider the subject, the packing company requesting the former to bring it about, and with knowledge of Dolan causing one of its employees to be in hiding where he could overhear whatever might be said, the arrangement being made on the part of the company by Mr. Layer the person in charge of its wholesale department. At such interview the accused proposed that Dolan should procure some packages of the company's meat to be placed on their loading platform, as was customary in delivering meat to customers, and that he should drive to such platform, ostensibly as a customer and remove such packages. Dolan agreed to the proposition and it was decided that the same should be consummated early the next morning, all of which was reported to Mr. Layer. He thereupon caused four barrels of meat to be packed and put in the accustomed condition for delivery to customers and placed on the platform in readiness for the accused to take them. He set a watch over the property and notified the person in charge of the platform, who was ignorant of the reason for so placing the barrels, upon his inquiring what they were placed there for, to let them go; that they were for a man who would call for them. About the time appointed for the accused to appear he drove to the platform and commenced putting the barrels in his wagon. The platform boss supposing, as the fact was, that the accused was the man Mr. Layer said was to come for the property, assumed the attitude of consenting to the taking. He did not actually help load the barrels onto the wagon, but he was by, consented by his manner and when the accused was ready to go, helped him arrange his wagon and inquired what was to be done with the fourth barrel. The accused replied that he wanted it marked and sent up to him with a bill. He told the platform boss that he ordered the stuff the night before through Dolan. He took full possession of the three barrels of meat with intent to deprive the owner permanently thereof and without compensating it therefor, wholly in ignorance, however, of the fact that Dolan had acted in the manner on behalf of such owner and that it had knowingly aided in carrying out the plan for obtaining the meat.

Marshall, J. (after stating the facts).

It will be noted that the plan for depriving the packing company of its property originated with the accused, but that it was wholly impracticable of accomplishment without the property being placed on the loading platform and the accused not being interfered with when he attempted to take it. When Dolan agreed to procure such placing the packing company in legal effect agreed thereto. Dolan did not expressly consent nor did the agreement he had with the packing company authorize him to do so, to the misappropriation of the property. Did the agreement in legal effect with the accused to place the property of the packing company on the loading platform, where it could be appropriated by the accused, if he was so disposed and was not interfered with in so doing, though his movements in that regard were known to the packing company, and his taking of the property, his efforts to that end being facilitated as suggested, constitute consent to such appropriation?

The case is very near the border line, if not across it, between consent and non-consent to the taking of the property. *Reg. v. Lawrence*, 4 Cox C. C. 438, it was held that if the property was delivered by a servant to the defendant by the master's direction the offense cannot be larceny, regardless of the purpose of the defendant. In this case the property was not only placed on the loading platform, as was usual in delivering such goods to customers, with knowledge that the accused would soon arrive, having a formed design to take it, but the packing company's employé in charge of the platform, Ernst Klotz, was instructed that the property was placed there for a man who would call for it. Klotz from such statement had every reason to infer, when the accused arrived and claimed the right to take the property, that he was the one referred to and that it was proper to make delivery to him and he acted accordingly. While he did not physically place the property, or assist in doing so, in the wagon, his standing by, witnessing such placing by the accused, and then assisting him in arranging the wagon, as the evidence shows he did, and taking the order, in the usual way, from the accused as to the disposition of the fourth barrel, and his conduct in respect thereto amounted, practically, to a delivery of the three barrels to the accused.

In *Rex v. Egginton*, 2 P. & P. 508, we have a very instructive case on the subject under discussion here. A servant informed his master that he had been solicited to aid in robbing the latter's house. By the master's discretion the servant opened the house, gave the would-be thieves access thereto and took them to the place where the intended subject of the larceny had been laid in order that they might take it. All this was done with a view to the apprehension of the guilty parties after the accomplishment of their purpose. The servant by direction of the master not only gave access to the house but afforded the would-be thieves every facility for taking the property, and yet the court held that the crime of larceny was complete, because there was no direction to the servant to deliver the property to the intruders or consent to their taking it. They were left free to commit the larceny, as they had purposed doing, and the way was made easy for them to do so, but they were neither induced to commit the crime, nor was any act essential to the offense done by any one but themselves.

...

We cannot well escape the conclusion that this case falls under the condemnation of the rule that where the owner of property by himself or his agent, actually or constructively, aids in the commission of the offense, as intended by the wrongdoer, by performing or rendering unnecessary some act in the transaction essential to the offense, the would-be criminal is not guilty of all the elements of the offense. Here Mr. Layer, acting for the owner of the property, packed or superintended the packing of the four barrels of meat as suggested by the owner's agent in the matter, Dolan, and caused the same to be placed on the platform, knowing that the accused would soon arrive to take them, under an arrangement between him and its agent, and directed its platform boss, when he inquired as to the purpose of so placing the barrels, "Let them go; They are for some man and he will call for them." He, from the standpoint of such employé, directed the latter to deliver the barrels to the man when he called. He substantially made such delivery, by treating the accused when he arrived upon the scene as having a right to take the property. In that the design to trap a criminal went a little too far, at least, in that it included the doing of an act, in effect preventing the taking of the property from being characterized by any element of trespass.

The logical basis for the doctrine above discussed is that there can be no larceny without a trespass. So if one procures his property to be taken by another intending to commit larceny, or delivers his property to such other, the latter purposing to commit such crime, the element of trespass is wanting and the crime not fully consummated however plain may be the guilty purpose of the one possessing himself of such property. That does not militate against a person's being free to set a trap to catch one whom he suspects of an intention to commit the crime of larceny, but the setting of such trap must not go further than to afford the would-be thief the amplest opportunity to carry out his purpose, formed without such inducement on the part of the owner of the property, as to put him in the position of having consented to the taking. If I induce one to come and take my property and then place it before him to be taken, and he takes it with criminal intent, or if knowing that one intends to take my property I deliver it to him and he takes it with such intent, the essential element of trespass involving nonconsent requisite to a completed offense of larceny does not characterize the transaction, regardless of the fact that the moral turpitude involved is no less than it would be if such essential were present. Some writers in treating this subject give so much attention to condemning the deception practiced to facilitate and encourage the commission of a crime by one supposed to have such a purpose in view, that the condemnation is liable to be viewed as if the deception were sufficient to excuse the would-be criminal, or to preclude his being prosecuted; that there is a question of good morals involved as to both parties to the transaction and that the wrongful participation of the owner of the property renders him and the public incapable of being heard to charge the person he has entrapped with the offense of larceny. That is wrong. It is the removal from the completed transaction, which from the mental attitude of the would-be criminal may have all the ingredients of larceny, from the standpoint of the owner of the property of the element of trespass or nonconsent. When such element does not characterize a transaction involving the full offense of larceny so far as concerns the mental purpose of such would-be criminal is concerned, is often not free from difficulty and courts of review should incline quite strongly to support the decision of the trial judge in respect to the matter and not disturb it except in a clear case. It seems that there is such a case before us.

If the accused had merely disclosed to Dolan, his ostensible accomplice, a purpose to improve the opportunity when one should present itself to steal barrels of meat from the packing company's loading platform, and that had been communicated by Dolan to the company and it had then merely furnished the accused the opportunity he was looking for to carry out such purpose, and he had improved it, the situation would be quite different. The mere fact that the plan for obtaining the property was that of the accused, under the circumstances of this case, is not controlling. Dolan, as an emissary of the packing company, as we have seen, was sent to the accused to arrange, if the latter were so disposed, some sort of a plan for taking some of the company's property with the intention of stealing it. Though the accused proposed the plan, Dolan agreed to it, which involved a promise to assist in carrying it out, ostensibly as an accomplice, but actually as an instrument of the packing company. That came very near, if it did not involve, solicitation by the company, in a secret way, for the accused to take its property as proposed. With the other element added of placing such property on the loading platform for the accused to take pursuant to the agreement, with directions, in effect, to the person in charge of the platform, to let the accused take it when he came for that purpose, we are unable to see any element of trespass in the taking which followed. The packing company went very significantly further than the owner of the property did in *Rex v. Egginton, supra*, which is regarded as quite an extreme case. It solicited the opportunity to be an ostensible accomplice in committing the offense of larceny instead of being solicited in that regard, and the property was in practical effect delivered to the would-be thief instead of its being merely placed where he could readily trespass upon the rights of the packing company by taking it. When one keeps in mind the plain distinction between merely furnishing opportunity for the execution of a formed design to commit larceny and negotiations for the purpose of developing a scheme to commit the offense, regardless of who finally proposes the plan jointly adopted, and not facilitating the execution of the plan by placing the property pursuant to the arrangement where it can readily be taken, but in practical effect, at least, delivering the same into the possession of the would-be thief, one can readily see that the element of trespass, involving consent, is present in the first situation mentioned and not in the last, and that the latter pretty clearly fits the circumstances of this case

The judgment is *reversed, and* the cause remanded for a new trial.

Fletcher, *The Metamorphosis of Larceny**

89 Harv. L. Rev. 469, 493–98 (1976)

In reversing Topolewski's conviction, the Wisconsin Supreme Court carefully separated out matters that were not in dispute. There was no question about Topolewski's intention to steal the barrels of meat. Nor was there any dispute about whether entrapment provided a rationale for reversing the conviction. The court specifically says that it is wrong to justify reversals in this sort of case on the ground that the owner's deception excused the would-be criminal, or, alternatively, that the owner's improper behavior should preclude a criminal prosecution. The proposition recurs repeatedly in the opinion that regardless of the actor's criminal intent there could be no conviction unless his conduct satisfied the objective elements in larceny. The

* (Footnotes omitted.) Copyright 1976 © by George P. Fletcher. Reprinted by permission.

central objective requirement was a trespass. All of the court's doctrinal arguments were designed to prove that the taking of the barrels with the intent to steal was not sufficient to constitute a trespass.

...

After its opening discussion of consent and delivery and the setting up of *Egginton* as the counterpoint to the facts before it, the court's opinion seeks to develop a systematic account of the difference between permissible and impermissible traps. The general claim is that undue facilitation of the crime undermines the element of trespass. The servant in *Egginton* had not unduly facilitated the theft; but Dolan and the company manager had. Undue facilitation occurs when the owner does "acts amounting to the constituents of the crime" or does "some act in the transaction essential to the offense." ...

What the Wisconsin court had in mind was that the "design to trap a criminal" went a little too far because the company's facilitation prevented "the taking of the property from being characterized by an element of trespass." The reference to "essential acts" helps us little in understanding why the "design ... went a little too far." The "essential act" wanting is the trespass and "trespass" in the context of larceny is not an act in the ordinary sense. It is a quality or an attribute of taking property. The difference between a trespass and a mere taking lies in the manner of acquisition. A trespass has to evoke associations with the ancient form of taking *vi et armis*. Thus the focus on undue facilitation and essential acts leads us back to the principle of manifest criminality. The undue facilitation eliminated the quality of trespass by converting the thieving into a taking in the ordinary course of business.

The important point to be drawn from *Topolewski* is that the principle of manifest criminality can still influence the outcome of larceny prosecutions.... Yet the shared image of the thief continues to affect the course of the law in but this remote corner of criminal prosecutions. The exclusive survival of manifest criminality in the context of staged larceny suggests that there is a deeper connection between the common law concept of criminality and the practice of designing a trap for a would-be thief. *Topolewski* invites us to consider what that deeper connection might be.

While we can grasp the concept of manifest larceny there is another element in the classical concept of criminality that is far more elusive. This additional element is expressed by describing crime as a breach of the peace or a socially disturbing event. An act of larceny is a frightening and unnerving episode in communal life. Yet this account of criminality is problematic, for larceny is not disturbing every time it occurs. The thief might work in secret with no one present. In what sense is that actually unnerving? What one has to say is that thieving is typically or paradigmatically disturbing; and in any event, the thought or anticipation of falling prey to thieves is always disturbing. This aspect of larceny may indeed be essential to the common law conceptualization of larceny as a public rather than a private harm.

Comments and Questions

(1) As the court recounts, the defendant in *Topolewski* "took full possession of the three barrels of meat with intent to deprive the owner permanently thereof" and moved them into his own wagon. Why did the court rule that the state had not established a trespassory taking?

(2) Professor Fletcher explains why the element of trespass was central to common law notions of larceny. How would you describe manifest criminality? What societal purpose did it serve?

(3) As commerce and trade grew, common law courts broadly interpreted the elements of larceny in order to reach more conduct. The rule of "breaking bulk" is one such construction. Consider the following facts:

A manufacturer delivers a truckload of furniture to the defendant with instructions to deliver it to a particular address. Instead of doing so, the defendant sells the furniture and pockets the proceeds. In this scenario, the defendant is a "bailee" in lawful possession of the furniture. Is he guilty of larceny? How has the defendant trespassed?

The common law bailment doctrine found a trespass if the bailee "broke the bail." That is, it was larceny if actors opened crates and removed contents; they had trespassed on the "bail." The theory was that what had been bailed were the crates, not what was contained within. *See The Carrier's Case*, Y.B. Pasch. 13 Edw. 4, f.9, pl. 5 (1473), *reprinted* in 64 Selden Soc'y 30 (1945). According to Professor Fletcher, the rule illustrates the principle of objective criminality:

> One characteristic of the thief was his taking swiftly and violently. That aspect of thieving is captured in the moment of breaking bulk. The thief breaking bulk could be caught in the deed, *in flagrante*. Lawyers of the time could perceive thieving in the act of breaking open the bales; they were less likely to sense thievery in the acts of selling or giving away the bales. Consequently, these other forms of misappropriation remained within the protection of possessorial immunity. The exception of breaking bulk was one that proved the rule: Conduct that at no point featured behavior characteristic of thieving remained immune from the jurisdiction of the criminal courts.

George P. Fletcher, *The Metamorphosis of Larceny*, 89 Harv. L. Rev. 469, 484–85 (1976).

Hufstetler v. State

Court of Appeals of Alabama
63 So. 2d 730 (1953)

Carr, Presiding Judge.

The accused was convicted by the court without a jury on a charge of petit larceny. The property involved was 6½ gallons of gasoline.

The defendant did not testify nor offer any evidence.

The undisputed facts are narrated by a witness as follows:

> My name is Porter Whorton. I live at Forney in Cherokee County, Alabama. I know the defendant, Thomas R. Hufstetler. I own and operate a store and service station at Forney, Alabama. On March 29, 1952, the defendant drove an automobile up to my gasoline tanks. There were some two or three other men in the car with him, and a man in the back seat got out and started in the store and asked if I had a telephone. When I told him I did not have a phone, he said he wanted some gasoline and went back and got in the car. I asked him how much and he said, "fill it up." I put 6½ gallons of gasoline in the car and this man said to get a quart of oil, and when I went for the oil, the defendant drove off in the automobile together with the man who ordered the gas and the others in the car without paying for the gasoline. This 6½ gallons of gas belonged to me and was of the value of $1.94, and this occurred in Cherokee County, Alabama, and within twelve months before the commencement of this prosecution.

The only question of critical concern is whether, on the basis of the above proof, the judgment of conviction can be sustained.... The obtaining of the property by the consent of the owner under such conditions will not necessarily prevent the taking from being larceny. In other words, an actual trespass is not always required to be proven. The trick or fraud vitiates the transaction, and it will be deemed that the owner still retained the constructive possession.

Comments and Questions

(1) As in *Topolewski*, the owner in *Hufstetler* consented to defendant's possession of the gas. Do any facts differ from the taking in *Topolewski*? Is the conduct in *Hufstetler* an example of "manifest criminality"? Which party had legal possession? Courts distinguished between actual possession and the owner's "constructive possession" to facilitate proof of trespass.

(2) The conduct in *Hufstetler* is known as larceny by trick, a form of common law larceny. A trick vitiates the owner's consent, and establishes a trespassory taking. What was the "trick" here?

(3) Did the defendant in *Hufstetler* gain title to the gasoline or merely possession? The distinction matters: larceny by trick is a crime against possession; if title was also transferred to the actor, the crime is obtaining property by false pretenses.

[2] "Take and Carry Away"

People v. Olivo

Court of Appeals of New York
420 N.E.2d 40 (1981)

Cooke, Chief Judge.

These cases present a recurring question in this era of the self-service store which has never been resolved by this court: may a person be convicted of larceny for shoplifting if the person is caught with goods while still inside the store? For reasons outlined below, it is concluded that a larceny conviction may be sustained, in certain situations, even though the shoplifter was apprehended before leaving the store.

I.

In *People v. Olivo*, defendant was observed by a security guard in the hardware area of a department store. Initially conversing with another person, defendant began to look around furtively when his acquaintance departed. The security agent continued to observe and saw defendant assume a crouching position, take a set of wrenches and secret [sic] it in his clothes. After again looking around, defendant began walking toward an exit, passing a number of cash registers en route. When defendant did not stop to pay for the merchandise, the officer accosted him a few feet from the exit. In response to the guard's inquiry, defendant denied having the wrenches, but as he proceeded to the security office, defendant removed the wrenches and placed them under his jacket. At trial, defendant testified that he had placed the tools under his arm and was on line at a cashier when apprehended. The jury returned a verdict of guilty on the charge of petit larceny. The conviction was affirmed by Appellate Term.

II.

In *People v. Gasparik*, defendant was in a department store trying on a leather jacket. Two store detectives observed him tear off the price tag and remove a "sensormatic" device designed to set off an alarm if the jacket were carried through a detection machine. There was at least one such machine at the exit of each floor. Defendant placed the tag and the device in the pocket of another jacket on the merchandise rack. He took his own jacket, which he had been carrying with him, and placed it on a table. Leaving his own jacket, defendant put on the leather jacket and walked through the store, still on the same floor, bypassing several cash registers. When he headed for the exit from that floor, in the direction of the main floor, he was apprehended by security personnel. At trial, defendant denied removing the price tag and the sensormatic device from the jacket, and testified that he was looking for a cashier without a long line when he was stopped. The court, sitting without a jury, convicted defendant of petit larceny.

III.

In *People v. Spatzier*, defendant entered a bookstore on Fulton Street in Hempstead carrying an attaché case. The two co-owners of the store observed the defendant in a ceiling mirror as he browsed through the store. They watched defendant remove a book from the shelf, look up and down the aisle, and place the book in his case. He then placed the case at his feet and continued to browse. One of the owners approached defendant and accused him of stealing the book. An altercation ensued and when defendant allegedly struck the owner with the attaché case, the case opened and the book fell out. At trial, defendant denied secreting the book in his case and claimed that the owner had suddenly and unjustifiably accused him of stealing. The jury found defendant guilty of petit larceny, and the conviction was affirmed by the Appellate Term.

IV.

The primary issue in each case is whether the evidence, viewed in the light most favorable to the prosecution, was sufficient to establish the elements of larceny as defined by the Penal Law. To resolve this common question, the development of the common-law crime of larceny and its evolution into modern statutory form must be briefly traced.

Larceny at common law was defined as a trespassory taking and carrying away of the property of another with intent to steal.... The early common-law courts apparently viewed larceny as defending society against breach of the peace, rather than protecting individual property rights, and therefore placed heavy emphasis upon the requirement of a *trespassory taking*.... Thus, a person such as a bailee who had rightfully obtained possession of property from its owner could not be guilty of larceny....

Gradually, the courts began to expand the reach of the offense, initially by subtle alterations in the common-law concept of possession.... Thus, for instance, it became a general rule that goods entrusted to an employee were not deemed to be in his possession, but were only considered to be in his custody, so long as he remained on the employer's premises....

As the reach of larceny expanded, the intent element of the crime became of increasing importance, while the requirement of a trespassory taking became less significant, [sic] As a result, the bar against convicting a person who had initially obtained lawful possession of property faded. In *King v. Pear*, (1 Leach 212, 168 Eng. Rep. 208), for instance, a defendant who had lied about his address and ultimate destination when renting a horse was found guilty of larceny for later converting the horse. Because of the fraudulent misrepresentation, the court reasoned, the defendant had never obtained legal possession.... Thus, "larceny by trick" was born....

Later cases went even further, often ignoring the fact that a defendant had initially obtained possession lawfully, and instead focused upon his later intent.... The crime of larceny then encompassed, not only situations where the defendant initially obtained property by a trespassory taking, but many situations where an individual, possessing the requisite intent, exercised control over property inconsistent with the continued rights of the owner. During this evolutionary process, the purpose served by the crime of larceny obviously shifted from protecting society's peace to general protection of property rights ...

Modern penal statutes generally have incorporated these developments under a unified definition of larceny.... Case law, too, now tends to focus upon the actor's intent and the exercise of dominion and control over the property....

This evolution is particularly relevant to thefts occurring in modern self-service stores. In stores of that type, customers are impliedly invited to examine, try on, and carry about the merchandise on display. Thus in a sense, the owner has consented to the customer's possession of the goods for a limited purpose.... That the owner has consented to that possession does not, however, preclude a conviction for larceny. If the customer exercises dominion and control wholly inconsistent with the continued rights of the owner, and the other elements of the crime are present, a larceny has occurred. Such conduct on the part of a customer satisfies the "taking" element of the crime.

It is this element that forms the core of the controversy in these cases. The defendants argue, in essence, that the crime is not established, as a matter of law, unless there is evidence that the customer departed the shop without paying for the merchandise.

Although this court has not addressed the issue, case law from other jurisdictions seems unanimous in holding that a shoplifter need not leave the store to be guilty of larceny.... This is because a shopper may treat merchandise in a manner inconsistent with the owner's continued rights—and in a manner not in accord with that of a prospective purchaser—without actually walking out of the store. Indeed, depending upon the circumstances of each case, a variety of conduct may be sufficient to allow the trier of fact to find a taking. It would be well-nigh impossible, and unwise, to attempt to delineate all the situations which would establish a taking. But it is possible to identify some of the factors used in determining whether the evidence is sufficient to be submitted to the fact finder.

In many cases, it will be particularly relevant that defendant concealed the goods under clothing or in a container.... Such conduct is not generally expected in a self-service store and may in a proper case be deemed an exercise of dominion and control inconsistent with the store's continued rights. Other furtive or unusual behavior on the part of the defendant should also be weighed. Thus, if the defendant surveys the area while secreting the merchandise or abandoned [sic] his or her own property in exchange for the concealed goods, this may evince larcenous rather than innocent behavior. Relevant too is the customer's proximity to or movement towards one of the store's exits. Certainly it is highly probative of guilt that the customer was in possession of secreted goods just a few short steps from the door or moving in that direction. Finally, possession of a known shoplifting device actually used to conceal merchandise, such as a specially designed outer garment or false bottomed carrying case, would be all but decisive.

Of course, in a particular case, any one or any combination of these factors may take on special significance. And there may be other considerations, not now identified, which should be examined. So long as it bears upon the principal issue—whether the shopper exercised control wholly inconsistent with the owner's continued rights—any attending circumstance is relevant and may be taken into account.

V.

Under these principles, there was ample evidence in each case to raise a factual question as to the defendants' guilt. In *People v. Olivo*, defendant not only concealed goods in his clothing, but he did so in a particularly suspicious manner. And, when defendant was stopped, he was moving towards the door, just three feet short of exiting the store. It cannot be said as a matter of law that these circumstances failed to establish a taking.

In *People v. Gasparik*, defendant removed the price tag and sensor device from a jacket, abandoned his own garment, put the jacket on and ultimately headed for the main floor of the store. Removal of the price tag and sensor device, and careful concealment of those items, is highly unusual and suspicious conduct for a shopper. Coupled with defendant's abandonment of his own coat and his attempt to leave the floor, those factors were sufficient to make out a *prima facie* case of a taking.

In *People v. Spatzier*, defendant concealed a book in an attaché case. Unaware that he was being observed in an overhead mirror, defendant looked furtively up and down the aisle before secreting the book. In these circumstances, given the manner in which defendant concealed the book and his suspicious behavior, the evidence was not insufficient as a matter of law....

VII.

In sum, in view of the modern definition of the crime of larceny, and its purpose of protecting individual property rights, a taking of property in the self-service store context can be established by evidence that a customer exercised control over merchandise wholly inconsistent with the store's continued rights. Quite simply, a customer who crosses the line between the limited right he or she has to deal with merchandise and the store owner's rights may be subject to prosecution for larceny. Such a rule should foster the legitimate interests and continued operation of self-service shops, a convenience which most members of society enjoy.

Comments and Questions

(1) The court, in passing, notes that the purpose of larceny is to protect individual property rights. What broader community purpose is served by protecting individual interests in property?

(2) Given the following facts, why did the court decide the defendant had taken the car?

> ... Evidence at trial showed that the car dealership had been closed since 7 p.m. and that the car lot was unlighted. Officer Rivera saw a blue Oldsmobile without lights being driven through the car lot. As he watched, the car was driven into a cable that extended between two poles at the entrance to the

> lot. The cable did not break and the car was not driven from the lot. Because the cable was caught between the grill and the bumper, the car could not be moved.... Officer Rivera placed the defendant under arrest.

People v. Rivera, 566 N.E.2d 220 (Ill. 1990). The court reasoned that:

> [t]he defendant took complete though unauthorized control of the car by getting in it, starting it, and driving it through the car lot without the owner's permission.... [T]his action of the defendant satisfied the requirements of theft. It cannot be said that the owner retained control of the car. The security cable did not serve as a chain to Burba's possession of the car; it simply prevented the defendant from driving off with it. *Id.* at 222.

(3) A taking is accomplished when the defendant acquires control of the property. A taking, however, often overlaps and merges with the element of asportation, or a "carrying away" of the property.

Caruso v. State

Supreme Court of Tennessee
326 S.W.2d 434 (1958)

Mr. Justice Tomlinson, delivered the opinion of the Court.

...

Around 2:00 A.M. on the morning of August 24, 1958, an officer of Greeneville, Lyle Doty, was informed that a robbery, or some such crime, was being committed in the business building of Greene County Producers. Mr. Doty reached this building within five minutes and heard three men running and could hear water "pouring," as he expressed it. There was a creek nearby. About ten minutes after that he saw a two-tone Nash automobile bearing a Unicoi County automobile license tag.

When he entered the building he saw that the back door was open. He likewise saw a safe just outside the office with a "dolly" or cart against it. This safe had fallen over and hit one of the counters. At closing time that evening this safe, which weighed 600 pounds, was left at its usual place in the office of the company. It had been moved by the intruder a distance of five feet out of that office into the main part of the building. The cart had been used in moving it. It contained about $34,000 in money and securities.

The first question is whether the aforementioned facts constitute the offense of larceny. That offense is defined by Section 39-4202, T.C.A., as being "the felonious taking and carrying away the personal goods of another". Essential elements of larceny are trespass and feloniously taking possession and carrying away. Whoever it was that entered the building on that night and sought the removal of the safe did commit a trespass. But does that which was done constitute a taking and carrying away of the safe within the meaning of the statute?

The expression "carry away" used in this statute is generally referred to in the texts and decisions as "asportation." We find no decision of this Court as to whether the removal of this safe as above described is an asportation within the meaning of our statute, but numerous decisions on the point from other jurisdictions are annotated in 19 A.L.R. 724 *et seq.*, and 144 A.L.R. 1383 *et seq.*

These decisions uniformly hold, and without an exception, in so far as we find, that the moving of this safe under the circumstances mentioned was an asportation thereof. In the 19 A.L.R. annotations there will be found a Nebraska case holding that "even if the removal were but a hair's breadth, it will do." *Gettinger v. State*, 13 Neb. 308, 14 N.W. 403, 404, and that "the slightest change of location—is sufficient." *Lundy v. State*, 60 Ga. 143. A number of such cases from various jurisdictions will be found in the annotations above cited. It follows that within the meaning of our statute there was a larceny of this safe.

Comments and Questions

(1) In its most pristine form, the asportation requirement is satisfied if "every part of the [object] was removed by the prisoner from that space which that particular part occupied ... before." *State v. Chambers*, 22 W. Va. 779, 799–800 (1883). "This fine distinction, which makes not a bit of sense today, has been described as the distinction between rotating a doughnut (every part moves, as is required for larceny) or rotating a pie (the exact center portion, infinitely small, does not move)." LaFave, Criminal Law 981, n. 11 (2010).

(2) As the *Caruso* case illustrates, it is not necessary that the accused remove the object from the victim's premises. In *Rogers v. State*, 458 S.W.2d 369 (Ark. 1970), conviction of larceny of a boat and trailer was affirmed where the evidence showed that the tongue of the trailer supporting the boat was lifted off a block even though it was never attached to a vehicle. The court held that "the requisite element of asportation in larceny cases may be found from the slightest removal of goods from the place where they were left by the owner. The fact that the property was not actually removed from the owner's premises does not make the thief's dominion over it incomplete nor preclude a finding that there was an asportation." *Id.* at 370.

(3) In *People v. Alamo*, 315 N.E.2d 446 (N.Y. 1974), the Court of Appeals held that larceny is committed, "where an automobile is entered, where the culprit positions himself behind the wheel, starts the engine, turns on the lights and starts to move the car *or is about to do so*." *Id.* at 457 (emphasis supplied). The same disposition is often created by statute, and many criminal statutes do not now include a separate element of asportation. *See* Model Penal Code § 223.2(1).

[3] "Personal Property"

Under common law, only movable, personal property that could be taken and carried away could be stolen. Land, "real" property and objects attached to it, such as trees and crops, were not subject to theft law; nor were animals or personal services, electricity, and other intangibles. Today, state criminal codes are likely to use a comprehensive definition of property that may include tangible and intangible property, real estate, contract rights, choses-in-action and other interests in or claims to wealth.

See e.g., Model Penal Code § 223.0(6). The broader statutes reflect a change in the purpose of theft law, to protect private property. Safeguarding private property has the effect of encouraging productive activity and investment.

Notwithstanding these changes, the constraints imposed by common law larceny continue to raise interesting questions. Does the use of another's personal property constitute larceny? Is intangible information a form of personal property? The cases that follow, examples of what are termed "white-collar" crimes, turn to those questions.

People v. Ashworth

Supreme Court, Appellate Division, Fourth Department, New York
220 A.D. 498 (1927)

Taylor, J.

The defendant Harry Ashworth was the mill superintendent and general manager of the A-O Worsted Company, Inc., and his brother, the defendant Alfred Ashworth, was the vice president and principal stockholder of the Midland Wool Combing Company, Inc. The Lockport Felt Company, of Newfane, N. Y., made an agreement with these defendants for the combing by the Midland Company of approximately 20,000 pounds of raw wool. The wool was subsequently shipped from Newfane, and delivered to the Midland Company at Salamanca, and combed.

Later an agreement was entered into between the Lockport Company and these defendants for spinning the same wool into yarn at a price of 20 cents a pound. The Midland Company had no facilities for spinning wool, and all of the yarn was spun in the plant of the A-O Company by the defendants, who used for that purpose the machinery, the spinning facilities, and the laborers of the A-O Company. The wool, when spun, was shipped to the Lockport Company, and that company paid the Midland Company by check for the work, upon invoices rendered.

As a result of this transaction, these defendants, with three others, were indicted for conspiracy and grand larceny, for conspiring to cheat and deprive the A-O Worsted Company, Inc., of its money and of its property and the use of it, and for stealing the money and the use of the property.... Upon the trial they were found guilty by a general verdict, and have appealed.

The verdict of the jury has established that the spinning was done without the knowledge of any of the A-O Company's officers (except Harry Ashworth, its mill superintendent), and that the defendants entered into and carried through a corrupt arrangement to spin the wool for the Lockport Felt Company secretly in the plant of the A-O Company, to conceal from the officers of the A-O Company the contract and the work done pursuant to it, and to appropriate to themselves the use of the plant, the spinning facilities, and the workmen of the A-O Company, a property right.

...

Defendants also claim that the spinning facilities were real property, certainly not personal property, and that no larceny has been proved.

The charge in count 4 of the indictment, that the $2,097.92 received by the Midland Company for spinning was stolen by defendants from the A-O Worsted Company, must be dismissed at the outset. The case was tried upon the theory that the spinning facilities of the A-O Company were surreptitiously used and "appropriated"—not that the proceeds of a permitted use were stolen. However, if the proof was sufficient under either larceny count, the general verdict of guilty is good.

The next question, then, for consideration, is this: Was the use of the spinning facilities of the A-O Worsted Company a subject of larceny, under section 1290 Penal Law? The defendants "used" the personal property of the A-O Company, and this is perhaps the only word which precisely and accurately characterizes their activities with respect to that company's factory equipment. The word "appropriate" means "to take to one's self; claim to the exclusion of others." *Webster's New International Dictionary*. The defendants appropriated the use of the A-O Company's property—even though temporarily—to the exclusion of others. Can it be fairly said that this appropriation of use of the plant constituted larceny of personal property within the meaning of the statute?

It will be noted that the verb "use" does not appear in section 1290 of the Penal Law. The significant words which characterize the crime defined—considering the instant facts—are "takes from the possession of the true owner," "withholds, or appropriates to his own use, or that of any person other than the true owner, any ... personal property." These expressions connote something more than merely *using* personal property of the true owner. They refer to physical taking or acquiring of some concrete article.

We must bear in mind, also, that asportation is an essential element of larceny. Asportation, in larceny, is any appreciable changing of the location of the property involved, with felonious intent, by the person charged with the commission of the crime. The taker, at some particular moment, must have obtained complete, independent, and absolute possession and control of the property, adverse to the rights of the owner.

It may be conceivable that, if these defendants stole the use of the spinning facilities of the A-O Company, they carried the "use" away, or appreciably changed its location, although the work was all done on the premises of the A-O Company. But to conceive this requires a certain intellectual flexibility which is probably not possessed by the average person.

This brings us to a consideration of the question whether a mere property right, as distinguished from physical property, is the subject of larceny; is [a mere property right] "personal property." Personal property is defined in paragraph (1) of section 39 of the General Construction Law as follows:

> The term "personal property" includes chattels, money, things in action, and all written instruments themselves, as distinguished from the rights or interests to which they relate, by which any right, interest, lien or incumbrance in, to or upon property, or any debt or financial obligation is created, acknowl-

> edged, evidenced, transferred, discharged or defeated, wholly or in part, and *everything, except real property, which may be the subject of ownership.*

Th[is] is a very comprehensive definition, for it includes intangible property as well as tangible. Electricity and gas have been held to be the subject of larceny. Perhaps some court may soon hold that a property right, through a license, in a radio wave length may be stolen. It is reasonably clear, nevertheless, that all intangible personal property is not the subject of larceny, at least under section 1290 of the Penal Law as now worded. For instance, the right to produce oil is personal property. But it seems that it would be impossible to steal such property. Good will is personal property. But, if an unscrupulous competitor steals the good will of a rival business, is he guilty of larceny under section 1290 of the Penal Law? A leasehold interest in land is personal property. But there can be no larceny of such an interest or right. A mere credit is not the subject of larceny at common law.

Take the case of a franchise. This is an incorporeal hereditament, intangible, invisible, "unseen without form or substance and, as it were, the mere breath of the Legislature." It is not easy to conceive of such a thing being the subject of larceny.

Personal property has been variously defined. That which may be the subject of larceny is well comprehended in the following statement:

> It should have corporeal existence, that is, be something the physical presence, quantity, or quality of which is detectable or measurable by the senses or by some mechanical contrivance; for a naked right existing merely in contemplation of law, although it may be very valuable to the person who is entitled to exercise it, is not a subject of larceny.

36 Corpus Juris 737....

Larceny, under section 1290 of the Penal Law, has not been proved. The judgment of conviction should be reversed, and the indictment dismissed.

Comments and Questions

(1) In contrast to common law larceny, today's theft statutes protect a broader range of interests, such as "things of value." You have encountered one example, the federal statute at issue in *Morissette, supra* Chapter 3. In another case involving the same offense, a federal court held that an academician's use of a federally funded research assistant for a personal research project was a "thing of value" under 18 U.S.C. § 641. *United States v. Croft*, 750 F.2d 1354 (7th Cir. 1984).

The Model Penal Code defines property, for purposes of theft offenses, as "anything of value, including real estate, tangible and intangible personal property, contract rights, choses-in-action and other interests in or claims to wealth, admission or transportation tickets, captured or domestic animals, food and drink, electric or other power." *See* MODEL PENAL CODE § 223.0(6). Does this formulation resolve the issue in *Ashworth*?

(2) The court in *Ashworth* declined to rule that *use* of property is a form of property. The court relied in part on the asportation element of larceny. What conception of

asportation did the court use, the traditional literal definition of "taking away" or the broader conception articulated by *Olivo*?

(3) What is the advantage of the common law position, which distinguishes between a "mere property right" and physical property? The court distinguished intangible rights in the machinery from its physical form. As the treatise cited by the court puts it, "a naked right"—that exists only because of a legal determination—is different from property with a physical existence that can be measured by the senses. What purpose does the distinction serve?

(4) How does the reasoning in *Ashworth* support the common law's preference for "manifest criminality"? According to the court, the state may have prevailed if the defendants could be considered to have "carried the 'use' away." But the court registered concern that "to conceive this requires a certain intellectual flexibility which is probably not possessed by the average person." Should criminal law be used to teach such lessons? Is there some value in using ordinary meanings of criminal terms?

Lund v. Commonwealth

Supreme Court of Virginia (*en banc*)
232 S.E.2d 745 (1977)

I'Anson, Chief Justice.

Defendant, Charles Walter Lund, was charged in an indictment with the theft of keys, computer cards, computer printouts and using "without authority computer operation time and services of Computer Center Personnel at Virginia Polytechnic Institute and State University (V.P.I. or University) ... with intent to defraud, such property and services having a value of one hundred dollars or more." Code §§ 18.1-100 and 18.1-118 were referred to in the indictment as the applicable statutes. Defendant pleaded not guilty and waived trial by jury. He was found guilty of grand larceny and sentenced to two years in the State penitentiary. The sentence was suspended, and defendant was placed on probation for five years.

Defendant was a graduate student in statistics and a candidate for a Ph.D. degree at V.P.I. The preparation of his dissertation on the subject assigned to him by his faculty advisor required the use of computer operation time and services of the computer center personnel at the University. His faculty advisor neglected to arrange for defendant's use of the computer, but defendant used it without obtaining the proper authorization.

The computer used by the defendant was leased on an annual basis by V.P.I. from the IBM Corporation. The rental was paid by V.P.I. which allocates the cost of the computer center to various departments within the University by charging it to the budget of that department. This is a bookkeeping entry, and no money actually changes hands. The departments are allocated "computer credits (in dollars) back for their use (on) a proportional basis of their (budgetary) allotments." Each department manager receives a monthly statement showing the allotments used and the running balance in each account of his department.

An account is established when a duly authorized administrator or department head fills out a form allocating funds to a department of the University and an individual. When such form is received, the computer center assigns an account number to this allocation and provides a key to a locked post office box which is also numbered to the authorized individual and department. The account number and the post office box number are the access code which must be provided with each request before the computer will process a deck of cards prepared by the user and delivered to computer center personnel. The computer print-outs are usually returned to the locked post office box. When the product is too large for the box, a check [mark] is placed in the box, and it is used to receive the print-outs at the computer center main window.

Defendant came under surveillance on October 12, 1974, because of complaints from various departments that unauthorized charges were being made to one or more of their accounts. When confronted by the University's investigator, defendant initially denied that he had used the computer service, but later admitted that he had. He gave to the investigator seven keys for boxes assigned to other persons. One of these keys was secreted in his sock. He told the investigating officer he had been given the keys by another student. A large number of computer cards and print-outs were taken from defendant's apartment.

The director of the computer center testified that the unauthorized sum spent out of the accounts associated with the seven post office box keys, amounted to $5,065. He estimated that on the basis of the computer cards and print-outs obtained from the defendant, as much as $26,384.16 in unauthorized computer time had been used by the defendant. He said, however, that the value of the cards and print-outs obtained from the defendant was "whatever scrap paper is worth."

Defendant testified that he used the computer without specific authority. He stated that he knew he was a large computer user, but, because he was doing work on his doctoral dissertation, he did not consider this use excessive or that "he was doing anything wrong."

Four faculty members testified in defendant's behalf. They all agreed that computer time "probably would have been" or "would have been" assigned to defendant if properly requested. Dr. Hinkleman, who replaced defendant's first advisor, testified that the computer time was essential for the defendant to carry out his assignment. He assumed that a sufficient number of computer hours had been arranged by Lund's prior faculty advisor.

The head of the statistics department, at the time of the trial, agreed with the testimony of the faculty members that Lund would have been assigned computer time if properly requested. He also testified that the committee which recommended the awarding of degrees was aware of the charges pending against defendant when he was awarded his doctorate by the University.

The defendant contends that his conviction of grand larceny of the keys, computer cards, and computer print-outs cannot be upheld under the provisions of Code § 18.1-

100 because (1) there was no evidence that the articles were stolen, or that they had a value of $100 or more, and (2) computer time and services are not the subject of larceny under the provisions of Code §§ 18.1-100 or 18.1-118. Code § 18.1-100 (now § 18.2-95) provides as follows:

> Any person who: ...
>
> (2) Commits simple larceny not from the person of another of goods and chattels of the value of one hundred dollars or more, shall be deemed guilty of grand larceny....

Section 18.1-118 (now § 18.2-178) provides as follows:

> If any person obtain, by any false pretense or token, from any person, with intent to defraud, money or other property which may be the subject of larceny, he shall be deemed guilty of larceny thereof....

The Commonwealth concedes that the defendant could not be convicted of grand larceny of the keys and computer cards because there was no evidence that those articles were stolen and that they had a market value of $100 or more. The Commonwealth argues, however, that the evidence shows the defendant violated the provisions of § 18.1-118 when he obtained by false pretense or token, with intent to defraud, the computer print-outs which had a value of over $5,000.

Under the provisions of Code § 18.1-118, for one to be guilty of the crime of larceny by false pretense, he must make a false representation of an existing fact with knowledge of its falsity and, on that basis, obtain from another person money or other property which may be the subject of larceny, with the intent to defraud.

At common law, larceny is the taking and carrying away of the goods and chattels of another with intent to deprive the owner of the possession thereof permanently. Code § 18.1-100 defines grand larceny as a taking ... not from the person of another goods and chattels of the value of $100 or more. The phrase "goods and chattels" cannot be interpreted to include computer time and services in light of the often repeated mandate that criminal statutes must be strictly construed.

At common law, labor or services could not be the subject of the crime of false pretense because neither time nor services may be taken and carried away. It has been generally held that, in the absence of a clearly expressed legislative intent, labor or services could not be the subject of the statutory crime of false pretense. Some jurisdictions have amended their criminal codes specifically to make it a crime to obtain labor or services by means of false pretense.

Furthermore, the unauthorized use of the computer is not the subject of larceny. Nowhere in Code § 18.1-100 or § 18.1-118 do we find the word "use." The language of the statutes connotes more than just the unauthorized use of the property of another. It refers to a taking and carrying away of a certain concrete article of personal property. *People v. Ashworth*, 222 N.Y.S. 24 (App. Div. 1927). There it was held that the unauthorized use of machinery and spinning facilities of another to process wool did not constitute larceny under New York's false pretense statute.

We hold that labor and services and the unauthorized use of the University's computer cannot be construed to be a subject of larceny under the provisions of Code §§ 18.1-100 and 18.1-118.

For the reasons stated, the judgment of the trial court is reversed, and the indictment is quashed.

Comments and Questions

(1) Lund was prosecuted for obtaining goods through false pretenses from the university. Why did the court frame its discussion in terms of larceny? The *Lund* case demonstrates that the tenets of larceny remain central to and significant in all theft crimes. The Virginia legislature, apparently unhappy with the holding in *Lund*, amended the statute. *See Evans v. Commonwealth*, 308 S.E.2d 126 (Va. 1983).

(2) Peter Collins was convicted of converting government property to his own use in violation of 18 U.S.C. § 641, which prohibits theft of federal property *See Morissette, supra*, Ch. 3. Collins worked for the Defense Intelligence Agency and had access to the agency's computer system. An avid amateur ballroom dancer, he wrote a newsletter for the local chapter of the Amateur Ballroom Dance Association. He used the agency's word processing function to construct a 17-page dance calendar and 12 computer folders. He also used agency photocopiers to produce an estimated 70,000 copies of the material. Collins appealed his conviction, arguing that section 641 applies only to tangible property.

> Nevertheless, while we hold section 641 prohibits the conversion of computer time and storage, we find the government here failed to meet its evidentiary burden in proving this charge....
>
> ... [W]e conclude the government provided insufficient evidence that appellant converted to his own use the government's computer time and storage. The cornerstone of conversion is the unauthorized exercise of control over property in such a manner that serious interference with ownership rights occurs....
>
> [T]he government did not provide a shred of evidence in the case at bar that appellant seriously interfered with the government's ownership rights in its computer system. While appellant concedes he typed in data and stored information on the computer regarding his personal activities, no evidence exists that such conduct prevented him or others from performing their official duties on the computer. The government did not even attempt to show that appellant's use of the computer prevented agency personnel from accessing the computer or storing information. Thus, appellant's use of the government computer in no way seriously interfered with the government's ownership rights.

United States v. Collins, 56 F.3d 1416, 1420 (D.C. Cir. 1995). The court found, however, that the government had established Collin's use of the photocopier, and upheld the conviction for conversion of that property.

(3) States have responded by enacting new statutes that specifically address these issues. For instance, consider the approach taken by Illinois:

> *Theft of Labor or Services or Use of Property.* (a) A person commits theft when he obtains the temporary use of property, labor or services of another which are available only for hire, by means of threat or deception or knowing that such use is without consent of the person providing the property, labor or services.

720 Ill. Comp. Stat. 5/16-3. The new legislation often addresses misuse or tampering with computers that belong to others. *See* 720 Ill. Com/ Stat. 5/26/-9; 18 U.S.C. § 1030 (federal crime of computer fraud and abuse).

Regina v. Stewart

Supreme Court of Canada
50 D.L.R.4th 1, 41 C.C.C.3d 481 (1988)

The judgment of the Court was delivered by LAMAR, J.

While one can steal a document containing confidential information, does obtaining without authorization the confidential information, by copying the document or memorizing its content, constitute theft? ...

...

A union attempting to organize the approximately 600 employees of the Constellation Hotel, in Toronto, was unable to obtain the names, addresses and telephone numbers of the employees because of a hotel policy that such information be treated as confidential.... The appellant, Wayne John Stewart, a self-employed consultant, was hired by somebody he assumed to be acting for the union to obtain the names and addresses of the employees. Stewart offered [Jan William Hart,] a security guard at the hotel a fee to obtain this information.... I should like to make it very clear at the outset of this opinion that we are not here dealing with an attempt to obtain a physical object. This case was argued throughout on an agreed statement of facts, in which it was agreed that no tangible object, such as a list containing the information sought, would have been taken had the scheme been carried out. The security guard reported the offer to his security chief and the police; as a result, a subsequent telephone conversation between [the security guard] and Stewart was recorded, and Stewart was indicted [for counseling another to commit fraud and theft of private property].... He elected trial by Judge alone and was acquitted on all three counts.... [In a procedure authorized by Canadian law, the Crown appealed; the appellate court reversed and entered a judgment of conviction. Stewart then appealed to the Supreme Court.] ...

I. Theft

... In order to be convicted of theft, one has to take or convert "anything whether animate or inanimate" with the requisite intent.... To determine whether confidential information can be the object of theft, the meaning of "anything" must be ascertained.

The word "anything" is very comprehensive and is not in itself restricted in any way. As such it could include both tangible things and intangibles....

We are here dealing not with the theft of a list or any other tangible object containing confidential information, but with the theft of confidential information per se, a pure intangible. As mentioned earlier, the assumption that no tangible object would have been taken was part of the agreed statement of facts, and the case was argued throughout on that basis. The word "anything" is not in itself a bar to including any intangible, whatever its nature. However, its meaning must be determined within the context of § 283 of the Code.

In my view, the wording of § 283 restricts the meaning of "anything" in two ways. First, whether tangible or intangible, "anything" must be of a nature such that it can be the subject of a proprietary right. Second, the property must be capable of being taken or converted in a manner that results in the deprivation of the victim....

[In my opinion, it is clear that to be the object of theft, "anything" must be property in the sense that to be stolen, it has to belong in some way to someone. For instance, no conviction for theft would arise out of a taking or converting of the air that we breathe, because air is not property.]

It can be argued that confidential information is property for the purposes of civil law. Indeed, it possesses many of the characteristics of other forms of property: for example, a trade secret, which is a particular kind of confidential information, can be sold, licensed or bequeathed, it can be the subject of a trust or passed to a trustee in bankruptcy. In the commercial field, there are reasons to grant some form of protection to the possessor of confidential information: it is the product of labor, skill and expenditure, and its unauthorized use would undermine productive efforts which ought to be encouraged. As the term "property" is simply a reference to the cluster of rights assigned to the owner, this protection could be given in the form of proprietary rights. The cases demonstrate that English and Canadian civil law protect confidential information. However, the legal basis for doing so has not been clearly established by the Courts. Some cases have treated confidential information as property, and thus have entitled the owner to exclude others from the use thereof. On the other hand, the Courts have recognized certain rights with respect to confidential information in the guise of an equitable obligation of good faith.

It appears that the protection afforded to confidential information in most civil cases arises more from an obligation of good faith or a fiduciary relationship than from a proprietary interest. No Canadian Court has so far conclusively decided that confidential information is property, with all the civil consequences that such a finding would entail. The case law is therefore of little assistance to us in the present case.

It is possible that, with time, confidential information will come to be considered as property in the civil law or even be granted special legal protection by statutory enactment. Even if confidential information were to be considered as property under civil law, it does not however automatically follow that it qualifies as property for the purposes of criminal law. Conversely, the fact that something is not property under civil law is likewise not conclusive for the purpose of criminal law. Whether or not confidential information is property under the *Criminal Code* should be decided in the perspective of the criminal law....

In civil law, the characterization of something as property triggers a series of legal consequences. That characterization has the same effect under the criminal law, although the consequences are somewhat different. If confidential information is considered as property for the purposes of the theft section, other sections of the *Criminal Code* relating to offences against property may also apply: §§ 27 (use of force to prevent commission of offence), 38 (defense of movable property), 39 (defense with claim of right), 302 (robbery), 312 (possession of property obtained by crime), 350 (disposal of property to defraud creditors), 616 (restitution of property), 653 (compensation for loss of property) and 654 (compensation to bona fide purchasers). For example, let us assume a person obtains confidential information by the commission of a crime, such as theft if it were possible. If, after having memorized the information, that person is incapable of erasing it from his memory, he could, one might argue, be charged with an offence under § 312 [possessing property obtained by crime] for each day that he is unable to forget the information.

Furthermore, the qualification of confidential information as property must be done in each case by examining the purposes and context of the civil and criminal law. It is understandable that one who possesses valuable information would want to protect it from unauthorized use and reproduction. In civil litigation, this protection can be afforded by the Courts because they simply have to balance the interests of the parties involved. However criminal law is designed to prevent wrongs against society as a whole. From a social point of view, whether confidential information should be protected requires a weighing of interest much broader than those of the parties involved. As opposed to the alleged owner of the information, society's best advantage may well be to favour the free flow of information and greater accessibility by all. Would society be willing to prosecute the person who discloses to the public a cure for cancer, although its discoverer wanted to keep it confidential?

The criminalization of certain types of conduct should not be done lightly. If the unauthorized appropriation of confidential information becomes a criminal offence, there would be far reaching consequences that the Courts are not in a position to contemplate. For instance, the existence of such an offence would have serious implications with respect to the mobility of labor. In "Theft of Information" (1984), 100 L.Q.R. 252, Hammond points out (at p. 260) the problem that would follow:

> [W]hat is significant for present purposes about the traditional civil law formulations with respect to such [employee] covenants is that, notwithstanding their difficulties of application, they do allow a balance to be struck in particular cases between the various interests at stake. The criminal law on the other hand allocates responsibility in black and white terms. There is either an offence or there is not. Every employee who leaves a position in Canada now faces criminal sanctions if he misjudges a line which judges have had enormous difficulty in drawing in civil law cases.

This indirect restriction on the mobility of labor is only one of the many undesirable consequences that could result from a hasty extension of criminal provisions by qualifying confidential information as property.

Moreover, because of the inherent nature of information, treating confidential information as property simpliciter for the purposes of the law of theft would create a host of practical problems. For instance, what is the precise definition of "confidential information"? Is confidentiality based on the alleged owner's intent or on some objective criteria? At what point does information cease to be confidential and would it therefore fall outside the scope of the criminal law? Should only confidential information be protected under the criminal law, or any type of information deemed to be of some commercial value? I am of the view that, given recent technological developments, confidential information, and in some instances, information of a commercial value, is in need of some protection through our criminal law. Be that as it may, in my opinion, the extent to which this should be done and the manner in which it should be done are best left to be determined by Parliament rather than by the Courts.

Indeed, the realm of information must be approached in a comprehensive way, taking into account the competing interests in the free flow of information and in one's right to confidentiality or again, one's economic interests in certain kinds of information. The choices to be made rest upon political judgments that, in my view, are matters of legislative action and not of judicial decision....

Although this conclusion is sufficient to dispose of the appeal..., I will also consider the second restriction to the scope of the word "anything", that is that property must be capable of being taken or converted in a manner that results in the deprivation of the victim. Tangible things present no difficulty in this regard, as it is easy to conceive how they can be both taken and converted. On the other hand, pure intangibles, as they have no physical existence, can obviously only be converted, not taken. The "taking" of an intangible could only occur where such intangible is embodied in a tangible object, for example a cheque, a share certificate or a list containing information. However, that would not result in the taking of the intangible per se, but rather of the physical object evidencing it.

The question is thus whether confidential information is of a nature such that it can be taken or converted. In my opinion, except in very rare and highly unusual circumstances, it is not. As we have seen, information per se cannot be the subject of a taking. As for conversion, it is defined as an act of interference with a chattel inconsistent with the right of another, whereby that other is deprived of the use and possession of it. Confidential information is not of a nature such that it can be converted because if one appropriates confidential information without taking a physical object, for example by memorizing or copying the information or by intercepting a private conversation, the alleged owner is not deprived of the use or possession thereof. Since there is no deprivation, there can be no conversion. The only thing that the victim would be deprived of is the confidentiality of the information. In my opinion, confidentiality cannot be the subject of theft because it does not fall within the meaning of "anything"....

In the case at Bar, the majority of the Court of Appeal held that if Hart had taken the information requested, the hotel would not have been deprived of the information, but of its character of confidentiality. As a result, the Court was of the opinion that Hart would have had the intent [to] ... deal[] with the information in such a manner that it could not be restored in its original, confidential, condition. With respect, the Court of Appeal did not properly consider the actus reus required for committing the offence, that is a taking or a conversion. As I said one cannot be deprived of confidentiality, because one cannot own confidentiality. One enjoys it. Therefore, appellant should not have been convicted on the sole basis that he might have had the intent ... since the commission of the actus reus was not and could not be established.

...

For all these reasons, I am of the opinion that confidential information does not come within the meaning of the word "anything" of § 283(1) of the Criminal Code.

Comments and Questions

(1) Tort law recognizes rights in information, and victims of misappropriation may sue for damages. Does that argue for treating misappropriation of information as a crime? The civil suits are usually based on breach of contract, a duty of good faith, or the duty of loyalty owed by employees to employers. What characteristics of criminal law make one pause to import civil standards into criminal law? Or is it a simple matter of deferring to the legislature? Or had the Canadian legislators endorsed the view that information was subject to theft in its use of the term "anything"?

(2) What did the court intend when it noted at the outset that the case concerned "pure information." The court in *Stewart* implied that the outcome might be different if Hart had copied the names onto paper and given the paper to Stewart. Why would that make a difference? Should it?

(3) In *Stewart*, to whom did the information about individual employees belong? Who is injured by the divulgence of such information, the employer or the employees? Why are largely subjective criteria problematic? Would protecting information affect the ability of employees to move from one employer to another?

(4) The National Stolen Property Act defines a federal crime that prohibits transporting stolen property across state lines:

> Whoever transports, transmits, or transfers in interstate or foreign commerce any goods, wares, merchandise, securities or money, of the value of $5000 or more, knowing the same to have been stolen, converted or taken by fraud ... [s]hall be fined not more than $10,000 or imprisoned not more than ten years or both.

18 U.S.C. § 2314.

The following case considers what the terms "goods, wares, or merchandise" mean for purposes of the statute.

United States v. Farraj

United States District Court, Southern District of New York
142 F. Supp. 2d 484 (2001)

Marrero, District Judge.

In summer of 2000, Said Farraj was a paralegal with the law firm of Orrick, Harrington & Sutcliffe LLP ("Orrick"). At the time, Orrick represented plaintiffs in a class action tobacco case. In preparation for the trial, the attorneys and paralegals at Orrick created a trial plan, exceeding 400 pages and including, among other things, trial strategy, deposition excerpts and summaries, and references to anticipated trial exhibits. Only Orrick employees assigned to the case were permitted access to the Trial Plan. The Indictment does not reveal whether Said was included among such employees.

The Government charges that Said, using the moniker "FlyGuyNYt," e-mailed an 80-page excerpt of the Trial Plan to the defendants' attorneys and offered to sell them the entire Plan. An FBI agent posing as one of the defendants' attorneys negotiated with Said via e-mail and ultimately agreed to purchase the Trial Plan for $2 million. On July 21, 2000, Yeazid, Said's brother, met with a second undercover FBI agent at a McDonald's restaurant in lower Manhattan to receive payment. Yeazid was arrested then and gave a statement to the FBI implicating his brother in the conspiracy charged in the Indictment.

DISCUSSION

The Government charges in count two that by e-mailing the Trial Plan excerpt across state lines, Said violated [the National Stolen Property Act].... Said moves to dismiss, arguing that 8 U.S.C. § 2314 applies only to the physical asportation of tangible goods or currency, not to "information" stored and transmitted electronically, such as the Trial Plan excerpt e-mailed here. Neither the Supreme Court nor the Second Circuit has addressed this question directly, and this appears to be an issue of first impression in this District.

...

The Second Circuit has held that the phrase "goods, wares, or merchandise" is " 'a general and comprehensive designation of such personal property or chattels as are ordinarily a subject of commerce.' " *In re Vericker*, 446 F.2d 244, 248 (2d Cir. 1971) (Friendly, J.). Said, relying on *Vericker*, argues that the Second Circuit has at times determined that documents fall outside the scope of § 2314. At other times, however, the Second Circuit and other courts have held that documents may be considered "goods, wares, [or] merchandise" under § 2314.

The FBI documents at issue in *Vericker* detailed the criminal activity of certain individuals. Judge Friendly reasoned that the FBI documents were not "goods, wares, [or] merchandise" within the meaning of the statute because the substance contained in the documents was not ordinarily the subject of commerce. The Trial Plan at issue here, however, as is true for trial plans generally, was the work product of a business relationship between client and attorney, and may thus be viewed as an ordinary subject of commerce, created for a commercial purpose and carrying inherent commercial value at least as to the persons directly interested in the matter.

Said argues that even if trial plans generally may be viewed as goods under § 2314, he is accused of transmitting an "intangible," an electronic form of the document, and therefore that it was not a good, but merely "information."

The text of § 2314 makes no distinction between tangible and intangible property, or between electronic and other manner of transfer across state lines. Indeed, in 1988, Congress amended § 2314 to include the term "transmits" to reflect its agreement with the Second Circuit and other courts which had held that § 2314 applied to money wire transfers, where the only interstate transportation took place electronically and where there was no transportation of any physical item.

...

The Second Circuit has also held that § 2314 was violated when the defendants stole documents containing some drug manufacturing process, copied and returned them, and then sent the copies abroad. The court noted that it did not matter that the item stolen was not the same as that transported. Rather, as observed by Judge Friendly,

> where the physical form of the stolen goods is secondary in every respect to the matter recorded in them, the transformation of the information in the stolen papers into a tangible object never possessed by the original owner should be deemed immaterial. It would offend common sense to hold that these defendants fall outside the statute simply because, in efforts to avoid detection, their confederates were at pains to restore the original papers to [the employer] and transport only copies or notes....

Bottone, 365 F.2d at 391–92.

...

Weighing the scant authority at hand, the Court is persuaded that the view most closely analogous to Second Circuit doctrine is that which holds that the transfer of electronic documents via the internet across state lines does fall within the purview of § 2314. The indictment is therefore upheld and the motion to dismiss count two is denied.

Comments and Questions

(1) According to *Farraj*, what are "goods"? Is a trial plan a "subject of commerce" if there is only one buyer for it? How is the trial plan in *Farraj* different from the FBI documents in *Vericker*, cited by the court. Presumably, money was paid for the creation of the trial plan and the FBI documents; there may be greater demand for the FBI material than for the trial plan. Why was the trial plan a "good" if the FBI documents were not?

(2) Did the *Farraj* court engage in "creative judicial interpretation of federal criminal statutes" in interpreting the NSPA to include information products?

(3) The Seventh Circuit considered a conviction that involved number codes that truck drivers used to obtain cash at truck stops. *United States v. Stafford*, 136 F.3d 1109 (7th Cir. 1998). Drivers wrote the code on a form, which was used like a check; defendants had used stolen numbers. The court, Judge Posner writing, held that the numbers were not goods, wares, or merchandise as required by the National Stolen Property Act.

> The government concedes that the codes are not securities or money, but it says that they are goods, wares, or merchandise.
>
> They're not; they're information. No doubt Allison wrote them down rather than committing them to memory, but he was not charged with having transported pieces of paper containing codes across state lines and we need not decide whether such transportation would violate the statute. He was charged with transferring the codes themselves, which are simply sequences of digits. The sequences have no value in themselves; they are information the possession of which enables a person to cash a check.... Given the statute's age (it was enacted in 1934 as the National Stolen Property Act) and wording, and the principle that the definition of federal crimes is a legislative rather than a judicial function—a principle that places some limits on creative judicial interpretations of federal criminal statutes—we don't think the first paragraph of section 2314 will stretch this far. The government presses on us cases that hold, very sensibly as it seems to us, that wire transfers of money can violate the statute. What is transferred is intangible, the claim represented by money rather than the rice paper itself, but it is money, and the statute expressly includes transfers of "money." The Comdata code has to be "goods, wares, [or] merchandise" to come within the statute. It is none of those things.

Stafford, 136 F.3d at 1114–15. With which court do you agree, *Farraj* or *Stafford*?

(4) An owner of personal property who takes his own property may be guilty of larceny if it is taken from a person in lawful possession of the property for the purposes of care or repair. The *mens rea* is an intent to deprive the holder of his rights or of seeking compensation. *See State v. Cohen*, 263 N.W. 922 (Minn. 1936).

(5) "Property of another" is defined by Nevada as follows:

> ... real, personal or intangible property in which any person other than the defendant has an interest which the defendant is not privileged to infringe, including, without limitation, property in which the defendant also has an interest, notwithstanding that the other person might be precluded from civil recovery because the property was used in an unlawful transaction or was subject to forfeiture as contraband. Property in the possession of the defendant in which another person has only a security interest shall be deemed not to be the property of that other person, even if that person holds legal title to the property pursuant to a security agreement.

NRS 205.082.

[4] "Intent to Deprive Permanently"

In *Morissette, supra* Chapter 3, the Supreme Court held that a sincere belief that the property at issue had been abandoned absolved the defendant of theft charges. This mistake of fact about ownership negated the *mens rea* of an intention to deprive the owner of property. To prove larceny, the state must establish that the defendant took the property with an additional, further purpose to deprive the owner of it permanently. In addition, this *mens rea* element applies to all of the other elements of larceny. In sum, the actor must knowingly take and carry away property of another with the further purpose of permanently depriving the owner of the property.

Larceny cannot be proved if the factfinder believes the accused intended to return the property to the owner. A defendant who wanted to get even with a boy who threw oranges at him took the boy's bicycle, intending to return it—but was caught before he could do so. The court held that, under these facts, the defendant was not guilty of larceny. *See People v. Brown*, 38 P. 518 (Cal. 1894). In another case, the defendant confiscated shopping carts from various supermarkets and held them for ransom. Here, the court concluded the defendant intended to permanently deprive the owners of their property if they failed to accede to his demand; the court upheld conviction. *See People v. Stay*, 19 Cal. App. 3d 166 (1971).

State v. McGraw

Supreme Court of Indiana
480 N.E.2d 552 (1985)

Prentice, Justice.

Defendant (Appellant-Petitioner) was charged with nine counts of theft under Ind. Code § 35-43-4-2 (Burns Supp. 1983), by information alleging that he knowingly exerted "unauthorized control over the property of the City of Indianapolis, Indiana, to-wit: the use of computers and computer services with intent to deprive the City of Indianapolis, ..." He was convicted upon two counts, following a trial by jury. The trial court, thereafter, granted his renewed motion to dismiss, citing, among other grounds, the insufficiency of the evidence. The Court of Appeals (First District) reversed the trial court and ordered the verdicts reinstated by decision and opinion published at 459 N.E.2d 61.

...

Defendant was employed by the City of Indianapolis, as a computer operator. The City leased computer services on a fixed charge or flat rate basis, hence the expense to it was not varied by the extent to which it was used. Defendant was provided with a terminal at his desk and was assigned a portion of the computer's information storage capacity, called a "private library," for his utilization in performing his duties. No other employees were authorized to use his terminal or his library.

Defendant became involved in a private sales venture and began soliciting his co-workers and using a small portion of his assigned library to maintain records associated with the venture. He was reprimanded several times for selling his products in the office and on "office time," and he was eventually discharged for unsatisfactory job performance and for continuing his personal business activities during office hours.

Defendant, at the time of his being hired by the City, received a handbook, as do all new employees, which discloses the general prohibition against the unauthorized use of city property. Other city employees sometimes used the computer for personal convenience or entertainment; and although Defendant's supervisor knew or suspected that Defendant was using the computer for his business records, he never investigated the matter or reprimanded Defendant in this regard, and such use of the computer was not cited as a basis for his discharge.

Defendant, following his discharge, applied for and received unemployment compensation benefits, over the protest of the City. He requested a former fellow employee to obtain a "print-out" of his business data and then to erase it from what had been his library. Instead, the "print-out" was turned over to Defendant's former supervisor and became the basis for the criminal charges.

Assuming that Defendant's use of the computer was unauthorized and that such use is a "property" under the theft statute, there remains an element of the offense missing under the evidence. The act provides: "A person who knowingly or intentionally exerts unauthorized control over property of another person with *intent* to deprive the other of any part of its value or use, commits theft, a class D felony." (Emphasis added.) Ind. Code § 35-43-4-2. It is immediately apparent that the res of the statute, the harm sought to be prevented, is a deprivation to one of his property or its use — not a benefit to one which, although a windfall to him, harmed nobody.

The Court of Appeals focused upon Defendant's unauthorized use of the computer for monetary gain and upon the definition of "property" as used in the statute and as defined by Ind. Code § 35-41-1-2 (Burns 1979 Repl.), which we may assume, arguendo, includes the "use" of a computer, although we think that it would be more accurate to say that the *information* derived by use of a computer is *property*. Having determined that Defendant's use was property, was unauthorized and was for his monetary benefit, it concluded that he committed theft. Our question is, "Who was deprived of what?"

Not only was there no evidence that the City was ever deprived of any part of the value or the use of the computer by reason of Defendant's conduct, the uncontradicted evidence was to the contrary. The computer was utilized for City business by means of terminals assigned to various employee-operators, including Defendant. The computer processed the data from the various terminals simultaneously, and the limit of its capacity was never reached or likely to have been. The computer service was leased to the City at a fixed charge, and the tapes or discs upon which the imparted data was stored were erasable and reusable. Defendant's unauthorized use cost the City nothing and did not interfere with its use by others. He extracted from the system only such information as he had previously put into it. He did not, for his own benefit, withdraw City data intended for its exclusive use or for sale. Thus, Defendant did not deprive the City of the 'use of computers and computer services' as the information alleged that he intended to do. We find no distinction between Defendant's use of the City's computer and the use, by a mechanic, of the employer's hammer or a stenographer's use of the employer's typewriter, for other than the employer's purposes. Under traditional concepts, the transgression is in the nature of a trespass, a civil matter—and a de minimis one, at that. Defendant has likened his conduct to the use of an employer's vacant bookshelf, for the temporary storage of one's personal items, and to the use of an employer's telephone facilities for toll-free calls. The analogies appear to us to be appropriate.

...

It is appropriate to note a companion statute to the theft statute is Ind. Code § 35-43-4-3 (Burns 1979 Repl.), proscribing *conversion*, which is as follows:

> A person who knowingly or intentionally exerts unauthorized control over property of another person commits criminal conversion, a class A misdemeanor.

The only difference between the statutory definitions of theft and criminal conversion is that the definition for conversion omits the words "with intent to deprive the other of any part of its value or use." At most, the evidence in this case warranted a conviction for criminal conversion.

Pivarnik, Justice, dissenting.

I must dissent from the majority opinion wherein the majority finds that Defendant did not take property of the City "with intent to deprive the owner of said property." In the first place, intent is clearly shown in that Defendant used the City computer system for his personal business, well knowing that he was doing so and well knowing that it was unauthorized. I think the Court of Appeals properly focused upon Defendant's unauthorized use of the computer for monetary gain and upon the definition of property as used in the statute and as defined by Ind. Code § 35-41-1-2 (Burns 1979 Repl.). Time and use are at the very core of the value of a computer system. To say that only the information stored in the computer plus the tapes and discs and perhaps the machinery involved in the computer system, are the only elements that can be measured as the value or property feature of that system, is incorrect.

I think it is irrelevant that the computer processed the data from various terminals simultaneously and the limit of its capacity was never reached by any or all of the stations, including the defendant's. It is also irrelevant that the computer service was leased to the City at a fixed charge and that the tapes or discs upon which the imparted data was stored were erasable and reusable. The fact is the City owned the computer system of all the stations including the defendant's. The time and use of that equipment at that station belonged to the City. Thus, when the defendant used the computer system, putting on data from his private business and taking it out on printouts, he was taking that which was property of the City and converting it to his own use, thereby depriving the City of its use and value. The majority says: "Thus, Defendant did not deprive the City of the 'use of computers and computer services' as the information alleged that he intended to do." I disagree. I feel that is exactly what he did and I think the Court of Appeals properly found so.

...

Comments and Questions

(1) Although the court assumed that the term "property" included using an employer's computer, it held that such use did not violate the statute. What element of the offense had the government failed to prove?

The *McGraw* court poses the issue as one of *mens rea*, an intention to deprive the city of the value and use of its property. Yet the decision focuses on whether the city was actually deprived of the use of its computer, and the dissent accepts that characterization. Is the court saying that the defendant could not have intended to deprive the city of computer use because it was impossible to do so?

(2) Does the court's description of a computer as a storage unit like a bookcase accurately account for the employer's interests? The dissent noted that use is a "core value" of a computer system. Should violating a workplace rule give rise to criminal punishment? Consider the workplace norms of personal use of telephones, faxes, copiers, and even computers.

(3) The state in *McGraw* failed to convince the court that use of an employer's computer established intent. Given the intangible nature of computer use, how could the government establish intent? In the absence of a commercial market for the computer system at issue, how can the value of lost use—and the harm to a victim—be measured?

(4) If a defendant honestly and sincerely believes that the property at issue belongs to her, a "claim of right" may be a defense to a charge of larceny. A good faith belief, even if unreasonable, negates the *mens rea* of larceny, acting with purpose to deprive another of property. Actors cannot intend to deprive another if they believe the property is theirs. The modern trend disallows the defense when it involves a forcible collection of money owed to the defendant. *See People v. Tufunga*, 987 P.2d 168 (Cal. 1999) (citing the need to discourage forcible or violent self-help remedies).

(5) Most states do not recognize the claim of right defense to forcible larcenies like robbery or burglary. The court in *State v. Miller*, 622 N.W.2d 782 (Iowa Ct. App. 2000), explained why it rejected the claim as a defense to burglary:

> Iowa public policy evinces the modern distaste for violent self-help.... [B]asic public policy dictates that even rightful owners should not be permitted to perpetrate break-ins or use force to regain their property, once it has been taken. As one court noted, to accept the claim of right defense in contexts where force has been used is "one step short of accepting lawless reprisal as an appropriate means of redressing grievances...." [O]ur own supreme court has stated that nothing in the code "approves of after-the-fact vigilante action." The same policy would presumably extend to one who breaks into a residence to retake property that was previously stolen from him.

...

> The crime of burglary was not designed to protect property rights, as the theft statutes are. Instead, the crime is considered to be an offense against the security of habitation or occupancy. While the law supports a claim-of-right defense, it does not condone the invasion of another's home to regain property rights, when viable legal channels exist to effect a remedy. Expanding the claim-of-right defense to burglary would undermine the purpose of the burglary statute.

Id. at 786.

[B] False Pretenses

In 1757, the English Parliament created the crime of taking property by false pretenses. Common law courts had limited the application of larceny by trick to takings of possession. The crime of false pretenses targeted tricks and lies (false pretenses) that led victims to convey title, that is, ownership of property. If the deception resulted in only a transfer of possession, the correct charge was larceny by trick; if the defendant gained both possession and title, the crime was false pretenses.

Although common law courts and the eighteenth-century Parliament did not conceive of them as such, larceny by trick, false pretenses, and embezzlement are white-collar offenses. That is, property is taken or misappropriated without an actual physical taking. Although there are many forms of white-collar offenses in the regulatory and administrative realm, the term "white collar" was first applied to deprivations of property by means of deception. The conduct or *actus reus* is a lie or misrepresentation; the *mens rea* is a purpose to defraud the victim of money or property. Victims of false pretenses and fraud willingly transfer title in reliance on the misrepresentation.

Brown v. Commonwealth

Supreme Court of Kentucky
656 S.W.2d 727 (1983)

Opinion of the Court

Thomas M. Brown was convicted by a jury in Jefferson Circuit Court of theft by deception of property valued over $100 (KRS 514.040), and was sentenced to two years' imprisonment....

In December, 1978, state and local law enforcement officials initiated an undercover operation to investigate automobile transmission shops in Jefferson County which were allegedly making unnecessary repairs on cars. In February, 1979, a 1968 Ford LTD was taken to a Kentucky State Police garage where the chief mechanic removed the transmission, disassembled and inspected its parts to insure they were in working order, marked the parts for later identification and reassembled the transmission. After driving the car to make sure it was working properly, the mechanic made a malfunction adjustment to the transmission by turning the band adjustment screw backwards three turns, causing the transmission to slip. To correct the problem, one needed only to turn the screw the opposite way three times, without disassembling or removing the transmission.

The car was then towed to Powers Transmission Shop where Thomas Brown worked as a manager. Detective Davis, posing as the owner of the car, was told by Brown that the transmission bands were broken due to overtightening and the entire transmission would have to be disassembled prior to knowing the extent of the damages. The next day, Brown told Detective Davis that his inspection revealed it would cost $372.82 to repair the transmission or it could be replaced for $415.00. Davis authorized the repair job only.

Four days later, Brown received $372.82 from Detective Davis for the alleged repairs. The car was then taken back to the Kentucky State Police garage where the transmission was thoroughly re-examined by the chief mechanic. It was at this juncture that the mechanic discovered the transmission had been replaced, not repaired as represented, and relayed the information to Davis.

Movant assigns several errors, only one of which has merit. That is the argument that the movant was entitled to a directed verdict, as the Commonwealth failed to prove an essential element in the offense to theft by deception, *i.e.*, reliance by the detective upon the misrepresentation of the movant.

The statute in question, KRS 514.040, in pertinent part, states:

> (1) A person is guilty of theft by deception when he obtains property of another by deception with intent to deprive him thereof. A person deceives when he intentionally; (a) creates or reinforces a false impression, including false impressions as to law, value, intention or other state of mind.

The former statute covering the offense herein was KRS 434.050. This statute was also silent on the question of the necessity of victim's reliance on the false impression, but this court, in *Rowland v. Commonwealth*, Ky., 355 S.W.2d 292 (1962), held that reliance was an essential part of the offense, and in our opinion it remains a necessary element under KRS 514.040.

However, in the instant case, the movant created two false impressions, viz., that the transmission was defective, which was not relied upon by the detective, and that he would repair the transmission, which was relied upon; and in fact a used transmission of dubious value was substituted. Because of the second misrepresentation, we affirm the conviction.

...

Comments and Questions

(1) The common law elements of obtaining property by false pretenses are: (1) a material misrepresentation of a present or past fact (2) which induces the victim (3) to part with title to (4) property (5) with knowledge of the misrepresentation and intent to defraud. According to the defendant, which elements are missing in *Brown*? Has the defendant committed larceny?

(2) States that follow the Model Penal Code may refer to false pretenses as "theft by deception." A deception includes creating or reinforcing a false impression, preventing the victim from obtaining correct information, or failing to correct a false impression created by the defendant. *See* Model Penal Code § 223.3.

(3) Recall that the defendant in *Lund, supra,* was convicted of grand larceny on the basis of the state's false pretenses statute. How had the defendant deceived the university?

State v. Clermont

Court of Appeals of Oregon
495 P.2d 305 (1972)

Thornton, Judge.

Defendant was convicted by a jury for obtaining money by false pretenses in violation of ORS 165.205....

This prosecution arose out of the following facts:

The Shrine Club for Josephine County sponsored a traveling circus to be held September 17, 1971. The contract provided that the circus would send in personnel to handle advance ticket sales. The ticket manager for the circus hired four telephone solicitors, who were to contact business firms in the area to sell tickets. When a sale was made over the telephone the manager would send out a collector to deliver the tickets and collect the money therefor. The tickets were printed by a printing firm in California. Each ticket contained an identification number.

Defendant applied for a job as a solicitor but was not hired. Defendant and a third party were staying with Mr. Evans, one of the hired solicitors.

Defendant and the third party arranged to have 2,000 spurious Shrine circus tickets printed up at a printing firm in Medford. The tickets were not individually numbered, however. Thereafter defendant caused 10 of the spurious tickets to be delivered to a Grants Pass shop whose owners paid $10 therefor. Defendant did not personally deliver the tickets, but was in the vicinity when delivery was made by his landlady's young son. A few days after the purchase, one of the owners of the shop turned the tickets over to the police. Neither the shop owners nor any of their customers ever had an opportunity to use them.

The secretary-treasurer of the Shrine Club testified that any child who had a ticket was admitted "regardless of whether the tickets were numbered." The Shrine Club also informed the police it would honor any ticket presented by a child.

Defendant's act of tendering the false tickets to the victim was a false written representation of a present fact, namely, that the tickets were valid, when in fact they were spurious. Thus the spurious tickets were false tokens.

When the victim paid the money for the tickets believing them to be bona fide the crime of obtaining money by false pretenses was complete notwithstanding the circus was to occur at a later date. The making of the false representation and the necessary intent to defraud must be decided at the date the tickets were delivered and the money received....

The fact that the Shrine Club later chose to admit to the circus any child presenting a ticket, whether bona fide or bogus, would not constitute a defense. It is a uniformly recognized and accepted proposition of the criminal law that, in the absence of statute, restitution is not a defense to crimes of this type, including false pretenses.... Just as this offense cannot be purged by subsequent restitution ... by the same reasoning we conclude that this offense cannot be "ratified" or wiped out by similar subsequent actions by third persons such as the Shrine Club, since the crime is against the laws of Oregon.

Comments and Questions

(1) Under common law, the defendant's misrepresentation must concern a present or past fact; misrepresentation about the future did not suffice. *See, e.g., People v. Cage*, 301 N.W.2d 819 (Mich. 1981). Frequently misrepresentations will involve *both* present and future facts. In such cases, courts may find it necessary to determine on *which* misrepresentation the victim relied. It is always necessary to show that the victim was in fact deceived. *See, e.g., Mullican v. State*, 360 S.W.2d 35 (Tenn. 1962).

On what ground did the *Clermont* court reject the defendant's argument that the misrepresentation involved a future event, that is, admittance to the circus?

(2) Would a prudent shop owner buy admittance tickets that did not include the number of the ticket? Should it be a defense that a reasonable person would not have relied upon the misrepresentation of the defendant? While an argument can be made for such an objective standard, the preferred approach focuses upon whether the victim of the deception was in fact deceived. The more gullible and trusting members of society are the most vulnerable, and therefore most in need of protection.

People v. Whight

California Court of Appeals
43 Cal. Rptr. 2d 163 (1995)

SPARKS, ACTING PRESIDING JUSTICE.

Defendant Theodore Whight discovered that the automated teller machine (ATM) card connected to his defunct checking account could still be used to obtain cash at four local Safeway stores. For several weeks he availed himself freely of this happenstance to obtain thousands of dollars. This led to his conviction by a jury of ... four counts of grand theft by false pretenses....

The Crimes

Defendant opened a regular checking account at Tri Counties Bank (the bank) in Chico in January 1991. He was issued an ATM card which bore no expiration date. This card did not offer any overdraft protection and could be used only with the checking account. Thereafter, monthly statements for his checking account were sent to defendant by the bank at his post office box. Defendant originally deposited $3,750.99 into the checking account. By June 1991, defendant's account was overdrawn by $6.17. In accordance with the bank's normal practice, defendant was mailed a letter stating that his account was overdrawn, that his bank statement and canceled checks would be held at the bank and if no deposits were made to cover the shortage, the account would be closed.... On July 10, 1991, no deposit having been made, the bank closed the account because of the negative balance. From the bank's viewpoint, when defendant's checking account was closed, his ATM card was simultaneously canceled and revoked.

Despite the cancellation by the bank, defendant continued to use his ATM card, mainly at local Safeway markets. Safeway allows customers to make purchases and receive cash back by using ATM cards. Safeway's practice was to verify the cards through the use of a computer system operated by Wells Fargo Bank (Wells Fargo)....

It appears that there was an error in the Wells Fargo computer, which repeatedly failed to notify Safeway that defendant's ATM card was invalid. In March and April 1992, defendant was able to use his ATM card at four different Safeway markets in Butte County. He would purchase a small item, then use his ATM card to pay for the item and to receive cash back, usually $200 at a time, often more than once a day. He received to total of over $19,000. During that time his ATM card was rejected at two other (non-Safeway) markets.

...

II. False Pretenses

Defendant next contends his convictions for grand theft by false pretense must be reversed because "Safeway relied on the code issued by Wells Fargo, rather than [defendant's] presentation of his ATM card, in approving [defendant's] request for money." This leaky contention cannot hold water.

Theft by false pretenses is committed by "[e]very person who knowingly and designedly, by any false or fraudulent representation or pretense, defrauds any other person of money, labor, or property, whether real or personal, ..." (§ 532, subd. (a).)

"To support a conviction of theft for obtaining property by false pretenses, it must be shown: (1) that the defendant made a false pretense or representation, (2) that the representation was made with intent to defraud the owner of his property, and (3) that the owner was in fact defrauded in that he parted with his property in reliance upon the representation." We are here concerned with causation or reliance.

The representation need not be in the form of an oral or written statement; it may also consist of conduct. "The false pretense may consist in any act, word, symbol, or token calculated and intended to deceive. It may be either express or implied from the words or conduct." Thus, when defendant proffered his ATM card he impliedly represented, falsely, that it was valid.... Reliance on a false representation may be, and in some cases must be, inferred form the evidence.... However, if the evidence establishes that the victim did not rely on the false pretense, a conviction cannot stand. Defendant maintains that because the Safeway employees did not merely hand him cash upon presentation of the card, but instead verified the card though the computer system, Safeway did not actually rely on his implied representation and therefore he did not commit the crime of theft by false pretenses. In short, he urges there was no substantial evidence of the reliance element of the crime.

It is true that "[f]or false pretenses it is necessary that the swindler's misrepresentation cause the victim to pass title to his property or money to the swindler...." Thus, "[e]ven though a false representation is made and property obtained by the person making the representation, no prosecution will lie where the complainant parted with his property to the accused from some cause other than such false representation since to constitute this offense the representation must have been a material element in proximately causing the complainant to part with his property and without which he would not have done so."

...

Defendant claims that Safeway relied upon the computer authorization rather than upon his implicit representation that his card was valid. Whether Safeway relied exclusively on the computer authorization would ordinarily pose a factual question to be resolved by the jury under proper instruction.... But in this case the record conclusively established that Safeway did not rely upon any computer authorization from Wells Fargo.

The ATM terminals in the Safeway stores were connected to a computer system operated by Wells Fargo. When a customer uses his ATM card in the ATM terminal at a checkstand in a Safeway store by swiping it through the terminal, the magnetic stripe on the back of the card is read. This information is then sent by modem via telephone lines to computers at Wells Fargo. These computers then pass the information to a banking network. As a banking supervisor for Safeway described it, the information "goes from that network to the card holder's bank for an authorization. If the money's in the account, the bank approves it, comes back in through the network, through our bank and back to the store." For the most part, the system generates a code either approving or disapproving the transaction. If approved, the transaction is consummated. On the other hand, if the transaction is denied, the screen at a checkstand states, "transaction declined" and sale and/or request for cash would be refused.

In addition to codes for approval and disapproval, the system generates what are called "stand-in" codes. Two types of "stand-in" codes were described by the banking supervisor.

> First one being if any place along the network, that phone path I have described may be down, the phone line may not be operational at any given point in time. That's one type.
>
> The other type where Safeway will stand in is if we don't get that authorization or that response through the system in a reasonable amount of time, then we will stand in for that transaction.

Safeway would then automatically resubmit the transaction at a later time for approval. Thus, a "stand-in" code meant that either Safeway could not make connection with the Wells Fargo Bank computers or Wells Fargo could not make connection with the bank it sought approval from. In short, a "stand-in" code simply tells the Safeway store that there has been no response to its request for authorization. In these circumstances, as a Safeway accountant explained it, Safeway "management has elected to take stand-in. They will do it after approximately 25 to 30 seconds. If the card is a card from an approved bank, from a bank that Safeway deals with, we will accept the card in stand-in, management made that decision, and then the system will keep trying to connect to the bank and then get the approval for the card and get the money from the person's account, but after 25 or 30 seconds, we will take the card and give the person the money for it rather than holding the customer up and making them stand there and wait."

As it turned out, there was a glitch in Wells Fargo's system concerning defendant's account. Rather than transmitting a code declining the transaction because defendant's account had been closed, Wells Fargo kept returning a code to Safeway indicating that there was no response. This, in turn, caused Safeway to treat each transaction as a "stand-in" without a verification or approval from the computer banking system. Given these facts, it can hardly be said that Safeway relied upon the Well [sic] Fargo's computer system instead of defendant's representation that his card was valid. Even assuming that the use of a computer verification system can be described as an investigation, the computer system in fact never approved defendant's transactions. As a result, Safeway had nothing to rely upon except defendant's implicit representation that his ATM card was valid. It elected to take the risk and to rely solely on defendant's representation. On this record, the element of reliance or causation was indisputably established.

Comments and Questions

(1) Evidence also revealed that the defendant knew the account was closed, used it anyway, went to different stores at different hours, and attempted to conceal the card so clerks could not see it. He engaged in false pretenses with an intent to defraud the store of money. What is the purpose of the element of reliance?

(2) Why did Safeway accept the debit card? Because the defendant represented it was valid? Because Wells Fargo could not confirm it was not valid? Because of its internal policy regarding customer service and its decision not to keep customers waiting? In what sense did the defendant "cause" the grocery store to honor the debit card? How was the victim induced by the defendant's conduct to part with money?

[C] Embezzlement

Embezzlement is the fraudulent appropriation of property by one lawfully entrusted with its possession.

Black's Law Dictionary (6th ed. 1990).

As with false pretenses, there was no common law crime that prohibited employees and agents from taking property from their employer or principal if they lawfully possessed it. Parliament created the offense by statute in 1799, and American states incorporated it into their criminal statutes upon independence.

Briggs v. State

Court of Criminal Appeals of Tennessee
463 S.W.2d 161 (1970)

HYDER, JUDGE.

James Daily Briggs was convicted of embezzlement of more than one hundred dollars, and he was sentenced to three years in the penitentiary. His motion for a new trial was overruled and he has appealed to this Court. He has been represented by employed counsel throughout the proceedings.

The defendant was employed by the City of Memphis to take the money from parking meters or coin boxes of a City parking lot in Memphis. The money was counted and turned into the city treasury. When a shortage was suspected a police investigation was made, and the boxes were unlocked by officers at about six o'clock in the morning, the money counted, and the boxes were then kept under constant surveillance until the defendant opened them during his routine work when he removed the money. He failed to turn in all of the money which had been found to be in the boxes, and the charge of embezzlement followed.

When the defendant was arrested he admitted to the police that he had been taking money from the boxes for a long time and using it for his own purposes, spending part of it on slot machines in Mississippi.

The first four assignments of error complain that there is no evidence to sustain the verdict of the jury; that the verdict is contrary to the law and the evidence and that the evidence preponderates against the verdict and in favor of defendant's innocence.

A reading of this record by a person with an unbiased mind does not lead one to believe that there is any merit whatever to the contention that the evidence preponderates against the verdict of guilty. On the contrary there is ample evidence of guilt.

Questions and Comments

(1) The elements of embezzlement are: (1) the defendant was entrusted with the property for a specific use, (2) the defendant came into possession of the property in a lawful manner, often as a result of his employment, and (3) the defendant intended to appropriate and convert the property to his own use and permanently deprive that person of the use. *State v. Oliveira*, 432 A.2d 664, 666 (R.I. 1981). Identify the facts in *Briggs* that establish each element.

(2) An employment or fiduciary relationship usually exists between the accused and the victim of embezzlement. *See, e.g., State v. Robinson*, 603 S.E.2d 345 (N.C. App. 2004) (rejecting defendant's argument that a fiduciary relationship did not exist between a saleswoman and TJ Maxx, Inc.; position of clerk or agent is sufficient); *Commonwealth v. Oliver*, 820 N.E.2d 194 (Mass. 2005) (finding the relationship be-

tween a contractor and homeowner was not of a "confidential or fiduciary" nature and thus defendant did not hold their deposit in trust).

(3) Embezzlement can be conceived as a kind of fraud or false pretense. Given the rule stated below, identify the deceptive act in *Briggs*.

> The elements necessary to establish embezzlement are a trust relation, possession or control of property by virtue of the trust relation, and a fraudulent appropriation of the property to a use or purpose not in the due and lawful execution of the trust.

State v. Gomez, 553 P.2d 1233, 1237 (Ariz. App. 1976).

Batin v. State

Supreme Court of Nevada
38 P.3d 880 (2002)

Leavitt, Judge.

Appellant Marlon Javar Batin was convicted of three counts of embezzlement for stealing money from his employer, John Ascuaga's Nugget Hotel and Casino. On direct appeal, Batin contended that his conviction was not supported by sufficient evidence. Specifically, Batin contended that there was no evidence establishing the entrustment element of the crime of embezzlement. In a divided decision, a three-justice panel of this court affirmed Batin's conviction. His petition for rehearing was likewise denied.

Batin then filed a petition for en banc reconsideration, arguing that he was actually innocent of the crime of embezzlement. This court determined that en banc consideration of Batin's case was warranted, and the petition was granted. Having considered the evidence presented in the light most favorable to the State, we now conclude that Batin did not commit embezzlement as a matter of law because there was no evidence presented of the entrustment element of that crime. Because we cannot sustain a conviction where there is no evidence of an essential element of the charged offense, we reverse the judgment of conviction.

Facts

In 1993, Batin moved to Sparks from the Philippines and began working as a dishwasher at the Nugget. After several years at the Nugget, Batin became a slot mechanic. Batin's job duties as a slot mechanic included fixing jammed coins and refilling the "hopper." Warren Reid Anderson, Batin's supervisor, explained that the "hopper" is the part of the slot machine that pays coins back, and is separate from the "bill validator" component of the slot machine where the paper currency is kept. Anderson further testified that Batin had no duties with respect to the paper currency in the bill validator, except to safeguard the funds, and that the cash in the bill validator "wasn't to be touched." Likewise, Anderson testified that if a customer had a problem with a machine that required a cash refund "it would require supervisory backup in order to take any money out of a slot machine and pass it back to a customer." Batin also testified about his job duties as a slot mechanic. Like Anderson, Batin testified that he was prohibited from handling the paper currency inside the bill validator.

As a slot mechanic, Batin was given an "SDS" card that was used both to access the inside of the slot machine and identify him as the employee that was opening the slot machine door. The computerized SDS system is physically connected to each slot machine and counts the paper currency placed into each machine's bill validator. The SDS actually records the different denominations of bills and runs numerous reports concerning the currency. The SDS also registers every time that the slot machine door is opened or closed. If the power is turned off to a particular slot machine, the SDS system will only record the opening and closing of the door; it cannot track what happens inside the machine.

Lori Barrington, soft count supervisor, explained that after the money is counted by SDS, it is then counted three more times by a minimum of three Nugget employees. Barrington further testified that there was not much variance between the amount of money SDS recorded that the casino was supposed to have and the amount of money the casino actually had. In fact, out of 1100 slot machines, there were perhaps three errors per month totaling approximately $100.00 in variance.

In March and early June 1999, however, there were larger discrepancies discovered between the amount of money that the SDS recorded had been put into the slot machines and the amount of money the slot machine actually contained. Kathleen Plambeck, the Nugget's Internal Auditor, testified to several shortages from four different slot machines, totaling approximately $40,000.00.

In reviewing the SDS reports, Plambeck testified that she found a pattern of conduct. Namely, prior to the time that a shortage had been detected on a slot machine, Batin inserted his SDS card into the slot machine, opened the door, turned off the power, and thereafter closed the door on the machine. Plambeck found this pattern of conduct unusual because it was not necessary to turn off the slot machine for most repairs, and no one other than Batin had been turning off the power on the slot machines with the shortages. Batin testified at trial, however, that he turned off the power on the slot machines so that he would not be electrocuted and that he had always turned off the power prior to working on the slot machines.

...

Although Batin adamantly denied taking the money, Batin was arrested and charged with three counts of embezzlement. The information alleged that Batin had been entrusted with money by his employer and converted the money for a purpose other than that for which it was entrusted. After a jury trial, Batin was convicted of all three counts of embezzlement.

Discussion

Batin contends that his convictions for embezzlement should be reversed because there was insufficient evidence of an essential element of the crime. We agree.

... To prove that a defendant committed the crime of embezzlement, the State must demonstrate beyond a reasonable doubt that the defendant was a "*person with whom any money, property, or effects ha[d] been deposited or entrusted,*" and that the defendant "use[d] or appropriate[d] the money, property, or effects ... in any manner or for any other purpose than that for which [it was] deposited or entrusted."

The key distinguishing element of the crime of embezzlement is the element of entrustment. In order to be guilty of embezzlement, a defendant must have been entrusted with lawful possession of the property prior to its conversion. For purposes of proving embezzlement, the lawful possession need not be actual; rather, the State may show that a defendant had constructive possession of the property converted. This court has defined constructive possession as "both the power and the intention at a given time to exercise dominion or control over a thing, either directly or through another person or persons." In proving constructive possession, a showing that a defendant was given mere access to the property converted is insufficient. Often, an individual is entrusted with access to a particular place or thing without being given dominion and control over the property therein.[13] This is particularly true in instances, like the present one, where the individual is expressly told that he is not allowed to touch the property in the place to which access is granted.

In the instant case, the record reveals that Batin was not entrusted with lawful possession, constructive or otherwise, of the currency he allegedly took from the bill validators. In fact, both Batin and his supervisor testified that Batin had no job duties whatsoever involving this currency and that it "wasn't to be touched." Further, Batin had absolutely no power to exercise control over this currency, as Batin was required to contact his supervisor for any job task involving possession of the currency inside the bill validator, such as a cash refund to a customer. Because the aforementioned testimony was not contradicted at trial, we conclude that there was insufficient evidence of an essential element of embezzlement, as Batin was never entrusted with actual or constructive possession of the currency taken.

Our dissenting colleagues conclude that there was sufficient evidence of constructive possession because Batin had access to the inside of the slot machine where the bill validator was located and, occasionally, observed non-employee slot repairmen work on the slot machine. As previously discussed, however, constructive possession requires a showing that the accused was entrusted with control over property. We cannot say that an individual exercises control over property when he is prohibited from touching it.

In light of the foregoing, we are compelled to reverse Batin's conviction. The State failed to prove the entrustment element of the crime of embezzlement beyond a reasonable doubt, and we cannot sustain a conviction where the record is devoid of an essential element of a charged offense. To do otherwise, would imperil our system of justice by undermining the presumption that those charged with crimes are innocent until proven guilty beyond a reasonable doubt.

---

13. For example, if a person gives a neighbor the key to their house to let the plumber in to fix a leaky faucet, and the neighbor steals the television set, the crime is larceny not embezzlement because the neighbor was never entrusted with possession of the television.

MAUPIN, C.J., with whom BECKER, J., agrees, dissenting.

...

To prove that a defendant committed the crime of embezzlement, the State must proffer evidence that the defendant was entrusted with lawful possession of the property which he converted. The State need not prove that the defendant actually possessed the property, but must merely prove that the defendant had constructive possession of the property alleged to have been embezzled.

In viewing the evidence in a light most favorable to the State, we conclude that there is ample evidence to support the jury's verdict that Batin had constructive possession of the paper currency inside the bill validator. The State proffered evidence that Batin's employer entrusted him with an SDS card, which allowed Batin to access the bill validator inside the slot machine where the currency was kept. Moreover, Batin's job, as prescribed by his employer included safeguarding the funds contained inside the bill validator when he made a slot machine repair and when supervising non-employee slot machine repairmen. In safeguarding the currency inside the bill validator, Batin was entrusted with dominion and control over that currency sufficient to support the jury's finding that Batin had constructive possession over the fund that he converted.

Accordingly, because we conclude that there was sufficient evidence of the crime of embezzlement, we would affirm the judgment of conviction.

Comments and Questions

(1) Who has the better case, the majority or the dissent? How did the majority define "constructive possession"?

(2) Given the facts of *Batin*, could the government establish a larceny?

State v. Lough

Supreme Court of Rhode Island
899 A.2d 468 (2006)

JUSTICE FLAHERTY, for the Court.

...

After a jury trial in May 2004, John Lough, a patrolman in the Providence Police Department, was convicted of embezzling and fraudulently converting a child's minibike, valued at approximately $350. Sometime around midnight on July 14, 2003, Lough stopped to aid a fellow officer, Thomas Teft. Officer Teft had detained a juvenile, Shane, because he suspected that the young man was operating a stolen minibike. Officer Teft's suspicions were further aroused because Shane was unable to produce proof of ownership and the vehicle identification number had been partially scratched off the surface of the bike.... [R]ather than arresting him, Officer Teft decided to confiscate the bike and hold it at the police station until Shane could produce proof of ownership.

When Lough arrived at the scene, Officer Teft explained to him that he was unsure about the protocol for confiscating the minibike.... [T]he more experienced Lough offered his assistance by volunteering to take possession of the bike and complete the necessary paperwork. Officer Teft accepted this offer and he loaded the bike into the back seat of Lough's police cruiser. After he and Officer Teft went their separate ways, Lough removed the bike from the back seat and placed it in the trunk of the vehicle because it smelled of fuel and had fallen forward against his seat.

A short time later, as Lough and several other officers were responding to a report of a stolen vehicle, his cruiser struck the back of another officer's patrol car, apparently because of faulty brakes. Lough's supervisor instructed him and the officer driving the other vehicle to return to the police station to complete paperwork related to the accident. After finishing the paperwork, Lough left the police station intending to bring his damaged cruiser to a repair facility known as the Bucklin Street Garage.

Lough said he remembered that Shane's minibike still was in the trunk of his car while he was on his way to the garage. Lough testified at trial that because he was aggravated by the evening's events and anxious to go home, he "made a wrong decision" and decided to rid himself of the bike by leaving it behind a dumpster. He assumed that the young man would never return to claim the bike, but this assumption proved to be wrong and Shane arrived at the police station the next morning with his mother to reclaim the confiscated bike.

...

As the case of the missing minibike continued, Lough eventually came forward with his story about the dumpster, asserting that he had discarded the bike because he believed that Shane would never return to claim it. In August 2003, Lough was indicted on one count of embezzlement and fraudulent conversion in violation of § 11-41-3. Following a four-day trial in May 2004, a jury returned a verdict of guilty and Lough was fined $1,000 and received a one-year suspended sentence....

On appeal, Lough contends that the trial justice misinterpreted § 11-41-3 and incorrectly instructed the jury that a person could violate the statute by disposing of the property of another. On the basis of this same alleged misinterpretation of the law, he maintains that the trial justice improperly denied his motions for judgment of acquittal and his motion for new trial. Lough's claims of error all hinge on one central issue: whether a person who is lawfully entrusted with property and throws the property away can be convicted of embezzlement and fraudulent conversion pursuant to § 11-41-3 in the absence of proof that he derived a benefit from using the property.

...

III. Analysis

... Section 11-41-3 provides in relevant part as follows:

> "Embezzlement and fraudulent conversion.—Every ... officer, agent, clerk, servant, or other person to whom any money or other property shall be entrusted for any specific purpose ... who shall embezzle or fraudulently convert

> to his or her own use ... any money or other property which shall have come into his or her possession or shall be under his or her care or charge virtue of his or her employment ... shall be deemed guilty of larceny...."

In *Oliveira*, this Court outlined the elements of proof required to sustain a conviction under § 11-41-3. We explained that the state must establish the following: "(1) that defendant was entrusted with the property for a specific use, (2) that he came into possession of the property in a lawful manner, often as a result of his employment, and (3) that defendant intended to appropriate and convert the property to his own use and permanently deprive that person of the use."

Lough concedes that he was lawfully entrusted with the minibike for the specific purpose of delivering it to the police station. Thus, there is no dispute that the state satisfied the first two elements required to sustain a conviction. He also admitted during trial that when he threw the bike away, he intended to permanently deprive the owner of its use. He maintains, however, that this is insufficient to sustain a conviction because the state also must establish that he "convert[ed] the property to his own use." According to him, this third element of proof requires evidence that he derived some personal gain from using the property.

...

Lough argues that by instructing the jury that a person converts property to his own use by disposing of it, the trial justice permitted the jury to return a guilty verdict in the absence of evidence that he derived a benefit from his use of the minibike. This distinction is of paramount importance because Lough conceded in his testimony that he threw the minibike away. Thus, if the act of throwing the minibike away constitutes conversion, Lough's testimony was essentially an admission of guilt.

This Court has not squarely addressed what it means to fraudulently convert property to one's "own use" under § 11-41-3.... [U]nder our holding in *Powers* and under the language of the statute, the relevant inquiry is not whether Lough derived a benefit from throwing the bike away, but rather, whether he put the property to " 'his own use.' "

...

In our opinion, a person puts property to his own use when he treats it as his own, and when a person discards property, he treats it as his own. This interpretation of the statute is consistent with the plain meaning of the words used by the Legislature. When Lough decided to dispose of the minibike that had been entrusted to him, he made a decision that was properly vested in its lawful owner; in other words, by discarding the property as if it were his own, Lough converted it to "his ... own use." We therefore hold that the trial justice correctly instructed the jury on the elements of proof necessary to sustain a conviction under § 11-41-3.

Comments and Questions

(1) In *Lough*, the court ruled that use of property could constitute embezzlement. How does this compare to the results in *Ashworth* and *McGraw*, *supra*, in which the

courts ruled that use of spinning machinery and a computer system, respectively, did not constitute larceny. How do you account for the different results?

(2) A defendant agreed to wear an electronic monitoring bracelet while on probation and signed an agreement accepting responsibility for the care and return of the device. Instead he removed it, damaged it, and threw it into a field. Had the state entrusted him with the device for purposes of embezzlement? *State v. Archie*, 943 P.2d 537 (N.M. Ct. App. 1997).

(3) An accounting clerk helped with payroll, performed data entry, printed checks, prepared cash receipts, wrote up and made bank deposits, cashed petty cash checks, and filed payroll items in a locked filing drawer. When she filed items, she asked for a key from the owner's wife or another employee. When out of town, the owner's wife left pre-signed but otherwise blank checks in the locked drawer. Was the defendant entrusted with the checks? *State v. Kovach*, 143 P.3d 192 (N.M. Ct. App. 2006).

(4) *The Scrap Fat Thief.*

> Defendant drove a truck for [Utah By-Products Company] picking up scrap fat, meat and bones from butcher shops and cafes on a daily route. He would give each customer a slip showing the poundage of the items picked up and turn in a copy to the company, which would issue checks to the customers in payment. There was one exception to this procedure. Hill Field Air Force Base required payment in cash rather than by check. So the company would issue a check for the value of scraps, payable to the defendant, who would cash the check and make the required payment.
>
> On October 31, 1961, the defendant made out a slip showing a pickup at Hill Field of bones and scraps totaling $84.25. It is undisputed that he delivered these items to the company, for which he received a check for that amount payable to himself. The difficulty exists because these particular scraps did not come from, and the proceeds of the check were not paid to, the Hill Field account. Inquiry brought forth a confession by the defendant that he had, by issuing shorted weight slips to other customers, accumulated that amount of scrap and turned it in to obtain the money for himself.

State v. Taylor, 378 P.2d 352 (Utah 1963).

The defendant was convicted of embezzlement. What result on appeal?

(5) The complexities of common law larceny and its progeny led drafters of the Model Penal Code to consolidate theft-related crimes into a single statute. Under this approach, theft is one offense that may be supported by evidence that it was committed in any manner that constitutes theft. *See* Model Penal Code § 223.1.

Thus, the government may establish theft by proving any form of theft, larceny, false pretense, embezzlement, etc., as long as defendants' rights to a fair trial are preserved. The drafters' goal was to avoid procedural problems, not to eliminate the need to specify with care the various forms of conduct meant to be included. *See* Comment 1, Model Penal Code § 223.1. For a critique of consolidation, see Stuart

P. GREEN, 13 WAYS TO STEAL A BICYCLE: THEFT LAW IN THE INFORMATION AGE 45–54 & 27 (2012) (noting 38 states have enacted theft statutes that, at a minimum, consolidate the crimes of larceny, false pretenses, and embezzlement).

§ 5.02 Robbery

State v. Sein

Supreme Court of New Jersey
590 A.2d 665 (1991)

CLIFFORD, J.

The narrow issue on this appeal ... is whether the sudden snatching of a purse from the grasp of its owner involves enough force to elevate the offense from theft from the person to robbery....

A.

On August 27, 1986, Edythe Williams cashed her unemployment check at Proper Check Cashing, a concession located in the Woolworth store on Main Street in Paterson. Mrs. Williams placed the proceeds in a zipped compartment in the strapless, clutch-type purse that she carried under her arm. After purchasing a notebook in Woolworth's, she left the store and headed for her car, which she had parked a couple of blocks away.

Mrs. Williams arrived at her car intending to drop off the notebook and continue shopping in the area. She went to the passenger side and put her key in the lock, all the while carrying the purse under her right arm. As Mrs. Williams stood in the street, defendant, Francisco Sein, walked up and stood close beside her on her left. Mrs. Williams turned to face the man, thinking he had approached to ask a question, but defendant said nothing. Instead, "he reached across [her] and just slid [her] pocketbook—which wasn't very hard to do—from under [her] arm and took off," running toward Main Street. There was no evidence that defendant used any force other than that required to slide the purse from beneath Mrs. Williams' arm.

The police apprehended defendant, who was subsequently indicted for robbery. The robbery statute, N.J.S.A. § 2C:15-1, reads as follows:

> **a. Robbery defined.** A person is guilty of robbery if, in the course of committing a theft, he:
>
> (1) Inflicts bodily injury or uses force upon another; or
>
> (2) Threatens another with or purposely puts him in fear of immediate bodily injury; or
>
> (3) Commits or threatens immediately to commit any crime of the first or second degree.
>
> An act shall be deemed to be included in the phrase "in the course of committing a theft" if it occurs in an attempt to commit theft or in immediate flight after the attempt or commission.

> **b. Grading.** Robbery is a crime of the second degree, except that it is a crime of the first degree if in the course of committing the theft the actor attempts to kill anyone, or purposely inflicts or attempts to inflict serious bodily injury, or is armed with, or uses or threatens the immediate use of a deadly weapon.

At trial, defendant moved at the conclusion of the State's case for a judgment of acquittal in respect of the robbery charge, contending that the case should proceed only on the lesser-included offense of theft from the person, defined by *N.J.S.A.* § 2C:20-3a as the "unlawful[] tak[ing], or exercis[ing of] unlawful control over, movable property of another with purpose to deprive him thereof." The crux of defendant's argument was that there was no evidence in the record that the taking of Mrs. Williams' purse was accompanied by the use of force against her person, a requirement for conviction under *N.J.S.A.* § 2C:15-1a(1). The State, on the other hand, urged that a judgment of acquittal would be improper because the Legislature intended that the force used to remove the purse from the victim was sufficient to elevate the unlawful taking to a robbery. The trial court denied defendant's motion, and the jury subsequently found defendant guilty of second-degree robbery.

...

B.

Cases involving "snatching" have required courts to determine where to draw the line between robbery and the lesser offense of larceny from the person. A certain amount of "force" is necessary to take property from the person of another, but whether the amount necessary merely to accomplish that taking is sufficient to warrant the more serious penalties associated with robbery has vexed those courts that have considered the question.

Some jurisdictions have construed the term "force" as used in the state's robbery statute to mean mere physical force or energy ... while others have rejected hypertechnical distinctions in favor of a view that acknowledges that snatching an object from the grasp of the owner increases the risk of danger to the victim and justifies enhanced punishment.... Those jurisdictions implicitly recognize that victims do not turn over their property willingly, even if they do not resist or struggle with a thief. Thus, the amount of physical energy necessary to take the property is deemed sufficient to support a robbery conviction.

The predominant view, however, is that there is insufficient force to constitute robbery when the thief snatches property from the owner's grasp so suddenly that the owner cannot offer any resistance to the taking.... This "majority rule" has been set forth in the following terms:

> [A] simple snatching or sudden taking of property from the person of another does not of itself involve sufficient force to constitute robbery, though the act may be robbery where a struggle ensues, the victim is injured in the taking, or the property is so attached to the victim's person or clothing as to create resistance to the taking.

People v. Patton, 389 N.E.2d 1174, 1175 (Ill. 1979).

...

The legislative history of New Jersey's robbery statute ... when read in the context of the Code Commentary on theft, reveals that our Legislature intended to adopt the majority rule.

C.

...

The standard we adopt today continues the focus of a robbery on the conduct of the perpetrator rather than on the nature of the property stolen or the characteristics of the victim and his or her actions. Furthermore, we do not agree with the State's contention that this standard is "inexact and unworkable." If in fact jurors will henceforth be required to resort to concepts founded in the science of physics to determine whether more force was used than that quantum necessary merely to remove the object, that is hardly a dismaying by-product of a correct interpretation of the statute. Such concepts are used frequently by juries in their deliberations and are entirely within their ken.

...

Wilentz, C.J., dissenting.

I would hold that, under the statutory amendment, all purse snatchings are robberies, regardless of the amount of force used. I believe this construction of the amendment achieves the overriding goal of the Legislature: to deter and to prevent purse snatchings, not some kind, one kind, or a particular kind, but all purse snatchings.

...

A literal application of the "uses force upon another" language to the offense of purse snatching suggests that force used solely upon a purse would be insufficient to elevate the crime from theft to robbery. Pursuant to such a construction, one who snatched a purse without touching the victim, even if he exerted a great deal of force in order to pull a purse tightly clutched under the victim's arm, would not be guilty of robbery. A robbery would result only if he pulled the owner's hand itself, pushed her arm to loosen the clutch, or in some way used force upon the *person* as well as on the purse. That reading of the statute, closely conforming to the statutory language, would remove a substantial portion of purse snatching offenses from the robbery statute, contrary to the Legislature's intent....

The majority's reliance on a so-called "majority rule" is misplaced. The concept of a "majority rule," while persuasive in matters of common law, is sometimes inappropriately applied to criminal law, a field dominated by statute. There exists no nationwide, uniform robbery statute. Many states have enacted statutes which differ slightly in their language. To the extent that other states have statutory language identical to our own, the legislative history of our statute, which differs from that of other states, and its explicit reference to purse snatching, must control our decision.

Comments

(1) At common law, robbery is "an aggravated larceny," the elements of which are (1) larceny, (2) from the person (or his presence), (3) by violence or intimidation. While larceny is an offense against property, robbery is an offense against person and property, the danger and apprehension posed to the victim making the crime more serious. Typically, the potential punishment will be greater if a deadly weapon is used.

(2) Courts are generally agreed that it is no defense to a robbery charge that the defendant lacked the capability to harm the victim so long as the latter was in fact intimidated. *See State v. Felix*, 737 P.2d 393 (Ariz. Ct. App. 1986) (nasal inhaler used to simulate barrel of gun pressed against victim's body); *Commonwealth v. Johnson*, 543 N.E.2d 22 (Mass. 1989) (hairbrush concealed in pocket and pointed at cashier); *People v. Lopez*, 535 N.E.2d 1328 (N.Y. 1989) ("By his gesture the defendant conspicuously and consciously conveyed the impression that he was reaching for something which, under the circumstances, the victim could reasonably conclude was a firearm."). In that vein, in a felony murder case, defendant's hands were not a "dangerous weapon" for purposes of aggravated robbery, but offense of common law robbery through use of force was proven. *See State v. Staten*, 616 S.E.2d 650 (N.C. App. 2005).

When a distinction is drawn between robbery and armed robbery the potential of the instrumentality may be determinative. *See Brooks v. State*, 552 A.2d 872 (Md. 1989) (defendant who used toy plastic pistol improperly convicted of armed robbery); *Handy v. State*, 730 A.2d 710 (Md. 1999) (pepper spray was deadly weapon). The presence of violence or intimidation is determined by examining the conduct of the accused; that the victim was frightened is not dispositive. *See Goodwine v. State*, 764 P.2d 680 (Wyo. 1988).

(3) In most instances, the violence or intimidation required for a robbery conviction precedes or is contemporaneous with the taking of property. When the violence or intimidation occurs *after* the taking, such as during an attempt to escape, states vary in their treatment of the crime. Some states follow the common law approach and hold that "the force used in the taking of property must 'precede or be concomitant or contemporaneous with the taking. Violence or intimidation by the thief *subsequent to the taking* will not render the act robbery.'" *State v. Owens*, 20 S.W.3d 634, 638 (Tenn. 2000). For example, in *Owens*, the defendant took an item of clothing from a store without paying and fled. A store supervisor chased the defendant, and eventually, the defendant dropped the article of clothing and brandished a box cutter. The *Owens* Court held that the defendant was guilty of theft—but not robbery—because the intimidation (brandishing the box cutter) did not precede the taking. *See also State v. Bateson*, 970 P.2d 1000 (Kansas 1998) (defendant's robbery conviction overturned because he took money from desk drawer without violence or intimidation; slamming door in victim's face after taking did not convert theft into robbery). A majority of states, though, have defined robbery in a way that rejects the common law timing requirement for violence or intimidation. *Owens*, 20 S.W.3d 634, 638–639 (collecting cases and statutes). These statutes embrace the "continuous offense"

theory of robbery. Under the continuous offense theory: "the use of force during the course of a larceny in order to take the property away from the custodian supplies the element of force necessary to sustain a robbery conviction. The mere fact that some asportation has occurred before the use of force does not mean that the perpetrator is thereafter not guilty of the offense of robbery. Rather, the totality of the circumstances that surround the taking must be considered. If ... the use of force enables the accused to retain possession of the property in the face of immediate resistance from the victim, then the taking is properly considered a robbery." *Ball v. State*, 699 A.2d 1170, 1185 (Ct. App. Md. 1997) (rejecting common law timing requirement); *see also Comm. v. Lashway*, 634 N.E.2d 930, 932 (Mass. App. Ct. 1994) ("the nexus between the force or fear and the taking may be relatively loose and yet encompass a robbery."); *State v. Ali*, 886 A.2d 449, 456 (Conn. App. Ct. 2005)("[I]f the use of force occurs during the continuous sequence of events surrounding the taking or attempted taking, even though some time immediately before or after, it is considered to be in the course of the robbery or the attempted robbery within the meaning of the statute.").

§ 5.03 Extortion

Rendelman v. State

Court of Special Appeals of Maryland
927 A.2d 468 (2007), *aff'd*, 947 A.2d 546 (2008)

Deborah S. Eyler, J.

Scott Lewis Rendelman mailed a letter to William Elmhirst threatening to sue him for damages if he did not pay a $100,000 "settlement demand." Rendelman's threat was made in bad faith, with actual knowledge that he had no factual or legal ground for the threatened suit. A jury in the Circuit Court for Montgomery County convicted Rendelman of one count of extortion by economic threat and one count of extortion in writing by economic threat. On appeal, Rendelman challenges the legal sufficiency of the evidence to support his convictions. Finding merit in this contention, we shall reverse.

In 1981, Elmhirst hired Rendelman to work as a bookkeeper for his company, Solarquest. Rendelman's duties included reconciling the books of account and paying bills. He was not a financial planner or a certified public accountant, and his job did not involve making investments or handling financial matters other than straight bookkeeping.

Three years later, in 1984, Kevin P. Fay, Elmhirst's lawyer, became suspicious that Rendelman might be embezzling money from the company. Fay reviewed Solarquest's books of account and found 22 checks made out to Rendelman, and ostensibly signed by Elmhirst. The checks totaled $246,000. All the reference lines on the checks bore the notation, "Loan."

As it turned out, Elmhirst knew nothing about the checks and had not authorized any of the so-called "loans." Fay and Elmhirst immediately reported the theft to the authorities, and obtained a court order that, among other things, froze certain of Rendelman's accounts.

...

... Rendelman was prosecuted on the felony theft charges in the Circuit Court for Montgomery County. On September 10, 1986, he was convicted on 15 counts. About six weeks later, he was sentenced to 10 years' incarceration, all but 18 months suspended, in favor of three years' supervised probation.

In late 1986, Rendelman stepped up his letter-writing campaign. He sent vitriolic and profane letters to Elmhirst, blaming him for the fact that his wife had divorced him and he was estranged from his young children. He also blamed Elmhirst for the physical and emotional pain he claimed he was suffering in prison. In some of the letters, Rendelman called Elmhirst a liar and a thief, and alleged that Elmhirst owed him $20,000. Over time, Rendelman's letters grew increasingly vulgar and included wishes that Elmhirst and his entire family would die.

All told, Rendelman sent one letter to Elmhirst in 1986; twelve in 1987; and four in 1988. In his third letter in 1988, he announced that he had decided to "play it safe" and stop writing, so he would not jeopardize an early release date. In March 1988 (apparently after being transferred into federal custody), Rendelman sent one more letter to Elmhirst, claiming that he had been raped in prison.

...

Rendelman finished serving his sentence in the felony theft case in February of 1988. He was released to federal authorities on a pending federal detainer, and began serving a federal sentence.[3]

On December 21, 2001, Rendelman finally was released from prison and began his three year period of supervised probation.

Exactly three years and one day later, on December 22, 2004, Rendelman sent a letter to Elmhirst, the first since 1988. The letter is typed and bears a letterhead with Rendelman's name and an address in Sacramento, California. Rendelman mailed a copy of the letter to Fay. The December 22, 2004 letter ("Letter") is the basis for the extortion convictions in the case at bar.

One only can fully appreciate the contents and flavor of the Letter by reading it in its entirety. We set it forth with the most exceptionally profane vulgarities deleted:

3. The record does not reflect the nature of his federal conviction. Public records reveal that, in 1988, Rendelman was convicted in federal court on seven counts of mailing threatening letters, in violation of 18 U.S.C. section 876. The letters were mailed to Elmhirst, the attorney who prosecuted the felony theft case, and certain appellate judges....

William K. Elmhirst, you filthy [expletives],

I've waited 20 years to write this letter. It was December 24, 1984, almost exactly 20 years ago, when you froze my bank accounts, ruined my Christmas with my family, and started the process that would put me in prison for 17 years. You're a [expletives] piece of dog shit. Thanks to you, my kids grew up without a father and my wife (or should I say my ex-wife) is a widow. [Expletives] I hate your guts. You will *NEVER* be able to give me back my lost years, return me to father my 6 and 2 year old kids, or give me back my wife. My life is ruined and it's all your doing. You made false claims against me, stole my money, and you don't give a shit. The only thing you could do is give me back my money. That won't make everything right again, but it's the best you can do. It's the only thing you can do.

I was released on December 21, 2001, and I've been on three years parole. During that time I was not allowed to contact you, I was not allowed to travel, and I couldn't change my residence. But now I am off of parole. Now there is nothing stopping me from coming back there. *NOTHING!!* You stole about $22,000 from me. It was actually a little more, and yes, I still have the exact amount in my records which have been sent to a third party who has kept them for me all these years. I can look it up if it becomes necessary, but for the purpose of settlement, let's just say it was $22,000. Twenty years at 9% compounded interest makes the current amount due $123,297.04. I will settle for $100,000 even. This is the amount I want. You give me back my money, and I swear, you will never see or hear from me again. I will take the money and leave this stinking fucking country and the United Fucking States can kiss my ass goodbye. This country breaks up families, puts innocent people in prison without fair trials, and no one cares. Well, fuck all you people. This is the wrong country to marry in and raise a family in. My son is in the army and is in Iraq and the government will probably have him killed and I never knew him beyond the age of 6 years old. Fuck all of you. Give me my money and I'm gone.

But if you don't give me my money, I swear, I will come back there and I will knock on your front door. I will demand my money, and if you refuse, I will sue you, and I will sue you for the entire $123,297.04. I will make your remaining years of your life miserable. I will sue you, I will file liens on your property, I will have the sheriff seize your assets. Don't think the statute of limitations will help you. I remember from my legal research that the time of the statute of limitations is tolled while I am involuntarily out of the state, and I have been involuntarily out of the State of Fucking Maryland since 1988. The statute didn't start running again until today. The way I figure, I still have another year to file on you, but I'm not going to wait that long. I will give you one, maybe two months, and if I don't have my money back, I will come back. I will quit my dead end job and move out of my one room studio and I will come back. I will find you. If I have to hunt for you door

> to door, I will find you, and when I find you, I will sue you. How old are you now, about 76? 77? I don't even know if you're still alive, but if you are, I WILL find you. If you're dead, I will search for your heirs, and when I find them, I will demand my money from them, because they did not inherit your money. It was *MINE!!!!* I will demand my money from them, and if they refuse, I will sue them. I will sue them and get my money, and then I will leave this stinking country and never come back. [Expletives].
>
> I want my money sent to me at the above address. If I do not hear from you, I will return. I will come to your house and look you in the eye. Don't think this is over. Far from it. It's just starting. All these years, you got away with it because I was locked up. I lost cases because I could not print copies of my appeal brief, I could not research State of Fucking Maryland issues in federal prisons on the other side of the fucking country, and I did not have access to my records. Well, all that changes. Now, you will never again win a case by my default. I will prosecute all my cases fully and to the end. You will not win by default. You will either give me back my money, or you will spend at least as much in legal fees trying to illegally keep it. Either way, God will not let you profit from what you did to me and my family. [Expletives]. How can you sleep at night and look yourself in the mirror in the morning??? You don't care. You ruined a man's life for what was a puny $22,000 which made no difference in your lifestyle at all. You did it just for the fun of it, didn't you?? I stole nothing from you. *YOU* are the thief. *YOU* are the menace to society. Its [sic] people like you who make society the shit that it is. You break up families and [expletives]. You [expletive]. All you had to do was come to my sentencing and say a few words on my behalf like Kevin P. Fucking Fay said you would do to get me to settle the civil suit with you. If you had done it, you would never have heard from me again. But you didn't, and you cost me 20 years of my life. Now, it's not over. Now I want my money back, and if you don't give it to me, I will make you wish you had come to my sentencing like you promised. I will sue you, I will file liens on your house and Solarquest property, and I will have the sheriff seize your assets. You will pay. You will pay $100,000 or your remaining years will be spent paying legal fees and going to court when I sue you for $123,297.04.
>
> By the way, Merry Fucking Christmas you [expletives].
>
> I'm sending a copy of this letter to Kevin Fay. I may sue him too for being a fucking piece of shit.

(Emphasis in original.) The appellant signed the Letter.

...

Maryland Law of Extortion

The word "extortion" has its root in the Latin "*torquere*," which means to wrench or twist. MERRIAM WEBSTER COLLEGIATE DICTIONARY at 444 (11th ed. 2003). Common law extortion, a misdemeanor, was a first cousin of the crimes of bribery and misconduct in office. Rollin M. Perkins & Ronald N. Boyce, *Criminal Law* 538 (3d ed. 1982) (stating that "[t]he dividing line between bribery and *extortion* is shadowy." (emphasis in original)). It was a limited crime that prohibited the corrupt collection by an officer of an unlawful fee, under color of office.

Beginning in the 19th century, many states enacted extortion statutes to criminalize conduct that was extortionate but did not fall within the ambit of the narrow crime of common law extortion. Generally, "statutory extortion," which may be committed by private people as well as by public officials, is "[t]he act or practice of obtaining something or compelling some action by illegal means, as by force or coercion." Black's Law Dictionary 623 (8th ed. 2004). "Blackmail," which is the act of obtaining money or something of value upon threat of disclosing incriminating or embarrassing information, even if true, is a subset of extortion.

...

Maryland's general extortion statute, presently codified at Md. Code (2002, 2006 Supp.) Section 3-701 of the Criminal Law Article ("CL"), was enacted in 1978 and remains substantively unchanged. It provides, at subsection (b):

> A person may not obtain or attempt to obtain money, property, or anything of value from another person with the person's consent, if the consent is induced by wrongful use of actual or threatened force or violence, or by wrongful threat of economic injury.

... No Maryland appellate case has interpreted or applied the phrase "wrongful threat of economic injury."

CL section 3-706 more specifically prohibits "Extortion by written threat." Presently (and when Rendelman mailed the Letter), that statute states, in pertinent part:

> (b) A person, with intent to unlawfully extort money [or thing of value] ... may not knowingly send or deliver ... a writing threatening to:
>
> (1) accuse any person of a crime or of anything that, if true, would bring the person into contempt or disrepute; or
>
> (2) *(iii) cause economic damage to a person; or*
>
> *(iv) cause damage to the property of a person.*

(Emphasis added.). This statute, like CL section 3-701, criminalizes the making of the threat; it is not necessary that the extortionist have obtained the money or thing of value to have committed the crime. The crime is complete upon the sending or delivery of the threatening writing....

...

Federal Hobbs Act

When the General Assembly enacted the Maryland general extortion statute in 1978, it patterned the legislation after the Hobbs Act, 18 U.S.C. § 1951 (2000), according to a memorandum in the bill file. The Hobbs Act, enacted in 1946, makes it a federal crime to affect commerce "by robbery or extortion," or by attempting or conspiring to do so. As pertinent to the case at bar, "extortion" under the Hobbs Act is, the obtaining of property from another, with his consent, induced by *wrongful* use of actual or threatened force, violence, or *fear*....

18 U.S.C § 1951(b)(2) (emphasis added).[13] To convict a defendant of extortion under the Hobbs Act, the government must show that he engaged in one of the statutorily identified means to obtain or attempt to obtain property: actual or threatened force, violence, or fear; and that his conduct affected, or was intended to affect, interstate commerce.

The word "wrongful" in subsection 1951(b)(2) modifies all of the language that follows it, not just the phrase "actual or threatened force." Thus, in a Hobbs Act extortion prosecution based upon threats that would instill fear, the defendant must have engaged in the wrongful use of fear or threats that would place the victim in fear. Also, the word "wrongful" in the statute "limits [its] coverage to those instances where the obtaining of the property would itself be 'wrongful' because the alleged extortionist has no lawful claim to that property."

Federal courts have interpreted the Hobbs Act to mean that the "fear" element of extortion can be satisfied by proof of acts by the defendant that were designed to put the victim in fear of economic loss. In this type of prosecution, the government's burden of proof is satisfied by evidence that the victim was put in fear of economic harm and that the fear was reasonable under the circumstances.

Regardless of the type of extortion alleged under the Hobbs Act, specific intent must be proven, *i.e.*, it must be shown that the defendant acted with the intent to compel the victim to part with his property. When the charge is attempted extortion under the Hobbs Act, the proof required is that the defendant have acted with the specific intent to instill fear in the victim that would compel him to part with his property.

Several federal courts of appeal have considered the question whether a threat to file a lawsuit if a settlement demand is not paid is "extortion" under the Hobbs Act. Some of these cases are appeals of criminal convictions under the Hobbs Act....

It is clear, and the cases so hold, that when the threat of litigation has some legitimate basis, *i.e.*, the person making the threat has a colorable legal claim of entitlement to damages, the conduct is not extortion.

Even when the threat of litigation absent settlement is made in bad faith (that is, when the threatener knows that he has no legal claim or entitlement to damages), a

13. The Hobbs Act also criminalizes ... the obtaining (or attempt to obtain, or conspiracy) of property "under color of official right," which is a special breed of extortion that harkens back to common law extortion. Because this type of extortion is not at issue in the case at bar, we shall not reference it in our general discussion of the Hobbs Act.

strong majority of federal courts have held that the threat likewise is not "extortion" under the Hobbs Act.

...

Analysis

...

The evidence most favorable to the State in the case at bar established that Rendelman had no colorable cause of action for damages against Elmhirst.... Rendelman was obsessed with hatred for Elmhirst and Fay, whom he blamed for his criminal theft convictions and for the 10 year sentence the court imposed; but that there was no factual basis to any assertion he ever made, at any time, that Elmhirst owed him money.

The evidence further showed that Rendelman's demands upon Elmhirst were carefully calculated, both in their timing and nature. As Rendelman acknowledged in the Letter, he waited precisely three years and one day after being released from prison to write to Elmhirst, so as not to violate his probation. In demanding a "settlement," Rendelman computed to the penny the exact amount of his bogus damages claim.

The evidence also showed, however, that as vulgar and obnoxious as Rendelman's Letter was..., [t]he sole threat (express or implied) by Rendelman in the Letter was to sue Elmhirst and use the processes the civil justice system makes available to enforce his claim, unless Elmhirst paid a $100,000 "settlement demand." We are persuaded that that demand, although made in bad faith, did not constitute extortion by threat of economic damage ... as a matter of law.

As discussed above, CL section 3-701 in pertinent part prohibits attempting to obtain money from another person, with his consent, "if the consent is induced by ... wrongful threat of economic injury." Because CL section 3-701 was patterned after the Hobbs Act, and there is a dearth of Maryland case law on the meaning of the statute's "wrongful threat" language, the federal cases interpreting similar language in the Hobbs Act are persuasive authority. We agree with the reasoning of the clear majority of the federal courts in holding that a threat to file suit unless a settlement is paid, even when made in bad faith, is not a "wrongful" threat.

A civil action is a lawful means for people to have their private disputes, including financial disputes, decided when they are unable to decide them on their own. Obviously, it is preferable that disputes be resolved lawfully, through litigation, than by resort to the "rough justice" of fistfights, retaliation, and other street solutions to disagreements.

The usual demand letter (which, to be sure, Rendelman's December 22, 2004 letter was not) serves notice to a potential defendant that the potential plaintiff plans to pursue litigation, unless the underlying dispute can be privately resolved, by an agreement to pay money or other legitimate consideration. If the dispute is not resolved privately, and suit is filed, it is routine that as the case develops through discovery, the plaintiff again will make demands for settlement that, in effect, are statements of his intention to continue the litigation through trial unless the parties agree to a payment that will resolve their dispute.

Settlement demands of this sort are overtures to negotiation, not threats to inflict economic injury. The action "threatened" is to place the dispute in the hands of those lawfully empowered to resolve it, in a civil justice system that, for actions at law, uses money as the medium of exchange. Thus, a threat that litigation will be initiated, or will be continued, to resolve a dispute, unless money is paid in settlement of the dispute, cannot be a wrongful means to obtain or attempt to obtain money, at least when a claim actually exists.

The same reasoning applies even when the threat of litigation is made in bad faith, with knowledge that there is no genuine claim. The extortionist uses intimidation to leverage gain. Intimidation can be achieved only when the victim reasonably believes (or, if the threat actually would have been communicated to him, reasonably would have believed) that the extortionist has the power to inflict harm (bodily injury, property damage, emotional injury, or economic injury). In other words, the nature of the threat must be such as to make the victim susceptible of being placed in fear of harm.

...

[A] threat to bring civil litigation does not have intrinsic extortionate value. The threat is to place the extortionist's claim against the victim in the hands of a neutral third party, the civil justice system, to decide. The threat is not such as to instill fear because, if it is carried out, the extortionist no longer has the power to affect its result. Without the capacity to instill fear, the threat, in and of itself, does not have the force to leverage payment of value from the victim merely to avoid a consequence.

The State argues that, because the evidence showed that Rendelman's threats "had a wrongful purpose," in that he had no valid claim for redress, then his use of an otherwise proper vehicle (litigation) to accomplish that purpose also would have been wrongful. We are not persuaded by this argument, for the reasons we have just explained. A wrongful purpose does not necessarily make the means threatened to accomplish it wrongful. The means threatened must be of a sort that will instill fear, and therefore produce coercion. The threat of litigation, being a lawful means in which a third party assigned by government to decide disputes will decide that very dispute, is not such a means.

The elements of extortion by writing are that the defendant, 1) with the intent to unlawfully extort property, 2) knowingly send or deliver "a writing threatening to" reveal incriminating or disreputable information about the victim (*i.e.*, blackmail), or to physically, emotionally, or economically injure the victim, or to harm his property. An unlawful extortion of property is the attainment of property for a wrongful purpose by a wrongful means. Thus, to prove an intent to unlawfully extort property, the State must show that the defendant intended to achieve a wrongful purpose by a wrongful means. For the reasons we have discussed above, litigation is not a wrongful means.

For the same reasons, a threat to sue, even when made in bad faith, is not a threat to inflict economic harm. If the threat is carried out, the claim will be decided in the civil justice system. If the claim is decided on its facts, by a court or jury, and is found to have merit, then any damages awarded to the plaintiff who "threatened" to bring suit to begin with is compensation due, not an injury to the defendant. If a court decides the claim has no legal merit, the court will dispose of it. If the claim is factually false, and was pursued in bad faith, the process of discovery and trial should make that known; and the court has tools available to it, such as Rule 1-341 sanctions, to compensate the defendant for economic harm that the plaintiff's pursuit of the claim caused. Likewise, ... in some instances, a civil action for abuse of process or malicious prosecution would lie.

Because the facts in evidence could not, as a matter of law, support any reasonable finding that Rendelman's Letter constituted extortion under CL sections 3-701 or 3-706, his convictions cannot be sustained.

Comments and Questions

(1) Extortion requires: (1) an improper threat (2) for the purpose of obtaining for oneself or another (3) something of value. *Iowa Supreme Court Atty. Disc. Bd. v. Stowers*, 823 N.W.2d 1, 13 (Iowa 2012). In *Rendelman*, the State satisfied only two of these three elements. The Court conceded that Mr. Rendelman may have had a wrongful purpose, in that he did not have a valid legal claim against Mr. Elmhirst, but the Court noted that a wrongful *purpose* is not the same thing as a wrongful *threat*. Obviously, something of value was at stake—the $100,000 that the defendant demanded of Mr. Elmhirst in order to avoid being sued.

(2) The Hobbs Act defines extortion as "obtaining of property from another, with his consent, induced by wrongful use of actual or threatened force, violence, or fear, or under color of official right." 18 U.S.C. § 1951(b)(2). Actual use of force, violence, and fear to prevent the professional staff of abortion clinics from practicing their professions does not violate the statute. Although the defendants can prevent the staff from exercising their property right, they do not "obtain" any property from the victims. *See Scheidler v. National Org. for Women, Inc.*, 537 U.S. 393 (2003).

(3) The *Rendelman* court reasoned that a threat to sue is neither wrongful nor a threat to inflict economic harm because litigation places the matter in the hands of a neutral third party, the judicial system. Should the same rationale apply to bad faith threats of criminal charges? The next case addresses that question.

State v. Greenspan

Court of Appeals of North Carolina
374 S.E.2d 884 (1989)

PARKER, JUDGE.

Defendant was tried and convicted of extortion under G.S. 14-118.4.

...

The State's evidence tended to show the following. In late September or early October of 1986, defendant contacted the Chapel Hill Police Department to complain of harassing telephone calls. Defendant told the police that he had contacted the telephone company and the company traced five calls to a Chapel Hill address through the use of a pen register. Ali Mobarakeh, a dental student at the University of North Carolina, resided at that address. Defendant previously had contacted the sheriff's office in Chatham County, where defendant resided, and the Chatham County authorities told defendant to take the matter to the Chapel Hill Police.

The police took no immediate action, but defendant continued to report that he was receiving harassing calls. On 14 January 1987, a meeting was arranged between defendant, Ali Mobarakeh, Mobarakeh's brother, and Lieutenant Arthur Summey of the Chapel Hill Police Department. The meeting was held to see if defendant could identify Mobarakeh's voice. Defendant identified Mobarakeh as the caller, and told Lieutenant Summey he wanted to wait overnight before signing an arrest warrant.

The next day, defendant called Mobarakeh and indicated that he would not press charges if Mobarakeh would offer him money. Mobarakeh refused, and he recorded defendant's call on his answering machine. Mobarakeh took the recording to Lieutenant Summey. Defendant had told Mobarakeh that he would call back at 11:00 P.M., and Summey instructed Mobarakeh to refuse any offers and to record that call as well. Mobarakeh returned the next morning, 16 January 1987, and gave Summey a recording of the second call. Later that morning, defendant signed three warrants for Mobarakeh's arrest.

The recordings of defendant's calls and transcripts of the calls were offered into evidence by the State. Defendant testified the Mobarakeh had initially offered a cash settlement but that this portion of the conversation had not been recorded. Defendant also testified that he had believed that he could settle the matter in the manner of a civil suit.

The jury found defendant to be guilty of extortion. The trial court made findings of factors in aggravation and mitigation of punishment and found that the factors in aggravation outweighed the factors in mitigation. From a judgment imposing a six year prison term, defendant appeals. Defendant first argues that the trial court erred in denying his motion to dismiss the charge against him at the close of all the evidence. The crime of extortion is defined by statute:

> Any person who threatens or communicates a threat or threats to another with the intention thereby wrongfully to obtain anything of value or any acquittance, advantage, or immunity is guilty of extortion and such person shall be punished as a Class H felon. G.S. 14-118.4....

Defendant does not contend that the State's evidence failed to show that he threatened to initiate criminal proceedings against Mobarakeh or offered to refrain from initiating those proceedings in exchange for cash. Rather, defendant contends that these actions do not constitute the elements of a threat and wrongful intent within the meaning of G.S. 14-118.4. Defendant argues that threatening an individual with criminal prosecution is not a threat within the meaning of the statute and, even if it is, such a threat is not made with wrongful intent if the maker of the threat reasonably believes that the threatened party is guilty. Defendant also argues that there is no wrongful intent where the maker of the threat reasonably believes that he is entitled to the property he seeks to obtain.

...

The common-law crime of extortion did not encompass threats to accuse the victim of a crime, but almost all jurisdictions have included such threats in statutory definitions of extortion.... The definition of extortion in G.S. 14-118.4 covers any threat made with the intention to wrongfully obtain "anything of value or any acquittance, advantage, or immunity." Defendant's action in making the telephone call in which he offered to refrain from pressing criminal charges in exchange for money amounted to threatening criminal prosecution and clearly comes within the purview of the broad language, "a threat."

...

Defendant's belief in the victim's guilt is not relevant. The wrongful intent required by the statute refers to the obtaining of property and not to the threat itself. Even if the victim were guilty, this would not entitle defendant to demand money in exchange for refraining from initiating criminal proceedings. The majority of jurisdictions that have considered the matter have held that the victim's guilt of the crime of which he is accused is no defense to a charge of extortion....

Defendant also argues that, because he believed he was entitled to the money he sought to obtain, he did not communicate a threat with the intent to "wrongfully" obtain the property. There is a split of authority on the question of whether a defendant's reasonable belief that he is entitled to the property he seeks to obtain constitutes a defense to a charge of extortion.... Those states that have refused to recognize the defense have done so on the theory that their statutes prohibit the means used to obtain the property and, therefore, it is no defense that the defendant believed he was entitled to the property.... Several states, however, have included the "claim of right" defense in their statutes.... In the absence of such a statutory provision, however, the majority of jurisdictions do not recognize the defense....

Among those jurisdictions that have recognized the defense, it has most often been recognized in cases where, assuming that the victim was in fact guilty, the defendant was clearly entitled to some form of compensation. The cases cited by defendant are illustrative. In *State v. Burns*, 161 Wash. 362, 297 P. 212 *aff'd per curiam on rehearing*, 161 Wash. 362, 1 P.2d 229 (1931), the defendant demanded the return of funds that had been embezzled by the victim. In *Mann v. State*, 47 Ohio St. 556, 26 N.E. 226 (1890), the defendant demanded compensation for property destroyed by the victim. In the present case, however, defendant's entitlement to any money from the victim would depend upon defendant's ability to prevail in a civil action for damages. Even assuming that defendant could prevail in such an action, the amount of damages he would recover is a matter of speculation; yet the evidence shows that defendant asked for the specific sums of $750 and $500.

...

For the foregoing reasons, we hold that defendant's trial and sentence were free of reversible error.

§ 5.04 Burglary

Burglary, one of the oldest common law crimes, is not strictly a theft offense.

> [Common law] burglary "stems from the common law policy of providing heightened protection to the residence. At common law, burglary was considered "an offense against habitation rather than against property." The peace of mind and security of the residents was sought to be protected, rather than the property. Burglary laws are "based primarily upon a recognition of the dangers to personal safety created by ... the danger that the intruder will harm the occupants in attempting to perpetrate the intended crime or to escape and the danger that the occupants will in anger or panic react violently to the invasion, thereby inviting more violence." As one court explained, "a person is more likely to react violently to burglary of his living quarters than to burglary of other places because in the former case persons close to him are more likely to be present, because the property threatened is more likely to belong to him, and because the home is usually regarded as a particularly private sanctuary, even as an extension of the person."

People v. Villalobos, 145 Cal. App. 4th 310, 51 Cal. Rptr. 3d 678 (2006).

At common law, burglary consisted of six elements: (1) breaking, (2) entering, (3) into the dwelling house, (4) of another, (5) at nighttime, (6) with intent to commit a felony therein. As the following materials illustrate, the offense has been significantly broadened in most jurisdictions by statutes. For example, the Illinois statute expands several of the common law elements of burglary:

> A person commits burglary when without authority he knowingly enters or without authority remains within a building, housetrailer, watercraft, aircraft, motor vehicle (as defined in the Illinois Motor Vehicle Law), railroad car, or any part thereof, with intent to commit therein a felony or theft.

720 Ill. Comp. Stat. 5/19-1.

(1) *Breaking*. Common law burglary required a "breaking"—a requirement analogous to the trespass element of larceny. Forcible entry indicates that subsequent entry is against the wishes of the occupants. But courts have varied widely on what kind of and how much physical action satisfies the "breaking" component of burglary. *Compare* Watson v. State, 123 So.3d 446 (Miss. 2013) (walking through open door did not satisfy breaking element) *with* Keller v. State, 987 N.E.2d 1099 (Ind. Ct. App. 2013)(" 'Using even the slightest force to gain unauthorized entry satisfies the breaking element of the crime.... For example, opening an unlocked door or pushing a door that is slightly ajar constitutes a breaking.' "

A breaking can occur when entry is by consent through three types of constructive breaking, threat, fraud, or conspiracy. Breaking by threat occurs, for instance, when the victim opens the door to his dwelling, and the culprit secures entry by brandishing a pistol. An example of breaking by fraud or artifice is when the occupant permits entry upon the misrepresentation that the party is a law enforcement officer, or a meter reader, or a sales person. The landmark decision is *LeMott's Case*, J. Kelyng 42, 84 Eng. Rep. 1073 (1650), in which thieves came to the entrance of a manor and told the servant they had come to see the master. She opened the door, whereupon they entered and robbed him. Artifice was employed in *Nichols v. State*, 32 N.W. 543 (Wis. 1887), in which the defendant concealed himself in a chest and had it shipped on a railroad express car with the intent to rob the express clerk while the train was en route. Breaking by conspiracy occurs when, for example, a servant agrees with another to leave the premises open to facilitate an entry to commit a felony. In *State v. Bray*, 365 S.E.2d 571 (N.C. 1988), a coconspirator broke into a house while the defendant hid in a nearby barn. Later, the defendant entered the house with the co-conspirator and stole several items. The defendant could be convicted of burglary under a constructive breaking theory. *Id.*

As the Illinois statute above indicates, some jurisdictions have dispensed with the breaking requirement altogether and only require "unlawful" entry or entry "without authority." *See also State v. Simonson*, 163 So. 3d 37, 41–42 (La. Ct. App. 2015) (referring to Louisiana burglary statute that requires unauthorized entry; of an inhabited dwelling; with the intent to commit a felony or theft).

(2) *Entry.* Must the defendant physically enter the building? In *People v. Tragni*, 113 Misc. 2d 852, 449 N.Y.S.2d 923 (Sup. Ct. 1982), the "gang that couldn't drill straight" had drilled one hole through and another hole partially through the exterior wall of the China Jade Company jewelry store. The state argued that entry was effected because one drill bit broke through the wall into the air space of the building.

> ... [A] careful perusal of the varied statutes and judicial pronouncements of sister states on the subject of breaking and/or entering reveals a hodgepodge of legal platitudes, of confusing technicalities, of erroneous common law recollections and of strained statutory interpretations which merely buttress the adage that "hard cases make bad law." Nevertheless, there at least emerges a consensus of opinion concerning common standards, which is supported by leading writers and commentators in the criminal law field.
>
> Initially, and obviously, full bodily entry within a building is sufficient to prove *prima facie* the entering element. Moreover, the penetration of air space in the premises by any portion of the body, whether by a hand, foot, finger, head or shoulder, is equally adequate as a demonstration of entry.
>
> ... With a bodily intrusion, it makes no difference whether it was intended actually to effect a crime within the premises or whether it was intended merely to aid in gaining entrance, by a breaking or otherwise, so that a crime could be committed therein.

> The instrumentality criterion of burglary, however, is different. When some instrument is used in connection with a criminal purpose in a building, it is absolutely essential—for an entry to take place—that the instrument or weapon employed is one actually used, or intended to be used to commit a crime within.
>
> Therefore, the splintering of a door with a bullet intended to kill or to injure someone inside (or even the violation of air space by a round propelled through an open door for the same purpose) ... [is an] example[] of the employment of an instrument or weapon to accomplish some crime in a building.
>
> ...
>
> However, the use of a weapon or instrument solely to create or enlarge an opening or to facilitate an entrance into a building cannot be designated an entering into the building or an entry within the commonly accepted legal definition. At most, such an instrumental utilization would constitute a breaking.
>
> Accordingly, no entry is effected when a bullet or rock is used merely to smash a lock or break open a window; ...
>
> ... [A] fair, predictable and workable definition, which accords with common custom, usual explanation and practical judgment, may be stated as follows:
>
> Any penetration of air space in a building—no matter how slight—by a person; by any part of his body; or by any instrument or weapon being used, or intended to be used, in the commission of a crime, constitutes an entering.

(3) *Nighttime.* At common law, burglary can only be perpetrated at nighttime, which was defined as a time when the countenance of a person could not be discerned by natural light. All of the acts constituting the offense must have occurred at night, but not necessarily on the same night. The nighttime requirement remains an element of burglary in most jurisdictions today, but only insofar as it affects the degree of the offense. Some jurisdictions now define the term astronomically, i.e., the period between sunset and sunrise.

(4) *Dwelling House of Another.* At common law, the "dwelling house" element of burglary was construed narrowly, as the crime was designed to prevent intrusions into the sanctuary of one's home. Thus, a "dwelling" was a place where someone regularly slept, including a store or other place of business. *State v. Hudson*, 430 P.2d 386 (N.M. 1967). In one recent case the Court found that an apartment and jewelry store were within a single structure and thus counted as a dwelling for the purpose of burglary. *State v. McPherson*, 344 P.3d 1283 (Wash. Ct. App. 2015). Sleeping on the premises occasionally was not sufficient, *Scott v. State*, 62 Miss. 781 (Miss. 1885), though the dwelling did not necessarily need to be occupied at the time of the breaking and entering. *State v. Bair*, 166 S.E. 369 (W.Va. 1932).

As the Illinois statute cited above indicates, modern statutes may prohibit breaking and entering into all kinds of buildings and certain modes of transportation—i.e., the focus of the burglary offense is no longer exclusively on dwelling places.

Leased premises, rented rooms, apartments, hotel accommodations, etc. are the dwellings of the occupants, unless the occupants are merely transients. *People v. Carr*, 99 N.E. 357 (Ill. 1912). In New York, when the rooms are occupied by transients, they are considered the dwelling of the landlord, whether or not the landlord lives on the premises. *Rodgers v. People*, 86 N.Y. 360 (N.Y. 1881). In California, a motel room rented only for one night to a transient is "inhabited" within the meaning of the statute. *People v. Villalobos*, 51 Cal. Rptr. 3d 678 (Cal. Ct. App. 2006).

When a defendant breaks into and enters a place under construction or renovation, courts have taken varying positions. *Compare Keller v. State*, 25 N.E.3d 807 (Ind. Ct. App. 2015) (farmhouse empty for years and under renovation for future occupation was not dwelling for purposes of burglary) *with Young v. State*, 141 So.3d 161 (Fla. 2013) (home under renovation had a roof, drywall, and locked door, thereby still was a dwelling for burglary purposes).

At common law, a person who breaks into his own dwelling is not guilty of burglary. *Clarke v. Comm.*, 66 Va. 908 (Va. 1874). If two people occupy the same dwelling, neither can commit burglary therein. Cases involving residential premises owned by estranged spouses have produced mixed results. *Compare State v. Lily*, 717 N.E.2d 322 (Ohio 1999) (collecting cases holding that entry of estranged spouse upon the property of other spouse supports burglary charge) *with State v. White*, 330 P.3d 482 (Nev. 2014) (defendant, separated husband of victim, could not burglarize home because he had absolute right to enter home).

(5) *Intent to Commit a Felony Therein.* Burglary requires a showing of intent to commit a felony within the building. If the objective is achieved, the perpetrator may be charged with both the felony committed within and the felony of burglary. Moreover, burglary is equally chargeable when the defendant breaks and enters with intent to commit larceny, murder, rape, arson—in fact *any* felony. State statutes have broadened this element even further. In *People v. Martinez*, 115 Cal. Rptr. 2d 574 (Cal. Ct. App. 2002), the court held that entry with intent to use minuscule amounts of soap, shampoo, and water necessary to shower were property with sufficient intrinsic value to satisfy the burglary statute.

Under New York law, the government is not required to prove the precise crime the defendant intended to commit. *See People v. Rivera*, 837 N.Y.S.2d 460. N.Y.App. Div. 2007). In Alabama, however, the state must prove, and an indictment must set forth and define, the crime the defendant intended to commit. *Payne v. State*, 915 So. 2d 1179 (Ala. Crim. App. 2005).

Intent may be established by circumstantial evidence. A Texas court held that evidence of unexplained possession of stolen guitars permitted inference that defendant had perpetrated a burglary. *Poncio v. State*, 185 S.W.3d 904 (Tex. Crim. App. 2006). In Georgia, an intent to steal may be inferred when evidence shows an unlawful entry into a building where valuable goods are stored or kept. *Jackson v. State*, 581 S.E.2d 382 (Ga. Ct. App. 2003); *Rivera, supra* (holding intent to commit crime may be inferred based upon the circumstances of the unlawful entry and other actions while inside the apartment). *But see State v. Sandoval*, 94 P.3d 323 (Wash. Ct. App. 2004) (evidence insufficient to allow inference of criminal intent from entering or remaining unlawfully in a building).

At common law, the intent must be to commit a felony in the dwelling that was entered. In *People v. Murphy*, the state charged the defendant with two counts of burglary, alleging that he entered a pawn shop with the intent to commit theft therein. The court held that the defendant did not commit burglary because he did not enter the pawn shop with an intent to commit theft; rather, defendant had purchased stolen property on the street and the theft had already been completed when he entered the pawn shop. 28 N.E.3d 1058 (Ill. App. Ct. 2015). Not all courts take the same approach to the "intent to commit a felony *therein*" requirement. In *State v. Syddall*, 433 P.2d 10 (Utah 1967), defendants broke into a furniture company with the intent of cutting through the wall of the building into an adjoining building, and through the wall of that building into a bank. They were caught when they were in the second building, beginning to cut their way into the bank. The court held that the evidence need not show that a felony was committed on the premises entered, but merely that the premises were entered with the intent to commit a felony.

§ 5.05 Arson

State v. Rosales

Supreme Court of South Dakota
860 N.W. 2d 251 (S.D. 2015)

Zinter, Justice.

...

In the early morning hours of November 21, 2012, Juan Rosales set fire to two vehicles owned by Amy Faehnrich and Toby Rolfe. The fire spread to their garage, which was located approximately four feet from the vehicles. The fire marshal's investigation indicated that the vehicle fires were started by the ignition of a flammable liquid on their hoods and windshields. The garage fire started because of its close proximity to the vehicles. Law enforcement officers were summoned. They interviewed several witnesses and, based on their investigation, began searching for Rosales.

...

Rosales was indicted on five counts: (1) reckless burning ... (2) intentional damage to property in the first degree (one vehicle).... (3) intentional damage to property in the first degree (the second vehicle)... [and two drug possession charges] ... A jury found Rosales guilty on all five counts....

Rosales raises two issues on appeal. He argues that, under the language of the intentional damage to property statute ... the crime does not occur if an unoccupied motor vehicle is damaged or destroyed by fire. Because Faehnrich's and Rolfe's vehicles were unoccupied, he contends that the circuit court erred in denying his motion to dismiss, motion for partial judgment of acquittal, and request for jury instructions on the two counts involving intentional damage to the vehicles....

Decision

Intentional Damage to Property

Rosales argues that "it is a legal impossibility ... to intentionally damage a vehicle by fire[.]" A person is guilty of intentional damage to property if he or she, "with specific intent to do so, injures, damages, or destroys ... [p]rivate property in which any other person has an interest, without the consent of the other person[.]" SDCL 22-34-1. However, that statute also provides that its provisions "*do not apply* if the intentional damage to property was accomplished by arson or reckless burning ... pursuant to chapter 22–33." *Id.* (emphasis added). Therefore, Rosales argues that the intentional damage to property statute and the arson statutes are mutually exclusive. And because Rosales also argues that setting the two cars on fire was arson or reckless burning, he contends that the circuit court erred in failing to grant his motions to dismiss and request for a jury instruction on the two intentional-damage-to-property counts.

The State argues that the "accomplished by arson or reckless burning" language in the intentional damage statute "is simply a provision requiring prosecutors to elect between arson or intentional damage to property." We disagree. There is no ambiguity in the statute. The text plainly provides that SDCL 22-34-1 does not apply if the predicate acts meet the statutory elements of arson or reckless burning under SDCL chapter 22–33. Therefore we must determine if Rosales's acts satisfied the elements of arson or reckless burning under chapter 22–33 to decide whether the offense of intentional damage to property occurred.

Rosales's acts did not satisfy the elements of first-degree arson or reckless burning. First-degree arson occurs when "[a]ny person ... starts a fire ... with the intent to destroy any occupied structure of another [.]" SDCL 22-33-9.1. Reckless burning occurs when "[a]ny person ... intentionally starts a fire..., whether on his or her own property or another's, and thereby recklessly: (1) Places another person in danger of death or serious bodily injury; or (2) Places a building or occupied structure of another in danger of damage or destruction[.]"SDCL 22-33-9.3. Under the criminal code, a motor vehicle is both "property," ... and a "structure," ... However, "[f]or the purposes of chapter 22–33, the term, occupied structure, means any structure, vehicle, or place adapted for overnight accommodation of persons, ... whether or not a person is actually present." SDCL 22-33-9.5. Because the State does not argue that the motor vehicles were adapted for the overnight accommodation of persons, the "occupied structure" elements of SDCL 22-33-9.1 and SDCL 22-33-9.3(2) were not satisfied. And because the State does not argue that Rosales placed any person in danger of death or serious bodily injury, that element of SDCL 22-33-9.3(1) was not satisfied. Therefore the damage to the vehicles was not accomplished by first-degree arson or reckless burning.

Rosales' acts, however, may have satisfied the elements of second-degree arson. SDCL 22-33-9.2 provides in relevant part: "Any person who starts a fire or causes an explosion with the intent to: (1) Destroy any unoccupied structure of another; or (2) Destroy or damage any property, whether his or her own or another's, to collect insurance for such loss; is guilty of second degree arson." The State does not argue that Rosales set fire to the vehicles in order to collect insurance, so that element of SDCL 22-33-9.2(2) was not satisfied. But the vehicles were "unoccupied structures," and Rosales may have intended to "destroy" them, which would satisfy the elements of SDCL 22-33-9.2(1). Therefore, if Rosales did intend to destroy the vehicles, the damage was accomplished by second-degree arson and he could not have been convicted of intentional damage to property.

We cannot, however, determine on this record whether Rosales acted with intent to destroy the vehicles. The jury's verdict on the intentional damage to property counts was premised on the circuit court's jury instruction, which required a finding that Rosales intended "to injure, damage, *or* destroy" the vehicles. (Emphasis added.) This instruction follows the language of the intentional damage to property statute. *See* SDCL 22-34-1 ("Any person who, with specific intent to do so, injures, damages, or destroys [private property of another] is guilty of intentional damage to property."). But second-degree arson does not occur if the actor starts a fire with the intent only to damage or injure an unoccupied structure; instead, second-degree arson requires proof of intent to destroy an unoccupied structure.

Because the jury did not determine this issue of fact, we are unable to determine whether Rosales's acts constituted second-degree arson under SDCL chapter 22–33. We reverse and remand for a new trial on the intentional damage charges so a jury may determine Rosales's intent. The jury should be instructed to determine whether Rosales intended to destroy the vehicles or whether he merely intended to injure or damage the vehicles. If the jury finds that he intended to destroy the vehicles and the damage was accomplished under circumstances constituting second-degree arson, he may not be convicted of intentional damage to property. If the jury finds that he intended only to injure or damage the vehicles, then the damage was not accomplished by second-degree arson, and he may be convicted of intentional damage to property.

. . .

Comments and Questions

(1) At common law, arson was defined as the malicious burning of the dwelling house of another. The primary purpose of arson law was to protect the security of individuals within the dwelling house, and protection of the dwelling itself was of secondary importance. *See generally* John Poulos, *The Metamorphosis of the Law of Arson*, 51 Mo. L. Rev. 295, 299–324 (1986) (discussing the elements of common law arson). Today nearly all states have arson statutes that treat arson as an offense against both people and property.

(2) As the *Rosales* case demonstrates, the South Dakota arson statute includes three felony arson offenses: first degree arson; second degree arson; and reckless burning. Re-read the language of each provision as cited by the court. Notice the way in which the three offenses are graded according to the requisite mental state and to the harm risked or caused. South Dakota also recognizes a misdemeanor arson offense for failing to control or report a dangerous fire under certain circumstances. *See* SDCL § 22-33-9.4.

(3) Rosales did not deny that he set fire to the two vehicles, but rather he argued that "it is a legal impossibility ... to intentionally damage a vehicle by fire[.]". How exactly does that argument go? Why would Rosales make such an argument? Does it matter whether he is charged with intentionally damaging property or with second degree arson?

§ 5.06 Sex Offenses

[A] Rape

[1] Context

Throughout the past four decades, states amended their rape statutes, slowly abandoning common law doctrine to better reflect changed societal values. Generally, two types of reforms were initiated. States passed evidentiary rules to safeguard the privacy of rape victims during investigation and trial. Second, many states amended substantive rape laws or state courts reinterpreted existing provisions. The materials in this chapter focus on changes in the substantive law.

An accurate sense of the scope of the problem and the evolution of rape law is a prerequisite to formulating laws that deter potential offenders and vindicate victims' injuries. Recent surveys have focused attention on unacceptably high incidences of rape, whether it occurs in dark alleys, on college campuses, in the military, or in prisons. The following paragraphs briefly outline what we now know.

Rape is underreported.

Only a minority of sexual assaults, between 16% to 42%, are reported to police.[1] The number of reported rapes varies by defendant's status: 46% of rapes by strangers were reported to police, 39% of acquaintance rapes, and 23% of rapes by a current or former husband or boyfriend.[2]

Rapes have also been underreported in the Uniform Crime Report (UCR), administered by the Federal Bureau of Investigation (FBI). Local police agencies forward

1. *See e.g.*, Callie Marie Rennison, *Rape and Sexual Assault: Reporting to Police and Medical Attention, 1992–2000*, Bureau of Justice Statistics at 1 (Aug. 2002); *see also* Michele C. Black, *et al.*, National Center for Disease Control and Injury Prevention, *National Intimate Partner and Sexual Violence Survey (NISVS): 2010 Summary Report* (disclosing 1.3 million women may be victims of rape or attempted rape, yet only 86,767 forcible rapes were reported in 2010).

2. Rennison, *supra*, n. 1.

the number of reported rapes in their district to the FBI. A recent study of rapes reported between 1995 and 2012 estimated that approximately 796,213 to 1,145,309 rape incidents reported by victims to police were not included in the UCR.[3]

This discrepancy might have been due to the definition of rape that the FBI had been using: "carnal knowledge of a female, forcibly and against her will." In 2012, the definition was amended to reflect conceptions of rape used by most states:

> The penetration, no matter how slight, of the vagina or anus with any body part or object, or oral penetration by a sex organ of another person, without the consent of the victim.[4]

The new definition for reporting purposes is said to account for the 8.7% increase in the UCR's reported rapes in January through June 2013.[5]

Other studies gather information through telephone surveys. One of these, a 2010 effort by the Centers for Disease Control (CDC), found that sexual violence is far more common than previously thought.[6] The CDC survey also found:

Sexual violence disproportionately affects women.

- One-third (33%) of the women surveyed said they were victims of a rape, beating, stalking, or combination of assaults.
- One in five women (20%) surveyed reported that they had been raped or the victim of attempted rape in their lifetime.
- One in 71 (1.4%) men reported they had been raped in their lifetime.

Youth is a risk factor.

- Approximately 50% of female victims were raped before they were 18. Eighty percent were raped before the age of 25.
- Approximately 28% of male victims of rape reported their first assault occurred before they were 11.

Most rapes are committed by partners and acquaintances.

- Over 50% of female rape victims were raped by an intimate partner; 41% were raped by an acquaintance.
- One in seven men experienced severe sexual violence by an intimate partner. Fifty-two per cent of male rape victims were raped by an acquaintance.

---

3. *See* Corey Rayburn Yung, *How to Lie with Rape Statistics: America's Hidden Rape Crisis*, 99 Iowa L. Rev. 1197, 1201–05 (2014) (finding that 22% of 210 police departments in districts of at least 100,000 residents have substantial irregularities in their rape data).

4. *See* Justice News, Dep't. of Justice, Office of Public Affairs, *Attorney General Eric Holder Announces Revisions to the Uniform Crime Report's Definition of Rape*, Jan. 6, 2012, http://www.justice.gov/opa/pr/2012/January/12-ag-018.html.

5. *See* Niraj Chokshi, *Rapes Are Up Under New FBI Definition*, Wash. Post, Feb. 18, 2014.

6. *See* Black, *supra*, n. 1; *see also* U.S. Dept. of Justice, Bureau of Justice Statistics, *Female Victims of Sexual Violence, 1994–2010* (March 2013) (data collected through telephone surveys).

With these facts in mind, the following excerpt reviews the evolution in rape law, begun in the 1960s, that continues today.

State in Interest of M.T.S.

Supreme Court of New Jersey
609 A.2d 1266 (1992)

The opinion of the Court was delivered by HANDLER, J.

...

The provisions proscribing sexual offenses found in the Code of Criminal Justice, *N.J.S.A.* 2C:14-2c(1), became effective in 1979, and were written against almost two hundred years of rape law in New Jersey. The origin of the rape statute that the current statutory offense of sexual assault replaced can be traced to the English common law. Under the common law, rape was defined as "carnal knowledge of a woman against her will." American jurisdictions generally adopted the English view, but over time states added the requirement that the carnal knowledge have been forcible, apparently in order to prove that the act was against the victim's will. As of 1796, New Jersey statutory law defined rape as "carnal knowledge of a woman, forcibly and against her will." Those three elements of rape—carnal knowledge, forcibly, and against her will-remained the essential elements of the crime until 1979.

Under traditional rape law, in order to prove that a rape had occurred, the state had to show both that force had been used and that the penetration had been against the woman's will. Force was identified and determined not as an independent factor but in relation to the response of the victim, which in turn implicated the victim's own state of mind. "Thus, the perpetrator's use of force became criminal only if the victim's state of mind met the statutory requirement. The perpetrator could use all the force imaginable and no crime would be committed if the state could not prove additionally that the victim did not consent." Although the terms "non-consent" and "against her will" were often treated as equivalent, under the traditional definition of rape, both formulations squarely placed on the victim the burden of proof and of action. Effectively, a woman who was above the age of consent had actively and affirmatively to withdraw that consent for the intercourse to be against her will. As a Delaware court stated, "If sexual intercourse is obtained by milder means, or with the consent or silent submission of the female, it cannot constitute the crime of rape."

The presence or absence of consent often turned on credibility. To demonstrate that the victim had not consented to the intercourse, and also that sufficient force had been used to accomplish the rape, the state had to prove that the victim had resisted. According to the oft-quoted Lord Hale, to be deemed a credible witness, a woman had to be of good fame, disclose the injury immediately, suffer signs of injury, and cry out for help. Courts and commentators historically distrusted the testimony of victims, "assuming that women lie about their lack of consent for various reasons: to blackmail men, to explain the discovery of a consensual affair, or because of psychological illness." Evidence of resistance was viewed as a solution to the credibility problem; it was the "outward manifestation of nonconsent, [a] device for determining whether a woman actually gave consent."

The resistance requirement had a profound effect on the kind of conduct that could be deemed criminal and on the type of evidence needed to establish the crime. *See, e.g., State v. Brown*, 127 Wis. 193, 106 N.W. 536 (1906) (overturning forcible rape conviction based on inadequate resistance by the victim). Courts assumed that any woman who was forced to have intercourse against her will necessarily would resist to the extent of her ability. *People v. Barnes*, 42 Cal. 3d 284, 228 Cal. Rptr. 228, 721 P. 2d 110, 117 (1986) (observing that "[h]istorically, it was considered inconceivable that a woman who truly did not consent to sexual intercourse would not meet force with force"). In many jurisdictions the requirement was that the woman have resisted to the utmost. "Rape is not committed unless the woman oppose the man to the utmost limit of her power." *People v. Carey*, 223 N.Y. 519, 119 N.E. 83 (N.Y. 1918). Other states followed a "reasonableness" standard, while some required only sufficient resistance to make non-consent reasonably manifest.

...

The judicial interpretation of the pre-reform rape law in New Jersey, with its insistence on resistance by the victim, greatly minimized the importance of the forcible and assaultive aspect of the defendant's conduct. Rape prosecutions turned then not so much on the forcible or assaultive character of the defendant's actions as on the nature of the victim's response. "[I]f a woman assaulted is physically and mentally able to resist, is not terrified by threats, and is not in a place and position that resistance would have been useless, it must be shown that she did, in fact, resist the assault." Under the pre-reform law, the resistance offered had to be "in good faith and without pretense, with an active determination to prevent the violation of her person, and must not be merely passive and perfunctory." That the law put the rape victim on trial was clear.

The resistance requirement had another untoward influence on traditional rape law. Resistance was necessary not only to prove non-consent but also to demonstrate that the force used by the defendant had been sufficient to overcome the victim's will. The amount of force used by the defendant was assessed in relation to the resistance of the victim. In New Jersey the amount of force necessary to establish rape was characterized as " 'the degree of force sufficient to overcome any resistance that had been put up by the female.' " Resistance, often demonstrated by torn clothing and blood, was a sign that the defendant had used significant force to accomplish the sexual intercourse. Thus, if the defendant forced himself on a woman, it was her responsibility to fight back, because force was measured in relation to the resistance she put forward. Only if she resisted, causing him to use more force than was necessary to achieve penetration, would his conduct be criminalized. Indeed, the significance of resistance as the proxy for force is illustrated by cases in which victims were unable to resist; in such cases the force incident to penetration was deemed sufficient to establish the "force" element of the offense.

The importance of resistance as an evidentiary requirement set the law of rape apart from other common-law crimes, particularly in the eyes of those who advocated reform of rape law in the 1970s. However, the resistance requirement was not the only special rule applied in the rape context. A host of evidentiary rules and standards of proof distinguished the legal treatment of rape from the treatment of other crimes. Many jurisdictions held that a rape conviction could not be sustained if based solely on the uncorroborated testimony of the victim. Often judges added cautionary instructions to jury charges warning jurors that rape was a particularly difficult charge to prove. Courts in New Jersey allowed greater latitude in cross-examining rape victims and in delving into their backgrounds than in ordinary cases. Rape victims were required to make a prompt complaint or have their allegations rejected or viewed with great skepticism. Some commentators suggested that there be mandatory psychological testing of rape victims.

During the 1970s feminists and others criticized the stereotype that rape victims were inherently more untrustworthy than other victims of criminal attack. Reformers condemned such suspicion as discrimination against victims of rape. They argued that "[d]istrust of the complainant's credibility [had] led to an exaggerated insistence on evidence of resistance," resulting in the victim rather than the defendant being put on trial. Reformers also challenged the assumption that a woman would seduce a man and then, in order to protect her virtue, claim to have been raped. If women are no less trustworthy than other purported victims of criminal attack, the reformers argued, then women should face no additional burdens of proving that they had not consented to or had actively resisted the assault.

To refute the misguided belief that rape was not real unless the victim fought back, reformers emphasized empirical research indicating that women who resisted forcible intercourse often suffered far more serious injury as a result. That research discredited the assumption that resistance to the utmost or to the best of a woman's ability was the most reasonable or rational response to a rape.

The research also helped demonstrate the underlying point of the reformers that the crime of rape rested not in the overcoming of a woman's will or the insult to her chastity but in the forcible attack itself—the assault on her person. Reformers criticized the conception of rape as a distinctly sexual crime rather than a crime of violence. They emphasized that rape had its legal origins in laws designed to protect the property rights of men to their wives and daughters. Although the crime had evolved into an offense against women, reformers argued that vestiges of the old law remained, particularly in the understanding of rape as a crime against the purity or chastity of a woman. The burden of protecting that chastity fell on the woman, with the state offering its protection only after the woman demonstrated that she had resisted sufficiently.

That rape under the traditional approach constituted a sexual rather than an assaultive crime is underscored by the spousal exemption. According to the traditional reasoning, a man could not rape his wife because consent to sexual intercourse was implied by the marriage contract. Therefore, sexual intercourse between spouses was lawful regardless of the force or violence used to accomplish it.

Critics of rape law agreed that the focus of the crime should be shifted from the victim's behavior to the defendant's conduct, and particularly to its forceful and assaultive, rather than sexual, character. Reformers also shared the goals of facilitating rape prosecutions and of sparing victims much of the degradation involved in bringing and trying a charge of rape. There were, however, differences over the best way to redefine the crime. Some reformers advocated a standard that defined rape as unconsented-to sexual intercourse; others urged the elimination of any reference to consent from the definition of rape. Nonetheless, all proponents of reform shared a central premise: that the burden of showing non-consent should not fall on the victim of the crime. In dealing with the problem of consent the reform goal was not so much to purge the entire concept of consent from the law as to eliminate the burden that had been placed on victims to prove they had not consented.

Similarly, with regard to force, rape law reform sought to give independent significance to the forceful or assaultive conduct of the defendant and to avoid a definition of force that depended on the reaction of the victim. Traditional interpretations of force were strongly criticized for failing to acknowledge that force may be understood simply as the invasion of "bodily integrity." In urging that the "resistance" requirement be abandoned, reformers sought to break the connection between force and resistance.

Comments and Questions

(1) The literature on rape is extensive. For an introduction, see SUSAN ESTRICH, REAL RAPE (1987); STEPHEN J. SCHULHOFER, UNWANTED SEX: THE CULTURE OF INTIMIDATION AND THE FAILURE OF LAW (1998). Additional articles are noted throughout this chapter.

The following comments review some of the developments in rape law since the 1970s that are not otherwise covered in this chapter.

(2) *Punishment.* The Supreme Court has spoken twice on whether the death penalty is an appropriate penalty for rape. In 1977, the Court ruled that the Eighth Amendment ban on cruel and unusual punishment barred the death penalty for the rape of an adult woman. *See Coker v. Georgia*, 433 U.S. 584 (1977). In 2008, the Supreme Court ruled that the Eighth Amendment prohibits the death penalty for aggravated rape of a child where the crime did not result, and was not intended to result, in the death of the victim. *See Kennedy v. Louisiana*, 554 U.S. 407 (2008).

(3) *"Of a woman."* Traditionally, only men could rape and only women could be the victims of rape. In *People v. Liberta*, 474 N.E.2d 567 (N.Y. 1984), the Court of Appeals of New York concluded the distinction is unconstitutional.

> Rape statutes historically applied only to conduct by males against females, largely because the purpose behind the proscriptions was to protect the chastity of women and thus their property value to their husbands.... A statute which treats males and females differently violates equal protection unless the classification is substantially related to the achievement of an im-

> portant governmental objective.... The People bear the burden of showing both the existence of an important objective and the substantial relationship between the discrimination in the statute and that objective.... This burden is not met in the present case, and therefore the gender exemption also renders the statute unconstitutional.
>
> The first argument advanced by the People in support of the exemption for females is that because only females can become pregnant, the State may constitutionally differentiate between forcible rapes of females and forcible rapes of males....
>
> There is no evidence, however, that preventing pregnancies is a primary purpose of the statute prohibiting forcible rape, nor does such a purpose seem likely.... Rather, the very fact that the statute proscribes "forcible compulsion shows that its overriding purpose is to protect a woman from an unwanted, forcible, and often violent sexual intrusion into her body....
>
> The People also claim that the discrimination is justified because a female rape victim "faces the probability of medical, sociological, and psychological problems unique to her gender". This same argument, when advanced in support of the discrimination in the statutory rape laws, was rejected by this court ... and it is no more convincing in the present case. "[A]n '"archaic and overbroad" generalization' ... which is evidently grounded in long-standing stereotypical notions of the differences between the sexes, simply cannot serve as a legitimate rationale for a penal provision that is addressed only to adult males." ...
>
> Finally, the People suggest that a gender-neutral law for forcible rape is unnecessary, and that therefore the present law is constitutional, because a woman either cannot actually rape a man or such attacks, if possible, are extremely rare. Although the "physiologically impossible" argument has been accepted by several courts ... it is simply wrong. The argument is premised on the notion that a man cannot engage in sexual intercourse unless he is sexually aroused, and if he is aroused then he is consenting to intercourse. "Sexual intercourse" however, "occurs upon any penetration, however slight" ...; this degree of contact can be achieved without a male being aroused and thus without his consent.
>
> ... Women may well be responsible for a far lower number of all serious crimes than are men, but such a disparity would not make it permissible for the State to punish only men who commit, for example, robbery.

(4) *Marital exemption.* Under common law, a wife could not be raped, in part because her consent was implied by the marriage contract. *See* Matthew Hale, The History of the Pleas of the Crown 629 (1736). In *Weishaupt v. Commonwealth*, 315 S.E.2d 847 (Va. 1984), the court held to the contrary and outlined circumstances in which marital rape is subject to criminal punishment. In addition, a rape statute that is neutral as to gender and relationship may be construed to encompass rape

within marriage. *See Jones v. State*, 74 S.W.3d 663 (Ark. 2002). Some states have removed the marital exemption by statute. *See e.g.*, Cal. Penal Code § 262.

(5) *Trial procedures.* Another set of reform measures addressed trial procedures that often focused more on victims' reactions than on defendants' conduct, and that opened the victim's personal life to examination. Both discourage reporting of the crime. *See* Vivian Berger, *Man's Trial, Woman's Tribulation: Rape Cases in the Courtroom*, 77 Colum. L. Rev. 1 (1977); *see also* Andrew E. Taslitz, Rape and the Culture of the Courtroom (2000). Most states have enacted statutes that seek to limit admissibility of victims' prior sexual behavior when it does not impinge on defendants' rights. *See e.g.*, State v. Pulizzano, 456 N.W.2d 325 (Wis. 1990) (setting out a five-part test to achieve constitutional balancing). These procedural reforms raise concern about defendants' right to challenge victim testimony in court. *See e.g.*, Richard Klein, *An Analysis of Thirty-Five Years of Rape Reform: A Frustrating Search for Fundamental Fairness*, 41 Akron L. Rev. 981, 1052 (2008); Joshua Dressler, *Where We Have Been, and Where We Might Be Going: Some Cautionary Reflections on Rape Law Reform*, 47 Cleveland St. L. Rev. 400 (1998).

Rape Statutes

The discussion in *M.T.S.* reviewed the evolution of the crime of rape in state laws. Many legislatures and state courts revised and reinterpreted their statutes to conform more closely to the profound changes regarding women's sexual autonomy and the unique harms of rape. This evolution is uneven, often inconsistent, and continues today. As a result, rape laws vary widely, as the materials in this chapter illustrate.

> (1) Under common law, rape was defined as (1) carnal knowledge of a woman not one's wife, (2) by force (3) and without consent. *See* 4 William Blackstone, Commentaries of the Law of England 210 (Univ. Chicago Press 1979) (1769). When states codified their criminal laws, most adopted the formulation of William Blackstone's eighteenth-century treatise.
>
> (2) The rape provisions of the Model Penal Code were based on research completed in the 1950s and, in many respects, reflect the common law. As you read the following provisions of the MPC, evaluate whether the code reflects contemporary social norms.

Model Penal Code

Section 213.1. Rape and Related Offenses.

(1) *Rape.* A male who has sexual intercourse with a female not his wife is guilty of rape if:

> (a) he compels her to submit by force or by threat of imminent death, serious bodily injury, extreme pain or kidnapping, to be inflicted on anyone; or
>
> (b) he has substantially impaired her power to appraise or control her conduct by administering or employing without her knowledge drugs, intoxicants or other means for the purpose of preventing resistance; or
>
> (c) the female is unconscious; or

(d) the female is less than 10 years old.

Rape is a felony of the second degree unless (i) in the course thereof the actor inflicts serious bodily injury upon anyone, or (ii) the victim was not a voluntary social companion of the actor upon the occasion of the crime and had not previously permitted him sexual liberties, in which cases the offense is a felony of the first degree. Sexual intercourse includes intercourse per os or per anum, with some penetration however slight; emission is not required.

(2) *Gross Sexual Imposition.* A male who has sexual intercourse with a female not his wife commits a felony of the third degree if:

(a) he compels her to submit by any threat that would prevent resistance by a woman of ordinary resolution; or

(b) he knows that she suffers from a mental disease or defect which renders her incapable of appraising the nature of her conduct; or

(c) he knows that she is unaware that a sexual act is being committed upon her or that she submits because she falsely supposes that he is her husband.

* * *

By the early 1970s, the MPC rape provisions had been overtaken by changes in cultural and societal norms. Many of its provisions, such as the gender limitation, emphasis on force and thus resistance, exemption of marital rape, the social companion provision, and the corroboration requirement were outdated. *See e.g.*, Deborah W. Denno, *Why the Model Penal Code's Sexual Offense Provisions Should Be Pulled and Replaced*, 1 Ohio St. J.Crim. Law 207 (2003).

(3) Tennessee's rape statute exemplifies a contemporary approach. In what ways dos it differ from the MPC? What more would you need to know to evaluate its efficacy?

Rape.—(a) rape is unlawful sexual penetration of a victim by the defendant or of the defendant by a victim accompanied by any of the following circumstances:

(1) force or coercion is used to accomplish the act;

(2) the sexual penetration is accomplished without the consent of the victim and the defendant knows or has reason to know at the time of the penetration that the victim did not consent.

(3) the defendant knows or has reason to know that the victim is mentally defective, mentally incapacitated or physically helpless; or

(4) The sexual penetration is accomplished by fraud.

Tenn. Code Ann. §39-13-503. Under Tennessee law, aggravated rape is an unlawful sexual penetration accompanied by force or coercion and use of a weapon resulting in bodily injury, or the defendant was aided and abetted by others. Tenn. Code Ann. §39-13-502.

(4) The American Law Institute (ALI) is now in the process of revising the sexual offense section of the MPC. *See* Reporter's Memorandum from Stephen J. Schulhofer,

Model Penal Code Article 213: Sexual Offenses, Discussion Draft No. 5 (Oct. 8, 2015) [hereinafter Fifth Draft], available at http://heinonline.org as (Preliminary Draft No. 5 of Sept. 8, 2015). When relevant, specific provisions from the Fifth Draft are provided herein. A cautionary note—the provisions are drafts only; after committee members have approved a draft, it is considered by all ALI members. The final form of the new MPC rape laws may differ from the provisions in the Fifth Draft.

[2] By Force

People v. Iniguez

Supreme Court of California
872 P.2d 1183 (1994)

Arabian, Justice.

Defendant Hector Guillermo Iniguez admitted that on the night before Mercy P.'s wedding, he approached her as she slept on the living room floor, removed her pants, fondled her buttocks, and had sexual intercourse with her. He further conceded that he had met Mercy for the first time that night, and that Mercy did not consent to any sexual contact or intercourse. The Court of Appeals reversed defendant's conviction for rape on the grounds that the evidence of force or fear of immediate and unlawful bodily injury was insufficient. We granted review to determine whether there was sufficient evidence to support the verdict, and to delineate the relationship between evidence of fear and the requirement under Penal Code section 261, subdivision (a)(2), that the sexual intercourse be "accomplished against a person's will," in a case where lack of consent is not disputed. We reverse the Court of Appeal.

I. Facts and Procedural Background

On June 15, 1990, the eve of her wedding, at approximately 8:30 p.m., 22-year-old Mercy P. arrived at the home of Sandra S., a close family friend whom Mercy had known for at least 12 years and considered an aunt. Sandra had sewn Mercy's wedding dress, and was to stand in at the wedding the next day for Mercy's mother who was unable to attend. Mercy was planning to spend the night at her home.

Mercy met defendant, Sandra's fiancé, for the first time that evening. Defendant was scheduled to stand in for Mercy's father during the wedding.

Mercy noticed that defendant was somewhat "tipsy" when he arrived. He had consumed a couple of beers and a pint of Southern Comfort before arriving at Sandra's. Mercy, Sandra, and defendant celebrated Mercy's impending wedding by having dinner and drinking some wine. There was no flirtation or any remarks of a sexual nature between defendant and Mercy at any time during the evening.

Around 11:30 p.m., Mercy went to bed in the living room. She slept on top of her sleeping bag. She was wearing pants with an attached skirt, and a shirt. She fell asleep at approximately midnight.

Mercy was awakened between 1:00 and 2:00 a.m. when she heard some movement behind her. She was lying on her stomach, and saw defendant, who was naked, approach her from behind. Without saying anything, defendant pulled down her pants fondled her buttocks, and inserted his penis inside her. Mercy weighed 105 pounds. Defendant weighed approximately 205 pounds. Mercy "was afraid, so I just laid there." "You didn't try to resist or escape or anything of that nature because of your fear?" "Right." Mercy further explained that she "didn't know how it was at first, and just want[ed] to get on with my wedding plans the next day." Less than a minute later, defendant ejaculated, got off her, and walked back to the bedroom. Mercy had not consented to any sexual contact.

Officer Fragoso, who interviewed Mercy several days after the attack, testified that she told him she had not resisted defendant's sexual assault because, "She said she knew that the man had been drinking. She hadn't met him before; he was a complete stranger to her. When she realized what was going on, she said she panicked, she froze. She was afraid that if she said or did anything, his reaction could be of a violent nature. So she decided just to lay still, wait until it was over with and then get out of the house as quickly as she could and get to her fiancee [*sic*] and tell him what happened."

Mercy immediately telephoned her fiancé Gary and left a message for him. She then telephoned her best friend Pam, who testified that Mercy was so distraught she was barely comprehensible. Mercy asked Pam to pick her up, grabbed her purse and shoes, and ran out of the apartment. Mercy hid in the bushes outside the house for approximately half an hour while waiting for Pam because she was terrified defendant would look for her. Pam arrived about 30 minutes later, and drove Mercy to Pam's house. Mercy sat on Pam's kitchen floor, her back to the wall, and asked Pam, "Do I look like the word 'rape' [is] written on [my] face?" Mercy wanted to take a shower because she "felt dirty," but was dissuaded by Pam. Pam telephoned Gary, who called the police.

Gary and his best man then drove Mercy to the hospital, where a "rape examination" was performed. Patricia Aiko Lawson, a blood typing and serology expert, testified that there was a large amount of semen present in Mercy's vagina and on the crotch area of her underpants. A deep vaginal swab revealed that many sperm were whole, indicating intercourse had occurred within a few hours prior to the rape examination. ABO blood group, blood type B, which was consistent with defendant's, but not Gary's or Mercy's blood type, was found on the internal and external vaginal swabs and on the underpants.

The following day, Mercy and Gary married. Gary picked up the wedding dress from Sandra while Mercy waited in the car. Neither Sandra nor defendant participated in the wedding.

Defendant was arrested the same day. When asked by the arresting officer if he had had sexual intercourse with Mercy, defendant replied, "I guess I did, yes."

Dr. Charles Nelson, a psychologist, testified as an expert on "rape trauma syndrome." He stated that victims respond in a variety of ways to the trauma of being raped. Some try to flee, and others are paralyzed by fear. This latter response he termed "frozen fright."

Defendant conceded at trial that the sexual intercourse was nonconsensual. Defendant testified that he fondled Mercy without her consent, pulled down her pants, had sexual intercourse, and thereafter ejaculated. However, defense counsel argued that the element of force or fear was absent. "So if he was doing anything, it wasn't force or fear ... It's a situation where it looks to him like he can get away with it and a situation where his judgment is flown out the window ... He keeps doing it, probably without giving much thought to it, but certainly there is nothing there to indicate using fear ever entered his mind. What he was doing was taking advantage, in a drunken way, of a situation where somebody appeared to be out of it."

The jury was instructed on both rape pursuant to then Penal Code section 261, subdivision (2), and sexual battery. Upon the jury's request for further instruction on the definition of fear of immediate and unlawful bodily injury, the court instructed in relevant part, "'[F]ear' means, a feeling of alarm or disquiet caused by the expectation of danger, pain, disaster or the like." "Verbal threats are not critical to a finding of fear of unlawful injury, threats can be implied from the circumstances or inferred from the assailant's conduct. A victim may entertain a reasonable fear even where the assailant does not threaten by words or deed."

The jury found defendant guilty of rape. He was sentenced to state prison for the midterm of six years.

The Court of Appeal reversed, concluding that there was insufficient evidence that the act of sexual intercourse was accomplished by means of force or fear of immediate and unlawful bodily injury. On the issue of fear, the court stated: "While the [defendant] was admittedly much larger than the small victim, he did nothing to suggest that he intended to injure her. No coarse or sexually suggestive conversation had taken place. Nothing of an abusive or threatening nature had occurred. The victim was sleeping in her aunt's house, in which screams presumably would have raised the aunt and interrupted the intercourse. Although the assailant was a stranger to the victim, she knew nothing about him which would suggest that he was violent. [The] event of intercourse is singularly unusual in terms of its ease of facilitation, causing no struggle, no injury, no abrasions or other marks, and lasting, as the victim testified, 'maybe a minute.'" The court modified the judgment, reducing defendant's conviction of rape under section 261, former subdivision 2, to the offense of sexual battery under section 243.4, subdivision (a) and remanded for sentencing.

We granted the Attorney General's petition for review.

II. Discussion

...

Prior to 1980, section 261, subdivision 2 and 3 "defined rape as an act of sexual intercourse under circumstances where the person resists, but where 'resistance is overcome by force or violence' or where 'a person is prevented from resisting by threats of great and immediate bodily harm, accompanied by apparent power of execution....'" (*People v. Barnes* (1986) 42 Cal. 3d 284, 292). Under the former law, a person was required to either resist or be prevented from resisting because of threats....

Section 261 was amended in 1980 to eliminate both the resistance requirement and the requirement that the threat of immediate bodily harm be accompanied by an apparent power to inflict the harm.... As the legislative history explains, "threat is eliminated and the victim need only fear harm. The standard for injury is reduced from great and immediate bodily harm to immediate and unlawful bodily injury." ...

In discussing the significance of the 1980 amendment in *Barnes*, we noted that "studies have demonstrated that while some women respond to sexual assault with active resistance, others 'freeze.'" ... In response to this information, "For the first time, the Legislature has assigned the decision as to whether a sexual assault should be resisted to the realm of personal choice." ... "By removing resistance as a prerequisite to a rape conviction, the Legislature has brought the law of rape into conformity with other crimes such as robbery, kidnapping and assault, which require force, fear, and nonconsent to convict. In these crimes, the law does not expect falsity from the complainant who alleges their commission and thus demand resistance as a corroboration and predicate to conviction."

...

In *Barnes*, we then addressed the question of the role of force or fear of immediate and unlawful bodily injury in the absence of a resistance requirement. We stated that "[a]lthough resistance is no longer the touchstone of the element of force, the reviewing court still looks to the circumstances of the case, including the presence of verbal or nonverbal threats, or the kind of force that might reasonably induce fear in the mind of the victim, to ascertain sufficiency of the evidence of a conviction under section 261, subdivision (2)." ... "Additionally, the complainant's conduct must be measured against the degree of force manifested or in light of whether her fears were genuine and reasonably grounded." ... "In some circumstances, even a complainant's unreasonable fear of immediate and unlawful bodily injury may suffice to sustain a conviction under section 261, subdivision (2), if the accused knowingly takes advantage of that fear in order to accomplish sexual intercourse." ... "[T]he trier of fact 'should be permitted to measure consent by weighing both the acts of the alleged attacker and the response of the alleged victim, rather than being required to focus on one or the other.'" ...

Thus, the element of fear of immediate and unlawful bodily injury has two components, one subjective and one objective. The subjective component asks whether a victim genuinely entertained a fear of immediate and unlawful bodily injury sufficient to induce her to submit to sexual intercourse against her will. In order to satisfy this component, the extent of seriousness of the injury feared is immaterial....

In addition, the prosecution must satisfy the objective component, which asks whether the victim's fear was reasonable under the circumstances, or, if unreasonable, whether the perpetrator knew of the victim's subjective fear and took advantage of it.... The particular means by which fear is imparted is not an element of rape....

Applying these principles, we conclude that the evidence that the sexual intercourse was accomplished against Mercy's will by means of fear of immediate and unlawful bodily injury was sufficient to support the verdict in this case. First, there was substantial evidence that Mercy genuinely feared immediate and unlawful bodily injury. Mercy testified that she froze because she was afraid, and the investigating police officer testified that she told him she did not move because she feared defendant would do something violent.

The Court of Appeals stated, however, "But most importantly, the victim was unable to articulate an experience of fear of immediate and unlawful bodily injury." This statement ignores the officer's testimony as to Mercy's state of mind. Moreover, even absent the officer's testimony, the prosecution was not required to elicit from Mercy testimony regarding what precisely she feared. "Fear" may be inferred from the circumstances despite even superficially *contrary* testimony of the victim....

In addition, immediately after the attack, Mercy was so distraught her friend Pam could barely understand her. Mercy hid in the bushes outside the house waiting for Pam to pick her up because she was terrified defendant would find her; she subsequently asked Pam if the word "rape" was written on her forehead, and had to be dissuaded from bathing prior to going to the hospital....

Second, there was substantial evidence that Mercy's fear of immediate and unlawful bodily injury was reasonable. The Court of Appeal's statements that defendant "did nothing to suggest that he intended to injure" Mercy, and that "[a]lthough the assailant was a stranger to the victim, she knew nothing about him which would suggest that he was violent" ignores the import of the undisputed facts. Defendant, who weighed twice as much as Mercy, accosted her while she slept in the home of a close friend, thus violating the victim's enhanced level of security and privacy....

Defendant, who was naked, then removed Mercy's pants, fondled her buttocks, and inserted his penis into her vagina for approximately one minute, without warning, without her consent, and without a reasonable belief of consent. Any man or woman awakening to find himself or herself in this situation could reasonably react with fear of immediate and unlawful bodily injury. Sudden, unconsented—to groping, disrobing, and ensuing sexual intercourse while one appears to lie sleeping is an appalling and intolerable invasion of one's personal autonomy that, in and of itself, would reasonably cause one to react with fear....

The Court of Appeal's suggestion that Mercy could have stopped the sexual assault by screaming and thus eliciting Sandra S.'s help, disregards both the Legislature's 1980 elimination of the resistance requirement and our express language in *Barnes* upholding that amendment.... It effectively guarantees an attacker freedom to intimidate his victim and exploit any resulting reasonable fear so long as she neither struggles nor cries out.... There is no requirement that the victim say, "I am afraid, please stop," when it is the defendant who has created the circumstances that have so paralyzed the victim in fear and thereby submission.... Moreover, it is sheer speculation that Mercy's assailant would have responded to screams by desisting the attack, and not by causing her further injury or death.

The jury could reasonably have concluded that under the totality of the circumstances, this scenario, instigated and choreographed by defendant, created a situation in which Mercy genuinely and reasonably responded with fear of immediate and unlawful bodily injury, and that such fear allowed him to accomplish sexual intercourse with Mercy against her will....

Comments

(1) As *Iniguez* indicates, force and resistance are historically related; resistance by the victim was necessary to establish force, an element of the offense. As of 2013, 32 states and the District of Columbia have abolished the resistance requirement completely, and six others expressly state that physical resistance is not required for a rape conviction. *See* Idaho v. Jones, 154 Idaho 412, 419 (2013) (providing citations and noting also Idaho has not followed the common law standard of "resistance to the utmost" for 105 years).

Fear of force satisfies the element of force in many states. As in *Inguez,* the state must typically establish that the victim was subjectively afraid and that her fear was reasonable.

(2) The defendant in *Iniguez* testified that the sexual intercourse was nonconsensual. What is the significance of the concession?

(3) *How much force?* In *People v. Griffin*, 94 P.3d 1089 (Cal. 2004), the California Supreme Court addressed this question in a case brought under the same statute as that in *Iniguez.*

> Rape is a general intent offense. Forcible rape is defined as "an act of sexual intercourse accomplished with a person not the spouse of the perpetrator ... where it is accomplished against a person's will by means of force, violence, duress, menace, or fear of immediate and unlawful bodily injury on the person or another."
>
> The term "force" as used in the rape statute is not specifically defined. Although trial courts, generally, have a duty to define technical terms that have meanings peculiar to the law, there is no duty to clarify, amplify, or otherwise instruct on commonly understood words or terms used in statutes or jury instructions....
>
> There are several nonlegal definitions of "force" that have been cited in the cases construing penal provisions that incorporate the term. "One nonlegal meaning of force is 'to press, drive, attain to, or effect as indicated against resistance ... by some positive compelling force or action.' (Webster's 3d New Internat. Dict. (1993)....) Another is 'to achieve or win by strength in struggle or violence.' ..." If we conclude the Legislature's use of the term "force" in the rape statute was not intended to have any specialized legal meaning significantly different from such common usage definitions, then trial courts are under no obligation to instruct sua sponte on the definition of the term.
>
> A plain reading of section 261 in its entirety supports a conclusion that the Legislature did not intend the term "force," as used in the rape statute, to be given any specialized legal definition....

Nor is there anything in the common usage definitions of the term "force," or in the express statutory language of section 261 itself, that suggests force in a forcible rape prosecution actually means force "*substantially* different from or *substantially* greater than" the physical force normally inherent in an act of consensual sexual intercourse. To the contrary, it has long been recognized that "in order to establish force within the meaning of section 261, subdivision (2), the prosecution need only show the defendant used physical force of a degree sufficient to support a finding that the act of sexual intercourse was against the will of the [victim]." Even prior to the pivotal 1980 amendment of the rape statute, when the victim's resistance to the rapist's attack and the rapist's act of overcoming that resistance by force or violence still had to be shown, it was nevertheless understood that "*The kind of physical force is immaterial;* ... it may consist in the taking of indecent liberties with a woman, or laying hold of and kissing her against her will."

...

Barnes's recognition that the element of force plays a similar role in robbery and rape prosecutions lends further support to our conclusion that the Legislature did not intend force to have a special meaning as used in the rape statute. "Robbery is the felonious taking of personal property in the possession of another, from his person or immediate presence, and against his will, accomplished by means of force or fear." As with the crime of rape, resistance by the victim is not a required element of robbery. As with rape, for purposes of the crime of robbery, the degree of force utilized is immaterial. Critically, this court has held that "The terms 'force' and 'fear' as used in the definition of the crime of robbery have no technical meaning peculiar to the law and must be presumed to be within the understanding of jurors." By parity of reasoning, the same conclusion must be reached regarding the requirement of force found in the rape statute.

(4) One commentator lists 32 state statutes that use force in their definition of rape; four more include the term in the definition of consent. *See* Deborah Tuerkheimer, *Rape On and Off Campus*, 65 Emory L.J. 1, 15 & n. 76 (2015). As *Inguez* and *Berkowitz* illustrate, the definition of force, fear of force, and threat of force vary among states, either through statutes or case law. Although statutory language tells only part of the story, the inclusion of force by so many states shows how closely tied rape law is to the common law.

(5) As you read the following Pennsylvania case (*Berkowitz*), consider whether the conduct in *Inguez* would have resulted in a rape conviction in that state.

Commonwealth v. Berkowitz

Supreme Court of Pennsylvania
641 A.2d 1161 (1994)

CAPPY, J.

The relevant facts of this case are as follows. The complainant, a female college student, left her class, went to her dormitory room where she drank a martini, and then went to a lounge to await her boyfriend. When her boyfriend failed to appear, she went to another dormitory to find a friend, Earl Hassel. She knocked on the door, but received no answer. She tried the doorknob and, finding it unlocked, entered the room and discovered a man sleeping on the bed. The complainant originally believed the man to be Hassel, but it turned out to be Hassel's roommate, Appellee. Appellee asked her to stay for a while and she agreed. He requested a back-rub and she declined. He suggested that she sit on the bed, but she declined and sat on the floor.

Appellee then moved to the floor beside her, lifted up her shirt and bra and massaged her breasts. He then unfastened his pants and unsuccessfully attempted to put his penis in her mouth. They both stood up, and he locked the door. He returned to push her onto the bed, and removed her undergarments from one leg. He then penetrated her vagina with his penis. After withdrawing and ejaculating on her stomach, he stated, "Wow, I guess we just got carried away," to which she responded, "No, we didn't get carried away, you got carried away."

The crime of rape is defined as follows:

> § 3121. Rape
>
> A person commits a felony of the first degree when he engages in sexual intercourse with another person not one's spouse;
>
> (1) by forcible compulsion;
>
> (2) by threat of forcible compulsion that would prevent resistance by a person of reasonable resolution;
>
> (3) who is unconscious; or
>
> (4) who is so mentally deranged or deficient that such person is incapable of consent.

18 Pa. Const. Stat. Ann. § 3121.

The victim of a rape need not resist. "The force necessary to support a conviction of rape ... need only be such as to establish lack of consent and to induce the [victim] to submit without additional resistance." ... The degree of force required to constitute rape is relative and depends on the facts and particular circumstance of the case.

In regard to the critical issue of forcible compulsion, the complainant's testimony is devoid of any statement which clearly or adequately describes the use of force or the threat of force against her. In response to defense counsel's question, "Is it possible that [when Appellee lifted your bra and shirt] you took no physical action to discourage him," the complainant replied, "It's possible." When asked, "Is it possible that [Appellee] was not making any physical contact with you ... aside from attempting to untie the knot [in the drawstrings of complainant's sweatpants]," she answered, "It's possible." She testified that, "He put me down on the bed. It was kind of like—He didn't throw me on the bed. It's hard to explain. It was kind of like a push but not—I can't explain what I'm trying to say." She concluded that "it wasn't much" in reference to whether she bounced on the bed, and further detailed that their movement to the bed "wasn't slow like a romantic kind of thing, but it wasn't a fast shove either. It was kind of in the middle." She agreed that Appellee's hands were not restraining her in any manner during the actual penetration, and that the weight of his body on top of her was the only force applied. She testified that at no time did Appellee verbally threaten her. The complainant did testify that she sought to leave the room, and said "no" throughout the encounter. As to the complainant's desire to leave the room, the record clearly demonstrates that the door could be unlocked easily from the inside, that she was aware of this fact, but that she never attempted to go to the door or unlock it.

As to the complainant's testimony that she stated "no" throughout the encounter with Appellee, we point out that, while such an allegation of fact would be relevant to the issue of consent, it is not relevant to the issue of force.... [W]here there is a lack of consent, but no showing of either physical force, a threat of physical force, or psychological coercion, the "forcible compulsion" requirement under 18 Pa.C.S. § 3121 is not met.

Moreover, we find it instructive that in defining the related but distinct crime of indecent assault under 18 Pa.C.S. § 3126, the Legislature did not employ the phrase "forcible compulsion" but rather chose to define indecent assault as "indecent contact with another ... without the consent of the other person." The phrase "forcible compulsion" is explicitly set forth in the definition of rape under 18 Pa.C.S. § 3121, but the phrase "without the consent of the other person," is conspicuously absent. The choice by the Legislature to define the crime of indecent assault utilizing the phrase "without the consent of the other" and to not so define the crime of rape indicates a legislative intent that the term "forcible compulsion" under 18 Pa.C.S. § 3121, be interpreted as something more than a lack of consent. Moreover, we note that penal statutes must be strictly construed to provide fair warning to the defendant of the nature of the proscribed conduct.

Reviewed in light of the above described standard, the complainant's testimony simply fails to establish that the Appellee forcibly compelled her to engage in sexual intercourse as required under 18 Pa.C.S. § 3121.... Accordingly, we hold that the Superior Court did not err in reversing Appellee's conviction of rape.

Comments and Questions

(1) In addition to reversing the rape conviction, the court reinstated the indecent assault conviction, for "indecent contact ... without the consent of the other person." *Berkowitz*, 642 A.2d at 1166. At the time, the offense was classified as a second degree misdemeanor.

(2) Following public controversy over the *Berkowitz* decision, Pennsylvania legislators revised the statutory scheme for sexual crimes by redefining sexual offenses and grouping them into categories. Sexual assault is committed when a "person engages in sexual intercourse ... without the complainant's consent." *See* 18 Pa. Cons. Stat. Ann. 3124.1 (1995).

(3) According to a 2007 study, one in five women reported being sexually assaulted while in college. *See* Campus Sexual Assault (CSA) (2007) (compiling data from a web-based survey of 5,466 women and 1,375 men at two large public universities).

A 2014 survey of undergraduates at M.I.T. reports that 17 percent of women and five percent of men at the university said they were victims of sexual contact, which ranged from touching to penetration and involved force, threat, or incapacitation. *See* Office of the Chancellor, *Survey Results: 2014 Community Attitudes on Sexual Assault*, Table 2.2 (2014).

(4) Students who reported sexual assaults to their university complained that their accounts were discouraged or brushed aside and that college procedures were cumbersome and often humiliating. *See* Jennifer Steinhauer, *Quietly Building a Focus on College Assaults*, N.Y. TIMES, April 30, 2014, at A18. Efforts by students to change college attitudes and procedures ultimately attracted the attention of legislators and the Department of Education. *See* Richard Perez-Pena and Kate Taylor, *Fight Against Sex Assaults Holds Colleges to Account*, N.Y. TIMES, May 4, 2014, at A1.

The combination of startling data and student activism led to action by the Department's Office of Civil Rights (OCR). In April 2014, the OCR updated a "Dear Colleague Letter," that emphasizes a school's independent responsibility to address sexual violence on campus and notes potential Title IX violations. *See* Office for Civil Rights, *Dear Colleague Letter from Assistant Secretary for Civil Rights Catherine E. Lhamon* (April 29, 2014), http://www.ed.gov/about/offics/list/ocr/letters/colleague-201 104.html.

(5) As colleges change the way they resolve complaints of sexual assaults, critics charge that new procedures sometimes treat those accused of sexual assault unfairly. *See* Ariel Kaminer, *A New Factor in Campus Assault Cases*, N.Y. TIMES, Nov. 20, 2014, at A22. Ironically, those accused of sexual assault complain about the same dismissive practices that spurred reactions of those subject to assault. *Id.*

It would appear that asking colleges to resolve complaints of sexual assault may be neither effective (as complainants argue) nor fair (as the accused argue). Does this state of affairs argue for enforcement by criminal law authorities? For reform of criminal laws? For seeking ways to encourage reporting to police instead of to campus authorities?

One commentator suggests that college sexual assault hearings should be integrated with law enforcement. This would include training both police officers and college administrators in sexual assault procedures and appointing law enforcement liaison officers who would attend college hearings. *See* Jeb Rubenfeld, *Mishandling Rape*, N.Y. TIMES, Nov. 16, 2014, at SR1.

(6) Without discounting the high incidence of campus rapes, it is instructive to recall that poor women are more likely to suffer sexual crimes than college women. *See* Claire Marie Rennison, *Privilege, Among Rape Victims*, N.Y. TIMES, Dec. 21, 2014 (citing research showing greater incidence of sexual assaults for women in the lowest income bracket, for single women with children in their home, and for women with low educational attainment).

(7) Consider section 213.1 of the Fifth Draft of the proposed revision of the Model Penal Code's sexual offense section. This provision is a draft whose final form may differ markedly. Nevertheless, the draft provides an alternate conception of rape and bears discussion. Based on this draft section, what would be the result in *Inguez* and *Berkowitz*?

> SECTION 213.1. FORCIBLE RAPE
>
> (1) *Aggravated Forcible Rape.* An actor is guilty of Aggravated Forcible Rape if he or she violates subsection (2) of this Section and in doing so knowingly or recklessly:
>
> (a) uses a deadly weapon to cause the other person to engage in the act of sexual penetration; or
>
> (b) acts with the active participation or assistance of one or more other persons who are present at the time of the act of sexual penetration; or
>
> (c) causes serious bodily injury to the other person or to anyone else.
>
> Aggravated Forcible Rape is a registrable offense and a felony of the first degree.
>
> (2) *Forcible Rape.* An actor is guilty of Forcible Rape if he or she knowingly or recklessly:
>
> (a) uses physical force, physical restraint, or an implied or express threat of physical force, bodily injury, or physical restraint to cause another person to engage in an act of sexual penetration; or
>
> (b) threatens to inflict bodily injury on someone other than such person or threatens to commit any other crime of violence to cause such person to engage in an act of sexual penetration.
>
> Forcible Rape is a registrable offense and a felony of the second degree.

In the Interest of M.T.S.

Supreme Court of New Jersey
609 A.2d 1266 (1992)

The opinion of the Court was delivered by HANDLER, J.

Under New Jersey law a person who commits an act of sexual penetration using physical force or coercion is guilty of second-degree sexual assault. The sexual assault statute does not define the words "physical force." The question posed by this appeal is whether the element of "physical force" is met simply by an act of non-consensual penetration involving no more force than necessary to accomplish that result.

...

I

... Fifteen year old C.G. was living with her mother, her three siblings, and several other people, including M.T.S. and his girlfriend....

C.G. testified that on May 22, at approximately 1:30 a.m., she awoke to use the bathroom. As she was getting out of bed, she said, she saw M.T.S., fully clothed standing in her doorway. According to C.G., M.T.S. then said that "he was going to tease [her] a little bit." C.G. testified that she "didn't think anything of it", she walked past him, used the bathroom, and then returned to bed, falling into a heavy sleep within fifteen minutes. The next event C.G. claimed to recall of that morning was waking up with M.T.S. on top of her, her underpants and shorts removed. She said "his penis was into [her] vagina." As soon as she realized what had happened, she said, she immediately slapped M.T.S. once in the face, then "told him to get off [her], and get out." She did not scream or cry out. She testified that M.T.S. complied in less than one minute after being struck.

...

M.T.S. testified that at exactly 1:15 a.m. on May 22, he entered C.G.'s bedroom as she was walking to the bathroom. He said ... the two began "kissing and all," eventually moving to the bed. Once they were in bed, he said, they undressed each other and continued to kiss and touch for about five minutes. M.T.S. and C.G. proceeded to engage in sexual intercourse. According to M.T.S. who was on top of C.G., he "stuck it in" and "did it [thrust] three times, and then the fourth time [he] stuck it in, that's when [she] pulled [him] off of her. M.T.S. said that as C.G. pushed him off, she said "stop, get off," and he "hopped off right away."

...

... [T]he court concluded that the victim had consented to a session of kissing and heavy petting with M.T.S. The trial court did not find that C.G. had been sleeping at the time of penetration, but nevertheless found that she had not consented to the actual sexual act. Accordingly, the court concluded that the State had proven second-degree sexual assault beyond a reasonable doubt.

II

The New Jersey Code of Criminal Justice, *N.J.S.A.* 2C:14-2c(1), defines "sexual assault" as the commission "of sexual penetration" "with another person" with the use of "physical force or coercion." An unconstrained reading of the statutory language indicates that both the act of "sexual penetration" and the use of "physical force or coercion" are separate and distinct elements of the offense. Neither the definitions section of *N.J.S.A.* 2C:14-1 to -8, nor the remainder of the Code of Criminal Justice provides assistance in interpreting the words "physical force." ...

...

The parties offer two alternative understandings of the concept of "physical force" as it is used in the statute. The State would read "physical force" to entail any amount of sexual touching brought about involuntarily. A showing of sexual penetration coupled with a lack of consent would satisfy the elements of the statute. The Public Defender urges an interpretation of "physical force" to mean force "used to overcome lack of consent." That definition equates force with violence and leads to the conclusion that sexual assault requires the application of some amount of force in addition to the act of penetration.

[Ed. *See supra* § 5.05[A], for the *MTS* court's review of the common law of rape.]

III

... The circumstances surrounding the actual passage of the current law reveal that it was conceived as a reform measure reconstituting the law to address a widely-sensed evil and to effectuate an important public policy. Those circumstances are highly relevant in understanding legislative intent and in determining the objectives of the current law.

...

Since the 1978 reform, the Code has referred to the crime that was once known as "rape" as "sexual assault." The crime now requires "penetration," not "sexual intercourse." It requires "force" or "coercion," not "submission" or "resistance." It makes no reference to the victim's state of mind or attitude, or conduct in response to the assault. It eliminates the spousal exception based on implied consent. It emphasizes the assaultive character of the offense by defining sexual penetration to encompass a wide range of sexual contacts, going well beyond traditional "carnal knowledge." Consistent with the assaultive character, as opposed to the traditional sexual character, of the offense, the statute also renders the crime gender-neutral: both males and females can be actors or victims.

...

The Legislature's concept of sexual assault and the role of force was significantly colored by its understanding of the law of assault and battery. As a general matter, criminal battery is defined as "the unlawful application of force to the person of another." The application of force is criminal when it results in either (a) a physical injury or (b) an offensive touching. Any "unauthorized touching of another [is] a battery." Thus, by eliminating all references to the victim's state of mind and conduct, and by broadening the definition of penetration to cover not only sexual intercourse between a man and a woman but a range of acts that invade another's body or compel intimate contact, the Legislature emphasized the affinity between sexual assault and other forms of assault and battery.

...

The understanding of sexual assault as a criminal battery, albeit one with especially serious consequences, follows necessarily from the Legislature's decision to eliminate non-consent and resistance from the substantive definition of the offense. Under the new law, the victim no longer is required to resist and therefore need not have said or done anything in order for the sexual penetration to be unlawful. The alleged victim is not put on trial, and his or her responsive or defensive behavior is rendered immaterial. We are thus satisfied that an interpretation of the statutory crime of sexual assault to require physical force in addition to that entailed in an act of involuntary or unwanted sexual penetration would be fundamentally inconsistent with the legislative purpose to eliminate any consideration of whether the victim resisted or expressed non-consent.

...

Because the statute eschews any reference to the victim's will or resistance, the standard defining the role of force in sexual penetration must prevent the possibility that the establishment of the crime will turn on the alleged victim's state of mind or responsive behavior. We conclude, therefore, that any act of sexual penetration engaged in by the defendant without the affirmative and freely-given permission of the victim to the specific act of penetration constitutes the offense of sexual assault. Therefore, physical force in excess of that inherent in the act of sexual penetration is not required for such penetration to be unlawful. The definition of "physical force" is satisfied if the defendant applies any amount of force against another person in the absence of what a reasonable person would believe to be affirmative and freely-given permission to the act of sexual penetration.

Under the reformed statute, permission to engage in sexual penetration must be affirmative and it must be given freely, but that permission may be inferred either from acts or statements reasonably viewed in light of the surrounding circumstances. Persons need not, of course, expressly announce their consent to engage in intercourse for there to be affirmative permission. Permission to engage in an act of sexual penetration can be and indeed often is indicated through physical actions rather than words. Permission is demonstrated when the evidence, in whatever form, is sufficient to demonstrate that a reasonable person would have believed that the alleged victim had affirmatively and freely given authorization to the act.

Our understanding of the meaning and application of "physical force" under the sexual assault statute indicates that the term's inclusion was neither inadvertent nor redundant. The term "physical force," like its companion term "coercion," acts to qualify the nature and character of the "sexual penetration." Sexual penetration accomplished through the use of force is unauthorized sexual penetration. That functional understanding of "physical force" encompasses the notion of "unpermitted touching" derived from the Legislature's decision to redefine rape as a sexual assault. As already noted, under assault and battery doctrine, any amount of force that results in either physical injury or offensive touching is sufficient to establish a battery. Hence, as a description of the method of achieving "sexual penetration," the term "physical force" serves to define and explain the acts that are offensive, unauthorized, and unlawful.

That understanding of the crime of sexual assault fully comports with the public policy sought to be effectuated by the Legislature. In redefining rape law as sexual assault, the Legislature adopted the concept of sexual assault as a crime against the bodily integrity of the victim. Although it is possible to imagine a set of rules in which persons must demonstrate affirmatively that sexual contact is unwanted or not permitted, such a regime would be inconsistent with modern principles of personal autonomy. The Legislature recast the law of rape as sexual assault to bring that area of law in line with the expectation of privacy and bodily control that long has characterized most of our private and public law. In interpreting "physical force" to include any touching that occurs without permission we seek to respect that goal.

Today the law of sexual assault is indispensable to the system of legal rules that assures each of us the right to decide who may touch our bodies, when, and under what circumstances. The decision to engage in sexual relations with another person is one of the most private and intimate decisions a person can make. Each person has the right not only to decide whether to engage in sexual contact with another, but also to control the circumstances and character of that contact. No one, neither a spouse, nor a friend, nor an acquaintance, nor a stranger, has the right or the privilege to force sexual contact.

We emphasize as well that what is now referred to as "acquaintance rape" is not a new phenomenon. Nor was it a "futuristic" concept in 1978 when the sexual assault law was enacted. Current concern over the prevalence of forced sexual intercourse between persons who know one another reflects both greater awareness of the extent of such behavior and a growing appreciation of its gravity. Notwithstanding the stereotype of rape as a violent attack by a stranger, the vast majority of sexual assaults are perpetrated by someone known to the victim. One respected study indicates that more than half of all rapes are committed by male relatives, current or former husbands, boyfriends or lovers. Similarly, contrary to common myths, perpetrators generally do not use guns or knives and victims generally do not suffer external bruises or cuts. Although this more realistic and accurate view of rape only recently has achieved widespread public circulation, it was a central concern of the proponents of reform in the 1970s.

...

IV

In a case such as this one, in which the State does not allege violence or force extrinsic to the act of penetration, the factfinder must decide whether the defendant's act of penetration was undertaken in circumstances that led the defendant reasonably to believe that the alleged victim had freely given affirmative permission to the specific act of sexual penetration. Such permission can be indicated either through words or through actions that, when viewed in the light of all the surrounding circumstances, would demonstrate to a reasonable person affirmative and freely-given authorization for the specific act of sexual penetration.

In applying that standard to the facts in these cases, the focus of attention must be on the nature of the defendant's actions.... The role of the factfinder is to decide ... only whether the defendant's belief that the alleged victim had freely given affirmative permission was reasonable.

In these cases neither the alleged victim's subjective state of mind nor the reasonableness of the alleged victim's actions can be deemed relevant to the offense. The alleged victim may be questioned about what he or she did or said only to determine whether the defendant was reasonable in believing that affirmative permission had been freely given. To repeat, the law places no burden on the alleged victim to have expressed non-consent or to have denied permission, and no inquiry is made into what he or she thought or desired or why he or she did not resist or protest.

In short, in order to convict under the sexual assault statute in cases such as these, the State must prove beyond a reasonable doubt that there was sexual penetration and that it was accomplished without the affirmative and freely-given permission of the alleged victim.... The State bears the burden of proof throughout the case.

...

Comments and Questions

(1) As the preceding cases illustrate, another theme of rape law is ambiguity about the nature of the crime; rape has been variously categorized as a crime of sex, of assault, and a violation of autonomy. Treating rape as an assault has several consequences, among them the rule that the victim cannot lawfully consent to an assault.

> [A]s a matter of law, no one has the right to beat another even though that person may ask for it. Assault and battery cannot be consented to by a victim, for the State makes it unlawful and is not a party to any such agreement between the victim and perpetrator. To allow an otherwise criminal act to go unpunished because of the victim's consent would not only threaten the security of our society but also might tend to detract from the force of the moral principles underlying the criminal law.

State v. Brown, 364 A.2d 27 (N.J. 1976) (assault of wife impinges on the community at large); *United States v. Arab*, 55 M.J. 508 (Army Ct. Crim. App. 2001).

(2) In *M.T.S.*, the court recounted the legislative effort to define rape as a crime of violence, an assault. The court notes the essence of assault, an unwanted touching. Does the court arrive at a third conception of rape, as a crime against autonomy? What are the implications of that conception?

(3) The *M.T.S.* court decided: (1) without affirmative permission of the victim, sexual penetration is a sexual assault, and (2) in the absence of affirmative consent, any amount of force against another person satisfies the requirement of physical force. The Idaho Supreme Court recently considered the force requirement in light of *M.T.S.*

> There are two primary approaches for addressing [the meaning of force]: the extrinsic force standard, which defines "force" as anything beyond that which is inherent or incidental to the sexual act itself and the intrinsic force

> standard, which deems the force inherent in intercourse as sufficient to substantiate a charge of forcible rape.
>
> The extrinsic force standard is the traditional view and is still the most commonly adopted.... [T]o establish second degree rape the evidence must be sufficient to show that the force exerted was directed at overcoming the victim's resistance and was more than that which is normally required to achieve penetration.
>
> The intrinsic force standard ... represents the more modern trend. It provides that any amount of force—even that which is inherent in intercourse—can substantiate a charge of rape....

Idaho v. Jones, 299 P.3d at 219, 228 (Ida. 2013).

(4) The statute at issue in the Idaho case provided:

> Rape is defined as the penetration, however slight, of the oral, anal or vaginal opening with the perpetrator's penis accomplished with a female under any one of the following circumstances:

...

> (3)Where she resists but her resistance is overcome by force or violence.
>
> I.C. § 18-6101(3).

The court held, based on plain language of the statute, that the extrinsic force standard applies in Idaho.

> Were we to construe "force" as encompassing the act of penetration itself, it would effectively render the force element moot. Force would always be present and never have to be proven, so long as there was sexual intercourse.... Thus, in order to give full effect to the complete text of the statute, we adopt the extrinsic force standard.

Jones, 299 P.3d at 229. (rejecting state's argument that intrinsic force of the sexual act was sufficient force to satisfy the statute).

(5) Florida law provides a counter-example. The state law provided:

> A person who commits sexual battery [on another] ... without that person's consent, and in the process thereof uses physical force and violence not likely to cause serious personal injury is guilty of a felony of the second degree.

Fl. St. § 794. 011(5).

Citing the legislature's intention that the only force necessary to convict is the force inherent in penetration, the court reinstated the rape charges. *See* Florida v. Sedia, 614 So.2d 533 (Fla.App.1993); *see also* Louisiana v. Chandler, 939 So. 2d 574, 580 (La. App. 2006) (relying on statutory text and holding that force other than the inherent force of the rape itself is not required).

(6) Florida, Vermont, and Wisconsin define consent as positive agreement. *See* Fla. Stat. Ann. § 794.011(1)(a);Vt. Stat. Ann. Tit. § 13 3251(3); Wis. Stat. Ann.

§ 940.225(4). Hawaii, like New Jersey, accomplished the same effect through judicial interpretation of existing law. *See* Hawaii v. Adams, 880 P.2d 226, 234 (Haw. Ct. App. 1994).

(7) A relevant section of the Fifth Draft proposed by the ALI committee charged with reforming the rape provision of the MPC is provided below. As noted earlier, it is provided here for discussion purpose because it may not be adopted in its present form. To what extent does it reflect the holding of *M.T.S.*?

SECTION 213.2. SEXUAL PENETRATION AGAINST THE WILL OR WITHOUT CONSENT

(1) *Sexual Penetration Against the Will.* An actor is guilty of Sexual Penetration Against the Will if he or she engages in an act of sexual penetration, and knows or recklessly disregards a risk that the other person has:

(a) expressed by words or conduct his or her refusal to consent to the act of sexual penetration; a verbally expressed refusal establishes such refusal in the absence of subsequent words or actions indicating positive agreement; or

(b) not given consent to the act of sexual penetration, and is wholly or partly undressed, or is in the process of undressing, for the purpose of receiving nonsexual professional services from the actor.

Sexual Penetration Against the Will is a felony of the third degree.

(2) *Sexual Penetration Without Consent.* An actor is guilty of Sexual Penetration Without Consent if the actor engages in an act of sexual penetration and knows or recklessly disregards a risk that the other person, not the actor's spouse or intimate partner, has not expressed consent to such act.

Sexual Penetration Without Consent is a misdemeanor.

SECTION 213.0. DEFINITIONS

(3) "Consent"

(a) "Consent" means a person's positive, freely given agreement to engage in a specific act of sexual penetration or sexual contact.

(b) Consent is absent until such agreement is communicated by conduct, words, or both.

(c) Consent can be revoked at any time by communicating unwillingness by conduct, words, or both. Any verbal expression of unwillingness suffices to establish the lack of consent, in the absence of subsequent words or actions indicating positive agreement.

(d) Lack of physical or verbal resistance does not by itself constitute consent to sexual penetration.

(e) Consent is not "freely given" when it is the product of force, restraint, threat, coercion, or exploitation under any of the circumstances described in this Article, or when it is the product of any force or restraint that inflicts serious bodily injury.

People v. Thompson

Court of Appeals of New York
530 N.E.2d 839 (1988)

Chief Judge Wachtler.

Defendant was convicted, after a trial by jury, of two counts of first degree sodomy. The Appellate Division reversed the judgment of conviction and remitted the matter for a new trial on the third degree sodomy counts not reached by the jury, on the ground that the People had failed to adduce sufficient evidence of forcible compulsion.

...

The events in question took place on August 6, 1981, while defendant and the victim were both inmates at the Albany County jail. The victim, a 16-year-old male, had been in the jail slightly less than three weeks, awaiting disposition of charges that he had sold hashish. He occupied a cell in the first east tier of the jail, a portion of the jail reserved for unsentenced juveniles. The juvenile tier consists of 25 cells which open to a common walkway known as the bullpen. The cells are routinely unlocked during most of the day, so that the bullpen area is accessible to all inmates on the tier. Beyond the bullpen, and separated from it by a set of bars, is a parallel walkway referred to in the testimony as the catwalk. The bullpen and the catwalk each end in a locked gate, tended by a correction officer, which separate the tier from the rest of the jail. Jail policy prohibits adult inmates from entering the juvenile tier.

The defendant, a 35-year-old male, was housed in one of the adult tiers. He had spoken to the victim on three occasions prior to the August 6 incident, twice in the mess hall, where they engaged in conversation about their backgrounds, and once in or near the weight-lifting room, where defendant commented on the victim's slight stature and demonstrated his own strength by lifting the victim over his head. The victim testified that he was about five feet, six inches tall and weighed approximately 120 pounds. He estimated that defendant was six-feet tall and weighed about 180 pounds.

Sometime between 11:00 a.m. and noon on August 6, defendant approached the correction officer on duty at the gate to the juvenile tier and asked to be permitted into the tier to speak to an inmate. Despite the policy prohibiting such access, defendant was admitted to the catwalk area. The guard then returned to his desk, from which point he was unable to view the tier.

Defendant called to the victim through the bars separating the catwalk from the rest of the tier. The victim exited his cell and approached the bars. Defendant then stated that he wanted the victim to perform an act of oral sex. When the victim refused, defendant issued the threats which are the focus of this appeal. According to the victim:

> He started to threaten me and say he could have people kick my ass if I didn't do it. He told me that anything could happen to me if I walked off the tier. It could happen anywhere, he said. I could get beat up anywhere, it could even be somebody on the tier if he wanted to. He said that he could put the word out on me if he wanted to and he could have anybody kick my ass. He said it was a matter of trusting him and if I did it with him I wouldn't have to worry about it. I wouldn't have to be worried about being bothered again and if I didn't do it, that, you know, the same thing would happen. He would make sure I would have a rough time while I was there. He just meant that, you know, he could have somebody kick my ass if he wanted to.

Another inmate on the tier testified that he viewed the incident and heard defendant state, "[I]f you don't give me no piece of ass I'll kick your ass."

Following these threats, the victim complied with defendant's requests that he submit to various acts of sodomy. Defendant renewed his threats between episodes. During the entire incident the two remained on opposite sides of the bars of the catwalk.

That afternoon the victim asked to be placed in protective custody, and the following day he reported the incident to officials. Defendant was charged in an indictment with two counts of first degree sodomy and two counts of third degree sodomy. Following a trial, a jury found defendant guilty of the two first degree counts but did not reach the third degree counts, pursuant to the court's instructions.

II.

First degree sodomy, as charged in the indictment against defendant, occurs when the actor "engages in deviate sexual intercourse with another person ... [b]y forcible compulsion" Penal Law § 130.50 [1]. At the time of the alleged crime, forcible compulsion was defined as follows: "physical force which is capable of overcoming earnest resistance; or a threat, express or implied, that places a person in fear of immediate death or serious physical injury to himself or another person, or in fear that he or another person will immediately be kidnapped."

The definition of forcible compulsion has since been amended to eliminate the requirements of "earnest resistance" and fear that a threatened physical injury be "serious."

The Appellate Division concluded that defendant's threats did not rise to the level of forcible compulsion because they were not "capable of immediately being carried out." We note at the outset that, although it may not have been so intended, to the extent that this standard would relieve a defendant of criminal liability simply because he is, in fact, incapable of making good on his threats, it must be rejected.

As we stated in a similar situation, the inquiry required in determining whether threats amount to forcible compulsion is not what the defendant would or could have done, "but rather what the victim, observing [the defendant's] conduct, feared [he] would or might do if [the victim] did not comply with [his] demands" The proper focus is on the state of mind produced in the victim by the defendant's conduct, because the *sine qua non* for criminal liability for sex offenses under our Penal Law is lack of consent, resulting from either forcible compulsion or incapacity to consent.

The impossibility or improbability of the defendant's assertions may be relevant considerations for the fact finder in determining whether the victim was actually placed in fear or whether the defendant intended such an effect. But the fact that a court may, in hindsight, determine that the threats were incapable of being executed cannot transform the victim's submission to them into consent. As the drafters of the Model Penal Code noted, "It seems clear ... that one who takes advantage of [a victim's] unreasonable fears of violence should not escape punishment any more than a swindler who cheats gullible people by false statements which they should have found incredible. Neither the blameworthiness of the actor nor the gravity of the insult to the victim is ameliorated by a finding that the threat was implausible or that the actor lacked capacity to carry it out" (ALI, Model Penal Code and Commentaries § 213.1, at 310). For that reason, the Model Penal Code rejected the requirement, common in many jurisdictions at the time, that the victim's reaction to threats be reasonable or that the actor have the present capacity to inflict the harm feared. Notably, New York's contemporaneous revision of its Penal Law, which was heavily influenced by the Model Penal Code, resulted in a new definition of forcible compulsion which eliminated the prior requirement that the victim have "reasonable cause to believe" that the threatened harm would be inflicted.

Thus, the proper question is not whether the defendant was capable of carrying out his threats, but rather whether the jury could reasonably infer that those threats placed the victim in fear of "immediate death or serious physical injury" We conclude that the trial evidence was sufficient to justify such an inference.

Defendant contends that the evidence failed to establish that there was a threat of immediate harm. According to defendant, the evidence established, at most, that the threats were to have the victim assaulted by someone else at some indefinite time in the future. This characterization of the evidence, however, ignores several important aspects of the testimony.

Most significantly, defendant fails to take into account his threat that the victim "could get beat up anywhere, it could even be somebody on the tier". With the cell doors unlocked, as they were throughout the day, the inmates within the juvenile tier had immediate access to the victim. The evidence also established that at least two of those inmates, including one considered by the victim to be a friend, viewed the incident without offering the victim any assistance. The victim was only 16 years old and a novice to the world of incarceration. The defendant was more than twice his age, powerfully built, and had made it clear to the victim that he held a position of power in the oppressive and unfamiliar environment the victim had recently entered. Indeed, defendant's mere presence in the restricted juvenile tier was evidence of the influence at his disposal. That the defendant was not specific about when the threats might be carried out is of little consequence. The breadth of his threats encompassed the possibility that the harm could be delivered by anyone, including those with immediate access to the victim, and at anytime, including the present. The evidence, therefore, viewed as a whole, provided a sufficient basis for the jury's conclusion that defendant's threats placed the victim in fear of immediate death or serious physical injury.

In light of this conclusion, we need not decide whether forcible compulsion can result from threats that put the victim in fear of retaliation—i.e., threats that the victim understands can only be accomplished in the future.

...

Accordingly, the order of the Appellate Division should be reversed and the case remitted for further proceedings in accordance with this opinion.

Comments and Questions

(1) Rape can also be accomplished by a threat of force, as *Thompson* illustrates. Was it reasonable for the victim to fear serious bodily injury? To fear immediate serious bodily injury? Should the standard focus on the victim's subjective state of mind, or should an objective standard of reasonableness govern? How does the force here compare to that in *Iniguez, supra*? Recall that the court in *Iniguez* stated that in some circumstances even an unreasonable fear may suffice to sustain a rape conviction if the defendant knew of the victim's subjective fear and took advantage of it. What if Thompson had honestly believed that the victim was not afraid?

(2) To satisfy the force or threat of force standard, courts may require that a victim's fear of death or serious bodily injury be objectively reasonable. *See State v. Rusk*, 424 A.2d 720 (Md. 1981) (stating the objective standard obviates the need for proof of actual force or physical resistance).

(3) Is acquiescence or submission obtained by threatening the victim with future harm a form of coercion? How should the law deal with evidence of past abuse and physical harm that may induce acquiescence? *See State v. Alston*, 312 S.E.2d 470 (N.C. 1984) (holding that general fear based on past experience was not sufficient to show that threat of force overcame the victim's will). A subsequent decision by the North Carolina Supreme Court held that the *Alston* rationale does not apply to intrafamilial sexual abuse where the defendant/father repeatedly coerced his son to submit to anal intercourse. *See State v. Etheridge*, 352 S.E.2d 673 (N.C. 1987) (holding that facts sufficiently proved element of force).

(4) Rapes and sexual assaults in prisons are endemic. The DOJ report for 2010–11 states that 4.0% of prison inmates and 3.2% of jail inmates experienced one or more sexual victimization incidents, either by another inmate or staff member, within the past 12 months or since admission to the facility if less than 12 months. *See* Allen J. Beck, Bureau of Justice Statistics, Sexual Victimization in Prisons and Jails Reported by Inmates, 2011–12, at 1, available at http://www.bjs.gov/index.cfm?ty=pbdetail&iid=4989; *see also* Benett Capers, *Real Rape Too*, 99 CAL. L. REV. 1259, 1266 (2011) (reporting studies).

[3] By Coercion and Fraud

Commonwealth v. Caracciola

Supreme Judicial Court of Massachusetts
569 N.E.2d 774 (1991)

ABRAMS, JUSTICE.

The defendant was indicted on a charge of rape under G.L. c. 265, §22.... [T]he defendant moved to dismiss the indictment, arguing that there was no evidence presented to the grand jury showing that he used force or the threat of force against the victim. The defendant claims that, at most, the evidence suggests fraudulent inducement to consent to sexual intercourse, but that *Commonwealth v. Goldenberg*, 338 Mass. 377, 155 N.E.2d 187 (1959), precludes the use of fraud as force as an element of rape.

The judge summarized the grand jury testimony as follows. The defendant, who is not a police officer, pulled his vehicle alongside the victim on a downtown Springfield street. He told the victim to get off the street. She noticed that he was wearing a gun. The victim left and went to the bus station to make a telephone call. After watching her for a while, the defendant approached the victim again and said, "I thought I told you to get lost." The defendant told the victim to get in the automobile, and she obeyed. The defendant drove in what the victim believed to be the direction of the police station. The victim began to cry and the defendant told her that if she did not stop crying he would "lock [her] up for more things than [he] was planning on."[1] The defendant started to drive her home but stopped in a school parking lot instead. He began to touch her and rub her legs. The victim told him she was scared and that police officers came by that area often. He said not to be afraid, because he was a police officer.[2] He made her get on top of him and have sexual intercourse. She said that she feared that if she did not do what he wanted, he would arrest her.[3]

The judge determined that there was no evidence presented to the grand jury that the defendant used force on the victim....

We do not agree with the judge's assessment that no evidence was presented to satisfy the statutory words "by force and against [her] will." The words of the statute

---

1. Although the judge does not specifically find this fact, the victim asserted in her statement to police read to the grand jury that, "He made me beg him not to lock me up." In considering the defendant's motion, we view the evidence in the light most favorable to the Commonwealth.

2. The victim's statement also indicates that she believed the defendant was a police officer because he knew many of the officers in the Crime Prevention Bureau. She also noted that the defendant asked her if she had heard of Carlo D'Amato. When she said no, he said, "That's me."

3. Although the judge did not report it as a fact, the transcript of the grand jury proceedings indicates that, after her statement had been read, the victim added the following comment: "I would just like to mention, it doesn't sound like I was in any fear there. I was really scared. I was petrified he was going to put me in jail. I had a prior criminal record and I felt if I got arrested one more time, I was going to go to Framingham."

are not limited solely to physical force.[5] We previously have recognized that a defendant can be guilty of rape without having used or threatened physical force if the consent of the complainant was obtained from the victim's fear arising from threats or conduct of a third party.... We also have held that a rape occurs where intercourse is had with only "such force as was necessary to accomplish the purpose" when the victim was "wholly insensible so as to be incapable of consenting." ... Likewise have we instructed that the jury is entitled to "consider the entire sequence of events and acts of [the] defendants as it affected the victim's ability to resist." ... We do not require victims to use physical force to resist an attack.... These cases are cited to illustrate the point that an examination of the circumstances or fear in which the victim is placed, the impact of those circumstances or fear on the victim's power to resist and the defendant's conduct all are relevant to the determination of whether conduct complained of by the victim was accomplished by force and against the victim's will. No case has held that rape is limited solely to the use of physical force. Indeed, the words of the statute are to the contrary....

Relying on *Commonwealth v. Goldenberg* ... the defendant asserts that, because he was not a police officer, his statements are merely fraudulent, and fraud is not force. Therefore, he concludes that his motion to dismiss should be allowed. We do not agree. We think the defendant's lie about being a police officer is irrelevant. The complainant was entitled to take the defendant's threatening words and his conduct at face value. Those threats and the circumstances created by his conduct and his words are sufficient to constitute the force contemplated by the statute. His words and conduct also distinguish this case from *Goldenberg*. In that case, there were no threats and no conduct which were calculated to instill fear in the complainant in order for the defendant to achieve his goal. There was no actual or constructive force in *Goldenberg*. As we read the statute, the force needed for rape may, depending on the circumstances, be constructive force, as well as physical force, violence, or the threat of bodily harm. Where, as here, the Commonwealth relies on constructive force, it also must prove that the sexual intercourse was against the will of the complainant.

...

Applying the statutory language to the evidence presented, we conclude there was evidence of force and constraint of the victim's will. The evidence indicates that the defendant wore a gun that he ordered the victim into his car; that he named a number of police officers; that he gave her a false name; and that he told her he was a police officer, and would imprison her if she did not obey him. The defendant made the complainant beg him not to "lock her up." The facts indicate that the woman was "petrified" by the defendant's threats that he would "lock her up." The issue whether,

5. The evidence before the grand jury did not focus on the question whether the defendant used his gun (which was in plain view) in any manner or displayed it so as to permit this case to go to the jury on the question of a threat of bodily injury. We therefore do not discuss that aspect of the case.

in light of the circumstances, the victim's obedience or submission to the defendant's threats was by force and against her will is for the petit jury....

O'CONNOR, JUSTICE (dissenting).

... [F]or several hundred years, a proper understanding of the word "force," as used in the Commonwealth's rape statutes, has been critical to their application, and nothing suggests that, as successor statutes or amendments were enacted, the Legislature intended a redefinition of that term. Nevertheless, not until today has this court discovered that the Legislature, presumably from the beginning, has intended "force" in rape to include constructive, as well as physical, force. The very lateness of the court's discovery makes it questionable. This is especially so when one considers the principle, deeply imbedded in our jurisprudence, that criminal statutes are to be strictly construed against the Commonwealth. I do not agree that the word "force," in G.L. c. 265, § 22, clearly refers to constructive, nonphysical, force.

...

Comments and Questions

(1) What is "constructive force"? If it is an act that so constrains the victim's will to make invalid any notion of consent, how does it differ from a threat of physical force?

(2) How would you characterize the following conduct? The defendant, a 63-year-old guardian, was convicted of rape and attempt to rape his 15-year-old charge. *See Commonwealth v. Mlinarich*, 542 A.2d 1335 (Pa. 1988). The victim had been released from a juvenile detention home in the care of the defendant and his wife. Over the course of four weeks, when alone with the victim in his house, the defendant threatened to return her to the juvenile detention home unless she engaged in sexual acts with the defendant, including disrobing, being fondled, performing oral sex, and submitting to intercourse. On appeal, the court held that the threat did not satisfy the element of "forcible compulsion," as required by the statute. Reviewing common law, the court noted that obtaining intercourse through physical intimidation could be punished as rape. But the court concluded that:

> This historical review of the offense of rape provides no support for the position that there has been any discontent with the essence of that crime being an *involuntary* submission to sexual intercourse. The changes in the language in the formulation set forth under the 1939 Crimes Code and the present statute were merely to accommodate the complaints that had been articulated. The focus of the inquiry has been removed from the victim's actions to a scrutiny of the conduct of the offender. Moreover, the test of the degree of compulsion is now judged on an objective standard as opposed to a subjective one. However, the conclusion that the will was overborne is still critical to a finding that the offense has been committed. We are therefore satisfied that the adjective "forceful" was employed to establish that the assault must be upon the will. Nor does the modification of the former requirement appearing in some of our earlier cases requiring that the victim resist "to the utmost"

> in any way undercut this conclusion. As previously noted, the compulsion to submit is still the requirement although we no longer require that involuntariness must be demonstrated by useless resistance which would further imperil the victim's safety.
>
> The critical distinction is where the compulsion overwhelms the will of the victim in contrast to a situation where the victim can make a deliberate choice to avoid the encounter even though the alternative may be an undesirable one. Indeed, the victim in this instance apparently found the prospect of being returned to the detention home a repugnant one. Notwithstanding, she was left with a choice and therefore the submission was a result of a deliberate choice and was not an involuntary act. This is not in any way to deny the despicable nature of appellee's conduct or even to suggest that it was not criminal. We are merely constrained to recognize that it does not meet the test of "forcible compulsion" set forth in subsections (1) and (2) of sections 3121 and 3123.
>
> In reaching its conclusion that the charges of rape and attempted rape were not established, the majority of the Superior Court erroneously inferred that the term "forcible compulsion" required physical violence. As we have indicated, the term "forcible compulsion" was employed to convey that the result produced must be non-voluntary rather than to describe the character of force itself. Certainly, psychological coercion can be applied with such intensity that it may overpower the will to resist as effectively as physical force. The purpose of the term was to distinguish between assault upon the will and the forcing of the victim to make a choice regardless how repugnant. Certainly difficult choices have a coercive effect but the result is the product of the reason, albeit unpleasant and reluctantly made. The fact cannot be escaped that the victim has made the choice and the act is not involuntary.

Mlinarich, *supra*, 542 A.2d at 1341–42.

(3) The Fifth Draft of the proposed revision of the Model Penal Code's rape provisions offers a relevant provision. Recall the caveat that this provision is a draft only, subject to change before final adoption by the American Law Institute; it is provided here for discussion purposes.

> (1) *Sexual Penetration by Coercion.* An actor is guilty of Sexual Penetration by Coercion if he or she engages in an act of sexual penetration with another person and
>
> (a) knowingly or recklessly obtains that person's consent by threatening to:
>
> (i) accuse anyone of a criminal offense or of a failure to comply with immigration regulations; or
>
> (ii) take or withhold action in an official capacity, whether public or private, or cause another person to take or withhold action in an official capacity, whether public or private; or

(iii) inflict any substantial economic or financial harm that would not benefit the actor; ...

Section 213.4. Sexual Penetration by Coercion or Exploitation. Conviction of sexual penetration through coercion is a third-degree felony.

Does the model draft provision adequately address the conduct in *Caracciola* and *Mlinarich*?

(4) The California rape statute prohibits public officials from obtaining sexual intercourse by threats of nonphysical harm, using the doctrines of duress or menace. Cal. Penal Code § 261(a)(7). Duress is defined as "a direct or implied threat of force, violence, danger, or retribution sufficient to coerce a reasonable person of ordinary susceptibilities to perform an act which otherwise would not have been performed, or acquiesce in an act to which one otherwise would not have submitted." Cal. Penal Code § 261(b). Menace means "any threat, declaration, or act which shows an intention to inflict an injury upon another." Cal. Penal Code § 261(c).

State v. Bolsinger

Supreme Court of Iowa
709 N.W.2d 560 (2006)

Larson, Justice.

John Michael Bolsinger appealed his convictions of third-degree sexual abuse under Iowa Code section 709.4(1) (2001), sexual exploitation by a counselor under Iowa Code section 709.15(2), and sexual misconduct with juvenile offenders under Iowa Code section 709.16(2). Bolsinger was sentenced to a combination of concurrent and consecutive sentences totaling a term not exceeding thirty-seven years. The court of appeals affirmed, and we granted further review. We vacate the decision of the court of appeals, reverse his conviction for sexual abuse, affirm the remainder of the convictions, and remand.

I. *Facts and Prior Proceedings.*

Bolsinger was the program supervisor of a highly structured state facility for delinquent boys, the Wittenmyer Youth Center, in August 2001 when the Iowa Department of Human Services (DHS) conducted an investigation into allegations of sexual abuse by Bolsinger. The investigation revealed, through interviews with past and present youth at the camp, that Bolsinger would take boys into a private room and touch their genitals, saying he was checking for bruises, scratches, hernias, and testicular cancer. The testimony of the boys revealed that Bolsinger asked permission to touch them in this way and that he did not appear to them to be gaining any sexual gratification from the touching. The boys testified that they were not aware that they were being touched in a sexual manner, and they would not have consented if they had known the true reason for the touching. However, they also testified that, given the nature of the structured program, it was almost impossible for them to make choices of their own or to refuse the request of an instructor.

...

III. *Interpretation of Iowa Code Section 709.4(1) (Third-Degree Sexual Abuse).*

Under Iowa Code section 709.4,

> [a] person commits sexual abuse in the third degree when the person performs a sex act under any of the following circumstances:
>
> 1. The act is done by force or against the will of the other person, whether or not the other person is the person's spouse or is cohabiting with the person.

In applying the "force or against the will" language of section 709.4, the court submitted Instruction No. 21:

> Concerning [the third-degree sexual abuse counts] the State must prove that the defendant committed a sex act "by force or against the will" of the alleged victim in that Instruction. In order to do so, however, the State does not have to prove that the alleged victim physically resisted the defendant's acts. The force used by the defendant does not have to be physical. *An act may be done "by force and against the will" of another if the other's consent or acquiescence is procured by:*
>
> *1. threats of violence; or*
>
> *2. deception, which may include deception concerning the nature of the act or deception concerning the defendant's right to exercise authority over the other under the circumstances.*
>
> You may consider all of the circumstances surrounding the defendant's act in deciding whether the act was done by force or against the will of the alleged victim. (Emphasis added.)

The court stated that its authority for giving this instruction was found in Iowa Code section 709.5, which provides:

> Under the provisions of this chapter it shall not be necessary to establish physical resistance by a person in order to establish that an act of sexual abuse was committed by force or against the will of the person. *However, the circumstances surrounding the commission of the act may be considered in determining whether or not the act was done by force or against the will of the other.* (Emphasis added).

The court also relied on the case of *State v. Vander Esch*, 662 N.W.2d 689 (Iowa Ct. App. 2002). In *Vander Esch* the defendant, an owner of a pizza restaurant, employed teenage boys. He informed two of these employees that he was doing a scientific research project and asked them to provide him semen samples for this purpose. He promised to pay $50 for the samples should their sperm count be high enough. Vander Esch was present during the procedure and took possession of the semen samples. Vander Esch was not authorized by any scientific body to collect semen samples, and the victims indicated that they would not have consented to these acts had they known that no scientific research existed. Vander Esch was charged with four counts of third-degree sexual abuse under Iowa Code section 709.4(1). He argued that the definition of sexual abuse, as set out in Iowa Code section 709.1(1), set forth the only means recognized in Iowa to negate consent and that neither fraud nor deceit did so.

Our examination of the issue must begin with Iowa Code section 709.1(1), which defines sexual abuse and provides that certain circumstances will vitiate a victim's consent:

> Any sex act between persons is sexual abuse by either of the persons when the act is performed with the other person in any of the following circumstances:
>
> 1. The act is done by force or against the will of the other. If the consent or acquiescence of the other is procured by threats of violence toward any person or if the act is done while the other is under the influence of a drug inducing sleep or is otherwise in a state of unconsciousness, the act is done against the will of the other.

In *Vander Esch* the district court ruled that, in view of the fact that Iowa Code section 709.5 permits the consideration of all surrounding circumstances, section 709.1(1) is not exclusive and fraud and deception may vitiate consent. The court of appeals upheld that decision, classifying the fraud in question as fraud in fact, as opposed to fraud in the inducement (concepts we later discuss), and therefore, the act was done "by force or against the will" of the boys. Bolsinger argues that the acts which occurred were hand-to-genital contact, which was expressly agreed to by the boys. He argues that his unexpressed purpose, apparently sexual gratification, was collateral to the act itself and, therefore, constituted fraud only in the inducement. As such, the fraud does not vitiate consent, according to him. Bolsinger also argues that *Vander Esch*, relied on by the court of appeals (which divided four to four on the question) and the district court in the present case, was incorrectly decided and should be overruled. Bolsinger argues that *Vander Esch* erroneously characterized the consent to semen sampling as being produced by fraud in fact, and therefore, any consent was vitiated.

If an act is done that is different from the act the defendant said he would perform, this is fraud in fact. If the act is done as the defendant stated it would be, but it is for some collateral or ulterior purpose, this is fraud in the inducement. Fraud in fact vitiates consent; fraud in the inducement does not. In other words, if deception causes a misunderstanding as to the fact itself (fraud in the *factum*) there is no legally-recognized consent because what happened is not that for which consent was given; whereas consent induced by fraud is as effective as other consent, so far as direct and immediate legal consequences are concerned, if the deception relates not to the thing done but merely to some collateral matter (fraud in the inducement).

Cases illustrating fraud in fact have often involved victims undergoing medical examination or treatment. In many cases, the victims consented to an examination, only to find that the doctor engaged in sex acts. One treatise discusses fraud in these cases:

> In some of these cases the doctor has not hesitated to make it clear that he intended to have sexual intercourse with the patient, his fraud being in the deceitful suggestion that this was necessary to cure some malady, which was fraud in the inducement, since the patient knew exactly what was to be done

> and was deceived only in regard to a collateral matter—the reason why it was to be done. And here as usual the direct and immediate consequence of consent obtained by fraud in the inducement is the same as consent given in the absence of fraud, and since the patient consented to the intercourse it was not rape so long as she was over the statutory age.

Bolsinger argues that each of these young men was told what the touching would consist of and that they were then touched in the exact manner they expected. Thus, he argues, any fraud was fraud in the inducement, not fraud in fact.

In Bolsinger's case, if the boys had consented to acts such as massaging their legs and instead Bolsinger had touched their genital area, this would clearly be fraud in fact; they would have consented to one act but subjected to a different one. That is not the case, however. We conclude that the consents given here were based on fraud in the inducement, not on fraud in fact, as the victims were touched in exactly the manner represented to them. The consents, therefore, were not vitiated.

...

... We now hold that *Vander Esch* is no longer controlling because the facts on which that case was based clearly show fraud in the inducement, not fraud in fact.

...

We reverse the convictions for third-degree sexual abuse and affirm the remaining convictions.

Comments and Questions

(1) Fraud is generally defined as a deception through which the actor obtains a pecuniary gain from the victim of the lie. The victim consents to the harmful transaction because of the misrepresentation. Fraudulent misrepresentations, although they may result in significant harm, are not encompassed by rape law, as *Bolsinger* makes clear. Only when the act the defendant said would be performed is different than what was done—known as fraud-in-fact—does rape law apply.

Further, the exception of fraud-in-fact is limited to two circumstances: when the actor misrepresents a medical procedure or when the actor impersonates a husband or person with whom the victim has an intimate relation. *See* Patricia J. Falk, *Rape by Fraud and Rape by Coercion*, 64 BROOK. L. REV. 39, 119 (1998); Jeb Rubenfeld, *The Riddle of Rape-by-Deception and the Myth of Sexual Autonomy*, 122 YALE L. J. 1372, 1396–98 (2013) (concluding that neither exception withstands scrutiny).

(2) In *Boro v. Superior Court*, 163 Cal. App. 3d 1224, 210 Cal. Rptr. 122 (1985), the defendant deceived the victim by posing as a doctor and telling her that she had a deadly disease that could be cured if she had intercourse with an anonymous "donor" who had been injected with a special serum. The state argued the victim was unconscious of the nature of the act because she thought it was a medical treatment. The defendant successfully argued that the victim was plainly aware of the nature of the act and her reason for engaging in it was irrelevant. What of the alternate doctrine

b/c Fraud in Inducement

of coercion? Do the misrepresentations by Boro—disease, donor, serum—amount to coercion that vitiates consent?

(3) Consider the following case of impersonation:

> Private First Class B had been drinking and was asleep in her barracks room at Camp Hovey, Korea. She left the door unlocked so that her boyfriend, Sergeant R, could enter. At some time during the night, appellant entered her barracks and had intercourse with B. She was not fully awake and called out R's name several times during the intercourse. After the intercourse was completed, B got out of bed, went to the bathroom, and then noticed that appellant and not R was sitting on her bunk.

United States v. Hughes, 48 M.J. 214, 215 (C.A.A.F. 1998) (holding evidence was sufficient to show the female soldier had not consented to sexual penetration).

[4] *Mens Rea*, Mistake, and Consent

At common law, rape was a general intent offense that required proof that the defendant acted in a morally blameworthy manner. Moral blameworthiness was inherent in the use of force and, indeed, in sexual intercourse outside of marriage. *See generally* Anne M. Coughlin, *Sex and Guilt*, 84 Va. L. Rev. 1 (1998). The combination of an ancient general intent offense and today's statutory element offense can produce confounding theories about the *mens rea* of rape. Defendants who claim an honest and reasonable belief that the victim had consented to the sexual act necessarily implicate the *mens rea* element of the crime, illustrated by the following cases.

Commonwealth v. Lopez

Supreme Judicial Court of Massachusetts
745 N.E.2d 961 (2001)

Spina, J.

...

1. *Background.* We summarize facts that the jury could have found. On May 8, 1998, the victim, a seventeen year old girl, was living in a foster home in Springfield. At approximately 3 P.M., she started walking to a restaurant where she had planned to meet her biological mother. On the way, she encountered the defendant. He introduced himself, asked where she was going, and offered to walk with her. The victim met her mother and introduced the defendant as her friend. The defendant said that he lived in the same foster home as the victim and that "they knew each other from school." Sometime later, the defendant left to make a telephone call. When the victim left the restaurant, the defendant was waiting outside and offered to walk her home. She agreed.

The two walked to a park across the street from the victim's foster home and talked for approximately twenty to thirty minutes. The victim's foster sisters were within earshot, and the victim feared that she would be caught violating her foster mother's rules against bringing "a guy near the house." The defendant suggested that they take a walk in the woods nearby. At one point, deep in the woods, the victim said that she wanted to go home. The defendant said, "trust me," and assured her that nothing would happen and that he would not hurt her. The defendant led the victim down a path to a secluded area.

The defendant asked the victim why she was so distant and said that he wanted to start a relationship with her. She said that she did not want to "get into any relationship." The defendant began making sexual innuendos to which the victim did not respond. He grabbed her by her wrist and began kissing her on the lips. She pulled away and said, "No, I don't want to do this." The defendant then told the victim that if she "had sex with him, [she] would love him more." She repeated, "No, I don't want to. I don't want to do this." He raised her shirt and touched her breasts. She immediately pulled her shirt down and pushed him away.

The defendant then pushed the victim against a slate slab, unbuttoned her pants, and pulled them down. Using his legs to pin down her legs, he produced a condom and asked her to put it on him. The victim said, "No." The defendant put the condom on and told the victim that he wanted her to put his penis inside her. She said, "No." He then raped her, and she began to cry. A few minutes later, the victim made a "jerking move" to her left. The defendant became angry, turned her around, pushed her face into the slate, and raped her again. The treating physician described the bruising to the victim's knees as "significant." The physician opined that there had been "excessive force and trauma to the [vaginal] area" based on his observation that there was "a lot of swelling" in her external vaginal area and her hymen had been torn and was "still oozing." The doctor noted that in his experience it was "fairly rare" to see that much swelling and trauma.

The defendant told the victim that she "would get in a lot of trouble" if she said anything. He then grabbed her by the arm, kissed her, and said, "I'll see you later." The victim went home and showered. She told her foster mother, who immediately dialed 911. The victim cried hysterically as she spoke to the 911 operator.

The defendant's version of the encounter was diametrically opposed to that of the victim. He testified that the victim had been a willing and active partner in consensual sexual intercourse. Specifically, the defendant claimed that the victim initiated intimate activity, and never once told him to stop. Additionally, the defendant testified that the victim invited him to a party that evening so that he could meet her friends. The defendant further claimed that when he told her that he would be unable to attend, the victim appeared "mildly upset."

Before the jury retired, defense counsel requested a mistake of fact instruction as to consent.[1] The judge declined to give the instruction, saying that, based "both on the law, as well as on the facts, that instruction is not warranted." ... [T]he judge

1. The defendant proposed the following instruction: "If the Commonwealth has not proved beyond a reasonable doubt that the defendant was not motivated by a reasonable and honest belief that the complaining witness consented to sexual intercourse, you must find the defendant not guilty."

concluded that the ultimate question for the jury was simply whether they believed the victim's or the defendant's version of the encounter. The decision not to give the instruction provides the basis for this appeal.

2. *Mistake of fact instruction.* The defendant claims that the judge erred in failing to give his proposed mistake of fact instruction. The defendant, however, was not entitled to this instruction. In *Commonwealth v. Ascolillo*, we held that the defendant was not entitled to a mistake of fact instruction, and declined to adopt a rule that "in order to establish the crime of rape the Commonwealth must prove *in every case* not only that the defendant intended intercourse but also that he did not act pursuant to an honest and reasonable belief that the victim consented" (emphasis added). Neither the plain language of our rape statute nor this court's decisions prior to the *Ascolillo* decision warrant a different result.

A fundamental tenet of criminal law is that culpability requires a showing that the prohibited conduct (actus reus) was committed with the concomitant mental state (mens rea) prescribed for the offense. *See*, e.g., *Morissette v. United States*.... The mistake of fact "defense" is available where the mistakes negates the existence of a mental state essential to a material element of the offense. In determining whether the defendant's honest and reasonable belief as to the victim's consent would relieve him of culpability, it is necessary to review the required elements of the crime of rape.

At common law, rape was defined as "the carnal knowledge of a woman forcibly and against her will." 4 W. Blackstone, Commentaries 210.... Since 1642, rape has been proscribed by statute in this Commonwealth.... While there have been several revisions to this statute, the definition and the required elements of the crime have remained essentially unchanged since the original enactment. The current rape statute, G.L. c. 265, § 22(b), provides in pertinent part:

> "Whoever has sexual intercourse or unnatural sexual intercourse with a person and compels such person to submit by force and against his will, or compels such person to submit by threat of bodily injury, shall be punished by imprisonment in the state prison for not more than twenty years."

This statute follows the common-law definition of rape, and requires the Commonwealth to prove beyond a reasonable doubt that the defendant committed (1) sexual intercourse (2) by force or threat of force and against the will of the victim....

Although the Commonwealth must prove lack of consent, the "elements necessary for rape do not require that the defendant intend the intercourse to be without consent." ... Historically, the relevant inquiry has been limited to consent in fact, and no mens rea or knowledge as to the lack of consent has ever been required.

A mistake of fact as to consent, therefore, has very little application to our rape statute. Because G.L. c. 265, § 22, does not require proof of a defendant's knowledge of the victim's lack of consent or intent to engage in nonconsensual intercourse as a material element of the offense, a mistake as to that consent cannot, therefore, negate a mental state required for commission of the prohibited conduct. Any perception (reasonable, honest, or otherwise) of the defendant as to the victim's consent is consequently not relevant to a rape prosecution....

This is not to say, contrary to the defendant's suggestion, that the absence of any mens rea as to the consent element transforms rape into a strict liability crime. It does not.... Rape, at common law and pursuant to G.L. c. 265, §22, is a general intent crime, ... and proof that a defendant intended sexual intercourse by force coupled with proof that the victim did not in fact consent is sufficient to maintain a conviction....

We also have concerns that the mistake of fact defense would tend to eviscerate the long-standing rule in this Commonwealth that victims need not use any force to resist an attack.... A shift in focus from the victim's to the defendant's state of mind might require victims to use physical force in order to communicate an unqualified lack of consent to defeat an honest and reasonable belief as to consent. The mistake of fact defense is incompatible with the evolution of our jurisprudence with respect to the crime of rape.

We are cognizant that our interpretation is not shared by the majority of other jurisdictions. States that recognize a mistake of fact as to consent generally have done so by legislation. Some State statutes expressly require a showing of a defendant's intent as to nonconsent. Alaska, for example, requires proof of a culpable state of mind. "... Because no specific mental state is mentioned in Alaska's statute governing sexual assault in the first degree," the State "must prove that the defendant acted 'recklessly' regarding his putative victim's lack of consent. So understood, an honest and reasonable mistake as to consent would negate the culpability requirement attached to the element of consent...."

The New Jersey statute defines sexual assault (rape) as "any act of sexual penetration engaged in by the defendant without the affirmative and freely-given permission of the victim to the specific act of penetration." *In re M.T.S.* a defendant by claiming that he had permission to engage in sexual intercourse, places his state of mind directly in issue. The jury must then determine "whether the defendant's belief that the alleged victim had freely given affirmative permission was reasonable."

The mistake of fact "defense" has been recognized by judicial decision in some States. In 1975, the Supreme Court of California became the first State court to recognize a mistake of fact defense in rape cases. Although the court did not make a specific determination that intent was required as to the element of consent, it did conclude that, "[i]f a defendant entertains a reasonable and bona fide belief that a prosecutrix voluntarily consented ... to engage in sexual intercourse, it is apparent he does not possess the wrongful intent that is a prerequisite under Penal Code section 20 to a conviction of ... rape by means of force or threat." Thus, the intent required is an intent to engage in nonconsensual sexual intercourse, and the State must prove that a defendant intentionally engaged in intercourse and was at least negligent regarding consent.

Other state courts have employed a variety of different constructions in adopting the mistake of fact defense. *See State v. Smith*, 210 Conn. 132, 142, 554 A.2d 713

(1989); *State v. Koonce*, 731 S.W.2d 431, 437 n. 2 (Mo. Ct. App. 1987) (construing rape statute to require defendant acted at least recklessly as to consent).

However, the minority of States sharing our view is significant.... [Ed. The court cites eight states that agree with its holding; Illinois, Iowa, Maine, New Hampshire, Pennsylvania, Michigan, Washington, and Wisconsin.] ... This case does not persuade us that we should recognize a mistake of fact as to consent as a defense to rape in *all* cases.... Whether such a defense might, in some circumstances, be appropriate is a difficult question that we may consider on a future case where a defendant's claim of reasonable mistake of fact is at least arguably supported by the evidence. This is not such a case.

Judgments affirmed.

Comments and Questions

(1) It is axiomatic that an honest and reasonable mistake about a fact essential to proof of an element of the offense negates proof of that element. *See Morissette, supra*, Ch. 3.01. Yet the court decided the defendant was not entitled to a jury instruction on mistake of fact. Do the statute's redundant terms, "submit by force and against his will" explain why a mistake of fact "has very little application to the rape statute at issue"?

(2) The government bears the burden of proving every element of the offense beyond a reasonable doubt. When a defendant raises a mistake regarding consent in states where consent is an element of the offense, the state bears the burden of proving that the victim did not "by either words or actions freely agree to have sexual contact or intercourse with the defendant." *See* Gates v. Wisconsin, 283 N.W. 2d 474, 477–78 (Wis. App. 1979) (holding that evidence of victim screaming and struggling for five minutes before succumbing was sufficient proof of lack of consent).

(3) The issue of consent can also be pertinent in casting doubt on whether consent existed, i.e., consent in fact. In that situation, defendant's claim that the victim actually consented may raise reasonable doubt that negates forcible assault. *See, e.g.*, Washington v. W.R., Jr., 336 P.3d 1134 (Wash. 2014) (*en banc*).

Commonwealth v. Fischer

Superior Court of Pennsylvania
721 A.2d 1111 (1998)

Beck, J.

This case prompts our consideration of the law with respect to forcible compulsion and consent in sexual assault cases. After a careful review of the record and an in-depth analysis of the issue at hand, we affirm.

Appellant, an eighteen year-old college freshman, was charged with involuntary deviate sexual intercourse (IDSI), aggravated indecent assault and related offenses in connection with an incident that occurred in a Lafayette College campus dormitory. The victim was another freshman student appellant met at school.

At trial, both the victim and appellant testified that a couple of hours prior to the incident at issue, the two went to appellant's dorm room and engaged in intimate contact. The victim testified that the couple's conduct was limited to kissing and fondling. Appellant, on the other hand, testified that during this initial encounter, he and the victim engaged in "rough sex" which culminated in the victim performing fellatio on him. According to appellant, the victim acted aggressively at this first rendezvous by holding appellant's arms above his head, biting his chest, stating "You know you want me," and initiating oral sex.

After the encounter, the students separated and went to the dining hall with their respective friends. They met up again later and once more found themselves in appellant's dorm room. While their accounts of what occurred at the first meeting contained significant differences, their versions of events at the second meeting were grossly divergent. The victim testified that appellant locked the door, pushed her onto the bed, straddled her, held her wrists above her head and forced his penis into her mouth. She struggled with appellant throughout the entire encounter and warned him that "someone would look for her" and "someone would find out." She also told him that she was scheduled to be at a mandatory seminar and repeatedly stated that she did not want to engage in sex, but her pleas went unheeded.

According to the victim, appellant forced his hands inside a hole in her jeans and penetrated her with his fingers. He then placed his penis inside the torn jeans, removed it and ejaculated on her face, hair and sweater. Thereafter, he turned her over onto her stomach, pulled down her underpants and attempted to penetrate her anally. Throughout the incident, appellant made various statements to the victim, including "I know you want it," "I know you want my dick in your mouth" and "Nobody will know where you are." When the victim attempted to leave, appellant blocked her path. Only after striking him in the groin with her knee was the victim able to escape.

Appellant characterized the second meeting in a far different light. He stated that as he led the victim into his room, she told him it would have to be "a quick one." As a result, appellant figured that their sexual liaison would be brief. Thereafter, according to appellant, he began to engage in the same type of behavior the victim had exhibited in their previous encounter. Appellant admitted that he held the young woman's arms above her head, straddled her and placed his penis at her mouth. He testified that at that point he told her "I know you want my dick in your mouth." When she replied "no," appellant answered "No means yes." After another verbal exchange that included the victim's statement that she had to leave, appellant again insisted that "she wanted it." This time she answered "No, I honestly don't." Upon hearing this, appellant no longer sought to engage in oral sex and removed himself from her body. However, as the two lay side by side on the bed, they continued to kiss and fondle one another.

Appellant admitted to touching the victim's genitalia and to placing his penis inside the hole in her jeans. According to appellant, the victim enjoyed the contact and responded positively to his actions. At some point, however, she stood up and informed appellant that she had to leave. When appellant again attempted to touch her, this time on the thigh, she told him she was "getting pissed." Before appellant could "rearrange himself," so that he could walk the victim to her class, she abruptly left the room.

At trial, both sides presented evidence to support their positions. Appellant's college friends testified that after the first encounter, but before the second, appellant showed them bite marks on his chest that he had received from the victim during the first encounter. Numerous character witnesses testified on appellant's behalf.

The Commonwealth offered physical evidence of sperm found on the victim's sweater. Medical personnel testified to treating the victim on the night in question. Many of the victim's friends and classmates described her as nervous, shaken and upset after the incident.

Defense counsel argued throughout the trial and in closing that appellant, relying on his previous encounter with the victim, did not believe his actions were taken without her consent. Presenting appellant as sexually inexperienced, counsel argued that his client believed the victim was a willing participant during their intimate encounters. In light of his limited experience and the victim's initially aggressive behavior, argued counsel, appellant's beliefs were reasonable. Further, the victim's conduct throughout the second encounter, as testified to by appellant, would not make appellant's actions "forcible" since it appeared that the victim was enjoying the encounter. Finally, as soon as appellant realized that the victim truly did not wish to engage in oral sex a second time, appellant stopped seeking same. As a result, appellant's actions could not be deemed forcible compulsion.

The jury returned a verdict of guilty on virtually all counts. Appellant was sentenced to two to five years in prison.... Specifically, appellant claims that counsel should have asked the court to instruct the jurors that if they found appellant reasonably, though mistakenly, believed that the victim was consenting to his sexual advances, they could find him not guilty.

...

The Commonwealth [relies] on an opinion by a panel of this court. *Commonwealth v. Williams* concerned the rape and assault of a Temple University student. The facts established that the victim accepted a ride from the appellant on a snowy evening in Philadelphia. Instead of taking the young woman to the bus station, appellant drove her to a dark area, threatened to kill her and informed her that he wanted sex. The victim told Williams to "go ahead" because she did not wish to be hurt.

After his conviction and sentence, appellant filed a direct appeal and argued, among other things, that the trial court erred in refusing to instruct the jury "that if the defendant reasonably believed that the prosecutrix had consented to his sexual advances that this would constitute a defense to the rape and involuntary deviate sexual intercourse charge." This court rejected Williams's claim and held:

> In so refusing the proffered charge the court acted correctly. The charge requested by the defendant is not now and has never been the law of Pennsylvania. When one individual uses force or the threat of force to have sexual

> relations with a person not his spouse and without the person's consent he has committed the crime of rape. *If the element of the defendant's belief as to the victim's state of mind is to be established as a defense to the crime of rape then it should be done by our legislature which has the power to define crimes and offenses. We refuse to create such a defense.*

...

The issues of consent and forcible compulsion raised in sexual assault prosecutions have always been complex. Unless the incident is witnessed by a third party, or is accompanied by conspicuous injury, a rape case is often reduced to a credibility battle between the complainant and the defendant. Our laws have sought continually to protect victims of sexual assault, and in the process, have undergone significant change. Although the rape and IDSI laws have always required the element of "forcible compulsion," that term was not initially defined. The definition of that term and its relation to the concept of consent have been the frequent topic of discussion among lawmakers, courts and scholars.

...

Less than one year after the *Berkowitz* decision, the legislature amended the sexual assault law by adding a definition for forcible compulsion....

> "Forcible Compulsion." Compulsion by use of physical, intellectual, moral, emotional or psychological force, either express or implied. The term includes, but is not limited to, compulsion resulting in another person's death, whether the death occurred before, during or after sexual intercourse.

18 Pa. Const. Stat. Ann. § 3101.

It is this broader definition, argues appellant in this case, that prompts the necessity for a mistake of fact jury instruction in cases where such a defense is raised. According to appellant:

> The language of the present statute inextricably links the issues of consent with *mens rea*. To ask a jury to consider whether the defendant used "intellectual or moral" force, while denying the instruction as to how to consider the defendant's mental state at the time of alleged encounter is patently unfair to the accused.

Appellant's argument is bolstered by the fact that the concept of "mistake of fact" has long been a fixture in the criminal law....

The notion that one charged with sexual assault may defend by claiming a reasonable belief of consent has been recognized in other jurisdictions. *In the Interest of M.T.S.*

Courts in other jurisdictions have likewise held that jury instructions regarding the defendant's reasonable belief as to consent are proper ...

Although the logic of these other cases is persuasive, we are unable to adopt the principles enunciated in them because of the binding precedent with which we are faced, namely, *Williams*. In an effort to avoid application of *Williams*, appellant directs our attention to the Subcommittee Notes of the Pennsylvania Criminal Suggested Standard Jury Instructions. The possible conflict between *Williams* and § 304 (Mistake of Fact) was not lost on the Subcommittee....

Appellant's insistence that *Williams* should be disregarded in light of the legislature's broader and more complex definition of forcible compulsion is echoed by the Subcommittee:

> In the opinion of the Subcommittee there may be cases, especially now that *Rhodes* has extended the definition of force to psychological, moral and intellectual force, where a defendant might non-recklessly or even reasonably, but wrongly, believe that his words and conduct do not constitute force or the threat of force and that a non-resisting female is consenting. An example might be "date rape" resulting from mutual misunderstanding. The boy does not intend or suspect the intimidating potential of his vigorous wooing. The girl, misjudging the boys' character, believes he will become violent if thwarted; she feigns willingness, even some pleasure. In our opinion the defendant in such a case ought not to be convicted of rape.

It is clear that the Subcommittee gave extensive thought to the ever-changing law of sexual assault and our understanding of sexual behavior in modern times. We agree with the Subcommittee that the rule in *Williams* is inappropriate in the type of date rape case described above. Changing codes of sexual conduct, particularly those exhibited on college campuses, may require that we give greater weight to what is occurring beneath the overt actions of young men and women. Recognition of those changes, in the form of specified jury instructions, strikes us an appropriate course of action.

Despite appellant's excellent presentation of the issues, there remain ... distinct problems precluding relief in this case. First is appellant's reliance on the evolution of our sexual assault laws to avoid the application of *Williams*. As is obvious from our discussion above, the changes in the statute are significant and have served to extend culpability in rape and IDSI cases to a variety of new circumstances, including incidents involving psychological, moral and intellectual force.

This case, however, is not one of the "new" varieties of sexual assault contemplated by the amended statute.... This is a case of a young woman alleging physical force in a sexual assault and a young man claiming that he reasonably believed he had consent.[4] In such circumstances, *Williams* controls.

We are keenly aware of the differences between *Williams* and this case. Most notable is the fact that Williams and his victim never met before the incident in question. Here, appellant and the victim not only knew one another, but had engaged in inti-

4. We observe that the facts of this case are not the same as those set out in the Subcommittee's "date rape" scenario. The victim in this case testified that she was physically forced to engage in sex against her will, that she resisted verbally and physically and that she had to strike appellant in order to leave the room. Appellant characterized the victim as a sexually experienced woman who initiated oral sex in the first encounter, declined it in the second and made a false rape claim thereafter.

mate contact just hours before the incident in question. It is clear however, that the *Williams* court's basis for denying the jury instruction was its conclusion that the law did not require it and, further, that the judiciary had no authority to grant it. Even if we were to disagree with those conclusions, we are powerless to alter them.

Comments and Questions

(1) Does a wider conception of force (threat, fear, and coercion) increase the significance of the consent element? If so, what is the effect at trial?

(2) How should the law balance the interest of the state in deterring rape, vindicating the harm to victims, and maintaining fairness to defendants? Should victims bear responsibility for communicating nonconsent in an unequivocal manner? On whom should the risk of error fall—the victim or the defendant?

[5] Post-Penetration Rape

State v. Robinson

Supreme Judicial Court of Maine
496 A.2d 1067 (1985)

McCusick, Chief Justice.

On June 21, 1984, a Penobscot County jury found defendant Gordon Robinson III guilty of Class A rape, 17-A M.R.S.A. § 252(1)(B) (1983). Finding no reversible error in his trial, we affirm the Superior Court's judgment of conviction.

I.

At trial the prosecutrix and defendant Robinson gave sharply divergent testimony as to what happened at her home in Garland on an October night in 1983. Defendant, who at that time lived in Dover-Foxcroft, said that he had driven to the prosecutrix's house in the early morning hours but had left when he saw through a window that she was talking on the telephone. Down the road he ran out of gasoline.

The prosecutrix testified that when she found Robinson at her door and heard that he had run out of gasoline and needed to use her telephone, she allowed him to come in to make his call. Rather than immediately using the telephone, however, defendant went into the living room with the prosecutrix and began watching the video cassette movie she was already playing.

The prosecutrix testified that defendant started a struggle with her and forced her against her will to have sexual intercourse with him. Defendant, by contrast, testified that the prosecutrix joined him in engaging in foreplay that culminated in consensual sexual intercourse. He recalled that during intercourse she suddenly declared, "I guess I don't want to do this anymore." He testified that he thereupon stopped, got dressed, and left.

During the jury's deliberations, it sent out the following question to the presiding justice:

> Concerning the law—if two people began consenting to an act, then one person says no and the other continues—is that rape?

In response, the justice instructed the jury in summary as follows:

> If a couple consensually engages in sexual intercourse and one or the other changes his or her mind, and communicates the revocation or change of mind of the consent, and the other partner continues the sexual intercourse by compulsion of the party who changes his or her mind, then it would be rape. The critical element there is the *continuation under compulsion.*

(*Emphasis added*). The justice also repeated his careful description of what constitutes the compulsion necessary for a conviction for rape under the Criminal Code. At trial counsel for neither the State nor defendant Robinson objected in any way when the justice gave the supplemental charge. On appeal, however, defense counsel contends that, once the initial penetration of sexual intercourse is made with the woman's consent, her subsequent revocation of consent cannot transform continued sexual intercourse, even if compelled by the man, into rape. At most, it is suggested, the crime is simple or aggravated assault.

We reject defendant's appellate attack on the justice's supplemental instruction. We agree with the apparent unanimous view of all the participants at the time the instruction was given that the legislative intent expressed in the controlling provision of the Maine Criminal Code, as well as common sense, establishes the correctness of that instruction.

Section 252 of the Criminal Code defines adult rape to have three elements: (1) "sexual intercourse" by the defendant (2) with a person not the defendant's spouse (3) in circumstances by which that other person submits to the sexual intercourse as a result of compulsion applied by the defendant.[1] Only elements (1) and (3) are involved in the challenged instruction. In anybody's lexicon, the continued penetration of the female sex organ by the male sex organ, after the time either party has withdrawn consent, is factually "sexual intercourse." At the same time, continued penetration is defined by section 251(1)(B) to be "sexual intercourse" in the sight of the law.[2] The presiding justice went on—we find entirely correctly—to charge the jury that the continuing sexual intercourse became rape if the prosecutrix submitted to

---

1. A.M.R.S.A. §251(1)(E) (1983) reads in full:

   Compulsion means physical force, a threat of physical force or a combination thereof which makes a person unable to physically repel the actor or which produces in that person a reasonable fear that death, serious bodily injury or kidnapping might be imminently inflicted upon that person or upon another human being.

2. 17-A M.R.S.A. §251(1)(B) (1983) provides in pertinent part:

   Sexual intercourse means any penetration of the female sex organ by the male sex organ.

(Emphasis added). The case law almost always focuses upon the threshold invasion of the female's body and declares that sexual intercourse "is complete upon proof of penetration of the female organ by the male organ, however slight." The fact that the overwhelming bulk of rape cases involve the question whether the threshold entry of the female sex organ occurred cannot blink the fact that in either everyday or legal parlance *any* continuing presence of the male sex organ in the female sex organ constitutes sexual intercourse.

the continuation only as a result of compulsion. We emphasize that the ongoing intercourse, initiated we here assume with the prosecutrix's consent, did not become rape merely because she revoked her consent. It became rape if and when the prosecutrix thereafter submitted to defendant's sexual assault only because "physical force, a threat of physical force or a combination thereof ... [made her] unable to physically repel the [defendant] or ... produce[d] in [her] a reasonable fear that death, serious bodily injury or kidnapping might be imminently inflicted upon [her]." As in any rape case, the State must prove beyond a reasonable doubt a whole lot more than mere absence of consent. The presiding justice was absolutely right in emphasizing:

The critical element there is the continuation under compulsion.

In his answer to the jury's question, he was also complete in explaining the Code's definition of "compulsion" in the exact terms of the Criminal Code, thereby repeating with emphasis the explanation that he had given as part of the main charge.

...

Practical, common sense considerations support our reading of Maine's rape statute. Defendant's argument in essence is that rape occurs only when a male's entry of the female sex organ is made as a result of compulsion. By that argument, the question of rape or no rape in fact situations like the present one would turn on whether the prosecutrix, on revoking her consent and struggling against the defendant's forcible attempt to continue intercourse, succeeds at least momentarily in displacing the male sex organ. That makes for a close evidentiary call. Furthermore, it hardly makes sense to protect from a rape prosecution the party whose compulsion through physical force or threat of serious bodily harm is so overwhelming that there is no possible withdrawal, however brief. At the same time, there is no reason to strain to limit the ordinary meaning of the language of our rape statute for fear of a flood of possibly trumped up charges that courts have to adjudicate on the basis of diametrically opposed testimony of the man and the woman. The legislative intent that we find expressed in the rape statute does not impose any undue factfinding burden upon the courts.... The dramatic change from the role of a voluntary participant to that of a victim compelled involuntarily to submit to the sexual intercourse is a distinct one.

...

Comments and Questions

(1) Courts in Maine, Kansas, and six other states have ruled that continued penetration after consent is withdrawn may be rape. *See Maryland v. Baby,* 946 A.2d 463 (Md. 2008); *In re John Z.*, 60 P.3d 183 (Cal. 2003); *McGill v. Alaska*, 18 P.3d 77 (Alaska Ct. App. 2001); *State v. Siering*, 35 Conn. App. 173 (1994); *Maddox v. State*, 170 Ga. App. 633 (1984); *Minnesota v. Crims*, 540 N.W.2d 860 (Minn. App.1995); *South Dakota v. Jones*, 521 N.W.2d 662 (S.D. 1994).

In North Carolina, however, continued intercourse after withdrawal of consent cannot constitute rape. *See State v. Way*, 254 S.E. 2d 760, 762 (N.C. 1979) (stating that if "the actual penetration is accomplished with the woman's consent, the accused is not guilty of rape").

Illinois adopted a specific statute: "A person who initially consents to sexual penetration or sexual conduct is not deemed to have consented to any sexual penetration or conduct that occurs after he or she withdraws consent during the course of that sexual penetration or sexual conduct." 720 Ill. Comp. Stat. Ann. 5/11-1.70 (2007 Supp.).

(2) Defendants argued the jury must also find the defendant did not cease sexual intercourse within a reasonable time. The following case traces the debate.

Kansas v. Flynn

Supreme Court of Kansas
329 P.3d 429 (2014)

The opinion of the court was delivered by MORITZ, J.:

...

On September 26, 2007, A.S. reported to friends, family, and police that Ira Flynn had raped her. The State ultimately prosecuted Flynn on six charges: one count each of kidnapping, aggravated kidnapping, and aggravated criminal sodomy and three counts of rape.

Flynn's Jury Trial

The evidence presented at trial established that Flynn and A.S. had known each other for several years and attended the same schools and that A.S. and her mother worked with Flynn's mother and sister. At trial, Flynn and A.S. testified consistently as to certain events that occurred the evening of September 25, 2007, and in the early morning hours of September 26, 2007. Namely, both Flynn and A.S. testified the two of them made plans to hang out at Jennie Townsend's house after A.S. got off work....

A.S.'s Testimony

A.S. testified Flynn took two wrong turns after leaving Townsend's house and, when A.S. pointed this out, Flynn responded, "'We're going out here to go fuck.'" A.S. objected, telling Flynn, "'No we're not. No we're not.'" A.S. immediately became afraid when Flynn took the first wrong turn. A.S. also testified Flynn had not previously behaved violently toward her or caused her any harm.

According to A.S., Flynn eventually stopped the car on a country road, yelled at her to get out, and forced her to remove her clothing. Flynn then forced her to engage in nonconsensual vaginal intercourse on the hood of the car, on the ground in front of the car, and again in the backseat of the car. During the sexual intercourse on the ground, A.S.'s "bottom part," vagina, legs, arms, back, elbows and knees came in contact with the gravel road. At some point, Flynn attempted anal intercourse and told A.S. if they did not have anal intercourse she would have to provide oral sex. Flynn later placed his penis in A.S.'s mouth without her permission and forced her to perform oral sex.

A.S. testified she was overcome by fear during each act of intercourse as well as when forced to perform oral sex. She twice tried to run from Flynn, but he caught her each time. After the second time, A.S. placed her hands over her face and told Flynn she would have to quit her job. According to A.S., at this point Flynn's "face just completely changed," and it appeared to her Flynn realized what he had done. Flynn then picked up A.S.'s clothing from around the car, A.S. got dressed, and Flynn helped her put on her shoes.

Flynn's Testimony

...

According to Flynn, after he parked the car, he and A.S. got out, met in front of the car, and removed each other's clothing before having sexual intercourse on the hood of the car. A.S. then got down from the hood and performed oral sex on him. Flynn testified these acts were consensual, but the intercourse was "rough." Next, he and A.S. attempted to reengage in sexual intercourse on the hood of the car but, according to Flynn, they "went down to the ground" instead and had intercourse in front of A.S.'s car. Flynn testified A.S. was not fighting and he did not try to control her, but A.S. hit her head when they "flopped to the ground."

Flynn testified that during the intercourse on the ground, A.S. told him, " 'No. Just stop. No. Not here on the ground.' " Flynn "slowed down" but did not immediately stop because he was not sure A.S. was serious. According to Flynn, the two continued having intercourse for "30 seconds, a minute, maybe two," but he stopped when A.S. again said, " 'Stop, I'm serious.' " Flynn then helped A.S. gather her clothing and get dressed, and he dressed himself. Flynn denied having intercourse with A.S. in the backseat of her car and testified A.S. did not try to run from him at any point during the incident.

...

Ultimately, the jury found Flynn guilty of the rape charge ... concerning the allegation Flynn raped A.S. on the ground in front of her car but acquitted Flynn of the five remaining charges.

...

The district court imposed an aggravated presumptive sentence of 186 months' imprisonment ...

Court of Appeals' Decision

In reversing Flynn's conviction and sentence, the Court of Appeals majority addressed only one of Flynn's four appeal issues—*i.e.*, Flynn's claim the district court violated his Sixth Amendment right to a fair trial and to present his theory of defense when the court failed to instruct the jury in accordance with *State v. Bunyard*, 281 Kan. 392, "that sex can cease to become consensual if the consent is withdrawn after penetration and the intercourse continues either by force or fear, however, the defendant is allowed a 'reasonable time' in which to act upon the withdrawal of consent."

Citing Flynn's testimony that he briefly continued the intercourse after A.S. withdrew consent, the majority concluded the district court clearly erred in failing to give a *Bunyard* instruction.

Discussion

In its petition for review, the State advocates a two-prong position ... *i.e.,* the facts of this case did not warrant a *Bunyard* instruction and this court should revisit and disapprove *Bunyard*'s holding that a defendant has a "reasonable time" to withdraw when consent is withdrawn. The State reasons *Bunyard*'s rule is unnecessary because the rape statute already requires nonconsensual intercourse to be accomplished by force or fear.

Court of Appeals decision in Bunyard.

Before revisiting *Bunyard,* we find it helpful to thoroughly discuss the rationale for both the Court of Appeals' decision in Bunyard, as well as this court's review of that decision in *Bunyard.*

Bunyard directly appealed his rape conviction to the Court of Appeals arguing ... the district court failed to properly respond to a jury question about the rape charge.

The victim in *Bunyard,* E.N., testified she and Bunyard were watching a movie in the backseat of Bunyard's car, when he put his arm around her and they began kissing while Bunyard removed E.N.'s clothing. E.N. testified she was " 'okay' " with kissing Bunyard, but she was not okay with his removal of her clothing or his touching her breasts. According to E.N., after Bunyard removed his pants, put on a condom, laid her down in the backseat, and achieved penetration, she told him to stop. But Bunyard did not stop, instead continuing the intercourse for 5 to 10 minutes. E.N. further testified she tried to move away from Bunyard after she told him to stop.

In contrast, Bunyard testified his entire encounter with E.N. was consensual and that in fact, E.N. was on top of him during intercourse. According to Bunyard, E.N. ended the intercourse by dismounting when he told her he did not plan to call her the next day and was not interested in a relationship.

In his direct appeal to the Court of Appeals, Bunyard challenged the sufficiency of the evidence, arguing the evidence showed he and E.N. had consensual intercourse until after penetration occurred, and "rape occurs at the time of penetration, or not at all." ... Ultimately, the panel adopted the view held by a majority of jurisdictions—*i.e.,* when intercourse begins as consensual, it can become rape in some circumstances....

Had the panel ended with this straightforward analysis, we probably would not be revisiting this issue today. Instead, the panel chose to address Bunyard's alternative argument that "even if rape can occur after consensual penetration, a defendant must have a reasonable time in which to act on the victim's withdrawal of consent." Citing *In re John Z.,* 29 Cal.4th 756, the *Bunyard* panel essentially adopted the "reasonable time" argument and applied it to the facts before it:

> The [*John Z.*] court noted that the defendant was given 'ample time' to withdraw, and that his failure to cease intercourse was not reasonable. In *John Z.,* the victim told the defendant three times that she 'needed to go home.' It was estimated that the intercourse continued for 4 to 5 minutes after the victim first told the defendant she needed to go home.

> In the instant case, E.N. estimated that it took Bunyard approximately 5 to 10 minutes to stop the intercourse. When consent is withdrawn, continuing sexual intercourse for 5 to 10 minutes is not reasonable and constitutes rape." *Bunyard,* 31 Kan.App.2d at 859.

Unfortunately, the panel's reliance on *John Z.* was misplaced as the California Supreme Court in *John Z.* specifically rejected the argument that "the male should be permitted a 'reasonable amount of time' in which to withdraw." *In re John Z.,* 29 Cal.4th at 762–63. Thus, the panel's consideration of Bunyard's alternative theory was both unnecessary and legally unsound.

In any event, the *Bunyard* panel ultimately concluded the evidence was sufficient to find Bunyard guilty of rape based on its determination that (1) rape can occur when consent is withdrawn post-penetration, (2) the victim withdrew her consent post-penetration, (3) Bunyard failed to withdraw from intercourse within a reasonable time after the victim withdrew her consent, and (4) Bunyard continued the intercourse by force or fear.

...

This court's review of the panel's decision in Bunyard.

After granting Bunyard's petition for review, this court in *Bunyard* reversed the Court of Appeals' decision, reversed Bunyard's rape convictions on grounds of prosecutorial misconduct, and remanded the case for a new trial.

Based on its decision to reverse and remand for a new trial, the court addressed two additional issues: "(1) Was the evidence insufficient as a matter of law to support the conviction of rape, *i.e.,* does the Kansas rape statute cover post-penetration conduct, and (2) if rape can occur after consensual penetration, must the defendant have a reasonable time in which to act?"

... [T]he court agreed with the panel's conclusion that Kansas' rape statute proscribes all nonconsensual intercourse accomplished by force or fear, not just the initial penetration. Thus, the court succinctly reasoned "a person may be convicted of rape if consent is withdrawn after the initial penetration but intercourse is continued by the use of force or fear."

In addressing the second question—whether a defendant is entitled to a reasonable time to withdraw from intercourse after the victim withdraws consent—the court pointed out that the panel relied on *In re John Z.* in finding Bunyard did not withdraw within a reasonable time. The *Bunyard* court then briefly discussed *John Z.* and specifically noted the defendant in that case had argued "the male should be permitted a reasonable amount of time in which to withdraw once the female raises an objection to intercourse" because:

> By essence of the act of sexual intercourse, a male's primal urge to reproduce is aroused. It is therefore unreasonable for a female and the law to expect a male to cease having sexual intercourse immediately upon her withdrawal of consent. It is only natural, fair and just that the male be given a reasonable amount of time in which to quell his primal urge....

Notably, this court in *Bunyard* pointed out that in impliedly adopting the "reasonable time to withdraw argument," the *Bunyard* panel failed to consider *John Z.'s* "clear rejection" of the defendant's "reasonable time" argument. But after pointing out the panel's misplaced reliance on *John Z.* and *John Z.'s* strong rejection of the defendant's "primal urge" rationale for his "reasonable time to withdraw" theory, this court in *Bunyard* inexplicably concluded:

> In the case of consensual intercourse and withdrawn consent, we agree that the defendant should be entitled to a reasonable time in which to act after consent is withdrawn and communicated to the defendant. However, we conclude that the jury should determine whether the time between withdrawal of consent and the interruption of intercourse was reasonable. This determination must be based on the particular facts of each case, taking into account the manner in which consent was withdrawn. We believe this conclusion balances our rejection of the primal urge theory per se with our recognition of the unique facts and circumstances of each individual case.
>
> ...
>
> We, thus, conclude that the trial court had a duty to instruct the jury that post-penetration rape can occur under Kansas law and that the defendant has a 'reasonable time' to respond to the withdrawal of consent.

...

We disapprove Bunyard's *"reasonable time" holding because it is contrary to the plain language of the rape statute and without legal support.*

...

Simply stated, *Bunyard*'s conclusion that a defendant should be entitled to a "reasonable time" to discontinue intercourse with a nonconsenting partner is contrary to the plain language of the rape statute, is inconsistent with *Bunyard*'s own interpretation of the rape statute as encompassing the crime of post-penetration rape, and is not supported by the authorities the *Bunyard* panel considered or relied upon to reach its conclusion. We therefore disapprove *Bunyard*'s holding on this point.

But as *Bunyard* recognized, Kansas' rape statute "proscribes *all* nonconsensual intercourse that is accomplished by force or fear, not just the initial penetration. Thus, a person may be convicted of rape if consent is withdrawn after the initial penetration but intercourse is continued by the use of force or fear." That portion of our holding in *Bunyard* is consistent with the plain language of K.S.A. 21-3502(a)(1)(A), and we reaffirm it today.

Our modification of *Bunyard*'s holding means that when a party presents evidence demonstrating the victim initially consented to sexual intercourse but later withdrew consent, the critical issue for the jury is whether the defendant continued the intercourse through compulsion despite the victim's withdrawal of consent. It is the continuation of nonconsensual intercourse by compulsion that makes the offender's act rape, not the offender's failure to immediately respond to the victim's withdrawal of consent.

...

In light of the conflicting evidence presented in this case; the severity and number of charges filed against Flynn based on the incident with A.S.; the jury's acquittal of Flynn on charges of aggravated kidnapping, kidnapping, two counts of rape, and one count of aggravated criminal sodomy; and the jury's verdict of guilt only on the rape count clearly involving the issue of withdrawn consent, we are not persuaded the error was harmless.

Accordingly, we affirm the Court of Appeals decision, reverse Flynn's rape conviction, and remand for a new trial with a supplemental instruction based on *Bunyard* as modified by this opinion.

Comments and Questions

(1) Draft a jury instruction that would reflect the reasoning of *Flynn*.

(2) Note the difficulty that the trial, appellate, and supreme court, which considered the issue twice, had in deciding the "reasonable time" matter. As a matter of law, did the Kansas Supreme Court reach a correct conclusion? A reasonable conclusion?

[B] Statutory Rape

The crime of statutory rape was enacted by the English Parliament in 1275 to protect young girls under the age of 12 from "ravish." Because the young were presumed to lack the judgment and maturity to give informed consent, conviction depended only on the act. *See* Russell Christopher & Kathryn H. Christopher, *The Paradox of Statutory Rape*, 87 Ind. L.J. 505, 509 (2012) (noting that American colonies imported the English statutory scheme). As a strict-liability offense, a defense based on *mens rea* is simply irrelevant, as was outlined in Chapter 3.03.

Statutory age-span provisions now temper this rule in a majority of jurisdictions. The laws typically specify that the perpetrator must be "x" years older (usually three to four) than the juvenile and at least "x" years of age (usually 18). *See id.* at 519 (noting the rationale is that "where the two parties are within the same age range, the prospect of coercion and exploitation is minimal").

The two cases that follow provide contrasting approaches to statutory rape.

People v. Hernandez

Supreme Court of California
393 P.2d 673 (1964)

Peek, Justice.

By information defendant was charged with statutory rape. (Penal Code, § 261, subd. 1.) Following his plea of not guilty he was convicted as charged by the court sitting without a jury and the offense determined to be a misdemeanor.

Section 261 of the Penal Code provides in part as follows: "Rape is an act of sexual intercourse, accomplished with a female not the wife of the perpetrator, under either of the following circumstances: 1. Where the female is under the age of 18 years; ..."

The sole contention raised on appeal is that the trial court erred in refusing to permit defendant to present evidence going to his guilt for the purpose of showing that he had in good faith a reasonable belief that the prosecutrix was 18 years or more of age.

The undisputed facts show that the defendant and the prosecuting witness were not married and had been companions for several months prior to January 3, 1961—the date of the commission of the alleged offense. Upon that date the prosecutrix was 17 years and 9 months of age and voluntarily engaged in an act of sexual intercourse with defendant.

In support of his contention defendant relies upon Penal Code, § 20, which provides that "there must exist a union, or joint operation of act and intent, or criminal negligence" to constitute the commission of a crime. He further relies upon section 26 of that code which provides that one is not capable of committing a crime who commits an act under an ignorance or mistake of fact which disapproves any criminal intent.

Thus the sole issue relates to the question of intent and knowledge entertained by the defendant at the time of the commission of the crime charged.

Consent of the female is often an unrealistic and unfortunate standard for branding sexual intercourse a crime as serious as forcible rape. Yet the consent standard has been deemed to be required by important policy goals. We are dealing here, of course, with statutory rape where, in one sense, the lack of consent of the female is not an element of the offense. In a broader sense, however, the lack of consent is deemed to remain an element but the law makes a conclusive presumption of the lack thereof because she is presumed too innocent and naive to understand the implications and nature of her act.... The law's concern with her capacity or lack thereof to so understand is explained in part by a popular conception of the social, moral and personal values which are preserved by the abstinence from sexual indulgence on the part of a young woman. An unwise disposition of her sexual favor is deemed to do harm both to herself and the social mores by which the community's conduct patterns are established. Hence the law of statutory rape intervenes in an effort to avoid such a disposition. This goal, moreover, is not accomplished by penalizing the naive female but by imposing criminal sanctions against the male, who is conclusively presumed to be responsible for the occurrence....

The assumption that age alone will bring an understanding of the sexual act to a young woman is of doubtful validity. Both learning from the cultural group to which she is a member and her actual sexual experiences will determine her level of comprehension. The sexually experienced 15-year old may be far more acutely aware of the implications of sexual intercourse than her sheltered cousin who is beyond the age of consent. A girl who belongs to a group whose members indulge in sexual intercourse at an early age is likely to rapidly acquire an insight into the rewards and penalties of sexual indulgence. Nevertheless, even in circumstances where a girl's actual comprehension contradicts the law's presumption, the male is deemed criminally responsible for the act, although himself young and naive and responding to advances which may have been made to him.

The law as presently constituted does not concern itself with the relative culpability of the male and female participants in the prohibited sexual act. Even where the young woman is knowledgeable it does not impose sanctions upon her. The knowledgeable young man, on the other hand, is penalized and there are none who would claim that under any construction of the law this should be otherwise. However, the issue raised by the rejected offer of proof in the instant case goes to the culpability of the young man who acts *without* knowledge that an essential factual element exists and has, on the other hand, a positive, reasonable belief that it does not exist....

Statutory rape has long furnished a fertile battleground upon which to argue that the lack of knowledgeable conduct is a proper defense. The law in this state now rests, as it did in 1896, with this court's decision in *People v. Ratz*, 115 Cal. 132, at pages 134 and, 135, 46 P. 915, at page 916, where it is stated:

> The claim here made is not a new one. It has frequently been pressed upon the attention of courts, but in no case, so far as our examination goes, has it met with favor. The object and purpose of the law are too plain to need comment, the crime too infamous to bear discussion. The protection of society, of the family, and of the infant, demand that one who has carnal intercourse under such circumstances shall do so in peril of the fact, and he will not be heard against the evidence to urge his belief that the victim of his outrage had passed the period which would make his act a crime.

The age of consent at the time of the *Ratz* decision was 14 years, and it is noteworthy that the purpose of the rule, as there announced, was to afford protection to young females therein described as 'infants'. The decision on which the court in *Ratz* relied was *The Queen v. Prince*. However England has now, by statute, departed from the strict rule, and excludes as a crime an act of sexual intercourse with a female between the ages of 13 and 16 years if the perpetrator is under the age of 24 years, has not previously been charged with a like offense, and believes the female "to be of the age of sixteen or over and has reasonable cause for the belief." ...

The rationale of the *Ratz* decision, rather than purporting to eliminate intent as an element of the crime, holds that the wrongdoer must assume the risk; that, subjectively, when the act is committed, he consciously intends to proceed regardless of the age of the female and the consequences of his act, and that the circumstances involving the female, whether she be a day or a decade less than the statutory age, are irrelevant. There can be no dispute that a criminal intent exists when the perpetrator proceeds with utter disregard of, or in the lack of grounds for, a belief that the female has reached the age of consent. But if he participates in a mutual act of sexual intercourse, believing his partner to be beyond the age of consent, with reasonable grounds for such belief, where is his criminal intent? In such circumstances he has not consciously taken any risk. Instead he has subjectively eliminated the risk by satisfying himself on reasonable evidence that the crime cannot be committed. If it occurs that he has been misled, we cannot realistically conclude that for such reason alone the intent with which he undertook the act suddenly becomes more heinous....

We are persuaded that the reluctance to accord to a charge of statutory rape the defense of a lack of criminal intent has no greater justification than in the case of other statutory crimes, where the Legislature has made identical provision with respect to intent. At common law an honest and reasonable belief in the existence of circumstances, which, if true, would make the act for which the person is indicted an innocent act, has always been held to be a good defense.... Our departure from the views expressed in *Ratz* is in no manner indicative of a withdrawal from the sound policy that it is in the public interest to protect the sexually naive female from exploitation. No responsible person would hesitate to condemn as untenable a claimed good faith belief in the age of consent of an "infant" female whose obviously tender years preclude the existence of reasonable grounds for that belief. However, the prosecutrix in the instant case was but three months short of 18 years of age and there is nothing in the record to indicate that the purposes of the law as stated in *Ratz* can be better served by foreclosing the defense of a lack of intent. This is not to say that the granting of consent by even a sexually sophisticated girl known to be less than the statutory age is a defense. We hold only that in the absence of a legislative direction otherwise, a charge of statutory rape is defensible wherein a criminal intent is lacking.

Comments

(1) Twenty states agree with the view expressed in *Hernandez* and have created a mistake of fact defense, usually available only when victims were above a certain age. *See* United States v. Wilson, 66 M.J. 39, n. 8 (C.A.A.F. 2008) (rejecting the *Hernandez* approach). The *Wilson* court noted that 22 states do not recognize a mistake of fact defense and that seven states and the District of Columbia expressly forbid the defense when the sexual activity involves children. *See id.* at 43 & nn.7 & 9 (providing cites to statutes).

(2) In addition to substantial penalties that may include mandatory sentences, defendants convicted of statutory rape may be subject to state sex offender laws that require registration and community notification. *See* Meredith J. Duncan, *Sex Crimes and Sexual Miscues: The Need for a Clearer Line Between Forcible Rape and Nonconsensual Sex*, 42 Wake Forest L. Rev. 1087 (2007); Catherine Carpenter, *On Statutory Rape, Strict Liability, and the Public Welfare Offense Model*, 53 Am. U. L. Rev. 313 (2003).

(3) A recent news item drew attention to state registration laws. After meeting online, a 19-year-old student had sex with a 14-year-old girl, who claimed to be 17. Upon pleading guilty to fourth-degree sexual misconduct, the student was sentenced to 90 days in jail, probation, and to remain on the Michigan sex offender registry for 25 years. The case gained national attention when, upon appeal, the sentence was

amended to probation without registration. *See* Julie Boxman, *Sex Registry Challenge Cuts Penalty for Man, 19,* N.Y. Times, Oct. 20, 2015 at A13.

Garrison v. Elo

United States District Court, Eastern District of Michigan
156 F. Supp. 2d 815 (2001), *overruled on other grounds,*
Friday v. Pitcher, 200 F. Supp. 2d 725 (2002)

O'Meara, District Judge.

...

Petitioner pleaded guilty to one count of committing third degree criminal sexual conduct upon a thirteen year old girl.

[Ed. The trial court accepted the plea and sentenced Garrison to three-and-a-half to fifteen years imprisonment. In a habeas corpus petition to the federal courts, Garrison alleged that he was being confined in violation of his constitutional rights.]

...

Petitioner contends that his conviction of third degree criminal sexual conduct violates the Fifth and Fourteenth Amendments, because he had no *mens rea* or scienter to commit the offense.

In general, the states are free to define the elements of crimes. The Michigan Supreme Court has held that "the Legislature intentionally omitted the defense of a reasonable mistake of age from its statutory definition of third-degree criminal sexual conduct involving a 13- to 16-year-old. Moreover, we hold that this defense is not constitutionally compelled."

Strict liability has been permitted in the criminal law in a very limited number of instances, one of which is having sexual relations with an underage person, often known as statutory rape. The most widely recognized form of strict liability outside the realm of public-welfare offenses probably is the doctrine, embodied in statute and upheld by courts in a majority of states, that the perpetrator of the crime of "statutory rape," that is, intercourse with a person below the age at which the law deems consent possible, cannot defend on the grounds that he did not know of or was mistaken as to the victim's age.

In defense of mens rea principles, a growing number of states have developed legislative or judge-made defenses applicable in statutory rape cases, usually requiring the defendant to prove a "reasonable" mistake of fact as to the victim's age.... The California Supreme Court prepared the ground on which these exculpatory doctrines have flourished in *People v. Hernandez.*

Imposition of strict liability has been justified on the grounds that, in certain instances, the prosecution otherwise would have difficulty proving the requisite mental state. H.L.A. Hart rejects this argument, stating,

> At present we have in strict liability clear exceptions to the principle [of responsibility], but no very persuasive evidence that the sacrifice of principle

> is warranted here by the amount of dishonest evasion of conviction which would ensue if liability were not strict.

H.L.A. Hart, *Punishment and Responsibility* 183 (1968). One observer has argued, that while heightened caution on the part of the individual actor can be achieved through a negligence standard, strict liability unnecessarily establishes a standard which can only breed frustration and disrespect for the law by imposing criminal sanctions irrespective of care.

The Michigan Supreme Court, however, has not chosen to abandon the strict liability standard in statutory rape prosecutions under the third degree criminal sexual conduct statute. The weight of authority in this country indicates that statutory rape has traditionally been viewed as a strict liability offense.

The long history of statutory rape as a recognized exception to the requirement of criminal intent undermines Petitioner's implied argument that the statute in question offends principles of justice deeply rooted in our traditions and conscience. The third degree criminal sexual conduct statute does not impinge on other protected constitutional rights. Moreover, the statute rationally furthers a legitimate governmental interest. It protects children from sexual abuse by placing the risk of mistake as to a child's age on an older, more mature person who chooses to engage in sexual activity with one who may be young enough to fall within the statute's purview. Such a strict rule may reasonably be expected to have some deterrent effect.

The effect of *mens rea* and mistake on state criminal law has generally been left to the discretion of the states. The *mens rea* principle is just that—a general principle—not a constitutionally mandated doctrine. "The [United States] Supreme Court has never held that an honest mistake as to the age of the prosecutrix is a constitutional defense to statutory rape, and nothing in the Court's recent decisions clarifying the scope of procreative privacy, suggests that a state may no longer place the risk of mistake as to the prosecutrix's age on the person engaging in sexual intercourse with a partner who may be young enough to fall with[in] the protection of the statute." Petitioner has cited and this Court has found no United States Supreme Court authority to the contrary.

For all of the above-stated reasons, Petitioner's challenge to the lack of proof of any *mens rea* or criminal intent element in his conviction for third degree criminal sexual conduct is denied.

Comments and Questions

(1) Although criminal law theory, whether from the common law or today's statutory schemes, places special emphasis on the *mens rea* element of crime, the Supreme Court has not given the concept constitutional status.

(2) Given the sexual sophistication of many teens and young adults, how would you assess statutory rape laws? How might they be adjusted to protect the unsophisticated and also account for the freedom of others to engage in sexual activity? *See* Michelle Oberman, *Regulating Consensual Sex with Minors: Defining a Role for Statu-*

tory Rape, 48 Buff. L. Rev. 703, 757 (2000) (noting difficulty of balancing the protective rationale of statutory rape law with patriarchal impulses).

[C] Prostitution

> Prostitution is not a crime against the prostitute; it is an offense against the "public decency and order" because it violates the moral values of society.

Dornbusch v. Texas, 156 S.W.3d 859, 871 (Tex. App. Corpus Christi 2005).

Commonwealth v. Dodge

Superior Court of Pennsylvania
429 A.2d 1143 (1981)

Spaeth, Judge.

This is an appeal from a judgment of sentence for prostitution and criminal conspiracy. Appellant argues that for numerous reasons, the provision of the Crimes Code making prostitution criminal is unconstitutional; she also argues that her motion for a mistrial should have been granted. Finding no merit in either argument, we shall affirm.

In June 1978 the Pennsylvania State Police were investigating prostitution in Pittsburgh. As part of this investigation, on June 15 Trooper Louis W. Gentile telephoned a woman later identified as Debbie Ross. Gentile told Ross that he was a businessman named "Tony" from Philadelphia, that he was attending a convention in Pittsburgh, and that a friend, Joe, had given him her telephone number and had said that if he wanted sexual services, he should call the number and "he would be satisfied."

Apparently suspicious, Ross questioned Gentile about the identity of Joe and his familiarity with Philadelphia. She then asked Gentile what "exactly" he wanted. Gentile said there were seven people in his party seeking sexual services. Ross instructed Gentile to come to her residence so that she could check his identification, and told him that if she "approved," it would cost $25 per man plus $25 for cab fare for the "lady."

Gentile went by cab to the address provided by Ross. After inspecting Gentile's driver's license and business card, Ross directed Gentile to a motel in Pittsburgh. Ross told Gentile that he would have to pay the $200 before any sexual services would be rendered. Gentile went to the designated room and was greeted by appellant, who was naked. She explained that "Debbie" had just called and she had not had time to get dressed. She asked Gentile if "Debbie" had told him that the $200 would have to be paid "up front." Gentile replied that Ross had told him, and that he would make the payment, but that it would have to be at his hotel room because he would have to get the money from the other members of the party. Appellant and Gentile then went by cab to Gentile's hotel. Upon arriving at Gentile's room, they were greeted by another Pennsylvania State Trooper, Gerald Fielder, who was in bed dressed only in his underwear. After discussing the specific services to be rendered, and after payment of the $200.00, appellant began to undress. Fielder then told appellant that she was under arrest, advised her of her Constitutional rights, and asked her how the money was to be divided. Appellant said that she and Ross divided the money evenly.

I.

Section 5902(a) of the Crimes Code provides:

> (a) Prostitution.—A person is guilty of prostitution; a misdemeanor of the third degree, if he or she:
>
> > (1) is an inmate of a house of prostitution or otherwise engages in sexual activity as a business; or
> >
> > (2) loiters in or within view of any public place for the purpose of being hired to engage in sexual activity.

...

A.

Several of appellant's arguments may be disposed of summarily.

Appellant was charged with violating section 5902(a)(1) of the Crimes Code in that she "engaged in sexual activity as a business."

...

Appellant does have standing to argue that the term "sexual activity as a business" in section 5902(a)(1) is so vague that to punish her for such activity violates the fifth and fourteenth amendments of the United States Constitution. However, we find no merit in the argument. The Constitution requires that a statute be definite enough to provide a person of ordinary intelligence with fair notice of the type of conduct proscribed. *Papachristou v. City of Jacksonville*.... In deciding whether such notice has been provided here, we are not limited to a consideration of the language of section 5902(a)(1) alone. For unless it involves an infringement of first amendment freedoms of speech, association, and assembly, the definiteness of a statute will be decided in light of the conduct in which the party challenging the statute has engaged.... Here that conduct consisted of appellant offering to engage in sexual intercourse with men she did not know, for the paid-in-advance consideration of $200. We conclude that the prohibition in section 5902(a)(1) against "engag[ing] in sexual activity as a business" provided appellant, and the arresting officers, with fair notice that appellant's conduct was proscribed....

Appellant's argument that section 5902 violates the equal protection clause of the fourteenth amendment of the United States Constitution and the equal rights amendment of the Pennsylvania Constitution because it provides for disproportionate punishments based on gender classification between the female prostitute and the male patron and promoter of prostitution has already been decided against her. In *Commonwealth v. Finnegan*, we held that the difference in punishment is

> based upon the separate roles played by the prostitute, client, and promoter [and that this] classification bears a rational relationship to the avowed ob-

> jective of eliminating this form of crime. Indeed an analogous dichotomy exists in the penalty provisions of the Controlled Substance, Drug, Device, and Cosmetic Act in this Commonwealth, in which a greater penalty is imposed upon the "pusher" or provider of the contraband than upon one who merely purchases or possesses the material. Thus, we believe that the legislatively-employed method of punishing the prostitute and promoter as the providers of the sexual services to a greater extent than the client who purchases such services is rationally related to the legitimate purpose of eliminating prostitution and maintenance of the public health, safety, morals and general welfare....

B.

... Here we have no difficulty in concluding that section 5902(a) does not violate appellant's right to privacy. Under the section, the proscribed activity is not sexual activity but the *business* of engaging in sexual activity for hire.... Whatever may be the "outer limits" of the right to privacy, the decision whether to enter the business of engaging in sexual activity for hire is not the "kind[] of important decision[]" included within the right. As a commercial regulation, section 5902(a) does not preclude any personal activity protected by the Constitution. It can hardly be maintained that appellant is deprived of a constitutional right to engage in intimate sexual relations merely because she is prohibited from charging a fee for such conduct.

Since section 5902(a) does not violate appellant's right to privacy, the Commonwealth is only required to show that the section bears some rational relationship to a valid state interest....

The evils that have been perceived as associated with prostitution are numerous. As stated in the Comment to the Model Penal Code:

> Prostitution is an important source of venereal disease.... [P]rostitution is a source of profit and power for criminal groups who commonly combine it with illicit trade in drugs and liquor, illegal gambling and even robbery and extortion. Prostitution is also a corrupt influence on government and law enforcement machinery. Its promoters are willing and able to pay for police protection; and unscrupulous officials and politicians find them an easy mark for extortion. Finally, some view prostitution as a significant factor in social disorganization, encouraging sex delinquency and undermining marriage, the home, and individual character.

Appellant characterizes these evils as "myths," and cites studies suggesting that it would be wiser to decriminalize prostitution than prohibit it. The arguments in favor of this position include:

> (1) Prostitution cannot be eliminated by law.
>
> (2) Sumptuary laws that cannot be generally enforced lend themselves to extortion and arbitrary and episodic prosecution.
>
> (3) Failure to provide a professional outlet for male sexuality will result in more rape and other sexual crimes.

> (4) Registration and periodic health inspection are the best means of controlling venereal disease; disease is much more likely to be spread by the promiscuous amateur than by professional prostitutes concerned and instructed to avoid infection.
>
> (5) Legalized prostitution offers less opportunity for official corruption than an unrealistic effort at total repression.
>
> (6) By confining prostitution to particular neighborhoods police surveillance is facilitated and the safety of the general community is promoted.

The weight to be given these arguments, however is not for us but the legislature. Certainly it may not be said that the legislature's rejection of them is irrational. The American Medical Association has concluded that the control of venereal disease requires the elimination of prostitution because, it found, medical inspection of prostitutes is ineffectual, and while giving a false sense of security, fails to prevent the spread of infection. Moreover, the legislature could rationally conclude that to legalize prostitution might imply that the state both recognized and condoned promiscuous sexual relations as a social necessity.... Such an attitude might be seen as inconsistent with the goal of discouraging sexual delinquency, for as prostitution was encouraged, more money might be invested in it, and more persons participate, both as prostitutes and as patrons of prostitutes. Such an outcome would have a deleterious effect not only on public health and morals but also because the business of prostitution would compete with other, more socially constructive, businesses for the limited resources of capital and labor. Finally, we note that an overwhelming majority of the states and the authors of the Model Penal Code have come to the conclusion that prostitution should be prohibited.

Comments and Questions

(1) In *Frieling v. State*, 67 S.W.3d 462 (Tex. App. 2002), the court considered the First Amendment implications of prostitution statutes. The issue was whether Texas's statute was so overbroad that it reached words like "okay" or "sure" that are harmless absent criminal intent.

> When governmental action implicates First Amendment rights, courts must balance those individual rights against governmental interest in limiting the activity in question. The protection available for the freedom of expression turns on the nature both of the expression and of the governmental interest served by the regulation. When an overbreadth claim is presented, it is the duty of the courts to determine which of the conflicting interests demands the greater protection under the particular circumstances.
>
> The First Amendment to the United States Constitution provides that Congress shall make no law abridging the freedom of speech, press, or assembly. It has, however, long been established that these freedoms are dependent upon the power of constitutional government to survive. These freedoms "do not give absolute protection to every individual to speak whenever or

> wherever he pleases, or to use any form of address in any circumstances that he chooses." The right to free speech is not an unlimited, unqualified right. On occasion the societal value of speech must be subordinated to other values and considerations.
>
> Statutes regulating activities in order to protect public health are considered to be a lawful exercise of the police power of a state. It has been held that the enactment of section 43.02 was to protect the health, safety and welfare of the population and was within the discretion of the legislature and the police power of the state....
>
> In balancing the interests, we conclude that the State's compelling interest in quelling prostitution outweighs the de minimis interest of an individual in uttering certain words as urged by appellant. We reject appellant's contention that 42.03(a)(1) is constitutionally overbroad as he claims.

Frieling, 67 S.W.3d at 473–75.

(2) In a suit for declaratory judgment brought by a prostitute and a patron, the court held that the statute did not violate the constitutional right of privacy. *Cherry v. Koch*, 129 Misc. 2d 346, 491 N.Y.S.2d 934 (Sup. Ct. 1985). The court stated:

> In New York, decisions voluntarily made by adults regarding indulgence in acts of sexual intimacy by unmarried persons are protected under the cloak of the right to privacy only when they are made in a non-commercial private setting.... [T]he Court of Appeals repeatedly emphasized the lack of a commercial component and recognized the evils commonly attached to the retailing of sexual pleasures. The Court of Appeals [has] also stated that "prostitution is criminal activity no matter where it occurs." Thus, where commerce is involved, such as the payment of a fee, personal sexual activity whether done privately or publicly, does not come within the sphere of privacy recognized for other types of conduct.

Cherry, 491 N.Y.S.2d at 942–44. The *Cherry* court also noted that "commercial sex demeans and exploits women, particularly the young and uneducated who require protection of their interests." *Id.*

(3) The link between child trafficking and prostitution provides another state interest in prohibiting prostitution. *See* Cheryl Nelson Butler, *Kids For Sale: Does America Recognize Its Own Sexually Exploited Minors as Victims of Human Trafficking?*, 44 Seton Hall L. Rev. 833, 840 (2014) (noting the legal conundrum that allows victims of trafficking to be prosecuted for prostitution).

(4) Some scholars argue that moral and constitutional rights justify decriminalizing prostitution. *See* David A.J. Richards, *Commercial Sex and the Rights of the Person: A Moral Argument for the Decriminalization of Prostitution,* 127 U. Penn. L. Rev. 1195 (1979); Tom DeFranco & Rebecca Stellato, *Prostitution and Sex Work*, 14 Geo. J. Gender & L. 553 (2013).

In 2002, the Supreme Court invalidated state laws that criminalized consensual sexual relations between persons of the same sex, basing the decision in part on the constitutional right of liberty. *See Lawrence v. Texas*, 539 U.S. 558 (2003), *supra*, Ch. 1, § 1.01. Courts that have considered whether that right includes prostitution have held that it does not. *See, e.g., United States v. Thompson*, 458 F. Supp. 2d 730,732 (N.D. Ind. 2006) (stating *Lawrence* held only that "a state cannot enact laws that criminalize homosexual sodomy, it did not address the constitutionality of prostitution statutes.").

(5) Nevada allows local government entities to legalize prostitution, subject to strict regulations that vary among communities. Licensed brothels are usually located outside city limits and prostitutes undergo mandatory health tests. *See* Micole Bingham, *Nevada Sex Trade: A Gamble for the Workers*, 10 Yale J.L. & Feminism 69 (1998).

In 1980, Rhode Island passed a law that prohibited soliciting sex on streets, which inadvertently decriminalized commercial sex activity that took place indoors. In 2009, the state legislature revised its prostitution law to close the loophole. *See* Max Ehrenfreund, *When Rhode Island Accidently Legalized Prostitution, Rape Decreased Sharply*, Wash. Post, July 17, 2014 (reporting that rape complaints declined sharply during the intervening years).

§ 5.07 Homicide

[A] The Killing of a Human Being

State v. Fierro

Supreme Court of Arizona
603 P.2d 74 (1979)

Cameron, Chief Justice.

Defendant David Madrid Fierro was adjudged guilty of first degree murder following trial to a jury in the Maricopa County Superior Court and was sentenced to life imprisonment.

The facts necessary for a resolution of this matter on appeal are as follows. Between 8 and 9 o'clock on the evening of 18 August 1977, Victor Corella was given a ride by Ray Montez and his wife Sandra as they were attempting to locate some marijuana. In the vicinity of 12th Street and Pima, Ray Montez heard his name called from another car. He stopped his car, walked over to the other car and saw that the passenger who had called his name was the defendant David Fierro. Defendant told Ray Montez that his brother in the "M," or "Mexican Mafia," had instructed the defendant to kill Corella. Ray Montez told defendant to do it outside the car because he and his wife "did not want to see anything."

Montez returned to his car. Defendant followed and began talking with Corella. Corella got out of the car. Montez started to drive away when defendant began shooting Corella. Corella was shot once in the chest and four times in the head. Following the shooting, Corella's body was taken to the emergency room at Maricopa County Hospital. His blood pressure was very low due to secondary bleeding from the gunshot wound to the chest area. Surgery was performed in an effort to control the bleeding. He was then taken to the surgical intensive care unit where a follow-up examination and evaluation revealed that he had suffered brain death. Corella was maintained on support systems for the next three days while follow-up studies were completed which confirmed the occurrence of brain death. The supportive measures were terminated and he was pronounced dead on 22 August 1977. Ray Montez, upon reading the day after the shooting that Corella was still alive, reported to his probation officer the details of the shooting. Ray Montez and his wife Sandra were the principal witnesses against the defendant.

Cause of Death

At the trial, Dr. Hugh McGill, a surgical resident at the Maricopa County Hospital, testified that:

> "A. After surgery he was taken to the intensive care unit. He was evaluated by a neurosurgeon who felt there was nothing we could do for his brain, he had brain death. He remained somewhat stable over the next two or three days. We had follow-up studies that confirmed our impression of brain death and because of that, supportive measures were terminated and he was pronounced dead, I believe, on the 22nd.
>
> "Q. Who pronounced him dead?
>
> "A. I did.
>
> "Q. Approximately what time?
>
> "A. 3:45 p.m. on the 22nd of August.
>
> "Q. How many days after he was brought in did you actually pronounce him dead?
>
> "A. Would have been four days."

Dr. Hugh McGill, who performed the surgery on Corella and later pronounced him dead, and Doctor Thomas B. Jarvis, a Deputy Medical Examiner who performed an autopsy on Corella, both testified the cause of death was multiple gunshot wounds to the head.

Defendant initially argues that the termination of support systems by attendant doctors three days after Corella had suffered "brain death" was the cause of Corella's death, and that the evidence supporting the judgment of guilt to the crime of murder was therefore insufficient to convict the defendant Fierro. We do not agree:

> ... It is not indispensable to a conviction that the wounds be fatal and the direct cause of death. It is sufficient that they cause death indirectly through a chain of natural effects and causes unchanged by human action....

By the phrase "unchanged by human action" we mean human action that changes or breaks the chain of natural events and of itself causes the death of the victim. In the instant case, the removal of life support systems did not change nor alter the natural progression of the victim's physical condition from the gunshot wounds in the head to his resulting death. There was no change "by human action."

> One who inflicts an injury on another is deemed by the law to be guilty of homicide if the injury contributes mediately or immediately to the death of such other. The fact that other causes contribute to the death does not relieve the actor of responsibility, provided such other causes are not the proximate cause of the death.

The removal of the life support systems was not the proximate cause of death, the gunshot wounds were, and it was not error to find that the defendant was the cause of the victim's death.

We also believe that the defendant was legally dead before the life support systems were withdrawn. Although our legislature has defined dead human remains and fetal death it has not adopted a definition of death. A statutory definition is not necessary, however. Both the fact of death and its cause can be apparent to an ordinary layman when the condition of the body or the nature of the wound is such that no other determination is reasonable. When these obvious factors are present, it is not necessary that experts be required to testify in order to establish death and its cause. It is only where the fact of death and its cause is beyond the understanding of the average layman that expert testimony may be necessary.

The common law definition of death was as follows:

> The cessation of life; the ceasing to exist; defined by physicians as a total stoppage of the circulation of the blood, and a cessation of the animal and vital functions consequent thereon, such as respiration, pulsation, etc.

Thus, according to common law, as long as the person was breathing and the blood was flowing through his veins he was not dead even though his brain was no longer able to function.

Because of the increased interest in organ transplants, it was felt by some that a new definition of death was necessary. As a result, the National Conference of Commissioners on Uniform State Laws proposed the Uniform Brain Death Act that stated, "for legal and medical purposes an individual who has sustained irreversible cessation of all functioning of the brain including the brain stem, is dead." The uniform law provides that a determination of brain death must be made "in accordance with the reasonable medical standards." The Report of the Ad Hoc Committee of the Harvard Medical School at 205 Journal of American Medical Association 337 (1968) defined "cessation of life" as "brain death" which takes place when there is (1) unresponsiveness to normally painful stimuli; (2) absence of spontaneous movements or breathing; and (3) absence of reflexes.

In the instant case, the body of the victim was breathing, though not spontaneously, and blood was pulsating through his body before the life support mechanisms were withdrawn. Because there was an absence of cardiac and circulatory arrest, under the common law rule he would not have been legally dead. Under the Harvard Medical

School test and Proposal of the National Conference of Commissioners on Uniform State Laws he was, in fact, dead before the life supports were withdrawn as he had become "brain" or "neurologically" dead prior to that time. We believe that while the common law definition of death is still sufficient to establish death, the test of the Harvard Medical School or the Commissioners on Uniform State Laws, if properly supported by expert medical testimony, is also a valid test for death in Arizona.

In the instant case, expert testimony was received which showed that the victim has suffered irreversible "brain death" before the life supports had been withdrawn. In effect, the doctors were just passively stepping aside to let the natural course of events lead from brain death to common law death. In either case, the victim was legally dead.

Comments and Questions

(1) Who killed Victor Corella? Was he killed before the life support systems were withdrawn? Would it matter if the surgeon had testified that the body could have continued to breathe, and blood would have been pulsated through the body, for years if the support systems had been maintained?

(2) Consider the following:

> Until approximately twenty years ago, human beings were not declared dead until they experienced an irreversible cessation of respiratory and circulatory functions. Use of these criteria—which are known as the heart-lung criteria for determining human death—was not problematic until modern medicine invented the means for artificially maintaining heart beat and respiration. With the development of artificial life-support mechanisms, patients who were irreversibly comatose could be kept "alive" indefinitely.

Humber, *Statutory Criteria for Determining Human Death*, 42 Mercer L. Rev. 1069 (1991).

In 1981 the President's Commission for the Study of Ethical Problems in Medicine and Biomedical and Behavioral Research recommended that the states adopt a uniform brain stem death standard.

> An individual who has sustained either 1) irreversible cessation of circulatory and respiratory functions, or 2) irreversible cessation of all functions of the entire brain, including the brain stem, is dead. A determination of death must be made in accordance with accepted medical standards.

In *People v. Eulo*, 472 N.E.2d 286, 296 (N.Y. 1984), the standard was set out in this way:

> ... when a determination has been made according to accepted medical standards that a person has suffered an irreversible cessation of heartbeat and respiration, or, when these functions are maintained solely by extraordinary mechanical means, an irreversible cessation of all functions of the entire brain, including the brain stem, no life traditionally recognized by law is present in that body.

(3) Another problem of defining death arises with the "year and a day" rule.

> To make the killing either murder or manslaughter it is requisite that the party die within a year and a day after the stroke received or the cause of death administered; in the computation of which the whole of the day on which the act was done, shall be reckoned first.

Idaho Code § 18-4008.

What is the rationale behind this rule? *See Commonwealth v. Lewis*, 409 N.E.2d 771, 772–73 (Mass. 1980):

> By the Eighteenth Century, and indeed much earlier, we find a general assumption that a homicide could be prosecuted as such only if the death occurred within a year and a day of the act; this was distinct from any question of the period of limitations for commencing a prosecution.... The standard, if perhaps unhistorical, explanation of the rule, often repeated in the books, is that, in the condition of medical science until recent times, it would have been hard to establish convincingly a line of causation between an act and a relatively distant death, and it was thus plausible to make the presumption ("conclusive" as well as arbitrary) that a death more than a year removed from the assault or similar antecedent arose from a natural rather than the criminal cause. Occasionally it has been surmised that the rule was linked in some way to the early function of the jury as reporters of the happenings of the vicinage who required no aid from witnesses—but the jury would not have had knowledge sufficient to trace cause to effect over a sizeable interval of time. Again we find a suggestion that the rule was intended simply to soften the old brutal law regarding homicides.

While some states retain the rule, others have weakened it (extending the time period to three years and a day, and only creating a rebuttable presumption that the killing was non-criminal, Cal. Penal Code § 194) or have eliminated it entirely. The Tennessee Supreme Court abolished the rule in *State v. Rogers*, 992 S.W.2d 393 (Tenn. 1999), writing:

> Medical science can now sustain the critically wounded for months and even years beyond what might have been imagined only a few decades ago. Comparable progress has been made in the development of diagnostic skills, so that problems of medical causation are more readily resolved. Modern pathologists are able to determine the cause of death with much greater accuracy than was possible in earlier times. Moreover, jurors today may rely upon expert testimony, even when the testimony relates to an ultimate issue of fact such as causation.... Finally, the death penalty is no longer indiscriminately imposed for all homicides.

In *Rogers v. Tennessee*, 532 U.S. 451 (2001), the Supreme Court sharply criticized the rule as an "outdated" relic of the common law and noted that most jurisdictions recently addressing the rule have legislatively or judicially abolished it. Is there any need for retaining some version of the rule? Consider the case of William J. Barnes who served 20 years for shooting and partially paralyzing a police officer. Forty-one years after the shooting, the district attorney filed murder charges against 71-year-old Barnes, alleging that the officer died from a urinary tract infection brought about by the bullet that lodged near his spine. Urbina, *41 Years After Crime, Prosecutor Says Assault Victim Is Now Murder Victim*, N.Y. Times, Sept. 19, 2007, at A19, cols. 1–6.

Another even more attenuated example is the case of Antonio Cicarello, whose death at 97 years old was determined to be a homicide. The medical examiner concluded that Mr. Cicarello's death was connected to a stabbing that had occurred roughly 55 years earlier. J. David Goodman, *Twist in 97-Year-Old's Murder: His Knifing Was 5 Decades Ago*, N.Y. Times, Jan. 25, 2015, at A1.

When Wisconsin abrogated the rule, it chose not to do so retroactively despite the obviously unlawful nature of the defendant's acts. *State v. Picotte*, 661 N.W.2d 381 (Wis. 2003).

(4) In *Cruzan v. Director, Missouri Department of Health*, 497 U.S. 261 (1990), Nancy Cruzan, after a serious automobile accident, suffered permanent brain damage; she remained in a coma for three weeks and then moved to an unconscious state in which she was able to ingest orally some nutrition. To assist in feeding, surgeons implanted a feeding and hydration tube in her, but she remained in "what is commonly referred to as a persistent vegetative state: generally, a condition in which a person exhibits motor reflexes but evinces no indications of significant cognitive function." Her parents asked doctors to withdraw the artificial nutrition and hydration procedures, but the request was refused without court approval as all agreed that such action would cause her death under any standard then in use. The Supreme Court was thus faced, for the first time, with the question of whether "the United States Constitution grants what is in common parlance referred to as a 'right to death.'" The Court explored in some detail the decision of the State of Missouri not to allow withdrawal unless there was clear and convincing evidence regarding Cruzan's wishes as to the withdrawal of treatment.

> The choice between life and death is a deeply personal decision of obvious and overwhelming finality. We believe Missouri may legitimately seek to safeguard the personal element of this choice through the imposition of heightened evidentiary requirements. It cannot be disputed that the Due Process Clause protects an interest in life as well as an interest in refusing life-sustaining medical treatment. Not all incompetent patients will have loved ones available to serve as surrogate decision makers. And even where family members are present, "[t]here will, of course, be some unfortunate situations in which family members will not act to protect the patient." A State is entitled to guard against potential abuses in such situations. Similarly, a State is entitled to consider that a judicial proceeding to make a determination regarding an incompetent's wishes may very well not be an adversarial one, with the added guarantee of accurate fact-finding that the adversary process brings with it. Finally, we think a State may properly decline to make judgments about the "quality" of life that a particular indi-

> vidual may enjoy, and simply assert an unqualified interest in the preservation of human life to be weighed against the constitutionally protected interests of the individual.

497 U.S. at 281–82.

Commenting on the case, Philosophy Professor Carl Cohen, University of Michigan Medical School, wrote the following letter to the *New York Times* on January 31, 1991:*

> Dead people do belong in cemeteries, not hospital beds, as your correspondent recently wrote, but what "dead" means is not a simple matter. Nancy Cruzan's brain was not entirely dead, although most of it was. Enough of it had been destroyed to ensure that, being in a persistent vegetative state, she did not and could not ever again have any awareness or experience of any kind. If we think that is what death ought to mean, we need to work for a change in the Uniform Determination of Death Act, which governs in most American states.
>
> The law, and medical practice that is respectful of the law, defines brain death as the irreversible cessation of function of the entire brain, lower as well as upper. All human experience will permanently cease with the destruction of the upper brain only, but the living lower brain will maintain temperature control, respiration, and some other functions below the level of consciousness. There is no doubt that Nancy Cruzan, while in a persistent vegetative state and until the disconnection of life-support equipment that led to her eventual demise, had a functioning lower brain and was by current standards alive.
>
> The definition of death, in law and medical practice, can be changed. Such change would require a widespread rethinking of what functions are sufficient to compel the judgment human life remains.

The Jahi McMath case presents a contrasting analogue to *Cruzan*. McMath was declared legally brain dead on December 12, 2013, after complications from a series of operations to remove her tonsils. According to McMath's family, new tests showed that the girl had regained brain activity. If proven true, McMath would have been the first person to regain consciousness after a declaration of brain death. Her family petitioned the court to reverse the finding that she is legally dead, an unprecedented action that would challenge the definition of death in America. David DeBolt & Kristin J. Bender, *Jahi McMath: Family Seeks to Have Brain-Death Ruling Overturned, Girl Declared Alive* (Oct. 1, 2014), http://www.mercurynews.com/science/ci_26644995/jahi-mcmath-family-seeks-have-brain-death-ruling. Although the petition was withdrawn, in March 2015 her family sued the hospital and surgeon for malpractice, arguing that McMath was still alive.

* Reprinted with the permission of the writer.

Washington v. Glucksberg

Supreme Court of the United States
521 U.S. 702 (1997)

Chief Justice Rehnquist delivered the opinion of the Court.

The question presented in this case is whether Washington's prohibition against "causing" or "aiding" a suicide offends the Fourteenth Amendment to the United States Constitution. We hold that it does not.

It has always been a crime to assist a suicide in the State of Washington. In 1854, Washington's first Territorial Legislature outlawed "assisting another in the commission of self-murder." Today, Washington law provides: "A person is guilty of promoting a suicide attempt when he knowingly causes or aids another person to attempt suicide." "Promoting a suicide attempt" is a felony, punishable by up to five years' imprisonment and up to a $10,000 fine. At the same time, Washington's Natural Death Act, enacted in 1979, states that the "withholding or withdrawal of life-sustaining treatment" at a patient's direction "shall not, for any purpose, constitute a suicide."

Petitioners in this case are the State of Washington and its Attorney General. Respondents are physicians who practice in Washington. These doctors occasionally treat terminally ill, suffering patients, and declare that they would assist these patients in ending their lives if not for Washington's assisted-suicide ban. In January 1994, respondents, along with three gravely ill, pseudonymous plaintiffs who have since died and Compassion in Dying, a nonprofit organization that counsels people considering physician-assisted suicide, sued in the United States District Court, seeking a declaration that Wash. Rev. Code § 9A.36.060(1) (1994) is, on its face, unconstitutional.

I.

We begin, as we do in all due-process cases, by examining our Nation's history, legal traditions, and practices. In almost every State—indeed, in almost every western democracy—it is a crime to assist a suicide. The States' assisted-suicide bans are not innovations. Rather, they are longstanding expressions of the States' commitment to the protection and preservation of all human life. Indeed, opposition to and condemnation of suicide—and, therefore, of assisting suicide—are consistent and enduring themes of our philosophical, legal, and cultural heritages.

More specifically, for over 700 years, the Anglo-American common-law tradition has punished or otherwise disapproved of both suicide and assisting suicide. In the 13th century, Henry de Bracton, one of the first legal-treatise writers, observed that "just as a man may commit felony by slaying another so may he do so by slaying himself." Thus, "the principle that suicide of a sane person, for whatever reason, was a punishable felony was ... introduced into English common law." Centuries later, Sir William Blackstone, whose Commentaries on the Laws of England not only provided a definitive summary of the common law but was also a primary legal authority for 18th and 19th century American lawyers, referred to suicide as "self-murder" and "the pretended heroism, but real cowardice, of the Stoic philosophers, who destroyed themselves to avoid those ills which they had not the fortitude to endure...." 4 W. Blackstone, Commentaries 189. Blackstone emphasized that "the law has ... ranked [suicide] among the highest crimes," ibid, although, anticipating later developments, he conceded that the harsh and shameful punishments imposed for suicide "border a little upon severity."

For the most part, the early American colonies adopted the common-law approach.

Over time, however, the American colonies abolished ... harsh common-law penalties. [H]owever, that the movement away from the common law's harsh sanctions did not represent an acceptance of suicide; rather, as Chief Justice Swift observed, this change reflected the growing consensus that it was unfair to punish the suicide's family for his wrongdoing. Nonetheless, although States moved away from Blackstone's treatment of suicide, courts continued to condemn it as a grave public wrong.

That suicide remained a grievous, though nonfelonious, wrong is confirmed by the fact that colonial and early state legislatures and courts did not retreat from prohibiting assisting suicide. Swift, in his early 19th century treatise on the laws of Connecticut, stated that "if one counsels another to commit suicide, and the other by reason of the advice kills himself, the advisor is guilty of murder as principal." This was the well established common-law view. And the prohibitions against assisting suicide never contained exceptions for those who were near death. Rather, "the life of those to whom life had become a burden—of those who [were] hopelessly diseased or fatally wounded—nay, even the lives of criminals condemned to death, [were] under the protection of law, equally as the lives of those who [were] in the full tide of life's enjoyment, and anxious to continue to live."

The earliest American statute explicitly to outlaw assisting suicide was enacted in New York in 1828, and many of the new States and Territories followed New York's example. By the time the Fourteenth Amendment was ratified, it was a crime in most States to assist a suicide.

Though deeply rooted, the States' assisted-suicide bans have in recent years been reexamined and, generally, reaffirmed. Because of advances in medicine and technology, Americans today are increasingly likely to die in institutions, from chronic illnesses. Public concern and democratic action are therefore sharply focused on how best to protect dignity and independence at the end of life, with the result that there have been many significant changes in state laws and in the attitudes these laws reflect. Many States, for example, now permit "living wills," surrogate health-care decisionmaking, and the withdrawal or refusal of life-sustaining medical treatment. At the same time, however, voters and legislators continue for the most part to reaffirm their States' prohibitions on assisting suicide.

Thus, the States are currently engaged in serious, thoughtful examinations of physician-assisted suicide and other similar issues. For example, New York State's Task Force on Life and the Law—an ongoing, blue-ribbon commission composed of doctors, ethicists, lawyers, religious leaders, and interested laymen—was convened in 1984 and commissioned with "a broad mandate to recommend public policy on issues raised by medical advances." Over the past decade, the Task Force has recommended laws relating to end-of-life decisions, surrogate pregnancy, and organ donation. After studying physician-assisted suicide, however, the Task Force unanimously concluded that "legalizing assisted suicide and euthanasia would pose profound risks to many individuals who are ill and vulnerable.... The potential dangers of this dramatic change in public policy would outweigh any benefit that might be achieved."

Attitudes toward suicide itself have changed since Bracton, but our laws have consistently condemned, and continue to prohibit, assisting suicide. Despite changes in medical technology and notwithstanding an increased emphasis on the importance of end-of-life decisionmaking, we have not retreated from this prohibition. Against this backdrop of history, tradition, and practice, we now turn to respondents' constitutional claim.

II.

The Due Process Clause guarantees more than fair process, and the "liberty" it protects includes more than the absence of physical restraint. The Clause also provides heightened protection against government interference with certain fundamental rights and liberty interests. In a long line of cases, we have held that, in addition to the specific freedoms protected by the Bill of Rights, the "liberty" specially protected by the Due Process Clause includes the rights to marry, to have children, to direct the education and upbringing of one's children, to marital privacy, to use contraception, to bodily integrity, and to abortion. We have also assumed, and strongly suggested, that the Due Process Clause protects the traditional right to refuse unwanted lifesaving medical treatment.

But we "have always been reluctant to expand the concept of substantive due process because guideposts for responsible decisionmaking in this unchartered area are scarce and open-ended." By extending constitutional protection to an asserted right or liberty interest, we, to a great extent, place the matter outside the arena of public debate and legislative action. We must therefore "exercise the utmost care whenever we are asked to break new ground in this field," lest the liberty protected by the Due Process Clause be subtly transformed into the policy preferences of the members of this Court.

Our established method of substantive-due-process analysis has two primary features: First, we have regularly observed that the Due Process Clause specially protects those fundamental rights and liberties which are, objectively, "deeply rooted in this Nation's history and tradition," and "implicit in the concept of ordered liberty," such that "neither liberty nor justice would exist if they were sacrificed." Second, we have required in substantive-due-process cases a "careful description" of the asserted fundamental liberty interest. Our Nation's history, legal traditions, and practices thus provide the crucial "guideposts for responsible decisionmaking," that direct and restrain our exposition of the Due Process Clause. [T]he Fourteenth Amendment "forbids the government to infringe ... 'fundamental' liberty interests at all, no matter what process is provided, unless the infringement is narrowly tailored to serve a compelling state interest."

Turning to the claim at issue here, the Court of Appeals stated that "properly analyzed, the first issue to be resolved is whether there is a liberty interest in determining the time and manner of one's death," or, in other words, "is there a right to die?" Similarly, respondents assert a "liberty to choose how to die" and a right to "control of one's final days," and describe the asserted liberty as "the right to choose a humane, dignified death," and "the liberty to shape death." As noted above, we have a tradition of carefully formulating the interest at stake in substantive-due-process cases. The Washington statute at issue in this case prohibits "aiding another person to attempt suicide," and, thus, the question before us is whether the "liberty" specially protected by the Due Process Clause includes a right to commit suicide which itself includes a right to assistance in doing so.

We now inquire whether this asserted right has any place in our Nation's traditions. Here, as discussed above, we are confronted with a consistent and almost universal tradition that has long rejected the asserted right, and continues explicitly to reject it today, even for terminally ill, mentally competent adults. To hold for respondents, we would have to reverse centuries of legal doctrine and practice, and strike down the considered policy choice of almost every State.

The history of the law's treatment of assisted suicide in this country has been and continues to be one of the rejection of nearly all efforts to permit it. That being the case, our decisions lead us to conclude that the asserted "right" to assistance in committing suicide is not a fundamental liberty interest protected by the Due Process Clause. The Constitution also requires, however, that Washington's assisted-suicide ban be rationally related to legitimate government interests. This requirement is unquestionably met here. As the court below recognized, Washington's assisted-suicide ban implicates a number of state interests.

First, Washington has an "unqualified interest in the preservation of human life." The State's prohibition on assisted suicide, like all homicide laws, both reflects and advances its commitment to this interest.

The State also has an interest in protecting the integrity and ethics of the medical profession. In contrast to the Court of Appeals' conclusion that "the integrity of the medical profession would [not] be threatened in any way by [physician-assisted suicide]," the American Medical Association, like many other medical and physicians' groups, has concluded that "physician-assisted suicide is fundamentally incompatible with the physician's role as healer."

Next, the State has an interest in protecting vulnerable groups—including the poor, the elderly, and disabled persons—from abuse, neglect, and mistakes. The Court of Appeals dismissed the State's concern that disadvantaged persons might be pressured into physician-assisted suicide as "ludicrous on its face." We have recognized, however, the real risk of subtle coercion and undue influence in end-of-life situations. Similarly, the New York Task Force warned that "legalizing physician-assisted suicide would pose profound risks to many individuals who are ill and vulnerable.... The risk of harm is greatest for the many individuals in our society whose autonomy and well-being are already compromised by poverty, lack of access to good medical care, advanced age, or membership in a stigmatized social group."

The State's interest here goes beyond protecting the vulnerable from coercion; it extends to protecting disabled and terminally ill people from prejudice, negative and inaccurate stereotypes, and "societal indifference." The State's assisted-suicide ban reflects and reinforces its policy that the lives of terminally ill, disabled, and elderly people must be no less valued than the lives of the young and healthy, and that a seriously disabled person's suicidal impulses should be interpreted and treated the same way as anyone else's.

Finally, the State may fear that permitting assisted suicide will start it down the path to voluntary and perhaps even involuntary euthanasia. The Court of Appeals struck down Washington's assisted-suicide ban only "as applied to competent, terminally ill adults who wish to hasten their deaths by obtaining medication prescribed by their doctors." Washington insists, however, that the impact of the court's decision will not and cannot be so limited. If suicide is protected as a matter of constitutional right, it is argued, "every man and woman in the United States must enjoy it." The Court of Appeals' decision, and its expansive reasoning, provide ample support for the State's concerns. The court noted, for example, that the "decision of a duly appointed surrogate decision maker is for all legal purposes the decision of the patient himself," that "in some instances, the patient may be unable to self-administer the drugs and ... administration by the physician ... may be the only way the patient may be able to receive them," and that not only physicians, but also family members and loved ones, will inevitably participate in assisting suicide. Thus, it turns out that what is couched as a limited right to "physician-assisted suicide" is likely, in effect, a much broader license, which could prove extremely difficult to police and contain. Washington's ban on assisting suicide prevents such erosion.

We need not weigh exactingly the relative strengths of these various interests. They are unquestionably important and legitimate, and Washington's ban on assisted suicide is at least reasonably related to their promotion and protection. We therefore hold that Wash. Rev. Code § 9A.36.060(1) (1994) does not violate the Fourteenth Amendment, either on its face or "as applied to competent, terminally ill adults who wish to hasten their deaths by obtaining medication prescribed by their doctors."

Throughout the Nation, Americans are engaged in an earnest and profound debate about the morality, legality, and practicality of physician-assisted suicide. Our holding permits this debate to continue, as it should in a democratic society. The decision of the en banc Court of Appeals is reversed, and the case is remanded for further proceedings consistent with this opinion.

It so ordered.

Justice O'Connor, concurring.

Death will be different for each of us. For many, the last days will be spent in physical pain and perhaps the despair that accompanies physical deterioration and a loss of control of basic bodily and mental functions. Some will seek medication to alleviate that pain and other symptoms.

The Court frames the issue in this case as whether the Due Process Clause of the Constitution protects a "right to commit suicide which itself includes a right to assistance in doing so," and concludes that our Nation's history, legal traditions, and practices do not support the existence of such a right. I join the Court's opinions because I agree that there is no generalized right to "commit suicide."

Every one of us at some point may be affected by our own or a family member's terminal illness. There is no reason to think the democratic process will not strike the proper balance between the interests of terminally ill, mentally competent individuals who would seek to end their suffering and the State's interests in protecting those who might seek to end life mistakenly or under pressure. As the Court recognizes, States are presently undertaking extensive and serious evaluation of physician-assisted suicide and other related issues. In such circumstances, "the ... challenging task of crafting appropriate procedures for safeguarding ... liberty interests is entrusted to the laboratory' of the States ... in the first instance."

In sum, there is no need to address the question whether suffering patients have a constitutionally cognizable interest in obtaining relief from the suffering that they may experience in the last days of their lives. There is no dispute that dying patients in Washington and New York can obtain palliative care, even when doing so would hasten their deaths. The difficulty in defining terminal illness and the risk that a dying patient's request for assistance in ending his or her life might not be truly voluntary justifies the prohibitions on assisted suicide we uphold here.

Justice Stevens, concurring in the judgments.

... [A]lthough the differences the majority notes in causation and intent between terminating life-support and assisting in suicide support the Court's rejection of the respondents' facial challenge, these distinctions may be inapplicable to particular terminally ill patients and their doctors. Our holding does not foreclose the possibility that some applications of the New York statute may impose an intolerable intrusion on the patient's freedom.

There remains room for vigorous debate about the outcome of particular cases that are not necessarily resolved by the opinions announced today. How such cases may be decided will depend on their specific facts. In my judgment, however, it is clear that the so-called "unqualified interest in the preservation of human life," is not itself sufficient to outweigh the interest in liberty that may justify the only possible means of preserving a dying patient's dignity and alleviating her intolerable suffering.

Justice Souter, concurring in the judgment.

... While an extensive literature on any subject can raise the hopes for judicial understanding, the literature on this subject is only nascent. Since there is little experience directly bearing on the issue, the most that can be said is that whichever way the Court might rule today, events could overtake its assumptions, as experimentation in some jurisdictions confirmed or discredited the concerns about progression from assisted suicide to euthanasia.

Legislatures, on the other hand, have superior opportunities to obtain the facts necessary for a judgment about the present controversy. Not only do they have more flexible mechanisms for factfinding than the Judiciary, but their mechanisms include the power to experiment, moving forward and pulling back as facts emerge within their own jurisdictions. There is, indeed, good reason to suppose that in the absence of a judgment for respondents here, just such experimentation will be attempted in some of the States.

I do not decide here what the significance might be of legislative foot-dragging in ascertaining the facts going to the State's argument that the right in question could not be confined as claimed. Sometimes a court may be bound to act regardless of the institutional preferability of the political branches as forums for addressing constitutional claims. Now, it is enough to say that our examination of legislative reasonableness should consider the fact that the Legislature of the State of Washington is no more obviously at fault than this Court is in being uncertain about what would happen if respondents prevailed today. We therefore have a clear question about which institution, a legislature or a court, is relatively more competent to deal with an emerging issue as to which facts currently unknown could be dispositive. The answer has to be, for the reasons already stated, that the legislative process is to be preferred. There is a closely related further reason as well.

One must bear in mind that the nature of the right claimed, if recognized as one constitutionally required, would differ in no essential way from other constitutional rights guaranteed by enumeration or derived from some more definite textual source than "due process." An unenumerated right should not therefore be recognized, with the effect of displacing the legislative ordering of things, without the assurance that its recognition would prove as durable as the recognition of those other rights differently derived. To recognize a right of lesser promise would simply create a constitutional regime too uncertain to bring with it the expectation of finality that is one of this Court's central obligations in making constitutional decisions.

Legislatures, however, are not so constrained. The experimentation that should be out of the question in constitutional adjudication displacing legislative judgments is entirely proper, as well as highly desirable, when the legislative power addresses an emerging issue like assisted suicide. The Court should accordingly stay its hand to allow reasonable legislative consideration. While I do not decide for all time that respondents' claim should not be recognized, I acknowledge the legislative institutional competence as the better one to deal with that claim at this time.

Justice Breyer, concurring in the judgments.

I believe that Justice O'Connor's views, which I share, have greater legal significance than the Court's opinion suggests. I join her separate opinion, except insofar as it joins the majority. And I concur in the judgments. I shall briefly explain how I differ from the Court.

I agree with the Court in *Vacco v. Quill*, that the articulated state interests justify the distinction drawn between physician assisted suicide and withdrawal of life-support. I also agree with the Court that the critical question in both of the cases before us is whether " 'the liberty' specially protected by the Due Process Clause includes a right" of the sort that the respondents assert. I do not agree, however, with the Court's formulation of that claimed "liberty" interest. The Court describes it as a "right to commit suicide with another's assistance." But I would not reject the respondents' claim without considering a different formulation, for which our legal tradition may provide greater support. That formulation would use words roughly like a "right to die with dignity." But irrespective of the exact words used, at its core would lie personal control over the manner of death, professional medical assistance, and the avoidance of unnecessary and severe physical suffering—combined.

I do not believe, however, that this Court need or now should decide whether or not such a right is "fundamental." That is because, in my view, the avoidance of severe physical pain (connected with death) would have to comprise an essential part of any successful claim and because, the laws before us do not force a dying person to undergo that kind of pain. Rather, the laws of New York and of Washington do not prohibit doctors from providing patients with drugs sufficient to control pain despite the risk that those drugs themselves will kill. And under these circumstances the laws of New York and Washington would overcome any remaining significant interests and would be justified, regardless.

Medical technology, we are repeatedly told, makes the administration of pain-relieving drugs sufficient, except for a very few individuals for whom the ineffectiveness of pain control medicines can mean, not pain, but the need for sedation which can end in a coma. We are also told that there are many instances in which patients do not receive the palliative care that, in principle, is available, but that is so for institutional reasons or inadequacies or obstacles, which would seem possible to overcome, and which do not include a prohibitive set of laws.

Were the legal circumstances different—for example, were state law to prevent the provision of palliative care, including the administration of drugs as needed to avoid pain at the end of life—then the law's impact upon serious and otherwise unavoidable physical pain (accompanying death) would be more directly at issue. And as Justice O'Connor, suggests, the Court might have to revisit its conclusions in these cases.

Vacco v. Quill

Supreme Court of the United States
521 U.S. 793 (1997)

Chief Justice Rehnquist delivered the opinion of the Court.

In New York, as in most States, it is a crime to aid another to commit or attempt suicide, but patients may refuse even lifesaving medical treatment. The question presented by this case is whether New York's prohibition on assisting suicide therefore violates the Equal Protection Clause of the Fourteenth Amendment. We hold that it does not.

Petitioners are various New York public officials. Respondents are physicians who practice in New York. They assert that although it would be "consistent with the standards of [their] medical practices" to prescribe lethal medication for "mentally competent, terminally ill patients" who are suffering great pain and desire a doctor's help in taking their own lives, they are deterred from doing so by New York's ban on assisting suicide. Respondents, and three gravely ill patients who have since died, sued the State's Attorney General in the United States District Court. They urged that because New York permits a competent person to refuse life-sustaining medical treatment, and because the refusal of such treatment is "essentially the same thing" as physician-assisted suicide, New York's assisted-suicide ban violates the Equal Protection Clause.

The Equal Protection Clause commands that no State shall "deny to any person within its jurisdiction the equal protection of the laws." This provision creates no substantive rights. Instead, it embodies a general rule that States must treat like cases alike but may treat unlike cases accordingly. If a legislative classification or distinction "neither burdens a fundamental right nor targets a suspect class, we will uphold [it] so long as it bears a rational relation to some legitimate end."

New York's statutes outlawing assisting suicide affect and address matters of profound significance to all New Yorkers alike. They neither infringe fundamental rights nor involve suspect classifications. *Washington v. Glucksberg*. These laws are therefore entitled to a "strong presumption of validity."

On their faces, neither New York's ban on assisting suicide nor its statutes permitting patients to refuse medical treatment treat anyone differently than anyone else or draw any distinctions between persons. Everyone, regardless of physical condition, is entitled, if competent, to refuse unwanted lifesaving medical treatment; no one is permitted to assist a suicide. Generally speaking, laws that apply evenhandedly to all "unquestionably comply" with the Equal Protection Clause.

The Court of Appeals, however, concluded that some terminally ill people—those who are on life-support systems—are treated differently than those who are not, in that the former may "hasten death" by ending treatment, but the latter may not "hasten death" through physician-assisted suicide. This conclusion depends on the submission that ending or refusing lifesaving medical treatment "is nothing more nor less than assisted suicide." Unlike the Court of Appeals, we think the distinction between assisting suicide and withdrawing life-sustaining treatment, a distinction widely recognized and endorsed in the medical profession and in our legal traditions, is both important and logical; it is certainly rational.

The distinction comports with fundamental legal principles of causation and intent. First, when a patient refuses life-sustaining medical treatment, he dies from an underlying fatal disease or pathology; but if a patient ingests lethal medication prescribed by a physician, he is killed by that medication.

Furthermore, a physician who withdraws, or honors a patient's refusal to begin, life-sustaining medical treatment purposefully intends, or may so intend, only to respect his patient's wishes and "to cease doing useless and futile or degrading things to the patient when [the patient] no longer stands to benefit from them." The same is true when a doctor provides aggressive palliative care; in some cases, painkilling drugs may hasten a patient's death, but the physician's purpose and intent is, or may be, only to ease his patient's pain. A doctor who assists a suicide, however, "must, necessarily and indubitably, intend primarily that the patient be made dead." Similarly, a patient who commits suicide with a doctor's aid necessarily has the specific intent to end his or her own life, while a patient who refuses or discontinues treatment might not.

The law has long used actors' intent or purpose to distinguish between two acts that may have the same result. Put differently, the law distinguishes actions taken "because of" a given end from actions taken "in spite of" their unintended but foreseen consequences.

Given these general principles, it is not surprising that many courts, including New York courts, have carefully distinguished refusing life-sustaining treatment from suicide. In fact, the first state-court decision explicitly to authorize withdrawing lifesaving treatment noted the "real distinction between the self-infliction of deadly harm and a self-determination against artificial life support." And recently, the Michigan Supreme Court also rejected the argument that the distinction "between acts that artificially sustain life and acts that artificially curtail life" is merely a "distinction without constitutional significance—a meaningless exercise in semantic gymnastics."

Similarly, the overwhelming majority of state legislatures have drawn a clear line between assisting suicide and withdrawing or permitting the refusal of unwanted lifesaving medical treatment by prohibiting the former and permitting the latter. And "nearly all states expressly disapprove of suicide and assisted suicide either in statutes dealing with durable powers of attorney in health-care situations, or in 'living will' statutes." Thus, even as the States move to protect and promote patients' dignity at the end of life, they remain opposed to physician-assisted suicide.

This Court has also recognized, at least implicitly, the distinction between letting a patient die and making that patient die. In *Cruzan v. Director, Mo. Dept. of Health*, 497 U.S. 261, 278 (1990), we concluded that "the principle that a competent person has a constitutionally protected liberty interest in refusing unwanted medical treatment may be inferred from our prior decisions," and we assumed the existence of such a right for purposes of that case. But our assumption of a right to refuse treatment was grounded not, as the Court of Appeals supposed, on the proposition that patients have a general and abstract "right to hasten death," but on well established, traditional rights to bodily integrity and freedom from unwanted touching. In fact, we observed that "the majority of States in this country have laws imposing criminal penalties on one who assists another to commit suicide." *Cruzan* therefore provides no support for the notion that refusing life-sustaining medical treatment is "nothing more nor less than suicide."

For all these reasons, we disagree with respondents' claim that the distinction between refusing lifesaving medical treatment and assisted suicide is "arbitrary" and "irrational." Granted, in some cases, the line between the two may not be clear, but certainty is not required, even were it possible. Logic and contemporary practice support New York's judgment that the two acts are different, and New York may therefore, consistent with the Constitution, treat them differently. By permitting everyone to refuse unwanted medical treatment while prohibiting anyone from assisting a suicide, New York law follows a longstanding and rational distinction.

New York's reasons for recognizing and acting on this distinction—including prohibiting intentional killing and preserving life; preventing suicide; maintaining physician's role as their patients' healers; protecting vulnerable people from indifference, prejudice, and psychological and financial pressure to end their lives; and avoiding a possible slide towards euthanasia—are discussed in greater detail in our opinion in *Glucksberg, ante.* These valid and important public interests easily satisfy the constitutional requirement that a legislative classification bear a rational relation to some legitimate end.

The judgment of the Court of Appeals is reversed.

It is so ordered.

[Separate opinions by JUSTICES O'CONNOR, STEVENS, SOUTER, GINSBURG, and BREYER are omitted.]

Comments and Questions

(1) The Chief Justice explicitly recognized the nation's ongoing "profound debate" over the difficult issues raised. Still, should the Court have so entirely deferred to this debate and the legislative process?

(2) One commentator, just months before the opinions were delivered, showed remarkable predictive abilities.

> In this Essay, I argue that the Supreme Court should not invalidate laws forbidding physician-assisted suicide. My basic claim is institutional: The Court should be wary of recognizing rights of this kind amid complex issues of fact and value, at least if reasonable people can decide those issues either way, and if the Court cannot identify malfunctions in the system of deliberative democracy that justify a more aggressive judicial role. The issues presented by a right to physician-assisted suicide are especially well-suited to a federal system, where appropriate experiments may be made, and where such experiments are likely to provide valuable information about underlying risks. It is particularly important that the issue of physician-assisted suicide is facing not neglect or indifference but intense discussion in many states. It is far too early for courts to preempt these processes of discussion, especially if we consider the fact that there is no systematic barrier to a fair hearing of any affected group. Despite appearances, the Court's current doctrines reflect this point. Thus a general theme of this Essay is that many cases involving "fundamental rights" including the key privacy cases and the key equal pro-

> tection cases are best seen not as flat declarations that the state interest was inadequate to justify the state's intrusion, but more narrowly as democracy-forcing outcomes designed to overcome problems of discrimination and desuetude.
>
> In short, the Court should say that even if it assumes that the right to physician-assisted suicide qualifies as "fundamental" under the Due Process Clause, a legal ban on physician-assisted suicide is constitutionally permissible in light of the state's legitimate and weighty interests in preventing abuse, protecting patient autonomy, and avoiding involuntary death. The Court should reach this conclusion partly because of appropriate judicial modesty in the face of difficult underlying questions of value and fact; it should emphasize these institutional concerns in explaining its conclusion.

Sunstein, *The Right to Die*, 106 Yale L.J. 1123, 1124 (1997).

(3) *Washington v. Glucksberg* held that assisting suicide could be criminalized by the states. In *Gonzales v. Oregon*, 546 U.S. 243 (2006), the issue was whether states could, over federal opposition, permit doctors to assist terminally ill patients to commit suicide by prescribing drugs. Oregon had declared that such prescriptions were for "legitimate medical purposes" under the Federal Controlled Substances Act, although the U.S. Attorney General had determined they were not. In a narrow ruling, the Court held that the Attorney General (as opposed perhaps to Congress) could not make that determination under the Act.

(4) The criminal law issues surrounding the withholding of life support and physician-assisted suicide are difficult ones indeed. Much of the public controversy has revolved around the actions of one individual, Dr. Jack Kevorkian, in Michigan. In response to his acquittal of a homicide charge, the American Medical Association issued the following statement on May 2, 1994.

> Over the past few years, Jack Kevorkian has convinced some very vulnerable patients that they have no alternative other than death. The American Medical Association understands the desperation that terminally and chronically ill patients can feel.
>
> We are surprised and disturbed that Mr. Kevorkian was acquitted today. He has violated the most basic of medical ethical principles—that physicians do no harm.
>
> We need to better treat pain and depression in terminally and chronically ill patients, rather than simply encourage people to kill themselves, as Kevorkian would do. There is great danger in allowing physician-assisted suicide to persist. Patients who feel they are burdens to their families and friends may be encouraged to ask for help committing suicide. In the only two referenda ever held on this issue in this country, voters in Washington state and California rejected the legalization of physician-assisted suicide. It seems that when Americans really do have time to think about physician-assisted suicide, they just cannot support it.

While it could not agree on whether physician-assisted suicide could ever be an allowable part of the physician-patient relationship, the Michigan State Medical Society presented a statement of agreement which outlined nine points of consensus on the issue.

1. The medical profession in Michigan should strive to provide the following strategies to enhance patient control over the dying process:

a) improved pain and symptom control;

b) assurance of the right to competent treatment refusal; and

c) utilization of advance directives (written and verbal).

Full utilization and emphasis on the above may reduce the number of patients expressing an interest in assistance in suicide.

2. Providing a patient with sufficient medications to relieve pain even if it ends up shortening life, is neither assisting a suicide nor performing active euthanasia. Such provision is an essential of compassionate care.

3. The so-called "right to die," i.e., right to refuse unwanted or burdensome medical treatment, does not extend to or embrace a right to die with a physician's assistance (through assisted suicide or active euthanasia).

4. A physician should never suggest or recommend suicide to a patient. The medical profession should not create nor allow a practice or specialty focused on or limited to assisting in suicide nor the development of specialized facilities for effecting assisted suicide. These could have the effect of advocating assisted suicide as a preferred or routine option.

5. Even if there are theoretical arguments which deny the existence of morally relevant differences among allowing a patient to die, assisting a patient's suicide and active euthanasia, there are strong prudential and clinical reasons to maintain these distinctions as a matter of policy.

6. A patient's mention of an intent or desire to commit suicide, or of a request for assistance, should result in a concerted effort to ascertain and ameliorate any factors contributing to the patient's suffering.

7. The physician's reluctance to assist in or to cause the death of a patient is rooted in the very basic principles of professional integrity having to do with healing and relief of suffering for the purposes of extending the life of the patient. Only the most pressing circumstances, if any at all, can justify abandoning this position.

8. Legal prohibition of (physician) assisted suicide would be difficult if not impossible to enforce, and it is likely to have undesirable effects upon medical practice.

9. Societal changes to improve the quality of life and the perceived value of the life of the ill and/or elderly and to eliminate the financial barriers to med-

ical (including hospice and comprehensive long term) care may serve to limit patient requests for assisted suicide.

June 1993, Michigan Medicine at 28.[19]

Keeler v. Superior Court

Supreme Court of California
470 P.2d 617 (1970)

Mosk, Justice.

In this proceeding for writ of prohibition we are called upon to decide whether an unborn but viable fetus is a "human being" within the meaning of the California statute defining murder (Pen. Code, § 187). We conclude that the Legislature did not intend such a meaning, and that for us to construe the statute to the contrary and apply it to this petitioner would exceed our judicial power and deny petitioner due process of law.

The evidence received at the preliminary examination may be summarized as follows: Petitioner and Teresa Keeler obtained an interlocutory decree of divorce on September 27, 1968. They had been married for 16 years. Unknown to petitioner, Mrs. Keeler was then pregnant by one Ernest Vogt, whom she had met earlier that summer. She subsequently began living with Vogt in Stockton, but concealed the fact from petitioner. Petitioner was given custody of their two daughters, aged 12 and 13 years, and under the decree Mrs. Keeler had the right to take the girls on alternate weekends.

On February 23, 1969, Mrs. Keeler was driving on a narrow mountain road in Amador County after delivering the girls to their home. She met petitioner driving in the opposite direction; he blocked the road with his car, and she pulled over to the side. He walked to her vehicle and began speaking to her. He seemed calm, and she rolled down her window to hear him. He said, "I hear you're pregnant. If you are you had better stay away from the girls and from here." She did not reply, and he opened the car door; as she later testified, "He assisted me out of the car.... [I]t wasn't roughly at this time." Petitioner then looked at her abdomen and became "extremely upset." He said, "You sure are. I'm going to stomp it out of you." He pushed her against the car, shoved his knee into her abdomen, and struck her in the face with several blows. She fainted, and when she regained consciousness petitioner had departed.

Mrs. Keeler drove back to Stockton, and the police and medical assistance were summoned. She had suffered substantial facial injuries, as well as extensive bruising of the abdominal wall. A Caesarian section was performed and the fetus was examined

19. Jack Kevorkian was paroled in 2007, from a 10- to 25-year prison sentence for his 1999 second degree murder conviction in the death of a patient suffering from Lou Gehrig's disease. He died in 2011.

in utero. Its head was found to be severely fractured, and it was delivered stillborn. The pathologist gave as his opinion that the cause of death was skull fracture with consequent cerebral hemorrhaging, that death would have been immediate, and that the injury could have been the result of force applied to the mother's abdomen. There was no air in the fetus' lungs, and the umbilical cord was intact.

Upon delivery the fetus weighed five pounds and was 18 inches in length. Both Mrs. Keeler and her obstetrician testified that fetal movements had been observed prior to February 23, 1969. The evidence was in conflict as to the estimated age of the fetus;[1] the expert testimony on the point, however, concluded "with reasonable medical certainty" that the fetus had developed to the stage of viability, *i.e.*, that in the event of premature birth on the date in question it would have had a 75 percent to 96 percent chance of survival.

I.

Penal Code section 187 provides: "Murder is the unlawful killing of a human being, with malice aforethought." The dispositive question is whether the fetus which petitioner is accused of killing was, on February 23, 1969, a "human being" within the meaning of this statute. If it was not, petitioner cannot be charged with its "murder" and prohibition will lie.

Section 187 was enacted as part of the Penal Code of 1872. Inasmuch as the provision has not been amended since that date, we must determine the intent of the Legislature at the time of its enactment.

It will be presumed, of course, that in enacting a statute the Legislature was familiar with the relevant rules of the common law, and, when it couches its enactment in common law language, that its intent was to continue those rules in statutory form.

We therefore undertake a brief review of the origins and development of the common law of abortional homicide. From that inquiry it appears that by the year 1850—the date with which we are concerned—an infant could not be the subject of homicide at common law *unless it had been born alive.* Perhaps the most influential statement of the "born alive" rule is that of Coke, in mid-17th century: "If a woman be quick with childe,[5] and by a potion or otherwise killeth it in her wombe, or if a

---

1. Mrs. Keeler testified, in effect, that she had no sexual intercourse with Vogt prior to August 1968, which would have made the fetus some 28 weeks old. She stated that the pregnancy had reached the end of the seventh month and the projected delivery date was April 25, 1969. The obstetrician, however, first estimated she was at least 31 1/2 weeks pregnant, then raised the figure to 35 weeks in the light of the autopsy report of the size and weight of the fetus. Finally, on similar evidence an attending pediatrician estimated the gestation period to have been between 34½ and 36 weeks. The average full-term pregnancy is 40 weeks.

5. "Quickening" is said to occur when movements of the fetus are first sensed or observed, and ordinarily takes place between the 16th and 18th week of pregnancy. Although much of the history of the law of abortion and abortional homicide revolves around this concept, it is of no medical significance and was never adopted into the law of California.

man beat her, whereby the childe dyeth in her body, and she is delivered of a dead childe, this is a great misprision [*i.e.*, misdemeanor], and no murder; but if the childe be born alive and dyeth of the potion, battery, or other cause, this is murder; for in law it is accounted a reasonable creature, *in rerum natura*, when it is born alive." (3 Coke, Institutes (1648)). In short, "By Coke's time, the common law regarded abortion as murder only if the fetus is (1) quickened, (2) born alive, (3) lives for a brief interval, and (4) then dies." Whatever intrinsic defects there may have been in Coke's work the common law accepted his views as authoritative. In the 18th century, for example, Coke's requirement that an infant be born alive in order to be the subject of homicide was reiterated and expanded by both Blackstone and Hale.

By the year 1850 this rule of the common law had long been accepted in the United States. As early as 1797 it was held that proof the child was born alive is necessary to support an indictment for murder, and the same rule was reiterated on the eve of the first session of our Legislature.

While it was thus "well settled" in American case law that the killing of an unborn child was not homicide, a number of state legislatures in the first half of the 19th century undertook to modify the common law in this respect. The movement began when New York abandoned the common law of abortion in 1830. The revisers' notes on that legislation recognized the existing rule, but nevertheless proposed a special feticide statute which, as enacted, provided that "The wilful killing of an unborn quick child, by any injury to the mother of such child, which would be murder if it resulted in the death of such mother, shall be deemed manslaughter in the first degree."

We conclude that in declaring murder to be the unlawful and malicious killing of a "human being" the Legislature of 1850 intended that term to have the settled common law meaning of a person who had been born alive, and did not intend the act of feticide—as distinguished from abortion—to be an offense under the laws of California.

It is the policy of this state to construe a penal statute as favorably to the defendant as its language and the circumstances of its application may reasonably permit; just as in the case of a question of fact, the defendant is entitled to the benefit of every reasonable doubt as to the true interpretation of words or the construction of language used in a statute. We hold that in adopting the definition of murder in Penal Code section 187 the Legislature intended to exclude from its reach the act of killing an unborn fetus.

II.

The People urge, however, that the sciences of obstetrics and pediatrics have greatly progressed since 1872, to the point where with proper medical care a normally developed fetus prematurely born at 28 weeks or more has an excellent chance of survival, *i.e.*, is "viable"; that the common law requirement of live birth to prove the fetus had become a "human being" who may be the victim of murder is no longer in accord with scientific fact, since an unborn but viable fetus is now fully capable of independent life; and that one who unlawfully and maliciously terminates such a life should therefore be liable to prosecution for murder under section 187. We may grant the premises of this argument; indeed, we neither deny nor denigrate the vast progress of medicine in the century since the enactment of the Penal Code. But we cannot join in the conclusion sought to be deduced: we cannot hold this petitioner to answer for murder by reason of his alleged act of killing an unborn—even though viable—fetus.

The first essential of due process is fair warning of the act which is made punishable as a crime. "That the terms of a penal statute creating a new offense must be sufficiently explicit to inform those who are subject to it what conduct on their part will render them liable to its penalties, is a well-recognized requirement, consonant alike with ordinary notions of fair play and the settled rules of law." "No one may be required at peril of life, liberty or property to speculate as to the meaning of penal statutes. All are entitled to be informed as to what the State commands or forbids."

This requirement of fair warning is reflected in the constitutional prohibition against the enactment of *ex post facto* laws (U.S. Const., art. I, §§ 9, 10; Cal. Const., art. I, § 16). When a new penal statute is applied retrospectively to make punishable an act which was not criminal at the time it was performed, the defendant has been given no advance notice consistent with due process. And precisely the same effect occurs when such an act is made punishable under a preexisting statute but by means of an unforeseeable *judicial* enlargement thereof.

Properly understood, the often cited case of *People v. Chavez* (1947) 77 Cal. App. 2d 621, 176 P.2d 92, does not derogate from this rule. There the defendant was charged with the murder of her newborn child, and convicted of manslaughter. She testified that the baby dropped from her womb into the toilet bowl; that she picked it up two or three minutes later, and cut but did not tie the umbilical cord; that the baby was limp and made no cry; and that after 15 minutes she wrapped it in a newspaper and concealed it, where it was found dead the next day. The autopsy surgeon testified that the baby was a full-term, nine-month child, weighing six and one-half pounds and appearing normal in every respect; that the body had very little blood in it, indicating the child had bled to death through the untied umbilical cord; that such a process would have taken about an hour; and that in his opinion "the child was born alive, based on conditions he found and the fact that the lungs contained air and the blood was extravasated or pushed back into the tissues, indicating heart action."

On appeal, the defendant emphasized that a doctor called by the defense had suggested other tests which the autopsy surgeon could have performed to determine the matter of live birth; on this basis, it was contended that the question of whether the infant was born alive "rests entirely on pure speculation." The Court of Appeal found only an insignificant conflict in that regard, and focused its attention instead on testimony of the autopsy surgeon admitting the possibility that the evidence of heart and lung action could have resulted from the child's breathing "after presentation of the head but before the birth was completed."

The court cited the mid-19th century English infanticide cases mentioned hereinabove, and noted that the decisions had not reached uniformity on whether breathing, heart action, severance of the umbilical cord, or some combination of these or other factors, established the status of "human being" for purposes of the law of homicide. The court then adverted to the state of modern medical knowledge, discussed the phenomenon of viability, and held that "a viable child *in the process of being born is a human being within the meaning of the homicide statutes*."

Chavez thus stands for the proposition—to which we adhere—that a viable fetus "in the process of being born" is a human being within the meaning of the homicide statutes. But it stands for no more; in particular it does not hold that a fetus, however viable, which is *not* "in the process of being born" is nevertheless a "human being" in the law of homicide. On the contrary, the opinion is replete with references to the common law requirement that the child be "born alive," however that term is defined, and must accordingly be deemed to reaffirm that requirement as part of the law of California.

We conclude that the judicial enlargement of section 187 now urged upon us by the People would not have been foreseeable to this petitioner, and hence that its adoption at this time would deny him due process of law.

BURKE, ACTING CHIEF JUSTICE (dissenting).

The majority hold that "Baby Girl" Vogt, who, according to medical testimony, had reached the 35th week of development, had a 96 percent chance of survival, and was "definitely" alive and viable at the time of her death, nevertheless was not a "human being" under California's homicide statutes. In my view, in so holding, the majority ignore significant common law precedents, frustrate the express intent of the Legislature, and defy reason, logic and common sense.

Penal Code section 187 defines murder as "the unlawful killing of a human being, with malice aforethought." Penal Code section 192 defines manslaughter as "the unlawful killing of a human being, without malice." The majority pursue the meaning of the term "human being" down the ancient hallways of the common law, citing Coke, Blackstone and Hale to the effect that the slaying of a "quickened" (i.e. stirring in the womb) child constituted "a great misprision," but not murder.

The majority opinion suggests that we are confined to common law concepts, and to the common law definition of murder or manslaughter. However, the Legislature, in Penal Code sections 187 and 192, has defined those offenses for us: homicide is the unlawful killing of a "human being." Those words need not be frozen in place as of any particular time, but must be fairly and reasonably interpreted by this court to promote justice and to carry out the evident purposes of the Legislature in adopting a homicide statute. Thus, Penal Code section 4, which was enacted in 1872 along with sections 187 and 192, provides: "The rule of the common law, that penal statutes are to be strictly construed, has no application to this Code. All its provisions are to be construed according to the fair import of their terms, with a view to effect its objects and to promote justice."

We commonly conceive of human existence as a spectrum stretching from birth to death. However, if this court properly might expand the definition of "human being" at one end of that spectrum, we may do so at the other end. Consider the following example: All would agree that "Shooting or otherwise damaging a corpse is not homicide...." In other words, a corpse is not considered to be a "human being" and thus cannot be the subject of a "killing" as those terms are used in homicide statutes. However, it is readily apparent that our concepts of what constitutes a "corpse" have been and are being continually modified by advances in the field of medicine, including new techniques for life revival, restoration and resuscitation such as artificial respiration, open heart massage, transfusions, transplants and a variety of life-restoring stimulants, drugs and new surgical methods. Would this court ignore these developments and exonerate the killer of an apparently "drowned" child merely because that child would have been pronounced dead in 1648 or 1850? Obviously not. Whether a homicide occurred in that case would be determined by medical testimony regarding the capability of the child to have survived prior to the defendant's act. And that is precisely the test which this court should adopt in the instant case.

The common law reluctance to characterize the killing of a quickened fetus as a homicide was based solely upon a presumption that the fetus would have been born dead. This presumption seems to have persisted in this country at least as late as 1876. Based upon the state of the medical art in the 17th, 18th and 19th centuries, that presumption may have been well-founded. However, as we approach the 21st century, it has become apparent that "This presumption is not only contrary to common experience and the ordinary course of nature, but it is contrary to the usual rule with respect to presumptions followed in this state."

There are no accurate statistics disclosing fetal death rates in "common law England," although the foregoing presumption of death indicates a significantly high death experience. On the other hand, in California the fetal death rate in 1968 is estimated to be 12 deaths in 1,000, a ratio which would have given Baby Girl Vogt a 98.8 percent chance of survival. (California Statistical Abstract (1969) Table E-3, p. 65.) If, as I have contended, the term "human being" in our homicide statutes is a fluid concept to be defined in accordance with present conditions, then there can be no question that the term should include the fully viable fetus.

The majority suggest that to do so would improperly create some new offense. However, the offense of murder is no new offense. Contrary to the majority opinion, the Legislature has not "defined the crime of murder in California to apply only to the unlawful and malicious killing of one who has been born alive." Instead, the Legislature simply used the broad term "human being" and directed the courts to construe that term according to its "fair import" with a view to effect the objects of the homicide statutes and promote justice. (Pen. Code, § 4.) What justice will be promoted, what objects effectuated, by construing "human being" as excluding Baby Girl Vogt and her unfortunate successors? Was defendant's brutal act of stomping her to death any less an act of homicide than the murder of a newly born baby? No one doubts that the term "human being" would include the elderly or dying persons whose potential for life has nearly lapsed; their proximity to death is deemed immaterial. There is no sound reason for denying the viable fetus, with its unbounded potential for life, the same status.

The majority also suggest that such an interpretation of our homicide statutes would deny defendant "fair warning" that his act was punishable as a crime. Aside from the absurdity of the underlying premise that defendant consulted Coke, Blackstone or Hale before kicking Baby Girl Vogt to death, it is clear that defendant had adequate notice that his act could constitute homicide. Due process only precludes prosecution under a new statute insufficiently explicit regarding the specific conduct proscribed, or under a pre-existing statute "by means of an unforeseeable *judicial* enlargement thereof."

Our homicide statutes have been in effect in this state since 1850. The fact that the California courts have not been called upon to determine the precise question before us does not render "unforeseeable" a decision which determines that a viable fetus is a "human being" under those statutes. Can defendant really claim surprise that a 5-pound, 18-inch, 34-week-old, living, viable child is considered to be a human being?

Comments and Questions

(1) Assuming it is correct, as a matter of scientific fact, that "an unborn but viable fetus is now fully capable of independent life," why did the court reach its result? Consider the dissenter's view that the "Legislature [could not have] intended a person such as defendant charged with malicious slaying of a fully viable child, to suffer only the mild penalties imposed upon common abortionists who, ordinarily, procure only the miscarriage of a nonviable fetus or embryo."

Quite a number of cases have been brought in which the *Keeler* question has been posed. The courts have split in response. Some of the cases in which the *Keeler* view is followed include: *Commonwealth v. Booth*, 766 A.2d 843 (Pa. 2001) (legislature did not intend for the term "person" to include a fetus in the homicide by vehicle statute); *State v. Beale*, 376 S.E.2d 1, 4 (N.C. 1989) ("We do not discern any legislative intent to include the act of killing a viable fetus within the murder statute."); *State ex rel. Atkinson v. Wilson*, 332 S.E.2d 807, 810 (W. Va. 1984) ("[T]here are fundamental policy reasons why it is appropriate for this Court to defer the creation of new crimes to the legislature."); *State v. Anonymous*, 516 A.2d 156, 159 (Conn. Super. Ct. 1986) ("For this court to explore new fields of crime is foreign to modern concepts of justice and raises serious questions of separation of powers between it and the legislature."). Other courts, however, have been willing to include the fetus within the criminal statutes: *Commonwealth v. Morris*, 142 S.W.3d 654 (Ky. 2004) (unborn viable fetus was a "human being" but abrogation of the common law rule was prospective only); *State v. MacGuire*, 84 P.3d 1171 (Utah 2004) (including an "unborn child" in the homicide statute did not make it void for vagueness); *Hughes v. Oklahoma*, 868 P.2d 730, 732 (Okla. Crim. App. 1994) ("Advances in medical and scientific knowledge and technology have abolished the need for the born alive rule."); *Commonwealth v. Cass*, 467 N.E.2d 1324, 1327 (Mass. 1984) ("We reject the suggestion that, in using the term 'person' in defining a statutory crime, the Legislature intended to crystallize the *pre-existing* common law with regard to who may be the victim of a homicide."); *State v. Horne*, 319 S.E.2d 703, 704 (S.C. 1984) ("If there was malice in appellant's heart, he was guilty of the crime charged, it matters not whether he killed his intended victim or a third person through mistake.").

(2) The *Keeler* majority relied on the *Chavez* case but distinguished its facts. Are the facts distinguishable? Was *Chavez* correctly decided?

(3) In response to the holding in *Keeler*, the Legislature subsequently amended Section 187 to provide that "Murder is the unlawful killing of a human being, *or a fetus*, with malice aforethought." [Ed. note: with exceptions in the lawful abortion context.] The statute was applied to the killing of a non-viable fetus. *People v. Davis*, 872 P.2d 591 (Cal. 1994) (fetus was 23–25 weeks old).

In *People v. Valdez*, 126 Cal. App. 4th 575, 23 Cal. Rptr. 3d 909 (2005), the court upheld a murder conviction of a nonviable fetus with a serious medical condition that would not have survived until birth, against a challenge of cruel and unusual punishment. The California statute was also applied in the Scott Peterson case in which Peterson was found guilty of murdering his pregnant wife, Lacey, and of murdering their unborn child.

Several statutes have created new offenses to deal with the problems created by cases such as *Keeler*. The Mississippi law was entitled "Feticide" before it was amended in 2011. Section 97-3-37 of the Mississippi Code Annotated provided:

> The willful killing of an unborn quick child, by an injury to the mother of such child, which would be murder if it resulted in the death of the mother, shall be manslaughter.

The Minnesota Statute, § 609.2661, is an even more particular effort:

> **Murder of an Unborn Child in the First Degree**
>
> Whoever does any of the following is guilty of murder of an unborn child in the first degree and must be sentenced to imprisonment for life:
>
> (1) causes the death of an unborn child with premeditation and with intent to effect the death of the unborn child or of another;
>
> (2) causes the death of an unborn child while committing or attempting to commit criminal sexual conduct in the first or second degree with force or violence, either upon or affecting the mother of the unborn child or another; or
>
> (3) causes the death of an unborn child with intent to effect the death of the unborn child or another while committing or attempting to commit burglary, aggravated robbery, kidnapping, arson in the first or second degree, tampering with a witness in the first degree, or escape from custody.

In New Mexico the legislature has attempted to deal with the broad physical abuse problem by enacting a law specifically protecting pregnant women.

> Injury to [a] pregnant woman consists of a person other than the woman injuring a pregnant woman in the commission of a felony causing her to suffer a miscarriage or stillbirth as a result of that injury.

Section 30-3-7(A).

[B] Murder

[1] Malice Aforethought

> Murder, in the sense in which it is now understood, is the killing of any person in the peace of the commonwealth, with *malice aforethought*, either express or implied by law. Malice, in this definition, is used in a technical sense, including not only anger, hatred, and revenge, but every other unlawful and unjustifiable motive. It is not confined to ill-will towards one or more individual persons, but is intended to denote an action flowing from any wicked and corrupt motive, a thing done *malo animo*, where the fact has been attended with such circumstances as carry in them the plain indications of a heart regardless of social duty, and fatally bent on mischief. And therefore malice is implied from any deliberate or cruel act against another, however sudden.
>
> Manslaughter is the unlawful killing of another without malice; and may be either voluntary, as when the act is committed with a real design and purpose to kill, but through the violence of sudden passion, occasioned by some great provocation, which in tenderness for the frailty of human nature the law considers sufficient to palliate the criminality of the offence; or involuntary, as when the death of another is caused by some unlawful act not accompanied by any intention to take life.
>
> From these two definitions, it will be at once perceived, that the characteristic distinction between murder and manslaughter is malice, express or implied. It therefore becomes necessary, in every case of homicide proved, and in order to an intelligent inquiry into the legal character of the act, to ascertain with some precision the nature of legal malice, and what evidence is requisite to establish its existence.

Commonwealth v. Webster, 59 Mass. 295, 304 (1850).

Well more than a century and a half after this analysis by Chief Justice Shaw, the pertinent homicide question remains: can the government show a killing with malice aforethought? Unfortunately, the question is simple to ask but extremely difficult to answer. First, "malice" does not really mean malice. Second, "aforethought" has "become either false or else superfluous." Report of the Royal Commission on Capital Punishment 26 (1953). Third, many modern statutes by definition do not even use the terms "malice" or "malice aforethought."

Still, the concept of malice aforethought must be confronted. Its generally accepted meaning is that the prosecution has shown, beyond a reasonable doubt, that the defendant intended to kill, intended to inflict great bodily harm, or acted in a grossly reckless fashion ("depraved heart," "abandoned and malignant heart"). See, for example, Illinois Compiled Statutes, ch. 720, 5/9-1, which defines murder in this way:

> A person who kills an individual without lawful justification commits murder if, in performing the acts which cause the death:
>
> (1) he either intends to kill or do great bodily harm to that individual or another, or knows that such acts will cause death to that individual or another; or
>
> (2) he knows that such acts create a strong probability of death or great bodily harm to that individual or another; or
>
> (3) he is attempting or committing a forcible felony other than second degree murder.[22]

The Wyoming Supreme Court in 2014 redefined the meaning of "malice" to include acts done recklessly under circumstances manifesting an extreme indifference to the value of human life and done without legal justification or excuse. This decision overruled the Court's previous precedent that had defined malice as acts committed with "hatred, ill will, or hostility," and, alternatively, acts "committed without legal justification or excuse." *Wilkerson v. State*, 336 P.3d 1188 (Wyo. 2014).

[a] Intent to Kill

State v. Myers

Supreme Court of New Jersey
81 A.2d 710 (1951)

WACHENFELD, J.

The interest created by the unusual circumstances here involved is accentuated by the assertion that the facts are unparalleled in this or any other jurisdiction.

The nub of the episode is a command by the husband to his wife to jump into the Passaic River. She did so and was drowned.

The defendant contends the proof did not establish that her entry into the water was intentional and in compliance with his order but indicates she slipped or fell. He says she had been "spanked" as presently narrated but he did not threaten her life with a weapon nor was he armed; there were no circumstances suggesting her life would be endangered by his violence if she did not jump, "nor was there evidence that he anticipated that, if she responded to the threat, anything more than a disciplinary dunking would result."

Whether the so-called "spanking" and the "disciplinary dunking" are properly termed or tenable under the proofs will be developed as we progress.

The defendant and his wife were married in 1946. He was then twenty-two years of age and she sixteen. He was employed as a boiler manufacturer and his wife was

22. See Section [2], *infra*, for a separate discussion of felony murder.

a part-time domestic. Their married life was stormy and controversial, with frequent violent quarrels and separations followed by reconciliations.

The deceased left her husband five days before the commission of the crime. On the night of April 8, 1950, the defendant, accompanied by his wife's stepfather, Frank Byrd, while trying to repair his car, noticed his wife, accompanied by two men, go into a tavern almost across the street at Market and VanBuren Streets. He got "mad." He went to the tavern and called her outside. They walked down Market Street and before she could explain where she had been, he "hit her in the face with my open right hand."

She broke away and fled, running toward the Jackson Street bridge. He chased "right behind her." When he caught up to her he "hit her three or four or five licks on the shoulder with my open hand, also with my fist." The wife muttered: "Don't, don't, let me explain," and again broke away. He caught her near the steps of the bridge, where "I started punching my wife again mostly on the shoulders and the side of the face and my wife was crying and hollering."

She again attempted to elude him. "I was after her. My wife is hollering, 'stop, stop,' and she is running and I catch up with her by a big rock that is near the bank of the river. I grabbed my wife by the collar and she is hollering she wants to explain everything, and I hit her again a half dozen or more times with both hands, fists and open hands both."

The wife sought to prevent the beating by holding his arms and legs. "I grabbed her by the collar and picked her up." She asked for forgiveness and was crying. "Then I told my wife to go ahead and jump in the goddam river and she put her foot in a hole into which some river water was seeping and she told me the water was too cold." There was some conversation as to where she had been during her absence. "Then I started to hit my wife again," and he accused her of staying at another man's house. He charged her with lying and called her many vile and filthy names, interwoven with intensive profanity.

"I was good and mad at this time. I then told my wife that if she did not jump in I would push her in. My wife and I are right at the edge of the river now, near the big rock. I am standing up and she is sitting down on the rock."

"My wife then got up from the rock and went to the side of the dock and I am standing on the side of her. I told my wife again and again that if she did not jump in the river I would push her in. At this time my wife is sitting on the edge of the dock and the third time I told her that if she did not jump in the river I would push her in. I am standing to my wife's right with my back to the bridge and at this time my wife is holding on to the edge of the planking along the river bank and the water is about three or four feet below her. The tide is high and after I told my wife the third time that if she did not jump in the river I would push her in she let go her hold and dropped in the river."

"I saw my wife go out about two or three feet into the river and she started to holler for me and asked me not to go away but to come and get her. She was struggling in the water and I saw that she was being carried away from the Jackson Street bridge downstream. I stayed there about a minute, I saw that my wife was being carried down the stream, I could just see the top of her head. I could not see her hands and I heard my wife still hollering, 'Don't go away.' I ran away to my mother's house thinking that my wife drowned."

The State proceeded on the theory that the deceased's jumping into the river was caused by the defendant's assaults and threats of physical violence, constituting well-grounded fear and apprehension on her part, and that the death amounted to a willful, deliberate and premeditated killing.

The defense moved for judgment at the close of the State's case and the denial of the motion is advanced as error principally because there was supposedly no evidence of an intent to kill the deceased.

Admittedly such intent is rarely provable by direct evidence and is generally inferred from other proof, but it is alleged there was no such proof here because the "spanking" administered, no matter how viewed, does not evidence such intention.

It is also argued that the threat to push the deceased into the river if she did not jump does not add a deadly quality to the blows, which were not otherwise of that character, nor did the defendant have knowledge that the river at that point was sufficiently deep to cause drowning.

The violent onslaughts, the numerous applications of force, the physical dragging by her hair or neck across the boulevard, plus the frightening threats, had reduced her to a groveling, pleading bit of abject humanity begging for mercy and humbly seeking a cessation of the repeated violence applied.

She was cornered between her assailant and the river, with no means of escape except past him. The terror created by his course of conduct forced her to select what she seemingly thought was the lesser of two evils in following his repeated command.

Perhaps she did so in the hope that his anger and hatred might then subside and, having proven himself complete master, he would relent and assist her out of the water, to another reconciliation; but he stood as silent as the night itself, calmly watching her struggle for life and listening to her repeated anguished cries. There was no thought or pretense of giving aid or attempting a rescue. He did not even raise his voice in a call for help which might have been heard and answered.

The death struggle took place only a few feet away from him, punctuated by pitiful calls for assistance. His failure to respond in any manner under these harrowing circumstances reveals how hardened his intention and determination had become. His behavior was not only diabolical but clearly proves the design he formulated—the riddance of his wife, who had angered him for the last time.

The jury had a right to believe, from the proof submitted, that the deceased's death was due to the defendant's unlawful conduct which, together with the assaults and threats of violence, caused her to commit an act resulting in her death, which the defendant intended within the meaning of our statute. We see no error in this respect nor do we think the jury's determination contrary to the weight of the evidence.

The defendant's theory that his physical remonstrances with his wife were merely disciplinary treatments administered by him for corrective purposes without realization or anticipation of the results which occurred, is so far out of line with and so foreign to the proven facts and their natural inferences as to be absurd.

The series of assaults with fists and open hands, the frequency, the way and manner of their occurrence and infliction, the time and place, the painful and violent dragging of the deceased across the boulevard, the vile and vituperative names uttered with hatred and venom, cannot all be shrugged off under the heading of a "spanking."

The "voluntary dunking" as a mild chastisement, which is now the mental operation of the defendant as an explanation of what transpired, has little merit in view of the circumstances preceding the wife's entry into the river. His conduct was irreconcilable with anything constructive or corrective. It smacks rather of a preconceived scheme to bring about her death in a manner which would still give him an opportunity to deny full responsibility if he could find a jury gullible enough to agree with him.

Photos S-3 and S-4, not in the printed record but made available to the court by stipulation, the originals being filed with the clerk, indicate clearly the sharp embankment three or four feet above the edge of the water, making apparent both the depth and the current of the river. It was not a location where one would go wading. When there is added the defendant's knowledge that his wife could not swim and his observation that "the tide was high," the pattern becomes significant. We are in accord with the jury's views.

Notes and Questions

(1) There seems little doubt that the jury could believe that the "death was due to the defendant's unlawful conduct." Did the government show, however, that the defendant intentionally or deliberately killed his wife? Can the government seek to prove an intent to kill through the testimony of a medical professional? That was the issue in *State v. Chambers*, 507 N.W.2d 237, 238–39 (Minn. 1993). There the pathologist testified as to the victim's cause of death. The prosecutor then asked, "Doctor, as a result of your examination ... do you have an opinion as to the intent of the person 'who inflicted the wounds?'" The witness stated that to a "reasonable medical certainty [he thought the wounds] were meant to cause the subject's death." Held to be error because the issue of the defendant's state of mind "is a legal construct, a medical opinion is being improperly elicited on a mixed question of law and fact."

> Though a subjective state of mind may at times be difficult to determine, there is no mystery to mens rea, the Latinism not withstanding. Jurors in their everyday lives constantly make judgments on whether the conduct of others was intentional or accidental, premeditated or not. Thus, to do something intentionally is to do it with a purpose of accomplishing that some-

thing.... [The witness] should not be allowed to make an "expert inference" of intent to kill.... That is for the jury to do.

(2) What would the result have been if the wife had been a good swimmer?

(3) *Transferred Intent:* The defendant intends to shoot and kill the victim. His aim is bad so that he misses the intended victim and instead shoots and kills the victim's daughter. Is the defendant guilty of murder even though he did not intend to kill the daughter? Under the doctrine of transferred intent, a murder conviction would be valid. As stated in *State v. Moffitt*, 431 P.2d 879, 895 (Kan. 1967), *overruled on other grounds*, *State v. Underwood*, 615 P.2d 153 (Kan. 1980):

> It is no defense to the crime of murder in the first degree that the appellant may have mistaken Mary Alice Downing for some other person; or that the victims of the assault were unknown to the appellant; or that the appellant may have been angry; or that he may have supposed himself wronged by some other person.
>
> The fact that the homicidal act was directed against one other than the person killed does not relieve the slayer of criminal responsibility. It is generally held that such a homicide partakes of the quality of the original act, so that the guilt of the perpetrator of the crime is exactly what it would have been had the assault followed upon the intended victim instead of another.

The California Supreme Court held that the defendant could be convicted of both the completed crime (unintended victim) and the attempted crime (intended victim).

> Contrary to what its name implies, the transferred intent doctrine does not refer to any actual intent that is "used up" once it has been employed to convict a defendant of a specific intent crime against an intended victim.

People v. Scott, 927 P.2d 288, 292 (1996).

(4) Can intent to kill be demonstrated without direct physical violence? The defendant locks his children in a closet in his home, initially only while he is away, or for disciplinary purposes, but he eventually permanently leaves the children in the closet, feeding them irregularly, until the children eventually starved to death. Is this sufficient evidence to prove the defendant intended to kill his children? Yes, said Arizona, in *State v. Payne*, 306 P.3d 17 (Ariz. 2013).

[b] Intent to Inflict Great Bodily Harm

State v. Thompson

Court of Appeal of Louisiana
578 So. 2d 1151 (1991)

Lanier, Judge.

The defendant, Arthur Thompson, was charged by grand jury indictment with first degree murder, in violation of La.R.S. 14:30. He pled not guilty and, after trial by jury, was found guilty as charged. He was sentenced to life imprisonment at hard labor without benefit of parole, probation, or suspension of sentence. This appeal followed.

Facts

On Sunday morning, January 8, 1989, the defendant climbed through a window and entered the rectory of the Sacred Heart Church in Lacombe, St. Tammany Parish, Louisiana. He looked inside a desk and found a cigar box containing approximately $550 cash. He placed this box under his arm and attempted to leave when the victim, Father William O'Brien, the pastor of Sacred Heart Church, confronted him. The victim grabbed the defendant, and a struggle took place. The defendant threw the victim against the wall and beat him with his right fist. Even after the victim fell to the floor, the defendant struck him twice with his fists before fleeing out the back door. The victim bled to death as a result of severe lacerations to his face. His body was discovered a short time later.

Meanwhile, after going home to change his bloody clothes, the defendant was subsequently stopped and arrested for several traffic violations. When the authorities learned of the victim's murder that morning, they immediately suspected the defendant. The defendant made a videotaped confession to the murder.

At the trial, the assistant coroner, Dr. Fraser MacKenzie, testified the victim bled to death as the result of "multiple traumatic injuries with extensive facial lacerations." These injuries were caused by a blunt force or trauma, and they were consistent with injuries which could have been caused by State Exhibit 9, an iron rod wrapped in duct tape which had been seized from the defendant's truck. This iron rod was fourteen inches long, one inch in diameter, and weighed approximately three pounds. However, Dr. MacKenzie testified that the victim's skull had not been fractured. Furthermore, both Dr. MacKenzie and the defendant's expert witness, Dr. Milton Cox, testified that if State Exhibit 9 had been used to inflict the victim's injuries, they would have expected more tissue to be found on this weapon. In fact, Dr. Cox's examination of State Exhibit 9 revealed that there was only a small amount of blood and no human tissue on the iron rod.

At the trial, the defendant testified that he did not enter the rectory with State Exhibit 9 and did not use this weapon against the victim. Instead, he explained that he threw the victim against the wall and struck him several times with his right fist in order to free himself from the victim's grasp. The defendant testified that he did not intend to kill the victim. In his videotaped confession, the defendant stated that the victim was still breathing when he fled through the back door.

Sufficiency of the Evidence

In his only assignment of error, the defendant contends that the evidence was insufficient to support his conviction.

The standard of review for the sufficiency of the evidence to uphold a conviction is whether or not, viewing the evidence in the light most favorable to the prosecution, a rational trier of fact could conclude that the State proved the essential elements of the crime beyond a reasonable doubt.

La.R.S. 14:30 provides, in pertinent part, as follows:

A. First degree murder is the killing of a human being:

(1) When the offender has specific intent to kill or to inflict great bodily harm ...

In his brief to this court, the defendant ... contends that he did not have the specific intent to kill the victim or inflict great bodily harm upon him and, therefore, the evidence supports only a conviction of second degree murder. We disagree.

At trial and on appeal, the main contention between the State and the defense is whether or not the victim's injuries were inflicted with the defendant's fists or with State Exhibit 9, the solid iron rod wrapped in gray duct tape which was retrieved from the defendant's truck. Of course, if the defendant used this iron rod to beat the victim, a specific intent to kill or inflict great bodily harm could easily be inferred from such conduct. However, the trial testimony of the expert witnesses for the State and the defense seem to negate the use of this iron rod. While the use of such a weapon would have been consistent with the type of injuries which caused the victim's death, the lack of tissue and the small amount of blood found on the iron rod suggest that it was not used to inflict these injuries. In any event, it is not the source of these injuries (whether the defendant's fists, the iron rod, or some other instrument), but the severity of the injuries, which we find to be sufficient proof of *a specific intent to inflict great bodily harm.*

Specific intent is the state of mind which exists when the circumstances indicate that the offender actively desired the prescribed criminal consequences to follow his act or failure to act. Specific intent may be proved by direct evidence, such as statements by a defendant, or by inference from circumstantial evidence, such as a defendant's actions or facts depicting the circumstances. The defendant testified that the victim grabbed him and a struggle took place. He stated that he did not intend to kill the victim, he only wished to free himself and escape. Yet, in his videotaped confession, the defendant admitted that he struck the victim twice after the victim was already on the floor. Such testimony is inconsistent with his explanation that he only struggled with the victim in an attempt to flee. Consequently, no matter what the defendant used to inflict the victim's injuries, the severity of these injuries and the fact that the defendant struck the victim at least twice after he had fallen is sufficient to prove that, at the very least, he had the specific intent to inflict great bodily harm upon the victim.

As previously indicated, the defendant took the witness stand in his own defense and testified he did not intend to kill the victim. The jury's verdict indicates that they did not accept this testimony as truthful.

Under the facts of the instant case, there are two possible factual hypotheses pertaining to the defendant's intent at the time he beat the victim; either he had the specific intent to kill or to inflict great bodily harm upon the victim, or he did not. The defendant testified that he did not have the requisite intent. The jury rejected this factual hypothesis. The only remaining hypothesis is that the defendant had the requisite intent.

Therefore, we believe that a rational trier of fact, viewing all of the evidence as favorably to the prosecution as any rational factfinder can, could have concluded that the State proved beyond a reasonable doubt that the defendant was guilty of first degree murder.

Comments and Questions

(1) In most of the "great bodily harm" cases, the evidentiary problems are somewhat minimal because the attack is made with a deadly weapon such as a gun or knife. How could the court reach its decision if it concluded that the evidence was insufficient as to the iron rod? What result if the defendant only hit the victim once and the victim fell over and dropped dead? "Every death resulting from a fist fight does not constitute murder.... Conviction of murder ... requires clear evidence of the existence of malice." *Commonwealth v. Buzard*, 76 A.2d 394, 396 (Pa. 1950). What evidence would satisfy the malice requirement? Would proof of "a protracted and continued beating with bare hands by a stronger person upon a weaker person"? Yes, *State v. Bias*, 195 S.E.2d 626, 629 (W. Va. 1973). Would proof of an assault "committed on ... a person enfeebled by old age or disease"? Yes, *Bishop v. People*, 439 P.2d 342, 346 (Colo. 1968).

(2) The principle of inferred malice based on a disparity in size or strength between the victim and the defendant is not limited to cases in which adults kill young children or the elderly. The Rhode Island Supreme Court upheld an instruction of inferred malice where the victim was in an overall "unhealthy condition," had a blood-alcohol level of 0.152 percent, and was 22 years older and 16 pounds lighter than the defendant. *State v. Payette*, 38 A.3d 1120 (R.I. 2010).

(3) In *State v. Ferreira*, 850 P.2d 541 (Wash. Ct. App. 1993), the defendant was charged with first degree assault which required the government to show an intent to inflict great bodily harm. The essence of the case involved a drive-by shooting in which a group of juveniles shot more than a dozen bullets into a house as the car in which they were being driven went slowly past the home. The trial court specifically found that the defendants did not actually see anyone inside the house and concluded that it was only "likely apparent that the house was occupied." Relying on the fact that the shots were fired into the kitchen and living room, not the bedroom, the court on appeal concluded that the government had not sustained its burden to demonstrate an intent to inflict great bodily harm. Do you agree with the court's conclusion? How significant is the fact that the shooting took place early in the evening?

People v. Geiger

Court of Appeals of Michigan
159 N.W.2d 383 (1968)

BURNS, JUDGE.

Sometime after 11 p.m., May 6, 1965, defendant confronted his estranged wife, Sharon Geiger, in the parking lot of a bar in Prudenville, Michigan, as she was about to enter the bar with Joan Greening. Joan Greening testified that she and Mrs. Geiger had had only one drink at another bar prior to meeting the defendant, that Mrs. Geiger's health appeared normal and that she observed no black and blue marks or abrasions upon Mrs. Geiger that evening. Joan Greening further testified that she was told by the defendant to wait for Mrs. Geiger in the bar, but that she waited in the parking lot and observed the defendant talking to his wife and trying to force her into the car; he then "threw" her into the car and drove away.

State police officers who had interrogated the defendant after the alleged offense testified that defendant told them the couple drove to the Prudenville elementary school playing field. They argued and got out of the car. Defendant struck his wife "two or three times" with his open hand and pushed her to the ground in such a manner that she bumped her head against the car. When Mrs. Geiger failed to get up and appeared unconscious, defendant picked her up and placed her in his car. He then allegedly attempted to clean her after driving a short distance to a house trailer which the Geigers had rented until May 1, 1965.

Early in the morning on May 7, defendant left his wife in the trailer and drove to James Meigs' house where defendant had been residing while he and his wife were separated. Meigs was awakened around 3:15 a.m., at which time defendant persuaded Meigs to help move the automobile which Mrs. Geiger had driven to the bar. After taking the vehicle to Mrs. Geiger's parents' home, defendant finally replied to Meigs' inquiries as to what was going on; defendant stated that he might be "facing a murder rap."

Between 3:30 a.m. and 4:30 a.m., May 7, defendant aroused his employer, asked for $100 and was given $50 in order to get away for a few days.

Defendant apparently returned to the house trailer, placed his wife in the front seat of his car and put a blanket over her. He drove south for approximately 186 miles and at 7:30 a.m. or 8 a.m., stopped at the Addison Community Hospital, Addison, Michigan, where his wife was pronounced dead.

Doctor Gordon J. Hammersley performed an autopsy and testified that Sharon Geiger had been struck about the face and body by a blunt object such as a hand or a fist. The deceased's external marks of violence included swelling around both eyes, the chin, both lips, the right forearm, the left hand, both shoulders and the neck. There were facial abrasions and dried blood covering the right side of her face. Also present were small hemorrhages in the covering of the brain. The medical cause of death was "aspiration of the gastric contents into the air passages with resultant shock, asphyxia, collapse and pulmonary edema." In other words, sometime after the beating Sharon Geiger had attempted to vomit and had choked to death on her own vomitus.

Defendant related the night's activities to the State police, but in so doing he neglected to mention that he had forced Sharon Geiger into the car at the Sands bar. He also failed to mention his visits to James Meigs' house and to his employer's home until the police confronted him with these omissions.

Defendant was charged with first-degree murder, but the jury was instructed only as to second-degree murder and manslaughter. Defendant contends that the instructions regarding second-degree murder should not have been submitted to the jury because there were no proofs showing malice.

Malice has been defined as "an intent to cause the very harm that results *or some harm of the same general nature, or an act done in wanton or wilful disregard of the plain and strong likelihood that some such harm will result.*"

> It is not necessary in all cases that one held for murder must have intended to take the life of the person he slays by his wrongful act. It is not always necessary that he must have intended a personal injury to such person. But it is necessary that *the intent with which he acted shall be equivalent in legal character to a criminal purpose aimed against life.* Generally the intent must have been to commit either a specific felony, or at least an act involving all the wickedness of a felony. And if the intent be directly to produce a bodily injury, it must be such an injury as may be expected to involve serious consequences, either periling life or leading to great bodily harm. There is no rule recognized as authority which will allow a conviction of murder where a fatal result was not intended, *unless the injury intended was one of a very serious character which might naturally and commonly involve loss of life, or grievous mischief.* (Emphasis supplied.)

The question before this Court is: was there evidence from which a jury could infer defendant's alleged intent to produce great bodily injury with the attendant likelihood that death would result therefrom?

It was legally possible for the jury in this case to find that the nature and extent of Sharon Geiger's injuries were reflective of an intent equivalent to a criminal purpose aimed against life. This consideration standing alone would be insufficient to establish malice, but the extent and nature of the injuries is not set against a solitary backdrop. Defendant "forced" or "pushed" the deceased into his car shortly before he severely beat her. After the beating decedent's unconsciousness and general physical appearance, as revealed to the jury from photographs and the autopsy report, showed a need for medical attention. Notwithstanding this need, defendant failed to immediately take his wife to a local hospital; instead he waited approximately 6 to 8 hours, during which time he traveled over 180 miles. Although by no means conclusive, defendant's statement to James Meigs that he "might be facing a murder rap" would give a jury additional insight into defendant's intent. An inference of intent to kill could be drawn from these and other facts presented in this case.

Defendant further argues, however, that the immediate cause of death, asphyxiation, renders a finding of malice impossible. It is true that the likelihood of death resulting from the head wounds *per se* was medically improbable. Nevertheless, the likelihood of death resulting as a natural and probable consequence of the beating was within the range of medical testimony from which a jury could find a causal connection between the assault and Mrs. Geiger's act of vomiting. The pathologist who performed the autopsy testified as follows:

"Q. [prosecuting attorney] Now my question to you is this: These blows on the head, these blows to the side of the face, or whatever the blows were, did they have anything to do with the asphyxiation?

"A. Yes, I think they did in that they indicated a trauma which resulted in minor brain and subarachnoid damage that probably caused some degree of cerebral concussion, probably a temporary thing. That would contribute to the diminution of laryngeal reflexes which would allow the asphyxiation.

"Q. In other words, if she hadn't had the blows to the head, blows to the side of the face, or the blows on the other parts of her body, would she have been able to—excuse my words—vomit and bring this content of the stomach up?

"A. I would think that she would have been able to vomit and remove it from her body in normal fashion.

26 Am. Jur. Homicide, § 52, p.195, states:

"It is not indispensable to a conviction that the wounds be necessarily fatal and the direct cause of death. It is sufficient that they cause death indirectly through a chain of natural effects and causes unchanged by human action."

The evidence in this case would permit a jury to find that the injuries were "'reasonably calculated to cause death'" and that the wounds "'contributed mediately or immediately to the death.'"

Comments and Questions

(1) In *Thompson*, the intent to inflict great bodily harm was fairly clear. In *Geiger*, however, did the government prove this intent beyond a reasonable doubt? Which evidence proved it? Was it the evidence indicating what was said and done by the defendant *after* the attack? Should this evidence have been allowed at trial?

(2) Why should Geiger be convicted of murder if there was no intent to kill? Should the penalty be as great as in the case where there is an intent to kill?

[c] Abandoned and Malignant (or Depraved) Heart

People v. Knoller

Supreme Court of California
158 P.3d 731 (2007)

KENNARD, JUSTICE.

On January 26, 2001, two dogs owned by defendant Marjorie Knoller and her husband, codefendant Robert Noel, attacked and killed Diane Whipple in the hallway of an apartment building in San Francisco. Defendant Knoller was charged with second degree murder and involuntary manslaughter; codefendant Noel, who was not present at the time of the attack on Whipple, was charged with involuntary manslaughter but not murder. Both were also charged with owning a mischievous animal that caused the death of a human being, in violation of section 399.

With respect to Knoller, whose conviction of second degree murder was based on a theory of implied malice, the trial court took the position that, to be guilty of that crime, Knoller must have known that her conduct involved *a high probability of resulting in the death of another.* Finding such awareness lacking, the trial court granted Knoller's motion for a new trial on the second degree murder conviction.

The Court of Appeals reversed the trial court's order granting Knoller a new trial on the second degree murder charge. It remanded the case to the trial court for reconsideration of the new trial motion in light of the Court of Appeal's holding that implied malice can be based simply on a defendant's conscious disregard of the risk of *serious bodily injury to another.* In all other respects, the Court of Appeal affirmed the convictions of both defendants.

Both defendants petitioned this court for review. We granted only Knoller's petition, limiting review to two questions: "(1) Whether the mental state required for implied malice includes only conscious disregard for human life or can it be satisfied by an awareness that the act is likely to result in great bodily injury," and (2) Whether the trial court abused its discretion in granting Knoller's motion for new trial.

. . .

Malice is implied when the killing is proximately caused by " 'an act, the natural consequences of which are dangerous to life, which act was deliberately performed by a person who knows that his conduct endangers the life of another and who acts with conscious disregard for life.' " In short, implied malice requires a defendant's awareness of engaging in conduct that endangers the life of another—no more, and no less.

Measured against that test, it becomes apparent that the Court of Appeal set the bar too low, permitting a conviction of second degree murder, based on a theory of implied malice, if the defendant knew his or her conduct risked causing death *or serious bodily injury*. But the trial court set the bar too high, ruling that implied malice requires a defendant's awareness that his or her conduct had a *high probability* of resulting in death, and that granting defendant Knoller a new trial was justified because the prosecution did not charge codefendant Noel with murder. Because the trial court used an incorrect test of implied malice, and based its decision in part on an impermissible consideration, we conclude that it abused its discretion in granting Knoller a new trial on the second degree murder count. It is uncertain whether the court would have granted the new trial had it used correct legal standards. We therefore remand the matter to the Court of Appeal, and direct it to return the case to the trial court with directions to reconsider defendant Knoller's new trial motion in light of the views set out in this opinion.

I. Facts and Proceedings

Defendants Knoller and Noel, who were attorneys representing a prison guard at Pelican Bay State Prison, met inmate Schneider at the prison sometime in 1999. In October 1999, defendants filed a lawsuit on behalf of Brenda Storey against Coumbs over the ownership and custody of the four dogs. Coumbs decided not to contest the lawsuit and to turn the dogs over to defendants. Coumbs warned Knoller that the dogs had killed Coumbs's sheep, but Knoller did not seem to care.

Defendant Knoller thereafter contacted Dr. Donald Martin, a veterinarian for 49 years, and on March 26, 2000, he examined and vaccinated the dogs. With his bill to Knoller, Dr. Martin included a letter, which said in part: "I would be professionally amiss [*sic*] if I did not mention the following, so that you can be prepared. These dogs are huge, approximately weighing in the neighborhood of 100 pounds each. They have had no training or discipline of any sort. They were a problem to even get to, let alone to vaccinate. You mentioned having a professional hauler gather them up and taking them.... Usually this would be done in crates, but I doubt one could get them into anything short of a livestock trailer, and if let loose they would have a battle. To add to this, these animals would be a liability in any household, reminding me of the recent attack in Tehama County to a boy by large dogs. He lost his arm and disfigured his face. The historic romance of the warrior dog, the personal guard dog, the gaming dog, etc. may sound good but hardly fits into life today." Knoller thanked Dr. Martin for the information and said she would pass it on to her client.

On April 1, 2000, both defendants and a professional dog handler took custody of the dogs from Coumbs. Bane then weighed 150 pounds and Hera 130 pounds. Coumbs told both defendants that she was worried about the dogs, that Hera and Fury should be shot, and that she was also concerned about Bane and Isis.

...

On April 30, 2000, defendants brought Hera to their sixth-floor apartment at 2398 Pacific Avenue in San Francisco. Bane arrived in September 2000. Codefendant Noel purchased dog licenses, registering himself and Knoller as the dogs' owners.

Between the time defendants Noel and Knoller brought the dogs to their sixth-floor apartment in San Francisco and the date of the fatal mauling of Diane Whipple on January 26, 2001, there were about 30 incidents of the two dogs being out of control or threatening humans and other dogs....

Mauling victim Diane Whipple and her partner Sharon Smith lived in a sixth-floor apartment across a lobby from defendants. Smith encountered defendants' two dogs as often as once a week. In early December 2000, Whipple called Smith at work to say, with some panic in her voice, that one of the dogs had bitten her. Whipple had come upon codefendant Noel in the lobby with one of the dogs, which lunged at her and bit her in the hand. Whipple did not seek medical treatment for three deep, red indentations on one hand. Whipple made every effort to avoid defendants' dogs, checking the hallway before she went out and becoming anxious while waiting for the elevator for fear the dogs would be inside. She and Smith did not complain to apartment management because they wanted nothing to do with defendants Knoller and Noel.

On January 26, 2001, Whipple telephoned Smith to say she was going home early. At 4:00 p.m., Esther Birkmaier, a neighbor who lived across the hall from Whipple, heard dogs barking and a woman's "panic-stricken" voice calling, "Help me, help me." Looking through the peephole in her front door, Birkmaier saw Whipple lying facedown on the floor just over the threshold of her apartment with what appeared to be a dog on top of her. Birkmaier saw no one else in the hallway. Afraid to open the door, Birkmaier called 911, the emergency telephone number, and at the same time heard a voice yelling, "No, no, no" and "Get off." When Birkmaier again approached her door, she could hear barking and growling directly outside and a banging against a door. She heard a voice yell, "Get off, get off, no, no, stop, stop." She chained her door and again looked through the peephole. Whipple's body was gone and groceries were strewn about the hallway. Birkmaier called 911 a second time.

At 4:12 p.m., San Francisco Police Officers Sidney Laws and Leslie Forrestal arrived in response to Birkmaier's telephone calls. They saw Whipple's body in the hallway; her clothing had been completely ripped off, her entire body was covered with wounds, and she was bleeding profusely. Defendant Knoller and the two dogs were not in sight.

An emergency medical technician administered first aid to Whipple, who had a large, profusely bleeding wound to her neck. The wound was too large to halt the bleeding, and Whipple's pulse and breathing stopped as paramedics arrived. She was revived but died shortly after reaching the hospital.

An autopsy revealed over 77 discrete injuries covering Whipple's body "from head to toe." The most significant were lacerations damaging her jugular vein and her carotid artery and crushing her larynx, injuries typically inflicted by predatory animals to kill their prey. The medical examiner stated that although earlier medical attention would have increased Whipple's chances of survival, she might ultimately have died anyway because she had lost one-third or more of her blood at the scene. Plaster molds of the two dogs' teeth showed that the bite injuries to Whipple's neck were consistent with Bane's teeth.

...

II. The Elements of Implied Malice

The statutory definition of implied malice, a killing by one with an "abandoned and malignant heart" (§ 188), is far from clear in its meaning. Indeed, an instruction in the statutory language could be misleading, for it "could lead the jury to equate the malignant heart with an evil disposition or a despicable character" instead of focusing on a defendant's awareness of the risk created by his or her behavior. "Two lines of decisions developed, reflecting judicial attempts 'to translate this amorphous anatomical characterization of implied malice into a tangible standard a jury can apply.'" Under both lines of decisions, implied malice requires a defendant's awareness of the risk of death to another.

The earlier of these two lines of decisions, originated in Justice Traynor's concurring opinion in *People v. Thomas* (1953) 41 Cal.2d 470, 480 [261 P.2d 1], which stated that malice is implied when "the defendant for a base, antisocial motive and with wanton disregard for human life, does an act that involves a high degree of probability that it will result in death." (We here refer to this as the *Thomas* test.) The later line dates from this court's 1966 decision in *People v. Phillips*, 64 Cal.2d at page 587: Malice is implied when the killing is proximately caused by "'an act, the natural consequences of which are dangerous to life, which act was deliberately performed by a person who knows that his conduct endangers the life of another and who acts with conscious disregard for life.'" (The *Phillips* test.)

III. The Court of Appeal's Test for Implied Malice

As discussed in the preceding part, the great majority of this court's decisions establish that a killer acts with implied malice only when acting with an awareness of *endangering human life*. This principle has been well settled for many years, and it is embodied in the standard jury instruction given in murder cases, including this one. The Court of Appeal here, however, held that a second degree murder conviction, based on a theory of implied malice, can be based simply on a defendant's awareness of the risk of causing *serious bodily injury* to another.

We conclude that a conviction for second degree murder, based on a theory of implied malice, requires proof that a defendant acted with conscious disregard of the danger to human life. In holding that a defendant's conscious disregard of the risk of serious bodily injury suffices to sustain such a conviction, the Court of Appeal erred.

IV. The Trial Court's Grant of a New Trial on the Second Degree Murder Charge

In granting Knoller a new trial, the trial court properly viewed implied malice as requiring a defendant's awareness of the danger that his or her conduct will result in another's *death* and not merely in serious bodily injury. But the court's ruling was legally flawed in other respects.

...

The court stated that a killer acts with implied malice when the killer "*subjectively knows*, based on everything, that the conduct that he or she is about to engage in has a *high probability of death* to another human being" and thus the issue in this case was "whether or not as a *subjective* matter and as a matter of law Ms. Knoller *knew* that there was a *high probability*" that her conduct would result in someone's death. (Italics added.) But "high probability of death" is the *objective*, not the *subjective*, component of the *Thomas* test, which asks whether the defendant's act or conduct "involves a high degree of probability that it will result in death." The *subjective* component of the *Thomas* test is whether the defendant acted with "a base, antisocial motive and with wanton disregard for human life." Nor does the *Phillips* test require a defendant's awareness that his or her conduct has a *high probability* of causing death. Rather, it requires only that a defendant acted with a "'conscious disregard for human life.'"

As just shown, in treating the objective component of the *Thomas* test as the subjective component of that test, the trial court applied an erroneous definition of implied malice in granting defendant Knoller a new trial on the second degree murder charge.

In sum, the trial court abused its discretion in granting defendant Knoller a new trial on the second degree murder charge. That court erroneously concluded both that Knoller could not be guilty of murder, based on a theory of implied malice, unless she appreciated that her conduct created a high probability of someone's death, and that a new trial was justified because the prosecution did not charge codefendant Noel with murder. It is uncertain whether the trial court would have reached the same result using correct legal standards. Moreover, the Court of Appeal, in reversing the trial court's order, also erred, mistakenly reasoning that implied malice required only a showing that the defendant appreciated the risk of serious bodily injury. Under these circumstances, we conclude that the matter should be returned to the trial court to reconsider its new trial order in light of the views set out in this opinion.

Comments and Questions

(1) In *Commonwealth v. Malone*, 47 A.2d 445, 447 (Pa. 1946), the defendant and his friend were playing "Russian Poker" with a pistol that had five chambers and a single cartridge, which he thought was in the final chamber. The defendant pulled the trigger three times and "did not 'expect to have the gun go off,'" but it did. He declared that he had no intention of harming Long, who was his friend and companion. Murder conviction affirmed. A murder conviction was affirmed also in *Commonwealth v. Ward*, 688 N.E.2d 227 (Mass. 1997), with similar facts. The court wrote: "The victim died in one of a series of encounters in which the defendant chose to gamble with the life of another."

(2) The modern statutes speak in terms of knowledge of "a strong probability of death," (720 Ill. Comp. Stat. 5/9-1) or actions "manifesting extreme indifference to human life" (Wash. Rev. Code 9A.32.030). Would the defendant in *State v. Bolsinger*, 699 P.2d 1214 (Utah 1985), be convicted? There the defendant and the victim were lovers who both became quite intoxicated. During the act of intercourse, the defendant wrapped a cord around the victim's neck and pulled as they both reached climax. The victim died as a result of strangulation. The defendant was charged with second degree murder. The court on appeal reversed his conviction finding that there was no indication of any fight or dispute, there was no showing the defendant was angry with the victim and that the evidence demonstrated that strangulation occurred with relatively little force due to the high alcohol content in the victim's blood.

(3) In *Commonwealth v. Bowden*, 309 A.2d 714, 718 (Pa. 1973), the defendant first injected himself and then his friend with heroin. His friend died from an adverse reaction to the dosage. Under *Knoller*, should Bowden's murder conviction be affirmed? The court reversed the conviction:

> Under the facts of the instant case, we do not believe the necessary element of malice can be implied from Bowden's act of injecting Saunders with the drug, heroin. Initially, although we recognize heroin is truly a dangerous drug, we also recognize that the injection of heroin into the body does not generally cause death. Unfortunately, there are thousands of individuals who use or abuse heroin daily.
>
> While there has recently been a substantial increase in deaths from narcotics, the proportion of such deaths to the numbers of times narcotics are currently being used by addicts and for legal medical treatment is not nearly great enough to justify an assumption by a person facilitating the injection of a

> narcotic drug by a user that the latter is thereby running a substantial and unjustified risk that death will result from that injection.
>
> Moreover, and more importantly, under the facts of the instant case, Bowden knew Saunders was an addict and had used heroin with him for a period of time, he knew the deceased's tolerance to heroin and knew the quantity of heroin he injected into Saunders was his normal dosage, and he knew this dosage had never adversely affected Saunders before in the times he had used the drug. Moreover, the medical testimony established that the amount of heroin taken by Saunders would not normally cause death in an addict. Hence, under the facts of the instant case, Bowden could not "reasonably anticipate that death to [Saunders was] likely to result."

(4) Consider whether evidence related to a defendant who was driving in the wrong direction on a highway was sufficient to support a conviction for depraved heart murder. Prior to the collisions, the defendant appeared steady on his feet and maintained conversations without slurring his speech even though he was intoxicated. While driving, the defendant maintained a steady speed, successfully negotiated curves, and stayed within one lane. Additionally, the defendant passed "wrong way" signs and at least five sets of headlights shining directly at him. *People v. Heidgen*, 87 A.D.3d 1016 (N.Y. App. Div. 2d Dep't 2011).

(5) Can a defendant claim that he was hired by the victim of a homicide to stage the victim's death as the result of a robbery, murder, or assisted suicide and use this as a defense against depraved heart murder? This situation arose in *People v. Minor*, 973 N.Y.S.2d 43 (N.Y. App. Div. 1st Dep't 2013), where the defendant claimed assisted suicide as his defense to second-degree murder, saying that the victim, who was financially troubled, wanted his death to look like a robbery so his family could collect on his life insurance policy. At trial, the jury was instructed that this defense was invalid if the defendant "actively caused" the victim's death, clarifying "active" as "[d]oing something, carrying out an actual process, or carrying out by involvement, energy, or action." On appeal, these instructions were considered confusing and conveying the wrong standard, especially as it would be impossible to aid someone in committing suicide without "doing something." The defendant's conviction was reversed and the case remanded for retrial.

(6) The defendant in *Regina v. Ward*, (1956) 1 Q.B. 351, 356, was convicted of murder after shaking a baby and thus causing the infant's death. His lawyer showed that the defendant was a man of sub-normal intelligence and did not appreciate the risk in shaking the child. The court rejected the argument:

> The jury considered their verdict for a long time, and sent a note to the judge asking for a further direction, and the final direction given by the judge to the jury was: "If, when the person did the act which he did do, he must as a reasonable man have contemplated that death or grievous bodily harm was likely to result, he was guilty of murder." The objection which Mr. Lyons takes to that is that it brings in the test of a reasonable man, and you have

> to say whether the particular man knew. Of course, the test must be applied to all alike, and the only measure that can be brought to bear in these matters is what a reasonable man would or would not contemplate. If the act is one as to which the jury can find that a reasonable man would say: "It would never occur to me that death would result or grievous bodily harm would result," then the jury can find him guilty of manslaughter; but if the jury come to the conclusion that any reasonable person, that is to say, a person who cannot set up a plea of insanity, must have known that what he was doing would cause at least grievous bodily harm, and the death is the result of that grievous bodily harm, then that amounts to murder in law and a verdict of murder is justified.

Parliament legislatively overruled *Ward* in the Criminal Justice Act of 1967, ch. 80, § 8:

> A court or jury, in determining whether a person has committed an offence—
>
> (a) shall not be bound in law to infer that he intended or foresaw a result of his actions by reason only of its being a natural and probable consequence of those actions; but
>
> (b) shall decide whether he did intend or foresee that result by reference to all the evidence, drawing such inferences from the evidence as appear proper in the circumstances.

Many commentators also disagree with *Ward*:

> Thus an English case ... approved the trial court's instruction to the jury that if the defendant's conduct (shaking a baby, thus suffocating it to death) was such that a reasonable man would have realized that death or serious bodily injury was likely to result, the defendant would be guilty of murder.
>
> No doubt most depraved-heart murder cases do not require a determination of the issue of whether the defendant actually was aware of the risk entailed by his conduct; his conduct was very risky and he himself was reasonable enough to know it to be so. It is only the unusual case which raises the issue—where the defendant is more absent-minded, stupid or intoxicated than the reasonable man.
>
> In the unusual case where the defendant is not aware of the risk, which view is the preferable, [the] objective view or [the] subjective one? It is a question of how much fault should be required for murder; and one who consciously creates risk is morally a worse person than one who unconsciously does so, though each of the two persons may constitute an equal danger to his fellow man. On balance, it would seem that, to convict of murder, with its drastic penal consequences, subjective realization should be required.

LaFave & Scott, *Criminal Law* 620–21 (2d ed. 2000).

State v. Hemphill

Court of Appeals of North Carolina
409 S.E.2d 744 (1991)

Defendant was charged with second degree murder for the death of defendant's four month old daughter, Kala Marie Hemphill. Evidence presented by the State tends to show the following: At approximately 3:50 on the afternoon of 20 April 1989 defendant brought his daughter to be examined by her pediatrician, Dr. Ora Wells. The examination revealed that the baby was dead, and Dr. Wells stated that in his opinion the child had been dead for three to four hours. Dr. William Dunn, a medical examiner in Henderson County, performed an autopsy on the body of Kala Hemphill on 21 April 1989. His examination revealed swelling of the infant's brain, bleeding into the skull around the brain substance, bruises on the brain and hemorrhage in the lungs. The bruises were on the frontal parts of the brain and on the back of the brain. Dunn stated that the bleeding in the lungs was caused by the injury to the brain.

Dr. Dunn testified that he considered such injuries to be severe, and that he believed the cause of death was "Shaken Baby Syndrome," which is an injury resulting from the brain being shaken inside of the skull in such a violent or vigorous manner that it tears blood vessels inside the brain and on the surface of the brain, between the brain and its coverings. Dr. Dunn testified that the injury typically occurs when an infant's head is shaken violently while being held so that the skull itself is maintained within the person's grasp and the brain is shaken inside the head. He stated that vigorous shaking would be required to produce the sort of injury he observed in his autopsy of the victim.

Dr. Dunn indicated that one of the results of the increased intercranial pressure resulting from the swelling of the brain was typically vomiting, and that he had found evidence that this child had breathed some aspirated gastric material down into her lungs. He testified that the victim was alive when the aspiration occurred, although he could not tell if the baby had aspirated prior or subsequent to being shaken, but that the conditions he observed about the child's brain and lungs was consistent with an intentional violent repeated shaking, and that the child had died as a result of "Shaken Baby Syndrome."

Tim Shook, a special agent with the North Carolina State Bureau of Investigation, testified that he took a statement from defendant at 3:16 p.m. on 21 April 1989. Defendant stated that he had fed Kala at about 2:00 p.m. on the date of her death, and that she seemed fine. He further stated that when he checked on her about 3:20 p.m., that she had vomited and was not breathing. He then took the child to Transylvania Community Hospital where she was pronounced dead.

Agent Shook further testified that he took another statement from defendant at 5:16 p.m. on 21 April 1989, after informing defendant that the cause of death was "Shaken Baby Syndrome." In this second statement, defendant recalled that he had shaken the child about four times around 11:30 a.m. on 20 April 1989 because she was throwing up and he thought she was choking. Shook testified that defendant had not mentioned shaking the child in his first statement.

Defendant testified at trial that he had shaken the child because she was choking, and that "I might have shook her too hard and I might have shook her too much but I shook her, but after I shook her, she was all right." Defendant also testified that he did not intentionally injure his daughter and denied shaking her by her head. Defendant also offered character testimony that he was kind and gentle to children.

Defendant was found guilty of second degree murder and appealed from a judgment imposing a sentence of thirty-five years.

Opinion By: Hedrick

Defendant's one assignment of error is that the trial court erred in denying his motion to dismiss the charge of second degree murder. He argues that the evidence is insufficient to support a finding of the element of malice.

In *State v. Wilkerson*, 295 N.C. 559, 247 S.E.2d 905 (1978), our Supreme Court defined malice as follows:

[I]t comprehends not only particular animosity "but also wickedness of disposition, hardness of heart, cruelty, recklessness of consequences and a mind regardless of social duty and deliberately bent on mischief, though there may be no intention to injure a particular person."

This Court has said that "[m]alice does not necessarily mean an actual intent to take human life; it may be inferential or implied, instead of positive, as when an act which imports danger to another is done so recklessly or wantonly as to manifest depravity of mind and disregard of human life." In such a situation "the law regards the circumstances of the act as so harmful that the law punishes the act as though malice did in fact exist."

We hold the evidence in the present case is sufficient to support a finding by the jury that defendant acted with malice as defined by *Wilkerson*. The evidence that defendant shook the baby as well as the expert testimony that the cause of death was "Shaken Baby Syndrome," which typically results from an infant's head being held and shaken so violently that the brain is shaken inside the skull causing bruising and tearing of blood vessels on the surface of and inside the brain, is sufficient to show that defendant acted with "recklessness of consequences, ... though there may be no intention to injure a particular person."

We hold the trial court properly denied defendant's motion to dismiss the charge of second degree murder, and that defendant had a fair trial free from prejudicial error.

No error.

Dissent: Judge Greene

I disagree with the majority's conclusion that the evidence is sufficient to support a finding that the defendant acted with "recklessness of consequences" and therefore with malice.

The evidence on the malice element of the second degree murder charge tends to show that the baby's death was caused by "Shaken Baby Syndrome," the "intentional violent repeated shaking" of the baby. As part of its case, the State introduced the defendant's two statements that he made to the police on 21 April 1989. In his second statement, the defendant stated that at approximately 11:30 a.m. on 20 April 1989, the baby was throwing up, and because he was scared and thought she was choking, he shook the baby hard about four times to try to clear her airway. This evidence is uncontradicted and must be taken as true. Indeed, the State's expert testimony tends to show that the baby died from intentional violent repeated shaking. Accordingly, the issue becomes whether the evidence, viewed in the light most favorable to the State, is sufficient to support a finding that the defendant acted with "recklessness of consequences" and therefore malice.

> According to our Supreme Court, any act evidencing "wickedness of disposition, hardness of heart, cruelty, recklessness of consequences, and a mind regardless of social duty and deliberately bent on mischief, though there may be no intention to injure a particular person" is sufficient to supply the malice necessary for second degree murder....
>
> An act that indicates a total disregard for human life is sufficient to supply the malice necessary to support the crime of second degree murder.

The evidence from the defendant's statement does not show wickedness of disposition, hardness of heart, cruelty, recklessness of consequences, a mind regardless of social duty and deliberately bent on mischief, or total disregard for human life. To the contrary, the evidence tends to show a person who, fearing for the welfare of his child, made a very poor decision about how to handle his child's apparent choking. Furthermore, the uncontradicted evidence shows that once the defendant realized that his child had stopped breathing, he took her to the hospital, and after learning that she was dead, "he was beside himself with grief" and requested that an autopsy be performed on her. His conduct may rise to the level of culpable negligence for a conviction of involuntary manslaughter, but it does not amount to second degree murder. Because there was no substantial evidence tending to support a determination of malice, the trial court should have allowed the defendant's motion to dismiss the charge of second degree murder. Accordingly, I would grant the defendant a new trial.

Comments and Questions

(1) Did the court in *Hemphill* apply an objective or subjective standard? In *People v. Drumheller*, 304 N.E.2d 455 (Ill. Ct. App. 2d Dist. 1973), a friend of the defendant and the friend's infant son moved in with the defendant. Several times, in attempting to teach the infant how to walk, the defendant lost his temper and struck the child. "Medical testimony established that the major causes of death were a rupture of 4 centimeters in length in the stomach, hemorrhaging in the left lung, and edema or swelling of the brain." (Brief and Argument of Defendant—Appellant at 14). Counsel for the defendant argued strenuously that the defendant could not be found guilty of murder:

> The evidence established that defendant had been raised in a strict and highly religious background. Defendant was raised to obey without question the dictates of his father. While the evidence does not indicate Mr. Drumheller's disciplinary techniques in raising his own children, the testimony of the defendant established that he was at home and present from his own son's birth until age two.
>
> Defendant testified that his own children had learned to walk long before David, and that in general, his own children matured more quickly. He stated that he had no animosity toward David, that his expectations for David were affected by his own children's progress, and that he was trying to teach David by discipline.
>
> Defendant expressed his shame and remorse at what had happened and said that he had never intentionally inflicted any harm to David.
>
> Finally, it is clear from the record here that this instance was not part of a continuing "propensity" of the defendant. He had no prior record of arrest or conviction, had honorably served in the armed forces, and had held several positions of responsibility since his leaving the service. His relationship to Mrs. Breitweiser was described as "kind" and "affectionate", and they never had fought physically.
>
> In short, defendant's actions were not those of a murderer but rather of a confused man attempting to fulfill the role of surrogate parent.

Id. at 20–21.

The government responded to this argument.

> Intent or knowledge may be determined by the facts and circumstances surrounding an act. In the case at bar testimony by witnesses for the State, testimony by the defendant himself, and photographs of the victim introduced as evidence established that the victim was repeatedly and seriously abused by the defendant and the result of that abuse was readily visible to the defendant.
>
> The jury could conclude that under these circumstances it was the defendant's conscious objective or purpose to inflict death or further serious bodily harm or that he was at least consciously aware that death or further great bodily harm was practically certain to result from further efforts to "discipline" the victim.
>
> The defendant contends that death is not a reasonable or probable consequence of a blow with a bare fist and intent to produce death is therefore not presumed. The cases relied upon by defendant involved combatants of similar size and strength. In one of those cases the Court noted "... There might be a case in which the disparity in size and strength of the parties might be so great that a blow delivered with a bare fist might reasonably be expected to result in dangerous or fatal consequences ..." It is difficult to imagine a greater disparity in size and strength than between a 26-year old man and a 14-month old infant.

Brief and Argument of Plaintiff—Appellee at 8–9. Should the murder conviction be affirmed?

(2) If the defendant had not admitted to shaking the baby, would the expert evidence of "shaken baby syndrome" be sufficient to sustain his conviction for murder? For involuntary manslaughter based on recklessness? In 2008, a Wisconsin appeals court ordered a new trial for a mother convicted of reckless homicide fifteen years earlier for the "shaking" death of a neighbor's infant daughter. It was the first time an appeals court had reexamined the scientific validity of shaken baby syndrome. Critics of the medical diagnosis contend it is questionable whether shaking alone could cause immediate unconsciousness or death from brain damage in an infant absent other causes or injuries. Mark Hansen, "Unsettling Science: Experts Are Still Debating Whether Shaken Baby Syndrome Exists," *available at* www.abajournal.com/magazine/article/unsettling_science_experts_are_still_debat ing_whether_shaken_baby_syndrome_/; *see also* Tuerkheimer, *The Next Innocence Project: Shaken Baby Syndrome and the Criminal Courts*, 87 Wash. U. L. Rev. 1 (2009).

(3) If the defendant started screaming at a five-year-old child, and the child ran into the street where he was killed by a car, would the defendant be guilty of murder under the opinions in *Hemphill*? What if the defendant also threatened the child? *Compare Parrish v. State*, 97 So. 2d 356, 358 (Fla. Dist. Ct. App. 1st Dist. 1957):

> Applying this rule we find that the jury in this case was justified in finding that the deceased was the former wife of the appellant who had divorced him because of extreme cruelty including brutal physical violence; that the appellant had stated in most solemn terms that if he could not "have" deceased, no one else would, that deceased had married another man, that appellant had told deceased "if you stay in Jacksonville I am going to kill you"; that in the City of Jacksonville in the early hours of the morning of September 22, 1955, appellant was one of four men riding in a car driven by Edward W. Ramsey who was taking instructions from defendant; that appellant was looking for deceased as she left her place of employment about 12:30 A.M.; that a few blocks from the place of deceased's employment they located deceased and another young lady riding in deceased's car and began to pursue them; that deceased attempted to flee by increasing the speed of her car but still retaining some regard for traffic regulations but this proved inadequate; Ramsey maneuvered his car in front of deceased's car forcing her to stop at a point where another car was immediately behind deceased making it impossible for her to get away; appellant left the car in which he was riding and approached deceased who had closed the window and locked the door of her car; deceased cried, "Oh! My God! There is Theo, he is going to kill me"; defendant having tried unsuccessfully to open the door of deceased's car began striking the glass of the window with a bayonet, with which he was then armed, with such force that shattered glass was hurled across deceased and upon the other young lady who was on the opposite side of the car; this young lady opened the door on her side of the car and both the girls at-

> tempted to escape in that way; appellant then came around the car and while the first young lady escaped deceased was unable to do so, but the car behind having moved, the deceased managed to get back under the wheel, evade the car in which appellant had been riding and renew her flight alone; appellant hurriedly reentered the car in which he had been riding and instructed Ramsey to give chase still holding the bayonet and refusing to surrender it to one of the other occupants of the car; during this pursuit Ramsey's car reached a speed of 70 miles per hour; appellant gave Ramsey instructions to "catch her and run into her if you have to but stop her, block her off"; Ramsey finally passed deceased again but deceased cut sharply to her left and entered another street; Ramsey turned his car so quickly that he ran upon the curb and began still further pursuit of deceased. Under these conditions deceased disregarded a stop sign and drove at a high rate of speed into a through street and in doing so ran into another car being operated in a lawful manner upon that street and in this accident received injuries of which she died within a few hours. The degree of the deceased's fear of appellant and her state of terror during her flight from him is demonstrated by the fact that immediately after the accident in which she had received the wounds of which she shortly died she cried to strangers, "Don't let them cut me. Don't let them cut me."

Should the defendant's murder conviction be affirmed? Would his former wife have been guilty of murder if she had survived but had hit and killed a pedestrian?

(4) In *Gibson v. State*, 476 P.2d 362 (Okla. Crim. App. 1970), the defendant, while in police custody, lunged across the front seat of the police car and grabbed the steering wheel, causing it to swerve across the highway. The car collided with another car, killing one of the police officers. The court upheld the defendant's murder conviction. Would it be murder if the defendant drove while intoxicated, swerved his car, and struck and killed someone else? Yes, said the court in *Pears v. State*, 672 P.2d 903 (Alaska Ct. App. 1983), for the defendant was aware of the dangerous nature of his driving (though the *sentence* was lowered on appeal, 698 P.2d 1198 (Alaska 1985)). No, found the court in *State v. Chalmers*, 411 P.2d 448, 452 (Ariz. 1966) (no showing of "vicious or brutal conduct which might support a finding of 'an abandoned and malignant heart' "). Most states have adopted statutes imposing somewhat lesser penalties for vehicular deaths. *See, e.g.*, §782.071, Florida Statutes:

> "Vehicular homicide" is the killing of a human being or the killing of an unborn child by an injury to the mother, caused by the operation of a motor vehicle by another in a reckless manner likely to cause the death of, or great bodily harm to, another. Vehicular homicide is a felony of the third degree [or] of the second degree.

[2] Felony Murder

The felony-murder rule as it was formulated in England was a doctrine of constructive malice. To make out a case of murder it was necessary only to establish that the defendant had committed a homicide while engaged in the

> commission of a felony. No other evidence had to be introduced to prove the essential element of malice aforethought. This was the only function which the rule performed; it obviated the necessity of establishing malice aforethought by other means.

Commonwealth v. Balliro, 209 N.E.2d 308, 312 (Mass. 1965). As stated by Chief Justice Traynor in *People v. Washington*, 402 P.2d 130, 133 (Cal. 1965), the "purpose of the felony-murder rule is to deter felons from killing negligently or accidentally by holding them strictly responsible for killings they commit."

Though the felony murder rule was formulated in England, the British rejected it in 1957. Most American jurisdictions, however, still adhere to it, normally in statutory form. *See, e.g.*, 720 Ill. Comp. Stat. 5/9-1(a): "A person who kills an individual without lawful justification commits first degree murder if, in performing the acts which cause the death:

> (3) He is attempting or committing a forcible felony other than second degree murder."

The felony murder rule has been the subject of intense criticism and has been restricted in a number of states. A "compromise" rule was suggested in § 210.2 of the Model Penal Code:

> [C]riminal homicide constitutes murder when:
>
> (a) it is committed purposely or knowingly; or
>
> (b) it is committed recklessly under circumstances manifesting extreme indifference to the value of human life. Such recklessness and indifference are presumed if the actor is engaged or is an accomplice in the commission of, or an attempt to commit, or flight after committing or attempting to commit robbery, rape or deviate sexual intercourse by force or threat of force, arson, burglary, kidnapping or felonious escape.

In this part of the chapter we shall explore the three main problems which have arisen under the felony murder rule: which felonies are within the scope of the rule; when is a felony being attempted or committed; and, what is the extent of criminal responsibility?

[a] Which Felonies

In some jurisdictions the issue of which felonies are within the scope of the rule never arises. In these states, the statutes are quite explicit. In the Illinois statute mentioned earlier, the rule is limited to a "treason, first degree murder, second degree murder, predatory criminal sexual assault of a child, aggravated criminal sexual assault, criminal sexual assault, robbery, burglary, residential burglary, aggravated arson, arson, aggravated kidnaping, kidnaping, aggravated battery resulting in great bodily harm or permanent disability or disfigurement and any other felony which involves the use or threat of physical force or violence against any individual." 720 Ill. Comp. Stat. 5/2-8.

In other states the problems remain.

People v. Howard

Supreme Court of California
104 P.3d 107 (2005)

Kennard, Justice.

Murder is the unlawful killing of a human being, with malice aforethought. But under the second degree felony-murder rule, the prosecution can obtain a conviction without showing malice if the killing occurred during the commission of an inherently dangerous felony. Is the crime of driving with a willful or wanton disregard for the safety of persons or property while fleeing from a pursuing police officer an inherently dangerous felony for purposes of the second degree felony-murder rule? We conclude it is not.

At 12:40 a.m. on May 23, 2002, California Highway Patrol Officer Gary Stephany saw defendant driving a Chevrolet Tahoe (a sport utility vehicle) without a rear license plate, and signaled him to pull over. Defendant stopped on the side of the road. But when Officer Stephany and his partner, Officer Wayne Bernard, got out of their patrol car, defendant restarted the engine and sped to a nearby freeway. The officers gave chase at speeds of up to 90 miles per hour and radioed for assistance. Defendant left the freeway and drove onto a surface street, turning off his car's headlights. He ran two stop signs and a red light, and he drove on the wrong side of the road. His speed was 15 to 20 miles over the posted speed limit of 50 miles per hour. At some point, he made a sharp turn onto a small dirt road and escaped.

Minutes later, Officer Anthony Arcelus and his partner, Officer Bret Boss, who had been monitoring the pursuit on their car radio, saw the Tahoe with its headlights on again and took up the chase. Officer Arcelus, who was driving, estimated the Tahoe's speed at more than 80 miles per hour, and he saw it run a stop sign and a traffic light. By then, the car's headlights were again turned off. Up to that point, the chase had taken place in rural parts of Fresno County. When the Tahoe started heading toward downtown Fresno, Officer Arcelus gave up the pursuit, fearing that the high-speed chase might cause an accident.

About a minute after Officer Arcelus stopped chasing the Tahoe, he saw it run a red light half a mile ahead of him and collide with a car driven by Jeanette Rodriguez. Rodriguez was killed and her husband, a passenger in the car, was seriously injured. It turned out that the Tahoe that defendant was driving had been stolen earlier that day. Defendant, who was also injured in the crash, was arrested and charged with murder, causing serious bodily injury while evading a police officer, and with evading a police officer in willful or wanton disregard for the safety of persons or property (§ 2800.2).

Because the second degree felony-murder rule is a court-made rule, it has no statutory definition. This court has described it thusly: "A homicide that is a direct causal result of the commission of a felony *inherently dangerous to human life* (other than the ... felonies enumerated in Pen. Code, § 189) constitutes at least second degree murder." The rule "eliminates the need for proof of malice in connection with a charge of murder." It is not an evidentiary presumption but a substantive rule of law which is based on the theory that "when society has declared certain inherently dangerous conduct to be felonious, a defendant should not be allowed to excuse himself by saying he was unaware of the danger to life because, by declaring the conduct to be felonious, society has warned him of the risk involved."

"In determining whether a felony is inherently dangerous [under the second degree felony-murder rule], the court looks to the elements of the felony *in the abstract*, 'not the "particular" facts of the case,' i.e., not to the defendant's specific conduct."

In concluding that section 2800.2 is an inherently dangerous felony, the Court of Appeal relied heavily on *People v. Johnson* (1993), 15 Cal. App. 4th 169 [18 Cal. Rptr. 2d 650]. There the Court of Appeal, construing an earlier version of section 2800.2 that was essentially the same as what is now subdivision (a) of that section, held that driving with "willful or wanton disregard for the safety of persons or property" was inherently dangerous to life. We need not decide, however, whether *Johnson* was correct, because in 1996, three years after *Johnson* was decided, the Legislature amended section 2800.2 to add subdivision (b). Subdivision (b) very broadly defines the term "willful or wanton disregard for the safety of persons or property," as used in subdivision (a), to include *any* flight from an officer during which the motorist commits three traffic violations that are assigned a "point count" under section 12810, or which results in "damage to property."

Violations that are assigned points under section 12810 and can be committed without endangering human life include driving an unregistered vehicle owned by the driver, driving with a suspended license, driving on a highway at slightly more than 55 miles per hour when a higher speed limit has not been posted, failing to come to a complete stop at a stop sign, and making a right turn without signaling for 100 feet before turning.

Subdivision (b) greatly expanded the meaning of the quoted statutory phrase to include conduct that ordinarily would not be considered particularly dangerous.

In the absence of any evidence of legislative intent, we assume that the Legislature contemplated that we would determine the application of the second degree felony-murder rule to violations of section 2800.2 based on our long-established decisions holding that the rule applies only to felonies that are inherently dangerous in the *abstract*.

As we have explained in this opinion, a violation of section 2800.2 is not, in the abstract, inherently dangerous to human life. Therefore, the second degree felony-murder rule does not apply when a killing occurs during a violation of section 2800.2. Nothing here should be read as saying that a motorist who kills an innocent person in a hazardous, high-speed flight from a police officer should *not* be convicted of murder. A jury may well find that the motorist has acted with malice by driving with conscious disregard for the lives of others, and thus is guilty of murder. But, as we have explained, not all violations of section 2800.2 pose a danger to human life. Therefore, the prosecution may not (as it did here) resort to the second degree felony-murder rule to remove from the jury's consideration the question whether a killing that occurred during a violation of section 2800.2 was done with malice.

We reverse the judgment of the Court of Appeal, which upheld defendant's conviction for second degree murder, and remand the matter to that court for further proceedings consistent with this opinion.

DISSENT, BAXTER, J.

... I respectfully dissent. In early morning darkness, defendant, driving a stolen vehicle, led police officers on a perilous and extended chase over Fresno County roads. He ran three stop signs and a red light, and even proceeded on the wrong side of a divided highway, while operating the vehicle far in excess of posted speed limits. Finally, as he dashed on city streets toward downtown Fresno at speeds between 80 and 90 miles per hour, he ran a second red light and collided with another vehicle. Both occupants of that car were ejected onto the street. One perished.

Subdivision (a) of section 2800.2 gives clear and specific notice that one who, in order to elude police pursuit, drives with reckless indifference to safety is guilty of a felony. Such reckless driving is, of course, inherently dangerous—by definition, it creates a substantial risk that someone will be killed. Moreover, there is no doubt that defendant committed exactly the reckless endangerment of human life forbidden by the statute. His conviction for violating section 2800.2, as well as his felony-murder conviction, were unambiguously based on the dangerous recklessness of his flight from the police.

Hence, the principal reason noted by the majority for limiting the second degree felony-murder rule should not bar a felony-murder finding here. The statute's express words placed defendant on notice that the particular conduct he was committing—recklessly unsafe driving to elude police pursuit—was both felonious and inherently dangerous, and thus a basis for murder liability if death resulted. This is a case where "'society has declared certain inherently dangerous conduct to be felonious,'" and "'defendant should [therefore] not be allowed to excuse himself by saying he was unaware of the danger to life because, by declaring the conduct to be felonious, society has warned him of the risk involved.'"

Conversely, the principal reason for applying the felony-murder rule is present. The purpose of the felony-murder doctrine "'is to deter those engaged in felonies from killing negligently or accidentally.'" Because the doctrine absolves the prosecution from proving malice, it properly applies when "'the killer is engaged in a felony whose inherent danger to human life renders logical an imputation of malice on the part of all who commit it.'"

Those requirements are met here. It is appropriate to deter persons from killing negligently or accidentally—as did defendant—while engaged—as was defendant—in recklessly unsafe driving to elude police pursuit, a specific form of conduct made felonious by section 2800.2, subdivision (a). Moreover, the inherent danger such conduct poses to human life is so clear that it is logical to impute malice to anyone who commits it.

Under such circumstances, it perverts reason to refuse to apply the felony-murder rule simply because subdivision (b) of section 2800.2 may additionally describe a nondangerous felony. Where society has warned, in plain statutory words, that the particular conduct committed by the defendant is both dangerous and felonious, it should not matter that the statute may forbid nondangerous conduct as well.

Comments and Questions

(1) The problem arises here, as in most situations, where the first degree murder statute is quite specific as to its underlying felonies, but the second degree murder statute is not. In *Ex parte Mitchell*, 936 So. 2d 1094 (Ala. Crim. App. 2006), the court adopted the "overwhelming consensus" that a fact-based approach should be used to determine whether a particular felony can be the predicate felony for felony-murder. *See Jenkins v. State*, 230 A.2d 262, 268–69 (Del. 1967):

> The California rule has been stated as follows: a homicide that is a direct causal result of the commission of a felony inherently dangerous to human life (except felonies enumerated in the first degree murder statute) constitutes at least second degree murder. In our judgment, the California rule is supported by logic, reason, history, and common sense. The only rational function of the felony-murder rule is to furnish an added deterrent to the perpetration of felonies which, by their nature or by the attendant circumstances, create a foreseeable risk of death. This function is not served by application of the rule to felonies not foreseeably dangerous. The rule should not be extended beyond its rational function. Moreover, application of the rule to felonies not foreseeably dangerous would be unsound analytically because there is no logical basis for imputing malice from the intent to commit a felony not dangerous to human life.

The Delaware court went on to note that there "are statutory felonies, such as forgery and counterfeiting, embezzlement, pandering, and pimping, as to which an unqualified felony-murder rule would be incongruous." Would it? *See People v. Williams*, 406 P.2d 647, 650 (Cal. 1965): "The purpose of the felony-murder rule is to deter felons from killing negligently or accidentally. This purpose may be well served with respect to felonies such as robbery or burglary, but it has little relevance to a felony which is not inherently dangerous. If the felony is not inherently dangerous it is highly improbable that the potential felon will be deterred; he will not anticipate that any injury or death might arise solely from the fact that he will commit the felony."

(2) In *Commonwealth v. Lopez*, 80 Mass. App. Ct. 390 (2011), the Court upheld a conviction for felony murder in an unarmed robbery in which the defendant phoned a restaurant to place a delivery order, waited for the delivery person to arrive, pushed the delivery person down the stairs, and took money from the delivery person as he lay on the pavement gasping for air and foaming at the mouth.

Which felonies are inherently dangerous? Is the crime of stealing a motor vehicle? Felony child endangerment? (No, *People v. Culuko*, 78 Cal. App. 4th 307, 92 Cal.

Rptr. 2d 789 (2000)). Grand theft? (No, *People v. Phillips*, 414 P.2d 353 (Cal. 1966); Yes, *State v. Garner*, 699 P.2d 468 (Kan. 1985).) Practicing medicine without a license? (Yes, *People v. Brown*, 234 Cal. App. 3d 918, 285 Cal. Rptr. 824 (1991).) Felony false imprisonment? (No, *People v. Henderson*, 560 P.2d 1180 (Cal. 1977).) How does one determine whether a felony is inherently dangerous? Is it a question of law for the judge, or a question of fact for the jury? *See People v. Satchell*, 489 P.2d 1361, 1369 (Cal. 1971):

> It bears emphasis that, in determining whether a felony is inherently dangerous for purposes of the felony-murder rule we assess that felony *in the abstract*. The felony here in question is possession of a concealable firearm by one who has previously been convicted of a (*i.e.*, another) felony. We do *not* look to the specific facts of the case before us in order to determine whether, in light of the nature of the particular felony of which defendant was previously convicted, his possession of a concealable firearm was inherently dangerous. Rather, we direct our attention to the genus of crimes known as felonies and determine whether the possession of a concealable firearm by one who has been convicted of *any crime within that genus* is an act inherently dangerous to human life which, as such, justifies the extreme consequence (*i.e.*, imputed malice) which the felony-murder doctrine demands.

But see *Fisher v. State*, 786 A.2d 706, 733 (Md. 2001), where the court decided that the risk is to be "determined by the nature of the crime *or* by the manner in which it was perpetrated in a given set of circumstances." The court explained its decision:

> In our view the abstract approach undermines one of the primary purposes of the modern felony murder rule. The modern version of the rule is intended to deter dangerous conduct by punishing as murder a homicide resulting from dangerous conduct in the perpetration of a felony, even if the defendant did not intend to kill. If the felonious conduct, under all of the circumstances, made death a foreseeable consequence, it is reasonable for the law to infer from the commission of the felony under those circumstances the malice that qualifies the homicide as murder. The abstract approach, however, eliminates this inference merely because death is not a *necessary* consequence of the felony, *i.e.*, because the felony *could have been* committed in a non-mortally-dangerous manner.

Barnett v. State

Court of Criminal Appeals of Oklahoma

263 P.3d 959 (2011)

Lewis, Vice-Presiding Judge.

ANALYSIS

* * * In Proposition Five, Appellant argues that his conviction for second degree felony murder violates the merger doctrine, or independent crime requirement, recognized by our case law in *Quillen v. State*, 2007 OK CR 22, 163 P.3d 587, and earlier

cases. Although the State charged Appellant in Count 2 with first degree malice aforethought murder, the trial court also instructed the jury on the lesser included offense of second degree felony murder in the commission of using a vehicle to facilitate the intentional discharge of a firearm. The jury acquitted Appellant of first degree murder, but convicted him of second degree murder in the commission of the underlying felony. Counsel's failure to object to the second degree felony murder instruction at trial waived all but plain error. We therefore consider whether Appellant's conviction of second degree murder in the commission of this underlying felony is plain error; that is, an error which goes "to the foundation of the case," or which takes from a defendant "a right which was essential to his defense."

Under this Court's merger doctrine, or independent crime requirement, "[i]n order for the taking of human life in the commission of a felony to constitute murder, the precedent felony must constitute an independent crime not included within the resulting homicide." The merger doctrine is a historical feature of our case law, and is not based on any statutory or constitutional text. This Court in *Quillen* recently reaffirmed its adherence to the merger doctrine as it "has been applied in Oklahoma for many years," first being mentioned in *Jewell v. Territory*, 4 Okla. 53, 43 P. 1075 (Okla.1896), and "a part of Oklahoma's jurisprudence ever since."

* * * The State charged the defendant with first degree child abuse murder. The trial court also instructed the jury on the lesser included offense of second degree murder, in the commission of the underlying felony of child neglect. The jury convicted the defendant of this lesser offense. The appellant in *Quillen* argued on appeal that this conviction violated the merger doctrine, because her commission of felony child neglect—failing to get medical care for her newborn child—was not a felony independent from the homicidal act. The State argued that the plain language of the second degree murder statute authorized a conviction where the killing of a human being results from the commission of any felony other than the unlawful acts enumerated in the first degree felony murder statute. The State reasoned that this Court's application of the merger doctrine to void a conviction authorized by the plain language of the statute would defeat legislative intent, and urged the Court to abandon the merger doctrine.

This Court in *Quillen* rejected the State's arguments, finding that the merger doctrine was "not based on statutory language" but derived from policy considerations:

> [W]ithout the merger doctrine, any person who commits a felony, other than one enumerated for First Degree Felony Murder, from which a death that is not excusable or justified results, can be prosecuted for Second Degree Felony Murder. Although the State argues that such concerns are no longer viable, we find this argument unpersuasive. We further disagree with the State's argument that the merger doctrine is contra to clear legislative intent. The fact that this Court has recognized the merger doctrine for over one hundred years without legislative intervention lends credibility to the conclusion that this Court's application of the merger doctrine is not at odds with legislative intent.

Based on the facts, the Court found that the merger doctrine required reversal of the murder conviction:

> [T]he felony charge upon which Appellant's Second Degree Felony Murder conviction is predicated, Child Neglect, was not separate from the act which caused the death. Therefore, we find that the underlying felony merged into the homicide and could not be used to sustain the Second Degree Felony Murder conviction.

The Court also held that the appropriate remedy was to modify appellant's conviction to the underlying felony of child neglect. In this regard, the Court reasoned:

> In finding the Appellant guilty of Second Degree Felony Murder the jury necessarily found the evidence sufficient to prove the felony of Child Neglect beyond a reasonable doubt. Therefore, we modify Appellant's sentence to this lesser crime and modify the sentence to fifteen years imprisonment.

Appellant argues persuasively that the predicate felony of using a vehicle to facilitate the intentional discharge of a firearm is *not* independent from the homicidal act of shooting Vernon Sutton, and that his conviction therefore violates the merger doctrine set forth in *Quillen.* This case sharply presents the question of whether the merger doctrine remains an appropriate limitation of the statutory definition of second degree felony murder. After careful consideration, the Court abandons this judicially created limitation on second degree felony murder and overrules *Quillen.*

* * * Today the Court finds that what began as an early judicial limitation on the harshness of felony murder at common law could readily usurp the modern Legislature's constitutional authority to reasonably define the crime of felony murder.

> The truth is that in this jurisdiction, no act is a crime unless made so by statute, and *where the crime is defined by statute such definition must be relied on rather than the common law* or some other definition of the act so classified as a crime.

(emphasis added). In interpreting and applying the criminal statutes, our purpose is to ascertain the intent of the Legislature, as evidenced primarily "in the ordinary meaning of the words of the statute construed in view of the connection in which they are used, and of the evil to be remedied."

The Legislature has defined second degree felony murder as the killing of a human being perpetrated by a person "engaged in the commission of any felony other than" the enumerated felonies in the first degree felony murder statute. The term "any" is defined by *Webster's Third New International Dictionary* 97(Unabridged ed., 1986) as:

> **1b:** one, no matter what one: EVERY—used as a function word esp. in assertions or denials to indicate one that is selected without **restriction or limitation of choice; 2b:** ALL—used as a function word to indicate the maximum or whole of a number or quantity.

We therefore interpret the phrase "any felony" in section 7018(2) to mean every felony other than those enumerated in the first degree felony murder statute.

We . . . conclude that the current legislative classification of criminal homicides by their respective degrees, defined by distinct factual elements, obviates the need for the merger doctrine.

The case before us today well illustrates the objectionable effects of the merger doctrine when applied to the facts. Riding from a protected position in a passing vehicle, Appellant repeatedly fired on an unsuspecting group of people standing near the street and killed a man. This fatal attack was neither excusable nor justifiable, and therefore it was a criminal homicide, either murder or manslaughter, under Oklahoma law. The jury at trial clearly rejected the charge of malice aforethought murder. However, when the jury found Appellant guilty of second degree felony murder, it *necessarily* concluded, beyond a reasonable doubt, that Appellant feloniously used a vehicle to facilitate the intentional discharge of a firearm; that he did so "in conscious disregard for the safety of any other person or persons"; and that he caused the death of a human being as a result.

Application of the merger doctrine in this case, by reversing Appellant's second degree murder conviction and modifying his conviction to the underlying felony, would be a miscarriage of justice. The *mens rea* associated with this type of drive-by shooting is either the malice aforethought of first degree murder, i.e., "that deliberate intention" unlawfully to take away the life of a human being which can be "inferred from the fact of killing," and "may be formed instantly" before the fatal act; or the "depraved mind" emblematic of second degree murder, i.e., perpetrating an imminently dangerous act, "regardless of human life, although without any premeditated design to effect the death of any particular individual." As a matter of history and policy, it is entirely reasonable for the Legislature to punish the killing of a person during the commission of this type of dangerous felony as murder in the first or second degree.

The felony crimes of assault and battery, child neglect, caretaker abuse and neglect, operation of a motor vehicle while intoxicated, unlawful possession and use of firearms and explosives, using a vehicle to facilitate intentional discharge of a firearm, and a host of other felonies, can have deadly consequences. The Legislature is well within reason to define killings during the commission of these dangerous felonies as murder, even when the felony is not "independent" of the act or acts resulting in death. Indeed, it is when such felonies destroy life that they are most deserving of the infamy and punishment of murder. Continued adherence to the merger doctrine, and the remedy as established in *Quillen*, would, in many instances, nullify the proper exercise of the Legislature's power to define and punish murder. We will not follow that course.

Appellant killed a human being in the commission of using a vehicle to facilitate intentional discharge of a firearm. He is, at the very least, guilty of second degree murder under the plain language of section 701.8(2) of Title 21. His conviction for that offense is authorized by statute, and no plain error occurred. To the extent that *Quillen*, and earlier cases recognizing the merger doctrine as a limitation on the statutory definition of second degree felony murder, including *Massie*, 1976 OK CR 174, ¶ 16, 553 P.2d 186, 191, *Tucker*, 1984 OK CR 36, ¶ 3, 675 P.2d 459, 461, *Sullinger*,

1984 OK CR 44, ¶3, 675 P.2d 472, 473, and *State v. McCann*, 1995 OK CR 70, ¶3, 907 P.2d 239, 240, are inconsistent with our ruling today, those cases are overruled. Proposition Five is denied.

* * *

DECISION

The Judgment and Sentence of the District Court of Okmulgee County is AFFIRMED....

A. Johnson, Presiding Judge, Specially Concurring.

I agree with the decision to abandon the merger doctrine as a limitation to second degree felony murder. The purpose of the merger limitation—to bring fairness to the potential harshness of the felony murder rule—is a sound one. A fair and consistent application of this particular limitation, however, is difficult. In *Quillen v. State*, 2007 OK CR 22, 163 P.3d 587, this Court extended the application of the merger doctrine to the non-assaultive crime of felony child neglect in an apparent attempt to achieve a fair and appropriate balance between moral culpability and criminal liability in that case. This broad application of the merger limitation and the difficulty of its application in *Quillen* lead me to reexamine the continued validity of the merger limitation in this case. There may be future cases that test the wisdom of this decision. Nevertheless, I am confident that this Court's expressed commitment to maintaining the distinction between the different degrees and forms of murder, manslaughter and other homicide crimes will resolve any issues of unfair over-charging and undeserved convictions and sentences.

C. Johnson, Judge, Specially Concurring.

It is with some hesitation that I concur in the Court's decision in this case to abandon the merger doctrine. The merger doctrine operates to preserve the different degrees of homicide crimes. I understand the position of the majority regarding the historical context in which the merger doctrine developed, but I do not agree that the problem the merger doctrine seeks to remedy has been eliminated by the legislative classification of differing degrees of homicide. Second Degree Felony Murder allows a person who commits any felony other than one enumerated for First Degree Felony Murder, from which a death results that is not excusable or justified, to be prosecuted for Second Degree Felony Murder. The prosecutors make the determination of which crime to charge and the abandonment of the merger doctrine allows them, under these circumstances, unrestrained discretion to charge the greater offense of Second Degree Felony Murder to the exclusion of lesser degrees of homicide. Thus, in the absence of the merger doctrine, it will be even more important that district courts give instructions on lesser forms of homicide where such instructions are supported by the evidence as is required by *Shrum v. State*, 1999 OK CR 41, 991 P.2d 1032.

Comments and Questions

(1) Only a few states accept the position that there is no merger of the felonious assault and the resulting homicide for felony murder. What is the rationale for the

rule? The more usual statement of the principle is found in *Barnett v. State*, 783 So. 2d 927 (Ala. Crim. App. 2000), and *People v. Morgan*, 758 N.E.2d 813 (2001). In *Barnett*, the State sought to use a felonious assault as the basis for the felony murder charge, while in *Morgan* the predicate felony was aggravated battery. Both courts rejected the felony murder convictions. The court in *Barnett* wrote that a contrary ruling would effectively eliminate the elements of murder and substitute the lower crime of assault. The *Morgan* court agreed:

> Potentially, then, all fatal shootings could be charged as felony murder based upon aggravated battery and/or aggravated discharge of a firearm. [The result would be to] effectively eliminate the second degree murder statute and also to eliminate the need for the State to prove an intentional or knowing killing in most murder cases. Given the foregoing considerations, we agree with the appellate court that where the acts constituting forcible felonies arise from and are inherent in the act of murder itself, those acts cannot serve as predicate felonies for a charge of felony murder.

In 2006, the Iowa Supreme Court overruled 24 years of precedent to join the majority of states adopting the merger doctrine. *State v. Heemstra*, 721 N.W.2d 549 (Iowa 2006). If a defendant is charged with felony hit-and-run, is it felony-murder if the victim dies? In contrast to *Heemstra*, in *Barnett* the Oklahoma Court of Criminal Appeals abandoned the merger doctrine after more than a century of using it to preclude felony-murder.

(2) "The People's evidence, if believed, established that the defendant went to Fennell's apartment uninvited and armed with a butcher knife and spray can; that when the apartment door was opened, he lunged across the threshold, sprayed Fennell with a choking gas, and attacked him with the knife; and that when Aleem came to Fennell's aid, the defendant fatally stabbed him."

Was the underlying felony here burglary—which in New York does not merge—or assault—which does merge? *See People v. Miller*, 297 N.E.2d 85, 86–87 (N.Y. 1973):

> It should be apparent that the Legislature, in including burglary as one of the enumerated felonies as a basis for felony murder, recognized that persons within domiciles are in greater peril from those entering the domicile with criminal intent, than persons on the street who are being subjected to the same criminal intent. Thus, the burglary statutes prescribe greater punishment for a criminal act committed within the domicile than for the same act committed on the street. Where, as here, the criminal act underlying the burglary is an assault with a dangerous weapon, the likelihood that the assault will culminate in a homicide is significantly increased by the situs of the assault. When the assault takes place within the domicile, the victim may be more likely to resist the assault; the victim is also less likely to be able to avoid the consequences of the assault, since his paths of retreat and escape may be barred or severely restricted by furniture, walls and other obstructions incidental to buildings.

(3) Suppose the defendant committed the dangerous felony, but he can disprove the particular state of mind requirement for the felony, will the felony murder conviction be valid? No, "specific intent to commit the underlying felony is necessary to the operation of the felony murder doctrine." *People v. Ireland*, 450 P.2d 580, 590 (Cal. 1969). This principle was also demonstrated in *Collins v. State*, 420 A.2d 170 (Del. 1980). The defendant there was given immunity from prosecution for robbery, but not for murder. The government then proved that the killing had occurred during the commission of the robbery. The Supreme Court of Delaware treated the immunity as an acquittal of the robbery charges. Therefore, "an acquittal of robbery requires a determination that defendant did not commit the predicate crime of robbery which is necessarily required for a finding of guilt of the offense of felony murder; hence, [the] felony murder prosecution ... is barred by defendant's acquittal through immunity of the underlying robbery." 420 A.2d at 176. *See also People v. Croy*, 710 P.2d 392 (Cal. 1985), where the court found that the reversal of the robbery conviction required striking down the felony murder conviction which had been predicated on the robbery. But most courts would not require that there be a conviction for the underlying felony, only that the government prove beyond a reasonable doubt all the elements of that crime. It would be difficult to find a case "where a felony murder conviction was overturned despite the fact that all the essential elements of the underlying felony had been proved, merely because a formal conviction had not been obtained." *United States v. Greene*, 834 F.2d 1067, 1072 (D.C. Cir. 1987).

[b] During the Commission of a Felony

People v. Johnson

Court of Appeal of California

5 Cal. App. 4th 552, 7 Cal. Rptr. 2d 23 (1992)

Reardon, Associate Justice.

A jury convicted appellant John Edward Johnson, Jr., of first degree murder with special circumstances. He pled guilty to charges of assault with a firearm, vehicle theft, being an ex-felon in possession of a deadly weapon, and two counts of robbery. Sentenced to a life term without possibility of parole for murder that is to be served consecutive to a determinate term of nine years, four months for the other offenses, Johnson appeals.

I. Facts

On May 13, 1989, Elaine Williams died as the result of an automobile accident. The car she was driving was struck by a car driven by appellant John Edward Johnson, Jr. Thirty minutes earlier, Johnson had robbed two men of cash and a ring and had fled in a stolen vehicle. The robberies had been immediately reported to police, who set up a county-wide roadblock in an attempt to apprehend the robber. Various law enforcement officers spotted Johnson's vehicle as he drove from the robbery site toward the San Francisco International Airport.

Before Williams' vehicle was hit, Johnson had lost control of the stolen car which was moving at least 58 miles per hour. After impact, Johnson left the car and entered a nearby marsh. He was arrested on the other side of it. Police later retrieved a revolver and cash from the marsh and found a ring and a warm-up suit in the car.

Johnson was advised of and waived his *Miranda* rights, agreeing to talk to San Mateo Police Officer Malcolm Laner. After a short interview, he sought counsel. Laner stopped the questioning and advised him that he would be charged with murder and armed robbery. Johnson then told Laner, "[i]t was just because I heard the sirens."

Johnson was charged with the murder of Williams, enhanced by the use of a firearm. The information also alleged two special circumstances: that Johnson killed Williams during the commission of the two robberies. It charged two counts of robbery, one count of assault with a deadly weapon and one count of attempted murder, each enhanced by the use of a firearm; and single counts of vehicle theft and being an ex-felon in possession of a firearm.

At trial, Johnson testified that after the San Mateo robberies, he drove south on Highway 101 to Highway 92 and saw no one follow him. He drove to Highway 280, but no one was chasing him. Driving north on Highway 280, he first saw what appeared to be a law enforcement officer in a vehicle. When the officer turned on his red and blue flashing lights, Johnson sped up. When he lost sight of the pursuing car, Johnson turned off the freeway and drove for eight or nine minutes in a residential area. During this period, he saw no police and thought he was safe. Johnson testified that he then drove through the residential area to El Camino Real in Burlingame and headed back to Highway 101. Heading north, Johnson thought he saw another police officer, so he got off the freeway at the Millbrae exit. Then, Johnson spotted the airport police, who began to pursue him. He drove on toward the airport, where another police vehicle began to follow him. Johnson testified that this vehicle did not have lights or sirens on. He passed a van and hit another car very hard. Dizzy and shaken, he fled the scene but was soon arrested.

Johnson admitted the robberies, assault and automobile theft charges, but denied making any statement about hearing sirens. On rebuttal, an officer who participated in the county-wide roadblock testified that if Johnson had taken the Millbrae exit off of Highway 101 north as he had testified, the officer would not have seen Johnson's car as he did. An officer had testified that he had driven from the robbery site to a location about 4 miles from the accident site by freeway—a distance of 22 miles—in 22 minutes and 40 seconds. Driving two slightly different routes took approximately one minute longer. The prosecution argued that the accident occurred within 30 minutes after Johnson fled the robbery site. Johnson countered that he had reached a place of temporary safety before police began to pursue him. Ultimately, the jury found Johnson guilty of first degree murder and found both of the special circumstances allegations to be true.

...

III. Sufficiency of Evidence

A. Generally

Johnson next contends that the evidence was insufficient to support both the first degree murder conviction or the special circumstances allegations. He argues that there was insufficient evidence to support the finding that the murder took place in the commission of the robberies. Both the first degree felony-murder verdict and the special circumstances aspects of the jury's verdict depend on a finding that the robberies continued until the homicide occurred. At trial, his motion for a judgment of acquittal on the special circumstances allegations, the success of which would have precluded a verdict of first degree felony murder, was denied. On appeal, he contends both that the motion was improperly denied—that the People's case-in-chief was insufficient to support the conviction and findings—and that the evidence in the record as a whole was insufficient to support the verdict.

B. Place of Temporary Safety

Johnson argues that the evidence established that the robberies had ended—that he had reached a place of temporary safety—before the homicide occurred. He urges that this determination turns on his state of mind, rather than on an objective, reasonable-person standard. Johnson testified at trial that he felt safe before police began to pursue him. On appeal, he argues that there was no evidence to contradict his testimony; thus, there was no substantial evidence to support the contrary finding that was necessarily made by the jury when it found him guilty of first degree murder and found the special circumstances allegations to be true.

The issue of whether the "place of temporary safety" is determined on an objective or subjective standard appears to be a case of first impression. However, the law of felony murder is well settled. One who kills another in the perpetration of a robbery is guilty of first degree murder, whether the killing is intentional or unintentional. To find a robbery—murder special circumstance allegation to be true, a jury must find that the murder was committed during the commission of a robbery. When an officer or citizen is murdered while in immediate pursuit of a robber who flees from the scene of the crime with the fruit of that offense, the killing is in perpetration of the robbery—a crime that is not legally complete until the robber has won his or her way even momentarily to a place of temporary safety. When the robber is still in flight, he or she has not yet achieved a place of temporary safety.

Whether a defendant has reached a place of temporary safety is a question of fact for the jury. Case law does not specifically address whether this determination is to be based on the defendant's subjective belief or whether objective criteria is also relevant to this inquiry. However, we are satisfied that an objective standard is to be applied. The black letter law announced in the relevant cases states the rule in terms of whether the defendant actually reached a place of temporary safety, rather than whether the defendant believed that he or she reached such a safe location.

Certainly, appellate courts have considered the defendant's belief about whether he or she reached a place of temporary safety. However, this does not indicate that the defendant's state of mind is dispositive on this issue. Objective criteria have also been considered relevant to this issue. The fact that Williams was killed 30 minutes after the robbery does not preclude a finding that the homicide occurred in the commission of the robbery.

Finally, in first degree felony-murder cases, the prosecution must prove only that the defendant intended to commit the underlying offense—it need not establish malice, premeditation or deliberation. To also require the People to establish an additional state of mind—that the defendant did not believe that he reached a place of temporary safety—would thwart application of the felony-murder rule. For all these reasons, we conclude that the issue to be resolved is whether a robber had actually reached a place of temporary safety, not whether the defendant thought that he or she had reached such a location.

Thus, the issue of whether Johnson believed that he reached a place of temporary safety is only one factor for the jury to consider. At trial, Johnson argued that he had driven in a residential area for eight or nine minutes before returning to the freeway where police pursuit began. The prosecution attempted to prove that this was not possible—that, given the time elapsed and distance between the robberies and the accident, Johnson must necessarily have been in constant flight. The prosecution bolstered its argument with other objective evidence: Johnson did not have time to dispose of the gun or the stolen property or to change into the warm-up suit that the state theorized he had placed in the stolen car to alter his appearance after the robberies. The jury's verdict of first degree felony murder and the two special circumstances findings imply that it found the prosecution's theory more plausible and therefore rejected Johnson's argument. This issue was within the jury's purview.

We may not set aside the trial court judgment for insufficiency of evidence unless it clearly appears that under no hypothesis whatever is there sufficient evidence to support it. Under the prosecution's hypothesis, the jury could have found that Johnson did not reach a place of temporary safety. Thus, there was sufficient evidence and reasonable inferences from that evidence to support the jury's verdict on both the special circumstances findings and the first degree murder conviction.

C. Continuing Transaction

Johnson also argues that the robbery and homicide were not parts of a continuing transaction. First degree felony murder does not require a strict causal relation between the felony and the killing. The only nexus required is that both are part of one continuous transaction. A fleeing robber's failure to reach a place of temporary safety is sufficient to establish the continuity of the robbery within the felony-murder rule. We have already found that there was sufficient evidence to support the jury's implied finding that Johnson did not reach a place of temporary safety before the killing occurred.

Robbery is not confined to a fixed location, but may be spread over a considerable distance and varying periods of time. Thus, the fact that Williams was killed 30 minutes after the robbery does not preclude a finding that the homicide occurred in the commission of the robbery. Likewise, the fact that the homicide occurred more than

22 miles from the robbery does not necessarily preclude a finding that the killing occurred in the commission of the robbery. A burglar fleeing from police may be prosecuted for felony murder when a high-speed chase leads to an automobile accident, killing the driver of the other vehicle. The jury had before it the evidence from which to properly determine that the killing of Elaine Williams was a continuing part of the robberies.

Comments and Questions

(1) Under California law, was the defendant guilty of murder? In what way was he attempting to perpetrate, or perpetrating, a robbery?

(2) The Ohio Supreme Court has held that attempted felony murder is not a recognized offense. The Court noted that an attempted crime requires a mens rea of purposely or knowingly, whereas no intent to kill is required in order for the state to obtain a conviction for felony murder. Moreover, a person could be convicted for felony murder even if the death was unintended, and the Court reasoned that it was impossible to purposefully or knowingly cause an unintended death. *State v. Nolan*, 995 N.E.2d 902 (Ohio 2014).

Many cases deal with the problem raised in *Johnson:* Is a felony being committed during an escape? The courts consistently agree with the California court and find the felony was still being committed. For a striking application of the principle, see *State v. Lopez*, 845 P.2d 478, 482 (Ariz. Ct. App. 1992), where the defendant argued that because he was arrested just after the attempted armed robbery, but before the police officer was shot, he could not be found guilty of felony murder. The court disagreed:

> Even if Lopez had been handcuffed or … ordered to lie on the ground, the jury still could have found him guilty of felony murder because his actions were the proximate cause of Richards' death.… Because Lopez set into action the chain of events leading to Richards' death, and did nothing to "indicate to those present that he had abandoned the robbery or that it was at an end," he cannot escape liability for the consequences of his actions.

See also People v. Auman, 67 P.3d 741 (Colo. App. 2002), *rev'd on other grounds*, 109 P.3d 647 (Colo. 2005) (felony murder even though police officer was shot five minutes after the defendant had surrendered to the police).

(3) In *State v. Metalski*, 185 A. 351, 353 (N.J.E. & A. 1936), the government proved the following:

> In the early morning of the date named, Yenser and Matey, state troopers, in a Ford sedan, were patrolling State Highway No. 25, just west of New Brunswick. Matey was driving and Yenser was sitting to Matey's right. A coupe, with Pennsylvania license plates, was traveling eastwardly at a high rate of speed, and the troopers endeavored to overtake it. They temporarily lost track of it, but again came up to it and pulled alongside of it, and Trooper Yenser blew his whistle. The testimony was that both cars were then traveling

> between 75 and 80 miles an hour; that the coupe again shot forward; that the troopers again pulled up alongside of the coupe; and that as Yenser was about to blow his whistle again, a shot was fired, which struck Yenser in the face, causing almost immediate death.
>
> It was undisputed that the coupe was occupied by the defendant and one Whitey Morton, who, at about 2 o'clock in the morning in question, had held up a tavern known as Palms Garden Café, on Ridge Avenue, in Philadelphia, and were fleeing in a car which they had taken from a garage in Philadelphia without the knowledge of the garage attendant.

Felony murder? See the dissenting opinion which would have reversed the conviction:

> Here, the police officers were unaware of the commission of the robbery; they were moved to action by the unlawful speed of the automobile. The state proved (the evidence was uncontroverted) that the robbery was committed at 2 a. m.; that at 4 a. m., or shortly thereafter, plaintiff in error and his accomplice, apparently under the influence of intoxicating liquor, entered a roadside diner near Plainsboro, where they remained for a half hour or more, that while eating, drinking, and conversing with the patrons; that they re-entered the automobile, and, after proceeding several miles in the direction of Newark (their destination was the home of accused's mother in that city), were hailed by the police officers. The fact that they then had possession of the money stolen is not, in the circumstances, material; the fatal resistance was designed to escape apprehension and punishment for the completed crime, not to consummate an uncompleted crime of the statutory class. As well might it be said that, if plaintiff in error and his accomplice had continued the journey, and, two or three days or a week or a month later, while in possession of the loot, or a part thereof, killed to escape arrest for the original robbery, the homicide occurred in the perpetration of the latter crime. "It is evident that, if the criminals had escaped and were a mile away from the place of the crime, it could not be said that they were then in the commission of a felony."

(4) The court in *Commonwealth v. Stelma*, 192 A. 906, 908 (Pa. 1937), made the following statement:

> The defendant's argument that the intention to rob originated subsequent to the assault upon the deceased need not be seriously considered in view of the verdict of the jury. Moreover, even though such were the case, it is immaterial when the design to rob was conceived, if the homicide occurred while defendant was perpetrating or attempting to perpetrate a robbery. Where the killing occurs in the perpetration of any of the crimes specifically named in the statute referred to, the intent to kill is immaterial. Such considerations do not affect the situation here presented because the circumstances leading up to the attack on Doyle indicate an assault with an intent to rob, and the defendant has twice confessed his crime in writing. The ques-

> tion of defendant's guilt and the degree of the crime are primarily for the jury to determine, and upon appeal this court will not arbitrarily substitute its judgment for that of the jury, even if it had the power to do so.

Under *Johnson*, was the defendant's argument valid? In *Commonwealth v. Legg*, 417 A.2d 1152, 1154 (Pa. 1980), the trial judge instructed the jury that "the intent to commit the felony of robbery may be formed by the actor, the robber, the one doing the acts, either before or after the infliction of the fatal wound."

The court agreed with the defendant that the instruction was an incorrect statement of law.

> When an actor engages in one of the statutorily enumerated felonies and a killing occurs, the law, via the felony-murder rule, allows the finder of fact to infer the killing was malicious from the fact that the actor engaged in a felony of such a dangerous nature to human life because the actor, as held to a standard of a reasonable man, knew or should have known that death might result from the felony. Additionally, a greater penalty is imposed for murder of the second degree or felony murder, than that imposed for murder of the third degree even though the latter also is malicious. In so providing, the law seeks to add a greater deterrent to engaging in particularly dangerous felonies.
>
> But, where an actor kills prior to formulating the intent to commit the underlying felony, we cannot say the actor knew or should have known death might occur from involvement in a dangerous felony because no involvement in a dangerous felony exists since the intent to commit the felony is not yet formulated. Also, the greater deterrent is not necessary, and the rule has no application.

The Supreme Court of Tennessee stated the "majority position":

> Given the fact that the felony-murder rule is a legal fiction in which the intent and the malice to commit the underlying felony is "transferred" to elevate an unintentional killing to first-degree murder, we are reluctant to extend the doctrine to include cases in which there was no intent to commit the felony at the time of the killing. Thus, in a felony-murder case, intent to commit the underlying felony must exist prior to or *concurrent with the commission of the act causing the death of the victim*."

State v. Buggs, 995 S.W.2d 102 (Tenn. 1999); *accord State v. Allen*, 875 A.2d 724 (Md. 2005); *Nay v. State*, 167 P.3d 430 (Nev. 2007) (adopting the majority view). *But see State v. Morganherring*, 517 S.E.2d 622 (N.C. 1999):

> Where there is a continuous transaction, the temporal order of the killing and the taking is immaterial. Provided that the theft and the killing are aspects of a single transaction, it is immaterial whether the intent to commit the theft was formed before or after the killing.

Morganherring, 517 S.E.2d at 641.

State v. Maudlin

Supreme Court of Kansas
529 P.2d 124 (1974)

KAUL, JUSTICE.

Omitting formalities the information reads as follows:

> ... [O]n or about the 27th day of November, 1973 one Robert Maudlin, did maliciously and wilfully kill and murder a certain Gary McCallon, while in the perpetration or attempt to perpetrate the crime of selling, administering, delivering, distributing or dispensing any opiates, opium, or narcotic drugs, a felony....

Our statute defining murder in the first degree reads as follows:

> Murder in the first degree. Murder in the first degree is the killing of a human being committed maliciously, willfully, deliberately and with premeditation or committed in the perpetration or attempt to perpetrate any felony.

Defendant filed a motion to dismiss taking the position that the deceased was not killed nor did he die while the defendant was alleged to have been perpetrating or attempting to perpetrate a felony.

The trial judge filed a well-reasoned memorandum decision setting forth the facts and thoroughly analyzing and discussing all of the issues and the cases from other jurisdictions cited by both parties. We believe the trial court's ruling was entirely correct. Therefore, we shall quote its memorandum decision in full:

> The defendant's motion to dismiss was argued to the court on March 22, 1974, and was taken under advisement. I have now reviewed the file and considered the briefs and arguments of counsel.
>
> The State contends that the evidence in this case will show that on the evening of November 27, 1974, Steve Cottrell and Gary McCallon purchased a quantity of heroin from the defendant Robert Maudlin. Thereafter, Steve and Gary went to Steve's apartment where Gary prepared and injected himself with a shot of the heroin. He subsequently died from an overdose. For the purpose of this motion, these facts must be accepted as true. The question presented, then, is whether the death of Gary McCallon under these circumstances was "the killing of a human being ... committed in the perpetration ... of any felony."
>
> The question has not been decided in this state. There is precedent from other states, however, although it is not in accord.
>
> This difference results primarily from a difference of opinion as to what constitutes a homicide committed in the perpetration or attempt to perpetrate a felony. Our court has defined this to mean that there must be "a direct causal relation between the commission of the felony and the homicide."
>
> The State relies rather strongly herein on the ruling in *State v. Moffitt* [199 Kan. 514, 431 P.2d 879]. The facts in that case were that the defendant, a

convicted felon, fired a pistol while assaulting two pedestrians and inadvertently killed a woman sitting on a motorcycle some distance down the street. The court held that the possession of a pistol, after conviction of a felony was a felony and was inherently dangerous to human life, and that there was a direct causal relation between the commission of such felony and the homicide. It further held that it was no defense to the felony murder that the defendant did not intend to kill the victim.

I have no quarrel with this reasoning. It is to be noted, however, that possession of a pistol by a convicted felon is a continuing offense.

It should be further noted that even more directly related to the homicide [than] mere possession of the pistol was the fact that Moffitt fired the pistol at two pedestrians in the perpetration of a felonious assault upon them. Thus direct causal relation was not dependent upon the concept of an illegal possession of a gun.

In the case before me, the defendant's only connection with the homicide was that he sold a quantity of heroin to the deceased who some time later, voluntarily and out of the presence of the defendant, injected himself with an overdose and died as a result. This is not a case where the defendant injected the heroin into the deceased, or otherwise determined the amount of the dose, or assisted in administering the dosage, where different considerations are involved.

Under the State's theory, the time element, or other conduct subsequent to or preceding the sale, are not necessarily relevant if death results from use of the drug. It is felony-murder whether the victim injected himself a few hours later, as here, or a few days later, or whether the purchaser sold or furnished the drug to another who took the overdose. The result is the controlling factor.

The objective of deterring the sale and use of heroin is, of course, very desirable, but an objective in itself does not justify a rule that is otherwise unsound. For example, there are many drugs other than heroin which are inherently dangerous if taken in excess. It is not only a felony to sell such drugs but to manufacture, prescribe, administer, deliver, distribute, dispense or compound these substances. It is also becoming increasingly accepted that alcohol can be as addictive and inherently dangerous as many drug[s]. The State regulates the sale and use of many things other than drugs, liquor and firearms in the interest of the public welfare and safety. Any one of these transactions could conceivably be encompassed under the State's theory where death resulted from the use of a controlled item. Such a drastic extension of the felony-murder rule by judicial decree is unwarranted, in my opinion.

What then, constitutes "a direct causal relation" within the meaning of the felony-murder rule? It seems to me that something more is required beyond the fact the death sequentially followed the sale of the heroin. I have not

> found, nor has counsel cited, a ruling by our Supreme Court on this precise point, but it has been discussed elsewhere.
>
> These cases hold in principle that there must be a closer and more direct causal connection between criminal conduct and a homicide than is required by the tort concept of proximate cause, and that to convict of felony-murder it must be shown that the conduct causing the death was done while in the commission of a felony or in furtherance of the design to commit the felony. I believe *State v. Moffitt* supports this view. In the case before me, the felony involved was the sale of heroin, and it was completed upon consummation of the sale.

We would note that on the facts presented here the sole act of defendant was selling the heroin. The injection by the purchaser was out of the presence of defendant. In the California cases, cited by the state, the accused actively participated in administering the drugs, or at least was present while the purchaser consumed an overdose of narcotic tablets.

Our statute explicitly requires that the killing be "committed in the perpetration or attempt to perpetrate any felony." Under the facts presented in the instant case the commission of the felony (the act of selling heroin) completely terminated when the seller and the purchaser parted company. As pointed out by the trial court, this is not a case such as *State v. Moffitt*, wherein the felony relied upon (possession of a pistol after conviction of a felony) was a continuing one.

The clear import of the language of the statute cannot be broadened so as to encompass felony murder upon the facts presented herein.

The judgment is affirmed.

Comments and Questions

(1) Is the result here consistent with *Johnson*? What result if the defendant had been in the presence of the deceased when the heroin was injected? In *Heacock v. Commonwealth*, 323 S.E.2d 90, 94 (Va. 1984), the defendant supplied cocaine to Wilson at a drug party. Wilson died from an overdose, and the defendant was convicted of felony murder:

> The underlying felony was distribution of cocaine, a drug the defendant should have known was inherently dangerous to human life; Wilson ingested that drug and, as we have said, it is immaterial who made the injection; Wilson died of "acute intravenous cocainism"; thus, cause and effect were proximately interrelated.

(2) In distinguishing the *Moffitt* case (possession of a pistol), the court noted that the instant case did not involve a "continuing felony." What is a continuing felony? What result if this were a continuing felony? Assume a defendant crashes the car he is driving into a pedestrian. If a robbery was committed by the defendant 20 minutes earlier, he is driving a stolen car, and five minutes earlier he had been chased briefly by a police officer for running a stop sign, is it felony-murder?

(3) In *Campbell v. State*, 227 So. 2d 873 (Fla. 1969), the defendant robbed a bank in Georgia and drove across the state line to Florida. Florida officers pursued him, and one Florida officer was killed in the pursuit by the defendant. Is this felony murder in Florida?

(4) This statement describes the important role jurors will play in applying the felony murder rule:

> [T]he question is to be submitted to the jury, under an appropriate charge. The jury should be instructed to give consideration to whether the homicide and the felony occurred at the same location or, if not, to the distance separating the two locations. Weight may also be placed on whether there is an interval of time between the commission of the felony and the commission of the homicide. The jury may properly consider such additional factors as whether the culprits had possession of the fruits of criminal activity, whether the police, watchmen or concerned citizens were in close pursuit, and whether the criminals had reached a place of temporary safety. These factors are not exclusive; others may be appropriate in differing factual settings. If anything, past history demonstrates the fruitlessness of attempting to apply rigid rules to virtually limitless factual variations. No single factor is necessarily controlling; it is the combination of several factors that leads to a justifiable inference.

People v. Gladman, 359 N.E.2d 420, 424 (N.Y. 1976).

Does the following instruction reflect the view set out by the Court of Appeals in *Gladman*?

> It is not enough that the killing occurred soon or presently after the felony was attempted or committed. There must be such a legal relationship between the two that it can be said that the killing occurred by reason and as a part of the felony, to—wit: rape; *or that it occurred before the felony was at an end;* so that the felony had a legal relationship to the killing and was concurrent with it in part, at least, and a part of it in an actual and natural sense. (Emphasis supplied.)

Parson v. State, 222 A.2d 326, 332 (Del. 1966), *cert. denied*, 386 U.S. 935 (1967).

[c] The Extent of Responsibility

Jackson v. State

Court of Appeals of Maryland

408 A.2d 711 (1979)

ORTH, JUDGE.

The issue for decision is whether the accidental killing of a hostage by a law enforcement officer attempting to apprehend robbers fleeing from an armed robbery while holding the hostage at gunpoint constitutes murder in the first degree on the part of the robbers under the Maryland felony murder statute. We hold that it does.

Bernard Sugar and Charlotte Farber operated a jewelry shop located in a shopping area in the 9100 block of the Baltimore National Pike in Howard County. About 9:30 a.m. on 29 April 1977 Jackson and Wells came in. Each brandished a handgun and forced Sugar and Farber to lie on the floor. The robbers took jewelry valued at more than $10,000 from a safe and display cabinets.

At 10:05 a.m. one Charlene Kelly entered the store, asked for Farber, and was told by Wells that she was not there but would return in half an hour. Suspicious, Kelly left the store and contacted the police. Leonard Shipley, a mailman, appeared on the scene. He also became suspicious, but as he attempted to leave the store Wells stopped him at gunpoint. The two men struggled, Wells struck Shipley on the head and forced him to join Sugar and Farber on the floor. At 10:15 a.m. Howard County policemen arrived on the scene and announced their presence. Wells started to leave by the front door, saw the police, and ran back in. Both Wells and Jackson attempted to leave by the rear door, were deterred by the police and retreated into the store.

Unable to find another escape route, Wells grabbed Farber, held his handgun to her neck and said, "You do what I do. I walk, you walk, I run, you run. If they shoot me, you're dead. If they shoot me I'm going to kill you." Wells held her in a headlock and kept the gun to her neck. Jackson grasped Sugar, holding him in a similar manner at gunpoint. Jackson and Wells, using Farber and Sugar as shields, left the store by the rear door, disregarding the order of the police to stop and release their hostages.

The robbers forced Farber and Sugar to get in a police car with them and drove away. Before the car reached the exit from the shopping area, gunfire by the police disabled it. The felons stole another police car, and with Jackson at the wheel and their hostages still held at gunpoint, drove away amid a fusillade of shots by the police. They pulled into the westbound lane of State Route 99, forced a civilian to stop his car, entered it with the hostages and, with Jackson driving, speeded away, pursued by members of the Howard County Police Department and the Maryland State Police. The fleeing felons evaded a roadblock by driving across a plowed field and eventually proceeded on Interstate 70 towards Baltimore with the police close behind. Wells, holding Farber by the neck and keeping his gun to her head, forced her to kneel on the back seat with her face in the rear window, thus exposing her to gunfire from the pursuing police cars. The chase continued on Interstate 70, on the Baltimore Beltway and east on Route 40 to Ingleside Avenue in Baltimore County. Gunshots by the police had punctured the fleeing vehicle's tires, and it was finally brought to a halt by a roadblock.

Police manning the roadblock, unaware of the presence of the hostages, fired at the car. Law enforcement officers of three counties and the State converged on the scene and placed the car under heavy gunfire. Officer Wayne White of the Howard County Police Department, armed with a shotgun, ran to the car and jumped on its hood. At that moment Wells had his arm out of a window of the car, waiving a revolver in his hand. White swung his shotgun across the top of the car in an attempt to strike Wells's arm and knock the revolver from his hand. The shotgun discharged. Sugar was lying on the front seat of the car. The pellets from the shotgun struck him in the back of his neck, and he died as a result of that wound. After a struggle, Jackson was seized from the driver's seat of the vehicle. Wells was taken from the rear seat. Two .38 caliber revolvers were recovered. The one located in the area in which Jackson was taken into custody contained five live rounds and one spent round. It was cocked. The other gun was found on the rear seat. It was fully loaded.

At the common law, to which the inhabitants of Maryland are entitled, homicide is the killing of a human being by another human being; criminal homicide is homicide without lawful justification or excuse; criminal homicide with malice aforethought is murder; malice aforethought is established, *inter alia*, upon commission of criminal homicide in the perpetration of, or in the attempt to perpetrate, a felony.[3]

The evidence as proffered was sufficient to prove the *corpus delicti* of murder in the first degree if the killing of Sugar may be attributed to Jackson and Wells. It is manifest that, at the time Sugar was killed, Jackson and Wells were perpetrating a felony. Their seizing Sugar and Farber and carrying them to some other place was the felony of kidnapping. The killing was, of course, homicide, as it was the killing of a human being by another human being. It was, as to Jackson and Wells, criminal, being neither justifiable nor excusable. Because the criminal homicide was committed in the perpetration of a felony, malice was established, making it murder. The murder was in the first degree because the felony being perpetrated in its commission was kidnapping. The issue for decision, therefore, boils down to whether Jackson and Wells were criminal agents in the murder.

As the trial judge observed, the case is unusual in that the fatal shot was fired accidently by a police officer and not by the felons perpetrating the kidnapping. But the case is not unique. Application of the felony-murder doctrine to circumstances other than those in which a death is directly caused by the felon perpetrating the underlying felony or his accomplice has harassed courts and excited commentators to critical analyses.

Courts have followed tortuous paths endeavoring to arrive at a sound rationale applicable to a variety of circumstances in determining whether those persons perpetrating the underlying felony are responsible for the lethal act. For example, California enunciated as a test to ascertain if a defendant is guilty of murder when, during the perpetration of a felony, someone is killed by a person other than the defendant or an accomplice, whether the killing was in response to malicious conduct additional to the underlying felony. But then it made the test inapplicable to cases where the victim was being used by the defendant or an accomplice as a shield. It declared that the function of the test was "to provide the trier of fact with a guideline for determining whether the malicious conduct, rather than the underlying felony, *proximately* caused the victim's death. In a shield case this determination may be made without employing that test."

3. There is suggestion that the common law rule ultimately required that the underlying felony be one "dangerous to human life."

Pennsylvania, on the other hand, went the other way. [A] defendant could be found guilty of murder even though the fatal bullet was fired by a police officer in opposition to the felony. The proximate cause theory of murder was applied. "[H]e whose felonious act is the *proximate cause* of another's death is *criminally* responsible for that death...." [This case of *Almeida*, 362 Pa. 596, 68 A.2d 595 (1949), *cert. denied*, 339 U.S. 950, 70 S. Ct. 798, 94 L. Ed. 1364 (1950)] changed the rule previously followed that in order to convict for felony-murder, the killing must have been done by the defendant or by an accomplice. In *Commonwealth ex rel. Smith v. Myers*, 438 Pa. 218, 261 A.2d 550 (1970), there was a prosecution for murder arising from the death of an off-duty policeman who was shot while attempting to thwart the escape of the defendant and co-participants in an armed robbery. The trial judge had charged the jury that even if the victim was killed by another policeman, who was attempting to prevent the robbery, or was returning the fire of the felons, the felons would be guilty of murder. A majority of the court, over vigorous dissent, held that the instruction denied a fair trial. The way had been paved for this ruling by extending *Almeida* in *Commonwealth v. Thomas*, 382 Pa. 639, 117 A.2d 204 (1955), and by overruling *Thomas* in *Commonwealth v. Redline*, 391 Pa. 486, 137 A.2d 472 (1958). So the court in *Myers* expressly overruled *Almeida*, stating that it gave "Almeida burial, taking it out of its limbo, and plunging it downward into the bowels of the earth." Thus *Myers* reverted the Pennsylvania law to the pre-*Almeida* rule—to convict of murder under the felony-murder doctrine, the killing must be done by the hand of the felon or an accomplice.

Four score years ago the Court of Criminal Appeals of Texas was faced with a case comparable to the one before us. Robbers stopped a train to rob the express car. They forced one of the trainmen to stand in a place of danger, where he was accidentally shot and killed by a passenger or by one of the robbers. Texas followed essentially the common law definition of murder and by statute made murder in the perpetration or attempted perpetration of certain felonies, including that of robbery, murder in the first degree. The court held that the causal connection was complete. It may not have been, the court observed, the primary object of the robber, Taylor, and his companions to have the trainman killed, but

> their act was unlawful. It was a felony. They chose to put deceased in a dangerous place, in order to consummate their purpose, regardless of whether he was killed or not. They put him there in order to effect the robbery, and while they required him to remain at the post assigned him, which was a place of danger, he was shot. His life was taken on account of their direct and lawless act, and they are responsible for his murder, whether it was occasioned by their own volition or by the shots of their adversaries; and their act was the proximate cause of the destruction of his life, and they cannot escape the consequences.

The holding was followed by the court with respect to the conviction for the same murder of another of the robbers, one Keaton. "[C]ertainly [Keaton] would be responsible for the reasonable, natural, and probable result of his act, to wit, placing deceased in a place of danger, where he would probably lose his life."

The basic premise is that "[a] person is only criminally liable for what he has caused, that is, there must be a causal relationship between his act and the harm sustained for which he is prosecuted." But

> [i]t is not essential to the existence of a causal relationship that the ultimate harm which has resulted was foreseen or intended by the actor. It is sufficient that the ultimate harm is one which a reasonable man would foresee as being reasonably related to the acts of the defendant.... It is not necessary that the defendant personally inflict harm upon the victim.... To constitute the cause of the harm, it is not necessary that the defendant's act be the sole reason for the realization of the harm which has been sustained by the victim. The defendant does not cease to be responsible for his otherwise criminal conduct because there were other conditions which contributed to the same result.

"An accused is not responsible for the death of another, unless that fatal harm was caused by the defendant's act or omission, or by the behavior of persons whose actions are attributable or chargeable to the defendant."

Actual causation may be examined in terms of the *sine qua non*. "In order that conduct be the actual cause of a particular result it is almost always sufficient that the result would not have happened in the absence of the conduct; or, putting it another way, that 'but for' the antecedent conduct the result would not have occurred." So examined here, there can be no doubt that 'but for' the acts of Jackson and Wells—committing the armed robbery, kidnapping Sugar and Farber to use them as hostages, forcing them against their will into a position of known grave danger, attempting to elude apprehension by fleeing in stolen automobiles, all the while purposely exposing their hostages to gunfire, and, when ultimately halted in their flight by police action, resisting arrest—"but for" those acts, Sugar would not have been killed. Although the lethal shot was through the actions of a police officer attempting to apprehend the felons, the behavior of that officer was chargeable to Jackson and Wells. They were just as much the cause of Sugar's death as if each had fired the fatal shot. Their acts themselves produced the intervening cause of Sugar's death, and the result is not to be considered remote and was foreseeable.

The causal relationship between the acts of Jackson and Wells and the death of Sugar for which they were prosecuted is clear and direct.

Comments and Questions

(1) If the defendants in *Jackson* "were just as much the cause of Sugar's death as if each had fired the fatal shot," why was the Pennsylvania court not convinced of this point in *Myers*?

> *We have gone into this lengthy discussion of the felony-murder rule not for the purpose of hereby abolishing it. That is hardly necessary in the instant case. But we do want to make clear how shaky are the basic premises on which it rests. With so weak a foundation, it behooves us not to extend it further and indeed, to restrain it within the bounds it has always known. As stated above, [we] de-*

molished the extension to the felony-murder rule made in Almeida: "In adjudging a felony-murder, it is to be remembered at all times that the thing which is imputed to a felon for a killing incidental to his felony is malice and not the act of killing.... The malice of the *initial* offense attaches to whatever else the criminal may do in connection therewith." ... And so, until the decision of this court in *Commonwealth v. Almeida, supra,* in 1949, the rule which was uniformly followed, whether by express statement or by implication, was that in order to convict for felony-murder, *the killing must have been done by the defendant or by an accomplice or confederate or by one acting in furtherance of the felonious undertaking.* [citing a long line of cases].

> Until the *Almeida* case there was no reported instance in this State of a jury ever having been instructed on the trial of an indictment for murder for a killing occurring contemporaneously with the perpetration of a felony that the defendant was guilty of murder regardless of the fact that the fatal shot was fired by a third person acting in hostility and resistance to the felon and in deliberate opposition to the success of the felon's criminal undertaking.

> Redline proceeded to discuss the cases, both within and without Pennsylvania, which establish the rule that murder is not present where the fatal shot is fired by a third person acting in opposition to the felon.

261 A.2d at 555 (emphasis added).

But see People v. Hickman, 319 N.E.2d 511, 513 (Ill. 1974):

> Here defendants planned and committed a burglary, which is a forcible felony under Illinois law. One of them was armed. It was their conduct which occasioned the presence of the police. When confronted by approaching officers, the defendants elected to flee. We have previously held that the period of time and activities involved in escaping to a place of safety are part of the crime itself. The defendants were repeatedly told to halt and the police identified themselves, but the defendants continued their attempt to escape. The commission of the burglary, coupled with the election by defendants to flee, set in motion the pursuit by armed police officers. The shot which killed Detective Loscheider was a shot fired in opposition to the escape of the fleeing burglars, and it was a direct and foreseeable consequence of defendants' actions. The escape invited retaliation, opposition and pursuit. Those who commit forcible felonies know they may encounter resistance, both to their affirmative actions and to any subsequent escape.

In a case remarkably similar to *Hickman*, the New York Court of Appeals in *People v. Hernandez*, 624 N.E.2d 661, 665 (N.Y. 1993), explained the rationale for the same result:

> The basic tenet of felony murder liability is that the mens rea of the underlying felony is imputed to the participant responsible for the killing. By operation of that legal fiction, the transferred intent allows the law to characterize a homicide, though unintended and not in the common design of the felons,

> as an intentional killing. Thus, the presence or absence of the requisite mens rea is an issue turning on whether the felon is acting in furtherance of the underlying crime at the time of the homicide, not on the proximity or attenuation of the death resulting from the felon's acts. Whether the death is an immediate result or an attenuated one, the necessary mens rea is present if the causal act is part of the felonious conduct.

In *People v. Lowery*, 687 N.E.2d 973, 978 (Ill. 1997), the state supreme court (relying on *Hickman*) allowed a felony murder prosecution. There the innocent bystander was shot by the robbery victim who used the defendant's dropped gun and was trying to kill the defendant.

(2) In *Jackson*, could the defendants have been successfully prosecuted for murder without the use of the felony murder doctrine?

(3) The defendant in *Commonwealth v. Waters*, 418 A.2d 312, 317 (Pa. 1980), did not fire the shots which killed the victim, though he did participate in the incident leading up to the shooting (burglary and theft). At trial defendant requested that the jury be instructed that the state was required to show "the conduct causing the death was done in furtherance of the design to commit the felony." The judge refused to so instruct the jury. On appeal the defendant's conviction was reversed with the court finding a "requirement that the slayer's act be in furtherance of the felony." But see the dissenter's view:

> I cannot agree with the conclusion that the jury instruction on the felony murder rule should include the charge that a defendant may be found guilty of murder of the second degree only if the homicide committed by his accomplice during the perpetration of the felony was "in furtherance of" the felony. I cannot agree that inserting this requirement into the felony murder charge adequately advances the stated policy of this Commonwealth with regard to felony murder liability. Whether the actions are in "furtherance" of the underlying felony unnecessarily clutters the issue.
>
> I am of the opinion that the jury should be charged to the effect that so long as the energy initiating the felonious undertaking continues to pervade the felonious atmosphere created by co-felons, then, any result engendered by that felonious energy is within the purview of the felony murder doctrine and all who participate therein are equally guilty of murder.

In contrast, the Delaware Supreme Court held that the phrase "in furtherance of" not only requires that the defendant or any accomplices commit the killing but also that the murder is done to advance the felony. Because the defendant burglarized the victim's residence solely to kill the victim, the felony was committed to further the murder rather than the murder being committed to further the felony. *Williams v. State*, 818 A.2d 906 (Del. 2002).

In *People v. Matos*, 634 N.E.2d 157 (N.Y. 1994), a police officer's death was caused when he fell while chasing a fleeing felon across city rooftops. The court found the defendant, who was running from the scene of an armed robbery, responsible under the felony murder doctrine. The court cited with approval the trial judge's instruction to the jury to determine whether the defendant's conduct was a sufficiently direct cause of the death based upon a finding of reasonable foreseeability. Is it felony murder if two news helicopters filming a police chase crash, and the pilots are killed?

(4) Are different considerations involved if the victim of the crime kills a co-felon? Relying on *Myers*, the New Jersey Supreme Court refused to apply the felony murder rule to this fact situation. "Most modern progressive thought in criminal jurisprudence favors restriction rather than expansion of the felony murder rule." *State v. Canola*, 374 A.2d 20, 29 (N.J. 1977). But see the dissenting opinion in *Jackson v. State*, 589 P.2d 1052, 1053–54 (N.M. 1979):

> I respectfully dissent from the majority opinion. The majority has adopted the view that the felony-murder doctrine may not be applied to a case in which the victim of a crime kills one of the perpetrators. I cannot concur in the absolute prohibition against the application of the felony-murder rule in all such cases.
>
> We held in *Harrison* [90 N.M. 439, 564 P.2d 1321 (1977)] that the acts of the defendant or his accomplice must be the *cause* of the death upon which a felony-murder charge is based. Causation was defined in terms of the physical acts of the defendant or his accomplice which initiated or led to the killing without the intervention of an independent force. Nothing we said in *Harrison* intimated that the fatal shot must be fired by the defendant himself or his accomplice. To the contrary, in Footnote 1, we cited an example of a situation in which a felon could be convicted of felony-murder even though the fatal shot was fired by an innocent third party. We said:
>
> A policeman who shoots at an escaping robber but misses and kills an innocent bystander would be considered a dependent, intervening force, and the robber would be criminally liable for felony murder.
>
> The majority opinion, read in the context of Footnote 1 in *Harrison*, establishes a distinction which has been rejected by most courts and commentators which have addressed the issue, including the courts in the jurisdictions relied on by the majority. The present rule in New Mexico, in light of the *Harrison* decision and the decision of the Court in the present case, is that if an innocent third party's aim is true and one of two robbers is killed, the surviving felon is not guilty of felony-murder. If the third party's aim is not accurate and an innocent person is killed, the surviving felon may be convicted of felony-murder. Thus, responsibility and accountability for the loss of life resulting from the commission of a crime rests not upon any well-reasoned principle of law, but rather, upon the accuracy of the aim of a party resisting a criminal act. Public respect for the law is not enhanced by courts engaging in distinctions based on such fortuitous circumstances as the marksmanship of victims.

> Any distinction based on the notion of causation is illusory. The shooting of a co-felon by the victim is no less "a dependent, intervening force" than is the policeman's accidental shooting of an innocent bystander. It is as foreseeable that a co-felon will be killed while committing a felony as it is that an innocent bystander will accidentally become the victim. In fact, it may be more likely that a bullet will hit the person it is aimed at rather than another person not aimed at.

The Louisiana Supreme Court agreed with the restriction on the felony-murder rule so that it would not apply when the co-felon was killed by a victim or police officer. An individual could not be found responsible under the doctrine "for remote and indirect consequences which a reasonable person could not have foreseen as likely to have flowed from his conduct or from those consequences which would have occurred regardless of his conduct." The codefendants had fled the police after seeking to manufacture drugs. The court found that the codefendants' flight "and his firing at his pursuers were intervening acts which weakened any causal relationship between defendant's manufacturing of drugs and the killing." *State v. Kalathakis*, 563 So. 2d 228, 231–32 (La. 1990). But see *State v. O'Dell*, 684 S.W.2d 453, 461 (Mo. Ct. App. 1984), where the court stated that "a felon attempting to commit robbery is guilty of the felony-murder of his co-felon shot by the intended victim." The key point for the court was that liability under the doctrine extends to "a death that is the proximate result of the act of the felon or felons ... whenever the death was the natural and proximate result...." The court in *State v. Oimen*, 516 N.W.2d 399 (Wis. 1994), followed the "minority position" in affirming the felon's conviction for the death of the co-felon, relying on the breadth of the state felony murder statute. The court emphasized that if the death was foreseeable, the fact that the decedent was the co-felon was irrelevant. See also *Palmer v. State*, 704 N.E.2d 124 (Ind. 1999), where the court's majority emphasized, over a strong dissent, the dangerous acts of the defendants which "clearly raised the foreseeable possibility that the intended victim might resist or that law enforcement would respond."

(5) In *State v. Williams*, 254 So. 2d 548, 549, 551 (Fla. Dist. Ct. App. 2d Dist. 1971), the co-felon "met death at his own hands from injuries suffered when he accidentally set fire to himself while attempting to burn certain buildings." The court held that the felony-murder statute is applicable only "when an innocent person is killed as a sequential result of events or circumstances set in motion by one or more persons acting in furtherance of an intent or attempt to commit one of the felonies specified in such statute. As noted, the facts herein are patently outside the scope of this rationale and, accordingly, the felony-murder statute is inapplicable." In *People v. Billa*, 79 P.3d 542 (Cal. 2003), the California court concluded that the accidental death of the co-conspirator arsonist was felony-murder because they were all actively engaged in furtherance of the arson.

(6) Consider also the case of Blake Layman. Layman was 16, with a clean criminal record. One day he decided to break into a neighbor's house with some friends, believing the homeowner was away. Layman and his friends were not armed. After en-

tering the home, the owner fired several shots from a handgun, wounding Layman and killing one of Layman's friends. Layman was charged and convicted of felony murder and sentenced to 55 years in a maximum-security prison. Is this a fair result? How could Layman have had the mens rea for the death when none of the robbers were armed and the fatal shot came from the homeowner? Does his age or lack of criminal record matter? Ed Pilkington, *Felony Murder: Why a Teenager Who Didn't Kill Anyone Faces 55 Years in Jail* (Feb. 26, 2015), http://www.theguardian.com/us-news/2015/feb/26/felony-murder-teenager-55-years-jail-indiana.

The final words are Chief Justice Traynor's:

> When a killing is not committed by a robber or by his accomplice but by his victim, malice aforethought is not attributable to the robber, for the killing is not committed by him in the perpetration or attempt to perpetrate robbery. It is not enough that the killing was a risk reasonably to be foreseen and that the robbery might therefore be regarded as a proximate cause of the killing. Section 189 requires that the felon or his accomplice commit the killing, for if he does not, the killing is not committed to perpetrate the felony. Indeed, in the present case the killing was committed to thwart a felony. To include such killings within section 189 would expand the meaning of the words "murder ... which is committed in the perpetration ... [of] robbery ..." beyond common understanding.
>
> The purpose of the felony-murder rule is to deter felons from killing negligently or accidentally by holding them strictly responsible for killings they commit. This purpose is not served by punishing them for killings committed by their victims.
>
> It is contended, however, that another purpose of the felony-murder rule is to prevent the commission of robberies. Neither the common-law rationale of the rule nor the Penal Code supports this contention. In every robbery there is a possibility that the victim will resist and kill. The robber has little control over such a killing once the robbery is undertaken as this case demonstrates. To impose an additional penalty for the killing would discriminate between robbers, not on the basis of any difference in their own conduct, but solely on the basis of the response by others that the robber's conduct happened to induce. An additional penalty for a homicide committed by the victim would deter robbery haphazardly at best. To "prevent stealing, [the law] would do better to hang one thief in every thousand by lot." (Holmes, *The Common Law*, p. 58.)
>
> Defendants who initiate gun battles may also be found guilty of murder if their victims resist and kill. Under such circumstances, "the defendant for a base, anti-social motive and with wanton disregard for human life, does an act that involves a high degree of probability that it will result in death," and it is unnecessary to imply malice by invoking the felony-murder doctrine. To invoke the felony-murder doctrine to imply malice in such a case is un-

> necessary and overlooks the principles of criminal liability that should govern the responsibility of one person for a killing committed by another.
>
> To invoke the felony-murder doctrine when the killing is not committed by the defendant or by his accomplice could lead to absurd results. Thus, two men rob a grocery store and flee in opposite directions. The owner of the store follows one of the robbers and kills him. Neither robber may have fired a shot. Neither robber may have been armed with a deadly weapon. If the felony-murder doctrine applied, however, the surviving robber could be convicted of first degree murder even though he was captured by a policeman and placed under arrest at the time his accomplice was killed.

People v. Washington, 402 P.2d 130, 133–34 (Cal. 1965).

[d] The Dissenting View

People v. Aaron

Supreme Court of Michigan
299 N.W.2d 304 (1980)

FITZGERALD, JUSTICE.

The existence and scope of the felony-murder doctrine have perplexed generations of law students, commentators and jurists in the United States and England, and have split our own Court of Appeals. In these cases, we must decide whether Michigan has a felony murder rule which allows the element of malice required for murder to be satisfied by the intent to commit the underlying felony or whether malice must be otherwise found by the trier of fact.

Defendant Aaron was convicted of first-degree felony murder as a result of a homicide committed during the perpetration of an armed robbery. The jury was instructed that they could convict defendant of first-degree murder if they found that defendant killed the victim during the commission or attempted commission of an armed robbery.

II. History of the Felony Murder Doctrine

Felony murder has never been a static, well-defined rule at common law, but throughout its history has been characterized by judicial reinterpretation to limit the harshness of the application of the rule. Historians and commentators have concluded that the rule is of questionable origin and that the reasons for the rule no longer exist, making it an anachronistic remnant, "a historic survivor for which there is no logical or practical basis for existence in modern law."

At early common law, the felony-murder rule went unchallenged because at that time practically all felonies were punishable by death. It was, therefore, "of no particular moment whether the condemned was hanged for the initial felony or for the death accidentally resulting from the felony." Thus, no injustice was caused directly by application of the rule at that time.

In this century, the felony-murder doctrine was comparatively rarely invoked in England and in 1957 England abolished the felony-murder rule. Section 1 of England's Homicide Act, 1957, 5 & 6 Eliz. 2, ch. 11, § 1, provides that a killing occurring in a felony-murder situation will not amount to murder unless done with the same malice aforethought as is required for all other murder.

Thus, an examination of the felony-murder rule indicates that the doctrine is of doubtful origin. Derived from the misinterpretation of case law, it went unchallenged because of circumstances which no longer exist. The doctrine was continuously modified and restricted in England, the country of its birth, until its ultimate rejection by Parliament in 1957.

III. Limitation of the Felony Murder Doctrine in the United States

While only a few states[45] have followed the lead of Great Britain in abolishing felony murder, various legislative and judicial limitations on the doctrine have effectively narrowed the scope of the rule in the United States. Perkins states that the rule is "somewhat in disfavor at the present time" and that "courts apply it where the law requires, but they do so grudgingly and tend to restrict its application where circumstances permit."

The draftsmen of the Model Penal Code have summarized the limitations imposed by American courts as follows:

(1) "The felonious act must be dangerous to life."

(2) and (3) "The homicide must be a natural and probable consequence of the felonious act." "Death must be 'proximately' caused." Courts have also required that the killing be the result of an act done in the furtherance of the felonious purpose and not merely coincidental to the perpetration of a felony. These cases often make distinctions based on the identity of the victim (*i.e.*, whether the decedent was the victim of the felony or whether he was someone else, *e.g.*, a policeman or one of the felons) and the identity of the person causing the death.

(4) "The felony must be *malum in se*."

(5) "The act must be a common-law felony."

(6) "The period during which the felony is in the process of commission must be narrowly construed."

(7) "The underlying felony must be 'independent' of the homicide."

Some courts, recognizing the questionable wisdom of the rule, have refused to extend it beyond what is required. "[W]e do want to make clear how shaky are the basic premises on which [the felony murder rule] rests. With so weak a foundation, it behooves us not to extend it further and indeed, to restrain it within the bounds it has always known." Commonwealth *ex rel.* Smith v. Myers, 438 Pa. 218, 227, 261 A.2d 550, 555 (1970). "We have thus recognized that the felony-murder doctrine

45. Hawaii, Kentucky and Ohio.

expresses a highly artificial concept that deserves no extension beyond its required application. Indeed, the rule itself has been abandoned by the courts of England, where it had its inception. It has been subjected to severe and sweeping criticism." *People v. Phillips*, 64 Cal. 2d 574, 582–83, 51 Cal. Rptr. 225, 414 P.2d 353, 360 (1966).

Other courts have required a finding of a separate *mens rea* connected with the killing in addition to the intent associated with the felony. In *State v. Millette*, 112 N.H. 458, 462, 299 A.2d 150, 153 (1972), the Court stated:

> Neither the legislature nor our court ever adopted a presumption of malice from the commission of an unlawful act whether felony or misdemeanor. While language in our cases defining murder may be construed to presume malice from a homicide occurring during the commission of the named inherently dangerous felonies [citations omitted] malice remains an indispensable element in the crime of murder. "Malice is not an inference of law from the mere act of killing; but like any other fact in issue, it must be found by the jury upon competent evidence."

This Court has held, at least with killings occurring during commission of non-enumerated felonies, that malice may be inferred but the nature of the felonious act must be considered. *People v. Carter*, 387 Mich. 397, 422, 197 N.W.2d 57 (1972). Similarly, New Mexico has declared that where a non-first-degree felony (this category would include many of Michigan's enumerated felonies) is involved, the presumption that the defendant has the requisite *mens rea* to commit first-degree murder "is a legal fiction we no longer can support." *State v. Harrison*, 90 N.M. 439, 442, 564 P.2d 1321 (1977). The Iowa Supreme Court has recently ruled that the issue of malice aforethought necessary for murder must be submitted to the jury and that it may not be satisfied by proof of intent to commit the underlying felony. *State v. Galloway*, 275 N.W.2d 736, 738 (Iowa 1979). Many state legislatures have also been active in restricting the scope of felony murder by imposing additional limitations.

Kentucky and Hawaii have specifically abolished the felony-murder doctrine. The commentary to Hawaii's murder statute is instructive as to that state's reasoning in abolishing the doctrine:

> Even in its limited formulation the felony-murder rule is still objectionable. It is not sound principle to convert an accidental, negligent, or reckless homicide into a murder simply because, without more, the killing was in furtherance of a criminal objective of some defined class. Engaging in certain penally-prohibited behavior may, of course, evidence a recklessness sufficient to establish manslaughter, or a practical certainty or intent, with respect to causing death, sufficient to establish murder, but such a finding is an independent determination which must rest on the facts of each case.
>
> ...
>
> In recognition of the trend toward, and the substantial body of criticism supporting, the abolition of the felony-murder rule, and because of the ex-

> tremely questionable results which the rule has worked in other jurisdictions, the Code has eliminated from our law the felony-murder rule.

Ohio has effectively abolished the felony-murder rule. It defines as *involuntary manslaughter* the death of another proximately resulting from the offender's commission or attempt to commit a felony.

Seven states have downgraded the offense and consequently reduced the punishment. Alaska, Louisiana, New York, Pennsylvania and Utah have reduced it to second-degree murder. Minnesota classifies felony murder as third-degree murder (with the exception of a killing in the course of criminal sexual conduct in the first or second degree committed with force or violence, which is punished as first-degree murder) which involves a sentence of not more than 25 years. Wisconsin makes felony murder a class B felony which is punishable by imprisonment not to exceed 20 years.

Three states require a demonstration of *mens rea* beyond the intent to cause the felony. The Arkansas statute states that the defendant must cause the death "under circumstances manifesting extreme indifference to the value of human life." Delaware's first-degree murder statute requires that the defendant cause death recklessly in the course of a felony or with at least criminal negligence in the course of one of the enumerated felonies. It defines as second-degree murder death caused with criminal negligence in the course of non-enumerated felonies. New Hampshire's capital and first-degree murder statutes require that death be caused knowingly in connection with certain enumerated felonies while its second-degree murder statute requires that death be caused "recklessly under circumstances manifesting an extreme indifference to the value of human life."

Some of the limitations on the felony-murder doctrine which have been imposed by the courts, as mentioned above, have been codified by statute. These limitations include restrictions on the underlying felony, requiring that it be forcible, violent or clearly dangerous to human life, that death be proximately caused, that death be a natural or probable consequence or a reasonably foreseeable consequence of the commission or attempted commission of the felony, that the felon must have caused the death, and that the victim must not be one of the felons.

Other restrictions of the common-law rule include the enumeration of felonies which are to be included within the felony-murder category, and the reduction to manslaughter of killings in the course of non-enumerated felonies. The commentary following New York's revision of its felony murder statute, deleting "any felony" and inserting specifically enumerated felonies, states: "The purpose of the indicated limitations is to exclude from felony murder, cases of accidental or not reasonably foreseeable fatality occurring in the course of a non-violent felony." The limitation is a response to a significant aspect of the common-law felony-murder rule—the fact that it ignores the relevance of factors, *e.g.*, accident, which mitigate culpability.

Finally, a limitation of relatively recent origin is the availability of affirmative defenses where a defendant is not the only participant in the commission of the underlying felony. The New York statute provides, as do similar statutes of nine other states, an affirmative defense to the defendant when he:

> (a) Did not commit the homicidal act or in any way solicit, request, command, importune, cause or aid the commission thereof; and
>
> (b) Was not armed with a deadly weapon, or any instrument, article or substance readily capable of causing death or serious physical injury and of a sort not ordinarily carried in public places by law-abiding persons; and
>
> (c) Had no reasonable ground to believe that any other participant was armed with such a weapon, instrument, article or substance; and
>
> (d) Had no reasonable ground to believe that any other participant intended to engage in conduct likely to result in death or serious physical injury.

The commentary to the New York statute states that the provision is premised "upon the theory that the felony murder doctrine, in its rigid automatic envelopment of all participants in the underlying felony, may be unduly harsh...." The comment acknowledges that there may be some cases where it would be "just and desirable to allow a non-killer defendant of relatively minor culpability a chance of extricating himself from liability for murder, though not, of course, from liability for the underlying felony."

The numerous modifications and restrictions placed upon the common-law felony-murder doctrine by courts and legislatures reflect dissatisfaction with the harshness and injustice of the rule. Even though the felony-murder doctrine survives in this country, it bears increasingly less resemblance to the traditional felony-murder concept. To the extent that these modifications reduce the scope and significance of the common-law doctrine, they also call into question the continued existence of the doctrine itself.

IV. The Requirement of Individual Culpability for Criminal Responsibility

"If one had to choose the most basic principle of the criminal law in general ... it would be that criminal liability for causing a particular result is not justified in the absence of some culpable mental state in respect to that result...."

The most fundamental characteristic of the felony-murder rule violates this basic principle in that it punishes all homicides, committed in the perpetration or attempted perpetration of proscribed felonies whether intentional, unintentional or accidental, without the necessity of proving the relation between the homicide and the perpetrator's state of mind. This is most evident when a killing is done by one of a group of co-felons. The felony-murder rule completely ignores the concept of determination of guilt on the basis of individual misconduct. The felony-murder rule thus "erodes the relation between criminal liability and moral culpability." *People v. Washington*, 62 Cal. 2d 777, 44 Cal. Rptr. 442, 402 P.2d 130 (1965).

The felony-murder rule's most egregious violation of basic rules of culpability occurs where felony murder is categorized as first-degree murder. All other murders carrying equal punishment require a showing of premeditation, deliberation and willfulness while felony murder only requires a showing of intent to do the underlying felony. Although the purpose of our degree statutes is to punish more severely the more culpable forms of murder, an accidental killing occurring during the perpetration of a felony would be punished more severely than a second-degree murder requiring intent to kill, intent to cause great bodily harm or wantonness and willfulness. Furthermore, a defendant charged with felony murder is permitted to raise defenses only to the mental element of the felony, thus precluding certain defenses available to a defendant charged with premeditated murder who may raise defenses to the mental element of murder (*e.g.*, self-defense, accident). Certainly, felony murder is no more reprehensible than premeditated murder.

LaFave and Scott explain the felony-murder doctrine's failure to account for a defendant's moral culpability as follows:

"The rationale of the doctrine is that one who commits a felony is a bad person with a bad state of mind, and he has caused a bad result, so that we should not worry too much about the fact that the fatal result he accomplished was quite different and a good deal worse than the bad result he intended. Yet it is a general principle of criminal law that one is not ordinarily criminally liable for bad results which differ greatly from intended results."

Termed as a "somewhat primitive rationale" it is deserving of the observation made by one commentator that "the felony-murder doctrine gives rise to what can only be described as an emotional reaction, not one based on logical and abstract principles."

Another writer states:

> It is an excuse based on the rough moral notion that a man who intentionally commits a felony must have a wicked heart, and therefore "ought to be punished" for the harm which he has done accidentally. It is to guard against this kind of reasoning that our modern rules of evidence exclude in most cases any communication to the jury of a prisoner's previous misdeeds.

While it is understandable that little compassion may be felt for the criminal whose innocent victim dies, this does not justify ignoring the principles underlying our system of criminal law.

"The underlying rationale of the felony-murder doctrine—that the offender has shown himself to be a 'bad actor,' and that this is enough to exclude the niceties bearing on the gravity of the harm actually committed—might have been defensible in early law. The survival of the felony-murder doctrine is a tribute to the tenacity of legal conceptions rooted in simple moral attitudes. For as long ago as 1771 the doctrine was severely criticized by Eden [Baron Auckland], who felt that it 'may be reconciled to the philosophy of slaves; but it is surely repugnant to that noble, and active confidence, which a free people ought to possess in the laws of their constitution, the rule of their actions.'" …

The United States Supreme Court has reaffirmed on several occasions the importance of the relationship between culpability and criminal liability.

[T]he criminal law ... is concerned not only with guilt or innocence in the abstract but also with the degree of criminal culpability.

The failure of the felony-murder rule to consider the defendant's moral culpability is explained by examining the state of the law at the time of the rule's inception. The concept of culpability was not an element of homicide at early common law. The early definition of malice aforethought was vague. The concept meant little more than intentional wrongdoing with no other emphasis on intention except to exclude homicides that were committed by misadventure or in some otherwise pardonable manner. Thus, under this early definition of malice aforethought, an intent to commit the felony would in itself constitute malice. Furthermore, as all felonies were punished alike, it made little difference whether the felon was hanged for the felony or for the death.

Thus, the felony-murder rule did not broaden the concept of murder at the time of its origin because proof of the intention to commit a felony met the test of culpability based on the vague definition of malice aforethought governing at that time. Today, however, malice is a term of art. It does not include the nebulous definition of intentional wrongdoing. Thus, although the felony-murder rule did not broaden the definition of murder at early common law, it does so today. We find this enlargement of the scope of murder unacceptable, because it is based on a concept of culpability which is "totally incongruous with the general principles of our jurisprudence" today.

"The modern tendency has been to oppose policy-formation such as that embodied in or extended from the felony-murder doctrine. It has insisted on a decent regard for the facts and on sanctions that represent fair evaluation of these facts and not of the supposed character of the offender. Most emphatically the progressive tendency has been to repudiate the imposition of severe penalties where bare chance results in an unsought harm."

V. The Felony-Murder Doctrine in Michigan

We believe that it is no longer acceptable to equate the intent to commit a felony with the intent to kill, intent to do great bodily harm, or wanton and willful disregard of the likelihood that the natural tendency of a person's behavior is to cause death or great bodily harm.

"Malice requires an intent to cause the very harm that results or some harm of the same general nature, or an act done in wanton or willful disregard of the plaintiff and strong likelihood that such harm will result." In a charge of felony murder, it is the murder which is the harm which is being punished. A defendant who only intends to commit the felony does not intend to commit the harm that results and may or may not be guilty of perpetrating an act done in wanton or willful disregard of the plain and strong likelihood that such harm will result. Although the circumstances surrounding the commission of the felony may evidence a greater intent beyond the intent to commit the felony, or a wanton and willful act in disregard of the possible consequence of death or serious injury, the intent to commit the felony, of itself, does not connote a "man-endangering-state-of-mind." Hence, we do not believe that it constitutes a sufficient *mens rea* to establish the crime of murder.

Accordingly, we hold today that malice is the intention to kill, the intention to do great bodily harm, or the wanton and willful disregard of the likelihood that the natural tendency of defendant's behavior is to cause death or great bodily harm. We further hold that malice is an essential element of any murder, as that term is judicially defined, whether the murder occurs in the course of a felony or otherwise. The facts and circumstances involved in the perpetration of a felony may evidence an intent to kill, an intent to cause great bodily harm, or a wanton and willful disregard of the likelihood that the natural tendency of defendant's behavior is to cause death or great bodily harm; however, the conclusion must be left to the jury to infer from all the evidence. Otherwise, "juries might be required to find the fact of malice where they were satisfied from the whole evidence it did not exist."

VI. Practical Effect of Abrogation of the Common-Law Felony-Murder Doctrine

From a practical standpoint, the abolition of the category of malice arising from the intent to commit the underlying felony should have little effect on the result of the majority of cases. In many cases where felony murder has been applied, the use of the doctrine was unnecessary because the other types of malice could have been inferred from the evidence.

Abrogation of this rule does not make irrelevant the fact that a death occurred in the course of a felony. A jury can properly *infer* malice from evidence that a defendant intentionally set in motion a force likely to cause death or great bodily harm. Thus, whenever a killing occurs in the perpetration or attempted perpetration of an inherently dangerous felony, in order to establish malice the jury may consider the "nature of the underlying felony and the circumstances surrounding its commission." If the jury concludes that malice existed, they can find murder and, if they determine that the murder occurred in the perpetration or attempted perpetration of one of the enumerated felonies, by statute the murder would become first-degree murder.

The difference is that the jury may not find malice from the intent to commit the underlying felony alone. The defendant will be permitted to assert any of the applicable defenses relating to *mens rea* which he would be allowed to assert if charged with premeditated murder. The latter result is reasonable in light of the fact that felony murder is certainly no more heinous than premeditated murder. The prosecution will still be able to prove first-degree murder without proof of premeditation when a homicide is committed with malice, as we have defined it, and the perpetration or attempted perpetration of an enumerated felony is established. Hence, our first-degree murder statute continues to elevate to first-degree murder a *murder* which is committed in the perpetration or attempted perpetration of one of the enumerated felonies.

As previously noted, in many circumstances the commission of a felony, particularly one involving violence or the use of force, will indicate an intention to kill, an intention to cause great bodily harm, or wanton or willful disregard of the likelihood that the natural tendency of defendant's behavior is to cause death or great bodily harm. Thus, the felony-murder rule is not necessary to establish *mens rea* in these cases.

In the past, the felony-murder rule has been employed where unforeseen or accidental deaths occur and where the state seeks to prove vicarious liability of co-felons. In situations involving the vicarious liability of co-felons, the individual liability of each felon must be shown. It is fundamentally unfair and in violation of basic principles of individual criminal culpability to hold one felon liable for the unforeseen and unagreed—results of another felon. In cases where the felons are acting intentionally or recklessly in pursuit of a common plan, the felony-murder rule is unnecessary because liability may be established on agency principles.

Finally, in cases where the death was purely accidental, application of the felony-murder doctrine is unjust and should be precluded. The underlying felony, of course, will still be subject to punishment. The draftsmen of the Model Penal Code report that juries are not disposed to accept unfounded claims of accident in Ohio where all first-degree murder requires a purpose to kill.

Thus, in the three situations in which the felony-murder doctrine typically has applied, the rule is either unnecessary or contrary to fundamental principles of our criminal law.

"It is submitted that this is one of the most persuasive arguments in favor of abolition of the doctrine: it is not necessary to the establishment of criminal liability in the majority of cases in which it has been applied, and its application to those cases in which death occurred wholly by accident—*i.e.*, without intent or likelihood of harm—is contrary to the modern trend toward establishment of culpability as the basis of criminal liability."

"[I]t is unsatisfactory and inelegant to have a rule of law which, whenever it is applied, is either unnecessary (as in the case where dangerous violence is knowingly used) or unjust (as in the case where the risk of death is not foreseen)."

The Pennsylvania Supreme Court has called the felony-murder rule "nonessential", and the commentators to the Hawaii statute abolishing felony murder concluded that "[t]he rule certainly is not an indispensable ingredient in a system of criminal justice." The penal code of India has done away with felony murder and the doctrine "is also unknown as such in continental Europe." England, the birthplace of the felony-murder doctrine, has been without the rule for over 20 years and "its passing apparently has not been mourned." One writer suggests that the experience in England demonstrates that its demise would have little effect on the rate of convictions for murders occurring in the perpetration of felonies.

We are in full agreement with the following conclusion of the Model Penal Code draftsmen:

"We are, in any case, entirely clear that it is indefensible to use the sanctions that the law employs to deal with murder, unless there is at least a finding that the actor's conduct manifested an extreme indifference to the value of human life. The fact that the actor was engaged in a crime of the kind that is included in the usual first degree felony-murder enumeration or was an accomplice in such crime will frequently justify such a finding.... But liability depends, as we believe it should, upon the crucial finding. The result may not differ often under such a formulation from that which would be reached under the present rule. But what is more important is that a conviction on this basis rests upon sound ground."

VII. Conclusion

Whatever reasons can be gleaned from the dubious origin of the felony-murder rule to explain its existence, those reasons no longer exist today. Indeed, most states, including our own, have recognized the harshness and inequity of the rule as is evidenced by the numerous restrictions placed on it. The felony-murder doctrine is unnecessary and in many cases unjust in that it violates the basic premise of individual moral culpability upon which our criminal law is based.

We conclude that Michigan has no statutory felony-murder rule which allows the mental element of murder to be satisfied by proof of the intention to commit the underlying felony. Today we exercise our role in the development of the common law by abrogating the common-law felony-murder rule. We hold that in order to convict a defendant of murder, as that term is defined by Michigan case law, it must be shown that he acted with intent to kill or to inflict great bodily harm or with a wanton and willful disregard of the likelihood that the natural tendency of his behavior is to cause death or great bodily harm. We further hold that the issue of malice must always be submitted to the jury.

Comments and Questions

(1) The court in *People v. Dillon*, 668 P.2d 697, 709 (Cal. 1983), rejected an attack on the state felony murder rule fashioned after *Aaron*. The justices relied on the California *codification* of the rule. The court went on, however, to discuss the basis for the rule:

> [O]ur opinions make it clear we hold no brief for the felony-murder rule. We have repeatedly stated that felony-murder is a "highly artificial concept" which "deserves no extension beyond its required application." And we have recognized that the rule is much censured "because it anachronistically resurrects from a bygone age a 'barbaric' concept that has been discarded in the place of its origin" and because "in almost all cases in which it is applied it is unnecessary" and "it erodes the relation between criminal liability and moral culpability."

That same court repeated the rationale for the felony-murder rule:

> The justification therefore is that, when society has declared certain inherently dangerous conduct to be felonious, a defendant should not be allowed to excuse himself by saying he was unaware of the danger to life because, by declaring the conduct to be felonious, society has warned him of the risk involved. The physical requirement, however, remains the same; by committing a felony inherently dangerous to life, the defendant has committed "an act, the natural consequences of which are dangerous to life," thus satisfying the physical component of implied malice.

People v. Patterson, 778 P.2d 549, 557–58 Cal. (1989). After *Aaron*, Michigan expanded and re-adopted the murder provision which includes killings in the perpetration of designated felonies as first degree murder. Mich. Penal Code § 750.316. The state supreme court has in fact given a broad interpretation to when a killing is "in the perpetration of" a felony to include the deaths in a police chase initiated 10 minutes after a home invasion. *People v. Gillis*, 712 N.W.2d 419 (Mich. 2006).

(2) Consider Marcus, *The Model Penal Code and Commentaries*, 73 J. Crim. L. & Criminology 811, 825 n.81 (1982):

> [There is] no evidence to demonstrate that the felony murder rule serves a useful purpose in actually deterring felons from killing negligently or accidentally. Indeed, the evidence is somewhat to the contrary. "There is no basis in experience for thinking that homicides *which the evidence makes accidental* occur with disproportionate frequency in connection with specified felonies." The statistical evidence shows that the number of all homicides which occur during the course of robbery, burglary, and rape is somewhat lower than might otherwise be expected. More substantially, "it remains indefensible in principle to use the sanctions that the law employs to deal with murder unless there is at least a finding that the actor's conduct manifested an extreme indifference to the value of human life."

(3) One commentator explored the continued viable presence of the felony-murder rule. In response to questions as to its applicability, he wrote:

> Also probably inextricable from the public consciousness is the idea that felons—by virtue of their choices to engage in felonies—have effectively forfeited any entitlement to close scrutiny of their blameworthiness. If a person with dirty hands causes a death he may not insist on the inquiry and finding of fault to which he would ordinarily be entitled. We are simply less sympathetic to, and not as inclined to listen to, felons' claims of innocent accident. It serves them right to have their pleas ignored; they asked for such treatment by deciding to violate the law.

Tomkovicz, *The Endurance of the Felony-Murder Rule: A Study of the Forces That Shape Our Criminal Law*, 51 Wash. & Lee L. Rev. 1429, 1475 (1994).

[3] The Degrees of Murder

California Penal Code Section 189:

> All murder which is perpetrated by means of a destructive device or explosive, a weapon of mass destruction, knowing use of ammunition designed primarily to penetrate metal or armor, poison, lying in wait, torture, or by any other kind of willful, deliberate, and premeditated killing or which is committed in the perpetration of, or attempt to perpetrate, arson, rape, carjacking, robbery, burglary, mayhem, kidnapping, train wrecking, is murder in the first degree. All other kinds of murders are of the second degree.

The Manual for Courts-Martial of the United States, Article 118 c.(2)(a):

> A murder is not premeditated unless the thought of taking life was consciously conceived and the act or admission by which it was taken was intended. Premeditated murder is murder committed after the formation of a specific intent to kill someone and consideration of the act intended. It is not necessary that the intention to kill had been entertained for any particular or considerable length of time. When a fixed purpose to kill has been deliberately formed, it is immaterial how soon afterwards it is put into execution. The existence of premeditation may be inferred from the circumstances.

Austin v. United States

United States Court of Appeals, District of Columbia Circuit
382 F.2d 129 (1967)

LEVENTHAL, CIRCUIT JUDGE.

Appellant Bernard Austin was indicted for murdering Nettie Scott with premeditation, deliberation, and malice aforethought. Appellant was convicted of first-degree murder.

First we review the Government's evidence and the rulings of the trial judge bearing on the issues of premeditation and deliberation. In Part II we consider how common law murder has been divided by the legislature into different statutory categories, the first degree reserved for deliberated murders, such as those committed with coolness of mind, and second degree used for murders committed on impulse, in frenzy or the heat of passion. We conclude that the Government's case in chief, though ample to permit a finding of intentional murder, did not present evidence of premeditation and deliberation sufficient to warrant retention of the charge of murder in the first degree when gauged by proper tests.

I.

The Government's evidence was as follows: Appellant was seen in the company of the deceased, Nettie Scott, for some period of time on the night in question. They were drinking together at an after-hours establishment called Will's Place, where appellant bought deceased a sandwich. During this period appellant was seen using a sharp pocket knife to repair the broken thumb nail of another female patron sitting at his table. At about 4:00 a.m. appellant left Will's Place together with the deceased and her acquaintance, Mabel Proctor, and went to an all-night carry-out shop. The sandwiches bought there were eaten in appellant's truck. Appellant then drove Mabel Proctor home, dropping her off at about 4:30 a.m., and drove off in his truck with deceased. The Government produced no witness as to what happened thereafter. However, at approximately 5:00 a.m. that morning, two policemen, cruising in an unmarked car, saw appellant's truck stopped in a parking bay off the Anacostia Parkway. As they approached to investigate they noticed some clothing lying on the grass near the truck. At that point appellant came up the bank from the river, got in his truck and drove away. Further investigation revealed bloody clothing and a pool of blood in the grassy area near the parking bay. The officers retrieved from the river the mutilated and nearly lifeless body of the deceased, nude except for a piece of clothing around her neck. She died almost immediately. Appellant was apprehended later that morning. Expert testimony revealed that deceased had suffered approximately 26 major stab wounds, culminating in a stab wound to the head, penetrating the brain, and lodging the broken blade in the skull. The body had suffered at least the same number of superficial lacerations. The expert concluded that the death had been caused by hemorrhage and shock from the multiple knife wounds.

The Government also produced evidence showing that the body of the deceased had been dragged from the grassy area where the bloody clothes were found to the sea wall, and that on the slope leading down to the river had been found a man's torn and bloody shirt, similar to one owned by appellant. There was no testimony as to any fights, quarrels, animosity, or threats between appellant and deceased.

Defense counsel moved for acquittal only of first degree murder at the close of the prosecution's case and again when defense rested. Although the District Court's denial of those motions was without opinion, its underlying views of the concepts of premeditation and deliberation are reflected in its rulings and actions on instructions. The court's charge on premeditation and deliberation[1] instructed the jury that premeditation is the formation of an intention to kill, and deliberation means a further thought upon the plan to kill. The judge charged the jury that "although some time" is required for deliberation, deliberation may be sufficient "though it be of an exceedingly brief duration," and that the time "may be in the nature of hours, minutes or seconds."

Appellant requested that the time required for deliberation be stated as "some appreciable period of time," rather than "some period of time" as originally proposed by the judge. The court not only declined this request but changed the instruction submitted to counsel ("it does not require the lapse of days or hours or even minutes") to include the reference to "seconds."

1. "Now as to the fourth element of first degree murder, that the defendant acted with premeditation and with deliberation. Now premeditation is the formation of the intent or plan to kill; the formation of a positive design to kill. Deliberation means further, or to put it another way—I am speaking now of deliberation—that deliberation means a further thought upon the plan or design to kill. It must have been considered by the defendant Bernard Austin.

"It is your duty to determine from all of the facts and the circumstances which have been presented to you in this case that you may find surrounding the killing on April 24, some time between four-forty and five o'clock, whether there was any reflection and consideration amounting to deliberation by the defendant Bernard Austin. Now if there was such deliberation, even though it be of an exceedingly brief duration, that is in itself, so far as the deliberation is concerned, is sufficient. Because it is the fact of deliberation rather than the length of time it required that is important. Although some time, that is there must be some time to deliberate and to create in the mind of the defendant Austin the premeditation and the deliberation. As I have told you before, the time itself may be in the nature of hours, minutes, or seconds. But there must be the deliberation and the premeditation."

II.

It may be helpful to approach the issues presented by this appeal with the perspective of history.

At common law, unlawful homicides were divided into two classes, murder and manslaughter, depending on whether the killing was with or without malice aforethought. Although the term malice aforethought was most probably intended to be applied literally when it was first introduced into the law of homicide, the courts soon converted it into a term of art. To the popular understanding of subjective malice was added an objective standard, by which negligence tantamount to recklessness might make a culpable homicide murder. The objective standard persists in the law, but what we are primarily concerned with here is not so much the extension of "malice" as the elimination of the literal significance of the word "aforethought." The courts held it sufficient to establish common law murder, subject to capital punishment, if the homicide was accompanied by the intention to cause death or grievous bodily harm, whether the slaying was calculated or only impulsive.

The nineteenth century ushered in a new approach. Beginning in 1794 with Pennsylvania, state legislatures began to separate murder into two degrees, reserving the death penalty for the first degree. These statutes typically defined murder in the first degree as an intended killing, accompanied by premeditation and deliberation (as well as malice aforethought); murder in the second degree was defined residually to include all other unlawful homicides with malice aforethought. In 1901 Congress passed such a statute for the District of Columbia.

As we have noted:

> Statutes like ours, which distinguish deliberate and premeditated murder from other murder, reflect a belief that one who meditates an intent to kill and then deliberately executes it is more dangerous, more culpable or less capable of reformation than one who kills on sudden impulse; or that the prospect of the death penalty is more likely to deter men from deliberate than from impulsive murder. The deliberate killer is guilty of first degree murder; the impulsive killer is not.

The reports reflect the effort of some courts to carry out the legislative conception, by interpreting "deliberation" to call for elements which the word normally signifies—that the determination to kill was reached calmly and in cold blood rather than under impulse or the heat of passion and was reached some appreciable time prior to the homicide. The more widespread judicial tendency was marked by a restrictive reading of the statutory terms. "The statutory scheme was apparently intended to limit administrative discretion in the selection of capital cases. As so frequently occurs, the discretion which the legislature threw out the door was let in the window by the courts."

In 1937, we abandoned an earlier conception that deliberation and premeditation may be instantaneous, and held "that some appreciable time must elapse in order that reflection and consideration amounting to deliberation may occur."

* * * There is nothing deliberate and premeditated about a killing which is done within a second or two after the accused first thinks of doing it....

The need for careful attention to the requirement of premeditation and deliberation, and for clear distinction between the first and second degrees of murder, remains a cardinal tenet of our jurisprudence.

This historical review underscores our concern over three aspects of the court's instruction on first degree murder. The rulings of this court and the Supreme Court establish the propriety of the defense's request for a charge that the design of the accused to kill must have preceded his actions by an "appreciable" period of time before deliberation can be found. The Government contends that this error was not prejudicial because the crux of the issue of premeditation and deliberation is not the time involved but whether defendant did engage in the process of reflection and meditation. Certainly the charge should focus primarily on the defendant's actual thought processes in terms of meditation and conscious weighing of alternatives. The "appreciable time" element is subordinate, necessary for but not sufficient to establish deliberation. Yet the "appreciable time" charge is a meaningful way to convey to the jury the core meaning of premeditation and deliberation and for that reason should be given, at least where specifically requested by the defense. Moreover, the court's refusal so to instruct was compounded here by the charge that the time to deliberate "may be in the nature of hours, minutes *or seconds*." [N]o particular length of time is necessary for deliberation, and the time required need not be longer than a span of minutes. But none of our opinions sanctions the reference to "or seconds" injected by the trial judge. The obvious problem with such a reference is that it tends to blur, rather than clarify, the critical difference between impulsive and deliberate killings.

Finally, we note that after giving this misleading first degree instruction, the court offered only a skimpy explanation of second degree murder. Our concern is that there was no straightforward explanation to the jury of the difference between the two degrees of murder—that first degree murder, with its requirement of premeditation and deliberation, covers calculated and planned killings, while homicides that are unplanned or impulsive, even though they are intentional and with malice aforethought, are murder in the second degree.

In homespun terminology, intentional murder is in the first degree if committed in cold blood, and is murder in the second degree if committed on impulse or in the sudden heat of passion. These are the archetypes, that clarify by contrast. The real facts may be hard to classify and may lie between the poles. A sudden passion, like lust, rage, or jealousy, may spawn an impulsive intent yet persist long enough and in such a way as to permit that intent to become the subject of a further reflection and weighing of consequences and hence to take on the character of a murder executed without compunction and "in cold blood". The term "in cold blood" does not necessarily mean the assassin lying in wait, or the kind of murder brilliantly depicted by Truman Capote in *In Cold Blood* (1965). Thus the common understanding might find both passion and cold blood in the husband who surprises his wife in adultery, leaves the house to buy a gun at a sporting goods store, and returns for a deadly sequel. The analysis of the jury would be illuminated, however, if it is first advised that a typical case of first degree is the murder in cold blood; that murder committed on impulse or in sudden passion is murder in the second degree; and then instructed that a homicide conceived in passion constitutes murder in the first degree only if the jury is convinced beyond a reasonable doubt that there was an appreciable time after the design was conceived and that in this interval there was a further thought, and a turning over in the mind—and not a mere persistence of the initial impulse of passion.

In our opinion the Government's evidence was insufficient to warrant submission to the jury of the issue of premeditation and deliberation....

* * * The judge is aware that many murders most brutish and bestial are committed in a consuming frenzy or heat of passion, and that these are in law only murder in the second degree. The Government's evidence sufficed to establish an intentional and horrible murder—the kind that could be committed in a frenzy or heat of passion. However, the core responsibility of the court requires it to reflect on the sufficiency of the Government's case. We conclude that, making all due allowance for the trial court's function, but applying proper criteria as to the elements of murder in the first degree, the Government's evidence in this case did not establish a basis for a reasoned finding, surpassing speculation, that beyond all reasonable doubt this was not murder committed in an orgy of frenzied activity, possibly heightened by drink, but the act of "one who meditates an intent to kill and then deliberately executes it."

That appellant used a knife to accomplish the murder is not probative of premeditation and deliberation because he did not procure it specifically for that purpose but rather carried it about with him as a matter of course. The violence and multiple wounds, while more than ample to show an intent to kill, cannot standing alone, support an inference of a calmly calculated plan to kill requisite for premeditation and deliberation, as contrasted with an impulsive and senseless, albeit sustained, frenzy. That there was a half-hour period (4:30 a.m. until 5:00 a.m.) during which appellant had ample time to premeditate and deliberate is not evidence that appellant actually did cogitate and mull over the intent to kill. Finally the Government was not able to show any motive for the crime or any prior threats or quarrels between appellant and deceased which might support an inference of premeditation and deliberation. Thus the jury could only speculate and surmise, without any basis in the testimony or evidence, that appellant acted with premeditation and deliberation. The office of the motion for acquittal is precisely to avoid such improper and unfounded conjecture.

The claim that appellant acted not merely intentionally but with deliberation when he stabbed the unfortunate woman to death is manifestly not established beyond a reasonable doubt by evidence showing that he acted with deliberation afterward, in an effort to avoid detection and punishment—dragging the victim on the point of death down to the river; then fleeing; then feigning lack of any knowledge when the officer arrived. These facts may intensify emotional recoil against appellant. But they do not provide a reasoned basis for concluding beyond a reasonable doubt that the crime appellant sought to wash away, and run away from, was a crime he had committed not merely intentionally, in sustained frenzy or heat of passion, but beyond that with premeditation and deliberation!

The cause is remanded to the District Court with directions to enter a judgment of guilty of murder in the second degree and sentence accordingly, unless the District Court determines that a new trial is in the interest of justice.

So ordered.

DANAHER, CIRCUIT JUDGE (dissenting).

Let us turn to the testimony of the coroner. Dr. Rayford testified that Nettie Scott had been 5 feet 7 inches tall and had weighed 195 pounds. The exact cause of her death was hemorrhage from multiple stab wounds. A blood test revealed a .24 per cent of alcohol from which the witness concluded, the victim could have been considered well under the influence of alcohol. She had suffered a broken nose which, in the doctor's opinion, could have been caused by the blow of a human fist.

The doctor's examination revealed some 26 stab wounds resulting from the use of a sharp-bladed instrument. Additionally, the doctor had found at least 20 smaller wounds.

Finally, the doctor testified that the stab wounds could have been inflicted by an assailant who used a knife of the type he had found in the victim's head. The assailant had struck his victim above the jaw angle in such fashion that the knife blade penetrated the cranium and broke off in the skull.

Previously, the woman had been stabbed in the area of her sexual organs. Carved on the victim's thigh was an intricate design, much resembling what the doctor called a "tic-tac-toe." That any such result could have been achieved, the testimony ran, the victim must have been recumbent and passive by that time. It fairly could have been inferred by the trial judge from all the evidence and from the doctor's testimony, as it was by defense counsel, that this appellant had fought with his stupefied victim, had knocked her out, had stripped her of her clothing and sexually assaulted her. That all of these events must have involved a substantial period of time would seem beyond question. Finally, Austin had to take whatever time was necessary to drag her body to the river and to throw her in as he sought to drown her.

Austin had earlier used and had in his pocket a sharp knife. He had to decide to take that knife from his pocket and to open it. That thought and that action without more resulted from deliberation. He had evolved a definite purpose to wield that knife upon the woman. His plan and his actions reflected his intent, deliberately pursued, the judge could have deduced. Stab wounds in the chest had led to massive bleeding. Austin had stabbed Nettie Scott no less than four times in the vicinity of her sexual organ. Over and over again the assailant stabbed and cut his victim, a total of more than fifty times, until she was helpless. The last blow from the knife had been into her skull where the blade broke off.

Seeing that she was still alive, determined to kill her, Austin dragged her body some thirty-five feet down the bank and into the river that as a last resort in the accomplishment of his purpose, she would drown.

Then he took flight, giving rise to an inference of consciousness of guilt. Apprehended within a few minutes, he lied to the arresting officers as to his earlier movements.

Only sketchily have I reviewed the salient facts and only briefly touched upon the inferences that the judge was free to draw from those facts. I submit that the judge could properly come to no other conclusion than that Austin had acted with that degree of deliberation which the law requires.[4]

It will be remembered that my colleagues find error in the ruling upon the motion for acquittal at the close of the Government's case. It was the duty of the judge at that point to determine credibility and the weight to be given to the evidence and the justifiable inferences to be drawn from the facts he deemed to have been established. Thinking thus, upon all that had gone before, he readily could have concluded that Austin, with premeditation, had decided upon the steps he intended to take and with deliberation undertook to execute his plan. From the moment Austin reached into his pocket, took out his knife, opened it and commenced slashing and stabbing his victim, the successive steps might have required only a short time. But as his victim resisted him, kicked him, struggled for her life, Austin's purpose, deliberately conceived, was accentuated down to where his knife became lodged in her skull. He took one more step, finally. He had to drag that woman's dying body down to the river and throw it in. Deliberation? A "second thought"?

Comments and Questions

(1) If the prosecution proved "an intentional and horrible murder"—as the majority conceded—why was the defendant not guilty of first degree murder? Consider the following:

> The intent to kill can also be inferred from the manner in which the killing was accomplished. One is presumed to intend the natural, reasonable and probable consequences of his voluntary acts. Appellant is thus presumed to have intended the natural, reasonable and probable consequences of repeatedly striking his victim about the head with a hammer and strangling her with his hands and, later, with a rope.
>
> It has been the law of this state for more than one hundred years that, if a person has actually formed the purpose to maliciously kill another and deliberated and premeditated upon it before he performed the act of killing, he is guilty of murder in the first degree, however short the time may have been between the purpose and the execution. It is not the time of deliberation and premeditation that is requisite, but the actual existence of the purpose,

4. My colleagues' "cold blood" theory finds support in Capote's work, to be sure: the criteria I deem applicable derive from our case law.

> malice, deliberation and premeditation, and it matters not how short the time, if the party has actually turned it over in his mind and has weighed and deliberated upon it. It makes no difference whether the deliberation was in forming the design maliciously to kill, or, in the continuance of such design after being formed, until the same was executed. Thus, the law fixes no time within which premeditation and deliberation must be had. The time can be a matter of seconds if the situation is such as to enable a person under the circumstances, whatever they may be in the particular case, to turn over and to plan and to execute in pursuance of the plan, a realization of what one is about to do.

State v. Stewart, 198 N.E.2d 439, 443 (Ohio 1964). Is this statement consistent with *Austin*? In *Hairston v. Commonwealth*, 230 S.E.2d 626, 628 (Va. 1976), the court stated:

> A wilful, deliberate and premeditated killing is murder of the first degree. That does not mean, however, that in order for a killing to be murder of the first degree that any measurable period of time for pondering must elapse before the killing occurs. The intent to kill may come into existence for the first time at the time of the killing, or at any time prior thereto. It is the will and purpose to kill and not the interval of time which determines the grade of the offense.

Is this a correct statement of the law? Note Judge Leventhal's comment in *Hemphill v. United States*, 402 F.2d 187, 189 (D.C. Cir. 1968):

> In considering whether premeditation is permissibly inferred from this evidence we revert to the opinions in *Austin v. United States*, and *Belton v. United States*. In *Austin* the evidence showed a killing caused by twenty-six major stab wounds from a pocket knife. There was no testimony indicating motive. The court held the evidence was as consistent with an impulsive and senseless frenzy as with premeditation, and did not permit a reasonable juror to find beyond reasonable doubt that there was premeditation. In *Belton*, the court upheld a first degree murder conviction where the evidence showed that defendant quarreled with his common law wife, brought a loaded gun with him to her apartment, and shot her soon after he entered.
>
> In the present case when the trial judge asked what evidence the Government was relying on to establish premeditation, the prosecutor referred only to the fact that the killer had climbed a flight of stairs to Phillip's room. Though the time to go upstairs is more likely to be measured in seconds than minutes, we may assume it was appreciable enough to have been consistent with a killing that was the product of deliberation rather than impulse. But the jury may not find premeditation solely from the fact that defendant had time to premeditate. This is established by *Austin*, where there was time enough for premeditation but the facts of the killing were equally consistent with a mind in the grip of a sustained frenzy. The prosecutor made no attempt to show animosity or any other motive for the killing by appellant.

(2) If the defendant brings a deadly weapon with him, encounters the victim, and uses the weapon to kill, does that establish first degree murder? In *Clarke v. State*, 402 S.W.2d 863, 867 (Tenn. 1966), *cert. denied*, 385 U.S. 942 (1966), the court wrote:

> Paula was shot to death and malice is inferred from the use of a deadly weapon. She was not only shot once but twice and then in the back while she lay face down on the floor in a semiconscious or unconscious condition from the results of a beating about the face. These facts, accepted by the jury, are enough to support a finding this murder was premeditated.
>
> The distinctive characteristic of murder in the first degree is premeditation. This element is super-added, by the statute, to the common law definition of murder. Premeditation involves a previously formed design, or actual intention to kill. But such design, or intention, may be conceived, and deliberately formed, in an instant. It is not necessary that it should have been conceived, or have preexisted in the mind, any definite period of time anterior to its execution. It is sufficient that it preceded the assault, however short the interval. The length of time is not of the essence of this constituent of the offense. The purpose to kill is no less premeditated, in the legal sense of the term, if it were deliberately formed but a moment preceding the act.

A similar finding of premeditation was based on evidence that the defendant had a romantic history with the victim, that tension developed when he became involved with another woman, that he retrieved a gun from his sister's home after being taunted by the victim, and that he walked toward the victim and fired multiple shots while she was unarmed and seated. *United States v. Thomas*, 664 F.3d 217 (8th Cir. 2011).

Would the facts in *Clarke* be sufficient under the statement of the military court in *United States v. Hoskins*, 36 M.J. 343, 346 (C.M.A. 1993)?:

> We must find that there is more than evidence of intent before we can affirm the decision below in this case: what we must also find is evidence of a "premeditated design to kill." Premeditation requires that one with a cool mind did, in fact, reflect before killing.

See also *Wells v. Commonwealth*, 57 S.E.2d 898, 901 (Va. 1950), where the court held that the defendant arming himself with a knife "suggests a fear of the deceased as readily as a purpose willfully to kill him," and *Hervey v. People*, 495 P.2d 204, 207 (Colo. 1972), where the court also held that "the use of a deadly weapon, of itself, is not a sufficient basis for the legal presumption that the killing was deliberate, premeditated."

(3) Following the common law tradition, some states have chosen not to divide murder into degrees. Other states, however, have attempted to refine the first degree murder rule, though using different terminology.

The newly amended statute reads:

> No person shall purposely, and with prior calculation and design, cause the death of another.

> Prior calculation and design sets up a more demanding standard than the old first degree murder standard of "deliberate and premeditated malice." Prior calculation and design requires the accused to have killed purposefully after devising a plan or scheme to kill. There must be some kind of studied analysis with its object being the means by which to kill. The kind of momentary deliberation or instantaneous premeditation that was the accepted standard under the old statute is no longer sufficient or acceptable.
>
> The trier of fact must look to the context in which the killing occurred to determine whether there was prior calculation and design. Some of the important factors to be examined and considered in deciding whether a homicide was committed with prior calculation and design include: whether the accused knew the victim prior to the crime, as opposed to a random meeting, and if the victim was known to him whether the relationship had been strained; whether thought and preparation were given by the accused to the weapon he used to kill and/or the site on which the homicide was to be committed as compared to no such thought or preparation; and whether the act was drawn out over a period of time as against an almost instantaneous eruption of events. These factors must be considered and weighed together and viewed under the totality of all circumstances of the homicide. When the evidence adduced at trial establishes that the victim was unknown to the accused prior to the crime, and that there was little or no preparation, but rather that the crime was an instantaneous eruption of events, then the trial court shall not charge the jury on aggravated murder. If the evidence adduced at trial is legally insufficient to establish any essential element of the crime charged the trial court shall not charge the jury as to that offense.

State v. Jenkins, 355 N.E.2d 825, 828 (Ohio Ct. App. 1976).

(4) Several cases illustrate the debate concerning the first degree murder statutes. The language in *Thomerson v. Lockhart*, 835 F.2d 1257, 1259 (8th Cir. 1987), is quite striking: "Although Thomerson may have begun to beat his girl friend out of anger over her unfaithfulness, a reasonable jury could infer from the evidence that as Thomerson continued to assault the woman his actions became calculated and deliberate … [and] could find the nature, extent, and location of these wounds in addition to Thomerson's conduct in inflicting them indicate he premeditated and deliberated the murder." The Tennessee Supreme Court, however, expressed its frustration with the inability of courts to maintain the distinctions between first and second-degree murder in *State v. Brown*, 836 S.W.2d 530, 542 (Tenn. 1992):

> Repeated blows can be delivered in the heat of passion with no design or reflection.… Certainly, more than the mere fact of "repeated blows" must be shown to establish first-degree murder … we conclude that it is prudent to abandon an instruction that tells the jury that "premeditation may be formed in an instant." [For first-degree murder requires proof] that the homicide was "committed with a 'cool purpose' and without passion or provocation,"

> which would reduce the offense to either second-degree murder or to manslaughter, respectively.

In *State v. Bingham*, 719 P.2d 109, 113 (Wash. 1986), the defendant caused the victim's death by strangling her over a 3- to 5-minute period. Held, such evidence shows only "the opportunity to deliberate," not actual "deliberation or reflection before or during the strangulation, only the strangulation." Also in a prosecution for first-degree murder, evidence that the victim suffered injuries consistent with prolonged strangulation was insufficient to establish premeditation where the state failed to prove that the injuries inflicted were such that the killer would have had sufficient time to reflect on his actions. *Balzourt v. State*, 75 So.3d 830 (Fla. Dist. Ct. App. 2011). The court in *Clozza v. Commonwealth*, 321 S.E.2d 273 (Va. 1984), took a different view: "A design to kill may be formed only a moment before the fatal act is committed provided the accused had time to think and did intend to kill."

The court in *Byford v. State*, 994 P.2d 700, 714–15 (Nev. 2000), approved the following instruction:

> Deliberation is the process of determining upon a course of action to kill as a result of thought, including weighing the reasons for and against the action and considering the consequences of the action. A deliberate determination may be arrived at in a short period of time. But in all cases the determination must not be formed in passion, or if formed in passion, it must be carried out after there has been time for the passion to subside and deliberation to occur. A mere unconsidered and rash impulse is not deliberate, even though it includes the intent to kill. Premeditation is a design, a determination to kill, distinctly formed in the mind by the time of the killing. Premeditation need not be for a day, an hour, or even a minute. It may be as instantaneous as successive thoughts of the mind. For if the jury believes from the evidence that the act constituting the killing has been preceded by and has been the result of premeditation, no matter how rapidly the act follows the premeditation, it is premeditated. The law does not undertake to measure in units of time the length of the period during which the thought must be pondered before it can ripen into an intent to kill which is truly deliberate and premeditated. The time will vary with different individuals and under varying circumstances. The true test is not the duration of time, but rather the extent of the reflection. A cold, calculated judgment and decision may be arrived at in a short period of time, but a mere unconsidered and rash impulse, even though it includes an intent to kill, is not deliberation and premeditation as will fix an unlawful killing as murder of the first degree.

As stated succinctly by the court in *State v. Guthrie*, 461 S.E.2d 163, 181 (W. Va. 1995),

> To allow the state to prove premeditation and deliberation by only showing that the intention came "into existence for the first time at the time of such killings" completely eliminates the distinction between the two degrees of murder.

Consider Justice Cardozo's view:

> There can be no intent unless there is choice, yet by the hypothesis, the choice without more is enough to justify the inference that the intent was deliberate and premeditated. The presence of a sudden impulse is said to mark the dividing line, but how can an impulse be anything but sudden when the time for its formation is measured by the lapse of seconds? Yet the decisions are to the effect that seconds may be enough.... If intent is deliberate and premeditated whenever there is choice, then in truth it is always deliberate and premeditated, since choice is involved in the hypothesis of the intent. What we have is merely a privilege offered to the jury to find the lesser degree when the suddenness of the intent, the vehemence of the passion, seems to call irresistibly for the exercise of mercy. I have no objection to giving them this dispensing power, but it should be given to them directly and not in a mystifying cloud of words.

Cardozo, "What Medicine Can Do for Law," *Law and Literature and Other Essays and Addresses* 70, 96–101 (1931).

[4] The Corpus Delicti

People v. Scott

California District Court of Appeal
176 Cal. App. 2d 458, 1 Cal. Rptr. 600 (1959)

SHINN, PRESIDING JUSTICE.

L. Ewing Scott was convicted of the murder of his wife Evelyn, who disappeared from her home May 16, 1955.

The principal contention is that there was insufficient evidence to establish the corpus delicti. The evidence was wholly circumstantial. It is not claimed that in a trial for murder the death of a missing person and the use of criminal means to accomplish death cannot be proved by circumstantial evidence, provided it is sufficient to preclude every reasonable theory of innocence of the accused. The principle is well established. If it were not so we would have to hold the evidence insufficient to support the verdict.

Mrs. Scott simply disappeared from her house, dropped out of sight, and has not been heard from. There was no evidence of violence or other means of death used upon her and no body, or part of a body has been found. Appellant did not testify at the trial. His only explanation of his wife's disappearance has been that she left home in her car about 4:30 p.m. during his temporary absence and that he has not seen or heard from her since that time. He asks where is there evidence as to when she died, where she died and how she died, or that she is dead. The People reply that the answers to these questions are to be found in a multitude of circumstances developed by the testimony of many witnesses and reported in some 6,000 pages of the reporter's transcript.

The case in hand is without precedent in this country. There is no reported case from our state or federal courts that in its facts bears close resemblance to the present one. For that reason we shall not abbreviate our statement of the evidence nor our analysis of it. In some respects the evidence was cumulative, but properly so. The jurors no doubt gained a better understanding of many occurrences and conditions described in detail by numerous witnesses than could have been conveyed to them by mere generalizations of only a few.

The theory of the People can be stated as follows: It would be utterly unreasonable to believe that Mrs. Scott would have run away from her home, her husband and her friends; it would have been an irrational thing for her to do. If it was unreasonable to believe that she would have left home voluntarily that would have been a circumstance tending logically to prove that she did not leave of her own accord. The People's theory then proceeds to the activities of appellant both before and after his wife's disappearance. It is contended that the evidence proved that he had a motive for doing away with his wife, he coveted her large estate, attempted to prepare her friends for an explanation of her disappearance at some future time, was pleased and satisfied when she disappeared, did everything in his power to deceive her friends and the authorities in order to prevent an investigation, promptly set about through forgeries and thefts to steal her property, and fled the country when he feared that he would be charged with her murder. Thus the evidence was centered in proof of the characters, the motives and the activities of two persons. More precisely, it was centered in proof of their respective states of mind which would tell whether Mrs. Scott had a reason or purpose for running away, whether appellant had a motive and a plan for making away with her and whether he knew after the 16th day of May, 1955, that she was dead.

Mrs. Scott was 63 years of age. Her marriage to appellant was her fifth. At the time of her marriage to appellant Evelyn had an estate of the value of some $400,000. Her yearly income was around $20,000. A few years after her marriage to appellant she converted securities worth in excess of $200,000 into cash and made no new investments. Her income thereafter was from her Milwaukee property and amounted to about $17,000 a year. Appellant, who was not a man of means, and was without income, depended upon his wife for support.

There was evidence of physicians and friends that Mrs. Scott was in good mental and physical health; she was intelligent, gay, devoted to many fine friends, leading a tranquil domestic life, possessed of a more than ample estate and income and quite satisfied with her way of life. The evidence tended to prove that if she went away it was without preparation, without money or extra clothing and leaving behind two pairs of eyeglasses and a denture which she habitually wore, and which were subsequently found on adjoining property buried under leaves and ashes. With respect to the conduct of appellant after his wife's disappearance it is contended that his attempts to frustrate an investigation and his every act and statement proved beyond question that he knew his wife was dead.

[Ed.: The court then recounted the evidence in great detail.]

Commencing immediately after May 16th appellant entered upon a course of concealment and deceit calculated to forestall an investigation of his wife's disappearance.

The first step in a calculated plan to account for Mrs. Scott's disappearance was the cancellation of her appointment at the beauty shop on May 17th and all future weekly appointments.

Mrs. Scott's friends soon became alarmed over their frequent unsuccessful attempts to communicate with her by telephone. Mrs. Baum had been calling early in the morning and late in the evening, but had received no answer. About the middle of June appellant telephoned her that he was returning a book that had been loaned to Mrs. Scott. He told Mrs. Baum that Mrs. Scott was ill and had been ill for two years, that he was closing the house and preparing to take her to Baltimore or New York for treatment. Mrs. Baum asked to speak to Evelyn and offered to help but was told that she was too ill to talk and there was nothing Mrs. Baum could do. Appellant promised to let Mrs. Baum know where Evelyn would be in the East but she heard nothing more from him. A letter she sent to Mrs. Scott expressing her distress over the latter's illness was not returned.

The controlling questions were whether Mrs. Scott left her home voluntarily and alone and whether appellant knew after the 16th of May that his wife was dead. If it was found that Mrs. Scott left home alone it would follow that appellant was not guilty of her murder. If she did not leave home voluntarily, her body was removed by some one who had already caused her death or she was taken by some one who had planned it. This could have been no one other than appellant. The verdict implies that the jury concluded that Mrs. Scott did not leave home by herself and that appellant knew after May 16th that she was dead. These were inferences which it would have been necessary for the jury to draw in order to reach the conclusion of appellant's guilt.

It is not enough that the jury should have believed that the proved circumstances tended strongly to establish the guilt of appellant. The final test to be applied was whether the facts found and the reasonable inferences from them proved the nonexistence of any reasonable hypothesis of innocence.

Appellant contends that since no body was produced, no direct evidence of death was introduced and there was no confession, the People's case was based upon mere suspicion and conjecture.

If this contention is valid it would mean that a man could commit a secret murder and escape punishment if he was able to completely destroy the body of his victim, however complete and convincing the circumstantial evidence of guilt. No one would say that the law should be powerless to uncover such a crime and inflict punishment unless the accused had made a confession. The question, however, is whether it is so inadequate. We hold that it is not.

The corpus delicti can be proved by circumstantial evidence. Can circumstantial evidence be sufficient to supply proof of guilt so convincing as to preclude every reasonable hypothesis of innocence? We hold that it can be sufficient.

All that is required to prove death is circumstantial evidence sufficient to convince the minds of reasonable men of the existence of the fact. The law employs the judgment of reasonable minds as the only means of arriving at the truth by inference from the circumstances in evidence. If this were not true, an infinite number of crimes involving the element of a specific intent would go unpunished.

In the reported cases of murder there was almost invariably proof of death consisting of (1) direct evidence of the use of the means of death upon the body of the missing person, as in some cases of death at sea; (2) production of a body or part of a body identified as that of the missing person; or (3) incriminating circumstances sufficient to prove the corpus delicti and an admission or confession of the fact of death. There may be added a few cases of the disappearance of infants under suspicious circumstances in which the fact of death was satisfactorily proved. These are of no assistance.

There are a great many cases of the third class which without exception hold that proof of the corpus delicti plus a confession is legally sufficient. The facts of the present case, in our opinion, bring it clearly within the principle of the confession cases.

It cannot be doubted that in the present case there was *prima facie* proof of death by criminal means. There remained the question of the quantum of the proof, which consisted entirely of circumstantial evidence. But it will be presently shown that the circumstantial evidence of the fact of death by criminal means was as strong and convincing as a confession would have been and much stronger than a confession of questionable validity.

Testimony that appellant had made statements that his wife was dead, if credited, would have constituted sufficient proof that he knew she was dead. The value of the testimony, however, would depend upon the credibility of the witnesses and the accuracy of their testimony as to what appellant had been overheard to say. But there could be no mistake as to the circumstances which pointed to the fact that after the 16th day of May, appellant knew his wife to be dead. The circumstances indicating the motives and state of mind of appellant prior to his wife's disappearance were created by him and no one else. He alone created the circumstances after the disappearance of his wife which indicated the state of his mind and his knowledge that she would not return.

Whether appellant knew that his wife was dead was a question of fact susceptible to proof by circumstantial evidence.

We could not declare the evidence legally insufficient except by holding that it furnished no good reason for believing that Mrs. Scott was murdered by appellant and that it was consistent only with his innocence. We entertain no such motion. We have searched the record in vain for a reason that could have caused the jury to doubt that Mrs. Scott was murdered on the 16th of May. In our opinion, the only reasonable material factual conclusions are those which the jury presumably reached.

The circumstances that were established without dispute furnished strong evidence that Mrs. Scott met her death on or about the 16th day of May, 1955. But, as we have said, the test was whether the evidence of death was so overpowering as to preclude every reasonable hypothesis that she did not die at that time. The task of the jury could not have been completed without an exhaustive search for a reasonable ground for believing that she was alive when she left her home.

Our review of the evidence takes into consideration certain implied factual findings of the jury based upon the circumstances in evidence and those inferences which were necessarily drawn in order to furnish support for the verdict.

There was evidence from which the jury could, and presumably did reach many factual conclusions consistent only with appellant's guilt, among them the following:

1. Mrs. Scott was in sound physical and mental health; she was intelligent, competent, poised and self-controlled; her domestic life was tranquil and her social life satisfying to an unusual extent; she had a large number of devoted friends for whom she had great affection and whose society she enjoyed almost daily; her friendships were intimate, constant and they continued to the date of her disappearance; they were her principal interest in life. She took pleasure in small benefactions for a few old friends, which were greatly appreciated. She was well to do and had an ample income; she had suffered no misfortune or upsetting experience; she had expressed no intention or desire to go away but had said she would not be happy away from her friends. The jury inferred that it would be unreasonable to believe that Mrs. Scott had any motive for running away or that she would have left home voluntarily. This was a reasonable inference. It would have been an irrational thing to do and Mrs. Scott was not irrational.

2. She would not have left home without her eyeglasses and her denture. She would not have thrown them away. Some one found them after her departure and threw them away. When she removed the denture at night she always replaced it with the retaining device, which has not been found. These circumstances indicated that she retired the night of May 16th after removing the denture and installing the retaining device.

3. If Mrs. Scott had intended to leave home she would have taken money, baggage and a wardrobe.

4. It would have been impossible for her to conceal herself for several years and find a way to live without drawing upon her bank accounts. It was incredible that if alive she would not have communicated with friends.

5. Appellant had a motive for doing away with his wife. It would give him a chance to steal her money through forgery of her name upon many documents. After her disappearance he displayed no sorrow, no regret or other human emotion. He spoke no kind word of her, only vilification and abuse. He appeared to be well satisfied to have her out of the way.

6. Appellant's purpose in persuading his wife to convert her securities into cash was to make it easier for him to obtain her property through forgeries.

7. Every act, every statement of appellant after the disappearance of his wife was consistent only with knowledge that Mrs. Scott was dead. His bold forgeries and thefts indicated that he knew she could not return to accuse him. On the morning of May 17th he canceled all her future appointments at the beauty shop; he gave to Mrs. Hanson his wife's belongings, including her favorite jacket; he showered gifts of his wife's jewelry and personal belongings upon a female bedroom guest in his

wife's home; he told Mrs. Livermore he planned to wait seven years until his wife could be declared legally dead; only he could have thrown away the eyeglasses and denture; he was the one who had ashes from the incinerator thrown onto the neighbor's property; he would not have canceled insurance of $6,500 upon his wife's jewelry, to be effective May 17th, unless he knew his wife was dead; his constant lies that his wife had been or was to be sent East for treatment proved that he feared an investigation of her disappearance. Why was it necessary "to spend most of the day" on May 17th cleaning up Mrs. Scott's car and why did he not notify the police of her disappearance at that time or at any time thereafter? The jury no doubt inferred that the car was in a condition that required the removal of something more than a few spots of dirt and that appellant did not want it to be seen until it had been thoroughly cleaned.

We must presume that all the material questions suggested by the evidence were answered by the jury in a manner which pointed toward appellant's guilt. The jury could reasonably have found, and no doubt did find, that every statement of appellant, every act and failure to act tended to prove that he was pleased to be rid of his wife.

Appellant has not mentioned and we have not found a single circumstance indicative of a belief on his part that Mrs. Scott was alive after her disappearance. Upon the contrary, every statement, every activity of his, was consistent with knowledge that she was dead.

Appellant has been content with the statement that his wife drove away in her car and did not return. He has made no attempt to give a reason for her disappearance. He has offered no explanation of his own conduct. It has been left to the jurors to determine what implications it carried. We can only conclude that appellant has felt immune from a conviction of murder in the belief that his wife's body lies where it cannot be found. This has been his attitude from the beginning.

It is our opinion that the circumstantial evidence forms a complete pattern of murder, from the first circumstance tending to prove appellant's motive, through his flight into Canada and his unwillingness to take the stand to deny, excuse or explain the conduct of which he stood accused. We have found in the evidence no rational explanation of the disappearance of Mrs. Scott other than her murder by appellant. We have been unable to reconcile the evidence with a theory that she was alive after May 16th.

In our study of the evidence we have found no reason for questioning the correctness of the verdict. Although, as we have said, the case is factually without precedent, it is not without precedent in principle or in the law, which allows death to be proved by circumstantial evidence. Appellant wove about himself a web of incriminating circumstances that was complete. He has evolved from the evidence no theory of innocence; the jury could not find such a theory, nor can we. Appellant merely says, and others may say, "But Mrs. Scott may still be alive." They would have to rest their belief upon some mythical or miraculous hypothesis, since it could not find support in any reasonable deduction from the established facts. But the law is reason; it does not proceed upon fantasy or remote and unrealistic possibilities.

Because of the multitude of material circumstances established by the testimony of many witnesses and documentary evidence, we have gone to unusual lengths in our statement of the record. The undisputed facts point unerringly to a single conclusion. The evidence of appellant's guilt was convincing. We can only regard the verdict as a reasonable and just disposition of the charge that appellant murdered his wife. He was accorded a fair trial. There is no reason for disturbing the judgment or order.

The judgment and the order denying motion for a new trial are *affirmed*.

Comments and Questions

(1) For a criminal conviction, our system requires proof beyond a reasonable doubt. Without "evidence as to when she (the victim) died, where she died and how she died" how did the prosecution prove beyond a reasonable doubt that she was dead? See *State v. Thompson*, 870 P.2d 1022 (Wash. Ct. App. 1994), where the court relied on evidence regarding the victim's habits for cleanliness, reliability, and punctuality, the failure to see anyone after making several appointments, the presence of dirty dishes in the house, and the fact that her cat was left for days without food and water.

(2) In accord with *Scott* is *Commonwealth v. Burns*, 187 A.2d 552, 555 (Pa. 1963):

> Marie Coleman borrowed money from a bank in April 1958, which required repayment in monthly installments which were made each month within the time prescribed by the loan conditions. The last payment was received by the bank on December 17, 1958 and there were no other payments made, although there was much more money due on the loan to be paid in future monthly installments. Her credit rating was excellent.
>
> The police made an extensive search in an attempt to find her or learn something of her whereabouts.
>
> An examination of the premises occupied by the defendant and Marie Coleman revealed all her apparel, jewelry, underclothing, medication, toothbrush, comb and luggage and several coats and all the articles she owned were intact in the premises.
>
> The Commonwealth's purpose in submission of its evidence was to establish the corpus delicti by showing the habits and way of life of Marie Coleman. The consistency of her practice of maintaining a close relationship with her family and friends, who were numerous, and with her daughter and grandchildren in Detroit. She had a good credit rating and a recognition of financial obligations to be met regularly and on time. Her employment enabled her to meet her obligations and enabled her to buy gifts and send greeting cards on holidays, birthdays and other times throughout the year to her relatives. She was able to spend time with her daughter and grandchildren in Detroit on her annual summer trip to be with them, when she brought gifts for her family. Any time Marie Coleman would make a trip she would advise members of her family she was leaving.
>
> Her customs were well known.

The Commonwealth advances its position of establishment of the corpus delicti by showing a well, healthy woman, with a consistent pattern of living for many years and a sudden and abrupt termination of such pattern without any prior preparation or discussion with any of her relatives or friends; her disappearance without natural or legitimate reason or cause established the corpus delicti by showing circumstantially (1) death; and (2) felonious circumstances surrounding her disappearance abruptly and without apparent cause. The last time she was seen was in the presence of the defendant in an apparently helpless condition on the floor of their common abode in circumstances that would indicate she was unconscious or incapable of moving herself.

"It is elementary that the term corpus delicti with respect to homicide does not require the Commonwealth to produce the body or part of the body of the victim. The rule is satisfied by evidence, other than the confession, from which the jury on proper instructions may find that the child's death resulted from a felonious act. The fact may be found on circumstantial evidence."

The Commonwealth then produced other evidence in addition to that submitted for the purpose of establishing the corpus delicti, the additional evidence to show the defendant as the party responsible for the homicide.

See also People v. Manson, 71 Cal. App. 3d 1, 139 Cal. Rptr. 275, 298 (1977), *cert. denied*, 435 U.S. 953 (1978):

Here Manson places great emphasis on the fact that Shea's body was never recovered. The fact that Shea's body was never recovered would justify an inference by the jury that death was caused by a criminal agency. It is highly unlikely that a person who dies from natural causes will successfully dispose of his own body. Although such a result may be a theoretical possibility, it is contrary to the normal course of human affairs.

The fact that a murderer may successfully dispose of the body of the victim does not entitle him to an acquittal. That is one form of success for which society has no reward. Production of the body is not a condition precedent to the prosecution for murder.

"Here the corpus delicti consists of two elements, the death of the alleged victims and the existence of some criminal agency as the cause, either or both of which may be proved circumstantially or inferentially. It is not necessary in order to support the conviction that the bodies actually be found.... Proof of the corpus delicti does not require identity of the perpetrators. It is not necessary that it connect the defendant with the commission of the crime although it may do so. Nor does motive form any part of the corpus delicti. It is the settled rule, however, that the corpus delicti must be established independently of admissions of the defendant. Conviction cannot be had on his extrajudicial admissions or confessions without proof *aliunde* of the corpus delicti; but full proof of the body of the crime, sufficient to convince the jury of its conclusive character, is not necessary before the admis-

> sions may be received. A *prima facie* showing that the alleged victims met death by a criminal agency is all that is required. The defendant's extrajudicial statements are then admissible, the order of proof being discretionary, and together with the *prima facie* showing must satisfy the jury beyond a reasonable doubt. The purpose of the rule is to protect the defendant against the possibility of fabricated testimony which might wrongfully establish the crime and the perpetrator."
>
> Here the prosecution's evidence established that Shea was dead and that he met death by criminal means; it established that Manson, and his family, had a significant motive to murder Shea. Manson's own admissible admissions establish guilt beyond a reasonable doubt. The evidence was clearly sufficient.

(3) "Corpus delicti," the body of the crime, is not literally limited to a human body for homicide. In one case, the evidence showed that the victim and the defendant were friends and had previously ingested drugs together. Additionally, the victim sent a picture of himself to the victim holding a handful of prescription pills and a bottle cap. The victim did not have a prescription for the pills, but the defendant did. Finally, the defendant filled her prescriptions the afternoon before the victim's death, but the bottles were almost empty the following day. Combined, the evidence was sufficient for the defendant's conviction for controlled substance homicide where circumstantial evidence established a reasonable inference that the defendant provided the victim with the pills that caused the victim's death. *State v. Zillyette*, 256 P.3d 1288 (Wash. Ct. App. 2011). In this context, corpus delicti means that the prosecution must prove a criminal act and a resulting injury. In Washington an incriminating statement cannot be sufficient alone for conviction, absent independent proof of the corpus delicti, which the defendant claimed was lacking on causation.

Tennessee abandoned the traditional corpus delicti rule for extrajudicial confessions in *State v. Bishop*, 431 S.W.3d 22 (Tenn. 2014), requiring that such confessions must meet a "modified trustworthiness" standard. Under this standard, when a defendant challenges the admission of a confession on lack-of-corroboration grounds, the trial court must begin by asking whether the charged offense is one that involves a tangible injury. If so, then the state must provide substantial independent evidence showing that the defendant's statement is trustworthy, plus independent *prima facie* evidence that the injury actually occurred.

[C] Manslaughter

[1] Voluntary Manslaughter

> A person commits the offense of voluntary manslaughter when he causes the death of another human being under circumstances which would otherwise be murder, and if he acts solely as the result of a sudden, violent, and irresistible passion resulting from serious provocation sufficient to excite such passion in a reasonable person; however, if there should have been an

> interval between the provocation and the killing sufficient for the voice of reason and humanity to be heard, of which the jury in all cases shall be the judge, the killing shall be attributed to deliberate revenge and be punished as murder.

Ga. Code Ann., Section 16-5-2.

> The elements of heat of passion are (1) adequate provocation; (2) a passion or emotion such as fear, terror, anger, rage or resentment; (3) [the] homicide occurred while the passion still existed and before a reasonable opportunity for the passion to cool; and (4) a causal connection between the provocation, passion, and homicide.

Hogan v. Gibson, 197 F.3d 1297, 1308 (10th Cir. 1999).

State v. Soto

Supreme Court of New Hampshire
34 A.3d 738 (2011)

LYNN, J.

I.

The defendant's conviction arises out of the fatal shooting of Aaron Kar in Manchester on the evening of January 2, 2007. On the previous day, a man named Bill threatened Roney White's young cousins with a knife at a 7-Eleven store close to Roney's home. When Roney learned of the incident from his cousins, he directed them to identify the man with the knife. Finding Bill standing outside the store, Roney punched him in the face in retaliation and fled the scene. Later that night, apparently in response to Roney's actions, Kar and his friends drove past a small group of people standing on the street, which included Roney, his brother Roscoe White, and their friend Anthony Clagon, and unsuccessfully attempted to hit one of them with a stick from the moving vehicle. No further encounter between the two groups occurred that night.

The next day, at around 2:30 p.m., Bill and another person attacked Roney with a baseball bat as he was walking alone on Nashua Street. Badly injured, Roney stumbled home to his mother and two brothers, Roscoe and Raymond Alleyene. Roney's mother took him to the hospital. Shortly thereafter, Alleyene, Clagon, and Roscoe met at Roscoe's house and discussed the possibility of an armed fight in retaliation for the attack on Roney. After Roscoe failed to get his own gun to work, he called some friends in Nashua, asking them to bring a gun.

That evening, the defendant, his brother Sergio, Andrew Gonzalez, and Clagon's cousin Kim and her children drove from Nashua to Manchester in a red Chevrolet Blazer. The men met Clagon, Alleyene, and Roscoe in the room Roscoe shared with Roney, smoked marijuana, and settled on a plan to find Roney's attackers and confront them. After Roscoe confirmed that the defendant had brought a gun, the six men set out in the Blazer to find Roney's attackers. A short time later, they found a group of people whom they suspected had been involved in Roney's attack gathered near a dumpster. After driving past the group once or twice, they parked the Blazer around the corner and discussed who would do the shooting. They settled on Roscoe as the shooter based on his blood relationship with Roney. The defendant then wiped the gun with his shirt, racked the slide to cock it, and handed it to Roscoe. Roscoe left with a mask on, shot Kar in the leg and abdomen, returned to the Blazer, and the men drove away. Kar later died from his wounds.

* * *

II.

The defendant first argues that the trial court should have instructed the jury to consider whether the defendant acted under an extreme mental or emotional disturbance caused by extreme provocation, thereby reducing his criminal liability from murder to manslaughter. He argues that "there was overwhelming evidence to support a jury determination that Soto had been adequately provoked within the meaning of [the provocation provision of the manslaughter statute]." We disagree.

* * *

"A person is guilty of manslaughter when he causes the death of another ... [u]nder the influence of extreme mental or emotional disturbance caused by extreme provocation but which would otherwise constitute murder." Under the common-law rule, to reduce the crime of murder to manslaughter, the provocation must be so severe or extreme as to provoke a reasonable person to kill another person out of passion.[1] Even if a reasonable person would have committed the act, still the defendant must have been actually provoked. And even a defendant so provoked will not be entitled to a manslaughter instruction where the time elapsing between the provocation and the killing is such that a reasonable person would have cooled. "[I]f, from any circumstances whatever, it appears that the party reflected, deliberated, or cooled any period of time before the fatal stroke was given, or if in legal presumption there was time or opportunity for cooling, the killing will amount to murder, being attributable to malice and revenge, and not to mental disturbance."

* * *

Turning now to the circumstances of the instant case, we conclude that the undisputed facts culminating in Kar's death reveal no evidence upon which a provocation instruction was warranted. At least two hours passed between the moment the defendant learned by telephone that Roney had been attacked and the moment the de-

1. Most modern formulations of the common-law "heat of passion" doctrine measure both the adequacy of the provocation and the severity of the response by a "reasonable person" standard. 2 W. LaFave, *Substantive Criminal Law* § 15.2(b)(10), at 504 (2d ed. 2003). Unlike in the tort context, however, the reasonable person standard in the provocation context is not a standard of acceptable, non-blameworthy conduct; rather it is a fiction that stands for a centuries-old recognition that, in certain extreme circumstances, even an average person of ordinary disposition may suffer a temporary loss of reason and control. *See id.* at 495 ("[T]he reasonable man, however greatly provoked he may be, does not kill."). Provocation manslaughter is, therefore, a "concession to human frailty," reflected in the fact that a person killing under an extreme mental or emotional disturbance in response to extreme provocation has committed a serious crime—manslaughter—but not as serious a crime as first or second-degree murder.

fendant and his friends found and killed Kar. In that time, the defendant located a loaded gun, drove with his friends from Nashua to Manchester, met with Roscoe and several others at Roscoe's home, smoked marijuana, and discussed how to avenge the attack on Roney. The drive to Manchester took about one-half hour and the discussion in Roney's home took at least an additional half-hour. Then, with the defendant's brother driving, they set out to find Roney's assailants on the street. When they found the men they were looking for, they drove past once or twice, parked around the corner, and discussed for about seven or eight minutes who would do the shooting. After the group settled on Roscoe as the shooter, the defendant pulled out a gun, wiped it off, cocked it, and gave it to Roscoe, telling him the gun was "smooth."

This sequence is not consistent with a sudden emotional disturbance from which the defendant had no time to regain control of his passions. Even assuming that Kar was the person with Bill during the attack on Roney the day before, and that such attack both actually and reasonably provoked the defendant, a reasonable person would not remain in that extreme emotional state after driving to a different city, meeting with several friends to discuss how to retaliate, taking the time to smoke marijuana, and again driving to search for one's provokers. The law is careful to distinguish a sudden rush of passion following extreme provocation, on the one hand, from a desire for revenge, on the other. A provocation manslaughter instruction is simply not appropriate where, as here, the defendant has killed after a period of reflection and deliberation during which a reasonable person's passions would have cooled. *See* LaFave, *supra* § 15.2(d), at 507; *see also State v. Ramirez*, 116 Ariz. 259, 569 P.2d 201, 213 (1977) (four and a half hours sufficient to show cool state of mind); *Com. v. Colon*, 449 Mass. 207, 866 N.E.2d 412, 425 (2007) ("[W]here the alleged provocation is followed by at least a few minutes during which the defendant and the victim are separated, and then the defendant *seeks out the victim*, a charge of voluntary manslaughter based on provocation is not warranted." (emphasis added)); *Com. v. Keohane*, 444 Mass. 563, 829 N.E.2d 1125, 1130 (2005) ("[E]ven where sufficient provocation exists, if a defendant leaves the scene of the provocation ... and then returns to attack the victim, the defendant is considered to have had adequate opportunity for his anger to subside."); *People v. Pouncey*, 437 Mich. 382, 471 N.W.2d 346, 351 (1991) (going to safe harbor and retrieving gun is sufficient cooling time).

Equally implausible is the defendant's contention that he had not actually cooled off. "[A defendant] cannot have his homicide reduced to voluntary manslaughter if ... he has actually cooled off by the time he commits his deadly act." LaFave, *supra* § 15.2(e), at 509. Anger alone is not sufficient to warrant a provocation instruction; the law requires an extreme emotional response to a sufficiently provoking event. Here, the defendant's actions leading up to the killing reveal a calm and calculating state of mind, guided not by a sudden, uncontrollable passion but by a desire to avenge the beating of his friend. *See* LaFave, *supra* § 15.2(a), at 494 ("A passion for revenge, of course, will not do." (quotation omitted)). Even after learning of the attack on Roney, driving from Nashua to Manchester with a gun, meeting his friends to plot a violent response, and locating Roney's assailants, the defendant had the presence of mind to wipe the gun down with his shirt, rack the slide, and advise Roscoe that the gun was "smooth." For these reasons, the trial judge acted well within his discretion in refusing to instruct the jury as to provocation manslaughter.

* * *

Affirmed.

Comments and Questions

(1) From the court's opinion, what are the four requirements which must be met for what would otherwise be murder to be reduced to manslaughter based on provocation? If only a half hour had elapsed between the defendant learning that Roney had been attacked and the killing of Kar? What result if only a few minutes had elapsed, but it turned out Kar was not Roney's attacker?

(2) Compare *Soto* to *People v. Bridgehouse*, 303 P.2d 1018 (Cal. 1956). Bridgehouse shot his wife's long-time lover upon seeing him seated on a couch in the house of his mother-in-law. The court found him guilty of manslaughter, not murder:

> To be sufficient to reduce a homicide to manslaughter, the heat of passion must be such as would naturally be aroused in the mind of an ordinary, reasonable person, under the given facts and circumstances, or in the mind of a person of ordinary self-control. The evidence here shows, without conflict, that defendant's wife was having an affair which had extended over a considerable period of time with the deceased; that she would neither approve of the defendant commencing an action for divorce nor would she forego seeing the victim of the crime; that the sight of the victim in his mother-in-law's home was a great shock to the defendant who had not expected to see him there or anywhere else. In the case at bar, there was no malice shown, either express or implied; there was no showing of any premeditation, either express or implied; there was no evidence of an "abandoned and malignant heart." There was ample, uncontradicted, evidence that defendant was a man of excellent character; that he was mentally and emotionally exhausted and was white and shaking. It appears to us, as a matter of law, that under the circumstances here presented there was adequate provocation to provoke in the reasonable man such a heat of passion as would render an ordinary man of average disposition likely to act rashly or without due deliberation and reflection.

What was the evidence proving "adequate provocation"? Stated another way, what was it that provoked the defendant? The prior affair? His seeing the victim Barr? For a defendant to claim sufficient provocation, normally he must demonstrate that he was provoked by the victim. Was Bridgehouse able to show that? Can *Bridgehouse* be reconciled with *Soto*? See also *Brown v. State*, 755 S.E.2d 699 (Ga. 2014), in which the defendant was prosecuted for murder after repeatedly striking his romantic partner with an axe. The Georgia court held that jury instructions on the lesser included charge of voluntary manslaughter were not warranted, as an argument between the defendant and victim, even when coupled with alleged sexual jealousy due to the victim's telephone contact with her husband, was insufficient to lead to a sudden irresistible passion necessary for voluntary manslaughter.

(3) In *State v. Munoz*, 827 P.2d 1303 (N.M. Ct. App. 1992), the court on appeal found that the defendant, charged with the murder of his wife's stepfather, was entitled to a voluntary manslaughter instruction. State law required that provocation come from the victim. The stepfather had sexually molested the defendant's wife several years earlier, but it was the wife's disclosure to the defendant which incited him. The court held that it was the sexual molestation which was the provocation rather than the wife's disclosure to the defendant.

(4) *See State v. Harwood*, 519 P.2d 177, 179 (Ariz. 1974):

> Appellant was a court reporter, employed by the Pima County Superior Court. Wanda C. Fiak worked for him as a part-time transcriber. On the evening of March 16, 1971, appellant went to a local bar where later Mrs. Fiak joined him. They stayed there for several hours. When they left, an argument occurred in the bar's parking lot concerning whether appellant was going directly home. Mrs. Fiak said that she would follow appellant and if he stopped or she lost him, she would go to his house and cause a commotion. When appellant left, Mrs. Fiak followed him. After a period of evasive driving with Wanda Fiak in pursuit, appellant drove up behind her at an A. J. Bayless Market and twice rammed her. He left his automobile and, with a pistol in his hand, approached her car. Mrs. Fiak laughed and appeared to be taunting him. Appellant then fired at her through the window of her automobile, striking her three times.

Is this murder or voluntary manslaughter?

People v. Najera

Court of Appeal of California
138 Cal. App. 4th 212, 41 Cal. Rptr. 3d 244 (2006)

Fybel, J.

Introduction

Defendant Abimael Flores Najera was charged with the first degree murder of Victor Hernandez. The jury convicted Najera of second degree murder, and the trial court sentenced him to an indeterminate term of 15 years to life. Najera contends the conviction for second degree murder should be reduced to voluntary manslaughter on several grounds....

...

Najera was not entitled to a manslaughter instruction. Voluntary manslaughter is the unlawful killing of a person without malice "upon a sudden quarrel or heat of passion." The sudden quarrel or heat of passion must be provoked by the victim's conduct or by conduct that the defendant reasonably believed was engaged in by the victim.

The provocative conduct Najera claims gave rise to a sudden quarrel or heat of passion was that Hernandez called Najera a "jota," translated at trial to mean "faggot." We hold calling Najera that name was insufficient to cause an average person to lose reason and judgment under an objective standard; therefore, Najera was not entitled to a voluntary manslaughter instruction.

Facts

During the late afternoon of August 28, 2003, Najera and Victor Hernandez were sitting, drinking beer, and talking in the front yard of a house on South Golden West in Santa Ana where they rented rooms. Hernandez's uncle, Javier Penaloza, also was in the yard talking, and Najera's brother, Elias Najera, walked back and forth between the yard and the house. According to Elias Najera, Hernandez and Najera were joking around and talking, when Hernandez called Najera a "jota" (translated as "faggot"). Najera said, "I don't want you to call me that." Hernandez replied, "You don't want me to call you a fag? Fag." Hernandez, who was seated, stood up and pushed Najera, who fell back. Najera got up, and he and Hernandez soon were on the ground wrestling and exchanging fists.

According to Penaloza, Hernandez said to Najera, "I want your sister[,] I like her," to which Najera responded, "well, my sister likes men, and you ain't." Hernandez then called Najera a "faggot." The name calling went back and forth, and Hernandez and Najera became increasingly angry. Penaloza went inside the house and heard Hernandez and Najera cussing and fighting. When Penaloza came out of the house, Hernandez and Najera had been separated.

Arturo Herrera, who lived in a rented house at the rear of the property, separated Najera and Hernandez. Najera angrily told Hernandez, "it's not going to end like this." The owner of the house told Najera and Hernandez he would contact the police if they did not stop fighting.

Hernandez sat down in a chair in the front yard. Najera went inside the house. He walked past Rosalba Velasquez, who was at the house visiting her mother, and asked her to tell Hernandez to pay the $50 Hernandez owed him. Najera went into the bathroom and shut the door. He emerged a few minutes later, went to the kitchen, and then went to his bedroom. A few minutes later, Najera emerged from his bedroom and walked outside into the front yard. He had been inside the house for about five to ten minutes.

Najera walked straight toward Hernandez, who was still sitting in the chair. Najera used a knife taken from the kitchen to slash Hernandez's stomach three times. Hernandez stood and cried, "what happened?" Najera then slashed Hernandez's left elbow with the knife and said, "I told you. I told you."

Hernandez, bleeding profusely, went inside the house and asked Velasquez to call the police or the paramedics. Hernandez went back outside and sat down near the driveway.

Velasquez dialed 911 on her cell phone, but was so scared she could not speak. She went outside and handed the telephone to Herrera, who spoke to the 911 operator.

Najera stood in the front yard with a beer in one hand and a bloody knife in the other. After Herrera announced the police were on their way, Najera left and started walking down the street. He passed four or five houses and then ran.

In the early evening of August 28, Santa Ana Police Officer Caprice Kirkpatrick received a call about a stabbing at a house on South Golden West. On her way to the scene, she saw a man matching the description given her of the stabbing suspect. It was Najera. She arrested him.

The paramedics arrived at the house and transported Hernandez to University of California, Irvine Medical Center. Hernandez had lacerations to his diaphragm and elbow, and a deep laceration to his liver. Surgical efforts to save Hernandez failed, and he died about nine hours later. The official cause of death was described as "sharp force injuries of the thorax and abdomen."

Proceedings in the Trial Court

The information charged Najera with first degree murder. The jury convicted Najera of second degree murder. The trial court denied Najera's motion to reduce the conviction to voluntary manslaughter.

Analysis

...

Sudden Quarrel or Heat of Passion Limited to Situation in Which Defendant's Conduct Was a Reasonable Response

Najera argues the prosecutor told the jury on two occasions the determination of heat of passion should be based on the defendant's conduct rather than the circumstances in which the defendant was placed. During closing argument, the prosecutor stated: "Heat of passion is not measured by the standard of the accused. We don't care what the accused did. We don't care what the standard is for the accused. As a jury, you have to apply a reasonable, ordinary person standard, okay. Going back to that intruder hypothetical. Any reasonable, ordinary person walking in on a child being molested, if they had a gun in their hand, would probably do the same thing. It's that same hypothetical that was given to you in voir dire by defense. Remember the spider in the sink, the reasonable spectrum? *Would a reasonable person do what the defendant did? Would a reasonable person be so aroused as to kill somebody? That's the standard.*"

During rebuttal, the prosecutor stated: "[*T*] *he reasonable, prudent person standard ... [is] based on conduct, what a reasonable person would do in a similar circumstance. Pull out a knife and stab him? I hope that's not a reasonable person standard.*" The italicized portions of the prosecutor's statements are incorrect. An unlawful homicide is upon a sudden quarrel or heat of passion if the killer's reason was obscured by a provocation sufficient to cause an ordinary person of average disposition to act rashly and without deliberation. The focus is on the provocation—the surrounding circumstances—and whether it was sufficient to cause a reasonable person to act rashly. How the killer responded to the provocation and the reasonableness of the response is not relevant to sudden quarrel or heat of passion.

The prosecutor interspersed correct statements of the law with the incorrect ones stating, for example, "[w]ould a reasonable person be so aroused as to kill somebody? That's the standard." The effect of the prosecutor's statements was, however, to create confusion. Does the jury determine sudden quarrel or heat of passion based on the level of provocation or on the defendant's conduct in response to the provocation? The jury was confused on that issue and submitted a written question to the trial court asking whether "[u]nder voluntary manslaughter rule does the reasonable person *test* apply not only to the 'aroused passions' but also apply to the '*conduct*' of this person. The act resulting from the passion." The court wrote in response: "If the Court is understanding your question, I believe the answer may be in Instruction 8.42, found on page 37 of the packet, to be considered ... with all the Court's instructions."

The trial court correctly instructed the jury to follow the court's instructions, not the attorneys' description of the law, to the extent there was a conflict. We presume the jury followed that instruction.

...

Defense Counsel Was Not Ineffective Because Najera Was Not Entitled to a Manslaughter Instruction

Najera argues his counsel was ineffective by failing to object to the prosecutor's misstatements or by failing to request the mistakes be corrected. To prevail on a claim of ineffective assistance of counsel, the defendant must prove: (1) his or her attorney's representation was deficient in that it fell below an objective standard of reasonableness under prevailing professional standards; and (2) his or her attorney's deficient representation subjected him or her to prejudice. Prejudice means a "reasonable probability that, but for counsel's unprofessional errors, the result of the proceeding would have been different." A reasonable probability means a "probability sufficient to undermine confidence in the outcome."

After oral argument, we requested supplemental briefing from the parties addressing two issues: "1. What was the provocative conduct, if any, justifying an instruction on voluntary manslaughter under Penal Code section 192, subdivision (a) 2. Was that conduct sufficiently provocative that it would cause an ordinary person of average disposition to act rashly or without due deliberation and reflection." Najera and the Attorney General submitted letter briefs in response. We have considered those briefs and conclude Najera suffered no prejudice from his counsel's failure to object to the prosecutor's misstatements because the evidence did not "properly present[ ]" the issue of sudden quarrel or heat of passion. In other words, Najera suffered no prejudice because he was not entitled to an instruction on voluntary manslaughter in the first place.

As explained above, voluntary manslaughter is an unlawful killing of a human being without malice "upon a sudden quarrel or heat of passion." Although [The Penal Code] refers to 'sudden quarrel or heat of passion,' the factor which distinguishes the 'heat of passion' form of voluntary manslaughter from murder is provocation. The provocation which incites the defendant to homicidal conduct in the heat of passion must be caused by the victim, or be conduct reasonably believed by the defendant to have been engaged in by the victim. The provocative conduct by the victim may be physical or verbal, but the conduct must be sufficiently provocative that it would cause an ordinary person of average disposition to act rashly or without due deliberation and reflection. The test for adequate provocation is objective.

What was the provocative conduct in this case? Hernandez called Najera a "faggot." That taunt would not drive any ordinary person to act rashly or without due deliberation and reflection. " 'A provocation of slight and trifling character, such as words of reproach, however grievous they may be, or gestures, or an assault, or even a blow, is not recognized as sufficient to arouse, in a reasonable man, such passion as reduces an unlawful killing with a deadly weapon to manslaughter.' "

In *People v. Manriquez*, 37 Cal. 4th 547, 586 (2005), the victim called the defendant a " 'mother fucker' " and taunted him by repeatedly asserting that if the defendant had a weapon, he "should take it out and use it." The California Supreme Court stated such declarations "plainly were insufficient to cause an average person to become so inflamed as to lose reason and judgment" and held "[t]he trial court properly denied defendant's request for an instruction on voluntary manslaughter based upon the theory of a sudden quarrel or heat of passion." Calling Najera a "faggot" was equally insufficient to cause an ordinary person to lose reason and judgment under an objective standard. Najera was not entitled to a voluntary manslaughter instruction; therefore, defense counsel's failure to object to the prosecutor's misconduct did not cause Najera to suffer any prejudice.

Comments and Questions

(1) Are words alone enough to constitute provocation for voluntary manslaughter? Some courts state that "words alone, however scurrilous or insulting, will not furnish the adequate provocation required." *State v. Castro*, 592 P.2d 185, 187 (N.M. Ct. App. 1979). *See also State v. Williams*, 252 S.E.2d 739, 745 (N.C. 1979): "[L]egal provocation must be circumstances amounting to an assault or threatened assault." Other courts disagree, and allow juries to consider voluntary manslaughter based upon "mere words." *State v. Shane*, 590 N.E.2d 272, 277–78 (Ohio 1992):

> Many courts have adopted a rule that "mere words" can not be sufficient provocation to reduce a murder charge to voluntary manslaughter, no matter how insulting or inciteful. This general rule usually applies even if the spoken words have the effect of informing the defendant of some provocative event that has taken place.
>
> While the "mere words" rule is attractive—it has the advantage of offering a bright line test which eliminates an entire class of cases—the rule has been criticized as imposing an "unnecessary limitation on the use of voluntary manslaughter as a mitigating defense." It is argued that such a rule ignores the fact that sometimes words may be even more inflammatory than aggres-

> sive actions, and that the rule keeps from the jury some situations that should qualify for a manslaughter instruction. Nevertheless, we do not believe that words alone are generally as inflammatory as aggressive actions. Further, it is only when a jury could reasonably find that the defendant was incited by sufficient provocation brought on by the victim that an instruction on voluntary manslaughter should be given in a murder prosecution.
>
> We disapprove of a rule which does not allow "mere words" to be sufficient provocation to reduce murder to manslaughter generally, but which makes a specific exception where the provocation consists of mere words by one spouse informing the other spouse of infidelity. This exception to the general rule has its foundation in the ancient common-law concept that the wife is the property of the husband.
>
> We hold that words alone will not constitute reasonably sufficient provocation to incite the use of deadly force in most situations. Rather, in each case, the trial judge must determine whether evidence of reasonably sufficient provocation occasioned by the victim has been presented to warrant a voluntary manslaughter instruction.

As stated succinctly by the Maryland Court of Appeals in *Girouard v. State*, 583 A.2d 718, 722 (Md. 1991),

> [The key issue is] whether the taunting words uttered by [the victim] were enough to inflame the passion of a reasonable man so that the man would be sufficiently infuriated to strike out in hot-blooded blind passion to kill her.

(2) It is not enough that the defendant be provoked and act in anger; there must be some instantaneous explosion in response to the provocation. The court in *United States v. Bordeaux*, 980 F.2d 534, 537–38 (8th Cir. 1992), explained:

> A defendant's anger with the victim, however, is not sufficient to establish heat of passion without an element of sudden provocation. Evidence of "a string of prior arguments and a continuing dispute," without an indication of some sort of instant incitement, does not constitute a sufficient showing to warrant a voluntary manslaughter instruction.
>
> It is well established that if the defendant had enough time between the provocation and the killing to reflect on his or her intended course of action, "then the mere fact of passion would not reduce the crime below murder."

In *People v. Wilson*, 278 N.E.2d 473, 475, 477 (Ill. App. Ct. 1972), the court refused a voluntary manslaughter claim:

> Hudson testified that there was bad blood between Farland and Wilson. Their quarrel was renewed on August 26, 1967, when they met about 1:45 a.m. on the corner of Pulaski Road and Gladys Avenue, Chicago. Farland said, "I heard you have been looking for me." Wilson replied, "What of it?" and placed his hand in his pocket as if he had a weapon. Farland, who was unarmed, reached for him but Wilson broke away, picked up two bottles and threw one which struck Farland. Hudson and Farland tried to restrain him but could not.

As Wilson ran away a police car passed by. Wilson hailed it and told the officers that Farland and Hudson were out to get him. He also said that Farland had pulled a knife and cut his clothes. The officers searched the three men but found no weapons. They were advised to forget about their altercation and go home. Several people had gathered, among them Wilson's stepfather who owned a nearby restaurant. Wilson was turned over to him and they walked away. Hudson testified that before Wilson left he said he was not willing to forget about the quarrel.

Farland and Hudson walked north on Pulaski. As they walked on, Hudson heard footsteps behind him, turned and saw Wilson with a butcher knife in his hand. Wilson exclaimed, "You know, I'm for real" and plunged the knife into Farland's chest. Hudson chased Wilson but he escaped. He surrendered to the police the next day.

Police officers came to the scene. No weapons were found. Farland was bleeding profusely and was rushed to a hospital. He was stabbed just above the center of his chest; his aorta artery was severed and his left hand was cut.

The evidence did not prove that Wilson was acting under a sudden passion at the time of the stabbing. He may have suffered provocation which aroused an intense passion during his first encounter with Farland but the lapse of time between the two encounters would prevent Wilson's provocation, if any, arising from the first to mitigate the second. To reduce an unlawful killing from murder to voluntary manslaughter, the sudden and intense passion resulting from serious provocation cannot be followed by a period of time sufficient for the passion to cool and the voice of reason to be heard.

But see People v. Berry, 556 P.2d 777, 780–81 (Cal. 1976):

Dr. Martin Blinder, a physician and psychiatrist, called by the defense, testified that Rachel was a depressed, suicidally inclined girl and that this suicidal impulse led her to involve herself ever more deeply in a dangerous situation with defendant. She did this by sexually arousing him and taunting him into jealous rages in an unconscious desire to provoke him into killing her and thus consummating her desire for suicide. Throughout the period commencing with her return from Israel until her death, that is from July 13 to July 26, Rachel continually provoked defendant with sexual taunts and incitements, alternating acceptance and rejection of him. This conduct was accompanied by repeated references to her involvement with another man; it led defendant to choke her on two occasions, until finally she achieved her unconscious desire and was strangled. Dr. Blinder testified that as a result of this cumulative series of provocations, defendant at the time he fatally strangled Rachel, was in a state of uncontrollable rage, completely under the sway of passion.

[W]e pointed out that "'passion' need not mean 'rage' or 'anger'" but may be any "[v]iolent, intense, high-wrought or enthusiastic emotion'" and con-

> cluded there "that defendant was aroused to a heat of 'passion' by a series of events over a considerable period of time...." Accordingly we declared that evidence of admissions of infidelity by the defendant's paramour, taunts directed to him and other conduct, "supports a finding that defendant killed in wild desperation induced by [the woman's] long continued provocatory conduct." We find this reasoning persuasive in the case now before us. Defendant's testimony chronicles a two-week period of provocatory conduct by his wife Rachel that could arouse a passion of jealousy, pain and sexual rage in an ordinary man of average disposition such as to cause him to act rashly from this passion. It is significant that both defendant and Dr. Blinder testified that the former was in the heat of passion under an uncontrollable rage when he killed Rachel.
>
> The Attorney General contends that the killing could not have been done in the heat of passion because there was a cooling period, defendant having waited in the apartment for 20 hours. However, the long course of provocatory conduct, which had resulted in intermittent outbreaks of rage under specific provocation in the past, reached its final culmination in the apartment when Rachel began screaming. Both defendant and Dr. Blinder testified that defendant killed in a state of uncontrollable rage, of passion, and there is ample evidence in the record to support the conclusion that this passion was the result of the long course of provocatory conduct by Rachel.

The court in *People v. Wharton*, 809 P.2d 290, 319 (Cal. 1991), stated:

> The key element is not the duration of the source of the provocation but "whether or not defendant's reason was, at the time of his act, so disturbed or obscured by some passion ... to such an extent as would render ordinary men of average disposition liable to act rashly or without due deliberation and reflection, and from this passion rather than judgment."

After reviewing the complicated and somewhat inconsistent case law regarding the element of sudden behavior, the court in *United States v. Martinez*, 988 F.2d 685, 696 (7th Cir. 1993), concluded that "it may be arguable that the 'sudden quarrel' term is an anachronism with no meaning not adequately served by a proper definition of heat of passion." Do you agree?

(3) The defendant in *Commonwealth v. Stasko*, 370 A.2d 350, 356 (Pa. 1977), attempted at trial to offer medical evidence to show his "tendency to have a short temper and erupt in sudden rages." Should the trial judge have allowed the testimony?

> The psychologist was introduced to testify concerning the appellant's tendency to have a short temper and erupt in sudden rages. The purpose of the testimony was to show that, in the case of this particular accused, there was sufficient provocation for the attack. This evidence was clearly inadmissible:
>
> "Our law is quite explicit that the determination of whether a certain quantum of provocation is sufficient to support the defense of voluntary manslaughter is purely an objective standard."

> The test for adequate provocation is "whether a reasonable man, confronted with this series of events, became impassioned to the extent that his mind was 'incapable of cool reflection.'"
>
> "The questions thus proposed were properly rejected, because, had the required answers been received, the court could have done nothing else than instruct the jury to disregard them. They were intended, not to establish the fact that Jacobs, when he committed the homicide, was constrained by an insane impulse which for the time destroyed his free agency, but only to show that he was of an excitable temperament; ... But a rule which would allow the justification of crime on such pretext would utterly pervert and subvert the moral order of things.... The phlegmatic man may be moved to anger as well as the most nervous; the only difference is that it requires more to affect the one than the other; but when passion is once aroused in either, it is the same unreasoning and unreasonable power. Why, then, should it not excuse crime in the one as well as in the other? If the murder of the latter may thus be reduced in degree, why not that of the former? Questions, such as these, at once show the utter inapplicability of the rule contended for, hence it must be rejected. The main object of the Penal Code is to compel men to restrain their evil passions and desires, hence the want of such restraint is rather an aggravation of than an excuse for crime."

Would the result change if the evidence were offered to show that the defendant was "a man with a low intelligence quotient and a history of mental disturbance"? This evidence was held inadmissible (with reliance on *Stasko*) in *State v. Jackson*, 597 P.2d 255, 259 (Kan. 1979), *cert. denied*, 445 U.S. 952 (1980). The court stated that the "objective standard precludes consideration of the innate peculiarities of the individual defendant." Compare the statements made in a widely publicized case in the British House of Lords, *Director of Public Prosecutions v. Camplin*, 2 All E.R. 168 (1978). Lord Diplock:

> In my opinion a proper direction to a jury on the question would be on the following lines. The judge should state what the question is, using the very terms of the section. He should then explain to them that the reasonable man referred to in the question is a person having the power of self-control to be expected of an ordinary person of the sex and age of the accused, but in other respects sharing such of the accused's characteristics as they think would affect the gravity of the provocation to him, and that the question is not merely whether such a person would in like circumstances be provoked to lose his self-control but also would react to the provocation as the accused did.
>
> I accordingly agree with the Court of Appeal that the judge ought not to have instructed the jury to pay no account to the age of the accused even though they themselves might be of opinion that the degree of self-control to be expected in a boy of that age was less than in an adult.

Lord Morris:

> It seems to me that a jury is fully entitled to consider whether an accused person, placed as he was, only acted as even a reasonable man might have acted if he had been in the accused's situation. There may be no practical difference between, on the one hand, taking a notional independent reasonable man, but a man having the attributes of the accused and subject to all the events which surrounded the accused, and then considering whether what the accused did was only what such a person would or might have done, and, on the other hand, taking the accused himself with all his attributes and subject to all the events and then asking whether there was provocation to such a degree as would or might make a reasonable man do what he (the accused) in fact did.
>
> In my view it would now be unreal to tell the jury that the notional "reasonable man" is someone without the characteristics of the accused: it would be to intrude into their province. A few examples may be given. If the accused is of particular colour or particular ethnic origin and things are said which to him are grossly insulting it would be utterly unreal if the jury had to consider whether the words would have provoked a man of different colour or ethnic origin, or to consider how such a man would have acted or reacted. The question would be whether the accused if he was provoked only reacted as even any reasonable man in his situation would or might have reacted. If the accused was ordinarily and usually a very unreasonable person, the view that on a particular occasion he acted just as a reasonable person would or might have acted would not be impossible of acceptance.
>
> In the instant case the considerations to which I have been referring have application to a question of age. The accused was a young man. Sometimes in the summing-up he was called a boy or a lad. He was at the time of the events described at the trial under 16 years of age: he was accountable in law for the charge preferred against him. More generally in the summing-up he was referred to as a young man; that would appear to me to have been appropriate. In his summing-up, however, the learned judge in referring to a reasonable man seemed to emphasize to the jury that the reasonable man with whom they must compare the accused could not be a young man of the age of the accused but had to be someone older and indeed had to be someone of full age and maturity. In my view that was not correct. The jury had to consider whether a young man of about the same age as the accused but placed in the same situation as that which befell the accused could, had he been a reasonable young man, have reacted as did the accused and could have done what the accused did. For the reasons which I have outlined the question so to be considered by the jury would be whether they considered that the accused, placed as he was, and having regard to all the things that they find were said, and all the things that they find were done, only acted as a reasonable young man might have acted, so that, in compassion, and

> having regard to human frailty, he could to some extent be excused even though he had caused death.

Lord Simon:

> In *Bedder*, the defendant, who was sexually impotent, had in vain attempted to have intercourse with a prostitute. The woman jeered at him for his impotence; when he tried to hold her she slapped his face and punched him in the stomach, and as he pushed her back she kicked him in the private parts. He took a knife from his pocket and struck her two blows with it, which killed her. It was argued on his behalf that the "reasonable man" (whom a long line of previous authorities since 1859 had established as the standard for measuring the self-control required where a defence of provocation was in question) should be invested with the physical qualities of the defendant (in that case, impotence), and that the question should be asked, what would be the reaction of an impotent reasonable man in the circumstances? But the judge directed the jury in these terms:
>
> The reasonable person, the ordinary person, is the person you must consider when you are considering the effect which any acts, any conduct, any words, might have to justify the steps which are taken in response thereto, so that an unusually excitable or pugnacious individual, or a drunken one or a man who is sexually impotent is not entitled to rely on provocation which would not have led an ordinary person to have acted in the way which was in fact carried out.
>
> I think that the standard of self-control which the law requires before provocation is held to reduce murder to manslaughter is still that of the reasonable person but that, in determining whether a person of reasonable self-control would lose it in the circumstances, the entire factual situation, which includes the characteristics of the accused, must be considered.

2 All E.R. at 175, 178, 179, 182.

(4) The fundamental question here is rarely offered or answered by the courts: "Why are some emotions worthy of protection (jealous rages), while others are not (ill-inspired greed)?" Nourse, *Passion's Progress: Modern Law Reform and the Provocation Defense*, 106 Yale L.J. 1331, 1336 (1997). What is the answer? Consider the Tex. Penal Code, § 19.02(d):

> At the punishment stage of a trial, the defendant may raise the issue as to whether he caused the death under the immediate influence of sudden passion arising from an adequate cause. If the defendant proves the issue in the affirmative by a preponderance of the evidence, the offense is a felony of the second degree.

Is this a more moderate view of provocation? A more effective view?

(5) In a prosecution for voluntary manslaughter (or, commonly, for murder with a jury instruction with manslaughter), does the defendant have to show the adequate

legal provocation? "We therefore hold that the Due Process Clause requires the prosecution to prove beyond a reasonable doubt the absence of the heat of passion on sudden provocation when the issue is properly presented in a homicide case." *Mullaney v. Wilbur*, 421 U.S. 684 (1975). If the defendant claims that he acted on sudden provocation, should he not have the burden of proving it?

State v. Faulkner

Court of Appeals of Maryland
483 A.2d 759 (1984)

COLE, JUDGE.

The twin issues we shall decide in this case are whether Maryland recognizes the mitigation defense of "imperfect self defense" and, if so, whether that defense applies to the statutory offense of assault with intent to murder.

We set forth a shortened version of the facts that give rise to these issues. On September 15, 1981, the Emanuel brothers, Jimmy and Rickey, became embroiled in an argument with Melvin J. Faulkner, Jr. outside a Baltimore City bar. This argument quickly escalated into a fight between Jimmy and Faulkner. Because Faulkner believed that Jimmy was armed with a knife, Faulkner produced a handgun and began firing. Faulkner, however, shot Rickey twice in the chest as Rickey tried to push his brother from the handgun's line of fire. The testimony reflects considerable conflict as to what led Faulkner to believe that Jimmy was armed with a knife, which participant was the aggressor at various stages of this imbroglio, who entered into the melee mutually and willfully, and who was simply acting in self defense.

Faulkner was charged with assault with intent to murder and related offenses. At his trial in the Criminal Court of Baltimore, the court instructed the jury as to the defenses of justification by way of self defense and mitigation by way of hot-blooded response to the provocation of mutual combat. The court, however, declined Faulkner's request that the jury also be instructed as to the defense of "imperfect self defense." The jury subsequently found Faulkner guilty of assault with intent to murder and related handgun offenses.

Initially, we note that the difference between murder and manslaughter is the presence or absence of malice. Self defense operates as a complete defense to either murder or manslaughter. A successful self defense, therefore, results in the acquittal of the defendant.

Imperfect self defense, by contrast, is not a complete defense. Its chief characteristic is that it operates to negate malice, an element the State must prove to establish murder. As a result, the successful invocation of this doctrine does not completely exonerate the defendant, but mitigates murder to voluntary manslaughter.

Imperfect self defense, however, is different from either self defense or the commonly recognized mitigation defenses. Because the doctrine of imperfect self defense has been subjected to different interpretations and regarded by some courts and scholars as being a recent theory not far advanced, we believe a brief examination of its history and development will help clarify its nature and scope and point out the differences.

[C]ourts [have] fashioned three variations of the doctrine.

First, some courts indicated that the doctrine would apply where the homicide would fall within the perfect self defense doctrine but for the fault of the defendant in provoking or initiating the difficulty at the non-deadly force level. Second, courts noted that the doctrine would apply when the defendant committed a homicide because of an honest but unreasonable belief that he was about to suffer death or serious bodily harm. Third, other courts recognized the doctrine when the defendant used unreasonable force in defending himself and, as a result, killed his opponent.

Many states that recognize the doctrine on the basis of statutory law have adopted the subjectively honest but objectively unreasonable standard of the imperfect self defense doctrine. For example, Pennsylvania, which has "long recognized" this mitigation defense, has a statute governing voluntary manslaughter that embodies the doctrine of imperfect self defense. *See* 18 Pa. Cons. Stat. Ann. § 2503(b) (Purdon 1983). This statute provides:

> (b) Unreasonable belief killing justifiable.—A person who intentionally or knowingly kills an individual commits voluntary manslaughter if at the time of the killing he believes the circumstances to be such that, if they existed, would justify the killing under Chapter 5 of this title (relating to general principles of justification), *but his belief is unreasonable.*

In a recent interpretation of this statute, the Supreme Court of Pennsylvania noted that homicide is mitigated from murder to voluntary manslaughter when the defendant subjectively believes circumstances exist to justify the killing, but objective reality negates that existence.

Our review of the development of the imperfect defense doctrine and examination of the jurisdictions that have addressed circumstances when the doctrine is applicable convinces us that the honest but unreasonable belief standard of imperfect self defense is the proper one to be followed in Maryland.

> Perfect self-defense requires not only that the killer subjectively believed that his actions were necessary for his safety but, objectively, that a reasonable man would so consider them. Imperfect self-defense, however, requires no more than a subjective honest belief on the part of the killer that his actions were necessary for his safety, even though, on an objective appraisal by a reasonable man, they would not be found to be so. If established, the killer remains culpable and his actions are excused only to the extent that mitigation is invoked.

We agree that this statement represents an analytically sound view, and reflects the position taken by a majority of those jurisdictions that have addressed and embraced this defense. Logically, a defendant who commits a homicide while honestly, though unreasonably, believing that he is threatened with death or serious bodily harm, does not act with malice. Absent malice he cannot be convicted of murder.

Nevertheless, because the killing was committed without justification or excuse, the defendant is not entitled to full exoneration. Therefore, as we see it, when evidence is presented showing the defendant's subjective belief that the use of force was necessary to prevent imminent death or serious bodily harm, the defendant is entitled to a proper instruction on imperfect self defense.

Based on [the facts in this case], the jury evidently concluded that a reasonable person would not have believed Jimmy to be so armed by virtue of the jury's rejection of the perfect self defense theory. Whether the jury would have concluded that Faulkner had a subjectively honest but objectively unreasonable belief that he was in deadly peril is an open question that the jury never had an opportunity to answer.

In sum, Faulkner produced evidence sufficient to generate a jury issue as to whether he had a subjectively honest but objectively unreasonable belief that he was in imminent danger of death or serious bodily injury, and the trial court should have granted his requested instruction on imperfect self defense.

Comments and Questions

(1) If the jury had been properly instructed on self-defense and had found no perfect self-defense claim, should the charge nevertheless be reduced from murder to manslaughter if the defendant, genuinely—but unreasonably—believed he needed to defend himself?*

(2) Suppose the defendant did have a self-defense claim, but he used excessive force, thereby losing his privilege to defend. Would the murder charge be reduced to manslaughter? If the defendant initiated the conflict, as in *United States v. Milk*, 447 F.3d 593 (8th Cir. 2006) (no mitigation)? Would it be reduced if, as in *Wentworth v. State*, 349 A.2d 421 (Md. Ct. Spec. App. 1975), the defendant claims an "imperfect" duress defense (being forced by another to commit a crime)?

(3) The court in *Faulkner* referred to jury instructions which should be given at the retrial of the case. How should the trial judge instruct the jury?

[2] Involuntary Manslaughter

> [V]oluntary manslaughter is committed intentionally while involuntary manslaughter is committed unintentionally.

State v. Dixon, 489 P.2d 225, 230 (Ariz. 1971).

> The state of mind, or *mens rea*, which characterizes involuntary manslaughter is recklessness or gross negligence: a great departure from the standard of ordinary care evidencing a disregard for human life or an indifference to the possible consequences of the actor's conduct.

Commonwealth v. Agnew, 398 A.2d 209, 211 (Pa. Super. Ct. 1979).

---

* Ed. See discussion of self-defense in Chapter 7, *infra*.

Commonwealth v. Welansky

Supreme Judicial Court of Massachusetts
55 N.E.2d 902 (1944)

[Opinion is set out in Chapter 3, *supra*.]

Comments and Questions

(1) If the defendant was not present at the time of the deaths, how could he be convicted of manslaughter? Which of his acts caused the deaths?

(2) In 2003, a fire caused by a band's pyrotechnic display, due to flammable sound proofing foam, killed 100 people and injured more than 200 in an overcrowded club in Rhode Island. Would the owners of the club be guilty of involuntary manslaughter? The band manager who set off the pyrotechnics? All three pled no contest to 100 counts of involuntary manslaughter. The owner who installed the foam and the band manager were sentenced to four years; the other owner was ordered to perform 500 hours of community service. Parker et al., *The Station Night Club Disaster*, The Providence Journal, Nov. 30, 2006, at A-01.

Also in 2003, involuntary manslaughter charges were brought against the owners of another overcrowded club that had been ordered to close for safety violations seven months before a stampede in the club killed 21 people. One of the owners, his son, and the club's floor managers were acquitted by a judge. The other owner convicted of criminal contempt is awaiting trial. Sadovi & Keller, *3 Acquitted in E2 Deaths*, Chi. Trib., Mar. 5, 2007, at A9.

(3) Would the government be able to base a manslaughter charge on a negligence claim? Consider *State v. Brubaker*, 385 P.2d 318, 319 (Wash. 1963), another of the Russian Roulette cases. The court stated clearly that "ordinary, as distinguished from aggravated or gross, negligence will support a conviction of manslaughter." See also *Smith v. State*, 370 S.W.2d 543, 545–46 (Tenn. 1963), where the defendant security guard was convicted on evidence that he carelessly shot at a robbery suspect.

> [D]efendant was acting under stress of excitement, and only to guard the property and protect himself, and not upon any sudden heat or passion with the intention of killing deceased; and he was, therefore, not guilty of the lesser included offense of voluntary manslaughter.
>
> We think, however, the evidence does show that defendant, in shooting at the figure in the dark with a flashlight, without waiting to ask any question or trying to ascertain the identity or purpose of that person, acted without proper precaution. Even though he was under the stress of excitement and in shooting intended only to guard the property and protect himself, he, nevertheless was guilty of such culpable negligence as to make the killing unlawful and to constitute involuntary manslaughter.

(4) New York has adopted the standard definitions for criminal negligence and recklessness.

> Section 125.10 of the Penal Law ("Criminally negligent homicide") provides that "a person is guilty of criminally negligent homicide when, with criminal negligence, he causes the death of another person." Section 125.15 of the Penal Law ("Manslaughter in the second degree") provides, *inter alia*, that "a person is guilty of manslaughter in the second degree when: 1. He recklessly causes the death of another person."
>
> "Recklessly" and "criminal negligence" are defined in section 15.05 of the Penal Law as follows:
>
> 3. *Recklessly.* A person acts recklessly with respect to a result or to a circumstance described by a statute defining an offense when he is aware of and consciously disregards a substantial and unjustifiable risk that such result will occur or that such circumstance exists. The risk must be of such nature and degree that disregard thereof constitutes a gross deviation from the standard of conduct that a reasonable person would observe in the situation....
>
> 4. *Criminal negligence.* A person acts with criminal negligence with respect to a result or to a circumstance described by a statute defining an offense when he fails to perceive a substantial and unjustifiable risk that such result will occur or that such circumstance exists. The risk must be of such nature and degree that the failure to perceive it constitutes a gross deviation from the standard of care that a reasonable person would observe in the situation.

People v. Warner-Lambert Co., 417 N.Y.S.2d 997, 1003 (N.Y. App. Div. 1979).

In *Welansky*, was the government required to prove recklessness or negligence? Would it have made any difference?

Under the following analysis in *McCreary v. State*, 371 So. 2d 1024, 1026 (Fla. 1979), would the convictions in *Brubaker* and *Smith* be affirmed?

> Manslaughter is the killing of a human being by the act, procurement, or culpable negligence of another, without lawful justification. We have repeatedly said that the culpable conduct necessary to sustain proof of manslaughter must be of *a gross and flagrant character, evincing reckless disregard of human life*, or of the safety of persons exposed to its dangerous effects, or there is that *entire want of care* which would raise the presumption of a *conscious indifference to consequences*, or which shows *wantonness or recklessness*, or a *grossly careless disregard of the safety and welfare of the public*, or that *reckless indifference to the rights of others which is equivalent to an intentional violation of them.*

(5) Does an individual commit manslaughter if she provides cocaine to a friend who then ingests the drug and dies of an overdose? The Court of Military Appeals addressed the issue in *United States v. Sargent*, 18 M.J. 331, 339 (C.M.A. 1984):

> [A] conviction for involuntary manslaughter cannot be sustained solely by evidence that an accused sold someone a drug and that the purchaser later died from an overdose of that drug. On the other hand, when the seller has

> gone further and assisted the purchaser in injecting or ingesting the drug, the sale becomes one which [can be the basis for the manslaughter conviction].

But see *Commonwealth v. Perry*, 607 N.E.2d 434, 436 (Mass. App. Ct. 1993), *aff'd*, 620 N.E.2d 44 (Mass. 1993), where, in a similar case, the court found that an involuntary manslaughter charge could be sustained as the defendant had a subjective awareness of the risk involved with the use of heroin. She had tested her own portion of the drugs before injecting herself and then, in response to the victim's collapse, said "that's what happens when you get good stuff."

(6) In the widely publicized homicide involving the shaking death of a young child, British *au pair* Louise Woodward was convicted of murder. At the trial in Massachusetts, her attorneys objected to the judge proposing to instruct the jury on the lesser offense of manslaughter; only a murder instruction was therefore given. After the jury determination of murder, the judge reduced the charge to manslaughter. Excerpts of his opinion follow.

> The law, John Adams told a Massachusetts jury while defending British citizens on trial for murder, is inflexible, inexorable, and deaf: inexorable to the cries of the defendant; "deaf as an adder to the clamours of the populace." His words ring true, 227 years later. Elected officials may consider popular urging and sway to public opinion polls. Judges must follow their oaths and do their duty, heedless of editorials, letters, telegrams, picketers, threats, petitions, panelists, and talk shows. In this country, we do not administer justice by plebiscite. A judge, in short, is a public servant who must follow his conscience, whether or not he counters the manifest wishes of those he serves; whether or not his decision seems a surrender to the prevalent demands.
>
> In seeking a directed acquittal or a new trial, Defendant argued that the evidence as to causation so strongly raised a reasonable doubt as to liability for Matthew Eappen's death that the conviction could not stand. Now Defendant urges a reduced assessment of her culpability, relying upon Massachusetts Rule of Criminal Procedure 25(b)(2):
>
> If a verdict of guilty is returned, the judge may on motion ... order the entry of a finding of guilty of any offense included in the offense charged in the indictment.
>
> The test here is no longer narrowly legal. The judge, formerly only an umpire enforcing the rules, now must determine whether, under the special circumstances of this case, justice requires lowering the level of guilt from murder to manslaughter (or even to battery). The facts, as well as the law, are open to consideration.
>
> In deciding this issue, the judge must, above all, use the power sparingly, taking care not to act arbitrarily or unreasonably. The judge does not sit as a second jury, or even as a thirteenth juror; he should not second-guess the jury. Nonetheless, he is entitled to consider testimony that the jury may have disbelieved, including such of Defendant's own testimony as he finds credible.

Because Rule 25(b)(2) is a kind of safety valve, a means of rectifying disproportionate verdicts, the test is not whether the evidence could support a verdict of second degree murder, but whether a lesser verdict more comports with justice.

In short, the court may reduce the level of the conviction, for any reason that justice may require. This in turn means that the judge must decide whether failing to reduce the verdict raises a substantial risk that justice has miscarried.

Having considered the matter carefully, I am firmly convinced that the interests of justice—as Rule 25(b)(2) and the cases construing it have defined them—mandate my reducing the verdict to manslaughter. I do this in accordance with my discretion and my duty. Viewing the evidence broadly, as I am permitted to do, I believe that the circumstances in which Defendant acted were characterized by confusion, inexperience, frustration, immaturity and some anger, but not malice (in the legal sense) supporting a conviction for second degree murder. Frustrated by her inability to quiet the crying child, she was "a little rough with him," under circumstances where another, perhaps wiser, person would have sought to restrain the physical impulse. The roughness was sufficient to start (or re-start) a bleeding that escalated fatally.

This sad scenario is, in my judgment after having heard all the evidence and considered the interests of justice, most fairly characterized as manslaughter, not mandatory-life-sentence murder. I view the evidence as disclosing confusion, fright, and bad judgment, rather than rage or malice.

Had the manslaughter option been available to the jurors, they might well have selected it, not out of compromise, but because that particular verdict accorded with at least one rational view of the evidence.

No one, of course, doubts that had the Court denied Defendant's request, and had the jury convicted of manslaughter, defense counsel would be arguing that the jurors had unfairly compromised. It seems, then, at first glance unfair that Defendant should be able to escape the consequences of a decision by her experienced lawyers which she personally and publicly approved.

In fact, it is not unfair. I do not criticize counsel's advice and Defendant's adopting it. Given the state of the evidence, it was a rational, appropriate position. Had it succeeded, the defense would be hailed for courage and foresight. Should Defendant now be permitted to second-guess herself and her lawyers? If one regards the trial of a criminal case as a high-stakes game of chance where losers must accept their losses, the answer is, Certainly Not.

Massachusetts, however, never has and does not now view Justice as a handmaiden to Tyche, the Goddess of Good Fortune. Of course chance plays a part in litigation, as it does in every aspect of life. A court, nonetheless, is not a casino. The only institutionalized luck in a courtroom is the random

> selection of the jury venire at the beginning of trial and the random choice of alternate jurors at the end.

Commonwealth v. Woodward, 694 N.E.2d 1277 (Mass. 1998). Do you agree with the judge's decision? Is Rule 25(b)(2) appropriate? The judge ultimately sentenced the defendant to "time served," less than one year in jail.

The Supreme Judicial Court of Massachusetts affirmed the trial court's ruling, but it emphasized the policy favoring instructing juries on lesser included offenses:

> The doctrine serves the public purpose of allowing the jury to convict of the offense established by the evidence, rather than forcing them to choose between convicting the defendant of an offense not fully established by the evidence or acquitting, even though the defendant is guilty of some offense. Here, it was peculiarly inappropriate for the judge to refuse to charge the jury on manslaughter when, as revealed by his subsequent order reducing the jury's verdict, in his view the evidence was not consonant with a conviction of murder. The jury, in reaching their verdict, surely must have concluded that the Commonwealth had proved beyond a reasonable doubt the element of causation—that Woodward's acts caused Matthew's fatal injury. By refusing to accede to the Commonwealth's request for a manslaughter instruction, the judge impermissibly prevented the jury from considering a lesser degree of culpability for Woodward.

The dissenting judges were even more critical.

> I conclude that we should vacate the sentence imposed and have Woodward resentenced by another Superior Court judge. This case presents circumstances unique to our rule 25(b)(2) jurisprudence. In no other case has the trial judge denied a request by the Commonwealth for an obviously necessary lesser included offense instruction at the request of the defendant, and subsequently reduced a verdict returned by the jury on the greater offense to the lesser offense which the jury had been precluded from considering. The court correctly points out that the judge's failure to instruct on manslaughter was error. The judge improperly acquiesced in Woodward's counseled position that such an instruction should not be given, and he did so in reliance on case law that did not support that position. This error created the basis for the judge's subsequent reduction of Woodward's conviction to manslaughter.

Id.

Commonwealth v. Konz

Supreme Court of Pennsylvania
450 A.2d 638 (1982)

Flaherty, Justice.

This is an appeal from an order of the Superior Court which reversed a decision of the Court of Common Pleas of the Thirty-First Judicial District granting a Motion in Arrest of Judgment to the appellants, Dorothy A. Konz and Stephen R. C. Erikson, subsequent to their being found guilty of involuntary manslaughter in a trial by jury. The prosecution of Dorothy Konz arose from her failure to comply with an alleged duty to seek medical assistance for Reverend David G. Konz, her husband, when he was stricken with a diabetic crisis which proved fatal. The prosecution of Erikson rested upon his alleged role as an accomplice in that breach of duty.

Viewed in the light most favorable to the Commonwealth, as verdict winner, the following facts were established at trial. In September, 1973, Reverend Konz, while serving as a teacher, counselor, and chaplain at United Wesleyan College, became acquainted with Erikson, a student at the College. A close friendship, based on their common interest in religion, formed between Erikson and Reverend Konz as the former became a regular visitor at the latter's residence.

Reverend Konz was a thirty-four year old diabetic and had, for seventeen years, administered to himself daily doses of insulin. On March 4, 1974, however, following an encounter on campus with a visiting evangelist speaker, Reverend Konz publicly proclaimed his desire to discontinue insulin treatment in reliance on the belief that God would heal the diabetic condition. He assured the president of the College and members of the student body that he would carefully monitor his condition and would, if necessary, take insulin. On only one or two occasions did the Reverend thereafter administer insulin. On March 18, 1974, however, Erikson and Reverend Konz formed a pact to pray together to enable the latter to resist the temptation to administer insulin.

Mrs. Konz was informed of the prayer pact, and, on the morning of Saturday, March 23, 1974, when her husband evidenced symptoms of insulin debt, she removed his insulin from the refrigerator and concealed it.[2] Later that day, the Reverend attempted to obtain insulin from the refrigerator, and, upon discovering that the medicine had been removed, strongly indicated that it should be returned. He then attempted to proceed from room to room but his passage was blocked by Erikson. Harsh words were exchanged, and Erikson, after kneeling in prayer, forced the Reverend into a bedroom where, accompanied by Mrs. Konz, Erikson and the Reverend conversed for approximately one half hour. During that time, the Reverend tried to telephone police to obtain assistance but was prevented from doing so by Erikson and Mrs. Konz, who, during a struggle with the Reverend, rendered at least that telephone permanently inoperable.[3] Immediately after this confrontation, the Reverend, his wife, and Erikson returned amicably to the kitchen for coffee, and no further request for insulin was ever made. In addition, the Reverend approached his aunt who resided in the same household and stated, in an apparent reference to the preceding confrontation with Erikson, that "It's all settled now," and told her that there was no cause for concern. He also told his eleven year old daughter that "Everything is fine," and indicated to her that he did not intend to take insulin. The Reverend then departed

2. The insulin was returned to the refrigerator sometime prior to Sunday night.

3. There was testimony as to the existence of two telephones in the residence.

from the house, accompanied by Erikson, and returned an hour later. As the day progressed, Reverend Konz canceled his speaking commitment for the following day and drove his wife to an institution having hospital facilities to pick up a close friend who was a practical nurse. Late on Saturday night, while waiting inside the institution for the nurse to complete her duties, the Reverend appeared very fatigued and complained that he was developing an upset stomach. Both of these conditions were symptomatic of lack of insulin, but neither the Reverend nor his wife requested that insulin, which was available at the institution, be administered. With regard to the Reverend's condition at that time, the nurse observed that he traveled with unimpaired mobility, and that he was conversant, rational, and cognizant of his environs. Nevertheless, he made no mention of a need for insulin, and the nurse made no inquiry as to such a need because the Reverend had on a previous day become very upset at her inquiry as to his diabetic condition.

Upon returning home from this errand, Reverend Konz experienced increasing illness, vomiting intermittently Saturday night and Sunday morning, and remained in bed all day Sunday except for trips into the bathroom. On Sunday afternoon visitors arrived at the Konz residence. The Reverend, recognizing their voices, called to them from his room to inquire whether they wished to see him; having been informed of the Reverend's nausea, however, the visitors declined to stay. As the Reverend's condition worsened and he became restless, his wife and Erikson administered cracked ice but did not summon medical aid. The Konz's eleven year old daughter then inquired as to why a doctor had not been summoned but Mrs. Konz responded that her husband was "going to be getting better." Late Sunday night or early Monday morning everyone in the household fell asleep. On Monday morning at approximately 6 a.m., while the others were still asleep, Reverend Konz died of diabetic ketoacidosis.

Appellants were found guilty by a jury of the crime of involuntary manslaughter pursuant to Section 2504 of the Pennsylvania Crimes Code, which provides: "A person is guilty of involuntary manslaughter when as a direct result of the doing of an unlawful act in a reckless or grossly negligent manner, or the doing of a lawful act in a reckless or grossly negligent manner, he causes the death of another person." 18 Pa. Cons. Stat. Ann. § 2504. To impose criminal liability for an omission as opposed to an act, the omission must be "expressly made sufficient by the law defining the offense." 18 Pa. Cons. Stat. Ann. § 301(b)(1), or "a duty to perform the omitted act [must be] otherwise imposed by law." 18 Pa. Cons. Stat. Ann. § 301(b)(2). Since the involuntary manslaughter provision of the Crimes Code does not expressly address omissions as a basis for liability, only 18 Pa. Cons. Stat. Ann. § 301(b)(2) has potential applicability. The determinative issue on appeal, therefore, is whether Mrs. Konz had a duty to seek medical attention for her spouse. Under the circumstances of this case, we find no such duty to have been present; hence, the conviction of Mrs. Konz, and that of Erikson as her accomplice, cannot be sustained.

Courts have, in limited circumstances, departed from the longstanding common law rule that one human being is under no *legal* compulsion to take action to aid another human being. One such circumstance is where there exists a requisite status of relationship between the parties, as is present in the relationship of parent to child. Hence, a parent has been held guilty of involuntary manslaughter for failure to seek medical assistance for his sick child. The inherent dependency of a child upon his parent to obtain medical aid, *i.e.*, the incapacity of a child to evaluate his condition and summon aid by himself, supports imposition of such a duty upon the parent.

The Commonwealth argues that the marital relationship gives rise to a similar duty to aid one's spouse. Spouses, however, do not generally suffer the same incapacity as do children with respect to the ability to comprehend their states of health and obtain medical assistance. We reject, therefore, the holding of the Superior Court that the marital relationship gives rise to an unrestricted duty for one spouse to summon medical aid whenever the other is in a serious or immediate need of medical attention. Recognition of such a duty would place lay persons in peril of criminal prosecution while compelling them to medically diagnose the seriousness of their spouses' illnesses and injuries. In addition, it would impose an obligation for a spouse to take action at a time when the stricken individual competently chooses *not* to receive assistance. The marital relationship gives rise to an expectation of reliance between spouses, and to a belief that one's spouse should be trusted to respect, rather than ignore, one's expressed preferences. That expectation would be frustrated by imposition of a broad duty to seek aid, since one's spouse would then be forced to ignore the expectation that the preference to forego assistance will be honored.

[T]he instant case is not one wherein there is evidence of the stricken spouse having unintentionally entered a helpless state, or of having been less than competent to consciously and rationally deny medical aid. Rather, the record supports only the conclusion that subsequent to the incident on Saturday, March 23, 1974, when Reverend Konz was briefly restrained in a bedroom by Erikson, the Reverend was in such mental condition as to fairly understand and appreciate his situation and had ample opportunity to request assistance but chose, instead, to forego medical treatment. Hence, assuming that one spouse owes the other a duty to seek aid when the latter is unwillingly rendered incompetent to evaluate the need for aid, or helpless to obtain it, that duty would not have been breached under the facts presented.

Subsequent to being restrained by Erikson in a bedroom for one half hour on the Saturday preceding his death, Reverend Konz elected on numerous occasions not to obtain insulin. The record does not support the inference raised by the Superior Court that the Reverend was, against his will, and until his death, continuously held incommunicado as an isolated captive of Erikson and Mrs. Konz while being denied the opportunity to secure medical assistance.

After announcing that the confrontation with Erikson was "settled," Reverend Konz could easily have addressed a request for insulin to his aunt, to his daughter, to the clergyman to whom he spoke to cancel a speaking engagement for Sunday, to persons at the hospital facility to which he drove Saturday night, to the nurse with whom he conversed late Saturday night, or to visitors to his home on Sunday. The Reverend not only remained silent as to a desire for insulin, however, but even took the initiative to reassure his aunt and daughter that there was no cause for concern. This course of behavior is inconsistent with any conclusion other than that the Reverend, by Saturday evening, had become firmly resolved to abstain from the administration of insulin. Had the Reverend been dissatisfied with his treatment, as a diabetic would be in the event of being forcibly denied insulin, he presumably would have attempted to obtain the medication or to call his dissatisfaction to the attention of persons with whom he came in contact. Yet, the record is devoid of any evidence that such an effort was made. Nor can the Reverend's acquiescence be attributed to a lack of mental competency to comprehend and militate against his plight. The testimony of the nurse with whom the Reverend conversed on Saturday night, as well as the Reverend's reaction to the presence of visitors in his home on Sunday, indicate clearly that the Reverend was in an alert and rational condition. Hence, the conclusion is inescapable that Reverend Konz, having been a diabetic for seventeen years, was aware of the importance of insulin to the preservation of his life but competently chose to forego treatment. Under this circumstance, we find no breach of duty to have been incurred by Mrs. Konz in her failure to seek medical aid for her husband.

Order reversed and appellants discharged.

NIX, JUSTICE, concurring.

This case raises the possibility of criminal liability as to both defendants as a consequence of their affirmative acts of Saturday, March 23, 1974. As to Mrs. Konz, it also raises the question of possible criminal liability for her *failure to act* between the events of Saturday evening and Monday morning (when Rev. Konz died) in view of the relationship she shared with the decedent. For the reasons that follow, I am satisfied the instant record does not support criminal liability under either theory.

In this appeal there is no causal connection between the acts of appellants and the death of Rev. Konz. The record is clear that the appellants' prevention of the decedent's attempt to administer insulin on Saturday was in no way causally connected with the death on Monday morning. Subsequent to the events of Saturday, the Reverend had numerous opportunities to seek help if he wanted an insulin injection. His conscious decision to continue to forego insulin after the events of Saturday constituted an intervening, superseding cause, thus cutting off any connection between appellants' affirmative actions on Saturday and Rev. Konz's death on Monday.

The more difficult question presented is whether there is a duty upon a spouse to seek medical aid for the other partner in contravention of the conscious decision of the ill spouse. The majority correctly notes that this is not a situation where one spouse is unable, because of a weakened condition, "to evaluate the need for [medical] aid, or helpless to obtain it...."

Without determining whether a healthy spouse has to seek medical aid for a physically infirm spouse in spite of the conscious choice of the ill spouse, it is clear that if such a duty were required it could not be operative in this case. The knowledge requisite to show criminal responsibility for failure to act must include knowledge of the risk of danger or life. Since the wife here had no superior knowledge of medicine and apparently shared her husband's religious views, the knowledge essential to the establishment of an affirmative duty is lacking and the requisite mental state does not exist.[2]

Thus, I concur in the result.

McDermott, Justice, dissenting.

I dissent from the Court's decision, which disregards the jury's verdict, as well as our own maxim that, upon appeal, the evidence adduced at trial must be viewed in the light most favorable to the verdict winner.

I believe that, on the evidence recited above, the jury could properly have found that the affirmative actions of appellants in purposely depriving Reverend Konz of his life-sustaining insulin, in violently restraining his attempts to obtain assistance, and in deliberately isolating him from others from whom he might have sought aid satisfies the factual requirements of Section 2504. The jury was certainly not obliged to view the situation as the majority chooses to frame it, *i.e.*, that there could be no "conclusion other than that the Reverend ... became firmly resolved to abstain from the administration of insulin," regardless of the consequences.

The majority's "inescapable" conclusion is rendered all the more astonishing in light of the charge of the trial judge, who put the issue squarely before the jury:

> In this regard it is the law that a rational person has a right to refuse medical treatment, and he has a right to refuse it for any reason whatsoever, and that includes religious convictions. *If Reverend Konz did refuse treatment or did not want treatment and refused the taking of insulin and that this was his choice, the defendants are clearly entitled to a verdict of not guilty.*

The jury's verdict demonstrates without a doubt that it did not credit the proposition, upon which the majority relies, that Reverend Konz chose to forego insulin and medical treatment. This court is in no position to second-guess the fact-finder on such a clear issue of fact.

It does not matter what the relationship between appellants and decedent may have been, spouse or friend, in the real world beyond the situation precipitating the crisis which cost Reverend Konz his life. What appellants' duties might be under different circumstances or in another context is not relevant. Appellants created their own circumstances and context and lived them out in a reckless, even ruthless, fashion. They did not simply stand by while Reverend Konz expired. Despite the majority's creative re-interpretation of the facts, the record shows deliberate steps taken by appellants to keep from Reverend Konz the vital substance which he *needed and wanted* to save his life. The jury, having been carefully instructed as to the elements of involuntary manslaughter, properly could have found on this record that appellants'

---

2. I reject the broad proposition, suggested by the majority, that a conscious decision of an ailing spouse to forego medical help would relieve the surviving spouse in all situations of the obligation to procure help.

actions were reckless or grossly negligent and that they directly caused Reverend Konz's death. No more is required to sustain a conviction under Section 2504.

I would affirm the order of the Superior Court, reinstating the jury's verdict.

Comments and Questions

(1) Why does the majority reject the lower court's view that "the marital relationship gives rise to an unrestricted duty for one spouse to summon medical aid whenever the other is in a serious or immediate need of medical attention"? Did the defendants here do more than fail to call a doctor? Why were the charges against them ultimately dropped? In *Herman v. State*, 472 So. 2d 770 (Fla. Dist. Ct. App. 1985), the defendant provided cocaine to his friend, the decedent. She took the cocaine and went into violent convulsions. The defendant did not seek medical care for her immediately, and she died. Held, the case presented sufficient evidence to support a conviction for manslaughter. Is the government's case stronger in *Herman* or *Konz*?

(2) *State v. Cabezuela*, 265 P.3d 705 (N.M. 2011), concerned intentional child abuse resulting in death, which required the jury to find that the defendant committed the physical acts of abuse that led to the child's death. Therefore, a jury instruction that permitted a guilty verdict for intentional child abuse if the jury found the defendant caused the victim's death "either by her actions or failure to act" was improper. The court noted that the distinction between intentional child abuse resulting in death and negligent child abuse resulting in death bore important practical consequences at sentencing, with the former carrying a life sentence and the latter having a maximum penalty of 18 years imprisonment, a sentencing structure designed by the legislature to give the harshest punishment to only the most deliberate and reprehensible forms of child abuse. Is this distinction relevant regarding *Konz*? How?

(3) The father of the three-year-old in *State v. Franklin*, 861 S.W.2d 181 (Mo. 1993), was convicted of murder after he severely beat the child. The mother was convicted of involuntary manslaughter for failing to seek medical treatment for the child. The evidence demonstrated that the mother had checked on the child frequently after the beating and found the little boy sleeping normally. The conviction was affirmed on appeal with the court finding that the mother had seen how severe the beating was, knew that the child had been seriously injured, had vomited several times, and had complained of pain. If the defendant genuinely—but unreasonably—believed that she could safely attend to the child's medical needs at home without going to the emergency room, would she be guilty of manslaughter?

See *State v. Williams*, 484 P.2d 1167, 1170 (Wash. Ct. App. 1971), where the trial court expressly found:

> That both defendants were aware that William Joseph Tabafunda was ill during the period September 1, 1968 to September 12, 1968. The defendants were ignorant. They did not realize how sick the baby was. They thought that the baby had a toothache and no layman regards a toothache as dangerous to life. They loved the baby and gave it aspirin in hopes of improving

> its condition. They did not take the baby to a doctor because of fear that the Welfare Department would take the baby away from them. They knew that medical help was available because of previous experience. They had no excuse that the law will recognize for not taking the baby to a doctor.
>
> The defendants Walter L. Williams and Bernice J. Williams were negligent in not seeking medical attention for William Joseph Tabafunda.
>
> That as a proximate result of this negligence, William Joseph Tabafunda died.

The convictions were affirmed, with the court finding that the defendants did not exercise the caution "by a man of reasonable prudence under the same or similar conditions." 484 P.2d at 1174. *See also Smith v. State*, 408 N.E.2d 614, 620–22 (Ind. Ct. App. 1980):

> Defendant knew of the nature of the situation in which she placed Eric and allowed him to remain. This is sufficient to establish the *corpus delicti* of the crime of neglect of a dependent. The insertion in the statute of the words "knowingly" or "intentionally" require the State only to prove that the defendant parent was aware of facts that would alert a reasonable parent under the circumstances to take affirmative action to protect the child. It is within the legitimate province of the trier to infer from the totality of the circumstances whether or not the requisite awareness was present, and whether or not the action of the parent was reasonable. Defendant's argument [is] that she committed no act resulting in Eric's death, either intentionally or negligently.... Defendant's position as a parent is not one of benign neutrality. She had an affirmative duty to care for and protect her child. The standard of care is what a reasonable parent would do or not do under the circumstances.

(4) The "failure to act" cases normally involve parent-child or spousal care situations. Sometimes, however, the principle is applied beyond the family setting. In *People v. Thomas*, 272 N.W.2d 157, 159 (Mich. Ct. App. 1978), the court described the facts:

> The victim, a 19 year old male "catatonic schizophrenic," was at the time of his death a resident of Oak Haven, a religious practical training school. When it appeared he was not properly responding to ordinary treatment, defendant, the work coordinator at Oak Haven, obtained permission from the victim's parents to discipline him if such seemed necessary. Thereafter defendant, together with another supervisor at Oak Haven, took decedent to the edge of the campus, whereupon decedent's pants were taken down, following which he was spanked with a rubber hose. Such disciplinary session lasted approximately 15 to 30 minutes. During a portion thereof decedent's hands were tied behind his back for failure to cooperate.
>
> Following the disciplinary session aforesaid, defendant testified that the young man improved for awhile but then commenced to backslide. Defendant again received permission from decedent's parents to subject him to further discipline. On September 30, 1976, defendant again took decedent to the approx-

> imate same location, removed his pants, bound his hands behind him with a rope looped over a tree limb and proceeded to beat him with a doubled-over rubber hose. This beating lasted approximately 45 minutes to an hour. While the evidence conflicted, it appears that the victim was struck between 30 to 100 times. The beating resulted in severe bruises ranging from the victim's waist to his feet. Decedent's roommate testified that decedent had open bleeding sores on his thighs. On the date of death, which was nine days after the beating, decedent's legs were immobile. At no time did defendant obtain medical attention for the victim.
>
> Defendant admitted he had exercised poor judgment, after seeing the bruises, in continuing the discipline. He further testified that in the two days following the discipline, decedent seemed to be suffering from the flu, but by Sunday was up and walking and was in apparent good health until one week following the beating, when decedent became sick with nausea and an upset stomach. These symptoms continued for two days, when decedent died.
>
> As a result of the autopsy, one Dr. Clark testified that the bruises were the result of a trauma and that decedent was in a state of continuous traumatization because he was trying to walk on his injured legs. Dr. Clark testified that decedent's legs were swollen to possibly twice their normal size. He further testified that the actual cause of death was acute pulmonary edema, resulting from the aspiration of stomach contents. Said aspiration caused a laryngeal spasm, causing decedent to suffocate on his own vomit. Although pulmonary edema was the direct cause of death, Dr. Clark testified that said condition usually had some underlying cause and that, while there were literally hundreds of potential underlying causes, it was his opinion that in the instant case the underlying cause was the trauma to decedent's legs.

Is this manslaughter?

> Involuntary manslaughter may be based on the failure to perform a legal duty. Defendant was a supervisor of Oak Haven, stood in a position of authority over the victim and, by talking with the victim's parents and obtaining their permission to discipline the decedent, he directly and voluntarily assumed a parental function, and stood in a position of *loco parentis* to the decedent. Under such circumstances, defendant's beating of the victim coupled with his failure to provide medical attention, when decedent was unable to obtain same himself, violated defendant's legal duty to care for the victim. The elements of involuntary manslaughter were adequately established.

272 N.W.2d at 160.

Could the state have obtained a manslaughter conviction against the decedent's roommate? His parents?

(5) California enacted an elder abuse statute which, in part, imposed criminal liability on

> any person who knows or reasonably should know that a person is an elder or dependent adult and who, under circumstances or conditions likely to produce great bodily harm or death, willfully causes or permits any elder or dependent adult to suffer, or inflicts thereon unjustifiable physical pain or mental suffering, or having the care or custody of an elder or dependent adult, willfully causes or permits the person or health of the elder or dependent adult to be injured, or willfully causes or permits the elder or dependent adult to be placed in a situation in which his or her person or health is endangered ...

Cal. Penal Code § 368(b)(1). The facts in *People v. Heitzman*, 886 P.2d 1229 (Cal. 1994), presented a dreadful situation of such abuse. The defendant's father had been paralyzed by a stroke. While living with the defendant's brother, he had not been given food and liquids for three days, as the brother "did not want his father, who no longer had control over his bowels and bladder, to defecate or urinate because it would further cause the house to smell." At the time of his death, the decedent had bed sores over one-sixth of his body caused by malnutrition, dehydration, and neglect. The brother was properly found guilty of violating the statute. The debate centered on his sister's responsibility.

The majority held that the statute could not be applied against her, for she was not "under an existing legal duty to take positive action."

> Furthermore, given defendant's failure to intercede on her father's behalf under the egregious circumstances presented here, we can well understand the prosecution's decision to charge defendant under section 368(a). Because the People presented no evidence tending to show that defendant had a legal duty to control the conduct of either of her brothers however, we reverse the judgment of the Court of Appeal with directions to reinstate the trial court's order dismissing the charges against defendant.
>
> We emphasize that our disposition of this case in no way signifies our approval of defendant's failure to repel the threat to her father's well-being. The facts underlying this case are indeed troubling, and defendant's alleged indifference to the suffering of her father cannot be condoned. The desire to impose criminal liability on this defendant cannot be accomplished, however, at the expense of providing constitutionally required clarity to an otherwise vague statute.

The dissenters disagreed:

> [D]efendant—formerly her father's caretaker—knew he was paralyzed, incontinent, and completely dependent upon others to feed, clean, and move him. For a period of at least six weeks before her father died defendant repeatedly visited and spent the night in the home where her brothers and father lived. Defendant had actual knowledge during this time that her father required, but did not receive, medical attention; that his person and physical surroundings had become filthy from human waste and debris; that the

> mattress from which he could not move without assistance was damp and rotted through; and that he was confined alone in his room for long stretches of time.
>
> Nevertheless, defendant did not take any steps to assist her father during this period. She did not attempt to obtain professional help (*e.g.* telephoning the doctor, social worker, or paramedics); to care for him while present in the home (*e.g.*, feeding or cleaning him); or to discuss with other family members the possibility of making different care arrangements (*e.g.*, hospitalization or professional caretaking assistance). The evidence further discloses that defendant's father died as a result of the deplorable conditions of which defendant was actually or presumably aware (septic shock from bed sores, malnutrition, and dehydration).

Heitzman, 37 Cal. Rptr. 2d at 257–58. Could the sister have been legitimately prosecuted under the statute? Under any other statute? If the sister could have been prosecuted, could anyone else have been charged as well?

People v. Nelson

Court of Appeals of New York
128 N.E.2d 391 (1955)

DYE, JUDGE.

The indictment upon which the conviction was based contained two counts: The first charged manslaughter in the first degree insofar as the death of two persons was caused by a fire which occurred in defendant's multiple dwelling. These persons were unable to escape because of lack of adequate fire protection which defendant had knowingly neglected to provide, as required by the Multiple Dwelling Law, a misdemeanor, affecting "the person or property" of the two persons killed. The second count charged manslaughter in the second degree by reason of the fact that under the same circumstances of ownership he "wilfully and wrongfully used said building" in an unlawful manner and "with gross and culpable negligence" owned, operated and neglected to render the "building safe for the tenants and occupants thereof" by failing to provide adequate fire protection as required by law, and thereby caused the death of two persons.

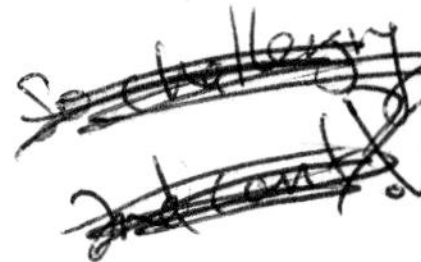

The appellant concedes that his premises were existing in violation of the safety provisions required by the Multiple Dwelling Law, and that such violations were the proximate cause of the death of two tenants. He, nonetheless, prays that his conviction on both counts be set aside on the ground that the trial court erred, as a matter of law, in ruling that lack of notice of the aforesaid violations afforded no defense, thereby depriving the jury of its right to determine as a question of fact, on the issue of culpable negligence, whether without such notice or knowledge he was "engaged in committing, or attempting to commit, a misdemeanor, affecting the person or property, either of the person killed" or whether such homicide when committed without a design to effect death, was the result of culpable negligence.

It is true defendant was not personally notified of the violations, but nothing turns on such omission for such notice is not required in a criminal proceeding. However, the record is replete with proof establishing that he had knowledge of the existence of the violations. There is evidence showing that the plaintiff had been a tenant of the subject premises for over fifteen years; that he was well familiar with its physical aspects, including lack of sprinkler system and secondary egress for use in case of fire. There came a time in 1951 when he negotiated with the then owner to purchase the premises. At the closing of title on June 15, 1951, the defendant was present and represented by attorneys. A report furnished by the company issuing the title insurance noted violations of the Multiple Dwelling Law and these were set forth in a deed which was given subject to such violation. While defendant now says that this reference to the violation was not brought to his attention, he nonetheless is bound thereby. In addition to such uncontroverted documentary proof, there is oral testimony to the effect that he had told a tenant that because boys were using the roof scuttle as a means of entrance, he had nailed it shut; that the real estate agent had told defendant of the need for fire escapes and that defendant had made measurements for such installation but that he "hadn't gotten to it yet."

On November 17, 1952, the defendant undertook to repair a leak in the roof. He heated a tar compound in a shallow pan over an open gas burner located in the basement. The tar caught fire and despite his best efforts spread to the building. He ran to give the alarm to the tenants. It was too late. Two tenants who were cut off jumped from the fourth-story window and were badly injured. One died and a third tenant trapped in her apartment was burned to death. An assistant fire marshal testified that on the day of the fire the defendant had told him that "he knew he was supposed to have fire escapes or a sprinkler."

In such a setting the defendant is chargeable with knowledge of the existence of the violation—and, even though such violations were committed without design to effect death, his act was culpable within the meaning of subdivision 3 of section 1052 of the Penal Law. This is so whether or not he knew the penal consequences of such culpability.

In the case at bar the conviction must be upheld. From the time of the appellant's acquisition of title to the date of the fire, a period of about one and one-half years, the lack of a secondary means of egress or a sprinkler system constituted a continuing misdemeanor "affecting the person ... killed." This continuing omission to provide proper fire protection was not merged in the homicide of the two deceased tenants as claimed by the appellant. The situation is not analogous to the assault homicide where a continuing assault against one resulting in death is merged in the homicide. It is undeniable that a tremendous duty is placed upon the owners and those in charge of property under the applicable section of the Multiple Dwelling Law; however, it is quite apparent that the Legislature intended the burden to be onerous so that owners would be impressed with the consequences flowing from violation of the statute, which violations could so readily endanger human life in the congested conditions under which people must live in the city of New York.

The judgment of conviction ... should be *affirmed*.

VAN VOORHIS, JUDGE (dissenting).

Appellant's defense was chiefly based upon his lack of knowledge or notice of the existence of these violations, but the trial court excluded such testimony upon the ground that the misdemeanors with which appellant was charged were *mala prohibita*, that he could be guilty of these violations of the Multiple Dwelling Law without having created or even knowing the condition of the building, and that, if the deaths of the persons named in the indictment resulted therefrom, he is automatically guilty of manslaughter regardless of culpable negligence and irrespective of any criminal intent. If the last conclusion is correct, it seems to me that the law has retreated a long distance into a stage of primitive formalism.

Appellant had himself been a tenant in these premises for a number of years. He is a Negro seventy-one years old whose education ended with the first grade in elementary school. His defense was that he had recently bought this real property; that he did so for a cash consideration of $1,000 and a purchase—money mortgage of $7,500, under threat of eviction by the former owner unless he became the owner; that these violations had been filed against the former owner without having been caused to be removed by the city department of housing and buildings, and were deliberately concealed from him by his vendor in order to induce him to purchase the property and to relieve the former owner of responsibility; that although there is a general recital in the deed that the conveyance is subject to building violations, he did not read it personally or know its full contents, and that the deed was recorded by the vendor's agent who procured it back from the register's office and kept it in his possession in order to prevent these matters from coming to appellant's attention. Appellant contends that he was in complete ignorance of these circumstances until he found himself confronted with a charge of manslaughter, but that the trial court withheld this defense from the jury upon the ground that criminal intent is unrelated to his guilt or innocence.

Manslaughter where death results from the commission of a misdemeanor is analogous to felony murder. "Felonious intention, as an element of the homicide, is supplied by the intention to do the unlawful act of which the homicide is a consequence. The intent is transferred by implication of law." As in the case of felony murder, no design to effect death is necessary but just as there must have been an intention to commit an independent felony in case of murder, so must there have been an intent to commit an independent misdemeanor in order to render a defendant guilty of manslaughter. Otherwise the whole underlying theory of criminality is withdrawn from the felony charge. At least, where the misdemeanor consists in a continuing offense which is *malum prohibitum*, a defendant must have been aware of its existence before being convicted of manslaughter. If awareness of the misdemeanor is held to be irrelevant, the basis for guilt of manslaughter is eliminated. "When there is a general intent to do evil, in other words, of which evil the wrong actually done may be looked upon as a probable incident, then the party having such general intent is to be regarded as having intended the particular wrong." If a criminal purpose is so large and necessary an element to fulfill the doctrine of "transferred intent" in case of felony murder, can it be true that one may become guilty of manslaughter in complete moral innocence without so much as knowing that a misdemeanor has occurred? If the People's witnesses testified truthfully, defendant is not morally guiltless, but that does not concern the outcome of this appeal inasmuch as the trial court did not give him his day in court on this issue by refusing to allow him to testify to his lack of knowledge of these building violations, and therefore his conviction can stand only upon the basis that his moral innocence is irrelevant.

Allied to the need of establishing a criminal intent in order to sustain a conviction of manslaughter, is the issue that has frequently arisen concerning whether manslaughter can be based on accidental homicides growing out of any and every kind of misdemeanor. In the able and exhaustive 1937 Report of the Law Revision Commission to the Legislature upon this subject, it was said: "Most other states include provisions in their statutes to the effect that homicide committed in the course of a misdemeanor or in the course of an 'unlawful act' less than a felony is manslaughter. Courts, called upon to construe these, have evinced a uniform reluctance to interpret the provision literally, and manage to read into it limitations which materially modify its rigor. As in the case of the felony murder rule, limitations have been affected in two ways—the imposition of the requirement of some causal connection between the underlying offense and the homicide, and a limitation of the kind of unlawful act which will be sufficient to furnish a basis for the charge of manslaughter. Both are encountered in various forms: it is variously stated merely that some causal connection must exist, or that the homicide must be the natural and probable consequence or the proximate result of the unlawful act. Still greater diversity exists in the statement of the law concerning the nature of the misdemeanor. Some authorities emphasize that the underlying offense must be intrinsically dangerous to human life; others, that it must be in violation of a statute designed to protect human life. By far the greatest number assert, however, that it must be *malum in se*, and that an act only *malum prohibitum* resulting in homicide is insufficient to subject the wrongdoer to liability for manslaughter. Among the misdemeanors which have been held to be insufficient under one criterion or another in cases where the defendant was charged with homicide, are hunting on another's land, carrying a concealed pistol, selling liquor, and driving past a tollgate to evade payment of toll. Infractions of laws regulating the operation of motor vehicles have been the subject of greater controversy, but such acts, though sometimes characterized as *mala prohibita*, are generally held to fall within the provisions of statutes on manslaughter committed in the course of unlawful acts."

No one questions that an owner is guilty of misdemeanor even though he is ignorant of the building violation. But to have been found guilty of misdemeanor manslaughter, a defendant should have known at least of the existence of the underlying offense, yet the trial court ruled and instructed the jury on this count in the indictment, that not only was this defendant held to strict compliance with this statute (which was correct so far as being guilty of the misdemeanor went), but that neither ignorance of the condition of the building nor of the Multiple Dwelling Law was a defense to first degree manslaughter.

Comments and Questions

(1) In some of the states which retain this rule, little guidance is given as to the state of mind requirement or the nature of the misdemeanor needed for conviction under the misdemeanor/manslaughter rule. As to the former point, what result in *Nelson* if it was clear that the defendant had absolutely no knowledge of the violations? In *People v. Stuart*, 302 P.2d 5, 9–10 (Cal. 1956), the defendant pharmacist mislabeled a prescription, without intent or negligence. The drug was given to a child who died as a result of taking it. The statute made it a strict liability offense to misbrand drugs. What result under *Nelson*? The California Supreme Court reversed Stuart's conviction:

> To be an unlawful act within the meaning of section 192, therefore, the act in question must be dangerous to human life or safety.
>
> It follows, therefore, that only if defendant had intentionally or through criminal negligence prepared, compounded, or sold an adulterated or misbranded drug, would his violation of section 26280 of the Health and Safety Code be an unlawful act within the meaning of section 192 of the Penal Code. When, as in this case, however, the defendant did not know, and could not reasonably be expected to know, that the sodium citrate bottle contained nitrite, those conditions are not met and there is therefore lacking the culpability necessary to make the act an unlawful act within the meaning of section 192.

(2) If the statute speaks inclusively of a death caused "by the commission of an unlawful act other than a felony" (Ga. Code Ann. 16-5-3(a)), could a manslaughter conviction be based upon the commission of *any* misdemeanor? Most courts impose the restriction that the act be "dangerous to human life or safety." Which misdemeanors are dangerous to human life or safety? To ask the question in another way, which misdemeanors are not? *See Comber v. United States*, 584 A.2d 26, 50–51 (D.C. 1990):

> Although some misdemeanors, at least when viewed in the abstract, prohibit activity which seems inherently dangerous, they may also reach conduct which might not pose such danger. A special difficulty arises in the case of simple assault, as presented here, because that misdemeanor is designed to protect not only against physical injury, but against all forms of offensive touching. To hold a defendant liable for involuntary manslaughter where a death freakishly results from spitting at another, putting one's hand on another in a sexually offensive manner, or lightly tapping another on the face, would create too severe an attenuation of the link between the criminal sanction imposed and the defendant's culpability. In such circumstances, there is no foreseeable risk of bodily injury of any appreciable sort.
>
> Accordingly, the fact that death results in the commission of what is classified as an inherently dangerous misdemeanor, is alone insufficient to establish guilt of misdemeanor involuntary manslaughter. Rather, the defendant must commit the misdemeanor in a way which is dangerous under the particular circumstances of the case. [The question] "ought to be not whether the crime

> is generally dangerous, but whether the defendant's conduct in the particular death-causing situation was under the circumstances dangerous." We think a misdemeanor will be dangerous under the circumstances if the manner of its commission entails a reasonably foreseeable risk of appreciable physical injury. If the manner in which an inherently dangerous misdemeanor is committed creates such a foreseeable risk of appreciable physical injury, the defendant should bear the consequences of criminal homicide if the result is not just bodily injury but death itself. A killing resulting from a misdemeanor which does not satisfy the standard just described will be excused.

(3) Often in these cases, the defendant cannot claim ignorance of the unlawful nature of his acts, but can only argue that the death caused was unforeseeable. In *State v. Frazier*, 98 S.W.2d 707 (Mo. 1936), the defendant struck the deceased once on the jaw. Unknown to the defendant, the decedent was a hemophiliac who died as a result of the punch. Manslaughter conviction affirmed. *See also State v. Lewis*, 824 S.W.2d 479, 483 (Mo. Ct. App. 1992):

> Ample evidence supported jury's finding that defendant convicted of involuntary manslaughter caused victim's death … it was immaterial that defendant did not know [that victim was a] "feeble person and was susceptible to bleeding of the brain" or that he did not anticipate his conduct would cause death.

(4) In *State v. Light*, 577 S.W.2d 134, 135 (Mo. Ct. App. 1979), the deceased and defendant were jointly engaged in an unsuccessful attempt to steal some wire. In pursuance of their common design, Bradshaw climbed a telephone pole, near an abandoned house in a remote rural area, for the purpose of stealing some wire attached to its top. In so doing, and before any larceny had been completed, Bradshaw came into contact with a high voltage line, received the fatal shock, and fell to the ground.

> The state's evidence showed that defendant was the originator of the larcenous plan. Defendant was present at the scene when Bradshaw climbed the pole and met his death. There was no claim nor proof by the state that either Bradshaw or defendant knew that any of the wires attached to the pole was energized.

Should defendant's manslaughter conviction be affirmed? Relying heavily on limitations imposed in the felony murder area, the court reversed.

(5) Is the misdemeanor-manslaughter rule needed? In what cases would the standard rules for involuntary manslaughter not work?

[D] Causation

In most homicide prosecutions the government will have no difficulty showing that the defendant killed the deceased and is criminally responsible for that killing. In some cases, however, two important questions emerge: (1) Did the death of the deceased result from the defendant's act? (2) Should the defendant be held criminally responsible if someone (or something) else contributed to the actions which killed the deceased?

Commonwealth v. Root

Supreme Court of Pennsylvania
170 A.2d 310 (1961)

Charles Alvin Jones, Chief Justice.

The appellant was found guilty of involuntary manslaughter for the death of his competitor in the course of an automobile race between them on a highway. We granted allocatur because of the important question present as to whether the defendant's unlawful and reckless conduct was a sufficiently direct cause of the death to warrant his being charged with criminal homicide.

The testimony, which is uncontradicted in material part, discloses that, on the night of the fatal accident, the defendant accepted the deceased's challenge to engage in an automobile race; that the racing took place on a rural 3-lane highway; that the night was clear and dry, and traffic light; that the speed limit on the highway was 50 miles per hour; that, immediately prior to the accident, the two automobiles were being operated at varying speeds of from 70 to 90 miles per hour; that the accident occurred in a no-passing zone on the approach to a bridge where the highway narrowed to two directionally-opposite lanes; that, at the time of the accident, the defendant was in the lead and was proceeding in his right hand lane of travel; that the deceased, in an attempt to pass the defendant's automobile, when a truck was closely approaching from the opposite direction, swerved his car to the left, crossed the highway's white dividing line and drove his automobile on the wrong side of the highway head-on into the oncoming truck with resultant fatal effect to himself.

This evidence would of course amply support a conviction of the defendant for speeding, reckless driving and, perhaps, other violations of The Vehicle Code. In any event, unlawful or reckless conduct is only one ingredient of the crime of involuntary manslaughter. Another essential and distinctly separate element of the crime is that the unlawful or reckless conduct charged to the defendant was the direct cause of the death in issue. The first ingredient is obviously present in this case but, just as plainly, the second is not.

While precedent is to be found for application of the tort law concept of "proximate cause" in fixing responsibility for criminal homicide, the want of any rational basis for its use in determining criminal liability can no longer be properly disregarded. When proximate cause was first borrowed from the field of tort law and applied to homicide prosecutions in Pennsylvania, the concept connoted a much more direct causal relation in producing the alleged culpable result than it does today. Proximate cause, as an essential element of a tort founded in negligence, has undergone in recent times, and is still undergoing, a marked extension. More specifically, this area of civil law has been progressively liberalized in favor of claims for damages for personal injuries to which careless conduct of others can in some way be associated. To persist in applying the tort liability concept of proximate cause to prosecutions for criminal homicide after the marked expansion of *civil* liability of defendants in tort actions for negligence would be to extend possible *criminal* liability to persons chargeable with unlawful or reckless conduct in circumstances not generally considered to present the likelihood of a resultant death.

The instant case is one of first impression in this State; and our research has not disclosed a single instance where a district attorney has ever before attempted to prosecute for involuntary manslaughter on facts similar to those established by the record now before us. In the instant case, the action of the deceased driver in recklessly and suicidally swerving his car to the left lane of a 2-lane highway into the path of an oncoming truck was not forced upon him by any act of the defendant; it was done by the deceased and by him alone, who thus directly brought about his own demise.

Legal theory which makes guilt or innocence of criminal homicide depend upon such accidental and fortuitous circumstances as are now embraced by modern tort law's encompassing concept of proximate cause is too harsh to be just.

Even if the tort liability concept of proximate cause were to be deemed applicable, the defendant's conviction of involuntary manslaughter in the instant case could not be sustained under the evidence. The operative effect of a supervening cause would have to be taken into consideration. But, the trial judge refused the defendant's point for charge to such effect and erroneously instructed the jury that "negligence or want of care on the part of [the deceased] is no defense to the criminal responsibility of the defendant...."

The Superior Court, in affirming the defendant's conviction in this case, approved the charge above mentioned, despite a number of decisions in involuntary manslaughter cases holding that the conduct of the deceased victim must be considered in order to determine whether the defendant's reckless acts were the proximate (*i.e.*, sufficiently direct) cause of his death. It did so on the ground that there can be more than one proximate cause of death. The point is wholly irrelevant. Of course there can be more than one proximate cause of death just as there can also be more than one *direct* cause of death. For example, in the so-called "shield" cases where a felon interposes the person of an innocent victim between himself and a pursuing officer, if the officer should fire his gun at the felon to prevent his escape and fatally wound the person used as a shield, the different acts of the policeman and the felon would each be a direct cause of the victim's death.

If the tort liability concept of proximate cause were to be applied in a criminal homicide prosecution, then the conduct of the person whose death is the basis of the indictment would have to be considered, not to prove that it was merely an *additional* proximate cause of the death, but to determine, under fundamental and long recognized law applicable to proximate cause, whether the subsequent wrongful act *superseded* the original conduct chargeable to the defendant. If it did in fact supervene, then the original act is so insulated from the ensuing death as not to be its proximate cause.

Under the uncontradicted evidence in this case, the conduct of the defendant was not the proximate cause of the decedent's death as a matter of law. "Where a second actor has become aware of the existence of a potential danger created by the negligence of an original tort-feasor, and thereafter, by an independent act of negligence, brings about an accident, the first tort-feasor is relieved of liability, because the condition created by him was merely a circumstance of the accident and not its proximate cause."

In the case now before us, the deceased was aware of the dangerous condition created by the defendant's reckless conduct in driving his automobile at an excessive rate of speed along the highway but, despite such knowledge, he recklessly chose to swerve his car to the left and into the path of an oncoming truck, thereby bringing about the head-on collision which caused his own death.

To summarize, the tort liability concept of proximate cause has no proper place in prosecutions for criminal homicide and more direct causal connection is required for conviction. In the instant case, the defendant's reckless conduct was not a sufficiently direct cause of the competing driver's death to make him criminally liable therefore.

The judgment of sentence is reversed and the defendant's motion in arrest of judgment granted.

EAGEN, JUSTICE (dissenting).

The opinion of the learned Chief Justice admits, under the uncontradicted facts, that the defendant, at the time of the fatal accident involved, was engaged in an unlawful and reckless course of conduct. Racing an automobile at 90 miles per hour, trying to prevent another automobile going in the same direction from passing him, in a no-passing zone on a two-lane public highway, is certainly all of that. Admittedly also, there can be more than one direct cause of an unlawful death. To me, this is self-evident. But, says the majority opinion, the defendant's recklessness was not a direct cause of the death. With this, I cannot agree.

If the defendant did not engage in the unlawful race and so operate his automobile in such a reckless manner, this accident would never have occurred. He helped create the dangerous event. He was a vital part of it. The victim's acts were a natural reaction to the stimulus of the situation. The race, the attempt to pass the other car and forge ahead, the reckless speed, all of these factors the defendant himself helped create. He was part and parcel of them. That the victim's response was normal under the circumstances, that his reaction should have been expected and was clearly foreseeable, is to me beyond argument. That the defendant's recklessness was a substantial factor is obvious. All of this, in my opinion, makes his unlawful conduct a direct cause of the resulting collision.

"He whose act causes in any way, directly or indirectly, the death of another, kills him, within the meaning of felonious homicide. It is a rule of both reason and the law that whenever one's will contributes to impel a physical force, whether another's, his own, or a combined force, proceeding from whatever different sources, he is responsible for the result, the same as though his hand, unaided, had produced it."

But, says the majority opinion, these are principles of tort law and should not in these days be applied to the criminal law. But such has been the case since the time of Blackstone. These same principles have always been germane to both crimes and tort. They have been repeatedly so applied throughout the years and were employed in a criminal case in Pennsylvania as long as one hundred and seventeen years ago. In that case, two separate bands of men were fighting each other with firearms in a public street and, as a result, an innocent citizen was shot and killed. The person firing the fatal shot could not be ascertained. Hare, one of the rioters, was convicted of homicide and the judgment was affirmed. Can anyone question the logic or correctness of this decision? Under the rationale of the majority opinion, what would be the result in the *Hare* case? Certainly, under its reasoning, if the truck driver met death under the circumstances the case at hand presents, the defendant would not be legally responsible. Again with this conclusion, I cannot agree.

While the victim's foolhardiness in this case contributed to his own death, he was not the only one responsible and it is not he alone with whom we are concerned. It is the people of the Commonwealth who are harmed by the kind of conduct the defendant pursued. Their interests must be kept in mind.

I, therefore, dissent and would accordingly affirm the judgment of conviction.

Comments and Questions

(1) Was not "the defendant's recklessness ... a substantial factor ... (and) a direct cause" of the homicide? As a matter of public policy, should Root's manslaughter conviction have been reversed? In *Commonwealth v. Atencio*, 189 N.E.2d 223, 224–25 (Mass. 1963), the deceased was killed when he voluntarily played "Russian Roulette" with the defendants. Their manslaughter convictions were affirmed:

> We are of opinion that the defendants could properly have been found guilty of manslaughter. This is not a civil action against the defendants by the personal representative of Stewart Britch. In such a case his voluntary act, we assume, would be a bar. Here the Commonwealth had an interest that the deceased should not be killed by the wanton or reckless conduct of himself and others.
>
> Such conduct could be found in the concerted action and cooperation of the defendants in helping to bring about the deceased's foolish act. The jury did not have to believe testimony that the defendants at the last moment tried to dissuade the deceased from doing that which they had just done themselves.
>
> The defendants argue as if it should have been ruled, as matter of law, that there were three "games" of solitaire and not one "game" of "Russian roulette." That the defendants participated could be found to be a cause and not a mere condition of Stewart Britch's death. It is not correct to say that his act could not be found to have been caused by anything which Marshall and Atencio did, nor that he would have died when the gun went off in his hand no matter whether they had done the same. The testimony does not require a ruling that when the deceased took the gun from Atencio it was an independent or intervening act not standing in any relation to the defendants' acts which would render what he did imputable to them. It is an oversimplification to contend that each participated in something that only one could do at a time.

> There could be found to be a mutual encouragement in a joint enterprise. In the abstract, there may have been no duty on the defendants to prevent the deceased from playing. But there was a duty on their part not to cooperate or join with him in the "game." Nor, if the facts presented such a case, would we have to agree that if the deceased, and not the defendants, had played first that they could not have been found guilty of manslaughter. The defendants were much more than merely present at a crime. It would not be necessary that the defendants force the deceased to play or suggest that he play.

What result under *Root*? Note the Massachusetts court's discussion of *Root*:

> In *Commonwealth v. Root*, the competitor drove on the wrong side of the road head-on into an oncoming truck and was killed. The court held that "the tort liability concept of proximate cause has no proper place in prosecutions for criminal homicide and more direct causal connection is required for conviction.... In the instant case, the defendant's reckless conduct was not a sufficiently direct cause of the competing driver's death to make him criminally liable therefor." In *Thacker v. State*, 103 Ga. App. 36, 117 S.E.2d 913 (1961), the defendant was indicted for the involuntary manslaughter of his competitor in a drag race who was killed when he lost control of his car and left the highway. The court said that the indictment "fails to allege any act or acts on the part of the defendant which caused or contributed to the loss of control of the vehicle driven by the deceased, other than the fact that they were engaged in a race at the time."
>
> Whatever may be thought of those two decisions, there is a very real distinction between drag racing and "Russian roulette." In the former much is left to the skill, or lack of it, of the competitor. In "Russian roulette" it is a matter of luck as to the location of the one bullet, and except for a misfire (of which there was evidence in the case at bar) the outcome is a certainty if the chamber under the hammer happens to be the one containing the bullet.

189 N.E.2d at 225.

The court in *Lewis v. State*, 474 So. 2d 766, 771 (Ala. Crim. App. 1985), reversed the homicide conviction in another Russian Roulette case. The key difference, according to the court, was that the victim had continued playing the "game" after the defendant had left the room.

> If the victim has shot himself while he and the appellant were playing Russian Roulette, or if the appellant was present when the victim was playing the game by himself, the appellant's conduct of influencing the victim to play would have been the cause-in-fact and the proximate cause of the victim's death. However, the key is the appellant's presence at the time the victim shot himself.

(2) In January 2000, professional basketball players Bobby Phills and David Wesley raced their cars after leaving an evening practice. Phills' Porsche went out of control, hitting another car and killing him. Wesley was going 107 m.p.h. behind Phills who

was going 110 m.p.h. in a 45 m.p.h. speed zone. Wesley's license had also been suspended indefinitely. Wesley was convicted of reckless driving but acquitted of involuntary manslaughter. Key to his defense was his assertion that they were not racing with each other but only racing their cars separately.

(3) The facts in *People v. Scott*, 185 N.W.2d 576, 577 (Mich. Ct. App. 1971), were set out by the court:

> The defendant, after engaging in an exchange of verbal hostilities with the occupants of a police patrol car, attempted to force the vehicle off the road. A chase ensued and a radio alert was relayed to other cars in the vicinity. An unmarked patrol car, in pursuit of defendant, collided at an intersection with a DSR bus, killing one of the officers in the patrol car.

The defendant's manslaughter conviction was reversed, with the court relying heavily on *Root*.

In *Cheung v. Commonwealth*, 753 S.E.2d 854 (Va. Ct. App. 2014), the defendant's conviction for involuntary manslaughter was upheld as supported by evidence that the defendant falling asleep while driving a bus was so gross and wanton as to show a reckless disregard of human life. Witnesses testified that the defendant was confused and agitated for hours before the crash, and a passenger overheard the defendant complaining over the telephone while driving that he was tired and that he did not get enough rest due to his work schedule. The bus had been on the road for seven hours at the time of the crash, and it was still three and one-half hours away from its destination. An experienced bus driver who was also a passenger testified that the defendant's driving was erratic for an hour before the crash.

(4) The defendant attacked the deceased, not inflicting serious harm. It turned out that the deceased suffered from a serious, pre-existing heart disease which was unknown to the defendant. Immediately after the attack, the deceased had an acute cardiac failure and died. Is the defendant guilty of a homicide offense? *See Commonwealth v. Hicks*, 396 A.2d 1183 (Pa. 1979). What result if the deceased had recently had two heart seizures, myocardial infarctions? *See State v. Williams*, 588 S.W.2d 70 (Mo. Ct. App. 1979). What if there was expert testimony that "the injury inflicted would not have killed a healthy person and ... the condition from which the victim was suffering would itself probably have been fatal"? *Wofford v. State*, 584 P.2d 227, 228 (Okla. Crim. App. 1978).

(5) The California Supreme Court upheld a jury finding that the murders of two rival gang members were the natural and probable consequences of the defendant's offenses of disturbing the peace and assault or battery in arranging for his brother to attempt to end his gang membership through a "jump out," because the defendant threatened to kill the gang members if they beat his brother too severely, brought fellow gang members for protection, and interrupted the jump out by pointing a gun at the participants. *People v. Smith*, 60 Cal.4th 603 (2014).

(6) The court in *State v. Foster*, 396 N.E.2d 246, 253 (Ohio C.P. 1979), attempted to shed light on the problem of causation:

> Proximate cause is an essential element of the offense charged, and proximate cause is an act or omission which in a natural and continuous sequence directly produces the death and without which it would not have occurred.
>
> Proximate cause exists when the death is the natural and probable result of the act or omission.
>
> There may be more than one proximate cause: however, if an act or omission of the defendant was one of the proximate causes, the existence of other causes is not a defense in this case.

The United States Supreme Court recently held that but-for causation is required to impose heightened sentences for drug sales causing death or serious bodily injury under 21 U.S.C. § 841(b). The language in that statute requires that the death "results from" the sale of illegal drugs. Thus, a defendant is not subject to the 20-year mandatory minimum sentence under 21 U.S.C. § 841(b) if the drug distribution is not an independently sufficient cause of the victims' death or serious bodily injury. *Burrage v. United States*, 134 S. Ct. 881 (2014).

Brackett v. Peters

United States Court of Appeals, Seventh Circuit
11 F.3d 78 (1993)

POSNER, CHIEF JUDGE.

Randy Brackett, an Illinois state prisoner who had been convicted after a bench trial of felony murder and given a long prison term, applied for federal *habeas corpus*, arguing that no rational finder of fact could have found that he had caused the death of his victim. The district judge, after reviewing the record of Brackett's trial, denied his application, precipitating this appeal, which raises interesting questions concerning the requirement of causation in criminal law.

Brackett, age 21 at the time, had raped and severely beaten an 85-year-old widow, Mrs. Winslow, for whom he had previously done yard work. She was admitted to the hospital with a broken arm, a broken rib, and extensive bruises. During her stay in the hospital, which lasted several weeks, she—described as "feisty" before the rape and beating—became depressed, resisted efforts to feed her, and became progressively weaker. Transferred to a nursing home, she continued to deteriorate, even though her physical injuries were healing. Her appetite was very poor. Her doctor ordered a nasal gastric feeding tube for her but the tube could not be inserted, in part because facial injuries inflicted by Brackett made insertion of the tube too painful. About ten days after her admission to the nursing home, she died while a nurse was feeding her some puréed food through a feeder syringe. An autopsy revealed that a large quantity of food, some six or seven ounces, had become lodged in Mrs. Winslow's trachea, asphyxiating her.

The question is whether Brackett's assault on Mrs. Winslow could be found to be a cause of her death. If so, Brackett is guilty of felony murder; if not, not. So far as bears on this case, an act is a cause of an event if two conditions are satisfied: the event would not have occurred without the act; the act made the event more likely. The first condition is necessary to distinguish the attempted from the completed crime, the second to rule out cases in which, while the event in question would not have occurred but for the act, the act did not create the kind of dangerous condition that would make such events more likely to occur. Suppose, for example, that Mrs. Winslow had been killed by a fire at the nursing home. She would not have been in the nursing home (in all likelihood), so would not have been killed, but for Brackett's assault. But as there would have been no greater danger of fire in a nursing home than in her own home, in our hypothetical case the assault would not have placed her in a situation of danger and therefore would not be considered a cause of her death.

Even with this qualification, which excludes from the concept of legally relevant causation certain purely adventitious "causes," every event has multiple causes. Mrs. Winslow's age was undoubtedly a cause of her death; a younger woman would have been much less likely to experience so rapid and complete a deterioration as a result of the assault. The autopsy revealed some signs of senility, and senility is a common cause of depression, loss of appetite, and general weakening—all additional causes of Mrs. Winslow's death, in the dual sense, which we have explained is the relevant sense, that had any of these conditions been absent she probably would not have died from the rape and beating *and* that each of the conditions made her death from the assault more likely. None of them was related to the death merely fortuitously, as in our example of the nursing-home fire, which would be deemed "a supervening act disconnected from any act of the defendant," so that the defendant would not be liable for the death.

The immediate cause of Mrs. Winslow's death was the action of the nurse in depositing food into Mrs. Winslow's trachea. Brackett's lawyer argues that the nurse was grossly negligent, but this is far from plain—Mrs. Winslow appears to have exhibited no signs of distress until she keeled over dead—and even if it is true all that it would mean is that the nurse's negligence was still another cause of Mrs. Winslow's death. An event is, as we have emphasized, typically the consequence of multiple causes. But a murderer does not avoid conviction by pointing out that his act was only one of many causes that concurred to bring about his victim's death. It is enough if his act was one of the causes—enough therefore if Brackett's assault made Mrs. Winslow's death more likely and if, but for the assault, she would not have died as soon as she did.

A rational finder of fact could find these conditions satisfied. The proposition that raping and beating an 85-year-old woman creates a risk of death requires no discussion, but we must also consider the first part of the dual test of cause, and thus ask whether she would have died anyway when she did. That is unlikely. Death was the last link in a continuous series of events that began with the assault. She died a month later, never having returned home. Her condition deteriorated from the start of her hospitalization, and when she was transferred to the nursing home her doctor already believed her to be near death. Of course she was very old and the autopsy revealed a condition of senile atrophy that must have existed before the assault. But judging from the description of her as "feisty" her senility could not have been so far advanced that death was imminent. It is more than unlikely that had she not been assaulted on October 21, 1981, she still would have entered the hospital the next day and died a month later. The assault appears to have precipitated her rapid decline. Of course there are dangers in inferring consequence from sequence. But they are slight when as in this case the event not only follows the act closely in time but is the kind of event frequently produced by the kind of act, and no persuasive evidence of an alternative causal sequence is presented....

Brackett's lawyer fastens on the statement in the state trial judge's otherwise uninformative opinion that the judge was rejecting the state's theory of "psychological murder." The theory had been advanced in a press conference called by the prosecutor. We are unable to determine exactly what the theory was or even whether it was pursued at the trial. Brackett's lawyer describes it as follows: the assault caused Mrs. Winslow to become clinically depressed, clinically depressed people (we know) are prone to suicide, Mrs. Winslow committed suicide by refusing to eat, and suicide is one of those "supervening acts disconnected from any act of the defendant" which cut off liability for causing death. If this is "psychological murder," we are puzzled by the trial judge's rejection of it. We think—to take a hypothetical case somewhat clearer than this case—that if a person, desiring the death of another whom he knew to suffer from depression, stole his intended victim's anti-depression medicine hoping to precipitate the victim's suicide, and his hope was fulfilled, this would be murder. The victim's depressive state would no more be a "supervening act" than any other vulnerability of the victim; in criminal law as in tort law, the injurer takes his victim as he finds him. It would be only a shade removed from a case of death by fright, but well removed from a case in which the defendant, not desiring the victim's death, made it more likely, for example by teaching him to play Russian roulette, as distinct from playing it with him. Well removed too from a case of assisted suicide, where ... the victim desires his death. In our hypothetical case the victim presumably was taking anti-depression medicine because he did *not* want to commit suicide, a recognized risk of depression. The fact that a psychiatric condition, whether or not by precipitating suicide, is one of the causes of a victim's death does not excuse his murderer. Otherwise it would be open season on sufferers from mental illness.

Courts worry, naturally, about problems of evidence and inference in *Gaslight*-type settings where cruel, deceptive, or even simply inconsiderate behavior might be claimed with more or less plausibility to have driven a susceptible person to suicide, or, as here, to loss of the "will to live." But we do not think that there is or should be a *categorical* bar to the imposition of criminal liability in such cases. It has long been the rule in tort law (the "thin-skull" or "eggshell-skull" rule) not only that the tortfeasor takes his victim as he finds him but also that psychological vulnerability is on the same footing with physical. If for example the victim is predisposed to schizophrenia, and the tortfeasor inflicts a minor injury which precipitates the schizophrenia, he is liable for the entire consequences even though they were both highly unlikely and unforeseen. In superficial tension with the eggshell-skull cases is the famous (or infamous) "taunting" case where one business rival taunted another into jumping into a deep trench filled with water, where he drowned, the taunter refusing to assist him—yet was held not liable for his death. The court emphasized, however, that there was no contention that the victim had not been in full possession of his mental faculties at the time of the incident. The analogy in criminal law would be to the pure assisted suicide, where the person who commits suicide is in full possession of his faculties. An intermediate case is *State v. Lassiter*, where the victim had been severely beaten by the defendant and when she threatened to jump out the window he said "go ahead and jump," she did, and his conviction of murder was affirmed. Other cases hold that the defendant cannot be guilty of murder in such circumstances, but they are not cases in which, as in our hypothetical case, the defendant deliberately induces a psychotic reaction in his victim. The fact that a normal person would not have had such a reaction does not excuse the defendant.

The eggshell-skull principle does not quite fit a case of intentional murder, for the murderer must intend his victim's death and ordinarily this will presuppose some awareness of the likely consequences of his act. It is not murder to kill a person by a slight blow harmless to an ordinary person if you do not know the person is unusually vulnerable; there is even a presumption in Illinois that one who beats another with his bare fists does not intend to kill him. But felony murder is different, and it is time to remind the reader that this a felony-murder case. No intent to kill, as in our hypothetical "psychological murder" case, is required; and though the Illinois cases do require that death be a "foreseeable" consequence of the felony, all they mean is that the death must be caused by the felony; for remember that "cause" in law means not just but-for cause but also an enhancement of the likelihood (what in law is often called "foreseeability") that the class of events would occur. (Some courts do not require proof of such enhancement in a felony-murder case. But the Illinois courts do.) Here the only issue is whether a rational finder of fact could conclude that the felonies which Brackett committed caused the death of his victim; the answer, we have seen, is yes.

... We have emphasized analogies from tort law because the doctrine of causation is more developed there than in criminal law. The reason is that tort law, which has compensatory as well as deterrent functions, focuses on injury, while criminal law, which emphasizes deterrence and incapacitation, focuses on the dangerousness of the defendant's conduct. There is no tort liability without proof of injury, but there are plenty of crimes that are punishable though no injury resulted—many attempts and conspiracies, for example. A victim's eggshell skull may require a refined adjustment in damages to reflect the likelihood that the victim would because of his vulnerability have been injured sooner or later nontortiously.

But a criminal assailant is punishable as a first-degree murderer "no matter how feeble the spark" of life that his blow extinguished. Uncompleted crimes are often punished severely; and when injury or death ensues from deliberate wrongdoing, even if (as in the case of felony murder) it is not an intended consequence, the criminal law comes down heavily on the defendant without worrying over much about the precise amount of harm inflicted.

Affirmed.

Comments and Questions

(1) Suppose the nurse's action in feeding was found to be negligent. Should that be significant? It was found irrelevant in *James v. State*, 366 So. 2d 1155 (Ala. Crim. App. 1979), where the defense lawyer unsuccessfully attempted to cross-examine the surgeon concerning the fact that he allegedly left the operating room to perform elective surgery on another patient. It was also found irrelevant in *People v. Dixon*, 397 N.E.2d 45 (Ill. App. Ct. 1965), where the trial court excluded the defense testimony of a doctor to show that medical negligence was the cause of death. *But see State v. Ulin*, 548 P.2d 19, 21 (Ariz. 1976):

> Generally, one who unlawfully wounds another is held to the consequences flowing from such injury. Other contributing causes relieve the wrongdoer of the death of a victim only if they are the proximate cause of death. The rationale is that everyone is held to contemplate, and to be responsible for, the natural consequences of his own act.
>
> Medical aid is a natural consequence flowing from a physical injury. Once an accused inflicts the injury which necessitates medical attention, he is held to assume certain risks attendant thereto.
>
> Before a physician can be substituted for an accused as the proximate cause of death, he must have committed medical malpractice.
>
> In a criminal setting, medical malpractice will break the chain of causation initiated by the accused, becoming the proximate cause of death, if it constitutes negligent and unskillful treatment and becomes the sole cause of death.

The Eleventh Circuit has held that the enhanced penalty for death resulting from healthcare fraud required nothing more than a factual causal connection. Reasonable foreseeability or legal proximate cause was not a required element. Nevertheless, in some cases the fraudulent healthcare conduct may be far too attenuated from the fact of the patient's death to impose liability on the defendant. *United States v. Webb*, 655 F.3d 1238 (11th Cir. 2011).

(2) In *People v. Funes*, 28 Cal. Rptr. 2d 758 (Cal. Ct. App. 1994), the family of the beating victim decided to withhold antibiotic treatment in order to allow him to die. In *People v. Velez*, 602 N.Y.S.2d 758 (Sup. Ct. 1993), the hospitalized victim pulled out his feeding tube, would not eat food, and ingested only ice water and liquids. He died two months after the gunshot wound. In *People v. Caldwell*, 692 N.E.2d 448 (Ill. App. Ct. 1998), the victim of the defendant's assault asked that life support systems be withdrawn. She died within minutes after their removal. In *Klinger v. State*, 816 So. 2d 697 (Fla. Dist. Ct. App. 2002), the victim was a Jehovah's Witness. For religious reasons he would not agree to have a blood transfusion. He was told that without the transfusion his chances of survival were very low, but that if he accepted the transfusion the chance of survival was 85%–90%. He continued to decline, and he soon died. Should the homicide convictions of these defendants be affirmed? All were. If a mother leaves a child in the car with the motor running, and a carjacker pushes the child out and runs over him, with what crimes should the mother be charged?

(3) Consider the following:

> "One other thing I must say to you in this connection, and that is that it does not necessarily follow that a wound is not the cause of a death simply because there was negligence in the treatment of the wound or of the wounded man. A dangerous wound, one which is calculated to endanger and destroy life and which naturally leads to a death, is the cause of the death even though it appears that the deceased might have recovered if he had taken proper care of himself, or that unskilled or negligent treatment has aggravated the wound or contributed to the death. As I have said before, it is not essential that the wound be the sole cause of the death. So where a wound, either operating directly or indirectly, by causing some other condition which produces death, has been a substantial factor in causing a death, it is still to be regarded as the cause of the death even though some negligence in the treatment of the wounded man by physicians and others is also a contributing factor." This part of the charge immediately followed a full and correct statement, as to which no error is assigned, of the relevant legal principles applicable to the determination of the issue of the cause of death. In the course of these instructions, the court said: "[E]ven though death follows a wound, in point of time, if the death is brought about by some cause independent of the wound, if it would have happened, that is, if there had been no wound, then of course the wound is not the cause of death.... [I]t is not essential that the wound be the sole cause of death. It is not essential that it be the immediate cause of death. It is essential that it be a substantial factor in bringing about the death."

State v. Tomassi, 75 A.2d 67, 70 (Conn. 1950). Are these instructions to the jury proper?

(4) The defendant in *People v. Hebert*, 39 Cal. Rptr. 539, 540–41 (Cal. Ct. App. 1964), struck the victim Swallow who was sitting on a barstool. The victim fell off the stool and hit his head on the floor. The police then arrived about 10 minutes later.

> Swallow was lying on the floor on his back, but apparently conscious. Officers assisted him to a sitting position and thought he was not seriously injured, but was intoxicated. They partly carried, partly dragged him to a patrol car and took him to the police station for booking for being intoxicated in a public place. Thelma McCord, the barmaid, testified that the two officers dragged Swallow from the place where he lay on the floor to the sidewalk; one officer lifted Swallow by holding onto his belt in the rear; the other lifted at his head; Swallow's feet were dragging; at the sidewalk the officers dropped him on his face; the drop was 12 to 14 inches; he was perfectly limp. The two officers testified that they partly carried, partly dragged Swallow to the sidewalk, sat him down in a sitting position and then laid him gently on his back; they did not drop him.
>
> The officers arrived at the station with the victim about 35 minutes after the altercation. According to the officers, during the booking procedure and just after Swallow was searched and as he was standing with his hands high against

> a wall, he was observed to fall over backwards with his arms at his sides and "completely rigid as though a plank were falling"; his buttocks hit the floor first and then the back of his head; his head bounced about six inches off the floor and fell back, striking the floor a second time. The floor was concrete with an asphalt tile covering. Immediately after hitting the floor he started bleeding from one ear and within a few seconds from both ears. He was removed to a hospital where he died that morning.

The autopsy surgeon testified at trial that

> there were three areas of injury to the head, each caused by a separate impact; one to the nasal area, causing a fracture of the nasal bones; one to the left rear of the skull, causing severe hemorrhaging; and a third to the right rear portion of the skull, causing additional fracturing and hemorrhaging. The nasal fracture was apparently due to the direct blows of defendant; the injury to the left rear of the skull was the most serious and the injury was more consistent with the decedent's having struck his head on the wooden barroom floor than with his falling and striking his head on the concrete floor at the police station. In the opinion of the witness, the injury to the left rear of the skull was received as the result of decedent's being knocked off the bar stool. Both these injuries to the brain caused hemorrhaging, and either one, in Dr. Kade's opinion, would have resulted in a loss of consciousness. It was the opinion of Dr. Kade that the injury to the right side of decedent's head was caused at the police station when decedent suddenly lost consciousness and fell backward. The opinion of Dr. Kade was stated on cross-examination as follows: "In my opinion, death was caused by the two blows to the rear of the head. Whether the injury causing the fracture of the nasal bone would have been enough to cause death in and of itself, is difficult for me to establish, since there were these two additional injuries to the back of the head."
>
> The witness was questioned further on cross-examination: "Q. You feel at this time, Doctor, that it is difficult for you to say that the damage to the nasal area and the front of the skull there, that would have been sufficient in and of itself to have brought about death; is that right? A. Well, it is difficult to say because it is a conjectural question. It is like saying, if a boat is on fire and there is an explosion on board and the boat sinks would the fire have been enough to destroy the boat by itself had there not been an explosion. It is trying to infer what would have happened or could have happened if something else didn't happen. But the something else did happen and so I would be hesitant to conjecture about what could or might have happened under other circumstances."

Based upon this testimony, the defendant was found guilty of involuntary manslaughter. On appeal, should his conviction be reversed?

(5) Can two persons, acting independently, be found guilty of the homicide of a single victim? *See Payne v. Commonwealth*, 75 S.W.2d 14, 19 (Ky. 1934):

According to the testimony of Ruby Nell Mathis, at least two of them were inflicted by Effie Payne on the porch at the home of Joe Payne, from which he was carried while in a helpless condition and placed in the car at the garage. The testimony of Ortkies corroborates that of the coroner and undertaker. It is undoubtful that at the moment he was jerked or pulled from the car by Higgs Payne was mortally wounded, if not dead. If one willfully and with malice aforethought mortally wounds another with a deadly weapon, the fact another immediately thereafter unlawfully, willfully, and maliciously inflicts a distinct wound, whether of itself mortal or not, on the wounded person, and thereby accelerates or hastens his death, both are guilty of murder. The terms "mortally wounded" and "mortal wound," as here used, means "deadly," "death-producing," and is defined by Webster as "destructive to life, causing or occasioning death." The acts of Effie Payne as described by Ruby Nell Mathis, corroborated by the wounds on the head of Joe Payne, and his profusely bleeding before he was jerked or pulled from the car and struck with a "car tool," leave no doubt the wounds inflicted by her were mortal and were sufficient to warrant the submission of the case to the jury on the question of her killing him with a blunt instrument.

Chapter 6

The Inchoate Offenses

§ 6.01 Solicitation

(a) Solicitation.

A person commits the offense of solicitation when, with intent that an offense be committed, other than first degree murder, he or she commands, encourages, or requests another to commit that offense. Illinois Compiled Statutes, 720 Ill. Comp. Stat. 5/8-1.

* * *

A person who endeavors to incite, procure, or hire another person to commit a felony, though a felony is not actually committed as a result of such inciting, hiring, or procuring, shall be imprisoned not more than five years or fined not more than $500.00, or both. Vt. Stat. Ann. tit. 13, § 7.

* * *

(a) Every person who, with the intent that the crime be committed, solicits another to offer, accept, or join in the offer or acceptance of a bribe, or to commit or join in the commission of carjacking, robbery, burglary, grand theft, receiving stolen property, extortion, perjury, subornation of perjury, forgery, kidnapping, arson or assault with a deadly weapon or instrument or by means of force likely to produce a great bodily injury ... shall be punished by imprisonment in a county jail for not more than one year or in the state prison, or by a fine of not more than ten thousand dollars ($10,000), or the amount which could have been assessed for commission of the offense itself, whichever is greater, or by both the fine and imprisonment.

(b) Every person who, with the intent that the crime be committed, solicits another to commit or join in the commission of murder shall be punished by imprisonment in the state prison for three, six, or nine years.

(c) Every person who, with the intent that the crime be committed, solicits another to commit rape by force or violence ... shall be punished by imprisonment in the state prison for two, three, or four years....

> (f) An offense charged in violation of subdivision (a), (b), or (c) shall be proven by the testimony of two witnesses, or of one witness and corroborating circumstances....

Cal. Penal Code § 653(f).

Dickerson v. City of Richmond

Court of Appeals of Virginia
346 S.E.2d 333 (1986)

Benton, Judge.

Clarence Dickerson was arrested on a warrant charging him with "loitering for the purpose of soliciting or engaging in prostitution or other lewd, lascivious or indecent act," a misdemeanor under the Richmond City Code. He was tried by a jury, found guilty of "loitering for the purpose of prostitution," and sentenced to twelve months in jail.

Detectives Steve Dalton and Richard Palmer, assigned to the Morals Squad of the Richmond Bureau of Police, Vice Division, were sitting in a parked car at Madison and Broad Streets on July 18, 1984, at 1:10 a.m., when they first observed Dickerson, dressed in blue jeans and a shirt tied above his navel, and carrying a tan purse. Dickerson occasionally stood with one foot on the curb and the other foot in the street and waved at passing vehicles with male occupants. Detectives Dalton and Palmer each testified to Dickerson's actions with respect to three vehicles; Dalton gave the license numbers for two of the three vehicles.

The detectives saw Dickerson wave at a vehicle on Broad Street. The vehicle circled the block and parked on the north side of Broad Street. Dickerson walked from the southeast corner of Broad and Madison Streets to the vehicle, entered it, and talked to the driver for approximately three minutes. Dickerson then left the vehicle and returned to the southeast corner of Broad and Madison Streets.

From this position Dickerson watched traffic on Broad Street and peered around the corner down Madison Street toward Grace Street. At 1:15 a.m., Dickerson approached a white Vega stopped in the 200 block of Madison Street. Leaning into the passenger side, Dickerson talked to the driver for approximately one minute. He then walked to the corner of Madison and Grace Streets, where he "just leaned on the light pole."

At 1:27 a.m., an unmarked police vehicle carrying uniformed officers drove up Madison Street. Detectives Dalton and Palmer saw Dickerson walk away and go behind a building on the northwest corner of Madison and Grace Streets. He remained there, "peering around," until the unmarked police vehicle passed.

At 1:30 a.m., Dickerson approached a Ford Fairmount which had stopped on Madison Street, and talked to the Ford's male driver from the driver's side for one or two minutes. Dickerson then returned to the corner of Madison and Grace Streets.

Detectives Dalton and Palmer asked a uniformed officer to detain Dickerson until they could leave their observation point. Detective Dalton approached Dickerson, identified himself, and asked how long Dickerson had been on the corner. Dickerson replied that he had been there a half hour. Detective Dalton asked what he had been doing on the corner. Dickerson said that he was just resting. Detective Dalton asked what he had been doing on the corner of Broad and Madison Streets. Dickerson said that he had been doing "nothing." He also told the detectives that he was not employed. The detectives then arrested Dickerson for "soliciting for the purpose of prostitution."

[W]e conclude that the evidence in this case was insufficient to sustain the conviction.

The offense for which the defendant was convicted contains two elements:

- to loiter, lurk, remain, or wander about in a public place, or in any place within view of the public or open to the public;
- [for] the purpose of engaging in prostitution, or of patronizing a prostitute, or of soliciting for or engaging in any other act which is lewd, lascivious or indecent.

To obtain a conviction under the ordinance the City must prove beyond a reasonable doubt *both* the act and mental state. Sufficient proof of one element, but not the other, will result in reversal.

Dickerson and the City concur that the mental state element of the ordinance requires proof of specific intent. We agree.

In most cases, of course, the City must satisfy its burden of proving specific intent by circumstantial evidence. Under familiar principles, such proof is insufficient if it creates merely a suspicion of guilt; the City's evidence must be consistent with guilt and exclude every reasonable hypothesis that the accused is innocent of the charged offense.

With these principles in mind, we turn to the circumstances of this case. Overruling a motion to set aside the verdict, the trial court summarized the City's evidence in this fashion:

> This happened with three cars, [waving] at other cars. It's late at night, quarter after one, quarter til two.... His only explanation was he was resting. He was standing. He did hide when the police came. My recollection is two uniformed officers came up in an unmarked car, and he went into the shadows and waited until they left, and then came back out. And, I think the strange thing about these cases is the appearance ... of the defendant, leads to what common sense tells you, that people that are soliciting for the purpose of this would dress differently than normal people.... I believe there was a conclusion he was dressed like a female, although the officer said he had on a blouse tied in a knot and his [navel] was exposed, and he had a pocketbook, which I think would be a consideration that the jury could consider.... It is a far cry from people just standing on the corner

> being arrested. And, really, [at] that hour of the night has a whole lot to do with it. And, it might have been an entirely different situation maybe if this was three o'clock in the afternoon. It is not likely that you would have three friends that would come by at one fifteen in the morning, quarter til two.

The court's summary accurately represents the totality of the City's evidence. On appeal, we view the evidence in a light most favorable to the City, granting all reasonable inferences that can be drawn from the evidence.

As the trial court's summary indicates, the jury was presented with proof of several circumstances which were consistent with a suspicion of guilt, including the time of the alleged offense, Dickerson's mode of attire, his ostensibly exclusive interest in vehicles with male occupants and the fact that he withdrew from his street-corner position when the unmarked police vehicle approached. In addition, the City proved that Dickerson more than once waved at motor vehicle operators, a circumstance which the ordinance expressly allows the trier of fact to consider with regard to specific intent.[3] The City also proved that Dickerson engaged in three brief conversations with the drivers of three vehicles. The City's evidence did not reveal the contents of these conversations, although the detectives took note of the license numbers of the three vehicles and the City presumably could have adduced the testimony of the drivers. The City's evidence also did not reveal any suggestive gestures or expressions by Dickerson, apart from his acts of waving.

We have defined "lascivious" to mean "a state of mind that is eager for sexual indulgence, desirous of inciting to lust or of inciting sexual desire and appetite." "Lewd" is a synonym of "lascivious" and "indecent." Webster's Third New International Dictionary 1301 (1969). As used in the ordinance, the terms refer to sexual conduct that is contrary to community standards of morality.

We believe the meaning of prostitution is generally understood and therefore requires no separate examination.

That Dickerson appeared to be dressed in female attire, as the detectives and the trial court concluded, and seemed to be drawn to only those vehicles with male occupants create a suspicion that his purpose in loitering was sexual in nature. Unlike the "direct statements, indirect suggestions, and salacious innuendoes" made [in other cases] however, the City's evidence does not prove beyond a reasonable doubt that Dickerson's intent was prostitution or other conduct of a lewd, lascivious or indecent nature. The City was not required to prove prostitution or attempted prostitution because "solicitation may be completed before an attempt is made to commit the solicited

3. The act of waving at motor vehicle operators is one of three illustrative circumstances which may be considered in determining specific intent. The jury was not limited to the three circumstances set out in the ordinance. We do not decide in this case whether proof of more than one of these circumstances is sufficient to convict under the ordinance.

crime." The evidence, however, must prove that Dickerson's specific intent was to engage in prostitution or to solicit or engage in any other lewd, lascivious or indecent act.

We conclude that the evidence, when viewed in a light most favorable to the City, did not prove beyond a reasonable doubt that Dickerson's actions manifested the purpose of engaging in prostitution or soliciting or engaging in other lewd, lascivious or indecent acts. Because one of the two elements of the ordinance was not proved, the evidence was not sufficient and the conviction must be reversed.

Comments and Questions

(1) What precisely did Dickerson do which was thought by the government to be criminal? Is it unlawful to ask a question which the listener can ignore? According to the appeals court, what did the government fail to prove? In *United States v. Mitchell*, 15 M.J. 214 (C.M.A. 1983), the defendant was a captain in the United States Army convicted by a general court-martial of soliciting another to commit a black-marketing offense while stationed in the Republic of Korea. The jury was instructed as to the state of mind requirement for the crime as follows:

> I caution you that solicitation refers to any statement, oral or written, or any other act or conduct which may reasonably be construed as a serious request or advice to bring about the offense....

(2) In *People v. Swimley*, 372 N.E.2d 887 (Ill. App. Ct.), *cert. denied*, 439 U.S. 911 (1978), much evidence was offered to show that the defendant tried to hire someone to kill her husband. One piece of evidence was particularly damaging.

> Defendant left the Continental and entered Saladino's car, seating herself on the front passenger's seat. The following conversation occurred:
>
> > JOSEPH SALADINO: I understand that you want to see me.
> >
> > MARLENE SWIMLEY: Yeah, you're a friend of Tom Mangione's right. Ah, my oldest one talked to Tom, and ah you said something about it could be done over there.
> >
> > JOSEPH SALADINO: It can be arranged. What is it exactly do you want, you know, what's, who is it. What's it about?
> >
> > MARLENE SWIMLEY: Well, it's my husband.
> >
> > JOSEPH SALADINO: And?
> >
> > MARLENE SWIMLEY: What do you mean?
> >
> > JOSEPH SALADINO: All I got, was I was supposed to contact you. In relation to what? But what is it? You want him what?
> >
> > MARLENE SWIMLEY: You know, kind of evaporated.
> >
> > JOSEPH SALADINO: What do you mean? What do you mean evaporated?
> >
> > MARLENE SWIMLEY: Well, you know, gone.
> >
> > JOSEPH SALADINO: Do you mean murder?

MARLENE SWIMLEY: Yeah.

JOSEPH SALADINO: You got a picture of him, identification?

Defendant then handed Saladino two photographs of her husband, who was in the Air Force Reserve on duty in Germany but would be returning February 3. Defendant indicated that she would pay five thousand dollars for the assassination. Saladino asked for a down payment, and defendant stated that she didn't want to give him too much since she had once paid $2,500 to a friend in Detroit to have Mr. Swimley killed and she never again heard from the man who was to accomplish the murder. Defendant agreed to pay $500 and asked if the slaying could be done in Germany. Defendant said Saladino could use the name of a friend of Mr. Swimley who sold paintings and guns, Hans Hagenaw, to lure him off the base, and that she didn't care so long as it was done quickly. Saladino asked why she wanted him killed and defendant replied that her husband was a "mean bastard." Defendant told Saladino that her husband would soon be worth about $500,000.00. Defendant stated that the only persons who knew of the plan were her son and Kevin.

Defendant wrote Mr. Swimley's address on the back of the photograph of her husband that she had shown and given to Saladino. Defendant gave Saladino two fifty dollar bills and agreed to pay four hundred dollars the following day.

Defendant explained this meeting.

Kevin came into the kitchen and told her that arrangements had been made to murder her husband and that she was to meet a man at Woodfield Mall at 11:00 a.m. the next morning and bring $1,500.00. Defendant, surprised, asked Kevin why he would do this. Kevin replied: "Well aren't you tired of getting beaten up all of the time."

Defendant responded that she and her husband would work out their problems alone. Kevin said he couldn't call the arranged meeting off because he didn't know where to call the man. Kevin became upset and stated that he was afraid that the man would do something to him if defendant didn't go. Defendant replied that she would try to think of something.

Defendant went to the Woodfield Mall at the arranged time not thinking anyone would be there to meet her. In case someone did appear, she asserted that she had brought along a ten-year-old photograph of her husband, taken of him in his military uniform and with the thought that perhaps a military uniform would be a deterrent to anyone involved in accomplishing her husband's death. Also, defendant testified that she did not believe her husband could be recognized from the old photograph. She asserted that she further discouraged the person she met by not taking any money with her, insisting on several days prior notice of the killing, telling him that she couldn't get money for a long time, insisting the act be done in Germany, and merely giving him the address of the air base. Defendant further stated that she

> never intended to kill her husband nor did she know how much money was in her purse when she left for the rendezvous. Defendant stated that she did not believe Saladino was actually a hit man.

The court concluded the conviction was proper:

> Furthermore, it must be borne in mind that the testimony of these and other witnesses served to explain the circumstances which led to defendant's meeting with Saladino. The central issue in this case was defendant's meaning and intent during this conversation. The meaning was so clear that the jury, without more, could have based its conviction upon Saladino's testimony and the tape recording and transcript of the conversation that occurred in the shopping center parking lot. Although defendant has raised the contention that the facts were insufficient to prove defendant guilty beyond a reasonable doubt, we must strongly disagree. The only testimony which contradicted the evidence of guilt was that of defendant. Her rendition of what occurred was palpably inconsistent with all of the circumstances proved. It is difficult to conceive that defendant would not intend to have her husband killed while at the same time giving money and information as to his whereabouts to someone representing to be a killer for hire. The transcript of the conversation belies her claim of innocence. The jury was well justified in disbelieving defendant's version and finding that the evidence supports a verdict of guilty.

Do you agree with the court or the defendant?

Suppose at a party, after hearing the defendant complain about her brother-in-law, a man said to her, "Do you really want him killed?" The defendant then said, "I'll pay you $1000 to kill him." Would it matter if they had not been drinking? If they shook hands on the deal?

(3) Could a state successfully prosecute based upon a solicitation to commit a crime in another state? See *Martin v. Kaiser*, 907 F.2d 931 (10th Cir. 1990), where the defendant was convicted in Oklahoma of soliciting a murder which was to take place in another state. He asserted that Oklahoma lacked jurisdiction to prosecute him for solicitation. The court disagreed:

> Martin contends that [the] solicitation statute does not extend to him because (1) any murders solicited were to have been performed outside the state of Oklahoma, and (2) the statute only covers solicitation of murders triable under Oklahoma law, i.e., committed in Oklahoma.
>
> This issue is easily disposed of.... The statute governs the solicitation in Oklahoma of first-degree murder, not the location of the murder itself. There is no dispute over the fact that the solicitations occurred within the state of Oklahoma, nor with the fact that murder is a crime in the states in which the solicited acts were to have been carried out.... Solicitation itself is "inimical to the public welfare and to the safety and morals of the inhabitants of [a] state, regardless of where the solicited acts are to be performed.... Oklahoma had jurisdiction to try Martin for solicitation...."

(4) The defendant in *State v. Keen*, 214 S.E.2d 242, 244 (N.C. App. 1975), attempted to hire undercover police officers to kill his wife.

> Defendant argues that there could have been no completion of the crime since all parties with whom he spoke were connected with law enforcement. The answer is that the interposition of a resisting will, by a law enforcement officer or anyone else, between the solicitation and the proposed felony is of no consequence. This is so "because the solicitation was complete before the resisting will of another had refused its assent and cooperation." Defendant was not charged with the crime of conspiracy, a crime which was not completed because of the failure of Bacon, in fact, to concur in defendant's scheme to murder defendant's wife. The crime of solicitation to commit a felony is complete with the solicitation even though there could never have been an acquiescence in the scheme by the one solicited.

Would the result change if Keen's wife had died in a car crash at the moment he solicited the officers? *See also Benson v. Superior Court of Los Angeles County*, 368 P.2d 116 (Cal. 1962):

> Purposeful solicitation presents dangers calling for preventive intervention and is sufficiently indicative of a disposition towards criminal activity to call for liability. Moreover, the fortuity that the person solicited does not agree to commit the incited crime plainly should not relieve the solicitor of liability.... The act solicited must, of course, be criminal. If the solicitor believes that the act can be committed "it is immaterial that the crime urged is not possible of fulfillment at the time when the words are spoken" or becomes impossible at a later time. Solicitation itself is the evil prohibited by the Legislature, and prosecution therefor is particularly appropriate for the very case in which the crime solicited does not take place.

People v. Gordon

Court of Appeal of California
47 Cal. App. 3d 465, 120 Cal. Rptr. 840 (1975)

COMPTON, ASSOCIATE JUSTICE.

Defendant was indicted by the grand jury of Los Angeles County for [solicitation of a bribe]. Prior to trial defendant moved under Penal Code section 995 to set aside the indictment. That motion was denied and in the jury trial which followed defendant was found guilty as charged. She appeals the judgment of conviction and among other things contends that her motion under section 995 should have been granted.

The indictment alleged that on or about the 3rd of January 1973, the defendant did "willfully and unlawfully and feloniously solicit another to offer, accept and join in the offer acceptance of a bribe." According to the evidence the person alleged to have been solicited was Officer Joseph Stanley of the Los Angeles Police Department who was at the time in question assigned to the narcotic detail.

Facts

Defendant was an attorney at law and shared office space with another practitioner, Mr. Bane. Mr. Bane had formerly been a member of the staff of the City Attorney of the City of Los Angeles. During that tenure he had become acquainted with Officer Stanley.

At some point late in the year 1972, defendant contacted Mr. Bane and stated that she knew where there was a two or three pound quantity of cocaine to be seized. She inquired whether Mr. Bane believed Officer Stanley would be interested and whether he could be trusted. Mr. Bane replied in the affirmative. Defendant asked Mr. Bane to contact Officer Stanley.

Mr. Bane mentioned the matter to Officer Stanley and the officer expressed an interest in seizing the cocaine. Mr. Bane advised the defendant of Officer Stanley's interest.

In late December of 1972, the defendant called Officer Stanley at the Administrative Narcotics Division of the Los Angeles Police Department and inquired if he had discussed with Mr. Bane the two or three pounds of cocaine and whether he was interested in seizing the cocaine and making an arrest. Officer Stanley stated that he was and arrangements were made for the defendant and Officer Stanley to meet. Defendant gave the officer her business and home telephone numbers.

On January 3, Officer Stanley called defendant at her office and a meeting was arranged at the building of the Los Angeles Community College Board of Trustees. That same afternoon Officer Stanley went to the agreed location. He saw the defendant sitting in the gallery observing a meeting of the board. Defendant nodded to Officer Stanley and the two went to a coffee shop located in the building.

In the conversation that followed defendant told the officer that she had a client who "wanted someone taken care of." The officer asked her if she meant "killed" and she replied "no" that she meant "discredited." She identified the person whom her client wanted discredited as Monroe Richman, a member of the Los Angeles Community College Board of Trustees. She stated that her client was highly politically oriented and that he, the client, had inquired of her if it could be arranged to have Mr. Richman "planted" with a quantity of narcotics and then arrested. Defendant also stated in that conversation that "she wouldn't even consider a situation like this unless it was worth money for everybody concerned." Defendant suggested that narcotics be planted either on Mr. Richman's person or in his car. Defendant offered to provide Officer Stanley with information upon which to effect the arrest of a person in possession of two or three pounds of cocaine and then asked if it would be possible to take a portion of that seized cocaine and plant it on Mr. Richman. Officer Stanley replied that it was possible. Defendant indicated that "it might be worth around $10,000." There were subsequent conversations between the two concerning the acquisition of the cocaine. On January 10, 1973, Officer Stanley called the defendant at her home and surreptitiously recorded the conversation which in part went as follows:

STANLEY: I wanna talk about the original 2 to 3 pounds.

GORDON: Um-hum.

STANLEY: All right. We gotta have that for our supply.

GORDON: I don't know if I'm gonna be able to get that.

STANLEY: You don't think—you don't think you're gonna be able to get that?

GORDON: I'm not sure about that. Assuming I can't get that, can we still do this other thing?

STANLEY: Well, assuming you can't get the 2–3 pounds of coke, I don't know how we can come up with any other cocaine.

GORDON: Maybe the price will just raise a little bit on the whole deal.

STANLEY: Well, can your man bear the traffic?

GORDON: I don't know what the traffic is.

STANLEY: Well, I don't either. What do you think?

GORDON: Well, *I'm thinking in terms of 10 grand.*

STANLEY: For the whole—For the whole thing 10 grand?

GORDON: Um-hum. That too little?

STANLEY: Well, then what do you and I do with it?

GORDON: *I don't care. I'll take a third, you can take three-quarters. You can take—give me a quarter. I don't care. Whatever you think is fair.*

STANLEY: All right.

GORDON: Uh—You know I'm not out to—to take 50. I'm not out to take very much at all. It depends.

STANLEY: Okay, well—

GORDON: I'd like—I'd like—uh—you know—a couple—$2500.

STANLEY: All right. But I—

GORDON: I didn't—matter of fact I would like to—if you think that's not enough we may have to go out and make a purchase and let's up it.

STANLEY: Well, I don't know. You're right. We may have to make a purchase.

The following day the officer called defendant at her office. In that conversation defendant told the officer that she had decided not to be a party to this scheme, that she felt she had a political career ahead of her and she did not want to take a chance on ruining that career. Subsequently the officer made several more contacts with the defendant in an effort to get her to introduce him to her client who originally proposed the scheme. Such meeting, however, was never consummated.

Contentions on Appeal

Defendant contends that there was insufficient evidence to sustain the conviction because there was no evidence that on January 3 she actually solicited the officer to accept the bribe, the argument being that she was "merely feeling out" the officer.

Solicitation consists of the asking of another to commit one of the specified crimes with intent that the crime be committed. The intent may be inferred from the circumstances of the asking.

The solicitation of a bribe need not be stated in any particular language; such a solicitation may be in the form of words which carry the import of a bribe and were evidently intended to be so understood.

The jury by its verdict found the defendant did in fact, and with the requisite intent, ask the officer to accept a bribe. On appeal from the judgment of conviction we view the evidence in the light most favorable to supporting the jury's determination and indulge in all reasonable inferences—which the evidence will support.

Officer Stanley testified to statements by the defendant from which it could be reasonably inferred that the defendant was asking the officer, in return for the lion's share of $10,000 to arrange to falsely arrest Monroe Richman for possession of narcotics. The jury's verdict is well supported by substantial evidence. The jury could consider defendant's statements subsequent to January 3, in determining her intent on that earlier date. In fact, since the indictment alleged that the crime was committed "on or about January 3," the jury could have based its verdict on the aggregate of the conversations between defendant and Officer Stanley.

Since the crime was fully committed on January 3, it is no defense that the defendant later withdrew or failed to consummate the crime which was the object of the solicitation. The offense of solicitation "is complete when [it] is made, and it is immaterial that the object of the solicitation is never consummated, or that no steps are taken toward its consummation."

Comments and Questions

(1) If the defendant truly did tell the officer the plan was off and did not go forward with the plan, why was the evidence sufficient for solicitation? Put another way, was she not "merely feeling out the officer"?

(2) The facts as disclosed by the State's principal witness, Wayne Pledger, show that appellant met with Pledger at a gas station and there told him that Dutch Thomas, a business agent for the Iron Workers Union, was getting too powerful and should be "gotten rid of." Appellant then stated that he did not want to be around when Thomas was "gotten rid of" and that he was looking for someone to help him. Pledger was asked how much it would cost to find someone to do the job. Although appellant suggested that there would be money in it for Pledger if he found someone, he did not mention an amount. Pledger told appellant that he would need a few days to think about the matter, but stated that he never intended to follow through with appellant's suggestion. He later reported the incident to the State Attorney's office.

Hutchinson v. State, 315 So. 2d 546, 547 (Fla. Dist. Ct. App. 1975). Are these facts sufficient for a solicitation conviction? *See also State v. Furr*, 235 S.E.2d 193 (N.C. 1977), "[S]uch a request constitutes the crime of solicitation to commit a felony in North Carolina."

(3) The defendant in *State v. Everett*, 330 P. 3d 22 (Ore. 2014) was convicted of soliciting an individual to commit murder. The case was somewhat unusual, for the evidence showed that the defendant asked another person [A] to deliver information to yet another person [B] in the belief that B [a member of an outlaw motorcycle gang] would then kill the defendant's enemy, someone who was prepared to testify against the defendant. The court rejected the defense view that the defendant's actual act was too far removed from any illicit action so as to be solicitation.

> That Van Alstine never delivered the information to the Outsiders is irrelevant. The crime of solicitation is complete upon the act of soliciting, regardless of what else does or does not transpire. "For the crime of solicitation to be completed, it is only necessary that the actor, with the intent that another person commit a crime, have enticed, advised, incited, ordered, or otherwise encouraged that person to commit a crime. The crime solicited need not be committed." That is because the underlying rationale for the offense is that the solicitation itself is considered sufficiently dangerous to justify punishment, regardless of whether the solicitation is successful....
>
> The crime of solicitation is complete when the defendant engages in the act of soliciting, regardless of whether anything actually happens as a result of the solicitation.
>
> [T]he fact that there is no evidence that the Outsiders, upon receipt of the DVD and the indictment, actually would have killed Piatt is also beside the point. Whether or not the Outsiders would have killed Piatt, the fact remains that the solicitation was complete at the moment that defendant asked Van Alstine to deliver the information for the purpose of causing the murder to occur.

Id. at 26.

(4) The court in *State v. Carr*, 110 A.3d 829, 835 (N.H. 2015), summed up the act requirement for solicitation:

> Solicitation "is the act of trying to persuade another to commit a crime that the solicitor desires and intends to have committed." "The mens rea of solicitation is a specific intent to have someone commit a completed crime." Solicitation is like conspiracy in that "disclosure of the criminal scheme to another party constitutes a part of the actus reus." "But, while the actus reus of a conspiracy is an agreement with another to commit a specific completed offense, the actus reus of a solicitation includes an attempt to persuade another to commit a specific offense." The crime of solicitation ordinarily implies the solicitant's rejection of the solicitor's request, "Thus, solicitation can be viewed as an attempt to conspire." [U]nlike conspiracy and attempt, it requires no overt act other than the offer itself.

(5) The defendant in *Gordon* clearly attempted to withdraw from her scheme, yet the court would not sanction such withdrawal. Why not? As explained in *People v. Burt*, 288 P.2d 503, 505 (Cal. 1955):

> Legislative concern with the proscribed soliciting is demonstrated not only by the gravity of the crimes specified but by the fact that the crime, unlike conspiracy, does not require the commission of any overt act. It is complete when the solicitation is made, and it is immaterial that the object of the solicitation is never consummated, or that no steps are taken toward its consummation. Section 653f is concerned not only with the prevention of the harm that would result should the inducements prove successful, but with protecting inhabitants of this state from being exposed to inducements to commit or join in the commission of the crimes specified.

(6) Some statutes do allow for successful withdrawal from the solicitation, following the lead of the Model Penal Code. Section 5.02(3) of the Code (1962), which provides:

> Renunciation of Criminal Purpose. It is an affirmative defense that the actor, after soliciting another person to commit a crime, persuaded him not to do so or otherwise prevented the commission of the crime, under circumstances manifesting a complete and voluntary renunciation of his criminal purpose.

Under § 5.02(3), would Gordon's conviction have been affirmed?

(7) As should be clear after reviewing the cases discussed above, the prosecutor in charging a defendant has considerable flexibility in this area. If the solicited crime is completed or attempted, the defendant can be charged under an accountability theory. If the offense is not completed or attempted, the government may still be able to obtain a solicitation conviction. At common law—and by statute in many states—the defendant cannot be convicted of both solicitation and the completed/attempted crime. The Court of Appeals of Maryland in *Lewis v. State*, 404 A.2d 1073, 1083 (Md. 1979), explained:

> [The] crime of solicitation contains no element which is not also present in the offense of being an accessory before the fact. Thus, we hold that under the required evidence test, solicitation of murder merges into the offense of being an accessory before the fact to the same murder. On retrial, if the defendant is again convicted of being an accessory before the fact to the murders of his wife and daughter, he may not also be convicted of solicitation.

(8) *Sentencing*. Assuming the defendant is not treated as an accomplice, should he nevertheless receive the sentence he would have received had the crime been completed? Compare the treatment by the drafters of the New York statute and the Illinois Code.

New York: § 100.05 Criminal solicitation in the fourth degree

> A person is guilty of criminal solicitation in the fourth degree when:
>
> 1. with intent that another person engage in conduct constituting a felony, he solicits, requests, commands, importunes or otherwise attempts to cause such other person to engage in such conduct; or
>
> 2. being over eighteen years of age, with intent that another person under sixteen years of age engage in conduct that would constitute a crime, he so-

licits, requests, commands, importunes or otherwise attempts to cause such other person to engage in such conduct.

Criminal solicitation in the fourth degree is a class A misdemeanor.

N.Y. Penal Law § 100.05

Illinois: § 5/8-1 Solicitation

(b) Sentence. A person convicted of solicitation may be fined or imprisoned or both not to exceed the maximum provided for the offense solicited.

Illinois Revised Statutes, 720 Ill. Comp. Stat. 5/8-1.

People v. Latsis

Supreme Court of Colorado
578 P.2d 1055 (1978)

LEE, JUSTICE.

An information in the district court charged defendant, Petros Demetrios Latsis, with six felony counts. The first four counts were dismissed after a preliminary hearing. The fifth and sixth counts charged the defendant with two separate offenses of criminal solicitation of the crime of aggravated robbery.

Defendant's motion to dismiss the solicitation counts on the ground that the statute is unconstitutional for reasons of vagueness and overbreadth was granted by the court. The district attorney appeals from this ruling.

The criminal solicitation statute provides:

> Criminal solicitation. (1) Except as to bona fide acts of persons authorized by law to investigate and detect the commission of offenses by others, a person is guilty of criminal solicitation if he commands, induces, entreats, or otherwise attempts to persuade another person to commit a felony, whether as principal or accomplice, with intent to promote or facilitate the commission of that crime, and under circumstances strongly corroborative of that intent.
>
> The district court's holding of unconstitutionality provided in pertinent part as follows:
>
> The portion of the statute which states, "... and under circumstances strongly corroborative of that intent" renders the statute unconstitutional for the following reasons:
>
> a. The legislature has not prohibited all solicitations of all criminal acts, but only solicitations of felonies "with intent to promote or facilitate the commission of that crime *and* under circumstances strongly corroborative of that intent."
>
> b. There is no standard in the statute which would enable a person of common intelligence to understand what circumstances are "strongly corroborative of that intent."

> c. Although the statute proscribes certain kinds of unprotected speech, it does not state in understandable terms what kinds of solicitations of felonies are prohibited and what kinds are not. There is no way that a citizen may know in advance what "circumstances" are "strongly corroborative of that intent." Determination of this critical issue, which is part of the statutory definition, is left to judges and juries on a case-by-case basis.
>
> d. Subsection (1) of the statute therefore includes an unconstitutional delegation to the judiciary of the legislative power to define a crime.

We do not agree with the court's ruling and hold that the criminal solicitation statute is constitutional.

In its ruling, the district court recognized the important interest of the state in "preserving the peace and preventing criminal activity" and noted that "there is no fundamental personal liberty to solicit another to commit a crime." The court then held the statute "does not prohibit solicitation of lawful acts and therefore does not purport to cover constitutionally protected speech."

The court then applied the long-standing test of vagueness as set forth in our several decisions—whether men of common intelligence can readily understand the statute and its application, or whether they must guess or speculate as to its meaning.

Nor do we agree with the court's conclusion that the use of the modifying phrase "and under circumstances strongly corroborative of that intent" makes unconstitutionally vague the operative portion of the statute which the court specifically found not to be vague. In our view, the modifying phrase relates to the burden upon the prosecution to present a quantum of evidence sufficient to demonstrate that the accused acted with the specific intent to promote or facilitate the commission of a crime. In other words, it is not sufficient to show merely that the accused solicited the commission of a crime; rather, sufficient circumstances surrounding the overt act of solicitation must be presented which corroborate that the act in fact was done with the requisite specific intent. This language of the statute is of benefit to an accused and protects those whose actions may have been innocently motivated or done in jest. It is, of course, for the jury to determine whether the circumstances shown by the prosecution were "strongly corroborative" of the alleged intent.

The district court also found that this language constituted an "unconstitutional delegation to the judiciary of the legislative power to define a crime." Due process of law requires that the legislature provide sufficiently precise standards to guide a judge and jury in deciding whether a crime has been committed. Failure to do so may well constitute an unlawful delegation of legislative power. There are an infinite variety of corroborating circumstances which could not reasonably have been catalogued by the legislature. The trier of fact is not being called upon to define a crime, but is rather only being told what quantum of evidence is sufficient to demonstrate that the requisite criminal intent was present. Thus, we conclude there has not been an unlawful delegation of legislative power.

GROVES, JUSTICE, dissenting:

I can understand a solicitation "with intent to promote or facilitate the commission of a certain crime." I do not understand it with the addition: "And under circumstances strongly corroborative of that intent."

Let us assume that the case has been tried and the jury has retired to consider its verdict. It finds that the defendant attempted to persuade another to commit a certain felony with intent to promote or facilitate the commission of that crime. It then perceives that it must also determine whether the acts of the defendant were "under circumstances strongly corroborative of that intent." It looks to the instructions to find the judge's definition of "circumstances strongly corroborative."

At that juncture, I imagine that I am the judge who submitted those instructions. What should I have written to define the additional element of "under circumstances strongly corroborative." I finally conclude that I am unable to perceive just what the legislative intent may have been. Therefore, to me the statute is unconstitutionally vague. "It is a basic principle of due process that an enactment is void for vagueness if its prohibitions are not clearly defined."

Comments and Questions

(1) How would a trial judge instruct as to the phrase "under circumstances strongly corroborative"? If the dissenter is correct that such a phrase is not readily defined, is the statute unconstitutional?

(2) Would Gordon be convicted under the Colorado statute? Would the woman who asked the man to kill her brother-in-law?

People v. Rubin

Court of Appeal of California

96 Cal. App. 3d 968, 158 Cal. Rptr. 488 (1979)

FLEMING, ASSOCIATE JUSTICE.

On March 16, 1978, Irving Rubin, a national director of the Jewish Defense League, held a press conference in Los Angeles, California, to protest a planned demonstration and march by the American Nazi Party to take place in Skokie, Illinois, on April 20, and to announce the organization of a counter demonstration to stop the march. During the press conference Rubin held up five $100 bills and offered the following reward:

> We are offering five hundred dollars, that I have in my hand, to any member of the community, be he Gentile or Jewish, who kills, maims, or seriously injures a member of the American Nazi Party. This offer is being made on the East Coast, on the West Coast. And if they bring us the ears, we'll make it a thousand dollars. The fact of the matter is, that we're deadly serious. This is not said in jest, we are deadly serious.

A criminal complaint was filed, Rubin was held to answer by the examining magistrate, and an information charged Rubin with solicitation of murder. At a hearing to set aside the information, the trial court found probable cause for Rubin's commitment for trial, in that his statements could be interpreted as solicitation to murder; but the court also concluded that the statements were protected as free speech under the First Amendment, in that although they solicited murder, their form and content indicated a desire to attract national media exposure and evidenced a lack of serious intent to solicit the commission of crime. The court ordered the information set aside, and the People have appealed.

Two issues are presented. First, whether the information should have been dismissed for lack of evidence of intent to solicit murder. Second, whether defendant's advocacy of crime is constitutionally protected speech and thus immune from prosecution as criminal solicitation.

I.
Probable Cause Supports the Information

Both the examining magistrate and the superior court found probable cause to believe Rubin had committed a public offense, and the trial court, apart from First Amendment grounds, denied the motion to set aside the information. Such a motion does not tender the issue of the guilt or innocence of the accused or the quantum of evidence necessary to sustain a conviction. Rather it presents the question whether the magistrate could entertain a reasonable suspicion that defendant had committed a crime.

...

Defendant argues there was no substantial evidence of his specific intent to solicit the crime of murder, that his only specific intent had been to stimulate action in defense of the Jewish community, that by reason of the lack of evidence of specific intent to solicit murder, probable cause to support the accusation did not exist as a matter of law. The trial court rejected this argument, concluding that Rubin's intent was susceptible to several interpretations, one of which was intent to solicit murder. Solicitation of murder to prevent a march through Skokie, said the judge, would constitute a crime.

We agree with this conclusion of the trial judge, in that under the standard of probable cause defendant's statements could be interpreted as a solicitation of murder. "Solicitation consists of the asking of another to commit one of the specified crimes with intent that the crime be committed." Defendant's true state of mind, his intent in offering a $500 reward to anyone "who kills, maims, or seriously injures a member of the American Nazi Party," presents a question of fact to be determined by the trier of fact on the basis of evidence produced at a trial. Neither the superior court nor this court is entitled to resolve that question as a matter of law. Accordingly, apart from First Amendment grounds, the information charging the crime of solicitation of murder is valid and is supported by probable cause.

II.
Solicitation of Crime as Protected Advocacy

The superior court, after concluding that probable cause existed to support the charge of solicitation of murder, went on to further conclude that Rubin's statements were protected as free speech by the First Amendment. The court arrived at this latter conclusion by deducing from the form and content of Rubin's statements that he had not seriously and truly intended to solicit murder, but had merely sought to attract national media attention. Rubin's statements, in the court's view, constituted no more than political hyperbole, and, as such, were protected against abridgement by the First Amendment. Accordingly, the court set aside the information. Patently, the trial court reached its decision by weighing the quality of Rubin's intent, determining it was not a truly serious intent, and thence concluding that the offer of reward for murder was advocacy rather than solicitation. The court arrived at this result even though Rubin himself at his press conference said he was not speaking in jest and was "deadly serious," and even though the specific intent with which an act is done presents an issue of fact.

In our view the trial court erred in undertaking to evaluate the quality of Rubin's intent.

We start with the demonstrable fact of Rubin's advocacy of violence in the form of murder, mayhem, and serious bodily injury. These acts are crimes, and their solicitation is a crime. Taken at face value, Rubin's statements invite political assassination. But we must also take into account a demonstrable proposition of law—under the First Amendment to the Constitution free speech may include advocacy of the use of force and violence. This latter proposition is not absolute, and advocacy of crime may be limited under various tests, including those of clear and present danger, of probable danger, of incitement, and of balance. Accordingly, solicitation of murder is not written off the books as a crime, but under certain circumstances its prosecution may be circumscribed by a constitutional freedom to advocate murder.

The facts and circumstances which differentiate advocacy of crime from solicitation of crime are those which differentiate advocacy of abstract doctrine from advocacy of incitement to unlawful action. Their application may be seen in *Brandenburg v. Ohio*, (1969) 395 U.S. 444, 89 S. Ct. 1827, 23 L. Ed. 2d 430, a conviction under Ohio's criminal syndicalism law of a leader of the Ku Klux Klan for advocating the general propriety of crime at a rally held for media reporters during which a cross had been burned and statements made derogatory to Negroes and Jews. In reversing the conviction the court declared that "the constitutional guarantees of free speech and free press do not permit a State to forbid or proscribe advocacy of the use of force or of law violation except where such advocacy is directed to inciting or producing imminent lawless action and is likely to incite or produce such action." Mere abstract teaching of the moral propriety of resort to force and violence, said the court, is not the same as preparing and steeling a group for violent action.

In *Brandenburg* the Supreme Court suggested evaluation of the language of advocacy in the light of two considerations: (1) its incitement to imminent lawless action; (2) its likelihood of producing such action. This particular formula parallels the test delineated by Justice Holmes on behalf of the Supreme Court in *Schenck v. United States*, (1919) 249 U.S. 47, 39 S. Ct. 247, 63 L. Ed. 470, in which, after saying that the most stringent protection of free speech would not protect a man in falsely shouting fire in a theatre and causing a panic, he refers to the test of clear and present danger and declares that protection of free speech is a question of *proximity* and *degree*. We consider the application of these factors to the cause at bench.

Proximity: Incitement to Imminent Lawless Action. Since murder is lawless action and an offer of reward for murder is, assuredly, an incitement, imminence is the critical element here in the factor of proximity. Imminence, a function of time, refers to an event which threatens to happen momentarily, is about to happen, or is at the point of happening. But time is a relative dimension and imminence a relative term, and the imminence of an event is related to its nature. A total eclipse of the sun next year is said to be imminent. An April shower thirty minutes away is not. The event which concerns us here was the scheduled Nazi Party demonstration and march to be held in Skokie in five weeks, an event which had already attracted national attention. We think that in terms of political assassination the demonstration could be said to have been proximate and imminent, just as a Papal visit to Belfast, a Soviet chief of state's visit to Rome, a Presidential campaign trip to Dallas, and a Presidential inauguration in Washington, can each be said to be proximate and imminent, even though occurrence may be some weeks away.

Degree: Likelihood of Producing Action. Here we are concerned with the practicality and feasibility of the solicitation—was it likely to incite or produce violence? We cannot, of course, answer this question with assurance, for the effect of emotional appeals for political violence on the actions of inherently unstable personalities remains obscure. But we think it a reasonable inference that serious reportage by respectable news media of a reward for murder tends in some degree to give respectability to what otherwise would remain an underground solicitation of limited credibility addressed to a limited audience, and thereby tends to increase the risk and likelihood of violence. Undoubtedly, the prosecution's case would be stronger if a specific Nazi Party member had been named as the target for assassination and if the demonstration had been one scheduled to take place in Los Angeles rather than in Skokie. Yet murder remains a crime, whether or not a specified victim is identified as the target, and solicitation in California of murder in Illinois is nonetheless solicitation of murder.

The solicitation to murder here was not made in a jesting or conditional manner, nor was it the outcome of an improvised piece of braggadocio. Its words and circumstances suggest the possibility it might incite or produce the violence sought. Rubin himself referred to earlier bloodshed in St. Louis, and he predicted bloodshed in Skokie unless the permit for the demonstration were revoked.

From the words and circumstances of Rubin's offer we conclude there was sufficient likelihood of his solicitation being interpreted as a call to arms, as a preparation and steelment of his group to violent action as a systematic promotion of future bloodshed in the streets, rather than as a communication of ideas through reasoned public discussion, to remove it from the category of protected speech and require Rubin to answer the charges against him.

The order setting aside the information is reversed.

ROTH, PRESIDING JUSTICE, dissenting.

At bench the trial judge, concluding his analysis of the facts, said in pertinent part:

> I have read your points and authorities ... [V]iewing the defendant's statement in its proper context I must agree with the comments that appear [in] the *Amicus* brief, where they state:
>
> *Amicus* contend that the form and contents of Rubin's communication were used solely to attract nationwide media exposure. The contents evidence *a lack of any serious intentions to solicit the commission of a crime.* His remarks constitute a political hyperbole and were merely a crude, offensive method of stating political opposition to the Nationalist Socialist Party.
>
> I feel in reading all of the statements made on March 16th, ... the language used by Mr. Rubin falls within the language protected by the First Amendment. (Emphasis added.)

The trial court's conclusion as a matter of law that Rubin's remarks were not a "true" solicitation ... but were embraced in the First Amendment as permitted speech, in my opinion follows the law.

I would affirm.

Comments and Questions

(1) Should Rubin's comments be permitted speech? What risks are involved if the speech is permitted without sanction? If it is not permitted? How helpful is this comment in *Pedersen v. City of Richmond*, 254 S.E.2d 95, 98–99 (Va. 1979):

> First Amendment protection is not afforded statements made in the solicitation of criminal acts. Laws prohibiting solicitation are not directed against words but against acts. A solicitation is, in itself, an act. It is an incitement to unlawful activity which goes beyond the permissible limits of the right of free expression. The social purposes underlying the First Amendment do not extend the protection of that amendment to verbal acts soliciting crimes.

Consider the following from the government's brief in *Rubin* (Appellant's Opening Brief at 12):

> Solicitation is not "mere advocacy." It is not only advocacy of a proposition to be believed; criminal solicitation encompasses action as its appropriate response. If the *Brandenburg* doctrine applies to all criminal solicitations, it follows that no person can be validly convicted of having solicited the commission of a crime ... unless it also constitutes an "incitement to imminent lawless action." If that is so, no person can be constitutionally convicted of having solicited the commission of a crime unless such solicitation occurred in close proximity (temporally and spatially) to the commission of the substantive offense so as to satisfy the imminency requirements.

> It must be remembered that the solicitor of a crime of murder is, when the solicited offense is actually committed, punishable for such solicitation ... as a principal in the crime of murder. If the *Brandenburg* doctrine is understood as being applicable to true solicitations to crime (necessarily entailing the intent that the solicited crime be committed), it is difficult to see how *Brandenburg* permits the conviction of a solicitor of murder as a principal unless the solicitation was directed to inciting or producing *imminent* murder or was likely to incite or produce such action.
>
> Finally, it should be pointed out that however politically or ideologically motivated respondent was in making his offer, his solicitation was framed in an appeal constituting the act of enticing or importuning on a personal basis for personal benefit because "[p]eople are motivated by money. Let's not kid around."

(2) The court in *United States v. White*, 698 F.3d 1005, 1008 (7th Cir. 2012) laid out the case against the defendant:

> William White was charged with soliciting the commission of a violent federal crime against a juror in violation of 18 U.S.C. § 373. The alleged solicitations at issue were messages that White posted to a website that he created to advance white supremacy, which included White's 2005 statement that "[e]veryone associated with the Matt Hale trial has deserved assassination for a long time," and his 2008 publication of information related to the foreperson, "Juror A," of the jury that convicted Hale. The 2008 post disclosed Juror A's home address and mobile, home, and work phone numbers, though it did not contain an explicit request for Juror A to be harmed. White was tried and convicted by a jury.

Protected speech, or criminal action? The court on appeal strongly rejected the speech claim, looking especially to the location of the messages.

> A reasonable jury cannot be expected to ignore the audience.... Readers of Overthrow.com were not casual Web browsers, but extremists molded into a community by the internet—loyal and avid readers who, whether or not they remember every specific solicitation to assassination, knew that Overthrow.com identified hateful enemies who should be assassinated. A reasonable jury could infer that members of the Party were regular readers of the Overthrow website, which prominently displayed links to the Party's own website, to its streaming radio, and to its hotline. One witness testified that he learned of the Party through Overthrow.com. White identified one reader in a post on the website as a "loyal soldier" and "fan of this website," and there is similar language in other posts. Two members of the party who testified made clear their familiarity with the contents of the website over a period of years. Though these members specifically denied interpreting White's post as an invitation to harm Juror A, a reasonable jury could have thought, based on White's reaching out

> to them for support following the search of White's home, that they were biased in White's favor and therefore skewed their testimony.

Id. at 1015. What result if the messages were put out to the general public, as in *Rubin*, rather than to the seemingly sympathetic website viewers?

(3) Consider also the facts in *Turner v. La Belle*, 251 F. Supp. 443, 444–45 (D. Conn. 1966).

> Charles Turner is director of the North End Community Action Project (NECAP), an organization described in the complaint as one "whose purpose is to help secure to Negro citizens in (Hartford) and in the State of Connecticut ... the rights guaranteed to them ... and to end all forms of discrimination and segregation ..." Earl Miller and Emanuel Williams are staff members of NECAP, and Ernest Russell is also Executive Director of the Connecticut Council on Human Rights.
>
> A relatively short time after the highly publicized violent disturbances and rioting in the Watts area of Los Angeles, NECAP, particularly Turner, scheduled a public civil rights meeting for 7:30 p.m. August 17, 1965. A handbill was distributed, saying, "NECAP will hold a protest demonstration to show our alliance with our black brothers in Los Angeles who died struggling against the very same evils of this society that we, right here in Hartford are faced with."
>
> The Hartford police were informed by NECAP of the proposed meeting and indicated that no permit was necessary. Captain Goldstein of the Hartford police visited Turner at NECAP headquarters on the night of August 16th, however, in an unsuccessful effort to dissuade Turner from holding the meeting at that time.
>
> The meeting was held in the North End, the center of Negro habitation in Hartford, and all four plaintiffs addressed the crowd, which numbered between 100 and 150. Police were present in abundance. Witnesses for plaintiffs described the atmosphere as relaxed; those for defendants said it was tense. Transcriptions of recordings of the speeches were placed in evidence. While most of the content of the speeches consisted of vague exhortations for "action, not talk," there were some more particular comments. Russell, according to the transcription, said, "Now I tell you, you treat every cop as your enemy, whether he's white or black until things in America wakes up, until America wakes up." Williams said, "If I can't be imported back, then kill me, kill me, or I'll kill you," and "anyone that's black is so very angry ... that he wants to fight, that he wants to shoot, well then, only turn your eyes to the left, to the blue shirts." (Apparently police in blue shirts were standing to the left of the crowd.)
>
> Following the speeches a symbolic coffin draped in black was carried through the streets to City Hall, accompanied by plaintiffs and 15 or 20 youths. Others joined them at City Hall, making a total of 40 to 50 demonstrators. Nearly

> the same number of police were present. Apparently there was some scuffling, and a Police Lieutenant was pulled into the crowd, and sustained injuries.
>
> Plaintiffs were then arrested on a charge of breach of the peace. Sent back by plaintiffs to the North End after the arrests, some of the demonstrators stoned cars and broke windows.

Under *Rubin*, would a solicitation conviction in this case be affirmed?

§ 6.02 Attempt

> The law surrounding criminal attempts has produced considerable commentary relating to the vagueness of its elements. Admittedly the elements are vague, but this results from the fact that an attempt to commit a crime covers a broad spectrum of different criminal offenses. Each criminal offense contains separate elements. Consequently, the type of facts necessary to prove an attempt to commit murder will not be the same as those necessary to prove an attempt to commit embezzlement or arson.
>
> Yet from a general definitional standpoint, two requirements must be met: (1) a specific intent to commit the underlying substantive crime; and (2) an overt act toward the commission of that crime, which falls short of completing the underlying crime.

State v. Starkey, 244 S.E.2d 219, 222–23 (W. Va. 1978), *overruled on other grounds* in *State v. Guthrie*, 461 S.E.2d 163 (W. Va. 1995).

[A] The Mental State

The culpability element of an attempt is a specific intention, in the sense of purposefulness, to commit the target offense.

> Where the substantive crime intended requires a specific intent ... it adds a culpability which mere general malevolence could not give. So that the indictable attempt exists only when the act, short of the substantive crime, proceeds from the specific intent to do the entire evil thing, thus imparting to so much as is done a special culpability. When we say that a man attempted to do a given wrong, we mean that he intended to do it specifically; and proceeded a certain way in the doing. The intent in the mind covers the thing in full; the act covers it only in part.

Merritt v. Commonwealth, 180 S.E. 395, 398–99 (Va. 1935).

Although the rule is, on its face, a straightforward matter, it leads to confusing and rather counter-intuitive results. Consider the following excerpts.

> If a person attempts to commit a murder and death ensues because of this act, that person is guilty of murder. However, merely because someone commits a murder does not mean that person is guilty of an attempt to commit

> murder. In other words, a person may recklessly commit murder but he cannot recklessly attempt to commit murder.

Free v. State, 455 So.2d 137, 147 (Ala. Crim. App. 1984).

> [I]f one from a house top recklessly throw down a billet of wood upon the sidewalk where persons are constantly passing, and it fall upon a person passing by and kill him, this would be, by the common law, murder; but if instead of killing him, it inflicts only a slight injury....

Moore v. State, 18 Ala. 532, 534 (1851). Under the rule summarized above, can the actor in the *Moore* court's hypothetical be convicted of attempted murder?

In *Thacker v. Commonwealth*, 114 S.E. 504, 505 (Va. 1922), the defendant and his friends got drunk at a church festival.

> They left the church between 10 and 11 o'clock at night, and walked down the county road about 1½ miles, when they came to a sharp curve. Located in this curve was a tent in which the said Mrs. J. A. Ratrie, her husband, four children, and a servant were camping for the summer. The husband, though absent, was expected home that night, and Mrs. Ratrie, upon retiring, had placed a lighted lamp on a trunk by the head of her bed. After 11 o'clock she was awakened by the shots of a pistol and loud talking in the road nearby, and heard a man say, "I am going to shoot that Goddamned light out;" and another voice said, "Don't shoot the light out." The accused and his friends then appeared at the back of the tent, where the flaps of the tent were open, and said they were from Bath county and had lost their way, and asked Mrs. Ratrie if she could take care of them all night. She informed them she was camping for the summer and had no room for them. One of the three thanked her, and they turned away, but after passing around the tent the accused used some vulgar language and did some cursing and singing. When they got back in the road, the accused said again he was going to shoot the light out, and fired three shots, two of which went through the tent, one passing through the head of the bed in which Mrs. Ratrie was lying, just missing her head and the head of her baby, who was sleeping with her. The accused did not know Mrs. Ratrie, and had never seen her before. He testified he did not know any of the parties in the tent, and had no ill will against either of them; that he simply shot at the light, without any intent to harm Mrs. Ratrie or anyone else; that he would not have shot had he been sober, and regretted his action.

Is Thacker guilty of attempted murder? The answer may depend on whether he acted recklessly, disregarding the risk of killing someone inside the tent (involuntary manslaughter), or with knowledge that death was a practical certainty (second degree murder), or purposefully to kill (first degree murder). The state supreme court reversed the conviction on a finding that "the evidence falls far short of proving that the shot was fired with the intent to murder her." Is Thacker entirely free of blame? Is he dangerous? Is there another crime with which he may be charged? Consider the facts in *People v. Stone*, 205 P.3d 272 (Cal. 2009). There the defendant—a member of a violent gang—pulled up to a group of rival gang members. He fired his gun into the group and left. No one was injured. Can he be convicted of attempted murder? Yes, said the California Supreme Court, as he had an intent to kill even though the government could not show any "primary target."

> [A] "defendant who intends to kill one person will be liable for multiple counts of murder where multiple victims die, but only one count of attempted murder where no one dies." But when no one dies that person *will* be guilty of attempted murder even if he or she intended to kill a random person rather than a specific one. [The only mental state required is] the intent to kill *a* human being, not a *particular* human being, [since an] indiscriminate would-be killer is just as culpable as one who targets a specific person.

State v. Casey

Supreme Court of Utah
82 P.3d 1106 (2003)

DURRANT, ASSOCIATE CHIEF JUSTICE:

This case concerns the mens rea that must be shown to convict a defendant of attempted murder. Specifically, we consider whether a conviction for attempted murder may rest upon a knowing mental state rather than an intentional mental state....

BACKGROUND

We recite the facts from the record ... in the light most favorable to the jury's verdict. In early 1999, Casey was involved in a relationship with Tresa Franz. On April 12, 1999, Casey and his friend, Terron Allred, met Franz at her home, where the three consumed some alcohol. Casey then drove Franz, Franz's four-year-old son, and Allred to tow Franz's truck to a friend's house. After dropping off the truck, Casey stopped at a liquor store where Franz purchased a bottle of rum. Though Franz and Allred had "a swig" of the rum, Casey consumed most of the bottle. Intoxicated, Casey became belligerent, and he and Franz began arguing. When Franz asked Casey to take her home, Casey refused, laughing at her and threatening to kill her.

Following this threat, Casey drove over to Tiffany Ribe's house, located in Salt Lake City. Once there, Casey got out of the vehicle and spoke with Ribe and others while Allred, Franz, and her child remained in the vehicle. When Casey returned to the vehicle, Allred got out to speak with Ribe, and Casey and Franz began arguing again. As Casey entered the driver's side of the vehicle, he reached behind the seat and grabbed a handgun from a camera bag. During the argument, Franz asked Casey if he was ready to go home. Casey responded, "F* * * you, bitch. I'm going to take you home alright," and pointed the gun at Franz's neck.

...

With Franz and Allred back in the vehicle, Casey began to pull out of Ribe's driveway. Casey and Franz began arguing again, and just after they pulled out of the driveway, Casey pointed the handgun at Franz's head. He pulled the trigger, but the handgun misfired; both Franz and Allred testified that they heard the click of the hammer when Casey pulled the trigger. Casey then pointed the gun at Franz's feet and successfully fired a round, which lodged in the floor of the vehicle. Once again, Casey pointed the gun at Franz's head. This time, Franz grabbed Casey's arm, pushed it away, and jumped out of the moving vehicle. As Franz jumped, Casey fired one more time. In total, Casey fired two shots from the gun in addition to the one misfire.

PROCEDURAL HISTORY

In August, 1999, following a three-day trial, a jury convicted Casey of attempted murder, aggravated assault, and domestic violence in the presence of a child....

Before the court of appeals, Casey argued, among other things, that the trial court improperly instructed the jury on the elements of attempted murder. He asserted that his conviction for attempted murder should be reversed because "the jury was improperly instructed that the required mental state was 'intentionally or knowingly.'" Following a discussion of our holdings in *Maestas* and *Vigil*, the trial court concluded that "*Vigil* explicitly allows a conviction [for attempted murder] for a 'knowing' mental state under" the "intentionally or knowingly" alternative of the murder statute.[2]

...

II. ATTEMPTED MURDER

On certiorari, Casey argues that a defendant cannot be convicted of attempted murder based merely on a "knowing" state of mind....

A. The Elements of Attempted Murder

Attempt crimes are derivatives of completed crimes, and the express language of both the completed crime statute and the attempt statute determines the elements of the attempt crime. Thus, a conviction for attempted murder must satisfy the elements of the murder statute, with the obvious exception that the murder need not be completed, and the attempt statute.

The murder statute at issue in this case allows for a conviction if a person "intentionally or knowingly causes the death of another." Both "intentionally" and "knowingly" are defined by statute. One acts intentionally "when it is his conscious objective or desire to engage in the conduct or cause the result." On the other hand, one acts knowingly "when he is aware of the nature of his conduct or the existing circumstances" and "aware that his conduct is reasonably certain to cause the result." A defendant can be convicted of murder under either level of culpability. To be convicted

---

2. Utah's murder statute contains several alternatives. The one at issue in this case, states that "[c]riminal homicide constitutes murder if the actor ... intentionally or knowingly causes the death of another."

of attempted murder, however, additional and different elements must be shown under the attempt statute. The attempt statute states as follows:

> (1) For purposes of this part a person is guilty of an attempt to commit a crime if, acting with the kind of culpability otherwise required for the commission of the offense, he engages in conduct constituting a substantial step toward commission of the offense.
>
> (2) For purposes of this part, conduct does not constitute a substantial step unless it is strongly corroborative of the actor's intent to commit the offense.

Thus, to be convicted of attempted murder, a defendant's actions must constitute a substantial step toward causing the death of another, and the substantial step must indicate his or her intent to commit the crime. In this case, Casey argues that the substantial step must indicate the intent to kill.... We must now decide whether a conviction for attempted murder in Utah requires a higher level of culpability than that required for murder.

B. Maestas, Vigil, and Other Utah Authority

Casey's challenge is not strictly one of first impression. We have addressed jury instructions regarding attempted murder in the past; two of these decisions, *Maestas* and *Vigil*, addressed jury instructions based on the same language at issue in the instant case. Additionally, when addressing attempted murder under other alternatives of the murder statute, we have consistently held that intentional conduct is required by the attempt statute.

1. *State v. Maestas*

In *Maestas*, the trial court granted the defendant's motion to dismiss his conviction for attempted first degree murder, ruling that "specific intent to kill could not properly be inferred from the evidence." The State appealed. On appeal, Maestas argued that, under the common law rule, "an 'attempt' crime must always consist of an intent to commit the corresponding completed crime accompanied by a substantial step toward realization of that crime." He derived this theory "from the common law rule that intent is a necessary element of every 'attempt' crime even where the corresponding completed crime does not require intent as an element." Expanding on this argument, the defendant asserted that "attempted first degree murder ... requires a 'specific intent' beyond that which would have been required in order to provide first degree murder itself." We noted that according to this argument, "the crime of attempted murder [would] require a *stronger* showing of intent than does the crime of murder itself." In other words, Maestas argued that the State must prove a greater degree of intent in order to obtain a conviction for attempted murder than to obtain a conviction for murder....

Though we concluded that a conviction for attempted murder only required the same mental state necessary to obtain a murder conviction, we failed to acknowledge the distinction between acting knowingly and intentionally. Instead, we merely examined "[t]he evidence tending to indicate that [Maestas] *intentionally* fired his revolver," and held that "substantial evidence supported the jury in finding that the state had established both the act and the *intent* components of attempted first degree murder." We focused on whether the evidence showed the defendant acted intentionally without considering whether he acted knowingly.

2. *State v. Vigil*

Ten years later we decided *Vigil*, holding that Utah does not recognize attempted second degree murder under the depraved indifference alternative of the murder statute. Using a plain language analysis to determine the meaning of "culpability" and "intent" in the two paragraphs of the attempt statute, we determined that

> to give the fullest possible effect to the terms of paragraphs (1) and (2), we construe the culpability requirement in paragraph (1) to refer to the attendant circumstances, if any, of the underlying offense and construe the intent language in paragraph (2) to limit the attempt statute to offenses with a mental state of "intent." In other words, *attempt can be found* for uncompleted *offenses that require "intent,"* even though those offenses have attendant circumstances that require lesser mental states.

We held that "the word 'intent' as used in ... the attempt statute should be read to mean 'conscious objective or desire.' This meaning of the word 'intent' obviously is distinguishable from *knowledge* of the proscribed conduct or result, which is the mental state required for depraved indifference homicide."

Following this analysis of the language of the attempt statute, we held "that to convict a defendant of attempted second degree murder, the prosecution must prove that the defendant had a conscious objective or desire to cause the death of another." Accordingly, in a footnote to the *Vigil* case, we overruled the *Maestas* decision to the extent it held that a defendant could be convicted for an attempt crime if he or she acted with the same level of culpability necessary to support a conviction for committing the completed crime.

However, we created some confusion by noting in the same footnote that the *Vigil* holding did not overrule the second rationale we used in *Maestas* to uphold the conviction for attempted murder.... Thus, the dicta in this footnote, contrary to the holding expressed in the main body of the opinion, provided that a person may be convicted of attempted murder if evidence showed that he or she acted knowingly or intentionally. Based on this footnote in *Vigil*, the trial court and the court of appeals denied Casey's challenges to the jury instructions concerning attempted murder.

...

C. The Model Penal Code and Attempt

Contrary to the State's argument, the Model Penal Code does not provide support for the contention that a knowing mens rea is sufficient to obtain an attempted murder conviction under Utah law. Though we have noted that the Utah attempt statute is based on the M.P.C. definition of attempt, our statute, in contradistinction to the M.P.C., requires intentional conduct.

The M.P.C. identifies four levels of culpability, providing that "a person is not guilty of an offense unless he acted purposely, knowingly, recklessly or negligently."[3] The commentary to the M.P.C. notes that the narrow distinction between "purposely" and "knowingly" is "one of the elements of ambiguity in legal usage of the term 'intent.' " ... While the difference between these two levels of culpability may be minimal, the M.P.C. commentary notes that the distinction becomes important in attempt crimes.

... According to the commentary, the M.P.C. definition is, in general, "designed to follow the conventional pattern of limiting the crime of attempt to purposive [or intentional] conduct." Nevertheless, while the M.P.C. expressly rejects the notion that an attempt can be committed recklessly or negligently, it does allow for attempts to be committed purposely or knowingly. "When ... a person actually believes that his behavior will produce the proscribed result, it is appropriate to treat him as attempting to cause the result, whether or not that is his purpose." ...

Though the M.P.C. would allow a conviction for attempt based on knowledge alone, Utah's attempt statute does not. Instead it allows convictions for attempt crimes only upon strong corroboration "of the actor's *intent* to commit the offense." Because the Utah legislature did not adopt the particular wording of the M.P.C. that would have allowed a knowing attempt, we assume that it did so deliberately in order to limit the reach of the attempt statute to intentional conduct.

D. Persuasive Authority from Other Jurisdictions

1. *Jurisdictions Allowing Conviction for "Knowing" Attempted Murder*

The State argues that allowing a conviction for attempted murder to stand on a knowing mens rea would be consistent with the decisions of other states. We do not find any of these cases cited by the State persuasive. Most of them only indirectly address the culpability required for attempt crimes. The few cases that directly address whether an attempted murder conviction may be obtained when a defendant acts knowingly are distinguishable.

...

2. *Jurisdictions Rejecting "Knowing" Attempted Murder*

On the other hand, we are persuaded by the reasoning of the numerous jurisdictions that hold a person cannot be convicted of attempted murder with only a "knowing" mens rea. The Maine Supreme Court, in a case similar to the instant case, held that "[b]efore a person can be convicted of attempted murder, he must act with the intent to cause the death of another human being." *State v. Huff*, 469 A.2d 1251, 1253 (Me. 1984)....

Examining a conviction for attempted murder under a definition of murder that allowed either an intentional or a knowing mens rea, the Illinois Appellate Court

---

3. When the Utah legislature adopted this section of the M.P.C., it decided, however, to substitute the word "intentionally" for the word "purposely." *See* Utah Code Ann. § 76-2-103 (1999).

held that "the difference between intent and knowledge should not be treated as a metaphysical distinction which can be ignored. Knowledge is not intent as defined by our statutes, and the jury instructions should reflect this distinction." *People v. Kraft*, 478 N.E.2d 1154, 1160 (Ill. App. 1985).

In sum, though the State cites several cases to support its argument that attempt crimes may be committed knowingly, we find them unpersuasive. However, several cases from other jurisdictions that directly address the attempt issue support our conclusion to disallow convictions for attempted murder based on the mens rea of knowledge alone.

E. An Attempted Murder Conviction Requires Proof of Intent

Contrary to these authorities, the State argues that "intentionally" and "knowingly" are functional equivalents. Although the distinction between intentional conduct and knowing conduct is narrow, the statutory definition of these terms creates a meaningful difference between the two. In addition, the Utah Code specifically states that acting "intentionally" encompasses acting "knowingly," but it does not provide for the reverse.

Indeed, we accept that it is difficult to conceptualize many examples where one could attempt to commit murder knowingly but not intentionally. However, it is certainly possible that a knowing crime can be committed unintentionally. That is, a person can know that a certain action will cause a certain result without that result being the person's conscious objective. For example, a person may know that blowing up a building will cause the death of people inside, but if his or her intent or conscious objective is only to destroy the building, there is no intent, for purposes of attempt, to kill. By acknowledging that a person may knowingly commit murder without committing the crime intentionally, we also recognize that such behavior is rare. Notwithstanding this observation, we conclude that a conviction for attempted murder must rest on intentional conduct.

... We now hold that a defendant may only be convicted of attempted murder when he or she acts intentionally. To the extent that our opinion in *Maestas* and our footnote in *Vigil* contradict this holding, they are overruled. In order to convict a defendant of attempted murder, the prosecution must show that the defendant acted intentionally.

...

CONCLUSION

We hold that in order to convict a defendant of attempted murder, the prosecution must establish that the defendant acted intentionally; it is not enough that he or she acted knowingly. However, we do not believe this holding significantly impacts Casey's conviction.... [W]e hold that the error was not of sufficient magnitude to affect Casey's substantial rights because no reasonable jury could have concluded that he acted knowingly without also concluding that he acted intentionally. For these reasons we conclude that no manifest injustice or plain error resulted from the use of the jury instructions in this case. Accordingly, we affirm.

Comments and Questions

(1) Why should the attempted murder conviction be set aside when Casey intended to fire the gun and fired it? It was fortuitous that a killing was prevented. Should the law of attempt distinguish between an incomplete attempt and a situation like that in *Casey*, in which the defendant has done all that needs to be done and only an accident or human intervention avoided the harm of homicide?

(2) Several states have ruled, in decisions the *Casey* court found unpersuasive, that attempted murder may be based on a knowing mens rea. *See, e.g., Bartlett v. State*, 711 N.E.2d 497, 499 (Ind. 1999); *Gentry v. State*, 881 S.W.2d 35, 40 (Tex. App. 1994). One court reasoned thus:

> One may be guilty of attempt without having engaged in the harmful conduct or having achieved the harmful result that ordinarily forms the basis for criminal liability; rather, culpability for criminal attempt rests primarily upon the actor's purpose to cause harmful consequences. Punishment is justified where the actor intends harm because there exists a high likelihood that his "unspent" intent will flower into harmful conduct at any moment. The probability of future dangerousness, however, is not confined to actors whose conscious purpose is to perform the proscribed acts or achieve the proscribed results, *i.e.*, those possessing the culpable mental state of specific intent. We believe that this danger is equally present when one acts knowingly.

People v. Krovarz, 697 P.2d 378, 381 (Colo. 1985) (knowledge is a proper state of mind for the attempt offense). Most states, however, require that intent be shown.

(3) *Attempted Involuntary Manslaughter*. Can a defendant be found guilty of attempted manslaughter? The law is clear with respect to involuntary manslaughter, which is based on reckless conduct. In this area the courts consistently find no attempt liability, as "it would be legally impossible to attempt to commit a crime which does not include culpable intent as an element, such as reckless manslaughter." *People v. Foy*, 587 N.Y.S.2d 111, 111 (N.Y. City Crim. Ct. 1992); *see State v. Howell*, 649 P.2d 91 (Utah 1982).

Attempted involuntary manslaughter was rejected by the Supreme Court of Nevada in *Bailey v. State*, 688 P.2d 320, 321 (Nev. 1984), for the following reason:

> Involuntary manslaughter is by definition an unintentional killing. The crime of attempt, however, requires that the accused formulate the intent to commit the crime attempted; absent proof of the element of intent, a conviction for attempt cannot stand. Appellant argues that it is logically impossible to attempt to commit an unintentional act. This contention has merit. Because "[t]here is no such criminal offense as an attempt to achieve an unintended result," the crime of "attempted involuntary manslaughter" is logically impossible.

See also, Free v. State, 455 So.2d 137,147 (Ala. Crim. App. 1984), *abrogated on other grounds by McKinney v. State*, 511 So.2d 220 (Ala. 1987):

> An attempt to commit murder requires the perpetrator to act with the specific intent to commit murder. One must intentionally or knowingly attempt to commit murder. A general felonious intent is not sufficient. Accordingly, one cannot recklessly attempt to commit murder.

Is the reason for rejecting the offense simply a matter of linguistics—that it is impossible to attempt to be reckless? Are there other, more substantive reasons?

(4) *Attempted Voluntary Manslaughter.* As to voluntary manslaughter, based on the heat of passion claim, the law has been much less certain. The modern trend is to allow liability.

> Cox contends that voluntary manslaughter does not require proof of intent, and therefore the crime of attempt does not arise. His argument, in effect, is that voluntary and involuntary manslaughter are the same crime. This is incorrect.... We define voluntary manslaughter as an intentional homicide, done in a sudden heat of passion, caused by adequate provocation, before there has been a reasonable opportunity for the passion to cool. Involuntary manslaughter, on the other hand, is defined as the unintentional killing done without malice, by doing some unlawful act endangering life, or in negligently doing some act lawful in itself, or by the negligent omission to perform a legal duty.
>
> Cases that apply the intent standard to crimes of attempt eliminate involuntary manslaughter, but acknowledge that attempt does attach to the generally accepted definition of voluntary manslaughter.
>
> In the several states that have rejected attempted voluntary manslaughter as a crime, the courts have indicated concern because of possible confusion with the crime of assault with intent to kill, or concern with lesser degrees of statutory manslaughter, or "because the specific crime of manslaughter invokes no intent and, accordingly, an intention to commit a crime whose distinguishing element is lack of intent is logically repugnant."
>
> ... [A]ssault with intent to murder and attempted murder are separate and distinct offenses in this state.
>
> We conclude that when an individual, engaged in an altercation, suddenly attempts to perpetuate a homicide caused by heat of passion in response to legally adequate provocation, and where the attempt results in something less than the actual wrongful killing, that person may be convicted of attempted voluntary manslaughter....

Cox v. State, 534 A.2d 1333, 1335–37 (Md. 1988).

Attempted voluntary manslaughter is a crime in limited circumstances, according to the New Mexico Supreme Court in *State v. Jernigan*, 127 P.3d 537 (N.M. 2006). The limited circumstances were those analogous to the situation in which a defendant fire bombed a mobile home intending to kill someone inside, knowing that this created the probability of death or great bodily harm with respect to unknown persons inside.

(5) If a victim of a felony is seriously injured in the course of that felony, can the defendant be charged with attempted felony murder? State courts are split on this matter. *Contrast White v. State*, 585 S.W.2d 952 (Ark. 1979), *with State v. Nolan*, 995

N.E.2d 902 (Ohio App. 2013). What are the impediments to a charge of attempted felony murder?

(6) The clearest illustration of the power of the intent requirement can be seen in a famous English case, *Gardner v. Akeroyd*, (1952) 2 Q.B. 743. The Justices there held that a regulation concerning the price of meat imposed strict (as well as vicarious) liability. To prove an attempted violation of the regulation, however, the government had to show intentional conduct.

(7) The intent issue can arise in other attempted crimes besides homicides. The crime of sexual abuse in the United States Code simply provides that one who "knowingly causes another person to engage in a sexual act" by threat or fear is guilty of sexual abuse. 18 U.S.C. § 2241 (2012). In *United States v. Sneezer*, 900 F.2d 177 (9th Cir. 1990), the defendant was convicted of attempted sexual abuse. The court found that all attempts include an element of intent even where the crime which was attempted does not.

(8) The defendant in *People v. Mitchell*, 473 N.E.2d 1270 (Ill. 1984), repeatedly slapped and punched her 16-month old daughter over a two-day period. When the child passed out, the defendant placed a cool cloth on the child's head. When she did not regain consciousness, the defendant took her to the hospital, stating that she (the defendant) was not the mother. Upon being arrested, the defendant told the police that she struck the child in anger after having an argument with her boyfriend and further explained that she wanted to give the child away because the child reminded her of the child's father, whom the defendant hated. Was the evidence sufficient on the attempted murder count? The court reversed the judgment relying on the fact that the defendant took the child to the hospital and further noting that there "was ample opportunity for her to complete her crime if, in fact, she intended to kill the child."

(9) *Proving the Mens Rea.* Intent may be established through circumstantial evidence.

> The defendant ... fired a single bullet into a slowly moving vehicle, narrowly missing a mother and her infant son. The evidence showed that the mother, who was known to defendant and was driving, and her baby, who was secured [in a back-facing] car seat directly behind her, were each in the defendant's line of fire when he fired a single .38-caliber round at them from behind the car as it pulled away from the curb. The bullet shattered the rear windshield, narrowly missed both the mother and baby, passed through the mother's headrest, and lodged in the driver's side door.

People v. Smith, 124 P.3d 730 (Cal. 2005).

The defendant was convicted of attempted murder of the mother and the baby; the court considered the conviction of attempted murder of the baby. Under California law, intent to kill the baby required proof that defendant purposefully shot at the baby with express malice. The court rejected the defense argument that firing a single bullet at two victims precluded a finding of express malice toward both victims. The court found that although defendant had no motive to kill the baby and had displayed overt hostility only toward the woman, he had acted with express malice. Evidence that the defendant was hostile to the mother, knew the baby was in the car, the baby was the child of a current boyfriend with whom he had an altercation moments before, and the determination to shoot when the baby was directly in the line of fire were sufficient to show express malice.

The dissent argued that the evidence did not prove the defendant intended to kill the baby.

> ... The majority is of course correct that intent may ordinarily be inferred from action. But to support the inference that defendant intended to kill the infant, the majority points to no aspect of defendant's action other than that he placed the infant's life in danger by shooting in his direction. The majority thus permits knowing endangerment, which establishes at most *implied* malice, to serve, by itself, as proof beyond a reasonable doubt of intent to kill. This result is contrary to fundamental concepts of California homicide law ... in particular the distinction between implied and express malice and the requirement that the latter be proven as an element of attempted murder.

Id. at 741–42.

(10) The commission of an important act by the accused may assist the state in proving intent, but it will not always do so.

> ... The [act] requirement does not mandate that the activity constituting a substantial step must be sufficient to prove that the defendant had the subjective, specific intent to commit a crime. The intent may need to be proven separately.
>
> This point is best illustrated by a hypothetical. A penniless young man, while walking through a city park, is asked to purchase drugs. To further his own misguided pursuit of personal amusement, the man engages in active negotiations with the drug dealer to purchase drugs, fully knowing that he could never consummate the sale. These negotiations, even though they would not establish the man's subjective intent to buy the drugs, no doubt do constitute a "substantial step" towards the commission of a crime of possession, for these negotiations would, objectively, corroborate the firmness of a defendant's criminal intent.
>
> This, of course, does not mean that the young man in our hypothetical is guilty of an attempt crime. The government must still fulfill its burden to establish that he had the specific intent to purchase the drugs. The young man would, no doubt, argue that the fact he was (1) penniless and (2) prone to amusing himself in unconventional ways served as strong evidence that he did not, in fact, intend to possess the drugs. The point is, however, that these two inquiries are, ultimately, separate ones. A defendant cannot argue that overt acts on his part did not constitute a "substantial step," even though a reasonable person would believe that they were strongly corrob-

> orative of the firmness of an actor's criminal intent, on the ground that his acts did not prove his subjective intent. The acts alleged need only corroborate (i.e., confirm) his intent; they are not the sole evidence on which the government can rely to establish that a defendant specifically intended to commit a crime.

United States v. Bilderbeck, 163 F.3d 971, 975–76 (6th Cir. 1999).

Problem

On June 20, 1975, the victim of the crime, Blakely Sower, together with his two brothers, Ronald and Cloyce, went to the home of the defendant Starkey, who had married Ronald's former wife. The purpose of the visit was to enable Ronald Sower to pick up his two minor children under a custody visitation arrangement embodied in a court order. There was testimony that on previous occasions Ronald had encountered trouble when picking up the children, and his attorney had advised him to take someone with him as a witness.

When the three brothers arrived at the premises the children were not ready to leave, and the brothers waited outside the house. The defendant Starkey appeared at the kitchen door and began to verbally abuse the Sowers, calling them "punks." He invited them to come around the house to the basement door where he said he would "take care of them."

The Sower brothers walked around the house to the basement door. On the way, the prosecuting witness Blakely picked up a stick. When they arrived at the basement door the defendant called at them to come in. When they declined to do so, the defendant reached behind the door and brought out a shotgun. He pointed it at Blakely Sower and, after threatening to shoot him, discharged the shotgun into the ground near where Blakely was standing and ordered the brothers off the premises.

The brothers then returned to the front of the house and by this time the children had come out of the house and their father, Ronald Sower, took them to his car. During this time an argument was ensuing between Ronald and his former wife. Ronald and his brother Cloyce got into their car with the children and began backing it down the driveway. The defendant was throwing gravel at them. Blakely Sower began to throw gravel at the defendant, who retaliated by throwing gravel back. Blakely then got into his truck and drove it through the driveway. As he passed the house, the defendant fired his shotgun. The pellets hit the right side of the topper on the truck bed, breaking the glass window.

The defendant argued that he did not intend to kill Blakely Sower; if "he wanted to kill Blakely Sower he could have done that when he fired the shotgun into the ground. The defendant testified he fired at the truck after he had pulled his wife from the path of the truck and it had gone past him."

> The obvious response to this point is that while there may have been no intent to kill formed at that time, this does not preclude the required intent from being present when he fired at Blakely Sower in his truck.
>
> Proof of intent in a criminal case can be developed from the circumstances surrounding the crime. This is the customary manner of proving malice in a murder case, since the defendant rarely admits this element of the crime.

State v. Starkey, 244 S.E.2d 219 (W. Va. 1978).

Would you affirm the attempted murder conviction?

[B] The Act Requirement

Courts generally agree that the conduct required to prove attempt must be greater than preparation but something less than perpetration. Consider the following:

> [T]o consummate an attempt to commit a crime there must be something more than mere intention or preparation. The attempt must be manifested by acts which would end in accomplishment, but for intervening circumstances occurring apart from, and independent of, the will of the defendant. There is a difference between preparation antecedent to an offense and the actual attempt to commit it. "The preparation consists in devising or arranging the means or measures necessary for the commission of the offense; the attempt is the direct movement toward the commission after the preparations are made." In other words, to constitute an attempt the acts of the defendant must go so far that they would result in the accomplishment of the crime unless frustrated by extraneous circumstances. "The reason for requiring evidence of a direct act, however slight, toward consummation of the intended crime, is ... that in the majority of cases up to that time the conduct of the defendant, consisting merely of acts of preparation, has never ceased to be equivocal; and this is necessarily so, irrespective of his declared intent. It is that quality of being equivocal that must be lacking before the act becomes one which may be said to be a commencement of the commission of the crime, or an overt act, or before any fragment of the crime itself has been committed, and this is so for the reason that, so long as the equivocal quality remains, no one can say with certainty what the intent of the defendant is."

State v. Martinez, 220 N.W.2d 530, 531 (S.D. 1974).

> "[C]riminal attempts require proof of an intent to bring about the consequences set forth in the crime attempted, and this is so even though no such intent is required for the completed crime." Likewise, with respect to the act, "a substantial step is less than what is necessary to complete the substantive crime, but more than mere preparation." The defendant's actions have to go beyond preparation and "corroborate strongly the firmness of the defendant's criminal intent." Put otherwise, the evidence must show that the crime "will take place unless interrupted by independent circumstances."

United States v. Astronomo, 183 F. Supp. 2d 158, 168–69 (D. Mass. 2001).

> In order to constitute an attempt, it is essential that the defendant, with the intent of committing the particular crime, should have done some overt act adapted to, approximating, and which in the ordinary and likely course of things would result in the commission thereof. Therefore, the act must reach far enough towards the accomplishment of the desired result to amount to the commencement of the consummation. It must not be merely preparatory. In other words, while it need not be the last proximate act to the consummation of the offense attempted to be perpetrated, it must approach sufficiently near to it to stand either as the first or some subsequent step in a direct movement towards the commission of the offense after the preparations are made.

State v. Dowd, 220 S.E.2d 393, 396 (N.C. Ct. App. 1975).

Over time, common law courts devised several tests to measure when a defendant's conduct exceeded that needed for preparation. Thus, you will see references in the cases that follow to "last act," "equivocality," "proximate danger," "substantial step," and so on. One court has helpfully distilled these various tests into three:

> Three legal standards exist in the United States by which the acts of an accused who is charged with having attempted to commit a crime may be judged. They are (i) the "slight acts" standard, (ii) the "substantial steps" standard, and (iii) the "dangerously close" standard.

People v. Sabo, 687 N.Y.S.2d 513, 517–18 (N.Y. Sup. Ct. 1998).

United States v. Lee

United States Court of Appeals, Eleventh Circuit
603 F.3d 904 (2010)

PRYOR, CIRCUIT JUDGE.

The question presented by this appeal is whether sufficient evidence supports the conviction of Van Buren Lee for attempted enticement of a minor, 18 U.S.C. § 2422(b).... For several months, Lee communicated online with a postal inspector who was posing as "Candi Kane," the "open-minded mother of two beautiful [minor] girls." Lee and Candi repeatedly discussed whether, how, and when Candi would grant Lee sexual access to her daughters, and Lee produced and sent Candi and her daughters sexually explicit images of him. Eventually Lee and Candi spoke by telephone. Lee also requested that Candi produce and send to him sexually explicit photographs of her daughters in specific poses, which, so far as Lee knew, she did. Lee argues that he communicated only with an adult intermediary.... We affirm.

I. BACKGROUND

At least as early as 2006, Jude Densley, a federal postal inspector, began investigating online predators. Densley created a profile on the social networking website hi5 using the pseudonym "Candi Kane." According to her profile, Candi was an "open-minded mother of two beautiful girls," ages seven and twelve. The profile also identified Candi as a member of online social groups called "Young Girls and Older Men Loving Each Other," "Dady's [sic] Favourite," and "Family Love is Best." At trial, Densley explained that the phrase "family love" is a euphemism for incest.

In September 2007, Lee, using the pseudonym "Doc," contacted Candi via hi5. In his first message to Candi, Lee stated, "I'm your man to handle all your needs." Lee closed his message by telling Candi to "[t]ake care … you and the girls."

On October 3, 2007, Lee and Candi interacted in two separate online conversations. During the first conversation, Lee asked Candi, "What's your sexual orientation and how old are your girls?" Lee asked Candi why she described herself in her profile as open minded and explained that he wanted to know more about Candi because "[t]here are a lot of things the police use the computer for these days to trap people if you know what I mean." Candi assured Lee that she was not a police officer and told him that when she was a child she was involved in a "loving sexual relationship" with her father. Lee responded by asking Candi if she wanted "[her] girls to learn the right way." Lee explained, "All I know is I love giving and receiving and I believe [in] giving 'til you reach orgasm. Can you handle that? Is that what you want for the girls too?" In the second online conversation, Lee again expressed his concern that Candi was a police officer. Lee explained that he had been charged once with a sex crime against a child. Candi had not mentioned her daughters during this conversation, but Lee explained that he feared "talk[ing] to [Candi] … about sex … especially concerning [her] daughters." Without prompting, Lee repeatedly asked her whether she wanted to "teach" her daughters in the same way that she had been "taught" when she was a child. Toward the end of the second conversation, Candi told Lee that she was "seeing someone so if you are really looking for your soul mate or something like that, maybe I'm not the one you should be talking with." At trial, Densley explained that she told Lee that Candi had a boyfriend to determine whether Lee was interested in Candi or Candi's daughters.

[Ed.—The court described in detail the numerous later contacts between Densley and Lee.]

…

Candi and Lee last communicated on March 7, 2008. On that day, a postal inspector in Georgia who had been working with Densley arranged to have government agents deliver to Lee a package that purported to contain photographs of Candi and her daughters. The package contained photographs of minors in sexually explicit poses. While Candi and Lee were conversing online on March 7, Lee exclaimed, "I think the mail just arrived!" Lee asked Candi to wait while he retrieved the mail. When Lee retrieved the package of child pornography from his porch, he was arrested. Candi never again heard from Lee.

In March 2008, a federal grand jury returned a three-count indictment against Lee.… Count three alleged that Lee had attempted to persuade, induce, entice, and coerce an individual under the age of eighteen to engage in child molestation, as defined by section 288 of the California Penal Code, id. § 2422(b). After trial, a jury convicted Lee on all three counts.

The district court sentenced Lee in December 2008. The presentence investigation report provided a total offense level of 41 and a criminal history of V. Lee's criminal history included three adult convictions. In 1980, Texas police investigated a report that Lee had exposed himself to a nine-year-old child. The investigation revealed that Lee had exposed himself to several other individuals during the preceding year: an adult female on a naval base in October 1979; a neighbor in January 1980; and a neighbor's twelve-year-old daughter in March 1980. A Texas jury convicted Lee of indecent exposure and Lee received a sentence of four years of probation. In October 1998, a Georgia jury convicted Lee of molesting his second wife's daughter—whom Lee had adopted—when the girl was under the age of sixteen. According to the investigation reports, Lee had exposed himself to the girl on several occasions. Lee's wife also caught him using a mirror to look underneath the bathroom door while his adopted daughter was showering. Moreover, in March 1997, while the girl was cooking, Lee exposed his genitals to her and touched her buttocks several times. For this conviction, Lee served five years in prison and began serving a five-year sentence of probation in October 2003. The terms of Lee's probation required him to, among other things, "not violate the criminal laws of any governmental unit," "not purchase or possess any pornographic, sexually explicit or stimulating material," and "not initiate contact with nor continue uninitiated contact with a child under the age of 16." Lee violated the terms of his probation in 2005 when he committed criminal trespass. Georgia police, responding to an anonymous tip, discovered Lee in an abandoned house, which was located across the street from a playground. Lee had a set of binoculars and had been watching the playground. After considering the advisory guidelines range and the sentencing factors set out at 18 U.S.C. § 3553(a), the district court sentenced Lee to a term of imprisonment of 300 months on each of the three counts, to be served concurrently....

III. DISCUSSION

[Ed.—The court explained why defendant could be convicted even though he never communicated directly with a minor or attempted to exploit real minors. *See* discussion, *infra*, on the impossibility defense.]

...

B. Sufficient Evidence Supports Each of Lee's Convictions.

...

1. Sufficient Evidence Supports Lee's Conviction Under Section 2422(b).

...

A reasonable jury also could have found that Lee took a substantial step toward causing Candi's daughters to assent to sexual contact with him. Lee's internet and telephone "conversations ... went beyond mere preparation," and constitute a substantial step sufficient to support his attempt conviction. Lee did not confide in a friend or write in his journal about his desire to have sex with Candi's daughters; he requested assistance from the one woman who had "influence and control over [the] daughters." Lee did more than suggest the possibility of having sex with Candi's daughters. Over the course of several months, he repeatedly discussed when and, in graphic detail, how he wanted to complete the act. Much of Lee's conduct—especially his sending graphic photographs to the girls and promising gifts—also supports a finding that he groomed the girls in an effort to facilitate a future sexual encounter. Lee stresses that he never made final plans to travel to California from Georgia to meet Candi and her daughters, but the government charged Lee with "an attempt to achieve the mental act of assent, for which physical proximity ... is not required." We will not require firm plans to travel where, as here, the defendant, for several months, took other steps sufficient to achieve the end that is the object of the attempt.

The dissent contends, without providing any support, that the government was required to prove that Lee "took a substantial step towards stimulating the occurrence of his intended goal of having sex with a child," and that Lee must have taken "a step to extend his relationship with Candi Kane or her daughters beyond the boundaries of his property in Georgia." But as we have explained, our precedent and the precedents of many of our sister circuits hold that section 2422(b) prohibits attempts to cause minors to agree to engage in illegal sexual conduct, not attempts to engage in illegal sexual conduct with minors. As we stated in Yost, "[W]e are not required to find Yost acted with the specific intent to engage in sexual activity." These decisions could not be any clearer: section 2422(b) does not require proof of an attempt at child molestation.

... So far as this appeal is concerned, what matters is that the grand jury indicted Lee for an attempt to "persuade, induce, entice, and coerce" a minor to engage in child molestation.

The dissent states that none of our precedents upheld a conviction where the defendant "made so little effort to consummate the crime," but our aim is not to decide whether Lee's conduct is at least as "criminal" as the conduct of others convicted under section 2422(b). Each of our precedents holds no more than that a reasonable jury could have found that the defendant at issue violated section 2422(b). Not surprisingly, none guesses at or purports to have identified the minimum conduct that section 2422(b) proscribes.

... [W]e consider the "totality" of Lee's conduct to determine whether the record supports a finding that he "committed a substantial step" toward persuading or enticing a minor to engage in a sex act. The "totality" of Lee's conduct includes the following acts:

> (1) initiating contact with Candi, who he believed to be interested in providing others with sexual access to her daughters;
>
> (2) asking more than once whether Candi was a police officer and expressing his concerns about falling into a trap;
>
> (3) during a conversation several months later, asking Candi whether she "would let him bring [her] children into womanhood";

(4) explaining that he had recently almost brought an eleven year old girl "into womanhood," but failed because he did not want to rush things and the girl eventually moved away;

(5) asking if he could meet Candi's daughters "any time soon" and asking whether Candi had "an age in mind for the girls to be deflowered or is now the time";

(6) sending a photograph of his penis to Candi, asking more than once that she share it with her daughters, and promising that his penis is not so large as to harm the girls;

(7) when he learned that the girls had seen the photograph, asking Candi how the girls had responded;

(8) requesting, more than once, from Candi photographs of the minor girls with "opened legs while lying on your back and doggie style with cheeks being held open with your hands";

(9) insisting, "I'm serious about this";

(10) giving Candi his phone number and asking that she call him;

(11) telling Candi that he was "ready to make a trip out to meet you guys," and later saying he wanted to meet the girls in their home so that they would feel comfortable around him;

(12) discussing with Candi travel details including easiest travel route and meeting in the summer when the girls would be out of school;

(13) speaking with Candi on the telephone and discussing when and how he might travel to California to meet the girls;

(14) again discussing with Candi his visiting the girls in California and discussing details, including his concern that Candi's boyfriend would complicate the plan;

(15) on more than one occasion, insisting to Candi that he was not interested in having sex with anyone other than the minor girls;

(16) asking Candi whether the oldest girl was menstruating and, if so, whether she was taking birth control pills because he is "not a condom user";

(17) inviting Candi to watch a live video stream of him masturbating, masturbating while Candi watched, and ending the event by "send[ing] [his] lov[e]" to the girls;

(18) later inviting Candi to watch a similar stream;

(19) promising to send gifts to the girls;

(20) in another conversation, promising that he had been shopping for coloring books, dolls, and necklaces;

(21) continuing to communicate with Candi after she told him that she had created and mailed him pornographic pictures of her minor daughters;

(22) excitedly accepting what he believed to be pornographic photographs of the minor girls;

(23) ending his pursuit of Candi's minor daughters only upon his arrest.

The evidence of "[t]hese acts, taken as a whole," allowed the jury to find that Lee's "conduct was criminal."

...

IV. CONCLUSION

We AFFIRM Lee's convictions.

MARTIN, CIRCUIT JUDGE, concurring in part, and dissenting in part:

I concur with the reasons given by the majority for affirming Mr. Lee's conviction for receiving child pornography and for attempting to produce child pornography. However, I write separately, and in dissent, because I do not believe the evidence supports Mr. Lee's conviction for attempting to entice a child to engage in illicit sexual activity, even when all inferences are made on the side of the government. In order for a person to be convicted of attempting to commit a crime, he must not only intend to commit the crime, he must also take a substantial step towards committing it. I believe the evidence against Mr. Lee fails on the substantial step requirement.

Because I address only whether the evidence presented at trial was sufficient to sustain Mr. Lee's conviction under 18 U.S.C. § 2422(b), I confine my discussion to the evidence actually presented to the jury. The majority opinion includes information from the Presentence Report—a court document prepared after Mr. Lee's trial and conviction. The court's probation officer prepared the Presentence Report and provided it to the district judge, under seal, as an aid in sentencing. The jury never saw nor had any knowledge of the information revealed about Mr. Lee's past. While the majority's recitation of Mr. Lee's prior convictions and alleged past conduct certainly casts an ugly light on Mr. Lee's character, sound policies caution against relying on these incidents when evaluating Mr. Lee's culpability in this case. Mr. Lee was not on trial for those admittedly perverse acts, and the bottom line is, of course, that the Presentence Report was not evidence in this case. In any event, I do not undertake to debate the manner in which Mr. Lee has chosen to live his life. I only mean to address the standard for what is legally required to convict any defendant of the crime of attempt.

As set forth by the majority, Mr. Lee communicated with United States Postal Service Inspector Jude Densley, known to him as Candi Kane, over a period of about six months. Candi Kane told Mr. Lee she was the mother of two girls, ages seven and twelve, living in California. Mr. Lee was in Georgia. It is undisputed that Mr. Lee never took any step, substantial or otherwise, to travel to California. He never bought a plane, bus or train ticket. He never set a date for a visit. He never left Georgia.

In order "[t]o sustain [Mr. Lee's] convictions, we must determine he (1) had the specific intent or mens rea to commit the underlying charged crimes, and (2) took actions that constituted a substantial step toward the commission of [each] crime." Precedent requires us to pay close attention to both requirements for an attempt conviction. We have said that the second element of an attempt charge—whether the defendant took a substantial step—requires the government to prove beyond a reasonable doubt that "the defendant's objective acts, without reliance on the accompanying mens rea, ... mark the defendant's conduct as criminal." "In other words, the defendant's acts, taken as a whole, must strongly corroborate the required culpability; they must not be equivocal."

I well understand that the act criminalized by 18 U.S.C. §2422(b) is to knowingly entice (or persuade, induce or coerce) a child to engage in criminal sexual activity. The majority describes the crime as attempting to cause assent on the part of the minor.... [Our prior holdings do not] obviate the need for proof that a defendant took a substantial step towards stimulating the occurrence of his intended goal of having sex with a child.

...

I do not press the view that travel is required for a conviction under 18 U.S.C. §2422(b). This Court has already decided that it is not. However, my review of the jurisprudence of this circuit does not reveal any defendant convicted under section 2422(b) after having made so little effort to consummate the crime.

For example, in United States v. Root, 296 F.3d 1222 (11th Cir. 2002), the defendant convicted under 18 U.S.C. §2422(b) introduced himself to a purported 13-year-old on the Internet, and three days later drove from North Carolina to the Mall of Georgia to meet her at the appointed time and place. In United States v. Yost, 479 F.3d 815 (11th Cir. 2007), the defendant convicted under this statute found Lynn—a fictitious 13-year-old—online, and within three days set a meeting with her at the McDonald's near her house for 9:30 a.m. the next day. Mr. Yost did not show up, but was arrested one week later, when he arrived at the time and location of another meeting he had planned with a second fictional child. In concluding that Mr. Yost's failure to arrive at the first meeting was not dispositive, we quoted the Tenth Circuit for the proposition that he had " 'crossed the line from "harmless banter" to inducement the moment he began making arrangements to meet [the minor], notwithstanding the lack of evidence that he traveled to the supposed meeting place.' " We found that Mr. Yost crossed that same line when he held online chats with the minor, talked to her on the telephone, posted pictures of his genitalia, and made arrangements to meet her at a certain time and place.

Mr. Lee communicated with Candi Kane beginning on September 26, 2007 until his arrest on March 7, 2008. To the extent there was conversation about meeting in person, the plans were never more than general talk about what could happen in the future. Inspector Densley testified at trial that during a telephone conversation on December 27, 2007, Mr. Lee said he would come ten months later, "around October," and he and Candi Kane discussed which airport would be closest. In the chats, there was nothing even as specific as that. It is quite true that Mr. Lee asked for pornography; sent photographs of his genitalia; and masturbated on a webcam for the purported mother. However, I see no fact in this case demonstrating that Mr. Lee ever took any step to extend his relationship with Candi Kane or her daughters beyond the boundaries of his property in Georgia. For that reason, I do not believe there was proof that Mr. Lee took a substantial step towards enticing a child to engage in illicit sexual conduct, and I would vacate his conviction for attempting that crime.

Furthering Mr. Lee's argument—even to the limited extent I do here[5]—is not an easy task. His interaction with Candi Kane is disturbing, and their conversations repugnant. I in no way intend to minimize the threat that sexual predators pose to children in our society or the life-shattering effects their actions have on their victims. Nevertheless, I write out of concern that the majority opinion does not clearly demarcate despicable but lawful talk from a criminal attempt punishable by up to thirty years in prison. For this reason, I respectfully dissent from the majority's decision to uphold Mr. Lee's conviction pursuant to 18 U.S.C. § 2422(b).

Comments and Questions

(1) The judges disagree with respect to the strength of the evidence and the dissenting judge does not join the majority opinion. How strong was the evidence here? Why does the dissenter distinguish among the attempt charges?

(2) Under the following statutes, what result in *Lee*?

N.Y. Penal Law § 110.00 states:

> A person is guilty of an attempt to commit a crime when, with intent to commit a crime, he engages in conduct which tends to effect the commission of such crime.

Nev. Rev. Stat. § 193.330 similarly requires:

> An act done with intent to commit a crime, and tending but failing to accomplish it, is an attempt to commit that crime.

Section 21a of the California Penal Code provides:

> An attempt to commit a crime consists of two elements: a specific intent to commit the crime, and a direct but ineffectual act done toward its commission.

(3) Determining what actions go beyond mere preparation and constitute an attempt is a difficult task for the courts. In *United States v. Candoli*, 870 F.2d 496, 503 (9th Cir. 1989), the defendants were seen driving by the retail store and parking up the street. Less than an hour later they were found to be in possession of plastic bottles with gasoline in their trunk. The court found that this conduct, as a matter of law, could not constitute the crime of attempted arson. The defendants in *State v. Fornino*, 539 A.2d 301 (N.J. Super. Ct. App. Div. 1988), planned to kill officers in a correctional institution. Pursuant to this plan they visited an office from which

---

5. As set forth by the majority, Mr. Lee was sentenced to 300 months of incarceration on each of three counts, to be served concurrently. This being the case, even if we were to reverse the section 2422(b) conviction, we would not change Mr. Lee's term of incarceration by a single day.

escape was to occur and surveyed a wooded area to determine where bodies could be hidden. In addition, one of the defendants accepted payment for aiding the escape efforts which were to take place. Held, these actions constituted substantial steps and supported a conviction for attempted murder. In *United States v. Garrett*, 948 F.2d 474, 477 (8th Cir. 1991), the defendant was convicted of attempted possession of cocaine. The court affirmed the conviction, responding to the defendant's arguments:

> Garrett contends that merely heading toward Room 117 is insufficient to constitute a substantial step toward possession of the crack cocaine.... [He] ignores the case's broader factual circumstances. After receiving the pager message, Garrett called Rodriguez to ascertain her location. He then expended a fair amount of time and energy in actually finding the motel, making three additional calls for directions and driving for approximately 45 minutes.

Are these three cases consistent with one another? Were they decided correctly?

(4) The defendant in *United States v. Duran*, 96 F.3d 1495, 1508 (D.C. Cir. 1996), was convicted of attempting to kill the President. He raised an issue of impossibility (*see* §6.02[E], *infra*), but the court rejected the claim.

> Duran had on numerous occasions expressed, both verbally and in writing, a strong desire to kill the President, and ... had purchased a rifle, ammunition clips, and an overcoat large enough to conceal the rifle (all of which he would eventually use in firing toward a man on the White House lawn who resembled the President), then traveled to Washington, D.C. and stood by the White House gate with the rifle and ammunition concealed.... [He] stood in front of the White House for several hours with the weapons and ammunition on his person, with the purpose of assassinating the President....
>
> Duran had already completed the crime of attempted assassination of the President before he began firing towards Dennis Basso.

(5) Two recent cases, each involving undercover sting operations targeting potential sex crime offenders, show the difficulties courts have in applying the attempt principles. The court laid out the basic facts in *United States v. Howard*, 766 F.3d 414, 415 (5th Cir. 2014):

> The government caught the Defendant-Appellant Jeffrey Howard ("Howard") in a sting operation. A government agent impersonated a mother offering up her two minor daughters for sex. Howard sent the agent sexually explicit photographs and asked that she show the photographs to the girls. He also suggested that the agent procure birth control for and perform sex acts on her daughters to get them ready for him. But Howard did not make travel arrangements to Corpus Christi, Texas—where the fictional mother and her two daughters lived. Further, the government agent tried to get Howard to commit to book a flight-instructing Howard to "take it or leave it," and Howard responded "okay, I'll leave it." Three months later, the police arrested Howard in California. Howard was convicted by bench trial of attempt to

> knowingly persuade, induce, entice, or coerce a minor to engage in illegal sexual activity in violation of 18 U.S.C. §2422(b).

In *Commonwealth v. Buswell*, 9 N.E.3d 276 (Mass. 2014) a similar undercover sting operation was conducted also involving sexual acts with a supposedly underage minor. Here, there were numerous text messages and phone conversations, and the defendant traveled to the place where he was supposed to meet the girl [actually a police officer]. The intent of the defendant was clear, according to the court, and he was arrested in the parking lot of the store where he was to meet the girl.

In *Howard* the court affirmed the conviction, emphasizing the clear intent shown.

> Accepting Howard's proposed bright-line rule—requiring an unequivocal commitment, like purchasing a plane ticket—would allow internet predators to look for vulnerable targets and escape criminal liability by simply avoiding concrete commitments through circumspection. We do not think that Congress ... intended that result.
>
> Here, we find that a reasonable trier of fact could conclude beyond a reasonable doubt that Howard's conduct approached the line between despicable lawful conduct and criminal attempt—through his sexually explicit conversations, transmission of sexual photographs, and discussion of specific travel details—and crossed it when he instructed the undercover police officer to perform sex acts on and procure birth control for the girls to get them ready for him.

Howard, 766 F.3d at 426.

The court in *Buswell* reversed, writing that in cases where "police officers have orchestrated the scene and no actual victim faces an immediate threat... the defendant must come 'very close' to committing the crime before he can be found guilty of the attempt." *Buswell*, 9 N.E.2d at 282.

Are these two cases consistent with *Lee*? With each other?

People v. Mahboubian

Court of Appeals of New York

543 N.E.2d 34 (1989)

KAYE, JUDGE.

In a case involving a staged theft of Persian antiquities, with the objective of recovering $18.5 million in insurance proceeds, the central issues on appeal are whether joint trial of the two defendants was proper, and whether the acts charged amounted to attempted grand larceny and burglary.

I.

Viewing the evidence in the light most favorable to the People, the proof was sufficient to show that the defendants entered into a conspiracy to stage a burglary of defendant Houshang Mahboubian's collection of gold and silver Persian antiquities.

Three art experts testified for the People that several pieces in the collection were of dubious authenticity, and indeed almost certainly modern forgeries. From the testimony of other witnesses, the jury could have concluded that Mahboubian became aware of this before the burglaries, and had been unsuccessful in his efforts to sell the collection.

In the summer of 1985, Mahboubian insured the collection with Lloyd's of London for $18.5 million, covering it while in transit for a 12-month period. The stated purpose for the insurance was to allow Mahboubian to ship the collection to the United States, where it would be offered for sale. In October, Mahboubian traveled to New York where he rented a vault at Morgan Brothers Manhattan Storage, a long-term storage facility. According to the assistant warehouse manager, co-defendant Nedjatollah Sakhai accompanied him to Morgan Brothers. A month later, the day after he returned from a trip to London, Sakhai, too, rented a vault at Morgan Brothers, attempting unsuccessfully to get space on the same floor as Mahboubian's vault.

In early December 1985, Sakhai contacted Abe Garabedian, who in turn spoke to several men experienced in robberies and burglaries of art storage facilities. Garabedian told them that Sakhai had "an insurance job" for them. Unbeknownst to the others, one of the men—Daniel Cardebat—had agreed to act as a police informant, and secretly recorded all of their conversations with Sakhai.

When Cardebat and the others first arrived at Sakhai's New York City antiques store to discuss the job, Sakhai was speaking in Farsi on the telephone to someone in London named Houshang about a "job" that "they will do." Telephone company records established that Sakhai placed a call to Mahboubian's London gallery at that time. After hanging up, Sakhai explained to them that the job involved stealing a number of crates that would be flown from Switzerland to New York City and that he was leaving that night to "finalize everything with the guy." They accepted his offer of $100,000 for the theft. Three days later, Sakhai flew to England.

A few weeks later, Mahboubian came to New York City and made arrangements for his collection to be handled upon arrival by W.R. Keating Company—a customs brokerage firm—and then stored at Regency Worldwide Packing, a secure art packing and customs warehouse, where customs inspection and clearance would be conducted. Mahboubian was given a full tour of the Regency, during which he was told that his shipment would not be stored in the open warehouse, but would be placed inside a special steel-vaulted room. While Mahboubian was in New York, telephone calls were made between his number and Sakhai's. In addition, right before Mahboubian's tour of the Regency warehouse, Sakhai met with Cardebat and Daniel Kohl, another of the hired thieves, and informed them that the shipment would be taken from Swissair to Regency for customs clearance, and then to Morgan Manhattan. During the meeting, Cardebat recorded another telephone conversation in Farsi in which Sakhai requested "the specifications from there." After hanging up, Sakhai told the others that the caller was "him" and that "he" was "going right now" to "find out where they're gonna be at the Regency."

Mahboubian then flew to Switzerland and visited the warehouse where his collection was stored. While there, in an unusual procedure, he marked his initials in red on the shipping crates in which it was packed; Sakhai had earlier told Cardebat and the others that that would be done. The crates were shipped to New York on December 24, 1985 and transferred to Regency the next day. Within 24 hours, two more telephone calls were made from Sakhai's house to Mahboubian's number, and Sakhai had met with Cardebat and the others to inform them that the marked boxes were at the Regency. There was an unresolved discussion concerning whether the theft would take place at the Regency or later at Morgan Manhattan. Sakhai drew the others a diagram showing where the collection would be stored at Morgan Manhattan in Mahboubian's seventh floor vault, and told them he had a key but preferred not to use it. The goods were cleared by customs the next day.

Sakhai met with the thieves again at the beginning of January. This time, he insisted that the burglary take place at the Regency, immediately. He also told them that it would ruin the entire plan even if one item went on the market, and that he had given his "word of honor that the whole thing is going to be returned to him." Sakhai showed the men a diagram of the Regency's warehouse floor, indicating that Mahboubian's crates were stored in the inner steel-vaulted room where Mahboubian had been told they would be placed when he toured the facility.

Two nights later, the burglary took place. Cardebat and his accomplice knocked down a retaining wall to gain entry. Inside, Cardebat found the room Sakhai had pointed out on his diagram and broke down its steel doors, but could not locate the boxes. He found them a few seconds later right outside the vault; Regency personnel had never in fact put the boxes inside the vault. Cardebat passed the boxes out of the warehouse to his colleagues, and the men began to remove the pieces from them. At that point, they were arrested by members of the Manhattan Robbery Task Force, who had been alerted by Cardebat and had observed the theft from the beginning. Cardebat telephoned Sakhai from the precinct on the pretext of arranging for delivery of the stolen goods, and agreed to meet him at La Guardia Airport. Sakhai was arrested on his way there. Mahboubian was not charged with participation in the crime until several months later, after he had been interviewed by an Assistant District Attorney and allegedly made a number of significant misrepresentations about his arrangements to ship and store his collection.

This evidence in our view was sufficient for the jury to find that both defendants had conspired, as charged, to stage a burglary and fraudulent theft in order to collect the insurance proceeds covering Mahboubian's collection. We therefore reject defendants' claims that their convictions for burglary, attempted grand larceny and conspiracy must be reversed for insufficiency and the indictment dismissed.

...

IV.

Wholly apart from the question of severance, both defendants contend that even if the People proved all of the allegations of the indictment, the acts they were charged with committing did not amount to an attempt to commit grand larceny or to a burglary.

With respect to the attempted grand larceny charge, defendants claim that the scheme to steal the proceeds of Mahboubian's insurance policy from Lloyd's not only was aborted short of fruition but also had not yet advanced to the point where, legally, their actions constituted an attempt. We disagree.

The substantive crime of attempt is a relatively recent development of the common law. The modern doctrine is said to date from Lord Mansfield's decision in the case of *Rex v. Scofield* (Cald 397) in 1784, and to have fully emerged in *Rex v. Higgins* (2 East 5), where, citing *Scofield*, the court said "[A]ll such acts or attempts as tend to the prejudice of the community, are indictable." As many commentators have noted, imposition of punishment for an attempt poses difficult questions for a criminal jurisprudence in which a basic premise is that bad thoughts alone do not constitute a crime. What justification, then, is there for punishing an attempt, when by definition the contemplated crime is not consummated?

Commonly given answers are that persons who engage in attempts to commit a crime are as dangerous as those who succeed, and it would be unjust to punish only the latter; that law enforcement agencies should be encouraged to act before a crime is actually committed; and that criminal attempts are in and of themselves substantively harmful to society. Nonetheless, the right to think bad thoughts undeterred or unpunished by the criminal law has been protected by the requirement that in order to be punishable as an attempt, conduct must have passed the stage of mere intent or mere preparation to commit a crime.

Defendants contend that under the law of New York demarcating the boundary where preparation ripens into punishable attempt, their conduct had not gone far enough to subject them to liability for an attempt to commit grand larceny, for they had not yet reported any loss to Lloyd's or filed an insurance claim when police intervention put an abrupt end to their scheme. According to defendants, their acts, including the forced entry into Regency and the removal of Mahboubian's collection, must be characterized as mere preparation for the larceny, and while perhaps punishable in themselves, may not be punished as an attempt to commit a crime that would not be complete until they had taken additional steps. In essence, the argument made by defendants is that their actions failed to reach the level of an attempt in two related respects, either compelling reversal: (1) several steps, requiring time, remained to be taken; and (2) defendants could still have changed their minds and abandoned the scheme after the warehouse break-in. The cases do not support defendants' contention.

The definition of a criminal attempt is found in Penal Law § 110.00: "A person is guilty of an attempt to commit a crime when, with intent to commit a crime, he engages in conduct which tends to effect the commission of such crime." On its face, the statute would appear applicable to defendants' conduct, but we made clear that the revised Penal Law definition was not intended to eliminate the preexisting requirement that an attempt come "'very near to the accomplishment of the intended crime'" before liability could be imposed. Thus, the precise issue presented is whether defendants' conduct came "very near" or "dangerously near" completion of the larceny, as that requirement has been interpreted. As is apparent, the boundary where preparation ripens into punishable conduct depends greatly on the facts of the particular case.

To be sure, the strictest possible approach to defining an attempt would be to require that the defendants have engaged in the last proximate act necessary to accomplish the intended crime. It is settled, however, that the defendants' act "need not be 'the final one towards the completion of the offense.' "

The necessity of further steps for completion of the crime and the possibility of abandonment or renunciation are factors to be considered in evaluating whether conduct has come "dangerously close" to success, but are not dispositive. Those factors do not call for reversal in this case.

Where the boundary line between preparation and attempt should be placed differs with different crimes. Here, it is significant that defendants' conduct went far beyond mere discussion of a crime, and beyond agreement to commit a crime, and even beyond arming themselves in preparation for a crime. Defendants hired professional burglars, provided them with tools, and caused them to break into a warehouse and steal property in the dead of night. These acts encompassed the most hazardous and difficult portion of their criminal scheme. What remained to be done was reporting of the supposed theft to the insurer.

Defendants' conduct had plainly "pass[ed] that point where most men, holding such an intention as defendant holds, would think better of their conduct and desist." Defendants' actions in causing the nighttime break-in were potentially and immediately dangerous—a factor we weigh in considering whether they were "dangerously close" to the completed crime. Their activities had reached the point where police intervention was called for, lest the burglars escape or the collection disappear. Most important, defendants' acts "had gone to the extent of placing it in their power to commit the offense unless interrupted."

We need not (and do not) adopt the Model Penal Code's definition of an attempt as a "substantial step" toward completion of the crime (*see* ALI Model Penal Code § 5.01) in order to conclude that some acts—even if preparatory in a dictionary sense—go sufficiently beyond "mere preparation" as to be properly characterized as an attempt for which criminal liability may be imposed.

Perhaps the real source of our disagreement with the dissent lies in the fact that defendants had planned a complex crime that necessarily had to proceed in several stages removed in time and space from one another. Thus, the fact pattern here is rather different from more typical attempts, where the would-be robber or burglar is apprehended on the premises, tools of the trade in hand. Simpler crimes proceed directly from preparation to completion, but defendants' scheme by its very nature involved a longer route.

Nevertheless, the principle remains the same: had defendants' acts reached the stage where they were very near or dangerously near completion of the larceny? Unlike a burglar or robber on the premises, defendants may not have been physically within striking distance of success, yet in all but the most literal sense, they were. The steps they had already taken were more than substantial: they had secured insurance, arranged for shipment of the goods from Europe and storage in a particular New York City warehouse, and hired thieves who actually broke in and removed the goods. These steps took defendants to the point where only a few comparatively minor acts—all wholly within defendants' own power—remained to be accomplished.

In the circumstances of this crime and this case, we therefore conclude that defendants' conduct went sufficiently beyond mere preparation and, as the jury found, constituted attempted grand larceny.

TITONE, JUDGE (concurring in part and dissenting in part).

I would go further and hold that the facts presented were not legally sufficient to establish the crime of attempted grand larceny. In my view, upholding an attempt prosecution on these facts requires a drastic departure from our prior case law and, in effect, makes our State's law virtually indistinguishable from the law of those jurisdictions that have adopted the Model Penal Code.

I. The Legal Standard

To establish an attempt, the prosecution must prove both the requisite intent to commit a specific object crime and an act "which tends to effect the commission of such crime" (Penal Law § 110.00). The standard for determining whether a particular act rose to the level of an attempt is well settled. "The act need not be 'the final one towards the completion of the offense' ... but it must 'carry the project forward within dangerous proximity to the criminal end to be attained.'" The requirement of "dangerous proximity" means that "[t]he act or acts must come or advance *very near* to the accomplishment of the intended crime."

In contrast, the drafters of the Model Penal Code have formulated the standard for attempts in terms of taking a "substantial step" toward the completion of the crime. Their purpose in doing so was to "shift the emphasis from what remains to be done—the chief concern of the proximity tests—to what the actor has *already done*" (ALI Model Penal Code § 5.01, Tent. Draft No. 10, comments, at 47). The underlying goal was to "broaden the scope of attempt liability" by permitting prosecution where "the steps already undertaken are substantial," notwithstanding that "major steps must be taken before the crime can be completed." However, as we have very recently reaffirmed, New York has not adopted the Model Penal Code drafters' approach, but has instead elected to adhere to the proximity analysis. Thus, the focus on the actor's proximity to the completion of the object crime is not merely archaic verbiage. To the contrary, it represents the current state of the law in New York.

Although, as the majority notes, the proper application of the proximity analysis is very much dependent on the facts of the particular case and the manner in which the intended crime is to be carried out, some general principles may be discerned. The cases have repeatedly stated, for example, that "dangerous proximity to the criminal end" exists when the defendant's acts have set in motion a chain of events that are likely to lead to the completion of the crime unless some external force intervenes. Other factors that have been considered are the temporal and geographic proximity between the act and the object crime, the existence of "several contingencies" standing between the act and the object crime and the remoteness or immediacy of the act in relation to that crime. Finally, the courts have often relied on the distinction between acts of "mere preparation" and those tending to effect commission of the crime. The concept of "mere preparation" has been persuasively defined by other courts as "the devising or arranging the means or measures necessary for the commission of the offense." Moreover, our own court has indicated that to be guilty of an attempt, the accused must have both acquired the wherewithal to commit the object crime and made some direct movement toward the ultimate object. Absent the latter step, the accused is guilty of no more than "mere preparation."

II. Analysis

As is evident from the foregoing, the set of facts presented here is unlike any other in which a conviction for attempt has been upheld. Defendants Mahboubian and Sakhai were charged with attempting to commit larceny by obtaining insurance proceeds under false pretenses. The act which formed the basis for this charge was the abortive staged theft of Mahboubian's collection from the Regency warehouse. However, this act constituted no more than "mere preparation" analogous to the gathering of equipment for a burglary or the obtaining of weapons for the effectuation of a planned robbery. In other words, by staging the warehouse break-in and theft, defendants were, in effect, merely laying the foundation for the crime they planned ultimately to commit: defrauding Lloyd's of London. They had not yet taken "a step in the direct movement towards th[at] crime," as the case law requires. Further, the "dangerous proximity" test is unsatisfied because (1) the act on which the People relied, the warehouse break-in, was remote, both in time and place, from the ultimate goal; (2) there remained "several contingencies" standing between the act and the effectuation of the crime; (3) even after the break-in, defendants still had complete freedom of action and could therefore have easily changed their minds before taking the next step toward their goal; and (4) the act was simply not "such as would naturally effect th[e intended] result [i.e., the wrongful obtaining of insurance money], unless prevented by some extraneous cause."

The majority's contrary conclusion seems to ignore these factors, particularly the last. Although the majority stresses, quite correctly, that the last act before interruption need not be the final step toward completion of the crime, the majority fails to address that the last act before interruption here, the break-in, did not even begin to set in motion the chain of events that would inevitably have led to defendants' fraudulent acquisition of the insurance proceeds if law enforcement authorities had not intervened. To the contrary, far more was required, including the safe disposition of the purportedly stolen goods, the collection of documents to establish the ownership and value of those goods, the filing of a loss claim with the insurance company and, finally, the successful avoidance of detection through the investigation that the insurer would unquestionably have undertaken. Hence, notwithstanding the majority's assertion to the contrary, defendants' acts had not "'gone to the extent of placing it in their power to commit the offense unless interrupted,'" except in the sense that *any* step taken in the direction of their goal would have increased the likelihood of its accomplishment.

Finally, the weight that the majority places on the fact that defendants' "activities had reached the point where police intervention was called for, lest the burglars escape or the collection disappear" is puzzling. While that observation would undoubtedly be helpful if the defendants had been charged with attempted theft of the art collection, its relevance in this context, where the ultimate object of the charged attempt crime was the theft of insurance proceeds through fraud, is difficult to discern.

In sum, by upholding an attempt prosecution in these circumstances, the court has significantly diluted the well-established requirements for proving an act rising to the level of an attempt. Moreover, by blurring the important distinction between a "substantial step" toward the completion of the object crime and an act "tend[ing] to effect commission of such crime" (Penal Law § 110.00), the court has brought the law of New York a giant step closer to the less stringent analysis adopted in the Model Penal Code, an analysis which our Legislature has deliberately rejected.

For all of these reasons, I cannot join in the majority's decision to permit a retrial on the attempted grand larceny counts. Accordingly, I dissent on this aspect of the majority's holding.

Comments and Questions

(1) Do the judges disagree on the test to be used, or simply on how to apply the test? How would you describe the "dangerously close" test as applied by the majority?

(2) The Model Penal Code defines a substantial step as conduct that "strongly" corroborates the actor's criminal purpose. The Code provides a non-exclusive list of examples of conduct that may constitute such a step. That list includes lying in wait, reconnoitering, unlawful entry, possession of tools, and soliciting an agent. *See* Model Penal Code § 5.01 (2). The courts have struggled in applying the substantial step standard. The court in *United States v. Sanchez*, 615 F.3d 836, 844 (7th Cir. 2010), made a valiant effort to provide guidance:

> A substantial step is "'some overt act adapted to, approximating, and which in the ordinary and likely course of things will result in, the commission of the particular crime.'" "[It is an act] strongly corroborative of the firmness of the defendant's criminal intent." It is "something more than mere preparation, but less than the last act necessary before the actual commission of the substantive crime." The line between mere preparation and a substantial step is inherently fact specific; conduct that would appear to be mere preparation in one case might qualify as a substantial step in another.
>
> Although there is no easy way to separate mere preparation from a substantial step, we are guided by two general principles. First, a substantial step must

> be "something that makes it reasonably clear that had [the defendant] not been interrupted or made a mistake ... [he] would have completed the crime." "To determine whether conduct is preparation or an attempt, a court must assess how probable it would have been that the crime would have been committed—at least as perceived by the defendant—had intervening circumstances not occurred." Second, we have said that the focus is on the actions already taken to complete the underlying crime, *not* on the acts that remain uncompleted at the time of the arrest.

(3) One court has characterized the federal standard (the Model Penal Code's substantial step test) as "considerably more liberal in establishing an attempt." *People v. Acosta*, 578 N.Y.S.2d 525, 526 (N.Y. Sup. Ct. 1991). Do you agree with this characterization? As the dissent in *Mahboubian* points out, the substantial step test focuses on what the defendant has done, whereas the common law tests tend to evaluate what remains to be done in order to commit the target offense. How is the MPC approach "more liberal in establishing an attempt"? Which approach to the crime of attempt do you prefer?

(4) Did the defendants in *Mahboubian* engage in a "direct act" as described in *Minshew v. State*, 594 So. 2d 703, 709 (Ala. Crim. App. 1991)?

> An "overt act," as an element in an attempt to commit a crime, must be something done that "directly moves towards the crime, and brings the accused nearer to its commission than mere acts of preparation or planning." Remote preparatory acts not reasonably in the chain of causation do not make out a case of attempt.
>
> The federal courts use the Model Penal Code "substantial step" test in defining an overt act.... In Alabama and other jurisdictions, the standard for the necessary overt act has been variously phrased as a "direct ineffective act done towards [the] commission [of the crime]" [or] "some appreciable fragment of the crime ... in such progress that it would be consummated unless interrupted by circumstances independent of the will of the attempter...."

(5) As *Mahboubian* indicates, courts can apply, for example, a dangerously close test so that it seems more like the substantial step test. The converse also occurs.

The government in *United States v. Joyce*, 693 F.2d 838 (8th Cir. 1982), was conducting a "reverse sting operation." A government agent informed the defendant that if he were to come to Missouri the agent would sell him cocaine. The defendant flew from Oklahoma City to St. Louis with over $20,000 in cash. At the assigned meeting place the defendant told the agent that he would only show the agent the cash after the agent showed the cocaine. The two argued and then the defendant walked out of the meeting in anger. The government contended that the defendant's conduct was sufficient to support a conviction for attempting to possess cocaine. The court disagreed:

> Here it is undisputed that Joyce, despite having both the opportunity and ability to purchase the cocaine at the agreed upon price, unambiguously re-

> fused either to produce his money or to purchase the cocaine. This effectively negated the government's effort to consummate the sale.

Id. at 842.

(6) In *State v. Dale*, 590 P.2d 1379, 1380 (Ariz. 1979), the defendants approached the victim and asked him for help in starting their car. The victim accompanied them to a distant parking lot where one of them said, "All we want is that wallet in your back pocket. If I hit you, I'll kill you." The victim then ran away and found the police who arrested the defendants. The defendants' conviction for attempted robbery was affirmed. What result under the substantial step test? Under the "dangerously close" test?

(7) As explained in *United States v. Williams*, 136 F.3d 547, 552 (8th Cir. 1998), "A substantial step is conduct such that if it had not been extraneously interrupted would have resulted in a crime." Is this a correct distillation of the substantial step test? Even in jurisdictions that have adopted the substantial step test, courts sometimes describe it in terms of one of the common law tests.

(8) The facts in two prison escape cases are quite similar. In *State v. Charbonneau*, 374 A.2d 321 (Me. 1977), the defendant was in an unauthorized spot in the prison, a "dummy" was in his cell, and a rope ladder was found close to where the defendant was hiding. Conviction of attempted escape affirmed. In *Commonwealth v. Skipper*, 294 A.2d 780 (Pa. Super. Ct. 1972), the evidence showed that the defendant had arranged for hacksaw blades to be smuggled into the prison. The officials found the blades and a file in his cell. Conviction reversed. Are these two cases consistent? If not, which is correct? Does the outcome depend on which test is used?

(9) Could the accused be convicted of attempted murder on proof that he bit and spit at someone else? Would the result change if the accused tested positive for Human Immunodeficiency Virus (H.I.V.)? What of the fact that "contact with saliva ... has never been shown to result in transmission of H.I.V."? http://www.cdc.gov/hiv/basics/transmission.html. In *State v. Smith*, 621 A.2d 493 (N.J. Super. Ct. App. Div. 1993), the court upheld a conviction for attempted murder stating that the key focus was on the steps taken, as intended by the individual. The court in *State v. Haines*, 545 N.E.2d 834, 839–41 (Ind. Ct. App. 1989), emphasized the same point.

> The State was not required to prove that Haines' conduct could actually have killed. It was only necessary for the State to show that Haines did all that he believed necessary to bring about an intended result, regardless of what was actually possible. Haines repeatedly announced that he had AIDS and desired to infect and kill others. At the hospital, Haines was expressly told by doctors that biting, spitting, and throwing blood was endangering others.... In addition to Haines' belief that he could infect others, there was testimony by physicians that the virus may be transmitted through the exchange of bodily fluids.... From the evidence in the record before us we can only conclude that Haines had knowledge of his disease and that he unrelentingly and unequivocally sought to kill the persons helping him by infecting them with AIDS, and that he took a substantial step towards killing them by his conduct

> believing that he could do so, all of which was more than a mere tenuous, theoretical, or speculative "chance" of transmitting the disease.

For a discussion of the issue as it relates to the broad state of mind question, see §2.02, *supra*; as to the claim of impossibility, see §6.02[E], *infra*.

(10) *Solicitation or Attempt?* Most courts hold that a mere solicitation cannot amount to a substantial step or be "dangerously close" to completing the crime and thus does not constitute an attempt. In one case, the court used a third test. The defendant had researched the underworld of professional killers, contracted with a supposed assassin to kill his sister, paid a down payment of $5000, and gave necessary information to the killer. When asked by the police officer acting as a hired killer if he was sure, Decker replied, "I am absolutely, positively 100 per cent sure ... I've never been so sure of anything in my entire life." Is this a solicitation or an attempt?

The court upheld an attempt conviction, relying on the "slight acts test." That test was appropriate because the defendant's intention to have his sister killed was proven by uncontradicted evidence. "Whenever the design of a person to commit crime is clearly shown, slight acts in furtherance of the design will constitute an attempt." The dissent argued that the defendant had not made a "direct movement toward consummation," as required by the state's standard. *People v. Superior Court (Decker)*, 157 P.3d 1017 (Cal. 2007). What result under the "dangerously close" or "substantial step" test? Does the slight acts test improperly conflate the *mens rea* and *actus reus* of an attempt? Do all attempt convictions do this to some degree?

In *United States v. Church*, 32 M.J. 70 (C.M.A. 1991), *cert. denied*, 501 U.S. 1231 (1991), the Court of Military Appeals stated the basic proposition but went on to hold that an attempt conviction was appropriate where there was a solicitation, plus payment, plus substantial planning, plus the provision of information to carry out the crime, and finally the ultimate approval for the "go ahead" on the crime. But see *State v. O'Neil*, 782 A.2d 209 (Conn. App. Ct. 2001), where the attempt conviction was reversed. The defendant sent a secret message from jail for the assailant to kill a witness. Finding that this was merely the first step in the unlawful process, the court held the action was a solicitation, not an attempt.

On similar facts regarding soliciting another to commit a crime, a New York court upheld a conviction for attempted arson, stating that the evidence met the state's standard that an attempt exists when the defendant comes "dangerously close" to the target offense. *People v. Sabo*, 687 N.Y.S.2d 513 (N.Y. Sup. Ct. 1998).

People v. Brown

Appellate Court of Illinois
394 N.E.2d 63 (1979)

STENGEL, JUSTICE.

Following a jury trial in the Circuit Court of Hancock County, defendant was convicted of attempted theft [of] under $150. He was sentenced to a two-year term of probation, with 30 days in jail, and fined $1,000. On appeal, defendant contends his conviction must be reversed because the State failed to prove he did an act constituting a substantial step toward the commission of the theft. We agree and reverse.

Taken in a light most favorable to the State, the evidence indicated that in the late evening hours of July 7, 1977, defendant, Leland Williamson and Randy Gossage left Williamson's home in Augusta and drove to Carthage, where they parked near the town square. During the ride defendant mentioned "finding some pop bottles" and upon their arrival in Carthage, the three men walked through an alley behind a supermarket where there was an enclosure containing such bottles. The topless fiberglass enclosure was eight feet wide, ten feet long and ten feet tall. Defendant jumped onto one side of the enclosure, observed its contents, and told his companions there were a lot of pop bottles inside it. Gossage, at defendant's suggestion, also climbed onto the enclosure and observed its contents.

The men then walked away from the pop bottle enclosure and subsequently met Brad Boyer, a prior acquaintance of defendant. The four men sat on a nearby curb and talked for about a half hour until defendant asked Boyer if he wanted to get the pop bottles. Boyer responded affirmatively and he, defendant, and Gossage returned to the enclosure while Williamson remained sleeping on the curb. While near the enclosure defendant asked Gossage to jump onto it and pass cases of bottles out to him. Gossage refused to do so, telling defendant to "forget it." Defendant made the same request of Williamson when he rejoined the men near the enclosure, but Williamson also declined.

All four men were walking away from the enclosure when they noticed a van pulling into the alley. Williamson continued walking toward defendant's auto, which was parked about a block away, but Gossage and defendant began to run. The van was driven by Deputy City Marshall Ed O'Neil, who pursued the fleeing men. Defendant and Gossage stopped and were arrested after O'Neil yelled "stop or I'll shoot." O'Neil said the men were about 27 feet away from the enclosure when he first observed them.

To convict a defendant of attempt, the State must prove two elements beyond a reasonable doubt: (1) that the defendant intended to commit a specific offense; and (2) that the defendant took a "substantial step" toward committing that offense. In the instant case defendant concedes there was sufficient evidence to establish his intent to commit the offense of theft, but claims the evidence was insufficient to prove that he took a substantial step toward the commission of that theft.

Determining what constitutes a "substantial step" under our attempt statute has been one of the most troublesome problems of our criminal law. On the one hand, it is clear that mere preparation to commit a criminal offense does not constitute a "substantial step" for purposes of the attempt statute. On the other hand, it is equally clear that to constitute an attempt it is not necessary to prove that the defendant performed the last deed immediately preceding that which would render the substantive crime complete. Each attempt case must be decided on its own unique facts, and the essential question which must be answered is whether, given the intent to commit a specific offense, the defendant performed acts bringing him in "dangerous proximity to success in carrying out his intent."

The facts of the instant case do not indicate that defendant Brown was within "dangerous proximity" of successfully carrying out his intended theft. There is no evidence that defendant actually attempted to remove any of the pop bottles from the enclosure. Defendant did climb on the enclosure and observe its contents and did solicit his friends to aid him in removing the pop bottles therein. But, these acts do not constitute a "substantial step" toward the commission of the theft.

In *People v. Ray*, (3d Dist. 1972), 3 Ill. App. 3d 517, 278 N.E.2d 170, we considered a case where the defendant was found in an alley behind a photography studio wearing gloves and carrying a pry bar and a flashlight. Gouge marks were found on the windows of the studio, but scientific evidence failed to establish that the gouge marks were made by defendant's pry bar. We held that these facts were insufficient to prove defendant had attempted to burglarize the studio. Similarly, in *People v. Peters*, (2d Dist. 1977), 55 Ill. App. 3d 226, 13 Ill. Dec. 461, 371 N.E.2d 156, the court reversed the defendant's conviction for attempt burglary, despite the fact defendants were apprehended at 2:30 a.m. on the roof of a tavern they apparently intended to burglarize. The court found the evidence insufficient to prove that defendants had taken a "substantial step" toward entry of the tavern.

Based on *Ray* and *Peters*, we do not believe the evidence was sufficient to prove that defendant in this case took the requisite step toward carrying out his intended theft. Defendant Brown was in a suspicious place at a suspicious hour with an improper intent. But mere presence at an inappropriate place is not sufficient to prove an attempt, even if it is established that defendant had a criminal intent at the time. To prove a defendant guilty of attempt, the State must prove that a defendant made a direct movement toward the commission of his intended crime after preparations for the commission of that crime were complete.

The State relies primarily on *People v. Burleson*, (4th Dist. 1977), 50 Ill. App. 3d 629, 8 Ill. Dec. 776, 365 N.E.2d 1162, but that case is distinguishable from the case at bar. In *Burleson* the defendants had previously "cased" and made a "practice run" of their approach to and escape from the bank they intended to rob. The defendants were arrested and convicted of attempted armed robbery when they approached the bank a second time with the intent to commit the robbery. The appellate court affirmed the defendant's attempt convictions. The State contends the instant case is analogous to *Burleson*, with defendant Brown being guilty of attempt when he returned to the pop bottle enclosure a second time after first observing or "casing" its contents. However, the basis of the court's decision in *Burleson* was not the mere fact that the defendants approached the bank a second time, but rather, the fact the defendants approached the bank *with* nylon disguises on and shotgun and suitcase in hand. The crux of the *Burleson* decision was the fact the defendants were at the site of their intended robbery with the tools necessary to carry out that robbery. The defendants in *Burleson* were dangerously close to carrying out their intended criminal objective.

Defendant in the instant case, on the other hand, although near the site of his intended theft, did not have the tools or assistance necessary to carry out that theft. The enclosure from which defendant intended to take the pop bottles was ten feet tall. Thus, it would have been impossible for defendant to remove the bottles from the enclosure without help from his companions, which was refused, or without a ladder, which he did not have. Also significant in this regard are the facts that defendant's car was parked a block away from the enclosure and that defendant and his companions were more than 20 feet away from the enclosure when observed by Officer O'Neil. Defendant was not in "dangerous proximity" of carrying out his intended theft for he had neither the tools nor the assistance necessary to do so. The evidence was insufficient to justify defendant's attempt conviction.

Comments and Questions

(1) Did the court properly apply the statutory substantial step test? Does it matter if Brown was within "dangerous proximity" of stealing the goods? The state's reliance on the *Burleson* case was quickly rejected by the court. Is that case so easily distinguished? What result in *Brown* if the defendant had made a third trip to the enclosure? Here are the arguments made by counsel in *Brown*. Brief and Argument for Defendant—Appellant at 14–15:

> In the instant case, the last physical act performed by the defendant was his climbing upon the enclosure for the purpose of viewing its contents. Thus the question at bar is whether this act of the defendant is a substantial step in *direct movement* toward the commission of a theft *after* the preparations were made. In making this determination one must look beyond the mere physical act of defendant to the limited purpose behind the act. It is clear from the facts that defendant's sole purpose in climbing the enclosure was to determine whether the enclosure contained pop bottles. This determination was a necessary prerequisite to the fulfillment of defendant's desire to take pop bottles.
>
> However, the defendant's preparations were not complete once he observed the contents of the enclosure. Since the enclosure was ten (10) feet tall it would have been impossible for the defendant to remove the bottles without any assistance. Therefore it was incumbent that the defendant enlist the aid of his friends in removing the bottles. Without their aid defendant was stymied from taking any action in direct movement toward the commission of a theft. Furthermore, it must be noted that the defendant's car was parked a block away from the enclosure. If the defendant were to take a significant number of bottles it would first be necessary for him to first bring his car within the vicinity of the enclosure. Based on these facts it is clear that all of the preparations for the offense had not been completed and that the defendant's act of climbing onto the enclosure was merely a step in preparation for the offense.

Brief and Argument for Plaintiff—Appellee at 8–9:

> The defendant's activities had gone beyond mere preparation to commit a theft. He had informed the others of his intent to procure pop bottles several

times that evening. He had driven to Carthage, a town in which he had lived for nineteen years. While there, he had directed the group down an alley behind one of the two grocery stores known to the defendant in that town. There he observed an enclosure and ascertained that it contained numerous pop bottles. At that point preparation to commit theft was completed. After leaving the alley and some discussion, the defendant, Boyer, and Gossage reentered the alley and returned to the enclosure. That return to the enclosure with the specific intent to commit a theft, after all preparation had been completed, constitutes a substantial step towards the commission of a theft.

(2) Consider the following facts:

> The key testimony against appellant, Mercer, came from Henson, an employee of a gasoline station. Henson testified that Mercer had been a customer at the gasoline service station for some months. On several occasions prior to September 21, 1975, Mercer had discussed with him the operation of the gas station, including the handling of the money and the shift transition in the morning. Mercer also learned that the manager had the only key to the safe. On the night of September 21, 1975, Mercer stopped in the station and talked to Henson. He sought to enlist Henson's help in robbing the station the following day. Henson refused, and Mercer left, but not before telling Henson: he was going to rob the station about 8:30 the next morning; he would have a machine gun; and he would shoot anyone who got in his way. Right on time the next day Mercer and another man drove into the station at 8:30 a.m. Mercer asked if the manager was there. Henson replied that he was not, and Mercer advised Henson he and his companion would return at 9:30 a.m.
>
> Although Mercer had mentioned the possibility of robbing the station before September 21, 1975, Henson had not taken him seriously. However, after Mercer departed at 8:30 on September 21st, Henson called the manager of the station and advised him of the threatened robbery and the manager notified the police. Shortly thereafter a deputy sheriff arrived at the station and interviewed Henson. During the interview, the deputy saw Mercer's car cruise by the station. The deputy pursued the car and stopped it several miles away where a frisk of the occupants revealed two live shotgun shells in Mercer's pocket. A search of the car revealed a sawed off shotgun and a shaving kit that contained gloves, binoculars, shoelaces, a rubber band, a knife, and a woman's stocking which was knotted on the end.

Mercer v. State, 347 So. 2d 733, 734 (Fla. Dist. Ct. App. 1977). Are the facts here closer to *Burleson* or *Brown*?

(3) In *United States v. Harper*, 33 F.3d 1143 (9th Cir. 1994), the defendants left money in an ATM causing a "bill trap" which would result in service people coming to the ATM and opening it up, presumably so that the defendants could then take money from the machine. Before the service people could arrive, police officers found

the defendants sitting in a rented car in the bank parking lot, near the ATM. The court reversed their attempt conviction (but affirmed their conspiracy conviction), noting that even though they had left money in the ATM which would cause service people to come to the machine, "that act ... is equivocal in itself. The robbery was in the future and ... the defendants never made a move toward the victims or the bank.... They had not taken a step of 'such substantiality that, unless frustrated, the crime would have occurred.'" Did the court correctly apply the substantial step test?

(4) Can a defendant be convicted of attempting to attempt a crime? The problem normally arises in jurisdictions that define assault as an attempted battery (rather than an act that places the victim in apprehension of injury). Do you agree with the following analysis?

> Wharton states that "as an assault is an attempt to commit a battery there can be no attempt to commit an assault."
>
> Since a simple assault is nothing more than attempt to commit a battery, and aggravated assaults are nothing more than attempts to commit murder, rape, or robbery, an attempt to commit an assault, whether simple or aggravated, is not a crime.
>
> Similar expressions can be found elsewhere. In none of these sources is it explained why this conclusion is inevitable. It appears to be assumed that logic permits no other conclusion. But is that so? Thurman Arnold, in an article in 40 Yale L.J. 53, 65 (1930) answers as follows:
>
> ... [It is said that] there can be no attempt at a direct attempt. But the query immediately arises, Why not? We do not punish attempts at ordinary assaults which carry light penalties. But suppose the accused is guilty of conduct tending toward an aggravated assault but which does not seem to require the heavier penalty. The court is confronted with the alternative of either discharging the accused or modifying the penalty to make it more nearly fit his conduct. An easy way to accomplish this is by making attempts at aggravated assaults punishable, and this is frequently done. It is academic to call such cases "wrong" because assault is in the nature of an attempt and hence cannot be attempted, particularly when a common sense result is reached. In short the generalization that there can be no attempt at a crime in the nature of an attempt tells us nothing and tends merely to divert the court's mind from the real issue.
>
> We agree with the foregoing analysis. The mere fact that assault is viewed as preceding a battery should not preclude us from drawing a line on one side of which we require the present ability to inflict corporal injury, denominating this an assault, and on the other side conduct which falls short of a present ability, yet so advanced toward the assault that it is more than mere preparation and which we denominate an attempt.

State v. Wilson, 346 P.2d 115, 121 (Or. 1959).

A Colorado court took the opposite view:

> [A]n assault (is) "[a]n unlawful *attempt* coupled with present ability to commit a violent injury on the person of another." An assault is therefore a particular type of an attempt, as defined by our statute, and accordingly, we have no occasion to determine the common law definition of an assault. What then is a criminal attempt? ... Criminal attempt is defined as follows:
>
> An attempt to commit a crime requires that the person has an intent to perform any act, and to obtain any result which, if accomplished, would constitute such crime, and that he does any act toward the commission of the crime which demonstrates, under the circumstances, that he formed that intent and would commit the crime except for the intervention of another person or some other extraneous factor.
>
> As above defined, the commission of a criminal attempt under our statutes requires the intent to commit a specific crime. Attempting an assault would require a person to *intend to "attempt* ... with present ability to commit a violent injury on the person of another." Perhaps philosophers or metaphysicians can intend to attempt to act, but ordinary people intend to act, not to attempt to act. As stated by one court, nearly one-hundred years ago, "[T]he refinement and metaphysical acumen that can see a tangible idea in the words 'an attempt to attempt to act is too great for practical use. It is like conceiving of the beginning of eternity or the starting point of infinity.' "
>
> As to crimes of this sort it is true as argued by defendant that "there can be no crime of an attempt to commit an attempt."
>
> The argument is made that an attempted assault should be construed to be an assault *without* the element of present ability. We note that in *Wilson* the Oregon court had no statute defining the crime of assault alone. The court went on to uphold the validity of the charge of attempted assault with a deadly weapon on the theory that an assault should be viewed as a "separate substantive crime and not as an attempted battery." Our statute defines an assault in terms of an attempt to injure another, or an attempt to commit a battery. We therefore do not regard this *Wilson* case as persuasive in our analysis of this issue.
>
> When a person is charged with an assault, it is clear that "present ability" must be construed in the light of the particular situation. The policy behind criminal statutes is to safeguard the public from harm from individuals. In construing the criminal assault statute therefore factors such as the gravity of the potential harm and the uncertainty of the result are to be included in appraising the actor's "present ability."

Allen v. People, 485 P.2d 886, 888 (Colo. 1971).

[C] The Completed Offense

When an attempt is successful, the crime of attempt "merges into the completed crime." *United States v. Ahmed*, 94 F.Supp.3d 394, 434 (E.D.N.Y. 2015). A defendant cannot be convicted of both crimes. But what about the converse? Is a conviction for attempt proper when evidence shows that the target offense was successfully completed?

Lightfoot v. State

Court of Appeals of Maryland
360 A.2d 426 (1976)

ELDRIDGE, JUDGE.

The question here is whether a criminal defendant may properly be convicted of *attempted* armed robbery upon evidence clearly establishing a consummated armed robbery.

On January 20, 1972, at approximately 8:30 p.m., Beulah Dorsey, employed as an assistant manager of the Gwynn Oak Fabric Center, a laundromat in Baltimore, Maryland, was working in the laundry room when three men entered. A few minutes later, she advised the men that they could not stay in the store; at this point, one of them questioned her about cleaning his coat. Shortly thereafter one of the men approached her and, according to her testimony, "poked a gun in my stomach and I went towards the cash register. I knew what he wanted." The man told her not to panic or run, to take it easy and give him the money.

Mrs. Dorsey accompanied the man to a back room where she gave him $77.00 from the cash register and desk drawer, together with $13.00 from her own pocketbook. He then placed the money into a bag. During this time one of the two remaining men was standing near the laundromat's security guard and the other was standing with two customers. Both of these men also displayed guns. Mrs. Dorsey, the security guard and the two customers were then herded into a rear bathroom and told to remain there for fifteen minutes.

Three hours later, Police Officer Birch, having heard a report over the police radio of the laundromat robbery, observed three men, one of whom matched the description of a participant in the robbery. After requesting a more detailed description of the alleged perpetrators, as well as additional police assistance, Officer Birch entered a tavern where the men had gone. The officer asked one of the men, who was the petitioner Thomas Lightfoot, to come outside, where he requested identification from him. As Lightfoot responded to the request for identification, the officer noticed a bulge in his pocket. A subsequent search of Lightfoot's person produced an automatic pistol, and he was then placed under arrest.

Lightfoot was subsequently tried before a jury in the Criminal Court of Baltimore on charges of, *inter alia*, robbery with a dangerous and deadly weapon, attempted robbery with a dangerous and deadly weapon, and carrying a concealed weapon. At the trial, Mrs. Dorsey positively identified Lightfoot as one of the three armed robbers, although not the one who held a pistol to her stomach. The security guard identified Lightfoot as being one of the three gunmen but believed that he was the one who had held the gun on Mrs. Dorsey. One of the customers identified Lightfoot as the one who "was standing there and told us to keep quiet and no one would get hurt."

Lightfoot was convicted of attempted robbery with a dangerous and deadly weapon, for which he was sentenced to a term of fifteen years, and of carrying a concealed weapon, for which he received a concurrent term of two years.

Upon appeal to the Court of Special Appeals, one of the grounds for reversal urged by Lightfoot was that "since the State's evidence established a consummated armed robbery, he could not be convicted of attempted armed robbery." The Court of Special Appeals, however, affirmed his conviction, holding in an extensive opinion by Judge Moore that an accused, charged with both a crime and an attempt to commit it, may be acquitted of the crime and yet convicted of the attempt where the evidence establishes that the crime was in fact committed.

We granted Lightfoot's petition for a writ of certiorari in this case, limited to the only question raised in the petition, namely the validity of an attempt conviction upon evidence establishing a consummated crime.

It is often stated that failure to consummate the crime is one of the essential elements of a criminal attempt. If this be so, it logically follows that if the uncontradicted evidence establishes the consummated crime, there can be no conviction for attempt, and the courts of several states have so concluded.

On the other hand, a majority of jurisdictions permit a conviction of attempt upon evidence showing a completed crime.

In *State v. Fox*, 159 N.W.2d at 495, the Supreme Court of Iowa set forth the rationale for permitting an attempt conviction upon evidence establishing the consummated offense:

> In a sense the commission of an offense involves an attempt to commit it. It may not be a degree of the main offense, nor be necessarily included therein, so as to require the court to charge with reference thereto in every case where the commission of an offense is charged. But, as the greater includes the less, it is manifest that in every case where an attempt is charged proof of the actual commission of the offense establishes the attempt. If the offender actually commits the offense, he necessarily attempted to do it, and proof of the commission of the actual offense does not constitute a variance.

The Indiana Supreme Court in *Crump v. State*, 287 N.E.2d at 345, emphasized that:

> It should make no difference whether the criminal conduct is successful or unsuccessful when determining an included offense. The conduct is the same in both cases; the actor's intent is the same in both cases.

And *see United States v. Fleming*, 215 A.2d at 840, 841, where the court, criticizing the authorities which would not permit an attempt conviction based upon evidence of a completed crime, pointed to "the anomalous situation of a defendant going free 'not because he was innocent, but for the very strange reason, that he was too guilty.'" Professor Perkins has set forth an excellent critique of the view that non-consummation of the offense is a necessary element of attempt, pointing to one absurd result if such view were carried to its logical conclusion:

> Much of the discussion and many of the definitions point to failure as of the very essence of a criminal attempt, but there is no factual background for such an approach. In the area of wrongdoing, as in the realm of law-abiding conduct, some attempts fail while many others are successful. Furthermore, nothing in the philosophy of juridical science requires that an attempt must fail in order to receive recognition. A successful attempt to commit a crime will not support two convictions and penalties—one for the attempt and the other for the completed offense. This is for the obvious reason that whatever is deemed the appropriate penalty for the total misconduct can be imposed upon conviction of the offense itself, but this does not require the unsound conclusion that proof of the completed offense disproves the attempt to commit it.... Suppose in ... a trial the uncontradicted evidence shows beyond doubt that defendant attempted to commit the offense charged, but there is conflict in the testimony as to whether the attempt succeeded or failed. Some of the statements on the subject, if carried to their logical conclusion, would entitle the defendant to an instruction which would tell the jury in substance: (1) they must acquit the defendant of the completed offense unless satisfied beyond a reasonable doubt that the attempt was successful; (2) they must acquit the defendant of an attempt to commit the offense unless satisfied beyond a reasonable doubt that the attempt failed. In other words the position would be that defendant is entitled to a verdict of not guilty if there is doubt in regard to success or failure although no doubt that the attempt was made. There is no proper basis for such a position, and probably no court would carry the unsound notion to such an absurd extreme.
>
> Where guilt is clear but there is doubt as to which of two grades or degrees the rule is not that defendant must be acquitted, but that conviction must be of the lower grade or degree. The same rule should apply in regard to an attempt to commit the offense charged. The attempt is a lower grade or degree of the offense because it is a part of it. It is not something separate and distinct.

This Court on two occasions has set forth the elements of an attempt to commit a crime as consisting of "an intent to commit it, the doing of some act towards its commission, *and the failure to consummate its commission.*"

The better view, we believe, is the one adopted by the Court of Special Appeals in the instant case, by the majority of other jurisdictions, and by Professor Perkins, that failure to consummate the crime is not an indispensable element of criminal attempt.

Consequently, where a defendant is charged with both the crime and the attempt to commit it, and where he is acquitted of the crime and convicted of the attempt, the attempt conviction may stand even though the evidence established that the crime was fully consummated.

Comments and Questions

(1) Consider the contrary argument, as summarized by the Court of Special Appeals of Maryland:

> An attempt to commit a crime consists of an intent to commit it, the performance of some act towards its commission and the failure to consummate its commission....
>
> A failure to consummate the crime is as much an essential element of an attempt as the intent and the performance of an overt act towards its commission. Evidence that a crime has been committed will not sustain a verdict on an attempt to commit it because the essential element of interception, or prevention of execution is lacking. Consummation of the crime can take the behavior out of the definition of an "attempt."

Boone v. State, 233 A.2d 476, 495 (Md. Ct. Spec. App. 1967), *abrogation recognized by In re Lakeysha*, 665 A.2d 264 (Md. 1995).

(2) When the target offense includes conduct that is tantamount to attempt, an attempt charge is improper. One example of this standard is found in *Foster v. State*, 875 So. 2d 1253 (Fla. Dist. Ct. App. 2004). A Wal-Mart employee tried to poison a coworker; she was caught when the security video camera recorded her putting what turned out to be rat poison into an opened can of Dr. Pepper that was sitting on the victim's desk. The court reversed the conviction because proof of the attempt would necessarily establish the crime of poisoning, defined as knowingly mingling poison with food or drink with the intent to kill.

In *People v. Lupinos*, 674 N.Y.S.2d 582 (N.Y. City Crim. Ct. 1998), the court considered an attempt to practice the profession of massage. The court held that the broad reach of the statute made it inconceivable that it also authorized prosecutions for attempt. Similarly, a New York court held that there was no such crime as attempted drunk driving because the detailed statutory scheme banned a sweeping breadth of conduct and the legislature had not provided a penalty for that offense. *See People v. Prescott*, 745 N.E.2d 1000 (N.Y. 2001); *see also People v. Jelke*, 135 N.E.2d 213 (N.Y. 1956).

(3) Can a defendant be convicted of attempting a criminal threat? *See People v. Toledo*, 26 P.3d 1051 (Cal. 2001) (yes, where the criminal threat statute requires specific intent to threaten death or bodily injury). Of carrying a concealed weapon without a license? *See People v. Pickett*, 175 N.W.2d 347 (Mich. Ct. App. 1970) (yes). Of attempted possession of burglary tools? *See State v. Thomas*, 362 So. 2d 1348 (Fla. 1978) (no). Of attempted possession of narcotics with intention to distribute? *See United States v. Valencia*, 907 F.2d 671 (7th Cir. 1990) (yes, where the defendant built a storage compartment for the drugs in anticipation of their purchase).

(4) *Sentencing—The Doctrinal View.* If the principal offense had not been completed, what sort of sentence should the defendant receive? The Model Penal Code drafters strongly argued that attempt sentences be generally treated the same as principal offenses. Section 5.05 so provides:

(1) *Grading.* Except as otherwise provided in this Section, attempt [is a crime] of the same grade and degree as the most serious offense which is attempted....

(2) *Mitigation.* If the particular conduct charged to constitute a criminal attempt ... is so inherently unlikely to result or culminate in the commission of a crime that neither such conduct nor the actor presents a public danger warranting the grading of such offense under this Section, the Court shall exercise its power under Section 6.12 to enter judgment and impose sentence for a crime of lower grade or degree or, in extreme cases, may dismiss the prosecution.

(5) *Sentencing—The Majority View.* Most states have not fully followed the lead of the Code and instead impose attempt punishments that are significantly weaker than the completed offense punishments. *See, e.g.*, Cal. Penal Code § 664.

Every person who attempts to commit any crime, but fails, or is prevented or intercepted in its perpetration, shall be punished where no provision is made by law for the punishment of those attempts, as follows:

(a) If the crime attempted is punishable by imprisonment in the state prison, the person guilty of the attempt shall be punished by imprisonment in the state prison for one-half the term of imprisonment prescribed upon a conviction of the offense attempted. However, if the crime attempted is willful, deliberate, and premeditated murder, as defined in Section 189, the person guilty of that attempt shall be punished by imprisonment in the state prison for life with the possibility of parole. If the crime attempted is any other one in which the maximum sentence is life imprisonment or death, the person guilty of the attempt shall be punished by imprisonment in the state prison for five, seven, or nine years. The additional term provided in this section for attempted willful, deliberate, and premeditated murder shall not be imposed unless the fact that the attempted murder was willful, deliberate, and premeditated is charged in the accusatory pleading and admitted or found to be true by the trier of fact.

(b) If the crime attempted is punishable by imprisonment in a county jail, the person guilty of the attempt shall be punished by imprisonment in a county jail for a term not exceeding one-half the term of imprisonment prescribed upon a conviction of the offense attempted.

(c) If the offense so attempted is punishable by a fine, the offender convicted of that attempt shall be punished by a fine not exceeding one-half the largest fine which may be imposed upon a conviction of the offense attempted.

The N.Y. Penal Code, section 110.05, also provides for lower punishment except in certain cases.

An attempt to commit a crime is a:

1. Class A-I felony when the crime attempted is the A-I felony of murder in the first degree, aggravated murder as defined in subdivision one of section

125.26 of this chapter, criminal possession of a controlled substance in the first degree, criminal possession of a chemical or biological weapon in the first degree, or criminal use of a chemical or biological weapon in the first degree;

2. Class A-II felony when the crime attempted is a class A-II felony;

3. Class B felony when the crime attempted is a class A-I felony except as provided in subdivision one hereof;

4. Class C felony when the crime attempted is a class B felony;

5. Class D felony when the crime attempted is a class C felony;

6. Class E felony when the crime attempted is a class D felony;

7. Class A misdemeanor when the crime attempted is a class E felony;

8. Class B misdemeanor when the crime attempted is a misdemeanor.

(6) *See* Kadish, *The Criminal Law and the Luck of the Draw*, 84 J. Crim. L. & Criminology 679, 681–82 (1994):

> Consider the case of a man who stabbed his son in anger, pleaded guilty and was convicted of a crime equivalent for our purposes to attempted murder. After serving several months of a two year sentence he was paroled. However, three months later his son, who had been hospitalized since the attack, took a turn for the worse and died, whereupon the prosecutor, quite within the law, charged the father with murder, a crime punishable with life imprisonment or death.
>
> What did the father do in jail or on parole that merited the greater punishment? Not a thing. If a good constitution or a good surgeon had saved the son, the father could not have been further punished. The occurrence of the resulting death alone raises the crime and the punishment. In most jurisdictions this same principle operates for all crimes, not just homicidal crimes. In California, for example, an attempt to commit a crime is punishable with half the punishment for the completed crime. Thus, the reward for failing, no matter how hard you try to succeed or how close you come, is a lesser punishment.

What accounts for a lower punishment? Is it the moral intuition that if conduct does not cause actual harm it is less blameworthy than the same conduct that does cause harm? Studies indicate that people generally reject the theoretical view that the punishment for attempt should be the same as for the target offense. *See* Robinson & Darley, *Justice, Liability, and Blame: Community Values and the Criminal Law* (1995).

(7) The Florida legislature drafted a rather odd attempt statute that classified attempted third-degree murder of a law enforcement officer as a higher crime (i.e., resulting in greater punishment) than the actual completed offense. Held, such a classification was irrational and unconstitutional. *Iacovone v. State*, 639 So. 2d 1108 (Fla. Dist. Ct. App. 1994). What purpose would such a statute serve?

[D] Abandonment

> Abandonment is a defense if the attempt to commit a crime is freely and voluntarily abandoned before the act is put in process of final execution, if there is no outside cause prompting the abandonment. On the other hand, a voluntary abandonment of an attempt which has proceeded beyond mere preparation will not bar a conviction for the attempt.
>
> We pause to point out that the law, like religion, holds out a promise to those who would commit crime and sin that if they voluntarily resist temptation so as to recant and desist before attempting to carry into effect their evil purpose, they will not be held accountable for mere evil intent.

Bucklew v. State, 206 So. 2d 200, 204 (Miss. 1968).

People v. Staples

Court of Appeal of California, Second Appellate District
6 Cal. App. 3d 61, 85 Cal. Rptr. 589 (1970)

Reppy, Associate Justice.

Defendant was charged in an information with attempted burglary. Trial by jury was waived, and the matter submitted on the testimony contained in the transcript of the preliminary hearing together with exhibits. Defendant was found guilty. Proceedings were suspended before pronouncement of sentence, and an order was made granting defendant probation. The appeal is from the order which is deemed a final judgment.

In October 1967, while his wife was away on a trip, defendant, a mathematician, under an assumed name, rented an office on the second floor of a building in Hollywood which was over the mezzanine of a bank. Directly below the mezzanine was the vault of the bank. Defendant was aware of the layout of the building, specifically of the relation of the office he rented to the bank vault. Defendant paid rent for the period from October 23 to November 23. The landlord had 10 days before commencement of the rental period within which to finish some interior repairs and painting. During this prerental period defendant brought into the office certain equipment. This included drilling tools, two acetylene gas tanks, a blow torch, a blanket, and a linoleum rug. The landlord observed these items when he came in from time to time to see how the repair work was progressing. Defendant learned from a custodian that no one was in the building on Saturdays. On Saturday, October 14, defendant drilled two groups of holes into the floor of the office above the mezzanine room. He stopped drilling before the holes went through the floor. He came back to the office several times thinking he might slowly drill down, covering the holes with the linoleum rug. At some point in time he installed a hasp lock on a closet, and planned to, or did, place his tools in it. However, he left the closet keys on the premises. Around the end of November, apparently after November 23, the landlord notified the police and turned the tools and equipment over to them. Defendant did not pay any more rent. It is not clear when he last entered the office, but it could have been after November 23, and even after the landlord had removed the equipment. On February 22, 1968, the police arrested defendant. After receiving advice as to his constitutional rights, defendant voluntarily made an oral statement which he reduced to writing.

Among other things which defendant wrote down were these:

> Saturday, the 14th ... I drilled some small holes in the floor of the room. Because of tiredness, fear, and the implications of what I was doing, I stopped and went to sleep.
>
> At this point I think my motives began to change. The actual commencement of my plan made me begin to realize that even if I were to succeed a fugitive life of living off of stolen money would not give the enjoyment of the life of a mathematician however humble a job I might have.
>
> I still had not given up my plan however. I felt I had made a certain investment of time, money, effort and a certain psychological commitment to the concept.
>
> I came back several times thinking I might store the tools in the closet and slowly drill down (covering the hole with a rug of linoleum square). As time went on (after two weeks or so), my wife came back and my life as bank robber seemed more and more absurd.

Defendant's position in this appeal is that, as a matter of law, there was insufficient evidence upon which to convict him of a criminal attempt. Defendant claims that his actions were all preparatory in nature and never reached a stage of advancement in relation to the substantive crime which he concededly intended to commit (burglary of the bank vault) so that criminal responsibility might attach.

In order for the prosecution to prove that defendant committed an attempt to burglarize, it was required to establish that he had the specific intent to commit a burglary of the bank and that his acts toward that goal went beyond mere preparation.

The required specific intent was clearly established in the instant case. Defendant admitted in his written confession that he rented the office fully intending to burglarize the bank, that he brought in tools and equipment to accomplish this purpose, and that he began drilling into the floor with the intent of making an entry into the bank.

There was definitely substantial evidence entitling the trial judge to find that defendant's acts had gone beyond the preparation stage. Without specifically deciding where defendant's preparations left off and where his activities became a completed criminal attempt, we can say that his "drilling" activity clearly was an unequivocal and direct step toward the completion of the burglary. It was a fragment of the substantive crime contemplated, i.e., the beginning of the "breaking" element. Further, defendant himself characterized his activity as the *actual commencement of his plan.* The drilling by defendant was obviously one of a series of acts which logic and ordinary experience indicate would result in the proscribed act of burglary.

The instant case provides an out-of-the-ordinary factual situation within the second category. Usually the actors in cases falling within that category of attempts are intercepted or caught in the act. Here, there was no direct proof of any actual interception. But it was clearly inferable by the trial judge that defendant became aware that the landlord had resumed control over the office and had turned defendant's equipment and tools over to the police. This was the equivalent of interception.

The inference of this nonvoluntary character of defendant's abandonment was a proper one for the trial judge to draw. However, it would seem that the character of the abandonment in situations of this type, whether it be voluntary (prompted by pangs of conscience or a change of heart) or nonvoluntary (established by inference in the instant case), is not controlling. The relevant factor is the determination of whether the acts of the perpetrator have reached such a stage of advancement that they can be classified as an attempt. Once that attempt is found there can be no exculpatory abandonment. "One of the purposes of the criminal law is to protect society from those who intend to injure it. When it is established that the defendant intended to commit a specific crime and that in carrying out this intention he committed an act that caused harm or sufficient danger of harm, it is immaterial that for some collateral reason he could not complete the intended crime."

The order is *affirmed.*

Comments and Questions

(1) Ultimately, the court's holding was a narrow one, for the judges concluded that the defendant's abandonment could be viewed as involuntary. Suppose that the abandonment had been clearly voluntary, would the California court allow a defense in that situation? *See United States v. Shelton*, 30 F.3d 702, 706 (6th Cir. 1994):

> We ... hold that withdrawal, abandonment and renunciation, however characterized, do not provide a defense to an attempt crime. As noted, the attempt crime is complete with proof of intent together with acts constituting a substantial step toward commission of the substantive offense. When a defendant withdraws prior to forming the necessary intent or taking a substantial step toward the commission of the offense, the essential elements of the crime cannot be proved. At this point, the question whether a defendant has withdrawn is synonymous with whether he has committed the offense. After a defendant has evidenced the necessary intent and has committed an act constituting a substantial step toward the commission of the offense, he has committed the crime of attempt, and can withdraw only from the commission of the substantive offense. We are not persuaded that the availability of a withdrawal defense would provide an incentive or motive to desist from the commission of an offense, especially since the success of the defense presupposes a criminal trial at which the issue would be submitted to the jury for decision. A remote chance of acquittal would appear to have an even more remote chance of deterring conduct. We recognize, of course, that attempt crimes pose unique issues. However, the interest of defendants in not being convicted for mere "thoughts, desires or motives" is adequately addressed by the government's burden of proving that the defendant took a substantial step toward the commission of the substantive offense.

If the defendant "voluntarily abandons the evil purpose" before he harms anyone else, should he have a defense to a charge of attempt?

(2) Consider Hoeber, *The Abandonment Defense to Criminal Attempt and Other Problems of Temporal Individuation*, 74 Cal. L. Rev. 377, 378 (1986):

> The traditional common law view is that abandonment cannot be a defense to attempt. This view is usually expressed in pronouncements that an attempt, like any other crime, is "complete" and that later abandonment can no more affect a defendant's attempt liability than later repentance or remorse can affect a defendant's liability for any other crime.
>
> This attitude towards the abandonment defense exhibits a fundamental misconception about criminalization decisions. The crime of attempt, like any other crime, is complete when we say it is. The temporal dimensions of attempt liability are defined differently depending on whether the law recognizes a defense for those who abandon their efforts after engaging in conduct otherwise constituting an attempt. Thus, to decide whether defendants who abandon have a defense is to decide (to that extent) what states of affairs the crime prohibits.

(3) In *People v. Crary*, 71 Cal. Rptr. 457, 460 (Cal. Ct. App. 1968), the defendant was convicted of robbery. He appealed, claiming he was entitled to a jury instruction dealing with attempted robbery.

> [R]obbery is defined as "the felonious taking of personal property in the possession of another, from his person or immediate presence, and against his will, accomplished by means of force or fear." Thus, if appellant and Pust had changed their minds about robbing the service station when Thorne put the gasoline in appellant's automobile, and if they left with the impression that they had paid for it with a pair of pliers, they did not have the felonious intent required to commit robbery. Moreover, if Thorne placed the gasoline in appellant's car voluntarily under the belief that he talked the boys out of robbing him, the gasoline was not taken by means of force or fear. But, even so, the boys would have been guilty of attempted robbery for "[i]t is generally held that when the defendant's acts go beyond mere preparation he is criminally liable for the attempt even though, before completion of the crime, he voluntarily abandons his purpose."
>
> There can be no doubt that mere intent by a single individual to commit a crime is not sufficient to amount to a criminal act. However, it is also unquestionable that after the intent has been formed and such intent has been coupled with an overt act toward the commission of the contemplated offense, the abandonment of the criminal purpose will not constitute a defense to a charge of attempting to commit a crime.

The court then went on to hold that abandonment was no defense to attempt, but the jury should have been "informed that a voluntary abandonment by [defendants] of their criminal purpose was a defense to the main charge." Why is abandonment a defense to robbery but not to attempted robbery?

(4) Several states have disavowed the *Staples* reasoning, relying on the provisions of the Model Penal Code.

> We ... hold that voluntary abandonment is an affirmative defense to a prosecution for criminal attempt. The burden is on the defendant to establish by a preponderance of the evidence that he or she has voluntarily and completely abandoned his or her criminal purpose. Abandonment is not "voluntary" when the defendant fails to complete the attempted crime because of unanticipated difficulties, unexpected resistance, or circumstances which increase the probability of detention or apprehension. Nor is the abandonment "voluntary" when the defendant fails to consummate the attempted offense after deciding to postpone the criminal conduct until another time or to substitute another victim or another but similar objective.

People v. Kimball, 311 N.W.2d 343, 349 (Mich. Ct. App. 1981). Abandonment will not work as a defense, however, "[o]nce the attempt has been completed by putting into motion forces the action can no longer stop." *O'Shaughnessy v. People*, 269 P.3d 1233, 1235 (Colo. 2012). Consider *State v. Cox*, 278 N.W.2d 62 (Minn. 1979), where the Minnesota Supreme Court discussed Minn. Stat. § 609.17(3), which provides:

> It is a defense to a charge of attempt that the crime was not committed because the accused desisted voluntarily and in good faith and abandoned the intention to commit the crime.

The defense was adopted because

> "[I]t is believed ... to be desirable to encourage the voluntary good faith withdrawal from the commission of the crime." An attempt is not voluntarily abandoned within the scope of § 609.17, subd. 3, if a defendant refrains from carrying out his criminal act because of intervening circumstances, such as being frightened by the arrival of law enforcement personnel.

278 N.W.2d at 66.

Michigan has adopted the standard, modern abandonment defense for attempt. The defendant must show that the abandonment was voluntary, and not "because of unanticipated difficulties, unexpected resistance, or circumstances which increase the probability of detention or apprehension." In *State v. McNeal*, 393 N.W.2d 907 (Mich. Ct. App. 1986), the defendant kidnapped the victim intending to have forced sexual intercourse with her. When he indicated his intent to her, the victim began talking with him and ultimately persuaded him not to have sexual relations with her. Did the defendant voluntarily abandon attempted criminal sexual conduct? Held, while it was a "close question," there was no abandonment because a "victim's entreaties or pleadings may constitute 'unanticipated difficulties' or 'unexpected resistance.'"

[E] Impossibility

> Factual impossibility denotes conduct where the objective is proscribed by the criminal law but a factual circumstance unknown to the actor prevents him from bringing it about. Factual impossibility traditionally has not been a defense to an attempt crime. There is no reason to exonerate a person who has demonstrated a willingness to commit a criminal act, but was unable to complete the dastardly deed because of an unknown outside circumstance. We join other circuits in holding that factual impossibility is not a defense to an attempt crime.... Legal impossibility is a defensive theory that the intended acts would not amount to a crime even if completed.

United States v. Hamrick, 995 F.2d 1267, 1273 (4th Cir. 1993).

The courts have faithfully and uniformly adhered to the principle that factual impossibility is no defense to an attempt charge but legal impossibility is. The application of this principle can be quite difficult, as explained in *United States v. Berrigan*, 482 F.2d 171, 188 n.35 (3d Cir. 1973):

> Wharton puts the following case: "Lady Eldon, when traveling with her husband on the Continent, bought what she supposed to be a quantity of French lace, which she hid, concealing it from Lord Eldon in one of the pockets of the coach. The package was brought to light by a custom officer at Dover. The lace turned out to be an English manufactured article, of little value, and of course, not subject to duty. Lady Eldon had bought it at a price vastly above its value, believing it to be genuine...."
>
> Wharton opined that Lady Eldon had the intent to smuggle this lace into England and was guilty of an attempt to smuggle. Professor Keedy suggests: "The fallacy of this argument is found in the fact that the particular lace which Lady Eldon intended to bring into England was not subject to duty and therefore, although there was the wish to smuggle, there was not the intent to do so."

Many of the impossibility cases are not nearly as difficult as *Lady Eldon*. "Thus a man who is physically impotent may be guilty of an attempt to commit rape." *Waters v. State*, 234 A.2d 147, 153 (Md. Ct. Spec. App. 1967). If it was an empty coin box which defendant was trying to open, his conviction for attempted larceny would still stand. *Gargan v. State*, 436 P.2d 968 (Alaska 1968). "[T]he fact that the gun was unloaded when Damms pointed it at his wife's head and pulled the trigger, did not absolve him of [attempted murder], if he actually thought at the time that it was loaded." *State v. Damms*, 100 N.W.2d 592, 597 (Wis. 1960).

In *Gargan, supra*, the court stated that "a factual impossibility which was not apparent to the actor at the time should not, as a matter of policy, insulate him from conviction for attempting the commission of the offense." 436 P.2d at 972. To what policy did the court refer? Were *Gargan, Damms*, and *Waters* correctly decided? How should the *Lady Eldon* case be decided?

Commonwealth v. Henley

Supreme Court of Pennsylvania
474 A.2d 1115 (1984)

PAPADAKOS, JUSTICE.

Appellant is the owner of the Henley Brothers Jewelry Store. On December 22, 1980, an informant, wired with a tape recording device, was given five (5) specially coated chains by the police, and sent to Appellant's jewelry store. The informant entered the store and offered to sell the five (5) gold chains to Appellant. He represented to Appellant that the chains were stolen. Appellant, believing them to be stolen, purchased the chains for $30.00, took possession of them, and expressed a willingness to buy more stolen goods in the future. This conversation was recorded.

[The defendant was convicted] of attempted theft by unlawful taking or disposition.

At the conclusion of the Commonwealth's case, Appellant demurred to the evidence, arguing that the chains were not stolen property because they were in police custody, and that, therefore, he could not be found guilty of an attempt to receive stolen property which was not stolen. The trial court found this defense of legal impossibility persuasive and granted the demurrer.

Impossibility defenses were usually classified as either legal or factual in nature. "Factual impossibility denotes conduct where the objective is proscribed by the criminal law but a circumstance unknown to the actor prevents him from bringing it about. The classic example is the thief who picks an empty pocket." *United States v. Conway*, 507 F.2d 1047, 1050 (5th Cir. 1975). Legal impossibility was said to occur where the intended acts would not amount to a crime even if completed. A frequently cited case standing for this proposition is *People v. Jaffe*, 185 N.Y. 497, 78 N.E. 169 (1906). The *Jaffe* Court held that where an element of the completed crime required the goods to be stolen, the fact that the goods were not stolen was a defense to the completed act. Consequently, an attempt to do an act which would not be criminal if completed could not itself be criminal regardless of the actor's intent.

Legal impossibility had been recognized in many jurisdictions as a defense to attempt charges, and this Court cited the *Jaffe* case approvingly, indicating that the defense of legal impossibility was available as a defense to attempt charges in this Commonwealth.

The reasoning in the *Jaffe* line of cases has come under considerable criticism in the last twenty-five years, and in response to the criticism the defense has been uniformly rejected by the highest courts in most states where the issue has been raised. Additionally, many states have passed legislation which specifically abrogated the defense.

Section 5.01 of the Model Penal Code abandons the defense of legal impossibility with the following language:

> 1. *Definition of Attempt*—A person is guilty of an attempt to commit a crime if acting with the kind of culpability otherwise required for the commission of the crime, he ...

2. purposely engages in conduct which would constitute the crime if the attendant circumstances were as he believes them to be.

Model Penal Code § 5.01 (1962).

Our Crimes Code is clear in defining the two (2) elements of the offense of attempt by providing: (1) that the actor intend to commit an offense; and (2) that the actor take a substantial step toward completion of the offense. The Code then specifically provides that impossibility is not a defense if the completed offense could have occurred had the circumstances been as the accused apprehended them to be. [I]mpossibility (factual or legal) is not a defense if the completed offense could have occurred had the circumstances been as the accused *believed* them to be.

We are thoroughly aware of the unsound basis for the legal impossibility defense and we hasten to add that the application of either of the impossibility defenses "is so fraught with intricacies and artificial distinctions that the defense has little value as an analytical method for reaching substantial justice."

The effort to compartmentalize factual patterns into these judicially created categories of factual or legal impossibilities is but an illusory test leading to contradictory and sometimes absurd results, because courts are left to evaluate an actor's beliefs or apprehensions in the light of the actual facts. Our statute abandons this out-dated approach with its former distinctions of legal and factual impossibilities and instead evaluates the actor's conduct according to his mental frame of reference alone.

Thus, if one forms intent to commit a substantive crime, then proceeds to perform all the acts necessary to commit the crime, and it is shown that completion of the substantive crime is impossible, the actor can still be culpable of attempt to commit the substantive crime. A defense based on the old legal or factual impossibility argument clearly is no longer available. Under the new code, an intent to commit an act which is not characterized as a crime by the laws of the subject jurisdiction cannot be the basis of a criminal charge and conviction even though the actor believes or misapprehends the intended act to be proscribed by the criminal laws. An example of this is where a fisherman believes he is committing an offense in fishing on a certain lake without a license when a fishing license is, in fact, not required in the subject jurisdiction. Since the conduct here would be perfectly legal, the actor could not be held accountable for any attempted crime. In all other cases, the actor should be held responsible for his conduct.

Since the defense of legal impossibility has been abrogated, it was not available to Appellant, and the demurrer was improperly granted.

Nix, Chief Justice, concurring.

I join the opinion and write in an attempt to further clarify an area which has proven over the years to be one elusive of satisfactory explication.

The inherent failing of the former concepts of legal and factual impossibility, aside from the difficulties encountered in attempting to make that distinction in a given factual setting, was that the use of this dichotomy tended to focus on the legal form rather than upon an evaluation of the substantive danger the defendant's actions posed for society. The latter concern is the only legitimate basis for assigning criminal liability to the conduct. Thus, where the crime charged to have been attempted would have constituted a violation of our criminal laws, had the attendant circumstances been such as the actor believed them to be, whether commission was factually or legally impossible is of no moment. Criminal liability should attach in either instance because the actor's mental frame of reference reflects the requisite dangerousness to society to justify that result.

[A]s the majority points out, we must be careful to distinguish situations where the intended conduct is not a crime. The mere fact that one thinks his conduct is criminal, but it is in fact lawful conduct, does not provide a basis for attaching criminal liability. The actor's willingness to perform an act which society has not deemed criminal does not reflect the dangerous disposition that would warrant a criminal sanction.

Up to this point in the development of our law, we have not accepted a willingness to break the law as the sole criterion for attaching criminal liability. The abstract inclination to violate the law must be concretized into an intent to engage in specific conduct which, if completed as intended, would amount to a violation of the criminal law. In both instances there is a subjective willingness to engage in the activity regardless of its legality. The justification for criminal sanction in the latter is that the conduct intended and entered upon is in fact a crime.

Comments and Questions

(1) The *Jaffe* case, discussed in *Henley*, was widely followed just after it was decided. Later, however, it became the subject of great and sustained criticism. What criticism may have caused many courts to reject *Jaffe*?

(2) In its conclusion, the court gives the example of the fisherman fishing without a license. Should that person's conduct be punished by our justice system?

(3) The rule in *Henley* is followed in a number of cases.

> An attempt requires only that the appellant have an intent to commit the crime and that he take a direct but ineffectual act toward the commission of the crime. Here, the evidence clearly indicates that appellant intended to and did receive goods he thought were stolen. The fact that the firearms had lost their "stolen" status was an extrinsic fact unknown to appellant and does not vitiate the criminality of the attempt.

Darnell v. State, 558 P.2d 624, 625–26 (Nev. 1976). *But see Booth v. State*, 398 P.2d 863, 871 (Okla. Crim. App. 1964):

> [T]he facts reveal a legal and not factual impossibility.
>
> In the case at bar the stolen coat had been recovered by the police for the owner and consequently had, according to the well-established law in this country, lost its character as stolen property. Therefore, a legal impossibility

> precluded defendant from being prosecuted for the crime of Knowingly Receiving Stolen Property.
>
> It would strain reasoning beyond a logical conclusion to hold contrary to the rule previously stated herein.
>
> If all which the accused person intended would, had it been done, constitute no substantive crime, it cannot be a crime under the name "attempt" to do, with the same purpose, a part of this thing.
>
> If a series of acts together will not constitute an offense, how can it be said that one of the acts alone will constitute an indictable offense?
>
> Steps on the way to the commission of what would be a crime, if the acts were completed, may amount to attempts to commit that crime, to which, unless interrupted, they would have led; but steps on the way to the doing of something, which is thereafter done, and which is no crime, cannot be regarded as attempts to commit a crime.
>
> ...
>
> It seems clear that cases (where none of the intended consequences is in fact criminal) cannot constitute criminal attempts. If none of the consequences which the defendant sought to achieve constitute a crime, surely his unsuccessful efforts to achieve his object cannot constitute a criminal attempt.

People v. Dlugash

Supreme Court of New York, Appellate Division
51 A.D.2d 974 (1976)

Defendant was charged, in a one-count indictment, with the crime of murder. The indictment alleged that "defendant, acting in concert with another person actually present, on or about December 22, 1973 ... with intent to cause the death of Michael Lawrence Geller caused [his] death ... by means of a deadly weapon, to wit: a loaded firearm." The prosecution's theory of the case was that one Joseph Bush had shot Geller in the chest several times with a .38 calibre revolver and that, "shortly thereafter," defendant had pulled out his own .25 calibre revolver and had shot Geller in the face five times.

At the close of the entire case, the trial court dismissed that portion of the indictment which charged that defendant had acted "in concert" with Bush and sent the case to the jury on the theory of common-law murder. The jury found defendant guilty.

Under the facts of this case, the People, in order to sustain a conviction, were required to prove beyond a reasonable doubt (1) that Geller was alive at the time the defendant shot him, and died from those shots and (2) that the defendant believed Geller to have been alive at that time and that defendant had intended to kill him when he fired the shots.

The People's evidence rested upon two confessions made by the defendant to an investigating detective and an Assistant District Attorney, respectively, and the testimony of two medical experts who had performed an autopsy upon the decedent. In his oral confession to the detective, the defendant stated that Bush had shot Geller three times; that Geller then fell to the floor; and that after a few minutes (the detective could not remember the precise number of minutes and testified that it could have been from two to five minutes) he went over to where Geller was lying, took out his revolver and fired five times into Geller's head and face. Defendant told the detective that he thought Geller was already dead when he fired the shots and that he had shot Geller notwithstanding such belief because he was afraid of Bush and feared for his life. In his statement to the Assistant District Attorney, defendant stated that he shot Geller "after Joe [Bush] had his .38 on him"; and that Geller was already dead when he, defendant, shot Geller.

The autopsy report states that the cause of decedent's death was "multiple bullet wounds of head and chest with brain injury and massive bilateral hemothorax with penetration of heart; homicidal." In response to a hypothetical question which posited that Geller had been shot in the chest by a .38 calibre revolver, and was shot three to five minutes later by defendant, both of the doctors who had performed the autopsy admitted that they could not, with any degree of medical certainty, state whether Geller had been alive at the time the latter shots were fired into his head. Under these circumstances, the People failed to prove beyond a reasonable doubt that Geller had been alive at the time he was shot by defendant; defendant's conviction of murder thus cannot stand. Upon the argument of this appeal the People, in effect, conceded such to be a fact. They contended, however, and urge in their brief, that, if the murder conviction is set aside, the judgment should be modified by reducing the conviction to one of attempted murder. Since the uncontradicted evidence is that the defendant, at the time that he fired the five shots into the body of the decedent, believed him to be dead, and as there is not a scintilla of evidence to contradict his assertion in that regard, section 110.10 of the Penal Law has no application.

People v. Dlugash

Court of Appeals of New York
363 N.E.2d 1155 (1977)

JASEN, JUDGE.

The criminal law is of ancient origin, but criminal liability for attempt to commit a crime is comparatively recent. At the root of the concept of attempt liability are the very aims and purposes of penal law. The ultimate issue is whether an individual's intentions and actions, though failing to achieve a manifest and malevolent criminal purpose, constitute a danger to organized society of sufficient magnitude to warrant the imposition of criminal sanctions. Difficulties in theoretical analysis and concomitant debate over very pragmatic questions of blameworthiness appear dramatically in reference to situations where the criminal attempt failed to achieve its purpose solely because the factual or legal context in which the individual acted was not as the actor supposed them to be. Phrased somewhat differently, the concern centers on whether an individual should be liable for an attempt to commit a crime when, unknown to him, it was impossible to successfully complete the crime attempted. For years, serious studies have been made on the subject in an effort to resolve the continuing controversy when, if at all, the impossibility of successfully completing the criminal act should preclude liability for even making the futile attempt. The 1967 revision of the Penal Law approached the impossibility defense to the inchoate crime of attempt in a novel fashion. The statute provides that, if a person engages in conduct which would otherwise constitute an attempt to commit a crime, "it is no defense to a prosecution for such attempt that the crime charged to have been attempted was, under the attendant circumstances, factually or legally impossible of commission, if such crime could have been committed had the attendant circumstances been as such person believed them to be." This appeal presents to us, for the first time, a case involving the application of the modern statute. We hold that, under the proof presented by the People at trial, defendant Melvin Dlugash may be held for attempted murder, though the target of the attempt may have already been slain, by the hand of another, when Dlugash made his felonious attempt.

Preliminarily, we state our agreement with the Appellate Division that the evidence did not establish, beyond a reasonable doubt, that Geller was alive at the time defendant fired into his body. To sustain a homicide conviction, it must be established, beyond a reasonable doubt, that the defendant caused the death of another person. Whatever else it may be, it is not murder to shoot a dead body. Man dies but once.

[I]t is quite unlikely and improbable that two persons, unknown and unconnected to each other, would attempt to kill the same third person at the same time and place. Thus, it is rare for criminal liability for homicide to turn on which of several attempts actually succeeded. In the case of coconspirators, it is not necessary to do so and the case of truly independent actors is unlikely. However, procedural developments make this case the unlikely one and we must now decide whether, under the evidence presented, the defendant may be held for attempted murder, though someone else perhaps succeeded in killing the victim.

The most intriguing attempt cases are those where the attempt to commit a crime was unsuccessful due to mistakes of fact or law on the part of the would-be criminal. A general rule developed in most American jurisdictions that legal impossibility is a good defense but factual impossibility is not. Thus, for example, it was held that defendants who shot at a stuffed deer did not attempt to take a deer out of season, even though they believed the dummy to be a live animal. The court stated that there was no criminal attempt because it was no crime to "take" a stuffed deer, and it is no crime to attempt to do that which is legal. These cases are illustrative of legal impossibility. A further example is Francis Wharton's classic hypothetical involving Lady Eldon and her French lace. The traditional view is that Lady Eldon is not liable for an attempt to smuggle.

On the other hand, factual impossibility was no defense. For example, a man was held liable for attempted murder when he shot into the room in which his target usually slept and, fortuitously, the target was sleeping elsewhere in the house that night.

Although one bullet struck the target's customary pillow, attainment of the criminal objective was factually impossible. On the same view, it was held that men who had sexual intercourse with a woman, with the belief that she was alive and did not consent to the intercourse, could be charged for attempted rape when the woman had, in fact, died from an unrelated ailment prior to the acts of intercourse.

The New York cases can be parsed out along similar lines. One of the leading cases on legal impossibility is *People v. Jaffe*, 185 N.Y. 497, 78 N.E. 169, in which we held that there was no liability for the attempted receipt of stolen property when the property received by the defendant in the belief that it was stolen was, in fact under the control of the true owner. Factual impossibility, however, was no defense. Thus, a man could be held for attempted grand larceny when he picked an empty pocket.

As can be seen from even this abbreviated discussion, the distinction between "factual" and "legal" impossibility was a nice one indeed and the courts tended to place a greater value on legal form than on any substantive danger the defendant's actions posed for society. The approach of the draftsmen of the Model Penal Code was to eliminate the defense of impossibility in virtually all situations. Under the code provision, to constitute an attempt, it is still necessary that the result intended or desired by the actor constitute a crime. However, the code suggested a fundamental change to shift the locus of analysis to the actor's mental frame of reference and away from undue dependence upon external considerations. The basic premise of the code provision is that what was in the actor's own mind should be the standard for determining his dangerousness to society and, hence, his liability for attempted criminal conduct.

In the belief that neither of the two branches of the traditional impossibility arguments detracts from the offender's moral culpability, the Legislature substantially carried the code's treatment of impossibility into the 1967 revision of the Penal Law. Thus, a person is guilty of an attempt when, with intent to commit a crime, he engages in conduct which tends to effect the commission of such crime. It is no defense that, under the attendant circumstances, the crime was factually or legally impossible of commission, "if such crime could have been committed had the attendant circumstances been as such person believed them to be." Thus, if defendant believed the victim to be alive at the time of the shooting, it is no defense to the charge of attempted murder that the victim may have been dead.

Turning to the facts of the case before us, we believe that there is sufficient evidence in the record from which the jury could conclude that the defendant believed Geller to be alive at the time defendant fired shots into Geller's head. Defendant admitted firing five shots at a most vital part of the victim's anatomy from virtually point blank range. Although defendant contended that the victim had already been grievously wounded by another, from the defendant's admitted actions, the jury could conclude that the defendant's purpose and intention was to administer the coup de grace. The jury never learned of defendant's subsequent allegation that Bush had a gun on him and directed defendant to fire at Geller on the pain of his own life. Defendant did not testify and this statement of duress was made only in a postverdict affidavit, which obviously was never placed before the jury. In his admissions that were related to the jury, defendant never made such a claim. Nor did he offer any explanation for his conduct, except for an offhand aside made casually to Detective Carrasquillo. Any remaining doubt as to the question of duress is dispelled by defendant's earlier statement that he and Joe Bush had peacefully spent a few days together on vacation in the country. Moreover, defendant admitted to freely assisting Bush in disposing of the weapons after the murder and, once the weapons were out of the picture, defendant made no effort at all to flee from Bush. Indeed, not only did defendant not come forward with his story immediately, but when the police arrived at his house, he related a false version designed to conceal his and Bush's complicity in the murder. All of these facts indicate a consciousness of guilt which defendant would not have had if he had truly believed that Geller was dead when he shot him.

His admissions are barren of any claim of duress and reflect, instead, an unstinting co-operation in efforts to dispose of vital incriminating evidence. Indeed, defendant maintained a false version of the occurrence until such time as the police informed him that they had evidence that he lately possessed a gun of the same caliber as one of the weapons involved in the shooting. From all of this, the jury was certainly warranted in concluding that the defendant acted in the belief that Geller was yet alive when shot by defendant.

The jury convicted the defendant of murder. Necessarily, they found that defendant intended to kill a live human being. Subsumed within this finding is the conclusion that defendant acted in the belief that Geller was alive. Thus, there is no need for additional fact findings by a jury. Although it was not established beyond a reasonable doubt that Geller was, in fact, alive, such is no defense to attempted murder since a murder would have been committed "had the attendant circumstances been as [defendant] believed them to be." The jury necessarily found that defendant believed Geller to be alive when defendant shot at him.

Comments and Questions

(1) In *State v. Guffey*, 262 S.W.2d 152, 156 (Mo. Ct. App. 1953), the court stated, "it is no crime to attempt to murder a corpse because it cannot be murdered." Is this not a correct statement of the law? How could Dlugash be convicted of attempted murder of a human being when that human being was already dead?

(2) How would the following cases be decided in New York:

(a) *State v. Porter*, 242 P.2d 984 (Mont. 1952), where the defendant was charged with attempting to influence a grand juror. When the influence efforts were made, the person contacted was no longer a grand juror.

(b) *United States v. Thomas*, 13 C.M.A. 278, 32 C.M.R. 278 (1962), where the defendant unlawfully had sexual intercourse with the victim and was convicted of rape. At the time of the intercourse, however, the victim was already dead.

(3) Suppose the defendant carefully planned to buy stolen firewood from a government forest preserve. Could he be convicted of an attempt offense if the govern-

ment had earlier changed its law to allow citizens to take as much firewood as they wished? *See State v. Davidson*, 584 P.2d 401, 404 (Wash. Ct. App. 1978):

> [O]ur statute eliminates both "factual" and "legal" impossibility as defenses to a prosecution for attempt, when the "conduct in which a person engages *otherwise* constitutes an attempt to commit a crime." (Italics ours.) The use of the word "otherwise" indicates that it is now a crime to attempt to do an act which would otherwise not be criminal because of the true facts not known to the actor. The apparent reason is to punish his culpable intent. The statute does not impose criminal liability, however, in a related situation: where the defendant intended to do an act which he mistakenly believed constituted a crime, but which has not been made criminal.
>
> In this case, defendant intended to buy and possess goods he believed were stolen. He intended to do what he believed to be a criminal act and what would have been criminal if the facts had been as he perceived them. [H]is conduct satisfied the elements of attempt: (1) intent to commit a specific crime; (2) an act which is a substantial step toward the commission of that crime. He intended to buy stolen property and he tendered money in exchange for the property offered to him. Under our statute and the modern decisional law, he has no defense that the property turned out not to be stolen.

The earlier discussion of cases in which an HIV-positive defendant bites a victim focused on the defendant's state of mind. Is it legal or factual impossibility if "there never has been a documented case of HIV transmission through saliva"? Hansen, *Biting, Spitting Bring Jail Terms*, A.B.A. J., Mar. 1994, at 30. *See also HIV and Its Transmission*, http://connection.ebscohost.com/c/articles/9501090766/biting-spitting-bring-jail-terms. As a state legislator, would you enact a law which simply makes it a crime to try to transmit the HIV infection? Is that a better, more direct way to handle the problem? Consider the Code of Virginia, Title 18.2-67.4:1, which while limited in scope, attempts to do just this: "Any person who, knowing he is infected with HIV, syphilis, or hepatitis B, has sexual intercourse, cunnilingus, fellatio, anallingus or anal intercourse with the intent to transmit the infection to another person shall be guilty of a Class 6 felony...." HIV "means the human immunodeficiency virus or any other related virus that causes acquired immunodeficiency syndrome (AIDS)."

(4) In an Internet chat room, the defendant met someone whom he thought was a teenage girl. Thereafter he sent nude photos to the "teenager" and invited her to meet him to have sex. At the meeting place, the defendant was arrested and charged with attempted distribution of obscene materials to a minor. The "teenager" was in fact an adult undercover police agent pretending to be a minor. The defendant was convicted, though he raised an impossibility defense. What result on appeal? Over a vigorous dissent, the Michigan Supreme Court upheld the conviction concluding that the state attempt statute does not allow for an impossibility defense. The holding did not distinguish between factual and legal impossibility. *People v. Thousand*, 631 N.W.2d

694, 702 (Mich. 2001). The court stated that "the notion that it would be 'impossible' for the defendant to have committed the *completed* offense is simply irrelevant to the analysis." All that was necessary was for the fact-finder to decide whether the defendant possessed specific intent and had engaged in some act "toward the commission" of it.

(5) Defendants accused of predatory sexual conduct toward children or actions involving child pornography caught in such stings argue that the crime of attempt was legally impossible; because no actual child or child pornography existed, no antecedent was legally impossible for them to have engaged in sex with a child. Courts have generally categorized the defense as one of factual impossibility and rejected it. *See United States v. Bauer*, 626 F.3d 1004 (8th Cir. 2010); *Hix v. Commonwealth*, 619 S.E.2d 80 (Va. 2005).

(6) According to the New York court in *Dlugash*, "if defendant believed the victim to be alive at the time of the shooting, it is no defense to the charge of attempted murder that the victim may have been dead." Does the court's analysis withstand the comments of Professors Williams and Hall and Judge Aldisert?

> It should need no demonstration that a person who commits or attempts to commit what is not a crime in law cannot be convicted of attempting to commit a crime, and it makes no difference that he thinks it is a crime.

G. Williams, *Criminal Law: The General Part* 611 (2d ed. 1961).

> Unless the intended end is a legally proscribed harm, causing it is not criminal, hence any conduct falling short of that is not a criminal attempt.

J. Hall, *General Principles of Criminal Law* 586 (2d ed. 1960).

> Simply stated, attempting to do that which is not a crime is not attempting to commit a crime.

United States v. Berrigan, supra, 482 F.2d at 190.

United States v. Oviedo

United States Court of Appeals, Fifth Circuit

525 F.2d 881 (1976)

DYER, CIRCUIT JUDGE.

Oviedo appeals from a judgment of conviction for the attempted distribution of heroin.

Oviedo was contacted by an undercover agent, who desired to purchase narcotics. Arrangements were made for the sale of one pound of heroin. The agent met Oviedo at the appointed time and place. Oviedo transferred the substance to the agent, and asked for his money in return. However, the agent informed Oviedo that he would first have to test the substance. A field test was performed with a positive result. Oviedo was placed under arrest.

Subsequent to the arrest, a search warrant was issued for Oviedo's residence. When the search was executed, two pounds of a similar substance was found hidden in a television set. Up to this point, the case appeared unexceptional.

A chemical analysis was performed upon the substances seized, revealing that the substances were not in fact heroin, but rather procaine hydrochloride, an uncontrolled substance.[4] Since any attempt to prosecute for distribution of heroin would have been futile, the defendant was charged with an attempt to distribute heroin.

At trial, Oviedo took the stand and stated that he knew the substance was not heroin, and that he, upon suggestion of his cohorts, was merely attempting to "rip off" the agent. It was, in his view, an easy way to pocket a few thousand dollars.

The court instructed the jury that they could find Oviedo guilty of attempted distribution if he delivered the substance thinking it to be heroin.[5] The jury rejected Oviedo's claimed knowledge of the true nature of the substance, and returned a verdict of guilty. Although Oviedo argues on appeal that there was insufficient evidence to establish that he thought the substance was heroin, this contention is without merit. We thus take as fact Oviedo's belief that the substance was heroin.

The facts before us are therefore simple—Oviedo sold a substance he thought to be heroin, which in reality was an uncontrolled substance. The legal question before us is likewise simple—are these combined acts and intent cognizable as a criminal attempt. The answer, however, is not so simple.

Oviedo and the government both agree the resolution of this case rests in an analysis of the doctrines of legal and factual impossibility as defenses to a criminal attempt. Legal impossibility occurs when the actions which the defendant performs or sets in motion, even if fully carried out as he desires, would not constitute a crime. Factual impossibility occurs when the objective of the defendant is proscribed by the criminal law but a circumstance unknown to the actor prevents him from bringing about that objective. The traditional analysis recognizes legal impossibility as a valid defense, but refuses to so recognize factual impossibility.

These definitions are not particularly helpful here, for they do nothing more than provide a different focus for the analysis. In one sense, the impossibility involved here might be deemed legal, for those *acts* which Oviedo set in motion, the transfer of the substance in his possession, were not a crime. In another sense, the impossibility is factual, for the *objective* of Oviedo, the sale of heroin, was proscribed by law, and failed only because of a circumstance unknown to Oviedo.[6]

---

4. Although not an opium derivative, procaine hydrochloride will give a positive reaction to the Marquis Reagent Field Test.

5. The court charged the jury on this issue: In other words, if you find beyond a reasonable doubt that Mr. Oviedo did knowingly and unlawfully and intentionally attempt to distribute what you have found beyond a reasonable doubt ... he believed to be one pound of heroin ... it would be no defense that the substance involved was not actually heroin. On the other hand, if you do not find beyond a reasonable doubt that the Defendant believed the substance involved to be heroin, even though you might find all of the other elements of the offense present beyond a reasonable doubt, then it would be your duty to acquit the Defendant.

6. At least one writer has recognized that legal impossibility is logically indistinguishable from factual impossibility. *See* Hall, *Criminal Attempt—A Study of Foundations of Criminal Liability*, 49 Yale L.J. 789, 836 (1940).

Although this issue has been the subject of numerous legal commentaries, federal cases reaching this question are few, and no consensus can be found.[7]

In *Roman* [356 F. Supp. 434 (S.D.N.Y.), *aff'd*, 484 F.2d 1271 (2d Cir. 1973), *cert. denied*, 415 U.S. 978 (1974)], the defendants were transporting a suitcase containing heroin. Through the aid of an informer and unknown to the defendants, the contents of the suitcase were replaced with soap powder. The defendants were arrested when they attempted to sell the contents of the suitcase, and were subsequently charged with *attempted* possession with intent to distribute. The court rejected defendants' contention that they could not be charged with attempted possession, since it was impossible for them to possess heroin. Recognizing the difficulty in distinguishing between legal and factual impossibility, the court never so categorized the case. Nevertheless, the court concluded that since the objective of the defendants was criminal, impossibility would not be recognized as a defense.

The defendants in *Berrigan* [482 F.2d 171 (3d Cir. 1973)] were charged with attempting to violate 18 U.S.C.A. § 1791, prohibiting the smuggling of objects into or out of a federal correctional institution. Since the evidence established that the warden had knowledge of the smuggling plan, and since lack of knowledge was a necessary element of the offense, the defendants could not be found guilty of violating the statute. The court held that such knowledge by the warden would also preclude conviction for the attempt, since "attempting to do that which is not a crime is not attempting to commit a crime."

The *Berrigan* court rested its determination on a strict view of legal impossibility. According to the court, such impossibility exists when there is an intention to perform a physical act, the intended physical act is performed, but the consequence resulting from the intended act does not amount to a crime. In this analysis, the intent to per-

7. State court cases are similarly divergent. State courts have labeled the following situations as involving legal impossibility, and concluded that there could be no attempt: (1) A person who accepts goods which he believes to be stolen, but which are not in fact stolen, is not guilty of attempting to receive stolen goods. People v. Jaffe, 1906, 185 N.Y. 497, 78 N.E. 169. (2) A person who offers a bribe to one whom he believes to be a juror, but who was not a juror, is not guilty of attempting to bribe a juror. State v. Taylor, 1939, 345 Mo. 325, 133 S.W.2d 336. (3) A hunter who shoots a stuffed deer, believing it to be alive, is not guilty of attempting to shoot a deer out of season. State v. Guffey, 1953 Mo. App. LEXIS 260, 262 S.W.2d 152.

In other apparently analogous situations, courts have concluded that the impossibility is factual, and therefore no defense to a charge of attempt: (1) A person who fires a gun at a bed, thinking it to be occupied by a man, is guilty of attempted murder, even though the bed is empty. State v. Mitchell, 1905, 170 Mo. 633, 71 S.W. 175. (2) A person who possesses a substance thinking it is narcotics, is guilty of attempted possession, notwithstanding that the substance is in fact talcum powder. People v. Siu, 1954, 126 Cal. App. 2d 41, 271 P.2d 575. (3) A person who introduces instruments into a woman for the purpose of producing an abortion is guilty of attempting an abortion, even though the woman is not pregnant. People v. Cummings, 1956, 141 Cal. App. 2d 193, 296 P.2d 610. We list these cases not to offer support to our conclusions, but rather to illustrate the inconsistency of approach which plagues this area of legal theory.

form a physical act is to be distinguished from the motive, desire or expectation to violate the law.[8]

The application of the principles underlying these cases leads to no clearer result than the application of our previous definitions of legal and factual impossibility. Applying *Roman*, we would not concern ourselves with any theoretical distinction between legal and factual impossibility, but would affirm the conviction, since the objective of Oviedo was criminal. Applying *Berrigan*, we would look solely to the physical act which Oviedo "intended," the transfer of the procaine in his possession, and we would conclude that since the transfer of procaine is not criminal, no offense is stated. The choice is between punishing criminal intent without regard to objective acts, and punishing objective acts, regarding intent as immaterial.

In our view, both *Roman* and *Berrigan* miss the mark, but in opposite directions. A strict application of the *Berrigan* approach would eliminate any distinction between factual and legal impossibility, and such impossibility would *always* be a valid defense, since the "intended" physical acts are never criminal.[9]

The *Roman* approach turns the attempt statute into a new substantive criminal statute where the critical element to be proved is *mens rea simpliciter.* It would allow us to punish one's thoughts, desires, or motives, through indirect evidence, without reference to any objective fact. The danger is evident.

We reject the notion of *Roman*, adopted by the district court, that the conviction in the present case can be sustained since there is sufficient proof of intent, not because of any doubt as to the sufficiency of the evidence in that regard, but because of the inherent dangers such a precedent would pose in the future.

When the question before the court is whether certain conduct constitutes mere preparation which is not punishable, or an attempt which is, the possibility of error is mitigated by the requirement that the objective acts of the defendant evidence commitment to the criminal venture and corroborate the *mens rea.* To the extent that this requirement is preserved it prevents the conviction of persons engaged in innocent acts on the basis of a *mens rea* proved through speculative inferences, unreliable forms of testimony, and past criminal conduct.

Courts could have approached the preparation-attempt determination in another fashion, eliminating any notion of particular objective facts, and simply could have asked whether the evidence at hand was sufficient to prove the necessary intent. But this approach has been rejected for precisely the reasons set out above, for conviction upon proof of mere intent provides too great a possibility of speculation and abuse.

8. This distinction is easily illustrated. If A takes a book which he thinks belongs to B, his desire or expectation is criminal. However, if the book turns out to belong to A, A does not have the requisite intent to be guilty of a criminal attempt, for his intent is to take the book, and it is not criminal to take one's own book.

9. If the "intended" physical acts were criminal, the defendant would be guilty of the completed crime, rather than the attempt.

In urging us to follow *Roman*, which found determinative the criminal intent of the defendants, the government at least implicitly argues that we should reject any requirement demanding the same objective evidentiary facts required in the preparation-attempt determination. We refuse to follow that suggestion.

When the defendant sells a substance which is actually heroin, it is reasonable to infer that he knew the physical nature of the substance, and to place on him the burden of dispelling the inference. However, if we convict the defendant of attempting to sell heroin for the sale of a non-narcotic substance, we eliminate an objective element that has major evidentiary significance and we increase the risk of mistaken conclusions that the defendant believed the goods were narcotics.

Thus, we demand that in order for a defendant to be guilty of a criminal attempt, the objective acts performed, without any reliance on the accompanying *mens rea*, mark the defendant's conduct as criminal in nature. The acts should be unique rather than so commonplace that they are engaged in by persons not in violation of the law.

Here we have only two objective facts. First, Oviedo told the agent that the substance he was selling was heroin, and second, portions of the substance were concealed in a television set. If another objective fact were present, if the substance were heroin, we would have a strong objective basis for the determination of criminal intent and conduct consistent and supportive of that intent. The test set out above would be met, and, absent a delivery, the criminal attempt would be established. But when this objective basis for the determination of intent is removed, when the substance is not heroin, the conduct becomes ambivalent, and we are left with a sufficiency-of-the-evidence determination of intent rejected in the preparation-attempt dichotomy. We cannot conclude that the objective acts of Oviedo apart from any indirect evidence of intent mark his conduct as criminal in nature. Rather, those acts are consistent with a noncriminal enterprise. Therefore, we will not allow the jury's determination of Oviedo's intent to form the sole basis of a criminal offense.

The government also argues that *United States v. Mandujano* [499 F.2d 370 (5th Cir. 1974)], although involving a preparation-attempt determination, compels a contrary result. In Mandujano, the defendant negotiated a sale of heroin with an undercover agent. After taking the agent's money, the defendant set about to find his source. He was unsuccessful, and returned a few hours later with the money and without the heroin. We found the evidence sufficient to take the case beyond preparation, and to support his conviction for attempted distribution.

In making that determination, we recognized that in order to be guilty of an attempt, the objective conduct of the defendant must strongly corroborate the firmness of the defendant's criminal intent. The objective acts must not be equivocal in nature. In that case, we had as objective facts defendant's act of taking money and his personal statements that he would purchase heroin with that money. Importantly, there were no objective facts which made these acts equivocal.

The situation in *Mandujano* is distinguishable from that now before us. Just as it is reasonable to infer a person's knowledge and criminal intent from the possession of a substance which is in fact narcotics, it is also reasonable to infer that same knowledge and intent from an individual's statements of future intention. However, just as it is impossible to infer that intent when the substance possessed is not in fact narcotics, it is also impossible to infer that intent when objective facts indicate that the person did not carry out his self-proclaimed intention.

Thus, when Mandujano stated that he would purchase heroin, we could infer that he intended to purchase heroin since there were no objective facts to the contrary. But here, Oviedo stated he would sell heroin and then sold procaine. Based on these objective facts, we cannot infer that he intended to do that which he said he was going to do, because he in fact did something else.

Reversed.

Comments and Questions

(1) Under *Dlugash*, would Oviedo's conviction be reversed? The court in *Oviedo* was concerned that affirming the conviction was improper "because of the inherent dangers such a precedent would pose in the future." What are those dangers? Are they outweighed by the government's proof of the defendant's culpable intent? What was the proof?

(2) The District Judge in the *Roman* case—discussed in *Oviedo*—wrote:

> Defendants claim their defense is one of legal impossibility. Although the categorization of a case as involving one type of impossibility or another is often difficult, the case at hand plainly involves factual not legal impossibility.
>
> There are apparently no federal cases in point, but "All courts are in agreement that what is usually referred to as 'factual impossibility' is no defense to a charge of attempt." Moreover, in light of the absence of controlling contrary federal case law, I hold that however this impossibility may be characterized, since the defendants' objective here was criminal, impossibility is no defense. This is in accord with the proposed revision of the federal criminal code.

United States v. Heng Awkak Roman, 356 F. Supp. 434, 438 (S.D.N.Y. 1973), *cert. denied*, 415 U.S. 978 (1974). Was he correct?

Consider *United States v. Sobrilski*, 127 F.3d 669, 675 (8th Cir. 1997), holding that the evidence demonstrated the defendants' intent to sell illegal drugs.

> Sobrilski negotiated to sell what he referred to as drugs, increased the previously negotiated price for what he described as pure "crank" because of its higher quality, and suggested that the buyer dilute it because otherwise people using it could harm themselves; stated that he could provide up to a pound and a half a week on two hours notice; when he was arrested stated "you got me" and offered to cooperate to secure leniency; during his five-hour automobile ride with the arresting officers to show them where he obtained the drugs, he did not tell them that the white powder he had attempted to sell to them was not amphetamine; and after his arrest he told Ellison that the police had overlooked some drugs in the trailer, which he hoped to sell to raise money for a lawyer.

> Martin ... also ... believed and intended that the substance they were attempting to sell was amphetamine. She told the purchaser that she liked the drug and did not have to pay for it; she retrieved the drug sample that had been left on the kitchen table; and after her arrest [said] that the police had overlooked some crank.

(3) The facts in *United States v. Korn*, 557 F.2d 1089, 1090 (5th Cir. 1977), were set out by the court:

> The appellee Peter Korn was indicted for knowingly and intentionally attempting to distribute a controlled substance, 40,000 units of methaqualone. The defense moved to dismiss the indictment, and for purposes of the motion admitted that Korn had entered into negotiations with a government undercover agent and a government informer for the purchase of 40,000 methaqualone tablets. The negotiations were "successful" and it was agreed that Korn would purchase the tablets from the informer for $20,000.
>
> The next day Korn gave the agent $20,000 and in return received four cartons which he (Korn) believed to contain genuine methaqualone tablets but actually contained only uncontrolled simulated methaqualone tablets. When Korn placed the cartons in his car he was arrested. The district court granted the defendant's motion to dismiss on the basis of this court's decision in Oviedo. The government appealed.

Should the Fifth Circuit have affirmed or reversed the trial judge's order?

> What the court did in *Oviedo* was to require that the objective acts of the defendant, taken as a whole, strongly corroborate the required culpability. The admitted facts in the case at bar meet this requirement. There are present all of the same objective facts which were present in *Oviedo*—negotiation for sale of a controlled substance, agreement, and transfer of a noncontrolled substance. However, there is an additional fact which makes Korn's conduct relatively unequivocal—the transfer by him of $20,000. Taken as a whole, these acts strongly corroborate Korn's subjective intent to purchase methaqualone tablets. Moreover, there is another distinction. In *Oviedo* the act which rendered the totality of the defendant's objective acts equivocal (transfer of a noncontrolled substance) was an act undertaken by the defendant. Thus, logically, it could either corroborate or nullify Oviedo's underlying culpability. Here, however, the act which Korn claims makes his conduct equivocal, was an act performed by the government, the transfer of a noncontrolled substance. Thus, it is not a relevant reflection of Korn's underlying intent.

Id. at 1091.

The court in *United States v. Lundy*, 676 F.3d 444, 448–49 (5th Cir. 2012) laid out the law on impossibility:

> This court has repeatedly held that factual impossibility to complete a criminal act does not preclude a conviction for attempting to break the law. Hence,

> Lundy's argument that he could not have committed statutory rape with a 'faux child' does not stop him from being charged with attempting to break the statutory law, if the facts had been as he thought they were. "Factual impossibility is not a defense if the crime could have been committed had the attendant circumstances been as the actor believed them to be." ...
>
> [T]his circuit has properly eschewed the semantical thicket of the impossibility defense in criminal attempt cases and has instead required proof of two elements: first, that the defendant acted with the kind of culpability otherwise required for the commission of the underlying substantive offense, and, second, that the defendant had engaged in conduct which constitutes a substantial step toward commission of the crime. The substantial step must be conduct which strongly corroborates the firmness of defendant's criminal attempt.

With these cases in mind, why was the evidence in *Oviedo* lacking?

(4) The Third Circuit determined whether the defense of legal impossibility is proper by evaluating the statute that prohibits the target crime. The court analyzed the text, congressional purpose, whether it was enacted after the doctrine became "mired" in fine distinctions, and damage to enforcement efforts to decide whether Congress intended to allow the defense of legal impossibility. *See United States v. Tykarsky*, 446 F.3d 458 (3d Cir. 2006) (considering the Child Protection and Sexual Predator Punishment Act); *United States v. Hsu*, 155 F.3d 189 (3d Cir. 1998) (reviewing the Economic Espionage Act). The *Tykarsky* decision was written by the judge who wrote the *Berrigan* opinion, *supra*, which had recognized the legal impossibility defense. The court noted that the Fifth, Ninth, Tenth, and Eleventh Circuits had also concluded that conviction under the same act does not require involvement of an actual minor. In determining this issue, should courts generally evaluate the attempt statute or the statute that defines the target crime?

(5) One final wrinkle to legal impossibility bears mentioning. Courts have noted that there are two types of legal impossibility. Hybrid legal impossibility, which may be easily conceptualized as factual impossibility, is increasingly rejected as a defense. The second is "pure" legal impossibility:

> "Pure" legal impossibility, which is always a defense, occurs when the law does not even "proscribe the goal that the defendant sought to achieve."

Tykarsky, 446 F.3d at 465 n.3 (citing *Hsu*).

> Pure legal impossibility applies when an actor engages in conduct that he believes is criminal, but is not actually prohibited by law.

Thousand, 631 N.W.2d 694, at 698.

Is it always easy to distinguish between hybrid and pure legal impossibility? If this inquiry leads to a "mire," would the reasons for invalidating the defense of hybrid legal impossibility apply equally to pure legal impossibility?

(6) For those students concerned with the state of affairs in the area of impossibility, the authors offer the following:

> In this country it is generally held that a defendant may be charged with an attempt where the crime was not completed because of "physical or factual impossibility" whereas a "legal impossibility" in the completion of the crime precludes prosecution for an attempt.
>
> What is a "legal impossibility" as distinguished from a "physical or factual impossibility" has over a long period of time perplexed our courts and has resulted in many irreconcilable decisions and much philosophical discussion by legal scholars in numerous articles and papers in law school publications and by text writers. Detailed discussion of the subject is unnecessary to make it clear that it is frequently most difficult to compartmentalize a particular set of facts as coming within one of the categories rather than the other.

People v. Rollino, 233 N.Y.S.2d 580, 582 (N.Y. Sup. Ct. 1962).

> The distinction between factual and legal impossibility is elusive at best ... the doctrine has become a "source of utter frustration" and a "morass of confusion." Most federal courts have repudiated the distinction or have at least openly questioned its usefulness.... [B]eyond the logical problem is the pragmatic: the difficulty of categorization [of the two impossibilities]. The tidy dichotomy of the theoretician becomes obscure in the courtroom.... [C]ategorizing a case as involving legal versus factual impossibility is difficult, if not pointless.

United States v. Farner, 251 F.3d 510, 512 (5th Cir. 2001).

> The distinctions made are ingenious, but they lead us either to absurd results or else to no results at all. It is contended that they do no more than illustrate the fact that the search for general principles underlying the abstraction "intent" in criminal attempts is useless.

Arnold, *Criminal Attempt—The Rise and Fall of an Abstraction*, 40 Yale L.J. 53, 71 (1930).

§ 6.03 Conspiracy

> Criminal conspiracy is an agreement between two or more persons formed for the purpose of committing a crime, [it serves two distinct purposes]. The first is inchoate: '[I]t serves a preventive function by stopping criminal conduct in its early stages of growth before it has a full opportunity to bloom ...' [The second] is the belief that serious group danger is present in the usual conspiracy situation ... We punish conspiracy because joint action is, generally, [thought to be] more dangerous than individual action.

Marcus, *Criminal Conspiracy Law: Time to Turn Back from an Ever Expanding, Ever More Troubling Area*, 1 Wm. & Mary Bill Rts. J. 1, 3 (1992).

> [C]ollective criminal agreement—partnership in crime—presents a greater potential threat to the public than individual delicts. Concerted action both increases the likelihood that the criminal object will be successfully attained

> and decreases the probability that the individuals involved will depart from their path of criminality. Group association for criminal purposes often, if not normally, make possible the attainment of ends more complex than those which one criminal could accomplish. Nor is the danger of a conspiratorial group limited to the particular end toward which it has embarked. Combination in crime makes more likely the commission of crimes unrelated to the original purpose for which the group was formed. In sum, the danger which a conspiracy generates is not confined to the substantive offense which is the immediate aim of the enterprise.

Callanan v. United States, 364 U.S. 587, 593–94 (1961).

> If there are still any citizens interested in protecting human liberty, let them study the conspiracy law of the United States.

Clarence Darrow, *The Story of My Life* 64 (1934).

[A] The Mental State

People v. McChristian

Appellate Court of Illinois
309 N.E.2d 388 (1974)

LEIGHTON, JUSTICE.

I.

On May 8, 1968, at about 9:30 P.M., near the intersection of East 65th Street and University Avenue in Chicago, three plain-clothes policemen stopped an automobile driven by David Barksdale, a youth who was known by the policemen as the leader of the Disciples, a street gang. In the automobile with Barksdale were four young men, William Gaddy, James Hall, Tyrone Withers and Mitchell Newton. The officers, who were members of the Chicago Police Gang Intelligence Unit, searched the five, found no weapons, said a few words to them and then released the youths. Barksdale drove on and the three policemen, in an unmarked car, followed him, approximately three car lengths behind.

After a number of turns in and out of several streets, Barksdale entered Ellis Avenue at East 66th Street and proceeded north. When he was at or near 6526 South Ellis, he slowed down, stopped and raced the motor of his automobile. At the time, but without knowing that Barksdale and his companions were coming there, defendant and Melvin Bailey were at or near 6526 South Ellis. They knew each other; in fact, they were members of the Blackstone Rangers, a youth gang that was a rival of the Disciples. They knew Barksdale, could recognize his car when they saw it; and on the evening in question, had arrived at 6526 South Ellis together. A short time before Barksdale drove up, defendant heard someone shout, "... here comes David!"

At about that moment, from the west side of Ellis Avenue, as they later testified, the three policemen heard someone shout, "D's!" They saw a number of youths on both sides of the street. They heard a shot. After a pause, several shots rang out from both sides of Ellis Avenue. One officer saw "... about ten or thirteen people firing [guns]." Two of the officers saw a young man run in front of their car and fire a gun four or five times directly at Barksdale's automobile. It was Melvin Bailey. The officers pursued him; and, while being chased, he threw away a .45 caliber gun that was recovered by the officers a moment or so before they arrested him.

While Bailey was being taken into custody, the third policeman saw a young man point a gun and fire it once at Barksdale's automobile. At the same time, that officer saw two other youths firing at Barksdale's car. The youth who was alone ran into a gangway and then to a porch, followed by the policeman. The youth ducked; and a short time later the policeman, using his flashlight, found him trying to unjam a .25 caliber automatic gun. He was the defendant, Andrew McChristian. On being ordered to do so, defendant dropped the gun and was placed under arrest. No one, either in or out of Barksdale's automobile was injured; no property was damaged.

A short time later, as defendant and Bailey were being put in the police car, Edward Dinkins approached the officers and asked why the two were being held. Dinkins was arrested. Barksdale, who had driven to the corner of East 65th Street and Ellis Avenue, stopped his car there and was asked by the three policemen to go with them to an area police station where they were taking defendant, Bailey and Dinkins. At the station, according to one policeman, Bailey and defendant had a conversation with Barksdale. Bailey said to Barksdale, "We didn't get you this time." Defendant, who was listening to the conversation, chuckled and said, "We will get him next time."

Defendant was acquitted of the attempts but was found guilty of conspiracy under the charge that on May 8, 1968, he, Bailey and Dinkins "... with the intent to commit the offense of murder, knowingly and intentionally agreed with each other and with divers other persons whose names are unknown to the Grand Jurors but who the said Grand Jurors believed to be members of an organization known as the Blackstone Rangers, to the commission of the offense of murder, that is to say, they knowingly and intentionally agreed to kill by shooting without lawful justification David Barksdale, William Gaddy, James Hall, Tyrone Withers and Mitchell Newton." In furtherance of the conspiracy, it was charged that on May 8, 1968, defendant and the two others intentionally discharged firearms in the direction of an automobile in which Barksdale, Gaddy, Hall, Withers and Newton were riding, with intent to kill or do great bodily harm to the occupants of the automobile. Therefore, in view of the specificity of the charge, the question we must decide is whether evidence which disclosed the facts in this record proved that on May 8, 1968, defendant, Bailey and Dinkins conspired to murder the five persons whose murder was the object of the alleged conspiracy.

II.

The offense with which defendant, Bailey and Dinkins were charged in the conspiracy count was a specific intent crime. The gist of that crime was the unlawful combination or agreement; one into which, according to the State, the three defendants had entered with intent to murder David Barksdale and the four named companions who were in his automobile on the evening of May 8, 1968.

To sustain a conviction for conspiracy, the object of the conspiracy has to be proved as laid out in the indictment. In this case, since the object of the conspiracy, according to the charge, was the murder of five named persons, the State had to prove that when defendant and Bailey fired guns in the direction of the automobile in which the five were riding, they did so with knowledge that the purported victims were in there.

An attempt to murder requires proof of specific intent to take human life. For example, in a charge of conspiracy to mutilate the face of a named person, the State must prove that it was the face of the named person which the conspirators intended to mutilate, not that of someone else. And where it is charged that a bulb of sulfuric acid was thrown into a cab with intent to maim a named individual who was seated in the rear seat of the cab, the State must prove that the defendants knew that the intended victim was in the cab. Therefore, in a case like this one, the State had to prove not only that the defendants knew David Barksdale, could recognize his automobile and shot at him the evening of May 8, 1968; it had to prove the defendants, as conspirators, had knowledge of Barksdale's four companions and shot at Barksdale's automobile with intent to murder them. A conspiracy against a number of individuals must be proved by evidence which shows that the conspiracy was against all as charged; a conspiracy against a single person cannot be sustained by proof of a conspiracy against the public generally.

With these principles in mind, we examine the evidence on which the jury found defendant guilty of conspiracy and which the State contends supports the judgment of conviction. We observe that this record does not show any of the defendants, at any time prior to May 8, 1968, knew that David Barksdale was going to drive his automobile past 6526 South Ellis Avenue with William Gaddy, James Hall, Tyrone Withers and Mitchell Newton as his companions. There is no evidence that defendant, at any time, agreed with Bailey and Dinkins to discharge firearms in the direction of Barksdale's automobile with intent to murder the persons who were objects of the conspiracy. It is true that to prove a conspiracy evidence of an express agreement is not necessary. A conspiracy is rarely susceptible of proof by direct evidence. Therefore, a conspiracy can be proved by direct evidence that discloses a common design by two or more persons. Or it can be proved by circumstantial evidence. However, circumstantial evidence that will support a conviction for conspiracy, as is true of circumstantial evidence generally, must be such that the conclusion drawn from it excludes every reasonable hypothesis other than guilt. It has been said that a conspiracy cannot be proved by mere suspicion, mere relationship of the defendants or association of the parties charged.

In this case, evidence of the alleged conspiracy consisted of proof that defendant and Bailey knew each other, were members of the same street gang, arrived together at 6526 South Ellis Avenue on the evening of May 8, 1968, were seen by three policemen (defendant firing a gun once and Bailey four or five times at Barksdale's automobile); and later, in a conversation with Barksdale, spoke of having missed him when they fired their guns. In our judgment, the statements did not admit a conspiracy to murder Barksdale and his four companions. At most, they expressed ill will toward Barksdale.

In determining whether the evidence proved that defendant and Bailey intended to murder five persons when they discharged firearms in the direction of Barksdale's automobile, it is significant that, according to the three policemen, as many as 13 people were seen firing guns, two youths were seen firing a weapon, defendant fired once and Bailey four or five times directly at the car; yet, when the automobile was examined, there were no bullet holes on it; when a picture of it was shown to an evidence technician of the Chicago Police Department, he could not tell what caused an indentation that could be seen on its roof.

As to defendant's conduct, according to one of three policemen, he was seen firing a gun once at Barksdale's automobile. This firing, by the State's theory, was defendant's overt act in furtherance of the conspiracy; it was also, by that theory, defendant's attempt to murder Barksdale, Gaddy, Withers, Hall and Newton. The jury, however, considered the charges of attempts to murder and found defendant not guilty. The jury could have found defendant guilty on the ground that he was accountable for Bailey's conduct in firing four or five times at the automobile, but it did not. There is no other evidence of any other act by the defendant. The crimes which the State charged were factually intertwined, and since each crime was covered by a separate count of the indictment, there is a logical inconsistency in the verdicts: five acquitted defendant of attempts to murder, one found him guilty of conspiracy to murder the same five persons. This does not make the verdicts legally inconsistent. However, this inconsistency tends to negate the existence of an element essential to proof of the crime of which defendant was convicted. That element, on the peculiar facts of this case, is the overt act of shooting which by its verdicts of acquittal the jury must have found defendant did not commit with intent to murder the five occupants of the automobile.

[W]e do not condone defendant's conduct nor that of Bailey. The evidence, in our judgment, proved that on the evening of May 8, 1968, according to three policemen whose testimony the jury chose to believe, defendant and Bailey acted in concert to endanger public safety and health by discharging firearms in one of the most densely populated areas of Chicago. However, the conviction for conspiracy in this case cannot be sustained by evidence that the defendants were guilty of some other charge or of generally bad and criminal conduct; the evidence must prove their guilt of the particular charge made in the indictment. Heinous as was their conduct, the evidence in this record did not prove a conspiracy to murder five persons, as was charged by the State. Therefore, the judgment is reversed.

Comments and Questions

(1) On appeal, the state supreme court affirmed. *People v. Bailey*, 322 N.E.2d 804 (Ill. 1975). Compare the majority and dissenting opinions. Justice Kluczynski:

> The State argues that the concerted efforts of Bailey and McChristian at the time of the shooting as well as their conversation in the police station after

their arrests is sufficient to permit a jury to conclude that a conspiracy existed. We do not agree.

The evidence does not establish beyond a reasonable doubt that Bailey, McChristian and others had agreed to murder Barksdale or any one else. Rather it clearly appears that Barksdale drove to the Ellis Avenue location in a car known to defendants and others, stopped and then raced the motor. The obvious purpose was to incite a rival and hostile street gang knowing that the police were a short distance behind in an unmarked squad car. Almost simultaneously with Barksdale's unexpected appearance and his recognition, gunfire erupted from both sides of the street.

While it might be argued that the defendants were members of a rival street gang, this mere relationship does not establish an intent to agree to kill Barksdale. Moreover, while the statements of Bailey and McChristian at the police station after the shooting might be construed as admitting to a conspiracy to shoot Barksdale, under the circumstances of this case, particularly the almost instantaneous or "knee jerk" reaction attributed to the defendants as well as other possible gang members, the evidence is sufficiently improbable and raises a reasonable doubt of a conspiracy to murder.

322 N.E.2d at 809.

Justice Ryan (dissenting):

Of course, it is not necessary, and in most cases not possible, to prove an agreement between co-conspirators by direct evidence. It is only necessary to show that they pursued a course tending toward the accomplishment of the objective of which complaint is made. Whether a scheme is a conspiracy or separate ventures is ordinarily a question of fact and may be proved not only by direct evidence but by inferences from conduct, statements, facts and circumstances which disclose a common design on the part of the accused and others to act in pursuance of a common criminal purpose. Examining the evidence of conspiracy in the light of these principles, we find that McChristian and Bailey knew each other; they were members of the same street gang; David Barksdale was a member of a rival street gang; McChristian and Bailey were sitting on a porch with some girls when someone shouted, "Here comes David"; the defendants knew David Barksdale and his automobile; the defendants were both seen by the officers firing shots at Barksdale's automobile as it left the scene and Officer Peck testified that at the police station, as noted above, Bailey said to Barksdale, "We didn't get you this time," and McChristian, who was chuckling, responded, "We will get him next time." In my opinion, these facts, particularly the statements of Bailey and McChristian made at the police station, clearly establish that a common design existed to murder Barksdale. In fact McChristian's reply, "We will get him next time," is strong evidence that the common design to murder him had not terminated.

Id. at 810.

(2) The trial judge gave the following instruction in the Watergate conspiracy trial, *United States v. Haldeman*, 559 F.2d 31, 113 (D.C. Cir. 1976), *cert. denied*, 431 U.S. 933 (1977):

> The Government must also prove, as part of the second element of the crime of conspiracy, that each Defendant who allegedly participated in the conspiracy charged did so with criminal intent.
>
> "Intent" means that a person had the purpose to do a thing; it means that he made an act of the will to do the thing; it means that the thing was done consciously and voluntarily and not inadvertently or accidentally.
>
> Now, some criminal offenses require only a general intent. Where this is so and it is shown that a person has knowingly committed an act which the law makes a crime, intent may be inferred from the doing of the act. Other offenses, *such as this one* [conspiracy], require a specific intent. Specific intent requires more than a mere general intent to engage in certain conduct or to do certain acts. A person who knowingly does an act which the law forbids intending with bad purpose either to disobey or disregard the law, may be found to act with specific intent.

(3) In *Commonwealth v. Mobley*, 359 A.2d 367, 367–68 (Pa. 1976), the court stated the facts:

> The evidence produced at trial consisted of appellant's statement to the police and the testimony of Cleveland Johnson, an eyewitness to the crime. This evidence indicated that on May 27, 1974, appellant and fellow members of the "Valley" gang were walking on a street in Philadelphia when they encountered members of the rival "Norris Street" gang. Words were exchanged and appellant and his friends became incensed at remarks made by members of the "Norris Street" gang concerning the killing of a "Valley" gang member the year before. Several members of the "Valley" gang shouted "Valley" and began chasing the "Norris Street" gang.
>
> In his statement to the police, appellant admitted that he engaged in a fight with Cleveland Johnson, a member of the "Norris Street" gang. When this individual affray ended, appellant turned and saw his brother, Anthony, and four other members of the "Valley" gang beating the decedent, Stephen Harris. Appellant noticed his brother with a knife and was with him when he discarded it into a sewer, but he denied witnessing the actual stabbing.
>
> Cleveland Johnson testified that appellant stabbed him with a knife and then joined the group assaulting Stephen Harris. He identified the appellant as the actual slayer. However, the Commonwealth volunteered that, based upon their information, Johnson was mistaken on this latter point and that appellant's brother, Anthony, committed the actual stabbing. However, the Commonwealth did not discredit the other portions of Johnson's testimony which indicated that the appellant had participated in the homicide.

> The trial judge found that appellant not only attacked Cleveland Johnson with a knife but also joined the group assaulting the decedent. As such, the trial judge concluded that appellant was part of a conspiracy to commit murder which was formed the moment the "Valley" gang began chasing the "Norris Street" gang.

Should the appellant's conviction for conspiracy be affirmed? It was. *But see State v. Mariano R.*, 934 P.2d 315, 317 (N.M. Ct. App. 1997):

> To be guilty of conspiracy the Child must have agreed with one or more other occupants of the car that one of the parties to the agreement would shoot a firearm recklessly from the vehicle. The agreement could be explicit or a "mutually implied understanding." On the other hand, mere passive submission or acquiescence in the conduct of others will not suffice. The conspirator must share the "purpose of committing [the] felony." "[I]t would not be sufficient ... if the actor only believed that the result would be produced but did not consciously plan or desire to produce it."
>
> The question before us is whether the evidence presented at trial was sufficient to establish beyond a reasonable doubt each element of the offense of conspiracy. Although the evidence must be viewed in the light most favorable to the verdict, the answer is "No." The evidence would suffice to establish that the Child knew that there were firearms in the vehicle and was present when one was fired. Beyond that, however, one must speculate. There is no evidence regarding what happened in the vehicle before the shot was fired. There is no evidence that the Child knew that anyone planned to fire a shot from the vehicle, much less that the Child joined in the planning.

(4) In *State v. Herrera*, 83 Cal. Rptr. 2d 307 (Cal. Ct. App. 1999), the conviction for conspiracy to commit murder was affirmed with strong reliance on evidence that the defendant was a member of a street gang, that the defendant told others that his fellow gang members "were after" a rival gang, and that he was going to "back up" his fellow gang members. Contrast with *United States v. Garcia*, 151 F.3d 1243, 1244 (9th Cir. 1998), where the court wrote:

> Because there is no direct evidence of an agreement to commit the criminal act which was the alleged object of the conspiracy, and because the circumstances of the shooting do not support the existence of an agreement, implicit or explicit, the government relied heavily on the gang affiliation of the participants to show the existence of such an agreement. We hold that gang membership itself cannot establish guilt of a crime, and a general agreement, implicit or explicit, to support one another in gang fights does not provide substantial proof of the specific agreement required for a conviction of conspiracy to commit assault.

United States v. Feola

United States Supreme Court

420 U.S. 671 (1975)

Mr. Justice Blackmun delivered the opinion of the Court.

This case presents the issue whether knowledge that the intended victim is a federal officer is a requisite for the crime of conspiracy, under 18 U.S.C. § 371, to commit an offense violative of 18 U.S.C. § 111,[1] that is, an assault upon a federal officer while engaged in the performance of his official duties.

Respondent Feola and three others were indicted for violations of §§ 371 and 111. A jury found all four defendants guilty of both charges. Because of a conflict among the federal Circuits on the scienter issue with respect to a conspiracy charge, we granted the Government's petition for a writ of certiorari in Feola's case.

I.

The facts reveal a classic narcotics "rip-off." The details are not particularly important for our present purposes. We need note only that the evidence shows that Feola and his confederates arranged for a sale of heroin to buyers who turned out to be undercover agents for the Bureau of Narcotics and Dangerous Drugs. The group planned to palm off on the purchasers, for a substantial sum, a form of sugar in place of heroin and, should that ruse fail, simply to surprise their unwitting buyers and relieve them of the cash they had brought along for payment. The plan failed when one agent, his suspicions being aroused, drew his revolver in time to counter an assault upon another agent from the rear. Instead of enjoying the rich benefits of a successful swindle, Feola and his associates found themselves charged, to their undoubted surprise, with conspiring to assault, and with assaulting, federal officers.

At the trial, the District Court, without objection from the defense, charged the jurors that, in order to find any of the defendants guilty on either the conspiracy count or the substantive one, they were not required to conclude that the defendants were aware that their quarry were federal officers.

The Court of Appeals reversed the conspiracy convictions on a ground not advanced by any of the defendants. Although it approved the trial court's instructions to the jury on the substantive charge of assaulting a federal officer, it nonetheless concluded that the failure to charge that knowledge of the victim's official identity must be proved in order to convict on the conspiracy charge amounted to plain error. The court perceived itself bound by a line of cases, commencing with Judge Learned

---

1. "§ 111. Assaulting, resisting, or impeding certain officers or employees.

Whoever forcibly assaults, resists, opposes, impedes, intimidates, or interferes with any person designated in section 1114 of this title while engaged in or on account of the performance of his official duties, shall be fined not more than $5,000 or imprisoned not more than three years, or both.

Whoever, in the commission of any such acts uses a deadly or dangerous weapon, shall be fined not more than $10,000 or imprisoned not more than ten years, or both.

Among the persons "designated in section 1114" of 18 U.S.C. is "any officer or employee ... of the Bureau of Narcotics and Dangerous Drugs."

Hand's opinion in *United States v. Crimmins*, 123 F.2d 271 (CA2 1941), all holding that scienter of a factual element that confers federal jurisdiction, while unnecessary for conviction of the substantive offense, is required in order to sustain a conviction for conspiracy to commit the substantive offense. Although the court noted that the *Crimmins* rationale "has been criticized," and, indeed, offered no argument in support of it, it accepted "the controlling precedents somewhat reluctantly."

II.

The Government's plea is for symmetry. It urges that since criminal liability for the offense described in 18 U.S.C. § 111 does not depend on whether the assailant harbored the specific intent to assault a federal officer, no greater scienter requirement can be engrafted upon the conspiracy offense, which is merely an agreement to commit the act proscribed by § 111. Consideration of the Government's contention requires us preliminarily to pass upon its premise, the proposition that responsibility for assault upon a federal officer does not depend upon whether the assailant was aware of the official identity of his victim at the time he acted.

That the "federal officer" requirement is anything other than jurisdictional is not seriously urged upon us; indeed, both Feola and the Court of Appeals concede that scienter is not a necessary element of the substantive offense under § 111.

We hold, therefore, that in order to incur criminal liability under § 111 an actor must entertain merely the criminal intent to do the acts therein specified. We now consider whether the rule should be different where persons conspire to commit those acts.

III.

Our decisions establish that in order to sustain a judgment of conviction on a charge of conspiracy to violate a federal statute, the Government must prove at least the degree of criminal intent necessary for the substantive offense itself. Respondent Feola urges upon us the proposition that the Government must show a degree of criminal intent in the conspiracy count greater than is necessary to convict for the substantive offense; he urges that even though it is not necessary to show that he was aware of the official identity of his assaulted victims in order to find him guilty of assaulting federal officers, in violation of 18 U.S.C. § 111, the Government nonetheless must show that he was aware that his intended victims were undercover agents, if it is successfully to prosecute him for conspiring to assault federal agents. And the Court of Appeals held that the trial court's failure to charge the jury to this effect constituted plain error.

The general conspiracy statute, 18 U.S.C. § 371,[20] offers no textual support for the proposition that to be guilty of conspiracy a defendant in effect must have known that his conduct violated federal law. The statute makes it unlawful simply to "conspire ... to commit any offense against the United States." A natural reading of these

---

20. Title 18 U.S.C. § 371 provides:

If two or more persons conspire either to commit any offense against the United States, or to defraud the United States, or any agency thereof in any manner or for any purpose, and one or more of such persons do any act to effect the object of the conspiracy, each shall be fined not more than $10,000 or imprisoned not more than five years, or both.

words would be that since one can violate a criminal statute simply by engaging in the forbidden conduct, a conspiracy to commit that offense is nothing more than an agreement to engage in the prohibited conduct. Then where, as here, the substantive statute does not require that an assailant know the official status of his victim, there is nothing on the face of the conspiracy statute that would seem to require that those agreeing to the assault have a greater degree of knowledge.

With no support on the face of the general conspiracy statute or in this Court's decisions, respondent relies solely on the line of cases commencing with *United States v. Crimmins*, 123 F.2d 271 (CA2 1941), for the principle that the Government must prove "antifederal" intent in order to establish liability under § 371. In *Crimmins*, the defendant had been found guilty of conspiring to receive stolen bonds that had been transported in interstate commerce. Upon review, the Court of Appeals pointed out that the evidence failed to establish that Crimmins actually knew the stolen bonds had moved into the State. Accepting for the sake of argument the assumption that such knowledge was not necessary to sustain a conviction on the substantive offense, Judge Learned Hand nevertheless concluded that to permit conspiratorial liability where the conspirators were ignorant of the federal implications of their acts would be to enlarge their agreement beyond its terms as they understood them. He capsulized the distinction in what has become well known as his "traffic light" analogy:

> While one may, for instance, be guilty of running past a traffic light of whose existence one is ignorant, one cannot be guilty of conspiring to run past such a light, for one cannot agree to run past a light unless one supposes that there is a light to run past.

Judge Hand's attractive, but perhaps seductive, analogy has received a mixed reception in the Courts of Appeals. The Second Circuit, of course, has followed it; others have rejected it. It appears that most have avoided it by the simple expedient of inferring the requisite knowledge from the scope of the conspiratorial venture. We conclude that the analogy, though effective prose, is, as applied to the facts before us, bad law.[24]

We hold here only that where a substantive offense embodies only a requirement of *mens rea* as to each of its elements, the general federal conspiracy statute requires no more.

The *Crimmins* rule rests upon another foundation: that it is improper to find conspiratorial liability where the parties to the illicit agreement were not aware of the fact giving rise to federal jurisdiction, because the essence of conspiracy is agreement and persons cannot be punished for acts beyond the scope of their agreement. This "reason" states little more than a conclusion, for it is clear that one may be guilty as a conspirator for acts the precise details of which one does not know at the time of

---

24. The Government rather effectively exposes the fallacy of the *Crimmins* traffic light analogy by recasting it in terms of a jurisdictional element. The suggested example is a traffic light on an Indian reservation. Surely, one may conspire with others to disobey the light but be ignorant of the fact that it is on the reservation. As applied to a jurisdictional element of this kind the formulation makes little sense.

the agreement. The question is not merely whether the official status of an assaulted victim was known to the parties at the time of their agreement, but whether the acts contemplated by the conspirators are to be deemed legally different from those actually performed solely because of the official identity of the victim. Put another way, does the identity of the proposed victim alter the legal character of the acts agreed to, or is it no more germane to the nature of those acts than the color of the victim's hair?

Our analysis of the substantive offense in Part II, *supra*, is sufficient to convince us that for the purpose of individual guilt or innocence, awareness of the official identity of the assault victim is irrelevant. We would expect the same to obtain with respect to the conspiracy offense unless one of the policies behind the imposition of conspiratorial liability is not served where the parties to the agreement are unaware that the intended target is a federal law enforcement official.

It is well settled that the law of conspiracy serves ends different from, and complementary to, those served by criminal prohibitions of the substantive offense. Because of this, consecutive sentences may be imposed for the conspiracy and for the underlying crime. Our decisions have identified two independent values served by the law of conspiracy. The first is protection of society from the dangers of concerted criminal activity. That individuals know that their planned joint venture violates federal as well as state law seems totally irrelevant to that purpose of conspiracy law which seeks to protect society from the dangers of concerted criminal activity. Given the level of criminal intent necessary to sustain conviction for the substantive offense, the act of agreement to commit the crime is no less opprobrious and no less dangerous because of the absence of knowledge of a fact unnecessary to the formation of criminal intent. Indeed, unless imposition of an "antifederal" knowledge requirement serves social purposes external to the law of conspiracy of which we are unaware, its imposition here would serve only to make it more difficult to obtain convictions on charges of conspiracy, a policy with no apparent purpose.

The second aspect is that conspiracy is an inchoate crime. This is to say, that, although the law generally makes criminal only antisocial conduct, at some point in the continuum between preparation and consummation, the likelihood of a commission of an act is sufficiently great and the criminal intent sufficiently well formed to justify the intervention of the criminal law. The law of conspiracy identifies the agreement to engage in a criminal venture as an event of sufficient threat to social order to permit the imposition of criminal sanctions for the agreement alone, plus an overt act in pursuit of it, regardless of whether the crime agreed upon actually is committed. Criminal intent has crystallized, and the likelihood of actual, fulfilled commission warrants preventive action.

Again, we do not see how imposition of a strict "antifederal" scienter requirement would relate to this purpose of conspiracy law. Given the level of intent needed to carry out the substantive offense, we fail to see how the agreement is any less blameworthy or constitutes less of a danger to society solely because the participants are unaware which body of law they intend to violate. Therefore, we again conclude that imposition of a requirement of knowledge of those facts that serve only to establish federal jurisdiction would render it more difficult to serve the policy behind the law of conspiracy without serving any other apparent social policy.

The judgment of the Court of Appeals with respect to the respondent's conspiracy conviction is reversed.

Mr. Justice Stewart, with whom Mr. Justice Douglas joins, dissenting.

I believe that before there can be a violation of U.S.C. § 111, an assailant must know or have reason to know that the person he assaults is an officer. It follows *a fortiori* that there can be no criminal conspiracy to violate the statute in the absence of at least equivalent knowledge. Accordingly, I respectfully dissent from the opinion and judgment of the Court.

Comments and Questions

Does § 111 require proof of scienter? If not, what of the intent requirement for conspiracy? Did the Court ignore the requirement?

United States v. Bruno

United States Court of Appeals, Second Circuit
105 F.2d 921, *rev'd on other grounds*, 308 U.S. 287 (1939)

Before L. Hand, Augustus N. Hand, and Clark, Circuit Judges.

Per Curiam.

Bruno and Iacono were indicted along with 86 others for a conspiracy to import, sell and possess narcotics; some were acquitted; others, besides these two, were convicted, but they alone appealed. They complain that if the evidence proved anything, it proved a series of separate conspiracies, and not a single one, as alleged in the indictment.

The first point was made at the conclusion of the prosecution's case; the defendants then moved to dismiss the indictment on the ground that several conspiracies had been proved, and not the one alleged. The evidence allowed the jury to find that there had existed over a substantial period of time a conspiracy embracing a great number of persons, whose object was to smuggle narcotics into the Port of New York and distribute them to addicts both in this city and in Texas and Louisiana. This required the cooperation of four groups of persons: the smugglers who imported the drugs; the middlemen who paid the smugglers and distributed to retailers; and two groups of retailers—one in New York and one in Texas and Louisiana—who supplied the addicts. The defendants assert that there were, therefore, at least three separate conspiracies; one between the smugglers and the middlemen, and one between the middlemen and each group of retailers. The evidence did not disclose any cooperation or communication between the smugglers and either group of retailers, or between the two groups of retailers themselves; however, the smugglers knew that the middlemen must sell to retailers, and the retailers knew that the middlemen must buy of importers of one sort or another. Thus the conspirators at one end of the chain knew that the unlawful business would not, and could not, stop with their buyers; and those at the other end knew that it had not begun with their sellers. That being true, a jury might have found that all the accused were embarked upon a venture, in all parts of which each was a participant, and an abettor in the sense that the success of that part with which he was immediately concerned, was dependent upon the success of the whole. That distinguishes the situation from that in *United States v. Peoni*, 2 Cir., 100 F.2d 401, where Peoni, the accused, did not know that Regno, his buyer, was to sell the counterfeit bills to Dorsey, and had no interest in whether he did, since Regno might equally well have passed them to innocent persons himself. It might still be argued that there were two conspiracies; one including the smugglers, the middlemen and the New York group, and the other, the smugglers, the middlemen and the Texas and Louisiana group, for there was apparently no privity between the two groups of retailers. That too would be fallacious. Clearly, quoad the smugglers, there was but one conspiracy, for it was of no moment to them whether the middlemen sold to one or more groups of retailers, provided they had a market somewhere. So too of any retailer; he knew that he was a necessary link in a scheme of distribution, and the others, whom he knew to be convenient to its execution, were as much parts of a single undertaking or enterprise as two salesmen in the same shop. We think therefore that there was only one conspiracy.

Comments and Questions

(1) If the defendant smuggler never met—or even heard of—the defendant retailer, how could this distinguished court find that the defendants all intended to agree to import and sell the narcotics? *See United States v. Agueci*, 310 F.2d 817, 827 (2d Cir. 1962), *cert. denied*, 372 U.S. 959 (1963):

> An individual associating himself with a "chain" conspiracy knows that it has a "scope" and that for its success it requires an organization wider than may be disclosed by his personal participation. Merely because the Government in this case did not show that each defendant knew each and every conspirator and every step taken by them did not place the complaining appellants outside the scope of the single conspiracy. Each defendant might be found to have contributed to the success of the overall conspiracy, notwithstanding that he operated on only one level.
>
> The nature of the enterprise determines whether the inference of knowledge of the existence of others in one overall conspiracy is justified. It is clear that in a narcotic conspiracy case of this nature no one member of the group can by himself insure the success of the venture; he must know that combined efforts are required.

(2) In *United States v. Peoni*, 100 F.2d 401 (2d Cir. 1938), decided just one year before *Bruno*, the government proved that the defendant knowingly sold counterfeit bills to Regno who sold them to Dorsey. Did Peoni conspire with Dorsey?

> Assuming that Peoni and Regno agreed that Regno should have possession of the bills, it is absurd to say that Peoni agreed that Dorsey should have

> them from Regno. Peoni knew that somebody besides Regno might get them, but a conspiracy also imports a concert of purpose, and again Peoni had no concern with the bills after Regno paid for them. At times it seemed to be supposed that, once some kind of criminal concert is established, all parties are liable for everything anyone of the original participants does, and even for what those do who join later. Nothing could be more untrue. Nobody is liable in conspiracy except for the fair import of the concerted purpose or agreement as he understands it; if later comers change that, he is not liable for the change; his liability is limited to the common purposes while he remains in it. The confusion is perhaps due to the fact that everything done by the conspirators—including the declarations of later entrants—is competent evidence against all, so far as it may fairly be thought to be in execution of the concert to which the accused is privy, though that doctrine too is abused.

Id. at 403.

Would the result change if Peoni had been dealing with Regno for a long period of time?

(3) Sometimes intent and agreement are proved through the use of the wheel/circle conspiracy metaphor:

> The multiple conspiracy problem is raised most frequently by what may be termed the "circle" conspiracy. This occurs when a number of persons (the spokes) are engaged in similar relationships with the same individual or group (the hub). Assuming that a criminal conspiracy exists between each spoke and the hub, the problem is whether the spokes can be drawn together into a single all-inclusive conspiracy.
>
> Although the hub may view his dealings with each spoke as part of a single large enterprise, the spoke is ordinarily concerned merely with his own transaction and is generally not held to have conspired with other spokes unless it can be inferred that their existence was known to him. When such knowledge is shown, it may be fairly said that the spoke was aware of, and thus consented to, the over-all plan as envisaged by the hub. To dispense with the requirement of demonstrating knowledge of the existence of other spokes is to refuse to distinguish between the agreement as seen by the hub and that viewed by the spokes. Under this approach, a finding of a single conspiracy is unduly facilitated by holding each spoke to the scope of the broader plan.

Note, *Federal Treatment of Multiple Conspiracies*, 57 Colum. L. Rev. 387, 388–89 (1957).

How helpful are these terms? Consider Judge Friendly's opinion in *United States v. Borelli*, 336 F.2d 376, 383–84 (2d Cir. 1964), *cert. denied*, 379 U.S. 960 (1965):

> As applied to the long term operation of an illegal business, the common pictorial distinction between "chain" and "spoke" conspiracies can obscure as much as it clarifies. The chain metaphor is indeed apt in that the links of a narcotics conspiracy are inextricably related to one another, from grower,

through exporter and importer, to wholesaler, middleman, and retailer, each depending for his own success on the performance of all the others. But this simple picture tends to obscure that the links at either end are likely to consist of a number of persons who may have no reason to know that others are performing a role similar to theirs—in other words the extreme links of a chain conspiracy may have elements of the spoke conspiracy. Moreover, whatever the value of the chain concept where the problem is to trace a single operation from the start through its various phases to its successful conclusion, it becomes confusing when, over a long period of time, certain links continue to play the same role but with new counterparts, as where importers who regard their partnership as a single continuing one, having successfully distributed one cargo through X distributing organization, turn, years later, to moving another cargo obtained from a different source through Y. Thus, however reasonable the so-called presumption of continuity may be as to all the participants of a conspiracy which intends a single act, such as the robbing of a bank, or even as to the core of a conspiracy to import and resell narcotics, its force is diminished as to the outer links—buyers indifferent to their sources of supply and turning from one source to another, and suppliers equally indifferent to the identity of their customers.

[B] The Agreement

Direct Sales Co. v. United States

United States Supreme Court
319 U.S. 703 (1943)

Mr. Justice Rutledge delivered the opinion of the Court.

Petitioner, a corporation, was convicted of conspiracy to violate the Harrison Narcotic Act. It challenges the sufficiency of the evidence to sustain the conviction. Because of asserted conflict with *United States v. Falcone*, 311 U.S. 205 [61 S. Ct. 204, 85 L. Ed. 128], certiorari was granted.

Petitioner is a registered drug manufacturer and wholesaler. It conducts a nationwide mail-order business from Buffalo, New York. The evidence relates chiefly to its transactions with one Dr. John V. Tate and his dealings with others. He was a registered physician, practicing in Calhoun Falls, South Carolina, a community of about 2000 persons. He dispensed illegally vast quantities of morphine sulphate purchased by mail from petitioner. The indictment charged petitioner, Dr. Tate, and three others, Black, Johnson and Foster, to and through whom Tate illegally distributed the drugs, with conspiring to violate Sections 1 and 2 of this Act over a period extending from 1933 to 1940. Foster was granted a severance, Black and Johnson pleaded guilty, and petitioner and Dr. Tate were convicted. Direct Sales alone appealed.

The parties here are at odds concerning the effect of the *Falcone* decision as applied to the facts proved in this case. The salient facts are that Direct Sales sold morphine sulphate to Dr. Tate in such quantities, so frequently and over so long a period it must have known he could not dispense the amounts received in lawful practice and was therefore distributing the drug illegally. Not only so, but it actively stimulated Tate's purchases.

He was a small-town physician practicing in a rural section. All of his business with Direct Sales was done by mail. Through its catalogues petitioner first made contact with him prior to 1933. Originally, he purchased a variety of pharmaceuticals. But gradually the character of his purchases narrowed, so that during the last two years of the period alleged for the conspiracy he ordered almost nothing but morphine sulphate. At all times during the period he purchased the major portion of his morphine sulphate from petitioner. The orders were made regularly on his official order forms. The testimony shows the average physician in the United States does not require more than 400 one-quarter grain tablets annually for legitimate use. Although Tate's initial purchases in 1933 were smaller, they gradually increased until, from November, 1937, to January, 1940, they amounted to 79,000 one-half grain tablets. In the last six months of 1939, petitioner's shipments to him averaged 5,000 to 6,000 half-grain tablets a month, enough as the Government points out to enable him to give 400 average doses every day.

These quantity sales were in line with the general mail-order character of petitioner's business. By printed catalogues circulated about three times a month, it solicits orders from retail druggists and physicians located for the most part in small towns throughout the country. Of annual sales of from $300,000 to $350,000 in the period 1936 to 1940, about fifteen per cent by revenue and two-and-a-half per cent by volume were in narcotics. The mail-order plan enabled petitioner to sell at prices considerably lower than were charged by its larger competitors, who maintained sales forces and traveling representatives. By offering fifty per cent discounts on narcotics, it "pushed" quantity sales. Instead of listing narcotics, like morphine sulphate, in quantities not exceeding 100 tablets, as did many competitors, Direct Sales for some time listed them in 500, 1000 and 5000 tablet units. By this policy it attracted customers, including a disproportionately large group of physicians who had been convicted of violating the Harrison Act.

All this was not without warning, purpose or design. In 1936 the Bureau of Narcotics informed petitioner it was being used as a source of supply by convicted physicians. The same agent also warned that the average physician would order no more than 200 to 400 quarter-grain tablets annually and requested it to eliminate the listing of 5000 lots. It did so, but continued the 1000 and 500 lot listings at attractive discounts. It filled no more orders from Tate for more than 1000 tablets, but continued to supply him for that amount at half-grain strength. On one occasion in 1939 he ordered on one form 1000 half and 100 quarter grains. Petitioner sent him the 1000 and advised him to reorder the 100 on a separate order form. It attached to this letter a sticker printed in red suggesting anticipation of future needs and taking advantage of discounts offered. Three days later Tate ordered 1000 more tablets, which petitioner sent out. In 1940, at the Bureau's suggestion, Direct Sales eliminated its fifty and ten per cent discounts. But on doing so it translated its discount into its net price.

Tate distributed the drugs to and through addicts and purveyors, including Johnson, Black and Foster. Although he purchased from petitioner at less than two dollars, he sold at prices ranging from four to eight dollars per 100 half-grain tablets and purveyors from him charged addicts as much as $25 per hundred.

On this evidence, the Government insists the case is in different posture from that presented in *United States v. Falcone.* It urges that the effort there was to connect the respondents with a conspiracy between the distillers on the basis of the aiding and abetting statute. The attempt failed because the Court held the evidence did not establish the respondents knew of the distillers' conspiracy. There was no attempt to link the supplier and the distiller in a conspiracy *inter sese.* But in this case that type of problem is presented. Direct Sales was tried, and its conviction has been sustained, according to the claim, on the theory it could be convicted only if it were found that it and Tate conspired together to subvert the order form provisions of the Harrison Act. As the brief puts the Government's view, "Petitioner's guilt was not made to depend at all upon any guilt of Dr. Tate growing out of his relationship to defendants other than petitioner or upon whether these other defendants were linked with the Tate-Direct Sales conspiracy."

On the other hand, petitioner asserts this case falls squarely within the facts and the ruling in the *Falcone* case. It insists there is no more to show conspiracy between itself and Tate than there was to show conspiracy between the respondent sellers and the purchasing distillers there. At most, it urges, there were only legal sales by itself to Dr. Tate, accompanied by knowledge he was distributing goods illegally. But this, it contends, cannot amount to conspiracy on its part with him, since in the *Falcone* case the respondents sold to the distillers, knowing they would use the goods in illegal distillation.

Petitioner obviously misconstrues the effect of the *Falcone* decision in one respect. This is in regarding it as deciding that one who sells to another with knowledge that the buyer will use the article for an illegal purpose cannot, under any circumstances, be found guilty of conspiracy with the buyer to further his illegal end. The assumption seems to be that, under the ruling, so long as the seller does not know there is a conspiracy between the buyer and others, he cannot be guilty of conspiring with the buyer, to further the latter's illegal and known intended use, by selling goods to him.

The *Falcone* case creates no such sweeping insulation for sellers to known illicit users. That decision comes down merely to this, that one does not become a party to a conspiracy by aiding and abetting it, through sales of supplies or otherwise, unless he knows of the conspiracy; and the inference of such knowledge cannot be drawn merely from knowledge the buyer will use the goods illegally. The Government did not contend, in those circumstances, as the opinion points out, that there was a conspiracy between the buyer and the seller alone. It conceded that on the evidence neither the act of supplying itself nor the other proof was of such a character as imported an agreement or concert of action between the buyer and the seller amounting to conspiracy. This was true, notwithstanding some of the respondents could be taken to know their customers would use the purchased goods in illegal distillation.

The scope of the concession must be measured in the light of the evidence with reference to which it was made. This related to both the volume of the sales and to casual and unexplained meetings of some of the respondents with others who were convicted as conspirators. The Court found this evidence too vague and uncertain to support a finding the respondents knew of the distillers' conspiracy, though not inadequate in some instances to sustain one that the seller knew the buyer would use the goods for illegal distilling. It must be taken also that the Government regarded the same evidence as insufficient to show the seller conspired directly with the buyer, by selling to him with knowledge of his intended illegal use.

Whether or not it was consistent making this concession and in regarding the same evidence as sufficient to show that the sellers knew of and joined the buyers' distilling ring is not material. Nor need it be determined whether the Government conceded too much. We do not now undertake to say what the Court was not asked and therefore declined to say in the *Falcone* case, namely, that the evidence presented in that case was sufficient to sustain a finding of conspiracy between the seller and the buyer *inter sese*. For, regardless of that, the facts proved in this case show much more than the evidence did there.

The commodities sold there were articles of free commerce, sugar, cans, etc. They were not restricted as to sale by order form, registration, or other requirements. When they left the seller's stock and passed to the purchaser's hands, they were not in themselves restricted commodities, incapable of further legal use except by compliance with rigid regulations, such as apply to morphine sulphate. The difference is like that between toy pistols or hunting rifles and machine guns. All articles of commerce may be put to illegal ends. But all do not have inherently the same susceptibility to harmful and illegal use. Nor, by the same token, do all embody the same capacity, from their very nature, for giving the seller notice the buyer will use them unlawfully. Gangsters, not hunters or small boys, comprise the normal private market for machine guns. So drug addicts furnish the normal outlet for morphine which gets outside the restricted channels of legitimate trade.

This difference is important for two purposes. One is for making certain that the seller knows the buyer's intended illegal use. The other is to show that by the sale he intends to further, promote and cooperate in it. This intent, when given effect by overt act, is the gist of conspiracy. While it is not identical with mere knowledge that another purposes unlawful action, it is not unrelated to such knowledge. Without the knowledge, the intent cannot exist. Furthermore, to establish the intent, the evidence of knowledge must be clear, not equivocal. This, because charges of conspiracy are not to be made out by piling inference upon inference, thus fashioning what, in that case, was called a dragnet to draw in all substantive crimes.

The difference between sugar, cans, and other articles of normal trade, on the one hand, and narcotic drugs, machine guns and such restricted commodities, on the other, arising from the latter's inherent capacity for harm and from the very fact they are restricted, makes a difference in the quantity of proof required to show knowledge that the buyer will utilize the article unlawfully. Additional facts, such as quantity sales, high-pressure sales methods, abnormal increases in the size of the buyer's purchases, etc., which would be wholly innocuous or not more than ground for suspicion in relation to unrestricted goods, may furnish conclusive evidence, in respect to restricted articles, that the seller knows the buyer has an illegal object and enterprise. Knowledge, equivocal and uncertain as to one, becomes sure as to the other. So far as knowledge is the foundation of intent, the latter thereby also becomes the more secure.

The difference in the commodities has a further bearing upon the existence and the proof of intent. There may be circumstances in which the evidence of knowledge is clear, yet the further step of finding the required intent cannot be taken. Concededly, not every instance of sale of restricted goods, harmful as are opiates, in which the seller knows the buyer intends to use them unlawfully, will support a charge of conspiracy. But this is not to say that a seller of harmful restricted goods has license to sell in unlimited quantities, to stimulate such sales by all the high-pressure methods, legal if not always appropriate, in the sale of free commodities; and thereby bring about subversion of the order forms, which otherwise would protect him, and violation of the Act's other restrictions. Such a view would assume that the market for opiates may be developed as any other market. But that is not true. Mass advertising and bargain-counter discounts are not appropriate to commodities so surrounded with restrictions. They do not create new legal demand and new classes of legitimate patrons, as they do for sugar, tobacco and other free commodities. Beyond narrow limits, the normal legal market for opiates is not capable of being extended by such methods. The primary effect is rather to create black markets for dope and to increase illegal demand and consumption.

When the evidence discloses such a system, working in prolonged cooperation with a physician's unlawful purpose to supply him with his stock in trade for his illicit enterprise, there is no legal obstacle to finding that the supplier not only knows and acquiesces, but joins both mind and hand with him to make its accomplishment possible. The step from knowledge to intent and agreement may be taken. There is more than suspicion, more than knowledge, acquiescence, carelessness, indifference, lack of concern. There is informed and interested cooperation, stimulation, instigation. And there is also a "stake in the venture" which, even if it may not be essential, is not irrelevant to the question of conspiracy. Petitioner's stake here was in making the profits which it knew could come only from its encouragement of Tate's illicit operations. In such a posture the case does not fall doubtfully outside either the shadowy border between lawful cooperation and criminal association or the no less elusive line which separates conspiracy from overlapping forms of criminal cooperation.

[I]t can make no difference the agreement was a tacit understanding, created by a long course of conduct and executed in the same way. Not the form or manner in which the understanding is made, but the fact of its existence and the further one of making it effective by overt conduct are the crucial matters. The proof, by the very nature of the crime, must be circumstantial and therefore inferential to an extent varying with the conditions under which the crime may be committed. But this does not mean either that the evidence may be equivocal or that petitioner is exempt from its effects when it is not so, merely because in the absence of excesses such as were committed and in other circumstances the order form would have given it protection. It follows the mere fact that none of petitioner's representatives ever met Dr. Tate face to face or held personal communion with him is immaterial. Conspiracies, in short, can be committed by mail and by mail-order houses. This is true, notwithstanding the overt acts consist solely of sales, which but for their volume, frequency and prolonged repetition, coupled with the seller's unlawful intent to further the buyer's project, would be wholly lawful transactions.

Accordingly, the judgment is affirmed.

Comments and Questions

(1) The application of the Supreme Court's doctrine by the Seventh Circuit is instructive.

> *Falcone* illustrates the doctrine that "mere" sellers and buyers are not automatically conspirators. If it were otherwise, companies that sold cellular phones to teen-age punks who have no use for them other than to set up drug deals would be in trouble, and many legitimate businesses would be required to monitor their customers' activities. Yet this does not get us very far, for no rule says that a supplier *cannot* join a conspiracy through which the product is put to an unlawful end. *Direct Sales* makes that point in holding that the jury may infer that a pharmaceutical house selling huge quantities of morphine to a physician over a seven-year span conspired with a physician to distribute the drug illegally.
>
> Where does the "mere" sale end, the conspiracy begin? One may draw a line, as *Falcone* and *Direct Sales* did, between knowledge of other persons' crimes and intent to join them, but this restates the elements of the offense without telling us when an inference of intent to join is permissible.... A long course of sales may permit a finding of conspiracy or aiding and abetting, for such conduct is both more dangerous (it is harder to ferret out crime when the criminals have a closed circle of suppliers) and more likely that the vendor's welfare is bound up with that of the organization to which he sells.... We come to the same conclusion as the Supreme Court did in *Falcone*. Lawrence knew what Zahm wanted to do in the trailer, but there is a gulf between knowledge and conspiracy. There is no evidence that Lawrence recognized, let alone that he joined and promoted, the full scope of the Nietupski organization's activities. He may have joined, or abetted, a more limited agreement to manufacture a quantity of methamphetamine, but he was not charged with that offense. Lawrence facilitated an attempted crime, and probably conspired to do this, but he did not subscribe to the broader agreement on which his conviction depends.

United States v. Blankenship, 970 F.2d 283, 285–89 (7th Cir. 1992).

(2) Should the conviction of the defendant in *People v. Lauria*, 59 Cal. Rptr. 628 (Cal. Ct. App. 1967), be affirmed? *See* Marcus, *Criminal Conspiracy: The State of Mind Crime—Intent, Proving Intent, and Anti-Federal Intent*, 1976 U. Ill. L. Rev. 627, 643:

> The Supreme Court has refrained from resolving these questions, but one California court has attempted to determine who can be charged as a conspirator in an arrangement similar to the situation in *Falcone*. Although most prosecutors will avoid charging a conspiracy when confronting facts similar to *Falcone*, the court in *California v. Lauria* reversed a conspiracy conviction of an owner of a telephone answering service. The defendant undoubtedly knew that his service was being used by prostitutes to continue their trade because he had personally used the services of at least one of the prostitutes. The state, however, offered no proof of an agreement between the defendant and the prostitutes, but sought to preserve the conspiracy conviction of Lauria by contending that his "knowledge alone of the continuing use of his telephone facilities for criminal purposes provided a sufficient basis from which his intent to participate in those criminal activities could be inferred."
>
> Lauria countered that he was like Falcone who provided a legitimate service with knowledge of its illegal use. The court responded to the defendant's argument with its explanation of the Supreme Court's *Direct Sales* opinion. The court believed that intent can be inferred when one of three conditions are present. First, when the provider of legitimate goods for illegal purposes has acquired a stake in the venture, the factfinder may infer the purveyor's intent. Second, the court may infer intent if the provided goods or service has no lawful use. Finally, sufficient evidence of the buyer's intent is present "when the volume of business ... is disproportionate to any legitimate demand ..." If these conditions are considered in light of the facts in *Lauria*, the conviction appears proper. Lauria knew of the illegal trade, and he also knew that the volume of business was beyond that of any legitimate business. Furthermore, the profits he received may have constituted a stake in the venture. Nevertheless, Lauria's conviction was reversed. In its opinion, however, the court did not rely upon the analysis of the *Falcone* court. The *Falcone* reasoning was that knowledge indicates only awareness whereas intent means purpose, and the two states of mind are not necessarily the same. The reasoning of the *Lauria* court, on the other hand, was that because the object crime of the "conspiracy" was only a misdemeanor, the factfinder could not infer the defendant's intent from his knowledge of the criminal use of his answering service. The object crime must be a felony before the court will allow the inference.

The author went on to raise some question concerning the holding in *Lauria:*

> The conclusion of the *Lauria* court is remarkable. Why can a factfinder infer intent if the object crime is a felony, but cannot if the crime is a misdemeanor? The distinction is difficult to understand. The nature of the defendant's conduct and state of mind rather than the category of the ultimate or object

> crime should determine if a court may infer intent. Whether the object crime is a felony or a misdemeanor is irrelevant in deciding if a defendant is a criminal conspirator.

Id. at 643–44.

(3) Other proof problems in the agreement area also present serious questions for judges. See, for example, *United States v. Bufalino*, 285 F.2d 408, 412–14 (2d Cir. 1960), which involved the famous Apalachin meeting of suspected gangland figures.

> **A. The Events on November 14**
>
> At 12:40 P.M. on November 14, Sergeant Edgar Croswell of the New York State Police, accompanied by another state trooper and two agents of the Alcohol and Tobacco Tax Unit of the U.S. Treasury Department, drove from a public road into the parking lot in front of Barbara's garage. Barbara's home was an estate of 130 acres in a rural section, and his house and garage were on a dead-end dirt road. After recording the license numbers of some of the eight or ten cars in the lot and observing several unidentified men, they drove away. Before leaving, however, Croswell noticed four or five men walking or running toward the house and saw at least 20 other cars parked away from the house. At 12:50, Croswell and his companions parked their car half a mile from Barbara's home and set up what amounted to a roadblock.
>
> When Croswell backed out of the Barbara driveway Mrs. Barbara saw his car and exclaimed, in the hearing of her maid, "There's the state troopers." A few minutes later Ignatius Cannone drove past the roadblock on his way to Barbara's. At about 1:15, Bartolo Guccia, in his pick-up truck, drove down from Barbara's past the parked police car and returned five minutes later. The jury could have concluded that Cannone and Guccia reported what they had seen, and that Guccia had been sent down the road to investigate.
>
> During the next few hours, 58 men were stopped and asked to identify themselves. Of these, 35 were more or less perfunctorily questioned by state troopers, occasionally assisted by federal officers. At 1:20 P.M. Emanuel Zicari and Dominic Alaimo drove past the roadblock and were stopped, on radioed instructions from Croswell, by other officers and asked to identify themselves. Next came Russell Bufalino in his Chrysler Imperial with Joseph Ida, Gerardo Catena, Dominick Oliveto and Vito Genovese. Upon being stopped at the roadblock, they all identified themselves. Bufalino said that he had come to visit his sick friend, Barbara. Vito Genovese remarked that he understood that he did not have to say anything and he said nothing. Ida, Catena, and Oliveto said nothing about the meeting and apparently were not asked about it. Other cars, driven by Joseph Magliocco, John Ormento, Pasquale Turrigiano, Anthony Riela, Pasquale Monachino, Joseph Falcone, Vincent Rao, Joseph Barbara, Jr., Cannone and Guccia, were stopped in the next few minutes. Passengers in these cars were Joseph Profaci, Sam Monachino, Pasquale

Sciortino, Anthony Guarnieri, Salvatore Falcone, Rosario Mancuso, Dominick D'Agostino and Sam Lagattuta.

After it began to rain, at about 2:30 P.M., the officers took those stopped at the roadblock to the Vestal barracks located about seven miles away. So treated were Santo Trafficante, James Osticco, Frank DeSimone, Joseph Civello, Simone Scozzari, Joseph Rosato, Natale Evola, Frank Cucchiara, Carmine Lombardozzi, Joseph Riccobono, Paul Castellano, Carlo Gambino, Michele Miranda, Armand Rava, Constanza Valenti, Frank Valenti, Angelo Sciandra, Charles Chiri, Mike Genovese, Gabriel Mannarino, and Salvatore Tornabe.

At about 1:45 P.M., A.T.U. agent Brown had seen eight or ten men walking in single file toward some woods and pastures behind Barbara's house, and A.T.U. agent Ruston had seen three or four running in the open away from the house. Four of these men were apprehended in the fields—John Montana, Antonio Magaddino, Joseph Bonanno and Giovanni Bonventre. Between 2 and 2:30 P.M., a villager named Glen Craig saw Frank Majuri and Louis Larasso hitchhiking about three quarters of a mile from Barbara's and he gave them a ride. Agent Brown stopped Craig's car at about 3:00 P.M. and took Majuri and Larasso to the barracks. A New York State trooper found Frank Zito on the stoop of a house about a mile from Barbara's, and James Colletti was found nearby. These eight and Roy Carlisi, John DeMarco, James LaDuca and John Scalish, on whom the record is not clear as to where they were apprehended, were also taken to the Vestal barracks for questioning.

B. The Statements Made on November 14 and Thereafter

Of the 58 men who were stopped by the officers on November 14, only 36 were then questioned beyond mere identification, and of these only 27 then gave some explanation for their presence in the area. None of them suggested that they had been invited to a gathering for other than social purposes and only three said that they had been invited at all. The most common explanation, given in one form or another by ten was that the purpose of the visit was to call upon Barbara, a sick friend. Eleven gave other explanations for their visit to Barbara's. Of these, three said they were invited to a party by Bufalino; three gave personal business reasons; two claimed that they came along with others for the trip; one, Profaci, said that he was visiting an old friend; one, Magaddino, stated that his companion's car had broken down nearby; and one, Guarnieri, insisted that he came for a good meal. Six denied being at Barbara's, and gave some other reason for their presence in the area.

Of the 58 men identified on November 14, forty-three were questioned after that date and of these 35 then gave some explanation for their presence in the Apalachin area. Most of the Apalachin visitors were questioned both on November 14 and on later occasions, many of them several times.

As on November 14, none stated that he had been invited for other than social purposes. Again, the most common explanation, given by fourteen,

> was that the purpose of the visit was to call upon a sick friend or to accompany someone doing so. A related explanation was given by one, Castellano, who said he had accompanied a relative who wanted to see Barbara to discuss a similar heart condition. Nineteen gave other explanations for their visit to Barbara's. Of these, seven said that they had a personal business reason for coming; three said that they had been invited to a party; two that they had accompanied friends on business trips; two that their car had broken down; one, Zicari, that he came to see a friend; one, Riccobono, that he went for a ride; and one, Lombardozzi, that he came to hunt. Three denied being at Barbara's and gave some other reason for their presence in the area.

Should the convictions for conspiracy to commit perjury have been affirmed?

> Indeed, the pervasive innuendo throughout this case that this was a gathering of bad people for an evil purpose would seem to us to rebut any possible argument that only as a result of group action would any individual lie. Even an otherwise law abiding citizen who is stopped and interrogated by police, and who is given no reason for his detention and questioning, may feel it his right to give as little information as possible and even perhaps to respond evasively if he believes he might thereby be earlier rid of police inquiry. That others may at times go to the brink of truth, or beyond, is likely, particularly when, as may have been true in the present case, they know that the existing law does not require them to give a truthful account to police officers.
>
> After November 14 there was every reason for each Apalachin attendant to decide on his own that he would give as little information as possible about the meeting. The Croswell discovery touched off nationwide publicity of such nature, intensity, and persistence, that there were few people in the United States who did not know, within a few days of November 14, about the Apalachin meeting and the suspicions of governmental authorities that it was a meeting of underworld overlords and their vassals, commonly credited with being members of the Mafia, called for various unknown but illegal purposes. The responses of the jury panel during the *voir dire* and the voluminous newspaper, magazine, and television extracts introduced by counsel for the defendants in support of motions for transfer or continuance of the trial attest to the notoriety of the Apalachin gathering. In the face of such a hue and cry, it is just as reasonable to suppose that each one present would of his own volition decide that the less he said about Apalachin, and the more innocent his statements made the occasion to be, the better for him.
>
> If a precisely similar explanation in support of a claim of casual attendance had been given by those present, rather than statements similar only in that they denied that presence was planned, this would be some evidence of agreement. But in our view the similarity of the stories told is insignificant under all the circumstances. Only a minority relied to any degree on Barbara's illness but even this is of little weight since Joseph Barbara, Sr., had in fact been suffering from a severe heart ailment from which he died before the trial.

> We therefore conclude that there was insufficient evidence for the jury to find the defendants had, on November 14, entered into an agreement to commit perjury.

Id. at 415.

State v. St. Christopher

Supreme Court of Minnesota
232 N.W.2d 798 (1975)

Rogosheske, Justice.

Defendant was found guilty by the court, sitting without a jury, of conspiracy to commit murder, and sentenced under the conspiracy conviction to a maximum indeterminate term of 20 years' imprisonment.

The facts in this case are relatively simple. On March 16, 1974, defendant (who formerly was named Marlin Peter Olson but legally changed his name to Daniel St. Christopher) stated to his cousin, Roger Zobel, that he wanted to kill his mother, Mrs. Marlin Olson, and that he wanted Zobel's help. He would pay him $125,000 over the years, money defendant would get from his father after his mother was dead. Zobel, the key witness against defendant at his trial on the charge of conspiracy, testified that at no time did he ever intend to participate in the murder but that he discussed the matter with defendant on that and subsequent occasions and acted as if he intended to participate in the plan. On March 18, Zobel contacted the police and told them of defendant's plan and they later told him to continue to cooperate with defendant. The plan, which became definite in some detail as early as March 20, was for Zobel to go to the Olson farmhouse on Saturday, March 23, when defendant's father was at the weekly livestock auction. Since defendant's mother was Zobel's aunt, Zobel could gain entrance readily. The idea was for Zobel to break her neck, hide her body in his automobile trunk, and then attach bricks to it and throw it in a nearby river after dark. Later it developed that defendant's father might not go to the sale on Saturday, so a plan was developed whereby defendant would feign car trouble, call his father for help, then signal Zobel when the father was on his way. Police followed defendant on Saturday when he left his apartment and observed him make a number of telephone calls. In one of these he called his father and told him he was having car trouble and asked him to come and help him pay the bill. In a call to Zobel, which was taped, defendant told Zobel that his father was coming and that Zobel should proceed with the plan. Shortly thereafter, police arrested defendant.

During the trial defense counsel, in a motion to dismiss, made it clear to the trial court that he felt defendant could not be convicted of conspiracy. He argued that since Zobel never intended to participate in a murder, he did not really conspire with defendant. The trial court was obviously troubled by this argument because, after the evidence was in and after he revealed that he believed the state's witnesses, he asked counsel what they thought of his finding defendant guilty of conspiracy, as charged, and of attempted murder as an included offense. The prosecutor at first expressed doubts at the fairness of convicting defendant of a crime with which he had not been charged but later agreed with the trial court that it could find defendant guilty of attempted murder. The prosecutor insisted, however, that he preferred that the trial court find defendant guilty of conspiracy. As it turned out, the trial court found defendant guilty of both conspiracy and attempted murder.

We have not found any Minnesota cases in point on the issue of the validity of the conspiracy conviction.

> There is extensive authority from other jurisdictions which supports defendant's contention.
>
> ... Conspiracy is the agreement of two or more to effect an unlawful purpose. Two people cannot agree unless they both intend to carry out the purpose which is stated to be the object of their combination. Therefore there is no agreement, and consequently no conspiracy, where one of the two never intends to carry out the unlawful purpose.

If there had been some evidence to suggest that, contrary to his testimony, Zobel in fact had intended to participate in the conspiracy and had not feigned agreement from the start, then the court as factfinder could have found defendant guilty of conspiracy without rejecting the rule followed in the cited cases. However, the only evidence that the state produced was that Zobel did not intend at any time to participate in the conspiracy and that his agreement was feigned, and the trial court believed this evidence. Therefore, if we accept the rule followed in these cases, we would have to reverse defendant's conviction.

We are persuaded not to accept this rule and base our decision on (a) our belief that the rule is unsound, and (b) our belief that the present conspiracy statute, § 609.175, subd. 2, authorizes a conviction in this situation.

(a) One criticism by a number of commentators of the rule followed in the cited cases is that the courts have reached their conclusion by using as a starting point the definition of conspiracy as an agreement between two or more persons, a definition which was framed in cases not involving the issue. As one commentator put it, "if a conspiracy is arbitrarily defined as 'an agreement of intentions and not merely of language (the intentions being unlawful)' the answer to the problem is undoubtedly that where there is no such agreement of intentions then there is no conspiracy." In other words, the basis for the rule is a strict doctrinal approach toward the conception of conspiracy as an agreement in which two or more parties not only objectively indicate their agreement but actually have a meeting of the minds.

Addressing the rule to be applied as a policy issue, a number of commentators have come to the conclusion that there should be no requirement of a meeting of the minds. Thus, Fridman points to cases holding that factual impossibility is no defense to a charge of attempt to commit a crime and argues that, because of close connections between the origins and purposes of the law of conspiracy and of attempt, a similar rule should obtain in conspiracy. Specifically, he argues that "[t]he fact that, unknown to a man who wishes to enter a conspiracy to commit some criminal purpose, the other person has no intention of fulfilling that purpose ought to be irrelevant as long as the first man does intend to fulfill it if he can" because "a man who believes he is conspiring to commit a crime and wishes to conspire to commit a crime has a guilty mind and has done all in his power to plot the commission of an unlawful purpose."

Professor Glanville Williams makes a somewhat similar argument, basing his opinion on the fact that conspiracy, like attempt, is an inchoate crime and that it is the act of conspiring by a defendant which is the decisive element of criminality, for it makes no difference in logic or public policy that the person with whom the defendant conspires is not himself subject to prosecution.

The draftsmen of the Model Penal Code take a slightly different approach. They recognize that conspiracy is not just an inchoate crime complementing the law of attempt and solicitation but that it is also a means of striking at the special dangers incident to group activity. A.L.I., Model Penal Code (Tent. Draft No. 10, 1960) § 5.03, Comment. In view of that recognition, it is probably not quite as easy to reject the approach taken by the cases cited, yet this is what the draftsmen have done. The provision which accomplishes this, § 5.03(1), reads as follows:

> A person is guilty of conspiracy with another person or persons to commit a crime if with the purpose of promoting or facilitating its commission he:
>
> (a) agrees with such other person or persons that they or one or more of them will engage in conduct which constitutes such crime or an attempt or solicitation to commit such crime; or
>
> (b) agrees to aid such other person or persons in the planning or commission of such crime or of an attempt or solicitation to commit such crime.

10 U.L.A., Model Penal Code, § 5.03(1). In comments explaining this provision, the reporters state as follows:

> 2. ***The Conspiratorial Relationship.***
>
> *Unilateral Approach of the Draft.* The definition of the Draft departs from the traditional view of conspiracy as an entirely bilateral or multilateral relationship, the view inherent in the standard formulation cast in terms of "two or more persons" agreeing or combining to commit a crime. Attention is directed instead to each individual's culpability by framing the definition in terms of the conduct which suffices to establish the liability of any given actor, rather than the conduct of a group of which he is charged to be a part—an approach which in this comment we have designated "unilateral."
>
> One consequence of this approach is to make it immaterial to the guilt of a conspirator whose culpability has been established that the person or all of the persons with whom he conspired have not been or cannot be convicted. Present law frequently holds otherwise, reasoning from the definition of conspiracy as an agreement between two or more persons that there must be at least two guilty conspirators or none. The problem arises in a number of contexts.
>
> ...

> *Second:* Where the person with whom the defendant conspired secretly intends not to go through with the plan. In these cases it is generally held that neither party can be convicted because there was no "agreement" between two persons. Under the unilateral approach of the Draft, the culpable party's guilt would not be affected by the fact that the other party's agreement was feigned. He has conspired, within the meaning of the definition, in the belief that the other party was with him; apart from the issue of entrapment often presented in such cases, his culpability is not decreased by the other's secret intention. True enough, the project's chances of success have not been increased by the agreement; indeed, its doom may have been sealed by this turn of events. But the major basis of conspiratorial liability—the unequivocal evidence of a firm purpose to commit a crime—remains the same. The result would be the same under the Draft if the only co-conspirator established a defense of renunciation under Section 5.03(6). While both the Advisory Committee and the Council support the Draft upon this point, it should be noted that the Council vote was 14–11, the dissenting members deeming mutual agreement on the part of two or more essential to the concept of conspiracy.

(b) We find the scholarly literature persuasive on this subject. The question is whether this court can take the recommended approach. We think the answer lies in the wording of our statute. The Minnesota statute formerly dealing with the crime of conspiracy reads as follows (Minn. St. 1961), § 613.70:

> When two or more persons shall conspire:
>
> (1) To commit a crime;
>
> ...
>
> Every such person shall be guilty of a misdemeanor.

This is the most common type of conspiracy statute and it is understandable that this type of statute lends itself easily to the result reached by the cases because the statute starts with the phrase, "When two or more persons shall conspire."

However, the Minnesota statute as it presently reads omits this phrase and is now phrased in unilateral terms similar to those used in the Model Penal Code. The provision, Minn. St. 609.175, subd. 2, reads in part:

> Whoever conspires with another to commit a crime and in furtherance of the conspiracy one or more of the parties does some overt act in furtherance of such conspiracy may be sentenced as follows.

Because of this wording, we hold that the trial court was free to convict defendant of conspiracy under the facts of this case.

Comments and Questions

(1) Consider Marcus, *The Prosecution and Defense of Criminal Conspiracy Cases* §2.04, at 2–31:*

> The so-called unilateral approach does make some sense. As the supporters say, the unsuccessful conspirator did try to conspire so his state of mind is clearly a criminal one. True enough, but did he enter into a conspiracy? After all, the conspiracy charge subjects a defendant to criminal liability at a stage earlier than other inchoate offenses and may raise grave procedural problems at the time of trial. And, the reason for such results is that there is a special, added danger resulting from group planning. Yet, in the unilateral situation there is no conspiracy, no added group danger, for the fact remains there was not an agreement between two persons. The defendant may have wanted to agree, may have intended to agree, and may have even believed he had agreed; but there was no agreement, no true planning by two or more persons, no meeting of the minds between the parties. Moreover, the requirement that there be such a true agreement is not strictly doctrinal. It serves a very real purpose; it isolates especially dangerous groups of persons so that the law may deal with such persons before it could otherwise deal with them and may sanction them in addition to punishing for an attempted or completed offense.
>
> The strongest proponents of conspiracy law argue that the reason the conspiracy offense can be punished wholly apart from the substantive offense is that conspirators acting together are dangerous. Group activities, it is said, are more likely to lead to serious anti-social acts than the acts of a single criminal. Reasonable people may disagree on such a rationale, but it is the rationale which has been accepted by the courts and commentators. With the unilateral approach, however, this grave risk will likely be lessened considerably or actually eliminated. Under such circumstances the rationale for the crime is destroyed, for there is no group danger.
>
> What rationale is there for punishing as a conspirator one who does not enter into a true agreement? A would-be conspirator may be guilty of a number of crimes, but surely conspiracy is not one of them. While the act taken in the unilateral situation—trying to entice someone else to assist in the criminal project—may be an attempt or a solicitation to commit the ultimate offense, it is not a conspiracy between two willing parties. It may be trite, but it is also undeniably true, one person cannot conspire with himself.
>
> Not only is the basic rationale for the crime destroyed, but the approach also sets a dangerous precedent generally with regard to the criminal sanction. That is, the defendant is being punished in the unilateral situation, under the M.P.C. approach, simply because he has demonstrated an evil, anti-social

> state of mind. Yet, one cannot be penalized only for demonstrating an evil state of mind. If he is to be punished, it should be for "attempting" a crime (the "agreement" perhaps being a substantial step); but then the basis for responsibility is that he has done *an act* which is anti-social, not simply that he has demonstrated his evil intent.
>
> As a practical matter, the unilateral approach has not had a significant impact on conspiracy prosecutions. The one area where it might have had an important impact—purchase and sale of narcotics—usually involves more than the one "true" conspirator and the informer or undercover agent; generally there are a great many more persons in the ring. Still the unilateral approach will have more than minimal impact on conspiracy prosecutions. With such an impact protestations about the traditional "strict doctrinal approach" of conspiracy do not answer the tough question of why the group danger rationale can be distorted to punish someone who, while perhaps dangerous, does not pose the sort of danger that should give rise to a conspiracy conviction. No one, not the American Law Institute, the Brown Commission, nor any of the legislatures which have adopted the unilateral approach has answered this; it is difficult to see any answer to it.

(2) Without the unilateral approach, the so-called Rule of Consistency applies. If a single jury trying X and Y for conspiracy were to find that X conspired with Y, but that Y did not conspire with X, X's conviction would not be allowed. What if the second conspirator, Y, is acquitted at a separate, later trial? A separate, earlier trial? What if Y receives a *nolle prosequi*? What if Y pleads guilty to a substantive offense in exchange for a dismissal of the conspiracy charge? What result if X is charged with conspiracy with "other persons unknown" at the time of the indictment, and still unknown at trial?

(3) Suppose the defendants agree to commit a crime which is impossible to commit. Can the defendants be convicted of conspiracy? *See United States v. Medina-Garcia*, 918 F.2d 4, 8 (1st Cir. 1990):

> The fact that both aliens were acting as INS informants and neither alien was remaining illegally in the United States at the time of the defendant's involvement in this case does not prevent the defendant from being prosecuted for conspiracy [to transport an alien into the United States]. "The crime of conspiracy ... is complete upon the agreement to do an unlawful act as implemented by one or more overt acts. Factual impossibility is no defense." This rule applies "even when the reason for the impossibility is that certain acts essential to the conspiracy's success are to be carried out by individuals who turn out to be government agents."

(4) In most jurisdictions the government must prove intent, agreement, and also some overt act in furtherance of the agreement.

> The federal conspiracy statute makes it a crime for two or more persons to agree, *inter alia*, to commit any offense against the United States, and one or

> more of them to do any act to effect the object of the conspiracy. Thus there are three essentials in a conspiracy indictment: the agreement, the offense-object toward which the agreement is directed, and an overt act. The agreement is the conspiring when it is to commit an offense against the United States. The offense-object need not be committed, for the crime is the agreement to do it. In that sense the crime of conspiracy is analogous to the offenses of "attempt." But if the offense-object is committed, the crime of conspiracy does not vanish or merge. The statutory crime differs from common-law conspiracy in that it requires an overt act. That is made an essential to give the conspirators a time, a place, and a chance to say that although we did agree, now that we are about to start, let's call it off. It also makes the indictment for, and the proof of, the illegal meeting of the minds more objective.

United States v. Offutt, 127 F.2d 336, 338 (D.C. Cir. 1942).

> All agree that the overt act requirement is satisfied by very little. The act in furtherance of the conspiracy need not itself be criminal; while some courts have argued that it should be criminal, no court has ever adopted this position, and indeed such a requirement might seriously affect the prosecution of conspiracy cases. No, the overt act need not be criminal nor need it be very substantial. The requirement is satisfied by "any step in preparation," "the slightest overt act," "any act," or just simply an "overt act." These requirements may appear minimal, and they appear that way because they are minimal. "[I]t is well settled that any act in pursuance of the conspiracy, however insignificant, is sufficient."

Marcus, *The Prosecution and Defense of Criminal Conspiracy Cases, supra*, § 2.08[3], at 2–82.

[C] Object of the Agreement

Commonwealth v. Donoghue

Court of Appeals of Kentucky
63 S.W.2d 3 (1933)

Stanley, Commissioner.

The opinion deals with the sufficiency of an indictment charging the common-law offense of conspiracy, and relates to what are popularly referred to by the invidious and iniquitous term of "loan sharks." We shall abridge the indictment by omitting terms and words usually regarded as essential to technical sufficiency. The instrument charges M. Donoghue, W. T. Day, and Vernon L. Buckman with the offense of criminal conspiracy, committed as follows: That they unlawfully and corruptly conspired with one another and others, to the grand jury unknown, "to engage in the business of lending money in small amounts to poor and necessitous wage earners at excessive, exorbitant and usurious rates of interest and to prevent the recovery of such interest paid by said borrowers."

The statute (Ky. St. § 1223) provides that if two or more persons shall "confederate or band themselves together" for certain specified purposes, "or to do any felonious act" they commit a felony.

[T]he broad definition or description everywhere accepted is that conspiracy is a combination between two or more persons to do or accomplish a criminal or unlawful act, or to do a lawful act by criminal or unlawful means.

> "A criminal conspiracy is (1) a corrupt combination (2) of two or more persons, (3) by concerted action to commit (4) a criminal or an unlawful act; (a) or an act not in itself criminal or unlawful, by criminal or unlawful means; (b) or an act which would tend to prejudice the public in general, to subvert justice, disturb the peace, injure public trade, affect public health, or violate public policy; (5) or any act, however innocent, by means neither criminal nor unlawful, where the tendency of the object sought would be to wrongfully coerce or oppress either the public or an individual...."
>
> "Every conspiracy to do an unlawful act, or to do a lawful act for an illegal, fraudulent, malicious, or corrupt purpose, or for a purpose which has a tendency to prejudice the public in general, is an indictable offense, regardless of the means whereby it is to be accomplished."

According to the overwhelming weight of authority the objects of the conspiracy need not be an offense against the criminal law for which an individual could be indicted or convicted, but it is sufficient if the purpose be unlawful. That term "unlawful" in this connection has been expanded beyond its original limits of being only some act punishable as a crime. It is now understood and regarded as covering an act not embraced in the crime of conspiracy as it originally existed. It cannot be said, however—and care must ever be exercised in the application, as all courts recognize—that the term "unlawful" includes every act which violates legal rights of another or such as may create a right of action.

A more specific distinction is noted by Wharton in his work on Criminal Law. There is a series of acts which have the essence but not the form of crime (e.g., immoral acts, undictable cheats), which, wanting the necessary objective constituents, escape judicial cognizance as being intrinsically criminal, but which are held to be invested by conspiracy with a garb that exposes them to the penalties of the law. Without the combination of men attempting to accomplish the objects, they had only the essence of crime, but, by means of the conspiracy, an unfair and mischievous advantage of the aggressors is recognized, and the acts are presented in such definiteness that they can be taken hold of and punished.

So it may be said that within the contemplation of the offense of criminal conspiracy are the acts which by reason of the combination have a tendency to injure the public, to violate public policy, or to injure, oppress, or wrongfully prejudice individuals collectively or the public generally.

Our current Statutes merely declare that the portions of contracts calling for payment of interest in excess of 6 per cent are void, authorize the recovery of the excess, and require the lender in an action to avoid payment to bear the entire costs of the proceeding. While in a degree this penalizes the usurer, the statute is remedial and cannot be regarded as making the act a criminal offense.

Turning our attention again to the indictment now before us. It is *much more* than merely a charge that the accused conspired to collect usury. The accusation is a conspiracy to carry on the business of lending money in small amounts from $5 to $50, to poor and necessitous wage-earners at rates of interest ranging from 240 to 360 per cent per annum, and then to prevent the recovery of the usury paid by such borrowers.

The indictment does not charge the accused with the mere exaction of usury, or of isolated instances of collecting slight excesses over the legal rate of interest. The objects of the conspiracy were not incidents to a legitimate business. If that were all, it might be doubted whether it could be regarded as an offense or an unlawful act within the meaning of that term in its relation to conspiracy. It charges *a nefarious plan for the habitual exaction of gross usury*, that is, in essence, the operation of the business of extortion. The import of the indictment is to charge systematic preying upon poor persons, of taking an unconscionable advantage of their needy conditions, of oppressing them, of extorting money from them through the disguise of interest, and, as an intrinsic part of the plan, to prevent restitution by obstructing public justice and the administration of the law. If ever there was a violation of public policy as reflected by the statutes and public conscience, or a combination opposed to the common weal, it is that sort of illegitimate business. It was extortioners of this class, called money changers, whom the Christ drove from the Temple on two occasions.

To willfully obstruct or prevent public justice or to do any act injurious to the administration of law is not only a misdemeanor but is obviously a violation of public policy. So a conspiracy which has that effect is clearly an indictable offense. The incessant activity and novel inventions of the unprincipled have given rise to unlimited schemes to effect that purpose. Whatever those means are, if that is their object, a conspiracy to use them is punishable.

Measuring the indictment by the foregoing considerations, the court is of the opinion that it states a public offense.

Wherefore, the judgment is *reversed.*

Clay, Justice (dissenting).

I am unable to concur in the majority opinion. However indefensible the exaction of usury may be, it is a matter that should be regulated by the Legislature and not by the courts. Already the conspiracy doctrine has been worked overtime, and should not be extended unless plainly required. When a court on the theory of conspiracy declares an act to be a crime, which was not recognized as a crime at the time it was done, its decision savors strongly of an ex post facto law. Briefly stated a criminal conspiracy is a combination of two or more persons by concerted action to accomplish some criminal or unlawful purpose, or to accomplish some purpose not in itself criminal or unlawful, by criminal or unlawful means. Stripped of surplusage, the indictment alleges a conspiracy to charge usury, and as part of the plan the failure of the defendants properly to file certain statements required by statute. At common law, as adopted in Kentucky, it was not a crime to charge usury, and it has never been made so by statute. Therefore, it was essential to a good indictment to allege that the defendants charged usury by criminal or unlawful means. That, of course, has reference to the method of obtaining the loan, and not to wholly disconnected steps which the lenders failed to take. It was not alleged that the defendants, for the purpose of effecting the loans, resorted to force, threats, intimidation, or fraud. On the contrary, the case is one where the borrowers were not imposed upon in any way, but willingly and freely entered into the arrangement. In the circumstances, the indictment does not allege facts showing that the defendants resorted to unlawful means.

The necessity of protecting the public, and particularly the laboring man, is much stressed, but that alone will not authorize the court to hold an indictment good. Moreover, it is not perceived how prosecutions like the one in question may help the situation, as separate individuals may still continue the business of lending money at exorbitant rates without being subject to punishment.

The decision not only presents a strained application of the conspiracy doctrine, but its chief danger lies in the fact that for all time to come it will be the basis for the creation of new crimes never dreamed of by the people.

Comments and Questions

(1) With loan sharking not a criminal offense, how could it be a crime to agree to engage in loan sharking?

(2) In contrast with *Donoghue* is *State v. Bowling*, 427 P.2d 928 (Ariz. Ct. App. 1967). The court there reversed a conviction under the conspiracy statute relating to an "act injurious to the public health or morals." It held that such "language is not sufficiently definite to satisfy due process requirements." What would the due process argument be? *See Musser v. Utah*, 333 U.S. 95 (1948), where the defendant was charged with having conspired to "commit acts injurious to public morals" (polygamous marriage).

> It is obvious that this is no narrowly drawn statute. We do not presume to give an interpretation as to what it may include. Standing by itself, it would seem to be warrant for conviction for agreement to do almost any act which a judge and jury might find at the moment contrary to his or its notions of what was good for health, morals, trade, commerce, justice or order. In some States the phrase "injurious to public morals" would be likely to punish acts which it would not punish in others because of the varying policies on such matters as use of cigarettes or liquor and the permissibility of gambling. This led to the inquiry as to whether the statute attempts to cover so much that it effectively covers nothing. Statutes defining crimes may fail of their purpose if they do not provide some reasonable standards of guilt. Legislation may run afoul of the Due Process Clause because it fails to give adequate guidance to those who would be law-abiding, to advise defendants of the nature of

> the offense with which they are charged, or to guide courts in trying those who are accused.

333 U.S. at 96–97.

[D] The Completed Offense

Adam and Eve, both former convicted armed robbers, agreed to rob Hooper's Grocery Store. They agreed expressly that they will not use weapons, they will simply threaten old Mr. Hooper. When they arrive at the store, while Adam takes money from the register, Eve uses a real gun to threaten Mr. Hooper. Adam—recalling the agreement—thought the gun was a black water pistol. Under the appropriate armed robbery statute, the act is defined *only* as committing a robbery while "actually armed with a dangerous weapon." Both Adam and Eve are convicted of armed robbery and conspiracy and receive consecutive sentences. Adam appeals. What result?

Albernaz v. United States

United States Supreme Court
450 U.S. 333 (1981)

Justice Rehnquist delivered the opinion of the Court.

Petitioners were convicted of conspiracy to import marihuana (Count I), in violation 21 U.S.C. § 963, and conspiracy to distribute marihuana (Count II), in violation of 21 U.S.C. § 846. Petitioners received consecutive sentences on each count. We granted certiorari to consider whether Congress intended consecutive sentences to be imposed for the violation of these two conspiracy statutes and, if so, whether such cumulative punishment violates the Double Jeopardy Clause of the Fifth Amendment of the United States Constitution.

[T]he petitioners were involved in an agreement, the objectives of which were to import marihuana and then to distribute it domestically. Petitioners were charged and convicted under two separate statutory provisions and received consecutive sentences. The length of each of their combined sentences exceeded the maximum five-year sentence which could have been imposed either for a conviction of conspiracy to import or for a conviction of conspiracy to distribute.

The statutes involved in this case are part of the Comprehensive Drug Abuse Prevention and Control Act of 1970, 84 Stat. 1236, 21 U.S.C. § 801 *et seq.* Section 846 is in Subchapter I of the Act and provides:

> Any person who attempts or conspires to commit any offense defined in this subchapter is punishable by imprisonment or fine or both which may not exceed the maximum punishment prescribed for the offense, the commission of which was the object of the attempt or conspiracy.

This provision proscribes conspiracy to commit any offense defined in Subchapter I, including conspiracy to distribute marihuana which is specifically prohibited in 21

U.S.C. § 841(a)(1). Section 846 authorizes imposition of a sentence of imprisonment or a fine that does not exceed the penalty specified for the object offense.

Section 963, which is part of Subchapter II of the Act, contains a provision identical to § 846 and proscribes conspiracy to commit any offense defined in Subchapter II, including conspiracy to import marihuana which is specifically prohibited by 21 U.S.C. § 960(a)(1). As in § 846, § 963 authorizes a sentence of imprisonment or a fine that does not exceed the penalties specified for the object offense. Thus, a conspiratorial agreement which envisages both the importation and distribution of marihuana violates both statutory provisions, each of which authorizes a separate punishment.

Petitioners do not dispute that their conspiracy to import and distribute marihuana violated both §§ 846 and 963. Rather, petitioners contend it is not clear whether Congress intended to authorize multiple punishment for violation of these two statutes in a case involving only a single agreement or conspiracy, even though that isolated agreement had dual objectives. Petitioners argue that because Congress has not spoken with the clarity required for this Court to find an "unambiguous intent to impose multiple punishment," we should invoke the rule of lenity and hold that the statutory ambiguity on this issue prevents the imposition of multiple punishment. Petitioners further contend that even if cumulative punishment was authorized by Congress, such punishment is barred by the Double Jeopardy Clause of the Fifth Amendment.

In resolving petitioners' initial contention that Congress did not intend to authorize multiple punishment for violations of §§ 846 and 963, our starting point must be the language of the statutes. Absent a "clearly expressed legislative intention to the contrary, that language must ordinarily be regarded as conclusive." Here, we confront separate offenses with separate penalty provisions that are contained in distinct Subchapters of the Act. The provisions are unambiguous on their face and each authorizes punishment for a violation of its terms. Petitioners contend, however, that the question presented is not whether the statutes are facially ambiguous, but whether consecutive sentences may be imposed when convictions under those statutes arise from participation in a single conspiracy with multiple objectives—a question raised, rather than resolved, by the existence of both provisions.

The answer to petitioners' contention is found, we believe, in application of the rule announced by this Court in *Blockburger v. United States*, 284 U.S. 299 (1932), and most recently applied last Term in *Whalen v. United States*, 445 U.S. 684 (1980). In *Whalen*, the Court explained that the "rule of statutory construction" stated in *Blockburger* is to be used "to determine whether Congress has in a given situation provided that two statutory offenses may be punished cumulatively." The Court then referenced the following test set forth in *Blockburger*:

> The applicable rule is that where the same act or transaction constitutes a violation of two distinct statutory provisions, the test to be applied to determine whether there are two offenses or only one, is whether each provision requires proof of a fact which the other does not.

Our decision in *Whalen* was not the first time this Court has looked to the *Blockburger* rule to determine whether Congress intended that two statutory offenses be punished cumulatively. We previously stated in *Brown v. Ohio*, 432 U.S. 161, 166 (1977), although our analysis there was of necessity based on a claim of double jeopardy since the case came to us from a state court, that "[t]he established test for determining whether two offenses are sufficiently distinguishable to permit the imposition of cumulative punishment was stated in *Blockburger v. United States* ..." Similarly, in *Iannelli v. United States*, 420 U.S. 770, 785 n.17 (1975), we explained:

> The test articulated in *Blockburger v. United States*, 284 U.S. 299 (1932), serves a generally similar function of identifying congressional intent to impose separate sanctions for multiple offenses arising in the course of a single act or transaction. In determining whether separate punishment might be imposed, *Blockburger* requires that courts examine the offenses to ascertain "whether each provision requires proof of a fact which the other does not." *Id.*, at 304. As *Blockburger* and other decisions applying its principle reveal, ... the Court's application of the test focuses on the statutory elements of the offense. If each requires proof of a fact that the other does not, the *Blockburger* test is satisfied, notwithstanding a substantial overlap in the proof offered to establish the crimes.

In *Gore v. United States*, 357 U.S. 386 (1958), the Court rejected the opportunity to abandon *Blockburger* as the test to apply in determining whether Congress intended to impose multiple punishment for a single act which violates several statutory provisions. In reaffirming *Blockburger*, the Court explained:

> The fact that an offender violates by a single transaction several regulatory controls devised by Congress as means for dealing with a social evil as deleterious as it is difficult to combat does not make the several different regulatory controls single and identic.

357 U.S. at 389.

Finally, in *American Tobacco Co. v. United States*, 328 U.S. 781 (1946), defendants who had been convicted of conspiracy in restraint of trade in violation of § 1 of the Sherman Act (15 U.S.C. § 1), and conspiracy to monopolize in violation of § 2 (15 U.S.C. § 2), sought review of their convictions contending that separate sentences for these offenses were impermissible because there was "but one conspiracy, namely, a conspiracy to fix prices." [*Id.*, at] 788. In rejecting this claim, the Court noted the presence of separate statutory offenses and then, relying on *Blockburger*, upheld the sentences on the ground that "§§ 1 and 2 of the Sherman Act require proof of conspiracies which are reciprocally distinguishable from and independent of each other although the objects of the conspiracies may partially overlap." [*Ibid.*]

The statutory provisions at issue here clearly satisfy the rule announced in *Blockburger* and petitioners do not seriously contend otherwise. Sections 846 and 963 specify different ends as the proscribed object of the conspiracy—distribution as opposed to importation—and it is beyond peradventure that "each provision requires proof of a fact

[that] the other does not." Thus, application of the *Blockburger* rule to determine whether Congress has provided that these two statutory offenses be punished cumulatively results in the unequivocal determination that §§ 846 and 963, like §§ 1 and 2 of the Sherman Act which were at issue in *American Tobacco*, proscribe separate statutory offenses the violations of which can result in the imposition of consecutive sentences.

Our conclusion in this regard is not inconsistent with our earlier decision in *Braverman v. United States*, 317 U.S. 49 (1942), on which petitioners rely so heavily. Petitioners argue that *Blockburger* cannot be used for divining legislative intent when the statutes at issue are conspiracy statutes. Quoting *Braverman*, they argue that whether the objective of a single agreement is to commit one or many crimes, it is in either case the agreement which constitutes the conspiracy which the statute punishes. "The one agreement cannot be taken to be several agreements and hence several conspiracies because it envisages the violation of several statutes rather than one." [*Id.*] at 53. *Braverman*, however, does not support petitioners' position. Unlike the instant case or this Court's later decision in *American Tobacco*, the conspiratorial agreement in *Braverman*, although it had many objectives, violated but a single statute. The *Braverman* Court specifically noted:

> Since the single continuing agreement, which is the conspiracy here, thus embraces its criminal objects, it differs from successive acts which violate a single penal statute and *from a single act which violates two statutes. See Blockburger v. United States*, 284 U.S. 299, 301–304; *Albrecht v. United States*, 273 U.S. 1, 11–12. The single agreement is the prohibited conspiracy, and however diverse its objects it violates but a single statute, § 37 of the Criminal Code. For such a violation, only the single penalty prescribed by the statute can be imposed.

Id., at 54 (emphasis added). Later in *American Tobacco*, the Court distinguished *Braverman*:

> *In contrast to the single conspiracy described in [Braverman]* in separate counts, all charged under the general conspiracy statute ... we have here separate statutory offenses, one a conspiracy in restraint of trade that may stop short of monopoly, and the other a conspiracy to monopolize that may not be content with restraint short of monopoly. One is made criminal by § 1 and the other by § 2 of the Sherman Act.

328 U. S. at 788. *See also Pinkerton v. United States*, 328 U.S. 640, 642–643 (1946).

The *Blockburger* test is a "rule of statutory construction" and because it serves as a means of discerning congressional purpose the rule should not be controlling where, for example, there is a clear indication of contrary legislative intent. Nothing, however, in the legislative history which has been brought to our attention discloses an intent contrary to the presumption which should be accorded to these statutes after application of the *Blockburger* test. In fact, the legislative history is silent on the question of whether consecutive sentences can be imposed for conspiracy to import and distribute drugs. Petitioners read this silence as an "ambiguity" over whether Congress intended to authorize multiple punishment. Petitioners, however, read much into nothing. Congress cannot be expected to specifically address each issue of statutory construction which may arise. But, as we have previously noted, Congress is "predominantly a lawyer's body," and it is appropriate for us "to assume that our elected representatives ... know the law." As a result, if anything is to be assumed from the congressional silence on this point, it is that Congress was aware of the *Blockburger* rule and legislated with it in mind. It is not a function of this Court to presume that "Congress was unaware of what it accomplished...."

Finally, petitioners contend that because the legislative history is "ambiguous" on the question of multiple punishment, we should apply the rule of lenity so as not to allow consecutive sentences in this situation. Last Term in *Bifulco v. United States*, 447 U.S. 381 (1980), we recognized that the rule of lenity is a principle of statutory construction which applies not only to interpretations of the substantive ambit of criminal prohibitions, but also to the penalties they impose. Quoting *Ladner v. United States*, 358 U.S. 169, 178 (1958), we stated: "'This policy of lenity means that the Court will not interpret a federal criminal statute so as to increase the penalty that it places on an individual when such an interpretation can be based on no more than a guess as to what Congress intended.'" We emphasized that the "touchstone" of the rule of lenity "is statutory ambiguity." And we stated: "where Congress has manifested its intention, we may not manufacture ambiguity in order to defeat that intent." Lenity thus serves only as an aid for resolving an ambiguity; it is not to be used to beget one. The rule comes into operation "at the end of the process of construing what Congress has expressed, not at the beginning as an overriding consideration of being lenient to wrongdoers."

In light of these principles, the rule of lenity simply has no application in this case; we are not confronted with any statutory ambiguity. To the contrary, we are presented with statutory provisions which are unambiguous on their face and a legislative history which gives us no reason to pause over the manner in which these provisions should be interpreted.

The conclusion we reach today regarding the intent of Congress is reinforced by the fact that the two conspiracy statutes are directed to separate evils presented by drug trafficking. "Importation" and "distribution" of marihuana impose diverse societal harms, and, as the Court of Appeals observed, Congress has in effect determined that a conspiracy to import drugs and to distribute them is twice as serious as a conspiracy to do either object singly. This result is not surprising for as we observed many years ago, the history of the narcotics legislation in this country "reveals the determination of Congress to turn the screw of the criminal machinery—detection, prosecution and punishment—tighter and tighter."

Having found that Congress intended to permit the imposition of consecutive sentences for violations of §§ 846 and 963, we are brought to petitioners' argument that notwithstanding this fact, the Double Jeopardy Clause of the Fifth Amendment of the United States Constitution precludes the imposition of such punishment. While the Clause itself simply states that no person shall "be subject for the same offence to be twice put in jeopardy of life or limb," the decisional law in the area is a veritable

Sargasso Sea which could not fail to challenge the most intrepid judicial navigator. We have previously stated that the Double Jeopardy Clause "protects against a second prosecution for the same offense after acquittal. It protects against a second prosecution for the offense after conviction. And it protects against multiple punishments for the same offense."

Last Term in *Whalen v. United States*, this Court stated that "the question whether punishments imposed by a court after a defendant's conviction upon criminal charges are unconstitutionally multiple cannot be resolved without determining what punishment the Legislative Branch has authorized." In determining the permissibility of the imposition of cumulative punishment for the crime of rape and the crime of unintentional killing in the course of rape, the Court recognized that the "dispositive question" was whether Congress intended to authorize separate punishments for the two crimes. This is so because the "power to define criminal offenses and to prescribe punishments to be imposed upon those found guilty of them, resides wholly with the Congress." As we previously noted in *Brown v. Ohio*, "[w]here consecutive sentences are imposed at a single criminal trial, the role of the constitutional guarantee is limited to assuring that the court does not exceed its legislative authorization by imposing multiple punishment for the same offense." Thus, the question of what punishments are constitutionally permissible is not different from the question of what punishment the Legislative Branch intended to be imposed. Where Congress intended, as it did here, to impose multiple punishment, imposition of such sentences does not violate the Constitution.[3]

The judgment of the Court of Appeals is accordingly *Affirmed.*

Comments and Questions

(1) Suppose the defendants entered into a single agreement, "whether express or by wink or handshake." Suppose also that this agreement had six objectives. Could the defendants be convicted of violating six separate conspiracy statutes and be given six consecutive sentences? Would this result be valid under *Braverman*? Under the Double Jeopardy Clause? Would it matter what the six objectives were?

(2) Did the Court answer the concerns expressed by dissenting Circuit Judge Ruben?

> One illegal agreement must be distinguished, as the Supreme Court has told us, "from a single act which violates two statutes." *Braverman v. United States.* My brethren acknowledge the authority of *Braverman* but make an effort to distinguish it, saying that it limits only "the Government's ability to frag-

3. Petitioners' contention that a single conspiracy which violates both §§ 846 and 963 constitute the "same offense" for double jeopardy purposes is wrong. We noted in *Brown v. Ohio*, that the established test for determining whether two offenses are the "same offense" is the rule set forth in *Blockburger*—the same rule on which we relied in determining congressional intent. As has been previously discussed, conspiracy to import marihuana in violation of § 963 and conspiracy to distribute marihuana in violation of § 846 clearly meet the *Blockburger* standard. It is well settled that a single transaction can give rise to distinct offenses under separate statutes without violating the Double Jeopardy Clause. This is true even though the "single transaction" is an agreement or conspiracy.

> ment a single conspiracy under the general conspiracy statute." This is not an adequate basis for reaching a different result from the one determined in *Braverman.* Here there was but one conspiracy regardless whether it is declared illegal by what my brethren consider two discrete laws, 21 U.S.C. §§ 846 and 963, or by one law, former 18 U.S.C. § 88, considered in *Braverman.* Moreover, I submit that the provisions we here consider are in fact but two parts of one law, Pub. L. No. 91-513 (1970), although that enactment was divided into multiple sections. However, whether there was one statute or two, there was one agreement and, as the court said in *Braverman:* "[t]he one agreement cannot be taken to be several agreements and hence several conspiracies because it envisages the violation of several statutes rather than one." I see little difference between fragmenting a conspiracy according to the number and diversity of its objectives in order to charge several violations of a single statute, and using the same technique to charge violations of two statutory provisions. The teaching of *Braverman* is that a conspiracy cannot be so fragmented.

United States v. Rodriguez, 612 F.2d 906, 926 (5th Cir. 1980).

(3) In addition to the conspiracy charge, the so-called RICO offense is used quite often in both federal and state jurisdictions. The Racketeer Influenced and Corrupt Organizations Act was first created as federal law in 1970. Since that time, many states have passed parallel laws. RICO provisions generally require that the government show that individuals conducted a pattern of racketeering activity through participation in an enterprise. Most of the RICO statutes also contain a conspiracy provision making it unlawful to agree to engage in such activities. In *United States v. Ford*, 21 F.3d 759, 762 (7th Cir. 1994), the defendants were residential counselors at the Illinois Department of Corrections Community Correctional Center in Chicago. They were convicted of conspiring to violate the federal RICO law after evidence was presented that the three had accepted bribes from residents (cash, drugs, and repair jobs) in exchange for various favors such as assigning preferable rooms, altering records, and tampering with drug testing samples. While the prosecution was not able to offer direct evidence regarding any sort of formal agreement, the court stated the standard rule that "an agreement to conspire may be established by circumstantial evidence, including reasonable inferences drawn from the defendants' conduct and overt acts.... The evidence presented at trial was clearly sufficient to support the inference of the defendants' acting in concert, pursuant to a mutual agreement."

United States v. Gardiner, 463 F.3d 445 (6th Cir. 2006), is another good illustration of the use of the RICO statute. The defendant there was convicted of violating the conspiracy portion of the federal RICO law, and also the Hobbs Act (robbery or extortion involving interstate commerce). He was the superintendent of public schools in a Michigan community. The evidence at trial showed that he and his family had received hundreds of thousands of dollars worth of gifts and cash from the head of a construction company, in exchange for his ensuring that this company would land lucrative contracts at the school district. With this evidence, the court found that the "defendant's agreement to participate in the RICO conspiracy may be inferred from his acts ... the government need not prove a formal agreement."

Numerous very high profile prosecutions have been brought based upon RICO charges (often linked with more standard conspiracy counts). Some of these include:

- Members of Congress, *United States v. Bustamante*, 45 F.3d 933 (5th Cir. 1995).
- Hells Angels gang members, http://www.signonsandiego.com/uniontrib/20050923/news_1m23hells.html
- Various police department officers, *United States v. Casayor*, 837 F.2d 1509 (1988).
- Financier Michael Milken, http://articles.philly.com/1989-03-30/news/26128942_1_michael-milken-bruce-l-newberg-98-count-indictment
- Several mob members, including the Gambino family, https://www.fbi.gov/newyork/press-releases/2012/four-gambino-crime-family-members-and-associates-plead-guilty-in-manhattan-federal-court
- Violent street gangs, http://articles.chicagotribune.com/2013-06-22/opinion/ct-edit-rico-0622-20130622_1_gang-leaders-black-souls-attorney-anita-alvarez

Pinkerton v. United States

United States Supreme Court
328 U.S. 640 (1946)

Mr. Justice Douglas delivered the opinion of the Court.

Walter and Daniel Pinkerton are brothers who live a short distance from each other on Daniel's farm. They were indicted for violations of the Internal Revenue Code. The indictment contained ten substantive counts and one conspiracy count. The jury found Walter guilty on nine of the substantive counts and on the conspiracy count. It found Daniel guilty on six of the substantive counts and on the conspiracy count. Walter was fined $500 and sentenced generally on the substantive counts to imprisonment for thirty months. On the conspiracy count he was given a two year sentence to run concurrently with the other sentence. Daniel was fined $1,000 and sentenced generally on the substantive counts to imprisonment for thirty months. On the conspiracy count he was fined $500 and given a two year sentence to run concurrently with the other sentence.

A single conspiracy was charged and proved. Some of the overt acts charged in the conspiracy count were the same acts charged in the substantive counts. Each of the substantive offenses found was committed pursuant to the conspiracy. Petitioners therefore contend that the substantive counts became merged in the conspiracy count, and that only a single sentence not exceeding the maximum two year penalty provided by the conspiracy statute could be imposed. Or to state the matter differently, they contend that each of the substantive counts became a separate conspiracy count but, since only a single conspiracy was charged and proved, only a single sentence for conspiracy could be imposed. They rely on *Braverman v. United States*, 317 U.S. 49. In the *Braverman* case the indictment charged no substantive offense. Each of the several counts charged a conspiracy to violate a different statute. But only one conspiracy was proved. We held that a single conspiracy, charged under the general conspiracy statute, however diverse its objects may be, violates but a single statute and no penalty greater than the maximum provided for one conspiracy may be imposed. That case is not apposite here. For the offenses charged and proved were not only a conspiracy but substantive offenses as well.

Nor can we accept the proposition that the substantive offenses were merged in the conspiracy. There are, of course, instances where a conspiracy charge may not be added to the substantive charge. One is where the agreement of two persons is necessary for the completion of the substantive crime and there is no ingredient in the conspiracy which is not present in the completed crime. Another is where the definition of the substantive offense excludes from punishment for conspiracy one who voluntarily participates in another's crime. But those exceptions are of a limited character. The common law rule that the substantive offense, if a felony, was merged in the conspiracy, has little vitality in this country. It has been long and consistently recognized by the Court that the commission of the substantive offense and a conspiracy to commit are separate and distinct offenses. The power of Congress to separate the two and to affix to each a different penalty is well established. A conviction for the conspiracy may be had though the substantive offense was completed. And the plea of double jeopardy is no defense to a conviction for both offenses. It is only an identity of offenses which is fatal. A conspiracy is a partnership in crime. It has ingredients, as well as implications, distinct from the completion of the unlawful project. As stated in *United States v. Rabinowich*, 238 U.S. 78, 88:

> For two or more to confederate and combine together to commit or cause to be committed a breach of the criminal laws, is an offense of the gravest character, sometimes quite outweighing, in injury to the public, the mere commission of the contemplated crime. It involves deliberate plotting to subvert the laws, educating and preparing the conspirators for further and habitual criminal practices. And it is characterized by secrecy, rendering it difficult of detection, requiring more time for its discovery, and adding to the importance of punishing it when discovered.

Moreover, it is not material that overt acts charged in the conspiracy counts were also charged and proved as substantive offenses. "If the overt act be the offense which was the object of the conspiracy, and is also punished, there is not a double punishment of it." The agreement to do an unlawful act is even then distinct from the doing of the act.[4]

---

4. The addition of a conspiracy count may at times be abusive and unjust. The Conference of Senior Circuit Judges reported in 1925:

> We note the prevalent use of conspiracy indictments for converting a joint misdemeanor into a felony; and we express our conviction that both for this purpose and for the purpose—or at least with the effect—of bringing in much improper evidence, the conspiracy statute is being much abused.

It is contended that there was insufficient evidence to implicate Daniel in the conspiracy. But we think there was enough evidence for submission of the issue to the jury.

There is, however, no evidence to show that Daniel participated directly in the commission of the substantive offenses on which his conviction has been sustained, although there was evidence to show that these substantive offenses were in fact committed by Walter in furtherance of the unlawful agreement or conspiracy existing between the brothers. The question was submitted to the jury on the theory that each petitioner could be found guilty of the substantive offenses, if it was found at the time those offenses were committed petitioners were parties to an unlawful conspiracy and the substantive offenses charged were in fact committed in furtherance of it.[6]

We have here a continuous conspiracy. There is here no evidence of the affirmative action on the part of Daniel which is necessary to establish his withdrawal from it. "Having joined in an unlawful scheme, having constituted agents for its performance, scheme and agency to be continuous until full fruition be secured, until he does some act to disavow or defeat the purpose he is in no situation to claim the delay of the law. As the offense has not been terminated or accomplished he is still offending. And we think, consciously offending, offending as certainly, as we have said, as at the first moment of his confederation, and consciously through every moment of its existence." And so long as the partnership in crime continues, the partners act for each other in carrying it forward. It is settled that "an overt act of one partner may be the act of all without any new agreement specifically directed to that act." Motive or intent may be proved by the acts or declarations of some of the conspirators in furtherance of the common objective. A scheme to use the mails to defraud, which is joined in by more than one person, is a conspiracy. Yet all members are responsible, though only one did the mailing. The governing principle is the same when the sub-

---

> Although in a particular case there may be no preconcert of plan, excepting that necessarily inherent in mere joint action, it is difficult to exclude that situation from the established definitions of conspiracy; yet the theory which permits us to call the aborted plan a greater offense than the completed crime supposes a serious and substantially continued group scheme for cooperative law breaking. We observe so many conspiracy prosecutions which do not have this substantial base that we fear the creation of a general impression, very harmful to law enforcement, that this method of prosecution is used arbitrarily and harshly. Further the rules of evidence in conspiracy cases make them most difficult to try without prejudice to an innocent defendant.

Annual Report of the Attorney General for 1925, pp. 5–6. But we do not find that practice reflected in this present case.

6. The trial court charged: "... after you gentlemen have considered all the evidence in this case, if you are satisfied from the evidence beyond a reasonable doubt that at the time these particular substantive offenses were committed, that is, the offenses charged in the first ten counts of this indictment if you are satisfied from the evidence beyond a reasonable doubt that the two defendants were in an unlawful conspiracy, as I have heretofore defined unlawful conspiracy to you, then you would have a right, if you found that to be true to your satisfaction beyond a reasonable doubt, to convict each of these defendants on all these substantive counts, provided the acts referred to in the substantive counts were acts in furtherance of the unlawful conspiracy or object of the unlawful conspiracy, which you have found from the evidence existed."

stantive offense is committed by one of the conspirators in furtherance of the unlawful project. The criminal intent to do the act is established by the formation of the conspiracy. Each conspirator instigated the commission of the crime. The unlawful agreement contemplated precisely what was done. It was formed for the purpose. The act done was in execution of the enterprise. The rule which holds responsible one who counsels, procures, or commands another to commit a crime is founded on the same principle. That principle is recognized in the law of conspiracy when the overt act of one partner in crime is attributable to all. An overt act is an essential ingredient of the crime of conspiracy. If that can be supplied by the act of one conspirator, we fail to see why the same or other acts in furtherance of the conspiracy are likewise not attributable to the others for the purpose of holding them responsible for the substantive offense.

A different case would arise if the substantive offense committed by one of the conspirators was not in fact done in furtherance of the conspiracy, did not fall within the scope of the unlawful project, or was merely a part of the ramifications of the plan which could not be reasonably foreseen as a necessary or natural consequence of the unlawful agreement. But as we read this record, that is not this case.

Affirmed.

Mr. Justice Rutledge, dissenting in part.

The judgment concerning Daniel Pinkerton should be reversed. In my opinion it is without precedent here and is a dangerous precedent to establish.

I think this ruling violates both the letter and the spirit of what Congress did when it separately defined the three classes of crime, namely, (1) completed substantive offenses; (2) aiding, abetting or counseling another to commit them; and (3) conspiracy to commit them. Not only does this ignore the distinctions Congress has prescribed shall be observed. It either convicts one man for another's crime or punishes the man convicted twice for the same offense.

The three types of offense are not identical. Nor are their differences merely verbal. The gist of conspiracy is the agreement; that of aiding, abetting or counseling is in consciously advising or assisting another to commit particular offenses, and thus becoming a party to them; that of substantive crime, going a step beyond mere aiding, abetting, counseling to completion of the offense.

These general differences are well understood. But when conspiracy has ripened into completed crime, or has advanced to the stage of aiding and abetting, it becomes easy to disregard their differences and loosely to treat one as identical with the other, that is, for every purpose except the most vital one of imposing sentence. And thus the substance, if not the technical effect, of double jeopardy or multiple punishment may be accomplished. Thus also may one be convicted of an offense not charged or proved against him, on evidence showing he committed another.

The old doctrine of merger of conspiracy in the substantive crime has not obtained here. But the dangers for abuse, which in part it sought to avoid, in applying the law of conspiracy have not altogether disappeared. There is some evidence that they may be increasing. The looseness with which the charge may be proved, the almost unlimited scope of vicarious responsibility for others' acts which follows once agreement is shown, the psychological advantages of such trials for securing convictions by attributing to one proof against another, these and other inducements require that the broad limits of discretion allowed to prosecuting officers in relation to such charges and trials be not expanded into new, wider and more dubious areas of choice. Daniel has been held guilty of the substantive crimes committed only by Walter on proof that he did no more than conspire with him to commit offenses of the same general character. There was no evidence that he counseled, advised or had knowledge of those particular acts or offenses. There was, therefore, none that he aided, abetted or took part in them. There was only evidence sufficient to show that he had agreed with Walter at some past time to engage in such transactions generally. As to Daniel this was only evidence of conspiracy, not of substantive crime.

The Court's theory seems to be that Daniel and Walter became general partners in crime by virtue of their agreement and because of that agreement without more on his part Daniel became criminally responsible as a principal for everything Walter did thereafter in the nature of a criminal offense of the general sort the agreement contemplated, so long as there was not clear evidence that Daniel had withdrawn from or revoked the agreement. Whether or not his commitment to the penitentiary had that effect, the result is a vicarious criminal responsibility as broad as, or broader than, the vicarious civil liability of a partner for acts done by a co-partner in the course of the firm's business.

Such analogies from private commercial law and the law of torts are dangerous, in my judgment, for transfer to the criminal field. Guilt there with us remains personal, not vicarious, for the more serious offenses. It should be kept so. The effect of Daniel's conviction in this case, to repeat, is either to attribute to him Walter's guilt or to punish him twice for the same offense, namely, agreeing with Walter to engage in crime. Without the agreement Daniel was guilty of no crime on this record. With it and no more, so far as his own conduct is concerned, he was guilty of two.

Comments and Questions

(1) An attempt (as well as a solicitation) and the completed offense merge into a single punishable crime. Why are conspiracy and the completed offense treated differently in the federal courts? Many states follow the federal rule against merger, but not all do. Some states require merger "if the conspiracy does not have objectives that go beyond the substantive offense." *State v. Le Furge*, 502 A.2d 35, 44 (N.J. 1986).

(2) In *United States v. Addo*, 989 F.2d 238, 244 (7th Cir. 1993), the court explained the giving of the common, so-called *Pinkerton* instruction:

> A *Pinkerton* instruction informs the jury members that if they initially determine beyond a reasonable doubt that a conspiracy existed and the defendant was a member of the conspiracy then they may find the defendant responsible for offenses committed by other co-conspirators in the furtherance of the conspiracy.

(3) Many states follow the *Pinkerton* complicity statute either by statute or case law. The North Dakota Criminal Code states simply that "a person may be convicted of an offense based upon the conduct of another person when ... he is a co-conspirator...." § 12.1-03-01. See the statement of the Supreme Court of Connecticut in *State v. Walton*, 630 A.2d 990, 1001 (Conn. 1993):

> All who join in a common design to commit an unlawful act ... are responsible.... Recognition of the *Pinkerton* principle in an appropriate case is not inconsistent with the notion of accessory liability, and does not mean, as the defendant argues, that the two are "collapsed into one."

This view has been subjected to criticism. As stated by the Supreme Judicial Court of Massachusetts:

> The fact of the conspiracy being proved against the prisoner is to be weighed as evidence in the case having a tendency to prove that the prisoner aided, but it is not in itself to be taken as a legal presumption of his having aided unless disproved by him.
>
> If the rule were otherwise, the fundamental distinction between a substantive offence and a conspiracy to commit that offence would be ignored. Each is a separate and distinct offence and each may be separately punished. The combination for the illegal purpose or for the use of illegal means is the essence of conspiracy. Punishment is imposed for entering into the combination. This is not the same thing as participating in the substantive offence which was the object of the conspiracy. While it has been said that a conspiracy is a "partnership in crime" that metaphor should not be pressed too far. It does not follow that such a partnership is governed by the same principles of vicarious liability as would apply in civil cases. Our criminal law is founded on the principle that guilt, for the more serious offences, is personal, not vicarious. One is punished for his own blameworthy conduct, not that of others. To ignore the distinction between the crime of conspiracy and the substantive offence would enable "the government through the use of the conspiracy dragnet to convict a conspirator of every substantive offense committed by any other member of the group even though he had no part in it or even knowledge of it."

Commonwealth v. Stasiun, 206 N.E.2d 672, 679 (Mass. 1965).

The Criminal Justice Section, American Bar Association (Aug. 1975), leveled a somewhat different criticism:

> The *Pinkerton* rule represents a form of vicarious criminal liability that, in essence, imposes liability for negligence. In the form of the rule adopted ... a person is liable for a co-conspirator's crime which was "reasonably foreseeable," or, stated another way, the person is criminally liable if he should have known, when he agreed to become a part of the conspiracy, that there was a risk that the collateral offense would be committed. This is clearly negligence liability, and should be imposed only if there is strong justification.

(4) At common law, as with attempt and solicitation, a conspirator could not escape responsibility for the conspiracy if he withdrew from the group. Here, too, *supra*, the modern rule—looking to the Model Penal Code § 5.03(6)—allows for withdrawal. See, for example, § 28-203 of the Nebraska Criminal Code, which provides:

> In a prosecution for criminal conspiracy, it shall be an affirmative defense that the defendant, under circumstances manifesting a voluntary and complete renunciation of his criminal intent, gave timely warning to law enforcement authorities or otherwise made a reasonable effort to prevent the conduct or result which is the object of the conspiracy.

The test for withdrawal was set out in *State v. Lobato*, 603 So. 2d 739, 746 (La. 1992):

> To prove withdrawal, a defendant must show affirmative actions made by him which are inconsistent with the conspiracy. Such affirmative actions include making a clean breast through confession to the authorities as well as notification to the co-conspirators of abandonment or withdrawal.

If a conspirator is jailed, has she—as a matter of law—withdrawn from the conspiracy?

> Leslie argues that his incarceration was prima facie evidence that he withdrew from the conspiracy ... it is well settled that withdrawal from a conspiracy is an affirmative defense....
>
> Mere cessation of the conspiratorial activity by the defendant is not sufficient to prove withdrawal. The defendant "must also show that he performed some act that affirmatively established that he disavowed his criminal association with the conspiracy, either the making of a clean breast to the authorities, or communication of the abandonment in a manner reasonably calculated to reach co-conspirators." "Unless a conspirator produces affirmative evidence of withdrawal, his participation in a conspiracy is presumed to continue until the last overt act by any of the conspirators."
>
> ... Leslie argues that imprisonment may be evidence of an affirmative act of withdrawal from a conspiracy; we agree. But "while arrest or incarceration *may* constitute a withdrawal from a conspiracy, it does not follow that in every instance it *must*." In the trial context, evidence of imprisonment during a conspiracy is merely a relevant fact that entitles the defendant to a jury instruction on withdrawal.

United States v. Leslie, 658 F.3d 140, 143–44 (2nd Cir. 2011).

(5) One of the most important discussions of conspiracy law is Justice Jackson's concurring opinion in *Krulewitch v. United States*, 336 U.S. 440, 445–54 (1949):

> This case illustrates a present drift in the federal law of conspiracy which warrants some further comment because it is characteristic of the long evolution of that elastic, sprawling and pervasive offense. Its history exemplifies the "tendency of a principle to expand itself to the limit of its logic." The unavailing protest of courts against the growing habit to indict for conspiracy

in lieu of prosecuting for the substantive offense itself, or in addition thereto, suggests that loose practice as to this offense constitutes a serious threat to fairness in our administration of justice.

The modern crime of conspiracy is so vague that it almost defies definition. Despite certain elementary and essential elements, it also, chameleon-like, takes on a special coloration from each of the many independent offenses on which it may be overlaid. It is always "predominantly mental in composition" because it consists primarily of a meeting of minds and an intent.

The crime comes down to us wrapped in vague but unpleasant connotations. It sounds historical undertones of treachery, secret plotting and violence on a scale that menaces social stability and the security of the state itself. "Privy conspiracy" ranks with sedition and rebellion in the Litany's prayer for deliverance. Conspiratorial movements do indeed lie back of the political assassination, the *coup d'etat*, the *putsch*, the revolution, and seizures of power in modern times, as they have in all history.

But the conspiracy concept also is superimposed upon many concerted crimes having no political motivation. It is not intended to question that the basic conspiracy principle has some place in modern criminal law, because to unite, back of a criminal purpose, the strength, opportunities and resources of many is obviously more dangerous and more difficult to police than the efforts of a lone wrongdoer. However, even when appropriately invoked, the looseness and pliability of the doctrine present inherent dangers which should be in the background of judicial thought wherever it is sought to extend the doctrine to meet the exigencies of a particular case.

A recent tendency has appeared in this Court to expand this elastic offense and to facilitate its proof. In *Pinkerton v. United States*, it sustained a conviction of a substantive crime where there was no proof of participation in or knowledge of it, upon the novel and dubious theory that conspiracy is equivalent in law to aiding and abetting.

Of course, it is for prosecutors rather than courts to determine when to use a scatter-gun to bring down the defendant, but there are procedural advantages from using it which add to the danger of unguarded extension of the concept.

An accused, under the Sixth Amendment, has the right to trial "by an impartial jury of the State and district wherein the crime shall have been committed." The leverage of a conspiracy charge lifts this limitation from the prosecution and reduces its protection to a phantom, for the crime is considered so vagrant as to have been committed in any district where any one of the conspirators did any one of the acts, however innocent, intended to accomplish its object. The Government may, and often does, compel one to defend at a great distance from any place he ever did any act because some accused confederate did some trivial and by itself innocent act in the chosen district. Circumstances may even enable the prosecution to fix the place of trial in Washington, D.C., where a defendant may lawfully be put to trial before a jury partly or even wholly made up of employees of the Government that accuses him.

When the trial starts, the accused feels the full impact of the conspiracy strategy. Strictly, the prosecution should first establish *prima facie* the conspiracy and identify the conspirators, after which evidence of acts and declarations of each in the course of its execution are admissible against all. But the order of proof of so sprawling a charge is difficult for a judge to control. As a practical matter, the accused often is confronted with a hodgepodge of acts and statements by others which he may never have authorized or intended or even known about, but which help to persuade the jury of existence of the conspiracy itself. In other words, a conspiracy often is proved by evidence that is admissible only upon assumption that conspiracy existed. The naive assumption that prejudicial effects can be overcome by instructions to the jury, all practicing lawyers know to be unmitigated fiction.

The trial of a conspiracy charge doubtless imposes a heavy burden on the prosecution, but it is an especially difficult situation for the defendant. The hazard from loose application of rules of evidence is aggravated where the Government institutes mass trials. Moreover, in federal practice there is no rule preventing conviction on uncorroborated testimony of accomplices, as there are in many jurisdictions, and the most comfort a defendant can expect is that the court can be induced to follow the "better practice" and caution the jury against "too much reliance upon the testimony of accomplices."

A co-defendant in a conspiracy trial occupies an uneasy seat. There generally will be evidence of wrongdoing by somebody. It is difficult for the individual to make his own case stand on its own merits in the minds of jurors who are ready to believe that birds of a feather are flocked together. If he is silent, he is taken to admit it and if, as often happens, co-defendants can be prodded into accusing or contradicting each other, they convict each other. There are many practical difficulties in defending against a charge of conspiracy which I will not enumerate.

Chapter 7

Defenses

§ 7.01 Privileges to Defend

[A] Self-Defense

People v. Goetz

New York Court of Appeals
497 N.E.2d 41 (1986)

Chief Judge Wachtler.

A Grand Jury has indicted defendant on attempted murder, assault, and other charges for having shot and wounded four youths on a New York City subway train after one or two of the youths approached him and asked for $5. The lower courts, concluding that the prosecutor's charge to the Grand Jury on the defense of justification was erroneous, have dismissed the attempted murder, assault and weapons possession charges. We now reverse and reinstate all counts of the indictment.

I.

On Saturday afternoon, December 22, 1984, Troy Canty, Darryl Cabey, James Ramseur, and Barry Allen boarded an IRT express subway train in The Bronx and headed south toward lower Manhattan. The four youths rode together in the rear portion of the seventh car of the train. Two of the four, Ramseur and Cabey, had screwdrivers inside their coats, which they said were to be used to break into the coin boxes of video machines.

Defendant Bernard Goetz boarded this subway train at 14th Street in Manhattan and sat down on a bench towards the rear section of the same car occupied by the four youths. Goetz was carrying an unlicensed .38 caliber pistol loaded with five rounds of ammunition in a waistband holster. The train left the 14th Street station and headed towards Chambers Street.

It appears from the evidence before the Grand Jury that Canty approached Goetz, possibly with Allen beside him, and stated "give me five dollars." Neither Canty nor any of the other youths displayed a weapon. Goetz responded by standing up, pulling out his handgun and firing four shots in rapid succession. The first shot hit Canty in the chest; the second struck Allen in the back; the third went through Ramseur's arm and into his left side; the fourth was fired at Cabey, who apparently was then standing in the corner of the car, but missed, deflecting instead off of a wall of the conductor's cab. After Goetz briefly surveyed the scene around him, he fired another shot at Cabey, who then was sitting on the end bench of the car. The bullet entered the rear of Cabey's side and severed his spinal cord.

All but two of the other passengers fled the car when, or immediately after, the shots were fired. The conductor, who had been in the next car, heard the shots and instructed the motorman to radio for emergency assistance. The conductor then went into the car where the shooting occurred and saw Goetz sitting on a bench, the injured youths lying on the floor or slumped against a seat, and two women who had apparently taken cover, also lying on the floor. Goetz told the conductor that the four youths had tried to rob him.

While the conductor was aiding the youths, Goetz headed towards the front of the car. The train had stopped just before the Chambers Street station and Goetz went between two of the cars, jumped onto the tracks and fled. Police and ambulance crews arrived at the scene shortly thereafter. Ramseur and Canty, initially listed in critical condition, have fully recovered. Cabey remains paralyzed, and has suffered some degree of brain damage.

On December 31, 1984, Goetz surrendered to police in Concord, New Hampshire, identifying himself as the gunman being sought for the subway shootings in New York nine days earlier. Later that day, after receiving *Miranda* warnings, he made two lengthy statements, both of which were tape recorded with his permission. In the statements, which are substantially similar, Goetz admitted that he had been illegally carrying a handgun in New York City for three years. He stated that he had first purchased a gun in 1981 after he had been injured in a mugging. Goetz also revealed that twice between 1981 and 1984 he had successfully warded off assailants simply by displaying the pistol.

According to Goetz's statement, the first contact he had with the four youths came when Canty, sitting or lying on the bench across from him, asked "how are you," to which he replied "fine." Shortly thereafter, Canty, followed by one of the other youths, walked over to the defendant and stood to his left, while the other two youths remained to his right, in the corner of the subway car. Canty then said "give me five dollars." Goetz stated that he knew from the smile on Canty's face that they wanted to "play with me." Although he was certain that none of the youths had a gun, he had a fear, based on prior experiences, of being "maimed."

Goetz then established "a pattern of fire," deciding specifically to fire from left to right. His stated intention at that point was to "murder [the four youths], to hurt them, to make them suffer as much as possible." When Canty again requested money, Goetz stood up, drew his weapon, and began firing, aiming for the center of the body of each of the four. Goetz recalled that the first two he shot "tried to run through the crowd [but] they had nowhere to run." Goetz then turned to his right to "go after the other two." One of these two "tried to run through the wall of the train, but ... he had nowhere to go." The other youth (Cabey) "tried pretending that he wasn't with [the others]" by standing still, holding on to one of the subway hand straps, and not looking at Goetz. Goetz nonetheless fired his fourth shot at him. He then ran back to the first two youths to make sure they had been "taken care of." Seeing that they had both been shot, he spun back to check on the latter two. Goetz noticed that the youth who had been standing still was now sitting on a bench and seemed unhurt. As Goetz told the police, "I said '[y]ou seem to be all right, here's another,'" and he then fired the shot which severed Cabey's spinal cord. Goetz added that "if I was a little more under self-control ... I would have put the barrel against his forehead and fired." He also admitted that "if I had had more [bullets], I would have shot them again, and again, and again."

II.

On March 27, 1985, the second Grand Jury filed a 10-count indictment, containing four charges of attempted murder, four charges of assault in the first degree, one charge of reckless endangerment in the first degree, and one charge of criminal possession of a weapon in the second degree. Goetz was arraigned on this indictment on March 28, 1985, and it was consolidated with the earlier three-count indictment.

Goetz moved to dismiss the charges contained in the second indictment alleging, among other things, that the prosecutor's instructions to that Grand Jury on the defense of justification were erroneous and prejudicial to the defendant so as to render its proceedings defective.

[The lower court held] that the prosecutor, in a supplemental charge elaborating upon the justification defense, had erroneously introduced an objective element into this defense by instructing the grand jurors to consider whether Goetz's conduct was that of a "reasonable man in [Goetz's] situation." The court concluded that the statutory test for whether the use of deadly force is justified to protect a person should be wholly subjective, focusing entirely on the defendant's state of mind when he used such force. It concluded that dismissal was required for this error because the justification issue was at the heart of the case.

III.

Penal Law article 35 recognizes the defense of justification, which "permits the use of force under certain circumstances." One such set of circumstances pertains to the use of force in defense of a person, encompassing both self-defense and defense of a third person. Penal Law 35.15(1) sets forth the general principles governing all such uses of force: "[a] person may ... use physical force upon another person when and to the extent he *reasonably believes* such to be necessary to defend himself or a third person from what he *reasonably believes* to be the imminent use of unlawful physical force by such other person." (Emphasis added).

Section 35.15(2) sets forth further limitations on these general principles with respect to the use of "deadly physical force": "A person may not use deadly physical force upon another person under circumstances specified in subdivision one unless (a) He *reasonably believes* that such other person is using or about to use deadly physical force ... or (b) He *reasonably believes* that such other person is committing or attempting to commit a kidnapping, forcible rape, forcible sodomy or robbery."

Thus, consistent with most justification provisions, Penal Law § 35.15 permits the use of deadly physical force only where requirements as to triggering conditions and the necessity of a particular response are met. As to the triggering conditions, the statute requires that the actor "reasonably believes" that another person either is using or about to use deadly physical force or is committing or attempting to commit one of certain enumerated felonies, including robbery. As to the need for the use of deadly physical force as a response, the statute requires that the actor "reasonably believes" that such force is necessary to avert the perceived threat.

Because the evidence before the second Grand Jury included statements by Goetz that he acted to protect himself from being maimed or to avert a robbery, the prosecutor correctly chose to charge the justification defense. The prosecutor properly instructed the grand jurors to consider whether the use of deadly physical force was justified to prevent either serious physical injury or a robbery, and, in doing so, to separately analyze the defense with respect to each of the charges. He elaborated upon the prerequisites for the use of deadly physical force essentially by reading or paraphrasing the language in Penal Law § 35.15. The defense does not contend that he committed any error in this portion of the charge.

When the prosecutor had completed his charge, one of the grand jurors asked for clarification of the term "reasonably believes." The prosecutor responded by instructing the grand jurors that they were to consider the circumstances of the incident and determine "whether the defendant's conduct was that of a reasonable man in the defendant's situation." It is this response by the prosecutor—and specifically his use of "a reasonable man"—which is the basis for the dismissal of the charges by the lower courts. As expressed repeatedly in the Appellate Division's plurality opinion, because section 35.15 uses the term "*he* reasonably believes," the appropriate test, according to that court, is whether a defendant's beliefs and reactions were "reasonable *to him*." Under that reading of the statute, a jury which believed a defendant's testimony that he felt that his own actions were warranted and were reasonable would have to acquit him, regardless of what anyone else in defendant's situation might have concluded. Such an interpretation defies the ordinary meaning and significance of the term "reasonably" in a statute, and misconstrues the clear intent of the Legislature to retain an objective element as part of any provision authorizing the use of deadly physical force.

Penal statutes in New York have long codified the right recognized at common law to use deadly physical force, under appropriate circumstances, in self-defense. These provisions have never required that an actor's belief as to the intention of another person to inflict serious injury be correct in order for the use of deadly force to be justified, but they have uniformly required that the belief comport with an objective notion of reasonableness. The 1829 statute, using language which was followed almost in its entirety until the 1965 recodification of the Penal Law, provided that the use of deadly force was justified in self-defense or in the defense of specified third persons "when there shall be a reasonable ground to apprehend a design to commit a felony, or to do some great personal injury, and there shall be imminent danger of such design being accomplished."

The provisions of the Model Penal Code with respect to the use of deadly force in self-defense reflect the position of its drafters that any culpability which arises from a mistaken belief in the need to use such force should be no greater than the culpability such a mistake would give rise to if it were made with respect to an element of a crime. Accordingly, under Model Penal Code 3.04(2)(b), a defendant charged with murder (or attempted murder) need only show that he "*believe*[*d*] that [the use of deadly force] was necessary to protect himself against death, serious bodily injury, kidnapping or [forcible] sexual intercourse" to prevail on a self-defense claim. (Emphasis added). If the defendant's belief was wrong, and was recklessly, or negligently formed, however, he may be convicted of the type of homicide charge requiring only a reckless or negligent, as the case may be, criminal intent.

The drafters of the Model Penal Code recognized that the wholly subjective test set forth in section 3.04 differed from the existing law in most States by its omission of any requirement of reasonableness. The drafters were also keenly aware that requiring that the actor have a "reasonable belief" rather than just a "belief" would alter the wholly subjective test. This basic distinction was recognized years earlier by the New York Law Revisions Commission and continues to be noted by the commentators.

New York did not follow the Model Penal Code's equation of a mistake as to the need to use deadly force with a mistake negating an element of a crime, choosing instead to use a single statutory section which would provide either a complete defense or no defense at all to a defendant charged with any crime involving the use of deadly force. The drafters of the new Penal Law adopted in large part the structure and content of Model Penal Code § 3.04, but, crucially, inserted the word "reasonably" before "believes."

The plurality below agreed with defendant's argument that the change in the statutory language from "reasonable ground," used prior to 1965, to "he reasonably believes" in Penal Law § 35.15 evinced a legislative intent to conform to the subjective standard contained in Model Penal Code § 3.04. This argument, however, ignores the plain significance of the insertion of "reasonably." Had the drafters of section 35.15 wanted to adopt a subjective standard, they could have simply used the language of section 3.04. "Believes" by itself requires an honest or genuine belief by a defendant as to the need to use deadly force. Interpreting the statute to require only that the defendant's belief was reasonable to *him*," as done by the plurality below, would hardly be different from requiring only a genuine belief; in either case, the defendant's own perceptions could completely exonerate him from any criminal liability.

We cannot lightly impute to the Legislature an intent to fundamentally alter the principles of justification to allow the perpetrator of a serious crime to go free simply because that person believed his actions were reasonable and necessary to prevent some perceived harm. To completely exonerate such an individual, no matter how aberrational or bizarre his thought patterns, would allow citizens to set their own standards for the permissible use of force. It would also allow a legally competent defendant suffering from delusions to kill or perform acts of violence with impunity, contrary to fundamental principles of justice and criminal law.

We can only conclude that the Legislature retained a reasonableness requirement to avoid giving a license for such actions. The plurality's interpretation, as the dissenters below recognized, excises the impact of the word "reasonably."

The change from "reasonable ground" to "reasonably believes" is better explained by the fact that the drafters of section 35.15 were proposing a single section which, for the first time, would govern both the use of ordinary force and deadly force in self-defense or defense of another. Under the 1909 Penal Law and its predecessors, the use of ordinary force was governed by separate sections which, at least by their literal terms, required that the defendant was *in fact* responding to an unlawful assault, and not just that he had a reasonable ground for believing that such an assault was occurring. Following the example of the Model Penal Code, the drafters of section 35.15 eliminated this sharp dichotomy between the use of ordinary force and deadly force in defense of a person. Not surprisingly then, the integrated section reflects the wording of Model Penal Code § 3.04, with the addition of "reasonably" to incorporate the long-standing requirement of "reasonable ground" for the use of deadly force and apply it to the use of ordinary force as well.

Goetz also argues that the introduction of an objective element will preclude a jury from considering factors such as the prior experiences of a given actor and thus require it to make a determination of "reasonableness" without regard to the actual circumstances of a particular incident. This argument, however, falsely presupposes that an objective standard means that the background and other relevant characteristics of a particular actor must be ignored. To the contrary, we have frequently noted that a determination of reasonableness must be based on the "circumstances" facing a defendant or his "situation." Such terms encompass more than the physical movements of the potential assailant. As just discussed, these terms include any relevant knowledge the defendant had about that person. They also necessarily bring in the physical attributes of all persons involved, including the defendant. Furthermore, the defendant's circumstances encompass any prior experiences he had which could provide a reasonable basis for a belief that another person's intentions were to injure or rob him or that the use of deadly force was necessary under the circumstances.

Accordingly, a jury should be instructed to consider this type of evidence in weighing the defendant's actions. The jury must first determine whether the defendant had the requisite beliefs under section 35.15, that is, whether he believed deadly force was necessary to avert the imminent use of deadly force or the commission of one of the felonies enumerated therein. If the People do not prove beyond a reasonable doubt that he did not have such beliefs, then the jury must also consider whether these beliefs were reasonable. The jury would have to determine, in light of all the "circumstances," as explicated above, if a reasonable person could have had these beliefs.[1]

---

1. Ed.—The defendant was acquitted of attempted murder, assault, and reckless endangerment

Comments and Questions

(1) The following instruction is a typical self-defense charge:

> Homicide is justifiable and not unlawful when committed by a person in the lawful defense of herself, when she has reasonable ground to apprehend that she is in danger of death or great bodily injury and that there is imminent danger of such a design being accomplished.
>
> In order to justify the taking of human life in self-defense, the slayer, as a reasonable person, must have reason to believe and must believe that she is in danger of death or of great bodily injury; and, further, the circumstances must be such that an ordinarily reasonable person, under similar circumstances, would believe that it was necessary for her to use, in her defense and to avoid death or great bodily injury to herself, such force or means as might cause the death of her adversary.
>
> A bare fear of death or great bodily injury is not sufficient to justify a homicide. To justify taking the life of another in self-defense, the circumstances must be such as to excite the fears of a reasonable person placed in a similar position, and the party killing must act under the influence of such fears alone. The danger must be apparent and must be present and imminent, or must so appear at the time to the slayer as a reasonable woman, and the killing must be done under a well-founded belief that it is necessary to save one's self from death or great bodily harm.

State v. Griffiths, 610 P.2d 522, 535 (Idaho 1980).

Why must the belief be reasonable? Why is it often said that a genuine belief in the imminence of danger does not entitle a person to kill if in fact the belief is unreasonable? At the conclusion of the *Goetz* opinion, the court discussed the defendant's argument which "falsely presupposes that an objective standard means that the background and other relevant characteristics of a particular actor must be ignored." Does the court mean that an elderly, enfeebled man who had been previously robbed several times could bring those facts out to the jury? Is that approach consistent with the objective standard the court sets out?

> The problem here, as always in the criminal law, is striking the balance between the defender's subjective perceptions and those of a hypothetical reasonable person. To apply a purely objective standard is unduly harsh because it ignores the characteristics which inevitably and justifiably shape the defendant's perspective, thus holding him (or her) to a standard he simply cannot meet. If the defender is young or crippled or blind, we should not expect him to behave like a strapping, sighted adult. On the other hand, if the reasonable person has all of the defender's characteristics, the standard loses any normative component and becomes entirely subjective. Applying a purely

---

charges but found guilty of the crime of having an unlicensed revolver. In 1996 a jury awarded Darrell Cabey $43 million in civil damages and Goetz later filed for bankruptcy.

> subjective standard in all cases would give free rein to the short-tempered, the pugnacious, and the foolhardy who see threats of harm where the rest of us would not and who blind themselves to opportunities for escape that seem plainly available. These unreasonable people may be not as wicked as (although perhaps more dangerous than) cold-blooded murderers—imperfect self-defense generally reduces murder to manslaughter—but neither are they, in practical or legal terms, justified in causing death.

Gillespie, *1990 Survey of Books Relating to the Law; II. Crime and Punishment: Defending Women. Justifiable Homicide: Battered Women, Self-Defense, and the Law*, 88 Mich. L. Rev. 1430, 1434–35 (1990).

(2) In *Rowe v. DeBruyn*, 17 F.3d 1047, 1052–53, 1055 (7th Cir. 1994), the state prisoner was disciplined for striking another prisoner. He claimed that he acted in self-defense in response to a physical attack and an attempted rape. The Indiana prison officials would not recognize the self-defense in such disciplinary hearings (though they did allow the officials to consider it in mitigation of penalty). The defendant argued that he had a constitutional right to raise a self-defense claim. Was he right? Contrast the majority and dissenting opinions.

Majority:

> [W]e believe that manufacturing such a right for application in non-criminal, prison proceedings is [not] justified. This is particularly so where prison authorities daily face an intractable problem of violence within the prison walls. A right that threatens to undermine prison discipline by encouraging inmates to combat violence with more violence subverts a core prison function of ensuring order and safety within the institution.

Dissent:

> It is indeed a novel proposition of constitutional law to hold that a state, having deprived a person of liberty according to law, can further punish that individual for attempting to stay alive, even when the state itself is not ready, willing, or capable of assuming that responsibility by substituting its own strong arm for that of the prisoner-victim.

(3) Should a self-defense instruction have been given in these cases? *Peals v. State*, 584 S.W.2d 1 (Ark. 1979), where,

> ... the appellant and several other persons were working on an automobile which had stalled in front of a store in close proximity to the home of William Murray, decedent-victim, and his sister, Susan Murray. The Murrays appeared and engaged appellant in an argument which resulted in Susan firing a gun at the appellant and William chasing him with a butcher knife. Shortly thereafter, appellant returned to the scene armed with a pistol and almost immediately the fracas was resumed. The testimony is greatly disputed as to whether Susan Murray opened fire the second time prior to the time appellant fired at her. Regardless of who started the firing, one of the shots from appellant's pistol proved fatal to William Murray. During the latter part of the episode

> the Murrays were standing on the balcony or stairways at their place of residence and the appellant was on the ground in the vicinity of the street below, near the stalled vehicle.

Villageliu v. State, 347 So. 2d 445, 447 (Fla. Dist. Ct. App. 3d Dist. 1977), where,

> after an altercation with the two victims, the defendant went to his car and returned with a baseball bat with which he beat one unarmed victim to death and injured the other.

(4) Could the trial court require the defendant to prove, by a preponderance of the evidence, that she acted in self-defense? The Supreme Court in *Martin v. Ohio*, 480 U.S. 228 (1987), held that such a requirement satisfied due process because the state did not "shift to [the defendant] any of [the] elements [of the offense]."

State v. Rupp

Supreme Court of Iowa
282 N.W.2d 125 (1979)

LEGRAND, JUSTICE.

The events in question started with a drinking party at a tavern known as the Hi-Lo Lodge. An argument ensued between Curtis Sederburg and a third party, Bud Wolf, concerning change for a $10.00 bill in connection with paying off a bet. Defendant became embroiled in the dispute, which continued outside after the parties left the Hi-Lo.

The argument became more and more heated. The record is in dispute as to who was the aggressor. Eventually Sederburg started toward defendant, who produced a .38 caliber revolver and shot him. Defendant fled the scene and was later arrested at his home.

I. Assault With Intention to Commit Murder

Defendant admitted he shot Sederburg. He claimed he was justified. As applicable in this case, justification—or self-defense—is a doctrine of the law permitting one, under certain circumstances, to use force in defending himself. The force used must be reasonable; and force should be resorted to at all only as a last resort.

We set out the relevant part of the applicable statute:

> 704.1 "*Reasonable force*" is that force which a reasonable person, in like circumstances, would judge to be necessary to prevent an injury or loss, and no more, except that the use of deadly force against another is reasonable only to resist a like force or threat. *Reasonable force, including deadly force, may be used even if an alternative course of action is available if the alternative entails a risk to one's life or safety....* (Emphasis added)

The problem in this case arises because of the italicized portion of the statute, which recognizes there may be circumstances when the attempt to take an alternative course of action will pose a serious threat to one's safety. In such a situation a party may use reasonable force, including deadly force, *without* first taking an available alternative course.

Defendant claimed he was in reasonable fear that Sederburg intended to do him serious injury. He gave detailed testimony of bad blood between them, of several prior assaults by Sederburg, and of Sederburg's threats to kill him.

He insisted he was justified in shooting without first taking an alternative course of action. The trial court refused to include this element in the instructions.

The relevant portions of the instructions on justification were as follows:

> You must find the defendant not guilty on grounds of justification unless the state has proved by evidence beyond a reasonable doubt any one of the following elements:
>
> 2. An alternative course of action was available as explained in [the following instruction].
>
> The trial court then gave this instruction:
>
> With regard to element number 2 (Alternative Course of Action) ... you are instructed that if a person is confronted with the use of unlawful force against himself, he is required to avoid the confrontation by seeking and using an alternative course of action. Thus, if there is evidence that, as a reasonable person, the defendant could have avoided the use of unlawful force, he must have taken or used the alternative course of action before he is justified in repelling the force used against him.

We have, then, these circumstances. The jury could have found defendant used deadly force by discharging his pistol and wounding Sederburg; that he did not first take an available alternative action; and that he is therefore not entitled to the doctrine of justification.

But defendant argues he was not obliged to take alternative action because of the exception in the statute which excuses him from doing so if the alternative involved a risk of his life or safety.

Defendant's testimony becomes vitally important here and we set it out at length.

> Q. How long have you known Curtis Sederburg?
>
> A. Approximately since 1963. That would be 15 years.
>
> Q. And during the time describe that relationship.
>
> A. It's always been quarrelsome.
>
> Q. Can you explain some of those problems you might have had?
>
> A. It started back right after I got to know Curtis in 1963.
>
> Q. What happened then?
>
> A. We got into a fight up in Red Oak, Iowa.
>
> Q. And can you tell me what happened in general on that?

A. After it was all over I ended up with a black eye and a fat lip.

Q. What was your next relationship?

A. Oh, it would be not until 1972.

Q. And what was that?

A. It was an incident at the Blue Spur Lounge in Shenandoah, Iowa.

Q. Can you tell me about that?

A. Curtis came down, well, he come down with another guy and Curtis came down and he wanted to fight and he was hollering at me and they stopped him before he could get me; the bouncer to the place did, and asked him to leave and he didn't want to leave so they throwed him out.

Q. What was the next occurrence?

A. It was later on in 1972.

Q. Okay, what was that?

A. This was the time when he come down and I was down at the bar ... and he come in and I was just getting off my bar stool because I saw him come through the door and he knocked over the bar stool and he got to me and hit me once and I started to go down and he kicked me and tore the cartilage loose on the right side of my chest.

Q. Did this disable you?

A. Yes.

Q. How?

A. I couldn't work. It tore all the cartilage loose in my chest so I had to be under doctor's care.

Q. Did any other incidents occur that you can think of?

A. Yeah, there was another time after this that happened at Jim's Lounge in Shenandoah, Iowa.

Q. Did anything unusual occur?

A. He come up to the end of the bar where I was standing up next to the owner of the bar and told me, you know, I wouldn't mind beating your head in. And says, killing you would be fun.

Q. Do you know the general reputation of Curtis Sederburg?

A. Yes.

Q. In the community?

A. I do.

Q. Do you know his general reputation for turbulence, violence, bad temper?

A. Yes, I do.

Q. Do you have an opinion [as to his] general reputation for turbulence, bad temper, violence in the community of Shenandoah and quarrelsomeness before the 14th day of February, 1978; yes or no?

A. Yes.

Q. And what is that opinion?

A. It's bad.

Q. Now, in doing this [work as a narcotics agent] where was it necessary for you to frequent?

A. Well, I was required to build cases against known drug pushers and drug sellers.

Q. Did anyone of these people ever find out about your position?

A. Yes, they did.

Q. And what were the results of this; people finding out?

A. Well, there was supposedly a contract put out on me. This is the word that was on the streets and still is.

Q. Did you hear this from anybody in particular?

A. Well, I first heard it from Curt Sederburg.

Q. What did Curtis Sederburg say to you about it?

A. Curtis came and told me.... He says, there is a contract out on you and, you know, I might just collect that.

Q. Did he make any threats to you later on, say, with or without a gun?

A. Yes, he did.

Q. Where was that?

A. This was one time me and my little brother went down to the house; going down to drink some beer. It was in the evening and when we walked in the house Curtis was standing out in the kitchen, which was straight through the house, and he reached in this drawer and pulled a gun and he pointed it at me and told me, he says, see how easy it would have been? You would have never got to your gun.

Q. He knew you had a gun?

A. Yes.

Q. Were there any threats made against you through a third party?

A. Yes, there was.

Q. And who was that?

A. My mother.

Q. And what was the nature of that?

A. She came down and told me that Curtis had told her that if he got the chance he was going to take the gun away from me and stick it up me.

Q. How apprehensive were you of Curtis Sederburg? What did you think he might do?

A. Well, it was really hard to say what Curtis would do. I was afraid he might kill me or he could seriously injure me; bodily.

Q. What do you mean by serious injury?

A. He could maim me; break an arm; break a leg. He could beat me senseless.

Q. At any of these times when you had previous fights were you injured seriously?

A. Yes, I was.

Q. At that time were you fearful of your life?

A. Yes, I was.

Q. What type of a fighter is Curtis from your own personal knowledge?

A. Animalistic.

Q. What went through your mind? What did you intend to do to him?

A. I intended to stop him so he couldn't hurt me. I didn't intend to kill him.

Q. And then what happened?

A. Then I kind of moved back off because I knew Curtis was mad and he approached Bud and told him, he says, Take everything out of your pockets again and put it up on the hood there. There was a pickup sitting there and he says, Put it all up on the pickup and give me your billfold. Bud said, I told you I don't have your money. I said, Curtis, Why don't you let it go. The man does not have your money. And he says, Well, I am not going to and you mind your own damn business. And I says, Okay, I will. And I turned around and started to walk away and I was going to my car. I was heading home and Curtis was starting an argument with Bud and I turned around and looked at Bud and says, That's stupid. Turned around and Curt heard me, he said, I have had enough of your bullshit. I looked over my shoulder when he said this and he started for me.

Q. And then what did you then do?

A. I then turned and I pulled my pistol.

Q. Did you say anything to Curt at this time?

A. Not at the particular time I did not.

Q. When you say you pulled your pistol what did you do?

A. I shot once in the air and I says, Curtis, don't come any further. I will use it Curtis to stop you.

Q. And then what happened?

A. He kept coming.

Q. What did you do?

A. I shot him.

Q. Where?

A. In the arm.

The instructions, considered together, omit a critical element of defendant's defense—his right to stand his ground without taking alternative action because of his fear of injury or death at Sederburg's hands.

Should defendant have backed away from the dispute at an earlier stage? Could he have retreated when Sederburg advanced upon him immediately before the shooting? Was he justified as a reasonable person in fearing death or injury at Sederburg's hands?

These are questions the jury should have decided. The trial court told them to consider the prior threats and altercations between Sederburg and defendant in deciding if defendant acted as a reasonable person under the circumstances. The defect in the instructions is that the jury was not told any place the circumstances under which defendant was legally entitled to use reasonable force without first taking alternative action. We hold this was reversible error and defendant is entitled to a new trial.

Comments and Questions

(1) What result in this case without the italicized portion of the statute? What alternative courses of action entail risks to one's life or safety? Would it matter that the defendant *knew* that Sederburg was not armed?

(2) Did the defendant use excessive force? How should the trial judge generally instruct if there is evidence of excessive force? *See Coleman v. Strohman*, 821 P.2d 88 (Wyo. 1991):

> This defense is established if you find both of the following: 1) The Defendant honestly and reasonably believed (although perhaps mistakenly) that under the circumstances it was necessary for him to use force to protect himself against an actual or apparent threatened harmful contact; 2) the Defendant used no more force than a reasonably prudent person would have used under the same or similar circumstances to protect himself against the actual or apparent threatened attack.

(3) In *State v. Marks*, 602 P.2d 1344 (Kan. 1979), the evidence showed that the decedent, a 65-year-old man disabled by a hip injury, was known to have a temper. On the night in question, he lost his temper with the defendant and said "'Nigger get out of my place' and raised his cane and started hitting the defendant." The defendant, a young man, then shot the decedent. Excessive force as a matter of law? See also *Neal v. State*, 597 P.2d 334 (Okla. Crim. App. 1979), where the "appellant, a 60-year-old man, called a woman a whore. Upon hearing this her husband, who was 38 years of age and weighed 240 pounds, struck the appellant, and the appellant

stabbed him." Excessive force as a matter of law? Held, in *Marks* the issue was a question of law, in *Neal* it was a question of fact. Are the cases distinguishable?

In *People v. Clark*, 136 Cal. Rptr. 3d 10 (2011), the court ruled that an adult could raise self-defense against a child when charged with child abuse. The court reasoned that self-defense is available to anyone who lawfully resists the application of force, regardless of the source of that force. Should an adult's use of force against a child be excessive as a matter of law?

Commonwealth v. Shaffer

Supreme Judicial Court of Massachusetts
326 N.E.2d 880 (1975)

Tauro, Chief Justice.

From the evidence, the jury could have found the following: The defendant, who was separated from her husband and in the process of being divorced, resided with her two children in a one-story ranch house in Sharon. The victim, to whom the defendant was engaged, had lived in the house since 1971. The defendant had received several severe beatings at the hands of the victim, and on at least one occasion he had threatened to kill her and the children when asked to leave the defendant's home. Although the defendant loved the victim, she feared for herself and the children, and had persuaded him to seek psychiatric help.

On the morning of the homicide, the defendant was having breakfast with the victim when an argument ensued. At one point, the victim rose, saying, "Never mind. I'll take care of you right now." The defendant threw a cup of tea at him and ran downstairs to the basement playroom, where the children were having breakfast and watching television.

Shortly thereafter, the victim opened the door at the top of the basement stairs and said, "If you don't come up these stairs, I'll come down and kill you and the kids." She started to telephone the police, but hung up the telephone when the victim said he would leave the house. Instead, he returned to the top of the stairs, at which time the defendant took a .22 caliber rifle from a rack on the wall and loaded it. She again started to telephone the police when the victim started down the stairs. She fired a fatal shot. More than five minutes elapsed from the time the defendant went to the basement until the shooting took place.

1. The defendant's principal argument for reversal is that the judge erred in his instructions to the jury regarding self-defense. She contends that the judge in effect instructed the jury that she had a duty to retreat from her home and that this was error. A review of the charge in its entirety discloses no error.

The defendant asks us in this case to adopt the majority rule that one assaulted in his own home need not retreat before resorting to the use of deadly force. This has never been the law of the Commonwealth, and we see no reason to adopt it now. We prefer instead to follow our long-established rule that the right to use deadly force by way of self-defense is not available to one threatened until he has availed himself of all reasonable and proper means in the circumstance to avoid combat, and hold that this rule has equal application to one assaulted in his own home.

This rule does not impose an absolute duty to retreat regardless of considerations of personal safety. The proper application of this doctrine does not require an innocent victim to increase his own peril out of regard for the safety of a murderous assailant, because one need only retreat as far as necessary in the circumstances, until there is "no probable means of escape." Our rule gives due recognition to the value of human life, and requires that all available means for escape be exhausted. "The right of self-defense arises from necessity, and ends when the necessity ends."

To what extent one who is threatened may go in defending himself and whether he has availed himself of all proper means of escape ordinarily are questions of fact for the jury, to be decided in light of all the existing circumstances. The jury must receive complete instructions from the trial judge, including an explanation of the proper factors to be considered in determining the issue of self-defense. The fact that one is threatened in his own home or in a place where he has exclusive right to be is one of the more important factors in making such determination, but this factor is not without limitations in its application.

"In passing upon the reasonableness of the force used by the defendant, ... the jury should consider evidence of the relative physical capabilities of the combatants, the characteristics of the weapons used,[2] and the availability of maneuver room in, or means of escape from, the ... area [in which the confrontation occurs]." We would add that in determining whether all proper means have been taken to avoid the use of deadly force, the jury should be instructed that the location of the assault is an element of major importance in their consideration. We hold that one assaulted in his own home does not have the unlimited right to react with deadly force without any attempt at retreat. However, the importance of the location of the assault and the surrounding circumstance should be stressed to the jury.

In the instant case, the judge charged the jury that, in order for there to have been a proper exercise of self-defense, "[i]t must appear that the defendant endeavored to avoid any further struggle and retreated as far as she could until there was no probable means of escape. In this connection, you may consider that the assault, if you find one took place, by the deceased took place in the home of the defendant where she had a right to be." This instruction, especially when considered with the charge as a whole, made clear that the location of the assault in the defendant's home was a proper

2. "As a practical consideration, it is important to bear in mind that the 20th century has introduced a multitude of deadly weapons ... [m]any of ... [which] are operative at long range, making attempts at escape by a prospective victim highly speculative and totally ineffectual." We believe that the nature of the weapons involved is a crucial consideration in determining both the reasonableness of the force exerted and the reasonableness of attempts to retreat.

factor to be considered. Reading the instructions as a whole, there is no merit to the defendant's argument that, in the circumstances of this case, they were misleading.

The defendant further argues that even if we do not adopt the majority rule, in the circumstances of the present case, the judge should have instructed the jury that the defendant, having already run to the basement, had no duty to retreat further.

In the instant case, the jury could have found that the defendant was not in imminent danger for her life or of serious injury at the hands of the victim. There was no evidence that he had a dangerous weapon at any time. He was only two or three steps from the top of the stairway when he was shot. The defendant had ample opportunity to call the police. She could have left the basement with her children. A period of five minutes had elapsed from the time the defendant first went down to the basement until the shooting occurred. The defendant did not warn the victim that she would shoot if he continued his descent down the stairway. There was evidence from the defendant's husband that she had considerable experience in the use of that rifle. One shot was sufficient to kill the victim.

In these circumstances, there was no error in the judge's instruction to the jury, on the question of reasonableness, that the jury could consider the "means of escape from the basement area." This is clearly a part of the totality of circumstances which must be considered in every case.

The judge's instructions were in keeping with our own rule that "[i]n order to create a right to defend oneself with a dangerous weapon likely to cause serious injury or death, it must appear that the person using the weapon had a reasonable apprehension of great bodily harm and a reasonable belief that no other means would suffice to prevent such harm."

Comments and Questions

(1) Why should a person have to retreat if she is assaulted in her own house? The majority rule on retreat was set out in *United States v. Peterson*, 483 F.2d 1222, 1234–37, *cert. denied*, 414 U.S. 1007 (1973):

> Within the common law of self-defense there developed the rule of "retreat to the wall," which ordinarily forbade the use of deadly force by one to whom an avenue for safe retreat was open. This doctrine was but an application of the requirement of strict necessity to excuse the taking of human life, and was designed to insure the existence of that necessity. Even the innocent victim of a vicious assault had to elect a safe retreat, if available, rather than resort to defensive force which might kill or seriously injure.
>
> In a majority of American jurisdictions, contrarily to the common law rule, one may stand his ground and use deadly force whenever it seems reasonably necessary to save himself.
>
> That is not to say that the retreat rule is without exceptions. Even at common law it was recognized that it was not completely suited to all situations. Today it is the more so that its precept must be adjusted to modern conditions non-

> existent during the early development of the common law of self-defense. One restriction on its operation comes to the fore when the circumstances apparently foreclose a withdrawal with safety. The doctrine of retreat was never intended to enhance the risk to the innocent; its proper application has never required a faultless victim to increase his assailant's safety at the expense of his own. On the contrary, he could stand his ground and use deadly force otherwise appropriate if the alternative were perilous, or if to him it reasonably appeared to be. A slight variant of the same consideration is the principle that there is no duty to retreat from an assault producing an imminent danger of death or grievous bodily harm. "Detached reflection cannot be demanded in the presence of an uplifted knife," nor is it "a condition of immunity that one in that situation should pause to consider whether a reasonable man might not think it possible to fly with safety or to disable his assailant rather than to kill him."
>
> The trial judge's charge to the jury incorporated each of these limitations on the retreat rule. Peterson, however, invokes another—the so-called "castle" doctrine. It is well settled that one who through no fault of his own is attacked in his home is under no duty to retreat therefrom. The oft-repeated expression that "a man's home is his castle" reflected the belief in olden days that there were few if any safer sanctuaries than the home. The "castle" exception, moreover, has been extended by some courts to encompass the occupant's presence within the curtilage outside his dwelling.
>
> Despite the practically universal acceptance of the "castle" doctrine in American jurisdictions wherein the point has been raised, its status in the District of Columbia has never been squarely decided. But whatever the fate of the doctrine in the District law of the future, it is clear that in absolute form it was inapplicable here. The right of self-defense, we have said, cannot be claimed by the aggressor in an affray so long as he retains that unmitigated role. It logically follows that any rule of no-retreat which may protect an innocent victim of the affray would like other incidents of a forfeited right of self-defense, be unavailable to the party who provokes or stimulates the conflict. Accordingly, the law is well settled that the "castle" doctrine can be invoked only by one who is without fault.

Massachusetts adopted the majority rule, effectively rejecting *Shaffer*, by enacting a statute which states there is no duty to retreat from one's dwelling. Mass. St. 278 § 8A. *See also State v. Glowacki*, 630 N.W.2d 392 (Minn. 2001):

> [A] duty to retreat rule recognizes the realities facing those persons, mostly women, living in situations of domestic violence. Battered spouses often have retreated in the past, only to be subjected to an increased risk of harm from their abuser. Additionally, despite clear language in a retreat rule, the complexities of battered spouse syndrome may lead juries to believe that a spouse could have left an abusive spouse at some time, even if she could not have retreated on a particular occasion....

> In addition to the increased threat of harm that abused spouses face when retreating from a domestic abuse situation, the duty to retreat also may force an abused spouse to choose between acting against the law or abandoning her children....
>
> We agree that when acting in self-defense in the home, a person should not be required to retreat from the home before using reasonable force to defend himself, regardless of whether the aggressor is also rightfully in the home. Thus we adopt the following rule: There is no duty to retreat from one's own home when acting in self-defense in the home, regardless of whether the aggressor is a co-resident. But the lack of a duty to retreat does not abrogate the obligation to act reasonably when using force in self-defense. Therefore, in all situations in which a party claims self-defense, even absent a duty to retreat, the key inquiry will still be into the reasonableness of the use of force and the level of force under the specific circumstances of each case.

(2) The no-retreat requirement for deadly force has created difficulties for the courts. Assuming that one follows the rule generally of no retreat from homes, what of: the defendant's office or club—*see State v. Davis*, 51 S.E.2d 86 (S.C. 1948); a common staircase shared by the defendant's apartment and other apartments—*see State v. Silva*, 684 A.2d 725 (Conn. App. Ct. 1996); the lobby in an apartment building—*see People v. Hernandez*, 774 N.E.2d 198 (N.Y. 2002); the hallway in an apartment building—*see State v. Devens*, 852 N.W.2d 255 (Minn. 2014); the front sidewalk of the defendant's house—*see State v. Menser*, 382 N.W.2d 18 (Neb. 1986); a home shared by both the defendant and the decedent—*see State v. Gartland*, 694 A.2d 564 (N.J. 1997); the defendant's home after he used force to repel an invited guest who had become violent—*see State v. Walton*, 615 A.2d 469 (R.I. 1992).

(3) Should a person be required to retreat in public places before using deadly force? The American Bar Association has found that so called "stand-your-ground" laws increase the number of homicides and have no deterrent effect on violent crimes in the states that have such laws, according to a two-year long study. The ABA House of Delegates adopted a formal resolution urging states to change or repeal existing no-retreat laws in public places. In addition, these laws have a discernible racial impact in their application. White defendants are acquitted 38 percent of the time when making a no-retreat defense based on a stand-your-ground law to a homicide charge when the victim is black. In contrast, black defendants were acquitted only three percent of the time in cases involving white victims. *Stand Your Ground Laws Increase Homicides ABA Task Force Says; Urges States to Repeal*, U.S.L.W., Feb. 17, 2015, at 1214.

(4) Can anyone stand their ground when committing an illegal activity? In *Dorsey v. State*, 149 So. 3d 144 (Fla. 2014), the court concluded yes. The court reasoned that the stand-your-ground law contained no requirement that the person claiming protection under the statute not be engaged in unlawful activity. Therefore, the defendant was allowed to raise the protections of the law even though he was engaged in unlawful activity at the time of the shooting (possession of a firearm by a convicted felon).

(5) The defendant in *People v. Williams*, 205 N.E.2d 749, 749–51 (Ill. App. Ct. 1st Dist. 1965), was convicted of involuntary manslaughter.

> On April 12, 1963, at about eight o'clock in the evening, defendant, while driving a Yellow Cab south on Princeton Avenue, stopped for a traffic light at the corner of 51st Street in Chicago. He observed a group of young men on the northeast corner, beating an old man, later identified as one Joseph Bell. The victim of the assault, while lying on the sidewalk, called to defendant for help. When defendant shouted to the boys to leave the victim alone, the boys shouted back insults. When the traffic light turned green, defendant turned west on 51st Street for about one half block, made a U-turn and drove east, back to the same corner. As he was re-crossing the intersection his cab was struck by a rock or brick. Defendant stopped his cab near the boys, who at this time were standing on the southeast corner. He fired two shots in their direction. The boys ran. Defendant drove away. One of the boys, Kenneth Boatner, age 16, was killed, the result of a bullet wound in the brain.
>
> A police officer, Thomas O'Malley, had a conversation with an eyewitness, one James Henley. Henley gave O'Malley the cab identification number. O'Malley, after checking with the cab garage, traced it to defendant. On April 13, 1964, defendant told the police he knew nothing of the shooting. He later agreed to tell the truth as to the happenings of April 12. He also gave the police his .380 Beretta revolver, which he admitted firing at the boys. In a signed statement, admitted into evidence, he stated:
>
> ... noticed the boys who were beating the man up, then standing on the corner, southeast corner, and one of them threw a rock at my cab. I then stopped the cab about twenty feet, opened the cab door on my side and took the gun from my belt in front of my pants and stepped out of the cab with one leg in the cab and the other out. I then held my hand with the gun in it and fired two shots over the roof of the cab in the direction of the boys on the corner.

Was the defendant entitled to use deadly force? Should/could he have retreated? The defendant's conviction was reversed.

> The State contends that the danger to defendant was not imminent. The State reasons that the deceased did not have the present ability of carrying out the alleged threat. This contention is invalid. There were several boys in the gang and they had just thrown a cement block and a brick at defendant's cab, the latter causing substantial damage to the right door (a picture of the damage to the cab was introduced in evidence). The gang was a short distance from defendant. They had the present ability to carry out the threatened ... use of force. The deceased, identified as part of the gang that damaged the cab, also had the present ability to carry out the threatened harm.
>
> The evidence that the gang threw a brick against the cab of defendant was sufficient to show that the threatened force was unlawful as such conduct

> is both criminal and tortious. Thus, we can proceed to the fifth and sixth elements.
>
> To satisfy the fifth and sixth elements it must be determined whether or not defendant actually believed that a danger existed; that the use of force was necessary to avert the danger; that the kind and amount of force used was necessary; and that such belief was reasonable. A belief is reasonable even if the defendant is mistaken. Defendant had just seen an elderly man beaten up. Furthermore, we again emphasize the fact that the gang, consisting of a number of young men, had just thrown a cement block and a brick at defendant's cab and that they caused substantial damage to the cab. Defendant testified that when he stopped his cab, the gang started to move toward him. There is only one conclusion that can be reached—defendant actually believed that a danger existed.

(6) What about victims? Should the prosecution get a jury instruction detailing whether or not the victim of a homicide had the right to stand their ground? The Kentucky Supreme Court in *Jones v. Kentucky*, 366 S.W.3d 376 (2011), ruled that the prosecution in a homicide trial was not entitled to a jury instruction that the victim had no duty to retreat. The court reasoned that the law was intended as a justification for those subject to criminal prosecution, not victims.

Bechtel v. State

Court of Criminal Appeals of Oklahoma
840 P.2d 1 (1992)

JOHNSON, JUDGE:

Donna Lee Bechtel, Appellant, was retried by jury for the crime of Murder in the First Degree. The jury returned a verdict of guilty and punishment at life imprisonment.

Facts

The following facts are primarily from the testimony of the Appellant who met the victim, Ken Bechtel, in June 1981. At that time he was married, but separated, and dating another woman with whom he had been living for seven years. Appellant saw him approximately five times after their first meeting but did not start seeing him on a regular basis until he got his divorce. They were married on August 25, 1982. Although there was great conflict between her testimony and that as presented by the State, most of the balance of the facts are as presented by Appellant. We are presenting her testimony to show facts necessary to meet the first prong of our guidelines under the Battered Woman Syndrome.

She recalled that the first incidence of violence perpetrated by the victim upon her was on July 4, 1982, when around midnight, he began crying about his deceased son and, in a drunken rage, grabbed her by the head and threw her into the windshield of his boat. As she tried to get to the telephone, he started to throw canned goods out of the closet at her. She left but was caught and put in a car by Ken; while they were stopped at a stop sign, she jumped out of the car. Mr. Bechtel came around the side of the car, threw her back in, and told her not to ever do that again. Inside the car, he grabbed her head by the hair and slammed her into the window and again, told her not to get out of the car. When they arrived at her home, Appellant jumped out of the car, ran into her house and locked the doors. When Ken Bechtel threatened to kick the "m-f-" door in, Appellant responded by telling him that she had guns in her home. Mr. Bechtel eventually left. This was the first of approximately 23 battering incidents leading to the fatal shooting on September 23, 1984.

Testimony at trial revealed that the deceased committed the batterings when intoxicated and without provocation. The batterings consisted of the deceased grabbing Appellant by either her ears or hair and pounding her head on the ground, wall, door, cabinet or other available object. During many of the episodes he would sob profusely and ramble about his deceased son who was born retarded. During all of the episodes, the deceased threatened or otherwise intimidated Appellant.[2] On three occasions, Appellant was treated in the Emergency Room. On each of the occasions, the deceased provided the information as to the cause of the injury. On one occasion, Appellant was treated for neck injury and provided with a neck collar. On the other occasions, she was treated for cuts to her hand and feet. On five occasions, Appellant sought police help. Each time the police arrived at her home, the deceased was made to leave. On one occasion, Appellant stopped at the scene of an accident and asked the policeman at the scene to remove the deceased who, in a drunken rage, was kicking the windshield and beating on the dashboard. The deceased was removed and taken to the residence and was there when Appellant arrived. Appellant was subsequently beaten by the deceased.

On several occasions, Appellant was able to escape her residence and stay overnight at various hotels. Appellant related the incidents to some of her close friends and the deceased's family. However, though some of the abuse occurred on business trips, she never told the deceased's business associates. Appellant also sought help from the deceased's family as to his alcohol problem. She made inquiries of several treatment facilities and made appointments for the deceased, who promised after later incidents to undergo treatment, but never did.

On September 23, 1984, the day of his death, the deceased had returned home unexpectedly at approximately 5:30 A.M. from a hunting trip, highly intoxicated. He awakened Appellant and ordered her to get out of the bed so they could have a drink. He ordered her out on the patio where the deceased related to her and her friend, Billy Bender, who was visiting from out of state, that he had been picked up for driving under the influence by the Nichols Hills Police. Ken Bechtel continued to drink coffee with liquor. He became angry when Appellant kept turning down the jukebox whenever he would turn it up.

---

2. We point out that Appellant was severely limited in her defense due to the trial court's refusal to allow her to relate any threats by the deceased or any conversations of whatever nature, which were necessary to explain or otherwise put into perspective the various relevant incidents. We address this problem below under Hearsay and the Battered Woman Syndrome.

After about three or four hours, Appellant decided to go back to bed. Once in her bedroom, she could hear Mr. Bechtel crying. She became afraid. Aware that Ms. Bender might be in difficulty, she went to the doors of the patio to try to get Ms. Bender's attention. Finally, Ms. Bender came inside to get some cigarettes. When she tried to return to the patio, Appellant admonished her not to go back but to leave Mr. Bechtel alone to sleep it off and for her to go to bed immediately. The next thing Appellant remembered was hearing the night table drawer opening and seeing the deceased with the .25 gun in his hand. He told Appellant that she would not need that "G-D-" gun anymore.

As he walked towards the door leading to the backyard, she jumped up and ran to the closet where she frantically looked for her purse and keys. After retrieving her purse, she turned to go to the kitchen when a naked Ken Bechtel pulled her by the hair and threw her back on the bed. He was rambling and crying about his son Kenny and questioning her about why she was not at home when he tried to call her earlier. He held his arm against her throat. Appellant raised her leg to free herself when they both fell onto the floor. The deceased threatened to "f-k you and kill your ass." He began pounding her head into the floor. He picked her up by the head and pulled her back on the bed. He pulled her gown off and rammed his fingers into her vagina. He then climbed on top of her, held her down by placing his knees on her arms and banged her head against the headboard. He ejaculated on her face and stomach, after which he slumped on top of her. She eased from under him and went to the bathroom to wash herself.

While in the bathroom, the deceased came up behind her, grabbed the back of her head, threw her down on the floor, bit her on the left breast and finally lay his head on her lower body. During this time, Appellant tried to calm him down by repeating it's okay, it's all right. Then the telephone rang. It was a friend inquiring about his luggage. During this time, Appellant vomited. As she was trying to put on some clothes, Ken returned, accusing her of taking the friend's luggage and betting that she thought it was her "G-D-" kids. He put her arm behind her back and his arm against her throat and forced her back onto the bed. At this point his eyes were glazed over and he was crying and rambling as he continued to beat her head against the headboard. He slumped on top of her.

Appellant tried to get from under him, but he would mumble whenever she made an effort. Finally, she eased herself from under him. As she sat on her knees on the floor beside the bed, she lit a cigarette, held it in one hand and her head with the other hand. As she got ready to smoke the cigarette, she heard a gurgling sound, looked up and saw the contorted look and glazed eyes of the deceased with his arms raised. Appellant reached for the gun under the bed and shot the deceased as she tried to get up and run.

Self-Defense and the Battered Woman

Appellant defended this case on the theory of self-defense. In Oklahoma, self-defense is the subject of statutory and case law.

Homicide is also justifiable when committed by any person in either of the following cases:....

2. When committed in the lawful defense of such person, ... when there is a reasonable ground to apprehend a design to commit a felony, or to do some great personal injury, and imminent danger of such design being accomplished;....

This Court has held that the bare belief that one is about to suffer death or great personal injury will not, in itself, justify taking the life of his adversary. There must exist reasonable grounds for such belief at the time of the killing. Further, the right to take another's life in self-defense is not to be tested by the honesty or good faith of the defendant's belief in the necessity of the killing, but by the fact whether he had reasonable grounds for such belief. Fear alone never justifies one person to take the life of another. Such fear must have been induced by some overt act, gesture or word spoken by the deceased at the time the homicide occurred which would form a *reasonable* ground for the belief that the accused is about to suffer death or great bodily harm.

For the purposes of deciding this appeal, we analyze two of the requirements of self-defense: (1) *reasonableness* and (2) *imminence*. These two requirements, as applied to this case, can be understood only within the framework of the Battered Woman Syndrome.

1. Admissibility of Testimony as It Relates to the Battered Woman Syndrome

On appeal, Appellant contends that the trial court erred in refusing to allow expert testimony on the Battered Woman Syndrome as such testimony would aid the trier of fact in assessing how her experiences as a battered woman affected her state of mind at the time of the killing. This, she argues, goes to the *reasonableness* of her belief that she was in *imminent* danger. We agree.

An offer of proof concerning the admissibility of testimony on the Battered Woman Syndrome was made in-camera where the trial judge heard testimony from Dr. Lenore Walker, a licensed, practicing psychologist and diplomate in clinical psychology who pioneered the research on the Battered Woman Syndrome, and the State's witness, Dr. Herbert C. Modlin, a licensed, practicing psychiatrist. Dr. Walker discussed the methodology used by her in diagnosing such syndrome and related that this is taught in the graduate schools and accepted in the entire scientific community of research.[3] On refusing to allow the testimony, the trial judge offered the following three reasons:

1. The lack of general acceptance of the theory in the psychological community based on the fact that the syndrome is not listed in the Diagnostic and

3. We note that the standards for evaluating the state of scientific knowledge in an area only require that the expert's *methodology* be *generally* accepted by the *relevant* scientific community, not that it be accepted unanimously or that the results of the methodology are infallible. Any disagreements about the specific methodology used or the accuracy of the expert's conclusions are left to the trier of fact, who will determine the weight to be given the expert's testimony. Additionally, the opposing party is given the opportunity to challenge and to rebut the expert's testimony and to present its own expert witness.

Statistical Manual of Mental Disorders-3R (DMS-3R), a publication of the American Psychiatric Association.

2. The testimony did not appear to be necessary or helpful to the jury since the jury was capable of making a decision based on all of the evidence.

3. The lapse of time between the incident and the psychological testing, which "would certainly permit time for manufacturing of a defense or for the healing of whatever emotional and personality abnormalities or wounds had been caused by the relationship."

We find no support for the trial court's first reason.[4] The relevant scientific community in this case is the psychological community and not the psychiatric community. Moreover, both experts acknowledged that the syndrome is considered a sub-category of Post-traumatic Stress Disorder, which is generally accepted and is listed in the DSM-3R. Based upon our independent review of the available sources on the subject, we believe that the syndrome is a mixture of both psychological and physiological symptoms but is not a mental disease in the context of insanity. Further, we believe that because psychologists see more battered women than psychiatrists, the psychological community has had the opportunity to be and, indeed, have been more responsive to the problems or symptoms experienced by those suffering from the syndrome.

Other courts have accepted the syndrome as a scientifically recognized theory. To date, thirty-one (31) states and the District of Columbia allow the use of expert testimony on the subject. Five (5) states acknowledged its validity, but held the testimony inadmissible based on the facts of the particular case. In addition, hundreds of books, articles and commentaries have been written and numerous studies have been done on the subject. Based on the aforesaid, we find that the Battered Woman Syndrome is a substantially scientifically accepted theory.

We next address the trial court's ruling that expert testimony does not appear to be necessary or helpful to the jury since Appellant's testimony concerning numerous drunken assaults and threats, including the vicious assault and threat to kill her on the night of the homicide, are, in the trial court's opinion, "easily within the common understanding of all the jurors and easily come[s] within the legal definition of self-defense. The jury may consider all the rest of the evidence offered and yet to be offered in conjunction with the Defendant's statement of the incident, and they can make the decision." We do not agree, especially in light of the two inquiries submitted by the jury during its deliberation. These inquiries demonstrate the lack of common understanding of the elements of self-defense, particularly where the defendant is a battered woman.

Expert testimony in Oklahoma is admissible if it will assist the trier of fact in search of the truth and augment the normal experience of the juror by helping him or her

---

4. The American Psychological Association, representing more than 55,000 psychologists, endorsed expert testimony on the syndrome in its Amicus Brief of the American Psychological Association, Hawthorne v. State, 408 So. 2d 801 (Fla. Dist. Ct. App. 1982) (No. VV-307).

draw proper conclusions concerning particular behavior of a victim in a particular circumstance or circumstances.

Appellant argues that expert testimony regarding the syndrome is admissible to help the jury understand the battered woman, and, why Appellant acted out of a reasonable belief that she was in imminent danger when considering the issue of self-defense. We agree.

While the Court does not, as a matter of law, adopt the definition of a "Battered Woman," it was first defined by Dr. Lenore Walker in her book, *The Battered Woman Syndrome* (1979), as follows:

> The battered woman is a woman who is repeatedly subjected to any forceful, physical or psychological behavior by a man in order to coerce her to do something he wants her to do without any concern for her rights. Battered women include wives or women in any form of intimate relationship with men. Furthermore, in order to be classified as a battered woman, the couple must go through the battering cycle at least twice. Any woman may find herself in an abusive relationship with a man once. If it occurs a second time, and she remains in the situation, she is defined as a battered woman.

Id. at XV.

Misconceptions regarding battered women abound, making it more likely than not that the average juror will draw from his or her own experience or common myths, which may lead to a wholly incorrect conclusion. Thus, we believe that expert testimony on the syndrome is necessary to counter these misconceptions.[8] We believe that the Battered Woman Syndrome has gained substantial scientific acceptance and will aid the trier of fact in determining facts in issue, i.e., *reasonableness and imminence* (discussed below), when testimony on the same is offered in cases of self-defense. However, before such testimony may be admitted, this Court today sets forth the following guidelines:

> 1. The defendant must offer evidence which establishes herself as a "battered woman."
>
> 2. The expert must establish herself/himself as one who is qualified by knowledge, skill, experience, training or education to diagnose the defendant as suffering from the Battered Woman Syndrome.
>
> 3. The defendant, who has submitted herself to psychological or psychiatric examination and who intends to use or otherwise rely on testimony resulting from said examination, may be ordered, at the discretion of the trial court, to submit to an examination by the State's expert witness, upon application

8. Dr. Walker writes: "Expert testimony on the battered woman syndrome would help dispel the ordinary lay person's perception that a woman in a battering relationship is free to leave at anytime. The expert evidence would counter any 'commonsense' conclusions by the jury that if the beatings were really that bad the woman would have left her husband much earlier. Popular misconceptions about battered women would be put to rest, including the beliefs that the women are masochistic and enjoy the beatings and that they intentionally provoke their husbands into fits of rage." *The Battered Woman Syndrome* (1979).

of the State. The defendant's expert is permitted to be present and observe the examination.

4. A report of the State's expert setting forth all relevant findings, opinions, conclusions and their factual bases shall be prepared and a copy provided to the defendant forthwith. Testimony of the State's witness shall be admitted only in rebuttal on matters covered by the expert for the defense and for the same purposes for which the defense expert's testimony was offered.

5. The expert may not give an opinion on whether the defendant acted reasonably in perceiving herself as being in imminent danger and whether the defendant acted in self-defense.

6. The trial court shall give in its charge to the jury the specific instruction on standard of reasonableness, which we adopt today (see below).

Thus, we conclude that the trial court erred in not allowing testimony on the syndrome. We find the trial court's failure to allow said testimony amounts to reversible error requiring a new trial.

2. Reasonableness and the Battered Woman Syndrome

The key to the defense of self-defense is reasonableness. A defendant must show that she had a *reasonable* belief as to the *imminence* of great bodily harm or death and as to the force necessary to compel it. Several of the psychological symptoms that develop in one suffering from the syndrome are particularly relevant to the standard of *reasonableness* in self-defense. One such symptom is a greater sensitivity to danger which has come about because of the intimacy and history of the relationship. Dr. Walker, in her offer of proof below, explained that the abuse occurs in a cycle (The Cycle Theory), which consists of three phases. The first phase is the "tension-building" period. The second stage is the "acute-explosion" period, where the abuse takes place. The third stage is the "loving, contrition" period.

It is during the tension-building period that the battered woman develops a heightened sensitivity to any kinds of cues of distress. Thus, because of her intimate knowledge of her batterer, the battered woman perceives danger faster and more accurately as she is more acutely aware that a new or escalated violent episode is about to occur.

What is or is not an overt demonstration of violence varies with the circumstances. Under some circumstances a slight movement may justify instant action because of reasonable apprehension of danger; under other circumstances this would not be so. And it is for the jury, and not for the judge passing upon the weight and effect of the evidence, to determine how this may be.

Indeed, considering her particular circumstances, the battered woman's perception of the situation and her belief as to the *imminence* of great bodily harm or death may be deemed *reasonable*.

During the loving, contrition period, the abuser makes amends by being loving, making promises to change and avowing that the abuse will never happen again. It is during this stage that the battered woman is being positively reinforced by her abuser. In most battering cases, this period is of the longest duration. The cultural characteristics of women influence the battered woman's belief that if she could only do something to help her abuser, then the bad part of him will go away. Thus, the battered woman learns to develop coping skills rather than escape skills and develops a "psychological paralysis" and "learned helplessness."

Thus, Dr. Walker's testimony as to how Appellant's particular experiences as a battered woman suffering from the Battered Woman Syndrome affected her perceptions of danger, its imminence, what actions were necessary to protect herself and the reasonableness of those perceptions are relevant and necessary to prove Appellant's defense of self-defense. However, it now becomes necessary to determine the standard of reasonableness against which the finder of fact must measure the accused's belief.

Standards of reasonableness have been traditionally characterized as either "objective" or "subjective." Under the objective standard of reasonableness, the trier of fact is required to view the circumstances, surrounding the accused at the time of the use of force, from the standpoint of the hypothetical reasonable person. Under the subjective standard of reasonableness, the fact finder is required to determine whether the circumstances, surrounding the accused at the time of the use of force, are sufficient to induce in the accused an honest and reasonable belief that he/she must use force to defend himself/herself against imminent harm.

A person is justified in using deadly force in self-defense if that person reasonably believed that use of deadly force was necessary to protect herself from imminent danger of death or great bodily harm. Self-defense is a defense although the danger to life or personal security may not

> have been real, if a reasonable person, in the circumstances and from the viewpoint of the defendant, would reasonably have believed that she was in imminent danger of death or great bodily harm.

The aforesaid instruction was given in this case. While the instruction explicitly states that the fact finder should assume the viewpoint and circumstances of the defendant in assessing the reasonableness of his or her belief, i.e., subjective, it also requires the defendant's viewpoint to be that of a reasonable person, in similar circumstances and with the same perceptions, i.e., objective. Thus, Oklahoma's standard is a hybrid, combining both the objective and subjective standards.

However, in light of the jury's inquiry and our decision today to allow testimony on the Battered Woman Syndrome[10] in appropriate cases, we hereby adopt a new OUJI-CR 743A instruction that will be given in all Battered Woman Syndrome cases. Such modified instruction shall read as follows:

A person is justified in using deadly force in self-defense if that person believed that use of deadly force was necessary to protect herself from imminent danger of

10. Under our present instructions, a fact finder conceivably may ponder whether the battered woman's perception should be viewed from the standpoint of a reasonable person in the circumstances of the battered woman or from the standpoint of a reasonable battered woman.

death or great bodily harm. Self-defense is a defense although the danger to life or personal security may not have been real, if a person, in the circumstances and from the viewpoint of the defendant, would reasonably have believed that she was in imminent danger of death or great bodily harm.

3. Imminence and the Battered Woman Syndrome

In addition to the reasonableness standard, Oklahoma's law of self-defense also imposes the temporal requirement of *imminence.* The thinking is that it is unreasonable to be provoked to the point of killing well after the provocative or assertive conduct has occurred.

Furthermore, the syndrome has been analogized to the classic hostage situation in that the battered woman lives under long-term, life-threatening conditions in constant fear of another eruption of violence. Robinson gives the example where the captor tells the hostage that he intends to kill him in three days. If on the first day, the hostage sees an opportunity to kill the captor and avoid the threat of his own death, a literal application of the requirement that the threat be "imminent" would prevent the hostage from using deadly force until the captor is standing over him with a knife. For the battered woman, if there is no escape or sense of safety, then the next attack, which could be fatal or cause serious bodily harm, is imminent. Based on the traditionally accepted definition of imminent and its functional derivatives,[11] a battered woman, to whom the threat of serious bodily harm or death is always imminent, would be precluded from asserting the defense of self-defense.

Under our "hybrid" reasonableness standard, the meaning of *imminent* must necessarily envelope the battered woman's perceptions based on all the facts and circumstances of his or her relationship with the victim. In *Women's Self-Defense Cases: Theory and Practice* (1981), Elizabeth Bochnak writes: "The battered woman learns to recognize the small signs that precede periods of escalated violence. She learns to distinguish subtle changes in tone of voice, facial expression, and levels of danger. She is in a position to know, perhaps with greater certainty than someone attacked by a stranger, that the batterer's threat is real and will be acted upon."

Thus, according to the author, an abused woman may kill her mate during the period of threat that precedes a violent incident, right before the violence escalates

---

11. *Black's Law Dictionary*, 5th ed. 1979, defines as follows:

"IMMINENT. Near at hand; mediate rather than immediate; close rather than touching; impending; on the point of happening; threatening; menacing; perilous."

"IMMINENT DANGER. In relation to homicide in self-defense, this term means immediate danger, such as must be instantly met, such as cannot be guarded against by calling for the assistance of others or the protection of the law. Or, as otherwise defined, such an appearance of threatened and impending injury as would put a reasonable and prudent man to his instant defense."

Webster's Third International Dictionary, Unabridged, (1986), defines as follows:

"IMMINENT ... impending; hanging threateningly over one's head; menacingly near ..."

OUJI-CR 752 defines:

IMMINENT DANGER: DANGER THAT IS PRESSING, URGENT, OR IMMEDIATE.

to the more dangerous levels of an acute battering episode. Or, she may take action against him during a lull in an assaultive incident, or after it has culminated, in an effort to prevent a recurrence of the violence. And so, the issue is not whether the danger was in *fact* imminent, but whether, given the circumstances as she perceived them, the defendant's *belief was reasonable that the danger was imminent.*

For the foregoing reasons, this case is *Reversed and Remanded* for a new trial, consistent with this opinion.

Concur: Parks, J., Concurring in Results:

I find that evidence concerning Battered Woman Syndrome was relevant to the jury's assessment of appellant's theory of the case self-defense. While I conclude that the syndrome should have been presented to the jury in this case, I disagree with the majority's decision to radically overhaul the laws pertaining to self-defense. The facts asserted by appellant, that the victim made a threatening movement and she shot him, constitute classic self-defense and do not necessitate the sweeping changes imposed by the majority. Our inquiry should be limited to an assessment of the syndrome's reliability and its relevance to the facts presented.

I find that appellant sufficiently demonstrated the syndrome's acceptance in the concerned scientific community during *in camera* hearings. Further, I find that evidence pertaining to the syndrome could have assisted the jury in determining whether appellant "reasonably and in good faith believed that she was in danger of losing her life or receiving great bodily injury at the hands of the deceased." The syndrome was pertinent to the jury's determination of whether a reasonable person, from the viewpoint of appellant, would have reacted as appellant did.

Allowing the jury to consider the circumstances from appellant's viewpoint in assessing reasonableness is not a novel concept and does not require the adoption of the standard of reasonableness set forth by the majority.

Currently, the jury is asked to view the circumstances as they appeared to the defendant and then is asked to determine whether a reasonable person, caught in the dynamics of those identical circumstances, would respond as the defendant did. I find that the syndrome should have been admitted as it sheds light on the circumstances surrounding the altercation *as they appeared to the appellant.* The facts before us require us to decide nothing more.

I find the majority's position regarding reasonableness puzzling. After stating that "we deem it necessary to modify OUJI-CR 743 by striking the words 'reasonably' and 'reasonable' from such instruction," the majority nevertheless includes the reasonableness requirement in the modified instruction. Thus, to the extent that the majority has correctly identified a deficiency in the current instruction, the problem survives the majority's attempt at a cure.

Lumpkin, Vice-presiding Judge: Dissents

I commend the Court regarding the extensive research which is reflected in this opinion. However, while I agree some revision regarding our application of self-defense might be warranted, the facts of this case do not present the evidentiary predicate which is required to adopt the changes proposed by the Court.

Domestic violence is appalling and each member of this Court empathizes with the victims of this degrading conduct. However, our empathy and distress with the violence which affects our society cannot be substituted for a rule of law which limits the scope of appellate review to the facts presented by the case. In addition, any rule of law must be applied equally to each citizen, regardless of gender.

The facts set forth by the Court reflect only Appellants' version of the evidence in the case without addressing the great conflict of this evidence with the evidence presented by the State. However, Appellant's evidence does define and restrict the nature and scope of the defense presented in this case. This evidence does not reveal the "Battered Woman Syndrome" was implicated on the night of September 23, 1984. The facts related by Appellant only raise a case of traditional self-defense based on the right of self-defense to resist any attempt to murder or commit a felony upon her, or the imminent threat as perceived by Appellant due to the victim's threats and actions committed that night. The "Cycle Theory" is not relevant based on the evidence. However, I recognize evidence regarding the victim's past trait of character for violence, which is admissible, is relevant as it goes to Appellant's perception as a reasonable person regarding the imminence of danger of death or great bodily harm. The admissibility of this evidence does not require the adoption of the "Battered Woman Syndrome." However, the Court appears bent upon embracing a sociological issue without regard to whether the facts support the legal concept it seeks to adopt. While I have great respect for the members of this Court, I cannot join in an abdication of the rules of appellate review in order to adopt a concept not presented on the record before the Court.

If and when a record on appeal is submitted to the Court which supports consideration of whether to adopt this type of concept as a part of the jurisprudence of this State, the Court should endeavor to adopt a rule of law which would apply equally to all citizens of the State, regardless of gender, who may be placed in a like situation. To do otherwise creates not only confusion as to its applicability but also question as to its validity if subjected to equal protection analysis. It is interesting to note the Court accurately identifies that the Diagnostic and Statistical Manual of Mental Disorders-3R (DSM-3R) recognizes the Post-traumatic Stress Disorder. However, rather than adopting a gender-neutral diagnostic criteria accepted by the entire scientific community, the Court seeks to adopt a gender-specific syndrome which has acceptance by only a subsection of the scientific community. If this disorder is such that it warrants this Court to review the reasonableness factor regarding action taken in self-defense, then it should be considered in a gender-neutral context. The information supplied to this Court reveals the Post-traumatic Stress Disorder, as does the proposed Battered Woman Syndrome, is a mixture of psychological and physiological symptoms which make it a medical issue. Psychologists do not have the medical training received by psychiatrists, therefore I cannot agree with the Court's unsupported statement that we should accept only the opinions of a sub-group of members of the psychological community as the gospel on this complex issue. This statement alone raises concern regarding the validity of the Court's determination and it creates a future problem for the Court when we are again required to determine if a proposed new "syndrome" of some type is generally accepted by the medical or scientific community.

If adoption of the proposed changes were proper in this case, I do agree that the application of the Post-traumatic Stress Disorder is most appropriately addressed within the context of self-defense rather than sanity at the time of the offense. Appellant's attorney acknowledged the concept is a part of self-defense during the oral argument and went further in his argument to state that there must be an imminent physical threat and delay waives the ability to raise self-defense. Therefore, the Court must first look to the defense of self-defense as defined by the Oklahoma Legislature.

Homicide is also justifiable when committed by any person in either of the following cases:

1. When resisting any attempt to murder such person, or to commit any felony upon him, or upon or in any dwelling house in which such person is; or

2. When committed in the lawful defense of such person, ... when there is a reasonable ground to apprehend a design to commit a felony, or to do some great personal injury, and imminent danger of such design being accomplished;

The fact that the Legislature has addressed the issue of self-defense within our statutory framework restricts the ability of the Court to act beyond the context of the statute. In the first instance, the language of Section 733 (1) is more applicable to the facts of this case than Section 733 (2). However, in discussing the provisions of Section 733 (2), the statute requires "imminent danger" of the threat to the person, therefore the Court cannot change that substantive element of the defense. In addition, the statute also allows the defense when there "is a reasonable ground to apprehend" the threat. It is within the Court's power and authority to interpret and determine the parameters of the application of a "reasonable ground to apprehend" and imminent threat to the person.

Many more questions are raised than answered by this opinion. The Court's discussion of "reasonableness," "imminence" and "hearsay" will be the source of much litigation and error at the trial court level for several years. This Court will be forced to address these same issues repeatedly in an effort to clear the legal quagmire which will develop as we attempt to explain what was meant by the opinion's analysis. The role of this Court should be to resolve issues, not create them. We should provide answers to the trial courts, not more questions. While the goal of this opinion is noble, it departs from the traditional rules of appellate review and embarks the Court on a course through much turbulent water in the future.

Regretfully, the Court seems to disregard the evidence of the case in a reaching attempt to adopt a syndrome which is not applicable to the facts and does not comport with the requirements of being generally accepted in the scientific/medical community. While I agree that evidence of the Post-traumatic Stress Disorder, which is accepted as a standard for diagnosis in the medical community, would be relevant evidence in a proper case to provide a jury with the medical and psychological diagnostic criteria required to determine the reasonableness of a defendant's actions, it is not relevant here. The appropriate resolution of the ills of society should be left to the Legislative and Executive branches of our government. This Court should restrict itself to the application of the law to the facts presented in the record. I therefore must dissent to the Court's actions in this case.

Comments and Questions

(1) Under a standard reasonable person self-defense test, were Bechtel's actions reasonable? Is the court creating a new defense? Why are the three judges in disagreement? Based on *Bechtel*, the Tenth Circuit Court of Appeals has held that expert testimony is necessary to assess the reasonableness of a battered woman's fear under Oklahoma law. *Paine v. Massie*, 339 F.3d 1194 (10th Cir. 2003).

As the court points out, quite a number of states have responded positively to defense requests regarding the battered woman syndrome. The response has not, however, been without sharp and often quite heated debate. Consider, for instance, these excerpts from a number of leading scholars in the field.

Burke, *Rational Actors, Self-Defense, and Duress: Making Sense, Not Syndromes, Out of the Battered Woman*, 81 N.C. L. Rev. 211, 214 (2002):

> The so-called battered woman syndrome ... has little empirical support, treats battered women as homogenous so that their self-defense claims rise and fall together, depicts battered women as cognitively impaired and irrational, and ultimately fails to explain why a battered woman might kill her sleeping husband. Moreover, it does nothing to jettison the faulty doctrinal rules that formed the impetus for the syndrome theory as a litigation strategy. An alternative approach is to change the rules themselves to reflect better the notion that force should be justified when and only when it is necessary. [We should be] treating (and judging) battered women who kill as rational actors, but changing doctrinal self-defense rules so that they more accurately justify all necessary uses of force.

Walker, *Battered Women Syndrome and Self-Defense*, 6 Notre Dame J.L. Ethics & Pub. Pol'y 321, 334 (1992):

> Since the introduction of what is often called the "battered woman self-defense" defense on behalf of those women who do kill in self-defense, many more women are receiving a fair trial. Often they are found not guilty by a jury who listens to what the women and other witnesses have to say, and the testimony of a psychologist who helps put the information into the context about what we know about the psychological effects of battering on the women's state of mind.... Newer applications of such testimony in cases such as battered children who kill parents in self-defense demonstrate the application of psychological theory to help understand victims' states of mind in a variety of situations.

Schneider, *Describing, and Changing: Women's Self-Defense Work and the Problem of Expert Testimony on Battering*, 14 Women's Rts. L. Rep. 213, 240 (1992):

> Defense efforts should focus on the battering experience as well as the reasonableness of the woman's actions. Expert testimony on battering should be proffered and admitted, but lawyers should be sensitive to the way in which they understand, characterize and explain the testimony and its relevance, and they should not rely on it to the exclusion of other defense strategies. Battered women who kill need not be portrayed solely as victims with a focus on the battering, but as actors and survivors whose acts are reasonable.... If battered women who kill are described as women who are victims but have fought back in order to survive, their actions in killing their batterers may be more effectively understood as reasonable.

Faigman & Wright, *The Battered Woman Syndrome in the Age of Science*, 39 Ariz. L. Rev. 67, 69–70 (1997):

> The battered woman syndrome ultimately fails because it was never a matter of science to begin with, and yet it was treated as a "scientific fact" by courts. Good science rarely serves the specific interests of any political viewpoint. Science has political consequences, but its results should remain untainted by political influence. Today, the majority of courts have accepted the scientific jargon of syndrome advocates, with ramifications not altogether salutary for battered women. Perhaps the most serious consequence of the use of syndrome evidence is the courts' tendency to pathologize battered women, referring to them as "sufferers" of the syndrome, as paralyzed by "learned helplessness," and, possibly, as victims of an identifiable psychological disability. Courts describe women who kill after suffering years of abuse, and who killed only after pursuing every reasonable alternative, as psychologically disabled and as deserving to be excused for their action. The pathology of the violent relationship has become the pathology of the battered woman. Other than archaic stereotypes about the weak character of women, there is no foundation for this characterization.

Mosteller, *Syndromes and Politics in Criminal Trials and Evidence Law*, 46 Duke L.J. 461, 485–86 (1996):

> I suggest an additional reason for broad admissibility, despite a debatable scientific foundation for the syndrome-politics. Society has arrived at a basic political judgment: the balance of advantage should be shifted in litigation in favor of battered women who respond violently to their batterers. Regardless of how it is technically labeled, my contention is that the substantive law of self-defense is being altered by changes in evidentiary rules designed, in large part, to aid women who have engaged in self-help.
>
> The motivation for admitting BWS is quite understandable. Domestic violence by husbands and boyfriends against women is an enormous social problem in the United States. In interspousal killings, well over half of those killed

are women. Of women who kill, a large percentage have been previously battered by the men they kill. Society may justifiably believe that the vast majority of women who die at the hands of their male domestic partners are the ultimate victims of widespread battering and that these women are largely, if not entirely, guiltless.

Coughlin, *Excusing Women*, 82 Cal. L. Rev. 1, 4–5, 91–92 (1994):

> While many feminist scholars conclude that the courts cannot justly blame an accused woman without considering abuse that she endured at the hands of her husband, several others have expressed uneasiness with the battered women syndrome defense because it institutionalizes within the criminal law negative stereotypes of women. I agree with this criticism: in particular, the defense is objectionable because it relieves the accused woman of the stigma and pain of criminal punishment only if she embraces another kind of stigma and pain: she must advance an interpretation of her own activity that labels that the irrational product of a "mental health disorder." ... Special excuses for women, in whatever form, reinforce incommensurable gender differences, in which the qualities characterized as male inevitably are privileged over those characterized as female; such excuses obscure feminist efforts to clarify our understanding of gender as a patriarchally constructed hierarchy of social differences and behavioral expectations. By the same token, our practice of excusing women reveals the inadequacy of the theory of responsibility presently endorsed by the criminal law.

Schopp, Sturgis & Sullivan, *Battered Woman Syndrome, Expert Testimony, and the Distinction Between Justification and Excuse*, 1994 U. Ill. L. Rev. 45, 112:

> The controversy regarding battered women who kill their batterers in the absence of occurrent attacks or threats demonstrates the critical importance to the criminal law of empirical rigor, careful attention to the jurisprudential foundations of legal doctrine, and the integration of the two. Although expert testimony regarding the battered woman syndrome has been widely endorsed by courts, commentators, and statutes, the battered woman syndrome lacks empirical support as a clinical syndrome. Furthermore, the battered woman syndrome bears almost no relevance to rigorously formulated and interpreted self-defense doctrine. If future research were to provide adequate empirical support for the battered woman syndrome, the syndrome could have limited relevance when admitted for the purposes of supporting the defendant's credibility or advancing an excuse for nonculpable mistake regarding justification.

Gillespie, *1990 Survey of Books Relating to the Law; II. Crime and Punishment: Defending Women. Justifiable Homicide: Battered Women, Self-Defense, and the Law*, 88 Mich. L. Rev. 1430, 1439 (1990):

> Whatever the statistics tell us about actual experience, more of us seem ready to identify and empathize actively as subway riders and mugging victims

> than as "battered women," just as more of us are willing to admit that we have been robbed than that we have been raped.
>
> I am not ready to abandon the requirements of self-defense because empathy is not always evenly applied; if I cannot always control juries with 'the law,' that is for me all the more reason to try to guide them with it. But I am not averse to trying to even the scales of injustice a bit. Admitting evidence of past batterings and expert testimony of battered women syndrome may not move us to try walking in that woman's shoes, but at least it tells us more about the person we are judging. It does not enforce empathy, but it may help us climb the barriers and traverse the distance that we place between ourselves and the victims of domestic and sexual abuse.

(2) Numerous states that allow the defense focus heavily on expert testimony:

> (A) The general assembly hereby declares that it recognizes both of the following, in relation to the "battered woman syndrome:"
>
> (1) That the syndrome currently is a matter of commonly accepted scientific knowledge;
>
> (2) That the subject matter and details of the syndrome are not within the general understanding or experience of a person who is a member of the general populace and are not within the field of common knowledge.
>
> (B) If a person is charged with an offense involving the use of force against another and the person, as a defense to the offense charged, raises the affirmative defense of self-defense, the person may introduce expert testimony of the "battered woman syndrome" and expert testimony that the person suffered from that syndrome as evidence to establish the requisite belief of an imminent danger of death or great bodily harm that is necessary, as an element of the affirmative defense, to justify the person's use of the force in question. The introduction of any expert testimony under this division shall be in accordance with the Ohio Rules of Evidence.

Ohio Stat. § 2901.06

(3) Congress passed, and the President signed, the Battered Women's Testimony Act of 1992. Section 2 provides that the State Justice Institute shall collect information regarding "the admissibility and quality of expert testimony on the experiences of battered women offered as part of the defense in criminal cases under state law" and also develop training materials to assist "battered women, operators of domestic violence shelters, battered women's advocates, and attorneys to use such expert testimony in appropriate cases, particularly appropriate cases involving indigent women defendants." The statute, and many of the court decisions, are gender specific. Should they be? The Australian High Court adopted the "battered wife syndrome" position in *Osland* (1999) 159 A.L.R. 170. Concurring, Justice Kirby encouraged legislators and judges to look beyond the more narrow gender specific confines.

> … However, unlike conception and childbirth, there is no inherent reason why a battering relationship should be confined to women as victims. In-

> stances exist where the reverse is the case, including in some same-sex relationships of analogous dependence and prolonged abuse. Moreover, it is important to be wary of the effects that BWS can have on the perception of women as fully independent and responsible individuals. What is at stake in reflecting the reality which may accompany long-term relationships of dependence is not 'gender loyalty or sympathy' but ethical and legal principle.
>
> There are particular reasons why "battered wife syndrome" is a complete misnomer. In my view that expression should not be used. Many women subjected to long-term battering are not wives. Although in an individual case a relationship of marriage might reinforce an abuser's notions of dominance, control and justification, the problem described in the literature extends beyond married couples. In the present case, for example, according to the appellant's evidence, it existed in her relationship with the deceased before their marriage. However understandable it may be, in its provenance and typical manifestations, to confine the notion involved in BWS to women in general, and to wives in particular, it is erroneous from the point of view of legal principle. What is relevant is not the sex or marital status of the victim of long-term abuse. Nor whether that abuse has been physical (battering) or otherwise. It is whether admissible evidence establishes that such a victim is suffering from symptoms or characteristics relevant in the particular case to the legal rules applicable to that case....

See also State v. Smullen, 844 A.2d 429 (Md. 2004) (in an appropriate case statutory "battered spouse" syndrome can apply to battered children); *People v. Colberg*, 182 Misc. 2d 798, 701 N.Y.S.2d 608 (County Ct. 1999) (expert testimony not limited to only women or children).

(4) In *People v. Humphrey*, 921 P.2d 1 (Cal. 1996), the trial judge allowed expert testimony on the issue of whether the defendant truly believed self-defense was necessary. The lower court would not, however, allow the testimony on the reasonableness of her belief. Held, the ruling was error, as such testimony "may help the jury understand the circumstances in which the defendant found herself at the time of the killing." In response to concerns that such a ruling would alter the substance of the self-defense claim in this area, the court wrote:

> ... [W]e are not changing the standard from objective to subjective, or replacing the reasonable "person" standard with a reasonable "battered woman" standard. Our decision would not, in another context, compel adoption of a "'reasonable gang member' standard." ... The jury must consider defendant's situation and knowledge, which makes the evidence relevant, but the ultimate question is whether a reasonable *person*, not a reasonable battered woman, would believe in the need to kill to prevent imminent harm. Moreover, it is the *jury*, not the expert, that determines whether defendant's belief and, ultimately, her actions, were objectively reasonable.

Id. at 151. The court concluded that such testimony was not only relevant in determining reasonableness, it is "critical in permitting the jury to evaluate [defendant's] testimony free of the misperceptions regarding battered women." *Id.* at 153.

Since 1992 when California enacted an evidentiary rule allowing for expert testimony on the battered wife syndrome, the lower courts in the state, as well as in other states, have struggled with whether a first-time battering victim may introduce such testimony. *See People v. Brown*, 94 P.3d 574 (Cal. 2004) (testimony admissible under general rule on expert testimony); *see also State v. Townsend*, 897 A.2d 316 (N.J. 2006) (diagnosis of battered woman syndrome not necessary for expert testimony to be admissible where woman had been beaten to death and made exculpatory statement for the defendant while in the hospital).

In 2002, California became the first state to allow women convicted of first or second degree murder to file habeas corpus petitions contending the outcome would have been different if evidence of battered women's syndrome had been permitted at trial, allowing for the possibility of a new trial. K. Edds, *Battered Women's New Day in Court*, Wash. Post, Nov. 22, 2002, at A3.

(5) Is expert testimony on battered women's syndrome relevant to whether the defendant acted recklessly for a crime requiring that mens rea? Would it be relevant in determining whether a defendant has an affirmative defense of duress to aggravated sexual assault of her child? In *State v. B.H.*, 183 N.J. 171, 870 A.2d 273 (2005), the Supreme Court of New Jersey concluded:

> We hold that in light of the particular requirements of our statute, courts must apply the standard of a "person of reasonable firmness" in determining whether duress excuses criminal conduct, and battered woman syndrome expert testimony is not relevant to that analysis. The evidence is relevant, however, to a defendant's subjective perception of a threat from her abuser and, in that respect, can be relevant to her credibility. It also helps in explaining why she would remain with her abuser and, therefore, why such a defendant ought not to be perceived as acting recklessly. In those important latter respects, our decision today permits the syndrome expert testimony to expand a juror's general knowledge about a battered defendant's circumstances. Moreover, if the complete defense of duress is rejected, the syndrome evidence may be relevant in connection with sentencing where it may be applicable to a defendant's mitigation argument under N.J. Stat. Ann. § 2C:44-1b(4). In this matter, battered woman syndrome expert testimony was admitted at trial, but its content and use inappropriately was restricted. We find too narrow the court's instruction that the expert testimony could be used only for evaluating defendant's recklessness. The court's trailing reference to use of the evidence to understand defendant's "state of mind," although correct, was inadequate to explain to the jury how the evidence may be used to assess the sincerity of defendant's perception of a threat from her alleged abuser. For that reason, we agree with the Appellate Division that defendant's conviction must be reversed. However, to the extent the Appellate Division

> held further that the evidence may be used to assist the jury in assessing the objective reasonableness of defendant's conduct in response to the purported threat, we disagree and reject that portion of the panel's direction to the trial court on remand.
>
> The jury charge must properly and completely explain how battered woman syndrome evidence may be considered in this matter.... [W]e are compelled to conclude that defendant's conviction cannot stand. We cannot treat the shortcoming in the charge as the equivalent of harmless error, particularly in light of the content restriction placed on the testimony of defendant's expert. Defendant's credibility was critical to her defense. Both the State and its expert called her credibility into question precisely because B.H. initially did not describe the coercive role that allegedly was played by S.H. (i.e., that his hand was on her throat as he forced her to engage in the sexual act with L.H.). The limitation imposed on the defendant's expert's testimony as it related to questions about defendant's credibility was significant.

183 N.J. at 201–02.

(6) The defendant in *State v. Hampton*, 558 N.W.2d 884 (Wis. Ct. App. 1996), *cert. denied*, 520 U.S. 1223 (1997), was charged with murder, and he claimed self-defense. The trial judge would not allow testimony as to his "psycho-social" history. In particular, the judge would not allow him to testify about particular instances in his past when he had experienced violence. He argued such evidence was relevant in determining the reasonableness of his actions, citing the Wisconsin battered spouse cases. The court on appeal rejected the argument.

> Hampton essentially is arguing that in order to determine the reasonableness of a defendant's belief "from the standpoint of the defendant" a jury must know the individual defendant's personal background and "psycho-social" history.... This "would eviscerate the objective, reasonable person requirement." The reasonableness of the belief is judged from the position of "a person of ordinary intelligence and prudence" in the same situation as the defendant, not of a person identical to the defendant placed in the same situation as the defendant. This is common sense because otherwise the privilege of self-defense would vary depending on the background or personal history of the person attempting to exercise the privilege. A person exposed to a lifetime of violence would have greater latitude to exercise the privilege of self-defense than a person raised in a life free from strife.... If the law were otherwise, every defendant who claimed an actual belief in the need to use force would escape conviction for first-degree murder.
>
> As such, none of Hampton's proffered "psycho-social" evidence that was rejected by the trial court is relevant to this objective standard of reasonableness....
>
> We acknowledge that Wisconsin law has recognized the relevance of some personal history evidence in the context of homicides in battered spouse situations. The trial court in the present case, however, rightfully recognized

> the difference in Hampton's "psycho-social" evidence from that admitted in the battered spouse cases where the evidence sought to be admitted is generally that of past instances of violence between the batterer-victim and the defendant. In such cases there is a direct connection between the pattern-of-abuse evidence and the homicide; that is, the actors in that evidence are the homicide victim and the defendant. Here, by contrast, none of the evidence excluded by the trial court involved past instances of violence exhibited by Storks towards Hampton. The proposed evidence all involved remote instances of alleged violence committed by third persons not involved in the events surrounding Storks's homicide.

Id. at 890–91. Do you agree with the court's distinction? Is it consistent with the New York court's decision in *Goetz*? Is it consistent with decisions which allow testimony of battered woman syndrome in situations where the defendant is *not* raising a self-defense claim? *See, e.g., Barrett v. State*, 675 N.E.2d 1112, 1117 (Ind. Ct. App. 1996) (relevant to show defendant did not have required intent); *State v. Grecinger*, 569 N.W.2d 189, 193 (Minn. 1997) (admissible to support credibility of victim if defendant has attacked credibility). Compare the majority and dissenting opinions in *State v. Mott*, 931 P.2d 1046 (Ariz. 1997), exploring the use of such testimony when offered to disprove required intent.

(7) Some courts allow other use of syndrome evidence in connection with self-defense. *See*, for instance, *State v. Janes*, 850 P.2d 495 (Wash. 1993) (battered child syndrome); *Frenzel v. State*, 849 P.2d 741 (Wyo. 1993) (child sexual abuse accommodation syndrome); *Commonwealth v. Kacsmar*, 617 A.2d 725 (Pa. Super. Ct. 1992) (battered persons syndrome). *But see Werner v. State*, 711 S.W.2d 639 (Tex. Crim. App. 1986). There the defendant was convicted of murder. His defense was that he acted to save his own life when he felt seriously threatened by the victim. At trial he offered the testimony of a psychiatrist who would have testified regarding the "Holocaust Syndrome." This would have been bolstered by further testimony that the doctor had been seeing the defendant as a patient, that the defendant had talked with him about many of the stories previously told to the defendant about the World War II concentration camps and the problems of individuals who did not fight back. The doctor would have further stated that it was the defendant's "state of mind to defend himself because he comes from a family that did not." Texas has a statute which provides:

> In all prosecutions for murder or voluntary manslaughter, the state or defendant shall be permitted to offer testimony as to all relevant facts and circumstances surrounding the killing and the previous relationship existing between the accused and the deceased, together with all relevant facts and circumstances going to show the condition of the mind of the accused at the time of the offense.

Tex. Code Crim. Proc. Art. 38.36 (1997).

The court on appeal found that the trial judge properly excluded the doctor's testimony. Compare the majority and dissenting opinions.

Majority:

> Even if the self-defense issue was validly before the jury the proffered testimony was still immaterial. The police officers related appellant spoke of the Holocaust, but his misgivings about the shooting and the effect upon his father were future oriented and did not necessarily explain appellant's state of mind at the time of the offense. Dr. Roden's testimony was that, although appellant continued to disclaim he was not thinking of the Holocaust at the time of the offense, he showed "some" characteristics of the syndrome associated with children of the survivors of the Holocaust, and the same might have had a subconscious effect on him. All that can be inferred from this evidence is that appellant may have been more susceptible to actions in self-defense.

Dissent:

> My understanding of the appellant's proffer of proof regarding Dr. Roden is that Dr. Roden would not have testified to any ultimate factual issue that had to be resolved by the jury, but, instead, would have merely supplied the jury with background data on the state of mind that the appellant had at the time in question in order to aid the jury in finding what the appellant's state or condition of his mind was at the time of the fatal shooting; thus, he would have explained to them that because the appellant was suffering from the effects of "The Holocaust Syndrome" this affected his state or condition of his mind at the time of the fatal shooting.
>
> The proffered testimony of Dr. Roden on "The Holocaust Syndrome," and how it affected the condition of the appellant's mind at the time he shot the deceased, should make it obvious to anyone that it comes within the rule that expert opinion testimony on issues to be decided by the jury is admissible where the conclusion of the expert is one which jurors would not ordinarily be able to draw for themselves. "But when the jurors are not competent to infer, without the aid of greater skill than their own, the probable existence of the facts to be ascertained, or the likelihood of their occurring from other facts actually proved, expert opinion evidence is rendered admissible."

State v. Pride

Missouri Court of Appeals
567 S.W.2d 426 (1978)

Smith, Judge.

On October 21, 1976, Ms. Mabel Stewart was traveling south on interstate highway I-55. She turned off the highway and parked her car on the truck parking side of the highway rest area in Cape Girardeau. She locked her car and went into the women's restroom. As she was leaving one of the stalls in the restroom, someone grabbed her around the neck and pushed her to the floor. Ms. Stewart testified that she was beaten about the head and robbed of her car keys and watch. She identified Roscoe James

Pittman as the robber. She further testified that appellant did not attack or threaten her, but did enter the restroom on one occasion.

Gary Lively, a truck driver, heard Ms. Stewart scream as he was coming out of the men's restroom. He testified that he saw Pittman standing inside the women's restroom and appellant standing "a foot or so away." Pittman and appellant then proceeded toward their car. Lively followed them and copied the license number of the car the two men were about to enter and called the police on his CB radio.

In the meantime, Ms. Stewart had gotten her pistol from her car and enlisted the aid of another truck driver, Phillip Wayne Brough, to help stop Pittman and appellant. Brough took the gun from Ms. Stewart and walked toward the car, holding the gun at his side. Brough testified that when he was within twenty or thirty yards, the man on the passenger side of the car (Pittman) leveled a .22 caliber rifle at him. Brough stopped and jumped behind a picnic table. Pittman and Brough exchanged shots. Then Pittman and appellant got in their car and drove off. Brough further testified that he fired one more shot as the car sped away. No one was seriously injured. Pittman and appellant were arrested later by the Jackson police.

[A]ppellant argues that the trial court erred in refusing to give instructions[2] to the jury on the law of self-defense and the lesser offense of assault without malice. Appellant argues there was sufficient evidence as a matter of law: the evidence showed Brough approached appellant with a gun in his hand and actually fired at the car as it drove away. Appellant contends this evidence established that appellant could have reasonably believed that his life or personal safety was immediately threatened and was therefore entitled to an instruction on self-defense. We disagree and find that appellant was not entitled to an instruction on self-defense as a matter of law.

---

2. "One of the issues in this case is whether the use of force on Phillip Brough was a justifiable assault. By 'justifiable assault' is meant the use of force on another in lawful self-defense. On that issue you are instructed as follows:

1. The State has the burden of proving beyond a reasonable doubt that the defendant did not act in lawful self-defense. If the evidence in this case leaves in your mind a reasonable doubt as to whether the defendant acted in lawful self-defense, then you must find the defendant not guilty.

2. If the defendant had reasonable cause to believe and did believe that he was in immediate danger of death or serious bodily harm and had reasonable cause to believe, and did believe, that it was necessary for him to act as he did to protect himself from such danger, then you are instructed that he acted in lawful self-defense and must be acquitted.

3. In determining whether or not the defendant acted in lawful self-defense you should consider all of the evidence in the case.

4. If the defendant had reasonable cause to believe and did believe that he was in immediate danger of death or serious bodily harm and that it was necessary for him to act as he did, it is of no consequence that the appearances later turned out to be false. If he acted in self-defense, as submitted in this instruction, he must be acquitted even though there was no purpose on the part of Phillip W. Brough to kill him or to do him serious bodily harm and no actual necessity to use the force which he did."

If there is any substantial evidence putting self-defense in issue, it is the duty of the trial court to instruct on self-defense as part of the law of the case. In such a situation the trial court must instruct on self-defense whether or not the defendant requested the instruction and even though the instruction requested or submitted by the defendant was defective. Under the so-called withdrawal doctrine, however, which is as applicable to assault as to homicide, one who was the aggressor or who provoked the difficulty in which he killed (or injured or assaulted) another cannot invoke the right of self-defense to excuse or justify the homicide (or injury or assault), unless he had previously withdrawn from the combat in such a manner as to have shown his intention in good faith to desist. Furthermore, "[t]here is a difference between 'withdrawal in good faith' from combat, and a mere 'retreat' which may be and often is a continuance of hostilities. A 'withdrawal' is an abandonment of the struggle by one of the parties and such abandonment must be perceived by the other."

In the present case it is true that Brough approached Pittman and appellant with a gun in his hand. Although at this point Brough became the aggressor, appellant is not entitled to the defense of self-defense because appellant was himself the aggressor in the robbery and had not indicated in any way that he was withdrawing from the combat so as to revive his right to self-defense. Because the robbery and the assault are so related in time, proximity and purpose, even though the victims are different, we view each as part of a single incident. Pittman and appellant were leaving the restrooms, the scene of the robbery, and walking toward their car when Brough started to approach them. In our view the action by Brough prevented Pittman and appellant from escaping with the stolen property and thus successfully completing the robbery. In other words, under these circumstances, appellant was merely retreating and not withdrawing in good faith. For this reason the trial court did not err in refusing to give an instruction on self-defense.

Comments and Questions

(1) Was the robbery still being committed at the time of the shot being fired by Brough? Why, then, did the court reject the instruction in the footnote?

(2) Was the defendant in *Hemphill v. State*, 387 N.E.2d 1324, 1326 (Ind. 1979), entitled to a self-defense instruction?

> Ron Deboe and John Muhlberger were working in Wally's Food Store, owned by Muhlberger. Shortly after midnight, three persons entered the store. One of the three, appellant Daniel Hemphill, had been in the store numerous times. Muhlberger ordered Hemphill to leave the store. After Hemphill left Muhlberger told the other two customers that he had thrown Hemphill out of the store because he was a thief. At this, Hemphill again appeared at the door and challenged Muhlberger's accusation. When Muhlberger repeated his statement that Hemphill was a thief, Hemphill said, "Man, I'm going to get you in a dark alley and waste you." Muhlberger then grabbed a billiard cue to chase Hemphill away from the store. Muhlberger followed Hemphill for a short distance down the street, but then turned around and started

> back to the store. At that point Hemphill appeared from the side of a nearby building with a handgun and was seen firing five rapid shots. Muhlberger was struck in the back and fell to the ground. Muhlberger later died from the bullet wound.

See generally United States v. Peterson, 483 F.2d 1222, 1231, *cert. denied*, 414 U.S. 1007 (1973):

> It has long been accepted that one cannot support a claim of self-defense by a self-generated necessity to kill. The right of homicidal self-defense is granted only to those free from fault in the difficulty; it is denied to slayers who incite the fatal attack, encourage the fatal quarrel or otherwise promote the necessitous occasion for taking life. The fact that the deceased struck the first blow, fired the first shot or made the first menacing gesture does not legalize the self-defense claim if in fact the claimant was the actual provoker. In sum, one who is the aggressor in a conflict culminating in death cannot invoke the necessities of self-preservation. Only in the event that he communicates to his adversary his intent to withdraw and in good faith attempts to do so is he restored to his right of self-defense.
>
> This body of doctrine traces its origin to the fundamental principle that a killing in self-defense is excusable only as a matter of genuine necessity. Quite obviously, a defensive killing is unnecessary if the occasion for it could have been averted, and the roots of that consideration run deep with us.
>
> [B]efore a person can avail himself of the plea of self-defense against the charge of homicide, he must do everything in his power, consistent with his safety, to avoid the danger and avoid the necessity of taking life. If one has reason to believe that he will be attacked, in a manner which threatens him with bodily injury, he must avoid the attack if it is possible to do so, and the right of self-defense does not arise until he has done everything in his power to prevent its necessity.

(3) Utah Code Ann. §§ 76-2-402(1) and (2) provide:

> (1)(a) A person is justified in threatening or using force against another when and to the extent that the person reasonably believes that force or a threat of force is necessary to defend the person or a third person against another person's imminent use of unlawful force.
>
> (b) A person is justified in using force intended or likely to cause death or serious bodily injury only if the person reasonably believes that force is necessary to prevent death or serious bodily injury to the person or a third person as a result of another person's imminent use of unlawful force, or to prevent the commission of a forcible felony.
>
> (2)(a) A person is not justified in using force under the circumstances specified in Subsection (1) if the person:
>
> (i) initially provokes the use of force against the person with the intent to use force as an excuse to inflict bodily harm upon the assailant;

(ii) is attempting to commit, committing, or fleeing after the commission or attempted commission of a felony; or

(iii) was the aggressor or was engaged in a combat by agreement, unless he withdraws from the encounter and effectively communicates to the other person his intent to do so and, notwithstanding, the other person continues or threatens to continue the use of unlawful force.

(b) For purposes of Subsection (2)(a)(iii) the following do not, by themselves, constitute "combat by agreement":

(i) voluntarily entering into or remaining in an ongoing relationship; or

(ii) entering or remaining in a place where one has a legal right to be.

In what situations would this statute, particularly 2(a), be important? *See State v. Sanders*, 245 S.E.2d 674, 679 (N.C. 1978):

> [A]lthough a party is privileged to use deadly force to defend against an attack by unarmed assailants of vastly superior size, strength or number, if the defendant precipitated the altercation intending to provoke a deadly assault by the victim in order that he might kill him, his subsequent killing of the victim in response to the attack is murder.

See also the instruction given in *State v. Robinson*, 360 P.2d 474, 478 (Ariz. 1961):

> The right of self-defense is not available to a person who has sought a quarrel with the design to force a deadly issue and thus through his fraud, contrivance or fault, to create a real or apparent necessity for making a felonious assault.

(4) As a matter of law, is a defendant considered an aggressor if he defends himself while committing a felony? *See State v. Marks*, 602 P.2d 1344, 1351 (Kan. 1979):

> We recognize that [our statute] authorizes a person to use force against an aggressor to the extent it appears reasonably necessary to defend himself against the aggressor's imminent use of unlawful force. However, it is well settled that a person cannot use greater force than is reasonably necessary to resist the attack and, furthermore, that self-defense is not available to a person who is committing or attempting to commit a forcible felony.

Another case raising the problem is *People v. Baker*, 372 N.E.2d 438, 440 (Ill. App. Ct. 1978):

> The plan was that the defendants would wait in the house and rob Ms. Tarro when she returned. Baker testified that he parked about two blocks from the Tarro residence and that when he heard gunfire, he drove to the house, stopped, picked up the defendants, and drove off. Several thousand dollars taken from Ms. Tarro and from in the house were later divided among the defendants and Baker.
>
> Defendants' theory is based upon the assumption that the jury could have believed that Joyce Tarro fired first and that she was not justified in doing so. They conclude that under those circumstances, they would have been justified in firing back in order to save their lives.

What result in *Baker* if the defendant, unarmed, hit Tarro over the head, killing her, after she had fired her gun at him?

People v. Cherry

Court of Appeals of New York
121 N.E.2d 238 (1954)

FULD, JUDGE.

Defendant, a plumber by trade, doing absolutely nothing improper, doing nothing, indeed, even to excite suspicion, was accosted and seized by two strangers in ordinary street attire, claiming to be police officers, late at night as he was about to enter his home. What citizen would do less, if resistance, concededly permissible, was to be effective, than defendant did in this case? He used no artificial or man-made weapon of any sort, relying solely on those supplied by nature, his hands and his teeth.

The police officers were, as everyone acknowledges, guilty of an illegal arrest and an unlawful assault. Defendant had the privilege, therefore, of resisting and using "force or violence" against his assailants, even though they were police officers, "to prevent an offense against his person ... if the force or violence ... [was] not more than sufficient to prevent such offense."

From the quiet vantage of a library, and after the event, one might look back and figure that defendant should not have done more than remonstrate with his captors or even that he should have submitted to the illegal arrest and the attendant assault. But defendant was not accorded time for calm thought or reflection; he was faced with a fact, not a hypothesis, in the form of two men, not in uniform but in ordinary garb who appeared out of the night on a deserted street in Brooklyn. It was not he who started the fight; according to the record, he tried to get away, and it was only after one of [the] officers (and this is the latter's testimony) "lunged from the rear and got him around the shoulders" that he fought back. And he reacted as any reasonable and quick-witted person might under the circumstances: having no weapon, he grabbed his assailant by the wrist and bit his thumb.

The consequences were, we have no doubt, painful to the officer, but we do not see how a court may say that defendant employed more force than was reasonable under the very frightening circumstances that suddenly confronted him. If defendant had any right to prevent his arrest, he was privileged to take effective steps toward that end and was not confined to words or pushes, or other futile gestures. Once the right to resist is acknowledged, it is impossible to conclude that this defendant used more force than—in the language of the statute—was "sufficient to *prevent*" his arrest, "[the] offense against his person," when, as we know, his efforts never even approached the point of success.

Whether or not the police officers exhibited their badges to defendant is completely beside the point. A badge may not substitute for a warrant of arrest, nor excuse its absence, when one is required. Lacking the essential warrant, having abused the authority which was their trust, the officers stood bereft of their usual prerogatives and whether or not defendant believed that they were police officers, he had a right to resist, and that quite apart from any fear or threat of physical harm and injury. For most people, an illegal arrest is an outrageous affront and intrusion—the more offensive because under color of law—to be resisted as energetically as a violent assault. In plain and unmistakable language, the legislature has recognized their right to do so.

The standard by which defendant must be judged is phrased solely in terms of the physical necessities of the situation presented. If force is necessary to prevent an unlawful arrest, then force may be employed, the one limitation on its exercise being that the victim may not pursue his counterattack merely for the sake of revenge or the infliction of needless injury. That, this defendant did not do.

The investigation of crime does not require and, certainly, does not justify a disregard of basic rights on the part of law enforcement officials. The legislature has deliberately and carefully enacted legislation authorizing an arrest without a warrant in limited fact situations, and police officers may not ignore the law's demands because they believe that effective policing or the end in view calls for such conduct. It may well have been misguided zeal, not deliberate violation of law, that underlay and accounted for what the officers here did. But, whichever it was, it would be a travesty to adjudge the very victim of the illegal arrest and the unprovoked attack guilty of the crime of assaulting his captors and assailants. The administration of justice would be ill served by such a result.

DESMOND, JUDGE (dissenting).

It is conceded that defendant bit the thumb of Gilchrist, a police officer. The witnesses against defendant were Gilchrist and another police officer named Pizzimenti. For the defense, Gilchrist was recalled, defendant testified in his own behalf, and his wife testified for him, as did a woman named Jordan and two character witnesses. Gilchrist testified that he is a city patrolman and that, about ten o'clock on the night of December 4, 1952, he was at the corner of Franklin Avenue and Madison Street in Brooklyn, on foot and not in uniform. He had defendant under observation for about a half hour. Beginning at about 9:30 P. M., he and Officer Pizzimenti had been seated in an automobile in the middle of the block on Madison Street, keeping a certain building under observation, and they observed defendant loitering about those premises. The witness saw two unknown men and a woman approach defendant and engage in a conversation, and then saw defendant enter a building which they were watching. Very shortly thereafter, defendant came out, according to Gilchrist, and walked to the corner, where Gilchrist approached defendant, told him that he (Gilchrist) was a police officer and asked defendant to show some identification. Patrolman Pizzimenti was with Gilchrist and Pizzimenti also announced to defendant that he was a police officer. He said that defendant looked at the officers, walked away a few steps and stopped, and said that he did not believe they were "cops," and asked them to show him their police shields again. Then he started to run, brushing against Officer Pizzimenti, whereupon Patrolman Gilchrist, from the rear, grabbed defendant around the shoulders and defendant took Gilchrist's left hand by the wrist, put

Gilchrist's thumb in his mouth and bit. Gilchrist testified that he received medical attention at a hospital and, as a result, was "out sick" for several days. In his cross-examination he said that he afterwards learned that defendant lived in the basement of 110 Madison Street, which was apparently the building the policemen were watching, that after they, from their automobile, had watched defendant for some time, they got out of the automobile, crossed over to defendant's side of the street, and then stopped him at the street corner. Gilchrist said that at first he put his hand on defendant's elbow, at the same time stating that he was a police officer and showing his badge. The other officer was standing nearby. Neither officer knew defendant. Gilchrist testified that at that first encounter he was not arresting defendant. He testified that the officers were taking defendant over to a building so that they could talk to him out of the stream of traffic since there were quite a few people passing by. He said that when defendant started to run away, which was just before the biting, Gilchrist then grabbed defendant and put him under arrest. When asked whether defendant had committed any crime, Gilchrist testified: "He bolted past my brother officer." He said that, after this, defendant was dragging Gilchrist along the street with Gilchrist's thumb in defendant's mouth, and that when Gilchrist freed his thumb defendant fell to the ground.

The next witness was Patrolman Pizzimenti, who, too, swore that the police officers twice showed their badges to defendant. Pizzimenti said that he secured the release of Gilchrist's thumb by punching defendant in the eye, that Pizzimenti then told defendant to get in the car but that defendant threw himself on the ground and the officers had to pick him up and put him in the car by force. He said that, after they got to the police station, he (Pizzimenti) told defendant that the latter was foolish since he had been told that the men were police officers, and that defendant replied that he knew he was wrong and that he was sorry. On cross-examination Pizzimenti said that both officers approached defendant from the side and rear, that defendant walked along with them for a few steps on the sidewalk, whereupon defendant stated that he did not believe they were police officers and they, for a second time, showed him their shields and then defendant attempted to brush past them. Then, according to Pizzimenti, Gilchrist threw his arms around defendant's arms or shoulders. Nowhere in the record is there any explanation of why the officers were watching the particular building or watching defendant.

The next witness was defendant himself who testified that, with his wife and four children, he lived in the basement and parlor floor at 110 Madison Street, that he had lived there about eight years, that he was a plumber by trade, that he had been convicted of petty larceny in 1946, but had never since been convicted of any crime. He said that on the evening in question he had come home from work about seven o'clock and had gone out again about 8:30 P.M. to make some collections, that he had collected some money for some jobs he had done, and that he had arrived home about a quarter of ten. He said that he had parked his car in a garage around the corner from his home and then, carrying some packages, went directly into the basement of his premises without making any stops or meeting anybody on the street.

He said that at his home were his wife and two visitors and that, at his wife's request, he went out, a few minutes after he had arrived home, to buy some ice cream, that he walked along Madison Street, and just before he got to Franklin Avenue, two men coming from behind grabbed hold of his arm and told him to get into a doorway. He had not seen them before. He tried to pull away from them. He saw no police badges. He was frightened because he had the money on his person and thought they were stick-up men. While he was pulling away from them, he testified, he was hit in the eye and began to yell for help. In the course of the struggle one man's hand "slipped past my face and I grabbed ahold of his thumb with my mouth." After that the men stopped trying to get him into the doorway and then tried to load him into a car. Then, he says, he was hit on the ear and went down and one of the men was over him. While he was lying there someone told him to get up because the men were policemen. Then a uniformed policeman came along, helped defendant up, got him into a car and told him that the others were police officers. The next witness was Mrs. Cherry, wife of defendant, who testified that her husband came home about a quarter of ten, then went out almost immediately to get the ice cream. Mrs. Jordan, who was a visitor at defendant's home that night, gave similar testimony.

The argument of defendant is based on section 177 of the Code of Criminal Procedure and subdivision 3 of section 246 of the Penal Law. Section 177 permits a peace officer without a warrant (there was, of course, no warrant here) to arrest a person for a crime committed or attempted in his presence, or when the person arrested has committed a felony although not in the peace officer's presence, or when a felony has, in fact, been committed and the officer has reasonable cause for believing the person arrested to have committed it. There is no showing that any of these conditions were present here. Subdivision 3 of section 246 of the Penal Law says that it is not unlawful to use force or violence on the person of another when the violence is done by a party about to be injured, in preventing or attempting to prevent an offense against his person "if the force or violence used is not more than sufficient to prevent such offense." In its memorandum opinion after reargument here, the Appellate Division said that, assuming that the detention of defendant was a false arrest, which he might resist, "he nevertheless had no right to use more force than such resistance required." Noting that the trial court had believed the testimony of the police officers, the Appellate Division said that, that being so, "there was no cause for appellant to apprehend bodily harm, and his violent conduct in biting a police officer supports the conclusion that thereby he committed an assault." In other words, the Appellate Division, assuming for the sake of argument that the conduct of the police officers amounted to an unlawful arrest, nevertheless, taking the facts, as found, that defendant had been informed that the two men were police officers and had been shown their police badges, held that there was no necessity for him to commit mayhem. In other words, we now have a finding by Special Sessions, affirmed by the Appellate Division (eight Justices authorized, unlike us, to pass on *facts*, unanimously so voting), that defendant did use more force than was sufficient to prevent the offense which police officers, we are bound by the findings of fact below and so we must start from that factual premise. Of course, we must assume, too, as the Appellate Division did, that the arrest or detention of this man was unlawful, since there was no showing of any of the elements required by the Code of Criminal Procedure for an arrest. However, the fact that the arrest or detention was illegal does no more than put the situation under the coverage of section 246 of the Penal Law, *supra*, and leaves us with the question of whether defendant used more than sufficient force, which is a question of fact. In most of the cases in which subdivision 3 of section 246 is discussed, the difficulty arises because of instructions to a jury, said to be erroneous. We do not have that situation here, but here we have a trial by court without a jury, a fact finding as to what occurred, and a finding that more than sufficient force was thereby used.

Although I have found no direct New York authority on the question, it seems obvious to me that the force "not more than sufficient" which a citizen may use in his own defense means not more than the amount of force that would have been deemed necessary by a reasonable person in a similar situation. The amount of force reasonably to be deemed necessary depends on the existing conditions, and one of those conditions here would be the fact, as found and affirmed below, that defendant knew these two men were policemen because he had been shown their official badges.

The whole of our law as to self-defense is limited to the use of "such force as might be reasonably necessary." Once an assault is prima facie proven, it is a matter of defense that the force used was reasonably necessary under the circumstances. It can hardly be said that such a defense was here established as matter of law and beyond dispute.

The judgment should be *affirmed*.

Comments and Questions

(1) While *Cherry* is now more than 60 years old, it remains one of the most influential decisions in the area, precisely because the majority opinion is so unyielding. Does Judge Fuld truly mean that whether the officers' badges were exhibited "is completely beside the point"? What would/should the result be if Cherry resisted a uniformed police officer? New York Penal Law § 35.27 was added in 1968:

> A person may not use physical force to resist an arrest, whether authorized or unauthorized, which is being effected or attempted by a police officer or peace officer when it would reasonably appear that the latter is a police officer or peace officer.

According to the Supreme Court of Washington, 30 states prohibit resisting even an unlawful arrest. As of 1997, only five states had taken that position. *State v. Valentine*, 935 P.2d 1294, 1301 (Wash. 1997). The court strongly supported the current majority view:

> In Washington today the law provides those arrested with numerous protections that did not exist when the common law rule arose. Reasonable bail is available. At any critical stage in a criminal prosecution a defendant has a right to appointed counsel.... [T]he Fourth Amendment requires a prompt

> judicial determination of probable cause as a prerequisite to an extended pretrial detention following a warrantless arrest. None of these rights was available in 1709. "[T]he right to resist developed when the procedural safeguards which exist today were unknown."
>
> Not only has criminal procedure advanced to protect the rights of the accused, jails themselves are no longer the pestilential death traps they were in eighteenth century England. Recent Eighth Amendment litigation of prisoners' claims of cruel and unusual punishment has established certain constitutional standards for prisons....
>
> More importantly, if the rule were, as the dissent suggests it should be, that a person being unlawfully arrested may always resist such an arrest with force, we would be inviting anarchy. While we do not, as the dissent appears to suggest, condone the unlawful use of state force, we can take note of the fact that in the often heated confrontation between a police officer and an arrestee, the lawfulness of the arrest may be debatable. To endorse resistance by persons who are being arrested by an officer of the law, based simply on the arrested person's belief that the arrest is unlawful, is to encourage violence that could, and most likely would, result in harm to the arresting officer, the defendant, or both. In our opinion, the better place to address the question of the lawfulness of an arrest that does not pose harm to the arrested person is in court and not on the street.

Id. at 1300, 1303. But see the vigorous dissent:

> This right to resist unlawful arrest "memorializes one of the principle elements in the heritage of the English revolution: the belief that the will to resist arbitrary authority in a reasonable way is valuable and ought not to be suppressed by the criminal law...."
>
> [T]he principle upon which the rule was founded that an individual may resist an unlawful arrest with reasonable force is rooted in political philosophy and is no way dependent upon a trivial factual inquiry into the conditions of one's local jail. Certainly we have repeated the rule in our jurisdiction in recent years when our jails were much the same as today....
>
> In America the tradition of resisting unlawful authority has been embraced from the early days of resisting imperial British power during the Revolution through the civil rights movement. It is fundamental.
>
> "In the face of obvious injustice, one ought not to be forced to submit and swallow one's sense of justice. More importantly, it is unconscionable to convict a man for resisting an injustice. This is indeed a value judgment, but the values are fundamental."
>
> ...
>
> When government agents commit assault and battery against the very citizens they are sworn to protect, the government is no longer our friend; it is our dangerous enemy....

> This rule has equal application in the twentieth and twenty-first centuries to the extent it is rooted in political theory and human nature. In a well-known passage in The Gulag Archipelago, at 13 n. 5 (English ed. 1973), Aleksandr Solzhenitsyn wonders what would have happened had the countless victims of Stalin's arbitrary state power resisted and whether the officers serving under Stalin might have acted with less zeal had they known they could face legitimate resistance and even harm in effectuating their unlawful arrests. Solzhenitsyn suggests that resistance would have been an effective deterrent; had the victims resisted, "notwithstanding all of Stalin's thirst, the cursed machine would have ground to a halt!"

Id. at 1310–11.

The debate continues. *See, e.g.*, Hemmens & Levin, *"Not a Law at all": A Call for a Return to the Common Law Right to Resist Unlawful Arrest*, 29 Sw. U. L. Rev. 1, 7 (1999). The authors argue that:

> [r]ecent attacks on the right [to resist unlawful arrest] are based on a misunderstanding of the right's original justifications, and that there remains a great need for the right, particularly as new police tactics increase the probability of arbitrary assertions of police authority. Such tactics often target individuals for questioning and arrest on the basis of race, leading to increased suspicion of the police and providing a new and important justification for a return....

(2) How much force can the defendant use in resisting an arrest under Judge Fuld's view? If an officer uses a billy club, can the defendant use a knife? If an officer reaches for a gun, can the defendant fire his first? Of course, in most states the question may turn on whether the officer's own use of force was lawful. *See State v. Wright*, 799 P.2d 642, 644 (Or. 1990):

> If a peace officer uses excessive force in making an arrest, the arrestee has a right to use physical force in self-defense against the excessive force being used by the officer. In that circumstance, the arrestee is not "resisting arrest," but, rather, is defending himself against the excessive force being used by the arresting officer. As noted, the state concedes that defendant presented evidence at trial that the arresting officers here used excessive force. Defendant, therefore, had a right to use physical force to defend himself against that excessive force.

As stated in *State v. Yeutter*, 566 N.W.2d 387, 391 (Neb. 1997): the question is whether the "officer used unreasonable force in making the arrest." In *State v. Williams*, 624 S.E.2d 443 (S.C. Ct. App. 2005), the court held that if the defendant fully complied with all the requirements of a citizen subject to lawful arrest, the defendant is entitled to resist to the extent necessary to protect against serious physical harm.

[B] Defense of Others

State v. Fair

Supreme Court of New Jersey
211 A.2d 359 (1965)

HANEMAN, J.

John B. Lynn (Lynn) and Dollie Fair (Fair) were charged in a single indictment with the murder of Aaron R. Rudesel. After a joint trial the jury returned a verdict of second degree murder against Lynn and manslaughter against Fair.

The facts surrounding the actual stabbing are very unclear, caused at least in part by the alcoholic condition of the eyewitnesses thereto. The pertinent testimony of the key witnesses is as follows:

Emily Williams testified that on the morning of September 2 she and Fair had been visiting in the neighborhood, and then went back to the Knox apartment. Lynn arrived shortly thereafter, followed by Rudesel. They were all sitting around the table in the kitchen when she suddenly saw Rudesel standing over Fair, and although she was not too clear, she thought that Rudesel had started an argument and a fight by hitting Fair. Fair picked up a paring knife from the table, went towards Rudesel and struck at him several times. She was unable to see whether Fair cut him with the knife because she was "scared and trying to get out." As Rudesel was reaching in his pocket for something, Lynn, who was at the other side of the table from Fair and Rudesel, picked up a knife and "came in and he got into it." At this point Lynn got between Fair and Rudesel and was "cutting at this man with a knife." After Lynn struck at him, Rudesel brushed past her and fell on the back porch. She ran downstairs out of the hallway door.

The defendant Lynn testified that he woke up about 4 A.M. on September 2 with a severe toothache. To alleviate his pain he started to drink gin, and by seven o'clock he had finished a pint. His brother-in-law came to his apartment about 7:30 with some vodka and he had several drinks of that. Lynn then went to a store to purchase food for the day and returned with a hen, which he proceeded to clean. Later that morning, on his way to the store to purchase additional food, he met Rudesel, who invited him to his apartment for a drink. Lynn accepted and accompanied him to the Knox apartment. Upon arrival there Rudesel asked Knox where Fair was. Upon learning that she had gone across the street Rudesel left to get her, leaving Lynn sitting at the table in the kitchen by himself. Lynn claims that his memory from that point on is a blank; he does not recall seeing Rudesel or Fair, or ever having met Emily Williams.

Dollie Fair testified that she and Rudesel had been sweethearts for about eight months prior to his death. On the night before Rudesel's death they had been to a tavern, and returned to the apartment at about 1:45 A.M. At about 8:00 or 8:30 Fair arose to fix Rudesel some breakfast. She then went across the street to another apartment and had several drinks. Rudesel came to get her and they returned to the Knox apartment. When they got there Lynn was in the kitchen and Emily Williams arrived shortly thereafter. All four of them had some drinks from a pint of whiskey which Rudesel had furnished. As she and Emily Williams were eating, Rudesel commenced to berate her for having gone across the street, and suddenly hit her in the mouth. She grabbed a paring knife and struck at Rudesel, with her eyes closed. Rudesel grabbed her hands and pushed her down in a chair, accusing her of having cut him on the shoulder. Rudesel said, "I will get even with you for that"; took a knife out of his pocket and cut her on the finger. At this point Lynn jumped up and said, "Man, you shouldn't cut your woman like that." He then intervened on her behalf, and she ran out the back door and up the stairs to another apartment to call the police. Fair stated that she did not see Lynn cut Rudesel nor did she ever see a knife in his hand, but when she came back downstairs from making the telephone call she saw Knox who told her that "Aaron [Rudesel] said Jake stabbed him." After learning of the stabbing she went to the home of her aunt. Later that day, at her aunt's suggestion, she surrendered herself to a detective, to whom she allegedly stated: "Aaron [Rudesel] hit me in the mouth and I may have cut him. I'm not sure. I didn't think I did, I had a knife."

The trial court charged only on self-defense, i.e., the right of each defendant to defend himself or herself, but did not charge on the right of Lynn to intervene in defense of Fair. Lynn argues that the trial judge had a duty to charge on his right to intervene in defense of Fair.

An essential element of the charge of murder is malice, and in order for criminal liability to attach there must be a concurrence of an "evil-meaning mind with an evil-doing hand." Basically, the so-called "affirmative defense" of defense of another in murder cases negates the existence of the essential element of malice.

> "There has been some uncertainty in the language of our cases upon the burden of proof. [A]lthough the burden is upon a defendant to adduce evidence to support the defense, yet if such evidence appears either in the State's case or upon the defendant's case, the issue must be left to the jury with this instruction: that the burden is upon the State to prove beyond a reasonable doubt that the defense is untrue, and hence there must be an acquittal if there is a reasonable doubt as to whether defendant did act within the definition of that defense...."

[The statute] provides:

> Any person who kills another by misadventure, or in his or her own defense, or in the defense of his or her husband, wife, parent, child, brother, sister, master, mistress or servant, or who kills any person attempting to commit arson, burglary, kidnapping, murder, rape, robbery or sodomy, is guiltless and shall be totally acquitted and discharged.

The right to use deadly force was not absolute at common law; the defender only had a privilege to use reasonable force to prevent the commission of the felony or to protect the member of his household who was endangered. The codification of those privileges did not change this result, as indicated by the judicial limitations which have been placed on the defense of self-defense, wherein it is settled that to give rise to the right of self-defense the defendant must act under a reasonable belief that he is in imminent danger of bodily harm, and the privilege is limited to the utilization of that amount of force which the defender reasonably believed necessary to overcome the risk of harm.

There are, however, two approaches as to the scope of the right of one person to intervene in defense of another. One is that the fault of the defended party is imputed to the one who intervenes on his behalf, while the other is that the intervening party is bound only by his own intent. The former, commonly referred to as the "*alter ego*" rule, emphasizes that the right of one person to defend another is co-extensive with the right of the other to defend himself. The latter categorized as the "objective test" theory, proceeds on the thesis that one who intervenes in a struggle under a reasonable but mistaken belief that he is protecting another who he assumes is being unlawfully assaulted is thereby exonerated from criminal liability.

> "What is absolute truth no man ordinarily knows. All act from what appears, not from what is. If persons were to delay their steps until made sure, beyond every possibility of mistake, that they were right, earthly affairs would cease to move.... All, therefore, must, and constantly do, perform what else they would not, through mistake of facts...."

New Jersey has aligned itself with the latter view; the test of whether a party may intervene in defense of a third person being determined by the subjective intent of the intervener, subject only to the qualification that a jury objectively find that he reasonably arrived at the conclusion that the apparent victim was in peril, and that the force he used was necessary. Thus, the so-called "reasonable mistake of fact" doctrine is given its due, both as to the amount of force and the initial lawfulness of the intervention, and precludes criminal liability even though it later appears that the person in whose behalf he intervened was in fact the aggressor or that no defensive measures on his part were actually necessary. Such a view has been recommended by the American Law Institute in its Model Penal Code. The test should, in theory, apply not only to non-fatal crimes committed in defense of a third person, as was the situation in that case, but as well to the killing of any person attempting to commit the felonies or attack the persons enumerated in [the statute].

The defense is founded upon, and strengthened by, persuasive policy considerations. Not only is it just that one should not be convicted of a crime if he selflessly attempts to protect the victim of an apparently unjustified assault, but how else can we encourage bystanders to go to the aid of another who is being subjected to an assault?

Applying these general principles to the facts herein, a jury may well have been justified in finding that Lynn became involved in the affray in order to defend Fair against what appeared to him to be the murderous onslaught of a drunken man wielding a knife. Whether such a mental state existed at all, and if so whether it was reasonably entertained, are necessarily jury questions which cannot be determined by this Court. In any event, this question was so essentially involved in the factual context of this case that the trial court's failure to charge the jury on that issue *sua sponte* was nothing less than plain error requiring a reversal.

Comments and Questions

(1) Most modern statutes have rejected the requirement that the victim of the initial assault be a member of the immediate family. But see *Blankenship v. State*, 719 P.2d 829 (Okla. Crim. App. 1986), where the court noted that the state rule allowed the protection, by deadly force, only of a spouse, parent, child, master, mistress, or servant. In addition, most modern statutes reject the "alter ego" limitation and adopt the more expansive view set out by the New Jersey court. *See, e.g.*, Iowa Code § 704.3:

> A person is justified in the use of reasonable force when he or she reasonably believes that such force is necessary to defend himself or herself or another from any imminent use of unlawful force.

(2) The court in *State v. Pendley*, 593 P.2d 755, 756–57 (N.M. Ct. App. 1979), set out the facts in the case:

> An office party, followed by a party at the country club, continued at defendant's residence. Defendant went upstairs to use the bathroom, then rested on a bed. Defendant's wife found him, inquired if he was all right and kissed him. As the door closed upon his wife leaving the bedroom, defendant heard the victim say, 'why don't you kiss me the way you did Jerry [defendant]'. Defendant got up and, as he opened the door, he saw the victim push defendant's wife against the wall of the stairs 'and start pawing and trying to kiss her.'
>
> The victim refused to accede to several requests to leave. Defendant "knocked me [his wife] to the bedroom." Defendant went downstairs, got a pistol and told the victim 'you will leave now. Again he refused and started toward me.' The evidence is conflicting as to whether the victim was shot before there was a struggle for the pistol, or was shot while defendant and the victim were struggling for the pistol. Defendant testified that he got the pistol in order to force the victim from defendant's house since the victim had refused to leave. Defendant also testified that the victim never threatened defendant and never threatened defendant's wife "other than when he pushed her up against the stairway" and "he tried to kiss her."

The trial judge refused to give an instruction on defense of others. The order was affirmed.

> Defendant's requested instruction, to the effect that he shot the victim in defense of his wife, was also properly refused. The evidence did not support the requested instruction, which would have required defending his wife "from an attack." Defendant had "defended" his wife, by knocking her into the bedroom, before he went after his pistol.

Was the court correct? Taking the evidence in the light most favorable to the defendant, should the instruction have been given?

[C] Defense of Property

People v. Ceballos

Supreme Court of California
526 P.2d 241 (1974)

Burke, Justice.

Don Ceballos was found guilty by a jury of assault with a deadly weapon. He appeals from the judgment, contending primarily that his conduct was not unlawful because the alleged victim was attempting to commit burglary when hit by a trap gun mounted in the garage of defendant's dwelling and that the court erred in instructing the jury. We have concluded that the former argument lacks merit, that the court did not commit prejudicial error in instructing the jury, and that the judgment should be affirmed.

Defendant lived alone in a home in San Anselmo. The regular living quarters were above the garage, but defendant sometimes slept in the garage and had about $2,000 worth of property there.

In March 1970 some tools were stolen from defendant's home. On May 12, 1970, he noticed the lock on his garage doors was bent and pry marks were on one of the doors. The next day he mounted a loaded .22 caliber pistol in the garage. The pistol was aimed at the center of the garage doors and was connected by a wire to one of the doors so that the pistol would discharge if the door was opened several inches.

The damage to defendant's lock had been done by a 16-year-old boy named Stephen and a 15-year-old boy named Robert. On the afternoon of May 15, 1970, the boys returned to defendant's house while he was away. Neither boy was armed with a gun or knife. After looking in the windows and seeing no one, Stephen succeeded in removing the lock on the garage doors with a crowbar, and, as he pulled the door outward, he was hit in the face with a bullet from the pistol.

Stephen testified: He intended to go into the garage "[f]or musical equipment" because he had a debt to pay to a friend. His "way of paying that debt would be to take [defendant's] property and sell it" and use the proceeds to pay the debt. He "wasn't going to do it [i.e., steal] for sure, necessarily." He was there "to look around," and "getting in, I don't know if I would have actually stolen."

Defendant, testifying in his own behalf, admitted having set up the trap gun. He stated that after noticing the pry marks on his garage door on May 12, he felt he should "set up some kind of a trap, something to keep the burglar out of my home." When asked why he was trying to keep the burglar out, he replied, "... Because somebody was trying to steal my property ... and I don't want to come home some night and have the thief in there ... usually a thief is pretty desperate ... and ... they just pick up a weapon ... if they don't have one ... and do the best they can."

When asked by the police shortly after the shooting why he assembled the trap gun, defendant stated that "he didn't have much and he wanted to protect what he did have."

As heretofore appears, the jury found defendant guilty of assault with a deadly weapon. An assault is "an unlawful attempt, coupled with a present ability, to commit a violent injury on the person of another."

Defendant contends that had he been present he would have been justified in shooting Stephen since Stephen was attempting to commit burglary [and] defendant had a right to do indirectly what he could have done directly, therefore any attempt by him to commit a violent injury upon Stephen was not "unlawful" and hence not an assault. The People argue that as a matter of law a trap gun constitutes excessive force, and that in any event the circumstances were not in fact such as to warrant the use of deadly force.

The issue of criminal liability where the instrument employed is a trap gun or other deadly mechanical device appears to be one of first impression in this state, but in other jurisdictions courts have considered the question of criminal and civil liability for death or injuries inflicted by such a device.

At common law in England it was held that a trespasser, having knowledge that there are spring guns in a wood, cannot maintain an action for an injury received in consequence of his accidentally stepping on the wire of such gun. That case aroused such a protest in England that it was abrogated seven years later by a statute, which made it a misdemeanor to set spring guns with intent to inflict grievous bodily injury, but excluded from its operation a spring gun set between sunset and sunrise in a dwelling house for the protection thereof.

In the United States, courts have concluded that a person may be held criminally liable under statutes proscribing homicides and shooting with intent to injure, or civilly liable, if he sets upon his premises a deadly mechanical device and that device kills or injures another. However, an exception to the rule that there may be criminal and civil liability for death or injuries caused by such a device has been recognized where the intrusion is, in fact, such that the person, were he present, would be justified in taking the life or inflicting the bodily harm with his own hands. The phrase "were he present" does not hypothesize the actual presence of the person but is used in setting forth in an indirect manner the principle that a person may do indirectly that which he is privileged to do directly.

Allowing persons, at their own risk, to employ deadly mechanical devices imperils the lives of children, firemen and policemen acting within the scope of their employment, and others. Where the actor is present, there is always the possibility he will realize that deadly force is not necessary, but deadly mechanical devices are without mercy or discretion. Such devices "are silent instrumentalities of death. They deal death and destruction to the innocent as well as the criminal intruder without the slightest warning. The taking of human life [or infliction of great bodily injury] by such means is brutally savage and inhuman."

It seems clear that the use of such devices should not be encouraged. Moreover, whatever may be thought in torts, the foregoing rule setting forth an exception to liability for death or injuries inflicted by such devices "is inappropriate in penal law for it is obvious that it does not prescribea workable standard of conduct; liability depends upon fortuitous results." We therefore decline to adopt that rule in criminal cases.

Furthermore, even if that rule were applied here, as we shall see, defendant was not justified in shooting Stephen. Penal Code section 197 provides: "Homicide is ... justifiable ... 1. When resisting any attempt to murder any person, or to commit a felony, or to do some great bodily injury upon any person: or, 2. When committed in defense of habitation, property, or person, against one who manifestly intends or endeavors, by violence or surprise, to commit a felony ..." Since a homicide is justifiable under the circumstances specified in section 197, *a fortiori* an attempt to commit a violent injury upon another under those circumstances is justifiable.

By its terms subdivision 1 of Penal Code section 197 appears to permit killing to prevent any "felony," but in view of the large number of felonies today and the inclusion of many that do not involve a danger of serious bodily harm, a literal reading of the section is undesirable.

[T]he rule developed at common law that killing or use of deadly force to prevent a felony was justified only if the offense was a forcible and atrocious crime.

Examples of forcible and atrocious crimes are murder, mayhem, rape and robbery. In such crimes "from their atrocity and violence human life [or personal safety from great harm] either is, or is presumed to be, in peril."

Burglary has been included in the list of such crimes. However, in view of the wide scope of burglary under Penal Code section 459, as compared with the common law definition of that offense, in our opinion it cannot be said that under all circumstances burglary under section 459 constitutes a forcible and atrocious crime.[2]

Where the character and manner of the burglary do not reasonably create a fear of great bodily harm, there is no cause for exaction of human life or for the use of deadly force. The character and manner of the burglary could not reasonably create such a fear unless the burglary threatened, or was reasonably believed to threaten, death or serious bodily harm.

In the instant case, the asserted burglary did not threaten death or serious bodily harm, since no one but Stephen and Robert was then on the premises. A defendant is not protected from liability merely by the fact that the intruder's conduct is such as would justify the defendant, were he present, in believing that the intrusion threatened death or serious bodily injury. There is ordinarily the possibility that the defendant, were he present, would realize the true state of affairs and recognize the intruder as one whom he would not be justified in killing or wounding.

2. At common law burglary was the breaking and entering of a mansion house in the night with the intent to commit a felony. Burglary under Penal Code section 459 differs from common law burglary in that the entry may be in the daytime and of numerous places other than a mansion house, and breaking is not required. For example, under section 459 a person who enters a store with the intent of committing theft is guilty of burglary. It would seem absurd to hold that a store detective could kill that person if necessary to prevent him from committing that offense.

We thus conclude that defendant was not justified under Penal Code section 197, subdivisions 1 or 2, in shooting Stephen to prevent him from committing burglary.

Comments and Questions

(1) The New York statute, Penal Law § 35.20, is a detailed attempt to deal with the defense of property claim.

> 1. Any person may use physical force upon another person when he reasonably believes such to be necessary to prevent or terminate what he reasonably believes to be the commission or attempted commission by such other person of a crime involving damage to premises. He may use any degree of physical force, other than deadly physical force, which he reasonably believes to be necessary for such purpose, and he may use deadly physical force if he reasonably believes such to be necessary to prevent or terminate the commission or attempted commission of arson.
>
> 2. A person in possession or control of any premises, or a person licensed or privileged to be thereon or therein, may use physical force upon another person when he reasonably believes such to be necessary to prevent or terminate what he reasonably believes to be the commission or attempted commission by such other person of a criminal trespass upon such premises. He may use any degree of physical force, other than deadly physical force, which he reasonably believes to be necessary for such purpose, and he may use deadly physical force in order to prevent or terminate the commission or attempted commission of arson, as prescribed in subdivision one, or in the course of a burglary or attempted burglary, as prescribed in subdivision three.
>
> 3. A person in possession or control of, or licensed or privileged to be in, a dwelling or an occupied building, who reasonably believes that another person is committing or attempting to commit a burglary of such dwelling or building, may use deadly physical force upon such other person when he reasonably believes such to be necessary to prevent or terminate the commission or attempted commission of such burglary.

Does this statute properly set out rules as to the use of force, especially deadly force, in defense of one's property?

(2) Mildred Emmons shot and seriously injured Edward Gray with her rifle. Seeing Gray tampering with her car—and believing he was about to steal the car—she fired her gun at him. In fact, Gray worked for a commercial garage and was checking the serial numbers. The court stated the question of the case as follows:

> Where in good faith and upon reasonable grounds, one believes her automobile is being stolen from where it was parked in broad daylight on an unopen street (or private way)—may one shoot the person believed to be the thief in order to prevent the supposed larceny?

The court gave a negative answer. Do you agree? *Commonwealth v. Emmons*, 43 A.2d 568, 569 (Pa. Super. Ct. 1945). What should Ms. Emmons have done? Suppose Gray really was a thief? Suppose he had been armed? Would the result in either situation change? What result if Ms. Emmons came upon Gray while he was engaged in a burglary of her home?

(3) Would you enact this portion of the Revised Code of Washington?

§ 9A.16.110. Defending against violent crime—Reimbursement

(1) No person in the state shall be placed in legal jeopardy of any kind whatsoever for protecting by any reasonable means necessary, himself or herself, his or her family, or his or her real or personal property, or for coming to the aid of another who is in imminent danger of or the victim of assault, robbery, kidnapping, arson, burglary, rape, murder, or any other violent crime as defined in RCW 9.94A.030.

(2) When a person charged with a crime listed in subsection (1) of this section is found not guilty by reason of self-defense, the state of Washington shall reimburse the defendant for all reasonable costs, including loss of time, legal fees incurred, and other expenses involved in his or her defense. This reimbursement is not an independent cause of action. To award these reasonable costs the trier of fact must find that the defendant's claim of self-defense was sustained by a preponderance of the evidence. If the trier of fact makes a determination of self-defense, the judge shall determine the amount of the award.

(3) Notwithstanding a finding that a defendant's actions were justified by self-defense, if the trier of fact also determines that the defendant was engaged in criminal conduct substantially related to the events giving rise to the charges filed against the defendant the judge may deny or reduce the amount of the award. In determining the amount of the award, the judge shall also consider the seriousness of the initial criminal conduct. Nothing in this section precludes the legislature from using the sundry claims process to grant an award where none was granted under this section or to grant a higher award than one granted under this section.

(4) Whenever the issue of self-defense under this section is decided by a judge, the judge shall consider the same questions as must be answered in the special verdict under subsection (4) [(5)] of this section.

(5) Whenever the issue of self-defense under this section has been submitted to a jury, and the jury has found the defendant not guilty, the court shall instruct the jury to return a special verdict in substantially the following form:

Answer yes or no.

1. Was the finding of not guilty based upon self-defense?
2. If your answer to question 1 is no, do not answer the remaining questions.
3. If you answer to question 1 is yes, was the defendant:
   a. Protecting himself or herself?
   b. Protecting his or her family?

c. Protecting his or her property?

d. Coming to the aid of another who was in imminent danger of a heinous crime?

e. Coming to the aid of another who was the victim of a heinous crime?

f. Engaged in criminal conduct substantially related to the events giving rise to the crime with which the defendant is charged?

[D] Defense of Habitation

C. Carpenter, *Of the Enemy Within, the Castle Doctrine, and Self-Defense**

86 Marq. L. Rev. 653 (2003)

Where the generalized duty to retreat is imposed, the Castle Doctrine—or the privilege of non-retreat—serves as an exception. A colorful reference to feudal times, the term invokes the maxim that has wound its way into idiomatic English: "Every man's house is his castle." Generally, under the Castle Doctrine, those who are unlawfully attacked in their homes have no duty to retreat, because their homes offer them the safety and security that retreat is intended to provide. They may lawfully stand ground instead and use deadly force if necessary to prevent imminent death or great bodily injury, or the commission of a forcible felony. In this limited situation, without a jury instruction mandating retreat, the Castle Doctrine serves to place the non-aggressor in the same relative position as if in a non-retreat jurisdiction.

But rather than providing a settled exception to the generalized duty to retreat, the Castle Doctrine has evolved into a confusing patchwork of rules on when, and against whom, one may assume the privilege of non-retreat. Partly because of the complications of modern society—gone are the days when deadly conflicts primarily originated from outside the home—and partly because of the increased awareness of the privilege's impact on intimate violence, courts regularly question whether the duty to retreat should be fashioned differently depending on the status of the parties involved. Debate over the Castle Doctrine's applicability to cohabitants and invited guests, it appears, is generated by three competing and intersecting policies. First, there remains the overriding desire to protect the sanctity of life whenever possible. Second, and in seeming conflict, is the principled belief that the sanctity of one's home must be recognized, even in the face of loss of life. Third, and possibly the most problematic, is the degree of importance that should be attached to the shared property rights of the parties involved in the deadly encounter.

And so, caught between conflicting principles of traditional notions of self-defense and concomitant rights of possession, divergent opinions have emerged on the Castle Doctrine's applicability to cohabitants.... At the heart of the matter is a fundamental

---

disagreement: flight from home base, it is suggested by those that support the duty to retreat, is not really fraught with the same danger that existed in the Nineteenth Century when the Castle Doctrine's privilege of non-retreat was established. The decreased degree of danger, coupled with the fact that the parties involved are cohabitants, rather than strangers, requires a "heightened obligation to treat each other with a degree of tolerance and respect." Therefore, as against a deadly cohabitant with equal possessory rights, courts that support the duty to retreat hold that the protection of sanctity of life outweighs the slight risk of peril that such flight may bring. In creating a cohabitant exception to the Castle Doctrine, these courts found that the reasonableness of retreat significantly outweighs the Castle Doctrine's applicability in the home.

. . .

As an exception to the generalized duty to retreat, the Castle Doctrine sits at the intersection of two distinct but interrelated defenses: defense of habitation and self-defense. Defense of habitation is primarily based on the protection of one's dwelling or abode, and stems from the common law belief that a man's home is his castle. Essentially, the defense provides that the use of deadly force may be justified to prevent the commission of a felony in one's dwelling, although there is considerable discussion on whether the intrusion must be accompanied by the intent to commit a violent felony. Some courts require that defense of habitation only be asserted as against an external threat, and if that is true, then the defense cannot be claimed as against a cohabitant in lawful possession. Because the threat is of the commission of a forcible felony in the home, courts agree that there is no duty to retreat when claiming the defense of one's habitation. As stated forcefully by the Minnesota Supreme Court, "mandating a duty to retreat for defense of dwelling claims will force people to leave their homes by the back door while their family members are exposed to danger and their houses burgled."

Derived from similar roots, and potentially overlapping, is self-defense in the home. Whereas in defense of habitation, deadly force may be used to prevent the commission of an atrocious felony, in self-defense, deadly force may be used when necessary in resisting or preventing an offense which reasonably exposes the person to death or serious bodily harm. The contemplated need for self-defense in the home, therefore, is in some sense broader—it can be an external or internal attack—but it is narrower in its requirement that the attacker intends death or serious bodily harm. Some jurisdictions, in a formalistic attempt to separate the two defenses, provide that defense of habitation occurs until the point of intrusion, at which time the claim becomes self-defense in the home.

Because of the defenses' commonalities, their distinctions have often been blurred, and while the privilege of non-retreat is provided in each of these defenses, their rationales are somewhat different. In the case of defense of habitation, the Castle Doctrine allows the resident to stand ground and use deadly force against the intruder to protect the sanctity of the home from the attempted atrocious felony because the duty to retreat would be incompatible with the goal of preventing the commission of the felony. In the claim of self-defense in the home, the Castle Doctrine is based on two articulated rationales. Like the defense of habitation, standing one's ground is allowed to protect the sanctity of defendant's home, which has been violated by someone who intends great bodily harm or death to the resident. To that extent, self-defense in the home shares the same goal of defense of habitation. But, an additional factor not relevant to defense of habitation also supports the Castle Doctrine. Retreat into the home is, in essence, a retreat to the wall. Having retreated as far as possible, the actor should not be compelled to leave the sanctuary.

Given that the defense of habitation generally presupposes an intrusion by a non-resident, it is appropriate to provide a resident with the privilege of non-retreat in order to protect the dwelling. The trespasser intending the atrocious felony is seen as a threat to the peaceful possessory interest held by the resident, and the resident should not be obligated to retreat. Marking as fundamental the element of the intrusion, the New Hampshire Supreme Court stated,

> In our view, this "defense of dwelling" exception to the general rule that the force used in response to a threat should be proportionate is based upon the defender's interest in the premises and the assailant's status as an intruder. Because "implicit in the defense of dwelling defense is the notion that the dwelling is being defended against an intruder," the exception does not apply where the assailant is a cohabitant.

Self-defense in the home, however, differs from the defense of habitation in two respects: first, there is no specific requirement of intrusion by the aggressor; and second, the force used by the occupant need not be to protect the sanctuary against an atrocious felony. Together, these differences raise an interesting question where cohabitants are involved. In defense of habitation, where an intrusion is presupposed, there may be a question of whether the defense applies to an assault by a cohabitant, whom the law presumes is lawfully present in the home. However, in a claim of self-defense in the home, where no intrusion is required, the cohabitant's rightful presence should be less relevant to a successful claim.

...

An examination of Florida case law over the last twenty years illuminates this tension of perspective between two important and competing principles: the power of the sanctuary, and the emphasis on shared property rights. As a retreat jurisdiction that supports the Castle Doctrine, Florida case law slowly expanded the reach of the Castle Doctrine, first as against the deadly invitee, and by supposition at the time, to cohabitants as well. Although the policy to preserve life was elevated above other worthy principles, these cases held that it was still secondary to the importance of the personal dignity attached to one's sanctuary. But in dramatic fashion, and over a relatively short time span, the Florida Supreme Court first invoked a cohabitant exception to the Castle Doctrine because of the lawful occupancy of both parties; and then in a striking reversal, eliminated the exception by shifting its focus to emphasize the defendant's personal relationship with the sanctuary.

Comments and Questions

(1) In 2005, Florida became the first of 15 states by April 2006 to adopt a so-called "stand-your-ground" law:

776.012 Use of force in defense of person.

A person is justified in the use of force, except deadly force, against another when and to the extent that the person reasonably believes that such conduct is necessary to defend himself or herself or another against the such other's imminent use of unlawful force. However, a person is justified in the use of deadly force and does not have a duty to retreat only if:

(1) He or she reasonably believes that such force is necessary to prevent imminent death or great bodily harm to himself or herself or another or to prevent the imminent commission of a forcible felony; or

(2) Under those circumstances permitted pursuant to §776.013.

776.013 Home protection; use of deadly force; presumption of fear of death or great bodily harm.

(1) A person is presumed to have held a reasonable fear of imminent peril of death or great bodily harm to himself or herself or another when using defensive force that is intended or likely to cause death or great bodily harm to another if:

(a) The person against whom the defensive force was used was in the process of unlawfully and forcefully entering, or had unlawfully and forcibly entered, a dwelling, residence, or occupied vehicle, or if that person had removed or was attempting to remove another against that person's will from the dwelling, residence, or occupied vehicle; and

(b) The person who uses defensive force knew or had reason to believe that an unlawful and forcible entry or unlawful and forcible act was occurring or had occurred.

The presumption set forth in subsection (1) does not apply if:

(a) The person against whom the defensive force is used has the right to be in or is a lawful resident of the dwelling, residence, or vehicle, such as an owner, lessee, or titleholder, and there is not an injunction for protection from domestic violence or a written pretrial supervision order of no contact against that person; or

(b) The person or persons sought to be removed is a child or grandchild, or is otherwise in the lawful custody or under the lawful guardianship of, the person against whom the defensive force is used; or

(c) The person who uses defensive force is engaged in an unlawful activity or is using the dwelling, residence, or occupied vehicle to further an unlawful activity; or

(d) The person against whom the defensive force is used is a law enforcement officer, as defined in § 943.10(14), who enters or attempts to enter a dwelling, residence, or vehicle in the performance of his or her official duties and the officer identified himself or herself in accordance with any applicable law or the person using force knew or reasonably should have known that the person entering or attempting to enter was a law enforcement officer.

(3) A person who is not engaged in an unlawful activity and who is attacked in any other place where he or she has a right to be has no duty to retreat and has the right to stand his or her ground and meet force with force, including deadly force if he or she reasonably believes it is necessary to do so to prevent death or great bodily harm to himself or herself or another or to prevent the commission of a forcible felony.

(4) A person who unlawfully and by force enters or attempts to enter a person's dwelling, residence, or occupied vehicle is presumed to be doing so with the intent to commit an unlawful act involving force or violence.

776.031 Use of force in defense of others. A person is justified in the use of force, except deadly force, against another when and to the extent that the person reasonably believes that such conduct is necessary to prevent or terminate the such other's trespass on, or other tortious or criminal interference with, either real property other than a dwelling or personal property, lawfully in his or her possession or in the possession of another who is a member of his or her immediate family or household or of a person whose property he or she has a legal duty to protect. However, the person is justified in the use of deadly force only if he or she reasonably believes that such force is necessary to prevent the imminent commission of a forcible felony. A person does not have a duty to retreat if the person is in a place where he or she has a right to be.

776.032 Immunity from criminal prosecution and civil action for justifiable use of force.

(1) A person who uses force as permitted in § 776.012, § 776.013, or § 776.031 is justified in using such force and is immune from criminal prosecution and civil action for the use of such force, unless the person against whom force was used is a law enforcement officer, as defined in § 943.10(14), who was acting in the performance of his or her official duties and the officer identified himself or herself in accordance with any applicable law or the person using force knew or reasonably should have known that the person was a law enforcement officer. As used in this subsection, the term "criminal prosecution" includes arresting, detaining in custody, and charging or prosecuting the defendant.

(2) A law enforcement agency may use standard procedures for investigating the use of force as described in subsection (1), but the agency may not arrest the person for using force unless it determines that there is probable cause that the force that was used was unlawful.

(3) The court shall award reasonable attorney's fees, court costs, compensation for loss of income, and all expenses incurred by the defendant in defense of any civil action brought by a plaintiff if the court finds that the defendant is immune from prosecution as provided in subsection (1).

2005 Fla. S.B. 436 (2005).

Generally these laws give individuals the right to protect their homes or vehicles with deadly force against any unlawful or forceful intrusion, even if they do not fear for their safety or the safety of others. The laws also abolish any obligation to retreat from a public place. A. Liptak, *15 States Expand Victims' Rights on Self-Defense*, N.Y. Times, Aug. 7, 2006, at A12, Col. 2–6. *See also George v. State*, 159 So. 3d 90 (Ala. Crim. App. 2014), noting the local "stand your ground" statute removed the previous self-defense statute's express duty to retreat, and that the "no-duty-to-retreat" provision was not limited to a place someone has an ownership interest in; *Dorsey v. State*, 149 So. 3d 144 (Fla. Dist. Ct. App. 2014), holding that there was no duty to retreat even for a defendant engaged in unlawful activity at the time of the shooting. But see *Bretherick v. State*, 135 So. 3d 337 (Fla. Dist. Ct. App. 2013), which held that a motorist coming to a complete stop in front of the defendant's car in the center lane of a busy highway did not constitute false imprisonment or any other forcible felony, and thus did not justify defendant pointing a firearm at the motorist and holding him at gunpoint under the stand-your-ground law. The Florida Supreme Court would later hold in *Bretherick v. State*, 170 So. 3d 766 (Fla. 2015), that it is the defendant's burden to prove, by a preponderance of the evidence, that he was entitled to "stand your ground" immunity.

The Florida "stand your ground" statute, the first in the country, received intense nationwide scrutiny as a result of the killing of Trayvon Martin by George Zimmerman in February of 2012. Zimmerman, a Hispanic neighborhood watch volunteer (and criminal justice major), reported a "suspicious" person to 911 in his gated community. What followed is disputed as to whether Zimmerman pursued Martin, a 17-year-old African-American, or Martin confronted Zimmerman, but Zimmerman shot and killed Martin. Martin was returning home from having bought a bottle of tea and Skittles candy and no weapon was found on him. The local police chief did not bring charges against Zimmerman, citing the Florida statute. After appointment of a special prosecutor, charges of second degree murder were brought against Zimmerman. Zimmerman was acquitted of murder and manslaughter, without utilization of the "stand your ground" provisions by defense counsel.

Since the Florida statute was passed, over 30 states have passed some part of the statute. Who should get the benefit of a legal presumption as to whether deadly force was or was not in self-defense—the decedent or the user of deadly force? Aside from this determination, should there be a heightened immunity from civil prosecution or criminal charges in these circumstances? Should Zimmerman's assertion that his neighborhood and he had experienced previous crimes in their neighborhood, either by teenagers or African-Americans, be relevant to his defense under *Goetz*?

[E] Prevention of Crime

Tennessee v. Garner

United States Supreme Court
471 U.S. 1 (1985)

JUSTICE WHITE delivered the opinion of the Court.

This case requires us to determine the constitutionality of the use of deadly force to prevent the escape of an apparently unarmed suspected felon. We conclude that such force may not be used unless it is necessary to prevent the escape and the officer has probable cause to believe that the suspect poses a significant threat of death or serious physical injury to the officer or others.

I.

At about 10:45 P.M. on October 3, 1974, Memphis Police Officers Elton Hymon and Leslie Wright were dispatched to answer a "prowler inside call." Upon arriving at the scene they saw a woman standing on her porch and gesturing toward the adjacent house. She told them she had heard glass breaking and that "they" or "someone" was breaking in next door. While Wright radioed the dispatcher to say that they were on the scene, Hymon went behind the house. He heard a door slam and saw someone run across the back yard. The fleeing suspect, who was appellee-respondent's decedent, Edward Garner, stopped at a 6-feet-high chain link fence at the edge of the yard. With the aid of a flashlight, Hymon was able to see Garner's face and hands. He saw no sign of a weapon, and though not certain, was "reasonably sure" and "figured" that Garner was unarmed. He thought Garner was 17 or 18 years old and about 5'5" or 5'7" tall.[2] While Garner was crouched at the base of the fence, Hymon called out "police, halt" and took a few steps toward him. Garner then began to climb over the fence. Convinced that if Garner made it over the fence he would elude capture, Hymon shot him. The bullet hit Garner in the back of the head. Garner was taken by ambulance to a hospital, where he died on the operating table. Ten dollars and a purse taken from the house were found on his body.

In using deadly force to prevent the escape, Hymon was acting under the authority of a Tennessee statute and pursuant to Police Department policy. The statute provides that "[i]f, after notice of the intention to arrest the defendant, he either flee or forcibly resist, the officer may use all the necessary means to effect the arrest." The Department policy was slightly more restrictive than the statute, but still allowed the use of deadly force in cases of burglary. The incident was reviewed by the Memphis Police Firearms Review Board and presented to a grand jury. Neither took any action.

2. In fact, Garner, an eighth-grader, was 15. He was 5'4" tall and weighed somewhere around 100 or 110 pounds.

Garner's father then brought this action in the Federal District Court for the Western District of Tennessee, seeking damages under 42 U.S.C. § 1983 for asserted violations of Garner's constitutional rights. The complaint alleged that the shooting violated the Fourth,[6] Fifth, Sixth, Eighth, and Fourteenth Amendments of the United States Constitution. It named as defendants Officer Hymon, the Police Department, its Director, and the Mayor and city of Memphis. After a 3-day bench trial, the District Court entered judgment for all defendants. It dismissed the claims against the Mayor and the Director for lack of evidence. It then concluded that Hymon's actions were authorized by the Tennessee statute, which in turn was constitutional. Hymon had employed the only reasonable and practicable means of preventing Garner's escape. Garner had "recklessly and heedlessly" attempted to vault over the fence to escape, thereby assuming the risk of being fired upon. The Court of Appeals reversed.[7]

II.

Whenever an officer restrains the freedom of a person to walk away, he has seized that person. While it is not always clear just when minimal police interference becomes a seizure, there can be no question that apprehension by the use of deadly force is a seizure subject to the reasonableness requirement of the Fourth Amendment.

A.

A police officer may arrest a person if he has probable cause to believe that person committed a crime. Petitioners and appellant argue that if this requirement is satisfied the Fourth Amendment has nothing to say about *how* that seizure is made. This submission ignores the many cases in which this Court, by balancing the extent of the intrusion against the need for it, has examined the reasonableness of the manner in which a search or seizure is conducted. To determine the constitutionality of a seizure, "[w]e must balance the nature and quality of the intrusion on the individual's Fourth Amendment interest against the importance of the governmental interests alleged to justify the intrusion." We have described "the balancing of competing interests" as

6. "The right of the people to be secure in their persons ... against unreasonable searches and seizures, shall not be violated...." U.S. Const., Amend. IV.

7. The Court of Appeals concluded that the rule set out in the Model Penal Code "accurately states Fourth Amendment limitations on the use of deadly force against fleeing felons." The relevant portion of the Model Penal Code provides:

> "The use of deadly force is not justifiable ... unless (i) the arrest is for a felony; and (ii) the person effecting the arrest is authorized to act as a peace officer or is assisting a person whom he believes to be authorized to act as a peace officer; and (iii) the actor believes that the force employed creates no substantial risk of injury to innocent persons; and (iv) the actor believes that (1) the crime for which the arrest is made involved conduct including the use or threatened use of deadly force; or (2) there is a substantial risk that the person to be arrested will cause death or serious bodily harm if his apprehension is delayed."

American Law Institute, Model Penal Code 3.07(2)(b) (Proposed Official Draft 1962).

"the key principle of the Fourth Amendment." Because one of the factors is the extent of the intrusion, it is plain that reasonableness depends on not only when a seizure is made, but also how it is carried out.

B.

The ... balancing process demonstrates ... that, notwithstanding probable cause to seize a suspect, an officer may not always do so by killing him. The intrusiveness of a seizure by means of deadly force is unmatched. The suspect's fundamental interest in his own life need not be elaborated upon. The use of deadly force also frustrates the interest of the individual, and of society, in judicial determination of guilt and punishment. Against these interests are ranged governmental interests in effective law enforcement. It is argued that overall violence will be reduced by encouraging the peaceful submission of suspects who know that they may be shot if they flee. Effectiveness in making arrests requires the resort to deadly force, or at least the meaningful threat thereof. "Being able to arrest such individuals is a condition precedent to the state's entire system of law enforcement."

Without in any way disparaging the importance of these goals, we are not convinced that the use of deadly force is a sufficiently productive means of accomplishing them to justify the killing of non-violent suspects. The use of deadly force is a self-defeating way of apprehending a suspect and so setting the criminal justice mechanism in motion. If successful, it guarantees that that mechanism will not be set in motion. And while the meaningful threat of deadly force might be thought to lead to the arrest of more live suspects by discouraging escape attempts, the presently available evidence does not support this thesis. The fact is that a majority of police departments in this country have forbidden the use of deadly force in arresting nondangerous felons, there is a substantial basis for doubting that the use of such force is an essential attribute of the arrest power in all felony cases. Petitioners and appellant have not persuaded us that shooting nondangerous fleeing suspects is so vital as to outweigh the suspect's interest in his own life.

It is not, however, unconstitutional on its face. Where the officer has probable cause to believe that the suspect poses a threat of serious physical harm, either to the officer or to others, it is not constitutionally unreasonable to prevent escape by using deadly force. Thus, if the suspect threatens the officer with a weapon or there is probable cause to believe that he has committed a crime involving the infliction or threatened infliction of serious physical harm, deadly force may be used if necessary to prevent escape, and if, where feasible, some warning has been given. As applied in such circumstances, the Tennessee statute would pass constitutional muster.

III.

A.

It is insisted that the Fourth Amendment must be construed in light of the common-law rule, which allowed the use of whatever force was necessary to effect the arrest of a fleeing felon, though not a misdemeanant. As stated in Hale's posthumously published Pleas of the Crown:

> "[I]f persons that are pursued by these officers for felony or the just suspicion thereof ... shall not yield themselves to these officers, but shall either resist or fly before they are apprehended or being apprehended shall rescue themselves and resist or fly so that they cannot be otherwise taken, it is no felony."

Most American jurisdictions also imposed a flat prohibition against the use of deadly force to stop a fleeing misdemeanant, coupled with a general privilege to use such force to stop a fleeing felon.

The State and city argue that because this was the prevailing rule at the time of the adoption of the Fourth Amendment and for some time thereafter, and is still in force in some States, use of deadly force against a fleeing felon must be "reasonable." It is true that this Court has often looked to the common law in evaluating the reasonableness, for Fourth Amendment purposes, of police activity. On the other hand, it "has not simply frozen into constitutional law those law enforcement practices that existed at the time of the Fourth Amendment's passage." Because of sweeping changes in the legal and technological context, reliance on the common-law rule in this case would be a mistaken literalism that ignores the purposes of a historical inquiry.

B.

It has been pointed out many times that the common-law rule is best understood in light of the fact that it arose at a time when virtually all felonies were punishable by death. Though effected without the protections and formalities of an orderly trial and conviction, the killing of a resisting or fleeing felon resulted in no greater consequences than those authorized for punishment of the felony of which the individual was charged or suspected. Courts have also justified the common-law rule by emphasizing the relative dangerousness of felons.

Neither of these justifications makes sense today. Almost all crimes formerly punishable by death no longer are or can be. And while in earlier times "the gulf between the felonies and the minor offences was broad and deep," today the distinction is minor and often arbitrary. Many crimes classified as misdemeanors, or nonexistent, at common law are now felonies. These changes have undermined the concept, which was questionable to begin with, that use of deadly force against a fleeing felon is merely a speedier execution of someone who has already forfeited his life. They have also made the assumption that a "felon" is more dangerous than a misdemeanant untenable. Indeed, numerous misdemeanors involve conduct more dangerous than many felonies.

There is an additional reason why the common-law rule cannot be directly translocated to the present day. The common-law rule developed at a time when weapons were rudimentary. Deadly force could be inflicted almost solely in a hand-to-hand struggle during which, necessarily, the safety of the arresting officer was at risk. Handguns were not carried by police officers until the latter half of the last century. Only then did it become possible to use deadly force from a distance as a means of apprehension. As a practical matter, the use of deadly force under the standard articulation of the common-law rule has an altogether different meaning—and harsher consequences—now than in past centuries.

In short, though the common-law pedigree of Tennessee's rule is pure on its face, changes in the legal and technological context mean the rule is distorted almost beyond recognition when literally applied.

C.

In evaluating the reasonableness of police procedures under the Fourth Amendment, we have also looked to prevailing rules in individual jurisdictions. Some 19 States have codified the common-law rule, though in two of these the courts have significantly limited the statute. Four States, though without a relevant statute, apparently retain the common-law rule. Two States have adopted the Model Penal Code's provision verbatim. Eighteen others allow, in slightly varying language, the use of deadly force only if the suspect has committed a felony involving the use or threat of physical or deadly force, or is escaping with a deadly weapon, or is likely to endanger life or inflict serious physical injury if not arrested. Louisiana and Vermont, though without statutes or case law on point, do forbid the use of deadly force to prevent any but violent felonies. The remaining States either have no relevant statute or caselaw, or have positions that are unclear.

It cannot be said that there is a constant or overwhelming trend away from the common-law rule. In recent years, some States have reviewed their laws and expressly rejected abandonment of the common-law rule. The Federal Bureau of Investigation and the New York City Police Department, for example, both forbid the use of firearms except when necessary to prevent death or grievous bodily harm. For accreditation by the Commission on Accreditation for Law Enforcement Agencies, a department must restrict the use of deadly force to situations where "the officer reasonably believes that the action is in defense of human life…, or in defense of any person in immediate danger of serious physical injury." A 1974 study reported that the police department regulations in a majority of the large cities of the United States allowed the firing of a weapon only when a felon presented a threat of death or serious bodily harm. Overall, only 7.5% of departmental and municipal policies explicitly permit the use of deadly force against any felon; 86.8% explicitly do not. In light of the rules adopted by those who must actually administer them, the older and fading common-law view is a dubious indicium of the constitutionality of the Tennessee statute now before us.

D.

Actual departmental policies are important for an additional reason. We would hesitate to declare a police practice of long standing "unreasonable" if doing so would severely hamper effective law enforcement. But the indications are to the contrary. There has been no suggestion that crime has worsened in any way in jurisdictions that have adopted, by legislation or departmental policy, rules similar to that announced today. *Amici* noted that "[a]fter extensive research and consideration, [they] have concluded that laws permitting police officers to use deadly force to apprehend unarmed, non-violent fleeing felony suspects actually do not protect citizens or law enforcement officers, do not deter crime or alleviate problems caused by crime, and do not improve the crime-fighting ability of law enforcement agencies." The submission is that the obvious state interests in apprehension are not sufficiently served to warrant the use of lethal weapons against all fleeing felons.

Nor do we agree with petitioners and appellant that the rule we have adopted requires the police to make impossible, split-second evaluations of unknowable facts. We do not deny the practical difficulties of attempting to assess the suspect's dangerousness. However, similarly difficult judgments must be made by the police in equally uncertain circumstances. Nor is there any indication that in States that allow the use of deadly force only against dangerous suspects, the standard has been difficult to apply or has led to a rash of litigation involving inappropriate second-guessing of police officers' split-second decisions. Moreover, the highly technical felony/misdemeanor distinction is equally, if not more, difficult to apply in the field. An officer is in no position to know, for example, the precise value of property stolen, or whether the crime was a first or second offense. Finally, as noted above, this claim must be viewed with suspicion in light of the similar self-imposed limitations of so many police departments.

IV.

The District Court concluded that Hymon was justified in shooting Garner because state law allows, and the Federal Constitution does not forbid, the use of deadly force to prevent the escape of a fleeing felony suspect if no alternative means of apprehension is available. This conclusion made a determination of Garner's apparent dangerousness unnecessary. The court did find, however, that Garner appeared to be unarmed, though Hymon could not be certain that was the case. Restated in Fourth Amendment terms, this means Hymon had no articulable basis to think Garner was armed.

In reversing, the Court of Appeals accepted the District Court's factual conclusions and held that "the facts, as found, did not justify the use of deadly force." We agree. Officer Hymon could not reasonably have believed that Garner—young, light, and unarmed—posed any threat. Indeed, Hymon never attempted to justify his actions on any basis other than the need to prevent an escape. The District Court stated in passing that "[t]he facts of this case did not indicate to Officer Hymon that Garner was 'non-dangerous.'" This conclusion is not explained, and seems to be based solely on the fact that Garner had broken into a house at night. However, the fact that Garner was a suspected burglar could not, without regard to the other circumstances, automatically justify the use of deadly force. Hymon did not have probable cause to believe that Garner, whom he correctly believed to be unarmed, posed any physical danger to himself or others.

The dissent argues that the shooting was justified by the fact that Officer Hymon had probable cause to believe that Garner had committed a nighttime burglary. While we agree that burglary is a serious crime, we cannot agree that it is so dangerous as automatically to justify the use of deadly force. The FBI classifies burglary as a "property" rather than a "violent" crime.[22] Although the armed burglar would present a

---

22. In a recent report, the Department of Corrections of the District of Columbia also noted that

different situation, the fact that an unarmed suspect has broken into a dwelling at night does not automatically mean he is physically dangerous. This case demonstrates as much. In fact, the available statistics demonstrate that burglaries only rarely involve physical violence. During the 10-year period from 1973–1982, only 3.8% of all burglaries involved violent crime.[23]

The judgment of the Court of Appeals is affirmed, and the case is remanded for further proceedings consistent with this opinion.

So ordered.

Justice O'Connor, with whom The Chief Justice and Justice Rehnquist join, dissenting.

Although the circumstances of this case are unquestionably tragic and unfortunate, our constitutional holdings must be sensitive both to the history of the Fourth Amendment and to the general implications of the court's reasoning. By disregarding the serious and dangerous nature of residential burglaries and the longstanding practice of many States, the Court effectively creates a Fourth Amendment right allowing a burglary suspect to flee unimpeded from a police officer who has probable cause to arrest, who has ordered the suspect to halt, and who has no means short of firing his weapon to prevent escape. I do not believe that the Fourth Amendment supports such a right, and I accordingly dissent.

The issue is not the constitutional validity of the Tennessee statute on its face or as applied to some hypothetical set of facts. Instead, the issue is whether the use of deadly force by Officer Hymon under the circumstances of this case violated Garner's constitutional rights. Thus, the majority's assertion that a police officer who has probable cause to seize a suspect "may not always do so by killing him," is unexceptionable but also of little relevance to the question presented here. The same is true of the rhetorically stirring statement that "[t]he use of deadly force to prevent the escape of all felony suspects, whatever the circumstances, is constitutionally unreasonable." The question we must address is whether the Constitution allows the use of such force to apprehend a suspect who resists arrest by attempting to flee the scene of a nighttime burglary of a residence.

"there is nothing inherently dangerous or violent about the offense," which is a crime against property.

23. The dissent points out that three-fifths of all rapes in the home, three-fifths of all home robberies, and about a third of home assaults are committed by burglars. These figures mean only that if one knows that a suspect committed a rape in the home, there is a good chance that the suspect is also a burglar. That has nothing to do with the question here, which is whether the fact that someone has committed a burglary indicates that he has committed, or might commit, a violent crime.

The dissent also points out that this 3.8% adds up to 2.8 million violent crimes over a 10-year period, as if to imply that today's holding will let loose 2.8 million violent burglars. The relevant universe is, of course, far smaller. At issue is only that tiny fraction of cases where violence has taken place and an officer who has no other means of apprehending the suspect is unaware of its occurrence.

The public interest involved in the use of deadly force as a last resort to apprehend a fleeing burglary suspect relates primarily to the serious nature of the crime. Household burglaries represent not only the illegal entry into a person's home, but also "pos[e] real risk of serious harm to others." According to recent Department of Justice statistics, "[t]hree-fifths of all rapes in the home, three-fifths of all home robberies, and about a third of home aggravated and simple assaults are committed by burglars." During the period 1973–1982, 2.8 million such violent crimes were committed in the course of burglaries. Victims of a forcible intrusion into their home by a nighttime prowler will find little consolation in the majority's confident assertion that "burglaries only rarely involve physical violence." Moreover, even if a particular burglary, when viewed in retrospect, does not involve physical harm to others, the "harsh potentialities for violence" inherent in the forced entry into a home preclude characterization of the crime as "innocuous, inconsequential, minor, or 'nonviolent.'"

Because burglary is a serious and dangerous felony, the public interest in the prevention and detection of the crime is of compelling importance. Where a police officer has probable cause to arrest a suspected burglar, the use of deadly force as a last resort might well be the only means of apprehending the suspect. With respect to a particular burglary, subsequent investigation simply cannot represent a substitute for immediate apprehension of the criminal suspect at the scene.

The Court unconvincingly dismisses the general deterrence effects by stating that "the presently available evidence does not support [the] thesis" that the threat of force discourages escape and that "there is a substantial basis for doubting that the use of such force is an essential attribute to the arrest power in all felony cases." There is no question that the effectiveness of police use of deadly force is arguable and that many States or individual police departments have decided not to authorize it in circumstances similar to those presented here. But it should go without saying that the effectiveness or popularity of a particular police practice does not determine its constitutionality.

Against the strong public interests justifying the conduct at issue here must be weighed the individual interests implicated in the use of deadly force by police officers. The majority declares that "[t]he suspect's fundamental interest in his own life need not be elaborated upon." This blithe assertion hardly provides an adequate substitute for the majority's failure to acknowledge the distinctive manner in which the suspect's interest in his life is even exposed to risk. For purposes of this case, we must recall that the police officer, in the course of investigating a nighttime burglary, had reasonable cause to arrest the suspect and ordered him to halt. The officer's use of force resulted because the suspected burglar refused to heed this command and the officer reasonably believed that there was no means short of firing his weapon to apprehend the suspect. Without questioning the importance of a person's interest in his life, I do not think this interest encompasses a right to flee unimpeded from the scene of a burglary.

A proper balancing of the interests involved suggests that use of deadly force as a last resort to apprehend a criminal suspect fleeing from the scene of a nighttime burglary is not unreasonable within the meaning of the Fourth Amendment. Admittedly, the events giving rise to this case are in retrospect deeply regrettable. No one can view the death of an unarmed and apparently nonviolent 15-year old without sorrow, much less disapproval. Nonetheless, the reasonableness of Officer Hymon's conduct for purposes of the Fourth Amendment cannot be evaluated by what later appears to have been a preferable course of police action. The officer pursued a suspect in the darkened backyard of a house that from all indications had just been burglarized. The police officer was not certain whether the suspect was alone or unarmed; nor did he know what had transpired inside the house. He ordered the suspect to halt, and when the suspect refused to obey and attempted to flee into the night, the officer fired his weapon to prevent escape. The reasonableness of this action for purposes of the Fourth Amendment is not determined by the unfortunate nature of this particular case; instead, the question is whether it is constitutionally impermissible for police officers, as a last resort, to shoot a burglary suspect fleeing the scene of the crime.

Comments and Questions

(1) Justice White discusses the "competing interests" in the balancing test required under the Fourth Amendment. What are those interests?

(2) Does the majority of the Court successfully resolve these competing interests? What of the dissenting Justices' point that "the effectiveness or popularity of a particular police practice does not determine its constitutionality"?

(3) Does section 18-4011 of the Idaho Criminal Code comply with *Garner*?

> **18-4011. Justifiable homicide by officer.**—Homicide is justifiable when committed by public officers and those acting by their command in their aid and assistance, either:
>
> 1. In obedience to any judgment of a competent court; or
>
> 2. When reasonably necessary in overcoming actual resistance to the execution of some legal process, or in the discharge of any other legal duty including suppression of riot or keeping and preserving the peace. Use of deadly force shall not be justified in overcoming actual resistance unless the officer has probable cause to believe that the resistance poses a threat of death or serious physical injury to the officer or to other persons; or
>
> 3. When reasonably necessary in preventing rescue or escape or in retaking inmates who have been rescued or have escaped from any jail, or when reasonably necessary in order to prevent the escape of any person charged with or suspected of having committed a felony, provided the officer has probable cause to believe that the inmate, or persons assisting his escape, or the person suspected of or charged with commission of a felony poses a threat of death or serious physical injury to the officer or other persons.

(4) Did the officer here have probable cause "to believe that the suspect pose[d] a threat of serious physical harm"? Why not? What result if the incident took place in the middle of the night, it was very dark and all the officer could see was that the suspect was a large, grown man?

(5) Could the officer have used deadly force to stop a burglary in progress? Could a homeowner?

Consider this scenario: An individual believes that an abortion clinic doctor is performing abortions that do not comply with all the applicable rules and regulations. The individual kills the doctor to prevent the crime of a technically illegal abortion. Is this a valid use of the defense of crime prevention? *See generally State v. Roeder*, 2014 WL 5408432 (Kan. 2014) for an analysis of this case under a necessity defense.

(6) Under *Garner*, what result would there be if a deputy terminated a high-speed car chase prompted by a speeding violation by pushing the car off the road, causing it to crash and killing the driver? In *Scott v. Harris*, 550 U.S. 372 (2007), the Supreme Court held that the deputy's use of deadly force was constitutional. The Court stated that car chase posed a "substantial and immediate risk of serious injury to others," and thus the use of force was reasonable whether or not the deputy's actions constituted deadly force.

In a per curiam decision, the Court also concluded that a police officer's firing at the engine block of a speeding car to disable it, which ultimately killed the driver, was not so unreasonable a use of force on the facts as to preclude the officer from having qualified immunity. The sole dissenting justice, Justice Sotomayor, noted that the officer fired six rounds in the dark at a car traveling 85 miles per hour, without any training in that tactic, despite the wait order of his superior officer, and less than a second before the car hit spike strips, which had been used to stop it. An officer has qualified immunity from a civil suit unless his conduct violated "clearly established statutory or constitutional rights of which a reasonable person would have known."

§ 7.02 Duress and Necessity

Problems

Killing of Others

(1) The defendant, following the mate's orders to spare women, children, and husbands, threw 14 male passengers from an overloaded life boat following a disaster at sea. Those remaining after the 14 males had been thrown overboard were saved and Holmes was prosecuted for manslaughter of one of the passengers. Holmes was convicted on an instruction of law that indicated that a seaman was obligated by his calling to sacrifice himself to save the passengers rather than vice versa.

(2) Three shipwrecked seamen killed a fourth member of their lifeboat to avoid starvation. Later the three survivors were rescued. The jury returned a special verdict reciting the facts and concluding that all four men would have died of starvation before rescue had they not sacrificed one to save the other three. The question of whether the facts established a charge of murder remained for the judgment of the

court. The court held that one was not justified in taking the life of another innocent person to save his own and found the persons guilty of capital murder.

Should the defendants be convicted of these crimes?

State v. Metcalf

Court of Appeals of Ohio
396 N.E.2d 786 (1977)

DOWD, JUDGE.

The defendant was convicted by a jury of a violation of R.C. 3719.44(D) in that "he did unlawfully sell, barter, exchange, give away or make offer therefor an hallucinogen, *i.e.*, marijuana."

The testimony was largely undisputed. On June 28, 1976, Thomas Berry, an undercover narcotics agent working with the Multi-County Narcotics Bureau, confronted Bart Luff about an earlier "bad drug" sale made by Luff to Berry. Berry was accompanied by Randy Imes. Imes, whose exact relationship with the Multi-County Narcotics Bureau was not disclosed, stands six feet two inches tall and weighs 275 pounds. He is the son of a deputy sheriff.

The issue raised on appeal arises from the defense of duress relied upon by the defendant who admitted to giving away a brick of marijuana to his cousin, Bart Luff, because of his fear for the safety of Bart Luff, his family, and himself. The trial court, despite the defendant's timely objection, limited the defense of duress to the fear which the defendant entertained on his own behalf, excluding the jury's consideration of the defendant's concern for the safety of his family.

Berry and Imes, after finding Luff, took him for a ride in Berry's automobile where he was physically manhandled by Imes, made to believe that his life was threatened, and told by Berry that Luff was to return the $120 previously paid by Berry for the bad drugs or, in the alternative, deliver good drugs. Berry and Imes were assisted in the threatening process by the appearance of a .357 magnum revolver admitted by Berry to be his weapon. Luff contended that he was threatened by Imes with the loaded .357 magnum. Imes and Berry both admitted that the weapon became evident when it slid onto the car floor and was recovered by Imes, but each denied that Luff was directly threatened with the weapon. Luff was led to believe that Berry had in turn sold the "bad drugs" to Imes and that Imes was demanding satisfaction. Berry referred to Imes as a wild man and, according to Imes' testimony, suggested that Imes was from Steubenville and a member of the "family" as in the "mafia."

After Luff, while still in the company of Berry and Imes, was unable to secure a loan from a friend, Charles Tony, or from his aunt, to make the demanded repayment, he suggested that his cousin, the defendant, might be of assistance. Berry and Imes drove Luff to the defendant's house. When Berry, Imes and Luff arrived at the defendant's house, the defendant, his wife, an adult relative, the three-year-old child of the defendant and his wife, and another three year old child were present. The Berry-Imes charade continued. Imes entered the defendant's home armed with the magnum wrapped in a jacket thrown over his arm. Luff begged his cousin, the defendant, for the money to save his life which he declared was threatened by Imes.

When the defendant and his wife indicated they had no available money to help Luff, the conversation turned to drugs as an alternative means of repayment for the "bad drugs" previously sold by Luff to Berry. Eventually the defendant agreed to produce a pound of marijuana if Imes would first leave the house. Imes left, going a short distance away. The defendant's wife then went outside to their van, secured a brick of marijuana and returned it to the defendant, who then, by his testimony, gave it to Luff and, by the testimony of Berry, gave it directly to Berry.

At trial, Berry, Imes, Luff, the defendant, his wife and an adult relative, Darrell Griffy, all present at the defendant's house where the delivery of the marijuana was made, testified to the events leading to the delivery. Luff, Griffy, the defendant and his wife each testified that they experienced fear for themselves and the children. Imes readily admitted the intimidation of Luff prior to the arrival at defendant's house and the fact of his armed presence in the house while the demand for money, or in the alternative, a demand for drugs, was made.

We begin with a consideration of whether the defense of duress for non-homicidal crimes may be predicated on fear for the safety of others. The common law defense of duress is long standing. It constitutes a claim that the defendant's apparent criminal conduct is negated by reason of the fact that he engaged in the conduct as a result of the threat of violence and from which threat he could not safely withdraw. However, the defense of duress is unavailable where one takes an innocent life.

Closely akin to the defense of duress is the common law defense of necessity.

> "[A]n act which would otherwise be a crime may be excused if the person accused can show that it was done only in order to avoid consequences which could not otherwise be avoided, and which, if they had followed, would have inflicted upon him, *or upon others whom he was bound to protect*, inevitable and irreparable evil; that no more was done than was reasonably necessary for that purpose; and that the evil inflicted by it was not disproportionate to the evil avoided."

[Ed.—The court's examples follow.]

> "1. A person is not guilty in joining a rebellion if it is necessary to save his life.
>
> "2. The crew of a vessel are not guilty of a crime in arising and deposing the master, if it is a case of necessity arising from the unseaworthiness of the vessel.
>
> "3. A vessel is not liable for a violation of the embargo laws where during a legitimate voyage she is obliged by stress of weather to take refuge in a proscribed port."

We set forth the law of the defense of necessity because it allows the defense to be invoked where the offender acts not only to protect himself but also to protect others whom he is bound to protect. Although only sparse authority exists on the issue of whether duress is available where the offender seeks to protect others such as the members of the family, we conclude that both reasoning and precedent in the context of the law of necessity dictate that the defense of duress may be invoked not only where the defendant fears for his own safety but, also, where he fears for the safety of others, in particular the members of his family. Accordingly, we find that the trial court erred to the prejudice of the defendant in failing to include in the instruction some reference to the defendant's concern for his wife, the children, his cousin and the guest in his house.

Comments and Questions

(1) In some ways *Metcalf* is an easy case, with Imes the large "Mafia" family man possessing a weapon. Suppose Imes was unknown to the defendant, did not have a weapon with him, and did not "manhandle" Luff. Would Imes' size and presence be sufficient to constitute duress? As noted in *State v. Harvill*, 234 P.3d 1166 (Wash. 2010), the threat looked at with the defense of duress need not be explicit: "So long as the defendant's perception of the implicit threat is reasonable under the circumstances, he is put to the choice between two evils through no fault of his own and should be allowed to argue the defense."

(2) The defendant in *United States v. Vasquez-Landaver*, 527 F.3d 798 (9th Cir. 2008), had an extensive immigration and criminal record and had frequently been deported. Coming back to the country unlawfully, he fought a criminal charge by contending that he had been threatened by police in his home town in El Salvador and was genuinely fearful of his safety if he remained there. The court rejected his duress defense, as "there was no evidence of a figurative gun to his head compelling his illegal entry." Did the judges there correctly apply the law? What if he could offer evidence of very real threats, though no "gun to his head"? The principles were laid out in *United States v. Sawyer*, 558 F.3d 705, 710–11 (7th Cir. 2009):

> The duress defense has its roots in common law, and excuses criminal conduct, even though the defendant engages in it with the requisite *mens rea*, because the defendant nevertheless acted under a threat of a greater immediate harm that could only be avoided by committing the crime charged.... [A] defendant attempting to present a defense of duress or coercion must show: (1) she reasonably feared immediate death or serious bodily harm unless she committed the offense; and (2) there was no reasonable opportunity to refuse to commit the offense and avoid the threatened injury. If the defendant had a reasonable alternative to violating the law, then the defense of duress will not lie. A defendant's fear of death or serious bodily injury is generally insufficient. Rather, "[t]here must be evidence that the threatened harm was present, immediate, or impending." [The] defendant must have ceased committing the crime as soon as the claimed duress lost its coercive force.

(3) The standard rule has always been that duress is no defense to the purposeful killing of another person. As stated in Blackstone, *Commentaries* 30: "He ought rather to die himself than escape by the murder of an innocent." Are there any situations in

which duress should be a defense to the purposeful killing of another? Reconsider the two problems at the start of this section. Consider also the facts in *State v. Glass*, 455 So. 2d 659 (La. 1984), where—according to the court—the jury could have found that the assailant put a loaded gun to the defendant's head and told him he would be killed immediately unless he shot the two victims. The defendant killed the two victims and was charged with first degree murder. At trial, he requested a jury instruction dealing with coercion. The trial court's refusal was affirmed on appeal.

> While coercion, or threats by Glass' accomplice (which we will accept as true for purpose of this argument), may in large part have affected Glass' motivation, i.e., to save his own life, this factor has no bearing on whether defendant had specific intent as required by the first degree murder statute.
>
> Under the facts of this case, the jury might properly conclude that by shooting both victims with the barrel of the pistol in contact with their heads, defendant had the specific intent to kill them. It is apparent that he "actively desired" to end their lives, regardless of the fact that his principal motivation may have been to save his own life.

In some jurisdictions, though, the defense of duress is permissible when the charge is *felony* murder. *See, e.g.*, *McMillan v. State*, 51 A.3d 623, 634–635 (Md. 2012) ("At common law, the rationale for barring the duress defense in a prosecution for murder was that a person 'ought rather to die himself than escape by the murder of an innocent.' ... This rationale disappears when the sole ground for the murder charge is that the defendant participated in an underlying felony, under duress, and the defendant's co-felons unexpectedly killed the victim, thereby elevating the charge to felony-murder. We conclude that if duress would serve as a defense to the underlying felony, it is also available as a defense to a felony-murder arising from that felony, assuming the criteria for such a defense are otherwise satisfied.").

(4) In two similar cases the trial court refused an instruction on duress. In *People v. Colgan*, 377 N.Y.S.2d 602 (App. Div. 1975), the defendant witnessed a killing. It was known that defendant was going to testify. Defendant received threats against his life as well as against his family. He informed the District Attorney of these threats and refused to testify. He was convicted of perjury (after changing his story). In *People v. Carradine*, 287 N.E.2d 670 (Ill. 1972), the defendant also witnessed a killing. She was found in contempt of court for refusing to testify, even after the following facts were adduced.

> [T]here seems little reason to doubt her refusal to testify resulted solely from her fear of harm to herself and her children if she testified against the defendants who apparently were members of the Blackstone Rangers, a youth gang.
>
> It is completely clear from the record that Mrs. Carradine understood the likely results of her refusal to testify and deliberately chose to incur imprisonment rather than expose herself and her family to what she considered to be the certainty of serious physical harm or death.

Should these defendants be punished for their actions?

(5) Can a defendant claim a duress defense if she has recklessly placed herself in a situation in which it was likely others would pressure her into committing a crime? In *Williams v. State*, 646 A.2d 1101 (Md. Ct. Spec. App. 1994), the Court held the defense is unavailable. Quoting the commentary to the Model Penal Code, the court found the defendant to be in a class "of persons who connect themselves with criminal activities, in which case too fine a line need not be drawn." The defendant had voluntarily become involved with a drug gang and the gang ordered him to be involved in a home break-in. *Cf. United States v. Zayac*, 765 F.3d 112 (2d Cir. 2014) (rejecting duress defense where defendant was accomplice to murder in course of drug deal and did not avail himself of reasonable opportunity to escape).

(6) As noted in *United States v. Sachdev*, 279 F.3d 25, 28–9 (1st Cir. 2002), several jurisdictions now allow judges to use evidence of duress to mitigate, even if the evidence is insufficient to establish a defense: "Even if the duress defense to criminal liability is rejected, a lesser showing of duress may still play a role at sentencing to permit a downward departure ... [That evidence] necessary to support a downward departure premised on duress is somewhat less than that necessary to support a defense of duress at trial."

(7) Can the state require the defendant to prove duress, or must the government disprove it? The Supreme Court in *Dixon v. United States*, 548 U.S. 1 (2006), conceded that Congress never actually considered the question of how the duress defenses should work. The Justices could find "no constitutional basis for placing upon the Government the burden of disproving petitioner's duress defense beyond a reasonable doubt."

United States v. Bailey

United States Supreme Court
444 U.S. 394 (1980)

MR. JUSTICE REHNQUIST delivered the opinion of the Court.

In the early morning hours of August 26, 1976, respondents Clifford Bailey, James T. Cogdell, Ronald C. Cooley, and Ralph Walker, federal prisoners at the District of Columbia Jail, crawled through a window from which a bar had been removed, slid down a knotted bed sheet, and escaped from custody. Federal authorities recaptured them after they had remained at large for a period of time ranging from one month to three and one-half months. Upon their apprehension, they were charged with violating 18 U.S.C. §751(a), which governs escape from federal custody. At their trials, each of the respondents adduced or offered to adduce evidence as to various conditions and events at the District of Columbia Jail, but each was convicted by the jury. The Court of Appeals for the District of Columbia Circuit reversed the convictions by a divided vote, holding that the District Court had improperly precluded consideration by the respective juries of respondents' tendered evidence. We granted certiorari, and now reverse the judgments of the Court of Appeals.

In reaching our conclusion, we must decide ... the elements that comprise defenses such as duress and necessity.

I.

All respondents requested jury trials and were initially scheduled to be tried jointly. At the last minute, however, respondent Cogdell secured a severance. Because the District Court refused to submit to the jury any instructions on respondents' defense of duress or necessity and did not charge the jury that escape was a continuing offense, we must examine in some detail the evidence brought out at trial.

The prosecution's case-in-chief against Bailey, Cooley, and Walker was brief. The Government introduced evidence that each of the respondents was in federal custody on August 26, 1976, that they had disappeared, apparently through a cell window at approximately 5:35 A.M. on that date, and that they had been apprehended individually between September 27 and December 13, 1976.

Respondents' defense of duress or necessity centered on the conditions in the jail during the months of June, July, and August 1976, and on various threats and beatings directed at them during that period. In describing the conditions at the jail, they introduced evidence of frequent fires in "Northeast One," the maximum-security cellblock occupied by respondents prior to their escape. Construed in the light most favorable to them, this evidence demonstrated that the inmates of Northeast One, and on occasion the guards in that unit, set fire to trash, bedding, and other objects thrown from the cells. According to the inmates, the guards simply allowed the fires to burn until they went out. Although the fires apparently were confined to small areas and posed no substantial threat of spreading through the complex, poor ventilation caused smoke to collect and linger in the cellblock.

Respondents Cooley and Bailey also introduced testimony that the guards at the jail had subjected them to beatings and to threats of death. Walker attempted to prove that he was an epileptic and had received inadequate medical attention for his seizures.

Consistently during the trial, the District Court stressed that, to sustain their defenses, respondents would have to introduce some evidence that they attempted to surrender or engaged in equivalent conduct once they had freed themselves from the conditions they described. But the court waited for such evidence in vain. Respondent Cooley, who had eluded the authorities for one month, testified that his "people" had tried to contact the authorities, but "never got in touch with anybody." He also suggested that someone had told his sister that the FBI would kill him when he was apprehended.

Respondent Bailey, who was apprehended on November 19, 1976, told a similar story. He stated that he "had the jail officials called several times," but did not turn himself in because "I would still be under the threats of death." Like Cooley, Bailey testified that "the FBI was telling my people that they was going to shoot me."

Only respondent Walker suggested that he had attempted to negotiate a surrender. Like Cooley and Bailey, Walker testified that the FBI had told his "people" that they would kill him when they recaptured him. Nevertheless, according to Walker, he called the FBI three times and spoke with an agent whose name he could not remember. That agent allegedly assured him that the FBI would not harm him, but was unable to promise that Walker would not be returned to the D. C. Jail.[2] Walker testified that he last called the FBI in mid-October. He was finally apprehended on December 13, 1976.

At the close of all the evidence, the District Court rejected respondents' proffered instruction on duress as a defense to prison escape.[3] The court ruled that respondents had failed as a matter of law to present evidence sufficient to support such a defense because they had not turned themselves in after they had escaped the allegedly coercive conditions. After receiving instructions to disregard the evidence of the conditions in the jail, the jury convicted Bailey, Cooley, and Walker of violating §751(a).

Two months later, respondent Cogdell came to trial before the same District Judge who had presided over the trial of his co-respondents. When Cogdell attempted to offer testimony concerning the allegedly inhumane conditions at the D. C. Jail, the District Judge inquired into Cogdell's conduct between his escape on August 26 and his apprehension on September 28. In response to Cogdell's assertion that he "may have written letters," the District Court specified that Cogdell could testify only as to "what he did ... [n]ot what he may have done." Absent such testimony, however, the District Court ruled that Cogdell could not present evidence of conditions at the jail. Cogdell subsequently chose not to testify on his own behalf, and was convicted by the jury of violating §751(a).

By a divided vote, the Court of Appeals reversed each respondent's conviction and remanded for new trials.

II.

Criminal liability is normally based upon the concurrence of two factors, "an evil-meaning mind [and] an evil-doing hand...." In the present case we must examine the circumstances under which the "evil-doing hand" can avoid liability because coercive conditions or necessity negate a conclusion of guilt even though the necessary *mens rea* was present.

Respondents contend that they are entitled to a new trial because they presented (or, in Cogdell's case, could have presented) sufficient evidence of duress or necessity to submit such a defense to the jury.

---

2. On rebuttal, the prosecution called Joel Dean, the FBI agent who had been assigned to investigate Walker's escape in August 1976. He testified that, under standard Bureau practice, he would have been notified of any contact made by Walker with the FBI. According to Dean, he never was informed of any such contact.

3. Respondents asked the District Court to give the following instruction:

Coercion which would excuse the commission of a criminal act must result from:

1) Threatening [*sic*] conduct sufficient to create in the mind of a reasonable person the fear of death or serious bodily harm;

2) The conduct in fact caused such fear of death or serious bodily harm in the mind of the defendant;

3) The fear or duress was operating upon the mind of the defendant at the time of the alleged act; and

4) The defendant committed the act to avoid the threatened [*sic*] harm.

Common law historically distinguished between the defenses of duress and necessity. Duress was said to excuse criminal conduct where the actor was under an unlawful threat of imminent death or serious bodily injury, which threat caused the actor to engage in conduct violating the literal terms of the criminal law. While the defense of duress covered the situation where the coercion had its source in the actions of other human beings, the defense of necessity, or choice of evils, traditionally covered the situation where physical forces beyond the actor's control rendered illegal conduct the lesser of two evils. Thus, where A destroyed a dike because B threatened to kill him if he did not, A would argue that he acted under duress, whereas if A destroyed the dike in order to protect more valuable property from flooding A could claim a defense of necessity.

Modern cases have tended to blur the distinction between duress and necessity. In the court below, the majority discarded the labels "duress" and "necessity," choosing instead to examine the policies underlying the traditional defenses. In particular, the majority felt that the defenses were designed to spare a person from punishment if he acted "under threats or conditions that a person of ordinary firmness would have been unable to resist," or if he reasonably believed that criminal action "was necessary to avoid a harm more serious than that sought to be prevented by the statute defining the offense." The Model Penal Code redefines the defenses along similar lines.

We need not speculate now, however, on the precise contours of whatever defenses of duress or necessity are available against charges brought under § 751(a). Under any definition of these defenses one principle remains constant: if there was a reasonable, legal alternative to violating the law, "a chance both to refuse to do the criminal act and also to avoid the threatened harm," the defenses will fail. Clearly, in the context of prison escape, the escapee is not entitled to claim a defense of duress or necessity unless and until he demonstrates that, given the imminence of the threat, violation of § 751(a) was his only reasonable alternative.

In the present case, the Government contends that respondents' showing was insufficient on two grounds. First, the Government asserts that the threats and conditions cited by respondents as justifying their escape were not sufficiently immediate or serious to justify their departure from lawful custody. Second, the Government contends that, once the respondents had escaped, the coercive conditions in the jail were no longer a threat and respondents were under a duty to terminate their status as fugitives by turning themselves over to the authorities.

Respondents, on the other hand, argue that the evidence of coercion and conditions in the jail was at least sufficient to go to the jury as an affirmative defense to the crime charged. As for their failure to return to custody after gaining their freedom, respondents assert that this failure should be but one factor in the overall determination whether their initial departure was justified. According to respondents, their failure to surrender "may reflect adversely on the bona fides of [their] motivation" in leaving the jail, but should not withdraw the question of their motivation from the jury's consideration.

We need not decide whether such evidence as that submitted by respondents was sufficient to raise a jury question as to their initial departures. This is because we decline to hold that respondents' failure to return is "just one factor" for the jury to weigh in deciding whether the initial escape could be affirmatively justified. On the contrary, several considerations lead us to conclude that, in order to be entitled to an instruction on duress or necessity as a defense to the crime charged, an escapee must first offer evidence justifying his continued absence from custody as well as his initial departure and that an indispensable element of such an offer is testimony of a bona fide effort to surrender or return to custody as soon as the claimed duress or necessity had lost its coercive force.

The Anglo-Saxon tradition of criminal justice, embodied in the United States Constitution and in federal statutes, makes jurors the judges of the credibility of testimony offered by witnesses. It is for them, generally, and not for appellate courts, to say that a particular witness spoke the truth or fabricated a cock-and-bull story. An escapee who flees from a jail that is in the process of burning to the ground may well be entitled to an instruction on duress or necessity, "'for he is not to be hanged because he would not stay to be burnt.'"

And in the federal system it is the jury that is the judge of whether the prisoner's account of his reason for flight is true or false. But precisely because a defendant is entitled to have the credibility of his testimony, or that of witnesses called on his behalf, judged by the jury, it is essential that the testimony given or proffered meet a minimum standard as to each element of the defense so that, if a jury finds it to be true, it would support an affirmative defense—here that of duress or necessity.

We therefore hold that, where a criminal defendant is charged with escape and claims that he is entitled to an instruction on the theory of duress or necessity, he must proffer evidence of a bona fide effort to surrender or return to custody as soon as the claimed duress or necessity had lost its coercive force. We have reviewed the evidence examined elaborately in the majority and dissenting opinions below, and find the case not even close, even under respondents' versions of the facts, as to whether they either surrendered or offered to surrender at their earliest possible opportunity. Since we have determined that this is an indispensable element of the defense of duress or necessity, respondents were not entitled to any instruction on such a theory. Vague and necessarily self-serving statements of defendants or witnesses as to future good intentions or ambiguous conduct simply do not support a finding of this element of the defense.

III.

In reversing the judgment of the Court of Appeals, we believe that we are at least as faithful as the majority of that court to its expressed policy of "allowing the jury to perform its accustomed role" as the arbiter of factual disputes. The requirement of a threshold showing on the part of those who assert an affirmative defense to a crime is by no means a derogation of the importance of the jury as a judge of credibility. Nor is it based on any distrust of the jury's ability to separate fact from fiction.

On the contrary, it is a testament to the importance of trial by jury and the need to husband the resources necessary for that process by limiting evidence in a trial to that directed at the elements of the crime or at affirmative defenses. If, as we here hold, an affirmative defense consists of several elements and testimony supporting one element is insufficient to sustain it even if believed, the trial court and jury need not be burdened with testimony supporting other elements of the defense.

These cases present a good example of the potential for wasting valuable trial resources. In general, trials for violations of § 751(a) should be simple affairs. The key elements are capable of objective demonstration; the *mens rea*, as discussed above, will usually depend upon reasonable inferences from those objective facts. Here, however, the jury heard five days of testimony. It was presented with evidence of every unpleasant aspect of prison life from the amount of garbage on the cellblock floor to the meal schedule to the number of times the inmates were allowed to shower. Unfortunately, all this evidence was presented in a case where the defense's reach hopelessly exceeded its grasp. Were we to hold, as respondents suggest, that the jury should be subjected to this potpourri even though a critical element of the proffered defenses was concededly absent, we undoubtedly would convert every trial under § 751(a) into a hearing on the current state of the federal penal system.

Because the juries below were properly instructed on the *mens rea* required by § 751(a), and because the respondents failed to introduce evidence sufficient to submit their defenses of duress and necessity to the juries, we reverse the judgments of the Court of Appeals and remand for reinstatement of the judgments of the District Courts.

Reversed.

MR. JUSTICE MARSHALL took no part in the consideration or decision of these cases.

MR. JUSTICE STEVENS concurred.

MR. JUSTICE BLACKMUN, with whom MR. JUSTICE BRENNAN joins, dissenting.

The Court's opinion, it seems to me, is an impeccable exercise in undisputed general principles and technical legalism: The respondents were properly confined in the District of Columbia jail. They departed from that jail without authority or consent. They failed promptly to turn themselves in when, as the Court would assert by way of justification, the claimed duress or necessity "had lost its coercive force." Therefore, the Court concludes, there is no defense for a jury to weigh and consider against the respondents' prosecution for escape violative of 18 U.S.C. § 751(a).

It is with the Court's assertion that the claimed duress or necessity had lost its coercive force that I particularly disagree. The conditions that led to respondents' initial departure from the D. C. jail continue unabated. If departure was justified—and on the record before us that issue, I feel, is for the jury to resolve as a matter of fact in the light of the evidence, and not for this Court to determine as a matter of law—it seems too much to demand that respondents, in order to preserve their legal defenses, return forthwith to the hell that obviously exceeds the normal deprivations of prison life and that compelled their leaving in the first instance. The Court, however, requires that an escapee's action must amount to nothing more than a mere and temporary gesture that, it is to be hoped, just might attract attention in responsive circles. But life and health, even of convicts and accused, deserve better than that and are entitled to more than pious pronouncements fit for an ideal world.

The Court, in its carefully structured opinion, does reach a result that might be a proper one were we living in that ideal world, and were our American jails and penitentiaries truly places for humane and rehabilitative treatment of their inmates. Then the statutory crime of escape could not be excused by duress or necessity, by beatings, and by guard—set fires in the jails, for these would not take place, and escapees would be appropriately prosecuted and punished.

But we do not live in an ideal world "even" (to use a self-centered phrase) in America, so far as jail and prison conditions are concerned. The complaints that this Court, and every other American appellate court, receives almost daily from prisoners about conditions of incarceration, about filth, and homosexual rape, and about brutality are not always the mouthings of the purely malcontent. The Court itself acknowledges, that the conditions these respondents complained about do exist. It is in the light of this stark truth, it seems to me, that these cases are to be evaluated. It must follow, then, that the jail-condition evidence proffered by respondent Cogdell should have been admitted, and that the jury before whom respondents Bailey, Cooley, and Walker were tried should not have been instructed to disregard the jail-condition evidence that did come in. I therefore dissent.

I.

The atrocities and inhuman conditions of prison life in America are almost unbelievable; surely they are nothing less than shocking. The dissent in the *Bailey* case in the Court of Appeals acknowledged that "the circumstances of prison life are such that at least a colorable, if not credible, claim of duress or necessity can be raised with respect to virtually every escape." And the Government concedes: "In light of prison conditions that even now prevail in the United States, it would be the rare inmate who could not convince himself that continued incarceration would be harmful to his health or safety."

A youthful inmate can expect to be subjected to homosexual gang rape his first night in jail, or, it has been said, even in the van on the way to jail. Weaker inmates become the property of stronger prisoners or gangs, who sell the sexual services of the victim. Prison officials either are disinterested in stopping abuse of prisoners by other prisoners or are incapable of doing so, given the limited resources society allocates to the prison system. Prison officials often are merely indifferent to serious health and safety needs of prisoners as well.

Even more appalling is the fact that guards frequently participate in the brutalization of inmates. The classic example is the beating or other punishment in retaliation for prisoner complaints or court actions.

The evidence submitted by respondents in these cases fit that pattern exactly. Respondent Bailey presented evidence that he was continually mistreated by correctional officers during his stay at the D. C. jail. He was threatened that his testimony in the Brad King case would bring on severe retribution. Other inmates were beaten by guards as a message to Bailey. An inmate testified that on one occasion, three guards displaying a small knife told him that they were going "to get your buddy, that nigger Bailey. We are going to kill him." The threats culminated in a series of violent attacks on Bailey. Blackjacks, mace and slapjacks (leather with a steel insert) were used in beating Bailey.

Respondent Cooley also elicited testimony from other inmates concerning beatings of Cooley by guards with slapjacks, blackjacks, and flashlights. There was evidence that guards threatened to kill Cooley.

It is society's responsibility to protect the life and health of its prisoners. "[W]hen a sheriff or a marshall [*sic*] takes a man from the courthouse in a prison van and transports him to confinement for two or three or ten years, *this is our act. We* have tolled the bell for him. And whether we like it or not, we have made him our collective responsibility. We are free to do something about him; he is not" (emphasis in original). Deliberate indifference to serious and essential medical needs of prisoners constitutes "cruel and unusual" punishment violative of the Eighth Amendment.

> An inmate must rely on prison authorities to treat his medical needs.... In the worst case, such a failure may actually produce physical "torture or a lingering death." ... In less serious cases, denial of medical care may result in pain and suffering which no one suggests would serve any penological purpose.... The infliction of such unnecessary suffering is inconsistent with contemporary standards of decency.

It cannot be doubted that excessive or unprovoked violence and brutality inflicted by prison guards upon inmates violates the Eighth Amendment. The reasons that support the Court's holding lead me to conclude that failure to use reasonable measures to protect an inmate from violence inflicted by other inmates also constitutes cruel and unusual punishment. Homosexual rape or other violence serves no penological purpose. Such brutality is the equivalent of torture, and is offensive to any modern standard of human dignity. Prisoners must depend, and rightly so, upon the prison administrators for protection from abuse of this kind.

There can be little question that our prisons are badly overcrowded and understaffed and that this in large part is the cause of many of the shortcomings of our penal systems. This, however, does not excuse the failure to provide a place of confinement that meets minimal standards of safety and decency.

Penal systems in other parts of the world demonstrate that vast improvement surely is not beyond our reach. "The contrast between our indifference and the programs in some countries of Europe—Holland and the Scandinavian countries in particular—is not a happy one for us." "It has been many years since Swedish prisoners were concerned with such problems as 'adequate medical treatments.'" Sweden's prisons are not overcrowded, and most inmates have a private cell. The prisons are small. The largest accommodate 300–500 inmates; most house 50–150. "There appears to be a relaxed atmosphere between staff and inmates, and a prevailing attitude that prisoners must be treated with dignity and respect."

II.

The real question presented in this case is whether the prisoner should be punished for helping to extricate himself from a situation where society has abdicated completely its basic responsibility for providing an environment free of life-threatening conditions such as beatings, fires, lack of essential medical care, and sexual attacks. To be sure, Congress in so many words has not enacted specific statutory duress or necessity defenses that would excuse or justify commission of an otherwise unlawful act. The concept of such a defense, however, is "anciently woven into the fabric of our culture." And the Government concedes that "it has always been an accepted part of our criminal justice system that punishment is inappropriate for crimes committed under duress because the defendant in such circumstances cannot fairly be blamed for his wrongful act."

Although the Court declines to address the issue, it at least implies that it would recognize the common law defenses of duress and necessity to the federal crime of prison escape, if the appropriate prerequisites for assertion of either defense were met. Given the universal acceptance of these defenses in the common law, I have no difficulty in concluding that Congress intended the defenses of duress and necessity to be available to persons accused of committing the federal crime of escape.

I agree with most of the Court's comments about the essential elements of the defenses. I, too, conclude that intolerable prison conditions are to be taken into account through affirmative defenses of duress and necessity, rather than by way of the theory of intent espoused by the Court of Appeals. That court's conclusion that intent to avoid the *normal* aspects of confinement is an essential element of the offense of escape means that the burden of proof is on the Government to prove that element. According to our precedents, the Government would have to prove that intent beyond a reasonable doubt. It is unlikely that Congress intended to place this difficult burden on the prosecution. The legislative history is sparse, and does not specifically define the requisite intent. Circumstances that compel or coerce a person to commit an offense, however, traditionally have been treated as an affirmative defense, with the burden of proof on the defendant. Although intolerable prison conditions do not fit within the standard definition of a duress or necessity defense they are analogous to these traditional defenses. I therefore agree that it is appropriate to treat unduly harsh prison conditions as an affirmative defense.

I also agree with the Court that the absence of reasonable less drastic alternatives is a prerequisite to successful assertion of a defense of necessity or duress to a charge of prison escape. One must appreciate, however, that other realistic avenues of redress seldom are open to the prisoner. Where prison officials participate in the maltreatment of an inmate, or purposefully ignore dangerous conditions or brutalities inflicted by other prisoners or guards, the inmate can do little to protect himself. Filing a complaint may well result in retribution, and appealing to the guards is a capital offense under the prisoners' code of behavior. In most instances, the question whether alternative remedies were thoroughly "exhausted" should be a matter for the jury to decide.

I, too, conclude that the jury generally should be instructed that, in order to prevail on a necessity or duress defense, the defendant must justify his continued absence from custody, as well as his initial departure. I agree with the Court that the very nature of escape makes it a continuing crime. But I cannot agree that the only way continued absence can be justified is by evidence "of a bona fide effort to surrender or return to custody." The Court apparently entertains the view, naive in my estimation, that once the prisoner has escaped from a life- or health-threatening situation, he can turn himself in, secure in the faith that his escape somehow will result in improvement in those intolerable prison conditions. While it may be true in some rare circumstance that an escapee will obtain the aid of a court or of the prison administration once the escape is accomplished, the escapee, realistically, faces a high probability of being returned to the same prison and to exactly the same, or even greater, threats to life and safety.

The rationale of the necessity defense is a balancing of harms. If the harm caused by an escape is less than the harm caused by remaining in a threatening situation, the prisoner's initial departure is justified. The same rationale should apply to hesitancy and failure to return. A situation may well arise where the social balance weighs in favor of the prisoner even though he fails to return to custody. The escapee at least should be permitted to present to the jury the possibility that the harm that would result from a return to custody outweighs the harm to society from continued absence.

Even under the Court's own standard, the defendant in an escape prosecution should be permitted to submit evidence to the jury to demonstrate that surrender would result in his being placed again in a life- or health-threatening situation. The Court requires return to custody once the "claimed duress or necessity had lost its coercive force." Realistically, however, the escapee who reasonably believes that surrender will result in return to what concededly is an intolerable prison situation remains subject to the same "coercive force" that prompted his escape in the first instance. It is ironic to say that that force is automatically "lost" once the prison wall is passed.

The Court's own phrasing of its test demonstrates that it is deciding factual questions that should be presented to the jury. It states that a "bona fide" effort to surrender must be proved. Whether an effort is "bona fide" is a jury question. The Court also states the "[v]ague and necessarily self-serving statements of defendants or witnesses as to future good intentions or ambiguous conduct simply do not support a finding of this element of the defense." Traditionally, it is the function of the jury to evaluate the credibility and meaning of "necessarily self-serving statements" and "ambiguous conduct."

Finally, I of course must agree with the Court that use of the jury is to be reserved for the case in which there is sufficient evidence to support a verdict. I have no difficulty, however, in concluding that respondents here did indeed submit sufficient evidence to support a verdict of not guilty, if the jury were so inclined, based on the necessity defense. Respondent Bailey testified that he was in fear for his life, that he was afraid he would still face the same threats if he turned himself in, and that "[t]he FBI was telling my people that they was going to shoot me." Respondent Cooley testified that he did not know anyone to call, and that he feared that the police would shoot him when they came to get him. Respondent Walker testified that he had been in "constant rapport," with an FBI agent, who assured him that the FBI would not harm him, but who would not promise that he would not be returned to the D. C. jail. Walker also stated that he had heard through his sister that the FBI "said that if they ran down on me they was going to kill me."

Perhaps it is highly unlikely that the jury would have believed respondents' stories that the FBI planned to shoot them on sight, or that respondent Walker had been in constant communication with an FBI agent. Nevertheless, such testimony, even though "self-serving," and possibly extreme and unwarranted in part, was sufficient to permit the jury to decide whether the failure to surrender immediately was justified or excused. This is routine grist for the jury mill and the jury usually is able to sort out the fabricated and the incredible.

In conclusion, my major point of disagreement with the Court is whether a defendant may get his duress or necessity defense to the jury when it is supported only by "self-serving" testimony and "ambiguous conduct." It is difficult to imagine any case, criminal or civil, in which the jury is asked to decide a factual question based on completely disinterested testimony and unambiguous actions. The very essence of a jury issue is a dispute over the credibility of testimony by interested witnesses and the meaning of ambiguous actions.

Ruling on a defense as a matter of law and preventing the jury from considering it should be a rare occurrence in criminal cases. "[I]n a criminal case the law assigns [the fact-finding function] solely to the jury." The jury is the conscience of society and its role in a criminal prosecution is particularly important. Yet the Court here appears to place an especially strict burden of proof on defendants attempting to establish an affirmative defense to the charged crime of escape. That action is unwarranted. If respondents' allegations are true, society is grossly at fault for permitting these conditions to persist at the D. C. jail. The findings of researchers and government agencies, as well as the litigated cases, indicate that in a general sense these allegations are credible. The case for recognizing the duress or necessity defenses is even more compelling when it is society, rather than private actors, that creates the coercive conditions. In such a situation it is especially appropriate that the jury be permitted to weigh all the factors and strike the balance between the interests of prisoners and that of society. In an attempt to conserve the jury for cases it considers truly worthy of that body, the Court has ousted the jury from a role it is particularly well-suited to serve.

Comments and Questions

(1) In order to raise the necessity defense, why must the defendant first show a "bona fide effort to surrender or return to custody as soon as the claimed duress or necessity had lost its coercive force"? What was the evidence showing such a bona

fide effort? Rejecting the *Bailey* approach is *State v. Baker*, 598 S.W.2d 540, 546 (Mo. Ct. App. 1980):

> The ... requirements of complaint to authorities and recourse to the courts have, of course, some reinforcing effect on the issue of credibility, but are likewise equally equated to policy arguments that, if another form of relief was available, escape should not be justified. No one could argue with the proposition that this is a valid policy—if effective relief is available, then escape is not justified.
>
> However, discussion of these conditions blunts the real thrust of the inquiry. The imminent danger of injury is the only basis for a defense of justification. That danger may arise suddenly and without opportunity for complaint or legal process....
>
> To summarize, the essential element which permits the submission of the defense of necessity is the imminence of danger to the person of the escapee. Voluntary return or attempts to do so and, in some instances of continued harassment, recourse to administrative and legal remedies will bear on issues of credibility. These issues bearing on the credibility of the prisoner's claim can be developed in the evidence and cross examination. All would be sources of argument to the jury based upon the record made at the trial. The jury can be trusted to separate the wheat from the chaff, and it is unlikely that escapes will be justified except in circumstances where the facts support the basic premise of immediate danger and the whole context of the situation supports the credibility of the claim made.

(2) Compare these two opinions in *United States v. Riffe*, 28 F.3d 565, 570, 571–72 (6th Cir. 1994):

Majority:

> The rule in *Bailey* is not a per se rule. *Bailey* recognizes that in most escape cases, an escapee will be able to remove himself from the threatened harm or duress by turning himself in to authorities. However, the case also recognizes that the escapee might be able to offer evidence "justifying his continued absence." In other words, there might be situations in which an escapee could offer evidence justifying his remaining at large because of the coercive force or duress that caused his initial escape. Similarly here, while the typical case will require a prisoner to attempt to seek help from prison authorities as an alternative to committing the crime, there may be cases in which the prisoner will be able to offer evidence justifying his decision not to go to prison authorities: that seeking help from prison authorities would not have been a reasonable legal alternative but instead would have subjected him to continued or additional physical harm.

Dissent:

> Under the majority's holding, if someone threatens a life and even though the threat is not immediate, the person threatened will be excused if he or

> she retaliates because society cannot guarantee that the threat will not be carried out. If we are to live in an ordered society, I believe the threatened person must take that chance and use legal means to stop the criminal from carrying out the threat. Defendant had a chance here to refuse to do the criminal act and avoid the threatened harm. He chose to commit further crimes over taking that chance. His evidence failed as a matter of law to reach the "minimum threshold" that would have required an instruction on duress.

(3) In *People v. White*, 397 N.E.2d 1246 (Ill. App. Ct. 1979), the defendant, while in jail, heard from a friend that his wife had been raped and his daughter beaten. He could not verify this by phone so he escaped and hitchhiked home. Two days later, he voluntarily turned himself in.

> The trial judge allowed an offer of proof by the defendant on the reasons for his escape, *i.e.*, that his wife had been raped and his daughter beaten. The offer was heard in order to determine the appropriateness of a necessity defense. The court then granted the prosecution's motion *in limine* and prohibited defendant from presenting to the jury evidence as to the reason for his escape and his subsequent voluntary surrender. The judge reasoned that defendant's wife had already been raped, the child already beaten, and they were already in the hospital. The court acknowledged the concern of the defendant but stated that that did not amount to necessity.

The trial judge's order was affirmed. Compare the argument made by defense counsel with that made by the government.

> A jury could have concluded that Mr. White's rushing to comfort his family in the hospital was a reasonable act of necessity in that his mental anguish outweighed any possible public harm that occurred. It was for the jury and not the trial judge to decide if the escape was "justified."

Brief and Argument for Defendant-Appellant at 7.

> The evidence offered by defendant wholly failed to establish that defendant *reasonably* believed that his escape was necessary to *avoid* a public or private injury greater than the injury which might reasonably result from his own conduct.

Brief and Argument for Plaintiff-Appellee at 7.

(4) For an interesting statutory response to the difficult questions involved with prison escapes, see N.C. Gen. Stat. 148-45(g):

> (1) Any person convicted and in the custody of the North Carolina Department of Correction and ordered or otherwise assigned to work under the work-release program, or any convicted person in the custody of the North Carolina Department of Correction and temporarily allowed to leave a place of confinement by the Secretary of Correction or his designee or other authority of law, who shall fail to return to the custody of the North Carolina Department of Correction, shall be guilty of the crime of escape and subject

> to the applicable provisions of this section and shall be deemed an escapee. For the purpose of this subsection, escape is defined to include, but is not restricted to, willful failure to return to an appointed place and at an appointed time as ordered.
>
> (2) If a person, who would otherwise be guilty of a first violation, voluntarily returns to his place of confinement within 24 hours of the time at which he was ordered to return, such person shall not be charged with an escape as provided in this section but shall be subject to such administrative action as may be deemed appropriate for an escapee by the Department of Correction; said escapee shall not be allowed to be placed on work release for a four-month period or for the balance of his term if less than four months; provided, however, that if such person commits a subsequent violation of this section then such person shall be charged with that offense and, if convicted, punished under the provisions of this section.

State v. Warshow

Supreme Court of Vermont
410 A.2d 1000 (1979)

Barney, Chief Justice.

The defendants were part of a group of demonstrators that traveled to Vernon, Vermont, to protest at the main gate of a nuclear power plant known as Vermont Yankee. The plant had been shut down for repairs and refueling, and these protestors had joined a rally designed to prevent workers from gaining access to the plant and placing it on-line.

They were requested to leave the private premises of the power plant by representatives of Vermont Yankee and officers of the law. The defendants were among those who refused, and they were arrested and charged with unlawful trespass.

The issue with which this appeal of their convictions is concerned relates to a doctrine referred to as the defense of necessity. At trial the defendants sought to present evidence relating to the hazards of nuclear power plant operation which, they argued, would establish that defense. After hearing the defendants' offer of proof the trial court excluded the proffered evidence and refused to grant compulsory process for the witnesses required to present the defense. The jury instruction requested on the issue of necessity was also refused, and properly preserved for appellate review.

In ruling below, the trial court determined that the defense was not available. It is on this basis that we must test the issue.

The defense of necessity is one that partakes of the classic defense of "confession and avoidance." It admits the criminal act, but claims justification.

In the various definitions and examples recited as incorporating the concept of necessity, certain fundamental requirements stand out:

(1) there must be a situation of emergency arising without fault on the part of the actor concerned;

(2) this emergency must be so imminent and compelling as to raise a reasonable expectation of harm, either directly to the actor or upon those he was protecting;

(3) this emergency must present no reasonable opportunity to avoid the injury without doing the criminal act; and

(4) the injury impending from the emergency must be of sufficient seriousness to outmeasure the criminal wrong.

It is the defendants' position that they made a sufficient offer of proof to establish the elements of the necessity defense to raise a jury question. The trial court rejected this contention on the ground, among others, that the offer did not sufficiently demonstrate the existence of an emergency or imminent danger.

This ruling was sound, considering the offer. The defendants wished to subpoena witnesses to testify to the dangers of nuclear accidents and the effect of low-level radiation. It was conceded that there had been no serious accident at Vermont Yankee, but defendants contended that the consequences could be so serious that the mere possibility should suffice. This is not the law.

There is no doubt that the defendants wished to call attention to the dangers of low-level radiation, nuclear waste, and nuclear accident. But low-level radiation and nuclear waste are not the types of imminent danger classified as an emergency sufficient to justify criminal activity. To be imminent, a danger must be, or must reasonably appear to be, threatening to occur immediately, near at hand, and impending. We do not understand the defendants to have taken the position in their offer of proof that the hazards of low-level radiation and nuclear waste build-up are immediate in nature. On the contrary, they cite long-range risks and dangers that do not presently threaten health and safety. Where the hazards are long term, the danger is not imminent, because the defendants have time to exercise options other than breaking the law.

Nor does the specter of nuclear accident as presented by these defendants fulfill the imminent and compelling harm element of the defense. The offer does not take the position that they acted to prevent an impending accident. Rather, they claimed that they acted to foreclose the "chance" or "possibility" of accident. This defense cannot lightly be allowed to justify acts taken to foreclose speculative and uncertain dangers. Its application must be limited to acts directly to the prevention of harm that is reasonably certain to occur. Therefore the offer fails to satisfy the imminent danger element. The facts offered would not have established the defense.

These acts may be a method of making public statements about nuclear power and its dangers, but they are not a legal basis for invoking the defense of necessity. Nor can the defendants' sincerity of purpose excuse the criminal nature of their acts.

Judgment affirmed.

HILL, JUSTICE, concurring.

While I agree with the result reached by the majority, I am unable to agree with their reasoning. As I see it, the sole issue raised by this appeal is whether the trial court erred in not allowing the defendants to present the defense of necessity.

Necessity has long been recognized at common law as a justification for the commission of a crime.

The defense of necessity proceeds from the appreciation that, as a matter of public policy, there are circumstances where the value protected by the law is eclipsed by a superseding value, and that it would be inappropriate and unjust to apply the usual criminal rule. The balancing of competing values cannot, of course, be committed to the private judgment of the actor, but must, in most cases, be determined at trial with due regard being given for the crime charged and the higher value sought to be achieved.

Determination of the issue of competing values and, therefore, the availability of the defense of necessity is precluded, however, when there has been a deliberate legislative choice as to the values at issue. The common law defense of necessity deals with imminent dangers from obvious and generally recognized harms. It does not deal with non-imminent or debatable harms, nor does it deal with activities that the legislative branch has expressly sanctioned and found not to be harms.

Both the state of Vermont and the federal government have given their imprimatur to the development and normal operation of nuclear energy and have established mechanisms for the regulation of nuclear power. Implicit within these statutory enactments is the policy choice that the benefits of nuclear energy outweigh its dangers.

If we were to allow defendants to present the necessity defense in this case we would, in effect, be allowing a jury to redetermine questions of policy already decided by the legislative branches of the federal and state governments. This is not how our system of government was meant to operate.

I express no opinion as to the relative merits or demerits of nuclear energy, nor do I question the sincerity of the defendants' beliefs. All that I would hold is that this Court is not the proper forum to grant defendants the relief they seek. Defendants still have the right to try to induce those forums that have made the policy choices at issue today to reconsider their decisions. But until that time I feel constrained to follow the law as it is, not as some would like it to be.

BILLINGS, JUSTICE, dissenting.

The majority states that the danger of low-level radiation and nuclear waste, which the defendants offered to prove, are "not the types of imminent danger classified as an emergency sufficient to justify criminal activity." Furthermore, the majority dismisses those portions of the proof dealing with the threat of a nuclear accident by characterizing them as mere "speculative and uncertain dangers." It is not for this Court to weigh the credibility of the evidence in this manner where there is evidence offered on the elements of the defense. While this case might stand in a different posture if, at the close of the defendants' evidence, they had failed to introduce evidence, as offered, on each and every element of the defense sufficient to make out a prima facie case, that situation is not before us. Furthermore, it is not for the trial judge to rule on the ultimate credibility and weight of the evidence. Where there is evidence offered which supports the elements of the defense, the question of reasonableness and credibility are for the jury to decide.

The defendants offered evidence on all the requisite elements of the defense of necessity. They stated as follows:

> [They had] a feeling that there was a situation of an emergency or imminent danger that would have occurred with the start up of the reactor on October 8th the time of [their] alleged crime ... the chance ... of the nuclear power plant having a serious accident which would cause ... great untold damage to property and lives and health for many generations.

The defendants also stated that "there was reasonable belief that it would have been an emergency had they started that reactor up ... there was a very good chance of an accident there for which there is no insurance coverage or very little." Specifically, the defendants offered to show by expert testimony that there were defects in the cooling system and other aspects of the power plant which they believed could and would result in a meltdown within seven seconds of failure on the start up of the plant. In addition, the defendant went to great lengths to base their defense on the imminent danger that would result from the hazardous radiation emitted from the plant and its wastes when the plant resumed operations.

While the offer made by the defendants was laced with statements about the dangers they saw in nuclear power generally, it is clear that they offered to show that the Vermont Yankee facility at which they were arrested was an imminent danger to the community on the day of the arrests; that, if it commenced operation, there was a danger of meltdown and severe radiation damage to persons and property. In support of this contention, the defendants stated that they would call experts familiar with the Vermont Yankee facility and the dangerous manner of its construction, as well as other experts who would testify on the effects of meltdown and radiation leakage on the results of governmental testing, and on the regulation of the Vermont Yankee facility. These witnesses were highly qualified to testify about the dangers at the Vermont Yankee facility based either on personal knowledge or on conditions the defendants offered to show existed at the time of the trespass.

Furthermore, the defendants offered to show that, in light of the imminent danger of an accident, they had exhausted all alternative means of preventing the start up of the plant and the immediate catastrophe it would bring. Under the circumstances of imminent danger arising from the start up of the plant, coupled with the resistance of Vermont Yankee and government officials, which the defendants offered to prove, nothing short of preventing the workers access to start up the plant would have averted the accident that the defendants expected.

Through this offer, it cannot be said, without prejudgment, that the defendants failed to set forth specific and concrete evidence, which, if proven, would establish the existence of an imminent danger of serious proportions through no fault of the defendants which could not be averted without the trespass. Whether the defendants' expectations and opportunities were reasonable under the circumstances of this case is not for the trial court to decide without hearing the evidence. From a review of the record, I am of the opinion that the offer here measured up to the standard required and that the trial court struck too soon in excluding the offered evidence.

I would also dissent from the concurring opinion in so far as it attempts to hide behind inferences that the legislature precluded the courts from hearing the defense of necessity in the instant case. Even assuming that such inferences can be drawn from the regulatory schemes cited, they have no bearing on this case. We were asked to infer under the facts, which the defendants offered to prove (that they were acting to avert an imminent nuclear disaster), that the legislative branch of government would not permit the courts of this state to entertain the defense of necessity because it had legislatively determined nuclear power to be safe. Were the defense raised without any offer to show an imminent danger of serious accident, it might fail both because defendants did not offer evidence on imminent danger and on the basis of legislative preclusion. But, where, as here, the defendants offer to prove an emergency which the regulatory scheme failed to avert, the inference of preclusion is unwarranted. The defendants are entitled to show that although there is a comprehensive regulatory scheme, it had failed to such an extent as to raise for them the choice between criminal trespass and the nuclear disaster which the regulatory scheme was created to prevent.

Comments and Questions

(1) What options were available to the defendants, other than breaking the law? Consider *State v. Cozzens*, 490 N.W.2d 184 (Neb. 1992); *United States v. Maxwell*, 254 F.3d 21 (1st Cir. 2001); *United States v. Kroncke*, 459 F.2d 697 (8th Cir. 1972); and *United States v. Richardson*, 588 F.2d 1235 (9th Cir. 1978), *cert. denied*, 440 U.S. 947 (1979). The defendant in *Cozzens* raised a "choice of evils" claim in a prosecution for failing to leave an abortion clinic. He contended that his moral belief dictated active opposition to such clinics.

To protest naval exercises off the coast of Puerto Rico, the defendant in *Maxwell* engaged in criminal trespass at the naval installation. He argued that the testing, and ultimate deployment of, Trident nuclear submarines was "a far greater evil than the commission of a criminal trespass." In *Kroncke*, the defendant violated the Military Service Act by attempting to destroy documents in a Selective Service office. He took these actions "in order to bring the evils of the Vietnam War to the attention of the public and Congress. He stated that this act was necessary because the Vietnamese War is immoral and illegal, and because the political leadership in the United States lacks the moral sensitivity and courage to bring an end to the war. On this basis, and also on the basis that the governmental institutions and political leadership are not responsive to the will of the majority of the people, Kroncke argued that his belief in the necessity of acting as he did was reasonable. He described his act as measured, dramatic, symbolic and religious."

In *Richardson* the defendants conspired to smuggle the drug laetrile into the United States from Mexico. Importation of the controversial cancer-treating drug was forbidden by law. Believing in the healing power of the drug the defendants conspired because laetrile "was needed in the United States to treat cancer patients."

Are these defendants entitled to offer evidence on a defense of necessity? In all four cases the defense claim was rejected.

(2) The position of the majority has been followed rather uniformly in cases in which the necessity claims are raised. *See, e.g.*, *Commonwealth v. Leno*, 616 N.E.2d 453 (Mass. 1993) (free needle exchange program as a response to the spread of AIDS); *Zal v. Steppe*, 968 F.2d 924 (9th Cir. 1992) (abortion protesters); *United States v. Schoon*, 971 F.2d 193 (9th Cir. 1992) (defendants entered an IRS office, splashed simulated blood in protest of America's involvement in El Salvador). *But see* Aldridge & Stark, *Nuclear War, Citizen Intervention, and the Necessity Defense*, 26 Santa Clara L. Rev. 299, 300 (1986):

> Courts have usually suppressed proof of this criteria when faced with citizen intervention cases. Nevertheless, a small but growing practice of allowing juries to hear a necessity defense can be gleaned from the decisions of non-reported citizen intervention trials. Furthermore, when such a defense has been put to a jury, the defendant has usually been acquitted. This fact raises the question of whether courts are really effecting justice by denying a necessity defense or whether the courts are acting upon political motivations.

(3) Should economic necessity be accepted as an affirmative defense? *See State v. Moe*, 24 P.2d 638, 640 (Wash. 1933):

> Economic necessity has never been accepted as a defense to a criminal charge. The reason is that, were it ever countenanced, it would leave to the individual the right to take the law into his own hands. In larceny cases economic necessity is frequently invoked in mitigation of punishment, but has never been recognized as a defense. Nor is it available as a defense to the charge of riot. The fact that a riot is spontaneous makes it none the less premeditated. Premeditation may, and frequently does, arise on the instant. A lawful assembly may turn into a riotous one in a moment of time over trivial incident or substantial provocation. When it does, those participating are guilty of riot, and neither the cause of the riot nor their reason for participation in it can be interposed as a defense. The causes, great or small, are available to the participants only in mitigation of punishment.

(4) Ted Patrick was convicted in 1975 of false imprisonment. *People v. Patrick*, 541 P.2d 320 (Colo. App. 1975).

> From that record it appears that the events which led to the prosecution of this action took place in the summer of 1973. At that time, defendant was contacted by a group of parents who believed their daughters were members of a "dangerous religious cult," and, at a meeting with the parents on July 16, 1973, defendant agreed to "deprogram" the women. Later defendant

> came to Denver and, as a result of arrangements made by the parents previously, on August 23, 1973, drove one of the parents' cars to the parking lot of a medical center in Denver, where Dena Thomas (age 21) worked. While Dena Thomas and Kathy Markis (age 23) were attempting to drive out of the parking lot in their automobile, defendant effectively blocked their exit with the car he was driving. This made it possible for Dena's father, (who had been chasing the women's car on foot) to unlock the door of the women's car, and, together with Kathy's father, to push their way into the car and drive the women away without their consent. The young women were driven to Eldorado Springs, Colorado, where they were detained for two days, while defendant undertook his "deprogramming" procedure.

What type of defense would Patrick be able to raise?

(5) A number of states passed legislation to legalize cannabis for medical use, and many more states enacted laws recognizing cannabis's medicinal value. In states which have not acted legislatively, or whose laws do not cover patients enduring serious pain, can a patient successfully assert a necessity defense if she contends that the use of marijuana is necessary to alleviate that pain? That was precisely the claim made by the defendant in *People v. Kratovil*, 815 N.E.2d 78 (Ill. App. Ct. 2004). She was convicted of possession of marijuana. She claimed she was entitled to the defense of medical necessity, for she was using cannabis to alleviate her eye pain.

Section 7-13 of the Illinois Criminal Code states:

> Necessity. Conduct which would otherwise be an offense is justifiable by reason of necessity if the accused was without blame in occasioning or developing the situation and reasonably believed such conduct was necessary to avoid a public or private injury greater than the injury which might reasonably result from his own conduct.

While recognizing the necessity defense, the court rejected the defense here.

> Necessity involves a choice between two admitted evils where other optional courses of action are unavailable. The conduct chosen must promote some higher value than the value of literal compliance with the law. Conduct that would otherwise be illegal is justified by necessity only if the conduct was the sole reasonable alternative available to the defendant under the circumstances. When other alternatives exist, which if carried out would cause less harm, then the accused is not justified in breaking the law.
>
> [O]ur state legislature clearly considered the possibility of medical reasons for cannabis possession when it enacted the Cannabis Control Act. Section 11 of the Cannabis Control Act allows for the possession, production, manufacture, and delivery of cannabis by persons engaged in medical research. In order for a patient to fall under this narrow exception and lawfully possess cannabis for medical reasons, a licensed physician engaged in medical research must consult the Department of Human Services and certify that his or her patient must possess cannabis for medical purposes. Certification by a physi-

> cian engaged in medical research and the authorization of the Department of Human Services are indispensable conditions for the lawful possession of cannabis for medical research.
>
> The defendant here did not fall under the narrow exception for cannabis possession by a medical research patient as provided for in section 11 of the Cannabis Control Act. The defendant's physician was not engaged in medical research and he did not obtain authorization from the Department of Human Services for the defendant to possess cannabis. Indeed, the defendant's physician did not even endorse or recommend that the defendant use cannabis to alleviate her pain. Accordingly, the defendant was not exempt from prosecution for her possession of cannabis.
>
> Similar to Illinois, other states recognize the exception of medical necessity only according to the narrow exceptions as defined by the legislatures in the respective statutes. Even in those states that statutorily recognize an affirmative defense of medial necessity for the possession of cannabis, the subject must adhere to the stringent statutory provisions. We note that these states uniformly require a physician's approval.

§ 7.03 Entrapment

Sherman v. United States

Supreme Court of the United States
356 U.S. 369 (1958)

Mr. Chief Justice Warren delivered the opinion of the Court.

The issue before us is whether petitioner's conviction should be set aside on the ground that as a matter of law the defense of entrapment was established. Petitioner was convicted under an indictment charging three sales of narcotics in violation of 21 U.S.C. § 174. A previous conviction had been reversed on account of improper instructions as to the issue of entrapment. In the second trial, as in the first, petitioner's defense was a claim of entrapment: an agent of the Federal Government induced him to take part in illegal transactions when otherwise he would not have done so.

In late August 1951, Kalchinian, a government informer, first met petitioner at a doctor's office where apparently both were being treated to be cured of narcotics addiction. Several accidental meetings followed, either at the doctor's office or at the pharmacy where both filled their prescriptions from the doctor. From mere greetings, conversation progressed to a discussion of mutual experiences and problems, including their attempts to overcome addiction to narcotics. Finally Kalchinian asked petitioner if he knew of a good source of narcotics. He asked petitioner to supply him with a source because he was not responding to treatment. From the first, petitioner tried to avoid the issue. Not until after a number of repetitions of the request, predicated on Kalchinian's presumed suffering, did petitioner finally acquiesce. Several times thereafter he obtained a quantity of narcotics which he shared with Kalchinian. Each time petitioner told Kalchinian that the total cost of narcotics he obtained was twenty-five dollars and that Kalchinian owed him fifteen dollars. The informer thus bore the cost of his share of the narcotics plus the taxi and other expenses necessary to obtain the drug. After several such sales Kalchinian informed agents of the Bureau of Narcotics that he had another seller for them. On three occasions during November 1951, government agents observed petitioner give narcotics to Kalchinian in return for money supplied by the Government.

At the trial the factual issue was whether the informer had convinced an otherwise unwilling person to commit a criminal act or whether petitioner was already predisposed to commit the act and exhibited only the natural hesitancy of one acquainted with the narcotics trade. The issue of entrapment went to the jury, and a conviction resulted. Petitioner was sentenced to imprisonment for ten years. The Court of Appeals for the Second Circuit affirmed. We granted certiorari.

In *Sorrells v. United States*, 287 U.S. 435, 53 S. Ct. 210, 77 L. Ed. 413 (1932), this Court firmly recognized the defense of entrapment in the federal courts. The intervening years have in no way detracted from the principles underlying that decision. The function of law enforcement is the prevention of crime and the apprehension of criminals. Manifestly, that function does not include the manufacturing of crime. Criminal activity is such that stealth and strategy are necessary weapons in the arsenal of the police officer. However, "a different question is presented when the criminal design originates with the officials of the Government, and they implant in the mind of an innocent person the disposition to commit the alleged offense and induce its commission in order that they may prosecute." Then stealth and strategy become as objectionable police methods as the coerced confession and the unlawful search. Congress could not have intended that its statutes were to be enforced by tempting innocent persons into violations.

However, the fact that government agents "merely afford opportunities or faculties for the commission of the offense does not" constitute entrapment. Entrapment occurs only when the criminal conduct was "the product of the creative activity" of law enforcement officials. To determine whether entrapment has been established, a line must be drawn between the trap for the unwary innocent and the trap for the unwary criminal. The principles by which the courts are to make this determination were outlined in *Sorrells.* On the one hand, at trial the accused may examine the conduct of the government agent; and on the other hand, the accused will be subjected to an "appropriate and searching inquiry into his own conduct and predisposition" as bearing on his claim of innocence.

We conclude from the evidence that entrapment was established as a matter of law. In so holding, we are not choosing between conflicting witnesses, nor judging credibility. Aside from recalling Kalchinian, who was the Government's witness, the defense called no witnesses. We reach our conclusion from the undisputed testimony of the prosecution's witnesses.

It is patently clear that petitioner was induced by Kalchinian. The informer himself testified that, believing petitioner to be undergoing a cure for narcotics addiction, he nonetheless sought to persuade petitioner to obtain for him a source of narcotics. In Kalchinian's own words we are told of the accidental, yet recurring, meetings, the ensuing conversations concerning mutual experiences in regard to narcotics addiction, and then of Kalchinian's resort to sympathy. One request was not enough, for Kalchinian tells us that additional ones were necessary to overcome, first, petitioner's refusal, then his evasiveness, and then his hesitancy in order to achieve capitulation. Kalchinian not only procured a source of narcotics but apparently also induced petitioner to return to the habit. Finally, assured of a catch, Kalchinian informed the authorities so that they could close the net. The Government cannot disown Kalchinian and insist it is not responsible for his actions. Although he was not being paid, Kalchinian was an active government informer who had but recently been the instigator of at least two other prosecutions.[2] Undoubtedly the impetus for such achievements was the fact that in 1951 Kalchinian was himself under criminal charges for illegally selling narcotics and had not yet been sentenced.[3] It makes no difference that the sales for which petitioner was convicted occurred after a series of sales. They were not independent acts subsequent to the inducement but part of a course of conduct which was the product of the inducement. In his testimony the federal agent in charge of the case admitted that he never bothered to question Kalchinian about the way he had made contact with petitioner. The Government cannot make such use of an informer and then claim disassociation through ignorance.

The Government sought to overcome the defense of entrapment by claiming that petitioner evinced a "ready compliance" to accede to Kalchinian's request. Aside from

---

2.

"Q. And it was your [Kalchinian's] job, was it not, while you were working with these agents to go out and try and induce somebody to sell you narcotics, isn't that true?

...

"A. No, it wasn't my job at all to do anything of the kind.

"Q. Do you remember this question [asked at the first trial]— ...

"'Q. And it was your job while working with these agents to go out and try and induce a person to sell narcotics to you, isn't that correct?

"A. I would say yes to that.'

"Q. Do you remember that?

"A. If that is what I said, let it stand just that way.

...

"Q. So when you testify now that it was not your job you are not telling the truth?

"A. I mean by job that nobody hired me for that. That is what I inferred, otherwise I meant the same thing in my answer to your question."

3.

"Q. But you had made a promise, an agreement, though, to cooperate with the Federal Bureau of Narcotics before you received a suspended sentence from the court?

"A. [Kalchinian]. I had promised to cooperate in 1951.

"Q. And that was before your sentence?

"A. Yes, that was before my sentence." Kalchinian received a suspended sentence in 1952 after a statement by the United States Attorney to the Judge that he had been cooperative with the Government.

a record of past convictions, which we discuss in the following paragraph, the Government's case is unsupported. There is no evidence that petitioner himself was in the trade. When his apartment was searched after arrest, no narcotics were found. There is no significant evidence that petitioner even made a profit on any sale to Kalchinian. The Government's characterization of petitioner's hesitancy to Kalchinian's request as the natural wariness of the criminal cannot fill the evidentiary void.

The Government's additional evidence in the second trial to show that petitioner was ready and willing to sell narcotics should the opportunity present itself was petitioner's record of two past narcotics convictions. In 1942 petitioner was convicted of illegally selling narcotics; in 1946 he was convicted of illegally possessing them. However, a nine-year-old sales conviction and a five-year-old possession conviction are insufficient to prove petitioner had a readiness to sell narcotics at the time Kalchinian approached him, particularly when we must assume from the record he was trying to overcome the narcotics habit at the time.

The case at bar illustrates an evil which the defense of entrapment is designed to overcome. The government informer entices someone attempting to avoid narcotics not only into carrying out an illegal sale but also into returning to the habit of use. Selecting the proper time, the informer then tells the government agent. The set-up is accepted by the agent without even a question as to the manner in which the informer encountered the seller. Thus the Government plays on the weaknesses of an innocent party and beguiles him into committing crimes which he otherwise would not have attempted. Law enforcement does not require methods such as this.

It has been suggested that in overturning this conviction we should reassess the doctrine of entrapment according to principles announced in the separate opinion of Mr. Justice Roberts in *Sorrells v. United States*. To do so would be to decide the case on grounds rejected by the majority in *Sorrells* and, so far as the record shows, not raised here or below by the parties before us. We do not ordinarily decide issues not presented by the parties and there is good reason not to vary that practice in this case.

At least two important issues of law enforcement and trial procedure would have to be decided without the benefit of argument by the parties, one party being the Government. Mr. Justice Roberts asserted that although the defendant could claim that the Government had induced him to commit the crime, the Government could not reply by showing that the defendant's criminal conduct was due to his own readiness and not to the persuasion of government agents. The handicap thus placed on the prosecution is obvious. Furthermore, it was the position of Mr. Justice Roberts that the factual issue of entrapment—now limited to the question of what the government agents did—should be decided by the judge, not the jury. Not only was this rejected by the Court in *Sorrells*, but where the issue has been presented to them, the Courts of Appeals have since *Sorrells* unanimously concluded that unless it can be decided as a matter of law, the issue of whether a defendant has been entrapped is for the jury as part of its function of determining the guilt or innocence of the accused.

To dispose of this case on the ground suggested would entail both overruling a leading decision of this Court and brushing aside the possibility that we would be creating more problems than we would supposedly be solving.

The judgment of the Court of Appeals is reversed and the case is remanded to the District Court with instructions to dismiss the indictment.

Reversed and remanded.

MR. JUSTICE FRANKFURTER, whom MR. JUSTICE DOUGLAS, MR. JUSTICE HARLAN, and MR. JUSTICE BRENNAN join, concurring in the result.

Although agreeing with the Court that the undisputed facts show entrapment as a matter of law, I reach this result by a route different from the Court's.

The first case in which a federal court clearly recognized and sustained a claim of entrapment by government officers as a defense to an indictment was, apparently, *Woo Wai v. United States*, 223 F. 412. Yet the basis of this defense, affording guidance for its application in particular circumstances, is as much in doubt today as it was when the defense was first recognized over forty years ago, although entrapment has been the decisive issue in many prosecutions. The lower courts have continued gropingly to express the feeling of outrage at conduct of law enforcers that brought recognition of the defense in the first instance, but without the formulated basis in reason that it is the first duty of courts to construct for justifying and guiding emotion and instinct.

Today's opinion does not promote this judicial desideratum, and fails to give the doctrine of entrapment the solid foundation that the decisions of the lower courts and criticism of learned writers have clearly shown is needed. Instead it accepts without re-examination the theory espoused in *Sorrells v. United States*, over strong protest by Mr. Justice Roberts, speaking for Brandeis and Stone, JJ., as well as himself. The fact that since the *Sorrells* case the lower courts have either ignored its theory and continued to rest decision on the narrow facts of each case, or have failed after penetrating effort to define a satisfactory generalization, is proof that the prevailing theory of the *Sorrells* case ought not to be deemed the last word. In a matter of this kind the Court should not rest on the first attempt at an explanation for what sound instinct counsels. It should not forego re-examination to achieve clarity of thought, because confused and inadequate analysis is too apt gradually to lead to a course of decisions that diverges from the true ends to be pursued.

It is surely sheer fiction to suggest that a conviction cannot be had when a defendant has been entrapped by government officers or informers because "Congress could not have intended that its statutes were to be enforced by tempting innocent persons into violations." In these cases raising claims of entrapment, the only legislative intention that can with any show of reason be extracted from the statute is the intention to make criminal precisely the conduct in which the defendant has engaged. That conduct includes all the elements necessary to constitute criminality. Without compulsion and "knowingly," where that is requisite, the defendant has violated the statutory command. If he is to be relieved from the usual punitive consequences, it is on no account because he is innocent of the offense described. In these circumstances, conduct is not less criminal because the result of temptation, whether the tempter is a private person or a government agent or informer.

The courts refuse to convict an entrapped defendant, not because his conduct falls outside the proscription of the statute, but because, even if his guilt be admitted, the methods employed on behalf of the Government to bring about conviction cannot be countenanced. As Mr. Justice Holmes said in *Olmstead v. United States* (dissenting) in another connection, "It is desirable that criminals should be detected, and to that end that all available evidence should be used. It also is desirable that the Government should not itself foster and pay for other crimes, when they are the means by which the evidence is to be obtained.... For my part I think it a less evil that some criminals should escape than that the Government should play an ignoble part." Insofar as they are used as instrumentalities in the administration of criminal justice, the federal courts have an obligation to set their face against enforcement of the law by lawless means or means that violate rationally vindicated standards of justice, and to refuse to sustain such methods by effectuating them. They do this in the exercise of a recognized jurisdiction to formulate and apply "proper standards for the enforcement of the federal criminal law in the federal courts," an obligation that goes beyond the conviction of the particular defendant before the court. Public confidence in the fair and honorable administration of justice, upon which ultimately depends the rule of law, is the transcending value at stake.

The formulation of these standards does not in any way conflict with the statute the defendant has violated, or involve the initiation of a judicial policy disregarding or qualifying that framed by Congress. A false choice is put when it is said that either the defendant's conduct does not fall within the statute or he must be convicted. The statute is wholly directed to defining and prohibiting the substantive offense concerned and expresses no purpose, either permissive or prohibitory, regarding the police conduct that will be tolerated in the detection of crime. A statute prohibiting the sale of narcotics is as silent on the question of entrapment as it is on the admissibility of illegally obtained evidence. It is enacted, however, on the basis of certain presuppositions concerning the established legal order and the role of the courts within that system in formulating standards for the administration of criminal justice when Congress itself has not specifically legislated to that end. Specific statutes are to be fitted into an antecedent legal system.

It might be thought that it is largely an academic question whether the court's finding a bar to conviction derives from the statute or from a supervisory jurisdiction over the administration of criminal justice; under either theory substantially the same considerations will determine whether the defense of entrapment is sustained. But to look to a statute for guidance in the application of a policy not remotely within the contemplation of Congress at the time of its enactment is to distort analysis. It is to run the risk, furthermore, that the court will shirk the responsibility that is necessarily in its keeping, if Congress is truly silent, to accommodate the dangers of overzealous law enforcement and civilized methods adequate to counter the ingenuity of modern criminals. The reasons that actually underlie the defense of entrapment can too easily be lost sight of in the pursuit of a wholly fictitious congressional intent.

The crucial question, not easy of answer, to which the court must direct itself is whether the police conduct revealed in the particular case falls below standards, to which common feelings respond, for the proper use of governmental power. For answer it is wholly irrelevant to ask if the "intention" to commit the crime originated with the defendant or government officers, or if the criminal conduct was the product of "the creative activity" of law enforcement officials. Yet in the present case the Court repeats and purports to apply these unrevealing tests. Of course in every case of this kind the intention that the particular crime be committed originates with the police, and without their inducement the crime would not have occurred. But it is perfectly clear ... where the police in effect simply furnished the opportunity for the commission of the crime, that this is not enough to enable the defendant to escape conviction.

The intention referred to, therefore, must be a general intention or predisposition to commit, whenever the opportunity should arise, crimes of the kind solicited, and in proof of such a predisposition evidence has often been admitted to show the defendant's reputation, criminal activities, and prior disposition. The danger of prejudice in such a situation, particularly if the issue of entrapment must be submitted to the jury and disposed of by a general verdict of guilty or innocent, is evident. The defendant must either forego the claim of entrapment or run the substantial risk that, in spite of instructions, the jury will allow a criminal record or bad reputation to weigh in its determination of guilt of the specific offense of which he stands charged. Furthermore, a test that looks to the character and predisposition of the defendant rather than the conduct of the police loses sight of the underlying reason for the defense of entrapment. No matter what the defendant's past record and present inclinations to criminality, or the depths to which he has sunk in the estimation of society, certain police conduct to ensnare him into further crime is not to be tolerated by an advanced society. And in the present case it is clear that the Court in fact reverses the conviction because of the conduct of the informer Kalchinian, and not because the Government has failed to draw a convincing picture of petitioner's past criminal conduct. Permissible police activity does not vary according to the particular defendant concerned; surely if two suspects have been solicited at the same time in the same manner, one should not go to jail simply because he has been convicted before and is said to have a criminal disposition. No more does it vary according to the suspicions, reasonable or unreasonable, of the police concerning the defendant's activities. Appeals to sympathy, friendship, the possibility of exorbitant gain, and so forth, can no more be tolerated when directed against a past offender than against an ordinary law-abiding citizen. A contrary view runs afoul of fundamental principles of equality under law, and would espouse the notion that when dealing with the criminal classes anything goes. The possibility that no matter what his past crimes and general disposition the defendant might not have committed the particular crime unless confronted with inordinate inducements, must not be ignored. Past crimes do not forever outlaw the criminal and open him to police practices, aimed at securing his repeated conviction, from which the ordinary citizen is protected. The whole ameliorative hopes of modern penology and prison administration strongly counsel against such a view.

This does not mean that the police may not act so as to detect those engaged in criminal conduct and ready and willing to commit further crimes should the occasion arise. Such indeed is their obligation. It does mean that in holding out inducements they should act in such a manner as is likely to induce to the commission of crime only these persons and not others who would normally avoid crime and through self-struggle resist ordinary temptations. This test shifts attention from the record and predisposition of the particular defendant to the conduct of the police and the likelihood, objectively considered, that it would entrap only those ready and willing to commit crime. It is as objective a test as the subject matter permits, and will give guidance in regulating police conduct that is lacking when the reasonableness of police suspicions must be judged or the criminal disposition of the defendant retrospectively appraised. It draws directly on the fundamental intuition that led in the first instance to the outlawing of "entrapment" as a prosecutorial instrument. The power of government is abused and directed to an end for which it was not constituted when employed to promote rather than detect crime and to bring about the downfall of those who, left to themselves, might well have obeyed the law. Human nature is weak enough and sufficiently beset by temptations without government adding to them and generating crime.

What police conduct is to be condemned, because likely to induce those not otherwise ready and willing to commit crime, must be picked out from case to case as new situations arise involving different crimes and new methods of detection. The *Sorrells* case involved persistent solicitation in the face of obvious reluctance, and appeals to sentiments aroused by reminiscences of experiences as companions in arms in the World War. Particularly reprehensible in the present case was the use of repeated requests to overcome petitioner's hesitancy, coupled with appeals to sympathy based on mutual experiences with narcotics addiction. Evidence of the setting in which the inducement took place is of course highly relevant in judging its likely effect, and the court should also consider the nature of the crime involved, its secrecy and difficulty of detection, and the manner in which the particular criminal business is usually carried on.

As Mr. Justice Roberts convincingly urged in the *Sorrells* case, such a judgment, aimed at blocking off areas of impermissible police conduct, is appropriate for the court and not the jury. "The protection of its own functions and the preservation of the purity of its own temple belongs only to the court. It is the province of the court and of the court alone to protect itself and the government from such prostitution of the criminal law. The violation of the principles of justice by the entrapment of the unwary into crime should be dealt with by the court no matter by whom or at what stage of the proceedings the facts are brought to its attention." Equally important is the consideration that a jury verdict, although it may settle the issue of entrapment in the particular case, cannot give significant guidance for official conduct for the future. Only the court, through the gradual evolution of explicit standards in accumulated precedents, can do this with the degree of certainty that the wise administration of criminal justice demands.

Comments and Questions

(1) Chief Justice Warren sets forth the Supreme Court's governing test for entrapment, and it is a subjective one, designed to sort out whether the government has set a "trap for the unwary innocent" or a "trap for the unwary criminal." Notice that Justice Frankfurter agrees that the facts present show entrapment as a matter of law, but he would have arrived at that conclusion using an objective test: "a test that looks to the character and predisposition of the defendant rather than the conduct of the police loses sight of the underlying reason for the defense of entrapment ... Permissible police activity does not vary according to the particular defendant concerned." What are the pros and cons of each test? Continue to ask that question as you read the next two cases in this section.

(2) States have codified the defense of entrapment using both subjective and objective formulations.

The Connecticut Statute, § 53a-15, applies the subjective test:

> In any prosecution for an offense, it shall be a defense that the defendant engaged in the proscribed conduct because he was induced to do so by a public servant, or by a person acting in cooperation with a public servant, for the purpose of institution of criminal prosecution against the defendant, and that the defendant did not contemplate and would not otherwise have engaged in such conduct.

Arkansas utilizes an objective approach in § 5-2-209:

> (a) It is an affirmative defense that the defendant was entrapped into committing an offense.
>
> (b) (1) Entrapment occurs when a law enforcement officer or any person acting in cooperation with him induces the commission of an offense by using persuasion or other means likely to cause normally law-abiding persons to commit the offense. (2) Conduct merely affording a person an opportunity to commit an offense does not constitute entrapment.

(3) Some states combine the two approaches, requiring the government to first "pass" the objective test before the judge. At that point, the question is for the jury under the predisposition test. Is this the ideal answer to the questions raised by the two tests, or does it create still further problems?

United States v. Russell

Supreme Court of the United States
411 U.S. 423 (1973)

Mr. Justice Rehnquist delivered the opinion of the Court.

Respondent Richard Russell was charged in three counts of a five-count indictment returned against him and co-defendants John and Patrick Connolly. After a jury trial in the District Court, in which his sole defense was entrapment, respondent was convicted on all three counts of having unlawfully manufactured and processed methamphetamine ("speed") and of having unlawfully sold and delivered that drug in violation of 21 U.S.C. §§ 331(q)(1), (2), 360a(a), (b) (1964 ed., Supp. V). On appeal, the United States Court of Appeals for the Ninth Circuit, one judge dissenting, reversed the conviction solely for the reason that an undercover agent supplied an essential chemical for manufacturing the methamphetamine which formed the basis of respondent's conviction. The court concluded that as a matter of law "a defense to a criminal charge may be founded upon an intolerable degree of governmental participation in the criminal enterprise." We granted certiorari and now reverse that judgment.

There is little dispute concerning the essential facts in this case. On December 7, 1969, Joe Shapiro, an undercover agent for the Federal Bureau of Narcotics and Dangerous Drugs, went to respondent's home on Whidbey Island in the State of Washington where he met with respondent and his two co-defendants, John and Patrick Connolly. Shapiro's assignment was to locate a laboratory where it was believed that methamphetamine was being manufactured illicitly. He told the respondent and the Connollys that he represented an organization in the Pacific Northwest that was interested in controlling the manufacture and distribution of methamphetamine. He then made an offer to supply the defendants with the chemical phenyl-2-propanone, an essential ingredient in the manufacture of methamphetamine, in return for one-half of the drug produced. This offer was made on the condition that Agent Shapiro be shown a sample of the drug which they were making and the laboratory where it was being produced.

During the conversation, Patrick Connolly revealed that he had been making the drug since May 1969 and since then had produced three pounds of it. John Connolly gave the agent a bag containing a quantity of methamphetamine that he represented as being from "the last batch that we made." Shortly thereafter, Shapiro and Patrick Connolly left respondent's house to view the laboratory which was located in the Connolly house on Whidbey Island. At the house, Shapiro observed an empty bottle bearing the chemical label.

By prearrangement, Shapiro returned to the Connolly house on December 9, 1969, to supply 100 grams of propanone and observe the manufacturing process. When he arrived he observed Patrick Connolly and the respondent cutting up pieces of aluminum foil and placing them in a large flask. There was testimony that some of the foil pieces accidentally fell on the floor and were picked up by the respondent and Shapiro and put into the flask.[3] Thereafter, Patrick Connolly added all of the necessary chemicals, including the propanone brought by Shapiro, to make two batches of methamphetamine. The manufacturing process having been completed the following morning, Shapiro was given one-half of the drug and respondent kept the remainder. Shapiro offered to buy, and the respondent agreed to sell, part of the remainder for $60.

About a month later, Shapiro returned to the Connolly house and met with Patrick Connolly to ask if he was still interested in their "business arrangement." Connolly replied that he was interested but that he had recently obtained two additional bottles of phenyl-2-propanone and would not be finished with them for a couple of days. He provided some additional methamphetamine to Shapiro at that time. Three days later Shapiro returned to the Connolly house with a search warrant and, among other items, seized an empty 500-gram bottle of propanone and a 100-gram bottle, not the one he had provided, that was partially filled with the chemical.

There was testimony at the trial of respondent and Patrick Connolly that phenyl-2-propanone was generally difficult to obtain. At the request of the Bureau of Narcotics and Dangerous Drugs, some chemical supply firms had voluntarily ceased selling the chemical.

At the close of the evidence, and after receiving the District Judge's standard entrapment instruction,[4] the jury found the respondent guilty on all counts charged. On appeal, the respondent conceded that the jury could have found him predisposed to commit the offenses but argued that on the facts presented there was entrapment as a matter of law. The Court of Appeals agreed, although it did not find the District Court had misconstrued or misapplied the traditional standards governing the entrapment defense. Rather, the court in effect expanded the traditional notion of entrapment, which focuses on the predisposition of the defendant, to mandate dismissal of a criminal prosecution whenever the court determines that there has been "an intolerable degree of governmental participation in the criminal enterprise." In this case the court decided that the conduct of the agent in supplying a scarce ingredient essential for the manufacture of a controlled substance established that defense.

In the instant case, respondent asks us to reconsider the theory of the entrapment defense as it is set forth in the majority opinions in *Sorrells* and *Sherman*. His principal contention is that the defense should rest on constitutional grounds. He argues that

---

3. Agent Shapiro did not otherwise participate in the manufacture of the drug or direct any of the work.

4. The District Judge stated the governing law on entrapment as follows: "Where a person already has the willingness and the readiness to break the law, the mere fact that the government agent provides what appears to be a favorable opportunity is not entrapment." He then instructed the jury to acquit respondent if it had a "reasonable doubt whether the defendant had the previous intent or purpose to commit the offense ... and did so only because he was induced or persuaded by some officer or agent of the government." No exception was taken by respondent to this instruction.

the level of Shapiro's involvement in the manufacture of the methamphetamine was so high that a criminal prosecution for the drug's manufacture violates the fundamental principles of due process. The respondent contends that the same factors that led this Court to apply the exclusionary rule to illegal searches and seizures and confessions should be considered here. But he would have the Court go further in deterring undesirable official conduct by requiring that any prosecution be barred absolutely because of the police involvement in criminal activity. The analogy is imperfect in any event, for the principal reason behind the adoption of the exclusionary rule was the Government's "failure to observe its own laws." Unlike the situations giving rise to the holdings in *Mapp* and *Miranda*, the Government's conduct here violated no independent constitutional right of the respondent. Nor did Shapiro violate any federal statute or rule or commit any crime in infiltrating the respondent's drug enterprise.

Respondent would overcome this basic weakness in his analogy to the exclusionary rule cases by having the Court adopt a rigid constitutional rule that would preclude any prosecution when it is shown that the criminal conduct would not have been possible had not an undercover agent "supplied an indispensable means to the commission of the crime that could not have been obtained otherwise, through legal or illegal channels." Even if we were to surmount the difficulties attending the notion that due process of law can be embodied in fixed rules, and those attending respondent's particular formulation, the rule he proposes would not appear to be of significant benefit to him. For, on the record presented, it appears that he cannot fit within the terms of the very rule he proposes.

The record discloses that although the propanone was difficult to obtain, it was by no means impossible. The defendants admitted making the drug both before and after those batches made with the propanone supplied by Shapiro. Shapiro testified that he saw an empty bottle labeled phenyl-2-propanone on his first visit to the laboratory on December 7, 1969. And when the laboratory was searched pursuant to a search warrant on January 10, 1970, two additional bottles labeled phenyl-2-propanone were seized. Thus, the facts in the record amply demonstrate that the propanone used in the illicit manufacture of methamphetamine not only *could* have been obtained without the intervention of Shapiro but was in fact obtained by these defendants.

While we may some day be presented with a situation in which the conduct of law enforcement agents is so outrageous that due process principles would absolutely bar the government from invoking judicial processes to obtain a conviction, the instant case is distinctly not of that breed. Shapiro's contribution of propanone to the criminal enterprise already in process was scarcely objectionable. The chemical is by itself a harmless substance and its possession is legal. While the Government may have been seeking to make it more difficult for drug rings, such as that of which respondent was a member, to obtain the chemical, the evidence described above shows that it nonetheless was obtainable. The law enforcement conduct here stops far short of violating that "fundamental fairness, shocking to the universal sense of justice," mandated by the Due Process Clause of the Fifth Amendment.

The illicit manufacture of drugs is not a sporadic, isolated criminal incident, but a continuing, though illegal, business enterprise. In order to obtain convictions for illegally manufacturing drugs, the gathering of evidence of past unlawful conduct frequently proves to be an all but impossible task. Thus in drug-related offenses law enforcement personnel have turned to one of the only practicable means of detection: the infiltration of drug rings and a limited participation in their unlawful present practices. Such infiltration is a recognized and permissible means of investigation; if that be so, then the supply of some item of value that the drug ring requires must, as a general rule, also be permissible. For an agent will not be taken into the confidence of the illegal entrepreneurs unless he has something of value to offer them. Law enforcement tactics such as this can hardly be said to violate "fundamental fairness" or "shocking to the universal sense of justice."

[E]ntrapment is a relatively limited defense. It is rooted, not in any authority of the Judicial Branch to dismiss prosecutions for what it feels to have been "overzealous law enforcement," but instead in the notion that Congress could not have intended criminal punishment for a defendant who has committed all the elements of a proscribed offense, but was induced to commit them by the Government.

Sorrells and *Sherman* both recognize "that the fact that officers or employees of the Government merely afford opportunities or facilities for the commission of the offense does not defeat the prosecution." Nor will the mere fact of deceit defeat a prosecution for there are circumstances when the use of deceit is the only practicable law enforcement technique available. It is only when the Government's deception actually implants the criminal design in the mind of the defendant that the defense of entrapment comes into play.

Respondent's concession in the Court of Appeals that the jury finding as to predisposition was supported by the evidence is, therefore, fatal to his claim of entrapment. He was an active participant in an illegal drug manufacturing enterprise which began before the Government agent appeared on the scene, and continued after the Government agent had left the scene. He was, in the words of *Sherman, supra*, not an "unwary innocent" but an "unwary criminal." The Court of Appeals was wrong, we believe, when it sought to broaden the principle laid down in *Sorrells* and *Sherman*. Its judgment is therefore

Reversed.

Mr. Justice Douglas, with whom Mr. Justice Brennan concurs, dissenting.

A federal agent supplied the accused with one chemical ingredient of the drug known as methamphetamine ("speed") which the accused manufactured and for which act he was sentenced to prison. His defense was entrapment, which the Court of Appeals sustained and which the Court today disallows. Since I have an opposed view of entrapment, I dissent.

In my view, the fact that the chemical ingredient supplied by the federal agent might have been obtained from other sources is quite irrelevant. Supplying the chemical ingredient used in the manufacture of this batch of "speed" made the United

States an active participant in the unlawful activity. As stated by Mr. Justice Brandeis, "I am aware that courts—mistaking relative social values and forgetting that a desirable end cannot justify foul means—have, in their zeal to punish, sanctioned the use of evidence obtained through criminal violation of property and personal rights or by other practices of detectives even more revolting. But the objection here is of a different nature. It does not rest merely upon the character of the evidence or upon the fact that the evidence was illegally obtained. The obstacle to the prosecution lies in the fact that the alleged crime was instigated by officers of the Government; that the act for which the Government seeks to punish the defendant is the fruit of their criminal conspiracy to induce its commission. The Government may set decoys to entrap criminals. But it may not provoke or create a crime and then punish the criminal, its creature."

Mr. Justice Frankfurter stated the same philosophy: "No matter what the defendant's past record and present inclinations to criminality, or the depths to which he has sunk in the estimation of society, certain police conduct to ensnare him into further crime is not to be tolerated by an advanced society." And he added: "The power of government is abused and directed to an end for which it was not constituted when employed to promote rather than detect crime...."

Mr. Justice Roberts in *Sorrells* put the idea in the following words: "The applicable principle is that courts must be closed to the trial of a crime instigated by the government's own agents. No other issue, no comparison of equities as between the guilty official and the guilty defendant, has any place in the enforcement of this overruling principle of public policy."

Federal agents play a debased role when they become the instigators of the crime, or partners in its commission, or the creative brain behind the illegal scheme. That is what the federal agent did here when he furnished the accused with one of the chemical ingredients needed to manufacture the unlawful drug.

MR. JUSTICE STEWART, with whom MR. JUSTICE BRENNAN and MR. JUSTICE MARSHALL join, dissenting.

It is common ground that "[t]he conduct with which the defense of entrapment is concerned is the *manufacturing* of crime by law enforcement officials and their agents." For the Government cannot be permitted to instigate the commission of a criminal offense in order to prosecute someone for committing it. As Mr. Justice Brandeis put it, the Government "may not provoke or create a crime and then punish the criminal, its creature." It is to prevent this situation from occurring in the administration of federal criminal justice that the defense of entrapment exists. But the Court has been sharply divided as to the proper basis, scope, and focus of the entrapment defense, and as to whether, in the absence of a conclusive showing, the issue of entrapment is for the judge or the jury to determine.

I.

In my view, this objective approach to entrapment advanced by the Roberts opinion in *Sorrells* and the Frankfurter opinion in *Sherman* is the only one truly consistent with the underlying rationale of the defense.[1]

Indeed, the very basis of the entrapment defense itself demands adherence to an approach that focuses on the conduct of the governmental agents, rather than on whether the defendant was "predisposed" or "otherwise innocent." I find it impossible to believe that the purpose of the defense is to effectuate some unexpressed congressional intent to exclude from its criminal statutes persons who committed a prohibited act, but would not have done so except for the Government's inducements. For, as Mr. Justice Frankfurter put it, "the only legislative intention that can with any show of reason be extracted from the statute is the intention to make criminal precisely the conduct in which the defendant has engaged." Since, by definition, the entrapment defense cannot arise unless the defendant actually committed the proscribed act, that defendant is manifestly covered by the terms of the criminal statute involved.

Furthermore, to say that such a defendant is "otherwise innocent" or not "predisposed" to commit the crime is misleading, at best. The very fact that he has committed an act that Congress has determined to be illegal demonstrates conclusively that he is not innocent of the offense. He may not have originated the precise plan or the precise details, but he was "predisposed" in the sense that he has proved to be quite capable of committing the crime. That he was induced, provoked, or tempted to do so by government agents does not make him any more innocent or any less predisposed than he would be if he had been induced, provoked, or tempted by a private person—which, of course, would not entitle him to cry "entrapment." Since the only difference between these situations is the identity of the tempter, it follows that the significant focus must be on the conduct of the government agents, and not on the predisposition of the defendant.

The purpose of the entrapment defense, then, cannot be to protect persons who are "otherwise innocent." Rather, it must be to prohibit unlawful governmental activity in instigating crime. As Mr. Justice Brandeis stated: "This prosecution should be stopped, not because some right of Casey's has been denied, but in order to protect the Government. To protect it from illegal conduct of its officers. To preserve the purity of its courts." If that is so, then whether the particular defendant was "predisposed" or "otherwise innocent" is irrelevant; and the important question becomes whether the Government's conduct in inducing the crime was beyond judicial toleration.

Moreover, a test that makes the entrapment defense depend on whether the defendant had the requisite predisposition permits the introduction into evidence of

1. Both the Proposed New Federal Criminal Code (1971), Final Report of the National Commission on Reform of Federal Criminal Laws § 702, and the American Law Institute's Model Penal Code § 2.13 (Proposed Official Draft, 1962), adopt this objective approach.

all kinds of hearsay, suspicion, and rumor—all of which would be inadmissible in any other context—in order to prove the defendant's predisposition. It allows the prosecution, in offering such proof, to rely on the defendant's bad reputation or past criminal activities, including even rumored activities of which the prosecution may have insufficient evidence to obtain an indictment, and to present the agent's suspicions as to why they chose to tempt this defendant. This sort of evidence is not only unreliable, as the hearsay rule recognizes; but it is also highly prejudicial, especially if the matter is submitted to the jury, for, despite instructions to the contrary, the jury may well consider such evidence as probative not simply of the defendant's predisposition, but of his guilt of the offense with which he stands charged.

More fundamentally, focusing on the defendant's innocence or predisposition has the direct effect of making what is permissible or impermissible police conduct depend upon the past record and propensities of the particular defendant involved. Stated another way, this subjective test means that the Government is permitted to entrap a person with a criminal record or bad reputation, and then to prosecute him for the manufactured crime, confident that his record or reputation itself will be enough to show that he was predisposed to commit the offense anyway.

Yet, in the words of Mr. Justice Roberts: "Whatever may be the demerits of the defendant or his previous infractions of law these will not justify the instigation and creation of a new crime, as a means to reach him and punish him for his past misdemeanors.... To say that such conduct by an official of government is condoned and rendered innocuous by the fact that the defendant had a bad reputation or had previously transgressed is wholly to disregard the reason for refusing the processes of the court to consummate an abhorrent transaction."

And as Mr. Justice Frankfurter pointed out: "Permissible police activity does not vary according to the particular defendant concerned; surely if two suspects have been solicited at the same time in the same manner, one should not go to jail simply because he has been convicted before and is said to have a criminal disposition. No more does it vary according to the suspicions, reasonable or unreasonable, of the police concerning the defendant's activities." *Sherman v. United States*, *supra*, at 383. In my view, a person's alleged "predisposition" to crime should not expose him to government participation in the criminal transaction that would be otherwise unlawful.

This does not mean, of course, that the Government's use of undercover activity, strategy, or deception is necessarily unlawful. Indeed, many crimes, especially so-called victimless crimes, could not otherwise be detected. Thus, government agents may engage in conduct that is likely, when objectively considered, to afford a person ready and willing to commit the crime an opportunity to do so. But when the agents' involvement in criminal activities goes beyond the mere offering of such an opportunity, and when their conduct is of a kind that could induce or instigate the commission of a crime by one not ready and willing to commit it, then—regardless of the character or propensities of the particular person induced—I think entrapment has occurred. For in that situation, the Government has engaged in the impermissible manufacturing of crime, and the federal courts should bar the prosecution in order to preserve the institutional integrity of the system of federal criminal justice.

II.

It is the Government's duty to prevent crime, not to promote it. Here, the Government's agent asked that the illegal drug be produced for him, solved his quarry's practical problems with the assurance that he could provide the one essential ingredient that was difficult to obtain, furnished that element as he had promised, and bought the finished product from the respondent—all so that the respondent could be prosecuted for producing and selling the very drug for which the agent had asked and for which he had provided the necessary component. Under the objective approach that I would follow, this respondent was entrapped, regardless of his predisposition or "innocence."

In the words of Mr. Justice Roberts: "The applicable principle is that courts must be closed to the trial of a crime instigated by the government's own agents. No other issue, no comparison of equities as between the guilty official and the guilty defendant, has any place in the enforcement of this overruling principle of public policy."

I would affirm the judgment of the Court of Appeals.

Comments and Questions

(1) Another well known decision of the Supreme Court in the area is *Hampton v. United States*, 425 U.S. 484 (1976), where a federal agent provided drugs, which the defendant was later charged with selling. The trial court refused to give an entrapment instruction based upon this transaction. The United States Supreme Court was split in its response to the facts. Justice Rehnquist's plurality opinion emphasized that Hampton's predisposition made the entrapment defense unavailable to him. Justices Powell and Blackmun concurred on this point, but would not join the plurality opinion which appeared to reject the possibility that outrageous police behavior in some cases might violate due process. The dissenting opinion of Justices Brennan, Stewart, and Marshall stated that either due process or entrapment should bar conviction where the defendant in a drug sale case received the narcotics from a government agent.

(2) The Court in *Mathews v. United States*, 485 U.S. 58 (1988), reaffirmed the subjective test for entrapment but also allowed the claim when inconsistent defenses were raised. The defendant there was convicted of accepting a bribe in exchange for an official act. The lower courts would not allow him to raise the entrapment defense at trial because he denied having the requisite mental state, "he believed it was a personal loan unrelated to his duties at the [government]." The majority opinion found that the defense should have been allowed, as inconsistent defenses were permitted in both civil and criminal actions and no special rule should be applied to entrapment cases. The dissenters claimed that raising inconsistent defenses in the entrapment setting means simply that "it is a proper defense only if the accused is lying."

Jacobson v. United States

Supreme Court of the United States
503 U.S. 540 (1992)

Justice White delivered the opinion of the Court.

In February 1984, petitioner, a 56-year-old veteran-turned-farmer who supported his elderly father in Nebraska, ordered two magazines and a brochure from a California adult bookstore. The magazines, entitled *Bare Boys I* and *Bare Boys II*, contained photographs of nude preteen and teenage boys. The contents of the magazines startled petitioner, who testified that he had expected to receive photographs of "young men 18 years or older." On cross-examination, he explained his response to the magazines:

> "PROSECUTOR: You were shocked and surprised that there were pictures of very young boys without clothes on, is that correct?
>
> "JACOBSON: Yes, I was.
>
> "PROSECUTOR: Were you offended?
>
> ...
>
> "JACOBSON: I was not offended because I thought these were a nudist type publication. Many of the pictures were out in a rural or outdoor setting. There was—I didn't draw any sexual connotation or connection with that."

The young men depicted in the magazines were not engaged in sexual activity, and petitioner's receipt of the magazines was legal under both federal and Nebraska law. Within three months, the law with respect to child pornography changed; Congress passed the Act illegalizing the receipt through the mails of sexually explicit depictions of children. In the very month that the new provision became law, postal inspectors found petitioner's name on the mailing list of the California bookstore that had mailed him *Bare Boys I* and *II*. There followed over the next 2½ years, repeated efforts by two Government agencies, through five fictitious organizations and a bogus pen pal, to explore petitioner's willingness to break the new law by ordering sexually explicit photographs of children through the mail.

The Government began its efforts in January 1985 when a postal inspector sent petitioner a letter supposedly from the American Hedonist Society, which in fact was a fictitious organization. The letter included a membership application and stated the Society's doctrine: that members had the right to read what we desire, the right to discuss similar interests with those who share our philosophy, and finally that we have the "right to seek pleasure without restrictions being placed on us by outdated puritan morality." Petitioner enrolled in the organization and returned a sexual attitude questionnaire that asked him to rank on a scale of one to four his enjoyment of various sexual materials, with one being "really enjoy," two being "enjoy," three being "somewhat enjoy," and four being "do not enjoy." Petitioner ranked the entry "preteen sex" as a two, but indicated that he was opposed to pedophilia.

For a time, the Government left petitioner alone. But then a new "prohibited mail specialist" in the Postal Service found petitioner's name in a file, and in May 1986, petitioner received a solicitation from a second fictitious consumer research company, "Midlands Data Research," seeking a response from those who "believe in the joys of sex and the complete awareness of those lusty and youthful lads and lasses of the neophite [sic] age." The letter never explained whether "neophite" referred to minors or young adults. Petitioner responded: "Please feel free to send me more information, I am interested in teenage sexuality. Please keep my name confidential."

Petitioner then heard from yet another Government creation, "Heartland Institute for a New Tomorrow" (HINT), which proclaimed that it was "an organization founded to protect and promote sexual freedom and freedom of choice. We believe that arbitrarily imposed legislative sanctions restricting your sexual freedom should be rescinded through the legislative process." The letter also enclosed a second survey. Petitioner indicated that his interest in "preteen sex-homosexual" material was above average, but not high. In response to another question, petitioner wrote: "Not only sexual expression but freedom of the press is under attack. We must be ever vigilant to counter attack right-wing fundamentalists who are determined to curtail our freedoms."

"HINT" replied, portraying itself as a lobbying organization seeking to repeal "all statutes which regulate sexual activities, except those laws which deal with violent behavior, such as rape. HINT is also lobbying to eliminate any legal definition of the age of consent." These lobbying efforts were to be funded by sales from a catalog to be published in the future "offering the sale of various items which we believe you will find to be both interesting and stimulating." HINT also provided computer matching of group members with similar survey responses; and, although petitioner was supplied with a list of potential "pen pals," he did not initiate any correspondence.

Nevertheless, the Government's "prohibited mail specialist" began writing to petitioner, using the pseudonym "Carl Long." The letters employed a tactic known as "mirroring," which the inspector described as "reflecting whatever the interests are of the person we are writing to." Petitioner responded at first, indicating that his interest was primarily in "male-male items." Inspector "Long" wrote back:

> "My interests too are primarily male-male items. Are you satisfied with the type of VCR tapes available? Personally, I like the amateur stuff better if its [sic] well produced as it can get more kinky and also seems more real. I think the actors enjoy it more."

Petitioner responded:

> "As far as my likes are concerned, I like good looking young guys (in their late teens and early 20's) doing their thing together."

Petitioner's letters to "Long" made no reference to child pornography. After writing two letters, petitioner discontinued the correspondence.

By March 1987, 34 months had passed since the Government obtained petitioner's name from the mailing list of the California bookstore, and 26 months had passed since the Postal Service had commenced its mailings to petitioner. Although petitioner had responded to surveys and letters, the Government had no evidence that petitioner had ever intentionally possessed or been exposed to child pornography. The Postal

Service had not checked petitioner's mail to determine whether he was receiving questionable mailings from persons—other than the Government—involved in the child pornography industry.

At this point, a second Government agency, the Customs Service, included petitioner in its own child pornography sting, "Operation Borderline," after receiving his name on lists submitted by the Postal Service. Using the name of a fictitious Canadian company called "Produit Outaouais," the Customs Service mailed petitioner a brochure advertising photographs of young boys engaging in sex. Petitioner placed an order that was never filled.

The Postal Service also continued its efforts in the *Jacobson* case, writing to petitioner as the "Far Eastern Trading Company Ltd." The letter began:

> "As many of you know, much hysterical nonsense has appeared in the American media concerning 'pornography' and what must be done to stop it from coming across your borders. This brief letter does not allow us to give much comments; however, why is your government spending millions of dollars to exercise international censorship while tons of drugs, which makes yours the world's most crime ridden country are passed through easily."

The letter went on to say:

> "We have devised a method of getting these to you without prying eyes of U.S. Customs seizing your mail." ... "After consultations with American solicitors, we have been advised that once we have posted our material through your system, it cannot be opened for any inspection without authorization of a judge."

The letter invited petitioner to send for more information. It also asked petitioner to sign an affirmation that he was "not a law enforcement officer or agent of the U.S. Government acting in an undercover capacity for the purpose of entrapping Far Eastern Trading Company, its agents or customers." Petitioner responded. A catalogue was sent and petitioner ordered *Boys Who Love Boys*, a pornographic magazine depicting young boys engaged in various sexual activities. Petitioner was arrested after a controlled delivery of a photocopy of the magazine.

When petitioner was asked at trial why he placed such an order, he explained that the Government had succeeded in piquing his curiosity: "Well, the statement was made of all the trouble and the hysteria over pornography and I wanted to see what the material was. It didn't describe the—I didn't know for sure what kind of sexual action they were referring to in the Canadian letter." ...

In petitioner's home, the Government found the *Bare Boys* magazines and materials that the Government had sent to him in the course of its protracted investigation, but no other materials that would indicate that petitioner collected or was actively interested in child pornography.

Petitioner was indicted for violating 18 U.S.C. § 2252(a)(2)(A). The trial court instructed the jury on the petitioner's entrapment defense, petitioner was convicted and a divided Court of Appeals for the Eighth Circuit, sitting en banc, affirmed, concluding that "Jacobson was not entrapped as a matter of law." We granted certiorari.

There can be no dispute about the evils of child pornography or the difficulties that laws and law enforcement have encountered in eliminating it. Likewise, there can be no dispute that the Government may use undercover agents to enforce the law. "It is well settled that the fact that officers or employees of the Government merely afford opportunities or facilities for the commission of the offense does not defeat the prosecution. Artifice and stratagem may be employed to catch those engaged in criminal enterprises."

In their zeal to enforce the law, however, Government agents may not originate a criminal design, implant in an innocent person's mind the disposition to commit a criminal act, and then induce commission of the crime so that the Government may prosecute. Where the Government has induced an individual to break the law and the defense of entrapment is at issue, as it was in this case, the prosecution must prove beyond reasonable doubt that the defendant was disposed to commit the criminal act prior to first being approached by Government agents.[2]

Thus, an agent deployed to stop the traffic in illegal drugs may offer the opportunity to buy or sell drugs, and, if the offer is accepted, make an arrest on the spot or later. In such a typical case, or in a more elaborate "sting" operation involving government—sponsored fencing where the defendant is simply provided with the opportunity to commit a crime, the entrapment defense is of little use because the ready commission of the criminal act amply demonstrates the defendant's predisposition. Had the agents in this case simply offered petitioner the opportunity to order child

---

2. Inducement is not at issue in this case. The Government does not dispute that it induced petitioner to commit the crime. The sole issue is whether the Government carried its burden of proving that petitioner was predisposed to violate the law before the Government intervened. The dissent is mistaken in claiming that this is an innovation in entrapment law and in suggesting that the Government's conduct prior to the moment of solicitation is irrelevant. The Court rejected these arguments six decades ago in *Sorrells*, when the Court wrote that the Government may not punish an individual "for an alleged offense which is the product of the creative activity of its own officials" and that in such a case the Government "is in no position to object to evidence of the activities of its representatives in relation to the accused ..." Indeed, the proposition that the accused must be predisposed prior to contact with law enforcement officers is so firmly established that the Government conceded the point at oral argument, submitting that the evidence it developed during the course of its investigation was probative because it indicated petitioner's state of mind prior to the commencement of the Government's investigation.

This long-established standard in no way encroaches upon Government investigatory activities. Indeed, the Government's internal guidelines for undercover operations provide that an inducement to commit a crime should not be offered unless:

> "(a) [T]here is a reasonable indication, based on information developed through informants or other means, that the subject is engaging, has engaged, or is likely to engage in illegal activity of a similar type; or
>
> "(b) The opportunity for illegal activity has been structured so that there is reason for believing that persons drawn to the opportunity, or brought to it, are predisposed to engage in the contemplated illegal activity." Attorney General's Guidelines on FBI Undercover Operations (Dec. 31, 1980), reprinted in S. Rep. No. 97-682, p. 551 (1982).

pornography through the mails, and petitioner—who must be presumed to know the law—had promptly availed himself of this criminal opportunity, it is unlikely that his entrapment defense would have warranted a jury instruction.

But that is not what happened here. By the time petitioner finally placed his order, he had already been the target of 26 months of repeated mailings and communications from Government agents and fictitious organizations. Therefore, although he had become predisposed to break the law by May 1987, it is our view that the Government did not prove that this predisposition was independent and not the product of the attention that the Government had directed at petitioner since January 1985.

The prosecution's evidence of predisposition falls into two categories: evidence developed prior to the Postal Service's mail campaign, and that developed during the course of the investigation. The sole piece of preinvestigation evidence is petitioner's 1984 order and receipt of the *Bare Boys* magazines. But this is scant if any proof of petitioner's predisposition to commit an illegal act, the criminal character of which a defendant is presumed to know. It may indicate a predisposition to view sexually-oriented photographs that are responsive to his sexual tastes; but evidence that merely indicates a generic inclination to act within a broad range, not all of which is criminal, is of little probative value in establishing predisposition.

Furthermore, petitioner was acting within the law at the time he received these magazines. Receipt through the mails of sexually explicit depictions of children for noncommercial use did not become illegal under federal law until May 1984, and Nebraska had no law that forbade petitioner's possession of such material until 1988. Evidence of predisposition to do what once was lawful is not, by itself, sufficient to show predisposition to do what is now illegal, for there is a common understanding that most people obey the law even when they disapprove of it. This obedience may reflect a generalized respect for legality or the fear of prosecution, but for whatever reason, the law's prohibitions are matters of consequence. Hence, the fact that petitioner legally ordered and received the *Bare Boys* magazines does little to further the Government's burden of proving that petitioner was predisposed to commit a criminal act. This is particularly true given petitioner's unchallenged testimony was that he did not know until they arrived that the magazines would depict minors.

The prosecution's evidence gathered during the investigation also fails to carry the Government's burden. Petitioner's responses to the many communications prior to the ultimate criminal act were at most indicative of certain personal inclinations, including a predisposition to view photographs of preteen sex and a willingness to promote a given agenda by supporting lobbying organizations. Even so, petitioner's responses hardly support an inference that he would commit the crime of receiving child pornography through the mails.[3] Furthermore, a person's inclinations and "fantasies ... are his own and beyond the reach of government."

3. We do not hold, as the dissent suggests that the Government was required to prove that petitioner knowingly violated the law. We simply conclude that proof that petitioner engaged in legal conduct and possessed certain generalized personal inclinations is not sufficient evidence to prove beyond a

...

On the other hand, the strong arguable inference is that, by waving the banner of individual rights and disparaging the legitimacy and constitutionality of efforts to restrict the availability of sexually explicit materials, the Government not only excited petitioner's interest in sexually explicit materials banned by law but also exerted substantial pressure on petitioner to obtain and read such material as part of a fight against censorship and the infringement of individual rights. For instance, HINT described itself as "an organization founded to protect and promote sexual freedom and freedom of choice" and stated that "the most appropriate means to accomplish [its] objectives is to promote honest dialogue among concerned individuals and to continue its lobbying efforts with State Legislators." These lobbying efforts were to be financed through catalogue sales. Mailings from the equally fictitious American Hedonist Society and the correspondence from the non-existent Carl Long endorsed these themes.

Similarly, the two solicitations in the spring of 1987 raised the spectre of censorship while suggesting that petitioner ought to be allowed to do what he had been solicited to do. The mailing from the Customs Service referred to "the worldwide ban and intense enforcement on this type of material," observed that "what was legal and commonplace is now an 'underground' and secretive service," and emphasized that "[t]his environment forces us to take extreme measures" to insure delivery. The Postal Service solicitation described the concern about child pornography as "hysterical nonsense," decried "international censorship," and assured petitioner, based on consultation with "American solicitors" that an order that had been posted could not be opened for inspection without authorization of a judge. It further asked petitioner to affirm that he was not a government agent attempting to entrap the mail order company or its customers. In these particulars, both government solicitations suggested that receiving this material was something that petitioner ought to be allowed to do.

Petitioner's ready response to these solicitations cannot be enough to establish beyond reasonable doubt that he was predisposed, prior to the Government acts intended to create predisposition, to commit the crime of receiving child pornography through the mails. The evidence that petitioner was ready and willing to commit the offense came only after the Government had devoted 2½ years to convincing him that he had or should have the right to engage in the very behavior proscribed by law. Rational jurors could not say beyond a reasonable doubt that petitioner possessed the requisite predisposition prior to the Government's investigation and that it existed independent of the Government's many and varied approaches to petitioner. As was explained in *Sherman*, where entrapment was found as a matter of law, "the Government [may not] play on the weakness of an innocent party and beguile him into committing crimes which he otherwise would not have attempted."

Law enforcement officials go too far when they "implant in the mind of an innocent person the disposition to commit the alleged offense and induce its com-

---

reasonable doubt that he would have been predisposed to commit the crime charged independent of the Government's coaxing.

mission in order that they may prosecute." Like the *Sorrels* court, we are "unable to conclude that it was the intention of the Congress in enacting this statute that its processes of detection and enforcement should be abused by the instigation by government officials of an act on the part of persons otherwise innocent in order to lure them to its commission and to punish them." When the Government's quest for convictions leads to the apprehension of an otherwise law-abiding citizen who, if left to his own devices, likely would have never run afoul of the law, the courts should intervene.

Because we conclude that this is such a case and that the prosecution failed, as a matter of law, to adduce evidence to support the jury verdict that petitioner was predisposed, independent of the Government's acts and beyond a reasonable doubt, to violate the law by receiving child pornography through the mails, we reverse the Court of Appeals' judgment affirming the conviction of Keith Jacobson.

It is so ordered.

JUSTICE O'CONNOR, with whom THE CHIEF JUSTICE and JUSTICE KENNEDY join, and with whom JUSTICE SCALIA joins except as to Part II, dissenting.

Keith Jacobson was offered only two opportunities to buy child pornography through the mail. Both times, he ordered. Both times, he asked for opportunities to buy more. He needed no Government agent to coax, threaten, or persuade him; no one played on his sympathies, friendship, or suggested that his committing the crime would further a greater good. In fact, no Government agent even contacted him face to face. The Government contends that from the enthusiasm with which Mr. Jacobson responded to the chance to commit a crime, a reasonable jury could permissibly infer beyond a reasonable doubt that he was predisposed to commit the crime. I agree.

The first time the Government sent Mr. Jacobson a catalog of illegal materials, he ordered a set of photographs advertised as picturing "young boys in sex action fun." He enclosed the following note with his order: "I received your brochure and decided to place an order. If I like your product, I will order more later." For reasons undisclosed in the record, Mr. Jacobson's order was never delivered.

The second time the Government sent a catalog of illegal materials, Mr. Jacobson ordered a magazine called "Boys Who Love Boys," described as: "11 year old and 14 year old boys get it on in every way possible. Oral, anal sex and heavy masturbation. If you love boys, you will be delighted with this." Along with his order, Mr. Jacobson sent the following note: "Will order other items later. I want to be discreet in order to protect you and me."

Government agents admittedly did not offer Mr. Jacobson the chance to buy child pornography right away. Instead, they first sent questionnaires in order to make sure that he was generally interested in the subject matter. Indeed, a "cold call" in such a business would not only risk rebuff and suspicion, but might also shock and offend the uninitiated, or expose minors to suggestive materials. Mr. Jacobson's responses to the questionnaires gave the investigators reason to think he would be interested in photographs depicting preteen sex.

The Court, however, concludes that a reasonable jury could not have found Mr. Jacobson to be predisposed beyond a reasonable doubt on the basis of his responses to the Government's catalogs, even though it admits that, by that time, he was predisposed to commit the crime. The Government, the Court holds, failed to provide evidence that Mr. Jacobson's obvious predisposition at the time of the crime "was independent and not the product of the attention that the Government had directed at petitioner." In so holding, I believe the Court fails to acknowledge the reasonableness of the jury's inference from the evidence, redefines "predisposition," and introduces a new requirement that Government sting operations have a reasonable suspicion of illegal activity before contacting a suspect.

I.

This Court has held previously that a defendant's predisposition is to be assessed as of the time the Government agent first suggested the crime, not when the Government agent first became involved. Until the Government actually makes a suggestion of criminal conduct, it could not be said to have "implanted in the mind of an innocent person the disposition to commit the alleged offense and induce its commission...." Even in *Sherman v. United States, supra*, in which the Court held that the defendant had been entrapped as a matter of law, the Government agent had repeatedly and unsuccessfully coaxed the defendant to buy drugs, ultimately succeeding only by playing on the defendant's sympathy. The Court found lack of predisposition based on the Government's numerous unsuccessful attempts to induce the crime, not on the basis of preliminary contacts with the defendant.

Today, the Court holds that Government conduct may be considered to create a predisposition to commit a crime, even before any Government action to induce the commission of the crime. In my view, this holding changes entrapment doctrine. Generally, the inquiry is whether a suspect is predisposed before the Government induces the commission of the crime, not before the Government makes initial contact with him. There is no dispute here that the Government's questionnaires and letters were not sufficient to establish inducement; they did not even suggest that Mr. Jacobson should engage in any illegal activity. If all the Government had done was to send these materials, Mr. Jacobson's entrapment defense would fail. Yet the Court holds that the Government must prove not only that a suspect was predisposed to commit the crime before the opportunity to commit it arose, but also before the Government came on the scene.

The rule that preliminary Government contact can create a predisposition has the potential to be misread by lower courts as well as criminal investigator as requiring that the Government must have sufficient evidence of a defendant's predisposition before it ever seeks to contact him. Surely the Court cannot intend to impose such a requirement, for it would mean that the Government must have a reasonable suspicion of criminal activity before it begins an investigation, a condition that we have never before imposed. The Court denies that its new rule will affect run-of-the-mill sting operations, and one hopes that it means what it says. Nonetheless, after this case, every defendant will claim that something the Government agent did before soliciting the crime "created" a predisposition that was not there before. For example, a bribe taker will claim that the description of the amount of money available was so enticing that it implanted a disposition to accept the bribe later offered. A drug buyer will claim that the description of the drug's purity and effects was so tempting that it created the urge to try it for the first time. In short, the Court's opinion could be read to prohibit the Government from advertising the seductions of criminal activity as part of its sting operation, for fear of creating a predisposition in its suspects. That limitation would be especially likely to hamper sting operations such as this one, which mimic the advertising done by genuine purveyors of pornography. No doubt the Court would protest that its opinion does not stand for so broad a proposition, but the apparent lack of a principled basis for distinguishing these scenarios exposes a flaw in the more limited rule the Court today adopts.

The Court's rule is all the more troubling because it does not distinguish between Government conduct that merely highlights the temptation of the crime itself, and Government conduct that threatens, coerces, or leads a suspect to commit a crime in order to fulfill some other obligation. For example, in *Sorrells*, the Government agent repeatedly asked for illegal liquor, coaxing the defendant to accede on the ground that "one former war buddy would get liquor for another." In *Sherman*, the Government agent played on the defendant's sympathies, pretending to be going through drug withdrawal and begging the defendant to relieve his distress by helping him buy drugs.

The Government conduct in this case is not comparable. While the Court states that the Government "exerted substantial pressure on petitioner to obtain and read such material as part of a fight against censorship and the infringement of individual rights," one looks at the record in vain for evidence of such "substantial pressure." The most one finds is letters advocating legislative action to liberalize obscenity laws, letters which could easily be ignored or thrown away. Much later, the Government sent separate mailings of catalogs of illegal materials. Nowhere did the Government suggest that the proceeds of the sale of the illegal materials would be used to support legislative reforms. While one of the HINT letters suggested that lobbying efforts would be funded by sales from a catalog, the catalogs actually sent, nearly a year later, were from different fictitious entities (Produit Outaouais and Far Eastern Trading Company), and gave no suggestion that money would be used for any political purposes. Nor did the Government claim to be organizing a civil disobedience movement, which would protest the pornography laws by breaking them. Contrary to the gloss given the evidence by the Court, the Government's suggestions of illegality may also have made buyers beware, and increased the mystique of the materials offered: "for those of you who have enjoyed youthful material ... we have devised a method of getting these to you without prying eyes of U.S. Customs seizing your mail." Mr. Jacobson's curiosity to see what "all the trouble and the hysteria" was about, is certainly susceptible of more than one interpretation. And it is the jury that is charged with the obligation of interpreting it. In sum, the Court fails to construe the evidence in the light most favorable to the Government, and fails to draw all reasonable inferences in the Government's favor. It was surely reasonable for the jury to infer that Mr. Jacobson was predisposed beyond a reasonable doubt, even if other inferences from the evidence were also possible.

II.

The second puzzling thing about the Court's opinion is its redefinition of predisposition. The Court acknowledges that "[p]etitioner's responses to the many communications prior to the ultimate criminal act were ... indicative of certain personal inclinations, including a predisposition to view photographs of preteen sex...." If true, this should have settled the matter; Mr. Jacobson was predisposed to engage in the illegal conduct. Yet, the Court concludes, "petitioner's responses hardly support an inference that he would commit the crime of receiving child pornography through the mails."

The Court seems to add something new to the burden of proving predisposition. Not only must the Government show that a defendant was predisposed to engage in the illegal conduct, here, receiving photographs of minors engaged in sex, but also that the defendant was predisposed to break the law knowingly in order to do so. The statute violated here, however, does not require proof of specific intent to break the law; it requires only knowing receipt of visual depictions produced by using minors engaged in sexually explicit conduct. Under the Court's analysis, however, the Government must prove more to show predisposition than it need prove in order to convict.

The Court ignores the judgment of Congress that specific intent is not an element of the crime of receiving sexually explicit photographs of minors. The elements of predisposition should track the elements of the crime. The predisposition requirement is meant to eliminate the entrapment defense for those defendants who would have committed the crime anyway, even absent Government inducement. Because a defendant might very well be convicted of the crime here absent Government inducement even though he did not know his conduct was illegal, a specific intent requirement does little to distinguish between those who would commit the crime without the inducement and those who would not. In sum, while the fact that Mr. Jacobson's purchases of *Bare Boys I* and *Bare Boys II* were legal at the time may have some relevance to the question of predisposition, it is not, as the Court suggests, dispositive.

The crux of the Court's concern in this case is that the Government went too far and "abused" the "processes of detection and enforcement" by luring an innocent person to violate the law. Consequently, the Court holds that the Government failed to prove beyond a reasonable doubt that Mr. Jacobson was predisposed to commit the crime. It was, however, the jury's task, as the conscience of the community, to decide whether or not Mr. Jacobson was a willing participant in the criminal activity here or an innocent dupe. The jury is the traditional "defense against arbitrary law enforcement." Indeed, in *Sorrells*, in which the Court was also concerned about overzealous law enforcement, the Court did not decide itself that the Government conduct constituted entrapment, but left the issue to the jury. There is no dispute that the jury in this case was fully and accurately instructed on the law of entrapment, and nonetheless found Mr. Jacobson guilty. Because I believe there was sufficient evidence to uphold the jury's verdict, I respectfully dissent.

Comments and Questions

(1) The Supreme Court has consistently held that entrapment is generally to be a question of fact for the jury. In both *Sherman* and *Jacobson*, however, the Court found entrapment as a matter of law. Did it correctly follow its own rulings?

(2) Justice O'Connor was concerned that some would view the Court's decision as requiring the government to "have sufficient evidence of a defendant's predisposition before it ever seeks to contact him." Is this a valid concern? Would that change the law? See the footnote in Justice White's opinion discussing the Justice Department's guidelines for FBI undercover operations.

(3) The dissent argued forcefully that the actions of the government agent here were far less egregious than in *Sorrells* or *Sherman*. Do you agree?

(4) Can a defendant raising the entrapment defense offer expert testimony to show her "unusual susceptibility to inducement"? Yes, said the court in *State v. Shuck*, 953 S.W.2d 662, 670 (Tenn. 1997): "[A] jury may not be able to properly evaluate the effect of a defendant's cognitive and psychological characteristics on the existence of inducement or predisposition without the considered opinion of an expert."

(5) The defendants in *United States v. Hollingsworth*, 27 F.3d 1196, 1200, 1216 (7th Cir. 1994) (en banc), were amateurs ("tyros" in the court's words) in the world of finance. One was a farmer, the other a dentist. They purchased an offshore bank and were solicited by an undercover agent to commit various money laundering crimes. They responded with enthusiasm and little hesitation. At the trial level the entrapment defense was rejected because the prosecution had showed considerable interest on the defendants' part in this criminal activity, though there had been no prior criminal behavior alleged. The Seventh Circuit, *en banc*, found entrapment as a matter of law relying on *Jacobson*. The court held that the government had not proved the defendants would likely have committed the crimes without government involvement.

> Predisposition is not a purely mental state, the state of being willing to swallow the government's bait. It has positional as well as disposition force. The dictionary definitions of the word include "tendency" as well as "inclination." ... [It must be shown] that it is likely that if the government had not induced him to commit the crime some criminal would have done so.

The dissenters, also looking to *Jacobson*, sharply disagreed and could not understand

> why a person who fully desires to break the law and is entirely willing to do what needs to be done to accomplish a criminal objective ought be excused from criminal liability simply because, for whatever reason, he does not have his act together when afforded an opportunity by an undercover agent.

Which opinion more correctly applies the Supreme Court's holding? Consider Marcus, *Presenting, Back from the [Almost] Dead, the Entrapment Defense*, 47 U. Fla. L. Rev. 205, 234 (1995):

> The better approach is to apply the tried and true criminal law notion of causation to entrapment. This principle asks whether the defendant is "a person who, but for the inducement offered, would not have conceived of or engaged in conduct of the sort induced." Under this approach, the government's behavior becomes of paramount importance vis-a-vis the defendant's mental state. This strategy is demonstrated in both *Sherman* and *Jacobson* where each Court asked whether the crime resulted from the agent's actions or from the defendant's prior inclinations.

(6) In the wake of *Jacobson*, lower courts continue to apply different understandings of what facts qualify as government inducement. One court recently emphasized the fact that the undercover officer "did not give [the defendant] an explicit directive or order and did not exert a persuasive or other force over the [defendant]." *Mobley v. State*, 27 N.E.3d 1191, 1197 (Ind. App. 2015). Another opinion indicated that "[i]nducement means more than 'mere government solicitation of the crime; the fact that government agents initiated contact with the defendant, suggested the crime, or furnished the ordinary opportunity to commit it is insufficient to show inducement.'" *United States v. Blitch*, 773 F. 3d 837, 844 (7th Cir. 2014). Still other judges wrote that the "touchstone of an illegitimate inducement is that it creates a risk that a person who otherwise would not commit the crime if left alone will do so in response to the government's persuasion." *United States v. Mayfield*, 771 F.3d 417, 434 (7th Cir. 2014).

§ 7.04 Intoxication

Heideman v. United States

United States Court of Appeals, District of Columbia Circuit
259 F.2d 943 (1958)

Burger, Circuit Judge.

The question is whether the trial court should have instructed the jury to return a verdict of not guilty if it found that appellant was so intoxicated as to be incapable of forming the intent to rob. The appellant asked for such an instruction, but the trial court denied it.

Drunkenness is not per se an excuse for crime, but nevertheless it may in many instances be relevant to the issue of intent. One class of cases where drunkenness may be relevant on the issue of intent is the category of crimes where specific intent is required. Robbery falls into this category, and a defendant accused of robbery is entitled to an instruction on drunkenness as bearing on intent if the evidentiary groundwork has been adequately laid. Such an instruction is necessary, however, only if sufficient evidence on the intoxication issue has been introduced so that a reasonable man could possibly entertain a doubt therefrom that the accused was able to form the necessary intent. The record before us does not reveal such a case.[8] Drunkenness, while efficient to reduce or remove *inhibitions*, does not readily negate *intent*.[10]

Appellant's careful advance preparation for the crime, before boarding the cab, by filling a sock with gravel to use as an efficient but silent weapon with which to render the cab driver helpless, the rifling of his pockets and taking of his wallet show that appellant's mind was working logically, rationally and efficiently to the execution of his criminal purpose. We might add to that the not insignificant fact that the seating arrangement, with Brennan in the front seat ready to apply the brake, and appellant in the rear seat where he could more readily use his "sandbag" on the victim, like the other carefully calculated steps, including prompt flight, is not the work of a man so intoxicated as to be unable to form the intent to rob. We hold that the evidence in this case could not create a reasonable doubt in the mind of any reasonable man as to whether appellant possessed the requisite intent as to each element of the crime of robbery.

Bazelon, Circuit Judge (dissenting).

I agree with the majority that "a defendant accused of robbery is entitled to an instruction on drunkenness as bearing on intent if the evidentiary groundwork has been adequately laid." I cannot, however, agree with the majority that the evidentiary groundwork was lacking in the instant case.

The testimony on the question of intoxication in the instant case came largely from co-defendant Brennan. He testified:

> We consumed quite a bit of whiskey, but I didn't consume enough that I was beyond the point that I didn't know what I was doing; but Heideman got a little drunker than me....
>
> ...
>
> **Q.** You say Heideman was drunk?
>
> **A.** Yes, sir; he had quite a bit to drink, quite a bit more than me.
>
> **Q.** But you mean to say he didn't know what he was doing?
>
> **A.** I wouldn't say what [sic] he knew what he was doing. I couldn't speak for him.

---

8. The evidence as to drunkenness showed no incapacitating state of intoxication; co-defendant Brennan testified that "I didn't consume enough that I was beyond the point that I didn't know what I was doing; but [appellant] got a little drunker than me...." Also, "[appellant] had quite a bit to drink, quite a bit more than me." On the other hand, the record reveals such statements as "he wasn't that drunk," and "you could tell they had been drinking, but they weren't what you would call drunk or intoxicated."

10. In first degree murder trials, the degree of drunkenness need not be so great. In addition to intent, first degree murder requires deliberation and premeditation, and drunkenness may more readily negate these elements, and may thus reduce the degree of the offense.

The victim of the robbery, on the other hand, testified that "you could tell they [appellant and Brennan] had been drinking, but they weren't what you call drunk or intoxicated."

The evidence in this case created an issue as to whether there was such drunkenness as to negate intent. I think that issue was one for the jury to determine. The trial judge denied the requested instruction on the theory, which this court now holds was erroneous, that "robbery, unlike larceny, does not require a specific intent." He did not, like my brethren, deem the evidence insufficient to permit the jury to entertain a reasonable doubt as to appellant's ability to form an intent to commit robbery. He simply thought that the degree of intoxication was irrelevant. He told the jury:

> The defendant Brennan further testified that both he and Heideman were intoxicated and apparently he would infer that neither one of them knew what they were doing.[3] He also denies that he saw Heideman put the gravel in his sock.
>
> Now, the taxi driver testified that when the two sailors got into his cab they were not drunk. He said they evidently had been drinking, but they were not drunk. So, as far as this case is concerned, ladies and gentlemen of the Jury, it makes no difference whether they were intoxicated or not, because the law is that intoxication is not an excuse for the commission of a crime. The law does not recognize intoxication as a defense to a criminal charge. You can see a good many reasons for that rule of law, because if the rule were otherwise any one could drink to excess and then go out and commit a crime without fear of punishment. That would be intolerable.[28]

This instruction was clearly wrong, even under my brethren's view.

As the majority points out, one can conclude from the circumstances of the crime that appellant was not too drunk to have intended to rob the victim. But that conclusion was one to be drawn by the jury under a proper instruction, not by an appellate court.

In my opinion the judgment must be reversed because the charge to the jury on the question of intoxication was erroneous and because the refusal to give the instruction requested by appellant was equally erroneous.

---

3. As may be seen from his testimony quoted above, Brennan did not say that he did not know what he was doing. He did, however, suggest that *appellant* may have been too drunk to know what he was doing.

28. [4] At the beginning of the trial, the judge served notice on appellant's counsel that he would refuse the requested instruction, which may account for the fact, though it does not excuse it, that appellant himself offered no evidence of his intoxication. The judge said:

> I will have to instruct the jury that intoxication is not a defense. I have no patience with intoxication anyway. Many people get drunk but when honest people get drunk they do not go out and commit crimes. In other words, you could say if a person committed a crime while drunk he must have a criminal instinct in him because they say, as you probably know, that in a state of intoxication a person exhibits his true desires.

State v. Stasio

Supreme Court of New Jersey
396 A.2d 1129 (1979)

SCHREIBER, J.

The major issue on this appeal is whether voluntary intoxication constitutes a defense to a crime, one element of which is the defendant's intent. Defendant Stasio was found guilty by a jury of assault with intent to rob and of assault while being armed with a dangerous knife.

The scene of this incident was the Silver Moon Tavern located at 655 Van Houten Avenue, Clifton. The date was October 7, 1975. The defendant having presented no evidence, what occurred must be discerned from the testimony of three witnesses for the State: Peter Klimek, a part owner of the Silver Moon; Robert Colburn, a patron; and Robert Rowan, a member of the Clifton police force.

Robert Colburn had frequented the Silver Moon Tavern not only for its alcoholic wares but also to engage in pool. On October 7, Colburn arrived at the Tavern about 11:00 A.M. and started to play pool. Sometime before noon the defendant joined him. They stayed together until about 3:00 P.M. when the defendant left the bar. Though the defendant had been drinking during this period, in Colburn's opinion the defendant was not intoxicated upon his departure. Neither the defendant's speech nor his mannerisms indicated drunkenness.

Peter Klimek arrived at the Tavern shortly before 5:00 P.M. and assumed his shift at tending bar. There were about eight customers present when, at approximately 5:40 P.M., the defendant entered and walked in a normal manner to the bathroom. Shortly thereafter he returned to the front door, looked around outside and approached the bar. He demanded that Klimek give him some money. Upon refusal, he threatened Klimek. The defendant went behind the bar toward Klimek and insisted that Klimek give him $80 from the cash register. When Klimek persisted in his refusal, the defendant pulled out a knife. Klimek grabbed the defendant's right hand and Colburn, who had jumped on, seized the defendant's hair and pushed his head toward the bar. The defendant then dropped the knife.

Almost immediately thereafter Police Officer Rowan arrived and placed the defendant in custody. He testified that defendant responded to his questions with no difficulty and walked normally. Klimek also stated that defendant did not appear drunk and that he had not noticed any odor of alcohol on defendant's breath.

At the conclusion of the State's case, the defendant elected not to take the stand. He made this decision because of an earlier conference in chambers at which defense counsel had advised the court that his defense would be that defendant had been so intoxicated that he was incapable of forming the intent to rob. The trial court responded by stating that it would charge that "voluntary intoxication was not a defense to any act by the defendant in this matter." The defendant on a *voir dire* made it clear that his decision not to testify was predicated upon the trial court's position.

This Court last considered the culpability of an individual who had committed an illegal act while voluntarily under the influence of a drug or alcohol in *State v. Maik*, 60 N.J. 203, 287 A.2d 715 (1972).

It is generally agreed that a defendant will not be relieved of criminal responsibility because he was under the influence of intoxicants or drugs voluntarily taken. This principle rests upon public policy, demanding that he who seeks the influence of liquor or narcotics should not be insulated from criminal liability because that influence impaired his judgment or his control. The required element of badness can be found in the intentional use of the stimulant or depressant. Moreover, to say that one who offended while under such influence was sick would suggest that his sickness disappeared when he sobered up and hence he should be released. Such a concept would hardly protect others from the prospect of repeated injury.

A difference of opinion has been expressed in the Appellate Division as to the meaning of *Maik*. In *State v. Del Vecchio*, 142 N.J. Super. 359, 361 A.2d 579 (App. Div.), *certif den.* 71 N.J. 501, 366 A.2d 657 (1976), a conviction for breaking and entering with intent to steal was reversed on the ground that the jury had improperly been charged that voluntary intoxication was not a defense to a crime requiring a specific intent. The Appellate Division reasoned that, when a specific intent was an element of an offense, voluntary intoxication may negate existence of that intent. Since intoxication may have prevented existence of that specific intent, an acquittal might be in order. The Appellate Division also held that the only principle to be derived from *Maik* was the proposition that voluntary intoxication may be relevant in determining whether a murder may be raised to first degree. In contrast, Judge Allcorn's dissent in *State v. Atkins*, 151 N.J. Super. 555, 573, 377 A.2d 718 (App. Div. 1977), *rev'd* 78 N.J. 454, 396 A.2d 1122 (1979), expresses the opinion that *Maik* stands for the proposition that voluntary intoxication is not a defense to any criminal offense irrespective of whether a specific or general intent is an element of the offense.

We reject the approach adopted by *Del Vecchio* because, although it has surface appeal, it is based on an unworkable dichotomy, gives rise to inconsistencies, and ignores the policy expressed in *Maik*.

Del Vecchio would permit the intoxication defense only when a "specific" as distinguished from a "general" intent was an element of the crime. However, that difference is not readily ascertainable. "The distinction thus made between a 'specific intent' and a 'general intent,'" "is quite elusive, and although the proposition [that voluntary intoxication may be a defense if it prevented formation of a specific intent] is echoed in some opinions in our State, it is not clear that any of our cases in fact turned upon it."

The current confusion resulting from diverse uses of "general intent" is aggravated by dubious efforts to differentiate that from "specific intent." Each crime ... has its distinctive *mens rea, e.g.*, intending to have forced intercourse, intending to break and enter a dwelling-house and to commit a crime there, intending to inflict a battery, and so on. It is evident that there must be as many *mentes reae* as there are crimes. And whatever else may be said about an intention, an essential characteristic of it is that it is directed towards a definite end. To assert therefore that an intention is "specific" is to employ a superfluous term just as if one were to speak of a "voluntary act."

The undeniable fact is "that neither common experience nor psychology knows any such actual phenomenon as 'general intent' that is distinguishable from 'specific intent.' "

Moreover, distinguishing between specific and general intent gives rise to incongruous results by irrationally allowing intoxication to excuse some crimes but not others. In some instances if the defendant is found incapable of formulating the specific intent necessary for the crime charged, such as assault with intent to rob, he may be convicted of a lesser included general intent crime, such as assault with a deadly weapon. In other cases there may be no related general intent offense so that intoxication would lead to acquittal. Thus, a defendant acquitted for breaking and entering with intent to steal because of intoxication would not be guilty of any crime-breaking and entering being at most under certain circumstances the disorderly persons offense of trespass. Similarly, if the specific intent to rob were not demonstrated because of intoxication, then the defendant may have no criminal responsibility since assault with intent to rob would also be excused.

Finally, where the more serious offense requires only a general intent, such as rape, intoxication provides no defense, whereas it would be a defense to an attempt to rape, specific intent being an element of that offense. Yet the same logic and reasoning which impels exculpation due to the failure of specific intent to commit an offense would equally compel the same result when a general intent is an element of the offense.

The *Del Vecchio* approach may free defendants of specific intent offenses even though the harm caused may be greater than in an offense held to require only general intent. This course thus undermines the criminal law's primary function of protecting society from the results of behavior that endangers the public safety. This should be our guide rather than concern with logical consistency in terms of any single theory of culpability, particularly in view of the fact that alcohol is significantly involved in a substantial number of offenses. The demands of public safety and the harm done are identical irrespective of the offender's reduced ability to restrain himself due to his drinking. "[I]f a person casts off the restraints of reason and consciousness by a voluntary act, no wrong is done to him if he is held accountable for any crime which he may commit in that condition. Society is entitled to this protection."

Until a stuporous condition is reached or the entire motor area of the brain is profoundly affected, the probability of the existence of intent remains. The initial effect of alcohol is the reduction or removal of inhibitions or restraints. But that does not vitiate intent. The loosening of the tongue has been said to disclose a person's true sentiments—"*in vino veritas.*"

The great majority of moderately to grossly drunk or drugged persons who commit putatively criminal acts are probably aware of what they are doing and the likely consequences. In the case of those who are drunk, alcohol may have diminished their perceptions, released their inhibitions and clouded their reasoning and judgment, but they still have sufficient capacity for the conscious mental processes required by the ordinary definitions of all or most specific *mens rea* crimes. For example, a person can be quite far gone in drink and still capable of the conscious intent to steal, which is an element of common law larceny. When a defendant shows that he was comatose and therefore could not have broken and entered into the home or committed some other unlawful activity, such stage of intoxication may be relevant in establishing a general denial. But short of that, voluntary intoxication, other than its employment to disprove premeditation and deliberation in murder, should generally serve as no excuse. In this fashion the opportunities of false claims by defendants may be minimized and misapplication by jurors of the effect of drinking on the defendant's responsibility eliminated.

The new Code of Criminal Justice provides that a person is not guilty of an offense unless he acted purposely, knowingly, recklessly or negligently, as the law may require. It also states that intoxication is not a defense "unless it negatives an element of the offense," and that "[w]hen recklessness establishes an element of the offense, if the actor, due to self-induced intoxication, is unaware of a risk of which he would have been aware had he been sober, such unawareness is immaterial." These provisions were taken from the Model Penal Code of the American Law Institute, § 2.08 (Prop. Off. Draft 1962). The American Law Institute Committee has explained that in those instances when the defendant's purpose or knowledge is an element of a crime, proof of intoxication may negate the existence of either. The distinction between specific and general intent has been rejected.

Purpose or knowledge has been made a component of many offenses so that voluntary intoxication will be an available defense in those situations. Thus, voluntary intoxication may be a defense to aggravated assaults consisting of attempts to cause bodily injury to another with a deadly weapon. Intoxication could exonerate those otherwise guilty of burglaries and criminal trespass. It would be an available defense to arson, robbery, and theft. It could reduce murder to manslaughter, and excuse shoplifting. The Code would also permit the incongruous result of permitting intoxication to be a complete defense to an attempted sexual assault (rape), but not of a completed sexual assault. Whether the Legislature will retain any or all these provisions remains to be seen.

Our holding today does not mean that voluntary intoxication is always irrelevant in criminal proceedings. Evidence of intoxication may be introduced to demonstrate that premeditation and deliberation have not been proven so that a second degree murder cannot be raised to first degree murder or to show that the intoxication led to a fixed state of insanity. Intoxication may be shown to prove that a defendant never participated in a crime. Thus it might be proven that a defendant was in such a drunken stupor and unconscious state that he was not a part of a robbery. His mental faculties may be so prostrated as to preclude the commission of the criminal act. Under some circumstances intoxication may be relevant to demonstrate mistake. However, in the absence of any basis for the defense, a trial court should not in its charge introduce that element. A trial court, of course, may consider intoxication as a mitigating circumstance when sentencing a defendant.

HANDLER, J., concurring.

If a defendant's state of mind is a material factor in determining whether a particular crime has been committed—and if a degree of intoxication so affects the defendant's mental faculties as to eliminate effectively a condition of the mind otherwise essential for the commission of a crime—intoxication should be recognized as a defense in fact.

When dealing with the issue of intoxication, the focus at trial should be upon the mental state which is required for the commission of the particular crime charged. This should not ordinarily call for desiccated refinements between general intent and specific intent.

Adherence to the distinction between specific and general intent crimes, and the availability of voluntary intoxication as a defense in terms of that distinction, has led to anomalous results.

The Model Penal Code of the American Law Institute has eschewed this distinction. It deals with *mens rea* primarily in terms of purpose and knowledge and calls for an analysis of the elements of the criminal offense in relation to these components. The recently enacted New Jersey Code of Criminal Justice, similarly abandons the distinctions between specific and general intent in addressing the area of the mental components of crime. This approach, in my view, enables a trier of fact to assimilate proof of a defendant's intoxication in a more realistic perspective and to reach a more rational determination of the effect of intoxication upon criminal responsibility, particularly in terms of consciousness and purpose.

On this point, the majority disapproves of the decision in *Del Vecchio.* I also disavow that decision to the extent it maintains the distinction between specific intent and general intent crimes and determines the availability of voluntary intoxication as a defense based upon that distinction. I do not think it follows, however, that if the separation between so-called specific and general intent crimes is rejected, voluntary intoxication as a factual defense must also be rejected.

The majority of this Court repudiates the intoxication defense on grounds of general deterrence and a ubiquitous need to protect society from drunken criminals. This approach mirrors a commendable impulse which I share. But, it fails to consider that enforcement of the criminal law must be fair and just, as well as strict and protective.

I would require, in order to generate a reasonable doubt as to a defendant's responsibility for his acts, that it be shown he was so intoxicated that he could not think, or that his mind did not function with consciousness or volition.

I disagree therefore with the suggestion by the Court that if voluntary intoxication is recognized as a defense, as it is under the recently enacted New Jersey Code of Criminal Justice, it will serve to excuse criminal conduct with respect to which purpose or knowledge is a component. I do not share the pessimism of the Court that voluntary intoxication as a recognized defense will wreak havoc in criminal law enforcement under the New Jersey Criminal Justice Code. The fear of condoning criminals, who are also drunks, can be addressed, I respectfully suggest, by imposing a heavy burden of proof upon defendants to show a degree of intoxication capable of prostrating the senses. Drunkenness which does not have this effect does not diminish responsibility and should not serve to excuse criminality. I think it amiss therefore for this Court to forewarn the Legislature, on the basis of its own dire prognostications as to the applications of the statutory intoxication defense contemplated under the New Jersey Criminal Justice Code.

In this case, the crime with which defendant was charged is denominated by the statute, as assault with intent to rob. It serves no useful end to describe the mental state necessary to sustain the charge as a "specific intent" in contradistinction to a "general intent" to do the particular acts revealed by the evidence. I am satisfied that under any formulation of the elements of the crime, defendant on these facts could not be exonerated for reasons of intoxication. The facts, which are fully set forth in the Court's opinion, reveal that defendant engaged in volitional, purposeful activity—he assaulted his victim with a knife and at the same time unmistakably expressed his purpose by demanding that his victim turn over $80 from the cash register. He had the requisite *mens rea* for affixing criminal responsibility. The evidence of defendant's drinking during the day and before the assault is relevant, of course, to the question of whether he was intoxicated when he committed this crime. But, in light of his unequivocal assault on the bartender with a knife and his loud and clear demand for money from the cash register, the evidence of intoxication was palpably insufficient to negate the volitional character of the defendant's behavior. Juxtaposed against such overwhelming and clear evidence of purposeful criminal conduct, only intoxication which prostrated the defendant's faculties or deprived him of will would justify his acquittal.

Was defendant nevertheless entitled to have the jury consider the evidence of intoxication as a factor relevant to his commission of the charged crime? Evidence of intoxication, which may under some circumstances be inferred from prolonged, continuous, heavy drinking, should ordinarily entitle a defendant to a charge of intoxication as a factual defense bearing upon his mental state and whether he acted without purpose or volition. The charge on intoxication, however, should explain to the jury that unless defendant's intoxication was sufficiently extreme so as to have deprived him of his will to act and ability to reason, and prevented him in fact from having a purpose to rob the bartender, he would not, on this ground, be entitled to an acquittal.

Pashman, J., concurring in result only and dissenting.

The majority rules that a person may be convicted of the crimes of assault *with intent* to rob and breaking and entering *with intent* to steal even though he never, in fact, intended to rob anyone or steal anything. The majority arrives at this anomalous result by holding that voluntary intoxication can never constitute a defense to any crime other than first-degree murder even though, due to intoxication, the accused may not have possessed the mental state specifically required as an element of the offense. This holding not only defies logic and sound public policy, it also runs counter to dictates of prior caselaw and the policies enunciated by our Legislature in the new criminal code. I therefore dissent from that holding.

II.

Today's holding by the majority not only departs from precedent, it also stands logic on its head. This Court and the Legislature have long adhered to the view that criminal sanctions will not be imposed upon a defendant unless there exists a "concurrence of an evil-meaning mind with an evil-doing hand." The policies underlying this proposition are clear. A person who intentionally commits a bad act is more culpable than one who engages in the same conduct without any evil design. The intentional wrongdoer is also more likely to repeat his offense, and hence constitutes a greater threat to societal repose. A sufficiently intoxicated defendant is thus subject to less severe sanctions not because the law "excuses" his conduct but because the circumstances surrounding his acts have been deemed by the Legislature to be less deserving of punishment.

It strains reason to hold that a defendant may be found guilty of a crime whose definition includes a requisite mental state when the defendant actually failed to possess that state of mind. Indeed, this is the precise teaching of cases allowing the intoxication defense in first-degree murder prosecutions. To sustain a first-degree murder conviction, the State must prove that the homicide was premeditated, willful, and deliberate. If the accused, due to intoxication, did not in fact possess these mental attributes, he can be convicted of at most second-degree murder. That offense, however, can be sustained on a mere showing of recklessness, and the necessary recklessness can be found in the act of becoming intoxicated.

Just as the lack of premeditation, willfulness, or deliberation precludes a conviction for first-degree murder, so should the lack of intent to rob or steal be a defense to assault and battery with intent to rob, or breaking and entering with intent to steal. The principle is the same in both situations. If voluntary intoxication negates an element of the offense, the defendant has not engaged in the conduct proscribed by the criminal statute, and hence should not be subject to the sanctions imposed by that statute.

IV.

The majority and the commentators have criticized as elusive the "specific intent—general intent" dichotomy. The majority's difficulty in distinguishing the various mental states should not, however, be sufficient reason to mandate that *all* intoxicated defendants be incarcerated. The proper approach is to try and outline a more rational rule for applying the defense. I believe that such a rule is that enunciated in our new Code of Criminal Justice, effective September 1, 1979, which provides that intoxication will be a defense whenever it negates an element of an offense. The Act defines four mental states—purpose, knowledge, recklessness and negligence—one of which is necessary to establish guilt depending on the particular offense involved. Purpose and knowledge may be negated by intoxication, whereas recklessness and negligence may not. Moreover, the elements of recklessness or negligence may, where required by the definition of the crime, be satisfied by the recklessness implicit in becoming voluntarily intoxicated.

Although our current criminal law does not neatly compartmentalize *mens rea* into four such categories, the same type of analysis can be applied. Whenever a defendant shows that he was so intoxicated that he did not possess the requisite state of mind, he may not be convicted. Intoxication would not be a defense, however, to criminal offenses which may be established by recklessness or negligence as the carelessness in getting intoxicated would of itself supply the necessary mental state. This analysis would leave intact the long-standing rule that intoxication is not a defense to second-degree murder as that crime may be established by showing recklessness.

Although the distinction between specific intent and general intent would be erased by the rule enunciated herein, this does not mean that the different mental states implicit in our criminal law would become irrelevant. Some crimes—battery, for example—only require that the defendant intend the act that he has committed, while others—such as assault and battery with intent to kill—require that he also intend to bring about certain consequences. Certainly it would take a greater showing of intoxication to convince one that defendant had no intent to strike the victim than to show that he did not intend to kill. In the former case, one might well conclude that he must have intended his act unless he was unconscious. Indeed, this is the main reason why the "specific intent/general intent" dichotomy was first formulated.

In as much as defendants in these two cases were charged with crimes requiring intent to rob or intent to steal, their convictions must be reversed and a new trial ordered at which they can attempt to persuade the jury that they lacked those mental states. We must respect the legislative judgment, made explicit in the new Criminal Code, that those persons who, due to intoxication, act without the intent required by law as an element of the crime, are not to be treated as those who willfully commit the same acts.

Comments and Questions

(1) To begin, it is important to note that there is a distinction between involuntary intoxication and voluntary intoxication. While the cases are rare, facts that demonstrate truly involuntary intoxication can relieve the defendant of criminal responsibility. *Sallahdin v. Gibson*, 275 F.3d 1211, 1235 (10th Cir. 2002) ("Involuntary intoxication results from fraud, trickery or duress of another, accident or mistake on defendant's part, pathological condition, or ignorance as to the effects of prescribed medication. 'Involuntary intoxication is a complete defense.'"). *See also Torres v. State*, 585 S.W.2d 746 (Tex. Crim. App. 1979) (defendant entitled to put on affirmative defense of involuntary intoxication when she drank Alka-Seltzer which—unknown to her—also contained Thorazine).

(2) In cases where the defendant argues voluntary intoxication, historically the law has been unforgiving. As the *Stasio* Court announced: "It is generally agreed that a defendant will not be relieved of criminal responsibility because he was under the influence of intoxicants or drugs voluntarily taken. This principle rests upon public policy, demanding that he who seeks the influence of liquor or narcotics should not be insulated from criminal liability because that influence impaired his judgment or his control." Beginning in the nineteenth century, though, courts began to recognize that even voluntary intoxication could negate the mens rea component of some

crimes. Thus, as both the *Heideman* and *Stasio* cases demonstrate, courts distinguished between general intent and specific intent crimes; the voluntary intoxication defense was permitted in relation to specific intent crimes but not general intent crimes. The *Heideman* case reflects general acceptance of this distinction, whereas the *Stasio* court holds that the distinction creates "an unworkable dichotomy." Consider the following crimes where courts have ruled on the admissibility of intoxication evidence. Does this list shed some light on the notion that the general intent/specific intent distinction is unworkable or arbitrary?

possession of unregistered fire arms—*United States v. Reed*, 991 F.2d 399 (7th Cir. 1993) (inadmissible).

attempted sexual abuse—*United States v. Sneezer*, 900 F.2d 177 (9th Cir. 1990) (admissible).

premeditated murder—*People v. Castillo*, 945 P.2d 1197 (Cal. 1997) (admissible).

second-degree murder—*Crozier v. State*, 723 P.2d 42 (Wyo. 1986) (inadmissible).

robbery—*United States v. Sewell*, 252 F.3d 647 (2d Cir. 2001); *United States v. Burdeau*, 168 F.3d 352 (9th Cir. 1999) (inadmissible).

rape—*People v. Brumfield*, 390 N.E.2d 589 (Ill. App. Ct. 1979) (inadmissible).

carnal abuse of a child—*Hatfield v. Commonwealth*, 473 S.W.2d 104 (Ky. 1971) (inadmissible).

assault—*State v. Galvin*, 514 A.2d 705 (Vt. 1986) (inadmissible).

aggravated assault—*Id.* (admissible); *People v. Harkey*, 386 N.E.2d 1151 (Ill. App. Ct. 1979) (inadmissible).

assault upon a police officer—*Galvin, supra* (admissible).

arson—*State v. Miller*, 600 P.2d 1123 (Ariz. Ct. App. 1979) (inadmissible).

attempted arson—*Id.* (admissible).

(3) Very soon after the *Stasio* case had been decided, the New Jersey Criminal Code became effective. That code's provision regarding intoxication was based upon the Model Penal Code § 2.08 on intoxication. The New Jersey Code permits evidence regarding intoxication under the following circumstances: "[U]nder the Code voluntary intoxication is a defense to a criminal charge that contains as an essential element proof that a defendant acted purposely or knowingly; (2) the Code definition of 'intoxication' contemplates a condition by which the mental or physical capacities of the actor, because of the introduction of intoxicating substances into the body, are so prostrated as to render him incapable of purposeful or knowing conduct." *State v. Cameron*, 514 A.2d 1302, 1310 (N.J. 1986). Notice that the New Jersey Code does not permit intoxication as a defense to crimes that require a showing of recklessness. *See also* Model Penal Code § 2.08(2) ("When recklessness establishes an element of the offense, if the actor, due to self-induced intoxication, is unaware of a risk of which he would have been aware had he been sober, such unawareness is immaterial.");

Conn. Gen. Stat. Ann. § 53a-7(evidence of intoxication permitted to negate mens rea of offense except when recklessness or negligence are an element of the crime charged).

(4) In some states, evidence of voluntary intoxication is not admissible as a defense to any criminal charge. *See, e.g., Wyant v. State*, 519 A.2d 649 (Del. 1986) (upholding statute that stated that voluntary intoxication is "no defense to any criminal charge"); White v. State, 717 S.W.2d 784 (Ark. 1986) (interpreting legislation to preclude voluntary intoxication as a defense to criminal prosecution).

Montana's statute on intoxication, Mont. Cod. Ann. § 45-2-203, says the following:

> A person who is in an intoxicated condition is criminally responsible for the person's conduct, and an intoxicated condition is not a defense to any offense and may not be taken into consideration in determining the existence of a mental state that is an element of the offense unless the defendant proves that the defendant did not know that it was an intoxicating substance when the defendant consumed, smoked, sniffed, injected, or otherwise ingested the substance causing the condition.

Defendant Egelhoff, convicted of two counts of homicide and barred from putting on evidence of his intoxication at the time of the crime, challenged the Montana law as violative of the Due Process Clause, and the Montana State Supreme Court upheld his challenge. *State v. Egelhoff*, 900 P.2d 260, 266 (Mont. 1995) ("[T]he defendant had a due process right to present and have considered by the jury all relevant evidence to rebut the State's evidence on all elements of the offense charged."). In *Montana v. Egelhoff*, 518 U.S. 37 (1996), a majority of the United States Supreme Court disagreed and found the statute valid.

Justice Scalia, writing for Chief Justice Rehnquist, and Justices Kennedy and Thomas, could not find that evidence of intoxication "was so deeply rooted at the time of the Fourteenth Amendment (or perhaps has become so deeply rooted since) as to be a fundamental principle which that Amendment enshrined." *Id.* at 48. Noting that several states had adopted similar restrictions, they did not find "surprising" such a legislative judgment.

> A large number of crimes, especially violent crimes, are committed by intoxicated offenders; modern studies put the number as high as half of all homicides, for example. Disallowing consideration of voluntary intoxication has the effect of increasing the punishment for all unlawful acts committed in that state, and thereby deters drunkenness or irresponsible behavior while drunk. The rule also serves as a specific deterrent, ensuring that those who prove incapable of controlling violent impulses while voluntarily intoxicated go to prison. And finally, the rule comports with and implements society's moral perception that one who has voluntarily impaired his own faculties shall be responsible for the consequences. *Id.* at 49–50.

Justice Ginsburg, in concurrence, cast the controlling vote. She found that the substantive statute in question essentially redefined the principal offense so that evidence of voluntary intoxication is irrelevant as to the requisite mental state. Because the legislature has broad powers to redefine *mens rea*, she could find no difficulty with the new statute.

The dissenting Justices sharply disagreed with the plurality and concurring opinions. Justice O'Connor, joined by Justices Stevens, Souter, and Breyer, thought the Due Process challenge was legitimate.

> Here, to impede the defendant's ability to throw doubt on the State's case, Montana has removed from the jury's consideration a category of evidence relevant to determination of mental state where that mental state is an essential element of the offense that must be proved beyond reasonable doubt. Because this disallowance eliminates evidence with which the defense might negate an essential element, the State's burden to prove its case is made correspondingly easier. The justification for this disallowance is the State's desire to increase the likelihood of conviction of a certain class of defendants who might otherwise be able to prove that they did not satisfy a requisite element of the offense. In my view, the statute's effect on the criminal proceeding violates due process. *Id.* at 61.

Justice Souter, also dissenting, wrote more narrowly to note that while states may choose to redefine mental elements of an offense, the Montana Supreme Court had found no such redefinition and the Court should feel "bound by the state court's statement of its domestic law." *Id.* at 73.

§7.05 The Insanity Defense

> Our criminal justice system punishes those it convicts for many reasons, chief among them being retribution against the criminal, deterrence of future crimes, and rehabilitation of the criminal. However, we hold accountable only those who are morally culpable for their conduct; historically we have not held "the very crazy" morally accountable for at least some of their actions. In principle, the insanity defense can be traced back through at least 1,000 years of British law, and perhaps back as far as Roman, Christian, and Judaic law.
>
> The point to be gleaned from this discussion is simple: whatever the specific formulation the defense has been throughout history, it has always been the case that the law has been loathe to assign criminal responsibility to an actor who was unable, at the time he or she committed the crime, to know either what was being done or that it was wrong. This basic tenet has apparently been unaffected by advances in medicine or psychology. As the first Justice Harlan noted nearly 100 years ago, while one of the goals of the criminal justice system is to punish criminals and to protect public safety, some "crimes of the most atrocious character" must not be the subject of criminal sanctions if the imposition of such sanctions would require the courts "to depart from

> principles fundamental in criminal law, and the recognition and enforcement of which are demanded by every consideration of humanity and justice."

United States v. Denny-Shaffer, 2 F.3d 999, 1012 (10th Cir. 1993).

As the Tenth Circuit recognized in *Denny-Shaffer*, it is a bedrock principle of American law that the insane cannot and should not be held legally accountable for criminal acts.

It is important to note that a criminal defendant's mental competence may be relevant at three stages of the proceeding. First, a defendant must be competent to stand trial. The Supreme Court in *Dusky v. United States*, 362 U.S. 402 (1960), set out the test for competency. In order for the state to proceed with its case against the defendant, the defendant must have a "sufficient present ability to consult with his lawyer with a reasonable degree of rational understanding and ... a rational as well as factual understanding of the proceedings against him." The competency question focuses on the defendant's mental state at the time of the criminal proceedings. Second, a defendant may argue that he was insane at the time of his crime and thus should be excused of responsibility for his criminal acts. The insanity inquiry focuses on defendant's mental state at the time of the alleged crime. Finally, if convicted, an inmate facing the death penalty may raise the issue of sanity again, as the Constitution forbids execution of the insane. *Ford v. Wainwright*, 477 U.S. 399 (1986).

This section of Chapter Seven focuses on the defense of insanity at trial, rather than the question of whether a defendant is competent to stand trial or whether he is sane for purposes of execution. How should insanity be defined and measured? Who may raise the issue of a defendant's sanity? What is the difference between insanity and other forms of diminished capacity? The following materials address these and related questions.

[A] The Formulations

M'Naghten's Case

House of Lords

10 Cl. & F. 200, 8 Eng. Rep. 718 (1843)

Simon, The Jury and the Defense of Insanity,* at 20–22 (1967):

The case of Daniel M'Naghten was a Scottish woodcutter who assassinated Edward Drummond, secretary to the Prime Minister, Sir Robert Peel, in the mistaken belief that the secretary was the Prime Minister. M'Naghten, "an extreme paranoiac entangled in an elaborate system of delusions," believed that the Prime Minister was responsible for the financial and personal misfortunes that were continually plaguing him. During the trial nine medical witnesses all testified that the defendant was insane. Although the form of the insanity was not officially designated by the medical witnesses, psychiatrists today who have read reports of the trial believe that M'-

Naghten was "under the influence of a form of mental disorder symptomized by delusions of persecution in which Peel appeared as one of the persecutors." So convincing was the defense's plea that at the end of the testimony Lord Chief Justice Tindal, sitting with two other judges, came close to directing the jury's verdict. He told the jury: "I cannot help remarking in common with my learned brethren that the whole of medical evidence is on one side—that it seems almost unnecessary that I should go through the evidence. I am, however, in your hands." He then instructed the jury:

> The point I shall have to submit to you is whether on the whole of the evidence you have heard, you are satisfied that at the time the act was committed ... the prisoner had that competent use of his understanding as that he knew that he was doing, by the very act itself, a wicked and a wrong thing? If the prisoner was not sensible at the time he committed the act, that it was a violation of the law of God or of man, undoubtedly he was not responsible for that act or liable to any punishment flowing from that act.... If on balancing the evidence in your minds, you think the prisoner capable of distinguishing between right and wrong, then he was a responsible agent and liable to all the penalties the law imposes. If not ... then you will probably not take upon yourselves to find the prisoner guilty. If this is your opinion, then you will acquit the prisoner.

The jury found the defendant "not guilty on the grounds of insanity." Daniel M'-Naghten was committed to Broadmoor mental institution, where he remained until his death in May, 1865, about twenty years later.

Queen Victoria, the House of Lords, and the newspapers of the day disapproved of the verdict in openly angry and bitter tones. M'Naghten's attempted assassination of the Prime Minister marked the fifth attack on English sovereigns and their ministers since the turn of the century. In 1800 Hadfield had attempted to kill King George III. In 1813 Bellingham had assassinated Spencer Perceval, Chancellor of the Exchequer and Lord of the Treasury. Between 1840 and 1842 two attempts had been made on Queen Victoria's life. Now Daniel M'Naghten, a defendant who admitted that he attempted to assassinate the Prime Minister, was declared not guilty on the grounds of insanity and was sent to Broadmoor, a place described by the press as a retreat for idlers. The government and newspapers interpreted the court's action to be a direct disregard of the dangerous and threatening state of affairs.

The case of Daniel M'Naghten probably would have had a place of distinction in English criminal law even if the uproar had ended on this note of public indignation. But more was still to come. The House of Lords called upon the fifteen judges of the common law courts to respond to a series of questions on the law that the Lords would ask them. In effect, the judges were being asked to account for a miscarriage of justice. Their actions had been severely criticized by the Crown, the House of Lords, and the press, and now they were being confronted directly with their misdeeds.

[The opinion of the House of Lords]

The prisoner had been indicted for that he, on the 20th day of January 1843, at the parish of Saint Martin in the Fields, in the county of Middlesex, and within the jurisdiction of the Central Criminal Court, in and upon one Edward Drummond, feloniously, wilfully, and of his malice aforethought, did make an assault; and that the said Daniel M'Naghten, a certain pistol of the value of 20s., loaded and charged with gunpowder and a leaden bullet (which pistol he in his right hand had and held), to, against and upon the said Edward Drummond, feloniously, wilfully, and of his malice aforethought, did shoot and discharge; and that the said Daniel M'-Naghten, with the leaden bullet aforesaid, out of the pistol aforesaid, by force of the gunpowder, etc., the said Edward Drummond, in and upon the back of him the said Edward Drummond, feloniously, etc. did strike, penetrate and wound, giving to the said Edward Drummond, in and upon the back of the said Edward Drummond, one mortal wound, etc., of which mortal wound the said E. Drummond languished until the 25th of April and then died; and that by the means aforesaid, he the prisoner did kill and murder the said Edward Drummond. The prisoner pleaded not guilty.

Evidence having been given of the fact of the shooting of Mr. Drummond, and of his death in consequence thereof, witnesses were called on the part of the prisoner, to prove that he was not, at the time of committing the act, in a sound state of mind. The medical evidence was in substance this: That persons of otherwise sound mind, might be affected by morbid delusions: that the prisoner was in that condition: that a person so labouring under a morbid delusion, might have a moral perception of right and wrong, but that in the case of the prisoner it was a delusion which carried him away beyond the power of his own control, and left him no such perception; and that he was not capable of exercising any control over acts which had connexion with his delusion: that it was of the nature of the disease with which the prisoner was affected, to go on gradually until it had reached a climax, when it burst forth with irresistible intensity: that a man might go on for years quietly, though at the same time under its influence, but would all at once break out into the most extravagant and violent paroxysms.

Some of the witnesses who gave this evidence, had previously examined the prisoner: others had never seen him till he appeared in Court, and they formed their opinions on hearing the evidence given by the other witnesses.

Lord Chief Justice Tindal (in his charge): The question to be determined is, whether at the time the act in question was committed, the prisoner had or had not the use of his understanding, so as to know that he was doing a wrong or wicked act.

Verdict, Not guilty, on the ground of insanity.

This verdict, and the question of the nature and extent of the unsoundness of mind which would excuse the commission of felony of this sort, having been made the subject of debate in the House of Lords, it was determined to take the opinion of the Judges on the law governing such cases.

On the 19th of June, the Judges again attended the House of Lords; questions of law were propounded to them.

The first question proposed by your Lordships is this: "What is the law respecting alleged crimes committed by persons afflicted with insane delusion in respect of one or more particular subjects or persons; as, for instance, where at the time of the commission of the alleged crime the accused knew he was acting contrary to law, but did the act complained of with a view, under the influence of insane delusion, of redressing or revenging some supposed grievance or injury, or of producing some supposed public benefit?"

In answer to which question, assuming that your Lordships' inquiries are confined to those persons who labour under such partial delusions only, and are not in other respects insane, we are of opinion that, notwithstanding the party accused did the act complained of with a view, under the influence of insane delusion, of redressing or revenging some supposed grievance or injury, or of producing some public benefit, he is nevertheless punishable according to the nature of the crime committed, if he knew at the time of committing such crime that he was acting contrary to law; by which expression we understand your Lordships to mean the law of the land.

Your Lordships are pleased to inquire of us, secondly, "What are the proper questions to be submitted to the jury, where a person alleged to be afflicted with insane delusion respecting one or more particular subjects or persons, is charged with the commission of a crime (murder, for example), and insanity is set up as a defence?" And, thirdly, "In what terms ought the question to be left to the jury as to the prisoner's state of mind at the time when the act was committed?" And as these two questions appear to us to be more conveniently answered together, we have to submit our opinion to be, that the jurors ought to be told in all cases that every man is to be presumed to be sane, and to possess a sufficient degree of reason to be responsible for his crimes, until the contrary be proved to their satisfaction; and that to establish a defence on the ground of insanity, it must be clearly proved that, at the time of the committing of the act, the party accused was labouring under such a defect of reason, from disease of the mind, as not to know the nature and quality of the act he was doing; or, if he did know it, that he did not know he was doing what was wrong. The mode of putting the latter part of the question to the jury on these occasions has generally been, whether the accused at the time of doing the act knew the difference between right and wrong: which mode, though rarely, if ever, leading to any mistake with the jury, is not, as we conceive, so accurate when put generally and in the abstract, as when put with reference to the party's knowledge of right and wrong in respect to the very act with which he is charged. If the question were to be put as to the knowledge of the accused solely and exclusively with reference to the law of the land, it might tend to confound the jury, by inducing them to believe that an actual knowledge of the law of the land was essential in order to lead to a conviction; whereas the law is administered upon the principle that every one must be taken conclusively to know it, without proof that he does know it. If the accused was conscious that the act was one which he ought not to do, and if that act was at the same time contrary to the law of the land, he is punishable; and the usual course therefore has been to leave the question to the jury, whether the party accused had a sufficient degree of reason to know that he was doing an act that was wrong: and this course we think is correct, accompanied with such observations and explanations as the circumstances of each particular case may require.

The fourth question which your Lordships have proposed to us is this: "If a person under an insane delusion as to existing facts, commits an offence in consequence thereof, is he thereby excused?" To which question the answer must of course depend on the nature of the delusion: but, making the same assumption as we did before, namely, that he labours under such partial delusion only, and is not in other respects insane, we think he must be considered in the same situation as to responsibility as if the facts with respect to which the delusion exists were real. For example, if under the influence of his delusion he supposes another man to be in the act of attempting to take away his life, and he kills that man, as he supposes, in self-defence, he would be exempt from punishment. If his delusion was that the deceased had inflicted a serious injury to his character and fortune, and he killed him in revenge for such supposed injury, he would be liable to punishment.

The question lastly proposed by your Lordships is: "Can a medical man conversant with the disease of insanity, who never saw the prisoner previously to the trial, but who was present during the whole trial and the examination of all the witnesses, be asked his opinion as to the state of the prisoner's mind at the time of the commission of the alleged crime, or his opinion whether the prisoner was conscious at the time of doing the act that he was acting contrary to law, or whether he was labouring under any and what delusion at the time?" In answer thereto, we state to your Lordships, that we think the medical man, under the circumstances supposed, cannot in strictness be asked his opinion in the terms above stated, because each of those questions involves the determination of the truth of the facts deposed to, which it is for the jury to decide, and the questions are not mere questions upon a matter of science, in which case such evidence is admissible. But where the facts are admitted or not disputed, and the question becomes substantially one of science only, it may be convenient to allow the question to be put in that general form, though the same cannot be insisted on as a matter of right.

Comments and Questions

(1) The insanity test articulated in *M'Naghten* became the prevailing American view. Under the rule, in order to establish the defense of insanity, the defendant needed to prove that he "was labouring under such a defect of reason, from disease of the mind, as not to know the nature and quality of the act he was doing; or if he did know it, that he did not know he was doing what was wrong."

(2) The *M'Naghten* test has been—and continues to be—heavily criticized. *See, e.g., United States v. Currens*, 290 F.2d 751, 765–67 (3d Cir. 1961):

> Our institutions contain many patients who are insane or mentally ill or mentally diseased and who know the difference between right and wrong.

A visit of a few hours at any one of our larger State institutions within this Circuit will convince even the lay visitor of the correctness of this statement. The test, therefore, of knowledge of right and wrong is almost meaningless.

Further the *M'Naghten* Rules are a sham, as Mr. Justice Frankfurter made plain in his testimony before the Royal Commission on Capital Punishment. He stated in part: "... The *M'Naghten* Rules were rules which the Judges, in response to questions by the House of Lords, formulated in the light of the then existing psychological knowledge.... I do not see why the rules of law should be arrested at the state of psychological knowledge of the time when they were formulated.... If you find rules that are, broadly speaking, discredited by those who have to administer them, which is, I think, the real situation, certainly with us—they are honoured in the breach and not in the observance—then I think the law serves its best interests by trying to be more honest about it.... I think that to have rules which cannot rationally be justified except by a process of interpretation which distorts and often practically nullifies them, and to say the corrective process comes by having the Governor of a State charged with the responsibility of deciding when the consequences of the rule should not be enforced, is not a desirable system.... I am a great believer in being as candid as possible about my institutions. They are in large measure abandoned in practice, and therefore I think the *M'Naghten* Rules are in large measure shams. That is a strong word but I think the *M'Naghten* Rules are very difficult for conscientious people and not difficult enough for people who say, 'We'll just juggle them'... I dare to believe that we ought not to rest content with the difficulty of finding an improvement in the *M'Naghten* Rules ..."

We state again that the *M'Naghten* Rules assume:

> ... the existence of a "... logic-tight compartment in which the delusion holds sway leaving the balance of the mind intact ..."; the criminal retains enough logic ... so that from this sanctuary of reason he may inform himself as to what the other part of his mind, the insane part, has compelled or permitted his body to do. If the sane portion of the accused's mind knows that what the insane part compels or permits the body to do is wrong, the body must suffer [by punishment].... The human mind, however, is an entity. It cannot be broken into parts, one part sane, the other part insane.

See also Morris & Haroun, *"God Told Me to Kill": Religion or Delusion?*, 38 San Diego L. Rev. 973, 1000 (2001): "The *M'Naghten* test has been severely criticized for its narrow and exclusive focus on the defendant's cognitive capacity to distinguish right from wrong. The test assumes that the mind is compartmentalized, although most psychiatrists believe that it is an integrated unit."

But see Livermore & Meehl, *The Virtues of* M'Naghten, 51 Minn. L. Rev. 789, 800, 856 (1967):

> Although the admonition has been uttered many times, it is always necessary to start any discussion of *M'Naghten* by stressing that the case does not state

> a test of psychosis or mental illness. Rather, it lists conditions under which those who are mentally diseased will be relieved from criminal responsibility. Thus, criticism of *M'Naghten* based on the proposition that the case is premised on an outdated view of mental disease is inappropriate. The case can only be criticized justly if it is based on an outdated view of the mental conditions that ought to preclude application of criminal sanctions.
>
> While more refined formulations may be possible, it is our contention that the 124-year-old *M'Naghten* rule with its focus on cognitive impairment is sounder from the standpoints of the purposes of the criminal law, of present psychiatric knowledge, and of ease of judicial administration than any of the newer tests. We have noted the difficulty of giving meaning to terms such as "mental disease," "substantial inability to conform," and "product." Whenever the effort is made to make these terms consistent with general social views of responsibility, a retreat to *M'Naghten* is required. If the drafters of rules of criminal responsibility for the deranged are to remain true to general principles of responsibility, they must take account of societal views on the blameworthiness of conduct engaged in by mentally abnormal persons and of the effect of ignoring those views on the utility of the criminal law. It may be that to do this is to embrace consistency at the expense of substance and that the policies thought to support criminal sanctions are merely myths which have held us in thrall too long. But this position is better addressed to the criminal law as such and not to a small, in this respect indistinguishable, portion of it.

(3) In response to the growing dissatisfaction with the *M'Naghten* test and states' attempts to improve upon it, the American Law Institute's (ALI's) 1962 Model Penal Code devoted a whole Article to "Responsibility." The Code, § 4.01, permitted mental disease or defect to excuse criminal responsibility in the following way:

> (1) A person is not responsible for criminal conduct if at the time of such conduct as a result of mental disease or defect he lacks substantial capacity either to appreciate the criminality [wrongfulness] of his conduct or to conform his conduct to the requirements of law.
>
> (2) As used in this Article, the terms "mental disease or defect" do not include an abnormality manifested only by repeated criminal or otherwise antisocial conduct.

State v. Johnson

Supreme Court of Rhode Island

399 A.2d 469 (1979)

Opinion by: Doris, J:

The sole issue presented by this appeal is whether this court should abandon the *M'Naghten* test in favor of a new standard for determining the criminal responsibility of those who claim they are blameless by reason of mental illness.[1] For the reasons stated herein, we have concluded that the time has arrived to modernize our rule governing this subject.

Before punishing one who has invaded a protected interest, the criminal law generally requires some showing of culpability in the offender. The requirement of a mens rea, or guilty mind, is the most notable example of the concept that before punishment may be exacted, blameworthiness must be demonstrated. That some deterrent, restraint, or rehabilitative purpose may be served is alone insufficient. It has been stated that the criminal law reflects the moral sense of the community. "The fact that the law has, for centuries, regarded certain wrongdoers as improper subjects for punishment is a testament to the extent to which that moral sense has developed. Thus, society has recognized over the years that none of the three asserted purposes of the criminal law—rehabilitation, deterrence, and retribution—is satisfied when the truly irresponsible, those who lack substantial capacity to control their actions, are punished." The law appreciates that those who are substantially unable to restrain their conduct are, by definition, incapable of being deterred and their punishment in a correctional institution provides no example for others.

The law of criminal responsibility has its roots in the concept of free will. As Mr. Justice Jackson stated:

> How far one by an exercise of free will may determine his general destiny or his course in a particular matter and how far he is the toy of circumstance has been debated through the ages by theologians, philosophers, and scientists. Whatever doubts they have entertained as to the matter, the practical business of government and administration of the law is obliged to proceed on more or less rough and ready judgments based on the assumption that mature and rational persons are in control of their own conduct.

Our law proceeds from this postulate and seeks to fashion a standard by which criminal offenders whose free will has been sufficiently impaired can be identified and treated in a manner that is both humane and beneficial to society at large. The problem has been aptly described as distinguishing between those cases for which a correctional—punitive disposition is appropriate and those in which a medical—custodial disposition is the only kind that is legally permissible.

Because language is inherently imprecise and there is a wide divergence of opinion within the medical profession, no exact definition of "insanity" is possible. Every legal definition comprehends elements of abstraction and approximation that are particularly difficult to apply in marginal cases. Our inability to guarantee that a new rule will always be infallible, however, cannot justify unyielding adherence to an outmoded standard, sorely at variance with contemporary medical and legal knowledge. Any legal standard designed to assess criminal responsibility must satisfy several objectives. It must accurately reflect the underlying principles of substantive law and

---

1. ... [W]e prefer to avoid use of the term "insanity defense." Therefore, throughout this opinion we shall use the phrase "[defense] of lack of criminal responsibility due to a mental illness."

community values while comporting with the realities of scientific understanding. The standard must be phrased in order to make fully available to the jury such psychiatric information as medical science has to offer regarding the individual defendant, yet be comprehensible to the experts, lawyers, and jury alike. Finally, the definition must preserve to the trier of facts, be it judge or jury, its full authority to render a final decision. These considerations are paramount in our consideration of the rule to be applied in this jurisdiction in cases in which the defense of lack of criminal responsibility due to a mental illness is raised.

I.

The historical evolution of the law of criminal responsibility is a fascinating, complex story. For purposes of this opinion, however, an exhaustive historical discussion is unnecessary; a brief sketch will therefore suffice. The renowned "right-wrong" test had antecedents in England as early as 1582. In that year the Eirenarcha, written by William Lambard of the Office of the Justices of Peace, laid down as the test for criminal responsibility "knowledge of good or evil." During the 1700's the language of the test shifted its emphasis from "good or evil" to "know." During the eighteenth century, when these tests and their progeny were evolving, psychiatry was hardly a profession, let alone a science. Belief in demonology and witchcraft was widespread and became intertwined with the law of responsibility. So eminent a legal scholar as Blackstone adamantly insisted upon the existence of witches and wizards as late as the later half of the eighteenth century. The psychological theories of phrenology and monomania thrived and influenced the development of the "right and wrong" test. Both of these compartmentalized concepts have been soundly rejected by modern medical science which views the human personality as a fully integrated system. By historical accident, however, the celebrated case of Daniel M'Naghten froze these concepts into the common law just at the time when they were beginning to come into disrepute.

II.

The *M'Naghten* rule has been the subject of considerable criticism and controversy for over a century. The test's emphasis upon knowledge of right or wrong abstracts a single element of personality as the sole symptom or manifestation of mental illness. *M'Naghten* refuses to recognize volitional or emotional impairments, viewing the cognitive element as the singular cause of conduct. One scholar has stated that:

> "[t]he principle behind M'Naghten, namely, that defect of cognition as a consequence of mental disease is the primary exculpating factor in the determination of legal insanity, has probably never been other than a legal fiction."

M'Naghten has been further criticized for being predicated upon an outmoded psychological concept because modern science recognizes that "insanity" affects the whole personality of the defendant, including the will and emotions. One of the most frequent criticisms of *M'Naghten* has been directed at its all-or-nothing approach, requiring total incapacity of cognition. We agree that:

> Nothing makes the inquiry into responsibility more unreal for the psychiatrist than limitation of the issue to some ultimate extreme of total incapacity, when clinical experience reveals only a graded scale with marks along the way.

> The law must recognize that when there is no black and white it must content itself with different shades of gray.

By focusing upon total cognitive incapacity, the *M'Naghten* rule compels the psychiatrist to testify in terms of unrealistic concepts having no medical meaning. Instead of scientific opinions, the rule calls for a moral or ethical judgment from the expert which judgment contributes to usurpation of the jury's function as decision maker.

Probably the most common criticism of *M'Naghten* is that it severely restricts expert testimony, thereby depriving the jury of a true picture of the defendant's mental condition. This contention has been seriously questioned by some commentators who find no support for the argument that *M'Naghten* inhibits the flow of testimony on the responsibility issue. As a matter of practice in this jurisdiction, expert testimony under *M'Naghten* has been unrestricted and robust. Nevertheless, we are convinced that this testimony would be more meaningful to the jury were it not for the narrow determination demanded by *M'Naghten*.

That these criticisms have had a pronounced effect is evidenced by the large and growing number of jurisdictions that have abandoned their former allegiance to *M'-Naghten* in favor of the Model Penal Code formulation. We also find these criticisms persuasive and agree that *M'Naghten's* serious deficiencies necessitate a new approach.

III.

Responding to criticism of *M'Naghten* as a narrow and harsh rule, several courts supplemented it with the "irresistible impulse" test. Under this combined approach, courts inquire into both the cognitive and volitional components of the defendant's behavior. Although a theoretical advance over the stringent right and wrong test, the irresistible impulse doctrine has also been the subject of wide-spread criticism. Similar to *M'Naghten's* absolutist view of capacity to know, the irresistible impulse is considered in terms of a complete destruction of the governing power of the mind. A more fundamental objection is that the test produces the misleading notion that a crime impulsively committed must have been perpetrated in a sudden and explosive fit. Thus, the irresistible impulse test excludes those "far more numerous instances of crimes committed after excessive brooding and melancholy by one who is unable to resist sustained psychic compulsion or to make any real attempt to control his conduct."

The most significant break in the century-old stranglehold of *M'Naghten* came in 1954 when the Court of Appeals for the District of Columbia declared that, "an accused is not criminally responsible if his unlawful act was the product of mental disease or mental defect." *Durham v. United States*, 214 F.2d 862, 874–75 (D.C. Cir. 1954). The "product" test was designed to facilitate full and complete expert testimony and to permit the jury to consider all relevant information, rather than restrict its inquiry to data relating to a sole symptom or manifestation of mental illness. *Durham* generated voluminous commentary and made a major contribution in recasting the law of criminal responsibility. In application, however, the test was plagued by significant deficiencies. The elusive, undefined concept of productivity posed serious problems of causation and gave the jury inadequate guidance. Most troublesome was the test's tendency to result in expert witnesses' usurpation of the jury function.

IV.

Responding to the criticism of the *M'Naghten* and irresistible impulse rules, the American Law Institute incorporated a new test of criminal responsibility into its Model Penal Code.[5] The Model Penal Code has received widespread and ever-growing acceptance. It has been adopted with varying degrees of modification in 26 states and by every federal court of appeals that has addressed the issue. Although no definition can be accurately described as the perfect or ultimate pronouncement, we believe that the Model Penal Code standard represents a significant, positive improvement over our existing rule. Most importantly, it acknowledges that volitional as well as cognitive impairments must be considered by the jury in its resolution of the responsibility issue. The test replaces *M'Naghten's* unrealistic all-or-nothing approach with the concept of "substantial" capacity. Additionally, the test employs vocabulary sufficiently in the common ken that its use at trial will permit a reasonable three-way dialogue between the law—trained judges and lawyers, the medical—trained experts, and the jury.

Without question the essential dilemma in formulating any standard of criminal responsibility is encouraging a maximum informational input from the expert witnesses while preserving to the jury its role as trier of fact and ultimate decision maker. As one court has aptly observed:

> At bottom, the determination whether a man is or is not held responsible for his conduct is not a medical but a legal, social or moral judgment. Ideally, psychiatrists—much like experts in other fields—should provide grist for the legal mill, should furnish the raw data upon which the legal judgment is based. It is the psychiatrist who informs as to the mental state of the accused—his characteristics, his potentialities, his capabilities. But once this information is disclosed, it is society as a whole, represented by judge or jury, which decides whether a man with the characteristics described should or should not be held accountable for his acts.

Because of our overriding concern that the jury's function remain inviolate, we today adopt the following formulation of the Model Penal Code test:

> A person is not responsible for criminal conduct if at the time of such conduct, as a result of mental disease or defect, his capacity either to appreciate the wrongfulness of his conduct or to conform his conduct to the requirements of law is so substantially impaired that he cannot justly be held responsible.

5.

"(1) A person is not responsible for criminal conduct if at the time of such conduct, as a result of mental disease or defect, he lacks substantial capacity either to appreciate the criminality [wrongfulness] of his conduct or to conform his conduct to the requirements of law. "(2) As used in this article, the terms 'mental disease or defect' do not include an abnormality manifested only by repeated criminal or otherwise antisocial conduct." Model Penal Code §4.01 (Final Draft, 1962).

The terms "mental disease or defect" do not include an abnormality manifested only by repeated criminal or otherwise antisocial conduct.[8]

There are several important reasons why we prefer this formulation. The greatest strength of our test is that it clearly delegates the issue of criminal responsibility to the jury, thus precluding possible usurpation of the ultimate decision by the expert witnesses. Under the test we have adopted, the jury's attention is appropriately focused upon the legal and moral aspects of responsibility because it must evaluate the defendant's blameworthiness in light of prevailing community standards. Far from setting the jury at large, as in the majority Model Penal Code test the defendant must demonstrate a certain form of incapacity. That is, the jury must find that a mental disease or defect caused a substantial impairment of the defendant's capacity to appreciate the wrongfulness of his act or to conform his conduct to legal requirements. Our new test emphasizes that the degree of "substantial" impairment required is essentially a legal rather than a medical question. Where formerly under *M'Naghten* total incapacity was necessary for exculpation, the new standard allows the jury to find that incapacity less than total is sufficient. Because impairment is a matter of degree, the precise degree demanded is necessarily governed by the community sense of justice as represented by the trier of fact.

Several other components of our new test require elucidation. Our test consciously employs the more expansive term "appreciate" rather than "know." Implicit in this choice is the recognition that mere theoretical awareness that a certain course of conduct is wrong, when divorced from appreciation or understanding of the moral or legal impact of behavior, is of little import. A significant difference from our former rule is inclusion in the new test of the concept that a defendant is not criminally responsible if he lacked substantial capacity to conform his conduct to the requirements of law. As we noted at the outset, our law assumes that a normal individual has the capacity to control his behavior; should an individual manifest free will in the commission of a criminal act, he must be held responsible for that conduct. Mental illness, however, can effectively destroy an individual's capacity for choice and impair behavioral controls.

The drafters of the Model Penal Code left to each jurisdiction a choice between the terms "wrongfulness" and "criminality." We prefer the word "wrongfulness" because we believe that a person who, knowing an act to be criminal, committed it because of a delusion that the act was morally justified, should not be automatically foreclosed from raising the defense of lack of criminal responsibility.

The second paragraph of our test is designed to exclude from the concept of "mental disease or defect" the so-called psychopathic or sociopathic personality. We have included this language in our test to make clear that mere recidivism alone does not

8. This test was proposed as an alternative by the minority of the American Law Institute Council that drafted the Model Penal Code. The majority of the A.L.I. Council rejected this alternative because they deemed it unwise to present questions of justice to the jury. As this opinion indicates, we believe that the jury's resolution of the responsibility issue is in the final analysis always predicated upon the community sense of justice and it is preferable to be forthright about the basis of that decision.

justify acquittal. We recognize that this paragraph has been the source of considerable controversy. Nevertheless, we believe that its inclusion in our test is necessary to minimize the likelihood of the improper exculpation of defendants who are free of mental disease but who knowingly and deliberately pursue a life of crime.

V.

As we have emphasized previously, preserving the respective provinces of the jury and experts is an important concern. Consonant with modern medical understanding, our test is intended to allow the psychiatrist to place before the jury all of the relevant information that it must consider in reaching its decision. We adhere to Dean Wigmore's statement that when criminal responsibility is in issue, "any and all conduct of the person is admissible in evidence." Nevertheless, the charge to the jury must include unambiguous instructions stressing that regardless of the nature and extent of the experts' testimony, the issue of exculpation remains at all times a legal and not a medical question. In determining the issue of responsibility the jury has two important tasks. First, it must measure the extent to which the defendant's mental and emotional processes were impaired at the time of the unlawful conduct. The answer to that inquiry is a difficult and elusive one, but no more so than numerous other facts that a jury must find in a criminal trial. Second, the jury must assess that impairment in light of community standards of blameworthiness. The jury's unique qualifications for making that determination justify our unusual deference to the jury's resolution of the issue of responsibility. For it has been stated that the essential feature of a jury "lies in the interposition between the accused and his accuser of the commonsense judgment of a group of laymen, and in the community participation and shared responsibility that results from that group's determination of guilt or innocence." Therefore, the charge should leave no doubt that it is for the jury to determine: 1) the existence of a cognizable mental disease or defect, 2) whether such a disability resulted in a substantial impairment at the time of the unlawful conduct of the accused's capacity either to appreciate the wrongfulness of his conduct or to conform his conduct to the requirements of the law, and consequently, 3) whether there existed a sufficient relationship between the mental abnormality and the condemned behavior to warrant the conclusion that the defendant cannot justly be held responsible for his acts.

VI.

So there will be no misunderstanding of the thrust of this opinion, mention should be made of the treatment to be afforded individuals found lacking criminal responsibility due to a mental illness under the test we have adopted. Unquestionably the security of the community must be the paramount interest. Society withholds criminal sanctions out of a sense of compassion and understanding when the defendant is found to lack capacity. It would be an intolerable situation if those suffering from a mental disease or defect of such a nature as to relieve them from criminal responsibility were to be released to continue to pose a threat to life and property. The General Laws provide that a person found not guilty because he was "insane" at the time of the commission of a crime shall be committed to the Director of the State Department of Mental Health for observation. At a subsequent judicial hearing if he is found to be dangerous, the person must be committed to a public institution for care and treatment. This procedure insures society's protection and affords the incompetent criminal offender necessary medical attention.

Our test as enunciated in this opinion shall apply to all trials commenced after the date of this opinion. The defendant in the instant case is entitled to a new trial solely on the issue of criminal responsibility.

The defendant's appeal is sustained and the case is remanded to the Superior Court for a new trial in accordance with the opinions expressed herein.

Comments and Questions

(1) The *Johnson* Court discusses four different tests for insanity. What are the tests and what are their various merits and drawbacks as described by the Court? Is the Model Penal Code test, or the Court's variation on it, a significant improvement over *M'Naghten*?

On July 20, 2012, James Holmes entered a movie theater in Aurora, Colorado, where moviegoers were watching the newly released Batman film, *The Dark Knight Rises*. Holmes shot at people and threw gas canisters into the crowd, killing 12 and injuring 70 people. At his trial for the mass shooting, Holmes pleaded not guilty by reason of insanity. The Colorado insanity provision, Colo. Rev. Stat. § 16-8-101.5, reads in relevant part:

> (1) The applicable test of insanity shall be:
>
> > (a) A person who is so diseased or defective in mind at the time of the commission of the act as to be incapable of distinguishing right from wrong with respect to that act is not accountable; except that care should be taken not to confuse such mental disease or defect with moral obliquity, mental depravity, or passion growing out of anger, revenge, hatred, or other motives and kindred evil conditions, for, when the act is induced by any of these causes, the person is accountable to the law; or
> >
> > (b) A person who suffered from a condition of mind caused by mental disease or defect that prevented the person from forming a culpable mental state that is an essential element of a crime charged, but care should be taken not to confuse such mental disease or defect with moral obliquity, mental depravity, or passion growing out of anger, revenge, hatred, or other motives and kindred evil conditions because, when the act is induced by any of these causes, the person is accountable to the law.
>
> (2) As used in subsection (1) of this section:
>
> > (a) "Diseased or defective in mind" does not refer to an abnormality manifested only by repeated criminal or otherwise antisocial conduct.
> >
> > (b) "Mental disease or defect" includes only those severely abnormal mental conditions that grossly and demonstrably impair a person's perception or understanding of reality and that are not attributable to the voluntary ingestion of alcohol or any other psychoactive substance but does not include

> an abnormality manifested only by repeated criminal or otherwise antisocial conduct.

Is this statute consistent with any of the tests set forth in *Johnson*?

The jurors in Holmes's case heard conflicting reports regarding his sanity at the time of the shooting, but they ultimately found him guilty. *See* Jack Healy and Julie Turkewitz, *Guilty Verdict for James Holmes in Aurora Attack*, N.Y. TIMES, July 17, 2015, at A1.

(2) Initially, the Model Penal Code test for insanity was well-received and widely accepted. As the *Johnson* Court noted, by 1979 that test had been adopted in some form in 26 states and by every federal court of appeals that had addressed the issue. In 1981, John Hinckley, Jr. attempted to assassinate President Reagan. He was tried in federal court, and he pleaded not guilty by reason of insanity. Applying the federal government's test for insanity, which was the Model Penal Code test at the time, the jury found Hinckley not guilty by reason of insanity.

There was public outrage at the outcome, and legislative change quickly followed at the state and federal level. *See generally* Lisa Callahan, Connie Mayer, and Henry J. Steadman, *Insanity Defense Reform in the United States-Post-*Hinckley, 11 MENTAL & PHYSICAL DISABILITY L. REP. 54 (1987). For example, The Insanity Defense Reform Act, codified at 18 U.S.C. 17 and Federal Rules of Evidence 704(b), was passed in 1984. The law introduced three major changes into federal law regarding the insanity defense. First, the ALI defense was rejected and replaced with a defense that eliminates the volitional prong of the claim. The defendant will be successful if there is a showing that he was "unable to appreciate the nature and quality or the wrongfulness of his act" at the time of the crime. Second, the burden of proof on this issue has shifted from the government to the defendant. Prior to the act, the government had to prove beyond a reasonable doubt that the defendant was sane at the time of the offense. Under the law, the defendant must prove insanity by clear and convincing evidence to escape criminal liability. The third change is that experts may not testify as to the ultimate issue of the defendant's insanity. By 2006, the Supreme Court noted that, in addition to the federal government, a clear majority of the states had returned to using a form of the M'Naghten test. *Clark v. Arizona*, 548 U.S. 735, 750–752 (2006).

(3) As a matter of policy, upon which side should the burden of proof rest with insanity claims? It has consistently been held that placing the burden on the defendant does not violate the Constitution, for sanity "is an independent fact and not an element of any existing criminal offense." *State v. Joyner*, 625 A.2d 791 (Conn. 1993).

(4) The proof problems in insanity prosecutions are quite severe. See, for instance, *Commonwealth v. Bruno*, 407 A.2d 413 (Pa. Super. Ct. 1979), where the defendant raised

> the defense of not guilty by reason of insanity, contending that he had committed the killings for which he was charged because he thought the killings would improve his mother's condition. To support his contention, he sought to introduce evidence describing his mother's mental condition and actions, psychiatric testimony relating the effect of his mother's mental condition

> upon himself and medical records from the 1966 Sanity Commission report. He asserts that the court erred in excluding this evidence. We believe the court correctly excluded this evidence as irrelevant.
>
> In Pennsylvania, the standard of insanity, called the *M'Naghten* test, is that an accused is legally insane if, because of mental disease, he either did not know the nature and quality of his act or did not know that it was wrong. The Commonwealth conceded that appellant suffered from mental illness, of which extensive evidence was entered. Under the *M'Naghten* test, the only remaining questions were whether appellant, because of his mental disease, knew the nature and quality of his acts or that they were wrong. On these points, the trial court permitted appellant to enter both lay and expert evidence. The excluded evidence, although it may have demonstrated that appellant was mentally ill or revealed the causes of the illness, did not bear on the question at issue.

Was this evidence properly excluded under the "right-wrong" test? Would it be admissible under the ALI formulation?

One lingering question related to the proof problem is what role experts should play when the defendant pleads not guilty by reason of insanity. *See*, for example, Judge Bazelon's concern in *United States v. Brawner*, 471 F.2d 969, 1017 (1972)(decision superseded by statute):

> Ever since this court announced its new test of responsibility in 1954, we have been struggling with the problem of distinguishing between the uniquely psychiatric elements of the determination of responsibility, and the legal and moral elements of that determination. We have repeatedly urged psychiatrists to avoid using the conclusory labels of either psychiatry or law. Testimony in terms of the legal conclusion that an act was or was not the product of mental disease invites the jury to abdicate its function and acquiesce in the conclusion of the experts. Testimony in terms of psychiatric labels obscures the fact that a defendant's responsibility does not turn on whether or not the experts have given his condition a name and the status of disease.

Commentators in the field remain quite critical of the role of mental health experts in trials raising the insanity defense. *See, e.g.*, Pincus, *The Problem of Gauguin's Therapist: Language, Madness and Therapy* 96–97 (Avebury Academic Press 1994):

> What better example of the ridiculousness of psychiatric diagnosis than the pitting of expert v. expert in the legal proceeding. And the bigger the trial, the more ridiculous the testimony. When John Hinckley, Jr., employed the insanity defense at his trial for the attempted assassination of Ronald Reagan, the top psychiatric experts in the country were called to testify. [One] recognized expert on the diagnosis of schizophrenia, asserted that Hinckley was a processed schizophrenic. [Another], forensic specialist, demurred: "Mr. Hinckley does not suffer from schizophrenia … Mr. Hinckley has not been psychotic at any time." [Still another] after studying Hinckley's CT scans, confidently averred that it was a "psychiatric fact that Hinckley was psychotic." But [a ra-

diology specialist] studied the same CT scans and concluded that the scans showed "no evidence of any significant abnormality whatsoever." There is nothing atypical about the contradictory testimony described above. Similar testimony can be heard in any court whenever Mental Health Professionals are called upon to testify. Even the most renowned experts cannot agree on an individual's mental status—even when looking at the same brain scans.

(5) Some states have statutes allowing defendants to be found guilty but mentally ill. Under these statutes, if the criminal is found guilty but mentally ill—and not legally insane—he would receive the same sentence as if there had been a guilty verdict, but the sentence would include treatment for mental illness. "'[M]ental illness' or 'mentally ill' means a substantial disorder of thought, mood, or behavior which afflicted a person ... and which impaired that person's judgment, but not to the extent that he is unable to appreciate the wrongfulness of his behavior." 720 Ill. Comp. Stat. 5/6-2(d).

(6) Is a trial judge obliged to advise jurors that a criminal defendant who is found not guilty by reason of insanity will be committed to a mental hospital? This instruction was initially adopted due to concerns that a jury, without this information, might find the defendant guilty in order to make sure that she would not go free. The Supreme Court in *Shannon v. United States*, 512 U.S. 573 (1994), found that such an instruction was not mandated by the federal Insanity Defense Reform Act, but it did not address whether such an instruction was constitutionally required as a matter of fundamental fairness. Lower courts are split on that question. *Compare State v. Becker*, 818 N.W.2d 135 (Iowa 2012) (trial court's refusal to instruct jury on consequences of not guilty by reason of insanity verdict—even when jury asks the question during deliberation—does not violate due process) *with Roberts v. State*, 335 So. 2d 285 (Fla. 1976) (failure to instruct jury on consequences of verdict of not guilty by reason of insanity was reversible error).

(7) Must a state afford defendants the right to present an insanity defense? Some states have abolished the insanity defense, although they typically allow expert testimony "on the issue of any state of mind which is an element of the offense." Idaho Code Ann. § 18-207(3). The court in *State v. Bethel*, 66 P.3d 840 (Kan. 2003), upheld such abolition, noting that the state law allowed evidence with respect to the defendant's mental state on competency to stand trial, proof of his state of mind, and sentencing. In contrast, the court in *Finger v. State*, 27 P.3d 66 (Nev. 2001), struck down such a statute, finding that it violated due process.

The United States Supreme Court has indicated that states' limitations on the insanity defense are permissible. For example, in *Clark v. Arizona*, 548 U.S. 735 (2006), the defendant shot and killed a police officer. He admitted shooting the officer but sought to put on evidence regarding his paranoid schizophrenia and his belief at the time that the state had been invaded by aliens whom he had to shoot. Arizona law permitted Clark to present the evidence only as it pertained to his defense of insanity and not for purposes of defeating the mens rea component of first degree murder. Clark argued that the state's restrictions on his mental illness evidence violated Due Process. The Supreme Court rejected Clark's challenge and upheld the Arizona insanity definition, which included only the moral incapacity prong of the *M'Naghten* test and which excluded evidence of mental illness for purposes of negating specific intent. Writing for the majority, Justice Souter explained that neither aspect of Arizona law violated the Due Process clause.

> State law says that evidence of mental disease and incapacity may be introduced and considered, and if sufficiently forceful to satisfy the defendant's burden of proof under the insanity rule it will displace the presumption of sanity and excuse from criminal responsibility. But mental-disease and capacity evidence may be considered only for its bearing on the insanity defense, and it will avail a defendant only if it is persuasive enough to satisfy the defendant's burden as defined by the terms of that defense. The mental-disease and capacity evidence is thus being channeled or restricted to one issue and given effect only if the defendant carries the burden to convince the factfinder of insanity; the evidence is not being excluded entirely, and the question is whether reasons for requiring it to be channeled and restricted are good enough to satisfy the standard of fundamental fairness that due process requires. We think they are. *Id.* at 770–771.

Justice Breyer concurred in part, but dissented regarding the ultimate disposition, as he would have remanded the case for the Arizona courts to clarify their own reading of the statute. Justices Kennedy, Stevens and Ginsburg dissented, maintaining: "the Court is incorrect in holding that Arizona may convict petitioner Eric Clark of first-degree murder for the intentional or knowing killing of a police officer when Clark was not permitted to introduce critical and reliable evidence showing he did not have that intent or knowledge." *Id.* at 781.

More recently, at least three members of the Supreme Court have indicated a willingness to consider whether an insanity defense, and in what form, may be constitutionally required. Delling was convicted of murder in Idaho, one of a handful of states that have abolished the insanity defense. Delling argued that Idaho's abolition of the defense was unconstitutional and that the Fourteenth and Eighth Amendments require the availability of an insanity defense in criminal cases. In *Delling v. Idaho*, the Supreme Court denied certiorari, but Justice Breyer, joined by Justices Ginsburg and Sotomayor, dissented from the denial of certiorari. 133 S. Ct. 504 (2012) (Breyer, J., dissenting). Justice Breyer wrote:

> [T]he difference between the traditional insanity defense and Idaho's standard is that the latter permits the conviction of an individual who knew *what* he was doing, but had no capacity to understand that it was wrong.
>
> To illustrate with a very much simplified example: Idaho law would distinguish the following two cases. *Case One* : The defendant, due to insanity, believes that the victim is a wolf. He shoots and kills the victim. *Case Two* : The defendant, due to insanity, believes that a wolf, a supernatural figure, has ordered him to kill the victim. In *Case One,* the defendant does not know he has killed a human being, and his insanity negates a mental element necessary

to commit the crime.... In *Case Two,* the defendant has intentionally killed a victim whom he knows is a human being; he possesses the necessary *mens rea.* In both cases the defendant is unable, due to insanity, to appreciate the true quality of his act, and therefore unable to perceive that it is wrong. But in Idaho, the defendant in *Case One* could defend the charge by arguing that he lacked the *mens rea,* whereas the defendant in *Case Two* would not be able to raise a defense based on his mental illness. Much the same outcome seems likely to occur in other States that have modified the insanity defense in similar ways. For example, in *State v. Bethel,* 275 Kan. 456, 459, 66 P.3d 840, 843 (Kan.2003), the prosecution and defense agreed that under a similar Kansas statute, evidence that a schizophrenic defendant's "mental state precluded him from understanding the difference between right and wrong or from understanding the consequences of his actions ... does not constitute a defense to the charged crimes."

The American Psychiatric Association tells us that "severe mental illness can seriously impair a sufferer's ability rationally to appreciate the wrongfulness of conduct." ... And other *amici* tell us that those seriously mentally ill individuals often possess the kind of mental disease that *Case Two* describes—that is to say, they know that the victim is a human being, but due to mental illness, such as a paranoid delusion, they wrongly believe the act is justified.... In view of these submissions, I would grant the petition for certiorari to consider whether Idaho's modification of the insanity defense is consistent with the Fourteenth Amendment's Due Process Clause.

(8) Given all the debate around the insanity defense, its availability and its formulation, it is worth noting that, as a practical matter, the defense is rarely successful, and when it is, it is not a "get out of jail free card." Consider the following reflection.

Drawing a Clear Line Between Criminals and the Criminally Insane, Stephen Lally:*

As a forensic psychologist, I am often asked to evaluate men and women accused of committing crimes in order to assess their competency and whether they can be held criminally responsible for their acts. The law sets fairly straightforward standards for criminal responsibility, and usually I have little difficulty in deciding whether an accused individual qualifies for the insanity defense.

Thus, I'm often struck by the public outcry accompanying a high-profile trial that raises the question of whether the defendant was legally sane when he or she committed the crime. Each time, there is the same focus on the possibility that the perpetrator might be "let off," often accompanied by a hue and cry about a criminal justice system that would permit such a thing to happen.

In fact, very few defendants actually succeed with the insanity defense. (It is raised in approximately about 1 percent of felony cases and is successful only

---

* Reprinted with permission.

about one-quarter of the time.) Among those who are found not guilty by reason of insanity, virtually none are "let off"—in the sense that they remain free. Indeed, some of those found not guilty by reason of insanity spend more time confined in a locked mental hospital than those sane criminals who are convicted of similar acts and imprisoned for them. People are "let off" in the sense that they escape being formally condemned as "responsible" for their acts, but that is small comfort, I suspect, to a defendant in his 10th or 15th year at St. Elizabeth's Hospital, where I used to work. That sort of escape brings to the fore issues of moral responsibility and personal responsibility that are very different—and much vaguer—matters, than criminal responsibility....

During the seven years that I worked at St. Elizabeth's, many of the cases I saw were straightforward in terms of criminal responsibility. Take the homeless man I evaluated several years ago. In a delusional rage, he had attacked a stranger in broad daylight. He was within a stone's throw of half a dozen police officers. From what I could tell, he had never seen his victim before, but he was convinced that she had been persecuting him for many years. Even the presence of police officers did not inhibit his actions (although it did prevent the victim from being seriously injured).

This homeless man is typical of those who are found to be not guilty by reason of insanity. According to the courts, to qualify for the insanity defense, defendants must suffer from a "serious mental disease or defect" that interferes with their understanding of what they did or impairs their controls. The homeless man I evaluated had been suffering from schizophrenia for years. His mental condition clearly interfered with his understanding of the situation (believing that his victim represented a threat to him). Oddly enough, the shorthand often used by experts to assess whether an individual's control is impaired is to ask whether he would commit the act with a policeman at his elbow. The homeless man did just that. He was, quite appropriately, found not guilty by reason of insanity and committed to hospital.

In this case, as in about 70 percent of insanity adjudications, the decision to commit this man was made by plea bargain, in which both prosecution and the defense agree to the plea and there is no trial.

But, like [John] Hinckley, the homeless man did not "get off." He is indefinitely confined to a locked psychiatric hospital. He will be released only when a judge is persuaded that he is no longer mentally ill and dangerous. The average length of stay at St. Elizabeth's is eight years. Some individuals remain confined for decades, if not for their entire lives.

In this way, courts have drawn a clear—if somewhat arbitrary—line to define criminal responsibility. If you meet the criteria for insanity, like the homeless man, you are viewed as not being *criminally* responsible: In other words, your thinking was too disordered or your actions too impaired to have formed the intention to commit a criminal act, and so it is unfair to inflict punishment on you. This singular exception justifies treating all other defendants as competent and criminally responsible: They rationally chose to commit a crime and should be punished for their actions.

While the legal system does provide clear guidelines for assessing criminal responsibility, mental health professionals are often left to wrestle with the vaguer questions of assessing an individual's moral responsibility. I once evaluated a man, accused of brutally murdering a woman, to determine whether he qualified for the insanity defense. My opinion was that he was not criminally responsible. I was convinced by his pattern of behavior that he was seriously ill. At the time of the crime, he was hearing voices that told him to kill the victim—and were threatening to kill him if he did not comply. His condition was severe and there was a clear link between his illness and his crime.

He was found not guilty by reason of insanity and indefinitely committed to the hospital until he could show that he was no longer mentally ill and dangerous.

Much later at the hospital, I saw the same man in therapy, and the focus of our sessions was this issue of responsibility—whether he was in some way morally responsible for his actions. What would have happened, I asked him, if the voices had told him to kill his brother? That he would never do, he told me. He would have killed himself first. In other words, his attachment to his brother would have controlled his actions. But he felt no such attachment or empathy for the women he had killed. It is only by developing that sense of moral responsibility that he could ever hope to be released. No such requirements are made of inmates before their release from prison.

[B] Raising the Question

Frendak v. United States

District of Columbia Court of Appeal
408 A.2d 364 (1979)

FERREN, ASSOCIATE JUDGE:

A jury found appellant Paula Frendak guilty of first-degree murder. Troubled by evidence introduced at Frendak's competency hearings and at trial, the court conducted hearings on her sanity at the time of the crime. As a result, the court decided—over Frendak's objection—to interpose the insanity defense at a second, "insanity" phase of the trial. The jury then found Frendak not guilty by reason of insanity on both counts.

On appeal, Frendak attacks the present validity of *Whalem v. United States*, 346 F.2d 812, 120 U.S. App. D.C. 331*(en banc), cert. denied*, 382 U.S. 862, 86 S. Ct. 124, 15 L. Ed. 2d 100 (1965), in which the United States Court of Appeals for the District of Columbia Circuit held that the trial judge has discretion to raise an insanity defense over the objection of a defendant found competent to stand trial.

We reinterpret *Whalem, supra.* We hold that the trial judge may not force an insanity defense on a defendant found competent to stand trial *if* the individual intelligently and voluntarily decides to forego that defense.

At approximately 2:15 on the afternoon of January 15, 1974, Willard Titlow left his office on the seventh floor of 1735 K Street, N.W. Appellant Paula Frendak, a co-worker, departed immediately afterwards, explaining to a secretary that she had an appointment with her attorney. Within minutes, Titlow was discovered fatally shot in the first floor hallway of the building.

Following the shooting, Frendak left Washington, traveling through Atlanta, Miami, Mexico City, Spain, and Turkey before she was arrested on February 11, 1974 in Abu Dhabi, United Arab Emirates, after refusing to surrender her passport at the airport. A later search of her baggage revealed that she was carrying a .38 caliber pistol, 45 rounds of ammunition, two empty cartridges, and a pocket knife. On March 13, 1974, authorities in Abu Dhabi surrendered Frendak to the United States Marshal, who brought her back to the District of Columbia to face charges relating to the murder of Willard Titlow. On May 29, 1974, Frendak was indicted for first-degree murder and carrying a pistol without a license.

In the months preceding her trial, Frendak underwent a series of psychiatric examinations to determine her competency. There were four competency hearings at which psychiatrists gave varying testimony about Frendak's mental condition and her ability to consult with counsel concerning the proceedings against her. Ultimately, after the fourth hearing, the court determined that appellant was suffering from a personality disorder, was able to cooperate with her counsel, possessed a rational as well as factual understanding of the proceedings against her, and was fully cognizant of the charges. Accordingly, the court concluded that she was competent to stand trial, although it reserved the right to raise the competency issue *sua sponte* at any point in the proceedings.

Although evidence of insanity had been introduced in the competency proceedings, Frendak refused to raise the insanity defense at trial. The court, therefore, appointed *amicus curiae* to aid it in deciding whether to raise the defense on its own motion, under authority of *Whalem v. United States, supra.* The court also ordered a mental examination of Frendak on the question of her criminal responsibility.

In a subsequent hearing, the court received reports by Dr. Edward C. Kirby of the staff of the Forensic Psychiatry Office and Dr. Leon Yochelson of the Psychiatric Institute stating that, at the time of Titlow's murder, Frendak had been suffering from a mental illness which impaired her behavioral controls to such an extent that she could not appreciate the wrongfulness of her conduct and could not conform her conduct to the requirements of the law.[2] Dr. Franklin J. Pepper, a psychiatrist from

2. Dr. Kirby described Frendak's illness as a "schizophrenic reaction, paranoid type," while Dr. Yochelson stated that she suffered from "paranoid psychosis, probably schizophrenic."

St. Elizabeth's Hospital, testified at the hearing, explaining that appellant had a "paranoid personality" with "some tendency to lap over into some psychotic thinking." When asked whether Titlow's murder had been a product of this condition, Dr. Pepper responded that "at some level in the workings of Miss Frendak's mind, at some level of psychodynamics ... there is a causal connection between her mental illness and the event." He testified, however, that he was "unable to discover the cause and effect relationship." Although neither Dr. Kirby nor Dr. Yochelson discussed appellant's present capability of considering the consequences of rejecting an insanity defense, Dr. Pepper specifically stated that appellant understood the consequences of her decision not to raise the insanity defense.[3]

Both Frendak and the prosecution opposed the trial court's imposition of the insanity defense. After hearing the evidence and arguments on both sides, the trial judge reaffirmed his prior ruling that appellant was competent to stand trial.

He then found that the psychiatric evidence adduced throughout the proceedings raised a sufficient question about appellant's mental responsibility at the time of the crime to require that the court raise the insanity defense under the *Whalem* rule, although he expressed reservations about the current validity of that rule.

The insanity phase of the case was tried before the same jury which had heard the trial on the merits.[4]

Dr. Pepper, on the other hand, believed that Frendak had only a personality disorder with at most a borderline tendency toward psychosis, a condition characterized by hyper-sensitivity, unwarranted suspicion, jealousy, excessive self-importance, and a tendency to blame others and ascribe evil motives to them. He found no connecting link between appellant's mental disease and the crime, explaining that he did not believe she was delusional at the time of the murder, since her actions before and after the crime indicated that she had known what she was doing throughout the entire period.

---

3. Dr. Pepper explained that the main reason appellant had given for refusing to raise the defense was that it would be an admission of guilt.

4. In the District of Columbia, a bifurcated proceeding may be conducted when a defendant raises an insanity defense; accordingly, the trier of fact does not consider the issue of insanity until the government has established the essential elements of the offense beyond a reasonable doubt. Only then, in the second phase, may the trier of fact reach the question of insanity. *Amicus* presented evidence supporting the insanity defense. He first called Mark Freedricks, a former neighbor of Ms. Frendak, who recounted several incidents demonstrating appellant's hostile conduct toward him, including spitting at him, avoiding him, and accusing him of being a CIA agent. Doctors Kirby, Yochelson, and Pepper again testified. Dr. Kirby and Dr. Yochelson stated that, in their view, Frendak had been suffering from a major psychotic illness, characterized by delusions, hallucinations and looseness of associations. In particular, she feared that there were plots against her, especially by persons associated with the CIA. Dr. Kirby did not find any specific, logical connection between the crime and Frendak's mental disease but expressed his belief that if she had committed the crime, it was because of "her reduced behavioral control on account of her mental illness." Dr. Yochelson did see a causal link between appellant's illness and the murder, explaining that she had great difficulty forming close attachments with other people, and that this caused great anxiety. She was, the doctor speculated, beginning to develop positive feelings about Titlow and was afraid of those feelings. Titlow's murder would have provided a means of eliminating a serious external source of her anxiety.

Ms. Frendak testified in her own behalf, stating that she had had little contact with her former neighbor, Mr. Freedricks, and did not bear him any grudge; that she did not kill Titlow; and that the murder was all part of what she described as a "Rand Corporation game plan." On April 29, 1976, the jury returned a verdict of not guilty by reason of insanity.

Evidence presented during the four competency hearings and at trial had suggested that Paula Frendak may have been insane at the time she shot Willard Titlow. Thus, after the jury had convicted Frendak of first-degree murder, the trial judge found himself squarely confronted with the question whether, apropos of *Whalem, supra*, he should raise an insanity defense over the opposition of a competent defendant. After conducting a thorough inquiry with the help of *amicus*, the judge concluded that *Whalem* required him, under the circumstances, to interpose the insanity defense, despite reservations.

In *Whalem*, the United States Court of Appeals for the District of Columbia Circuit, sitting en banc, held that

> When there is sufficient question as to a defendant's mental responsibility at the time of the crime, that issue must become part of the case.... [I]n the pursuit of justice, a trial judge must have the discretion to impose an unwanted defense on a defendant....

[T]here are persuasive reasons why defendants convicted of an offense may choose to accept the jury's verdict rather than raise a potentially successful insanity defense. First, a defendant may fear that an insanity acquittal will result in the institution of commitment proceedings which lead to confinement in a mental institution for a period longer than the potential jail sentence. Although a judge may not automatically commit an accused to a mental institution if the judge, rather than the defendant, has raised the insanity defense, the state has a right to initiate civil commitment proceedings against an insanity acquittee. The risk of civil commitment following a conviction could be substantial, especially if the crime involved violence.

Second, the defendant may object to the quality of treatment or the type of confinement to which he or she may be subject in an institution for the mentally ill. If in need of psychiatric care, the individual may prefer the prospect of receiving whatever treatment is available in the prison. There are, moreover, "numerous restrictions and routines in a mental hospital which differ significantly from those in a prison."

[H]ospitalization itself interferes with privacy, since the patient cannot shield himself from constant observation by both his fellow patients and the staff of the institution. Furthermore, patients in hospitals risk brutality at the hands of their fellow residents and even their attendants, and may be subject to life in an institution which is overcrowded, inadequately staffed, poorly maintained, and unsanitary. Ms. Frendak, in particular, has indicated that she considers the hospital worse than any prison and, in order to avoid institutionalization there, has gone on hunger strikes, attempted suicide, and refused medication.

Third, a defendant, with good reason, may choose to avoid the stigma of insanity. In the District of Columbia, a jury may consider an insanity defense only after it has found the accused guilty of an offense beyond a reasonable doubt. Although an insanity acquittal officially absolves the defendant of all moral blame, in the eyes of many some element of responsibility may remain. Thus, the insanity acquittee found to have committed criminal acts and labeled insane may well see oneself "twice cursed." In addition, many persons do not understand mental illness, and some have an irrational fear of the mentally ill. Thus, an individual once labeled insane may be socially ostracized and victimized by employment or educational discrimination.

Fourth, other collateral consequences of an insanity acquittal can also follow the defendant throughout life. In some states, an adjudication of insanity may affect a person's legal rights, for example, the right to vote or serve on a federal jury, and may even restrict his or her ability to obtain a driver's license. Such an adjudication also may adversely affect the defendant in any interaction with the legal system. For instance, it may be used to attack his or her capacity as a trial witness, or could be admissible in a criminal trial to attack the character of a defendant who has put his or her character in issue. Furthermore, the record of such an adjudication would surely be used in any subsequent proceeding for civil commitment.

Finally, a defendant also may oppose the imposition of an insanity defense because he or she views the crime as a political or religious protest which a finding of insanity would denigrate. In any event, a defendant may choose to forego the defense because of a feeling that he or she is not insane, or that raising the defense would be equivalent to an admission of guilt.

In our view, these reasons substantially outweigh the express purpose of *Whalem:* to ensure that some abstract concept of justice is satisfied by protecting one who may be morally blameless from a conviction and punishment which he or she might choose to accept. Because the defendant must bear the ultimate consequences of any decision, we conclude that if a defendant has acted intelligently and voluntarily, a trial court must defer to his or her decision to waive the insanity defense.

It follows, however, that the underlying protective rationale of *Whalem* is sufficiently compelling that the trial court still must have the discretion to raise an insanity defense, *sua sponte*, when a defendant does not have the capacity to reject the defense. We acknowledge that a defendant who chooses to forego an insanity defense relinquishes important safeguards intended to protect persons who are not legally responsible for their acts from punishment and culpability in the eyes of society. We conclude that a trial judge must seek assurance when a defendant chooses to reject an insanity defense. The court must ensure that the defendant understands the consequences of his or her choice and makes the decision voluntarily. Moreover, because the court is dealing with an individual whose mental health was once in question, it is especially important to ensure that the defendant is capable of intelligently refusing to make the defense. Thus, the trial court need only respect the defendant's choice when it determines that the defendant "knows what he is doing and his choice is made with eyes open."

In accordance with *Whalem*, a trial judge will still have the duty to confront the insanity issue if the evidence adduced in the proceedings raises a "sufficient question as to a defendant's mental responsibility at the time of the crime." The judge will also continue to have the discretion to interpose an insanity defense *sua sponte* against the will of a defendant competent to stand trial. That discretion, however, is limited. Rather than permit a trial judge (as in *Whalem*) to raise an insanity defense whenever there is a sufficient quantum of evidence supporting the defense, we require the judge to respect the choice of a defendant capable of voluntarily and intelligently making that choice. The court will have the discretion to raise an insanity defense *sua sponte* only if the defendant is not capable of making, and has not made, an intelligent and voluntary decision.

Comments and Questions

(1) As the *Frendak* decision indicates, the question whether the trial judge should be able to raise the insanity defense over a competent defendant's objection is complex, to say the least. On one hand, the trial court judge has an obligation to preserve the fundamental fairness of the trial itself. On the other hand, as the *Frendak* court recognizes, there are "persuasive reasons why defendants convicted of an offense may choose to accept the jury's verdict rather than raise a potentially successful insanity defense." What are those reasons? Do you find them compelling?

(2) In *United States v. Marble*, the United States Court of Appeals for the District of Columbia Circuit overruled *Whalem* and held that "a district court must allow a competent defendant to accept responsibility for a crime committed when he may have been suffering from a mental disease." 940 F.2d 1543, 1547 (D.C. Cir. 1991). That ruling is consistent with the argument of Cohn in *Offensive Use of the Insanity Defense: Imposing the Insanity Defense over the Defendant's Objection*, 15 Hastings Const. L.Q. 295, 318 (1988).

> Although society has a legitimate interest in refusing to subject to criminal punishment those whom it considers morally blameless by virtue of their mental illness, that interest is not of constitutional dimension. In contrast, a competent defendant has a substantial interest and fundamental right to conduct his defense as he deems most appropriate. Though not explicit in the Bill of Rights, the right to choose one's manner of defense is implicit in our Anglo-American concept of criminal justice. Accordingly, a trial judge should not substitute her judgment for the judgment of a competent defendant on this basic trial decision unless the defendant's competence is so marginal that his decisions cannot be considered voluntary and intelligent. The defendant has the ultimate right to make those decisions, even if they are foolish or disastrous, and they should not be forced upon him, even in his supposed best interest.

Most, but not all, courts are in accord with the *Marble* decision. For the alternative view *see, e.g., State v. Pautz*, 217 N.W. 2d 190, 192 (Minn. 1974) (trial judge has a function and a role in the fair administration of justice and thus should be able to raise insanity issue sue sponte); *Walker v. State*, 321 A.2d 170, 174 (Ct. Sp. App. Md. 1974) (upholding trial court judge's refusal to permit withdrawal of insanity plea when "the court ha[d]before it uncontradicted, competent evidence that the accused was insane at the time of the commission of the offenses").

(3) The *Frendak* court acknowledged that defendants may strategically decide to not to plead insanity because they fear that they will be confined to a mental institution for a period longer than whatever prison sentence they face. A few years after the *Frendak* decision, the Supreme Court confirmed that such a fear is well-grounded. Defendant Jones established at trial that he was insane at the time of the crime; he was found not guilty by reason of insanity; and he was then confined to a mental institution. In *Jones v. United States*, 463 U.S. 354 (1983), the Supreme Court addressed the question whether his confinement in a mental institution for a period longer than he could have been kept in prison if he had been found guilty was constitutional. The Court held that this confinement was constitutional. As stated by Justice Powell:

> In light of the congressional purposes underlying commitment of insanity acquittees, we think petitioner clearly errs in contending that an acquittee's hypothetical maximum sentence provides the constitutional limit for his commitment. A particular sentence of incarceration is chosen to reflect society's view of the proper response to commission of a particular criminal offense, based on a variety of considerations such as retribution, deterrence, and rehabilitation.
>
> The State may punish a person convicted of a crime even if satisfied that he is unlikely to commit further crimes.
>
> Different considerations underlie commitment of an insanity acquittee. As he was not convicted, he may not be punished. His confinement rests on his continuing illness and dangerousness. Thus, under the District of Columbia statute, no matter how serious the act committed by the acquittee, he may be released within 50 days of his acquittal if he has recovered. In contrast, one who committed a less serious act may be confined for a longer period if he remains ill and dangerous. There simply is no necessary correlation between severity of the offense and length of time necessary for recovery. The length of the acquittee's hypothetical criminal sentence therefore is irrelevant to the purposes of his commitment.

Justice Brennan strongly disagreed.

> In many respects, confinement in a mental institution is even more intrusive than incarceration in a prison. Inmates of mental institutions, like prisoners, are deprived of unrestricted association with friends, family, and community; they must contend with locks, guards, and detailed regulation of their daily activities. In addition, a person who has been hospitalized involuntarily may to a significant extent lose the right enjoyed by others to withhold consent to medical treatment. The treatments to which he may be subjected include physical restraints such as straightjacketing, as well as electroshock therapy,

> aversive conditioning, and even in some cases psychosurgery. Administration of psychotropic medication to control behavior is common.

(4) In *Foucha v. Louisiana*, 504 U.S. 71 (1992), the Supreme Court held unconstitutional a Louisiana statute which allowed for the continued confinement of insanity acquittees on the ground of danger even after the individuals had been cured of mental illness. The state argued that *Jones* did not require the patient's release. The Court rejected this reliance on *Jones* stating that it stood for the proposition that "the acquittee may be held as long as he is both mentally ill and dangerous, but no longer."

[C] Diminished Capacity

> The concept [of "diminished capacity"] is directed at the evidentiary duty of the State to establish those elements of the crime charged requiring a conscious mental ingredient. There is no question that it may overlap the insanity defense in that insanity itself is concerned with mental conditions so incapacitating as to totally bar criminal responsibility. The distinction is that diminished capacity is legally applicable to disabilities not amounting to insanity, and its consequences, in homicide cases, operate to reduce the degree of the crime rather than to excuse its commission. Evidence offered under this rubric is relevant to prove the existence of a mental defect or obstacle to the presence of a state of mind which is an element of the crime, for example: premeditation or deliberation.

State v. Smith, 396 A.2d 126, 130 (Vt. 1978).

> [The] appellant must have a *fully informed intent to kill* and in determining whether or not appellant committed the crime of *intentional* killing required for first degree murder, [the jury] should consider the testimony of the expert witnesses as well as all the other evidence, which might shed light on *what was going on in the appellant's mind* at the time of the alleged killing.

Commonwealth v. Larkins, 489 A.2d 837, 843 (Pa. Super. Ct. 1985).

State v. Joseph

Supreme Court of Appeals of West Virginia
590 S.E.2d 718 (2003)

Davis, Justice:

Mr. Robert Joseph, defendant below and appellant herein, appeals from a conviction of first degree murder with mercy. He contends that the circuit court erred in excluding expert testimony offered by the defense to show that he suffered from a diminished capacity that prevented him from forming the requisite mental state for the commission of first or second degree murder. We first conclude that the diminished capacity defense is available in West Virginia to permit a defendant to introduce expert testimony regarding a mental disease or defect that rendered the defendant incapable, at the time the crime was committed, of forming a mental state that is an element of the crime charged. In addition, we find that the evidence offered by Mr. Joseph was sufficient to allow his diminished capacity theory to go to the jury. Accordingly, his conviction is reversed and this case is remanded for a new trial.

I. FACTUAL AND PROCEDURAL HISTORY

Stated briefly, the relevant facts are as follows. On the night of Wednesday, March 28, 2001, the defendant, Robert Bradley Joseph (hereinafter "Mr. Joseph"), was socializing in his home with Jessica Martin (hereinafter "Ms. Martin"), an eighteen year-old female, and Duane Lucas (hereinafter "Mr. Lucas"). The three spent the evening drinking beer and listening to music until the early hours of the morning. During the course of the evening, Ms. Martin rejected advances made by Mr. Joseph and she began flirting with Mr. Lucas. At approximately 4:00 a.m., Mr. Joseph became angry at the rejection and ordered Ms. Martin to leave the house. She left accompanied by Mr. Lucas. As the two departed, Mr. Joseph went out onto the porch of his home and fired two shots. No one was injured by the shots.

Mr. Joseph testified that he became concerned about Ms. Martin and decided to look for her. He first drove to her grandmother's house where he encountered Ms. Martin's boyfriend, Richard Hackney (hereinafter "Mr. Hackney"). The two men then drove to the home of the victim, Mr. Scott Light (hereinafter "Mr. Light"). Mr. Light was not home, but his girlfriend explained that he had driven Ms. Martin and Mr. Lucas "down the road." Mr. Joseph then drove away from the house, but saw Mr. Light's vehicle approaching and turned around and followed Mr. Light into his driveway. Messrs. Joseph and Hackney got out of their vehicle and Mr. Joseph questioned Mr. Light about Ms. Martin's whereabouts. Mr. Light first denied that he knew where Ms. Martin was, but then admitted that he had driven Ms. Martin and Mr. Lucas to the mouth of the hollow. Upon hearing this, Mr. Joseph returned to his truck and spun his tires in Mr. Light's driveway. Mr. Light yelled at him to stop the truck. Mr. Light then walked over to Mr. Joseph's truck, pulled the driver's door open, and the two men argued. During the argument, Mr. Light pointed his finger at Mr. Joseph and Mr. Joseph slapped his hand away. According to Mr. Joseph, Mr. Light then struck or slapped him on the left side of the head. Mr. Joseph testified that, upon being slapped, he saw a "blue flash," and his hand landed on a .22 caliber pistol that was lying on the seat of his truck. Mr. Joseph grabbed the pistol and fired five shots into Mr. Light, mortally wounding him.

Several years before the above described incident, in July 1989, Mr. Joseph was involved in a motorcycle accident. Among the serious injuries Mr. Joseph sustained in the accident was a crush injury to his left frontal skull.

Mr. Joseph was charged with first-degree murder in connection with Mr. Light's death, and was tried by jury. Mr. Joseph sought to assert the defense of diminished capacity resulting from the brain injury sustained in his motorcycle accident of 1989. He offered the testimony of three doctors in support of this defense.

The circuit court heard testimony from each of these doctors *in camera*. The circuit court then ruled that, although West Virginia has recognized the defense of diminished capacity, the testimony of the three doctors was insufficient upon which to base the defense. Therefore, the court excluded the testimony of these three witnesses.

At the close of all the evidence, Mr. Joseph was convicted of first degree murder with a recommendation of mercy.

III. DISCUSSION

At the core of this appeal is the question of whether the circuit court properly applied the diminished capacity defense asserted by Mr. Joseph in reaching its conclusion to exclude the medical testimony offered by Mr. Joseph in support of that defense. Before deciding this issue, however, we must first determine whether the defense of diminished capacity is available in West Virginia.

A. *Diminished Capacity*

Generally stated, what is sometimes referred to as the diminished capacity defense allows "a defendant to offer evidence of his mental condition with respect to his capacity to achieve the mens rea or intent required for commission of the offense charged (" 'diminished capacity is a "failure of proof" defense: evidence of defendant's mental illness or defect serves to negate the *mens rea* element of the crime.' ") ("Diminished capacity is a mental condition not amounting to insanity which prevents the defendant from possessing the requisite mental state necessary to commit the crime charged").

[As several courts have written:]

> Due process requires that the government prove every element of a criminal offense beyond a reasonable doubt. The defendant's right to present a defense to one of those elements generally includes the right to the admission of competent, reliable, exculpatory evidence.... [A] rule barring evidence on the issue of mens rea may be unconstitutional so long as we determine criminal liability in part through subjective states of mind.
>
> [A]lthough an accused has no absolute right to present evidence relevant to his defense, a limitation on his ability to present a defense may, under some circumstances, violate due process.... Rules excluding evidence contravene the due process right to present a defense when they infringe a weighty interest of an accused or significantly undermine a fundamental element of the defense. A jury considers evidence of diminished capacity in relation to the State's burden to prove the essential elements of the crime.

Thus, it is somewhat confusing to refer to diminished capacity as a "defense." As one court has observed, "the term ... 'diminished capacity' does not have a clearly accepted meaning in the courts ... although this principle has sometimes been phrased as a version of the 'diminished capacity defense,' it does not provide any ground for acquittal not provided in the definition of the offense. Properly understood, [diminished capacity is] not a defense at all but merely a rule of evidence." Indeed, it is important to note that, unlike the insanity defense, evidence of diminished capacity does not establish a complete defense. As one commentator has explained,

> It has been said that diminished capacity is not considered a justification or excuse for a crime, but rather an attempt to prove that the defendant, incapable of the requisite intent of the crime charged, is innocent of that crime but is most likely guilty of a lesser included offense; thus, a defendant claiming diminished capacity contemplates full responsibility, but only for the crime he or she actually committed.

In asserting a diminished capacity defense, a defendant is attempting to prove that his [or her] mental condition at the time of the crime was such that he [or she] was *incapable* of forming the specific intent to kill. If the defendant is successful, first degree murder is mitigated to third degree.

Numerous courts have allowed some form of diminished capacity defense. *See generally* Model Penal Code § 4.02(1) (1985) ("Evidence that the defendant suffered from a mental disease or defect is admissible whenever it is relevant to prove that the defendant did or did not have a state of mind that is an element of the offense.").

A review of West Virginia case law reveals that this Court has all but expressly recognized the use of evidence of a diminished capacity resulting from a mental disease or defect to negate the mental state of the crime charged. We have, heretofore, allowed evidence of voluntary intoxication to show that a defendant was incapable of forming the required mental state for first degree murder. "While it is true that voluntary drunkenness does not ordinarily excuse a crime, ... it may reduce the degree of the crime or negative a specific intent." The Court also commented that it had generally held that "the level of intoxication must be 'such as to render the accused incapable of forming an intent to kill, or of acting with malice, premeditation or deliberation.'"

It would be inequitable to allow evidence of a diminished capacity where voluntary intoxication is involved, yet deny such evidence where an organic brain injury or other brain injury or disease is involved.

The reason for allowing a defendant to assert the defense of diminished capacity is to permit the jury to determine if the defendant should be convicted of some lesser degree of homicide because the requisite mental intent to commit first-degree or second degree murder is not present by virtue of the defendant's mental disease or defect.

[An earlier decision] cautioned, however, that "the existence of a mental illness is not alone sufficient to trigger a diminished capacity defense. It must be shown by psychiatric testimony that some type of mental illness rendered the defendant incapable of forming the specific intent elements."

We hold that the diminished capacity defense is available in West Virginia to permit a defendant to introduce expert testimony regarding a mental disease or defect that rendered the defendant incapable, at the time the crime was committed, of forming a mental state that is an element of the crime charged. This defense is asserted ordinarily when the offense charged is a crime for which there is a lesser included offense. This is so because the successful use of this defense renders the defendant not guilty of the particular crime charged, but does not preclude a conviction for a lesser included offense. We now apply this holding to the case *sub judice*.

B. *Expert Testimony*

Mr. Joseph argues that the circuit court erred in excluding the testimony of his treating physicians and expert witness, Dr. Solomon. The State contends that the circuit court did not err in excluding the doctors' testimony in this case as their testimony failed to establish that Mr. Joseph suffered from a diminished capacity.

Dr. Solomon made the following relevant comments during his *in camera* testimony:

> All the indications ... pointed to me that he had suffered frontal lobe damage, that his long-term knowledge was intact but he underwent tremendous personality change along with the other things I talked about.
>
> ...
>
> He knows where he is, who he is, what time of day it is, what month it is. All of those things are within normal limits. It's the executive functions that I found to be diminished to show a great loss.
>
> ...
>
> Under the circumstances that existed there that morning, I think his ability to plan, organize, carry out decision-making processes were extremely flawed due to his brain injury. In other circumstances the situation might be different.
>
> ...
>
> Given those circumstances, I think his ability to plan and carry out a premeditated plan of action would have been diminished.
>
> ...

I can say yes, I think within a scientific certainty that his capacity was diminished during that particular time frame.

> Q. And that was the capacity to premeditate, to intend, and to have malice; is that correct?
>
> A. Yes. Given those circumstances, that's correct.

Dr. Solomon also acknowledged that in his report he expressed his opinion that "within a reasonable scientific probability ... Mr. Robert Joseph was operating under an involuntary state of diminished capacity and that this tragic shooting happened without malice due to his diminished capacity." Finally, the circuit court asked Dr. Solomon to clarify his position, and stated "you're saying ... that he's suffering from some mental defect which precludes him from being able to formulate intent or malice or to premeditate under these circumstances. Is that correct?" To which Dr. Solomon answered, "I think that's a pretty correct phrases (phonetic) of what I'm trying to say."

We find that the circuit court erred in its application of the diminished capacity doctrine. The circuit court apparently interpreted the diminished capacity defense as requiring a complete inability to form the necessary mental elements of a crime. On the contrary, "[a] defendant who raises a diminished capacity defense ... challenges his capacity to premeditate and deliberate *at the time of the criminal act.*"

While the circuit court misperceived the rule, we note that it was not necessarily unreasonable for the court to reach its conclusion given that there was no explicit statement of the rule in West Virginia at the time the circuit court ruled on the issue. We have corrected this absence by our holding today. Since it was proper for Dr. Solomon to offer an opinion as to Mr. Joseph's mental abilities at the time of the commission of the crime charged, we must now determine whether Dr. Solomon's conclusions regarding Mr. Joseph's mental capacity were sufficient to support a claim of diminished capacity.

Dr. Solomon's testimony was addressed directly to Mr. Joseph's mental capacity at the time of his criminal offense and Dr. Solomon opined that Mr. Joseph was, due to his mental defect, unable "to formulate intent or malice or to premeditate under these circumstances." Thus, in the instant case, there plainly was sufficient evidence to allow Dr. Solomon to testify before the jury. Accordingly, the circuit court was clearly wrong in excluding this evidence and prohibiting Mr. Joseph from presenting his defense attacking the State's case in chief. For this reason, Mr. Joseph's conviction must be overturned and this case remanded for a new trial.

Reversed and remanded.

Comments and Questions

(1) At several points the opinion refers to the defense of diminished capacity. Is there such a defense? In a case such as this, should there be a special jury instruction dealing with the subject of diminished capacity? *See* Mendez, *Diminished Capacity in California: Premature Reports of Its Demise*, 3 Stan. L. & Pol'y Rev. 216, 222 (1991):

> Some [jurisdictions] reject diminished capacity entirely; others accept it, although at times with limitations. Opposition stems from misunderstandings as well as from serious concerns about the doctrine's application.
>
> The misunderstanding can be traced to the belief held by some judges that evidence of mental disorders should be limited to claims of insanity. Defendants who claim diminished capacity, however, are not seeking an acquittal on insanity grounds. Rather, they seek to escape conviction by raising a reasonable doubt as to whether they possess the requisite mental state required for conviction. Because diminished capacity does not fit the insanity defense, these judges find such evidence inadmissible.

The courts continue to give less than helpful guidance here. Consider, for instance, *United States v. Vela*, 624 F.3d 1148 (9th Cir. 2010), where the opinion discussed "the defense of diminished capacity" and noted that this defense "is ordinarily available only when a crime requires proof of a specific intent ... [not a] general intent."

(2) In *Fisher v. United States*, the defendant argued that he should have been entitled to an instruction as to evidence regarding his mental deficiency, short of insanity, during his murder trial. The Supreme Court rejected this argument, finding "it is the established law in the District that an accused in a criminal trial is not entitled to an instruction based upon evidence of mental weakness, short of legal insanity, which

would reduce his crime from first to second degree murder." 328 U.S. 463, 473 (1946). Writing for the Court, Justice Reed further held

> No one doubts that there are more possible classifications of mentality than the sane and the insane ... Criminologists and psychologists have weighed the advantages and disadvantages of the adoption of the theory of partial responsibility as a basis of the jury's determination of the degree of crime of which a mentally deficient defendant may be guilty. Congress took a forward step in defining the degrees of murder so that only those guilty of deliberate and premeditated malice could be convicted of the first degree. It may be that psychiatry has now reached a position of certainty in its diagnosis and prognosis which will induce Congress to enact the rule of responsibility for crime for which petitioner contends. For this Court to force the District of Columbia to adopt such a requirement for criminal trials would involve a fundamental change in the common law theory of responsibility.

328 U.S. at 475–76. But see the dissenting opinion of Justice Murphy:

> More precisely, there are persons who, while not totally insane, possess such low mental powers as to be incapable of the deliberation and premeditation requisite to statutory first degree murder. Yet under the rule adopted by the court below, the jury must either condemn such persons to death on the false premise that they possess the mental requirements of a first degree murderer or free them completely from criminal responsibility and turn them loose among society. The jury is forbidden to find them guilty of a lesser degree of murder by reason of their generally weakened or disordered intellect.
>
> Common sense and logic recoil at such a rule. And it is difficult to marshal support for it from civilized concepts of justice or from the necessity of protecting society. When a man's life or liberty is at stake he should be adjudged according to his personal culpability as well as by the objective seriousness of his crime. That elementary principle of justice is applied to those who kill while intoxicated or in the heat of passion; if such a condition destroys their deliberation and premeditation the jury may properly consider that fact and convict them of a lesser degree of murder. No different principle should be utilized in the case of those whose mental deficiency is of a more permanent character. Society, moreover, is ill-protected by a rule which encourages a jury to acquit a partially insane person with an appealing case simply because his mental defects cannot be considered in reducing the degree of guilt.
>
> It is undeniably difficult, as the Government points out, to determine with any high degree of certainty whether a defendant has a general mental impairment and whether such a disorder renders him incapable of the requisite deliberation and premeditation. The difficulty springs primarily from the present limited scope of medical and psychiatric knowledge of mental disease. But this knowledge is ever increasing. And juries constantly must judge the baffling psychological factors of deliberation and premeditation, Congress

> having entrusted the ascertainment of those factors to the good sense of juries. It seems senseless to shut the door on the assistance which medicine and psychiatry can give in regard to these matters, however inexact and incomplete that assistance may presently be. Precluding the consideration of mental deficiency only makes the jury's decision on deliberation and premeditation less intelligent and trustworthy.
>
> It is also said that the proposed rule would require a revolutionary change in criminal procedure in the District of Columbia and that this Court should therefore leave the matter to local courts or to Congress. I cannot agree. Congress has already spoken by making the distinction between first and second degree murder turn upon the existence of deliberation and premeditation. It is the duty of the courts below to fashion rules to permit the jury to utilize all relevant evidence directed toward those factors. But when the courts below adopt rules which substantially impair the jury's function in this respect, this Court should exercise its recognized prerogative.

328 U.S. at 492–93.

(3) Congress in 1984 greatly altered federal law concerning the insanity defense, as noted above. 18 U.S.C. § 17 provides:

> *Affirmative Defense*—It is an affirmative defense to a prosecution under any Federal Statute that, at the time of the commission of the acts constituting the offense, the defendant, as a result of a severe mental disease or defect, was unable to appreciate the nature and quality or the wrongfulness of his acts. *Mental disease or defect does not otherwise constitute a defense.*

(Emphasis supplied.) Some courts took the view that the statute eliminated all diminished capacity evidence at trial, but most courts did not. As stated in *United States v. Westcott*, 83 F.3d 1354, 1358 (11th Cir. 1996):

> The Act does not, however, completely eliminate the use of mental disease or defect evidence outside of attempts to establish the affirmative defense of insanity. The Act does not, by its terms, prohibit psychiatric evidence relevant to issues other than excuse or justification of otherwise criminal conduct. If a subjective state of mind is an element of a crime, evidence regarding the existence or absence of that state of mind is evidence relevant to whether a crime was in fact committed. Psychiatric evidence which negates *mens rea* thus negates an element of the offense rather than constituting a justification or excuse. The plain language of the Act, as well as its legislative history, indicates that Congress did not intend to exclude psychiatric evidence which negates the element of a charged crime.

See also United States v. Schneider, 111 F.3d 197, 201 (1st Cir. 1997): "[I]f state of mind is a potential issue—as it is in most but not all criminal cases—why should expert medical evidence be excluded out of hand?"

(4) States are split on the question whether mental deficiency short of insanity should be a "defense." Some states have taken a very strict approach to the question

and have rejected the doctrine of diminished responsibility. *See, e.g.*, *People v. Carpenter*, 627 N.W.2d 276, 277 (Mich. 2001) (interpreting state insanity law to preclude "evidence of mental abnormalities short of legal insanity to avoid or reduce criminal responsibility by negating specific intent"); *State v. Burton*, 464 So.2d 421, 427 (La. App. 1985) (state does not recognize doctrine of diminished responsibility and "a mental defect short of legal insanity cannot serve to negate specific intent and reduce the degree of the crime"); *State v. Wilcox*, 436 N.E.2d 523 (Ohio 1982) (rejecting diminished responsibility and finding that "Ohio's test for criminal responsibility adequately safeguards the rights of the insane" and "an alternative defense ... could swallow up the insanity defense and its attendant commitment provisions"). Other courts are more permissive. *See, e.g., State v. McVey*, 376 N.W. 2d 585 (Iowa 1985) (diminished responsibility defense is available but only with respect to specific intent crimes); *People v. Gellagos*, 628 P.2d 999 (Co. 1981) ("diminished responsibility attributable to a lack of mental capacity is the statutory equivalent of the affirmative defense of impaired mental condition" and is distinct from claim of insanity).

(5) Should a state court's determination regarding diminished capacity hinge on the nature of the crime with which defendant is charged? In *McCarthy v. State*, 372 A.2d 180, 183–184 (Del. 1977), the Delaware Supreme Court held that the defendant could not avail himself of the diminished responsibility doctrine because of the nature of his alleged crimes—rape, attempted rape, and kidnapping. The McCarthy court explained:

> Our rejection of the doctrine in the instant case is based primarily upon its basic inconsistency to the offenses here involved. As previously noted, the salient aspect of the diminished responsibility doctrine is that it does not relieve the defendant of criminal responsibility. Like "extreme emotional distress," it is a defense of mitigation only. Criminal responsibility exists, but only for an offense for which the general *mens rea* can be found. In practice under the doctrine, while conviction for an offense requiring a specific intent was foreclosed, conviction for a lesser-included crime, requiring only a general criminal intent, was not. This specific intent—general intent dichotomy explains not only the application of the doctrine in the first degree murder cases wherein the specific intent element of premeditation and deliberation are negated, but also the seemingly more liberal application of the doctrine in cases such as assault and battery with intent to kill; first degree forgery, requiring intent to defraud; assault with intent to commit murder; and entering a building with intent to commit theft. In each of these instances, the requisite specific intent constituted an aggravating factor to an otherwise general *mens rea* offense and the doctrine was applied to permit a finding of the lesser offense.
>
> As the above cases illustrate, acceptance of the doctrine requires that there be some lesser-included offense which lacks the requisite specific intent of the greater offense charged. Otherwise, the doctrine of diminished responsibility becomes an impermissible substitute test of criminal responsibility.

> In the instant case, there are no such lesser-included offenses within those for which the defendant was charged and tried. The acceptance of the doctrine in this case, therefore, would be inconsistent with the theory's basic purpose.

Compare the McCarthy court's reasoning with that of the court in *State v. Booth*, 588 P.2d 614, 614 (Or. 1978). In *Booth*, the defendant was charged with theft, an offense for which there was no lesser included offense. The state urged that an instruction of diminished responsibility is only proper where the charged offense contains a lesser included offense. The Court rejected this argument:

> ORS 161.300 allows the jury to consider evidence of a defendant's mental disease or defect in determining "whether he did or did not have the intent which is an element of the crime." The State argues that a "partial responsibility" instruction based on ORS 161.300 is proper only in cases where acquittal of the crime charged will result in conviction of a lesser included offense, and that it was not intended to allow a complete acquittal. The state relies on our opinion that partial responsibility "is not a complete defense to the crime charged but results in a conviction on a lesser-included offense." That statement was correct on the facts involved. There, the defendant was charged with arson in the first degree. A lesser included offense would be reckless burning. Thus, we were addressing a situation where, if the State failed to prove the intent to damage property because of a partial responsibility defense or any other evidence of lack of intent, it would not result in an acquittal, but instead, the jury would be instructed on the lesser offense of reckless burning which does not involve the intent element necessary to convict for first degree arson.
>
> In the instant case, we agree with the conclusion of the Court of Appeals that if the State failed to prove the intent element because of defendant's partial responsibility defense, defendant would be acquitted. There is nothing novel about this conclusion, because even prior to the enactment of the partial responsibility defense statute, if the State failed to prove intent in a theft charge for any reason, the defendant would be entitled to an acquittal.
>
> We hold, therefore, that the partial responsibility defense is available whether or not the crime charged includes a lesser offense. If a lesser offense is available, a successful partial responsibility defense may reduce the crime to the lesser offense. If there is no lesser included offense, a successful partial responsibility defense will result in an acquittal.

(6) As discussed, *supra*, in *Clark v. Arizona*, 548 U.S. 735 (2006), the Supreme Court upheld a state's refusal to consider mens rea evidence outside the context of an insanity defense. Revisit that issue and consider whether you agree with that decision as a matter of fundamental fairness. What values does such a ruling promote?

Index

[References are to sections.]